P9-EGC-785

Sound Ideas

Michael Krasny
San Francisco State University
KQED Public Radio

M.E. Sokolik
University of California at Berkeley

 **Higher Education**

Boston   Burr Ridge, IL   Dubuque, IA   New York   San Francisco   St. Louis
Bangkok   Bogotá   Caracas   Kuala Lumpur   Lisbon   London   Madrid   Mexico City
Milan   Montreal   New Delhi   Santiago   Seoul   Singapore   Sydney   Taipei   Toronto

 **Higher Education**

Published by McGraw-Hill, a business unit of The McGraw-Hill Companies, Inc., 1221 Avenue of the Americas, New York, NY, 10020. Copyright © 2010 by The McGraw-Hill Companies, Inc. All rights reserved. No part of this publication may be reproduced or distributed in any form or by any means, or stored in a database or retrieval system, without the prior written consent of The McGraw-Hill Companies, Inc., including, but not limited to, in any network or other electronic storage or transmission, or broadcast for distance learning.

Some ancillaries, including electronic and print components, may not be available to customers outside the United States.

This book is printed on acid-free paper.

1 2 3 4 5 6 7 8 9 0 DOC/DOC 0 9

ISBN 978-0-07-353325-4
MHID 0-07-353325-4

Editor in Chief: *Michael Ryan*
Editorial Director: *Beth Mejia*
Publisher: *David Patterson*
Sponsoring Editor: *John Kindler*
Developmental Editor: *Adam Beroud*
Editorial Coordinator: *Jesse Hassenger*
Marketing Manager: *Allison Jones*
Project Manager: *Meghan Durko*
Production Supervisor: *Tandra Jorgensen*
Designer: *Laurie Entringer*
Cover Image: *Paul Tearle, Getty Images*
Media Project Manager: *Thomas Brierly*
Photo Researcher: *Kim Adams, Roaring Lion Image Research LLC*
Compositor: *10/12 Palatino by Laserwords*
Printer: *45# New Era Matte by R. R. Donnelley & Sons Company*

Library of Congress Cataloging-in-Publication Data

Krasny, Michael
  Sound ideas / Maggie Sokolik and Michael Krasny.—1st ed.
    p. cm.
  ISBN-13: 978-0-07-353325-4 (acid-free paper)
  ISBN-10: 0-07-353325-4 (acid-free paper)
 1.   College readers. 2. English language—Rhetoric—Problems, exercises, etc. I. Krasny, Michael, 1944- II. Title.
    PE1417.S6135 2008
    808′ .0427—dc22

                                                                                    2008043944

www.mhhe.com

About the Authors

Michael Krasny earned his BA and MA from Ohio University and his PhD from the University of Wisconsin. He is a professor of English at San Francisco State University and a widely published critic and scholar who hosts *Forum*, a daily news and public affairs radio program for KQED Radio, the San Francisco National Public Radio affiliate. This award-winning program can also be heard on Sirius/XM Radio, i-Tunes, and on the Internet at www.kqed.org. Krasny is the author of *Off Mike: A Memoir of Talk Radio and Liferary Life* (Stanford University Press, 2008) and has taught at Stanford, the University of California, and the University of San Francisco, as well as in the Fulbright Institutes. He has taught a wide range of literature courses in modern and contemporary periods, as well as literary theory, literature, and psychoanalysis. For many years, he taught composition and writing courses and was a composition coordinator who authored a text for the California State University system on composition skills. He produced a course for The Teaching Company (available on DVD, audio, and with accompanying two volumes on *Short Story Masterpieces*). A veteran interviewer for nationally broadcasted *City Arts and Lectures*, Krasny resides in Northern California.

M.E. (Maggie) Sokolik received her BA from Reed College in Portland, Oregon and her MA and PhD from UCLA. She taught at several universities including MIT, Harvard, and Texas A&M before settling in at the University of California, Berkeley, where she taught composition, digital storytelling, and composition pedagogy in College Writing Programs for 14 years. In 2006 she took over direction of the university's Technical Communication Program within the College of Engineering's Technology and Leadership Studies program. She currently teaches engineering education and engineering ethics and supervises technical communication courses. A textbook author and journal editor, Sokolik is especially concerned with multilingual writers' issues, and writes and speaks widely on topics concerning English language education. She lives with her husband and cats near Berkeley, California.

Contents

Chapter 3   Ideas about Education: Stories from School   218

Preface

Sound Ideas has as its main premise that reading goes beyond the written text. Reading involves interpreting texts of many sorts—not just the fiction, non-fiction, and poetry of the typical anthology, but also visual texts, the spoken word, and more. The differing learning styles of students and teaching styles of instructors help direct this approach: students learn best when exposed to information that is presented in a variety ways.

Sound Ideas also has as its premise that today's classroom may look different from the classroom of fifty years ago, or even just a decade ago. Students have a wide variety of linguistic backgrounds and types of preparation for college-level studies. This is not an obstacle to overcome, but a wealth of experience to explore. *Sound Ideas* strives to address the needs as well as the interests of an increasingly diverse student population, while maintaining strong connections to a history of ideas.

Main Features

A Multimedia Approach to Text.   The readings in *Sound Ideas* are complemented by links to suggested audio texts, primarily from San Francisco's National Public Radio station KQED's *Forum* with Michael Krasny, and by visual texts that are closely related to the themes. Since today's students are keenly attuned to both visual and audio texts, this multimedia approach will appeal to a variety of learners and enrich their understanding of the readings. As Eric H. Hobson* writes in "Seeing Writing in a Visual World," "Acknowledging the connections between visual and verbal literacy is the first step. Enacting that understanding in the classroom follows logically, yet as we know from our own experiences in making this perceptual transition, engaging a process of change is not easy." Our hopes for this book are that both the instructor and student become more fluent at discussing and writing about visual, spoken, and written texts.

Thematic Structure.   *Sound Ideas* is organized into ten theme-based chapters. These themes, such as gender, education, and war, do not present oppositions (i.e., pros and cons of issues) but rather multilayered and complex views of interconnected ideas. The goal in presenting themes in this way is to help students think more deeply about complex issues, and to move beyond the idea of merely agreeing or disagreeing with an idea.

Creative Thinking.   Critical thinking is at the core of the questions following each text. However, we hope to push students beyond the merely critical, and

*Eric H. Hobson, "Seeing Writing in a Visual World," in *ARTiculating: Teaching Writing in a Visual World,* Pamela B. Childres, Eric H. Hobson, and Joan A. Mullin, Eds. Portsmouth, NH: Boynton/Cook Publishers, 1998.

into drawing unique connections between readings, audio texts, and visual texts. In the same vein, our goal is to ask students to think not only critically about what they read, but also creatively in recognizing and evaluating ideas that we may not even have intended in putting these texts together. To this end, creative options for writing are provided at the end of each chapter. In addition, questions for discussion often ask students to synthesize information from various sources and media, encouraging them to think beyond the text at hand.

Concern for Multilingual Readers.   Most textbooks written for composition courses fall into two categories: those intended for native speakers of English in "traditional" classrooms, and those intended for English as a second language speakers, either in separate ESL programs or ESL courses within composition programs. However, as most instructors will report, these categories are less apparent in today's colleges and universities.

Many so-called traditional composition classes contain a blend of native, nonnative, and Generation 1.5 speakers.* Not only do these speakers come from a variety of linguistic backgrounds, they also come with varying levels of academic preparation, cultural understanding, and knowledge of academic expectations. As a result, instructors often find that the "tried and true" readings and assignments are not as effective as they once were. These students benefit from the multimedia approach taken here. Additionally, we have chosen texts that will appeal to students from a broad variety of backgrounds. We also offer some in-text support in defining cultural concepts that may be unfamiliar to students from different cultural or educational backgrounds. In addition, at least one cultural question is included in the questions that follow each text, encouraging students from all backgrounds to consider the multicultural implications of the text. These questions are not directed at particular groups of students—that is, the intention is not to spotlight students from various cultures as representatives of a particular cultural group or experience, but to ask all students to reflect on how culture and personal experience have informed their understanding of certain concepts.

Reading-Writing Connections.   *Sound Ideas* also includes student discussion and writing activities that focus on the production and analysis of different types of texts, including visual texts, as well as the traditional composition.

Organization

Each of the ten thematic chapters includes texts in the following genres or formats: nonfiction, fiction, poetry, graphic fiction, visual texts, and links to audio texts. Each text, in turn, concludes with follow-up questions broken into three categories: (1) *Questions for Discussion and Writing*, (2) *On Technique and Style*, and (3) *Cultural Questions*. Each chapter also begins with an essay introducing its theme and concludes with *Connections*, questions that ask readers to compare

---

*Generation 1.5 refers to nonnative speakers who migrate into English-speaking environments during their early K–12 school years, and receive some or all of their K–12 education in English-speaking schools. The academic and linguistic needs of these students have been shown to be different than those of ESL or native speakers.

and contrast the texts in the chapter, and *For Writing*, writing topics broken out by creative, narrative/expository, argumentative, and research choices.

Resources for Students and Instructors

Forum. The discussion incorporates excerpts and interviews, audio selections aired on a live, daily talk program, *Forum*, produced at KQED radio, Northern California's National Public Radio affiliate. An award-winning broadcast, which includes the nation's largest and most multicultural and diverse local public radio listenership, *Forum* features many leading thinkers, policy makers, writers, and artists in spontaneous and unedited discussions of current issues and events, and it includes a live listener call-in segment. The addition of audio from a live interactive talk-radio program will enhance the opportunity for students to confront major ideas by hearing them discussed in a format with which many are acquainted and at ease. It will provide the additional benefit of their hearing and absorbing high levels of rhetorically spoken English. Often students who grapple unsuccessfully with ideas and content in a text gain greater success and cognition when they can listen to ideas being discussed and analyzed. All students of English, regardless of their backgrounds or abilities, read and write as well as speak better with the benefit of hearing spoken English. Hearing ideas discussed will provide an excellent tool for instructors to facilitate classroom discussions.

Instructor's Manual. The instructor's manual for *Sound Ideas* offers information on how to use the audio materials effectively in conjunction with the readings, ways to develop assignments that will address the needs of a diverse student population, and ideas for writing assignments that go beyond the standard expository essay. This information will include ways to scaffold assignments and meaningfully integrate audiovisual materials, with the aim of improving the student success rate.

Companion Website. A companion website (www.mhhe.com/soundideas1e), addressing both student and instructor needs, and supplying additional materials supplements the text. Special focus in the instructor's materials is placed on how to integrate multimedia texts into the composition classroom successfully, and how to address the needs of multilingual readers.

Acknowledgments

The authors would like to thank the following reviewers whose suggestions and comments helped make this a better text: Michelle Adkerson, Nashville State Community College; Elisabeth Bloomer, Virginia Polytechnic Institute and State University; Dominic Delli Carpini, York College of Pennsylvania; Marc DiPaolo, Alvernia College; Andrew Fleck, San Jose State University; David Kaloustian, Bowie State University; Amy Lawlor, Pasadena City College; Agnetta Mendoza, Nashville State Community College; Anthony Mulholland, College of Southern Nevada; John Padgett, Brevard College; Linda Rosekrans, SUNY Cortland; Lisa Schuchter, Naugatuck Valley Community College; Greg Underwood, Pearl River Community College; Scott Warnock, Drexel University; Barbara Witucki, Utica College; Joseph Zeppetello, Marist College.

Introduction

Dear Reader,

While the art of reading is as old as the printed word, the act of reading is fresh each time we undertake it. As readers, we bring our attitudes, our moods, and our experiences to the act of reading each time we sit down with a text. Through reading, reacting, and thinking, we develop *sound ideas*.

Of course, "reading" is more than processing words on a page. Reading is also a multimedia experience. Because many readers benefit greatly from hearing ideas discussed, we include audio content, including discussions from *Forum*, a feature of KQED, San Francisco's National Public Radio affiliate and the country's most popular and listened to public radio station. You will find these audio programs complement and enhance your understanding of the readings and images found in this book.

Readers also benefit from seeing photographs or illustrations of ideas. You will find an arresting selection of photographs and illustrations that will highlight the themes of the readings in the book. You will also find selections from graphic novels, which bring image and story together in fresh ways.

The ideas generated by the text, the photos, the graphics, and the sounds are relevant to our lives, timely, contemporary and often exciting and controversial, worth exploring and working through for themselves in prose composition. Embedded in *Sound Ideas* are the ideals of a well-rounded education, one that connects you to the world you are in.

In the process of understanding the texts we have assembled here—whether nonfiction, fiction, poetry, audio programs, or images—we hope you will bring your own experiences and knowledge to bear on your understanding.

In this process, we hope you will . . .

. . . understand.

The complexity of a single topic goes beyond being "for" or "against" an idea. Sound ideas are by nature multifaceted, and we chose texts, images, and audio programs that we hope illustrate this idea.

. . . react.

Think seriously about what you have read, and how you feel about it. Did it ring true for you? Seem completely alien? Think beyond whether you enjoyed reading a particular text, seeing an image, or listening to an interview or panel discussion. Consider the elements of each that engaged, or failed to engage you.

. . . discuss.

Sound ideas are refined through the process of discussion. Discussion is not just a way to show you have understood the contents of what you have read or listened to; it is a way for you to understand more fully the ideas behind the words.

. . . write.

The details of ideas are often worked out in writing. In fact, many writers claim that they don't know what they think until they write it down. Find ways to respond to these selections in writing—whether informally in a journal, or formally through class assignments. You will find that the act of writing is intricately tied to the acts of reading, viewing, and listening.

As you think through the ideas and respond to what you hear and read, you will find a clarity of thought that initiates, and even ensures clarity in your own writing.

Synthesizing what you learn from reading and listening involves understanding the past and anticipating your own future. Situate yourself within the reading, visual, and audio selections. This will help you not only understand the ideas of others, but also understand yourself. In the process, we hope you discover your own sound ideas while experiencing these different types of texts.

Sincerely,

Michael Krasny, San Francisco State University and KQED Radio

Maggie Sokolik, University of California, Berkeley

THE READING-WRITING PROCESS

Reading and writing go hand-in-hand. At the end of each chapter in this text, you will find several topics for writing, or your instructor may give you other writing assignments.

The assignments in this text are divided into four categories: creative choices, narrative/expository choices, rhetorical choices, and research choices.

Creative Choices

Writing creatively about what you read can help you form important connections between your own experience and the experiences written about by the authors in the chapters. Writing in a journal, writing poetry, or even drawing images of the ideas you encounter in your reading can help refine your thinking. Your instructor may not ask for these types of assignments for your class work, but nonetheless, they may be ways for you to find a connection between reading and writing.

Narrative/Expository Choices

These choices are the more "traditional" responses to reading, often asking you to take a position with respect to the ideas you find in a reading, and back up your position with clear, concrete examples and argumentation.

Rhetorical Choices

Fashioning an argument or a position, persuading your reader of your point of view, is fundamental to good expository and effective critical writing. Argumentation and persuasion is, in fact, a rhetorical model for structuring your ideas, as are such rhetorical approaches as analysis, illustration, classification, definition, comparison and contrast, and diction and tone. You will have a separate set of questions following each of the selections that are designed to help you organize your ideas around argument and the use of various rhetorical methods of organization.

Research Choices

These writing choices ask you to go beyond what is found in the book and investigate a question or idea further. Research, in this case, however, does not mean just a trip to the library or some searching on the Internet. It might entail interviewing those with different experiences than yours, or observing behaviors or objects in your own environment.

The following selections expand on the idea of academic reading and writing, and can help guide you in your efforts to become a successful reader and writer.

READING AND THINKING

The beginning of good writing comes from critical reading and thinking about ideas. Critical reading and thinking means an *active* participation in the process—considering the strengths and weaknesses of ideas, relating them to your own observations or experience, and questioning the completeness or truth of what you've been presented.

In the first reading, the authors of the classic text *How to Read a Book* talk about the critical reading process. This text also talks about different kinds of reading, and how each serves a different purpose. As you read this selection, think about your own reading process, and how it may or may not fit in with the process the authors Adler and Van Doren describe.

The Activity and Art of Reading

Mortimer J. Adler and Charles Van Doren

Mortimer J. Adler was an author, educator, and philosopher. He was born in New York City in 1902 and moved to California, where he lived much of his life. He died in 2001. Adler wrote over fifty books, including How to Read a Book *(1940, revised 1972) (from which the following excerpt is taken);* The American Testament *(1975);* The Common Sense of Politics *(1971);* Aristotle for Everyone *(1978);* Ten Philosophical Mistakes *(1985); and* Art, the Arts and the Great Ideas *(1994). Adler was the editor of the* Encyclopedia Britannica, *and also editor of the sixty-volume* The Great Books of the Western World. *He helped create the Great Books reading program, a book discussion program with chapters throughout the United States in which participants read and discuss classic texts. He was a professor at several universities including Columbia University and the University of Chicago. He received his PhD before getting a high school diploma. Adler was also the founder of the Institute for Philosophical Research and was instrumental in founding the Aspen Institute, an organization that engages leaders in business, academics, and politics.*

   Charles Van Doren *(born 1926) is an American intellectual and former TV quiz show contestant. In the late 1950s, Van Doren was involved in a scandal and confessed that the show's producers had given him the answers, an event depicted in the film* Quiz Show *(1994). Van Doren is the son of Pulitzer Prize–winning poet Mark Van Doren and novelist and writer Dorothy Van Doren. He earned a bachelor's degree in liberal arts from St. John's College in Annapolis, Maryland, and a master's degree in astrophysics and a doctorate in English, both at Columbia University. He became a professor at Columbia University as well, but after the scandal, Van Doren resigned from his position. He eventually became an editor of the* Encyclopedia Britannica *and the author of several books.* A History of Knowledge *(1991) is probably his most famous. In this, and other older selections in this section, the authors use the generic "he" to refer to all readers and writers. This is not current usage, and in your own writing, you should find ways to avoid referring to all people as "he" or "men."*

Reprinted with the permission of Simon & Schuster, Inc., from *How to Read a Book*, Revised Edition by Mortimer J. Adler and Charles Van Doren. Copyright 1940, and renewed © 1967, by Mortimer J. Adler. Copyright © 1972 by Mortimer J. Adler and Charles Van Doren.

The Goals of Reading:
Reading for Information and Reading for Understanding

You have a mind. Now let us suppose that you also have a book that you want to read. The book consists of language written by someone for the sake of communicating something to you. Your success in reading it is determined by the extent to which you receive everything the writer intended to communicate.

   That, of course, is too simple. The reason is that there are two possible relations between your mind and the book, not just one. These two relations are exemplified by two different experiences that you can have in reading your book.

   There is the book; and here is your mind. As you go through the pages, either you understand perfectly everything the author has to say or you do not. If you do, you may have gained information, but you could not have increased your understanding. If the book is completely intelligible to you from start to finish, then the author and you are as two minds in the same mold. The symbols on the page merely express the common understanding you had before you met.

Let us take our second alternative. You do not understand the book perfectly. Let us even assume—what unhappily is not always true—that you understand enough to know that you do not understand it all. You know the book has more to say than you understand and hence that it contains something that can increase your understanding.

What do you do then? You can take the book to someone else who, you think, can read better than you, and have him explain the parts that trouble you. ("He" may be a living person or another book—a commentary or textbook.) Or you may decide that what is over your head is not worth bothering about, that you understand enough. In either case, you are not doing the job of reading that the book requires.

That is done in only one way. Without external help of any sort, you go to work on the book. With nothing but the power of your own mind, you operate on the symbols before you in such a way that you gradually lift yourself from *a state of understanding less to one of understanding more.* Such elevation, accomplished by the mind working on a book, is highly skilled reading, the kind of reading that a book which challenges your understanding deserves.

Thus we can roughly define what we mean by the art of reading as follows: the process whereby a mind, with nothing to operate on but the symbols of the readable matter, and with no help from outside,* elevates itself by the power of its own operations. The mind passes from understanding less to understanding more. The skilled operations that cause this to happen are the various acts that constitute the art of reading.

To pass from understanding less to understanding more by your own intellectual effort in reading is something like pulling yourself up by your bootstraps. It certainly feels that way. It is a major exertion. Obviously, it is a more active kind of reading than you have done before, entailing not only more varied activity but also much more skill in the performance of the various acts required. Obviously, too, the things that are usually regarded as more difficult to read, and hence as only for the better reader, are those that are more likely to deserve and demand this kind of reading.

The distinction between reading for information and reading for understanding is deeper than this. Let us try to say more about it. We will have to consider both goals of reading because the line between what is readable in one way and what must be read in the other is often hazy. To the extent that we can keep these two goals of reading distinct, we can employ the word "reading" in two distinct senses.

The first sense is the one in which we speak of ourselves as reading newspapers, magazines, or anything else that, according to our skill and

---

*There is one kind of situation in which it is appropriate to ask for outside help in reading a difficult book. This exception is discussed in Chapter 18 [Adler and Van Doren's note].

talents, is at once thoroughly intelligible to us. Such things may increase our store of information, but they cannot improve our understanding, for our understanding was equal to them before we started. Otherwise, we would have felt the shock of puzzlement and perplexity that comes from getting in over our depth—that is, if we were both alert and honest.

The second sense is the one in which a person tries to read something that at first he does not completely understand. Here the thing to be read is initially better or higher than the reader. The writer is communicating something that can increase the reader's understanding. Such communication between unequals must be possible, or else one person could never learn from another, either through speech or writing. Here by "learning" is meant understanding more, not remembering more information that has the same degree of intelligibility as other information you already possess.

There is clearly no difficulty of an intellectual sort about gaining new information in the course of reading if the new facts are of the same sort as those you already know. A person who knows some of the facts of American history and understands them in a certain light can readily acquire by reading, in the first sense, more such facts and understand them in the same light. But suppose he is reading a history that seeks not merely to give him some more facts but also to throw a new and perhaps more revealing light on *all* the facts he knows. Suppose there is greater understanding available here than he possessed before he started to read. If he can manage to acquire that greater understanding, he is reading in the second sense. He has indeed elevated himself by his activity, though indirectly, of course, the elevation was made possible by the writer who had something to teach him.

What are the conditions under which this kind of reading—reading for understanding—takes place? There are two. First, there is *initial inequality in understanding.* The writer must be "superior" to the reader in understanding, and his book must convey in readable form the insights he possesses and his potential readers lack. Second, *the reader must be able to overcome this inequality in some degree,* seldom perhaps fully, but always approaching equality with the writer. To the extent that equality is approached, clarity of communication is achieved.

In short, we can learn only from our "betters." We must know who they are and how to learn from them. The person who has this sort of knowledge possesses the art of reading in the sense with which we are especially concerned in this book. Everyone who can read at all probably has some ability to read in this way. But all of us, without exception, can learn to read better and gradually gain more by our efforts through applying them to more rewarding materials.

We do not want to give the impression that facts, leading to increased information, and insights, leading to increased understanding, are always easy to distinguish. And we would admit that sometimes a mere recital of

facts can itself lead to greater understanding. The point we want to emphasize here is that this book is about the art of reading for the sake of increased
understanding. Fortunately, if you learn to do that, reading for information will
usually take care of itself.

Of course, there is still another goal of reading, besides gaining information and understanding, and that is entertainment. However, this book will not
be much concerned with reading for entertainment. It is the least demanding
kind of reading, and it requires the least amount of effort. Furthermore, there
are no rules for it. Everyone who knows how to read at all can read for entertainment if he wants to.

In fact, any book that can be read for understanding or information can
probably be read for entertainment as well, just as a book that is capable of
increasing our understanding can also be read purely for the information it
contains. (This proposition cannot be reversed: it is *not* true that *every* book
that can be read for entertainment can also be read for understanding.) Nor
do we wish to urge you never to read a good book for entertainment. The
point is, if you wish to read a good book for understanding, we believe we
can help you. Our subject, then, is the art of reading good books when understanding is the aim you have in view.

Reading as Learning:
The Difference Between Learning by Instruction and Learning by Discovery

Getting more information is learning, and so is coming to understand what
you did not understand before. But there is an important difference between
these two kinds of learning.

To be informed is to know simply that something is the case. To be
enlightened is to know, in addition, what it is all about: why it is the case,
what its connections are with other facts, in what respects it is the same, in
what respects it is different, and so forth.

This distinction is familiar in terms of the differences between being able
to remember something and being able to explain it. If you remember what
an author says, you have learned something from reading him. If what he
says is true, you have even learned something about the world. But whether
it is a fact about the book or a fact about the world that you have learned,
you have gained nothing but information if you have exercised only your
memory. You have not been enlightened. Enlightenment is achieved only
when, in addition to knowing what an author says, you know what he means
and why he says it.

It is true, of course, that you should be able to remember what the author
said as well as know what he meant. Being informed is prerequisite to being
enlightened. The point, however, is not to stop at being informed.

Montaigne speaks of "an abecedarian ignorance that precedes knowledge, and a doctoral ignorance that comes after it." The first is the ignorance of those who, not knowing their ABC's, cannot read at all. The second is the ignorance of those who have misread many books. They are, as Alexander Pope rightly calls them, bookful blockheads, ignorantly read. There have always been literate ignoramuses who have read too widely and not well. The Greeks had a name for such a mixture of learning and folly which might be applied to the bookish but poorly read of all ages. They are all *sophomores.*

To avoid this error—the error of assuming that to be widely read and to be well-read are the same thing—we must consider a certain distinction in types of learning. This distinction has a significant bearing on the whole business of reading and its relation to education generally.

In the history of education, men have often distinguished between learning by instruction and learning by discovery. Instruction occurs when one person teaches another through speech or writing. We can, however, gain knowledge without being taught. If this were not the case, and every teacher had to be taught what he in turn teaches others, there would be no beginning in the acquisition of knowledge. Hence, there must be discovery—the process of learning something by research, by investigation, or by reflection, without being taught.

Discovery stands to instruction as learning without a teacher stands to learning through the help of one. In both cases, the activity of learning goes on in the one who learns. It would be a mistake to suppose that discovery is active learning and instruction passive. There is no inactive learning, just as there is no inactive reading.

This is so true, in fact, that a better way to make the distinction clear is to call instruction "aided discovery." Without going into learning theory as psychologists conceive it, it is obvious that teaching is a very special art, sharing with only two other arts—agriculture and medicine—an exceptionally important characteristic. A doctor may do many things for his patient, but in the final analysis it is the patient himself who must get well—grow in health. The farmer does many things for his plants or animals, but in the final analysis it is they that must grow in size and excellence. Similarly, although the teacher may help his student in many ways, it is the student himself who must do the learning. Knowledge must grow in his mind if learning is to take place.

The difference between learning by instruction and learning by discovery—or, as we would prefer to say, between aided and unaided discovery—is primarily a difference in the materials on which the learner works. When he is being instructed—discovering with the help of a teacher—the learner acts on something communicated to him. He performs operations on discourse, written or oral. He learns by acts of reading or listening. Note here the close relation between reading and listening. If we ignore the minor differences between these two ways of receiving communication, we can say that reading and listening are the same art—the art of being taught. When, however, the learner proceeds without the help of any sort of teacher, the operations of learning are performed on nature or the world rather than on discourse. The rules of such learning constitute the art of unaided discovery. If we use the word "reading" loosely, we can say that discovery—strictly, unaided discovery—is the art of reading nature or the world, as instruction (being taught, or aided discovery) is the art of reading books or, to include listening, of learning from discourse.

What about thinking? If by "thinking" we mean the use of our minds to gain knowledge or understanding, and if learning by discovery and learning by instruction exhaust the ways of gaining knowledge, then thinking must take place during both of these two activities. We must think in the course of reading and listening, just as we must think in the course of research. Naturally, the kinds of thinking are different—as different as the two ways of learning are.

The reason why many people regard thinking as more closely associated with research and unaided discovery than with being taught is that they suppose reading and listening to be relatively effortless. It is probably true that one does less thinking when one reads for information or entertainment than when one is undertaking to discover something. Those are the less active sorts of reading. But it is not true of the more active reading—the effort to understand. No one who has done this sort of reading would say it can be done thoughtlessly.

Thinking is only one part of the activity of learning. One must also use one's senses and imagination. One must observe, and remember, and construct imaginatively what cannot be observed. There is, again, a tendency to stress the role of these activities in the process of unaided discovery and to forget or minimize their place in the process of being taught through reading or listening. For example, many people assume that though a poet must use his imagination in writing a poem, they do not have to use their imagination in reading it. The art of reading, in short, includes all of the same skills that are involved in the art of unaided discovery: keenness of observation, readily available memory, range of imagination, and, of course, an intellect trained in analysis and reflection. The reason for this is that reading in this sense is discovery, too—although with help instead of without it.

Present and Absent Teachers

We have been proceeding as if reading and listening could both be treated as learning from teachers. To some extent that is true. Both are ways of being instructed, and for both one must be skilled in the art of being taught. Listening to a course of lectures, for example, is in many respects like reading a book; and listening to a poem is like reading it. Many of the rules to be formulated in this book apply to such experiences. Yet there is good reason to place primary emphasis on reading, and let listening become a secondary concern. The reason is that listening is learning from a teacher who is present—a living teacher—while reading is learning from one who is absent.

If you ask a living teacher a question, he will probably answer you. If you are puzzled by what he says, you can save yourself the trouble of thinking by asking him what he means. If, however, you ask a book a question, *you must answer it yourself.* In this respect a book is like nature or the world. When you question it, it answers you only to the extent that you do the work of thinking and analysis yourself.

This does not mean, of course, that if the living teacher answers your question, you have no further work. That is so only if the question is simply one of fact. But if you are seeking an explanation, you have to understand it or nothing has been explained to you. Nevertheless, with the living teacher available to you, you are given a lift in the direction of understanding him, as you are not when the teacher's words in a book are all you have to go by.

Students in school often read difficult books with the help and guidance of teachers. But for those of us who are not in school, and indeed also for those of us who are when we try to read books that are not required or assigned, our continuing education depends mainly on books alone, read without a teacher's help. Therefore if we are disposed to go on learning and discovering, we must know how to make books teach us well. That, indeed, is the primary goal of this book.

QUESTIONS FOR DISCUSSION AND WRITING

1. The authors claim that if you read and understand everything "perfectly" then you have not increased your understanding. Explain this claim. Do you agree? Can you give examples from your own experience?
2. According to the authors, what does it mean to be "enlightened"? How is the Montaigne quotation related to the idea of enlightenment?
3. What do the authors mean by the phrase "active reading"? Are you an active reader? What activities do you think might help your reading process (for example, outlining, note taking, etc.)?
4. What is the relationship between imagination and reading, according to the authors? In your own reading, do you find you use your imagination and creativity? How?

ON TECHNIQUE AND STYLE

1. Do you find the authors' style simple or complex? Give two or three examples from the reading to support your claim.
2. How do the authors organize this part of their book? Is it effective? What other options did they have?

CULTURAL QUESTION

1. The authors argue that a teacher can help students, but the student "must do the learning." What do you think of this idea? How do you see your role as a student with respect to your instructor? What role does a teacher play in learning? Is there a cultural component to this attitude—that is, how does the role of teacher vary in different cultures you know about?

WRITING AND REVISION

Although there are as many opinions about writing as there are writers, nearly all writers will agree that three ingredients are needed for success: practice, persistence, and revision. Just as no tennis player expects to ace every serve, and no singer expects to sing every note perfectly every time, writers grow to expect that some of their efforts will not be elegant or successful. It is through practice and revision that meaning becomes clear in writing.

This section is intended to help you consider some issues involved in writing and revision. However, it is not a comprehensive guide to crafting good essays. Your instructor may have assigned a style guide such as the well-known Strunk and White's *The Elements of Style,* or Joseph Williams's *Style: Ten Lessons in Clarity and Grace.* Alternatively, you may be using a handbook, which will give detailed information about writing essays—from drafting to revision to proper citation of sources. If English isn't your first language, you may want to refer to grammar guides or idiom guides in addition to the texts assigned by your instructor. All of these tools will help you become a more confident writer.

And confidence is part of the battle of writing—self-doubt and perfectionism often prevent newer writers from enjoying the act of crafting an argument or narrative. The following reading makes such a claim. The author, with her bold title "Everybody Is Talented, Original, and Has Something Important to Say," takes a position about talent and persistence that you may applaud, or you may not agree with. As you read this selection, think about how your own creativity has grown or been silenced since you were a child. How have teachers or family affected your attitude toward writing?

Everybody Is Talented, Original and Has Something Important to Say

Brenda Ueland

Brenda Ueland was born in Minneapolis, Minnesota, in 1891. For a lot of her adult life she lived in New York, working as a freelance writer. After returning to Minneapolis, she taught writing in various settings. She reported that she was born on Lake Calhoun "in a happier time before automobiles." Ueland was the author of two books, If You Want to Write *(1938), and* Me: A Memoir *(1939), and as well as many articles and short stories. She was knighted by the king of Norway and set an international swimming record for swimmers over eighty years old. She lived by two rules: tell the truth, and never do anything you don't want to do. She died in 1985 at the age of ninety-three. The following essay appears in her book* If You Want to Write *(Graywolf Press, 1987); however, it was written in 1938.*

I have been writing a long time and have learned some things, not only from my own long hard work, but from a writing class I had for three years. In this class were all kinds of people: prosperous and poor, stenographers, housewives, salesmen, cultivated people and little servant girls who had never been to high school, timid people and bold ones, slow and quick ones.

This is what I learned: that everybody is talented, original and has something important to say.

And it may comfort you to know that the only people you might suspect of *not* having talent are those who write very easily and glibly, and without inhibition or pain, skipping gaily through a novel in a week or so. These are the only ones who did not seem to improve much, to go forward. You cannot get much out of them. They give up working presently and drop out. But these, too, were talented underneath. I am sure of that. It is just that they did not break through the shell of easy glibness to what is true and alive underneath,—just as most people must break through a shell of timidity and strain.

Everybody Is Talented

Everybody is talented because everybody who is human has something to express. Try *not* expressing anything for twenty-four hours and see what happens. You will nearly burst. You will want to write a long letter or draw a picture or sing, or make a dress or a garden. Religious men used to go into the wilderness and impose silence on themselves, but it was so that they would talk to God and nobody else. But they expressed something: that is to say they had thoughts welling up in them and the thoughts went out to someone, whether silently or aloud.

Writing or painting is putting these thoughts on paper. Music is singing them. That is all there is to it.

Everybody Is Original

Everybody is original, if he tells the truth, if he speaks from himself. But it must be from his *true* self and not from the self he thinks he *should* be. Jennings at Johns Hopkins, who knows more about heredity and the genes and chromosomes than any man in the world, says that no individual is exactly like any other individual, that no two identical persons have ever existed. Consequently, if you speak or write from *yourself* you cannot help being original.

So remember these two things: you are talented and you are original. Be sure of that. I say this because self-trust is one of the very most important things in writing and I will tell why later.

This creative power and imagination is in everyone and so is the need to express it, i.e., to share it with others. But what happens to it?

It is very tender and sensitive, and it is usually drummed out of people early in life by criticism (so-called "helpful criticism" is often the worst kind), by teasing, jeering, rules, prissy teachers, critics, and all those unloving people who forget that the letter killeth and the spirit giveth life.* Sometimes I think of life as a process where everybody is discouraging and taking everybody else down a peg or two.

You know how all children have this creative power. You have all seen things like this: the little girls in our family used to give play after play. They wrote the plays themselves (they were very good plays too, interesting, exciting and funny). They acted in them. They made the costumes themselves, beautiful, effective and historically accurate, contriving them in the most ingenious way out of attic junk and their mothers' best dresses. They constructed the stage and theater by carrying chairs, moving the piano, carpentering. They printed the tickets and sold them. They made their own advertising. They drummed up the audience, throwing out a drag-net for all the hired girls, dogs, babies, mothers, neighbors within a radius of a mile or so. For what reward? A few pins and pennies.

Yet these small ten-year-olds were working with feverish energy and endurance. (A production took about two days.) If they had worked that hard for school it probably would have killed them. They were working for nothing but fun, for that glorious inner excitement. It was the creative power working in them. It was hard, hard work but there was no pleasure or excitement like it and it was something never forgotten.

But this joyful, imaginative, impassioned energy dies out of us very young. Why? Because we do not see that it is great and important. Because we let dry obligation take its place. Because we don't respect it in ourselves and keep it alive by using it. And because we don't keep it alive in others by *listening* to them.

For when you come to think of it, the only way to love a person is not, as the stereotyped Christian notion is, to coddle them and bring them soup when they are sick, but by listening to them and seeing and believing in the god, in the poet, in them. For by doing this, you keep the god and the poet alive and make it flourish.

*This phrase is a reference to 2 Corinthians 3:6.

How does the creative impulse die in us? The English teacher who wrote fiercely on the margin of your theme in blue pencil: "Trite, rewrite," helped to kill it. Critics kill it, your family. Families are great murderers of the creative impulse, particularly husbands. Older brothers sneer at younger brothers and kill it. There is that American pastime known as "kidding,"—with the result that everyone is ashamed and hang-dog about showing the slightest enthusiasm or passion or sincere feeling about anything. But I will tell more about that later.

You have noticed how teachers, critics, parents and other know-it-alls, when they see you have written something, become at once long-nosed and finicking and go through it gingerly sniffing out the flaws. AHA! a misspelled word! as though Shakespeare could spell! As though spelling, grammar and what you learn in a book about rhetoric has anything to do with freedom and the imagination!

A friend of mine spoke of books that are dedicated like this: "To my wife, by whose helpful criticism . . ." and so on. He said the dedication should really read: "To my wife. If it had not been for her continual criticism and persistent nagging doubt as to my ability, this book would have appeared in *Harper's* instead of *The Hardware Age.*"

So often I come upon articles written by critics of the very highest brow, and by other prominent writers, deploring the attempts of ordinary people to write. The critics rap us savagely on the head with their thimbles, for our nerve. No one but a virtuoso should be allowed to do it. The prominent writers sell funny articles about all the utterly crazy, fatuous, amateurish people who *think* they can write.

Well, that is all right. But this is one of the results: that all people who try to write (and all people long to, which is natural and right) become anxious, timid, contracted, become perfectionists, so terribly afraid that they may put something down that is not as good as Shakespeare.

And so no wonder you don't write and put it off month after month, decade after decade. For when you write, if it is to be any good at all, you must feel free,—free and not anxious. The only good teachers for you are those friends who love you, who think you are interesting, or very important, or wonderfully funny; whose attitude is:

"Tell me more. Tell me all you can. I want to understand more about everything you feel and know and all the changes inside and out of you. Let more come out."

And if you have no such friend,—and you want to write,—well then you must imagine one.

Yes, I hate orthodox criticism. I don't mean great criticism, like that of Matthew Arnold and others, but the usual small niggling, fussy-mussy criticism, which thinks it can improve people by telling them where they are wrong, and results only in putting them in strait-jackets of hesitancy and self-consciousness, and weazening all vision and bravery.

I hate it not so much on my own account, for I have learned at last not to let it balk me. But I hate it because of the potentially shining, gentle, gifted people of all ages, that it snuffs out every year. It is a murderer of talent. And because the most modest and sensitive people are the most talented, having the most imagination and sympathy, these are the very first ones to get killed off. It is the brutal egotists that survive.

Of course, in fairness, I must remind you of this: that we writers are the most lily-livered of all craftsmen. We expect more, for the most peewee efforts, than any other people.

A gifted young woman writes a poem. It is rejected. She does not write another perhaps for two years, perhaps all her life. Think of the patience and love that a tap-dancer or vaudeville acrobat puts into his work. Think of how many times Kreisler* practiced trills. If you write as many words as Kreisler has practiced trills I prophesy that you will win the Nobel Prize in ten years.

But there is an important thing: you must practice not perfunctorily, but with all your intelligence and love, as Kreisler does. A great musician once told me that one should never play a single note without hearing it, feeling that it is true, thinking it beautiful.

And so now you will begin to work at your writing. Remember these things. Work with all your intelligence and love. Work freely and rollickingly as though you were talking to a friend who loves you. Mentally (at least three or four times a day) thumb your nose at all know-it-alls, jeerers, critics, doubters.

And so that you will work long hours and not neglect it, I will now prove that it is important for *yourself* that you do so.

QUESTIONS FOR DISCUSSION AND WRITING

1. Ueland claims, "Everybody is talented, original, and has something important to say." Discuss how this may or may not be true.
2. You are probably taking a course in which your writing will be criticized in some way. How can you follow Ueland's advice to "thumb your nose at all . . . critics" and improve and even enjoy writing? Or, can you?
3. Why does Ueland believe that fear of writing results in perfectionism? Does fear of making mistakes prevent you from writing? What is the result of trying to be perfect in writing? What techniques can a writer use to avoid trying to be "perfect"?
4. Summarize Ueland's point about the value of practice in writing. How can you apply this advice to your own writing habits?

*Fritz Kreisler (1875–1962) was an Austrian violinist and composer, one of the most famous of his day.

ON TECHNIQUE AND STYLE

1. Ueland varies the length of paragraphs here significantly. Look at the short paragraphs. Why are they short? Look at the long paragraphs. Why are they so long?
2. Identify a passage you find effective. What makes it effective, in your opinion?

CULTURAL QUESTION

1. Ueland's prose indicates a particular time and place (we know it was written in the United States in 1938). What words, ideas, or phrases tell us that this piece is from a different time? What in it seems contemporary?

In the following reading, writer William Stafford explains his method of writing. This is a useful exercise for any writer—what exactly do you need to write successfully? Do you need a quiet place, music playing, a computer, a pad of paper? As you read Stafford, think about your own writing methods. Are they different from his? If so, do you find value in any of his suggestions?

A Way of Writing

William Stafford

William Stafford (1914–1993) was born in Hutchinson, Kansas. He received degrees from the University of Kansas and a PhD from the University of Iowa. In 1948 he began teaching at Lewis & Clark College in Portland, Oregon, where he would remain until his retirement. His first book of poetry, West of Your City (1960), *was published when he was forty-six. Through the course of his life, he went on to publish fifty more books. In the following essay, he examines the process of writing and what it means to be a writer. This essay was published in* Field, *No. 2 (Spring 1970), pp. 10–15.*

A writer is not so much someone who has something to say as he is someone who has found a process that will bring about new things he would not have thought of if he had not started to say them. That is, he does not draw on a reservoir; instead, he engages in an activity that brings to him a whole succession of unforeseen stories, poems, essays, plays, laws, philosophies, religions, or—but wait!

Back in school,, from the first when I began to try to write things, I felt this richness. One thing would lead to another; the world would give and give. Now, after twenty years or so of trying, I live by that certain richness, an idea hard to pin, difficult to say, and perhaps offensive to some. For there are strange implications in it.

One implication is the importance of just plain receptivity. When I write, I like to have an interval before me when I am not likely to be interrupted. For me, this means usually the early morning, before others are awake. I get pen and paper, take a glance out the window (often it is dark out there), and wait. It is like fishing. But I do not wait very long, for there is always a nibble—and this is where receptivity comes in. To get started I will accept anything that occurs to me. Something always occurs, of course, to any of us. We can't keep from thinking. Maybe I have to settle for an imme-diate impression: it's cold, or hot, or dark, or bright, or in between! Or—well, the possibilities are endless. If I put down something, that thing will help the next thing come, and I'm off. If I let the process go on, things will occur to me that were not at all in my mind when I started. These things, odd or trivial as they may be, are somehow connected. And if I let them string out, surprising things will happen.

If I let them string out. . . . Along with initial receptivity, then there is another readiness: I must be willing to fail. If I am to keep on writing, I cannot bother to insist on high standards. I must get into action and not let anything stop me, or even slow me much. By "standards" I do not mean "correct-ness"—spelling, punctuation, and so on. These details become mechanical for anyone who writes for a while. I am thinking about such matters as social significance, positive values, consistency, etc. I resolutely disregard these. Something better, greater, is happening! I am following a process that leads so wildly and originally into new territory that no judgment can at the moment be made about values, significance, and so on. I am making something new, something that has not been judged before. Later others—and maybe I myself—will make judgments. Now, I am headlong to discover. Any distrac-tion may harm the creating.

So, receptive, careless of failure, I spin out things on the page. And a wonderful freedom comes. If something occurs to me, it is all right to accept it. It has one justification: it occurs to me. No one else can guide me. I must follow my own weak, wandering, diffident impulses.

A strange bonus happens. At times, without my insisting on it, my writings become coherent; the successive elements that occur to me are clearly related. They lead by themselves to new connections. Sometimes the language, even the syllables that happen along, may start a trend. Sometimes the materials alert me to something waiting in my mind, ready for sustained attention. At such times, I allow myself to be eloquent, or intentional, or for great swoops (treach-erous! not to be trusted!) reasonable. But I do not insist on any of that; for I know that back of my activity there will be the coherence of my self, and that indulgence of my impulses will bring recurrent patterns and meanings again.

This attitude toward the process of writing creatively suggests a problem for me, in terms of what others say. They talk about "skills" in writing. Without denying that I do have experience, wide reading, automatic orthodoxies and maneuvers of various kinds, I still must insist that I am often baffled about what "skill" has to do with the precious little area of confusion when I do not know what I am going to say and then I find out what I am going to say. That precious interval I am unable to bridge by skill. What can I witness about it? It remains mysterious, just as all of us must feel puzzled about how we are so inventive as to be able to talk along through complexities with our friends, not needing to plan what we are going to say, but never stalled for long in our confident forward progress. Skill? If so, it is the skill we all have, something we must have learned before the age of three or four.

A writer is one who has become accustomed to trusting that grace, or luck, or—skill.

Yet another attitude I find necessary: most of what I write, like most of what I say in casual conversation, will not amount to much. Even I will realize, and even at the time, that it is not negotiable. It will be like practice. In conversations I allow myself random remarks—in fact, as I recall, that is the way I learned to talk—so in writing I launch many expendable efforts. A result of this free way of writing is that I am not writing for others, mostly; they will not see the product at all unless the activity eventuates in something that later appears to be worthy. My guide is the self, and its adventuring in the language brings about communication.

This process-rather-than-substance view of writing invites a final, dual reflection:

1. Writers may not be special—sensitive or talented in any usual sense. They are simply engaged in sustained use of a language skill we all have. Their "creations" come about through confident reliance on stray impulses that will, with trust, find occasional patterns that are satisfying.

2. But writing itself is one of the great, free human activities. There is scope for individuality, and elation, and discovery, in writing. For the person who follows with trust and forgiveness what occurs to him, the world remains always ready and deep, an inexhaustible environment, with the combined vividness of an actuality and flexibility of a dream. Working back and forth between experience and thought, writers have more than space and time can offer. They have the whole unexplored realm of human vision.

QUESTIONS FOR DISCUSSION AND WRITING

1. What is Stafford's main point? Do you agree with his point of view about writing?
2. What in Stafford's argument do you find consoling? What worries you?

3. What is Stafford's claim about form (e.g., punctuation, spelling, etc.)? Do you agree? Do you find that this echoes your own writing process?
4. What does Stafford have to say about skill? Do you agree?
5. Are there any pieces of advice Stafford gives that you will try in your own writing process? Which ones?
6. In what ways do you see Stafford and Ueland in agreement? Where might they disagree?

ON TECHNIQUE AND STYLE

1. Does this reading seem tightly organized, or more "loose" in its approach? Give specific examples from the text to support your opinion.
2. What is the *tone* of this piece? Optimistic? Depressing? Funny? Serious? Again, give specific examples showing this tone.

CULTURAL QUESTION

1. Stafford claims that writing is one of the "great, free human activities." What role does writing play, in your experience, in cultures outside the U.S. context? Is writing universally a great activity?

In a college composition class, you are often asked to do specific types of writing, frequently analyses, or critical analyses, in which you respond in some way to a piece of writing. Students often find this type of writing daunting initially, feeling like they have nothing of importance to say about the reading they've done, or that they don't understand "what the teacher wants." You may have had the experience of seeing the comment "too much summary" on something you've written, and not known how to revise your writing to be more analytical. In the following essay, the author and professor, John Trimble, demystifies some aspects of analytical writing. As you read his advice, think about your experience with analytical writing.

How to Write a Critical Analysis

John Trimble

John Trimble grew up in Buffalo, New York. He received degrees in English from Princeton University and the University of California, Berkeley. The following reading is from Writing with Style: Conversations on the Art of Writing, *written in 1975, a first-year composition textbook used at more than 280 colleges. A new edition was published in 2000. He is professor emeritus of Rhetoric & Writing at the University of Texas, Austin, where he began teaching in 1970.*

> *A writer's job is sticking his neck out.*
>
> *—Sloan Wilson*

> *The art of writing has for backbone some fierce attachment to an idea.*
>
> *—Virginia Woolf*

From *Writing with Style: Conversations on the Art of Writing*, 2nd Edition, © 2000, pp. 94–98. Reprinted by permission of Pearson Education, Inc., Upper Saddle River, NJ.

Teacher: This first paragraph reads a lot like plot summary, David, not a critical analysis. And so does the next one. David, you want to be *analyzing*.
David: Well, I thought I *was* analyzing.
Teacher: But you're merely giving the reader the story here.
David: Well, the reader's got to know what happens, doesn't he?

Chances are you've been in David's shoes yourself. His confusion is typical. He's been hearing the phrase "critical analysis" for years now but to him it's still incomprehensible. No one has ever bothered to explain to him precisely what it involves. As far as he can figure, the whole business is peculiar. How, he wants to know, can you analyze a story without discussing the plot? But if you discuss the plot, it seems you're immediately guilty of "plot summary." It's like *Catch-22,* he decides.

Actually it isn't, although it may seem that way. The difference between a plot summary and a critical analysis is like the difference between (a) an account of the highlights of the Vietnam War and (b) an explanation of how the U.S. happened to get into it, why we stayed in it, and what its effects were on us. A plot summary begins with no thesis or point of view; it merely recapitulates the facts. A critical analysis, on the other hand, *takes a viewpoint and attempts to prove its validity;* its object is to help readers make better sense of something they're *already* familiar with.

"Something they're *already* familiar with" holds the all-important assumption. If you look again at David's last comment—"Well, the reader's got to know what happens, doesn't he?"—you'll note that he's been operating from a quite different assumption, an assumption of ignorance. From ninth grade onward he was taught, "Never assume that your reader is familiar with your subject." While this may be sound advice to writers of book reports, it's fatal to apprentice critics, not to mention their hapless readers. The critic's job is to *explain and evaluate*—that is, to bring his readers to a *better* understanding of his subject. Plainly, he can't do this if he assumes that his readers are completely ignorant.

Knowing what you can and should assume is not, however, enough. You'll still slip into plot summarizing if you neglect to formulate an interesting, gutty thesis. Novelist Sloan Wilson's remark couldn't be more on target. "A writer's job is sticking his neck out." If you don't stick your neck out, your essay won't have a strong thesis; and if it lacks a strong thesis, you'll have nothing to assert, hence nothing to substantiate. Since nothing can come of nothing, your sole recourse will be to summarize large sections of plot under the guise of "analyzing" it.

If, on the other hand, you muster the courage and perceptiveness to formulate a strong position on your subject, you're already well on the way to a genuine critical analysis, since you have obliged yourself to offer the careful argumentation required to make your position convincing. This normally entails ranging back and forth through the plot in pursuit of textual evidence. In the process, of course, you'll find yourself drawing on many details of the plot . . . , but unlike the mechanical plot summarizer, you will always be using those details to *demonstrate a point.* In other words, it is their larger significance that always concerns you, not the details for their own sake. They are *illustrations* of something—a recurring pattern, a character trait, or whatever.

David might interrupt here: "OK, I follow you, but how do I come up with that 'genuinely interesting, gutty thesis' you talk about? I always have trouble thinking up things to write about."

Answer: As you read, and later as you prepare to write, get in the habit of thinking in terms of *how* and *why* questions. These are the questions a critical analysis usually deals with. They are more intrinsically interesting than *what* questions because they are *interpretive* rather than dryly descriptive. But, equally important, they are more likely to stimulate fresh ideas. Here are some examples:

"How is Hamlet like Horatio—and unlike him?"

"Why does Hamlet delay his promised revenge?"

"Why is the play-within-a-play scene pivotal?"

"How does King Claudius win over the enraged Laertes?"

Well-reasoned answers to questions such as these make for exciting reading because they help the reader to see clearly what before he had seen only dimly, if at all. And thinking out answers to such questions makes for exciting writing because it involves discovery.

Another suggestion: Pay close attention to the *form* of the work. One of the chief goals of critical analysis, said the poet W.H. Auden, is to "throw light on the process of artistic 'Making.'"

If the work is a poem, for example, you might begin by analyzing the rhyme scheme and ask yourself how it reinforces the poem's content, thematic movement, and so on. Look, too, at the punctuation for what it may reveal. (You may assume that very little is accidental in a poem.) It's also helpful to ponder these three questions:

1. What's the emotional effect of the poem?

2. How does it get its emotional power—that is, how does the poet manage to make us respond the way we do?
3. How does the poem give us a sense of wholeness (i.e., completed emotion or effect)?

If it's a play, begin by paying close attention to the opening scene, which usually strikes many of the major themes. Also, analyze each scene in relation to the scenes immediately preceding and following it. Adjacent scenes frequently point up ironies, significant contrasts, and the like. Further, be alert to repeated words and phrases, stage directions, and characters' names (often symbolic or ironic).

If it's a novel, start by analyzing it in terms of beginning, middle, and end to get a clearer sense of its movement. Ask yourself what each chapter accomplishes. Read closely the initial description of the various characters for clues to their essence, and be alert to verbal signatures in their speeches. Look for repeated words and images. Ponder especially well the final paragraph: What kind of concluding statement does it make?

For inspiration as well as instruction, read some master critics themselves. I'd recommend, for starters, Pauline Kael's* various collections of movie reviews and John Mason Brown's superb collection of theater reviews, *Dramatis Personae.* Reading them is like hitching a ride in the Daytona 500.

One other question concerns tenses. In analyzing works of literature and film, novice writers often employ the past tense. Experienced critics, however, almost invariably use the *present* tense. This is partly because of the force of convention and partly because dramatic characters are considered as "alive" now as when they were first conceived. Thus, say "Hamlet is," not "Hamlet was." The convention usually applies to authors, too: say "Keats observers," not "Keats observed." Here are two exceptions to the rule, though:

1. If you wish to refer to something that occurred earlier than the time span covered by the play or novel, use the past tense. Examples: "Hamlet and Horatio were school chums at Wittenberg." "Reared in the aristocratic home of General Gabler, Hedda was taught to value propriety at all costs."
2. If you wish to refer to something that has occurred before the thing you are now discussing but still within the time span of the work, use the present perfect tense. Example: "Although Hamlet has declared his readiness to avenge his father's murder, he seems here to betray a strong aversion to the deed."

In closing, let me take my major points and recast them as good working assumptions:

1. Assume that your audience is a well-informed reader, not the ignorant world.

*Pauline Kael (1919–2001) was a film critic who wrote for *The New Yorker* magazine. Her fourth book, *Deeper Into Movies* (1973), won a National Book Award.

2. Assume that since he's already read the work you're discussing, he'll be bored with vapid perceptions—as you yourself would be—and will feel insulted if you retell the plot.
3. Assume that he prefers reading arguments to mere chat, and that he won't really begin reading with interest until he sees you courageously crawling out on the interpretive limb—like this: "Love Story will not be the first disgraceful movie that has laid waste the emotions of a vast audience, though it may be one of the most ineptly made of all the lump-and-phlegm hits" (Pauline Kael).

QUESTIONS FOR DISCUSSION AND WRITING

1. Based on your reading of Trimble, how would you describe a "critical analysis"? What should it contain? What shouldn't it contain?
2. According to Trimble, what's necessary for a "strong thesis"? Have you encountered problems with crafting good thesis statements? In what ways might Trimble's advice help, if so?
3. Why should you assume an audience of well-informed readers, according to the author? What difference can this make in your writing?
4. What is meant by Trimble's use of the word "argument" in the last paragraph of this reading? How can you ensure that your writing contains an argument? Is all analytical writing somehow an argument? Explain your answer.

ON TECHNIQUE AND STYLE

1. Why does Trimble begin with the short dialog between the teacher and David? Is this an effective technique? Why or why not?
2. Trimble uses metaphors and similes to make his point. Find an example of this. How is the example effective or ineffective?

CULTURAL QUESTION

1. In different educational contexts, does the focus on analysis vary? In what ways? What is your experience with analysis in other educational systems, such as high school or other college courses?

A newspaper reporter on her first job writes an article and takes it to her editor. The editor has it for a day and then asks the reporter, "Is this the best you can do?" The reporter apologizes, goes back to her computer, and revises her article. She gives it to her editor again, who again keeps it for a day, then asks, "Is *this* the best you can do?" The reporter, in frustration, takes the story back, revises and revises it, gives it back to the editor, who after a while asks her the same question: "Is this really the best you can do?" The reporter, exasperated, says, "Yes! It's the best I can do." "Good," the editor replies. "Now I'll read it."

Oftentimes, a writer will go through many cycles of revision before what is written is readable. Unfortunately, many students will confess they don't undertake revision, or if they do, it consists only of checking their grammar and spelling, and maybe changing a few words "here and there." In the following selection, the author Anne Lamott discusses the process of writing a first draft. As you read her description, think about how your drafting process and your revision process work for you. Do you write bad first drafts then fix them up, or, are you still struggling with pefectionism, as Ueland discusses in an earlier reading in this chapter?

Shitty First Drafts

Anne Lamott

Anne Lamott was born in San Francisco, California, in 1954. She attended Goucher College in Maryland before dropping out to write. She is the author of several books, including Operating Instructions: A Journal of My Son's First Year *(1993), and* Bird by Bird: Some Instructions on Writing and Life *(1995), from which the following selection was taken. Lamott was a 1985 recipient of a Guggenheim Fellowship. She lives in northern California.*

Now, practically even better news than that of short assignments is the idea of shitty first drafts. All good writers write them. This is how they end up with good second drafts and terrific third drafts. People tend to look at successful writers, writers who are getting their books published and maybe even doing well financially, and think that they sit down at their desks every morning feeling like a million dollars, feeling great about who they are and how much talent they have and what a great story they have to tell; that they take in a few deep breaths, push back their sleeves, roll their necks a few times to get all the cricks out, and dive in, typing fully formed passages as fast as a court reporter. But this is just the fantasy of the uninitiated. I know some very great writers, writers you love who write beautifully and have made a great deal of money, and not *one* of them sits down routinely feeling wildly enthusiastic and confident. Not one of them writes elegant first drafts. All right, one of them does, but we do not like her very much. We do not think that she has a rich inner life or that God likes her or can even stand her. (Although when I mentioned this to my priest friend Tom, he said you can safely assume you've created God in your own image when it turns out that God hates all the same people you do.)

Very few writers really know what they are doing until they've done it. Nor do they go about their business feeling dewy and thrilled. They do not type a few stiff warm-up sentences and then find themselves bounding along like huskies across the snow. One writer I know tells me that he sits down every morning and says to himself nicely, "It's not like you don't have a choice, because you do—you can either type or kill yourself." We all often feel like we are pulling teeth, even those writers whose prose ends up being the most natural and fluid. The right words and sentences just do not come pouring out like ticker tape most of the time. Now, Muriel Spark is said to have felt that she was taking dictation from God every morning—sitting there, one supposes, plugged into a Dictaphone, typing away, humming. But this is a very hostile and aggressive position. One might hope for bad things to rain down on a person like this.

For me and most of the other writers I know, writing is not rapturous. In fact, the only way I can get anything written at all is to write really, really shitty first drafts.

The first draft is the child's draft, where you let it all pour out and then let it romp all over the place, knowing that no one is going to see it and that you can shape it later. You just let this childlike part of you channel whatever voices and visions come through and onto the page. If one of the characters wants to say, "Well, so what, Mr. Poopy Pants?," you let her. No one is going to see it. If the kid wants to get into really sentimental, weepy, emotional territory, you let him. Just get it all down on paper, because there may be something great in those six crazy pages that you would never have gotten to by more rational, grown-up means. There may be something in the very last line of the very last paragraph on page six that you just love, that is so beautiful or wild that you now know what you're supposed to be writing about, more or less, or in what direction you might go—but there was no way to get to this without first getting through the first five and a half pages.

I used to write food reviews for *California* magazine before it folded. (My writing food reviews had nothing to do with the magazine folding, although every single review did cause a couple of canceled subscriptions. Some readers took umbrage at my comparing mounds of vegetable puree with various ex-presidents' brains.) These reviews always took two days to write. First I'd go to a restaurant several times with a few opinionated, articulate friends in tow. I'd sit there writing down everything anyone said that was at all interesting or funny. Then on the following Monday I'd sit down at my desk with my notes, and try to write the review. Even after I'd been doing this for years, panic would set in. I'd try to write a lead, but instead I'd write a couple of dreadful sentences, XX them out, try again, XX everything out, and then feel despair and worry settle on my chest like an x-ray apron. It's over, I'd think, calmly. I'm not going to be able to get the magic to work this time. I'm ruined. I'm through. I'm toast. Maybe, I'd think, I can get my old job back as a clerk-typist. But probably not. I'd get up and study my teeth in the mirror for a while. Then I'd stop, remember to breathe, make a few phone calls, hit the kitchen and chow down. Eventually I'd go back and sit down at my desk, and sigh for the next ten minutes. Finally I would pick up my one-inch picture frame, stare into it as if for the answer, and every time the answer would come: all I had to do was to write a really shitty first draft of, say, the opening paragraph. And no one was going to see it.

So I'd start writing without reining myself in. It was almost just typing, just making my fingers move. And the writing would be *terrible.* I'd write a lead paragraph that was a whole page, even though the entire review could only be three pages long, and then I'd start writing up descriptions of the food, one dish at a time, bird by bird, and the critics would be sitting on my shoulders, commenting like cartoon characters. They'd be pretending to snore, or rolling their eyes at my overwrought descriptions, no matter how hard I tried to tone those descriptions down, no matter how conscious I was of what a friend said to me gently in my early days of restaurant reviewing. "Annie," she said, "it is just a piece of *chick*en. It is just a bit of *cake.*"

But because by then I had been writing for so long, I would eventually let myself trust the process—sort of, more or less. I'd write a first draft that was maybe twice as long as it should be, with a self-indulgent and boring beginning, stupefying descriptions of the meal, lots of quotes from my black-humored friends that made them sound more like the Manson girls than food lovers, and no ending to speak of. The whole thing would be so long and incoherent and hideous that for the rest of the day I'd obsess about getting creamed by a car before I could write a decent second draft. I'd worry that people would read what I'd written and believe that the accident had really been a suicide, that I had panicked because my talent was waning and my mind was shot.

The next day, though, I'd sit down, go through it all with a colored pen, take out everything I possibly could, find a new lead somewhere on the second page, figure out a kicky place to end it, and then write a second draft. It always turned out fine, sometimes even funny and weird and helpful. I'd go over it one more time and mail it in.

Then, a month later, when it was time for another review, the whole process would start again, complete with the fears that people would find my first draft before I could rewrite it.

Almost all good writing begins with terrible first efforts. You need to start somewhere. Start by getting something—anything—down on paper. A friend of mine says that the first draft is the down draft—you just get it down. The second draft is the up draft—you fix it up. You try to say what you have to say more accurately. And the third draft is the dental draft, where you check every tooth, to see if it's loose or cramped or decayed, or even, God help us, healthy.

What I've learned to do when I sit down to work on a shitty first draft is to quiet the voices in my head. First there's the vinegar-lipped Reader Lady, who says primly, "Well, *that's* not very interesting, is it?" And there's the emaciated German male who writes these Orwellian memos detailing your thought crimes. And there are your parents, agonizing over your lack of loyalty and discretion; and there's William Burroughs, dozing off or shooting up because he finds you as bold and articulate as a houseplant; and so on. And there are also the dogs: let's not forget the dogs, the dogs in their pen who will surely hurtle and snarl their way out if you ever *stop* writing, because writing is, for some of us, the latch that keeps the door of the pen closed, keeps those crazy ravenous dogs contained.

Quieting these voices is at least half the battle I fight daily. But this is better than it used to be. It used to be 87 percent. Left to its own devices, my mind spends much of its time having conversations with people who aren't there. I walk along defending myself to people, or exchanging repartee with them, or rationalizing my behavior, or seducing them with gossip, or pretending I'm on their TV talk show or whatever. I speed or run an aging yellow light or don't come to a full stop, and one nanosecond later am explaining to imaginary cops exactly why I had to do what I did, or insisting that I did not in fact do it.

I happened to mention this to a hypnotist I saw many years ago, and he looked at me very nicely. At first I thought he was feeling around on the floor for the silent alarm button, but then he gave me the following exercise, which I still use to this day.

Close your eyes and get quiet for a minute, until the chatter starts up. Then isolate one of the voices and imagine the person speaking as a mouse. Pick it up by the tail and drop it into a mason jar. Then isolate another voice, pick it up by the tail, drop it in the jar. And so on. Drop in any high-maintenance parental units, drop in any contractors, lawyers, colleagues, children, anyone who is whining in your head. Then put the lid on, and watch all these mouse people clawing at the glass, jabbering away, trying to make you feel like shit because you won't do what they want—won't give them more money, won't be more successful, won't see them more often. Then imagine that there is a volume-control button on the bottle. Turn it all the way up for a minute, and listen to the stream of angry, neglected, guilt-mongering voices. Then turn it all the way down and watch the frantic mice lunge at the glass, trying to get to you. Leave it down, and get back to your shitty first draft.

A writer friend of mine suggests opening the jar and shooting them all in the head. But I think he's a little angry, and I'm sure nothing like this would ever occur to you.

QUESTIONS FOR DISCUSSION AND WRITING

1. Why do you think Lamott chose the title "Shitty First Drafts" for this chapter of her book? What effect does using the word "shitty" have on the reader?
2. What is the "fantasy of the uninitiated" according to Lamott? Have you ever been guilty of this kind of belief?
3. What is Lamott's advice about writing? Do you find her way of giving advice effective? Why or why not?

4. Do you experience the "voices in your head" in the way Lamott describes? If so, explain their effect on your writing.
5. What relationship do you see between Lamott's ideas and Ueland's and/or Stafford's? Which of these writers do you find has the most helpful ideas for your own writing process? Why?

ON TECHNIQUE AND STYLE

1. How would you describe the *tone* of this reading? Give examples to support your opinion.
2. Lamott refers to several other writers by name. Do you know who these writers are? Why does she use them as examples? Could she have achieved the same outcome some other way?

CULTURAL QUESTION

1. Some researchers have said there are distinctive cultural styles in writing. Others dismiss this idea as a shallow understanding of the writing process. What is your experience? If you have read or written in another language, do you find it different from reading or writing in English? In what ways?

In the final reading selection of this chapter, William Zinsser talks about some revision practices, and the reasons that revision is so important.

Simplicity

William Zinsser

William Zinsser (born 1922) is a writer, editor, and teacher. He began his career with the New York Herald Tribune *and has long been a freelance writer for leading magazines. During the 1970s he taught writing at Yale, where he was master of Branford College. From 1979 to 1987 he was general editor of the Book-of-the-Month Club. His fifteen books, ranging from jazz to baseball, include* Speaking of Journalism *(1995),* American Places *(2007), and the influential* On Writing Well *(1985) from which the following excerpt was taken. He now teaches at the New School in New York, his hometown.*

Clutter is the disease of American writing. We are a society strangling in unnecessary words, circular constructions, pompous frills and meaningless jargon.

Who can understand the viscous language of everyday American commerce and enterprise: the business letter, the interoffice memo, the corporation report, the notice from the bank explaining its latest "simplified" statement? What member of an insurance or medical plan can decipher the brochure that tells him what his costs and benefits are? What father or mother can put together a child's toy—on Christmas Eve or any other eve—from the instructions on the box? Our national tendency is to inflate and thereby sound important. The airline pilot who wakes us to announce that he is presently anticipating experiencing considerable weather wouldn't dream of saying that there's a storm ahead and it may get bumpy. The sentence is too simple—there must be something wrong with it.

But the secret of good writing is to strip every sentence to its cleanest components. Every word that serves no function, every long word that could be a short word, every adverb which carries the same meaning that is already in the verb, every passive construction that leaves the reader unsure of who is doing what—these are the thousand and one adulterants that weaken the strength of a sentence. And they usually occur, ironically, in proportion to education and rank.

During the late 1960s the president of a major university wrote a letter to mollify the alumni after a spell of campus unrest. "You are probably aware," he began, "that we have been experiencing very considerable potentially explosive expressions of dissatisfaction on issues only partially related." He meant that the students had been hassling them about different things. I was far more upset by the president's English than by the students' potentially explosive expressions of dissatisfaction. I would have preferred the presidential approach taken by Franklin D. Roosevelt when he tried to convert into English his own government's memos, such as this blackout order of 1942:

> Such preparations shall be made as will completely obscure all Federal buildings and non-Federal buildings occupied by the Federal government during an air raid for any period of time from visibility by reason of internal or external illumination.

"Tell them," Roosevelt said, "that in buildings where they have to keep the work going to put something across the windows."

Simplify, simplify. Thoreau said it, as we are so often reminded, and no American writer more consistently practiced what he preached. Open *Walden* to any page and you will find a man saying in a plain and orderly way what is on his mind:

> I love to be alone. I never found the companion that was so companionable as solitude. We are for the most part more lonely when we go abroad among men than when we stay in our chambers. A man thinking or working always alone, let him be where he will. Solitude is not measured by the miles space that intervene between a man and his fellows. The really diligent student in of the crowded hives of Cambridge College is as solitary as a dervish in the desert.

How can the rest of us achieve such enviable freedom from clutter? The answer is to clear our heads of clutter. Clear thinking becomes clear writing: one can't exist without the other. It is impossible for a muddy thinker to write good English. He may get away with it for a paragraph or two, but soon the reader will be lost, and there is no sin so grave, for he will not easily be lured back.

Who is this elusive creature the reader? He is a person with an attention span of about twenty seconds. He is assailed on every side by forces competing for his time: by newspapers and magazines, by television and radio and stereo, by his wife and children and pets, by his house and his yard and all the gadgets that he has bought to keep them spruce, and by that most potent of competitors, sleep. The man snoozing in his chair with an unfinished magazine open on his lap is a man who was being given too much unnecessary trouble by the writer.

It won't do to say that the snoozing reader is too dumb or too lazy to keep pace with the train of thought. My sympathies are with him. If the reader is lost, it is generally because the writer has not been careful enough to keep him on the path.

This carelessness can take any number of forms. Perhaps a sentence is so excessively cluttered that the reader, hacking his way through the verbiage, simply doesn't know what it means. Perhaps a sentence has been so shoddily constructed that the reader could read it in any of several ways. Perhaps the writer has switched pronouns in mid-sentence, or has switched tenses, so the reader loses track of who is talking or when the action took place. Perhaps Sentence B is not a logical sequel to Sentence A—the writer, in whose head the connection is clear, has not bothered to provide the missing link. Perhaps the writer has used an important word incorrectly by not taking the trouble to look it up. He may think that "sanguine" and "sanguinary" mean the same thing, but the difference is a bloody big one. The reader can only infer (speaking of big differences) what the writer is trying to imply.

Faced with these obstacles, the reader is at first a remarkably tenacious bird. He blames himself—he obviously missed something, and he goes back over the mystifying sentence, or over the whole paragraph, piecing it out like an ancient rule, making guesses and moving on. But he won't do this for long. The writer is making him work too hard, and the reader will look for one who is better at his craft.

The writer must therefore constantly ask himself: What am I trying to say? Surprisingly often, he doesn't know. Then he must look at what he has written and ask: Have I said it? Is it clear to someone encountering the subject for the first time? If it's not, it is because some fuzz has worked its way into the machinery. The clear writer is a person clear-headed enough to see this stuff for what it is: fuzz.

I don't mean that some people are born clear-headed and are therefore natural writers, whereas others are naturally fuzzy and will never write well.

Thinking clearly is a conscious act that the writer must force upon himself, just as if he were embarking on any other project that requires logic: adding up a laundry list or doing an algebra problem. Good writing doesn't come naturally, though most people obviously think it does. The professional writer is forever being bearded by strangers who say that they'd like to "try a little writing sometime" when they retire from their real profession. Good writing takes self-discipline and, very often, self-knowledge.

Many writers, for instance, can't stand to throw anything away. Their sentences are littered with words that mean essentially the same thing and with phrases which make a point that is implicit in what they have already said. When students give me these littered sentences I beg them to select from the surfeit of words the few that most precisely fit what they want to say. Choose one, I plead, from among the three almost identical adjectives. Get rid of the unnecessary adverbs. Eliminate "in a funny sort of way" and other such qualifiers—they do no useful work.

The students look stricken—I am taking all their wonderful words away. I am only taking their superfluous words away, leaving what is organic and strong.

"But," one of my worst offenders confessed, "I never can get rid of anything—you should see my room." (I didn't take him up on the offer.) "I have two lamps where I only need one, but I can't decide which one I like better, so I keep them both." He went on to enumerate his duplicated or unnecessary objects, and over the weeks ahead I went on throwing away his duplicated and unnecessary words. By the end of the term—a term that he found acutely painful—his sentences were clean.

"I've had to change my whole approach to writing," he told me. "Now I have to think before I start every sentence and I have to think about every word." The very idea amazed him. Whether his room also looked better I never found out.

Writing is hard work. A clear sentence is no accident. Very few sentences come out right the first time. Or the third. Keep thinking and rewriting until you say what you want to say.

QUESTIONS FOR DISCUSSION AND WRITING

1. What does Zinsser mean when he says that cluttered sentences "usually occur, ironically, in proportion to education and rank"? Do you agree? What examples can you think of from your own experience? What function might overly complex language serve in your examples?
2. Look at something you've written recently. Does it suffer from any of the symptoms that Zinsser describes? How might you go about revising accordingly?
3. Examine the sample of revised text that the author provides. What do you notice most here? What kinds of things has he excised, and what has he kept? Why do you think he made these choices?

4. What connections do you see between Zinsser's advice about revising and Lamott's characterization of the drafting process? Are there other selections in this chapter that you see as connected with Zinsser's?

ON TECHNIQUE AND STYLE

1. Look at the language used to describe writing, readers, and the like. Are they effective? Strong? How would you describe these descriptors?
2. Why does Zinsser include the example of his own edited writing? What does this tell you about his style? His process?

CULTURAL QUESTION

1. In the various educational environments in which you may have participated, how was revision in writing treated? Was it taught? Required? Ignored? Describe your experience.

VISUAL TEXTS

Writing about visual texts—drawings, comics, artwork—may be a new undertaking for you. However, like reading written texts, reading visual texts requires understanding of the many forms that a visual text can take. It also requires looking closely at what you're seeing, and trying to relate what is before you on the page or screen, with what you know from other sources.

In the following selection, comic book artist and theorist Scott McCloud looks at some of our assumptions about what we see. He presents this information in the medium with which he is most known for—comics. As you read this text, think not only about the ideas he presents, but also how reading them in comic format changes your understanding of the information.

QUESTIONS FOR DISCUSSION AND WRITING

1. What is McCloud's point about the Magritte painting *The Treachery of Images?* Why do you think he chose this image? Why is it called *The Treachery of Images?*
2. What does McCloud mean by "amplification through simplification"? Why is it important to visual understanding?

3. What do you think about McCloud's claim that the reason we like comics is that we see ourselves in the images? How does simplification help this process? Can you think of other examples where this takes place, such as in advertising?
4. Are you a fan of comics? Which ones? (If not, why not?) Do you see the connection between what McCloud has written and anything you see in the comics you read?

ON TECHNIQUE AND STYLE

1. Try to read the passage again without looking at the pictures. How do pictures support the text?
2. McCloud places himself as a visual narrator in this text. How does this affect you as a reader?

CULTURAL QUESTION

1. Are you aware of comics from other cultures or countries? How are they similar or different from comics from the United States? What purpose do these comics serve?

The Vocabulary of Comics

Scott McCloud

Scott McCloud (born Scott McLeod on June 10, 1960, in Boston, Massachusetts) is a cartoonist and a scholar of comics. He created the science fiction/superhero comic book series Zot! *in 1984. Seen as a reaction to the darker superhero comics of the 1980s, it became a cult classic. He is best known as the author of* Understanding Comics *(1993), from which the following selection is taken. This volume is widely considered one of the definitive works about the medium of comics. He followed its publication with* Reinventing Comics *(2000) and* Making Comics *(2006).*

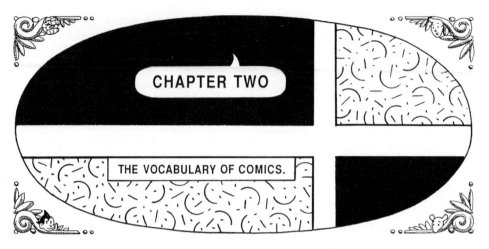

CHAPTER TWO

THE VOCABULARY OF COMICS.

THIS IS NOT A MAN.

THESE ARE NOT IDEAS.

THIS IS NOT A COUNTRY.

THIS IS NOT
A LEAF

THESE ARE NOT PEOPLE.

THIS IS NOT MUSIC.

THIS IS NOT A COW.

THIS IS NOT MY VOICE.

THIS IS NOT SOUND.

THESE ARE NOT FLOWERS.

THIS IS NOT ME.

THIS IS NOT LAW.

THIS IS NOT A PLANET.

THIS IS NOT FOOD.

THIS IS NOT A CAR.

THIS IS NOT A
COMPANY.

THIS IS NOT A
FACE.

THESE ARE NOT SEPARATE
MOMENTS.

NOW, THE WORD *ICON* MEANS MANY THINGS.

THIS IS PAPER

THIS IS *INK* ON PAPER

FOR THE PURPOSES OF THIS CHAPTER, I'M USING THE WORD *"ICON"* TO MEAN ANY IMAGE USED TO REPRESENT A A PERSON, PLACE, THING OR *IDEA*.

ICON

THAT'S A BIT BROADER THAN THE DEFINITION IN MY DICTIONARY, BUT IT'S THE CLOSEST THING TO WHAT I NEED HERE.

"SYMBOL" IS A BIT TOO *LOADED* FOR ME.

THE SORTS OF IMAGES WE USUALLY *CALL* SYMBOLS ARE ONE *CATEGORY* OF ICON, HOWEVER.

THESE ARE THE IMAGES WE USE TO REPRESENT *CONCEPTS, IDEAS* AND *PHILOSOPHIES*.

THEN THERE ARE THE ICONS OF *LANGUAGE, SCIENCE* AND *COMMUNICATION*.

ICONS OF THE *PRACTICAL* REALM.

AND FINALLY, THE ICONS WE CALL *PICTURES*: IMAGES DESIGNED TO ACTUALLY *RESEMBLE* THEIR SUBJECTS.

BUT AS RESEMBLANCE VARIES, SO DOES THE LEVEL OF ICONIC CONTENT.

OR TO PUT IT SOMEWHAT *CLUMSILY*, SOME PICTURES ARE JUST MORE ICONIC THAN OTHERS.

WHY-- --ARE-- --WE-- --SO-- --INVOLVED?

WHY WOULD *ANYONE*, YOUNG OR OLD, RESPOND TO A CARTOON AS MUCH OR MORE THAN A *REALISTIC IMAGE?*

WHY IS OUR CULTURE *SO IN THRALL* TO THE *SIMPLIFIED REALITY* OF THE *CARTOON?*

DEFINING THE CARTOON WOULD TAKE UP AS MUCH SPACE AS DEFINING *COMICS,* BUT FOR *NOW,* I'M GOING TO EXAMINE CARTOONING AS A FORM OF *AMPLIFICATION THROUGH SIMPLIFICATION.*

WHEN WE *ABSTRACT* AN IMAGE THROUGH *CARTOONING,* WE'RE NOT SO MUCH *ELIMINATING* DETAILS AS WE ARE *FOCUSING* ON *SPECIFIC DETAILS.*

BY *STRIPPING DOWN* AN IMAGE TO ITS ESSENTIAL *"MEANING,"* AN ARTIST CAN *AMPLIFY* THAT MEANING IN A WAY THAT REALISTIC ART *CAN'T.*

FILM CRITICS WILL SOMETIMES DESCRIBE A *LIVE-ACTION* FILM AS A "CARTOON" TO ACKNOWLEDGE THE STRIPPED-DOWN *INTENSITY* OF A SIMPLE STORY OR VISUAL STYLE.

THOUGH THE TERM IS OFTEN USED *DISPARAGINGLY*, IT CAN BE EQUALLY WELL APPLIED TO MANY *TIME-TESTED CLASSICS*. SIMPLIFYING CHARACTERS AND IMAGES TOWARD A *PURPOSE* CAN BE AN EFFECTIVE TOOL FOR STORYTELLING IN *ANY* MEDIUM.

CARTOONING ISN'T JUST A WAY OF *DRAWING*, IT'S A WAY OF *SEEING!*

FOLLOW! FOLLOW!

THE ABILITY OF CARTOONS TO *FOCUS* OUR ATTENTION ON AN IDEA IS, I THINK, AN IMPORTANT PART OF THEIR SPECIAL POWER, BOTH IN COMICS AND IN DRAWING GENERALLY.

ONE   A FEW   THOUSANDS   MILLIONS   (NEARLY) ALL

ANOTHER IS THE *UNIVERSALITY* OF CARTOON IMAGERY. THE MORE CARTOONY A FACE IS, FOR INSTANCE, THE MORE PEOPLE IT COULD BE SAID TO *DESCRIBE*.

BUT I BELIEVE THERE'S SOMETHING *MORE* AT WORK IN OUR MINDS WHEN WE VIEW A CARTOON-- ESPECIALLY OF A HUMAN FACE-- WHICH WARRANTS FURTHER INVESTIGATION.

WHAT   ARE YOU

REALLY   SEEING?

THE FACT THAT YOUR MIND IS *CAPABLE* OF TAKING A *CIRCLE, TWO DOTS* AND A *LINE* AND TURNING THEM INTO A *FACE* IS NOTHING SHORT OF *INCREDIBLE!*

BUT STILL *MORE* INCREDIBLE IS THE FACT THAT YOU CANNOT *AVOID* SEEING A FACE HERE. YOUR MIND WON'T *LET* YOU!

ASK A FRIEND TO DRAW YOU SOME SHAPES ON A PIECE OF PAPER. THEY SHOULD BE *CLOSED CURVES,* BUT OTHER-WISE CAN BE AS *WEIRD* AND *IRREGULAR* AS HE OR SHE *WANTS.*

LET'S SAY THE RESULTS LOOK SOMETHING LIKE *THIS.*

NOW-- YOU'LL FIND THAT NO MATTER WHAT THEY *LOOK* LIKE, EVERY SINGLE *ONE* OF THOSE SHAPES *CAN* BE MADE INTO A FACE WITH ONE SIMPLE ADDITION.

YOUR MIND HAS NO TROUBLE AT ALL CONVERTING SUCH SHAPES INTO FACES, YET WOULD IT EVER MISTAKE *THIS*--

--FOR *THIS?*

WE HUMANS ARE A SELF-CENTERED RACE.

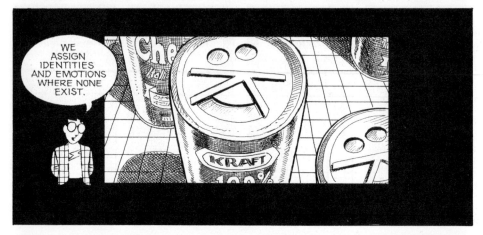

EACH ONE *ALSO* SUSTAINS A CONSTANT AWARENESS OF HIS OR HER *OWN* FACE, BUT *THIS* MIND-PICTURE IS NOT NEARLY SO VIVID; JUST A SKETCHY ARRANGEMENT... A SENSE OF SHAPE... A SENSE OF *GENERAL PLACEMENT.*

SOMETHING AS *SIMPLE* AND AS *BASIC*--

--AS A *CARTOON.*

THUS, WHEN YOU LOOK AT A PHOTO OR REALISTIC DRAWING OF A FACE--

--YOU SEE IT AS THE FACE OF *ANOTHER.*

BUT WHEN YOU ENTER THE WORLD OF THE *CARTOON*--

-- YOU SEE *YOURSELF.*

I BELIEVE THIS IS THE *PRIMARY CAUSE* OF OUR CHILDHOOD FASCINATION WITH *CARTOONS,* THOUGH OTHER FACTORS SUCH AS *UNIVERSAL IDENTIFICATION, SIMPLICITY* AND THE *CHILDLIKE FEATURES* OF MANY CARTOON CHARACTERS ALSO PLAY A PART.

THE CARTOON IS A *VACUUM* INTO WHICH OUR *IDENTITY* AND *AWARENESS* ARE PULLED...

...AN *EMPTY SHELL* THAT WE INHABIT WHICH *ENABLES* US TO TRAVEL IN *ANOTHER REALM.*

WE DON'T JUST *OBSERVE* THE CARTOON, WE *BECOME* IT!

THAT'S WHY I DECIDED TO *DRAW* MYSELF IN SUCH A SIMPLE *STYLE.*

WOULD YOU HAVE *LISTENED* TO ME IF I LOOKED LIKE *THIS*??

I *DOUBT* IT! YOU WOULD HAVE BEEN FAR TOO AWARE OF THE *MESSENGER* TO FULLY RECEIVE THE *MESSAGE!*

APART FROM WHAT LITTLE I TOLD YOU ABOUT MYSELF IN *CHAPTER ONE,* I'M PRACTICALLY A *BLANK SLATE!*

IT WOULD NEVER EVEN *OCCUR* TO YOU TO WONDER WHAT MY *POLITICS* ARE, OR WHAT I HAD FOR *LUNCH* OR WHERE I GOT THIS *SILLY OUTFIT!*

I'M JUST A LITTLE VOICE INSIDE YOUR *HEAD.*

A *CONCEPT.*

YOU GIVE ME LIFE BY READING THIS BOOK AND BY *"FILLING UP"* THIS VERY *ICONIC* (CARTOONY) *FORM.*

WHO I AM IS IRRELEVANT. I'M JUST A LITTLE PIECE OF *YOU.*

BUT IF WHO I AM MATTERS *LESS,* MAYBE WHAT I *SAY* WILL MATTER *MORE.*

THAT'S THE *THEORY,* ANYWAY.

SO FAR, WE'VE ONLY DISCUSSED *FACES,* BUT THE PHENOMENON OF *NON-VISUAL SELF-AWARENESS* CAN, TO A *LESSER DEGREE,* STILL APPLY TO OUR *WHOLE BODIES.* AFTER ALL, DO WE NEED TO *SEE* OUR HANDS TO KNOW WHAT THEY'RE DOING?

THERE'S *MORE,* TOO!

AUDIO TEXTS   To hear these conversations, go to www.mhhe.com/soundideas1e

Listening to spoken text taps into different skills than reading does. Whereas in reading you are able to skim ahead, review sections, skip over parts that look boring or redundant, and so forth, in listening you are typically unaware of what will come next, unless you have listened to the text before. Dealing with spoken text often requires notetaking, as well as close attention. As you encounter the spoken texts accompanying this book, think about the strategies for listening that work best for you.

In the following short audio selections, the authors Anne Lamott and Louise Erdrich make comments about their writing. Lamott discusses the influence her parents had on her as a writer, and Erdrich talks about her writing process. Listen to the *Forum* interview excerpts with writers Louise Erdrich and Anne Lamott.

Track 0.1

(date: March 29, 2005; running time: 2:49 min.)

*See this chapter for **Anne Lamott's** biography.*

Track 0.2

(date: October 16, 2005; running time: 1:44 min.)

Louise Erdrich (1954–   ) is the daughter of an Ojibwa Indian mother and a German American father, and her work is often focused on Native American themes. The eldest of seven children, she was born in Little Falls, Minnesota, and grew up in Wahpeton, North Dakota, where her parents taught at the Bureau of Indian Affairs school. She graduated from Dartmouth College in 1976, and earned her master of arts degree in writing from John Hopkins University in 1979. She is the 1987 O. Henry Award winner for her short story "Fleur" published in Esquire *magazine in August of 1986. Erdrich has also won the Pushcart Prize in Poetry, the Western Literary Association Award, received a Guggenheim Fellowship, and several of her stories have appeared in* The Best American Short Stories *series. Erdrich's short fiction has also appeared in* The New Yorker, Harper's Magazine, Atlantic Monthly, *and* The Paris Review. *From 1981 until his suicide in 1997, she was married to the author Michael Dorris. The couple had six children, three of them adopted. In 1991, their oldest child was killed in a car accident.*

QUESTIONS FOR DISCUSSION AND WRITING

1. What do Erdrich's comments about persistence mean for a new writer?

2. How do her comments about her process relate to any of the readings in this chapter?
3. Discuss Lamott's comments about her mother in light of Ueland's essay. What connections do you see between Lamott's experience and Ueland's characterizations of family influences on writers?

ON TECHNIQUE AND STYLE

1. How would you characterize Erdrich's speaking style? What do you like or dislike about it?
2. How does Lamott's speaking style compare to Erdrich's? Give specific examples.

CULTURAL QUESTION

1. Lamott talks about pressure from her mother to excel in her education. Do her observations seem tied to a particular social class or culture, or are they universal? How do parents encourage or discourage their children to excel in different cultures, from your experience?

FOR WRITING

CREATIVE CHOICES

1. Start a journal. In it, write about your past writing experiences. Do you consider yourself a good writer? What struggles have you had? How do you see yourself overcoming these struggles?
2. What kind of reader are you? Write a short memoir about a key experience you have had as a reader. How did this experience affect your academic success?
3. Copy or cut out a frame from a comic and paste it in your journal. Write about what you see, and why.

NARRATIVE/EXPOSITORY CHOICES

1. How would you describe the method the "typical" writer uses to craft an essay or other piece of writing? Describe, in a short paper, the process of writing, as you understand it from your reading. Use examples from your own experience where appropriate.

2. Write a narrative account of your writing process, from start to finish, when writing something assigned for a class. Use information from the reading to critique or comment on your process.

RHETORICAL CHOICES

1. Based on your reading in this chapter, what are the best strategies for becoming a good writer? Write an essay in which you present these ideas, quoting from the readings where appropriate.
2. Write a short, persuasive essay in which you agree or disagree with Ueland's claim that everyone has something unique and important to say. Use examples from your own experience to back up your claims.

RESEARCH CHOICES

1. What do other researchers have to say about the writing process? Conduct some research on the Internet or in a library. Write a short bibliography of what you found, summarizing briefly what each researcher believes about the process. What do you conclude from your research? (Hint: You may want to look at Richard Lanham's *Revising Prose,* or Donald M. Murray's *The Craft of Revision.*)
2. Interview three friends or classmates about their writing process. Summarize their statements in a short essay, using quotations from your interviews.
3. Look into what others have said about visual rhetoric, or writing about images. Give a summary account of your findings. List your sources in a bibliography.
4. What is plagiarism? What are the penalties for plagiarism at your institution? Research your school's policies on plagiarism online or at the appropriate office on campus. Write a short report in which you define plagiarism and discuss its penalties.

chapter *1*

On Gender Differences
Separating the Boys from the Girls

INTRODUCTION

The famous nursery rhyme tells us girls are made of "sugar and spice and everything nice" and boys of "snakes and snails and puppy dog tails." The stereotyping of sex roles is an enduring reality wrought by real and imagined gender differences. Those differences are seen through different lenses in different cultures but many believe they are innate and hardwired—based on neurological or hormonal differences—while others argue for the imperative of gender equity. This chapter exposes you to some of the differences, both real and imagined, as well as to a range of self- and society-imposed differences that separate girls from boys and men from women. There are two major questions upon which the selections in the chapter are built. One is the extent to which gender differences should or ought to matter. That is where stereotyping comes in. Is all stereotyping harmful or toxic or is a good deal of it simply a necessary byproduct of culture and of innate human behavior and the way the sexes are wired? The other major question has to do with the kinds of men and women boys and girls become. Related to that question are weighty issues of power and equity and similarities and differences in the ways men and women think and act. Freud once asked, what do women want, as if what women want is different. We will explore in this chapter the wants of girls and boys and women and men—how they differ and how they connect.

In this chapter you will encounter many ideas related to sexual identity as well as the ongoing debate about what gender differences mean. A feminist revolution, a liberation for both men and women, occurred in the United States. Its results and where it has led and the nature of gender differences resulting from influences of both nature and nurture thematically link the major selections.

A larger question looms over this chapter. In the early 1990s the American Association of University Women released a report that put the spotlight in education on girls. The report contended that girls have lower self-esteem than boys and are not given equal encouragement in school to study science and math. A decade later the spotlight shifted to boys being at greater risk because of the preponderance of women teachers and the fact that boys were more likely than girls to drop out or fail in school as well as to have far more serious disciplinary problems.

From leading psychologists Mary Pipher, Carol Gilligan, and William Pollack, we see and hear some of the difficulties both girls and boys face in their psychological development. Pipher, one of America's leading experts on the psychological development of girls, shows in her book, *Reviving Ophelia,* how social pressures and the demands of a popular culture that overemphasizes appearance and beauty in girls can cause damage and pain. However, in the selection included in *Sound Ideas,* we read about a woman who, by the time we meet her in her late twenties, has found strength in spite of these impediments. Famed Harvard psychologist and feminist writer Carol Gilligan talks in an interview of how the psychological views of girls, by others as well as by themselves, have changed and are continuing to change. Gilligan strongly believes girls were long undermined in finding their true voices and are only now beginning to discover what those real voices are. We also meet William Pollack's Adam, in a selection from the book *Real Boys,* a boy who needs to appear strong because of what Pollack calls "the boy code," a fact of life for boys which Pollack argues explains much of boys' emotional turmoil and their academically falling behind. A leading authority on boys as well as a Harvard professor, Pollack also talks in an interview. We hear him and other men who work with and advocate for boys in a roundtable, spirited discussion on what sets boys apart from girls and what boys want and need.

The other essays in this chapter give us a broad picture of how boys and girls are shaped by differences or perceived differences. Katha Pollitt, a well-known feminist essayist and poet, sees gender stereotyping as an ongoing battle; she offers a strong argument for the kind of sound ideas needed to win, through revitalizing feminism, gender battles that lie ahead. In a couple of excerpts from conservative philosopher Christina Hoff Sommers's book *The War Against Boys* we get a distinctly antifeminist argument by a writer strongly critical of the work of writers like Gilligan, Pollack, and Pipher, who argues that these and other contemporary feminist writers are creating arguments to support crises in gender that do not exist.

In the fiction in this chapter gender differences and how boys and girls grow into men and women are presented through traditional stories by John Updike, Alice Munro, and through two short, vivid, impressionistic, nontraditional narrative pieces by Jamaica Kincaid ("Girl") and Rick Moody ("Boys"). The more traditionally told stories by Updike ("A&P") and Munro ("Boys and Girls") consider what separates the sexes as well as what appears to define them. Sammy, Updike's narrator, is at the cusp between childhood and adulthood. He feels compelled to follow an impulse in defense of three girls who enter the A & P in their bathing suits. His protectiveness toward them has consequences, but taking on decisions that bear consequences appears to be what it means to take on the mantle of being a man in this tale and we see that being a man appears to involve being protective and chivalrous to females.

Munro takes us to a rural Canadian fox farm in her powerful story "Boys and Girls" to reveal the formative and indelible establishment of gender identity where children learn, especially the young girl at the center of the story, preset gender roles. In Kincaid's "Girl," we see the extraordinary effects a mother can have on shaping the gender identity of a girl growing into young womanhood and understand the manner in which, in a postcolonial setting, a girl is trained by her mother to think both in terms of her sexuality and her survival. In Moody's "Boys," we see the extraordinary effect of a father on his sons and the dramatic differences that separate boys from girls.

Marge Piercy, in "Barbie Doll," takes the well-known Barbie doll girls often play with and shows how it can be turned into a symbol of gender oppression. Her portrait of the influences of gender differences on a young girl is a disturbing and damning one. The African America poet Lucille Clifton moves us in another direction in her angry-sounding ironic poem "Wishes for Sons," in which she makes clear the nature of unfair gender differences stemming from biological facts of life. The photos and the cartoon we have included expand upon motifs related to gender differences and evoke strong responses and reactions that we trust will lead, like all the writing and audio selections in the first chapter, to what makes for sound writing—sound ideas.

NONFICTION

Reviving Ophelia

Mary Pipher

Mary Pipher, PhD, is a clinical psychologist and adjunct professor at the University of Nebraska. Her background is in both psychology and anthropology. The author of Reviving Ophelia: Saving the Selves of Adolescent Girls *(1994), Pipher is recognized as one of the nation's preeminent experts on the struggles, demands, and challenges young girls face socially, culturally, and psychologically and the reasons that contribute to low self-esteem and a range of contemporary maladies in girls including the rising rates in eating disorders, depression, addiction, and suicide. The title of her book is hopeful, drawn from the idea of reviving girls' inner Ophelia, the despairing and suicidal female character in Shakespeare's* Hamlet. *Pipher received the American Psychological Association Presidential Citation in 1998 and was a Rockefeller Foundation Scholar. Her other books include* The Shelter of Each Other, Another Country, Hunger Pains, *and* The Middle of Everywhere. *In* Reviving Ophelia, *from which we have taken part of a single section, Pipher profiles young girls she has treated in her clinical practice, revealing reasons why they suffer and the obstacles that cause them to lose themselves. The selection we have included gives a picture of what Pipher believes makes for psychologically strong and healthy girls. She uses a twenty-seven-year-old woman, June, who came to see her only once, as an example of how even a girl who was ridiculed and rejected for unattractiveness can still become a woman of strong character and sound mental health.*

Strong girls know who they are and value themselves as multifaceted people. They may see themselves as dancers, musicians, athletes or political activists. These kinds of identities hold up well under pressure. Talent allows girls some continuity between past childhood and current adolescent lives. Being genuinely useful also gives girls something to hold on to. Girls who care for ill parents or who help the disadvantaged have a hedge against the pain of adolescence.

Strong girls generally manage to stay close to their families and maintain some family loyalty. Even if they come from problem families, they usually have someone in the family whom they love and trust. Through all the chaos of adolescence, they keep the faith with this person.

Almost all girls have difficulty with their families. Even the healthiest girls push their parents to validate them as adults before the parents are ready to accept the new situation. All girls do some distancing as part of their individuation process. But healthy girls know that their parents love them and stay connected in important ways. They keep talking and seeking contact. Even as they rage at their parents on the surface, a part of them remains loyal and connected to them.

While no girls look or feel strong at this time, often there are signs that they are fighting to save themselves. It's a good sign if they maintain some memory of their preteen selves and are able to keep the interests and relationships of elementary school years. It's good if they resist pressure to become ultrafeminine.

Often strong girls can articulate a sense that things are much tougher and not quite right in the outside world. They are aware that they're being pressured to act in ways that aren't good for them. The premature sexualization of their lives makes them nervous. They may be involved in cliques, but a part of them hates the snobbishness and actively resists hurting other girls.

Healthy girls, like all girls, are scared of many things. They lose perspective and are more likely to be conformists than at any other time in their lives. They are more likely to blame their parents for their troubles and to do things they really don't believe in. They want to be pretty and well liked, but it's a matter of degree. They won't sell their souls to be popular. When push comes to shove, they'll stand up for themselves. There are certain lines they will not cross.

Positive signs include beliefs in causes or interests in anything larger than their own lives. Girls who have some special passions can call on something that is greater than their experiences in the halls of junior highs. Often their passion can give them some perspective and sustain them through the toughest times. Strong girls manage to avoid heavy chemical use and deal with pain in more adaptive ways. Often they have healthy stress-relieving habits such as reading, running or playing the piano.

In *Smart Girls, Gifted Women,* Barbara Kerr explores the common experiences of girls who grew into strong women. She studied the adolescent years of Marie Curie, Gertrude Stein, Eleanor Roosevelt, Margaret Mead, Georgia O'Keeffe, Maya Angelou and Beverly Sills, and she found that they had in common time by themselves, the ability to fall in love with an idea, a refusal to acknowledge gender limitations and what she called "protective coating." None of them were popular as adolescents and most stayed separate from their peers, not by choice, but because they were rejected. Ironically, this very rejection gave them a protected space in which they could develop their uniqueness.

Many strong girls have similar stories: They were socially isolated and lonely in adolescence. Smart girls are often the girls most rejected by peers. Their strength is a threat and they are punished for being different. Girls who are unattractive or who don't worry about their appearance are scorned. This isolation is often a blessing because it allows girls to develop a strong sense of self. Girls who are isolated emerge from adolescence more independent and self-sufficient than girls who have been accepted by others.

Strong girls may protect themselves by being quiet and guarded so that their rebellion is known by only a few trusted others. They may be cranky and irascible and keep critics at a distance so that only people who love them know what they are up to. They may have the knack of shrugging off the opinions of others or they may use humor to deflect the hostility that comes their way.

Many strong girls have found protected space in which they could grow. There are various ways to find that space. For example, athletics can be protective. Girls in sports are often emotionally healthy. They see their bodies as functional, not decorative. They have developed discipline in the pursuit of excellence. They have learned to win and lose, to cooperate, to handle stress and pressure. They are in a peer group that defines itself by athletic ability rather than popularity, drug or alcohol use, wealth or appearance.

Protective space can be created by books, interests, families, churches and physical or social isolation. It's a blessing. Girls who grow up unprotected, adrift in mass culture with little protective coating and no private territory are vulnerable to many kinds of problems.

This business of protected space is very complicated, however. Too much protection leads to the "princess and the pea syndrome," girls who are hothouse flowers unable to withstand stress. Too little protection often leads to addictions and self-destructive behaviors. The same stresses that help some girls grow, cripple others.

All lives have ups and downs. For most women, early adolescence is a big dip down. Strong girls, like all girls, do crazy things in junior high. They feel unstable and out of control. It's important to look beyond surface behavior to understand what's happening. For example, a girl can be depressed in junior high because she's bright enough to recognize our girl-poisoning culture and to feel defeated by it. A girl who withdraws may be acting adaptively. She may know that she's not ready to drink or be sexual and she may drop out of social life for a time while her friends grow up. Things are often different from the way they look on the surface.

Strong girls strive to define themselves as women and adults. They are trying to break away from family and remain close at the same time. They are trying to have friends without sacrificing themselves to do it. They attempt to define themselves as moral people and to take responsibility for their choices. They are trying to make good choices, often without much help. All of this is so difficult that weak often looks strong and strong looks weak. The girls who seem the happiest in junior high are often not the healthiest adults. They may be the girls who have less radar with which to pick up signals about reality. While this may be protective when the signals come fast and furious, later they may miss information. Or they may be the girls who don't even try to resolve contradictions or make sense of reality. They may be relatively comfortable, but they will not grow.

June

The morning we met, June had worked a double shift at the Kawasaki plant, gone out for breakfast and driven across town to my office. June was big-boned with a round, pockmarked face. She wore her hair short and was dressed in a gray sweat suit. She lumbered into my office and sank onto the couch. She was so physically imposing that I was surprised by her delicate sensibilities.

Her language was personal, precise and earthy. She talked about herself softly and carefully as if psychotherapy, like dentistry, might hurt. She did not, thank goodness, talk like someone who had read too many self-help books.

June said, "I'm here because I am dating someone for the first time in my life. I'm twenty-seven and I've never been kissed. I thought I might need some coaching."

She'd been at Kawasaki for ten years. Her closest friend worked next to her on the assembly line. Dixie was a single parent and June helped her with her kids. She pulled out their school pictures to show me and said they called her Aunt June. "They're real good kids," she said, "once you get to know them."

June had met her boyfriend, Marty, at work too. He was the union representative for her group of workers. The last three Saturday nights he had dropped by with a pizza and a video. Last Saturday night he put his arm around June. That's when she decided to call me.

I asked her about her family and June sighed, "I was afraid you would bring them up."

"We can wait," I say gently.

"I might as well get it out," she said. "After you hear about my teenage years, you'll understand why I haven't dated much."

June's father was a farm laborer who "never had much to do with me." Her mother was a cook at a rest home. "She was hard-working and fun. She'd bring me treats from the rest home—cookies and crafts that the residents made for me. She showed them my pictures and kept them posted on my activities. Everyone at the home loved her."

June paused and looked at me. "Mom died at the start of my freshman year in high school. It was an awful time to lose her. I had just started my periods. I was clumsy and had bad acne. I had been slightly chubby and then I got fat. I was totally alone."

June blew her nose before continuing. "The year Mom died, I watched the Miss America pageant all by myself. I stared at those thin, poised girls and knew I would never be like that. I had no looks and no talents. Only my mom had loved me as I was. I thought about giving up."

She rubbed her forehead as if to erase some memories too painful to consider. "I don't know how I made it through that year. Dad was never home. I had hardly any clothes. I did what housework and cooking got done and that was precious little. Dad almost never gave me money for groceries. I was fat and hungry at the same time."

I asked her about the kids at school. "They were terrible. Not so much mean, as totally indifferent. I didn't exist for them. I was too ugly and too sad to even be part of the class. I ate by myself and walked to and from school alone. No one would be my lab partner."

She rubbed her big face and continued. "One time a boy approached me in the cafeteria, in front of all the other kids, and asked me to go to a football game. I was such a goof that I thought be meant it. I thought maybe he could see past my appearance and like the real me. So I said sure, if I could get Dad's permission. Then he started laughing. His buddies all whooped it up too. They'd dared him to do it for a joke. He collected ten bucks for just asking me out."

June sighed. "After that I steered clear of boys."

Her father married Mercene a year after June's mother died. They took a honeymoon trip to Sun City and brought June salt and pepper shakers for her hope chest. "By then I had no hope," she said flatly.

"My stepmother was tight with money. She only let me wash my hair once a week. I needed to wash it daily it was so greasy, but she didn't want to pay for the water. My teeth were crooked and the school recommended braces. Mercene said, 'I've heard that can cost a thousand dollars. No way we'll spend that kind of money for straight teeth.' Once I cut my foot pretty badly when I was walking beans. She wouldn't pay for the doctor. I limped a little because of that."

I worked hard to remain neutral as June talked about this neglect. June herself had no anger. She continued matter-of-factly, "I was the black sheep. Once my stepbrother asked me why I lived with his family."

I asked how she survived those years when she was rejected at home and at school. "I thought about my mother and how she would have wanted me to behave. I decided that other people's bad behavior was no excuse for mine. I would do the best I could. I talked to Mom in bed at night. I told her about my days. I always tried to have something I was proud of to report to her. I knew she had really loved me, and that got me through a lot. I knew I was lovable and that the people around me were too blind to see it."

She rubbed her broad face with a handkerchief. "At the time I desperately wanted friends. Now I think I learned a lot those years. I learned to take care of myself. I got so that other people's rejection didn't faze me. I had my ideas about right and wrong.

"After high school my life really improved. I started working at Kawasaki. Immediately I felt more accepted. I worked hard and people noticed. Women invited me to eat with them. The men joked around with me. My supervisor took an interest in me. He encouraged me to get my teeth worked on and have my foot evaluated. I wear a brace now that corrected the limp."

June smiled when she spoke of work. "I have a Halloween party every year for all the workers in my area. Fridays I bowl on the union team. I have earned merit raises every year I've worked there. I make good money.

"I've forgiven Dad and Mercene. I'm happy, so what is there to be angry about now? I am happier than they are. I try to do something for them every weekend, I take over a pie or mow their yard."

I asked how she gets along with her father. "Dad can't forgive me for being fat. He really wanted a beautiful daughter."

I thought of June's life. She has a spirit as delicate and strong as a spiderweb. She is gifted at forgiving and loving. Because she is unattractive by our cultural standards, she has been devalued by many, including her own father. But somehow she has managed to survive and even thrive through all this adversity. She reminds me of those succulent desert flowers that remain dormant for so many seasons and then bloom lavishly when there is a smattering of rain.

I said to her, "Your father has missed an opportunity to love someone who is marvelous."

We talked about Marty. He's a bulky man who is prematurely balding. June said, "His looks don't matter. I know how hard he works and that he doesn't put anyone down. He's not a complainer."

I suggested that daily she imagine herself successfully kissing him. "It's hard to do what you can't even imagine doing. Once you have the images down, the reality will be easier." I encouraged her to keep her expectations for that first kiss low. "Bells may not ring and the sky may not light up." I quoted Georgia O'Keeffe, totally out of context: "Nobody's good at the beginning."

I pointed out that the relationship was going well. Physical affection was only a small part of a relationship. She was already gifted at loving and forgiving, which were much more important qualities. I predicted that kissing would be easy once she was ready.

When I saw June again, she reported that kissing was great. She asked me if I thought she needed more therapy. "No," I said. "I think you could teach me some lessons about strength through adversity and the importance of forgiveness."

June is a good example of someone who, with almost no luck at all, fashioned a good life for herself. Almost all our psychological theories would predict that June would turn out badly. But as happens more frequently than we psychologists generally acknowledge, adversity built her character. What saved her was her deep awareness of her mother's love. Even though her mother was dead, June felt her mother's spirit was with her. That enabled her to feel valued at a time when she was rejected by everyone. June's belief in her mother's love gave her a sense of purpose. She was determined to live in a way that would make her mother proud.

June had the gift for appreciating what was good in her life. Once she told me, "I always get what I want." Then she winked and said, "But I know what to want." Her life, which might strike some people as difficult or dull, is rich and rewarding. She has friends, money, a boyfriend and the respect of her peers. She has that pride in her life that so many self-made people have. She has no bitterness or anger because she is basically happy. She's a desert flower opening to the rain.

QUESTIONS FOR DISCUSSION AND WRITING

1. Pipher believes strong girls have self-value and a view of themselves as connected to a talent, or to an identity, or to an interest outside of themselves.

What other attributes do you believe make young girls strong both in character and in the strength that life demands? In what ways do we as a society define strength in girls differently from that in boys?

2. For Pipher, strength in girls also seems to be linked to family love and family loyalty; although she argues that all girls go through some form of rebellion or distancing of themselves from their parents. If you are a young woman: To what extent does this reflect your own experience? Do you believe it is different for boys? How? Why? If you are a young man: How is the need to *individuate*—that is, to separate for a period of time from your parents—different for you than for girls? Or is it?

3. Do you agree with the idea in this reading selection that as girls, strong women appear to have experienced rejection, isolation, loneliness, and lack of popularity? If this is true, what does it suggest about how we value social acceptance and popularity? How important are acceptance and popularity for girls' psychological development? How important should they be?

4. Pipher writes about the difficulty of choices for girls and for their parents. Parents, she says, often walk a thin line between being too protective and not being protective enough. Daughters, she asserts, often need to break away from their families but also want to stay close to them. Is there a happy medium, or do these kinds of choices depend on the parents and the girls involved?

5. What are your reactions to June, "the desert flower" Pipher writes about, the twenty-seven-year-old woman who had never been kissed? Pipher seems certain that June was well adjusted and content, that she did not require any additional psychotherapy, largely because she saw June as a loving and forgiving woman who was fortunate enough to have had a loving mother. Do you believe that a woman like June, who was ridiculed socially and was unaccepted by her father because of her physical unattractiveness, can be happy? Do you agree with Pipher that because June has romance, friends, money, and self-pride she can be happy despite her looks and regardless of how her father treated her?

ON TECHNIQUE AND STYLE

1. Does Pipher present a convincing and persuasive argument? What specific methods does she employ in her writing to make her argument most convincing?

2. Analyze the logic behind Pipher's presentation of ideas. Do you see patterns to the way she sets her ideas forward that suggest a roadmap or a plan for her readers? What are they?

3. Compare and contrast the authority Pipher evokes in us as readers. Does her gender affect your overall response as a reader? Should it?

CULTURAL QUESTION

1. Sociologic research reveals that African American girls generally have the highest self-esteem among girls of different racial and ethnic groups. Assuming that this is the case, what kinds of conclusions might you draw?

Inside the World of Boys

William Pollack

William Pollack, PhD, is a clinical psychologist who codirects the Center for Men at McLean Hospital/Harvard Medical School. He is an assistant clinical professor of psychiatry at Harvard Medical School and a founding member and Fellow of the Society for the Psychological Study of Men and Masculinity of the American Psychological Association. His best-known work, from which we have taken the selection included here, is Real Boys: Rescuing Our Sons from the Myths of Boyhood *(1998). He is also the author of* Real Boys' Voices. *Like Pipher, he uses his clinical practice to harvest observations about a national crisis, a "gender strait-jacketing" of boys. Pollack makes the case, both in his essay and in the interview on the weblink, that boys often suffer low self-esteem, in large part due to what he calls "the boy code," a set of unspoken rules that compel them to feel they need to hide their emotions and keep their vulnerability from exposure. However, again like Pipher, Pollack is hopeful. In the selection included here from* Real Boys *he calls to our attention, through the example of a patient of his named Adam, the importance of ameliorating the increasing problem of the gender gap between boys and girls in academic performance. Once a good student, Adam is suddenly performing poorly in school because of "the boy code." The assumption is that if the boy code is diminished or broken, academic and social performances of boys will heighten.*

The Boy Code "Everything's Just Fine"

Adam is a fourteen-year-old boy whose mother sought me out after a workshop I was leading on the subject of boys and families. Adam, she told me, had been performing very well in school, but now she felt something was wrong.

Adam had shown such promise that he had been selected to join a special program for talented students, and the program was available only at a different—and more academically prestigious—school than the one Adam had attended. The new school was located in a well-to-do section of town, more affluent than Adam's own neighborhood. Adam's mother had been pleased when her son had qualified for the program and even more delighted that he would be given a scholarship to pay for it. And so Adam had set off on this new life.

At the time we talked, Mrs. Harrison's delight had turned to worry. Adam was not doing well at the new school. His grades were mediocre, and at midterm he had been given a warning that he might fail algebra. Yet Adam continued to insist, "I'm fine. Everything's just fine." He said this both at home and at school. Adam's mother was perplexed, as was the guidance counselor at his new school. "Adam seems cheerful and has no complaints," the counselor told her. "But something must be wrong." His mother tried to talk to Adam, hoping to find out what was troubling him and causing him to do so poorly in school. "But the more I questioned him about what was going on," she said, "the more he continued to deny any problems."

Adam was a quiet and rather shy boy, small for his age. In his bright blue eyes I detected an inner pain, a malaise whose cause I could not easily fathom. I had seen a similar look on the faces of a number of boys of different ages, including many boys in the "Listening to Boys' Voices" study. Adam looked wary, hurt, closed-in, self-protective. Most of all, he looked alone.

One day, his mother continued, Adam came home with a black eye. She asked him what had happened. "Just an accident," Adam had mumbled. He'd kept his eyes cast down, she remembered, as if he felt guilty or ashamed. His mother probed more deeply. She told him that she knew something was wrong, something upsetting was going on, and that— whatever it was—they could deal with it, they could face it together. Suddenly, Adam erupted in tears, and the story he had been holding inside came pouring out.

Adam was being picked on at school, heckled on the bus, goaded into fights in the schoolyard. "Hey, White Trash!" the other boys shouted at him. "You don't belong here with *us*!" taunted a twelfth-grade bully. "Why don't you go back to your own side of town!" The taunts often led to physical attacks, and Adam found himself having to fight back in order to defend himself. "But I never throw the first punch," Adam explained to his mother. "I don't show them they can hurt me. I don't want to embarrass myself in front of everybody."

I turned to Adam. "How do you feel about all this?" I asked. "How do you handle your feelings of anger and frustration?" His answer was, I'm sad to say, a refrain I hear often when I am able to connect to the inner lives of boys.

"I get a little down," Adam confessed, "but I'm very good at hiding it. It's like I wear a mask. Even when the kids call me names or taunt me, I never show them how much it crushes me inside. I keep it all in."

"What do you do with the sadness?" I asked.

"I tend to let it boil inside until I can't hold it any longer, and then it explodes. It's like I have a breakdown, screaming and yelling. But I only do it inside my own room at home, where nobody can hear. Where nobody will know about it." He paused a moment. "I think I got this from my dad, unfortunately."

Adam was doing what I find so many boys do: he was hiding behind a mask, and using it to hide his deepest thoughts and feelings—his real self—from everyone, even the people closest to him. This mask of masculinity enabled Adam to make a bold (if inaccurate) statement to the world: "I can handle it. Everything's fine. I am invincible."

Adam, like other boys, wore this mask as an invisible shield, a persona to show the outside world a feigned self-confidence and bravado, and to hide the shame he felt at his feelings of vulnerability, powerlessness, and isolation. He couldn't handle the school situation alone—very few boys or girls of fourteen could—and he didn't know how to ask for help, even from people he knew loved him. As a result, Adam was unhappy and was falling behind in his academic performance.

Boys Today Are Falling Behind

While it may seem as if we live in a "man's world," at least in relation to power and wealth in adult society we do not live in a "boy's world." Boys on the whole are not faring well in our schools, especially in our public schools. It is in the classroom that we see some of the most destructive effects of society's misunderstanding of boys. Thrust into competition with their peers, some boys invest so much energy into keeping up their emotional guard and disguising their deepest and most vulnerable feelings, they often have little or no energy left to apply themselves to their schoolwork. No doubt boys still show up as small minorities at the top of a few academic lists, playing starring roles as some teachers' best students. But, most often, boys form the majority of the bottom of the class. Over the last decade we've been forced to confront some staggering statistics. From elementary grades through high school, boys receive lower grades than girls. Eighth-grade boys are held back 50 percent more often than girls. By high school, boys account for two thirds of the students in special education classes. Fewer boys than girls now attend and graduate from college. Fifty-nine percent of all master's degree candidates are now women, and the percentage of men in graduate-level professional education is shrinking each year.

So, there is a gender gap in academic performance, and boys are falling to the bottom of the heap. The problem stems as much from boys' lack of confidence in their ability to perform at school as from their actual inability to perform.

When eighth-grade students are asked about their futures, girls are now twice as likely as boys to say they want to pursue a career in management, the professions, or business. Boys experience more difficulty adjusting to school, are up to ten times more likely to suffer from "hyperactivity" than girls, and account for 71 percent of all school suspensions. In recent years, girls have been making great strides in math and science.

Boys' Self-Esteem—and Bragging

The fact is that *boys' self-esteem as learners is far more fragile than that of most girls.* A recent North Carolina study of students in grades six to eight concluded that "Boys have a much lower image of themselves as students than girls do." Conducted by Dr. William Purkey, this study contradicts the myth that adolescent boys are more likely than girls to see themselves as smart enough to succeed in society. Boys tend to brag, according to Purkey, as a "shield to hide deep-seated lack of confidence." It is the mask at work once again, a façade of confidence and bravado that boys erect to hide what they perceive as a shameful sense of vulnerability. Girls, on the other hand, brag less and do better in school. It is probably no surprise that a recent U.S. Department of Education study found that among high school seniors fewer boys than girls expect to pursue graduate studies, work toward a law degree, or go to medical school.

What we really need for boys is the same upswing in self-esteem as learners that we have begun to achieve for girls—to recognize the specialized academic needs of boys and girls in order to turn us into a more gender-savvy society.

Overwhelmingly, recent research indicates that girls not only outperform boys academically but also feel far more confident and capable. Indeed the boys in my study reported, over and over again, how it was not "cool" to be too smart in class, for it could lead to being labeled a nerd, dork, wimp, or fag. As one boy put it, "I'm not stupid enough to sit in the front row and act like some sort of teacher's pet. If I did, I'd end up with a head full of spitballs and then get my butt kicked in." Just as girls in coeducational environments have been forced to suppress their voices of certainty and truth, boys feel pressured to hide their yearnings for genuine relationships and their thirst for knowledge. To garner acceptance among their peers and protect themselves from being shamed, boys often focus on maintaining their masks and on doing whatever they can to avoid seeming interested in things creative or intellectual. To distance themselves from the things that the stereotype identifies as "feminine," many boys sit through classes with-out contributing and tease other boys who speak up and participate. Others pull pranks during class, start fights, skip classes, or even drop out of school entirely.

QUESTIONS FOR DISCUSSION AND WRITING

1. Pollack uses Adam, the fourteen-year-old boy who was being bullied, as an example of how boys often feel compelled to wear masks to hide their true thoughts and feelings, their real selves. Can you show, through specific examples, how or why you believe this is true? Is this the way boys tend to

behave, especially when they need to appear confident or strong in the face of adversity?

2. Adam, Pollack writes, "didn't know how to ask for help, even from people he knew loved him." Is the way Adam feels generally more the pattern for boys than for girls? Jokes are made about how men are supposedly less willing even to ask for directions. If, as the British poet William Wordsworth said, "the child is father to the man," might one conclude that men begin to hide their need for help as boys because asking for help supposedly shows weakness? Are girls less inclined to hide their feelings?

3. Pollack argues that boys are much worse off than girls academically, especially in public schools. On the other hand, there have been many arguments that girls are more often ignored by educators than boys are, and that they are given less attention and less validation. Pollack contends that much of the poorer performance by boys in school is the result of boys needing to wear masks and disguising their feelings and keeping up their emotional guards. What do you think? From your own observations and experience are boys really "more fragile learners" than girls? Is it largely because of lower self-esteem?

4. Pollack writes, "What we really need for boys is the same upswing in self-esteem as learners that we have begun to achieve for girls—to recognize the specialized academic needs of boys and girls in order to turn us into a more gender-savvy society." If boys are afraid of revealing real interest in learning out of fear of being thought nerdy or uncool, how can we best achieve what Pollack says should and must be achieved? What characteristics would exist in a more gender-savvy society? What might a gender-savvy society look like?

ON TECHNIQUE AND STYLE

1. Evaluate Pollack as an essayist. Can you sum up how or why you believe him to be effective in establishing and supporting his position? Does he present his position in an overall effective way? Why or why not?

2. Pollack has had a great deal of experience as a practicing psychologist who has worked with boys. Analyze how his experiential background comes through in his writing. How does it add to the weight and credibility of his ideas?

3. How well structured or organized does Pollack appear to be in the method he uses to bring us into the world of boys and their inner lives? How does the method of organization he imposes on his ideas affect the overall flow and reasonableness of his argument?

CULTURAL QUESTION

1. Do you believe boys from different cultural backgrounds wear different kinds of masks? How might these be set apart or distinguished without stereotyping?

Why Boys Don't Play with Dolls

Katha Pollitt

Katha Pollitt (1949–   ) is an American feminist writer and an award-winning poet known for her column "Subject to Debate" in The Nation, *where she writes mainly about culture and politics. She has also written for* The New Yorker, Harper's Maga-zine, MS, *and* The New York Times—*where the essay included here, "Why Boys Don't Play with Dolls," first appeared in 1995. She has published a number of volumes of essays including* Reasonable Creatures, Subject to Debate, *and* Sense and Dis-sents on Women, Politics and Culture. *Known for her sharp and provocative writing she also won a National Book Critics Circle Award for her poetry. She was educated at Barnard College and the Columbia School of the Arts and has taught at Barnard. In "Why Boys Don't Play with Dolls" she raises important sex role questions about gender differences from her perspective as a feminist and she focuses, to hearken back to Pollack's phrase, on the gender strait-jacketing of boys. Her diagnosis is serious. However, she clearly believes change can emerge if only change in consciousness lights the way. "Why Boys Don't Play with Dolls" was published in* The New York Times, *October 8, 1995.*

It's 28 years since the founding of NOW,[1] and boys still like trucks and girls still like dolls. Increasingly, we are told that the source of these robust pref-erences must lie outside society—in prenatal hormonal influences, brain chemistry, genes—and that feminism has reached its natural limits. What else could possibly explain the love of preschool girls for party dresses or the desire of toddler boys to own more guns than Mark from Michigan.[2]

True, recent studies claim to show small cognitive differences between the sexes: he gets around by orienting himself in space; she does it by remembering landmarks. Time will tell if any deserve the hoopla with which each is invariably greeted, over the protests of the researchers themselves. But even if the results hold up (and the history of such research is not encour-aging), we don't need studies of sex-differentiated brain activity in reading, say, to understand why boys and girls still seem so unalike.

The feminist movement has done much for some women, and something for every woman, but it has hardly turned America into a playground free of sex roles. It hasn't even got women to stop dieting or men to stop interrupting them.

[1] National Organization for Women.
[2] "Mark from Michigan" refers to Mark Koernke, a member of the Michigan Militia-at-Large, among other "patriot" movement militias. He was mistakenly linked to the bombing of the Mur-rah Federal Building in Oklahoma City.

Instead of looking at kids to "prove" that differences in behavior by sex are innate, we can look at the ways we raise kids as an index to how unfinished the feminist revolution really is, and how tentatively it is embraced even by adults who fully expect their daughters to enter previously male-dominated professions and their sons to change diapers.

I'm at a children's birthday party. "I'm sorry," one mom silently mouths to the mother of the birthday girl, who has just torn open her present—Tropical Splash Barbie. Now, you can love Barbie or you can hate Barbie, and there are feminists in both camps. But *apologize* for Barbie? Inflict Barbie, against your own convictions, on the child of a friend you know will be none too pleased?

Every mother in that room had spent years becoming a person who had to be taken seriously, not least by herself. Even the most attractive, I'm willing to bet, had suffered over her own body's failure to fit the impossible American ideal. Given all that, it seems crazy to transmit Barbie to the next generation. Yet to reject her is to say that what Barbie represents—being sexy, thin, stylish—is unimportant, which is obviously not true, and children know it's not true.

Women's looks matter terribly in this society, and so Barbie, however ambivalently, must be passed along. After all, there are worse toys. The Cut and Style Barbie styling head, for example, a grotesque object intended to encourage "hair play." The grown-ups who give that probably apologize, too.

How happy would most parents be to have a child who flouted sex conventions? I know a lot of women, feminists, who complain in a comical, eyeball-rolling way about their sons' passion for sports: the ruined weekends, obnoxious coaches, macho values. But they would not think of discouraging their sons from participating in this activity they find so foolish. Or do they? Their husbands are sports fans, too, and they like their husbands a lot.

Could it be that even sports-resistant moms see athletics as part of manliness? That if their sons wanted to spend the weekend writing up their diaries, or reading, or baking, they'd find it disturbing? Too antisocial? Too lonely? Too gay?

Theories of innate differences in behavior are appealing. They let parents off the hook—no small recommendation in a culture that holds moms, and sometimes even dads, responsible for their children's every misstep on the road to bliss and success.

They allow grown-ups to take the path of least resistance to the dominant culture, which always requires less psychic effort, even if it means more actual work: just ask the working mother who comes home exhausted and nonetheless finds it easier to pick up her son's socks than make him do it himself. They let families buy for their children, without *too* much guilt, the unbelievably sexist junk that the kids, who have been watching commercials since birth, understandably crave.

But the thing the theories do most of all is tell adults that the *adult* world—in which moms and dads still play by many of the old rules even as they question and fidget and chafe against them—is the way it's supposed to be. A girl with a doll and a boy with a truck "explain" why men are from Mars and women are from Venus, why wives do housework and husbands just don't understand.

The paradox is that the world of rigid and hierarchical sex roles evoked by determinist theories is already passing away. Three-year-olds may indeed insist that doctors are male and nurses female, even if their own mother is a physician. Six-year-olds know better. These days, something like half of all medical students are female and male applications to nursing school are inching upwards. When tomorrow's 3-year-olds play doctor, who's to say how they'll assign the roles?

With sex roles, as in every area of life, people aspire to what is possible, and conform to what is necessary. But these are not fixed, especially today. Biological determinism may reassure some adults about their present, but it is feminism, the ideology of flexible and converging sex roles, that fits our children's future. And the kids, somehow, know this.

That's why, if you look carefully, you'll find that for every kid who fits a stereotype, there's another who's breaking one down. Sometimes it's the same kid—the boy who skateboards *and* takes cooking in his after-school program; the girl who collects stuffed animals *and* A-pluses in science.

Feminists are often accused of imposing their "agenda" on children. Isn't that what adults always do, consciously and unconsciously? Kids aren't born religious, or polite, or kind, or able to remember where they put their sneakers. Inculcating these behaviors, and the values behind them, is a tremendous amount of work, involving many adults. We don't have a choice, really, about *whether* we should give our children messages about what it means to be male and female—they're bombarded with them from morning till night.

The question is, as always, what do we want those messages to be?

QUESTIONS FOR DISCUSSION AND WRITING

1. Pollitt titles her essay "Why Boys Don't Play with Dolls." Does she provide an answer? Pollitt is clearly a feminist who, consistent with feminist thought, argues for an ongoing "ideology of flexible and converging sex roles." Yet she also argues that the feminist movement "hasn't even got women to stop dieting or men to stop interrupting them." Do you think feminism, which Pollitt calls "an unfinished revolution," has failed despite the changes it has brought? Or does "an unfinished revolution" simply mean there is much work still to be done by everyone, including feminists?

2. Pollitt reasons that the gender gap continues to exist to a great degree because of the ease with which parents fall back on theories of innate gender differences and what she calls "biological determinism." Do you agree or disagree?

3. Can you think of other examples to support Pollitt's point of view or to challenge it?

4. Pollitt asks a central question: "When tomorrow's 3-year-olds play doctor, who's to say how they'll assign their roles?" She is punning on the phrase "play doctor," which is often used to describe what children do when they show each other their sexual anatomy. What is she indicating about the changing nature of sexual differences between boys and girls? How hopeful is her view?

5. Pollitt concludes her essay with a question concerning what we, as a society, should want gender differences between boys and girls to be. What should some of those messages ideally be for boys? For girls? For both?

ON TECHNIQUE AND STYLE

1. What techniques does Pollitt use to convince us as readers of the position she fashions in her essay? Do you feel they are successful techniques? Why or why not?

2. Assume for the moment that Pollitt also wants those who do not share her political and feminist views to agree with her ideas about gender. What devices does she use to persuade readers who might not agree with her or who might not be entirely sympathetic to her position?

3. Focus on examples and evidence Pollitt uses to support her notion that there is still much to be critical of in the ongoing feminist revolution. What is the overall effect of using such examples or evidence on her argument in favor of an ongoing vital feminism? Does it diminish the strength of her position or add to it?

CULTURAL QUESTION

1. Do the kinds of sex roles Pollitt writes about differ among boys and girls of varied cultural backgrounds? Based on your own experiences and observations, what gender differences reflect different cultural attitudes among boys and girls of different backgrounds? Be as specific as you can.

From The War Against Boys

Christina Hoff Sommers

Christina Hoff Sommers (1953–   ), a graduate of New York University, has a PhD in philosophy from Brandeis and is a resident scholar at the American Enterprise Institute in Washington, DC. She was a professor of philosophy at Clark University. Her work has appeared in The American Scholar, New Journal of Medicine, Atlantic Monthly, Partisan Review, National Review, *and* Chronicles of Higher

Education. *The coeditor of* Virtue and Vice in Everyday Life and Right and Wrong: Basic Readings in Ethics, *she is the author of* Who Stole Feminism? How Women Have Betrayed Women, One Nation Under Therapy: How the Helping Culture Is Eroding Self-Reliance, *and* The War Against Boys: How Misguided Feminism Is Harming Our Young Men *(2001). The two short selections from* The War Against Boys *make arguments designed to counter both the perceived feminist need to construct a paradigm for both sexes based on not acknowledging essential, innate gender differences and on the notion of a gender crisis. Footnotes have been deleted from this selection. See the original source for full documentation.*

Reprinted with the permission of Simon & Schuster, Inc., from *The War Against Boys* by Christina Hoff Sommers. Copyright © 2000 by Christina Hoff Sommers. All rights reserved.

Where the Equity Enthusiasts Go Wrong

The idea that girls and boys are the same and that masculinity and femininity are simply a matter of social conditioning have the status of first principles in schools of education, women's studies and gender studies departments, and the U.S. Department of Education. What follows from this is the notion that what society has constructed amiss can be torn down and reconstructed—in the right way. It is assumed that, at bottom, we are all essentially androgynous.

The feminist philosopher Sandra Lee Bartky speaks for many gender scholars when she says that human beings are born "bisexual" into our patriarchal society and then, through social conditioning, are "transformed into male and female gender personalities, the one destined to command, the other to obey."

Even the so-called difference feminists—Carol Gilligan and her school, Sara Ruddick, and other feminist philosophers who celebrate certain feminine qualities, such as caring, nurturing, and social sensitivity—believe that these differences are socially constructed and should be constructed differently.

This doctrine does not stand up well under critical scrutiny. A growing body of empirical data that is rarely if ever mentioned in the gender equity training seminars strongly supports the experience of parents and the wisdom of the ages: that many basic male-female differences are innate, hardwired, and not the result of conditioning. In the past few years, there have been important developments in neuroscience, evolutionary psychology, genetics, and neuroendocrinology that all but refute the social constructionist thesis and point to certain inborn gender differences.

Males, for instance, are, on average, better at spatial reasoning than females. They are more adept at rotating three-dimensional geometric figures in their minds, and they perform better on spatial manipulation tests. Males' superior skills in this area give them an advantage in math, engineering, and architecture. Of course, there are females with exceptional abilities in spatial reasoning, but, taken as a whole, males have a slight but distinct edge.

Females, on the other hand, have better verbal skills. It has long beenknown that girls begin talking earlier and that speech and reading disorders such as dyslexia are more common in males. On most national assessment tests, females are well ahead of males in reading and writing. Unsurprisingly, many more females than males major in English, comparative literature, and foreign languages.

Girls' verbal skills may be responsible for their superior emotional expressiveness. Daniel Goleman, a science writer at *The New York Times* and author of *Emotional Intelligence,* reports on one explanation that ties early language facility to emotional style: "Because girls develop language more quickly than do boys, this leads them to be more experienced at articulating their feelings and more skilled than boys at using words to explore and substitute for emotional reactions such as physical fights." Although Goleman believes girls' verbal skills may give them an emotional edge, he does not believe it makes them nicer than boys. As he sees it, girls' more rapid development of interpersonal skills and boys' physical superiority make for different styles of aggression: "By age 13 . . . girls become more adept than boys at artful aggressive tactics like ostracism, vicious gossip, and indirect vendettas . . . Boys, by and large, simply continue being confrontational when angered, oblivious to these more covert strategies."

Go to any large toy mart and you will find sections for boys and sections for girls answering to their different preferences. For boys, gadgets and action are the things, while girls prefer dolls, glamour, and playhouses. Many a parent will tell you of failed efforts to get daughters interested in Lincoln logs and sons in sewing kits. Being differently talented and differently driven, the sexes have characteristically different behavior preferences. The gender-equity specialists believe that gender-distinct play preferences are purely a matter of social conditioning. But researchers have confirmed what parents experience all the time: even without conditioning (indeed, even with counter-conditioing), boys and girls show different preferences and gravitate toward different toys.

The exceptions only go to prove the rule. One group of girls does consistently prefer trucks over dolls: girls with congenital adrenal hyperplasia (CAH). This is a genetic defect that results when the female fetus is subjected to abnormally large quantities of male hormones called adrenal androgens. CAH girls tend to grow up to be more aggressive than their non-CAH sisters. UCLA psychologists Sheri Berenbaum and Melissa Hines set up an experiment in which they observed the play behavior of both CAH and non-CAH girls. They found that "the CAH girls spent significantly more time playing with boys' toys than did control girls." CAH girls, incidentally, are also better at spatial rotation tests than their unaffected sisters.

These sorts of findings, while not definitive, certainly do not square with the crude view that "gender is a social construct." If all gender differences were culturally determined, you would expect to find some societies where females are the risk takers and males play with dolls. There would be societies in which females, on average, would do better in math and young males would be more verbally adept than females. But where are they? The social constructionists have no plausible explanation for the absence of such societies. But there are many plausible explanations for the distinctive gender differences in special aptitudes and characteristic behaviors that are grounded in biology, endocrinology, and evolutionary psychology. Quite apart from the sexual difference in reproductive functions, men and women are innately distinguished in "gender." Mother Nature is not a feminist.

The natural gender differences between men and women mean we cannot hope to get statistical male-female parity of competence and aptitude in all fields. The same seems true of preferences: there will always be far more women than men who want to stay home with children; there will always be more women than men who want to be kindergarten teachers rather than helicopter mechanics. Boys will always be less interested than girls in dollhouses. This does not mean that our sex rigidly determines our future. The anthropologist Lionel Tiger has it right when he says, "Biology is not destiny, but it is good statistical probability."

. . .

A Nation of Hamlets and Ophelias

In regarding seemingly normal children as abnormally afflicted, Pollack was taking the well-trodden path pioneered by Carol Gilligan and Mary Pipher. Gilligan had described the nation's girls as drowning, disappearing, traumatized, and undergoing various kinds of "psychological foot-binding." Following Gilligan, Mary Pipher, in Reviving Ophelia, had written of the selves of girls going down in flames, "crashing and burning." Pollack's Real Boys continues in this vein: "Hamlet fared little better than Ophelia. . . . He grew increasingly isolated, desolate, and alone, and those who loved him were never able to get through to him. In the end he died a tragic and unnecessary death."

By using Ophelia and Hamlet as symbols, Pipher and Pollack paint a picture of American children as disturbed and in need of rescue. But once one discounts the anecdotal and scientifically ineffectual reports on the inner turmoil of adolescents that have issued from the Harvard Graduate School of Education and the McLean Hospital's Center for Men, there remains no reason to believe that girls or boys are in crisis. Mainstream researchers see no evidence of it. American children, boys as well as girls, are on the whole psychologically sound. They are not isolated, full of despair, or "hiding parts of themselves from the world's gaze"—no more so, at least, than any other age group in the population.

One wonders why the irresponsible and baseless claims that girls and boys are psychologically impaired have been so uncritically received by the media and the public. One reason, perhaps, is that Americans seem all too ready to entertain almost any suggestion that a large group of outwardly normal people are suffering from some pathological condition. By 1999, best-selling books had successively identified women, girls, and boys as being in crisis and in need of rescue. Late in 1999, Susan Faludi's *Stiffed: The Betrayal of the American Male* called our attention to yet another huge segment of the population that no one had realized was in serious trouble: adult men. Faludi claims to have unmasked "masculinity crisis" so severe and pervasive that she finds it hard to understand why men do not rise up in rebellion.

Although Faludi seems to have arrived at her view of men without having read Pollack's analysis of boys, her conclusions about men are identical to his about boys. She claims that men are suffering because the culture imposes stultifying myths and ideals of manliness on them. *Stiffed* shows us the hapless baby-boomer males, burdened "with dangerous prescriptions of manhood," trying vainly to cope with a world in which they are bound to fail. Men have been taught that "to be a man means to be at the controls and at all times to feel yourself in control." They cannot live up to this stoical ideal of manliness. At the same time, our "misogynist culture" now imposes its humiliating "ornamental" demands on men as well as women. "No wonder," says Faludi, "men are in such agony."

What is Faludi's evidence of an "American masculinity crisis"? She talked to dozens of unhappy men, among them wife batterers in Long Beach, California, distressed male pornography stars, teenage sex predators known as the Spur Posse (how did she miss the Menendez brothers?). Most of Faludi's subjects have sad stories to tell about inadequate fathers, personal alienation, and feelings of helplessness. Unfortunately, the reader never learns why the disconsolate men Faludi selected for attention are to be regarded as representative.

If men are experiencing the agonies Faludi speaks of, they are doing so with remarkable equanimity. The National Opinion Research Center at the University of Chicago, which has been tracking levels of general happiness and life satisfaction in the general population since 1957, consistently finds that approximately 90 percent of Americans describe themselves as happy with their lives, with no significant differences between men and women. I recently asked its survey director, Tom Smith, if there had been any unusual signs of distress among men in the last few decades (the years in which Faludi claims that a generation of men have seen "all their hopes and dreams burn up on the launch pad"). Smith replied, "There have been no trends in a negative direction during those years." But Faludi believes otherwise and joins Gilligan, Pollack, and the others in calling for a "new paradigm" of how to be men.

Faludi cites the work of Dr. Darrel Regier, director of the Division of Epidemiology at the National Institute of Mental Health, to support her thesis that men are increasingly unhappy. I asked Dr. Regier what he thought of her men-are-in-distress claim. "I am not sure where she gets her evidence for any substantial rise in male distress," he replied. He was surprised that one of his own 1988 studies had been cited by Faludi as evidence of an increase in "anxiety, depressive disorders, suicide." "Well," Dr. Regier said, "that is a fallacy. The article shows no such thing." What does he think of these false mental health scares? I asked. "I guess they sell books," he said.

Apocalyptic alarms about looming mental health disasters do sell well. In a satirical article entitled "A Nation of Nuts," *New York Observer* editor Jim Windolf tallied the number of Americans allegedly suffering from some kind of mental disorder. He sent away for brochures and literature of dozens of advocacy agencies and mental health organizations. Then he did the math. Windolf reported, "If you believe the statistics, 77 percent of America's adult population is a mess. . . . And we haven't even thrown in alien abductees, road ragers, and internet addicts." If you factor in Gilligan's and Pipher's hapless girls, Pollack's suffering and dangerous boys, and Faludi's agonized men, we seem to be a country going to Hell in a handbasket.

Perhaps this fin de siècle fashion in identifying large groups as mentally infirm will soon wane—it has nothing left to feed on. With women, girls, boys, and now men all identified as stricken populations, the genre seems to have run out of victims.

Gilligan, Pollack, and Faludi are the preeminent crisis writers. Each finds abnormality and inner anguish in an outwardly normal and happy population. Each traces the malaise to the "male culture," which is blamed for forcing harmful gender stereotypes, myths, or "masks" on the population in crisis (be it women, girls, boys, or men). Girls and women, they say, are constrained to be "nice and kind"; boys and men are constrained to be "in control" and emotionally disconnected. Each writer projects an air of sympathy; each sincerely wants to help the casualties of our patriarchal culture. Nevertheless, by taking an unhappy minority as representative of a whole group, each of these writers is less than respectful to the allegedly afflicted population. Pollack, who wants to rescue boys from the myths of boyhood, unwittingly harms them by arousing public fear, dismay, and suspicion. In characterizing boys as "Hamlets," he stigmatizes an entire sex and a particular age group. His seemingly benign project of rescuing boys from "the myths of boyhood" by reconnecting them to their nurturers puts pressure on boys to be more like girls. The unintended effect is to put boys on the defensive. Gilligan, Pipher, and Faludi portray their disconsolate multitudes sympathetically—but at the price of presenting them as pitiable.

QUESTIONS FOR DISCUSSION AND WRITING

1. The essential idea that Christina Hoff Sommers is attacking in the chapter titled "Where the Equity Enthusiasts Go Wrong" is the notion that gender differences can somehow be refashioned or remade. Do you agree that the statistical gender differences she cites tend to be hardwired differences?

2. Hoff Sommers writes, "Mother Nature is not a feminist." Is she simply saying feminists believe in inborn gender equity or is she intimating stronger views of meaning by her choice of what author Margaret Atwood calls "the F word"?

3. At a number of points throughout her book *The War Against Boys* Hoff Sommers attempts to refute Carol Gilligan, William Pollack, and Mary Pipher as bad researchers who come to incorrect conclusions about gender

differences. Do you agree with her basic premise that these writers have placed too much emphasis on gender victimization and that the result is "regarding normal children as abnormally afflicted"? Is she correct in her position that there is "no reason to believe that girls or boys are in crisis"?

4. Hoff Sommers also advances the argument that misery sells and that if we believed all we read we would be a nation of afflicted victims. Do you agree that media and publishers, film and television, tend to overhype "apocalyptic alarms" that increase the overall sense that gender inequity and gender differences cause misery for both boys and girls? Do you think those kinds of approaches tend to sell well in the media? Are they perhaps what many people want or need to hear?

5. Hoff Sommers contends that writers like Pollack, Gilligan, and Pipher (as well as famed feminist Susan Faludi) ultimately do harm— Pollack by putting pressure on boys to be more like girls and the women writers by making girls and women "pitiable." Do you agree or disagree? Why?

ON TECHNIQUE AND STYLE

1. How effective do you feel Hoff Sommers is in her attacks on other writers? What specific methods or techniques, in going after well-known writers with whom she disagrees, does she use to make her arguments persuasive or convincing?

2. In the chapter titled "Where the Equity Enthusiasts Go Wrong" Hoff Sommers supports her position of innate gender differences with the example of a group of girls with a genetic defect of an abnormally large male hormone who prefer playing with trucks to playing with dolls. In "A Nation of Hamlets and Ophelias" she cites a research group in Chicago and an epidemiologist at the National Institute of Mental Health to validate the idea that most of us, with no significant gender differences, are satisfied and happy with our lives and that men as a rule are not unhappy. How well do these examples serve to support her positions?

3. Focus on the tone and diction used by Hoff Sommers in the two short excerpts from her book. How does her use of tone and language compare and contrast to any of the other essayists in the chapter—Pipher, Pollack, Pollitt? She has a chapter in her book *The War Against Boys* called "Gilligan's Island." How does the voice she creates as a writer compare and contrast to the voice we hear in Gilligan's responses on the web link interview?

CULTURAL QUESTION

1. Does Hoff Sommers's emphasis on boys and girls being portrayed as victims apply to an even greater extent to the picture often conveyed of boys and girls from cross-cultural backgrounds? In your opinion, is too much made of victimization?

FICTION

A&P

John Updike

John Updike (1932–2009) was one of America's most celebrated, prolific, and popular contemporary writers. He was born in Reading, Pennsylvania, to a low-income family and grew up in the nearby town of Shillington. He went on a scholarship to Harvard where he edited The Harvard Lampoon. *He then accepted a fellowship to study painting at Oxford, worked as a cartoonist, and ultimately joined the staff of* The New Yorker. *He has published a rich and voluminous oeuvre of stories, novels, poetry, essays, children's stories, and memoirs. His novels including the quartet about Harry Angstrom (*Rabbit Run, Rabbit Redux, Rabbit Is Rich, *and* Rabbit at Rest*).* Rabbit Run *and* Rabbit at Rest *both received the Pulitzer Prize. He was also awarded a National Book Award, the O'Henry Prize, the American Book Award, the National Book Critic's Circle Award, and a National Medal of the Arts. His other work includes* The Poorhouse Fair, The Captured Hen and Other Tame Creatures, The Same Door, The Centaur, Bech: A Book, A Month of Sundays, Marry Me, The Witches of Eastwick, Roger's Version, Trust Me, Brazil, The Afterlife and Other Stories, In the Beauty of the Cities, Gertrude and Claudius, *and* Villages. *"A&P" was part of an early (1962) volume of stories called* Pigeon Feathers. *In it one can see the debt Updike has acknowledged to J. D. Salinger, the author of* The Catcher in the Rye, *from whom he said he learned a lot about the pain of adolescence. "A&P" is a realistic, bittersweet, boy's coming-of-age story featuring Sammy who, like Updike, is a son of the working class. Also, like the author who created him, Sammy greatly appreciates the physical attributes of females. That appreciation inspires this story and provides us with a tender yet graphic sense of a young male's yearnings.*

In walks these three girls in nothing but bathing suits. I'm in the third checkout slot, with my back to the door, so I don't see them until they're over by the bread. The one that caught my eye first was the one in the plaid green two-piece. She was a chunky kid, with a good tan and a sweet broad soft-looking can with those two crescents of white just under it, where the sun never seems to hit, at the top of the backs of her legs. I stood there with my hand on a box of HiHo crackers trying to remember if I rang it up or not. I ring it up again and the customer starts giving me hell. She's one of these cash-register-watchers, a witch about fifty with rouge on her cheekbones and no eyebrows, and I know it made her day to trip me up. She'd been watching cash registers forty years and probably never seen a mistake before.

By the time I got her feathers smoothed and her goodies into a bag—she gives me a little snort in passing, if she'd been born at the right time they would have burned her over in Salem—by the time I get her on her way the girls had circled around the bread and were coming back, without a push-cart, back my way along the counters, in the aisle between the check-outs and the Special bins. They didn't even have shoes on. There was this chunky one, with the two-piece—it was bright green and the seams on the bra were still sharp and her belly was still pretty pale so I guessed she just got it (the suit)—there was this one, with one of those chubby berry-faces, the lips all bunched together under her nose, this one, and a tall one, with black hair that hadn't quite frizzed right, and one of these sunburns right across under the eyes, and a chin that was too long—you know, the kind of girl other girls think is very "striking" and "attractive" but never quite makes it, as they very well know, which is why they like her so much—and then the third one, that wasn't quite so tall. She was the queen. She kind of led them, the other two peeking around and making their shoulders round. She didn't look around, not this queen, she just walked straight on slowly, on these long white prima donna legs. She came down a little hard on her heels, as if she didn't walk in her bare feet that much, putting down her heels and then letting the weight move along to her toes as if she was testing the floor with every step, putting a little deliberate extra action into it. You never know for sure how girls' minds work (do you really think it's a mind in there or just a little buzz like a bee in a glass jar?) but you got the idea she had talked the other two into coming in here with her, and now she was showing them how to do it, walk slow and hold yourself straight.

She had on a kind of dirty-pink—beige maybe, I don't know—bathing suit with a little nubble all over it and, what got me, the straps were down. They were off her shoulders looped loose around the cool tops of her arms, and I guess as a result the suit had slipped a little on her, so all around the top of the cloth there was this shining rim. If it hadn't been there you wouldn't have known there could have been anything whiter than those shoulders. With the straps pushed off, there was nothing between the top of the suit and the top of her head except just her, this clean bare plane of the top of her chest down from the shoulder bones like a dented sheet of metal tilted in the light. I mean, it was more than pretty.

She had sort of oaky hair that the sun and salt had bleached, done up in a bun that was unravelling, and a kind of prim face. Walking into the A&P with your straps down, I suppose it's the only kind of face you *can* have. She held her head so high her neck, coming up out of those white shoulders, looked kind of stretched, but I didn't mind. The longer her neck was, the more of her there was.

She must have felt in the corner of her eye me and over my shoulder Stokesie in the second slot watching, but she didn't tip. Not this queen. She kept her eyes moving across the racks, and stopped, and turned so slow it made my stomach rub the inside of my apron, and buzzed to the other two, who kind of huddled against her for relief, and they all three of them went up the cat-and-dog-food-breakfast-cereal-macaroni-rice-raisins-seasonings-spreads-spaghetti-soft drinks-crackers-and-cookies aisle. From the third slot I look straight up this aisle to the meat counter, and I watched them all the way. The fat one with the tan sort of fumbled with the cookies, but on second thought she put the packages back. The sheep pushing their carts down the aisle—the girls were walking against the usual traffic (not that we have one-way signs or anything)—were pretty hilarious. You could see them, when Queenie's white shoulders dawned on them, kind of jerk, or hop, or hic-cup, but their eyes snapped back to their own baskets and on they pushed. I bet you could set off dynamite in an A&P and the people would by and large keep reaching and checking oatmeal off their lists and muttering "Let me see, there was a third thing, began with A, asparagus, no, ah, yes, applesauce!" or whatever it is they do mutter. But there was no doubt, this jiggled them. A few house-slaves in pin curlers even looked around after pushing their carts past to make sure what they had seen was correct.

You know, it's one thing to have a girl in a bathing suit down on the beach, where what with the glare nobody can look at each other much any-way, and another thing in the cool of the A&P, under the fluorescent lights, against all those stacked packages, with her feet paddling along naked over our checkerboard green-and-cream rubber-tile floor.

"Oh Daddy," Stokesie said beside me. "I feel so faint."

"Darling," I said. "Hold me tight." Stokesie's married, with two babies chalked up on his fuselage already, but as far as I can tell that's the only dif-ference. He's twenty-two, and I was nineteen this April.

"Is it done?" he asks, the responsible married man finding his voice. I forgot to say he thinks he's going to be manager some sunny day, maybe in 1990 when it's called the Great Alexandrov and Petrooshki Tea Company or something.

What he meant was, our town is five miles from a beach, with a big sum-mer colony out on the Point, but we're right in the middle of town, and the women generally put on a shirt or shorts or something before they get out of the car into the street. And anyway these are usually women with six children and varicose veins mapping their legs and nobody, including them, could care less. As I say, we're right in the middle of town, and if you stand at our front doors you can see two banks and the Congregational church and the newspaper store and three real-estate offices and about twenty-seven old free-loaders tearing up Central Street because the sewer broke again. It's not as if we're on the Cape; we're north of Boston and there's people in this town haven't seen the ocean for twenty years.

The girls had reached the meat counter and were asking McMahon some-thing. He pointed, they pointed, and they shuffled out of sight behind a pyra-mid of Diet Delight peaches. All that was left for us to see was old McMahon patting his mouth and looking after them sizing up their joints. Poor kids, I began to feel sorry for them, they couldn't help it.

Now here comes the sad part of the story, at least my family says it's sad but I don't think it's sad myself. The store's pretty empty, it being Thursday afternoon, so there was nothing much to do except lean on the register and wait for the girls to show up again. The whole store was like a pinball machine and I didn't know which tunnel they'd come out of. After a while they come around out of the far aisle, around the light bulbs, records at discount of the Caribbean Six or Tony Martin Sings or some such gunk you wonder they waste the wax on, sixpacks of candy bars, and plastic toys done up in cellophane that fall apart when a kid looks at them anyway. Around they come, Queenie still leading the way, and holding a little gray jar in her hand. Slots Three through Seven are unmanned and I could see her wondering between Stokes and me, but Stokesie with his usual luck draws an old party in baggy gray pants who stumbles up with four giant cans of pineapple juice (what do these bums *do* with all that pineapple juice' I've often asked myself) so the girls come to me. Queenie puts down the jar and I take it into my fingers icy cold. Kingfish Fancy Herring Snacks in Pure Sour Cream: 49¢. Now her hands are empty, not a ring or a bracelet, bare as God made them, and I wonder where the money's coming from. Still with that prim look she lifts a folded dollar bill out of the hollow at the center of her nubbled pink top. The jar went heavy in my hand. Really, I thought that was so cute.

Then everybody's luck begins to run out. Lengel comes in from haggling with a truck full of cabbages on the lot and is about to scuttle into that door marked MANAGER behind which he hides all day when the girls touch his eye. Lengel's pretty dreary, teaches Sunday school and the rest, but he doesn't miss that much. He comes over and says, "Girls, this isn't the beach."

Queenie blushes, though maybe it's just a brush of sunburn I was noticing for the first time, now that she was so close. "My mother asked me to pick up a jar of herring snacks." Her voice kind of startled me, the way voices do when you see the people first, coming out so flat and dumb yet kind of tony, too, the way it ticked over "pick up" and "snacks." All of a sudden I slid right down her voice into her living room. Her father and the other men were standing around in ice-cream coats and bow ties and the women were in sandals picking up herring snacks on toothpicks off a big plate and they were all holding drinks the color of water with olives and sprigs of mint in them. When my parents have somebody over they get lemonade and if it's a real racy affair Schlitz in tall glasses with "They'll Do It Every Time" cartoons stencilled on.

"That's all right," Lengel said. "But this isn't the beach." His repeating this struck me as funny, as if it had just occurred to him, and he had been thinking all these years the A&P was a great big dune and he was the head lifeguard. He didn't like my smiling—as I say he doesn't miss much—but he concentrates on giving the girls that sad Sunday-school-superintendent stare.

Queenie's blush is no sunburn now, and the plump one in plaid, that I liked better from the back—a really sweet can—pipes up, "We weren't doing any shopping. We just came in for the one thing."

"That makes no difference," Lengel tells her, and I could see from the way his eyes went that he hadn't noticed she was wearing a two-piece before. "We want you decently dressed when you come in here."

"We are decent," Queenie says suddenly, her lower lip pushing, getting sore now that she remembers her place, a place from which the crowd that runs the A&P must look pretty crummy. Fancy Herring Snacks flashed in her very blue eyes.

"Girls, I don't want to argue with you. After this come in here with your shoulders covered. It's our policy." He turns his back. That's policy for you. Policy is what the kingpins want. What the others want is juvenile delinquency.

All this while, the customers had been showing up with their carts but, you know, sheep, seeing a scene, they had all bunched up on Stokesie, who shook open a paper bag as gently as peeling a peach, not wanting to miss a word. I could feel in the silence everybody getting nervous, most of all Lengel, who asks me, "Sammy, have you rung up this purchase?"

I thought and said "No" but it wasn't about that I was thinking. I go through the punches, 4, 9, GROC, TOT—it's more complicated than you think, and after you do it often enough, it begins to make a lttle song, that you hear words to, in my case "Hello *(bing)* there, you *(gung)* hap-py pee-pul *(splat)*"—the splat being the drawer flying out. I uncrease the bill, tenderly as you may imagine, it just having come from between the two smoothest scoops of vanilla I had ever known were there, and pass a half and a penny into her narrow pink palm, and nestle the herrings in a bag and twist its neck and hand it over, all the time thinking.

The girls, and who'd blame them, are in a hurry to get out, so I say "I quit" to Lengel quick enough for them to hear, hoping they'll stop and watch me, their unsuspected hero. They keep right on going, into the electric eye; the door flies open and they flicker across the lot to their car, Queenie and Plaid and Big Tall Goony-Goony (not that as raw material she was so bad), leaving me with Lengel and a kink in his eyebrow.

"Did you say something, Sammy?"

"I said I quit."

"I thought you did."

"You didn't have to embarrass them."

"It was they who were embarrassing us."

I started to say something that came out "Fiddle-de-doo." It's a saying of my grandmother's, and I know she would have been pleased.

"I don't think you know what you're saying," Lengel said.

"I know you don't," I said. "But I do." I pull the bow at the back of my apron and start shrugging it off my shoulders. A couple customers that had been heading for my slot begin to knock against each other, like scared pigs in a chute.

Lengel sighs and begins to look very patient and old and gray. He's been a friend of my parents for years. "Sammy, you don't want to do this to your Mom and Dad," he tells me. It's true, I don't. But it seems to me that once you begin a gesture it's fatal not to go through with it. I fold the apron, "Sammy" stitched in red on the pocket, and put it on the counter, and drop the bow tie on top of it. The bow tie is theirs, if you've ever wondered. "You'll feel this for the rest of your life," Lengel says, and I know that's true, too, but remembering how he made that pretty girl blush makes me so scrunchy inside I punch the No Sale tab and the machine whirs "pee-pul" and the drawer splats out. One advantage to this scene taking place in summer, I can follow this up with a clean exit, there's no fumbling around getting your coat and galoshes, I just saunter into the electric eye in my white shirt that my mother ironed the night before, and the door heaves itself open, and outside the sunshine is skating around on the asphalt.

I look around for my girls, but they're gone, of course. There wasn't anybody but some young married screaming with her children about some candy they didn't get by the door of a powder-blue Falcon station wagon. Looking back in the big windows, over the bags of peat moss and aluminum lawn furniture stacked on the pavement, I could see Lengel in my place in the slot, checking the sheep through. His face was dark gray and his back stiff, as if he'd just had an injection of iron, and my stomach kind of fell as I felt how hard the world was going to be to me hereafter.

QUESTIONS FOR DISCUSSION AND WRITING

1. Sammy, the would-be hero of this story, is a boy. His name suggests it, as does his having a job because of his parents' friendship with Lengel, the store manager, as does the fact that he wears a shirt his mother ironed for him just the night before. How does the action Sammy decides to take reveal a transition from boyhood to manhood? What is the story telling us about the consequences of acting on one's own? What of the fact that the action Sammy decides on is sad to his family but not to him?

2. Discuss the effect of the young girls in the story on the boys, including Stokesie who, though twenty-two and the father of two, is seen by Sammy as being no different in his attitude toward the girls. Images of bathing suits and straps down and key signifiers like "naked" and "bare" seem to capture the effect the girls have on both Sammy and Stokesie. What is the nature of the overall visual effect of the exposure of girls' flesh on boys? Are girls apt to act as excited and stimulated by the sight of boys less clothed or in bathing suits?

3. How would you define Sammy's character (not just in terms of his willingness to follow through on his initial gesture and act like a protector toward the girls with Lengel)? What about the attitude in how he views the girls, as well as how he views Lengel and the customers in the A&P, whom he refers to with such pejoratives as "women with six children and varicose veins," or whom he calls "sheep," and "house-slaves"? What about Sammy's imagination and

the kind of boy he is—the way he describes how the shelves are set up or how the cash register sounds? Do you think Updike intends us to like him?

4. Sammy compares Queenie's chest, down from her shoulder bones, as being "like a dented sheet of metal tilted in the light." Does that imagery strike you as the kind a boy might actually use? What about Sammy's comparing girls' minds to "a little buzz like a bee in a glass jar" or asking if girls even have minds? Is this rank sexism or an example of the way boys think?

5. Nowadays a trio of girls in bathing suits would likely not appear as shocking or create a stir as they might have in the early 1960s, particularly in a puritanical New England community like the one in the story. What kinds of behaviors or dress do you think might shock staid suburbanites in today's world? How important, in terms of what shocked people then or might shock them today, is the setting?

6. Focus on the class differences between Sammy and the girl he calls the Queen, reflected especially in the passage in which he imagines what the Queen's family looks like compared to his own family. How important is the class gap in affecting Sammy's ultimate decision, the fact that he is a working-class kid reacting to the treatment of a girl he sees as a queen, perhaps not just as a Queen Bee?

7. "A&P," in addition to being a rites of passage story, is in many ways a generation gap story. Yet what are we to make of Sammy saying "fiddle-de-doo" to Lengel and adding that it is a saying of his grandmother's and one she would have been pleased to hear him use? Is Sammy perhaps being connected toward story's end to something not only more old-fashioned but female?

ON TECHNIQUE AND STYLE

1. How successful is Updike in capturing the voice of a real boy? What kind of language or techniques does he use to achieve that end?

2. Describe Updike's style. How would you characterize the way he uses language to enliven the story and ensure its flow?

3. How much does the story persuade us of the importance for young boys to take risks and to define themselves and establish their own individual identity?

CULTURAL QUESTION

1. The attitudes toward girls that appear in Updike's story are those of white lower-middle-class boys of that time period in New England. Do boys from other cultural backgrounds have different attitudes toward girls? Or should one avoid generalizing altogether about such cultural attitudes of one gender toward the other?

Boys and Girls

Alice Munro

Alice Munro (1931–   ) was born in the small rural Canadian town of Wingham,
Ontario, and educated at the University of Western Ontario. Considered one of the finest
contemporary short story writers, she has won two Giller Prizes and three Governor's
General Awards for her short fiction as well as a National Book Critic's Circle Award
and an O'Henry Award. Her published work includes Dance of the Happy Shades;
Lives of Girls and Women; Something I've Been Meaning to Tell You; Who Do
You Think You Are ?; The Moons of Jupiter; The Progress of Love; Friend of My
Youth; Open Secrets; Hateship, Courtship, Loveship, Marriage ; *and* Runaway.
"Boys and Girls," which appeared in Dance of the Happy Shades, *was first published*
in The Montrealer *in 1968. It is a sweet but disturbing tale that highlights how gender*
differences can be preestablished and sex roles made inevitable. The young girl's identity
in the story is initially linked more to the farm where the men work than to the kitchen,
her mother's domain. She feels more tied to bold deeds of war and adventure than the
far different identity her society is shaping for her as a girl. Despite a moment of rebel-
lion in which she identifies completely with the escape and liberation of the female mare,
Flora—she ultimately learns she must become the girl she is expected to be.

My father was a fox farmer. That is, he raised silver foxes, in pens; and in the
fall and early winter, when their fur was prime, he killed them and skinned
them and sold their pelts to the Hudson's Bay Company or the Montreal Fur
Traders. These companies supplied us with heroic calendars to hang, one
on each side of the kitchen door. Against a background of cold blue sky
and black pine forests and treacherous northern rivers, plumed adventures
planted the flags of England and or of France; magnificent savages bent their
backs to the portage.

For several weeks before Christmas, my father worked after supper in
the cellar of our house. The cellar was whitewashed, and lit by a hundred-
watt bulb over the worktable. My brother Laird and I sat on the top step and
watched. My father removed the pelt inside-out from the body of the fox,
which looked surprisingly small, mean, and rat-like, deprived of its arrogant
weight of fur. The naked, slippery bodies were collected in a sack and buried
in the dump. One time the hired man, Henry Bailey, had taken a swipe at me
with this sack, saying, "Christmas present!" My mother thought that was not
funny. In fact she disliked the whole pelting operation—that was what the
killing, skinning, and preparation of the furs was called—and wished it did
not have to take place in the house. There was the smell. After the pelt had
been stretched inside-out on a long board my father scraped away delicately,
removing the little clotted webs of blood vessels, the bubbles of fat; the smell

of blood and animal fat, which the strong primitive odor of the fox itself, penetrated all parts of the house. I found it reassuringly seasonal, like the smell of oranges and pine needles.

Henry Bailey suffered from bronchial troubles. He would cough and cough until his narrow face turned scarlet, and his light blue, derisive eyes filled up with tears; then he took the lid off the stove, and, standing well back, shot out a great clot of phlegm—hss—straight into the heart of the flames. We admired his for this performance and for his ability to make his stomach growl at will, and for his laughter, which was full of high whistlings and gurglings and involved the whole faulty machinery of his chest. It was sometimes hard to tell what he was laughing at, and always possible that it might be us.

After we had sent to bed we could still smell fox and still hear Henry's laugh, but these things reminders of the warm, safe, brightly lit downstairs world, seemed lost and diminished, floating on the stale cold air upstairs. We were afraid at night in the winter. We were not afraid of outside though this was the time of year when snowdrifts curled around our house like sleeping whales and the wind harassed us all night, coming up from the buried fields, the frozen swamp, with its old bugbear chorus of threats and misery. We were afraid of inside, the room where we slept. At this time upstairs of our house was not finished. A brick chimney went up one wall. In the middle of the floor was a square hole, with a wooden railing around it; that was where the stairs came up. On the other side of the stairwell were the things that nobody had any use for anymore—a soldiery roll of linoleum, standing on end, a wicker baby carriage, a fern basket, china jugs and basins with cracks in them, a picture of the Battle of Balaclava, very sad to look at. I had told Laird, as soon as he was old enough to understand such things, that bats and skeletons lived over there; whenever a man escaped from the county jail, twenty miles away, I imagined that he had somehow let himself in the window and was hiding behind the linoleum. But we had rules to keep us safe. When the light was on, we were safe as long as we did not step off the square of worn carpet which defined our bedroom-space; when the light was off no place was safe but the beds themselves. I had to turn out the light kneeling on the end of my bed, and stretching as far as I could to reach the cord.

In the dark we lay on our beds, our narrow life rafts, and fixed our eyes on the faint light coming up the stairwell, and sang songs. Laird sang "Jingle Bells," which he would sing any time, whether it was Christmas or not, and I sang "Danny Boy." I loved the sound of my own voice, frail and supplicating, rising in the dark. We could make out the tall frosted shapes of the windows now, gloomy and white. When I came to the party, the cold sheets but by pleasurable emotions almost silenced me. You'll kneel and say an Ave there above me—What was an Ave? Every day I forgot to find out.

Laird went straight from singing to sleep, I could hear his long, satisfied, bubbly breaths. Now for the time that remained to me, the most perfectly private and perhaps the best time of the whole day, I arranged myself tightly under the covers and went on with one of the stories I was telling myself from night to night. These stories were about myself, when I had grown a little older; they took place in a world that was recognizably mine, yet one that presented opportunities for courage, boldness, and self-sacrifice, as mine never did. I rescued people from a bombed building (it discouraged me that the real war had gone on so far away from Jubilee). I shot two rabid wolves who were menacing the schoolyard (the teachers cowered terrified at my back). Rode a fine horse spiritedly down the main street of Jubilee, acknowledging the townspeople's gratitude for some yet-to-be-worked-out piece of heroism (nobody ever rode a horse there, except King Billy in the Orangemen's Day parade). There was always riding and shooting in these stories, though I had only been on a horse twice—the first because we did not own a saddle—and the second time I had slid right around and dropped under the horse's feet; it had stepped placidly over me. I really was learning to shoot, but could not hit anything yet, not even tin cans on fence posts.

Alive, the foxes inhabited a world my father made for them. It was surrounded by a high guard fence, like a medieval town, with a gate that was padlocked at night. Along the streets of this town were ranged large, sturdy pens. Each of them had a real door that a man could go through, a wooden ramp along the wire, for the foxes to run up and down on, and a kennel—sometimes like a clothes chest with airholes—where they slept and stayed in winter and had their young. There were feeding and watering dishes attached to the wire in such a way that they could be emptied and cleaned from the outside. The dishes were made of old tin cans, and the ramps and kennels of odds and ends of old lumber. Everything was tidy and ingenious; my father was tirelessly inventive and his favorite book in the world was Robinson Crusoe. He had fitted a tin drum on a wheelbarrow, for bringing water down to the pens. This was my job in the summer, when the foxes had to have water twice a day. Between nine and ten o'clock in the morning, and again after supper. I filled the drum at the pump and trundled it down through the barnyard to the pens, where I parked it, and filled my watering can and went along the streets. Laird came too, with his little cream and green gardening can, filled too full and knocking against his legs and slopping water on his canvas shoes. I had the real watering can, my father's, though I could only carry it three-quarters full.

The foxes all had names, which were printed on a tin plate and hung beside their doors. They were not named when they were born, but when they survived the first year's pelting and were added to the breeding stock. Those my father had named were called names like Prince, Bob, Wally, and Betty. Those I had named were called Star or Turk, or Maureen or Diana. Laird named one Maude after a hired girl we had when he was little, one Harold after a boy at school, and one Mexico, he did not say why.

Naming them did not make pets out of them, or anything like it. Nobody but my father ever went into the pens, and he had twice had blood-poisoning from bites. When I was bringing them their water they prowled up and down on the paths they had made inside their pens, barking seldom—they saved that for nighttime, when they might get up a chorus of community frenzy—but always watching me, their eyes burning, clear gold, in their pointed, malevolent faces. They were beautiful for their delicate legs and heavy, aristocratic tails and the bright fur sprinkled on dark down their back—which gave them their name—but especially for their faces, drawn exquisitely sharp in pure hostility, and their golden eyes.

Besides carrying water I helped my father when he cut the long grass, and the lamb's quarter and flowering monkey-musk, that grew between the pens. He cut with the scythe and I raked into piles. Then he took a pitchfork and threw fresh-cut grass all over the top of the pens to keep the foxes cooler and shade their coats, which were browned by too much sun. My father did not talk to me unless it was about the job we were doing. In this he was quite different from my mother, who, if she was feeling cheerful, would tell me all sorts of things—the name of a dog she had had when she was a little girl, the names of boys she had gone out with later on when she was grown up, and what certain dresses of hers had looked like—she could not imagine now what had become of them. Whatever thoughts and stories my father had were private, and I was shy of him and would never ask him questions. Nevertheless I worked willingly under his eyes, and with a feeling of pride. One time a feed salesman came down into the pens to talk to him and my father said, "Like to have you meet my new hired hand." I turned away and raked furiously, red in the face with pleasure.

"Could of fooled me," said the salesman. "I thought it was only a girl."

After the grass was cut, it seemed suddenly much later in the year. I walked on stubble in the earlier evening aware of the reddening skies, on entering silence of fall. When I wheeled the tank out of the gates and put padlocks on. It was almost dark. One night at this time I saw my mother and father standing talking on the little rise of ground we called the gangway, in front of the barn. My father had just come from the meathouse; he had his stiff bloody apron on, and a pail of cut-up meat in his hand.

It was an odd thing to see my mother down at the barn. She did not often come out of the house unless it was to do something—hang out the wash or dig potatoes in the garden. She looked out of place, with her bare lumpy legs, not touched by the sun, her apron still on and damp across the stomach from the supper dishes. Her hair was tied up in a kerchief, wisps of it falling out. She would tie her hair up like this in the morning, saying she did not have time to do it properly, and it would stay tied up all day. It was true, too; she really did not have time. These days our back porch was piled with baskets of peaches and grapes and pears, bought in town, and onions and tomatoes and cucumbers grown at home, all waiting to be made into jelly and jam and preserves, pickles and chili sauce. In the kitchen there was a fire in the stove all day, jars clinked in boiling water, sometimes a cheesecloth bag was strung on a pole between two chairs straining blue-black grape pulp for jelly. I was given jobs to do and I would sit at the table peeling peaches that had been soaked in hot water, or cutting up onions, my eyes smarting and streaming. As soon as I was done I ran out of the house, trying to get out of earshot before my mother thought of what she wanted me to do next. I hated the hot dark kitchen in summer, the green blinds and the flypapers, the same old oilcloth table and wavy mirror and bumpy linoleum. My mother was too tired and preoccupied to talk to me, she had no heart to tell about the Normal School Graduation Dance; sweat trickled over her face and she was always counting under breath, pointing at jars, dumping cups of sugar. It seemed to me that work in the house was endless, dreary, and peculiarly depressing; work done out of doors, and in my father's service, was ritualistically important.

I wheeled the tank up to the barn, where it was kept, and I heard my mother saying, "Wait till Laird gets a little bigger, then you'll have a real help."

What my father said I did not hear. I was pleased by the way he stood listening, politely as he would to a salesman or a stranger, but with an air of wanting to get on with his real work. I felt my mother had no business down here and I wanted him to feel the same way. What did she mean about Laird? He was no help to anybody. Where was he now? Swinging himself sick on the swing, going around in circles, or trying to catch caterpillars. He never once stayed with me till I was finished.

"And then I can use her more in the house," I heard my mother say. She had a dead-quiet regretful way of talking about me that always made me uneasy. "I just get my back turned and she runs off. It's not like I had a girl in the family at all."

I went and sat on a feed bag in the corner of the barn, not wanting to appear when this conversation was going on. My mother, I felt, was not to be trusted. She was kinder than my father and more easily fooled, but you could not depend on her, and the real reasons for the things she said and did were not to be known. She loved me, and she sat up late at night making a dress of the difficult style I wanted, for me to wear when school started, but she was also my enemy. She was always plotting. She was plotting now to get me to stay in the house more, although she knew I hated it (because she knew I hated it) and keep me from working for my father. It seemed to me she would do this simply out of perversity, and to try her power. It did not occur to me that she could be lonely, or jealous. No grown-up could be; they were too fortunate. I sat and kicked my heels monotonously against a feed bag, raising dust, and did not come out till she was gone.

At any rate, I did not expect my father to pay any attention to what she said. Who could imagine Laird doing my work—Laird remembering the padlock and cleaning out the watering dishes with a leaf on the end of a stick, or even wheeling the tank without it tumbling over? It showed how little my mother knew about the way things really were.

I had forgotten to say what the foxes were fed. My father's bloody apron reminded me. They were fed horsemeat. At this time most farmers still kept horses, and when a horse got too old to work, or broke a leg or got down and would not get up, as they sometimes did, the owner would call my father, and he and Henry went out to the farm in the truck. Usually they shot and butchered the horse there, paying the farmer from five to twelve dollars. If they had already too much meat on hand, they would bring the horse back alive, and keep it for a few days or weeks in our stable, until the meat was needed. After the war the farmers were buying tractors and gradually getting rid of horses, that there was just no use for any more. If this happened in the winter we might keep the horse in our stable till spring, for we had plenty of hay and if there was a lot of snow—and the plow did not always get our roads cleared—it was convenient to be able to go to town with a horse and cutter.

The winter I was eleven years old we had two horses in the stable. We did not know what names they had had before, so we called them Mack and Flora. Mack was an old black workhorse, sooty and indifferent. Flora was a sorrel mare, a driver. We took them both out in the cutter. Mack was slow and easy to handle. Flora was given to fits of violent alarm, veering at cars and even at other horses, but we loved her speed and high-stepping, her general air of gallantry and abandon. On Saturdays we went down to the stable and as soon as we opened the door on its cozy, animal-smelling darkness Flora threw up her head, rolled her eyes, whinnied despairingly, and pulled herself through a crisis of nerves on the spot. It was not safe to go into her stall, she would kick.

This winter also I began to hear a great deal more on the theme my mother had sounded when she had been talking in front of the barn. I no longer felt safe. It seemed that in the minds of the people around me there was a steady undercurrent of thought, not to be deflected, on this one subject. The word girl had formerly seemed to me innocent and unburdened like the word child; now it appeared that it was no such thing. A girl was not, as I had supposed, simply what I was; it was what I had to become. It was a definition, always touched with emphasis, with reproach and disappointment. Also it was a joke on me. Once Laird and I were fighting, and for the first time ever I had to use all my strength against him; even so, he caught and pinned my arm for a moment, really hurting me. Henry saw this, and laughed, saying, "Oh, that there Laird's gonna show you, one of these days!" Laird was getting a lot bigger. But I was getting bigger too.

My grandmother came to stay with us for a few weeks and I heard other things. "Girls don't slam doors like that." "Girls keep their knees together when they sit down." And worse still, when I asked some questions, "That's none of girls' business." I continued to slam the doors and sit as awkwardly as possible, thinking that by such measures I kept myself free.

When spring came, the horses were let out in the barnyard. Mack stood against the barn wall trying to scratch his neck and haunches, but Flora trotted up and down and reared at the fences, clattering her hooves against the rails. Snow drifts dwindled quickly, revealing the hard gray and brown earth, the familiar rise and fall of the ground, plain and bare after the fantastic landscape of winter. There was a great feeling of opening-out, of release. We just wore rubbers now, over our shoes; our feet felt ridiculously light. One Saturday we went out to the stable and found all the doors open, letting in the unaccustomed sunlight and fresh air. Henry was there, just idling around looking at his collection of calendars which were tacked up behind the stalls in a part of the stable my mother probably had never seen.

"Come say goodbye to your old friend Mack?" Henry said. "Here, you give him a taste of oats." He poured some oats into Laird's cupped hands and Laird went to feed Mack. Mack's teeth were in bad shape. He ate very slowly, patiently shifting the oats around in his mouth, trying to find a stump of a molar to grind it on. "Poor old Mack," said Henry mournfully. "When a horse's teethes gone, he's gone. That's about the way."

"Are you going to shoot him today?" I said. Mack and Flora had been in the stables so long I had almost forgotten they were going to be shot.

Henry didn't answer me. Instead he started to sing in a high, trembly, mocking-sorrowful voice. Oh, there's no more work, for poor Uncle Ned, he's gone where the good darkies go. Mack's thick, blackish tongue worked diligently at Laird's hand. I went out before the song was ended and sat down on the gangway.

I had never seen them shoot a horse, but I knew where it was done. Last summer Laird and I had come upon a horse's entrails before they were buried. We had thought it was a big black snake, coiled up in the sun. That was around in the field that ran up beside the barn. I thought that if we went inside the barn, and found a wide crack or a knothole to look through, we would be able to see them do it. It was not something I wanted to see; just the same, if a thing really happened it was better to see, and know.

My father came down from the house, carrying a gun.

"What are you doing here?" he said.

"Nothing."

"Go on up and play around the house."

He sent Laird out of the stable. I said to Laird, "Do you want to see them shoot Mack?" and without waiting for an answer led him around to the front door of the barn, opened it carefully, and went in. "Be quiet or they'll hear us," I said. We could hear Henry and my father talking in the stable; then the heavy shuffling steps of Mack being backed out of his stall.

In the loft it was cold and dark. Thin crisscrossed beams of sunlight fell through the cracks. The hay was low. It was rolling country, hills and hollows, slipping under our feet. About four feet up was a beam going around the walls. We piled hay up in one corner and I boosted Laird up and hoisted myself. The beam was not very wide; we crept along it with our hands flat on the barn walls. There were plenty of knotholes, and I found one that gave me the view I wanted—a corner of the barnyard, the gate, part of the field. Laird did not have a knothole and began to complain.

I showed him a widened crack between two boards. "Be quiet and wait. If they hear you you'll get us in trouble."

My father came in sight carrying the gun. Henry was leading Mack by the halter. He dropped it and took out his cigarette papers and tobacco; he rolled cigarettes for my father and himself. While this was going on Mack nosed around in the old, dead grass along the fence. Then my father opened the gate and they took Mack through. Henry led Mack away from the path to a patch of ground and they talked together, not loud enough for us to hear. Mack again began to searching for a mouthful of fresh grass, which was not found. My father walked away in a straight line, and stopped short at a distance which seemed to suit him. Henry was walking away from Mack too, but sideways, still negligently holding on to the halter. My father raised the gun and Mack looked up as if he had noticed something and my father shot him.

Mack did not collapse at once but swayed, lurched sideways, and fell, first on his side; then he rolled over on his back and, amazingly, kicked his legs for a few seconds in the air. At this Henry laughed, as if Mack had done a trick for him. Laird, who had drawn a long, groaning breath of surprise when the shot was fired, said out loud, "He's not dead." And it seemed to me it might be true. But his legs stopped, he rolled on his side again, his muscles quivered and sank. The two men walked over and looked at him in a businesslike way; they bent down and examined his forehead where the bullet had gone in, and now I saw his blood on the brown grass.

"Now they just skin him and cut him up," I said. "Let's go." My legs were a little shaky and I jumped gratefully down into the hay. "Now you've seen how they shoot a horse," I said in a congratulatory way, as if I had seen it many times before. "Let's see if any barn cats had kittens in the hay." Laird jumped. He seemed young and obedient again. Suddenly I remembered how, when he was little, I had brought him into the barn and told him to climb the ladder to the top beam. That was in the spring, too, when the hay was low. I had done it out of a need for excitement, a desire for something to happen so that I could tell about it. He was wearing a little bulky brown and white checked coat, made down from one of mine. He went all the way up just as I told him, and sat down from one of the beams with the hay far below him on one side, and the barn floor and some old machinery on the other. Then I ran screaming to my father. "Laird's up on the top beam!" My father came, my mother came, my father went up the ladder talking very quietly and brought Laird down under his arm, at which my mother leaned against the ladder and began to cry. They said to me, "Why weren't you watching him?" but nobody ever knew the truth. Laird did not know enough to tell. But whenever I saw the brown and white checked coat hanging in the closet, or at the bottom of the rag bag, which was where it ended up, I felt a weight in my stomach, the sadness of unexorcised guilt.

I looked at Laird, who did not even remember this, and I did not like the look on his thin, winter-paled face. His expression was not frightened or upset, but remote, concentrating. "Listen," I said in an unusually bright and friendly voice, "you aren't going to tell, are you?"

"No," he said absently.

"Promise."

"Promise," he said. I grabbed the hand behind his back to make sure he was not crossing his fingers. Even so, he might have a nightmare; it might come out that way. I decided I had better work hard to get all thoughts of what he had seen out of his mind—which, it seemed to me, could not hold very many things at a time. I got some money I had saved and that afternoon we went into Jubilee and saw a show, with Judy Canova, at which we both laughed a great deal. After that I thought it would be all right.

Two weeks later I knew they were going to shoot Flora. I knew from the night before, when I heard my mother ask if the hay was holding out all right, and my father said, "Well, after tomorrow there'll just be the cow, and we should be able to put her out to grass in another week." So I knew it was Flora's turn in the morning.

This time I didn't think of watching it. That was something to see just one time. I had not thought about it very often since, but sometimes when I was busy, working at school, or standing in front of the mirror combing my hair and wondering if I would be pretty when I grew up, the whole scene would flash into my mind: I would see the easy, practiced way my father raised the gun, and hear Henry laughing when Mack kicked his legs in the air. I did not have any great feelings of horror and opposition, such as a city child might have had; I was too used to seeing the death of animals as a necessity by which we lived. Yet I felt a little ashamed, and there was a new wariness, a sense of holding-off, in my attitude to my father and his work.

It was a fine day, and we were going around the yard picking up tree branches that had been torn off in winter storms. This was something we had been told to do, and also we wanted to use them to make a teepee. We heard Flora whinny, and then my father's voice and Henry's shouting, and we ran down to the barnyard to see what was going on.

The stable door was open. Henry had just brought Flora out, and she had broken away from him. She was running free in the barnyard, from one end to the other. We climbed on the fence. It was exciting to see her running, whinnying, going up on her hind legs, prancing and threatening like a horse in a Western movie, an unbroken ranch horse, though she was just an old driver, an old sorrel mare. My father and Henry ran after her and tried to grab the dangling halter. They tried to work her into a corner, and they had almost succeeded when she made a run between them, wild-eyed, and disappeared round the corner of the barn. We heard the rails clatter down as she got over the fence, and Henry yelled. "She's into the field now!"

That meant she was in the long L-shaped field that ran up by the house. If she got around the center, heading towards the lane, the gate was open; the truck had been driven into the field this morning. My father shouted to me, because I was on the other side of the fence, nearest the lane, "Go shut the gate!"

I could run very fast. I ran across the garden, past the tree where our swing was hung, and jumped across a ditch into the lane. There was the open gate. She had not got out, I could not see her up on the road; she must have run to the other end of the field. The gate was heavy. I lifted it out of the gravel and carried it across the roadway. I had it halfway across when she came in sight, galloping straight toward me. There was just time to get the chain on. Laird came scrambling through the ditch to help me.

Instead of shutting the gate, I opened it as wide as I could. I did not make any decision to do this, it was just what I did. Flora never slowed down; she galloped straight past me, and Laird jumped up and down, yelling, "Shut it, shut it!" even after it was too late. My father and Henry appeared in the field a moment too late to see what I had done. They only saw Flora heading for the township road. They would think I had not got there in time.

They did not waste any time asking about it. They went back to the barn and got the gun and the knives they used, and put these in the truck; then they turned the truck around and came bounding up the field toward us. Laird called to them, "Let me go too, let me go too!" and Henry stopped the truck and they took him in. I shut the gate after they were all gone.

I supposed Laird would tell. I wondered what would happen to me. I had never disobeyed my father before, and I could not understand why I had done it. I had done it. Flora would not really get away. They would catch up with her in the truck. Or if they did not catch her this morning somebody would see her and telephone us this afternoon or tomorrow. There was no wild country here for her, we needed the meat to feed the foxes, we needed the foxes to make our living. All I had done was make more work for my father who worked hard enough already. And when my father found out about it he was not going to trust me any more; he would know that I was not entirely on his side. I was on Flora's side, and that made me no use to anybody, not even to her. Just the same, I did not regret it; when she came running at me I held the gate open, that was the only thing I could do.

I went back to the house, and my mother said, "What's all the commotion?" I told her that Flora had kicked down the fence and got away. "Your poor father," she said, "now he'll have to go chasing over the countryside. Well, there isn't any use planning dinner before one." She put up the ironing board. I wanted to tell her, but thought better of it and went upstairs and sat on my bed.

Lately I had been trying to make my part of the room fancy, spreading the bed with old lace curtains, and fixing myself a dressing table with some leftovers of cretonne for a skirt. I planned to put up some kind of barricade between my bed and Laird's, to keep my section separate from his. In the sunlight, the lace curtains were just dusty rags. We did not sing at night any more. One night when I was singing Laird said, "You sound silly," and I went right on but the next night I did not start. There was not so much need to anyway, we were no longer afraid. We knew it was just old furniture over there, old jumble and confusion. We did not keep to the rules. I still stayed away after Laird was asleep and told myself stories, but even in these stories something different was happening, mysterious alterations took place. A story might start off in the old way, with a spectacular danger, a fire or wild animals, and for a while I might rescue people; then things would change around, and instead, somebody would be rescuing me. It might be a boy from our class at school, or even Mr. Campbell, our teacher, who tickled girls under the arms. And at this point the story concerned itself at great length with what I looked like—how long my hair was, and what kind of dress I had on; by the time I had these details worked out the real excitement of the story was lost.

It was later than one o'clock when the truck came back. The tarpaulin was over the back, which meant there was meat in it. My mother had to heat dinner up all over again. Henry and my father had changed from their bloody overalls into ordinary working overalls in the barn, and they washed arms and necks and faces at the sink, and splashed water on their hair and combed it. Laird lifted his arm to show off a streak of blood. "We shot old Flora," he said, "and cut her up in fifty pieces."

"Well I don't want to hear about it," my mother said. "And don't come to my table like that."

My father made him go wash the blood off.

We sat down and my father said grace and Henry pasted his chewing gum on the end of his fork, the way he always did; when he took it off he would have us admire the pattern. We began to pass the bowls of steaming, overcooked vegetables. Laird looked across the table at me and said proudly distinctly, "Anyway it was her fault Flora got away."

"What?" my father said.

"She could of shut the gate and she didn't. She just open' it up and Flora ran out."

"Is that right?" my father said.

Everybody at the table was looking at me. I nodded, swallowing food with great difficulty. To my shame, tears flooded my eyes.

My father made a curt sound of disgust. "What did you do that for?"

I didn't answer. I put down my fork and waited to be sent from the table, still not looking up.

But this did not happen. For some time nobody said anything, then Laird said matter-of-factly, "She's crying."

"Never mind," my father said. He spoke with resignation, even good humor the words which absolved and dismissed me for good. "She's only a girl," he said.

I didn't protest that, even in my heart. Maybe it was true.

QUESTIONS FOR DISCUSSION AND WRITING

1. The young girl in "Boys and Girls" grows up on a fox farm, exposed from an early age to a great deal of blood and guts. How does that, along with the fact that she helps her father with his work-related tasks rather than helping her mother with household chores, help shape her early gender identity? Why is she "red in the face with pleasure" when her father introduces her to a salesman as his "new hired man"? What makes the duties in the world outside the house with her father so much more appealing to her than what lies within the house with her mother?

2. The pelting, the calendars on each side of the family's kitchen door, the picture of the battle on the other side of the stairwell, even the bronchial "real" hired man, Henry Bailey, and the way he spits out phlegm into flames—how are all these masculine images tied to our unnamed narrator's heroic fantasies of "courage, boldness and self-sacrifice"? Is it significant that a real war is going on, even though it is far away and remote from Jubilee, the Canadian town? How and why do her fantasies change and become more girl-like? Do the changes have to do largely with her concern over what she looks like and how pretty she is?

3. Discuss the changes in Laird, our narrator's younger brother. How do they contrast with the changes that occur in her? How does she regard her younger brother? What of Laird, at the story's end, telling on his older sister? Do you think he feels sibling rivalry toward her because she is a girl?

4. Emily Hancock, a psychologist and author of a book called *The Girl Within*, writes about how young girls, around the age of menstruation, turn from thinking and acting like boys to taking on traditional female traits, which often results in a loss of the kinds of strengths associated more with boys and their activities. This, Hancock asserts, is largely due to social pressures. Our narrator, who is eleven, declares: "A girl was not, as I had supposed, simply what I was; it was what I had to become." Why must she succumb to becoming a girl? What does the word "girl" signify to her?

5. When Flora, the skittish female sorrel mare, breaks free, the narrator holds the gate open and admits, "I did not make any decision to do this, it was just what I did." She also says, as she heads back to the house for dinner, "I held the gate open, that was the only thing I could do." Why does her decision to help the mare seem to her beyond her control, especially since she has always been obedient and knows her action will hurt her father, whom she loves?

6. Consider the line that comes from her father at the story's end, "She's only a girl." The words, she tells us, absolve and dismiss her "for good." Why? Why does she accept them?

ON TECHNIQUE AND STYLE

1. How convincing is the girl's voice in this story? Do you believe you are hearing the voice of a young girl?

2. Focus on the pacing in the story. Is it set up effectively to mirror the young protagonist's development and the changes in her views toward life?

3. How able is Munro at giving us a full sense of the other characters in the story aside from the narrator? Do we get a clear and full picture of her parents and her brother? Of Henry Bailey? What techniques does Munro use to try to make these other characters vivid or real?

CULTURAL QUESTION

1. Though this story takes place in a remote rural area of Canada the gender roles dramatized in it could occur anyplace. Or could they? Do different cultural attitudes toward gender exist that you are aware of that are not apparent in Munro's story?

Girl

Jamaica Kincaid

Jamaica Kincaid (1949–   ) was born Elaine Potter Richardson on the Caribbean island of St. John's, Antigua, in the West Indies. During her girlhood St. John's was a British colony. At seventeen she went to the United States and worked briefly as a nanny. After graduating from high school she attended at night, she briefly attended the New School for Social Research in New York City, then spent a year on scholarship at Franconia College in New Hampshire, dropping out in 1974 to educate herself in becoming a writer after finding college "a dismal failure." She began publishing stories in Rolling Stone, The Paris Review, *and* The New Yorker, *where she became a staff member and where "Girl" first appeared in 1978. In addition to short story collections, Kincaid has also published novels and a memoir about her brother's death from AIDS. Her published work includes* At the Bottom of the River, Annie John, A Small Place, Lucy, The Autobiography of My Mother, My Garden, Talk Stories, *and* Mr. Potter. *Like "Boys," "Girl" is an inventive, rhythmic poetic prose piece with few of the conventions we associate with the traditional short story. Yet it is a powerful, evocative representation of how a mother tries to make a good girl of the daughter she suspects will defy her by being a bad girl. It has become a kind of modern classic example of the hectoring and repetitive ways a colonized mother tries to shape the gender identity of her young daughter, and it reveals the enduring power of perceived and real gender differences.*

Wash the white clothes on Monday and put them on the stone heap; wash the color clothes on Tuesday and put them on the clothesline to dry; don't walk barehead in the hot sun; cook pumpkin fritters in very hot sweet oil; soak your little cloths right after you take them off; when buying cotton to make yourself a nice blouse, be sure that it doesn't have gum on it, because that way it won't hold up well after a wash; soak salt fish overnight before you cook it; is it true that you sing benna[1] in Sunday school?; always eat your food in such a way that it won't turn someone else's stomach; on Sundays

[1] Calypso music.

try to walk like a lady and not like the slut you are so bent on becoming; don't sing benna in Sunday school; you mustn't speak to wharf-rat boys, not even to give directions; don't eat fruits on the street—flies will follow you; *but I don't sing benna on Sundays at all and never in Sunday school;* this is how to sew on a button; this is how to make a button-hole for the button you have just sewed on; this is how to hem a dress when you see the hem coming down and so to prevent yourself from looking like the slut I know you are so bent on becoming; this is how you iron your father's khaki shirt so that it doesn't have a crease; this is how you iron your father's khaki pants so that they don't have a crease; this is how you grow okra—far from the house, because okra tree harbors red ants; when you are growing dasheen, make sure it gets plenty of water or else it makes your throat itch when you are eating it; this is how you sweep a corner; this is how you sweep a whole house; this is how you sweep a yard; this is how you smile to someone you don't like too much; this is how you smile to someone you don't like at all; this is how you smile to someone you like completely; this is how you set a table for tea; this is how you set a table for dinner; this is how you set a table for dinner with an important guest; this is how you set a table for lunch; this is how you set a table for breakfast; this is how to behave in the presence of men who don't know you very well, and this way they won't recognize immediately the slut I have warned you against becoming; be sure to wash every day, even if it is with your own spit; don't squat down to play marbles—you are not a boy, you know; don't pick people's flowers—you might catch something; don't throw stones at blackbirds, because it might not be a blackbird at all; this is how to make a bread pudding; this is how to make doukona;[2] this is how to make pepper pot; this is how to make a good medicine for a cold; this is how to make a good medicine to throw away a child before it even becomes a child; this is how to catch a fish; this is how to throw back a fish you don't like, and that way something bad won't fall on you; this is how to bully a man; this is how a man bullies you; this is how to love a man; and if this doesn't work there are other ways, and if they don't work don't feel too bad about giving up; this is how to spit up in the air if you feel like it, and this is how to move quick so that it doesn't fall on you; this is how to make ends meet; always squeeze bread to make sure it's fresh; *but what if the baker won't let me feel the bread?;* you mean to say that after all you are really going to be the kind of woman who the baker won't let near the bread?

QUESTIONS FOR DISCUSSION AND WRITING

1. The litany of advice and admonitions that make up this rhythmic and didactic piece of writing center on a mother trying to prepare her daughter

---

[2] Spicy plantain pudding.

for womanhood, kneading her daughter into it as a baker kneads bread. What are the mother's main ideas of what a woman needs to know?

2. The mother of the girl often sounds harsh. She even repeats the charge that her daughter is bent on becoming a "slut." The girl speaks out in only two instances—one about not singing benna music in Sunday school, and the other to ask what she should do if the baker doesn't allow her to feel the bread. What do we conclude about the relationship between mother and daughter?

3. In terms of power, does the relationship of mother and daughter mirror the mother's relationship to her husband or of a colonized, darker race to colonial masters? (Remember that the piece is set in the colonial world of Antigua in the West Indies.)

4. The characters in this story are poor people faced with the exigencies of survival. How much of the mother's advice is based on or rooted in folklore or superstition? Is there a maternal feeling behind the dispensing of the mother's advice? How much of the advice is sound, practical, or realistic?

5. The mother warns her daughter against speaking to "wharf-rat boys." How do you imagine the mother views these boys, and why do you think she insists her daughter steer clear of them? The mother tells her daughter not to "squat down to play marbles" because "you are not a boy, you know." Why is it important for the mother that her daughter not do what boys do or not appear to be like a boy? What about the mother's advice to her daughter on men? In general, what views come across toward gender differences of boys or men in "Girl"?

6. There is a fine division in the mother's creed to her daughter between acting like a lady and acting like a slut. What is the nature of the divide? Is there an ongoing similar divide in the views held toward girls in today's Western culture? Are appearances and reputation as important to girls today who grow up in what some believe to be a sex-saturated American culture?

ON TECHNIQUE AND STYLE

1. The writing style in this story is what is often described as impressionistic—memories conjured by details and associations that are more subjective than objective. How else would you define the style? Is it successful?

2. How would you characterize the effect of the mother's voice in this story? Is it too harsh? Too nagging?

3. To what extent does the use by Kincaid of local and generally unfamiliar references, such as "benna" and "doheen" and "doukona," enhance or take away from the story?

CULTURAL QUESTION

1. "Girl" contains strong embedded cultural attitudes. How do attitudes toward the upbringing of girls in the piece differ from attitudes toward the upbringing of girls you are familiar with in other cultures?

Boys

Rick Moody

Rick Moody (1961–   ) is an American writer best known for his novel The Ice
Storm, *which was made into a motion picture in 1997, directed by Ange Lee. Also
highly regarded for his short fiction and memoir, he was born Hiram Frederick Moody
III in New York City to a privileged middle-class family and grew up largely in the
suburbs of Connecticut. Educated at Brown and Columbia, he worked as an editor and
taught at the State University of New York at Purchase. In addition to* The Ice Storm
his novels include Garden State, Purple America, *and* The Diviners. *"Boys" is a
different kind of short fiction, a poignant and poetic prose piece capturing the cycle
from boyhood to manhood and distinguishing for its readers what it means to be a boy.
Published in a 2001 collection called* Demonology, *"Boys" is, on the surface, the story
of two brothers, their relationship to their parents, and the gender differences that exist
between them and their sister. At the same time, through its nearly incantatory and
rhythmic repetition, it is the story of archetypal boys and gender roles that distinguish
boys, boys who enter over and over until, inevitably, they exit.*

Boys enter the house, boys enter the house. Boys, and with them the ideas of
boys (ideas leaden, reductive, inflexible), enter the house. Boys, two of them,
wound into hospital packaging, boys with infant pattern baldness, slung in the
arms of parents, boys dreaming of breasts, enter the house. Twin boys, kettles
on the boil, boys in hideous vinyl knapsacks that young couples from Edison,
NJ, wear on their shirt fronts, knapsacks coated with baby saliva and staphy-
lococcus and milk vomit, enter the house. Two boys, one striking the other
with a rubberized hot dog, enter the house. Two boys, one of them striking the
other with a willow switch about the head and shoulders, the other crying,
enter the house. Boys enter the house, speaking nonsense. Boys enter the
house, calling for Mother. On a Sunday, in May, a day one might nearly
describe as *perfect,* an ice cream truck comes slowly down the lane, chimes
inducing salivation, and children run after it, not long after which boys dig a
hole in the backyard and bury their younger sister's dolls *two feet down,* so
that she will never find these dolls and these dolls will *rot in hell,* after which
boys enter the house. Boys, trailing after their father like he is the Second
Goddamned Coming of Christ Goddamned Almighty, enter the house, repair
to the basement to watch baseball. Boys enter the house, site of devastation,
and repair immediately to the kitchen, where they mix lighter fluid, vanilla pudding, drain-opening lye, balsamic vinegar, blue food coloring, calamine lotion,
cottage cheese, ants, a plastic lizard that one of them received in his Xmas
stocking, tacks, leftover mashed potatoes, Spam, frozen lima beans, and
chocolate syrup in a medium-sized saucepan and heat over a low flame until

thick, afterwards transferring the contents of this saucepan into a Pyrex lasagna dish, baking the Pyrex lasagna dish in the oven for nineteen minutes
before attempting to persuade their sister that she should *eat the mixture;* later
they smash three family heirlooms (the last, a glass egg, *intentionally*) in a two-
and-a-half hour stretch, whereupon they are sent to their bedroom, until freed,
in each case thirteen minutes after. Boys enter the house, starchy in pressed
shirts and flannel pants that *itch so bad,* fresh from Sunday School instruction,
blond and brown locks (respectively) plastered down, but even so with a number of cowlicks protruding at odd angles, disconsolate and humbled, uncertain
if boyish things—such as shooting at the neighbor's dog with a pump action
bb gun and gagging the fat boy up the street with a bandanna and showing
their shriveled boy-penises to their younger sister—are exempted from the
commandment to *Love the Lord thy God with all thy heart and with all thy soul,
and with all thy might, and thy neighbor as thyself.* Boys enter the house in
baseball gear (only one of the boys can hit): in their spikes, in mismatched
tube socks that smell like Stilton cheese. Boys enter the house in soccer gear.
Boys enter the house carrying skates. Boys enter the house with lacrosse
sticks, and, soon after, tossing a lacrosse ball lightly in the living room they
destroy a lamp. One boy enters the house sporting basketball clothes, the
other wearing jeans and a sweatshirt. One boy enters the house bleeding profusely and is taken out to get stitches, the other watches. Boys enter the
house at the end of term carrying report cards, sneak around the house like
spies of foreign nationality, looking for a place to hide the report cards for the
time being (under the toaster? in a medicine cabinet?). One boy with a black
eye enters the house, one boy without. Boys with acne enter the house and
squeeze and prod large skin blemishes in front of their sister. Boys with acne
treatment products hidden about their persons enter the house. Boys, standing just up the street, sneak cigarettes behind a willow in the Elys' yard, wave
smoke away from their natural fibers, hack terribly, experience nausea, then
enter the house. Boys call each other *retard, homo, geek,* and, later, *Neckless
Thug, Theater Fag,* and enter the house exchanging further epithets. Boys
enter the house with nose hair clippers, chase sister around the house threatening to depilate her eyebrows. She cries. Boys attempt to induce girls to
whom they would not have spoken only six or eight months prior to enter the
house with them. Boys enter the house with girls efflorescent and homely, and
attempt to induce girls to sneak into their bedroom, as they still share a single
bedroom; girls refuse. Boys enter the house, go to separate bedrooms. Boys,
with their father (an arm around each of them), enter the house, but of the
monologue preceding and succeeding this entrance, not a syllable is preserved. Boys enter the house having masturbated in a variety of locales. Boys
enter the house having masturbated in train station bathrooms, in forests, in
beach houses, in football bleachers at night under the stars, in cars (under a
blanket), in the shower, backstage, on a plane, the boys masturbate constantly, identically, three times a day in some cases, desire like a madness
upon them, at the mere sound of certain words, words that sound like other

words, *interrogative* reminding them of *intercourse, beast* reminding them of *breast, sects* reminding them of *sex,* and so forth, the boys are not very smart yet, and, as they enter the house, they feel, as always, immense shame at the scale of this *self-abusive cogitation,* seeing a classmate, seeing a billboard, seeing a fire hydrant, seeing things that should not induce thoughts of mastur-bation (their sister, e.g.) and then thinking of masturbation anyway. Boys enter the house, go to their rooms, remove sexually explicit magazines from hidden stashes, put on loud music, feel despair. Boys enter the house worried; they argue. The boys are ugly, they are failures, they will never be loved, they enter the house. Boys enter the house and kiss their mother, who feels differently, now they have outgrown her. Boys enter the house, kiss their mother, she explains the seriousness of their sister's difficulty, *her diagnosis.* Boys enter the house, having attempted to locate the spot in their yard where the dolls were buried, eight or nine years prior, without success; they go to their sister's room, sit by her bed. Boys enter the house and tell their completely bald sister jokes about baldness. Boys hold either hand of their sister, laying aside differ-ences, having trudged grimly into the house. Boys skip school, enter house, hold vigil. Boys enter the house after their parents have both gone off to work, sit with their sister and with their sister's nurse. Boys enter the house carrying cases of beer. Boys enter the house, very worried now, didn't know more worry was possible. Boys enter the house carrying controlled substances, nei-ther having told the other that he is carrying a controlled substance, though an intoxicated posture seems appropriate under the circumstances. Boys enter the house *weeping* and hear weeping around them. Boys enter the house, embarrassed, silent, anguished, keening, afflicted, angry, woeful, *griefstricken.* Boys enter the house on vacation, each clasps the hand of the other with gen-uine warmth, the one wearing dark colors and having shaved a portion of his head, the other having grown his hair out longish and wearing, uncharacteristi-cally, a tie-dyed shirt. Boys enter the house on vacation and argue bitterly about politics (other subjects are no longer discussed), one boy supporting the Maoist insurgency in a certain Southeast Asian country, one believing that *to change the system you need to work inside it;* one boy threatens to *beat the living shit out of the other,* refuses crème brûlée, though it is created by his mother in order to keep the peace. One boy writes home and thereby enters the house only through a mail slot: he argues that the other boy is *crypto-fascist,* believing that *the market can seek its own level on questions of ethics and morals;* boys enter the house on vacation and announce future professions; boys enter the house on vacation and change their minds about professions; boys enter the house on vacation and one boy brings home a *sweetheart,* but throws a tantrum when it is suggested that the *sweetheart* will have to retire on the folding bed in the basement; the other boy, having no *sweetheart,* is dis-tant and withdrawn, preferring to talk late into the night about family members gone from this world. Boys enter the house several weeks apart. Boys enter the house on days of heavy rain. Boys enter the house, in different calendar years, and upon entering, the boys seem to do nothing but compose manifestos, for the benefit of parents; they follow their mother around the place, having fashioned their manifestos in celebration of brand-new independence: *Mom, I like to lie in bed late into the morning watching game shows,* or, *I'm never going to date anyone but artists from now on, mad girls, dreamers, practicers of black magic,* or *A man should eat bologna, sliced meats are important,* or, *An American should bowl at least once a year,* but these manifestos apply only for brief spells, after which they are reversed or discarded. Boys don't enter the house, at all, except as ghostly afterimages of younger selves, fleeting images of sneakers dashing up a staircase; soggy towels on the floor of the bathroom; blue jeans coiled like asps in the basin of the washing machine; boys as an absence of boys, blissful at first, you put a thing down on a spot, put this book down, come back later, *it's still there;* you buy a box of cookies, eat three, later three are missing. Nevertheless, when boys next enter the house, which they ultimately must do, it's a relief, even if it's only in preparation for weddings of acquaintances from boyhood, one boy has a beard, neatly trimmed, the other has rakish sideburns, one boy wears a hat, the other boy thinks hats are ridiculous, one boy wears khakis pleated at the waist, the other wears denim, but each changes into his suit (one suit fits well, one is a little tight), as though suits are *the* liminary marker of adulthood. Boys enter the house after the wedding and they are slapping each other on the back and yelling at anyone who will listen, *It's a party!* One boy enters the house, carried by friends, having been arrested (after the wedding) for driving while intoxicated, complexion ashen; the other boy tries to keep his mouth shut: the car is on its side in a ditch, the car has the top half of a tree broken over its bonnet, the car has struck another car which has in turn struck a third, *Everyone will have seen.* One boy misses his brother horribly, misses the past, misses a time worth being nostalgic over, *a time that never existed,* back when they set their sister's playhouse on fire; the other boy avoids all mention of that time; each of them is once the boy who enters the house alone, missing the other, each is devoted and each callous, and each plays his part on the telephone, over the course of months. Boys enter the house with fishing gear, according to prearranged date and time, arguing about whether to use *lures* or *live bait,* in order to meet their father for the *fishing adventure,* after which boys enter the house again, almost immediately, with live bait, having settled the question; boys boast of having caught fish in the past, though no fish has ever been caught: *Remember when the blues were biting?* Boys enter the house carrying their father, slumped. Happens so fast. Boys rush into the house leading EMTs to the couch in the living room where the body lies, boys enter the house, boys enter the house, boys enter the house. Boys hold open the threshold, awesome threshold that has welcomed them when they haven't even been able to welcome themselves, that threshold which welcomed them when they *had* to be taken in, here is its tarnished knocker, here is its euphonious bell, here's where the boys had to sand the door down because it never would hang right in the frame, here are the scuffmarks from when boys were on the wrong side of the door *demanding,* here's where there were once milk bottles for the milkman, here's where the newspaper always landed, here's the mail slot, here's the light on the front step, illuminated, here's where the boys are standing, as that beloved man is carried out. Boys, no longer boys, exit.

QUESTIONS FOR DISCUSSION AND WRITING

1. The portrait Moody provides in "Boys" is of two brothers. Even though the two brothers turn out to be quite different from each other, what is the overall picture that emerges of boys, especially of young boys whose ideas (or the ideas about them) are, according to Moody, "leaden, reductive, inflexible"? How do those adjectives contribute to the picture that emerges?
2. How does Moody contrast what we might characterize as the energy of boys, especially when compared or contrasted to girls? Much of this is reflected in the piece in the way the boys relate to their sister. How and why does that relationship change? How does the energy in the boys change?
3. Moody describes "boyish things" as the brothers shooting a neighbor's dog with a pump action BB gun, gagging a fat boy and exposing themselves to their sister. The boys use a rubberized hot dog and a willow to strike others. Such behavior is violent, perhaps antisocial. Or is it? Are boys inclined to act violently and perhaps even outside the law? Is that what is meant by the cliché "boys will be boys"?
4. When the boys are young they follow their father, Moody writes, as if "he is the Second Goddamned Coming of Christ Goddamned Almighty." Why does Moody use such irreverent, impious, perhaps even sarcastic language to describe their father at this point in the boys' lives? How much has to do with the reality of loss and grief? The boys lose their sister. They ultimately lose their omnipotent seeming father. Is that some of what Moody suggests boys must suffer in order to become men?

ON TECHNIQUE AND STYLE

1. This is a story told in an unconventional style, in a kind of poetic prose. How does the story's style affect or make an impact on us?
2. How persuaded are you that "Boys" crystallizes the experiences of many boys rather than only a few? Does Moody use specific techniques to make the story general rather than specific?
3. Is there a specific definition in "Boys" of what boys are like or how they behave?

CULTURAL QUESTION

1. Could the boys Moody writes about be boys of color or boys of all ethnic groups?

POETRY

Barbie Doll

Marge Piercy

Poet, novelist, and social activist **Marge Piercy** *(1936–   ) was born in Detroit and raised Jewish (her mother was a Jew) in a working-class family, a child of the Great Depression. She went to the University of Michigan on a scholarship, the first in her family to attend college, and completed graduate work at Northwestern. A feminist with a long-time, passionate involvement in a wide range of social and political issues, she is known especially for writing on women's issues, particularly on the expectations and stereotypes society places and imposes on women. She has published fifteen novels, a play, and seventeen volumes of poetry including* Breaking Camp, The Moon Is Always Female, *and* The Art of Blessing the Day. *"Barbie Doll" is from the 1999 volume of poetry called* Circles on the Water: The Selected Poems of Marge Piercy. *It gives a clear, unvarnished picture of the pressures girls feel to be beautiful and the feelings of worthlessness they endure when they feel they are not.*

This girlchild was born as usual
and presented dolls that did pee-pee
and miniature GE stoves and irons
and wee lipsticks the color of cherry candy.
Then in the magic of puberty, a classmate said:
You have a great big nose and fat legs.

She was healthy, tested intelligent,
possessed strong arms and back,
abundant sexual drive and manual dexterity.
She went to and fro apologizing.
Everyone saw a fat nose on thick legs.

She was advised to play coy,
exhorted to come on hearty,
exercise, diet, smile and wheedle.
Her good nature wore out
like a fan belt.
So she cut off her nose and her legs
and offered them up.

In the casket displayed on satin she lay
with the undertaker's cosmetics painted on,
a turned-up putty nose,
dressed in a pink and white nightie.
Doesn't she look pretty? everyone said.
Consummation at last.
To every woman a happy ending.

QUESTIONS FOR DISCUSSION AND WRITING

1. The poem begins by telling us of the ways girls are conditioned into rigid sex roles by the consumer goods they are given to play with—dolls, miniature GE stoves and irons, wee lipsticks. How do such objects create social expectations for girls as they grow into women? Do they contribute to the low level of self-esteem girls like "this girlchild" seem plagued by in this poem?

2. Is it really so important for girls, as Piercy's poem suggests, to have social approval, especially for the way they look? To be, in effect, like Barbie dolls, rather than flesh and blood, real girls? Tie this to the imagery Piercy uses in the poem's second stanza, imagery often associated more with boys— "strong arms and back," "abundant sexual drive," "manual dexterity." What happens to traits like these as the girlchild tries to be like a Barbie doll and goes "to and fro apologizing"? Why is she apologizing?

3. Piercy uses sustained irony throughout the poem. A fine example of the cutting nature of her irony is in the third stanza where we read of the conflicting and dehumanizing advice the fanless girlchild receives: how "Her good nature wore out" like the mechanical failure of a fan belt, how she cut off her nose (rhinoplasty) to spite her face and cut her legs. Piercy tells us she "offered them up." To whom did she offer them and why?

4. In the final stanza of the poem Piercy's irony is complete. The girlchild has come to a happy ending as a woman, an everywoman. She has found "consummation," a word that means perfection but is also identifiable with the sexual union that completes the wedding vows. She looks pretty with an undertaker's cosmetics, a putty-fashioned nose and a pink and white nightie. What does this final image convey? What is Piercy saying, at poem's end, about how girls live and how they die?

ON TECHNIQUE AND STYLE

1. The poem has a story, a narrative embedded in it. Do you prefer poetry that uses narrative technique and actually tells a story? Is it more accessible?

2. "Barbie Doll" is a poem replete with much irony. Where do we see the poet being especially ironic? How does she make use of irony in the poem?

CULTURAL QUESTION

1. Compare and contrast the picture of the pressures we see from a cultural perspective on the girl in Piercy's poem to the girl in Kincaid's "Girl."

Wishes for Sons

Lucille Clifton

Lucille Clifton (1936–   ) was born in Depew, New York, and educated at the State University of New York at Fredonia. In addition to writing poetry she has published fiction and produced screenplays. She is an Emmy recipient and teaches at St. Mary's College in Maryland. Her volumes of poetry include Good Times *(1969);* Good News about the Earth *(1972);* An Ordinary Woman *(1974);* Two-Headed Woman *(1980);* Good Woman: Poems and a Memoir 1969–1980 *(1987);* Quilting Poems 1987–1990 *(1991);* The Book of Light *(1993);* The Terrible Stories *(1996); and* Blessing the Boats: New and Selected Poems 1988–2000 *(2000). "Wishes for Sons" is from the volume* Blessing the Boats. *As the poem's title implies, it is directed with pointed and poignant irony to all sons, all males, in the hope that they can be made to empathize with women and truly understand some of the more painful biological gender differences.*

i wish them cramps.
i wish them a strange town
and the last tampon.
I wish them no 7-11.
i wish them one week early
and wearing a white skirt.
i wish them one week late.
later i wish them hot flashes
and clots like you
wouldn't believe. let the
flashes come when they
meet someone special.
let the clots come
when they want to.
let them think they have accepted
arrogance in the universe,
then bring them to gynecologists
not unlike themselves.

QUESTIONS FOR DISCUSSION AND WRITING

1. Does Clifton really wish these things she writes about in her poem, burdens associated with menstruation and menopause, on her sons?
2. What is Clifton saying in the poem's last stanza about what she wishes for her sons? Why does she mention "arrogance" and "gynecologists" in this final stanza?
3. Clifton is an African American. Does that play any role in what she is communicating to us in this poem? Is it significant or is it merely a fact?
4. What advantages are there in Clifton using poetry as her means of expression? Could she as easily have written an essay and been more explicit about gender differences? How does poetry better serve or suit her purposes?

ON TECHNIQUE AND STYLE

1. "Wishes for Sons" has a good deal of humor. Is it effective humor? How does the humor in the poem affect us as readers?
2. Is the argument implicit in the poem about men's arrogance and their lack of sensitivity to women's biology convincing? How does Clifton try to ensure her argument?

CULTURAL QUESTION

1. Clifton once remarked, "I am a Black woman poet and I sound like one." Do you agree or disagree?

GRAPHIC FICTION

Gum of Mystery

Lynda Barry

*One of the more popular contemporary cartoonists, **Lynda Barry** (1956–   ) was born in Seattle, Washington, the daughter of a mixed race white and Filipina couple. A graduate of The Evergreen State College, she is best known for her syndicated weekly comic* Ernie Pook's Comeek. *Her published work includes many collections such as* The Good Times Are Killing Me, The Greatest of Marlys, The Freddie Stories, *and* 100 Demons. *Her cartoons, like the one we have included, often deal with the view and perspective of adolescent girls.*

QUESTIONS FOR DISCUSSION AND WRITING

1. The cartoon is obviously meant to make us laugh. Why is it funny? How is it serious? Certainly private property and unpleasant pranks are serious subjects, aren't they? Is their seriousness dimmed by the humor and fact that it comes to us in the form of a cartoon?

2. The three suspects (for putting gum in coat underarms) are caricatures, distorted or exaggerated portraits. Do they seem real types as well? What about the teacher, Miss Martles, who is referred to as Mrs. Martles by the boy in the first cartoon frame—who easily could be suspect Dewey M? Have you known teachers like her? What about Pammy, the real silent culprit—does she seem like a real person? Are Miss Martles and Pammy gender stereotypes?

3. Pammy is the quietest and smartest girl in the class. She never talks and wears glasses. (The great wit Dorothy Parker once said, "Boys don't make passes at girls who wear glasses.") What do you believe Barry was trying to reveal to us about the ways certain girls behave and appear, as opposed to what might be behind their appearances? Does this seem to you a reliable observation about the chasm that might exist between how girls appear and what may be their hidden secret lives?

4. What is Barry satirizing in this cartoon? How seriously are we to take her satire? What is she conveying about the nature of gender differences?

ON TECHNIQUE AND STYLE

1. What is the effect of Barry using language right away like "evil mystery" and "a secret juvenile delinquent"? What kind of tone is she trying to establish?

2. The figures in the cartoon are barely representational of real human beings. What is the effect of Barry's technique with characters who are literally sketchy and more like caricatures?

3. Does the revelation at the end of Pammy as the culprit pack a surprise punch?

CULTURAL QUESTION

1. Dewey M., "the new boy," is identified as having a Spanish name. He also appears darker than the other characters. Is there any reason behind these facts or anything that sets Dewey M. culturally apart from the other "suspects"?

VISUAL TEXTS

Quinceañera

Janet Jarman

*Tokyo-based **Janet Jarman** is a freelance photojournalist best known for her work in news, culture, and environmental issues and her internationally exhibited Latin American photos. We took the photograph included in this chapter from* Crossings: Stories of a Mexican Migrant Family *(2003). Educated at the University of Chile, her pictures have been in* Pictures of the Year *and have been cited for the best of photojournalism awards.*

Hannah, 13 Years Old
(third from the left)

Lauren Greenfield

*An internationally acclaimed photographer, **Lauren Greenfield** has had her work shown all over the world, especially the exhibit "Girl Culture" (2002) from which the selection in this chapter was taken. Educated at Harvard, she is an Infinity Award–*

winning documentary photographer who also directed the 2004 HBO film Thin, *about young women with eating disorders. She was named one of the twenty-five most influential photographers by American Photo Award.*

Shacktown Child

Dorothea Lange

Documentary photographer **Dorothea Lange**, *who was known during the Great Depression as "the photographer of the people," was born in 1895 in Hoboken, New Jersey. She began her career in New York City and wound up settling in San Francisco. The most widely published photographer of the 1930s, and prolific during the New Deal and the Second World War, Lange became associated with photographing migrant agricultural workers and society's "cast asides," the marginal, voiceless, and impoverished Americans, such as the girl shown in "Shacktown Child" (1936). In 1941 she gave up a Guggenheim Award to record the forced extradition of Japanese Americans to relocation camps in the American West.*

Boy and Girl at Debutante Ball

Catherine Karnow

Born and raised in Hong Kong and educated at Brown University, full-time photojournalist Catherine Karnow, who is presently based in San Francisco, gave us "Boy and Girl at Debutante Ball." One of seventy world journalists selected to work on the book

Passage to Vietnam, *her work has been exhibited in the Smithsonian museum and is included in the* Day in the Life *series. Her books include* Various Insight Guides *and* Adventures on the Scotch Whiskey Trail.

QUESTIONS FOR DISCUSSION AND WRITING

1. Pictures, like these photos, are often like Rorschach tests (the inkblot tests psychologists use that reveal a lot about the viewer of the photo and what he or she sees in it). When you first look at these photos what feelings do they emote in you? What do the photos communicate? Do feelings or ideas come across as fully or as effectively as they do in print or from sound? How are photographic images different from print or sound? How do they affect us differently and what can they convey about gender differences that cannot be conveyed in words?

2. Add some information to these photos. The photo of the girl in Lange's "Shacktown Child" was taken in 1936 during the Great Depression in Oklahoma. The so-called Okies, who were living during this period of American history and were captured in John Steinbeck's famous Depression-based novel *The Grapes of Wrath*, were dirt poor. The girl in the photo is a "shacktown child"; in other words, a child of poverty. What of the girl herself? Her facial expression? The look in her eyes? What do her features and the backdrop of the photo reveal to us about the girl that convey cross-cultural as well as gender differences?

3. In the photo titled "Boy and Girl at Debutante Ball," we are at a festive event in the Dominican Republic, a nation usually associated more with

poverty than debutante balls, events normally reserved for the rich. What does this photograph tell us? For example, what do the expressions on the children's faces communicate? What about the manner in which they are dressed and how they are standing? What does the fact that they are biracial communicate to us? What about the photo's backdrop? What does the picture communicate to you about cross-cultural and gender differences?

4. Look at the "Quinceañera" photo having to do with the dreams of Mexicans who want to cross the border to a better life in the United States. The children in the photo are at a Quinceañera, the Mexican version of a "sweet sixteen" party, held for those of *quince* (fifteen) years of age. What does the way the children are dressed and their being in a limousine tell us about who they are and who they hope or dream they will one day become? What do their attire and the expressions on their faces, as well as their body language, communicate? Can border crossings be culture- and age-related as well as geographic? What gender differences are revealed?

5. In the Lauren Greenfield photo, we see a seventh-grade party for thirteen-year-olds. What does the way the girls are dressed tell us about them? What do we learn about them from the way they look and pose? Tie in your impressions from the photo to the words of the girl, Hannah, who tells us how they have prepared for the party and what is important to the members of the clique, the members of the group of four pictured in the photograph. What feelings does Hannah express about how she looks as opposed to how she feels beneath her appearance? What gender differences are most evident?

ON TECHNIQUE AND STYLE

1. The photos of the children from Jarman and Greenfield project strong images of children trying to look older than they are. Compare and contrast the effect of what these two strong visual images project and create.

2. "Shacktown Child" and "Boy and Girl at Debutante Ball" are both evocative titles. How do the titles of either or both inform the content of the photograph(s)?

CULTURAL QUESTION

1. Each of these photos projects an image of a subculture. Which of the four projects the most vivid representation of a subculture?

AUDIO TEXTS To hear these conversations, go to www.mhhe.com/soundideas1e

Track 1.1

(date: May 20, 2002; running time: 50:50 min.)

Pioneer feminist psychologist **Carol Gilligan** *was born in New York City in 1936 and educated at Swarthmore College, Radcliffe College, and Harvard University. An internationally acclaimed author of* In a Different Voice: Psychological Theory and Women's Development *(1982) and* The Birth of Pleasure, *Gilligan served as the first professor of gender studies at Harvard and has been visiting professor at Cambridge University as well as professor at New York University. She also edited five books on gender. Her work has served to create a major shift in the views of girls' moral development and how women develop self-identity and values in a patriarchal society. She is a recipient of the Grawemeyer Award in Education and the Heinz Award for Knowledge. In 1996* Time *magazine named her one of America's twenty-five most influential people.*

Track 1.2

(date: November 22, 1999; running time: 50:50 min.)

Paul Kivel *is a violence prevention educator and community activist who cofounded the Oakland Men's Project, an organization whose mission is to help boys develop into responsible and caring, nonviolent men. The author of many articles on boys, men, and violence, his book is titled* Boys Will Be Men: Raising Our Sons for Courage, Caring and Community.

Track 1.3

(date: November 22, 1999; running time: 50:50 min.)

See **William Pollack's** *biography.*

Track 1.4

(date: November 22, 1999; running time: 50:50 min.)

Joseph Marshall Jr. was born in St. Louis in 1947. He spent much of his youth in South Central Los Angeles and received his BA from the University of San Francisco, his MA from San Francisco State University, and his PhD from the Wright Institute. A lifetime teacher and mentor to underprivileged and troubled urban youth, he formed the Omega

Boys Club in 1987, an organization dedicated to getting young people, including gang members, out of trouble and on to a college track. The coauthor of Street Soldier, *Marshall served on the planning board of the Surgeon General's Report on Youth Violence and as an adviser for the Community Violence Prevention Project at Harvard University's School of Public Health. He received the Freedom Works Award from Congress and a MacArthur "genius" Award.*

QUESTIONS FOR DISCUSSION AND WRITING

1. In Track 1.1, Gilligan speaks about her role in shifting the conversation about gender from leaving girls out of psychological research. She wrote of resistance girls appeared to have to speaking in their own voices. Her work, she said, was essentially about differences between boys and girls. How have the norms changed? Do girls now have voices equal to those of boys? Are they generally willing to speak in their own voices?

2. In Track 1.1, Gilligan seems to feel the classroom continues to be a place where girls are tacitly encouraged to be more passive. Is this what you have observed as a student? How might classroom teachers act to encourage all students to participate?

3. We need to talk, Gilligan states in Track 1.1, about what really goes on in girls, what they really think as opposed to what they *say* they think. Do you agree that girls are "meaner" now that there are fewer constraints on them? Is Gilligan correct when she declares that girls around the seventh grade form cliques and often do cruel things to one another? Is this, as she suggests, part of some kind of initiation process? Explain your answers to these questions.

4. In Track 1.2, Kivel argues that we need to get boys "out of the box" of trying to act like men. He believes boys don't really want to be in that box, and that they can unlearn in-the-box conditioning in classes, after-school programs, and through peer support. Do you believe such changes can occur? Are boys willing, as Kivel says, to make different choices? How can adults, families, and communities facilitate change?

5. In Track 1.3, Pollack talks about emotional disconnection being a root cause for boys feeling they need to wear masks; he claims boys push to be men rather than being "real boys." He adds that they push or are pushed away from their mothers. "Adults need to give different messages about what it means to be a real boy," Pollack says. He suggests the messages ought to have to do with love, care, and nurture rather than avoiding feelings of loss of masculinity. Do you agree? Does this mean boys ought not to be taught to be strong, independent, and "manly"? Explain your answer.

6. In Track 1.3, Pollack argues that we need to find ways to help boys open up. He also says we understand girls but that we need a new way of understanding boys. Do you agree? Are we failing boys more than girls? Explain your answer.

7. In Track 1.4, Marshall talks about shame and how boys are bombarded with images of what it takes to be a man—by peers and movies. He says

also that boys start early wanting to be known, to get recognition, or to make a mark, even in negative ways. He suggests that boys and girls need to start thinking of what they want to be without feeling the need to prove their manhood or womanhood. Is this a realistic view? Is it one worth striving toward even if it isn't entirely attainable?

ON TECHNIQUE AND STYLE

1. How persuasive is Gilligan in Track 1.1? What kinds of techniques does she employ that enhance or take away from her overall persuasiveness?
2. Gilligan argues in Track 1.1 that children see the world with acuity—the boy who acts as his mother's emotional barometer or the boy who asks the father who is hitting him if he (the father) fears his son will hit his children. What is Gilligan saying here about what Pollack calls "real boys"?
3. Which of the speakers in Tracks 1.2, 1.3, and 1.4 struck you as most effective? How much does effectiveness have to do with style? Is how things are said as important as what is said?
4. In a roundtable discussion from which Tracks 1.2, 1.3, and 1.4 were taken, how important is the give and take of ideas among the participants?

CULTURAL QUESTIONS

1. Famed feminist Germaine Greer once spoke of females having a separate culture. Does that seem to be what Gilligan is arguing in Track 1.1? Do you think the idea is a viable one? Explain your answer.
2. Marshall is an African American who works largely with African American youth. Are there cultural differences worth noting in what he expresses about boys in Track 1.4 as opposed to what we hear from the other participants?

CONNECTIONS

1. Adam, the boy Pollack writes about, is failing academically because he is being taunted and picked on and forced to fight—unfortunately, all too common for many boys. He also appears to have loving and caring parents. Compare his situation to that of June's in Pipher's selection "Strong Girls." June, Pipher believes, is happy. To what extent can we predict success or happiness for Adam? On what would that depend?
2. In what ways is Barry's comic a reflection of Pipher's and Pollack's writings? Considering June's story, do you think Pammy Lyons will find success in her future? What is your opinion based on?

3. In Munro's "Boys and Girls" we get a strong sense of what separates one gender from the other. How does this sense of what separates the boys from the girls differ in Updike's story "A&P" or in Clifton's poem "Wishes for Sons"?

4. The boys in Moody's story "Boys" bury their sister's dolls and hope the dolls will "rot in hell." How does this tie in with Pollitt's essay "Why Boys Don't Play with Dolls"?

5. In "Boys," recall that Moody tells us that at that point in their lives, the boys in the story feel they are ugly and failures and will never be loved. Does this link to what Pollack, in "Inside the World of Boys," says about the reasons that boys are academic underachievers?

6. What is Pollitt saying in her essay about Barbie dolls? Why do Barbie dolls matter to Pollitt? Compare her point of view that "Barbie must be passed along" to Piercy's in the poem "Barbie Doll."

7. Do boys and girls continue to this day, as Pollitt argues in her essay, to play differently in ways suggested in the poem by Piercy?

8. How does the spatial arrangement in Clifton's poem "Wishes for Sons" create a different kind of visual experience for readers accustomed to words as they are presented in "Barbie Doll" by Piercy?

9. Look again at the photographs related to this chapter. For each of the photos, which reading selection do you think is most closely related? Why?

10. Are there common themes or ideas about gender differences set forth in the Gilligan interview and in the roundtable discussion with Pollack, Marshall, and Kivel? What are the main connections?

FOR WRITING

CREATIVE CHOICES

1. Create a comic that illustrates one of the main themes of this chapter. (Keep in mind that you need not be an accomplished artist to create a comic. Simple drawings, such as those found in Barry's comic, can be very effective.)

2. Start a journal. In it, write a memory of a childhood event that recounts a story related to your own identity as a boy or girl and a moment of realizing gender differences. Think about the importance of the event, and what you learned from it that stays with you today. If you prefer, create an audio or video journal, recording your spoken ideas onto a tape or digital recorder.

3. Write a poem related to gender identity or childhood struggle with gender difference. Keeping in mind that poems are typically best appreciated in the spoken form, record yourself reading your poem, either on tape or digital recorder.

NARRATIVE/EXPOSITORY CHOICES

1. Consider the readings that focus on the issues of dolls. Did you play with dolls, or action figures, as a child? Did you do harm to a sibling's (or your own) dolls or action figures? Did you reject playing with dolls, or collect them obsessively? Write an essay in which you reflect on your own experience as confirming or contrasting with the experiences and ideas in these passages. Be sure to quote and cite the stories that you relate to your own experiences.

2. Choose the reading passage that interests you most from this chapter. Then, choose a photo from those connected to this chapter that illustrates either the same gender-related theme, or a theme that contradicts it. Write an essay in which you explore the themes of both the reading passage and the photo you chose, explaining the connection between them.

3. Choose two readings from this chapter from the Fiction and/or Poetry section. Make your choice based on a shared theme. What theme do these two readings share? How is the theme illustrated in the stories? Develop a thesis based on your reading of these stories, and write an analytical essay in which you use extensively passages from the readings to support your thesis.

RESEARCH CHOICES

1. Based on the Pipher and Pollack readings, develop a set of questions that interest you about gender differences. Interview a female and a male friend or classmate, using your questions. Record their responses. Write an essay in which you relate their experiences to those explained by Pipher and Pollack in both the reading passages and the *Forum* interviews. Use quotations both from your own interviews and from the readings and *Forum* interviews. If you have the tools and skills, create an "audio essay" in which you incorporate relevant clips from your interviews and/or audio clips from the *Forum* interviews with Pipher and Pollack with your writing.

2. Consider the images of boys and girls as offered by today's advertising media. Identify images from print or video advertising that reflect or reinforce gender differences. Write an essay in which you show how gender differences are represented in advertising media. Incorporate the images you found to support your thesis. If you have the tools and skills, create a web page essay for this research project.

VIDEO SUGGESTIONS

These videos feature stories by the authors introduced in this chapter, or are related to the chapter themes.

1. *The Ice Storm* (1997). Based on Moody's novel of the same name. In 1973, suburban Connecticut middle-class families find their lives out of control.
2. *Mean Girls* (2004). Cady Heron is popular with The Plastics, a clique at her new school, until she makes the mistake of falling for Aaron Samuels, the ex-boyfriend of Plastic leader Regina.
3. *Stand by Me* (1986). Based on a Stephen King novel. After the death of a friend, a writer tells the story of a boyhood journey to find the corpse of a missing boy.
4. *A&P* (1996). Based on the Updike story.
5. *Hamlet* (1996). Hamlet, the prince of Denmark, returns home to find his father murdered and his mother remarrying the murderer, his uncle. This Shakespearean story introduces us to the character Ophelia, played in this version by Kate Winslet.

 chapter **2**

Ideas about Family

Parents and Children

INTRODUCTION

The opening sentence of Tolstoy's *Anna Karenina* is one of the best known of any novel: "All happy families are alike; each unhappy family is unhappy in its own way." Families, in fact, continue to be the greatest source of stories, self-examination, and reflection.

Most of the writings in this chapter focus on what appear to be "unhappy" families. As you read, though, we encourage you to look beneath the apparent surfaces of the narratives and memoirs, and think about other truths that might lie there. Similarly, think about Tolstoy's idea: Are each of these families unique in their unhappiness, or do common themes emerge?

The first reading, "Nothing Lasts a Hundred Years," a section from Richard Rodriguez's *Days of Obligation: An Argument with My Mexican Father*, looks at Rodriguez's relationship with his mother, with his father, with their home country of Mexico, and with their community in Sacramento, California. Rodriguez, a controversial writer about issues of immigration and bilingualism, considers the history of California as it affects his family's history as well. Although addressing a different time and family situation, you may find parallels between Rodriguez's story and that of James Baldwin in "Notes of a Native Son." Baldwin, an important African American writer, has written extensively about race and racism. In this passage, the connection between his other writings and his home life become more apparent. Paul Theroux, a prolific writer of fiction and nonfiction, takes an unflinching look at his large family of "savages" in the ironically titled "Mother of the Year." In the final nonfiction piece, Sarah Vowell, a writer and comic, writes fondly about her father, and her family's relationship with guns and politics.

The four short stories presented next may, in some ways, seem nearly indistinguishable from the memoir and nonfiction pieces that precede them. Their themes and struggles would be familiar territory to any of the nonfiction writers. Grace Paley's very short story "Mother" examines a small conflict that becomes a large one between a mother and teenage child. Earl, the narrator of Russell Banks's "My Mother's Memoirs, My Father's Lie, and Other True Stories," tries to untangle what is true and what is not among the family stories. "Everyday Use," one of Alice Walker's better-known short stories, shows the conflict between daughters as they try to understand how best to honor their family's history. Finally, Dorothy Allison, in "River of Names," offers a picture of family death and violence and the need to cover up the truths about one's family history.

These themes carry over to two poems you will find in this chapter, dealing with themes of family happiness and unhappiness. In Kitty Tsui's "A Chinese Banquet: For the One Who Was Not Invited" the narrator addresses her lesbian partner, and contemplates homophobia and the weight and danger of silence. Nikki Giovanni's poem "Nikki-Rosa" examines the relationship between love and wealth, reflecting on the presence of love despite the family's poverty.

The graphic selection included is considered a "classic" of graphic fiction: the comic strip *Jimmy Corrigan: The Smartest Kid on Earth*, by Chris Ware. This selection deals with the difficult relationship of Jimmy Corrigan and his parents, especially his mother.

The images included in this chapter show a 1974 photo of parents in support of their gay children by Komi Chen, a classic portrait of mother and child by Edward S. Curtis, and a stereotypical 1950s family having dinner by William Gottlieb. As you look at these images, think about how they reinforce or contradict Tolstoy's observation about happy families.

The audio selections include parts of interviews with Richard Rodriguez, Paul Theroux, Alice Walker, and Grace Paley. In these selections you will find ideas that will help you put the readings into greater context.

As you read the selections in this chapter, you will no doubt be making comparisons with your own family, or other families you know. This strategy will help in your analysis of the readings, and in your understanding of what makes a family happy, or unhappy.

NONFICTION

Nothing Lasts a Hundred Years

Richard Rodriguez

Richard Rodriguez is the author of Brown: The Last Discovery of America *(2003),*
Hunger of Memory *(1983), and* Days of Obligation: An Argument with My
Mexican Father *(1992), from which the following excerpt is taken. He is also an
associate editor with Pacific News Service in San Francisco, a contributing editor of*
Harper's *and the* Los Angeles Times, *and a regular essayist on the* Jim Lehrer
News Hour *on PBS.*

*Rodriguez was born in San Francisco, California, and raised in Sacramento. He received
a bachelor's degree at Stanford University, and then spent two years at Union Theo-
logical Seminary in New York. He later spent time in England, at London's Warburg
Institute and Oxford University, before returning to the United States. He earned his
doctorate in Renaissance Literature at the University of California, Berkeley.*

*In 1997, Rodriguez received one of television's top honors, a George Foster Peabody
Award for his* News Hour *essays on American life. His other awards include the
Frankel Medal from the National Endowment for the Humanities and the International Journalism Award from the World Affairs Council of California. In the passage
that follows, Rodriguez takes a look at his family's history as it relates to the history of
the California community around them.*

A waiter bowed. The dining room was flooded with sunlight. I saw my mother
sitting alone at a table near the window.

Where's Papa?

I turned to see my father enter the dining room. His hand moved to adjust
his tie. Some pleasure tempted his lips.

He had gotten up early. He had taken a walk. He had gone to the Capu-
chin church on the Via Veneto. I remembered the church—the monk murmuring at the drop of a coin—and, several flights down, I remembered the
harvest of skulls.

For years I had dreamed of this trip with my parents. We were many years
from Sacramento. We were in Rome at the Eden Hotel. This was to have been
my majority—the grand tour—proof of my sophistication, my easy way with
the world. This was to have been the culmination of our lives together, a kind
of antiheaven. My father should have been impressed.

But nothing I could show my father, no Michelangelo, no Bernini, no cathedral or fountain or square, would so rekindle an enthusiasm in my father's eyes as that paltry catacomb he had found on his own. He had seen the final things. He was confirmed in his estimate of nature. He was satisfied.

. . .

I was born in the year 1632, in the city of York, of a good family, though not of that country, my father being a foreigner of Bremen. . . . I was called Robinson Kreutznaer; but by the usual corruption of words in England we are now called, nay, we call ourselves, and write our name 'Crusoe' . . .

Being the third son of the family, and not bred to any trade, my head began to be filled very early with rambling thoughts. . . . My father, a wise and grave man, gave me serious and excellent counsel against what he foresaw was my design.

When I was fourteen and my father was fifty, we toyed with the argument that had once torn Europe, South from North, Catholic from Protestant, as we polished the blue DeSoto.

"Life is harder than you think, boy."

"You're thinking of Mexico, Papa."

"You'll see."

. . .

We arrived late on a summer afternoon in an old black car. The streets were arcades of elm trees. The houses were white. The horizon was flat.

Sacramento, California, lies on a map around five hundred miles from the ruffled skirt of Mexico. Growing up in Sacramento, I found the distance between the two countries to be farther than any map could account for. But the distance was proximate also, like the masks of comedy and tragedy painted over the screen at the Alhambra Theater.

Both of my parents came from Mexican villages where the bells rang within an hour of the clocks of California. I was born in San Francisco, the third of four children.

When my older brother developed asthma, the doctors advised a drier climate. We moved one hundred miles inland to Sacramento.

Sacramento was a ladies' town—"the Camellia Capital of the World." Old ladies in summer dresses ruled the sidewalks. Nature was rendered in Sacramento, as in a recipe, through screens—screens on the windows; screens on all the doors. My mother would close the windows and pull down the shades on the west side of the house "to keep out the heat" through the long afternoons.

My father hated Sacramento. He liked an open window. When my father moved away from the ocean, he lost the hearing in one ear.

Soon my mother's camellias grew as fat and as waxy as the others on that street. She twisted the pink blossoms from their stems to float them in shallow bowls.

Because of my mother there is movement, there is change in my life. Within ten years of our arrival in Sacramento, we would leap from one sociological chart onto another, and from house to house to house—each house larger than the one before—all of them on the east side of town. By the time I went to high school, we lived on "Eve" Street, in a two-story house. We had two cars and a combination Silvertone stereo-television. My bedroom was up in the trees.

I am not unconscious. I cherish our fabulous mythology. My father makes false teeth. My father received three years of a Mexican grammar-school education. My mother has an American high-school diploma. My mother types eighty words per minute. My mother works in the governor's office, where the walls are green. Edmund G. "Pat" Brown is governor. Famous people walk by my mother's desk. Chief Justice Earl Warren says hi to my mother.

After mass on Sundays, my mother comes home, steps out of her high-heel shoes, opens the hatch of the mahogany stereo, threads three Mexican records onto the spindle. By the time the needle sinks into the artery of memory, my mother has already unwrapped the roast and is clattering her pans and clinking her bowls in the kitchen.

It was always a man's voice. Mexico pleaded with my mother. He wanted her back. Mexico swore he could not live without her. Mexico cried like a woman. Mexico raged like a bull. He would cut her throat. He would die if she didn't come back.

My mother hummed a little as she stirred her yellow cake.

My father paid no attention to the music on the phonograph. He was turning to stone. He was going deaf.

I am trying to think of something my father enjoyed.

Sweets.

Any kind of sweets. Candies. Nuts. Especially the gore oozing from the baker's wreath. Carlyle writes in *The French Revolution* about the predilection of the human race for sweets; that so much of life is unhappiness and tragedy. Is it any wonder that we crave sweets? Just so did my father, who made false teeth, love sweets. Just so does my father, to this day, disregard warnings on labels. Cancer, Cholesterol. As though death were the thing most to be feared in life.

My mother remembered death as a girl. When a girl of my mother's village died, they dressed the dead girl in a communion dress and laid her on a high bed. My mother was made to look; whether my mother was made to kiss that cold girl I do not know, but probably she did kiss her, for my mother remembered the scene as a smell of milk.

My mother would never look again. To this day, whenever we go to a funeral, my mother kneels at the back of the church.

But Mexico drew near. Strangers, getting out of dusty cars, hitching up their pants, smoothing their skirts, turned out to be relatives, kissing me on the front porch. Coming out of nowhere—full-blown lives—staying a month

(I couldn't remember our lives before they came), then disappearing when back-to-school ads began to appear in the evening paper.

Only my Aunt Luna, my mother's older sister, lives in Sacramento. Aunt Luna is married to my uncle from India, his name an incantation: Raja Raman. We call him Raj. My uncle and aunt came to the Valley before us. Raj is a dentist and he finds work where he can, driving out on weekends to those airless quonset-hut villages where farmworkers live. His patients are men like himself—dark men from far countries—men from India, from Mexico, from the Philippines.

One Sunday in summer my father and I went with my Uncle Raj and my Aunt Luna to Lodi, about thirty miles south of Sacramento. There was a brown lake in the center of Lodi where blond teenagers skied. We stopped to eat lunch in the shade of a tree and then we drove on, past dust-covered vineyards.

We stopped at an old house. I remember the look on my Aunt Luna's face. My father and my uncle got out of the car. There was some question about whether or not I should go with them. Aunt Luna fretted. "Don't be afraid of anything you'll see," she said. "It's just an old house where some men live." Aunt Luna stayed in the car.

Inside, the house is dark. The front-room windows are painted over. There are cots along the walls. On several cots men recline. They are dressed. Are they sick? They watch as we pass. We hear only the sound of our steps on the boards of the floor.

A crack of light shines from behind a door at the rear of the house. My uncle pushes open the door. A man wearing an apron is stirring a pot.

Romesh!

Romesh quickly covers the pot. He kisses my uncle on the mouth. He shakes hands with my father. Then, turning to me, he salutes: "General."

Romesh was Raj's older brother. Every Christmas, when Romesh came to my uncle's house, he called me the general. My brother was the colonel. Romesh came with his sister—"the doctor." One time he stood on his head. Every Christmas, Romesh and his sister gave me presents that either had no sex or should have gone to a girl. Once, a green cup; another year, a string of pearls. I was never sure if there was menace in Romesh.

Uncle Raj offered my father a job managing a "boardinghouse"—like the one in Lodi—where derelicts slept.

In private my mother said no, Leo, no.

My father ended up working in the back room of my uncle's office on J Street, making false teeth for several dentists. My father and Uncle Raj became closest friends.

My classmates at Sacred Heart School, two blocks from our house, belong to families with names that come from Italy and Portugal and Germany. We carry aluminum lunch boxes decorated with scenes from the lives of Hopalong Cassidy and Roy Rogers. We are an American classroom. And yet we are a dominion of Ireland, the Emerald Isle, the darling land. "Our lovely Ireland," the nuns always call her.

During the hot Sacramento summers, I passed afternoons in the long reading gallery of nineteenth-century English fiction. I took an impression of London and of the English landscape. Ireland held no comparable place in my literary imagination. But from its influence on my life I should have imagined Ireland to be much larger than its picayune place on the map. As a Catholic schoolboy I learned to put on the brogue in order to tell Catholic jokes, of grave diggers and drunkards and priests. Ireland sprang from the tongue. Ireland set the towering stalks of the litanies of the Church to clanging by its inflection. Ireland was droll, Ireland was omniscient, Ireland seeping through the screen of the confessional box.

And did your mother come from Ireland? Around March 17, a Catholic holiday, my Mexican mother—that free-floating patriot—my mother begins to bristle a bit. "If it's so wonderful, why did they all leave?" But it is her joke sometimes, too, that we are Irish. My mother's surname is Moran, her father a black Irishman? Her father was tall with eyes as green as leaves. There were Irish in nineteenth-century Mexico, my mother says. But there is no family tree to blow one way or the other. The other way would lead to Spain. For Moran is a common enough name in Spain, as throughout Latin America. Could it have been taken, not from Ireland but to Ireland, by Spaniards—Spanish sailors shipwrecked by Elizabeth's navy?

When my younger sister asked me to help her with an essay for school (the topic was Ireland), I dictated a mouthful of clover about Dublin's Jewish mayor and Ed Sullivan, Dennis Day, Mayor Daley, Carmel Quinn. "Ireland, mother of us all."

The essay won for my sister an award from the local Hibernian society. I taunted my sister the night she had to dress up for the awards banquet. My mother, though, returned from the banquet full of humor. They had all trooped into the hall behind the Irish colors—my sister, my mother, my father, an assortment of ladies, and some white-haired priests.

When Father O'Neil came back from his first trip home to Ireland, I was in third grade. There was a general assembly at school so we could see his slides, rectangles of an impossible green bisected by a plane's wing. The relations lined up in front of white houses, waving to us or just standing there. There was something so sad about Father then, behind the cone of light from the projector, in Sacramento, at Sacred Heart School, so far from the faces of home and those faces so sad.

In those days, people were leaving their villages and their mothers' maiden names to live among strangers in tract houses and God spoke to each ambition through the GI Bill. Highways swelled into freeways. If you asked, people in Sacramento said they were from Arkansas or from Portugal. Somewhere else.

It was my father who told me that an explorer with my surname, Juan Rodríguez Cabrillo, had been the first European to see California, rising and falling on the sea. The Irish nun at school confirmed the sighting. California was the farthest outpost of the Spanish colonial empire, Sister said. "Mexico City was the capital of the New World."

Mexico was the old country. In the basement of my Aunt Luna's house, I'd seen the fifty-gallon drums destined for Mexico, drums filled with blankets, flannel shirts, wrinkled dresses, faded curtains. When things got old enough they went to Mexico, where the earth shook and buildings fell down and old people waited patiently amid the rubble for their new old clothes.

I was repelled by Mexico's association with the old. On the map in Sister Mary Regis's classroom, Mexico was designated OLD MEXICO. In my imagination, Mexico was a bewhiskered hag huddled upon an expanse of rumpled canvas that bore her legend: Old Mexico.

Mexico City had universities and printing presses, cathedrals, palanquins, periwigs, long before there were British colonies in New England, Sister said. Long before there were cathedrals in Mexico, or periwigs or palanquins, there had been Indians in California. They had long hair. They wore no clothes. They ate acorns. They moved camp often. The fifth-grade textbook couldn't remember much else about them. (They looked like me.)

Alongside the duck pond at Sutter's Fort was a replica of an Indian teepee, but the wrong kind—a Plains Indian teepee—a tripod covered with painted leather.

Tall silvery grasses were bound into sheaflike water boats. California Indians paddled up and down the watery marshes of the Central Valley, which at that time looked very much like a duck-hunting print, said Sister, holding one up: a wedge of ducks driven into a rosy dawn.

In the nineteenth century, an unnamed Spanish explorer had come over the foothills from San Francisco Bay. The unnamed explorer nevertheless brought names; he flung names like blue-rocks; he consigned names to every creek and river. He named the valley Sacramento to honor the sacramental transformation of bread and wine into the body and blood of Christ. The river, which Californians would later call the Sacramento, the explorer named Jesús María. There were saints' names and Mary's name all up and down California.

In the 1950s, it seemed odd to me that non-Catholics went along with all this. They mispronounced the Spanish words, it's true. In Spanish, Sacramento gets a pinwheel in the middle—a twirling "r." Valley pronunciation flattened the word—trampled the "sack"—but then the Valley was flat. And Sacramento was a Protestant town.

My school was named to honor the Sacred Heart, which symbolized the ardor of Christ for His people—a heart with an open valve, spewing flame. Public schools in town were named to honor nineteenth-century American men, adventurers and civilizers, men crucial to the Protestant novel: Kit Carson, John Frémont, C. K. McClatchy, James Marshall. The most common naming name was that of John Sutter, Sacramento's founding father. Sutter's name attached to two hospitals in town; a boulevard; a men's club across from the state capitol; a public park; a tennis club.

Sutter's Fort was our historical landmark. Sutter's Fort was across the street from the new Stop'n'Shop, a ten-minute bicycle ride from my house. Sutter's Fort held no mystery for me. The grass was mowed once a week. The fort was surrounded on weekdays by yellow school buses. Not that Sacramento's memory of John Sutter was an unmixed pride. Sutter was a founding father notable for his failure. His story spelled a lesson in the Protestant annals.

Johann Sutter arrived in the 1830s, when California was Mexican territory. He had come from a low, delftish sky, from Bavaria, from Calvin, from Zwingli. When Sutter arrived in Monterey, he proposed to Mexican officials that he would build a fort in the great valley over the coastal hills. The fort would be a European settlement—New Helvetia he called it—a wall against the Indians. Mexico granted permission. Sutter paid no money to become a duke of wind and grass, the last European in a nineteenth-century opera.

As a young man, as a silent man, courting my mother, my father spent what little money he had on opera tickets, purchasing the extravagant gesture. When my father was seven years old, his mother died giving birth to a baby named Jesús. My father remembered lightning. How it rained that night! His father bundled up the blood-soaked sheets and the shift she wore, and with his son (my father carried the lantern), he went out into the storm to bury them. A few months later the baby died.

My father remembered the funeral of his father—the coffin floating on the shoulders of the men of the village, as if on a river, down the hill to the cemetery. As the casket was lowered into the pit, my father stepped forward to look down and he saw the bones of a hand reaching upward. My father never afterward passed up an opportunity to look into an open casket.

Infrequently, after dinner, my father told ghost stories.

"It doesn't happen here," my mother would say to her children, leaning into the story like an unwanted shaft of sunlight. "It happened in Mexico. Those things happen in old countries. During the Revolution, people used to bury their gold. When they died, they needed to come back to tell their children to dig up the money, so they could rest in peace. It doesn't happen here."

At the Saturday matinee at the Alhambra Theater we sat in the dark, beneath proximate grimaces of comedy and tragedy, laughing at death—we laughed at that pathetic tourist, the Creature from the Black Lagoon. For we were the sons and daughters of Arkies and Okies and the Isles of the Azores. Parents, grandparents—someone near enough to touch, someone close enough to whisper—had left tragedy behind. Our parents had crossed the American River, had come to Sacramento where death had no dominion. To anyone who looked back from the distance of California, the words of the dead were like mouths opening and closing in a silent film.

· · ·

Sacramento's ceremonial entrance was the Tower Bridge, where a sign proclaimed the town's population as 139,000. From the bridge you could see the state capitol—a wedding cake topped by a golden dome. Then, for six blocks, Sacramento posted BAIL BONDS; WEEKLY RATES; JESUS SAVES, Skid Row was what remained of the nineteenth-century river town, the Sacramento one sees in the early lithographs—a view from the river in the 1850s: young trees curling upward like calligraphic plumes; wooden sidewalks; optimistic store-fronts; saloons; hotels; the Eagle Theater.

In the 1950s, Sacramento had begun to turn away from the land. Men who "worked for the state" wore white short-sleeved shirts downtown. There were office buildings, hotels, senators. Sacramento seemed to me a long way from the Okie evangelists at the far end of the car radio. Except for Mexican farmworkers, I rarely saw men wearing cowboy hats downtown.

The urban progress of Sacramento in the 1950s—the pouring of cement and of asphalt—imitated, even as it attempted to check, the feared reclama-tion of California by nature. But in the 1950s there was plenty of nature left. On summer evenings, houses became intolerable. We lolled on blankets on the grass. We were that much closer to becoming Indians.

Summer days were long and warm and free and I could make of them what I liked. America rose, even as the grasses, even as the heat, even as planes rose. America opened like a sprinkler's fan, or like a book in summer. At Clunie Library the books which pleased me most were about boyhood and summer and America; synonyms.

I hate the summer of Sacramento. It is flat and it is dull. Though it is not yet noon, the dry heat of Sacramento promises to rise above the leaves to a hundred degrees. Just after noon, the California Zephyr cuts through town, pauses for five minutes, stopping traffic on K and L, and for those five minutes I inhabit the train's fabulous destination. But then the train sweeps aside like the curtain at the Memorial Auditorium, to reveal the familiar stage set for a rural comedy. A yellow train station.

Yet something about the Valley summer is elemental to me and I move easily through it—the cantaloupe-colored light, the puddles of shade on the street as I bicycle through. There is a scent of lawn.

When I think of Sacramento, I think of lawns—force-fed, prickling rect-angles of green. Lawns are not natural to California. Even one season without water, without toil, is ruinous to a garden, everyone knows. The place that had been before—before California—would come back; a place the Indians would recognize. Lovely tall grasses of dandelion or mustard in spring would inevitably mean lapsarian weeds, tinder grass and puncture vines come summer.

On Saturdays I mow the front lawn. On my knees I trim the edges. After-ward I take off my shoes to water down the sidewalk. Around noontime, as I finish, the old ladies of Sacramento, who have powdered under their arms and tied on their summer straw hats, walk by and congratulate me for "keep-ing your house so pretty and clean. Whyn't you come over to my house now," the ladies say.

I smile because I know it matters to keep your lawn pretty and green. It mattered to me that my lawn was as nice as the other lawns on the block. Behind the American facade of our house, the problem was Ireland. The problem was India. The problem was Mexico.

Mexico orbited the memory of my family in bitter little globes of sorrow, rosary beads revolving through the crushing weight of my mother's fingers. Mexico. Mexico. My mother said Mexico had skyscrapers. "Do not judge Mexico by the poor people you see coming up to this country." Mexico had skyscrapers, pyramids, blonds.

Mexico is on the phone—long-distance.

Juanito murdered!

My mother shrieks, drops the phone in the dark. She cries for my father. For light.

A crow alights upon a humming wire, bobs up and down, needles the lice within his vest, surveys with clicking eyes the field, the cloud of mites, then dips into the milky air and flies away.

The earth quakes. The peso flies like chaff in the wind. The Mexican police chief purchases his mistress a mansion on the hill.

The doorbell rings.

I split the blinds to see three nuns standing on our front porch.

Mama. Mama.

Monsignor Lyons has sent three Mexican nuns over to meet my parents. The nuns have come to Sacramento to beg for Mexico at the eleven o'clock mass. We are the one family in the parish that speaks Spanish. As they file into our living room, the nuns smell pure, not sweet, pure, like candles or like laundry.

The nun with a black mustache sighs at the end of each story the other two tell: Orphan. Leper. Crutch. One-eye. Casket.

Qué lástima!

"Someday you will go there," my mother would say. "Someday you'll go down and with all your education you will be 'Don Ricardo.' All the pretty girls will be after you." We would turn magically rich in Mexico—such was the rate of exchange—our fortune would be multiplied by nine, like a dog's age. We would be rich, we would be happy in Mexico.

. . .

Of Mexico my father remembered the draconian, the male face—the mustache parted over the false promises of the city.

"What is there to miss?" My father leaned over the map of Mexico I had unfolded on my desk.

"Tell me about the village."

"It's not on the map." His finger moved back and forth across the desert, effacing.

"Tell me names, Papa, your family."

He was an orphan in Mexico. My father had no private Mexico, no feminine corner. From the age of eight my father worked for rich relatives, a poor relation on the sufferance of his uncle. He remembers a cousin, a teenage girl, who went to bed when the sun went down and wept all night. And there were aunts, young aunts with their hair packed into gleaming loaves; old aunts whose hair had shriveled into dry little buns. My father appears in none of the family photographs he has kept in a cigar box in the closet.

The family was prominent, conservative, Catholic in the Days of Wrath— years of anti-Catholic persecution in Mexico. My father saw a dead priest twirling from the branch of a tree. My father remembered a priest hiding in the attic of his uncle's house. My father heard crowds cheering as the haughty general approached. My father remembered people in the crowd asking one another which general was passing, which general had just passed.

The church was my father's home; both of his parents were in heaven; the horizon was my father's home. My father grew up near the sea and he dreamed of sailing away. One day he heard a sailor boast of Australia. My father decided to go there.

My father's hand rests upon the map, a solitary continent, veined, unmoored. His native village was near enough to the town of Colima so that at night, as a boy, he saw the new electric glow of Colima instead of the stars. Colima, the state capital, has grown very large (a star on the map); per- haps what had been my father's village is now only a suburb of Colima?

He shrugs.

My father made false teeth for Dr. Wang. Mrs. Wang was the recep- tionist. Mrs. Wang sat at a bare table in an empty room. An old Chinese man, Dr. Wang's father, climbed the stairs at intervals to berate his son and his son's wife in Chinese.

Because of my mother, we lived as Americans among the middle class. Because of my father, because of my uncle from India, we went to Chinese wedding receptions in vast basement restaurants downtown, near the Grey- hound station. We sat with hundreds of people; we sat in back; we used forks. When the waiter unceremoniously plopped wobbly pink desserts in front of us, my mother pushed my plate away. "We'll finish at home."

My father and my uncle worked among outsiders. They knew a hand- some black doctor who sat alone in his office on Skid Row, reading the news- paper in his chair like a barber.

Sacramento was filling with thousands of new people each year—people fleeing the tanks of Hungary, people fleeing their father's debts or their fathers' ghosts or their fathers' eyes.

One of my aunts went back to Mexico to visit and she returned to tell my mother that the wooden step—the bottom step—of their old house near Guadalajara was still needing a nail. Thirty years later! They laughed.

My father said nothing. It was as close as he came to praising America.

We have just bought our secondhand but very beautiful blue DeSoto. "Nothing lasts a hundred years," my father says, regarding the blue DeSoto, as regarding all else. He says it all the time—his counsel. I will be sitting fat and comfortable in front of the TV, reading my *Time* magazine. My mother calls for me to take out the garbage. *Now!* My father looks over the edge of the newspaper and he says it: Nothing lasts a hundred years.

Holiday magazine published an essay about Sacramento by Joan Did- ion. The essay, an elegy for old Sacramento, was about ghostly ladies who perched on the veranda of the Senator Hotel and about their husbands, who owned the land and were selling the land. Joan Didion's Sacramento was nothing to do with me; families like mine meant the end of them. I so thoroughly missed the point of the essay as to be encouraged that a national magazine should notice my Sacramento.

Whenever Sacramento made it into the pages of *Time* magazine, I noticed the editors always affixed the explanatory *Calif.,* which I took as New York City's reminder. We were nothing. Still, that caliphate had already redeemed our lives. My mother, my father, they were different in California from what history had in store for them in Mexico. We breathed the air, we ate the cereal, we drank the soda, we swam in the pools.

My father was surprised by California and it interested him. It interested him that Sacramento was always repairing itself. A streetlight would burn out, a pothole would open in the asphalt, a tree limb would crack, and someone would come out from "the city" to fix it. The gringos were always ready to fix things, my father said.

In high school I worked as a delivery boy for Hobrecht Lighting Company. I delivered boxes of light fixtures to new homes on the north side of the river.

I remember standing outside a house near Auburn, waiting for the contractor to come with a key. I stood where the backyard would be. The March wind blew up from the fields and I regretted the loss of nature—the fields, the clear distance.

Yet California was elemental to me and I could no more regret California than I could regret myself. Not the dead California of Spaniards and forty-niners and Joan Didion's grandmother, but Kodachrome, CinemaScope, drive-in California—freeways and new cities, bright plastic pennants and spinning whirligigs announcing a subdivision of houses; hundreds of houses; houses where there used to be fields. A mall opened on Arden Way and we were first-nighters. I craved ALL-NEW and ALL-ELECTRIC, FREE MUGS, and KOOL INSIDE and DOUBLE GREEN STAMPS, NO MONEY DOWN, WHILE-U-WAIT, ALL YOU CAN EAT.

At a coffee shop—open 24 hours, 365 days a year—I approved the swipe of the waitress's rag which could erase history.

Through the years I was growing up there, Sacramento dreamed of its own redevelopment. Plans were proposed every few months to convert K Street downtown into a mall and to reclaim a section of Skid Row as "Old Town." The *Bee* published sketches of the carnival future—an expansive street scene of sidewalk cafés with banners and clouds and trees that were also clouds and elegant ladies with their purse arms extended, pausing on sidewalks that were made of glass.

A few years later, the future was built. Old Sacramento became a block of brick-front boutiques; some squat glass buildings were constructed on Capital Avenue; and K Street, closed to traffic for several blocks, got a concrete fountain and some benches with winos asleep in the sun.

Never mind. Never mind that the future did not always meet America's dream of itself. I was born to America, to its Protestant faith in the future. I was going to be an architect and have a hand in building the city. There was only my father's smile that stood in my way.

It wasn't against me; his smile was loving. But the smile claimed knowledge. My father knew what most of the world knows by now—that tragedy wins; that talent is mockery. In the face of such knowledge, my father was mild and manly. If there is trouble, if there is a dead bird to pick up, or when the lady faints in church, you want my father around. When my mother wants water turned into wine, she nudges my father, for my father is holding up the world, such as it is.

My father remains Mexican in California. My father lives under the doctrine, under the very tree of Original Sin. Much in life is failure or compromise; like father, like son.

For several years in the 1950s, when one of my family makes a First Holy Communion, we all go to Sutter's Fort to have our pictures taken. John Sutter's wall against the Indians becomes a gauge for the living, a fixed mark for the progress of my mother's children. We stand in formal poses against the low white wall of the fort. One of my sisters wears a white dress and veil and a little coronet of seed pearls. Or, when it is a boy's turn, one of us wears a white shirt, white pants, and a red tie. We squint into the sun. My father is absent from all the photographs.

The Sacramento Valley was to have been John Sutter's Rhineland. He envisioned a town rising from his deed—a town he decided, after all, to name for himself—Sutterville. Sutter imagined himself inventing history. But in the Eastern cities of Boston and Philadelphia and New York, Americans were imagining symmetry. They were unrolling maps and fixing them with weights set down upon the Pacific Ocean. Newcomers—Americans—were arriving in Mexican territory.

Already there were cracks in the sidewalk where the roots of the elm tree pushed up.

My father smiled.

Ask me what it was like to have grown up a Mexican kid in Sacramento and I will think of my father's smile, its sweetness, its introspection, its weight of sobriety. Mexico was most powerfully my father's smile, and not, as you might otherwise imagine, not language, not pigment. My father's smile seemed older than anything around me. Older than Sutter's Fort.

QUESTIONS FOR DISCUSSION AND WRITING

1. Describe the differences between Rodriguez's mother and his father— think particularly about the way he describes their history with Mexico and death. Are these differences important? Why or why not?
2. Rodriguez says, "I was never sure if there was menace in Romesh." What prompts him to say this? What does it say about Rodriguez?
3. Characterize Rodriguez's views of Mexico, as presented in this reading. In particular, why was he "repelled" by Mexico's "association with the old"?
4. Rodriguez refers to an article by Joan Didion. He says, "Joan Didion's Sacramento was nothing to do with me; families like mine meant the end of them." What does Rodriguez mean? What is happening in Sacramento?
5. What is the significance of Rodriguez's father's saying, "Nothing lasts a hundred years"?

ON TECHNIQUE AND STYLE

1. Rodriguez tells the story of Johann Sutter, then immediately moves to a story of his father purchasing opera tickets for his mother. Why are these two stories put in juxtaposition, in your opinion? What can you say about his style of writing? Is it effective?
2. Rodriguez can be said to relate his family's history closely to the history of the community. What examples of this do you find in the reading? Why do you think he has chosen to tell his family's history in this way (as opposed to narrating a family story without its historical context)?

CULTURAL QUESTION

1. Rodriguez describes a community in which we see many different cultural influences—notably Mexican, Irish, and Indian. He also says, "We are an American classroom. And yet we are a dominion of Ireland." How do you think Rodriguez views the effect of various cultures on his community and his education? Find passages in the reading that support your idea.

Notes of a Native Son

James Baldwin

James Baldwin gained fame with his very first novel, Go Tell It on the Mountain *(1953), an autobiographical story about growing up in Harlem, New York City, where he was born in 1924. He was the oldest of nine children. He never met his biological father. Instead, he considered his stepfather, David Baldwin, a factory worker and a storefront preacher, his only father.*

Baldwin became an important African American author of his generation, known for novels and essays that confronted issues of race and of sexuality. Although he had written as a child and student, Baldwin started writing seriously after being encouraged by fellow African American writer Richard Wright. Baldwin's strained relations with his stepfather, problems over sexual identity, suicide of a friend, and racism drove him, as it did Wright, to Paris in 1948. He returned to the United States in 1957 and became involved with the fight against racial segregation. Baldwin was a noted essayist during the Civil Rights movement of the 1960s. African American poet Langston Hughes said of Baldwin in a review, "Few American writers handle words more effectively in the essay form than James Baldwin" (The New York Times, February 26, 1958).

His novels, including Giovanni's Room *(1956),* Another Country *(1962), and* Just
Above My Head *(1979), deal with themes of individuality in conflict with intoler-
ance. He also wrote several plays, including* Blues For Mister Charlie *(1964) and*
Evidence of Things Not Seen *(1986), one of his last pieces of writing, a book about
racially motivated child murders in Atlanta.*

*In 1983, Baldwin became a professor in the Afro-American Studies Department of the
University of Massachusetts, Amherst. He spent the last years of his life in St. Paul
de Vence, France, where he died of cancer in 1987. The following selection is from his
1955 book* Notes of a Native Son.

On the 29th of July, in 1943, my father died. On the same day, a few hours
later, his last child was born. Over a month before this, while all our energies
were concentrated in waiting for these events, there had been, in Detroit,
one of the bloodiest race riots of the century. A few hours after my father's
funeral, while he lay in state in the undertaker's chapel, a race riot broke out
in Harlem. On the morning of the 3rd of August, we drove my father to the
graveyard through a wilderness of smashed plate glass.

The day of my father's funeral had also been my nineteenth birthday.
As we drove him to the graveyard, the spoils of injustice, anarchy, discontent, and hatred were all around us. It seemed to me that God himself had
devised, to mark my father's end, the most sustained and brutally dissonant
of codas. And it seemed to me, too, that the violence which rose all about
us as my father left the world had been devised as a corrective for the pride
of his eldest son. I had declined to believe in that apocalypse which had
been central to my father's vision; very well, life seemed to be saying, here
is something that will certainly pass for an apocalypse until the real thing
comes along. I had inclined to be contemptuous of my father for the conditions of his life, for the conditions of our lives. When his life had ended I
began to wonder about that life and also, in a new way, to be apprehensive
about my own.

I had not known my father very well. We had got on badly, partly because
we shared, in our different fashions, the vice of stubborn pride. When he was
dead I realized that I had hardly ever spoken to him. When he had been dead
a long time I began to wish I had. It seems to be typical of life in America,
where opportunities, real and fancied, are thicker than anywhere else on the
globe, that the second generation has no time to talk to the first. No one,
including my father, seems to have known exactly how old he was, but his
mother had been born during slavery. He was of the first generation of free
men. He, along with thousands of other Negroes, came North after 1919 and
I was part of that generation which had never seen the landscape of what
Negroes sometimes call the Old Country.

He had been born in New Orleans and had been a quiet young man there
during the time that Louis Armstrong, a boy, was running errands for the dives
and honky-tonks of what was always presented to me as one of the most

wicked of cities—to this day, whenever I think of New Orleans, I also helplessly think of Sodom and Gomorrah. My father never mentioned Louis Armstrong, except to forbid us to play his records; but there was a picture of him on our wall for a long time. One of my father's strong-willed female relatives had placed it there and forbade my father to take it down. He never did, but he eventually maneuvered her out of the house and when, some years later, she was in trouble and near death, he refused to do anything to help her.

He was, I think, very handsome. I gather this from photographs and from my own memories of him, dressed in his Sunday best and on his way to preach a sermon somewhere, when I was little. Handsome, proud, and ingrown, "like a toe-nail," somebody said. But he looked to me, as I grew older, like pictures I had seen of African tribal chieftains: he really should have been naked, with war-paint on and barbaric mementos, standing among spears. He could be chilling in the pulpit and indescribably cruel in his personal life and he was certainly the most bitter man I have ever met; yet it must be said that there was something else in him, buried in him, which lent him his tremendous power and, even, a rather crushing charm. It had something to do with his blackness, I think—he was very black—with his blackness and his beauty, and with the fact that he knew that he was black but did not know that he was beautiful. He claimed to be proud of his blackness but it had also been the cause of much humiliation and it had fixed bleak boundaries to his life. He was not a young man when we were growing up and he had already suffered many kinds of ruin; in his outrageously demanding and protective way he loved his children, who were black like him and menaced, like him; and all these things sometimes showed in his face when he tried, never to my knowledge with any success, to establish contact with any of us. When he took one of his children on his knee to play, the child always became fretful and began to cry; when he tried to help one of us with our homework the absolutely unabating tension which emanated from him caused our minds and our tongues to become paralyzed, so that he, scarcely knowing why, flew into a rage and the child, not knowing why, was punished. If it ever entered his head to bring a surprise home for his children, it was, almost unfailingly, the wrong surprise and even the big watermelons he often brought home on his back in the summertime led to the most appalling scenes. I do not remember, in all those years, that one of his children was ever glad to see him come home. From what I was able to gather of his early life, it seemed that this inability to establish contact with other people had always marked him and had been one of the things which had driven him out of New Orleans. There was something in him, therefore, groping and tentative, which was never expressed and which was buried with him. One saw it most clearly when he was facing new people and hoping to impress them. But he never did, not for long. We went from church to smaller and more improbable church, he found himself in less and less demand as a minister, and by the time he died none of his friends had come to see him for a long time. He had lived and died in an intolerable bitterness of spirit and it frightened me, as we drove him to the graveyard through those unquiet, ruined streets, to see how powerful and overflowing this bitterness could be and to realize that this bitterness now was mine.

When he died I had been away from home for a little over a year. In that year I had had time to become aware of the meaning of all my father's bitter warnings, had discovered the secret of his proudly pursed lips and rigid carriage: I had discovered the weight of white people in the world. I saw that this had been for my ancestors and now would be for me an awful thing to live with and that the bitterness which had helped to kill my father could also kill me.

He had been ill a long time—in the mind, as we now realized, reliving instances of his fantastic intransigence in the new light of his affliction and endeavoring to feel a sorrow for him which never, quite, came true. We had not known that he was being eaten up by paranoia, and the discovery that his cruelty, to our bodies and our minds, had been one of the symptoms of his illness was not, then, enough to enable us to forgive him. The younger children felt, quite simply, relief that he would not be coming home anymore. My mother's observation that it was he, after all, who had kept them alive all these years meant nothing because the problems of keeping children alive are not real for children. The older children felt, with my father gone, that they could invite their friends to the house without fear that their friends would be insulted or, as had sometimes happened with me, being told that their friends were in league with the devil and intended to rob our family of everything we owned. (I didn't fail to wonder, and it made me hate him, what on earth we owned that anybody else would want.)

His illness was beyond all hope of healing before anyone realized that he was ill. He had always been so strange and had lived, like a prophet, in such unimaginably close communion with the Lord that his long silences which were punctuated by moans and hallelujahs and snatches of old songs while he sat at the living-room window never seemed odd to us. It was not until he refused to eat because, he said, his family was trying to poison him that my mother was forced to accept as a fact what had, until then, been only an unwilling suspicion. When he was committed, it was discovered that he had tuberculosis and, as it turned out, the disease of his mind allowed the disease of his body to destroy him. For the doctors could not force him to eat, either, and, though he was fed intravenously, it was clear from the beginning that there was no hope for him.

In my mind's eye I could see him, sitting at the window, locked up in his terrors; hating and fearing every living soul including his children who had betrayed him, too, by reaching towards the world which had despised him. There were nine of us. I began to wonder what it could have felt like for such a man to have had nine children whom he could barely feed. He used to make little jokes about our poverty, which never, of course, seemed very funny to us; they could not have seemed very funny to him, either, or else our all too feeble response to them would never have caused such rages. He spent great energy and achieved, to our chagrin, no small amount of success in keeping us away from the people who surrounded us, people who had all-night rent parties to which we listened when we should have been sleeping, people who cursed and drank and flashed razor blades on Lenox Avenue. He could not understand why, if they had so much energy to spare, they could not use it to make their lives better. He treated almost everybody on our block with a most uncharitable asperity and neither they, nor, of course, their children were slow to reciprocate.

The only white people who came to our house were welfare workers and bill collectors. It was almost always my mother who dealt with them, for my father's temper, which was at the mercy of his pride, was never to be trusted. It was clear that he felt their very presence in his home to be a violation: this was conveyed by his carriage, almost ludicrously stiff, and by his voice, harsh and vindictively polite. When I was around nine or ten I wrote a play which was directed by a young, white schoolteacher, a woman, who then took an interest in me, and gave me books to read and, in order to corroborate my theatrical bent, decided to take me to see what she somewhat tactlessly referred to as "real" plays. Theater-going was forbidden in our house, but, with the really cruel intuitiveness of a child, I suspected that the color of this woman's skin would carry the day for me. When, at school, she suggested taking me to the theater, I did not, as I might have done if she had been a Negro, find a way of discouraging her, but agreed that she should pick me up at my house one evening. I then, very cleverly, left all the rest to my mother, who suggested to my father, as I knew she would, that it would not be very nice to let such a kind woman make the trip for nothing. Also, since it was a schoolteacher, I imagine that my mother countered the idea of sin with the idea of "education," which word, even with my father, carried a kind of bitter weight.

Before the teacher came my father took me aside to ask *why* she was coming, what *interest* she could possibly have in our house, in a boy like me. I said I didn't know but I, too, suggested that it had something to do with education. And I understood that my father was waiting for me to say something—I didn't quite know what; perhaps that I wanted his protection against this teacher and her "education." I said none of these things and the teacher came and we went out. It was clear, during the brief interview in our living room, that my father was agreeing very much against his will and that he would have refused permission if he had dared. The fact that he did not dare caused me to despise him: I had no way of knowing that he was facing in that living room a wholly unprecedented and frightening situation.

Later, when my father had been laid off from his job, this woman became very important to us. She was really a very sweet and generous woman and went to a great deal of trouble to be of help to us, particularly during one awful winter. My mother called her by the highest name she knew: she said she was a "christian." My father could scarcely disagree but during the four or five years of our relatively close association he never trusted her and was always trying to surprise in her open, Midwestern face the genuine, cunningly hidden, and hideous motivation. In later years, particularly when it began to be clear that this "education" of mine was going to lead me to perdition, he became more explicit and warned me that my white friends in high school were not really my friends and that I would see, when I was older, how white people would do anything to keep a Negro down. Some of them could be nice, he admitted, but none of them were to be trusted and most of them were not even nice. The best thing was to have as little to do with them as possible. I did not feel this way and I was certain, in my innocence, that I never would.

But the year which preceded my father's death had made a great change in my life. I had been living in New Jersey, working in defense plants, work-ing and living among southerners, white and black. I knew about the south, of course, and about how southerners treated Negroes and how they expected them to behave, but it had never entered my mind that anyone would look at me and expect *me* to behave that way. I learned in New Jersey that to be a Negro meant, precisely, that one was never looked at but was simply at the mercy of the reflexes the color of one's skin caused in other people. I acted in New Jersey as I had always acted, that is as though I thought a great deal of myself—I had to *act* that way—with results that were, simply, unbelievable. I had scarcely arrived before I had earned the enmity, which was extraordinarily ingenious, of all my superiors and nearly all my co-workers. In the beginning, to make matters worse, I simply did not know what was happening. I did not know what I had done, and I shortly began to wonder what *anyone* could pos-sibly do, to bring about such unanimous, active, and unbearably vocal hostility. I knew about jim-crow but I had never experienced it. I went to the same self-service restaurant three times and stood with all the Princeton boys before the counter, waiting for a hamburger and coffee; it was always an extraordinarily long time before anything was set before me; but it was not until the fourth visit that I learned that, in fact, nothing had ever been set before me: I had simply picked something up. Negroes were not served there, I was told, and they had been waiting for me to realize that I was always the only Negro present. Once I was told this, I determined to go there all the time. But now they were ready for me and, though some dreadful scenes were subsequently enacted in that restaurant, I never ate there again.

It was the same story all over New Jersey, in bars, bowling alleys, din-ers, places to live. I was always being forced to leave, silently, or with mutual imprecations. I very shortly became notorious and children giggled behind me when I passed and their elders whispered or shouted—they really believed that I was mad. And it did begin to work on my mind, of course; I began to be afraid to go anywhere and to compensate for this I went places to which I really should not have gone and where, God knows, I had no desire to be. My reputation in town naturally enhanced my reputation at work and my working day became one long series of acrobatics designed to keep me out of trouble. I cannot say that these acrobatics succeeded. It began to seem that the machinery of the organization I worked for was turning over, day and night, with but one aim: to eject me. I was fired once, and contrived, with the aid of a friend from New York, to get back on the payroll; was fired again, and bounced back again. It took a while to fire me for the third time, but the third time took. There were no loopholes anywhere. There was not even any way of getting back inside the gates.

That year in New Jersey lives in my mind as though it were the year during which, having an unsuspected predilection for it, I first contracted some dread, chronic disease, the unfailing symptom of which is a kind of blind fever, a pounding in the skull and fire in the bowels. Once this disease is contracted, one can never be really carefree again, for the fever, without an instant's warning, can recur at any moment. It can wreck more important things than race relations. There is not a Negro alive who does not have this rage in his blood—one has the choice, merely, of living with it consciously or surrendering to it. As for me, this fever has recurred in me, and does, and will until the day I die.

My last night in New Jersey, a white friend from New York took me to the nearest big town, Trenton, to go to the movies and have a few drinks. As it turned out, he also saved me from, at the very least, a violent whipping. Almost every detail of that night stands out very clearly in my memory. I even remember the name of the movie we saw because its title impressed me as being so patly ironical. It was a movie about the German occupation of France, starring Maureen O'Hara and Charles Laughton and called *This Land Is Mine.* I remember the name of the diner we walked into when the movie ended: it was the "American Diner." When we walked in the counterman asked what we wanted and I remember answering with the casual sharpness which had become my habit: "We want a hamburger and a cup of coffee, what do you think we want?" I do not know why, after a year of such rebuffs, I so completely failed to anticipate his answer, which was, of course, "We don't serve Negroes here." This reply failed to discompose me, at least for the moment. I made some sardonic comment about the name of the diner and we walked out into the streets.

This was the time of what was called the "brown-out," when the lights in all American cities were very dim. When we re-entered the streets something happened to me which had the force of an optical illusion, or a nightmare. The streets were very crowded and I was facing north. People were moving in every direction but it seemed to me, in that instant, that all of the people I could see, and many more than that, were moving toward me, against me, and that everyone was white. I remember how their faces gleamed. And I felt, like a physical sensation, a *click* at the nape of my neck as though some interior string connecting my head to my body had been cut. I began to walk. I heard my friend call after me, but I ignored him. Heaven only knows what was going on in his mind, but he had the good sense not to touch me—I don't know what would have happened if he had—and to keep me in sight. I don't know what was going on in my mind, either; I certainly had no conscious plan. I wanted to do something to crush these white faces, which were crushing me. I walked for perhaps a block or two until I came to an enormous, glittering, and fashionable restaurant in which I knew not even the intercession of the Virgin would cause me to be served. I pushed through the doors and took the first vacant seat I saw, at a table for two, and waited.

I do not know how long I waited and I rather wonder, until today, what I could possibly have looked like. Whatever I looked like, I frightened the waitress who shortly appeared, and the moment she appeared all of my fury flowed towards her. I hated her for her white face, and for her great, astounded, frightened eyes. I felt that if she found a black man so frightening I would make her fright worth-while.

She did not ask me what I wanted, but repeated, as though she had learned it somewhere, "We don't serve Negroes here." She did not say it with the blunt, derisive hostility to which I had grown so accustomed, but, rather, with a note of apology in her voice, and fear. This made me colder and more murderous than ever. I felt I had to do something with my hands. I wanted her to come close enough for me to get her neck between my hands.

So I pretended not to have understood her, hoping to draw her closer. And she did step a very short step closer, with her pencil poised incongruously over her pad, and repeated the formula: ". . . don't serve Negroes here."

Somehow, with the repetition of that phrase, which was already ringing in my head like a thousand bells of a nightmare, I realized that she would never come any closer and that I would have to strike from a distance. There was nothing on the table but an ordinary water-mug half full of water, and I picked this up and hurled it with all my strength at her. She ducked and it missed her and shattered against the mirror behind the bar. And, with that sound, my frozen blood abruptly thawed, I returned from wherever I had been, I *saw,* for the first time, the restaurant, the people with their mouths open, already, as it seemed to me, rising as one man, and I realized what I had done, and where I was, and I was frightened. I rose and began running for the door. A round, potbellied man grabbed me by the nape of the neck just as I reached the doors and began to beat me about the face. I kicked him and got loose and ran into the streets. My friend whispered, "*Run!*" and I ran.

My friend stayed outside the restaurant long enough to misdirect my pursuers and the police, who arrived, he told me, at once. I do not know what I said to him when he came to my room that night. I could not have said much. I felt, in the oddest, most awful way, that I had somehow betrayed him. I lived it over and over and over again, the way one relives an automobile accident after it has happened and one finds oneself alone and safe. I could not get over two facts, both equally difficult for the imagination to grasp, and one was that I could have been murdered. But the other was that I had been ready to commit murder. I saw nothing very clearly but I did see this: that my life, my *real* life, was in danger, and not from anything other people might do but from the hatred I carried in my own heart.

II

I had returned home around the second week in June—in great haste
because it seemed that my father's death and my mother's confinement
were both but a matter of hours. In the case of my mother, it soon became
clear that she had simply made a miscalculation. This had always been her
tendency and I don't believe that a single one of us arrived in the world, or
has since arrived anywhere else, on time. But none of us dawdled so intoler-
ably about the business of being born as did my baby sister. We sometimes
amused ourselves, during those endless, stifling weeks, by picturing the
baby sitting within in the safe, warm dark, bitterly regretting the necessity of
becoming a part of our chaos and stubbornly putting it off as long as possible. I understood her perfectly and congratulated her on showing such good
sense so soon. Death, however, sat as purposefully at my father's bedside as
life stirred within my mother's womb and it was harder to understand why he
so lingered in that long shadow. It seemed that he had bent, and for a long
time, too, all of his energies towards dying. Now death was ready for him but
my father held back.

All of Harlem, indeed, seemed to be infected by waiting. I had never
before known it to be so violently still. Racial tensions throughout this country
were exacerbated during the early years of the war, partly because the labor
market brought together hundreds of thousands of ill-prepared people and
partly because Negro soldiers, regardless of where they were born, received
their military training in the south. What happened in defense plants and army
camps had repercussions, naturally, in every Negro ghetto. The situation in
Harlem had grown bad enough for clergymen, policemen, educators, politicians, and social workers to assert in one breath that there was no "crime
wave" and to offer, in the very next breath, suggestions as to how to combat
it. These suggestions always seemed to involve playgrounds, despite the fact
that racial skirmishes were occurring in the playgrounds, too. Playground
or not, crime wave or not, the Harlem police force had been augmented
in March, and the unrest grew—perhaps, in fact, partly as a result of the
ghetto's instinctive hatred of policemen. Perhaps the most revealing news
item, out of the steady parade of reports of muggings, stabbings, shootings,
assaults, gang wars, and accusations of police brutality, is the item concerning six Negro girls who set upon a white girl in the subway because, as they
all too accurately put it, she was stepping on their toes. Indeed she was, all
over the nation.

I had never before been so aware of policemen, on foot, on horseback,
on corners, everywhere, always two by two. Nor had I ever been so aware of
small knots of people. They were on stoops and on corners and in doorways,
and what was striking about them, I think, was that they did not seem to be
talking. Never, when I passed these groups, did the usual sound of a curse or
a laugh ring out and neither did there seem to be any hum of gossip. There
was certainly, on the other hand, occurring between them communication

extraordinarily intense. Another thing that was striking was the unexpected diversity of the people who made up these groups. Usually, for example, one would see a group of sharpies standing on the street corner, jiving the passing chicks; or a group of older men, usually, for some reason, in the vicinity of a barber shop, discussing baseball scores, or the numbers, or making rather chilling observations about women they had known. Women, in a general way, tended to be seen less often together—unless they were church women, or very young girls, or prostitutes met together for an unprofessional instant. But that summer I saw the strangest combinations: large, respectable, churchly matrons standing on the stoops or the corners with their hair tied up, together with a girl in sleazy satin whose face bore the marks of gin and the razor, or heavy-set, abrupt, no-nonsense older men, in company with the most disreputable and fanatical "race" men, or these same "race" men with the sharpies, or these sharpies with the churchly women. Seventh Day Adventists and Methodists and Spiritualists seemed to be hobnobbing with Holyrollers and they were all, alike, entangled with the most flagrant disbelievers; something heavy in their stance seemed to indicate that they had all, incredibly, seen a common vision, and on each face there seemed to be the same strange, bitter shadow.

The churchly women and the matter-of-fact, no-nonsense men had children in the Army. The sleazy girls they talked to had lovers there, the sharpies and the "race" men had friends and brothers there. It would have demanded an unquestioning patriotism, happily as uncommon in this country as it is undesirable, for these people not to have been disturbed by the bitter letters they received, by the newspaper stories they read, not to have been enraged by the posters, then to be found all over New York, which described the Japanese as "yellow-bellied Japs." It was only the "race" men, to be sure, who spoke ceaselessly of being revenged—how this vengeance was to be exacted was not clear—for the indignities and dangers suffered by Negro boys in uniform; but everybody felt a directionless, hopeless bitterness, as well as that panic which can scarcely be suppressed when one knows that a human being one loves is beyond one's reach, and in danger. This helplessness and this gnawing uneasiness does something, at length, to even the toughest mind. Perhaps the best way to sum all this up is to say that the people I knew felt, mainly, a peculiar kind of relief when they knew that their boys were being shipped out of the south, to do battle overseas. It was, perhaps, like feeling that the most dangerous part of a dangerous journey had been passed and that now, even if death should come, it would come with honor and without the complicity of their countrymen. Such a death would be, in short, a fact with which one could hope to live.

It was on the 28th of July, which I believe was a Wednesday, that I visited my father for the first time during his illness and for the last time in his life. The moment I saw him I knew why I had put off this visit so long. I had told my mother that I did not want to see him because I hated him. But this was not true. It was only that I *had* hated him and I wanted to hold on to this hatred. I did not want to look on him as a ruin: it was not a ruin I had hated. I imagine that one of the reasons people cling to their hates so stubbornly is because they sense, once hate is gone, that they will be forced to deal with pain.

We traveled out to him, his older sister and myself, to what seemed to be the very end of a very Long Island. It was hot and dusty and we wrangled, my aunt and I, all the way out, over the fact that I had recently begun to smoke and, as she said, to give myself airs. But I knew that she wrangled with me because she could not bear to face the fact of her brother's dying. Neither could I endure the reality of her despair, her unstated bafflement as to what had happened to her brother's life, and her own. So we wrangled and I smoked and from time to time she fell into a heavy reverie. Covertly, I watched her face, which was the face of an old woman; it had fallen in, the eyes were sunken and lightless; soon she would be dying, too.

In my childhood—it had not been so long ago—I had thought her beautiful. She had been quick-witted and quick-moving and very generous with all the children and each of her visits had been an event. At one time one of my brothers and myself had thought of running away to live with her. Now she could no longer produce out of her handbag some unexpected and yet familiar delight. She made me feel pity and revulsion and fear. It was awful to realize that she no longer caused me to feel affection. The closer we came to the hospital the more querulous she became and at the same time, naturally, grew more dependent on me. Between pity and guilt and fear I began to feel that there was another me trapped in my skull like a jack-in-the-box who might escape my control at any moment and fill the air with screaming.

She began to cry the moment we entered the room and she saw him lying there, all shriveled and still, like a little black monkey. The great, gleaming apparatus which fed him and would have compelled him to be still even if he had been able to move brought to mind, not beneficence, but torture; the tubes entering his arm made me think of pictures I had seen when a child, of Gulliver, tied down by the pygmies on that island. My aunt wept and wept, there was a whistling sound in my father's throat; nothing was said; he could not speak. I wanted to take his hand, to say something. But I do not know what I could have said, even if he could have heard me. He was not really in that room with us, he had at last really embarked on his journey; and though my aunt told me that he said he was going to meet Jesus, I did not hear anything except that whistling in his throat. The doctor came back and we left, into that unbearable train again, and home. In the morning came the telegram saying that he was dead. Then the house was suddenly full of relatives, friends, hysteria, and confusion and I quickly left my mother and the children to the care of those impressive women, who, in Negro communities at least, automatically appear at times of bereavement armed with lotions, proverbs, and patience, and an ability to cook. I went downtown. By the time I returned, later the same day, my mother had been carried to the hospital and the baby had been born.

III

For my father's funeral I had nothing black to wear and this posed a nagging problem all day long. It was one of those problems, simple, or impossible of solution, to which the mind insanely clings in order to avoid the mind's real trouble. I spent most of that day at the downtown apartment of a girl I knew, celebrating my birthday with whiskey and wondering what to wear that night. When planning a birthday celebration one naturally does not expect that it will be up against competition from a funeral and this girl had anticipated taking me out that night, for a big dinner and a night club afterwards. Sometime during the course of that long day we decided that we would go out anyway, when my father's funeral service was over. I imagine *I* decided it, since, as the funeral hour approached, it became clearer and clearer to me that I would not know what to do with myself when it was over. The girl, stifling her very lively concern as to the possible effects of the whiskey on one of my father's chief mourners, concentrated on being conciliatory and practically helpful. She found a black shirt for me somewhere and ironed it and, dressed in the darkest pants and jacket I owned, and slightly drunk, I made my way to my father's funeral.

The chapel was full, but not packed, and very quiet. There were, mainly, my father's relatives, and his children, and here and there I saw faces I had not seen since childhood, the faces of my father's one-time friends. They were very dark and solemn now, seeming somehow to suggest that they had known all along that something like this would happen. Chief among the mourners was my aunt, who had quarreled with my father all his life; by which I do not mean to suggest that her mourning was insincere or that she had not loved him. I suppose that she was one of the few people in the world who had, and their incessant quarreling proved precisely the strength of the tie that bound them. The only other person in the world, as far as I knew, whose relationship to my father rivaled my aunt's in depth was my mother, who was not there.

It seemed to me, of course, that it was a very long funeral. But it was, if anything, a rather shorter funeral than most, nor, since there were no overwhelming, uncontrollable expressions of grief, could it be called—if I dare to use the word—successful. The minister who preached my father's funeral sermon was one of the few my father had still been seeing as he neared his end. He presented to us in his sermon a man whom none of us had ever seen—a man thoughtful, patient, and forbearing, a Christian inspiration to all who knew him, and a model for his children. And no doubt the children, in their disturbed and guilty state, were almost ready to believe this; he had been remote enough to be anything and, anyway, the shock of the incontrovertible, that it was really our father lying up there in that casket, prepared the mind for anything. His sister moaned and this grief-stricken moaning was taken as corroboration. The other faces held a dark, non-committal thoughtfulness. This was not the man they had known, but they had scarcely expected to be confronted with *him;* this was, in a sense deeper than questions of fact, the man they had not known, and the man they had not known may have been the real one. The real man, whoever he had been, had suffered and now he was dead: this was all that was sure and all that mattered now. Every man in the chapel hoped that when his hour came he, too, would be eulogized, which is to say forgiven, and that all of his lapses, greeds, errors, and strayings from the truth would be invested with coherence and looked upon with charity. This was perhaps the last thing human beings could give each other and it was what they demanded, after all, of the Lord. Only the Lord saw the midnight tears, only He was present when one of His children, moaning and wringing hands, paced up and down the room. When one slapped one's child in anger the recoil in the heart reverberated through heaven and became part of the pain of the universe. And when the children were hungry and sullen and distrustful and one watched them, daily, growing wilder, and further away, and running headlong into danger, it was the Lord who knew what the charged heart endured as the strap was laid to the backside; the Lord alone who knew what one *would* have said if one had had, like the Lord, the gift of the living word. It was the Lord who knew of the impossibility every parent in that room faced: how to prepare the child for the day when the child would be despised and how to *create* in the child—by what means?—a stronger antidote to this poison than one had found for oneself. The avenues, side streets, bars, billiard halls, hospitals, police stations, and even the playgrounds of Harlem—not to mention the houses of correction, the jails, and the morgue—testified to the potency of the poison while remaining silent as to the efficacy of whatever antidote, irresistibly raising the question of whether or not such an antidote existed; raising, which was worse, the question of whether or not an antidote was desirable; perhaps poison should be fought with poison. With these several schisms in the mind and with more terrors in the heart than could be named, it was better not to judge the man who had gone down under an impossible burden. It was better to remember: *Thou knowest this man's fall; but thou knowest not his wrassling.*

While the preacher talked and I watched the children—years of changing their diapers, scrubbing them, slapping them, taking them to school, and scolding them had had the perhaps inevitable result of making me love them, though I am not sure I knew this then—my mind was busily breaking out with a rash of disconnected impressions. Snatches of popular songs, indecent jokes, bits of books I had read, movie sequences, faces, voices, political issues—I thought I was going mad; all these impressions suspended, as it were, in the solution of the faint nausea produced in me by the heat and liquor. For a moment I had the impression that my alcoholic breath, inefficiently disguised with chewing gum, filled the entire chapel. Then someone began singing one of my father's favorite songs and, abruptly, I was with him, sitting on his knee, in the hot, enormous, crowded church which was the first church we attended. It was the Abyssinia Baptist Church on 138th Street. We had not gone there long. With this image, a host of others came. I had forgotten, in the rage of my growing up, how proud my father had been of me when I was little. Apparently, I had had a voice and my father had liked to show me off before the members of the church. I had forgotten what he had looked like when he was pleased but now I remembered that he had always been grinning with pleasure when my solos ended. I even remembered certain expressions on his face when he teased my mother—had he loved her? I would never know. And when had it all begun to change? For now it seemed that he had not always been cruel. I remembered being taken for a haircut and scraping my knee on the footrest of the barber's chair and I remembered my father's face as he soothed my crying and applied the stinging iodine. Then I remembered our fights, fights which had been of the worst possible kind because my technique had been silence.

I remembered the one time in all our life together when we had really spoken to each other.

It was on a Sunday and it must have been shortly before I left home. We were walking, just the two of us, in our usual silence, to or from church. I was in high school and had been doing a lot of writing and I was, at about this time, the editor of the high school magazine. But I had also been a Young Minister and had been preaching from the pulpit. Lately, I had been taking fewer engagements and preached as rarely as possible. It was said in the church, quite truthfully, that I was "cooling off."

My father asked me abruptly, "You'd rather write than preach, wouldn't you?"

I was astonished at his question—because it was a real question. I answered, "Yes."

That was all we said. It was awful to remember that that was all we had *ever* said.

The casket now was opened and the mourners were being led up the aisle to look for the last time on the deceased. The assumption was that the family was too overcome with grief to be allowed to make this journey alone and I watched while my aunt was led to the casket and, muffled in black, and shaking, led back to her seat. I disapproved of forcing the children to look on their dead father, considering that the shock of his death, or, more truthfully, the shock of death as a reality, was already a little more than a child could bear, but my judgment in this matter had been overruled and there they were, bewildered and frightened and very small, being led, one by one, to the casket. But there is also something very gallant about children at such moments. It has something to do with their silence and gravity and with the fact that one cannot help them. Their legs, somehow, seem *exposed,* so that it is at once incredible and terribly clear that their legs are all they have to hold them up.

I had not wanted to go to the casket myself and I certainly had not wished to be led there, but there was no way of avoiding either of these forms. One of the deacons led me up and I looked on my father's face. I cannot say that it looked like him at all. His blackness had been equivocated by powder and there was no suggestion in that casket of what his power had or could have been. He was simply an old man dead, and it was hard to believe that he had ever given anyone either joy or pain. Yet, his life filled that room. Further up the avenue his wife was holding his newborn child. Life and death so close together, and love and hatred, and right and wrong, said something to me which I did not want to hear concerning man, concerning the life of man.

After the funeral, while I was downtown desperately celebrating my birthday, a Negro soldier, in the lobby of the Hotel Braddock, got into a fight with a white policeman over a Negro girl. Negro girls, white policemen, in or out of uniform, and Negro males—in or out of uniform—were part of the furniture of the lobby of the Hotel Braddock and this was certainly not the first time such an incident had occurred. It was destined, however, to receive an unprecedented publicity, for the fight between the policeman and the soldier ended with the shooting of the soldier. Rumor, flowing immediately to the streets outside, stated that the soldier had been shot in the back, an instantaneous and revealing invention, and that the soldier had died protecting a Negro woman. The facts were somewhat different—for example, the soldier had not been shot in the back, and was not dead, and the girl seems to have been as dubious a symbol of womanhood as her white counterpart in Georgia usually is, but no one was interested in the facts. They preferred the invention because this invention expressed and corroborated their hates and fears so perfectly. It is just as well to remember that people are always doing this. Perhaps many of those legends, including Christianity, to which the world clings began their conquest of the world with just some such concerted surrender to distortion. The effect, in Harlem, of this particular legend was like the effect of a lit match in a tin of gasoline. The mob gathered before the doors of the Hotel Braddock simply began to swell and to spread in every direction, and Harlem exploded.

The mob did not cross the ghetto lines. It would have been easy, for example, to have gone over Morningside Park on the west side or to have crossed the Grand Central railroad tracks at 125th Street on the east side, to wreak havoc in white neighborhoods. The mob seems to have been mainly interested in something more potent and real than the white face, that is, in white power, and the principal damage done during the riot of the summer of 1943 was to white business establishments in Harlem. It might have been a far bloodier story, of course, if, at the hour the riot began, these establishments had still been open. From the Hotel Braddock the mob fanned out, east and west along 125th Street, and for the entire length of Lenox, Seventh, and Eighth avenues. Along each of these avenues, and along each major side street—116th, 125th, 135th, and so on—bars, stores, pawnshops, restaurants, even little luncheonettes had been smashed open and entered and looted—looted, it might be added, with more haste than efficiency. The shelves really looked as though a bomb had struck them. Cans of beans and soup and dog food, along with toilet paper, corn flakes, sardines and milk tumbled every which way, and abandoned cash registers and cases of beer leaned crazily out of the splintered windows and were strewn along the avenues. Sheets, blankets, and clothing of every description formed a kind of path, as though people had dropped them while running. I truly had not realized that Harlem *had* so many stores until I saw them all smashed open; the first time the word *wealth* ever entered my mind in relation to Harlem was when I saw it scattered in the streets. But one's first, incongruous impression of plenty was countered immediately by an impression of waste. None of this was doing anybody any good. It would have been better to have left the plate glass as it had been and the goods lying in the stores.

It would have been better, but it would also have been intolerable, for Harlem had needed something to smash. To smash something is the ghetto's chronic need. Most of the time it is the members of the ghetto who smash each other, and themselves. But as long as the ghetto walls are standing there will always come a moment when these outlets do not work. That summer, for example, it was not enough to get into a fight on Lenox Avenue, or curse out one's cronies in the barber shops. If ever, indeed, the violence which fills Harlem's churches, pool halls, and bars erupts outward in a more direct fashion, Harlem and its citizens are likely to vanish in an apocalyptic flood. That this is not likely to happen is due to a great many reasons, most hidden and powerful among them the Negro's real relation to the white American. This relation prohibits, simply, anything as uncomplicated and satisfactory as pure hatred. In order really to hate white people, one has to blot so much out of the mind—and the heart—that this hatred itself becomes an exhausting and self-destructive pose. But this does not mean, on the other hand, that love comes easily: the white world is too powerful, too complacent, too ready with gratuitous humiliation, and, above all, too ignorant and too innocent for that. One is absolutely forced to make perpetual qualifications and one's own reactions are always canceling each other out. It is this, really, which has driven so many people mad, both white and black. One is always in the position of having to decide between amputation and gangrene. Amputation is swift but time may prove that the amputation was not necessary—or one may delay the amputation too long. Gangrene is slow, but it is impossible to be sure that one is reading one's symptoms right. The idea of going through life as a cripple is more than one can bear, and equally unbearable is the risk of swelling up slowly, in agony, with poison. And the trouble, finally, is that the risks are real even if the choices do not exist.

"But as for me and my house," my father had said, "we will serve the Lord." I wondered, as we drove him to his resting place, what this line had meant for him. I had heard him preach it many times. I had preached it once myself, proudly giving it an interpretation different from my father's. Now the whole thing came back to me, as though my father and I were on our way to Sunday school and I were memorizing the golden text: *And if it seem evil unto you to serve the Lord, choose you this day whom you will serve; whether the gods which your fathers served that were on the other side of the flood, or the gods of the Amorites, in whose land ye dwell: but as for me and my house, we will serve the Lord.* I suspected in these familiar lines a meaning which had never been there for me before. All of my father's texts and songs, which I had decided were meaningless, were arranged before me at his death like empty bottles, waiting to hold the meaning which life would give them for me. This was his legacy: nothing is ever escaped. That bleakly memorable morning I hated the unbelievable streets and the Negroes and whites who had, equally, made them that way. But I knew that it was folly, as my father would have said, this bitterness was folly. It was necessary to hold on to the things that mattered. The dead man mattered, the new life mattered; blackness and whiteness did not matter; to believe that they did was to acquiesce in one's own destruction. Hatred, which could destroy so much, never failed to destroy the man who hated and this was an immutable law.

It began to seem that one would have to hold in the mind forever two ideas which seemed to be in opposition. The first idea was acceptance, the acceptance, totally without rancor, of life as it is, and men as they are: in the light of this idea, it goes without saying that injustice is a commonplace. But this did not mean that one could be complacent, for the second idea was of equal power: that one must never, in one's own life, accept these injustices as commonplace but must fight them with all one's strength. This fight begins, however, in the heart and it now had been laid to my charge to keep my own heart free of hatred and despair. This intimation made my heart heavy and, now that my father was irrecoverable, I wished that he had been beside me so that I could have searched his face for the answers which only the future would give me now.

QUESTIONS FOR DISCUSSION AND WRITING

1. Describe Baldwin's father, as portrayed by Baldwin. What is their relationship like?
2. What does Baldwin mean by this: "It seemed to me that God himself had devised, to mark my father's end, the most sustained and brutally dissonant of codas." What does it tell us about his feelings for his father?
3. To what does Wright attribute his father's bitterness? Identify one or more passages that illustrate this.
4. After the scene in the restaurant, in which Baldwin throws a glass and breaks it, why do you think he reacted with: "I realized what I had done, and where I was, and I was frightened"?
5. Who are the "race men" and the "sharpies"? What significance do they play?
6. Baldwin writes, "This was not the man they had known, but they had scarcely expected to be confronted with *him;* this was, in a sense deeper than questions of fact, the man they had not known, and the man they had not known may have been the real one." Explain this quotation, and its significance in light of Baldwin's relationship with his father.

ON TECHNIQUE AND STYLE

1. How does the historical context influence Baldwin's relating of these stories about his father? Give specific examples from the text.
2. Consider the metaphor of *gangrene* and *amputation* Baldwin uses. What does this metaphor refer to? Is this an effective way to present his argument? In what ways?

CULTURAL QUESTION

1. Baldwin says, "It seems to be typical of life in America, where opportunities, real and fancied, are thicker than anywhere else on the globe, that the second generation has no time to talk to the first." Is this really an American trait? Is it true of other cultures? Is it *not* true of America? Give examples from your own experience or from other readings.

Mother of the Year

Paul Theroux

Paul Theroux was born in 1941 in Medford, Massachusetts. He attended the University of Maine, where he wrote anti-Vietnam War editorials. He transferred to the University of Massachusetts, where he completed his education. Theroux then joined the Peace Corps and taught in the African nation of Malawi. He was involved in a failed coup d'état of the Malawi president-dictator, and was thrown out of the country and the Peace Corps. He then moved to Uganda to teach at Makerere University. When political trouble hit Uganda, Theroux left for Singapore, teaching at the University of Singapore.

Theroux is both a travel writer and novelist, whose most famous book is The Great Railway Bazaar *(1975). This travelogue documents his train trip from Great Britain through Europe, south Asia, Southeast Asia, Japan, and across Russia. He has since written other travel books, including descriptions of train travel from Boston to Argentina* (The Old Patagonian Express, *(1979) and visiting China* (Riding the Iron Rooster, *1988). Other nonfiction works by Theroux includes* Sir Vidia's Shadow *(1998), an account of his friendship with Nobel laureate V. S. Naipaul, which ended publicly and suddenly after thirty years. In 1986, two of his novels became films:* Doctor Slaughter *(1984) was made into the film* Half Moon Street, *and* The Mosquito Coast *(1981) was made into a film of the same name. Theroux is married and divides his time between homes in Cape Cod, Massachusetts, and Hawaii. The following story was published in* Granta 88 *in 2004.*

The words "big family" have the same ring for me as "savage tribe," and I now know that every big family is savage in its own way. There were altogether eight of us children, and one of us was dead. Our parents were severe and secretive, and seemed ancient to us, but as long as they were alive, no matter how doddering, we remained their much younger and unformed children. That was how we behaved towards one another, too, childishly, with pettiness and envy. The taunting was endless, and later, all these big stumbling teasers, bulking and bullying, middle-aged pot-bellied kids, mocking each other with fat fingers.

Each of us had the same father—he was solid, though he was often ill. Because of Mother's fickleness, her injustice, her disloyalty, and her unshakeable favouritism, each of us—dealing with our own version of her—had a different mother. Father's illnesses made her impatient and competitive—he was burdened by rotting lungs and arthritic joints and clotted eyes—and at last he was worn out. He said, "When you're old you never have a good day." Mother countered that she was ill in retaliatory moans. But Mother was healthy, a robust complainer; she declaimed her ailments with the whining defiance I later came to associate with all hypochondriacs.

Mother's stories and confidences varied, according to which child she was talking to. I should have guessed this early on, because her habit was to see each of us alone, like a wicked tyrant conspiring in a dark fable. She did not entertain us as a group. She encouraged us to visit her separately and hinted that she loved to be surprised with presents. But the phone call was her preferred medium of communication; it allowed for secretness and manipulation. She liked the unexpectedness of a ring, the power of hanging up. In seven phone calls—needy people are chronic phoners—she would tell seven different versions of her day, depending on which of her children she was talking to.

It might be Fred, the eldest, the only child she deferred to and respected. He was a lawyer. She poured out her heart to him and he responded, "This is what you should do, Ma." Or it might be Floyd, second oldest, whom she despised and feared, saying, "He never was right." He was a university professor and a poet. Or the sisters, Franny and Rose, both of them hoggishly fat and conspiratorial, both of them teachers of small children. Or Hubby, the gloomy one, of whom she said, "He's so good with his hands." He was a hospital technician, with a fund of gruesome stories. Or Gilbert, her favourite, a diplomat. "He's so busy, poor kid, but I'm proud of him." Or me, known from birth as JP. Mother was circumspect with me, blinking in uncertainty when I visited her and always eager for me to leave. She had wanted me to be a doctor—she had never liked my being a writer and when someone praised a book of mine, she said, "Oh?" and made a face as though she'd been poked with a stick. Mother spoke to Angela, too, though through the power of prayer, not on the phone; Angela was the dead one.

This infant girl had died at birth, her life snuffed out when she was hours old, yet she had a name ("She was like an angel"), she had a personality and certain lovable quirks and was part of the family. She was often mentioned as the perfect one, whom we should emulate. Angela was more conspicuous and present, much more available for advice and consolation—and even guidance—because of her being a spectre. Such ghostly presences often dominate the daily life of savage tribes. When Mother needed an ironclad excuse or a divine intervention, it came from Angela, who was the most powerful and prescient, warning Mother of disloyal whispers or dangerous portents. Angela not only had a name and a personality, she even had a history. She was mourned every January 8, a day when Mother was paralysed with grief and needed to be visited or phoned, in order to pour out her sorrow and the story of her difficult pregnancy, fifty years ago. Dead Angela was also necessary in helping to plump out the family, like the fictional dead souls in the Gogol novel, making our big family even bigger.

"Big family" does not mean a congenial crowd to me; it suggests disorder, treachery, greed and cruelty, an old-fashioned clan of close relations that is the nearest thing in civilization to a cluster of cannibals. I am generalizing here, using the words "savages" and "cannibals" for emphasis and for the colour of melodrama, and I know unfairly. Reading those words you are immediately put in mind of comic, half-naked bone-in-the-nose jungle dwellers, bow-and-arrow people, beating drums and dangerous only to themselves in their recreational violence; and of course hollering and jumping on big feet and showing their teeth. Such people don't exist in the real world. I once lived in the Equatorial regions where these belittled stereotypes are said to live, and I found the folk there to be anything but savage; they were subtle, chivalrous, open-hearted, dignified and generous. It was in suburban America that I encountered savagery in its riskiest form and recognized all the mythical characteristics associated with cannibals in my own big flesh-and-blood family.

My father was the henpecked chief, my mother his tyrant consort of the cannibal tribe that went under the name of a big family. Dissatisfied and frustrated, we were a collection of unruly people struggling for dominance, relentless rivals getting away with murder. We had our own language and customs, our peculiar pieties, grievances and anniversaries, all of them incomprehensible except to the family members themselves. Also, though we were moody, merciless and full of envy, we were always pretending to be the opposite. The solid seamless hypocrisy of religion was an asset: big families are nearly always attached to a fanatic and unforgiving faith. Ours was. You don't think happy or sad, you think of the fury of survival and of damnation and blame.

Such families hardly exist any more in the planning-conscious western world of tiny houses and limited space and rising costs. The birth rate in Europe is recorded in negative numbers, hinting at shrinking populations and small families. This is why the story of any large family is worth telling, because such families have been forgotten. Yet the members of these complex and crazed clans have helped shape the world we know now, probably for the worse.

"Big happy family," people used to say of us, and we smiled, for we believed there was no such thing. Yet happy was how we advertised our-selves, because we had so much to hide. Cynicism is another big family attribute. Some of our desperation must have arisen from the fact that we knew our family was a dinosaur, too big to survive, too clumsy to flourish, too embarrassing to expose to strangers. We were a grotesque phenomenon from another century, a furious and out of date tribe at war with itself, ruled over by a demented queen.

When I read or hear about a mother who dotes on her children, who works her fingers to the bone (Mother's self-regarding catchphrase); who often invites her children to visit her, or who visits them with presents—a kindly-seeming woman, full of solemn, stern advice—I think: What on earth does the senten-tious old woman want? She can only be wicked and manipulative to be so persistent; and whoever trusts her has got to be a fool. She will eat you alive.

As a child I believed my mother was a saintly and self-sacrificing woman—a little tedious and repetitive, but virtuous and on my side. For a long time I went on believing it. Of course, she fostered this fiction, she worked at shaping it, she did not tolerate dissent. And I was also influenced by her public image, for she was something of a local celebrity: a former schoolteacher respected by her students, active in church affairs, shrewd about money, insightful in matters of the heart, a pious busybody beloved by everyone except us, who only feared her unreasonable demands. To the world at large my mother was a resourceful and hardworking woman who had raised seven children (and nurtured the memory of the eighth) and put them through college, the matriarch of a big happy family. She identified with wise and long-suffering Mother figures in the news, especially the annual Mother of the Year, whom she never saw as a role model but always as a rival. She even compared herself with the mothers depicted in the comics—"Mary Worth" was one—and also the sensible grey-bunned soul in the early TV series, *I Remember Mama.* But she also prayed hard to the Virgin Mary, and in all her piety there was the presumption that she and the Mother of God had much in common as nurturers and advice-givers.

I marvel at my innocence, for Mother was the nearest thing to a witch I have ever known. She seldom told the truth—no, she never told the truth. To be fair, I don't think she knew what the truth was. Even Wittgenstein said, "Why tell the truth when it is to your advantage to lie." In her perversity, what-ever she wanted you to believe that day was the truth. She would do anything to get your attention—be angry, upset, abusive, even gentle in a foxy way. Sick, too: she could make herself noticeably ill so that we would listen to her. She might also offer us presents, but they were the sorts of simple tokens that simple folk exchanged in the jungle.

She never gave us money, for to do that would reveal to us that she had some, and her mantra was that she had none. Money did not exist in our fam-ily as a fact, only as an abstraction, something whispered about, so hard won it was almost unattainable. I might see a few dollars in a wallet or some coins in a purse but I never saw more than that. A wad of money, a thick roll of bills, was absurd fantasy. And because it was unseen, magic was attached to money, but a wicked magic, a kind of curse. We did not think we deserved to have money, and if by chance we got some we could not spend it, because spending was wasteful. Money in your pocket tripped you up, made you fail; you were better off without it.

Money was a thing of darkness; always put away. Money was something that was saved—stacked up, hoarded, stashed for a rainy day, but always small amounts scraped into a pile, like Father winding knotted lengths of string into a ball; but why? We didn't ask.

Money was whispered about because it was tainted. Other people had it—we did not; we would never have it. We had no idea where money came from. We did not know anyone who had it. The ways in which other people got money were a mystery to us.

Money did not grow on trees. Money was the root of all evil. Money was filthy lucre. A fool and his money were soon parted. Most people had more money than brains. They spent money like a drunken sailor. They knew the price of everything and the value of nothing.

We were so in awe of the rich that we were forbidden to use the word. Instead of "They're rich," we had to say, "They're comfortably off." Rich families were like members of another species, but a dangerous one that needed to be propitiated with our being submissive. We saw them as conquering tribes; the world belonged to them. We were moneyless and so powerless.

At first, when Mother claimed to have no money, we took her at her word, and pitied her a little. We got part-time jobs and gave her half our weekly pay. "This will go towards the electric bill," Mother would say, "This will help pay for your food." That was her way of saying it would never be enough. We went on owing her, paying off a debt that had no end.

Later, from vague hints and chance remarks, we suspected that Mother had some money, somewhere. Perhaps her bleak insistence that she was poor was the giveaway. "I'm wearing a dead woman's dress," she once said, to emphasize her poverty—a morbid hand-me-down, with the stink of death still on it. That shocked us. If she paid for something for us, she made such a fuss we felt so bad we never asked again. She had no chequebook; she never used credit. She paid in cash, though she always concealed these transactions from us to maintain the fiction that she had no money. Paying for something in cash was probably the most solemn of her secret ceremonies.

Father had nothing to do with money. He handed over his pay to Mother at the end of the week. He never mentioned money.

Mother set us against one another, played favourites, mocked one to another, and when hectoring didn't work she belittled us. I found a ghastly joy in this mockery. I would visit and without any cue from me she would talk about Fred's wife, who had just called to wish her well. What a slattern she was, very messy, never cooked a proper meal, always kept Fred waiting—and

Fred always came home from work to a bad meal and an unappreciative wife. Or she would tell a long satirical story of Fred's wedding day, what a charade it had been, how his in-laws had undermined him. Or Floyd had just sent her a nasty letter, much too abusive for her to show it to me. "Do I deserve that?" Mother rolled her eyes when Hubby's name was mentioned—Hubby was fat and slow and was always making conspicuous and needless improvements to his house, "his castle," Mother said, and pulled a face. Rose was not only the victim of her two children but of her husband, as well, a fanatical baseball fan. "When the Red Sox lose he's impossible." Gilbert was her favourite, "but he never visits." Franny she jeered at for being over-affectionate and care-less with money and a soft touch—a sucker: she was a fool for catering to her ungrateful children.

Mother resented all the spouses and disliked her grandchildren. She was particularly hard on Janine, Franny's eldest—memories of tantrums, howling fits, stubbornness, scenes. "Remember Janine kicked the windshield out of the car by bracing herself on the front seat?" One of the other daughters took ballet lessons. "Grace is a reindeer," Franny said. "In *The Nutcracker*." But even these dancing lessons were regarded by Mother as a foolish expense and she found humour in "Grace is a reindeer." Franny's husband was a security guard. He was a big frightened man with fat pale cheeks and a belly swollen with doughnuts, so Mother said. He had a habit of locking himself in the bathroom for hours on end. He patrolled a local shopping mall and car-ried a cellphone in a holster as though it was a pistol. Mother mocked him for his belly, his fear, his ulcers, his sweet tooth, his lack of ambition. He did not deserve Franny.

In the canniest way, she asked me what I had heard; pretended not to know anything so as to compare my version of a story with the one she had already been told, and was hungry for the smallest detail of frailty or foolish-ness. Her eyes glittered with pleasure at a choice piece of gossip, and hearing something truly wicked she could not prevent herself from laughing out loud.

My reward for visiting her was that she confided these things. Sometimes the betrayals took my breath away. Hubby had just visited for lunch. He had asked for seconds. "He's put on so much weight. His clothes are almost bursting. If he keeps on like this he's going to explode." Or it was Fred's ex-wife, who had brought her a lamp. "She must have found it in a thrift shop. There was a crack in the base. I think she wants to electrocute me." Or Rose's overbearing husband: "I understand they're in family counselling. Do you think he still drinks?" She jeered at her own children for their pretensions, and at their spouses for incompetence or greed. Her cruellest remarks were aimed at members of her family, Angela excepted.

None of this seemed particularly unfair to me; all of it was the cruel com-edy of a normal visit or phone call. And somehow I felt uplifted, for I was always flattered to think that she was singling me out to disclose these truths to me. I never defended any of these people—in fact, I added more gossip to it; I piled it on. It was as though in gossiping to me and running the other

children down Mother understood my resentments, my rivalry, all my hurts.
They deserved it.

The disclosures about the others made me happy in many petty ways; I
felt wanted, I felt secure, hearing Mother's secrets. It did not ever occur to me
that, with another member of the family, she would ever speak in this reckless
way about me—my spending, my size, my children, my ex-wives.

All that is horrible, but here is something I regard as more shameful still. This
woman was quite old before I was able to admit to myself who she really was.

But nothing was obvious to me about my family, or the world around it,
until Father died.

We were all summoned from our homes and told Father was ill—seven phone
calls as well as a prayer to Angela. Mother called each of us in turn. She said
something different to each of us. "I think you should be here," she told me.
To Fred: "As the eldest it's up to you to take charge." To Floyd: "Dad's ill. I
think he'd like you to be there." To Franny, "I don't think I can manage without you." To Rose: "Franny will need your help." To Hubby: "We'll need you
to do the driving." To Gilbert: "Your Father's been so difficult lately. I've felt
like hitting him."

We did not know until it was too late that we had been asked to gather in
order to witness him die.

The sterility of the hospital was like a preparation for his going—the
cold place seemed like an appropriate antechamber to a tomb. Though the
antiseptic smell made me think only of ill health, nothing was familiar in this
unornamented place, nothing at all that I could associate with Father, who
was untidy, and frugal, and like many frugal people not a minimalist but a
pack rat. Father was a hoarder and piler of junk, a collector of oddments, a
rifler of dumpsters. His garage had the stacked shelves you see in a Chinese
shop, and the same dense and toppling asymmetry too. He would take two
barrels of trash to the landfill and return with three barrels of items he had
rescued—old pots, broken tools, jelly jars, kindling wood, coils of old rope.
"That'll come in handy some day," he would say.

The hospital room was neat and bare, except for the man in the bed,
who lay like wreckage under the complex apparatus monitoring his heart
and lungs. Mother remained in the corridor, signalling for each of us to slip in
and greet Father. We had not been together this way for years, and towards
evening, we grouped around his bed to pray for him, looking less like children
than like superstitious jungle dwellers muttering to the gods, the first intimation I had after so many years that we were at heart nothing but savages.

Father struggled to speak, then gasped on his ventilator, "What a lovely
reunion." Barely had we recovered from the shock of seeing him reduced in
this way when Mother ordered us all into the hospital corridor. Standing there,
looking strong, she took charge and said, "We think it's best to take him off
his ventilator. He's so uncomfortable." Taking him off the ventilator meant: Let
him die. I started to object, but she interrupted. "The doctor says he doesn't

have long." She was glassy-eyed and seemed determined, not herself but a cast-iron version of herself, so nerved for the occasion and standing so straight she seemed energized, even a bit crazed, as though defying any of us to oppose her. She was eighty years old, though she was so sure of herself you would have taken her for a lot less. I did not know her. She was a stranger, a substitute—fierce, deaf to advice, domineering, wilful, sure of herself. She was not the tremulous old woman who had suffered through Father's illness; she was someone else entirely, a woman I scarcely recognized.

I said, lamely, "Where there's life there's hope"—and thought, "uncomfortable" is better than "dead."

"Don't you see this is for the best?" she said, in a peevish tone that implied I was being unreasonable. It was the tone she used when she said, "The TV is on the fritz. Junk it."

Her implication was that I was being weak and obstructive. He ought to be allowed to die, she was saying, in a merciful way; while I was urging her to let him live, something she regarded as cruel, inhumane and insensitive. And I was misinformed.

"What's the point of letting him suffer?"

"Why don't we all go out for a meal?" Gilbert said.

Franny and Rose stood on either side of Mother, less like daughters than like newly appointed ladies-in-waiting. They were bent over in grief. They were enormous, humpbacked with fat, panting and draped in sweat-stained clothes.

"I think I'll stay with Dad," I said.

"We should keep together," Mother said.

"We could all stay with Dad."

She said, "Let's just leave him in peace," again, in that tone that implied I was being uncooperative and cruel.

"Let's do what Ma says," Franny said.

"It's not asking too much," Rose added.

Mother just smiled her challenging smile.

"I don't know."

Fred said, "You should do what you think is right."

Floyd said, "I don't get this at all. This is like climbing Everest with Sherpas, and traversing the edge of the crevasse, all roped together. Dad slips and he's dangling on a rope way down there, and we don't know whether to cut him loose and leave him or drag him down the mountain. And there's a blizzard. And we can't hear what he's saying."

Hubby said, "That's it, make a big drama."

"Oh, right, sorry, it's not dramatic. It's only Dad dying. I forgot, Hubby."

"Asshole," Hubby said.

"I'd like to kick you through that wall," Floyd said.

Franny said, "Let's not fight."

"You're all upsetting Ma," Rose said.

"God knows I do my best," Mother said, not in her usual self-pitying whine but defiantly.

We went to a nearby restaurant. Fred whipped off his eyeglasses, sur-veyed the menu and, as the eldest of us, and being Fred, ordered the set meal for everyone. We sat like mourners, though Father was four blocks away, still alive. I looked at the faces around the table, Mother at the head of it, between Gilbert and Fred, the girls Franny and Rose close by, all of them watching Mother in a way I can only describe as loyal and submissive, squin-nying at the rest of us, while Hubby and Floyd sat with their heads down, looking torn.

"It's going to be all right," Franny said.

"This is for the best," Rose said.

I had been listening to such clichés my whole life, but I think it was there in the restaurant, knowing how Father was dying and we were here eating with Mother, that I realized how clichés always reveal the deepest cynicism.

Franny and Rose heaved themselves towards Mother and said, "Have some bread, Ma."

"Dad would have wanted it this way," Mother said. "All of us together."

I quietly excused myself, an easy thing to do, everyone at the table assuming I was going to the men's room. I had often done that as a small boy in Sunday school. "Please, Father." And the priest in the middle of a pep talk would wave me on my way; and I would go home.

I went back to the hospital and found Father alone. The nurse told me that he had been taken off his ventilator and, in place of the saline IV, was on a morphine drip. The fearful look in his eyes appalled me. He was like a terrified captive being dragged away to an unknown place against his will—which was exactly what was happening. I held his hand; it was warm and had the softness of someone very ill. The morphine dulled the pain but it also weakened him and loosened his grip on life—I could feel resignation in the slackness of his fingers.

The gauges beside his bed showed his heart rate in a jumping light, the pattern on the screen like that of a depth sounder in a boat tracing the troughs in an irregular ocean floor. The lights and beeps all seemed to me indications of his life, but the pace of them revealed his diminishing strength.

And there was his breathing. What had begun as slow exhalation became laborious and harsh, as though he was not propped up (which he was) but flat on his back, with a demon kneeling on his chest. His breathing gave him no relief, but was like a punishment, seeming to provide no air at all. He fought to inhale but the air stayed in his mouth, did not fill his lungs, and so he went on gasping, getting nowhere, his staring eyes filled with tears. He was wordless with fear.

The nurse stepped in and leaned towards the monitors.

"Is he feeling any pain?" I asked.

"I can increase the morphine," she said, and I took this to mean yes, he was having a bad time.

"He seems to be struggling."

"Agonal breathing."

She said it casually yet it seemed to me an awful expression and much more horrible for being exact.

Father laboured to stay alive but I could see from the lazier lines on one monitor that his strength was ebbing. Still I held his hand. I had no sense of time passing, but at one point his breathing became shallow, and all the needles and indicators faltered and fell. Father's jaw dropped, his mouth fell open. I clutched his hand and pressed it to my face. I kissed his stubbly cheek.

Take me with you, I thought.

The nurse returned soon after. She quickly summed up what had happened.

"Are you all right?" she asked.

"No," I said.

I walked back to the restaurant, and found that all of them had gone. Of course, four hours had passed. I called Mother.

She said, "Where have you been? You left the restaurant without telling anyone. You didn't even touch your meal. Fred and the girls ate your fried clams. Everyone's here now. We're talking about Dad, telling stories. So many wonderful memories. Gilbert was just about to call the hospital to see how things are going."

"He's gone," I said.

The crowded wake at the funeral home in Osterville was a muddle—tragedy and farce combined; all the distant relations meeting after a long time and making jokes in the form of greetings, remarking on how fat or how thin or how bald we had become. And the pieties about Father. Then tears. Then they just hung around and leafed through the albums of snapshots that cousins had brought—children's marriages, grandchildren, vacations, pets and gardens, even pictures of prize possessions, cars and houses, the sort of pictures that boastful and proud savages would haul out at a feast, if savages had cameras.

Mother sat near the casket, enthroned as it were, receiving people who paid their respects—and they too seemed like emissaries from other tribes, the big families who were our relations, several of them even bigger than ours. The look on Mother's face I recognized from the hospital: exalted, even somewhat crazed, with a snake's glittering stare. She sat upright, weirdly energized by the whole business.

More tribal rituals: the funeral mass at the church, the platitudes, the handling of the shiny coffin, the sprinkling of holy water on its lid, the processions and prayers. I kept thinking of naked people in New Guinea performing similar rites: preparing the corpse of an elder and calling upon the gods to protect him and to hurry his soul into the next world. Mother was the sole surviving dignitary, bestowing a kiss on the polished lid of the coffin and walking past the banks of flowers with a slight and smiling hauteur.

We drove to the cemetery in a long line of cars behind the hearse. Mother was in the back seat of the lead car between Franny and Rose, Fred at the wheel, Gilbert next to him. Hubby and his family in the next one; Floyd and I, the divorced sons, behind them.

I asked Floyd about the meal I had missed at the restaurant, when I had snuck out to be with Father.

"I didn't stay," he said. "I went for a walk. So did Hubby, but in a different direction. It was just Ma and the others, I guess."

"I think Ma was pissed off that I didn't stay. Like it was a test of loyalty."

Floyd wasn't listening. He said, "This is uncanny," and turned the radio up: *"Bye-bye, Miss American Pie,/Drove my Chevy to the levee . . ."*

"Remember Grandma's funeral?" Floyd said, and he laughed and shook his head.

One of the footnotes to our family history was that in the procession to Grandma's funeral our cousin Louie, a goofball, had the radio on, and that same song, "American Pie," was playing, while he sang along with it, drumming on the steering wheel with his grease-monkey's fingers, following Grandma's hearse. None of us ever remarked on it as an insult to the dead woman, only as an extemporized piece of hilarity.

At the cemetery we plodded past gravestones to the hole of the freshly dug grave of Father. The mourners consisted of a procession of mostly members of our own family—spouses, ex-spouses, children, grandchildren, even some great-grandchildren. The rest were near-relations. Hardly any were friends, for my parents were at the age when most of their friends were dead or too ill to show up.

Perhaps this is the place to stress that a big family does not welcome friends, and has no room for strangers; is uncomfortable when they penetrate the privacy of the family and become witnesses and listeners, privy to outbursts and secrets. Even outsiders who are frank admirers are kept at a distance—especially them, for there is so much that must be withheld from them in order to keep their admiration intact. In much the same way, a savage tribe is not just suspicious of strangers but overtly hostile.

As Mother emphasized in her gossip, spouses were outsiders and all of them were mocked, always behind their backs. It could be awkward when one of them caused trouble, but it was worse when they tried to be generous—offered presents, cooked a meal, paid for something. "Imagine, paying good money for this!" The present was laughable, the meal was a joke, and if they could so easily afford to pay for something, where was the sacrifice? But a dark angry spouse might inspire a measure of respect, if the person was strong, and especially so if the person was a crazy threat, because fear was all that mattered to us. At best, spouses were tolerated, but none of them was liked.

At the time of Father's funeral, neither Floyd nor I was married, and our ex-spouses and children were not present. I wasn't innocent any more. I tried to imagine what my family whispered about each of my two wives, but I knew I would never succeed in capturing the malice; I would underestimate it, and no one would tell me to my face. I knew what hideous things we said about the other spouses, the other children, nephews and nieces. I was relieved to be at the funeral alone, my ex-wives and two children elsewhere. In each case, after we split up, they went far away from me and my big family. Perhaps they always suspected that they were unwelcome, and maybe they also knew how they had been satirized.

The priest stood in the wind, his cloak blowing as he spoke. What he said seemed more like a formula of recited lines than sincere prayers. They were hackneyed and over-rehearsed and it was hard to take him seriously—"Dust to dust, ashes to ashes"—we had all heard them before, and now it was Father's turn. Much of what the priest said was drowned out by the traffic speeding along the road that ran past the cemetery wall.

". . . Father, Son and Holy Ghost," the priest was saying.

"I took the next plane from the coast," Floyd intoned, wagging his head. Then he said, "Remember, Grandma used to dig for salad here?"

Mother's mother was a frugal Italian, from another big disorderly family. She dug for dandelions as though they were a great delicacy that only ignorant people would spurn. A cemetery was a good place to dig them because of the wall and the gates that kept dogs out.

Floyd was reminiscing, but he could easily have been trying to make me laugh. Getting someone to laugh at a funeral was one of the skills we had acquired as altar boys. Even Father's funeral was not so solemn an event we wouldn't try to raise a laugh somehow. That wasn't a reflection on our love for Father. Our excuse was, "He'd have found that funny!"

Our heads were down, we were praying or pretending to. Floyd was humming and murmuring, *This'll be the day that I die*—yes, he was trying to get me to laugh by reminding me of "American Pie." I glanced sideways and saw that something else had happened to Mother's face. She wore an expression I had never seen before. Her pious posture, head bowed, shoulders rounded, was that of a mourner, yet her face startled me. The look of hauteur was gone, so were the glittering snake eyes. Hers was a look of relief, of weird jubilation, almost rapture, like someone who has survived an ordeal—weary yet triumphant, full of life and strength.

Father's coffin was not lowered. It remained covered with a velvet cloth. Dropping it into the hole while we watched was probably considered too dramatic and depressing—indelicate, anyway.

A last prayer by the priest, whom I noticed kept mispronouncing Father's name—did this invalidate the prayer?—and we filed back to our cars.

Most accounts of family funerals end here—are in fact an ending. But filing out and leaving Father behind was a beginning, and it began right away, before we left the cemetery.

Mother had been walking slowly towards the parking lot between Franny and Rose, looking small and propped up by her two big daughters, whose fat faces, exaggeratedly solemn, shook with each step.

"Take your time, Ma," they were saying.

"I got such a lot of guidance this morning talking to Angela. 'Be strong, Ma,' she said. You know how she is."

Seeing me about to join the procession, Mother turned and broke away from the girls, and looked herself again, fairly large and confident. She approached me, she squeezed my hands hard.

"I want you to get married. Find someone nice. I want you to do it for me. Will you do that?"

She had that same crazed look in her eyes as when in the hospital corridor she had demanded that Father be taken off the ventilator and said, "We think it's for the best."

I didn't know what to say. She had power. The death of her husband—of Father—had transformed her. The king was dead and she, as queen, was absolute monarch of the whole realm. She was eighty years old but in every sense a new life was beginning for her. It would be a long one, too, and eventful enough to fill a book.

"Maybe we should have a little get-together," Hubby said.

We were standing in the parking lot of the cemetery. Spouses and children stayed a little way off, with the wincing looks of wary people expecting to be abused.

"Dad would have wanted it—something like a family dinner, like the other night," Hubby said.

"I don't think he would have wanted that," Rose said. "He hated restaurants. He always said they were a waste of money."

"You had your chance and you blew it," Franny said. "You walked out of the restaurant the other night. So did Floyd. So did JP. So what's the point?"

"It's up to Ma," Fred said.

We looked at her; for an instant she didn't look strong any more. She made a theatrical gesture, touching her gloved hand to her forehead, and said, "I've got a splitting headache."

Franny and Rose rushed to assist her, Gilbert carried her purse, Fred fussed.

The rest of us went our separate ways. In the car, Floyd said, "Fred's such an asshole. 'It's up to Ma.' What about his wife? Did you ever see anyone so ugly?"

I called Mother that night, but she did not answer the phone, Franny did.

"She's tired," Franny said. "Rose and I are staying here a few more days to look after her. She's had an awful shock. Her nerves are shot."

But it seemed to me that she had had no shock at all, just a great reward, of health and strength, a renewed vigour, and confidence. She had been proud at the wake, queenly at the cemetery, surrounded by her big family. Her look of power had filled me with apprehension.

I called her the next day and she said she was feeling better, with Franny and Rose staying with her for a few days. Their presence seemed odd, for both of them had jobs that they were obviously neglecting.

Some days later, when she was alone, she called me back: "I'm sending you a little something. There was money left over from Dad's funeral expenses."

Mother paid a neighbour to clean out Father's shed—where the tools had been. The garage, too. All of Father's accumulated possessions were junked. The paint cans, the jars of nails, the rope, the wire, the rusty screwdrivers. The yellowed newspaper clippings went. They had been nailed to the wall and some of them were very old: one said WAR IS OVER, another said PEACE AT LAST, the Boston papers from 1945. Some were newspaper pictures of us. Floyd shooting a basket in a high-school gym. Fred bundled up in a hockey uniform, his stick poised and pretending to slap a puck. Me holding a trophy from the Science Fair. Hubby in a group of serious-faced Boy Scouts, en route to a jamboree. Clipped-out mentions of events, such as band concerts and ball games. Others were snapshots. Of Franny and her terrified prom date. Of Franny when she was a nun, draped in her penguin outfit, looking even fatter in her piety. Of Rose, an enormous child in a white dress, hands folded: First Communion. Of Gilbert smiling across the bridge of his violin. Several were attempts at group family photos, but they were amateurish and awkward—there were too many of us, the camera was cheap, we looked a discontented mob.

Father's wood stove was ripped out of the living room. He had kept it burning until the night he was taken to the hospital. No one wanted the old stove. It was so full of ashes when it was moved that they spilled out and the grey dust powdering the floor was a grotesque reminder of him.

"He never did clean it out thoroughly," Mother said.

I went back to the cemetery about a month later. Father's grave looked new and colourless. I planted some geraniums in front of it, and a small pointed juniper on either side. I told Mother this.

She smiled in pity, as she always did when I made a mistake. She said, "He's not there, you know."

She sent me a cheque for $500. I did not need it, and yet I did not know what to do with it, for the dark secret of receiving money from Mother so confused me I kept it to myself.

Franny and Rose were bigger and busier than ever. On their way to Mother's, they stopped off to see me sometimes, bringing me candy and doughnuts, the sort of things they imagined that everyone ate.

"We visit Ma every Sunday," Franny said one day. Rose just smiled. They were enormous, settled into the cushions of my furniture. The chairs spoke to me; the upholstery groaned, the frames grunted. I was fascinated by the way these pieces seemed so unsuitable, offering so little support, announcing danger. "We know how busy you are. You don't have to come if you don't want."

Soon after that, each of them bought a new car.

That year for Mother was the beginning of everything. She had another fifteen vigorous years to live. "My golden years," she said, sounding more than ever like a queen.

QUESTIONS FOR DISCUSSION AND WRITING

1. How does Theroux characterize big families? Find passages in the reading to support your answer. Do you agree with this assessment? Why or why not?
2. What role does the dead baby Angela play for Theroux's mother? For the rest of the family?
3. Why does Theroux refer to his mother as "the nearest thing to a witch I had ever known"?
4. What did Theroux learn about his family when his father died?

ON TECHNIQUE AND STYLE

1. Theroux refers to his family as a "tribe" in several places, even sometimes referring to them as a "savage tribe" or a "cannibal tribe." What is the connotation of the word *tribe* in these instances? What is Theroux trying to convey through the use of this word? How does he contrast it with the "real" tribes he has lived with?
2. Why do you think Theroux has written such an unflattering view of his mother, in fact, of most of his family?
3. The title of this piece is clearly ironic. What does the use of irony here relate to you as the reader?

CULTURAL QUESTION

1. What are the features of an "ideal mother"? Is the idea of an ideal mother culturally constructed, or is it more or less universal? Think of as many examples as you can to support your opinion.

Shooting Dad

Sarah Vowell

Sarah Jane Vowell was born December 27, 1969, in Muskogee, Oklahoma. She is an American author, journalist, humorist, and commentator. Vowell earned a BA from Montana State University in 1993, and an MA at the School of the Art Institute of Chicago in 1996. She received the Music Journalism Award in 1996.

Often referred to as a "social observer," Vowell has written several books, including Take the Cannoli: Stories From the New World *(2000), from which the following reading is taken. She also wrote* The Partly Cloudy Patriot *(2002),* Assassination Vacation *(2005) and* The Wordy Shipmates *(2008). She is a regular contributor to the public radio program* This American Life. *She was also the voice of Violet in the animated film* The Incredibles.

Vowell is part Cherokee, about which she has said, "Being at least a little Cherokee in northeastern Oklahoma is about as rare and remarkable as being a Michael Jordan fan in Chicago." She retraced the path of the forced removal—known as the Trail of Tears—of the Cherokee from the southeastern United States to Oklahoma with her twin sister Amy. This American Life *told her story on July 4, 1998. Vowell lives in Chelsea, a residential neighborhood in Manhattan in New York City.*

Reprinted with the permission of Simon & Schuster, Inc., from *Take the Cannoli* by Sarah Vowell. Copyright © 2000 by Sarah Vowell. All rights reserved if you were passing by the house where i grew up during my teenage years and it happened to be before Election Day, you wouldn't have needed to come inside to see that it was a house divided. You could have looked at the Democratic campaign poster in the upstairs window and the Republican one in the downstairs window and seen our home for the Civil War battleground it was. I'm not saying who was the Democrat or who was the Republican—my father or I—but I will tell you that I have never subscribed to *Guns & Ammo,* that I did not plaster the family vehicle with National Rifle Association stickers, and that hunter's orange was never my color.

About the only thing my father and I agree on is the Constitution, though I'm partial to the First Amendment, while he's always favored the Second.

I am a gunsmith's daughter. I like to call my parents' house, located on a quiet residential street in Bozeman, Montana, the United States of Firearms. Guns were everywhere: the so-called pretty ones like the circa 1850 walnut muzzleloader hanging on the wall. Dad's clients' fixer-uppers leaning into corners, an entire rack right next to the TV. I had to move revolvers out of my way to make room for a bowl of Rice Krispies on the kitchen table.

I was eleven when we moved into that Bozeman house. We had never lived in town before, and this was a college town at that. We came from Oklahoma—a dusty little Muskogee County nowhere called Braggs. My parents' property there included an orchard, a horse pasture, and a couple of acres of woods. I knew our lives had changed one morning not long after we moved to Montana when, during breakfast, my father heard a noise and jumped out of his chair. Grabbing a BB gun, he rushed out the front door. Standing in the yard, he started shooting at crows. My mother sprinted after him screaming, "Pat, you might ought to check, but I don't think they do that up here!" From the look on his face, she might as well have told him that his American citizenship had been revoked. He shook his head, mumbling. "Why, shooting crows is a national pastime, like baseball and apple pie." Personally, I preferred baseball and apple pie. I looked up at those crows flying away and thought, I'm going to like it here.

Dad and I started bickering in earnest when I was fourteen, after the 1984 Democratic National Convention. I was so excited when Walter Mondale chose Geraldine Ferraro as his running mate that I taped the front page of the newspaper with her picture on it to the refrigerator door. But there was some sort of mysterious gravity surge in the kitchen. Somehow, that picture ended up in the trash all the way across the room.

Nowadays, I giggle when Dad calls me on Election Day to cheerfully inform me that he has once again canceled out my vote, but I was not always so mature. There were times when I found the fact that he was a gunsmith horrifying. And just *weird.* All he ever cared about were guns. All I ever cared about was art. There were years and years when he hid out by himself in the garage making rifle barrels and I holed up in my room reading Allen Ginsberg poems, and we were incapable of having a conversation that didn't end in an argument.

Our house was partitioned off into territories. While the kitchen and the living room were well within the DMZ, the respective work spaces governed by my father and me were jealously guarded totalitarian states in which each of us declared ourselves dictator. Dad's shop was a messy disaster area, a labyrinth of lathes. Its walls were hung with the mounted antlers of deer he'd bagged, forming a makeshift museum of death. The available flat surfaces were buried under a million scraps of paper on which he sketched his mechanical inventions in blue ball-point pen. And the floor, carpeted with spiky metal shavings, was a tetanus shot waiting to happen. My domain was the cramped, cold space known as the music room. It was also a messy disaster area, an obstacle course of musical instruments—piano, trumpet, baritone horn, valve trombone, various percussion doodads (bells!), and recorders. A framed portrait of the French composer Claude Debussy was nailed to the wall. The available flat surfaces were buried under piles of staff paper, on which I penciled in the pompous orchestra music given titles like "Prelude to the Green Door" (named after an O. Henry short story by the way, not the watershed porn flick *Behind the Green Door*) I starting writing in junior high.

It has been my experience that in order to impress potential suitors, skip the teen Debussy anecdotes and stick with the always attention-getting line "My dad makes guns." Though it won't cause the guy to like me any better, it will make him handle the inevitable breakup with diplomacy—just in case I happen to have any loaded family heirlooms lying around the house.

But the fact is, I have only shot a gun once and once was plenty. My twin sister. Amy, and I were six years old—six—when Dad decided that it was high time we learned how to shoot. Amy remembers the day he handed us the gun for the first time differently. She liked it.

Amy shared our father's enthusiasm for firearms and the quick-draw cowboy mythology surrounding them. I tended to daydream through Dad's activities—the car trip to Dodge City's Boot Hill, his beloved John Wayne Westerns on TV. My sister, on the other hand, turned into Rooster Cogburn Jr., devouring Duke movies with Dad. In fact, she named her teddy hear Duke, hung a colossal John Wayne portrait next to her bed, and took to wearing one of those John Wayne shirts that button on the side. So when Dad led us out to the backyard when we were six and, to Amy's delight, put the gun in her hand, she says she felt it meant that Daddy trusted us and that he thought of us as "big girls."

But I remember holding the pistol only made me feel small. It was so heavy in my hand. I stretched out my arm and pointed it away and winced. It was a very long time before I had the nerve to pull the trigger and I was so scared I had to close my eyes. It felt like it just went off by itself, as if I had no say in the matter, as if the gun just had this *need.* The sound it made was as big as God. It kicked little me back to the ground like a bully, like a foe. It hurt. I don't know if I dropped it or just handed it back over to my dad, but I do know that I never wanted to touch another one again. And, because I believed in the devil, I did what my mother told me to do every time I felt an evil presence. I looked at the smoke and whispered under my breath, "Satan, I rebuke thee."

It's not like I'm saying I was traumatized. It's more like I was decided. Guns: Not For Me. Luckily, both my parents grew up in exasperating house-holds where children were considered puppets and/or slaves. My mom and dad were hell-bent on letting my sister and me make our own choices. So if I decided that I didn't want my father's little death sticks to kick me to the ground again, that was fine with him. He would go hunting with my sister, who started calling herself "the loneliest twin in history" because of my reluc-tance to engage in family activities.

Of course, the fact that I was allowed to voice my opinions did not mean that my father would silence his own. Some things were said during the Rea-gan administration that cannot be taken back. Let's just say that I blamed Dad for nuclear proliferation and Contra aid. He believed that if I had my way, all the guns would be confiscated and it would take the commies about fif-teen minutes to parachute in and assume control.

We're older now, my dad and I. The older I get, the more I'm interested in becoming a better daughter. First on my list: Figure out the whole gun thing.

Not long ago, my dad finished his most elaborate tool of death yet. A can-non. He built a nineteenth-century cannon. From scratch. It took two years.

My father's cannon is a smaller replica of a cannon called the Big Horn Gun in front of Bozeman's Pioneer Museum. The barrel of the original has been filled with concrete ever since some high school kids in the '50s pointed it at the school across the street and shot out its windows one night as a prank. According to Dad's historical source, a man known to scholars as A Guy at the Museum, the cannon was brought to Bozeman around 1870, and was used by local white merchants to fire at the Sioux and Cheyenne Indians who blocked their trade access to the East in 1874.

"Bozeman was founded on greed," Dad says. The courthouse cannon, he continues, "definitely killed Indians. The merchants filled it full of nuts, bolts, and chopped-up horseshoes. Sitting Bull could have been part of these engagements. They definitely ticked off the Indians, because a couple of years later, Custer wanders into them at Little Bighorn. The Bozeman mer-chants were out to cause trouble. They left fresh baked bread with cyanide in it on the trail to poison a few Indians."

Because my father's sarcastic American history yarns rarely go on for long before he trots out some nefarious ancestor of ours—I come from a long line of moonshiners, Confederate soldiers, murderers, even Democrats—he cracks that the merchants hired some "community-minded Southern soldiers from North Texas." These soldiers had, like my great-great-grandfather John Vowell, fought under pro-slavery guerrilla William C. Quantrill. Quantrill is most famous for riding into Lawrence, Kansas, in 1863 flying a black flag and com-manding his men pharaohlike to "kill every male and burn down every house."

"John Vowell," Dad says, "had a little rep for killing people." And since he abandoned my great-grandfather Charles, whose mother died giving birth to him in 1870, and wasn't seen again until 1912, Dad doesn't rule out the possibility that John Vowell could have been one of the hired guns on the Bozeman Trail. So the cannon isn't just another gun to my dad. It's a map of all his obsessions—firearms, certainly, but also American history and family history, subjects he's never bothered separating from each other.

After tooling a million guns, after inventing and building a rifle barrel boring machine, after setting up that complicated shop filled with lathes and blueing tanks and outmoded blacksmithing tools, the cannon is his most ambitious project ever. I thought that if I was ever going to understand the ballistic bee in his bonnet, this was my chance. It was the biggest gun he ever made and I could experience it and spend time with it with the added bonus of not having to actually pull a trigger myself.

I called Dad and said that I wanted to come to Montana and watch him shoot off the cannon. He was immediately suspicious. But I had never taken much interest in his work before and he would take what he could get. He loaded the cannon into the back of his truck and we drove up into the Bridger Mountains. I was a little worried that the National Forest Service would object to us lobbing fiery balls of metal onto its property. Dad laughed, assuring me that "you cannot shoot fireworks, but this is considered a fire*arm*."

It is a small cannon, about as long as a baseball bat and as wide as a coffee can. But it's heavy—110 pounds. We park near the side of the hill. Dad takes his gunpowder and other tools out of this adorable wooden box on which he has stenciled "PAT G. VOWELL CANNONWORKS." Cannonworks: So that's what NRA members call a metal-strewn garage.

Dad plunges his homemade bullets into the barrel, points it at an embankment just to be safe, and lights the fuse. When the fuse is lit, it resembles a cartoon. So does the sound, which warrants Ben Day dot words along the lines of *ker-pow!* There's so much Fourth of July smoke everywhere I feel compelled to sing the national anthem.

I've given this a lot of thought—how to convey the giddiness I felt when the cannon shot off. But there isn't a sophisticated way to say this. It's just really, really cool. My dad thought so, too.

Sometimes, I put together stories about the more eccentric corners of the American experience for public radio. So I happen to have my tape recorder with me, and I've never seen levels like these. Every time the cannon goes off, the delicate needles which keep track of the sound quality lurch into the bad, red zone so fast and so hard I'm surprised they don't break.

The cannon was so loud and so painful, I had to touch my head to make sure my skull hadn't cracked open. One thing that my dad and I share is that we're both a little hard of hearing—me from Aerosmith, him from gunsmith.

He lights the fuse again. The bullet knocks over the log he was aiming at. I instantly utter a sentence I never in my entire life thought I would say. I tell him, "Good shot, Dad."

Just as I'm wondering what's coming over me, two hikers walk by. Apparently, they have never seen a man set off a homemade cannon in the middle of the wilderness while his daughter holds a foot-long microphone up into the air recording its terrorist boom. One hiker gives me a puzzled look and asks, "So you work for the radio and that's your dad?"

Dad shoots the cannon again so that they can see how it works. The other hiker says, "That's quite the machine you got there." But he isn't talking about the cannon. He's talking about my tape recorder and my microphone—which is called a *shotgun* mike. I stare back at him, then I look over at my father's cannon, then down at my microphone, and I think, Oh. My. God. My dad and I are the same person. We're both smart-alecky loners with goofy projects and weird equipment. And since this whole target practice outing was my idea, I was no longer his adversary. I was his accomplice. What's worse, I was liking it.

I haven't changed my mind about guns. I can get behind the cannon because it is a completely ceremonial object. It's unwieldy and impractical, just like everything else I care about. Try to rob a convenience store with this 110-pound Saturday night special, you'd still be dragging it in the door Sunday afternoon.

I love noise. As a music fan, I'm always waiting for that moment in a song when something just flies out of it and explodes in the air. My dad is a one-man garage band, the kind of rock 'n' roller who slaves away at his art for no reason other than to make his own sound. My dad is an artist—a pretty driven, idiosyncratic one, too. He's got his last *Gesamtkunstwerk* all planned out. It's a performance piece. We're all in it—my mom, the loneliest twin in history, and me.

When my father dies, take a wild guess what he wants done with his ashes. Here's a hint: It requires a cannon.

"You guys are going to love this," he smirks, eyeballing the cannon. "You get to drag this thing up on top of the Gravellies on opening day of hunting season. And looking off at Sphinx Mountain, you get to put me in little paper bags. I can take my last hunting trip on opening morning."

I'll do it, too. I will have my father's body burned into ashes. I will pack these ashes into paper bags. I will go to the mountains with my mother, my sister, and the cannon. I will plunge his remains into the barrel and point it into a hill so that he doesn't take anyone with him. I will light the fuse. But I will not cover my ears. Because when I blow what used to be my dad into the earth, I want it to hurt.

QUESTIONS FOR DISCUSSION AND WRITING

1. Describe the key differences between Vowell and her father. Which differences are most important? How would you characterize their relationship?
2. Would you describe the Vowell family as a happy one, or an unhappy one? What leads you to this conclusion? Has it changed, or has it always been happy or unhappy?
3. Although set against the backdrop of politics, Vowell's dislike of guns seems to have a more complex and interesting background than politics alone. Explain her dislike of guns. Why do you think her twin sister, on the other hand, enjoyed shooting?

ON TECHNIQUE AND STYLE

1. How does Vowell use irony to make her point? Is this effective?
2. Vowell also uses a fair amount of humor in her writing. Identify two or three places where she does this. How does this affect your reaction to the story? Do you think your reaction would be different if she had written in a more serious tone? Explain.
3. How does Vowell use a shift in language to signal a type of resolution of the difference between her and her father? Find specific passages to support your ideas.

CULTURAL QUESTION

1. Vowell says: "About the only thing my father and I agree on is the Constitution, though I'm partial to the First Amendment, while he's always favored the Second." Explain this quotation. In what ways does this encapsulate possible divides in American society in general? How do attitudes toward guns and "the right to bear arms" vary in different cultures, both within the United States and outside it?

FICTION

Mother

Grace Paley

Grace Paley was born Grace Goodside in 1922, in the Bronx, New York. Her Jewish parents, Isaac and Manya Ridnyik Goodside, Anglicized the family name from "Gutseit" upon emigrating from Ukraine. Grace was the youngest of three children (she was fourteen years younger than her next eldest brother). As a child, she was interested in the struggles her immigrant neighborhood experienced, topics that would come to influence her fiction. In 1938 and 1939, Paley attended Hunter College, then, briefly, New York University, but she never received a degree. In the early 1940s, Paley studied with poet W. H. Auden at the New School for Social Research. In 1942, Grace Paley married Jess Paley, a movie camera operator, and they had two children, Nora and Danny. Paley divorced Jess Paley and later married author Robert Nichols. Paley's first collection of short stories was The Little Disturbances of Man *(1959). The collection introduces the semiautobiographical character Faith Darwin, who appears in several stories of her later collections* Enormous Changes at the Last Minute *(1985; written with the help of friend and neighbor Donald Barthelme, whose work appears in this book) and* Later the Same Day *(1986). Paley has taught at Columbia University, Syracuse, City College of New York, and Sarah Lawrence College; she also won a 1961 Guggenheim Fellowship for Fiction. Paley lives and works in Thetford, Vermont.*

One day i was listening to the AM radio. I heard a song: "Oh, I Long to See My Mother in the Doorway." By God! I said, I understand that song. I have often longed to see my mother in the doorway. As a matter of fact, she did stand frequently in various doorways looking at me. She stood one day, just so, at the front door, the darkness of the hallway behind her. It was New Year's Day. She said sadly, If you come home at 4 A.M. when you're seventeen, what time will you come home when you're twenty? She asked this question without humor or meanness. She had begun her worried preparations for death. She would not be present, she thought, when I was twenty. So she wondered.

Another time she stood in the doorway of my room. I had just issued a political manifesto attacking the family's position on the Soviet Union. She said, Go to sleep for godsakes, you damn fool, you and your Communist ideas. We saw them already, Papa and me, in 1905. We guessed it all.

At the door of the kitchen she said, You never finish your lunch. You run around senselessly. What will become of you?

Then she died.

Naturally for the rest of my life I longed to see her, not only in doorways, in a great number of places—in the dining room with my aunts, at the window looking up and down the block, in the country garden among zinnias and marigolds, in the living room with my father.

They sat in comfortable leather chairs. They were listening to Mozart. They looked at one another amazed. It seemed to them that they'd just come over on the boat. They'd just learned the first English words. It seemed to them that he had just proudly handed in a 100 percent correct exam to the American anatomy professor. It seemed as though she'd just quit the shop for the kitchen.

I wish I could see her in the doorway of the living room.

She stood there a minute. Then she sat beside him. They owned an expensive record player. They were listening to Bach. She said to him, Talk to me a little. We don't talk so much anymore.

I'm tired, he said. Can't you see? I saw maybe thirty people today. All sick, all talk talk talk talk. Listen to the music, he said. I believe you once had perfect pitch. I'm tired, he said.

Then she died.

QUESTIONS FOR DISCUSSION AND WRITING

1. What is the father's occupation? What tells you this?
2. What is the significance of the doorway, or the narrator's seeing his or her mother in the doorway?
3. What is the significance of Mother saying, "you and your Communist ideas. We saw them already, Papa and me, in 1905. We guessed it all"?

4. Look at the setting of this story. What does it tell us about the family?
5. Why do the parents look at one another "amazed"? What is the source of that amazement?

ON TECHNIQUE AND STYLE

1. Who is the narrator of this story? Is the narrator male or female? How do you know? Cite specific examples from the story. Do you think it is ambiguous from this context? Why or why not?
2. The narrator says twice, "Then she died." Is there a difference between the first and second time? How do you interpret this statement?

CULTURAL QUESTION

1. This story, like many American stories, tells a tale of immigrant parents. In what ways do you see these parents as typical of immigrant parents? Different than immigrant parents? Are there typical conflicts that arise from having immigrant parents, or are these typical parent–child conflicts? Support your answer with your own experience or other readings.

My Mother's Memoirs, My Father's Lie, and Other True Stories

Russell Banks

Russell Banks was born in 1940 in Newton, Massachusetts, the oldest of four children. He attended Colgate University for less than a semester, and later graduated Phi Beta Kappa from the University of North Carolina at Chapel Hill. He is a writer of both fiction and poetry. He is president of the International Parliament of Writers and a member of the American Academy of Arts and Letters. His work has been translated into twenty languages and has received numerous international prizes and awards. His main works include the novels Continental Drift *(1985),* Rule of the Bone *(1995),* Cloudsplitter *(1998),* The Sweet Hereafter *(1991), and* Affliction *(1989). The latter two novels were made into feature films.* Continental Drift *and* Cloudsplitter *were finalists for the Pulitzer Prize. Banks has also written poetry and short stories. Banks has taught at a number of colleges and universities, including Columbia University, Sarah Lawrence, University of New Hampshire, New England College, New York University, and Princeton University. He lives in upstate New York, and has been named a New York State Author. The following story is taken from* Success Stories *(1986).*

My mother tells me stories about her past, and I don't believe them, I interpret them.

She told me she had the female lead in the Catamount High School senior play and Sonny Tufts had the male lead. She claimed that he asked her to the cast party, but by then she was in love with my father, a stagehand for the play, so she turned down the boy who became a famous movie actor and went to the cast party with the boy who became a New Hampshire carpenter.

She also told me that she knew the principals in Grace Metalious's novel *Peyton Place.* The same night the girl in the book murdered her father, she went afterwards to a Christmas party given by my mother and father in Cata-mount. "The girl acted strange," my mother said. "Kind of like she was on drugs or something, you know? And the boy she was with, one of the Gold-ens. He just got drunk and depressed, and then they left. The next day we heard about the police finding the girl's father in the manure pile. . . ."

"Manure pile?"

"She buried him there. And your father told me to keep quiet, not to tell a soul they were at our party on Christmas Eve. That's why our party isn't in the book or the movie they made of it," she explained.

She also insists, in the face of my repeated denials, that she once saw me being interviewed on television by Dan Rather.

I remembered these three stories recently when, while pawing through a pile of old newspaper clippings, I came upon the obituary of Sonny Tufts. Since my adolescence, I have read two and sometimes three newspapers a day, and frequently I clip an article that for obscure or soon forgotten reasons attracts me; then I toss the clipping into a desk drawer, and every once in a while, without scheduling it, I am moved to read through the clippings and throw them out. It's an experience that fills me with a strange sadness, a kind of grief for my lost self, as if I were reading and throwing out old diaries.

But it's my mother I was speaking of. She grew up poor and beauti-ful in a New England mill town, Catamount, New Hampshire, the youngest of the five children of a machinist whose wife died ("choked to death on a porkchop bone"—another of her stories) when my mother was nineteen. She was invited the same year, 1933, to the Chicago World's Fair to compete in a beauty pageant but didn't accept the invitation, though she claims my father went to the fair and played his clarinet in a National Guard marching band. Her father, she said, made her stay in Catamount that summer, selling dresses for Grover Cronin's Department Store on River Street. If her mother had not died that year, she would have been able to go to the fair. "And who knows," she joked, "you might've ended up the son of Miss Chicago World's Fair of 1933."

To tell the truth, I don't know very much about my mother's life before 1940, the year I was born and started gathering material for my own stories. Like most people, I pay scant attention to the stories I'm told about lives and events that precede the remarkable event of my own birth. We all seem to tell and hear our own memoirs. It's the same with my children. I watch their adolescent eyes glaze over, their attention drift on to secret plans for the evening and weekend, as I point out the tenement on Perley Street in Catamount where I spent my childhood. Soon it will be too late, I want to say. Soon I, too, will be living in exile, retired from the cold like my mother in San Diego, alone in a drab apartment in a project by the bay, collecting social security and wondering if I'll have enough money at the end of the month for a haircut. Soon all you'll have of me will be your memories of my stories.

Everyone knows that the death of a parent is a terrible thing. But because our parents usually have not been a part of our daily lives for years, most of us do not miss them when they die. When my father died, even though I had been seeing him frequently and talking with him on the phone almost every week, I did not miss him. Yet his death was for me a terrible thing and goes on being a terrible thing now, five years later. My father, a depressed, cynical alcoholic, did not tell stories, but even if he had told stories—about his childhood in Nova Scotia, about beating out Sonny Tufts in the courtship of my mother, about playing the clarinet at the Chicago World's Fair—I would not have listened. No doubt, in his cynicism and despair of ever being loved, he knew that.

The only story my father told me that I listened to closely, visualized, and have remembered, he told me a few months before he died. It was the story of how he came to name me Earl. Naturally, as a child I asked, and he simply shrugged and said he happened to like the name. My mother corroborated the shrug. But one Sunday morning the winter before he died, three years before he planned to retire and move to a trailer down south, I was sitting across from my father in his kitchen, watching him drink tumblers of Canadian Club and ginger ale, and he wagged a finger in my face and told me that I did not know who I was named after.

"I thought no one," I said.

"When I was a kid," he said, "my parents tried to get rid of me in the summers. They used to send me to stay with my uncle Earl up on Cape Breton. He was a bachelor and kind of a hermit, and he stayed drunk most of the time. But he played the fiddle, the violin. And he loved me. He was quite a character. But then, when I was about twelve, I was old enough to spend my summers working, so they kept me down in Halifax after that. And I never saw Uncle Earl again."

He paused and sipped at his drink. He was wearing his striped pajamas and maroon bathrobe and carpet slippers and was chain-smoking Parliaments. His wife (his second—my mother divorced him when I was twelve, because of his drinking and what went with it) had gone to the market as soon as I arrived, as if afraid to leave him without someone else in the house. "He died a few years later," my father said. "Fell into a snowbank, I heard. Passed out. Froze to death."

I listened to the story and have remembered it today because I thought it was about *me,* my name, Earl. My father told it, of course, because it was about *him,* and because for an instant that cold February morning he dared to hope that his oldest son would love him.

At this moment, as I say this, I do love him, but it's too late for the saying to make either of us happy. That is why I say the death of a parent is a terrible thing.

After my father died, I asked his sister Ethel about poor old Uncle Earl. She said she never heard of the man. The unofficial family archivist and only a few years younger than my father, she surely would have known of him, would have known how my father spent his summers, would have known of the man he loved enough to name his firstborn son after.

The story simply was not true. My father had made it up.

Just as my mother's story about Sonny Tufts is not true. Yesterday, when I happened to come across the article about Sonny Tufts from the *Boston Globe,* dated June 8, 1970, and written by the late George Frazier, I wouldn't have bothered to reread it if the week before I had not been joking about Sonny Tufts with a friend, a woman who lives in Boston and whose mother died this past summer. My friend's mother's death, like my father's, was caused by acute alcoholism and had been going on for years. What most suicides accomplish in minutes, my father and my friend's mother took decades to do.

The death of my friend's mother reminded me of the consequences of the death of my father and of my mother's continuing to live. And then our chic joke about the 1940s film star ("Whatever happened to Sonny Tufts?"), a joke about our own aging, reminded me of my mother's story about the senior play in 1932, so that when I saw Frazier's obituary for Tufts, entitled "Death of a Bonesman" (Tufts had gone to Yale and been tapped for Skull and Bones), instead of tossing it back in the drawer or into the wastebasket, I read it through to the end, as if searching for a reference to my mother's having brushed him off. Instead, I learned that Bowen Charlton Tufts III, scion of an old Boston banking family, had prepped for Yale at Exeter. So that his closest connection to the daughter of a machinist in Catamount, and to me, was probably through his father's bank's ownership of the mill where the machinist ran a lathe.

I had never believed the story anyhow, but now I had proof that she made it up. Just as the fact that I have never been interviewed by Dan Rather is proof that my mother never saw me on television in her one-room apartment in San Diego being interviewed by Dan Rather. By the time she got her friend down the hall to come and see her son on TV, Dan had gone on to some depressing stuff about the Middle East.

As for Grace Metalious's characters from *Peyton Place* showing up at a Christmas party in my parents' house in Catamount, I never believed that, either. *Peyton Place* indeed based on a true story about a young woman's murder of her father in Gilmanton, New Hampshire, a village some twenty-five miles from Catamount, but in the middle 1940s people simply did not drive twenty-five miles over snow-covered back roads on a winter night to go to a party given by strangers.

I said that to my mother. She had just finished telling me, for the hundredth time, it seemed, that someday, based on my own experiences as a child and now as an adult in New Hampshire, I should be able to write another *Peyton Place.* This was barely two months ago, and I was visiting her in San Diego, an extension of a business trip to Los Angeles, and I was seated rather uncomfortably in her one-room apartment. She is a tiny, wrenlike woman with few possessions, most of which seem miniaturized, designed to fit her small body and the close confines of her room, so that when I visit her I feel huge and oafish. I lower my voice and move with great care.

She was ironing her sheets, while I sat on the unmade sofa bed, unmade because I had just turned the mattress for her, a chore she saves for when I or my younger brother, the only large-sized people in her life now, visits her from the East. "But we *weren't* strangers to them," my mother chirped. "Your father knew the Golden boy somehow. Probably one of his local drinking friends," she said. "Anyhow, that's why your father wouldn't let me tell anyone, after the story came out in the papers, about the murder and the incest and all. . . ."

"Incest? What incest?"

"You know, the father who got killed, killed and buried in the manure pile by his own daughter because he'd been committing incest with her. Didn't you read the book?"

"No."

"Well, your father, he was afraid we'd get involved somehow. So I couldn't tell anyone about it until after the book got famous. You know, whenever I tell people out here that back in New Hampshire in the forties I knew the girl who killed her father in *Peyton Place,* they won't believe me. Well, not exactly *knew,* her, but you know. . . ."

There's always someone famous in her stories, I thought. Dan Rather, Sonny Tufts, Grace Metalious (though my mother can never remember her name, only the name of the book she wrote). It's as if she hopes you will love her more easily if she is associated somehow with fame.

When you know a story isn't true, you think you don't have to listen to it. What you think you're supposed to do is interpret, as I was doing that morning in my mother's room, converting her story into a clue to her psychology, which in turn would lead me to compare it to my own psychology and, with relief, disapprove. (*My* stories don't have famous people in them.) I did the same thing with my father's drunken fiddler, Uncle Earl, once I learned he didn't exist. I used the story as a clue to help unravel the puzzle of my father's dreadful psychology, hoping no doubt to unravel the puzzle of my own.

One of the most difficult things to say to another person is I hope you will love me. Yet that is what we all want to say to one another—to our children, to our parents and mates, to our friends and even to strangers.

Perhaps especially to strangers. My friend in Boston, who joked with me about Sonny Tufts as an interlude in the story of her mother's awful dying, was showing me her hope that I would love her, even when the story itself was about her mother's lifelong refusal to love her and, with the woman's death, the absolute removal of any possibility of that love. I have, at least, my father's story of how I got my name, and though it's too late for me now to give him what, for a glimmering moment, he hoped and asked for, by remembering his story I have understood a little more usefully the telling of my own.

By remembering, as if writing my memoirs, what the stories of others have reminded me of, what they have literally brought to my mind, I have learned how my own stories function in the world, whether I tell them to my mother, to my wife, to my children, to my friends or, especially, to strangers. And to complete the circle, I have learned a little more usefully how to listen to the stories of others, whether they are true or not.

As I was leaving my mother that morning to drive back to Los Angeles and then fly home to New Hampshire, where my brother and sister and all my mother's grandchildren live and where all but the last few years of my mother's past was lived, she told me a new story. We stood in the shade of palm trees in the parking lot outside her glass-and-metal building for a few minutes, and she said to me in a concerned way, "You know that restaurant, the Pancake House, where you took me for breakfast this morning?"

I said yes and checked the time and flipped my suitcase into the back seat of the rented car.

"Well, I always have breakfast there on Wednesdays, it's on the way to where I baby-sit on Wednesdays, and this week something funny happened there. I sat alone way in the back, where they have that long, curving booth, and I didn't notice until I was halfway through my breakfast that at the far end of the booth a man was sitting there. He was maybe your age, a young man, but dirty and shabby. Especially dirty, and so I just looked away and went on eating my eggs and toast.

"But then I noticed he was looking at me, as if he knew me and didn't quite dare talk to me. I smiled, because maybe I did know him, I know just about everybody in the neighborhood now. But he was a stranger. And dirty. And I could see that he had been drinking for days.

"So I smiled and said to him, 'You want help, mister, don't you?' He needed a shave, and his clothes were filthy and all ripped, and his hair was a mess. You know the type. But something pathetic about his eyes made me want to talk to him. But honestly, Earl, I couldn't. I just couldn't. He was so dirty and all.

"Anyhow, when I spoke to him, just that little bit, he sort of came out of his daze and sat up straight for a second, like he was afraid I was going to complain to the manager and have him thrown out of the restaurant. 'What did you say to me?' he asked. His voice was weak but he was trying to make it sound strong, so it came out kind of loud and broken. 'Nothing,' I said, and I turned away from him and quickly finished my breakfast and left.

"That afternoon, when I was walking back home from my baby-sitting job, I went into the restaurant to see if he was there, but he wasn't. And the next morning, Thursday, I walked all the way over there to check again, even though I never eat breakfast at the Pancake House on Thursdays, but he was gone then too. And then yesterday, Friday, I went back a third time. But he was gone." She lapsed into a thoughtful silence and looked at her hands.

"Was he there this morning?" I asked, thinking coincidence was somehow the point of the story.

"No," she said. "But I didn't expect him to be there this morning. I'd stopped looking for him by yesterday."

"Well, why'd you tell me the story, then? What's it about?"

"About? Why, I don't know. Nothing, I guess. I just felt sorry for the man, and then because I was afraid, I shut up and left him alone." She was still studying her tiny hands.

"That's natural," I said. "You shouldn't feel guilty for that," I said, and I put my arms around her.

She turned her face into my shoulder. "I know, I know. But still . . ." Her blue eyes filled, her son was leaving again, gone for another six months or a year, and who would she tell her stories to while he was gone? Who would listen?

QUESTIONS FOR DISCUSSION AND WRITING

1. The narrator says, "Everyone knows that the death of a parent is a terrible thing. But because our parents usually have not been a part of our daily lives for years, most of us do not miss them when they die." Do you imagine this to be true? Why or why not?

2. How did the narrator come to be named Earl? Who tells him this story? What is the importance of the story to the narrator?

3. How does the narrator hope that his "interpretations" of his parents' stories will help to "unravel the puzzle" of their psychology? Does it?

4. What is the point of his mother's story of the homeless man at the Pancake House? What is its significance?

5. The narrator claims that he has "learned a little more usefully how to listen to the stories of others, whether they are true or not." What has he learned? Cite specific passages in the story that show this.

6. In a single word, what is the theme of this story? How did you arrive at that theme?

ON TECHNIQUE AND STYLE

1. The title distinguishes the narrator's mother's "memoirs" from his father's "lie." What is the difference? Are the memoirs also lies? How do we know? Does it matter?

2. In many ways, this reading may seem more like memoir than fiction. Can you identify elements that seem purely fictional? Which ones seem more like nonfiction or memoir? Why?

CULTURAL QUESTION

1. The narrator states: "I have learned how my own stories function in the world." Discuss the ways in which his stories function. In what ways do personal stories function culturally? That is, what is the function of a personal story within a family? A neighborhood? A cultural group? Give specific examples from your own experience.

Everyday Use

Alice Walker

Alice Walker was born in Eatonton, Georgia, in 1944. As a child, she was involved in a shooting accident that left her blind in one eye. Walker's writings include novels, stories, essays, and poems. They focus on the struggles of African Americans, and particularly African American women, against societies that are racist, sexist, and often violent. Her writings tend to emphasize the strength of black women and the importance of African American heritage and culture. Her most famous novel, The Color Purple *(1982), won both the Pulitzer Prize and the American Book Award. It was made into a movie directed by Steven Spielberg which was nominated for eleven Oscars, and a Broadway musical produced by Oprah Winfrey. Walker attended Spelman College in Atlanta, Georgia, and graduated in 1965 from Sarah Lawrence College in New York. Her first book of poetry was written while she was a senior at Sarah Lawrence. Walker was also an editor for* Ms. *magazine. An article she published in 1975 was largely responsible for the renewal of interest in the work of African American writer Zora Neale Hurston. Walker won the 1986 O. Henry Award for her short story "Kindred Spirits" published in* Esquire *magazine in August 1985. "Everyday Use" (1973) is a widely studied short story, which originally appeared in* In Love & Trouble: Stories of Black Women.

I will wait for her in the yard that Maggie and I made so clean and wavy yesterday afternoon. A yard like this is more comfortable than most people know. It is not just a yard. It is like an extended living room. When the hard clay is swept clean as a floor and the fine sand around the edges lined with tiny, irregular grooves, anyone can come and sit and look up into the elm tree and wait for the breezes that never come inside the house.

Maggie will be nervous until after her sister goes: she will stand hopelessly in corners, homely and ashamed of the burn scars down her arms and legs, eyeing her sister with a mixture of envy and awe. She thinks her sister has held life always in the palm of one hand, that "no" is a word the world never learned to say to her.

You've no doubt seen those TV shows where the child who has "made it" is confronted, as a surprise, by her own mother and father, tottering in weakly from backstage. (A pleasant surprise, of course: What would they do if parent and child came on the show only to curse out and insult each other?) On TV mother and child embrace and smile into each other's faces. Sometimes the mother and father weep, the child wraps them in her arms and leans across the table to tell how she would not have made it without their help. I have seen these programs.

Sometimes I dream a dream in which Dee and I are suddenly brought together on a TV program of this sort. Out of a dark and soft-seated limousine I am ushered into a bright room filled with many people. There I meet a smiling, gray, sporty man like Johnny Carson who shakes my hand and tells me what a fine girl I have. Then we are on the stage and Dee is embracing me with tears in her eyes. She pins on my dress a large orchid, even though she has told me once that she thinks orchids are tacky flowers.

In real life I am a large, big-boned woman with rough, man-working hands. In the winter I wear flannel nightgowns to bed and overalls during the day. I can kill and clean a hog as mercilessly as a man. My fat keeps me hot in zero weather. I can work outside all day, breaking ice to get water for washing; I can eat pork liver cooked over the open fire minutes after it comes steaming from the hog. One winter I knocked a bull calf straight in the brain between the eyes with a sledge hammer and had the meat hung up to chill before nightfall. But of course all this does not show on television. I am the way my daughter would want me to be: a hundred pounds lighter, my skin like an uncooked barley pancake. My hair glistens in the hot bright lights. Johnny Carson has much to do to keep up with my quick and witty tongue.

But that is a mistake. I know even before I wake up. Who ever knew a Johnson with a quick tongue? Who can even imagine me looking a strange white man in the eye? It seems to me I have talked to them always with one foot raised in flight, with my head turned in whichever way is farthest from them. Dee, though. She would always look anyone in the eye. Hesitation was no part of her nature.

"How do I look, Mama?" Maggie says, showing just enough of her thin body enveloped in pink skirt and red blouse for me to know she's there, almost hidden by the door.

"Come out into the yard," I say.

Have you ever seen a lame animal, perhaps a dog run over by some careless person rich enough to own a car, sidle up to someone who is ignorant enough to be kind to him? That is the way my Maggie walks. She has been like this, chin on chest, eyes on ground, feet in shuffle, ever since the fire that burned the other house to the ground.

Dee is lighter than Maggie, with nicer hair and a fuller figure. She's a woman now, though sometimes I forget. How long ago was it that the other house burned? Ten, twelve years? Sometimes I can still hear the flames and feel Maggie's arms sticking to me, her hair smoking and her dress falling off her in little black papery flakes. Her eyes seemed stretched open, blazed open by the flames reflected in them. And Dee. I see her standing off under the sweet gum tree she used to dig gum out of; a look of concentration on her face as she watched the last dingy gray board of the house fall in toward the red-hot brick chimney. Why don't you do a dance around the ashes? I'd wanted to ask her. She had hated the house that much.

I used to think she hated Maggie, too. But that was before we raised the money, the church and me, to send her to Augusta to school. She used to read to us without pity; forcing words, lies, other folks' habits, whole lives upon us two, sitting trapped and ignorant underneath her voice. She washed us in a river of make-believe, burned us with a lot of knowledge we didn't necessarily need to know. Pressed us to her with the serious way she read, to shove us away at just the moment, like dimwits, we seemed about to understand.

Dee wanted nice things. A yellow organdy dress to wear to her graduation from high school; black pumps to match a green suit she'd made from an old suit somebody gave me. She was determined to stare down any disaster in her efforts. Her eyelids would not flicker for minutes at a time. Often I fought off the temptation to shake her. At sixteen she had a style of her own: and knew what style was.

I never had an education myself. After second grade the school was closed down. Don't ask me why: in 1927 colored asked fewer questions than they do now. Sometimes Maggie reads to me. She stumbles along good-naturedly but can't see well. She knows she is not bright. Like good looks and money, quickness passed her by. She will marry John Thomas (who has mossy teeth in an earnest face) and then I'll be free to sit here and I guess just sing church songs to myself. Although I never was a good singer. Never could carry a tune. I was always better at a man's job. I used to love to milk till I was hooked in the side in '49. Cows are soothing and slow and don't bother you, unless you try to milk them the wrong way.

I have deliberately turned my back on the house. It is three rooms, just like the one that burned, except the roof is tin; they don't make shingle roofs any more. There are no real windows, just some holes cut in the sides, like the portholes in a ship, but not round and not square, with rawhide holding the shutters up on the outside. This house is in a pasture, too, like the other one. No doubt when Dee sees it she will want to tear it down. She wrote me once that no matter where we "choose" to live, she will manage to come see us. But she will never bring her friends. Maggie and I thought about this and Maggie asked me, "Mama, when did Dee ever *have* any friends?"

She had a few. Furtive boys in pink shirts hanging about on washday after school. Nervous girls who never laughed. Impressed with her they worshiped the well-turned phrase, the cute shape, the scalding humor that erupted like bubbles in lye. She read to them.

When she was courting Jimmy T she didn't have much time to pay to us, but turned all her faultfinding power on him. He *flew* to marry a cheap city gal from a family of ignorant flashy people. She hardly had time to recompose herself.

When she comes I will meet—but there they are!

Maggie attempts to make a dash for the house, in her shuffling way, but I stay her with my hand. "Come back here," I say. And she stops and tries to dig a well in the sand with her toe.

It is hard to see them clearly through the strong sun. But even the first glimpse of leg out of the car tells me it is Dee. Her feet were always neat-looking, as if God himself had shaped them with a certain style. From the other side of the car comes a short, stocky man. Hair is all over his head a foot long and hanging from his chin like a kinky mule tail. I hear Maggie suck in her breath. "Uhnnnh," is what it sounds like. Like when you see the wriggling end of a snake just in front of your foot on the road. "Uhnnnh."

Dee next. A dress down to the ground, in this hot weather. A dress so loud it hurts my eyes. There are yellows and oranges enough to throw back the light of the sun. I feel my whole face warming from the heat waves it throws out. Earrings gold, too, and hanging down to her shoulders. Bracelets dangling and making noises when she moves her arm up to shake the folds of the dress out of her armpits. The dress is loose and flows, and as she walks closer, I like it. I hear Maggie go "Uhnnnh" again. It is her sister's hair. It stands straight up like the wool on a sheep. It is black as night and around the edges are two long pigtails that rope about like small lizards disappearing behind her ears.

"Wa-su-zo-Tean-o!" she says, coming on in that gliding way the dress makes her move. The short stocky fellow with the hair to his navel is all grinning and he follows up with "Asalamalakim, my mother and sister!" He moves to hug Maggie but she falls back, right up against the back of my chair. I feel her trembling there and when I look up I see the perspiration falling off her chin.

"Don't get up," says Dee. Since I am stout it takes something of a push. You can see me trying to move a second or two before I make it. She turns, showing white heels through her sandals, and goes back to the car. Out she peeks next with a Polaroid. She stoops down quickly and lines up picture after picture of me sitting there in front of the house with Maggie cowering behind me. She never takes a shot without making sure the house is included. When a cow comes nibbling around the edge of the yard she snaps it and me *and* the house. Then she puts the Polaroid in the back seat of the car, and comes up and kisses me on the forehead.

Meanwhile Asalamalakim is going through the motions with Maggie's hand. Maggie's hand is as limp as a fish, and probably as cold, despite the sweat, and she keeps trying to pull it back. It looks like Asalamalakim wants to shake hands but wants to do it fancy. Or maybe he don't know how people shake hands. Anyhow, he soon gives up on Maggie.

"Well," I say. "Dee."

"No, Mama," she says. "Not 'Dee,' Wangero Leewanika Kemanjo!"

"What happened to 'Dee'?" I wanted to know.

"She's dead," Wangero said. "I couldn't bear it any longer being named after the people who oppress me."

"You know as well as me you was named after your aunt Dicie," I said. Dicie is my sister. She named Dee. We called her "Big Dee" after Dee was born.

"But who was *she* named after?" asked Wangero.

"I guess after Grandma Dee," I said.

"And who was she named after?" asked Wangero.

"Her mother," I said, and saw Wangero was getting tired. "That's about as far back as I can trace it," I said. Though, in fact, I probably could have carried it back beyond the Civil War through the branches.

"Well," said Asalamalakim, "there you are."

"Uhnnnh," I heard Maggie say.

"There I was not," I said, "before 'Dicie' cropped up in our family, so why should I try to trace it that far back?"

He just stood there grinning, looking down on me like somebody inspecting a Model A car. Every once in a while he and Wangero sent eye signals over my head.

"How do you pronounce this name?" I asked.

"You don't have to call me by it if you don't want to," said Wangero.

"Why shouldn't I?" I asked. "If that's what you want us to call you, we'll call you."

"I know it might sound awkward at first," said Wangero.

"I'll get used to it," I said. "Ream it out again."

Well, soon we got the name out of the way. Asalamalakim had a name twice as long and three times as hard. After I tripped over it two or three times he told me to just call him Hakim-a-barber. I wanted to ask him was he a barber, but I didn't really think he was, so I didn't ask.

"You must belong to those beef-cattle peoples down the road," I said. They said "Asalamalakim" when they met you, too, but they didn't shake hands. Always too busy: feeding the cattle, fixing the fences, putting up salt-lick shelters, throwing down hay. When the white folks poisoned some of the herd the men stayed up all night with rifles in their hands. I walked a mile and a half just to see the sight.

Hakim-a-barber said, "I accept some of their doctrines, but farming and raising cattle is not my style." (They didn't tell me, and I didn't ask, whether Wangero [Dee] had really gone and married him.)

We sat down to eat and right away he said he didn't eat collards and pork was unclean. Wangero, though, went on through the chitlins and corn bread, the greens and everything else. She talked a blue streak over the sweet potatoes. Everything delighted her. Even the fact that we still used the benches her daddy made for the table when we couldn't afford to buy chairs.

"Oh, Mama!" she cried. Then turned to Hakim-a-barber. "I never knew how lovely these benches are. You can feel the rump prints," she said, running her hands underneath her and along the bench. Then she gave a sigh and her hand closed over Grandma Dee's butter dish. "That's it!" she said. "I knew there was something I wanted to ask you if I could have." She jumped up from the table and went over in the corner where the churn stood, the milk in it clabber by now. She looked at the churn and looked at it.

"This churn top is what I need," she said. "Didn't Uncle Buddy whittle it out of a tree you all used to have?"

"Yes," I said.

"Uh-huh," she said happily. "And I want the dasher, too."

"Uncle Buddy whittle that, too?" asked the barber.

Dee (Wangero) looked up at me.

"Aunt Dee's first husband whittled the dash," said Maggie so low you almost couldn't hear her. "His name was Henry, but they called him Stash."

"Maggie's brain is like an elephant's," Wangero said, laughing. "I can use the churn top as a centerpiece for the alcove table," she said, sliding a plate over the churn, "and I'll think of something artistic to do with the dasher."

When she finished wrapping the dasher the handle stuck out. I took it for a moment in my hands. You didn't even have to look close to see where hands pushing the dasher up and down to make butter had left a kind of sink in the wood. In fact, there were a lot of small sinks; you could see where thumbs and fingers had sunk into the wood. It was beautiful light yellow wood, from a tree that grew in the yard where Big Dee and Stash had lived.

After dinner Dee (Wangero) went to the trunk at the foot of my bed and started rifling through it. Maggie hung back in the kitchen over the dishpan. Out came Wangero with two quilts. They had been pieced by Grandma Dee and then Big Dee and me had hung them on the quilt frames on the front porch and quilted them. One was in the Lone Star pattern. The other was Walk Around the Mountain. In both of them were scraps of dresses Grandma Dee had worn fifty and more years ago. Bits and pieces of Grandpa Jarrell's Paisley shirts. And one teeny faded blue piece, about the size of a penny matchbox, that was from Great Grandpa Ezra's uniform that he wore in the Civil War.

"Mama," Wangero said sweet as a bird. "Can I have these old quilts?"

I heard something fall in the kitchen, and a minute later the kitchen door slammed.

"Why don't you take one or two of the others?" I asked. "These old things was just done by me and Big Dee from some tops your grandma pieced before she died."

"No," said Wangero. "I don't want those. They are stitched around the borders by machine."

"That'll make them last better," I said.

"That's not the point," said Wangero. "These are all pieces of dresses Grandma used to wear. She did all this stitching by hand. Imagine!" She held the quilts securely in her arms, stroking them.

"Some of the pieces, like those lavender ones, come from old clothes her mother handed down to her," I said, moving up to touch the quilts. Dee (Wangero) moved back just enough so that I couldn't reach the quilts. They already belonged to her.

"Imagine!" she breathed again, clutching them closely to her bosom.

"The truth is," I said, "I promised to give them quilts to Maggie, for when she marries John Thomas."

She gasped like a bee had stung her.

"Maggie can't appreciate these quilts!" she said. "She'd probably be backward enough to put them to everyday use."

"I reckon she would," I said. "God knows I been saving 'em for long enough with nobody using 'em. I hope she will!" I didn't want to bring up how I had offered Dee (Wangero) a quilt when she went away to college. Then she had told me they were old-fashioned, out of style.

"But they're *priceless!*" she was saying now, furiously; for she has a temper. "Maggie would put them on the bed and in five years they'd be in rags. Less than that!"

"She can always make some more," I said. "Maggie knows how to quilt."

Dee (Wangero) looked at me with hatred. "You just will not understand. The point is these quilts, *these* quilts!"

"Well," I said, stumped. "What would *you* do with them?"

"Hang them," she said. As if that was the only thing you *could* do with quilts.

Maggie by now was standing in the door. I could almost hear the sound her feet made as they scraped over each other.

"She can have them, Mama," she said, like somebody used to never winning anything, or having anything reserved for her. "I can 'member Grandma Dee without the quilts."

I looked at her hard. She had filled her bottom lip with checkerberry snuff and it gave her face a kind of dopey, hangdog look. It was Grandma Dee and Big Dee who taught her how to quilt herself. She stood there with her scarred hands hidden in the folds of her skirt. She looked at her sister with something like fear but she wasn't mad at her. This was Maggie's portion. This was the way she knew God to work.

When I looked at her like that something hit me in the top of my head and ran down to the soles of my feet. Just like when I'm in church and the spirit of God touches me and I get happy and shout. I did something I never had done before: hugged Maggie to me, then dragged her on into the room, snatched the quilts out of Miss Wangero's hands and dumped them into Maggie's lap. Maggie just sat there on my bed with her mouth open.

"Take one or two of the others," I said to Dee.

But she turned without a word and went out to Hakim-a-barber.

"You just don't understand," she said, as Maggie and I came out to the car.

"What don't I understand?" I wanted to know.

"Your heritage," she said. And then she turned to Maggie, kissed her, and said, "You ought to try to make something of yourself, too, Maggie. It's really a new day for us. But from the way you and Mama still live you'd never know it."

She put on some sunglasses that hid everything above the tip of her nose and her chin.

Maggie smiled; maybe at the sunglasses. But a real smile, not scared. After we watched the car dust settle I asked Maggie to bring me a dip of snuff. And then the two of us sat there just enjoying, until it was time to go in the house and go to bed.

QUESTIONS FOR DISCUSSION AND WRITING

1. What is her mother's reaction when Dee tells her,"Dee is dead"?
2. What are Dee's intentions on the visit? How do they set up a central conflict in the story?
3. Dee and Maggie are very different from one another. Do they, however, share any characteristics with their mother? If so, what are these traits? In what ways are they different from their mother?
4. Why do you think the quilts are given to Maggie instead of Dee?
5. What is the source of Maggie's "real smile" at the end of the story?
6. Explain how the characters see their connections to their ancestral roots. Cite specific passages from the story to support your answer. Do you sympathize with one character over another? Why?

ON TECHNIQUE AND STYLE

1. Walker is often considered a feminist writer. Is this story a feminist story? Why or why not? Cite specific passages to support your claim.
2. This story is not only filled with symbols, it is a story about symbols. Besides the quilts, what other symbols are there in the story, and what do they represent?
3. In what way is Grandma Dee a character in the story, although dead?
4. How does the narrator relate details of their family history early in the story? How does this family history reflect the relationship between Dee and Maggie?

CULTURAL QUESTION

1. What is the cultural significance of the name "Hakim-a-barber"? How does this illustrate the difference between rural African American life and black nationalist ideas that were current at the time of this story's writing?

River of Names

Dorothy Allison

Dorothy Allison (1949–   ) was born in Greenville, South Carolina. Raised in pov-
erty, she is the oldest child of a fifteen-year-old single mother. Like Alice Walker, she
is blind in one eye. In the early 1970s, Allison attended Florida Presbyterian College.
While in college, she joined the feminist movement. She credits the "militant femi-
nists" for encouraging her to write. After receiving her BA, she did graduate work
in anthropology at Florida State University and the New School for Social Research.
Allison's work includes such themes as class struggle, child and sexual abuse, women,
lesbianism, feminism, and family. Her first novel, the semiautobiographical Bastard
Out of Carolina, *was published in 1992 and was a finalist for the 1992 National Book*
Award. It is graphic in its depiction of Southern poverty, child abuse, and rape. It won
the Ferro-Grumley and Bay Area Reviewers Award for Fiction. A film version was
directed by Anjelica Huston, and premiered in 1996 on Showtime *amid controversy*
for its disturbing content. Allison is active in feminist and lesbian communities. She
lives in California with her partner, Alix Layman, and adopted son, Wolf. Allison was
chosen as Writer in Residence for Columbia College in 2006. The following story is
from Trash *(2002).*

At a picnic at my aunt's farm, the only time the whole family ever gathered, my sister Billie and I chased chickens into the barn. Billie ran right
through the open doors and out again, but I stopped, caught by a shadow
moving over me. My Cousin Tommy, eight years old as I was, swung in
the sunlight with his face as black as his shoes—the rope around his neck
pulled up into the sunlit heights of the barn, fascinating, horrible. Wasn't
he running ahead of us? Someone came up behind me. Someone began
to scream. My mama took my head in her hands and turned my eyes
away.

Jesse and I have been lovers for a year now. She tells me stories about
her childhood, about her father going off each day to the university, her
mother who made all her dresses, her grandmother who always smelled of
dill bread and vanilla. I listen with my mouth open, not believing but wanting,
aching for the fairy tale she thinks is everyone's life.
"What did your grandmother smell like?"
I lie to her the way I always do, a lie stolen from a book. "Like lavender,"
stomach churning over the memory of sour sweat and snuff.
I realize I do not really know what lavender smells like, and I am for a
moment afraid she will ask something else, some question that will betray me.

But Jesse slides over to hug me, to press her face against my ear, to whisper, "How wonderful to be part of such a large family."

I hug her back and close my eyes. I cannot say a word.

I was born between the older cousins and the younger, born in a pause of babies and therefore outside, always watching. Once, way before Tommy died, I was pushed out on the steps while everyone stood listening to my Cousin Barbara. Her screams went up and down in the back of the house. Cousin Cora brought buckets of bloody rags out to be burned. The other cousins all ran off to catch the sparks or poke the fire with dogwood sticks. I waited on the porch making up words to the shouts around me. I did not understand what was happening. Some of the older cousins obviously did, their strange expressions broken by stranger laughs. I had seen them helping her up the stairs while the thick blood ran down her legs. After a while the blood on the rags was thin, watery, almost pink. Cora threw them on the fire and stood motionless in the stinking smoke.

Randall went by and said there'd be a baby, a hatched egg to throw out with the rags, but there wasn't. I watched to see and there wasn't; nothing but the blood, thinning out desperately while the house slowed down and grew quiet, hours of cries growing soft and low, moaning under the smoke. My Aunt Raylene came out on the porch and almost fell on me, not seeing me, not seeing anything at all. She beat on the post until there were knuckle-sized dents in the peeling paint, beat on that post like it could feel, cursing it and herself and every child in the yard, singing up and down, "Goddamn, goddamn that girl . . . no sense . . . goddamn!"

I've these pictures my mama gave me—stained sepia prints of bare dirt yards, plank porches, and step after step of children—cousins, uncles, aunts; mysteries. The mystery is how many no one remembers. I show them to Jesse, not saying who they are, and when she laughs at the broken teeth, torn overalls, the dirt, I set my teeth at what I do not want to remember and cannot forget.

We were so many we were without number and, like tadpoles, if there was one less from time to time, who counted? My maternal great-grandmother had eleven daughters, seven sons; my grandmother, six sons, five daughters. Each one made at least six. Some made nine. Six times six, eleven times nine. They went on like multiplication tables. They died and were not missed. I come of an enormous family and I cannot tell half their stories. Somehow it was always made to seem they killed themselves: car wrecks, shotguns, dusty ropes, screaming, falling out of windows, things inside them. I am the point of a pyramid, sliding back under the weight of the ones who came after, and it does not matter that I am the lesbian, the one who will not have children.

I tell the stories and it comes out funny. I drink bourbon and make myself drawl, tell all those old funny stories. Someone always seems to ask me, which one was that? I show the pictures and she says, "Wasn't she the one in the story about the bridge?" I put the pictures away, drink more, and someone always finds them, then says, "Goddamn! How many of you were there, anyway?"

I don't answer.

Jesse used to say, "You've got such a fascination with violence. You've got so many terrible stories."

She said it with her smooth mouth, that chin that nobody ever slapped, and I love that chin, but when Jesse said that, my hands shook and I wanted nothing so much as to tell her terrible stories.

So I made a list. I told her: that one went insane—got her little brother with a tire iron; the three of them slit their arms, not the wrists but the bigger veins up near the elbow; she, now she strangled the boy she was sleeping with and got sent away; that one drank lye and died laughing soundlessly. In one year I lost eight cousins. It was the year everybody ran away. Four disappeared and were never found. One fell in the river and was drowned. One was run down hitchhiking north. One was shot running through the woods, while Grace, the last one, tried to walk from Greenville to Greer for some reason nobody knew. She fell off the overpass a mile down from the Sears, Roebuck warehouse and lay there for hunger and heat and dying.

Later sleeping, but not sleeping, I found that my hands were up under Jesse's chin. I rolled away, but I didn't cry. I almost never let myself cry.

Almost always, we were raped, my cousins and I. That was some kind of joke, too.

"What's a South Carolina virgin?"

" 'At's a ten-year-old can run fast."

It wasn't funny for me in my mama's bed with my stepfather; not for my Cousin Billie in the attic with my uncle; nor for Lucille in the woods with another cousin; for Danny with four strangers in a parking lot; or for Pammy, who made the papers. Cora read it out loud: "Repeatedly by persons unknown." They stayed unknown since Pammy never spoke again. Perforations, lacerations, contusions, and bruises. I heard all the words, big words, little words, words too terrible to understand. DEAD BY AN ACT OF MAN. With the prick still in them, the broom handle, the tree branch, the grease gun . . . objects, things not to be believed . . . whiskey bottles, can openers, grass shears, glass, metal, vegetables . . . not to be believed, not to be believed.

Jesse says, "You've got a gift for words."

"Don't talk," I beg her, "don't talk." And this once, she just holds me, blessedly silent.

I dig out the pictures, stare into the faces. Which one was I? Survivors do hate themselves, I know, over the core of fierce self-love, never understanding, always asking, "Why me and not her, not him?" There is such mystery in it, and I have hated myself as much as I have loved others, hated the simple fact of my own survival. Having survived, am I supposed to say something, do something, be something?

I loved my Cousin Butch. He had this big old head, pale thin hair and enormous, watery eyes. All the cousins did, though Butch's head was the largest, his hair the palest. I was the dark-headed one. All the rest of the family seemed pale carbons of each other in shades of blond, though later on everybody's hair went brown or red, and I didn't stand out so. Butch and I stood out—I because I was so dark and fast, and he because of that big head and the crazy things he did. Butch used to climb on the back of my Uncle Lucius's truck, open the gas tank and hang his head over, breathe deeply, strangle, gag, vomit, and breathe again. It went so deep, it tingled in your toes. I climbed up after him and tried it myself, but I was too young to hang on long, and I fell heavily to the ground, dizzy and giggling. Butch could hang on, put his hand down into the tank and pull up a cupped palm of gas, breathe deep and laugh. He would climb down roughly, swinging down from the door handle, laughing, staggering, and stinking of gasoline. Someone caught him at it. Someone threw a match. "I'll teach you."
Just like that, gone before you understand.

I wake up in the night screaming, "No, no, I won't!" Dirty water rises in the back of my throat, the liquid language of my own terror and rage. "Hold me. Hold me." Jesse rolls over on me; her hands grip my hipbones tightly.
"I love you. I love you. I'm here," she repeats.
I stare up into her dark eyes, puzzled, afraid. I draw a breath in deeply, smile my bland smile. "Did I fool you?" I laugh, rolling away from her. Jesse punches me playfully, and I catch her hand in the air.
"My love," she whispers, and cups her body against my hip, closes her eyes. I bring my hand up in front of my face and watch the knuckles, the nails as they tremble, tremble. I watch for a long time while she sleeps, warm and still against me.

James went blind. One of the uncles got him in the face with home-brewed alcohol.
Lucille climbed out the front window of Aunt Raylene's house and jumped. They said she jumped. No one said why.
My Uncle Matthew used to beat my Aunt Raylene. The twins, Mark and Luke, swore to stop him, pulled him out in the yard one time, throwing him between them like a loose bag of grain. Uncle Matthew screamed like a pig coming up for slaughter. I got both my sisters in the toolshed for safety, but I hung back to watch. Little Bo came running out of the house, off the porch, feetfirst into his daddy's arms. Uncle Matthew started swinging him like a scythe, going after the bigger boys, Bo's head thudding their shoulders, their hips. Afterward, Bo crawled around in the dirt, the blood running out of his

ears and his tongue hanging out of his mouth, while Mark and Luke finally got their daddy down. It was a long time before I realized that they never told anybody else what had happened to Bo.

Randall tried to teach Lucille and me to wrestle. "Put your hands up." His legs were wide apart, his torso bobbing up and down, his head moving constantly. Then his hand flashed at my face. I threw myself back into the dirt, lay still. He turned to Lucille, not noticing that I didn't get up. He punched at her, laughing. She wrapped her hands around her head, curled over so her knees were up against her throat.

"No, no!" he yelled. "Move like her." He turned to me. "Move." He kicked at me. I rocked into a ball, froze.

"No, no!" He kicked me. I grunted, didn't move. He turned to Lucille. "You." Her teeth were chattering but she held herself still, wrapped up tighter than bacon slices.

"You move!" he shouted. Lucille just hugged her head tighter and started to sob.

"Son of a bitch," Randall grumbled, "you two will never be any good."

He walked away. Very slowly we stood up, embarrassed, looked at each other. We knew.

If you fight back, they kill you.

My sister was seven. She was screaming. My stepfather picked her up by her left arm, swung her forward and back. It gave. The arm went around loosely. She just kept screaming. I didn't know you could break it like that.

I was running up the hall. He was right behind me. "Mama! Mama!" His left hand—he was left-handed—closed around my throat, pushed me against the wall, and then he lifted me that way. I kicked, but I couldn't reach him. He was yelling, but there was so much noise in my ears I couldn't hear him.

"Please, Daddy. Please, Daddy. I'll do anything, I promise. Daddy, anything you want. Please, Daddy."

I couldn't have said that. I couldn't talk around that fist at my throat, couldn't breathe. I woke up when I hit the floor. I looked up at him.

"If I live long enough, I'll fucking kill you."

He picked me up by my throat again.

"What's wrong with her?"

"Why's she always following you around?"

Nobody really wanted answers.

A full bottle of vodka will kill you when you're nine and the bottle is a quart. It was a third cousin proved that. We learned what that and other things could do. Every year there was something new.

You're growing up. My big girl.

There was codeine in the cabinet, paregoric for the baby's teeth, whiskey, beer, and wine in the house. Jeanne brought home MDA, PCP, acid; Randall, grass, speed, and mescaline. It all worked to dull things down, to pass the time.

Stealing was a way to pass the time. Things we needed, things we didn't, for the nerve of it, the anger, the need. You're growing up, we told each other. But sooner or later, we all got caught. Then it was When Are You Going to Learn?

Caught, nightmares happened. "Razorback desperate" was the conclusion of the man down at the county farm where Mark and Luke were sent at fifteen. They both got their heads shaved, their earlobes sliced.

What's the matter, kid? Can't you take it?

Caught at sixteen, June was sent to Jessup County Girls' Home, where the baby was adopted out and she slashed her wrists on the bedsprings.

Lou got caught at seventeen and held in the station downtown, raped on the floor of the holding tank.

Are you a boy or are you a girl?

On your knees, kid, can you take it?

Caught at eighteen and sent to prison, Jack came back seven years later blank-faced, understanding nothing. He married a quiet girl from out of town, had three babies in four years. Then Jack came home one night from the textile mill, carrying one of those big handles off the high-speed spindle machine. He used it to beat them all to death and went back to work in the morning.

Cousin Melvina married at fourteen, had three kids in two and a half years, and welfare took them all away. She ran off with a carnival mechanic, had three more babies before he left her for a motorcycle acrobat. Welfare took those, too. But the next baby was hydrocephalic, a little waterhead they left with her, and the three that followed, even the one she used to hate so— the one she had after she fell off the porch and couldn't remember whose child it was.

"How many children do you have?" I asked her.

"You mean the ones I have, or the ones I had? Four," she told me, "or eleven."

My aunt, the one I was named for, tried to take off for Oklahoma. That was after she'd lost the youngest girl and they told her Bo would never be "right." She packed up biscuits, cold chicken, and Coca-Cola; a lot of loose clothes; Cora and her new baby, Cy; and the four youngest girls. They set off from Greenville in the afternoon, hoping to make Oklahoma by the weekend, but they only got as far as Augusta. The bridge there went out under them.

"An Act of God," my uncle said.

My aunt and Cora crawled out downriver, and two of the girls turned up in the weeds, screaming loud enough to be found in the dark. But one of the girls never came up out of that dark water, and Nancy, who had been holding Cy, was found still wrapped around the baby, in the water, under the car.

"An Act of God," my aunt said. "God's got one damn sick sense of humor."

My sister had her baby in a bad year. Before he was born we had talked about it. "Are you afraid?" I asked.

"He'll be fine," she'd replied, not understanding, speaking instead to the other fear. "Don't we have a tradition of bastards?"

He was fine, a classically ugly healthy little boy with that shock of white hair that marked so many of us. But afterward, it was that bad year with my sister down with pleurisy, then cystitis, and no work, no money, having to move back home with my cold-eyed stepfather. I would come home to see her, from the woman I could not admit I'd been with, and take my infinitely fragile nephew and hold him, rocking him, rocking myself.

One night I came home to screaming—the baby, my sister, no one else there. She was standing by the crib, bent over, screaming red-faced. "Shut up! Shut up!" With each word her fist slammed the mattress fanning the baby's ear.

"Don't!" I grabbed her, pulling her back, doing it as gently as I could so I wouldn't break the stitches from her operation. She had her other arm clamped across her abdomen and couldn't fight me at all. She just kept shrieking.

"That little bastard just screams and screams. That little bastard. I'll kill him."

Then the words seeped in and she looked at me while her son kept crying and kicking his feet. By his head the mattress still showed the impact of her fist.

"Oh no," she moaned, "I wasn't going to be like that. I always promised myself." She started to cry, holding her belly and sobbing. "We an't no different. We an't no different."

Jesse wraps her arm around my stomach, presses her belly into my back. I relax against her. "You sure you can't have children?" she asks. "I sure would like to see what your kids would turn out to be like."

I stiffen, say, "I can't have children. I've never wanted children."

"Still," she says, "you're so good with children, so gentle."

I think of all the times my hands have curled into fists, when I have just barely held on. I open my mouth, close it, can't speak. What could I say now? All the times I have not spoken before, all the things I just could not tell her, the shame, the self-hatred, the fear; all of that hangs between us now—a wall I cannot tear down.

I would like to turn around and talk to her, tell her . . . "I've got a dust river in my head, a river of names endlessly repeating. That dirty water rises in me, all those children screaming out their lives in my memory, and I become someone else, someone I have tried so hard not to be." But I don't say anything, and I know, as surely as I know I will never have a child, that by not speaking I am condemning us, that I cannot go on loving you and hating you for your fairy-tale life, for not asking about what you have no reason to imagine, for that soft-chinned innocence I love.

Jesse puts her hands behind my neck, smiles and says, "You tell the funniest stories."

I put my hands behind her back, feeling the ridges of my knuckles pulsing.

"Yeah," I tell her. "But I lie."

QUESTIONS FOR DISCUSSION AND WRITING

1. The narrator says that her relationship with Jesse eventually will end. Do you think she is right? Explain your answer.
2. The narrator says, "The mystery is how many no one remembers." Explain what she means.
3. Why doesn't the narrator want to have children?
4. In the final sentence, the narrator tells Jesse that she lies. Why? How do you imagine Jesse interprets this admission? What does the narrator tell us about Jesse, and what can you infer about her?
5. Do you think Allison implies that the narrator's experiences are typical of poor white Southern families? Defend your response with examples from the story. Do you think this is true, or is the family of this story somehow unusual?
6. The narrator states in different ways that patterns of the rural poor are passed down through the generations. Can the social class of a family change from one generation to the next, or are people too affected by the way they are raised to change? Give examples from real life or from fiction to support your answer.

ON TECHNIQUE AND STYLE

1. Reread the opening paragraph. Why did Allison choose to start "River of Names" with this incident?
2. Although this story may be considered dark and depressing, the narrator says, "I tell the stories and it comes out funny." How does she make these stories "funny"?
3. Does Allison's story imply that being lower class makes a person more vulnerable to abuse, violence, rape, and early death? If so, why do you think this may be?

CULTURAL QUESTION

1. This story comes from a collection titled *Trash*, as in "white trash." What does Allison mean by this term? What is usually meant by this term in U.S. culture? Do other cultures have similar concepts?

POETRY

A Chinese Banquet
For the one who was not invited

Kitty Tsui

Kitty Tsui was born in Hong Kong in 1953. She lived in Hong Kong and England before coming to the United States in 1969. She has been an actor, artist, and professional bodybuilder as well as a writer. Tsui (pronounced "choy") is a noted lesbian poet and writer of erotica. In the early 1980s, Tsui emerged as one of a few published Asian American lesbian writers and role models. In The Words of a Woman Who Breathes Fire *(1983), a collection of poetry and prose, Tsui offers an image of a proud, defiant woman. She also writes on issues of family, culture, and being Asian. The following poem is from* The Very Inside *(1994). Her other writings include* Nightvision *(1984),* Breathless: Erotica *(1996), and* Sparks Fly *(1997). Tsui played a role in the 1997 film* Stolen Moments, *a documentary on lesbian lifestyles in the Western world. The film combines historical drama with commentary on lesbian contemporary life. Tsui lives in the Midwest.*

it was not a very formal affair but
all the women over twelve
wore long gowns and a corsage,
except for me.

it was not a very formal affair, just
the family getting together,
poa poa, kuw fu without *kuw mow*[1]
(her excuse this year is a headache).

aunts and uncles and cousins,
the grandson who is a dentist,
the one who drives a mercedes benz,
sitting down for shark's fin soup.

they talk about buying a house and
taking a two week vacation in beijing.
i suck on shrimp and squab,

---

[1]*Poa poa* means grandmother; *kuw fu* means uncle; and *kuw now* means aunt.

dreaming of the cloudscape in your eyes.

my mother, her voice beaded with sarcasm:
you're twenty six and not getting younger.
it's about time you got a decent job.
she no longer asks when I'm getting married.

you're twenty six and not getting younger.
what are you doing with your life?
you've got to make a living.
why don't you study computer programming?

she no longer asks when i'm getting married.
one day, wanting desperately to
bridge the boundaries that separate us,
wanting desperately to touch her,

tell her: mother, i'm gay,
mother i'm gay and so happy with her.
but she will not listen,
she shakes her head.

she sits across from me,
emotions invading her face.
her eyes are wet but
she will not let tears fall.

mother, i say,
you love a man.
i love a woman.
it is not what she wants to hear.

aunts and uncles and cousins,
very much a family affair.
but you are not invited,
being neither my husband nor my wife.

aunts and uncles and cousins
eating longevity noodles
fragrant with ham inquire:
sold that old car of yours yet?

i want to tell them: my back is healing,
i dream of dragons and water.
my home is in her arms,
our bedroom ceiling the wide open sky.

QUESTIONS FOR DISCUSSION AND WRITING

1. How is the narrator's family portrayed in this poem? What are the specific elements that tell you this?
2. How are the narrator's values different from those of her family?
3. What is the central conflict of this poem? Do you find it obvious or predictable? Why or why not?
4. Why does the narrator insist "it was not a very formal affair"? Does anything tell you otherwise?

ON TECHNIQUE AND STYLE

1. What imagery makes an impression on you as the reader? Give specific examples, and explain how this imagery works for the poem.
2. The poet has not used capitalization in this poem. What effect does this have on you as a reader? Why do you think writers sometimes abandon this convention?

CULTURAL QUESTION

1. Although this poem's characters are Chinese, does culture play an overarching role in this poem? What if the characters had been European Americans? African Americans? Would the narrative of the story be the same, or different? Support your answer with examples from other readings or real life.

Nikki-Rosa

Nikki Giovanni

Nikki Giovanni was born in 1943, and grew up in Cincinnati, Ohio. She and her sister returned to Knoxville, Tennessee each summer to visit their grandparents. In 1960, Giovanni began her studies at Fisk University in Nashville, Tennessee, and graduated in history in 1967. She gave birth to Thomas Watson Giovanni, her only child, in 1969. She has been a professor of writing and literature at Virginia Polytechnic Institute and State University since 1987, and continues to speak and travel nationwide.

Giovanni has written more than twenty books, including volumes of poetry, illustrated children's books, and three collections of essays. The civil rights and black power movements informed her early poetry, including "Nikki-Rosa" which is

included here, and was published in Black Feeling, Black Talk *(1968). Other early
work includes* Black Judgment *(1968) and* Re: Creation *(1970). Quilting the
Black-Eyed Pea: Poems and Not Quite Poems *was published in 2002. Giovanni
has recently written a children's book about the civil rights leader Rosa Parks (Rosa,
2005). Giovanni received an NAACP Image Award for Literature in 1998, 2000,
and 2003. The poem presented here, one of her most read and studied, was inspired
by her childhood.*

childhood remembrances are always a drag
if you're Black
you always remember things like living in Woodlawn
with no inside toilet
and if you become famous or something
they never talk about how happy you were to have your mother
all to yourself and
how good the water felt when you got your bath from one of those
big tubs that folk in Chicago barbecue in
and somehow when you talk about home
it never gets across how much you
understood their feelings
as the whole family attended meetings about Hollydale
and even though you remember
your biographers never understand
your father's pain as he sells his stock
and another dream goes
and though you're poor it isn't poverty that
concerns you
and though they fight a lot
it isn't your father's drinking that makes any difference
but only that everybody is together and you
and your sister have happy birthdays and very good
Christmases
and I really hope no white person ever has cause to write about me
because they never understand that Black love is Black wealth and
    they'll
probably talk about my hard childhood and never understand that
all the while I was quite happy.

QUESTIONS FOR DISCUSSION AND WRITING

1. What is the main conflict presented by the narrator of this poem?
2. How would you describe the speaker's feelings toward her childhood? Why do you think she is concerned that a biographer will "never
   understand"?

3. Why does the narrator "really hope no white person ever has cause to write about" her?
4. What are the elements of a happy childhood, according to the narrator? How do these elements differ from what might be written if the writer is to "become famous or something"?
5. How did you interpret the lines "and though you're poor it isn't poverty that / concerns you"? If poverty doesn't concern the narrator, what does?

ON TECHNIQUE AND STYLE

1. Why do you think Giovanni chooses to address the reader directly as "you"? What effect did this have on you as a reader? What assumption is Giovanni making about her readers through the use of second person?
2. Like the previous poem, this one does not use standard capitalization practices, though it does use some. How does it differ from "A Chinese Banquet" in this regard? Which words does the poet capitalize, and which ones doesn't she capitalize? Why?

CULTURAL QUESTION

1. The last lines of the poem say that if a white person writes about the narrator, they'll talk about her "hard childhood." Is the theme of overcoming a hard childhood particularly American? Give examples to support your response.

GRAPHIC FICTION

From Jimmy Corrigan—
The Smartest Kid on Earth

Chris Ware

Chris Ware was born in Omaha, Nebraska in 1967. He moved to San Antonio, Texas, at age sixteen and went to the University of Texas in Austin. There he began publishing a weekly comic strip in the local paper. Pulitzer Prize–winning graphic

(continued on pg. 208)

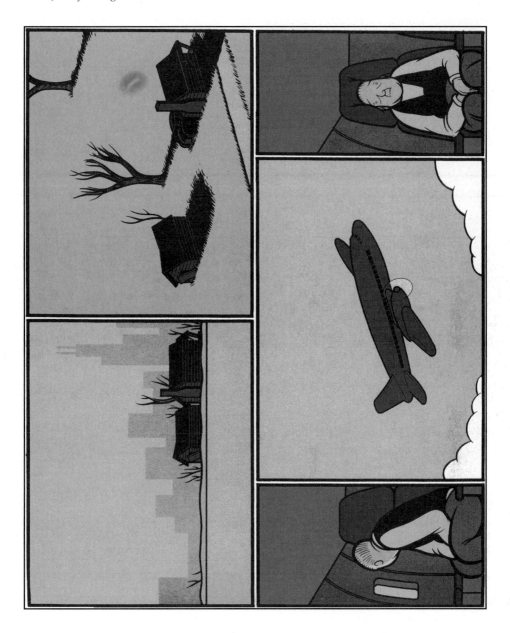

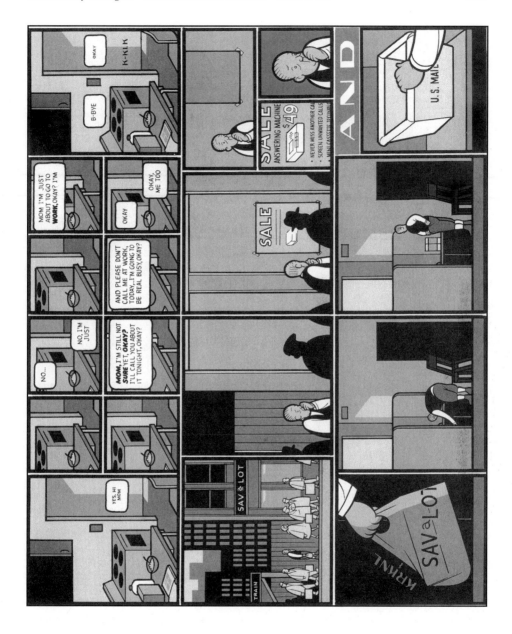

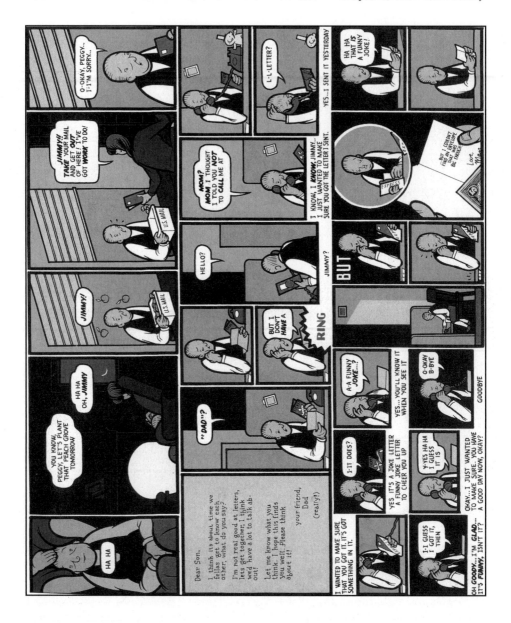

fiction artist Art Speigelman (Maus) saw Ware's work and called him (then a soph-omore) and gave him four pages of the highly regarded annual anthology RAW.

Ware moved to Chicago in the early 1990s and began publishing in the pages of the Chicago alt-weekly New City *the strip known as* The Acme Novelty Library. *This critically acclaimed strip won several comics awards during the 1990s, and is where the author developed his unique style. From this strip came the graphic novel* Jimmy Corrigan—The Smartest Kid on Earth *(2000). This selection is excerpted from Ware's novel.* Jimmy Corrigan *received the American Book Award in 2000, the Guardian First Book Award in 2001, and the prestigious French award L'Alph Art in 2003. In fact, in his short career, Ware has already received more awards than he has published comics.*

Ware is also a respected popular artist, whose work has appeared in many national and international exhibitions, including the Whitney Art Museum of New York in 2002. His work appeared in serial form in The New York Times *in 2005–2006. He continues to publish* Acme Novelty Library *every week in Chicago where he lives with his wife.*

QUESTIONS FOR DISCUSSION AND WRITING

1. This excerpt is taken from the early pages of the novel. How many conflicts are established here? How are they established?
2. What is the confusion over the letters—the one from Jimmy's father and the one from his mother?
3. What details does Ware give us about Jimmy Corrigan as a character? Identify any frames that are key in characterizing him.

ON TECHNIQUE AND STYLE

1. What is distinctive about Ware's style, in your experience? How does his work look the same or different from other works of graphic fiction that you know, or that you find in this book?
2. There are several frames that do not include words. How do these frames work to move the story forward? How, for example, do they show the passage of time?

CULTURAL QUESTION

1. How are the family themes presented in *Jimmy Corrigan* culture-specific? Universal? Give examples from other readings or your own experience.

VISUAL TEXTS

For Dragonboat Festival

Komi Chen

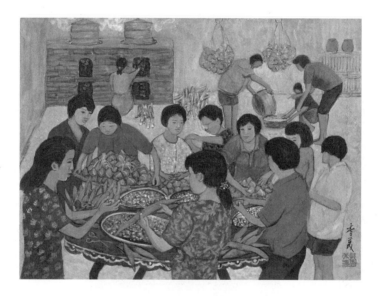

Komi Chen was born in Taipei, Taiwan. Her father, Kuo Hsueh-Hu, is one of Taiwan's top visual artists. Her father began Chen's training in classical Chinese painting and calligraphy.

Chen attended the College of Fine and Applied Arts at Taiwan's training college for teachers, the National Taiwan Normal University. There she mastered traditional Chinese fine arts techniques and was first exposed to Western styles. After graduation in 1966, she began teaching fine arts at a local middle school.

After graduation, Chen moved to Pittsburgh, Pennsylvania, to pursue an advanced degree in library science. She began teaching traditional Chinese painting techniques in local community colleges. At the same time, she began to take on the visual styles of her adopted country, especially Western realism. Chen became involved in the local arts community and exhibited at regional art shows.

During her early years in the United States, Chen's paintings were primarily tradi-tional mountain-and-water landscapes and still lifes of flowers and fruit. As her style evolved, however, she added more color and interest to her work, reflecting an interest in cultures and landscapes from around the world: temples in Japan, farms in South Africa, glaciers in Canada, and religious ceremonies in Thailand, among many others.

For Dragonboat Festival (1994) shows preparations for a holiday celebrated in China—one with a very long history. The Dragon Boat Festival is celebrated with races among boats built in the shape of dragons.

Mother and Child

Edward S. Curtis

Edward Sheriff Curtis *was born in Wisconsin in 1868. His sister, Eva, was born in 1870 and his brother, Asahel, in 1874. Edward also had an older brother, Ray, born in 1861. After Asahel's birth, the family moved to Cordova, a rural settlement in Minnesota, where Curtis's father worked as a preacher. As a boy, Edward often accompanied his father on canoe trips to visit members of the congregation. His experience camping outdoors with his father helped prepare him for the extensive fieldwork he would do later in his career.*

As an adolescent Edward built his own camera by consulting a popular manual. He may also have worked for a photographer in St. Paul before his family moved west. In the fall of 1887, Edward and his father traveled to the Washington Territory and by winter, had settled in the Puget Sound region. In 1892, he married Clara Phillips and opened a portrait studio in Seattle with partner Thomas Guptill. While their business was very successful, Guptill and Curtis parted ways in 1897 and Curtis renamed the business Edward S. Curtis, Photographer and Photoengraver.

Curtis is best known for his portraits of Native Americans, and his twenty-volume history of Native Americans called The North American Indian. *The photo here is from Volume 3 of that collection (1905). Curtis also did some work in Hollywood, taking still photographs of Elmo Lincoln as Tarzan and working on such films as* The Ten Commandments, Adam's Rib, King of Kings, *and* The Plainsman.

Curtis died of a heart attack on October 19, 1952, in Los Angeles.

Family Eating Dinner in Kitchen

William Gottlieb

William Paul Gottlieb (1917–2006) was an American photographer and newspaper columnist. He was born in Brooklyn, New York, and grew up in Bound Brook, New Jersey, where his father was in the building and lumber business. He was best known for his photographs of the leading performers of the golden age of American jazz in the 1930s and 1940s.

Gottlieb attended Lehigh University in Pennsylvania, majoring in economics. While at Lehigh, Gottlieb wrote for the college newspaper and became editor in chief of The Lehigh Review. *In his last year of university, he wrote a weekly jazz column for the* Washington Post. *After the* Post *said it could not afford a photographer for Gottlieb's jazz column, Gottlieb bought a camera and took pictures himself.*

Gottlieb was drafted into the Army Air Corps in 1943, and he served as a photo officer during World War II. After the war, Gottlieb went to New York City to pursue his interest in journalism. He worked as a writer-photographer for Down Beat *(a jazz magazine), and his work also appeared frequently in other major magazines. In 1948, Gottlieb retired from jazz in order to spend more time with his family. Gottlieb died of a stroke in Great Neck, New York, in 2006.*

The photograph here, "Family Eating Dinner in Kitchen" was taken around 1960.

QUESTIONS FOR DISCUSSION AND WRITING

1. What view of family is shown by Chen's painting? How does it reflect or negate the ideas of family found in this chapter?
2. The Gottlieb photo illustrates what is often known as the stereotypical white nuclear family. How does this photograph portray, or fail to portray that? How has this image of the middle-class white family affected ideals about family life overall?
3. Relate the Gottlieb photo to the Tolstoy quotation found early in this chapter. In what way might this portray the "happy family" Tolstoy refers to?

ON TECHNIQUE AND STYLE

1. Curtis's photograph could be said to focus on the people in the portrait, while Gottlieb's photo of the 1960s family seems as much about setting as the individuals. How so? Explain the difference in the way these two photos are taken, and what each photographer achieves by making these "editing" choices.
2. What is your impression of the Curtis portrait? Are the subjects of this photograph "exoticized" in any way? Explain your answer.
3. Which image do you find more "realistic"—Chen's painting or Gottlieb's photo? Why?

CULTURAL QUESTION

1. Photographs are often used as illustrations of "other" cultures. How do the photos of Gottlieb and Curtis fulfill that use? Which is the most effective? The least? Why? How do they present the family as "other"?

AUDIO TEXTS   To hear these conversations, go to www.mhhe.com/soundideas1e

Track 2.1

(date: June 1, 2004; running time: 10:20 min.)

See **Richard Rodriguez's** *biography*.

Track 2.2

(date: April 5, 2004; running time: 2:00 min.)

See **Paul Theroux's** *biography*.

Track 2.3

(date: March 26, 2003; running time: 4:22 min.)

See **Grace Paley's** *biography*.

Track 2.4

(date: March 27, 2003; running time: 2:45 min.)

See **Alice Walker's** *biography*.

QUESTIONS FOR DISCUSSION AND WRITING

1. Although Rodriguez talks about his previous book, *Hunger of Memory*, many of the themes apply to the reading from his later book, excerpted in this chapter. In what ways? What themes are similar? What are different?
2. What is the importance of social class to Rodriguez? What is its relationship to Rodriguez's criticism of the "liberal left"?

3. How is the "tribalism" that Theroux mentions in this excerpt related to the tribalism he discusses in "Mother of the Year"?
4. What does Theroux mean about the "narcissism of minor differences"? How does this relate to the Theroux reading?
5. Paley discusses here parents' influence on her stories. What connections do you see between her discussion and the story "Mother" in this chapter?
6. "To Be a Woman," the short poem she reads, is related to issues of feminism. Michael Krasny talks about the "spirit of the poem." What is the theme of this poem? How does it relate to the characters in the story "Everyday Use"?

ON TECHNIQUE AND STYLE

1. Paley says that after the first line or two, she decides whether what she's writing will be a poem or a story. Look at the first two lines of "Mother." Could this have been a poem? What makes it more of a story or narrative?
2. The first poem that Walker reads, "Thousands of Feet Below You," deals with issues of war and family. Do you react differently to poems read aloud, or ones that you read yourself? Explain any differences or similarities.

CULTURAL QUESTION

1. In what ways do our parents or families affect how we see political events, or events in the outside world? How do you see this in the way these writers talk about themselves or their families and travels? How does culture enter into the way the writers describe their stories?

Additional Audio Resources

1. You can find selections from Sarah Vowell on "This American Life," at www.thisamericanlife.org.
2. In 1987, James Baldwin gave his last speech and interview at the National Press Club in Washington, DC. *Gibbs Magazine* offers an audio file of this speech, at www.gibbsmagazine.com/james_baldwin__audio_file.htm.
3. Chris Ware has a free podcast at "Here and Now," at www.here-now.org/shows/2005/12/20051209_17.asp.
4. Nikki Giovanni's website, at www.nikki-giovanni.com/imulti.shtml, contains multimedia performances of some poetry by Giovanni herself.

CONNECTIONS

1. Rodriguez and Baldwin both discuss their family relationships in the context of local and current history. Theroux and Vowell treat their stories as more "internal" affairs. Why do you think they make these choices? How do these choices affect the style of writing and the stories that are eventually told?

2. Baldwin and Theroux don't seem particularly happy with their families, or at least certain aspects of their families. What common themes are there in these two readings? What makes them different from the other nonfiction pieces?

3. What makes some writers want to reveal such intimate details of their families, such as Vowell discussing her family's political differences, Baldwin's father's violence, or Theroux's mother's unflattering qualities? What purpose do these kinds of "confessionals" serve, for both the writer and the reader?

4. What connections do you find between Banks's short story and Theroux's nonfiction essay? In what ways does Banks's story seem like nonfiction? Does Theroux's seem like fiction?

5. Can you identify ways in which race affects the stories (say, comparing Baldwin, Rodriguez, Giovanni, and Walker to Paley, Allison, Theroux, and Banks) told in this chapter? In what ways does it *not* play a role? Could Baldwin have written the same story Banks did, for example?

6. Both the Giovanni and the Tsui poems address the issue of being happy in spite of what others think. How are these conditions of happiness different for the narrators in each of the poems?

7. Look again at the images related to this chapter. For each of these images, which reading selection do you think is most closely related to it? Why?

8. Which story, poem, or piece of nonfiction does the graphic fiction selection *Jimmy Corrigan* most closely relate to, in your opinion?

FOR WRITING

CREATIVE CHOICES

1. Create a comic that illustrates one of the main themes of this chapter. (Keep in mind that you need not be an accomplished artist to create a comic. Simple drawings can be very effective.)

2. Continue work in your journal. In it, write a memory of a family event or scene that had an impact on your growth and development. Think about the importance of the event, and what you learned from it that stays with you today. If you prefer, create an audio or video journal, recording your spoken ideas onto a tape or digital recorder.

3. Write a poem or short story related to your family and its history or identity. Keeping in mind that poems are typically best appreciated in the spoken form, record yourself reading your poem.

NARRATIVE/EXPOSITORY CHOICES

1. Choose the reading passage that interests you most from this chapter. Then, choose a photo from those connected to this chapter that illustrates either the same family-related theme, or a theme that contradicts it. Write an essay

in which you explore the themes of both the reading passage and the photo you chose, explaining the connection between them.

2. Choose two readings from this chapter from the fiction and/or poetry sections. Make your choice based on a shared theme. What theme do these two readings share? How is the theme illustrated in the stories? Develop a thesis based on your reading of these stories, and write an analytical essay in which you extensively use passages from the readings to support your thesis.

3. What is the role of *lying* in family history and stories? Choose two or more of the selections included in this chapter and explain the role of lying. Use examples from the readings to defend your thesis.

ARGUMENT CHOICES

1. Consider the readings that focus on the issues of family happiness. Is there such a thing as a truly "happy family"? What makes a happy family happy? Write a persuasive paper in which you argue for your view of family happiness. Reflect on the Tolstoy quotation in your argument.

2. Review "Everyday Use." In your opinion, who should get the quilts, Maggie or Dee? Defend your argument with sound reasoning.

3. "Shooting Dad" shows a family divided by politics. Can a family whose members hold very different political views from one another be considered a happy family? Support your opinion with examples from your own experience as well as your reading.

RESEARCH CHOICES

1. Think about your own family's history, and any areas you may not feel you know enough about. Identify a family member, if possible, who could answer the questions you have about your family history. Develop a set of questions to ask. Write a paper in which you explain the background for your questions, the family member's responses, and what you learned from your interview.

2. Consider the images of family as offered by today's advertising media. Identify images from print or video advertising. Write an essay in which you show how family is represented in advertising media. How do these portrayals corroborate or undermine the images presented in the readings from this chapter? Incorporate the images you found to support your thesis. If you have the tools and skills, create a web page essay for this research project.

3. Look at some online sites regarding genealogy. Look in particular at message boards, or other areas where individuals are trying to find out more

information about their own family histories. What kinds of questions arise most often? What else can you learn from these sites? Write a short overview of what you find.

VIDEO SUGGESTIONS

These videos feature stories by the authors introduced in this chapter, or are related to the chapter themes.

1. *Go Tell It on the Mountain* (1985). A made-for-television movie based on James Baldwin's novel, starring Paul Winfield, Alfre Woodard, Ruby Dee, among others. Baldwin appears in the film as well.
2. *The Sweet Hereafter* and *Affliction* (both 1997). Based on books by Russell Banks.
3. *Enormous Changes at the Last Minute* (1983). Based on the stories by Grace Paley, starring Kevin Bacon and Ellen Barkin.
4. *The Color Purple* (1985). Steven Spielberg's classic interpretation of Alice Walker's novel, starring Danny Glover and Whoopi Goldberg.
5. *Bastard Out of Carolina* (1996). Based on Dorothy Allison's novel. Directed by Anjelica Huston, starring Jennifer Jason Leigh.

 chapter *3*

Ideas about Education
Stories from School

INTRODUCTION

The American author Ambrose Bierce defined education in *The Devil's Diction-ary* as "that which discloses to the wise and disguises from the fool their lack of understanding." Understanding, through lessons, is often what education is all about. Most of our formal education comes through classroom lessons that exciting teachers can make inspiring. Fortunately, such teachers can and do enter our lives. But bad or misguided education can be toxic and harmful.

In this chapter we look at ideas about education and begin with two famed feminist, lesbian poets who considered themselves outsiders and who write about education from that point of view. Both Adrienne Rich and Audre Lorde look at education as providing different lessons to the outsider that enable both of them to grapple with inequities in education and bring into focus wrongs that need righting. From "Claiming an Education," a graduation speech delivered by Rich at an all-women's college, and from Lorde's narrative of her childhood experience of being mishandled by public and parochial classroom teachers, we go to two late 1960s school reformers, Neil Postman and Charles Weingarten, and an excerpt from their book *Teaching as a Subversive Activity.* With a crazy quilt of proposals these educators offer a different kind of classroom teaching that embodies, in the proposals they offer for reform, the enduring spirit of the sixties and ongoing in the present to turn educational institutions upside down, to change and to subvert them. This section concludes with "The Gradu-ation," another personal memoir excerpt from Maya Angelou's famous auto-biography, *I Know Why the Caged Bird Sings.* Maya and her brother Bailey feel they have had a rewarding education in their small Arkansas town but, since this is before civil rights and integration, the lesson from Maya's graduation speaker's address to them seems to be, "If you're black get back." The dream of upward mobility and self-realization, education appears to them a dream limited to those with white skin. That is until the lesson in "The Graduation" changes to one of uplift and hope as the poetic words of the Negro anthem are absorbed and understood.

The fiction section continues to reveal important motifs of education, learning, and the classroom experience. We are back in the Harlem Audre Lorde wrote about in Toni Cade Bambara's "The Lesson." Sylvia, the story's protagonist, is not as much an outsider as Lorde, who is a large-sized child of immigrants with a visual impairment, but we see Sylvia chafe at the good-intentioned Miss Moore, a woman trying to instill values into the black children through educational fieldtrip outings. Donald Barthelme's classroom in the postmodern story "The School" seems weird and bizarre but also has a real lesson in it: what occurs when deep and imponderable questions must be faced in school about matters such as death, tragedy, reproduction, hope, value, and nothingness. The two other stories included in this section, by Louise Erdrich and Willa Cather, continue the critique of education through portrayals of two additional outsiders, the part Indian girl Marie Lazarre in "Saint Marie" and the effeminate and psychologically disturbed boy, Paul, in "Paul's Case." Both appear to suffer because of their education. The main lesson Marie learns from her abusive nun teacher, Sister Leopolda, is one of needing to elude Satan and trying to create herself into a saint. For Paul, the main lesson he draws from his schooling is of a drab conformity that he refuses to follow. Instead he follows his own tragic-bound drummer beat.

The poetry section presents us with black youth and the outsider roles they play in Gwendolyn Brooks's simple, famous poem "We Real Cool." Life in the fast lane and the risk of early death tells us about the failure of formal education to provide the boys with the sense of a future. In Billy Collins's "The History Teacher" we see another form of miseducation, the kind that, like the old cliché about the road to hell, is paved with good intentions.

Also included in this chapter is a page from the graphic novel of Marcel Proust's *Remembrance of Things Past: Combray*, adapted by Stephane Heuet. The young protagonist, based on Proust himself, is spending the summer away from school in Combray. Yet he is in love with books, intoxicated with learning. The ideals of education appear to have been somehow deeply imbued in him.

Two evocative photographs and one painting of schools provide a historic context for the classroom and education as we see children being protected by marshals as they integrate a Southern school, view activities within a nineteenth-century American schoolroom, and absorb the sight of a rural old-fashioned one-room schoolhouse.

The audio section in this chapter includes discussion with academics and a student about educational convergence and interdisciplinarity as innovative and positive ways of enhancing learning. There is, as well, a rare interview with the poet Adrienne Rich following the publication of her poetry volume *School Among the Ruins*.

This chapter should make you think about your own education and where it went well and where it did not. It also ought to make you increasingly aware of some of the inequities and failures in education and classroom learning, and of ways to reform and even redirect education failures.

NONFICTION

Claiming an Education

Adrienne Rich

Adrienne Rich's most recent books of poetry are Telephone Ringing in the Labyrinth: Poems 2004–2006 *and* The School Among the Ruins: 2000–2004. *A selection of her essays,* Arts of the Possible: Essays and Conversations *appeared in 2001. She edited Muriel Rukeyser's* Selected Poems *for the Library of Congress. In spring 2009, Norton will publish* A Human Eye: Essays on Art in Society. *She is a recipient of the National Book Foundation's 2006 Medal of Distinguished Contribution to American Letters, among other honors. She lives in California.*

"Claiming an Education" was a commencement speech delivered by Rich in the late 1970s at the all-women's Douglass College. She makes the case for education having been hijacked by white patriarchal power and for students, particularly women students, to seek their own identities as they prospect for knowledge and establish a new kind of contract for what institutional learning can provide.

For this convocation, I planned to separate my remarks into two parts: some thoughts about you, the women students here, and some thoughts about us who teach in a women's college. But ultimately those two parts are indivisible. If university education means anything beyond the processing of human beings into expected roles, through credit hours, tests, and grades (and I believe that in a women's college especially it *might* mean much more), it implies an ethical and intellectual contract between teacher and student. This contract must remain intuitive, dynamic, unwritten; but we must turn to it again and again if learning is to be reclaimed from the depersonalizing and cheapening pressures of the present-day academic scene.

The first thing I want to say to you who are students, is that you cannot afford to think of being here to *receive* an education: you will do much better to think of being here to *claim* one. One of the dictionary definitions of the verb *"to claim"* is: *to take as the rightful owner; to assert in the face of possible contradiction.* "To receive" is *to come into possession of: to act as receptacle or container for; to accept as authoritative or true.* The difference is that between acting and being acted-upon, and for women it can literally mean the difference between life and death.

One of the devastating weaknesses of university learning, of the store of knowledge and opinion that has been handed down through academic training, has been its almost total erasure of women's experience and thought from the curriculum, and its exclusion of women as members of the academic community. Today, with increasing numbers of women students in nearly every branch of higher learning, we still see very few women in the upper levels of faculty and administration in most institutions. Douglass College itself is a women's college in a university administered overwhelmingly men, who in turn are answerable to the state legislature, again composed predominantly of men. But the most, significant fact for you is that what you learn here, the very texts you read, the lectures you hear, the way your studies are divided into categories and fragmented one from the other—all this reflects, to a very large degree, neither objective reality, nor an accurate picture of the past, nor a group of rigorously tested observations about human behavior. What you can learn here (and I mean not only at Douglass but any college in any university) is how *men* have perceived and organized their experience, their history, their ideas of social relationships, good and evil, sickness and health, etc. When you read or hear about "great issues," "major texts," "the mainstream of Western thought," you are hearing about what men, above all white men, in their male subjectivity, have decided is important.

Black and other minority peoples have for some time recognized that their racial and ethnic experience was not accounted for in the studies broadly labeled human: and that even the sciences can be racist. For many reasons, it has been more difficult for women to comprehend our exclusion, and to realize that even the sciences can be sexist. For one thing, it is only within the last hundred years that higher education has grudgingly been opened up to women at all, even to white, middle-*class* women. And many of us have found ourselves poring eagerly over books with titles like: *The Descent of Man; Man and His Symbols; Irrational Man; The Phenomenon of Man; The Future of Man; Man and the Machine; From Man to Man; May Man Prevail?; Man, Science and Society;* or *One Dimensional Man*—books pretending to describe a "human" reality that does not include over one-half the human species.

Less than a decade ago, with the rebirth of a feminist movement in this country, women students and teachers in a number of universities began to demand and set up women's studies courses—to *claim* a women-directed education. And, despite the inevitable accusations of "unscholarly," "group therapy," "faddism," etc. . . . despite backlash and budget cuts, woman's studies are still growing, offering to more and more women a new intellectual grasp on their lives, new understanding of our history, a fresh vision of the human experience, and also a critical basis for evaluating what they hear and read in other courses, and in the society at large.

But my talk is not really about women's studies, much as I believe in their scholarly, scientific, and human necessity. While I think that any Douglass student has everything to gain by investigating and enrolling in women's studies courses, I want to suggest that there is a more essential experience that you owe yourselves, one which courses in women's studies can greatly enrich, but which finally depends on you in all your interactions with yourself and your world. This is the experience of *taking responsibility toward yourselves.* Our upbringing as women has so often told us that this should come second to our relationships and responsibilities to other people. We have been offered ethical models of the self-denying wife and mother; intellectual models of the brilliant but slapdash dilettante who never commits herself to anything the whole way, or the intelligent woman who denies her intelligence in order to seem more "feminine," or who sits in passive silence even when she disagrees inwardly with everything that is being said around her.

Responsibility to yourself means refusing to let others do your thinking, talking, and naming for you; it means learning to respect and use your own brains and instincts; hence, grappling with hard work. It means that you do not treat your body as a commodity with which to purchase superficial intimacy or economic security; for our bodies to be treated as objects, our minds are in mortal danger. It means insisting that those to whom you give your friendship and love are able to respect your mind. It means being able to say, with Charlotte Bronte's *Jane Eyre:* "I have an inward treasure born with me, which can keep me alive if all the extraneous delights should be withheld or offered only at a price I cannot afford to give."

Responsibility to yourself means that you don't fall for shallow and easy solutions—predigested books and ideas, weekend encounters guaranteed to change your life, taking "gut" courses instead of ones you know will challenge you, bluffing at school and life instead of doing solid work, marrying early as an escape from real decisions, getting pregnant as an evasion of already existing problems. It means that you refuse to sell your talents and aspirations short, simply to avoid conflict and confrontation. And this, in turn, means resisting the forces in society which say that women should be nice, play safe, have low professional expectations, drown in love and forget about work, live through others, and stay in the places assigned to us. It means that we insist on a life of meaningful work, insist that work be as meaningful as love and friendship in our lives. It means, therefore, the courage to be "different"; not to be continuously available to others when we need time for ourselves and our work; to be able to demand of others—parents, friends, roommates, teachers, lovers, husbands, children—that they respect our sense of purpose and our integrity as persons. Women everywhere are finding the courage to do this, more and more, and we are finding that courage both in our study of women in the past who possessed it, and in each other as we look to other women for comradeship, community, and challenge. The difference between a life lived actively, and a life of passive drifting and dispersal of energies, is an immense difference. Once we begin to feel committed to our lives, responsible to ourselves, we can never again be satisfied with the old, passive way.

Now comes the second part of the contract. I believe that in a women's college you have the right to expect your faculty to take you seriously. The education of women has been a matter of debate for centuries, and old, negative attitudes about women's role, women's ability to think and take leadership, are still rife both in and outside the university. Many male professors (and I don't mean only at Douglass) still feel that teaching in a women's college is a second-rate career. Many tend to eroticize their women students—to treat them as sexual objects—instead of demanding the best of their minds. (At Yale a legal suit [*Alexander v. Yale*] has been brought against the university by a group of women students demanding a stated policy against sexual advances toward female students by male professors.) Many teachers, both men and women, trained in the male-centered tradition, are still handing the ideas and texts of that tradition on to students without teaching them to criticize its antiwoman attitudes, it's omission of women as part of the species. Too often, all of us fail to teach the most important thing, which is that clear thinking, active discussion, and excellent writing are all necessary for intellectual freedom, and that these require *hard work.* Sometimes, perhaps in discouragement with a culture which is both antiintellectual and antiwoman, we may resign ourselves to low expectations for our students before we have given them half a chance to become more thoughtful, expressive human beings. We need to take to heart the words of Elizabeth Barrett Browning, a poet, a thinking woman, and a feminist, who wrote in 1845 of her impatience with studies which cultivate a "passive recipiency" in the mind, and asserted that "women want to be made to *think actively:* their apprehension is quicker than that of men, but their defect lies for the most part in the logical faculty and in the higher mental activities." Note that she implies a defect which can be remedied by intellectual training; *not* an inborn lack of ability.

I have said that the contract on the student's part involves that you demand to be taken seriously so that you can also go on taking yourself seriously. This means seeking out criticism, recognizing that the most affirming thing anyone can do for you is demand that you push yourself further, show you the range of what you can do. It means rejecting attitudes of "take-it-easy," "why-be-so-serious," "why-worry-you'll-probably-get-married-anyway." It means assuming your share of responsibility for what happens in the classroom, because that affects the quality of your daily life here. It means that the student sees herself engaged *with* her teachers in active, ongoing struggle for a real education. But for her to do this, her teachers must be committed to belief that women's minds and experience are intrinsically valuable and indispensable to any civilization worthy the name: that there is no more exhilarating and intellectually fertile place in the academic world today than a women's college—if both students and teachers in large enough numbers are trying to fulfill this contract. The contract is really a pledge of mutual seriousness about women, about language, ideas, method, and values. It is our shared commitment toward a world in which the inborn potentialities of so many women's minds will no longer be wasted, raveled-away, paralyzed, or denied.

QUESTIONS FOR DISCUSSION AND WRITING

1. Rich's audience is the students and faculty of Douglass College. Her challenges on the role of education are geared largely to women from a feminist perspective. How much do the main points in her essay concerning students claiming their education apply in equal measure to both male and female students?

2. What does Rich mean when she talks about education being an "ethical and intellectual contract between teacher and student"? Can you provide examples from your own education that highlight how and when such a contract is or is not being fulfilled?

3. What does Rich mean when she speaks of "depersonalizing and cheapening pressures of the present-day academic scene"? How significant, in your judgment, are such pressures in interfering with or thwarting the best possible and most satisfactory kinds of educational experiences?

4. Rich speaks of self-responsibility in education and sees it in opposition to self-denying roles or allegiance to others. Are there risks in our visualizing education from such a divided, perhaps even polarized perspective?

5. Rich emphasizes "hard work" and being active versus being passive; she sees both as integral to the reclaiming of one's education and she highlights the importance of the role of faculty in the educational contract. Although her essay is mainly addressed to students, how do hard work and being active apply to educators? What exactly is their role or what should it be in the reclaiming of education?

ON TECHNIQUE AND STYLE

1. How persuasive is Rich's essay, especially in light of her argument that most knowledge taught is inaccurate because it is what men, mostly white men, have deemed important? Remember that this essay was delivered in 1977.

2. Much of Rich's essay rests on the idea of claiming. She uses the dictionary as a means of helping define the verb. How else does she create a working definition for us of claiming so we know what she means when she speaks of both "claiming" and "reclaiming"?

3. How important and effective are the examples of the two women writers Rich uses in her essay—the novelist Charlotte Brontë and the poet Elizabeth Barrett Browning—in giving breadth and credibility to her position on education? Does the choice of two women writers enhance central points in the essay? How does the content in the lines from the two women writers support Rich's stance?

CULTURAL QUESTION

1. Rich singles out white men as being largely responsible for education, for the foundation of our knowledge and our laws. To what extent are women and people of color still excluded from or not yet equitable partners in today's educational contracts?

From Zami:
A New Spelling of My Name

Audre Lorde

Audre Lorde (1934–1992) was a black, lesbian feminist poet. A social and political activist, she was a friend of Adrienne Rich. Dialogues of the two on the subject of conflicts and connections between black and white feminism were published in "Sister Outsider." Her background was socially and economically far different than that of her friend and fellow lesbian poet. The daughter of West Indian immigrants, Lorde grew up in Harlem. She did not speak until she was four and she was born nearly sightless, though she was able to learn to read before starting school. She published her first poem in Seventeen *magazine when she was still a teenager. A graduate of Hunter College, she received a master's degree from Columbia University in library science and went on to marriage and motherhood before "coming out" as a lesbian. In 1968 she published her first volume of poetry,* The First Cities, *followed by* Cables to Rage, From a Land Where Other People Live, The New York Head Shop and Museum, Coal, *and* The Black Unicorn.

The excerpt included here is from her autobiography Zami: A New Spelling of My Name *(1982), a work she called a biomythography. In the selection we see the formidable difficulties she faced growing up as a young Harlem black girl who was the child of immigrants and who also was large sized and nearly blind. But the piece is truly an indictment of much that was (and unfortunately in many cases may still be) wrong and harmful about early education.*

When I was five years old and still legally blind, I started school in a sight-conservation class in the local public school on 135th Street and Lenox Avenue. On the corner was a blue wooden booth where white women gave away free milk to Black mothers with children. I used to long for some Hearst Free Milk Fund milk, in those cute little bottles with their red and white tops, but my mother never allowed me to have any, because she said it was charity, which was bad and demeaning, and besides the milk was warm and might make me sick.

The school was right across the avenue from the catholic school where my two older sisters went, and this public school had been used as a threat against them for as long as I could remember. If they didn't behave and get good marks in schoolwork and deportment, they could be "transferred." A "transfer" carried the same dire implications as "deportation" came to imply decades later.

Of course everybody knew that public school kids did nothing but "fight," and you could get "beaten up" every day after school, instead of being marched out of the schoolhouse door in two neat rows like little robots, silent but safe and unattacked, to the corner where the mothers waited.

But the catholic school had no kindergarten, and certainly not one for blind children.

Despite my nearsightedness, or maybe because of it, I learned to read at the same time I learned to talk, which was only about a year or so before I started school. Perhaps *learn* isn't the right word to use for my beginning to talk, because to this day I don't know if I didn't talk earlier because I didn't know how, or if I didn't talk because I had nothing to say that I would be allowed to say without punishment. Self-preservation starts very early in West Indian families.

I learned how to read from Mrs. Augusta Baker, the children's librarian at the old 135th Street branch library, which has just recently been torn down to make way for a new library building to house the Schomburg Collection on African-American History and Culture. If that was the only good deed that lady ever did in her life, may she rest in peace. Because that deed saved my life, if not sooner, then later, when sometimes the only thing I had to hold on to was knowing I could read, and that that could get me through.

My mother was pinching my ear off one bright afternoon, while I lay spreadeagled on the floor of the Children's Room like a furious little brown toad, screaming bloody murder and embarrassing my mother to death. I know it must have been spring or early fall, because without the protection of a heavy coat, I can still feel the stinging soreness in the flesh of my upper arm. There, where my mother's sharp fingers had already tried to pinch me into silence. To escape those inexorable fingers I had hurled myself to the floor, roaring with pain as I could see them advancing toward my ears again. We were waiting to pick up my two older sisters from story hour, held upstairs on another floor of the dry-smelling quiet library. My shrieks pierced the reverential stillness.

Suddenly, I looked up, and there was a library lady standing over me. My mother's hands had dropped to her sides. From the floor where I was lying, Mrs. Baker seemed like yet another mile-high woman about to do me in. She had immense, light, hooded eyes and a very quiet voice that said, not damnation for my noise, but "Would you like to hear a story, little girl?"

Part of my fury was because I had not been allowed to go to that secret feast called story hour since I was too young, and now here was this strange lady offering me my own story.

I didn't dare to look at my mother, half-afraid she might say no, I was too bad for stories. Still bewildered by this sudden change of events, I climbed up upon the stool which Mrs. Baker pulled over for me, and gave her my full attention. This was a new experience for me and I was insatiably curious.

Mrs. Baker read me *Madeline,* and *Horton Hatches the Egg,* both of which rhymed and had huge lovely pictures which I could see from behind my newly acquired eyeglasses, fastened around the back of my rambunctious head by a black elastic band running from earpiece to earpiece. She also read me another storybook about a bear named Herbert who ate up an entire family, one by one, starting with the parents. By the time she had finished that one, I was sold on reading for the rest of my life.

I took the books from Mrs. Baker's hands after she was finished reading, and traced the large black letters with my fingers, while I peered again at the beautiful bright colors of the pictures. Right then I decided I was going to find out how to do that myself. I pointed to the black marks which I could now distinguish as separate letters, different from my sisters' more grown-up books, whose smaller print made the pages only one grey blur for me. I said, quite loudly, for whoever was listening to hear, "I want to read."

My mother's surprised relief outweighed whatever annoyance she was still feeling at what she called my whelpish carryings-on. From the background where she had been hovering while Mrs. Baker read, my mother moved forward quickly, mollified and impressed. I had spoken. She scooped me up from the low stool, and to my surprise, kissed me, right in front of everybody in the library, including Mrs. Baker.

This was an unprecedented and unusual display of affection in public, the cause of which I did not comprehend. But it was a warm and happy feeling. For once, obviously, I had done something right.

My mother set me back upon the stool and turned to Mrs. Baker, smiling.

"Will wonders never cease to perform!" Her excitement startled me back into cautious silence.

Not only had I been sitting still for longer than my mother would have thought possible, and sitting quietly. I had also spoken rather than screamed, something that my mother, after four years and a lot of worry, had despaired that I would ever do. Even one intelligible word was a very rare event for me. And although the doctors at the clinic had clipped the little membrane under my tongue so I was no longer tongue-tied, and had assured my mother that I was not retarded, she still had her terrors and her doubts. She was genuinely happy for any possible alternative to what she was afraid might be a dumb child. The ear-pinching was forgotten. My mother accepted the alphabet and picture books Mrs. Baker gave her for me, and I was on my way.

I sat at the kitchen table with my mother, tracing letters and calling their names. Soon she taught me how to say the alphabet forwards and backwards as it was done in Grenada. Although she had never gone beyond the seventh grade, she had been put in charge of teaching the first grade children their letters during her last year at Mr. Taylor's School in Grenville. She told me stories about his strictness as she taught me how to print my name.

I did not like the tail of the Y hanging down below the line in Audrey, and would always forget to put it on, which used to disturb my mother greatly.

I used to love the evenness of AUDRELORDE at four years of age, but I remembered to put on the Y because it pleased my mother, and because, as she always insisted to me, that was the way it had to be because that was the way it was. No deviation was allowed from her interpretations of correct.

So by the time I arrived at the sight-conservation kindergarten, braided, scrubbed, and bespectacled, I was able to read large-print books and write my name with a regular pencil. Then came my first rude awakening about school. Ability had nothing to do with expectation.

There were only seven or eight of us little Black children in a big classroom, all with various serious deficiencies of sight. Some of us were cross-eyed, some of us were nearsighted, and one little girl had a patch over one of her eyes.

We were given special short wide notebooks to write in, with very widely spaced lines on yellow paper. They looked like my sister's music notebooks. We were also given thick black crayons to write with. Now you don't grow up fat, Black, nearly blind, and ambidextrous in a West Indian household, particularly my parents' household, and survive without being or becoming fairly rigid fairly fast. And having been roundly spanked on several occasions for having made that mistake at home, I knew quite well that crayons were not what you wrote with, and music books were definitely not what you wrote in.

I raised my hand. When the teacher asked me what I wanted, I asked for some regular paper to write on and a pencil. That was my undoing. "We don't have any pencils here," I was told.

Our first task was to copy down the first letter of our names in those notebooks with our black crayons. Our teacher went around the room and wrote the required letter into each one of our notebooks. When she came around to me, she printed a large A in the upper left corner of the first page of my notebook, and handed me the crayon.

"I can't," I said, knowing full well that what you do with black crayons is scribble on the wall and get your backass beaten, or color around the edges of pictures, but not write. To write, you needed a pencil. "I can't!" I said, terrified, and started to cry.

"Imagine that, a big girl like you. Such a shame, I'll have to tell your mother that you won't even try. And such a big girl like you!"

And it was true. Although young, I was the biggest child by far in the whole class, a fact that had not escaped the attention of the little boy who sat behind me, and who was already whispering "fatty, fatty!" whenever the teacher's back was turned.

"Now just try, dear. I'm sure you can try to print your A. Mother will be so pleased to see that at least you tried." She patted my stiff braids and turned to the next desk.

Well, of course, she had said the magic words, because I would have walked over rice on my knees to please Mother. I took her nasty old soft smudgy crayon and pretended that it was a nice neat pencil with a fine point, elegantly sharpened that morning outside the bathroom door by my father, with the little penknife that he always carried around in his bathrobe pocket.

I bent my head down close to the desk that smelled like old spittle and rubber erasers, and on that ridiculous yellow paper with those laughably wide spaces I printed my best AUDRE. I had never been too good at keeping between straight lines no matter what their width, so it slanted down across the page something like this: A

        U

          D

            R

              E

The notebooks were short and there was no more room for anything else on that page. So I turned the page over, and wrote again, earnestly and laboriously, biting my lip, L

        O

          R

        D

          E

half-showing off, half-eager to please.

By this time, Miss Teacher had returned to the front of the room.

"Now when you're finished drawing your letter, children," she said, "Just raise your hand high." And her voice smiled a big smile. It is surprising to me that I can still hear her voice but I can't see her face, and I don't know whether she was Black or white. I can remember the way she smelled, but not the color of her hand upon my desk.

Well, when I heard that, my hand flew up in the air, wagging frantically. There was one thing my sisters had warned me about school in great detail: you must never talk in school unless you raised your hand. So I raised my hand, anxious to be recognized. I could imagine what teacher would say to my mother when she came to fetch me home at noon. My mother would know that her warning to me to "be good" had in truth been heeded.

Miss Teacher came down the aisle and stood beside my desk, looking down at my book. All of a sudden the air around her hand beside my notebook grew very still and frightening.

"Well I never!" Her voice was sharp. "I thought I told you to draw this letter? You don't even want to try and do as you are told. Now I want you to turn that page over and draw your letter like everyone . . ." and turning to the next page, she saw my second name sprawled down across the page.

There was a moment of icy silence, and I knew I had done something terribly wrong. But this time, I had no idea what it could be that would get her so angry, certainly not being proud of writing my name.

She broke the silence with a wicked edge to her voice. "I see," she said. "I see we have a young lady who does not want to do as she is told. We will have to tell her mother about that." And the rest of the class snickered, as the teacher tore the page out of my notebook.

"Now I am going to give you one more chance," she said, as she printed another fierce A at the head of the new page. "Now you copy that letter exactly the way it is, and the rest of the class will have to wait for you." She placed the crayon squarely back into my fingers.

By this time I had no idea at all what this lady wanted from me, and so I cried and cried for the rest of the morning until my mother came to fetch me home at noon. I cried on the street while we stopped to pick up my sisters, and for most of the way home, until my mother threatened to box my ears for me if I didn't stop embarrassing her on the street.

That afternoon, after Phyllis and Helen were back in school, and I was helping her dust, I told my mother how they had given me crayons to write with and how the teacher didn't want me to write my name. When my father came home that evening, the two of them went into counsel. It was decided that my mother would speak to the teacher the next morning when she brought me to school, in order to find out what I had done wrong. This decision was passed on to me, ominously, because of course I must have done something wrong to have made Miss Teacher so angry with me.

The next morning at school, the teacher told my mother that she did not think that I was ready yet for kindergarten, because I couldn't follow directions, and I wouldn't do as I was told.

My mother knew very well I could follow directions, because she herself had spent a good deal of effort and arm-power making it very painful for me whenever I did not follow directions. And she also believed that a large part of the function of school was to make me learn how to do what I was told to do. In her private opinion, if this school could not do that, then it was not much of a school and she was going to find a school that could. In other words, my mother had made up her mind that school was where I belonged.

That same morning, she took me off across the street to the catholic school, where she persuaded the nuns to put me into the first grade, since I could read already, and write my name on regular paper with a real pencil. If I sat in the first row I could see the blackboard. My mother also told the nuns that unlike my two sisters, who were models of deportment, I was very unruly, and that they should spank me whenever I needed it. Mother Josepha, the principal, agreed, and I started school.

My first grade teacher was named Sister Mary of Perpetual Help, and she was a disciplinarian of the first order, right after my mother's own heart. A week after I started school she sent a note home to my mother asking her not to dress me in so many layers of clothing because then I couldn't feel the strap on my behind when I was punished.

Sister Mary of Perpetual Help ran the first grade with an iron hand in the shape of a cross. She couldn't have been more than eighteen. She was big, and blond, I think, since we never got to see the nuns' hair in those days. But her eyebrows were blonde, and she was supposed to be totally dedicated, like all the other Sisters of the Blessed Sacrament, to caring for the Colored and Indian children of america. Caring for was not always caring about. And it always felt like Sister MPH hated either teaching or little children.

She had divided up the class into two groups, the Fairies and the Brownies. In this day of heightened sensitivity to racism and color usage, I don't have to tell you which were the good students and which were the baddies. I always wound up in the Brownies, because either I talked too much, or I broke my glasses, or I perpetrated some other awful infraction of the endless rules of good behavior.

But for two glorious times that year, I made it into the Fairies for brief periods of time. One was put into the Brownies if one misbehaved, or couldn't learn to read. I had learned to read already, but I couldn't tell my numbers. Whenever Sister MPH would call a few of us up to the front of the room for our reading lesson, she would say, "All right, children, now turn to page six in your readers," or, "Turn to page nineteen, please, and begin at the top of the page."

Well, I didn't know what page to turn to, and I was ashamed of not being able to read my numbers, so when my turn came to read I couldn't, because I didn't have the right place. After the prompting of a few words, she would go on to the next reader, and soon I wound up in the Brownies.

This was around the second month of school, in October. My new seatmate was Alvin, and he was the worst boy in the whole class. His clothes were dirty and he smelled unwashed, and rumor had it he had once called Sister MPH a bad name, but that couldn't have been possible because he would have been suspended permanently from school.

Alvin used to browbeat me into lending him my pencil to draw endless pictures of airplanes dropping huge penile bombs. He would always promise to give me the pictures when he was finished. But of course, whenever he was finished, he would decide that the picture was too good for a girl, so he would have to keep it, and make me another. Yet I never stopped hoping for one of them, because he drew airplanes very well.

He also would scratch his head and shake out the dandruff onto our joint spelling book or reader, and then tell me the flakes of dandruff were dead lice. I believed him in this, also, and was constantly terrified of catching cooties. But Alvin and I worked out our own system together for reading. He couldn't read, but he knew all his numbers, and I could read words, but I couldn't find the right page.

The Brownies were never called up to the front of the room; we had to read in anonymity from our double seats, where we scrunched over at the edges, ordinarily, to leave room in the middle for our two guardian angels to sit. But whenever we had to share a book our guardian angels had to jump around us and sit on the outside edge of our seats. Therefore, Alvin would show me the right pages to turn to when Sister called them out, and I would whisper the right words to him whenever it came his turn to read. Inside of a week after we devised this scheme of things, we had gotten out of the Brownies together. Since we shared a reader, we always went up together to read with the Fairies, so we had a really good thing going there for a while.

But Alvin began to get sick around Thanksgiving, and was absent a lot, and he didn't come back to school at all after Christmas. I used to miss his dive-bomber pictures, but most of all I missed his page numbers. After a few times of being called up by myself and not being able to read, I landed back in the Brownies again.

Years later I found out that Alvin had died of tuberculosis over Christmas, and that was why we all had been X-rayed in the auditorium after Mass on the first day back to school from Christmas vacation.

I spent a few more weeks in the Brownies with my mouth almost shut during reading lesson, unless the day's story fell on page eight, or ten, or twenty, which were the three numbers I knew.

Then, over one weekend, we had our first writing assignment. We were to look in our parents' newspaper and cut out words we knew the meaning of, and make them into simple sentences. We could only use one "the." It felt like an easy task, since I was already reading the comics by this time.

On Sunday morning after church, when I usually did my homework, I noticed an ad for White Rose Salada Tea on the back of the *New York Times Magazine* which my father was reading at the time. It had the most gorgeous white rose on a red background, and I decided I must have that rose for my picture—our sentences were to be illustrated. I searched through the paper until I found an "I," and then a "like," which I dutifully clipped out along with my rose, and the words "White," "Rose," "Salada," and "Tea." I knew the brand-name well because it was my mother's favorite tea.

On Monday morning, we all stood our sentence papers up on the chalk-channels, leaning them against the blackboards. And there among the twenty odd "The boy ran," "it was cold," was "I like White Rose Salada Tea" and my beautiful white rose on a red background.

That was too much coming from a Brownie. Sister Mary of PH frowned.

"This was to be our own work, children," she said. "Who helped you with your sentence, Audre?" I told her I had done it alone.

"Our guardian angels weep when we don't tell the truth, Audre. I want a note from your mother tomorrow telling me that you are sorry for lying to the baby Jesus."

I told the story at home, and the next day I brought a note from my father saying that the sentence had indeed been my own work. Triumphantly, I gathered up my books and moved back over to the Fairies.

The thing that I remember best about being in the first grade was how uncomfortable it was, always having to leave room for my guardian angel on those tiny seats, and moving back and forth across the room from Brownies to Fairies and back again.

This time I stayed in the Fairies for a long time, because I finally started to recognize my numbers. I stayed there until the day I broke my glasses. I had taken them off to clean them in the bathroom and they slipped out of my hand. I was never to do that, and so I was in disgrace. My eyeglasses came from the eye clinic of the medical center, and it took three days to get a new pair made. We could not afford to buy more than one pair at a time, nor did it occur to my parents that such an extravagance might be necessary. I was almost sightless without them, but my punishment for having broken them was that I had to go to school anyway, even though I could see nothing. My sisters delivered me to my classroom with a note from my mother saying I had broken my glasses despite the fact they were tied to me by the strip of elastic.

I was never supposed to take my glasses off except just before getting into bed, but I was endlessly curious about these magical circles of glass that were rapidly becoming a part of me, transforming my universe, and remaining movable. I was always trying to examine them with my naked, nearsighted eyes, usually dropping them in the process.

Since I could not see at all to do any work from the blackboard, Sister Mary of PH made me sit in the back of the room on the window seat with a dunce cap on. She had the rest of the class offer up a prayer for my poor mother who had such a naughty girl who broke her glasses and caused her parents such needless extra expense to replace them. She also had them offer up a special prayer for me to stop being such a wicked-hearted child.

I amused myself by counting the rainbows of color that danced like a halo around the lamp on Sister Mary of PH's desk, watching the starburst patterns of light that the incandescent light bulb became without my glasses. But I missed them, and not being able to see. I never once gave a thought to the days when I believed that bulbs were starburst patterns of color, because that was what all light looked like to me.

It must have been close to summer by this time. As I sat with the dunce cap on, I can remember the sun pouring through the classroom window hot upon my back, as the rest of the class dutifully entoned their Hail Marys for my soul, and I played secret games with the distorted rainbows of light, until Sister noticed and made me stop blinking my eyes so fast.

QUESTIONS FOR DISCUSSION AND WRITING

1. Lorde's portrait of her early school experiences is a disturbing one that highlights her difficulties as a large-sized black child with a visual impairment who desperately seeks her mother's approval. But we also get a picture of two classrooms—one public and one parochial. How would you characterize the overall picture of her early education? What is her attitude about her schooling from the perch of time as an adult remembering her childhood?

2. Lorde writes that her first "rude awakening" about school was that "ability had nothing to do with expectation." What exactly does she mean by this? What does the fact that she already knows how to read and how to write her name have to do with the assertion?

3. The kindergarten teacher (Miss Teacher) Lorde writes about appears to be concerned in the extreme with children following her directives as stated,

doing as they are told, and conforming. Is that too harsh a picture of primary education, or does it seem to you an accurate portrayal of what often goes on? What about the consequences of so much importance placed by a teacher on students following directions, even at the cost of the teacher being blind to the student's needs and abilities?

4. The Catholic school teacher (Sister Mary of Perpetual Help) accuses Lorde of turning in work that is not her own and, later on in the narrative, makes her sit in the back of the classroom with a dunce cap. She divides the children into Fairies and Brownies, a good versus bad classroom tracking. Also, she clearly favors (as does Lorde's mother) the use of corporal punishment. What would you conclude might be the net effects of such negative tactics on a child? What is Lorde communicating to us?

5. Alvin, Lorde's classmate who makes pictures of penile bomb dropping airplanes, fails to keep his promise of giving her one of his pictures. In fact, he tells her they are "too good for a girl." Another boy in Lorde's kindergarten ridicules her because of her weight. Lorde was both a feminist and a lesbian. What do you think she wants to tell us in these instances from those perspectives? What is she suggesting about the nature of gender differences in classrooms?

ON TECHNIQUE AND STYLE

1. Focus on the tone and use of language in this excerpt from Lorde's autobiography. How do Lorde's tone and diction differ from Angelou's selection later in this chapter? Who seems closer to the material she is writing about and who makes the narrative more immediate and experiential to us as readers? How is this done?

2. Lorde identifies herself as being black and from a heritage outside the United States (Grenada) as well as being heavy and visually impaired and relatively poor. How do all of these identifying characteristics provide us with a picture of her and how do they ultimately affect us as readers?

3. Lorde uses many illustrations to enhance the overall picture of her early schooling. How effective are the examples she draws? Would she have been better served in her overall presentation if she had not used only negative examples of classroom experiences?

CULTURAL QUESTION

1. How significant is color in this excerpt of Lorde's, the fact that these are black children being schooled? Lorde tells us that the big, blonde Catholic school teacher claims to care about the "colored and Indian children of america" but then adds, "Caring for was not always caring about." Of Miss Teacher, the kindergarten teacher who is so insistent on Lorde's using a crayon and

a music book and printing an *A*, she tells us she cannot recall if that teacher was black or white. How important is race in this piece?

From Teaching as a Subversive Activity

Neil Postman and Charles Weingartner

Neil Postman (1931–2003) and **Charles Weingartner** *are the coauthors of* Teaching as a Subversive Activity, *which was published in 1969. Both were prominent New York educators and authors and Postman was a prominent media and cultural critic. The book they coauthored in 1969 was a manifesto on reforming education and making it more relevant and student centered. Based on the work of Marshall McLuhan ("the media is the message") and the central importance of what became known as "the inquiry method of teaching," the ideas in* Teaching as a Subversive Activity *are based on students asking questions rather than receiving answers, the notion being that questions are more important than answers and that it matters not how hard or impossible it might be to find answers so long as questions are being raised.*

The excerpt from Teaching as a Subversive Activity *is a list of proposals the authors offer that would change and reform the school environment. Some of these may seem "far out," but they are geared to inspire a more creative and less learn-by-rote method of teaching, a subversive style of pedagogy.*

And so we will now put before you a list of proposals that attempt to change radically the nature of the existing school environment. Most of them will strike you as thoroughly impractical but only because you will have forgotten for the moment that the present system is among the most impractical imaginable, if the facilitation of learning is your aim. There is yet another reaction you might have to our proposals. You might concede that they are "impractical" and yet feel that each one contains an idea or two that might be translated into "practical" form. If you do, we will be delighted. But as for us, none of our proposals seems impractical or bizarre. They seem, in fact, quite conservative, given the enormity of the problem they are intended to resolve. As you read them, imagine that you are a member of a board of education, or a principal, or supervisor, or some such person who might have the wish and power to lay the groundwork for a new education.

1. *Declare a five-year moratorium on the use of all textbooks.*
Since with two or three exceptions all texts are not only boring but based on the assumption that knowledge exists prior to, independent of, and altogether outside of the learner, they are either worthless or harmful. If it is impossible

to function without textbooks, provide every student with a notebook filled with blank pages, and have him compose his own text.

2.   *Have "English" teachers "teach" Math, Math teachers English, Social Studies teachers Science, Science teachers Art, and so on.*

One of the largest obstacles to the establishment of a sound learning environment is the desire of teachers to get something they think they know into the heads of people who don't know it. An English teacher teaching Math would hardly be in a position to fulfill this desire. Even more important, he would be forced to perceive the "subject" as a learner, not a teacher. If this suggestion is too impractical, try numbers 3 and 4.

3.   *Transfer all the elementary-school teachers to high school and vice versa.*

4.   *Require every teacher who thinks he knows his "subject" well to write a book on it.*

In this way, he will be relieved of the necessity of inflicting *his* knowledge on other people, particularly his students.

5.   *Dissolve all "subjects," "courses," and especially "course requirements."*

This proposal, all by itself, would wreck every existing educational bureaucracy. The result would be to deprive teachers of the excuses presently given for their failures and to free them to concentrate on their learners.

6.   *Limit each teacher to three declarative sentences per class, and 15 interrogatives.*

Every sentence above the limit would be subject to a 25-cent fine. The students can do the counting and the collecting.

7.   *Prohibit teachers from asking any questions they already know the answers to.*

This proposal would not only force teachers to perceive learning from the learner's perspective, it would help them to learn how to ask questions that produce knowledge.

8.   *Declare a moratorium on all tests and grades.*

This would remove from the hands of teachers their major weapons of coercion and would eliminate two of the major obstacles to their students' learning anything significant.

9.   *Require all teachers to undergo some form of psychotherapy as part of their in-service training.*

This need not be psychoanalysis; some form of group therapy or psychological counseling will do. Its purpose: to give teachers an opportunity to gain insight into themselves, particularly into the reasons they are teachers.

10. *Classify teachers according to their ability and make the lists public.*

There would be a "smart" group (the Bluebirds), an "average" group (the Robins), and a "dumb" group (the Sandpipers). The lists would be published each year in the community paper. The I.Q. and reading scores of teachers would also be published, as well as the list of those who are "advantaged" and "disadvantaged" by virtue of what they know in relation to what their students know.

11. *Require all teachers to take a test prepared by students on what the students know.*

Only if a teacher passes this test should he be permitted to "teach." This test could be used for "grouping" the teachers as in number 10 above.

12. *Make every class an elective and withhold a teacher's monthly check if his students do not show any interest in going to next month's classes.*

This proposal would simply put the teacher on a par with other professionals, e.g., doctors, dentists, lawyers, etc. No one forces you to go to a particular doctor unless you are a "clinic case." In that instance, you must take what you are given. Our present system makes a "clinic case" of every student. Bureaucrats decide who shall govern your education. In this proposal, we are restoring the American philosophy: no clients, no money; lots of clients, lots of money.

13. *Require every teacher to take a one-year leave of absence every fourth year to work in some "field" other than education.*

Such an experience can be taken as evidence, albeit shaky, that the teacher has been in contact with reality at some point in his life. Recommended occupations: bartender, cab driver, garment worker, waiter. One of the common sources of difficulty with teachers can be found in the fact that most of them simply move from one side of the desk (as students) to the other side (as "teachers") and they have not had much contact with the way things are outside of school rooms.

14. *Require each teacher to provide some sort of evidence that he or she has had a loving relationship with at least one other human being.*

If the teacher can get someone to say, "I love her (or him)," she should be retained. If she can get two people to say it, she should get a raise. Spouses need not be excluded from testifying.

15. *Require that all the graffiti accumulated in the school toilets be reproduced on large paper and be hung in the school halls.*

Graffiti that concern teachers and administrators should be chiseled into the stone at the front entrance of the school.

16. *There should be a general prohibition against the use of the following words and phrases:* teach, syllabus, covering ground, I.Q., makeup, test, disadvantaged, gifted, accelerated, enhancement, course, grade, score, human nature, dumb, college material, and administrative necessity.

QUESTIONS FOR DISCUSSION AND WRITING

1. The authors tell us their proposals for radically changing the school environment are really conservative. As you read through the proposals, do they seem conservative to you? What might the response to them be from a member of a board of education or from a principal or supervisor?
2. What is the nature of what the authors would like to take place? What do their proposals reveal to us about their attitudes toward the kind of

education they believe young people are getting versus the kind of education they could receive?

3. The excerpt is from a book about learning how to teach subversively, meaning to undermine or overthrow what is already established. What is your sense of the importance or the need for subversive teaching, for subverting the status quo?

4. Some of the proposals the authors make seem outrageous, such as classifying some teachers into a dumb group and publishing teacher IQs, or requiring teachers to prove they have had a loving relationship. How seriously are we to take the authors' proposals? Are they intentionally trying to be outrageous and to shock us? To subvert? Or is there underlying seriousness to such proposals?

5. How might implementing some of the proposals suggested in this excerpt affect education?

ON TECHNIQUE AND STYLE

1. In this excerpt there is intention to persuade us of the necessity for change based on the system of learning being impractical. Do you feel, by their offering us a set of proposals "to lay the groundwork for a new education," the authors persuade us of the practicality and the necessity of moving from an old style of teaching to a new one, one that is obviously more relevant, more creative, and student rather than teacher centered?

2. Which of the proposals offered by the authors strike you as most worthwhile? Which least worthwhile? What is the effect on us as readers of the ways the authors list and classify their choices for "a new education"?

3. We so often hear the argument that teachers deserve better pay and more appreciation and respect for the work they do, especially teachers who are dedicated and inspiring. How does the view we get of teachers in this excerpt from Postman and Weingartner's book counter the one that emphasizes elevating the importance of teachers? Do the authors demean the profession of classroom teaching, or are they simply trying to create a different view of the profession?

CULTURAL QUESTION

1. Surely, as the authors argue, a more creative and less bureaucratic method of teaching students is more desirable. But how much of the authors' proposed loosening up of education ultimately seems a luxury for students who are from privileged or from all-white backgrounds than for students, say, of the inner city or the barrio? Are the kinds of proposals they offer for all kinds of students or for a limited few?

The Graduation*

Maya Angelou

Maya Angelou (1928–   ) was born Marguerite Johnson in St. Louis and grew up there and in Stamps, Arkansas. Best known for her autobiographical works and her poetry, she is also a songwriter, dancer, actor, and the first black woman Hollywood director. A college professor and long-time civil rights activist, she has also been an editor for papers in Egypt and Ghana and was a member of the Bicentennial Commission (appointed by President Gerald Ford) and the Commission for International Women (appointed by President Jimmy Carter). In 1993 she wrote and read a poem, "On the Pulse of the Morning," at the inauguration of President Bill Clinton.

I Know Why the Caged Bird Sings *(1970) is the first volume of a number of auto-biographical volumes that include* Gather Together in My Name, Singin' and Swingin' and Getting' Merry Like Christmas, The Heart of a Woman, *and* All God's Children Need Traveling Shoes. *The excerpt included here from* Caged Bird, *"The Graduation," captures the excitement and thrill of graduation day for young Maya and those in her small black community of Stamps—until a speaker from the world of the white establishment delivers a speech that casts a temporary shadow over the education she and the other black children worked so hard to achieve.*

The children in Stamps trembled visibly with anticipation. Some adults were excited too, but to be certain the whole young population had come down with graduation epidemic. Large classes were graduating from both the grammar school and the high school. Even those who were years removed from their own day of glorious release were anxious to help with preparations as a kind of dry run. The junior students who were moving into the vacating classes' chairs were tradition-bound to show their talents for leadership and management. They strutted through the school and around the campus exerting pressure on the lower grades. Their authority was so new that occasionally if they pressed a little too hard it had to be overlooked. After all, next term was coming, and it never hurt a sixth grader to have a play sister in the eighth grade, or a tenth-year student to be able to call a twelfth grader Bubba. So all was endured in a spirit of shared understanding. But the graduating classes themselves were the nobility. Like travelers with exotic destinations on their minds, the graduates were remarkably forgetful. They came to school without their books, or tablets or even pencils. Volunteers fell over themselves to secure replacements for the missing equipment. When accepted, the willing workers might or might not be

*This title does not appear in the original Random House, Inc. edition.

thanked, and it was of no importance to the pregraduation rites. Even teachers were respectful of the now quiet and aging seniors, and tended to speak to
them, if not as equals, as beings only slightly lower than themselves. After tests
were returned and grades given, the student body, which acted like an extended
family, knew who did well, who excelled, and what piteous ones had failed.

Unlike the white high school, Lafayette County Training School distinguished itself by having neither lawn, nor hedges, nor tennis court, nor
climbing ivy. Its two buildings (main classrooms, the grade school and home
economics) were set on a dirt hill with no fence to limit either its boundaries or
those of bordering farms. There was a large expanse to the left of the school
which was used alternately as a baseball diamond or a basketball court.
Rusty hoops on the swaying poles represented the permanent recreational
equipment, although bats and balls could be borrowed from the P. E. teacher
if the borrower was qualified and if the diamond wasn't occupied.

Over this rocky area relieved by a few shady tall persimmon trees the
graduating class walked. The girls often held hands and no longer bothered to speak to the lower students. There was a sadness about them, as if
this old world was not their home and they were bound for higher ground.
The boys, on the other hand, had become more friendly, more outgoing. A
decided change from the closed attitude they projected while studying for
finals. Now they seemed not ready to give up the old school, the familiar
paths and classrooms. Only a small percentage would be continuing on to
college—one of the South's A & M (agricultural and mechanical) schools,
which trained Negro youths to be carpenters, farmers, handymen, masons,
maids, cooks and baby nurses. Their future rode heavily on their shoulders,
and blinded them to the collective joy that had pervaded the lives of the boys
and girls in the grammar school graduating class.

Parents who could afford it had ordered new shoes and ready-made
clothes for themselves from Sears and Roebuck or Montgomery Ward. They
also engaged the best seamstresses to make the floating graduating dresses
and to cut down secondhand pants which would be pressed to a military
slickness for the important event.

Oh, it was important, all right. Whitefolks would attend the ceremony, and
two or three would speak of God and home, and the Southern way of life, and
Mrs. Parsons, the principal's, wife, would play the graduation march while the
lower-grade graduates paraded down the aisles and took their seats below
the platform. The high school seniors would wait in empty classrooms to
make their dramatic entrance.

In the Store I was the person of the moment. The birthday girl. The center.
Bailey had graduated the year before, although to do so he had had to forfeit
all pleasures to make up for his time lost in Baton Rouge.

My class was wearing butter-yellow piqué dresses, and Momma
launched out on mine. She smocked the yoke into tiny crisscrossing puck-
ers, then shirred the rest of the bodice. Her dark fingers ducked in and out of
the lemony cloth as she embroidered raised daisies around the hem. Before

she considered herself finished she had added a crocheted cuff on the puff sleeves, and a pointy crocheted collar.

I was going to be lovely. A walking model of all the various styles of fine hand sewing and it didn't worry me that I was only twelve years old and merely graduating from the eighth grade. Besides, many teachers in Arkansas Negro schools had only that diploma and were licensed to impart wisdom.

The days had become longer and more noticeable. The faded beige of former times had been replaced with strong and sure colors. I began to see my classmates' clothes, their skin tones, and the dust that waved off pussy willows. Clouds that lazed across the sky were objects of great concern to me. Their shiftier shapes might have held a message that in my new happiness and with a little bit of time I'd soon decipher. During that period I looked at the arch of heaven so religiously my neck kept a steady ache. I had taken to smiling more often, and my jaws hurt from the unaccustomed activity. Between the two physical sore spots, I suppose I could have been uncomfortable, but that was not the case. As a member of the winning team (the graduating class of 1940) I had outdistanced unpleasant sensations by miles. I was headed for the freedom of open fields.

Youth and social approval allied themselves with me and we trammeled memories of slights and insults. The wind of our swift passage remodeled my features. Lost tears were pounded to mud and then to dust. Years of withdrawal were brushed aside and left behind, as hanging ropes of parasitic moss.

My work alone had awarded me a top place and I was going to be one of the first called in the graduating ceremonies. On the classroom blackboard, as well as on the bulletin board in the auditorium, there were blue stars and white stars and red stars. No absences, no tardinesses, and my academic work was among the best of the year. I could say the preamble to the Constitution even faster than Bailey. We timed ourselves often: "Wethepeopleofthe UnitedStatesinordertoformamoreperfectunion . . ." I had memorized the Presidents of the United States from Washington to Roosevelt in chronological as well as alphabetical order.

My hair pleased me too. Gradually the black mass had lengthened and thickened, so that it kept at last to its braided pattern, and I didn't have to yank my scalp off when I tried to comb it.

Louise and I had rehearsed the exercises until we tired out ourselves. Henry Reed was class valedictorian. He was a small, very black boy with hooded eyes, and long, broad nose and an oddly shaped head. I had admired him for years because each term he and I vied for the best grades in our class. Most often he bested me, but instead of being disappointed I was pleased that we shared top places between us. Like many Southern Black children, he lived with his grandmother, who was as strict as Momma and as kind as she knew how to be. He was courteous, respectful and soft-spoken to elders, but on the playground he chose to play the roughest games. I admired him. Anyone, I reckoned, sufficiently afraid or sufficiently dull could be polite. But to be able to operate at a top level with both adults and children was admirable.

His valedictory speech was entitled "To Be or Not to Be." The rigid tenth-grade teacher had helped him write it. He'd been working on the dramatic stresses for months.

The weeks until graduation were filled with heady activities. A group of small children were to be presented in a play about buttercups and daisies and bunny rabbits. They could be heard throughout the building practicing their hops and their little songs that sounded like silver bells. The older girls (nongraduates, of course) were assigned the task of making refreshments for the night's festivities. A tangy scent of ginger, cinnamon, nutmeg and chocolate wafted around the home economics building as the budding cooks made samples for themselves and their teachers.

In every corner of the workshop, axes and saws split fresh timber as the woodshop boys made sets and stage scenery. Only the graduates were left out of the general bustle. We were free to sit in the library at the back of the building or look in quite detachedly, naturally, on the measures being taken for our event.

Even the minister preached on graduation the Sunday before. His subject was, "Let your light so shine that men will see your good works and praise your Father, Who is in Heaven." Although the sermon was purported to be addressed to us, he used the occasion to speak to backsliders, gamblers and general ne'er-do-wells. But since he had called our names at the beginning of the service we were mollified.

Among Negroes the tradition was to give presents to children going only from one grade to another. How much more important this was when the person was graduating at the top of the class. Uncle Willie and Momma had sent away for a Mickey Mouse watch like Bailey's. Louise gave me four embroidered handkerchiefs. (I gave her three crocheted doilies.) Mrs. Sneed, the minister's wife, made me an underskirt to wear for graduation, and nearly every customer gave me a nickel or maybe even a dime with the instruction "Keep on moving to higher ground," or some such encouragement.

Amazingly the great day finally dawned and I was out of bed before I knew it. I threw open the back door to see it more clearly, but Momma said, "Sister, come away from that door and put your robe on."

I hoped the memory of that morning would never leave me. Sunlight was itself still young, and the day had none of the insistence maturity would bring it in a few hours. In my robe and barefoot in the backyard, under cover of going to see about my new beans, I gave myself up to the gentle warmth and thanked God that no matter what evil I had done in my life He had allowed me to live to see this day. Somewhere in my fatalism I had expected to die, accidentally, and never have the chance to walk up the stairs in the auditorium and gracefully receive my hard-earned diploma. Out of God's merciful bosom I had won reprieve.

Bailey came out in his robe and gave me a box wrapped in Christmas paper. He said he had saved his money for months to pay for it. It felt like a box of chocolates, but I knew Bailey wouldn't save money to buy candy when we had all we could want under our noses.

He was as proud of the gift as I. It was a soft-leather-bound copy of a collection of poems by Edgar Allan Poe, or, as Bailey and I called him, "Eap." I turned to "Annabel Lee" and we walked up and down the garden rows, the cool dirt between our toes, reciting the beautifully sad lines.

Momma made a Sunday breakfast although it was only Friday. After we finished the blessing, I opened my eyes to find the watch on my plate. It was a dream of a day. Everything went smoothly and to my credit. I didn't have to be reminded or scolded for anything. Near evening I was too jittery to attend to chores, so Bailey volunteered to do all before his bath.

Days before, we had made a sign for the Store, and as we turned out the lights Momma hung the cardboard over the doorknob. It read clearly: CLOSED. GRADUATION.

My dress fitted perfectly and everyone said that I looked like a sunbeam in it. On the hill, going toward the school, Bailey walked behind with Uncle Willie, who muttered, "Go on, Ju." He wanted him to walk ahead with us because it embarrassed him to have to walk so slowly. Bailey said he'd let the ladies walk together, and the men would bring up the rear. We all laughed, nicely.

Little children dashed by out of the dark like fireflies. Their crepe-paper dresses and butterfly wings were not made for running and we heard more than one rip, dryly, and the regretful "uh uh" that followed.

The school blazed without gaiety. The windows seemed cold and unfriendly from the lower hill. A sense of ill-fated timing crept over me, and if Momma hadn't reached for my hand I would have drifted back to Bailey and Uncle Willie, and possibly beyond. She made a few slow jokes about my feet getting cold, and tugged me along to the now-strange building.

Around the front steps, assurance came back. There were my fellow "greats," the graduating class. Hair brushed back, legs oiled, new dresses and pressed pleats, fresh pocket handkerchiefs and little handbags, all home-sewn. Oh, we were up to snuff, all right. I joined my comrades and didn't even see my family go in to find seats in the crowded auditorium.

The school band struck up a march and all classes filed in as had been rehearsed. We stood in front of our seats, as assigned, and on a signal from the choir director, we sat. No sooner had this been accomplished than the band started to play the national anthem. We rose again and sang the song, after which we recited the pledge of allegiance. We remained standing for a brief minute before the choir director and the principal signaled to us, rather desperately I thought, to take our seats. The command was so unusual that our carefully rehearsed and smooth-running machine was thrown off. For a full minute we fumbled for our chairs and bumped into each other awkwardly. Habits change or solidify under pressure, so in our state of nervous tension we had been ready to follow our usual assembly pattern: the American national anthem, then the pledge of allegiance, then the song every Black person I knew called the Negro National Anthem. All done in the same key, with the same passion and most often standing on the same foot.

Finding my seat at least, I was overcome with a presentiment of worse things to come. Something unrehearsed, unplanned, was going to happen, and we were going to be made to look bad. I distinctly remember being explicit in the choice of pronoun. It was "we," the graduating class, the unit, that concerned me then.

The principal welcomed "parents and friends" and asked the Baptist minister to lead us in prayer. His invocation was brief and punchy, and for a second I thought we were getting back on the high road to right action. When the principal came back to the dais, however, his voice had changed. Sounds always affected me profoundly and the principal's voice was one of my favorites. During assembly it melted and lowed weakly into the audience. It had not been in my plan to listen to him, but my curiosity was piqued and I straightened up to give him my attention.

He was talking about Booker T. Washington, our "late great leader," who said we can be as close as the fingers on the hand, etc. . . . Then he said a few vague things about friendship and the friendship of kindly people to those less fortunate than themselves. With that his voice nearly faded, thin, away. Like a river diminishing to a stream and then to a trickle. But he cleared his throat and said, "Our speaker tonight, who is also our friend, came from Texarkana to deliver the commencement address, but due to the irregularity of the train schedule, he's going to, as they say, 'speak and run.' " He said that we understood and wanted the man to know that we were most grateful for the time he was able to give us and then something about how we were willing always to adjust to another's program, and without more ado—"I give you Mr. Edward Donleavy."

Not one but two white men came through the door offstage. The shorter one walked to the speaker's platform, and the tall one moved over to the center seat and sat down. But that was our principal's seat, and already occupied. The dislodged gentleman bounced around for a long breath or two before the Baptist minister gave him his chair, then with more dignity than the situation deserved, the minister walked off the stage.

Donleavy looked at the audience once (on reflection, I'm sure that he wanted only to reassure himself that we were really there), adjusted his glasses and began to read from a sheaf of papers.

He was glad "to be here and to see the work going on just as it was in the other schools."

At the first "Amen" from the audience I willed the offender to immediate death by choking on the word. But Amens and Yes, sir's began to fall around the room like rain through a ragged umbrella.

He told us of the wonderful changes we children in Stamps had in store. The Central School (naturally, the white school was Central) had already been granted improvements that would be in use in the fall. A well-known artist was coming from Little Rock to teach art to them. They were going to have the newest microscopes and chemistry equipment for their laboratory. Mr. Donleavy didn't leave us long in the dark over who made these improvements available to Central High. Nor were we to be ignored in the general betterment scheme he had in mind.

He said that he had pointed out to people at a very high level that one of the first-line football tacklers at Arkansas Agricultural and Mechanical College had graduated from good old Lafayette County Training School. Here fewer Amen's were heard. Those few that did break through lay dully in the air with the heaviness of habit.

He went on to praise us. He went on to say how he had bragged that "one of the best basketball players at Fisk sank his first ball right here at Lafayette County Training School."

The white kids were going to have a chance to become Galileos and Madame Curies and Edisons and Gauguins, and our boys (the girls weren't even in on it) would try to be Jesse Owenses and Joe Louises.

Owens and the Brown Bomber were great heroes in our world, but what school official in the white-goddom of Little Rock had the right to decide that those two men must be our only heroes? Who decided that for Henry Reed to become a scientist he had to work like George Washington Carver, as a bootblack, to buy a lousy microscope? Bailey was obviously always going to be too small to be an athlete, so which concrete angel glued to what country seat had decided that if my brother wanted to become a lawyer he had to first pay penance for his skin by picking cotton and hoeing corn and studying correspondence books at night for twenty years?

The man's dead words fell like bricks around the auditorium and too many settled in my belly. Constrained by hard-learned manners I couldn't look behind me, but to my left and right the proud graduating class of 1940 had dropped their heads. Every girl in my row had found something new to do with her handkerchief. Some folded the tiny squares into love knots, some into traingles, but most were wadding them, then pressing them flat on their yellow laps.

On the dais, the ancient tragedy was being replayed. Professor Parsons sat, a sculptor's reject, rigid. His large, heavy body seemed devoid of will or willingness, and his eyes said he was no longer with us. The other teachers examined the flag (which was draped stage right) or their notes, or the windows which opened on our now-famous playing diamond.

Graduation, the hush-hush magic time of frills and gifts and congratulations and diplomas, was finished for me before my name was called. The accomplishment was nothing. The meticulous maps, drawn in three colors of ink, learning and spelling decasyllabic words, memorizing the whole of *The Rape of Lucrece*—it was for nothing. Donleavy had exposed us.

We were maids and farmers, handymen and washerwomen, and anything higher that we aspired to was farcical and presumptuous.

Then I wished that Gabriel Prosser and Nat Turner had killed all whitefolks in their beds and that Abraham Lincoln had been assassinated before the signing of the Emancipation Proclamation, and that Harriet Tubman had been killed by that blow on her head and Christopher Columbus had drowned in the *Santa María.*

It was awful to be Negro and have no control over my life. It was brutal to be young and already trained to sit quietly and listen to charges brought against my color with no chance of defense. We should all be dead. I thought I should like to see us all dead, one on top of the other. A pyramid of flesh with the whitefolks on the bottom, as the broad base, then the Indians with their silly tomahawks and teepees and wigwams and treaties, the Negroes with their mops and recipes and cotton sacks and spirituals sticking out of their mouths. The Dutch children should all stumble in their wooden shoes and break their necks. The French should choke to death on the Louisiana Purchase (1803) while silk worms ate all the Chinese with their stupid pigtails. As a species, we were an abomination. All of us.

Donleavy was running for election, and assured our parents that if he won we could count on having the only colored paved playing field in that part of Arkansas. Also—he never looked up to acknowledge the grunts of acceptance—also, we were bound to get some new equipment for the home economics building and the workshop.

He finished, and since there was no need to give any more than the most perfunctory thank-you's, he nodded to the men on the stage and the tall white man who was never introduced joined him at the door. They left with the attitude that now they were off to something really important. (The graduation ceremonies at Lafayette County Training School had been a mere preliminary.)

The ugliness they left was palpable. An uninvited guest who wouldn't leave. The choir was summoned and sang a modern arrangement of "Onward, Christian Soldiers," with new words pertaining to graduates seeking their place in the world. But it didn't work. Elouise, the daughter of the Baptist minister, recited "Invictus," and I could have cried at the impertinence of "I am the master of my fate, I am the captain of my soul."

My name had lost its ring of familiarity and I had to be nudged to go and receive my diploma. All my preparations had fled. I neither marched up to the stage like a conquering Amazon, nor did I look in the audience for Bailey's nod of approval. Marguerite Johnson, I heard the name again, my honors were read, there were noises in the audience of appreciation, and I took my place on the stage as rehearsed.

I thought about colors I hated: ecru, puce, lavender, beige and black.

There was shuffling and rustling around me, then Henry Reed was giving his valedictory address, "To Be or Not to Be." Hadn't he heard the whitefolks? We couldn't *be,* so the question was a waste of time. Henry's voice came out clear and strong. I feared to look at him. Hadn't he got the message? There was no "nobler in the mind" for Negroes because the world didn't think we had minds, and they let us know it. "Outrageous fortune"? Now, that was a joke. When the ceremony was over I had to tell Henry Reed some things. That is, if I still cared. Not "rub," Henry, "erase." "Ah, there's the erase." Us.

Henry had been a good student in elocution. His voice rose on tides of promise and fell on waves of warnings. The English teacher had helped him to create a sermon winging through Hamlet's soliloquy. To be a man, a doer, a builder, a leader, or to be a tool, an unfunny joke, a crusher of funky toadstools. I marveled that Henry could go through with the speech as if we had a choice.

I had been listening and silently rebutting each sentence with my eyes closed; then there was a hush, which in an audience warns that something unplanned is happening. I looked up and saw Henry Reed, the conservative, the proper, the A student, turn his back to the audience and turn to us (the proud graduating class of 1940) and sing, nearly speaking,

"Life ev'ry voice and sing
Till earth and heaven ring
Ring with the harmonies of Liberty . . ."[1]

It was the poem written by James Weldon Johnson. It was the music composed by J. Rosamond Johnson. It was the Negro national anthem. Out of habit we were singing it.

Our mothers and fathers stood in the dark hall and joined the hymn of encouragement. A kindergarten teacher led the small children onto the stage and the buttercups and daisies and bunny rabbits marked time and tried to follow:

"Stony the road we trod
Bitter the chastening rod
Felt in the days when hope, unborn, had died.
Yet with a steady beat
Have not our weary feet
Come to the place for which our fathers sighed?"

Every child I knew had learned that song with his ABC's and along with "Jesus Loves Me This I know." But I personally had never heard it before. Never heard the words, despite the thousands of times I had sung them. Never thought they had anything to do with me.

On the other hand, the words of Patrick Henry had made such an impression on me that I had been able to stretch myself tall and trembling and say, "I know not what course others may take, but as for me, give me liberty or give me death."

And now I heard, really for the first time:

"We have come over a way that with tears
has been watered,
We have come, treading our path through
the blood of the slaughtered."

While echoes of the song shivered in the air, Henry Reed bowed his head, said "Thank you," and returned to his place in the line. The tears that slipped down many faces were not wiped away in shame.

We were on top again. As always, again. We survived. The depths had been icy and dark, but now a bright sun spoke to our souls. I was no longer

[1] "Lift Ev'ry Voice and Sing"—words by James Weldon Johnson and music by J. Rosamond Johnson. Copyright by Edward B. Marks Music Corporation. Used by permission.

simply a member of the proud graduating class of 1940; I was a proud member of the wonderful, beautiful Negro race.

Oh, Black known and unknown poets, how often have your auctioned pains sustained us? Who will compute the lonely nights made less lonely by your songs, or by the empty pots made less tragic by your tales?

If we were a people much given to revealing secrets, we might raise monuments and sacrifice to the memories of our poets, but slavery cured us of that weakness. It may be enough, however, to have it said that we survive in exact relationship to the dedication of our poets (include preachers, musicians and blues singers).

QUESTIONS FOR DISCUSSION AND WRITING

1. Describe the initial picture Maya Angelou (Marguerite Johnson) provides as well as the mood of the black people in Stamps in 1940 as graduation day arrives. What does the celebratory sense of this "great day" and the view of the graduates as being "nobility" reveal about the attitudes in this black community toward getting an education and graduating from school?

2. Maya's brother Bailey gives her a collection of Edgar Allan Poe's poetry. She and Bailey take pride in memorizing the preamble of the Constitution and Maya in the high quality of her academic work and of having no absences or tardiness. How do this sister and brother personally feel about their education?

3. Why does the appearance of the white political candidate Donleavy cast a shadow over the entire graduation ceremony? Why does his speech incense Angelou and fill her with hatred and futility and make her feel as if the ceremony has been turned into "ugliness"?

4. Describe what occurs once Henry Reed, the class valedictorian, sings the words of the poet James Weldon Johnson, which are the words of the Negro National Anthem. Why do things suddenly shift so dramatically to spirit and hope?

5. By the end of her piece on graduation Angelou tells us how the words of poets like Johnson have taken on real personal meaning for her; she ends the chapter with praise to "Black known and unknown poets." What has the graduation experience taught her about the value of words? Could such a lesson have been learned in school?

ON TECHNIQUE AND STYLE

1. There are major shifts that occur in this selection by Angelou—from elation to depression and ultimately to hope and pride. Do they occur with enough narrative detail and a completely credible kind of pacing? Are there enough details in each of the shifts that occur?

2. Do you think Angelou really felt the kind of anger and despair that she reveals to us on her hearing the speaker's disappointing statements about the expectations white society has for black people and their individual futures? If she seems to be exaggerating her reactions from the perch of time, what effect does that have on us as readers?

3. Some have criticized Angelou's writing style. A critic named Francine Prose, for example, set forth an argument that Angelou is a bad writer and her work should not be taught in classrooms throughout the country. How do you feel Angelou succeeds or fails as a stylist? Is her writing a good or a poor example for students to learn from?

CULTURAL QUESTION

1. Angelou's world of education is a black and white one centered in Arkansas in 1940 before the Civil Rights movement led to school integration. There is her all-black school, Lafayette, and the all-white school, Central. Education for white youth, Angelou tells us, means greater likelihood of their becoming Galileos, Gaugins, Madame Curies, or Edisons. At least, that is the message from Donleavy, the graduation speaker. The black boys can look to being athletes and the girls appear excluded from aspiration altogether, destined to be maids or washerwomen. To what extent do you believe such inequity still exists in the form of institutional racism? A long-time social reformer and author named Jonathan Kozol writes passionately of the ongoing economic inequities that exist between black and white schools. Many other writers continue to point out the ongoing imbalances between what white and black children believe their future possibilities can be. If there indeed still are such inequities and imbalances, what should be done? What can be done?

FICTION

The Lesson

Toni Cade Bambara

Toni Cade Bambara (1939–1995) was an African American teacher, civil rights activist, editor, and fiction writer who was born and grew up in Harlem and Bedford-Stuyvesant in New York. A graduate of Queens College, she received a master's degree from the City University of New York. She published her first short story the year she graduated from Queens College and went on to publish two short story volumes, Gorilla My Love

(1972) and The Seabirds Are Still Alive *(1977).* The Salt Eaters, *a novel, appeared in 1982 and won the American Book Award.* If Blessing Comes *was published in 1987.*

"The Lesson," which is from the volume Gorilla My Love, *is a portrait of young inner-city black girls and their view of education in an encounter with their would-be mentor, the schoolmarm-like Miss Moore. The story sets up a dynamic of the learning that comes from the streets and tenements and the formal learning that is supposed to provide the ticket out. An exuberant and spirited first-person narration, "The Lesson" nevertheless has serious and important lessons about education.*

Back in the days when everyone was old and stupid or young and foolish and me and Sugar were the only ones just right, this lady moved on our block with nappy hair and proper speech and no makeup. And quite naturally we laughed at her, laughed the way we did at the junk man who went about his business like he was some big-time president and his sorry-ass horse his secretary. And we kinda hated her too, hated the way we did the winos who cluttered up our parks and pissed on our handball walls and stank up our hallways and stairs so you couldn't halfway play hide-and-seek without a goddamn gas mask. Miss Moore was her name. The only woman on the block with no first name. And she was black as hell, cept for her feet, which were fish-white and spooky. And she was always planning these boring-ass things for us to do, us being my cousin, mostly, who lived on the block cause we all moved North the same time and to the same apartment then spread out gradual to breathe. And our parents would yank our heads into some kinda shape and crisp up our clothes so we'd be presentable for travel with Miss Moore, who always looked like she was going to church though she never did. Which is just one of the things the grownups talked about when they talked behind her back like a dog. But when she came calling with some sachet she'd sewed up or some gingerbread she'd made or some book, why then they'd all be too embarrassed to turn her down and we'd get handed over all spruced up. She'd been to college and said it was only right that she should take responsibility for the young ones' education, and she not even related by marriage or blood. So they'd go for it. Specially Aunt Gretchen. She was the main gofer in the family. You got some ole dumb shit foolishness you want somebody to go for, you send for Aunt Gretchen. She been screwed into the go-along for so long, it's a blood-deep natural thing with her. Which is how she got saddled with me and Sugar and Junior in the first place while our mothers were in a la-de-da apartment up the block having a good ole time.

So this one day Miss Moore rounds us all up at the mailbox and it's pure-dee hot and she's knockin herself out about arithmetic. And school suppose to let up in summer I heard, but she don't never let up. And the starch in my pinafore scratching the shit outta me and I'm really hating this nappy-head bitch and her goddamn college degree. I'd much rather go to the pool or to the show where it's cool. So me and Sugar leaning on the mailbox being surly, which is a Miss Moore word. And Flyboy checking out what everybody brought for lunch. And Fat Butt already wasting his peanut-butter-and-jelly sandwich like the pig he is. And Junebug punchin on Q.T.'s arm for potato chips. And Rosie Giraffe shifting from one hip to the other waiting for somebody to step on her foot or ask her if she from Georgia so she can kick ass, preferably Mercedes'. And Miss Moore asking us do we know what money is like we a bunch of retards. I mean real money, she say, like it's only poker chips or monopoly papers we lay on the grocer. So right away I'm tired of this and say so. And would much rather snatch Sugar and go to the Sunset and terrorize the West Indian kids and take their hair ribbons and their money too. And Miss Moore files that remark away for next week's lesson on brotherhood, I can tell. And finally I say we oughta get to the subway cause it's cooler an' besides we might meet some cute boys. Sugar done swiped her mama's lipstick, so we ready.

So we heading down the street and she's boring us silly about what things cost and what our parents make and how much goes for rent and how money ain't divided up right in this country. And then she gets to the part about we all poor and live in the slums which I don't feature. And I'm ready to speak on that, but she steps out in the street and hails two cabs just like that. Then she hustles half the crew in with her and hands me a five-dollar bill and tells me to calculate 10 percent tip for the driver. And we're off. Me and Sugar and Junebug and Flyboy hangin out the window and hollering to everybody, putting lipstick on each other cause Flyboy a faggot anyway, and making farts with our sweaty armpits. But I'm mostly trying to figure how to spend this money. But they are fascinated with the meter ticking and Junebug starts laying bets as to how much it'll read when Flyboy can't hold his breath no more. Then Sugar lays bets as to how much it'll be when we get there. So I'm stuck. Don't nobody want to go for my plan, which is to jump out at the next light and run off to the first bar-b-que we can find. Then the driver tells us to get the hell out cause we there already. And the meter reads eighty-five cents. And I'm stalling to figure out the tip and Sugar say give him a dime. And I decide he don't need it bad as I do, so later for him. But then he tries to take off with Junebug foot still in the door so we talk about his mama something ferocious. Then we check out that we on Fifth Avenue and everybody dressed up in stockings. One lady in a fur coat, hot as it is. White folks crazy.

"This is the place," Miss Moore say, presenting it to us in the voice she uses at the museum. "Let's look in the windows before we go in."

"Can we steal?" Sugar asks very serious like she's getting the ground rules squared away before she plays. "I beg your pardon," say Miss Moore, and we fall out. So she leads us around the windows of the toy store and me and Sugar screamin, "This is mine, that's mine, I gotta have that, that was made for me, I was born for that," till Big Butt drowns us out.

"Hey, I'm goin to buy that there."

"That there? You don't even know what it is, stupid."

"I do so," he say punchin on Rosie Giraffe. "It's a microscope."

"Whatcha gonna do with a microscope, fool?"

"Look at things."

"Like what, Ronald?" ask Miss Moore. And Big Butt ain't got the first notion. So here go Miss Moore gabbing about the thousands of bacteria in a drop of water and the somethinorother in a speck of blood and the million and one living things in the air around us is invisible to the naked eye. And what she say that for? Junebug go to town on that "naked" and we rolling. Then Miss Moore ask what it cost. So we all jam into the window smudgin it up and the price tag say $300. So then she ask how long'd take for Big Butt and Junebug to save up their allowances. "Too long," I say. "Yeh," adds Sugar, "outgrown it by that time." And Miss Moore say no, you never outgrow learning instruments. "Why, even medical students and interns and," blah, blah, blah. And we ready to choke Big Butt for bringing it up in the first damn place.

"This here costs four hundred eighty dollars," say Rosie Giraffe. So we pile up all over her to see what she pointin out. My eyes tell me it's a chunk of glass cracked with something heavy, and different-color inks dripped into the splits, then the whole thing put into a oven or something. But for $480 it don't make sense.

"That's a paperweight made of semi-precious stones fused together under tremendous pressure," she explains slowly, with her hands doing the mining and all the factory work.

"So what's a paperweight?" asks Rosie Giraffe.

"To weigh paper with, dumbbell," say Flyboy, the wise man from the East.

"Not exactly," say Miss Moore, which is what she say when you warm or way off too. "It's to weigh paper down so it won't scatter and make your desk untidy." So right away me and Sugar curtsy to each other and then to Mercedes who is more the tidy type.

"We don't keep paper on top of the desk in my class," say Junebug, figuring Miss Moore crazy or lyin one.

"At home, then," she say. "Don't you have a calendar and a pencil case and a blotter and a letter-opener on your desk at home where you do your homework?" And she know damn well what our homes look like cause she nosys around in them every chance she gets.

"I don't even have a desk," say Junebug. "Do we?"

"No. And I don't get no homework neither," says Big Butt.

"And I don't even have a home," say Flyboy like he do at school to keep the white folks off his back and sorry for him. Send this poor kid to camp posters, is his specialty.

"I do," says Mercedes. "I have a box of stationery on my desk and a picture of my cat. My godmother bought the stationery and the desk. There's a big rose on each sheet and the envelopes smell like roses."

"Who wants to know about your smelly-ass stationery," say Rosie Giraffe fore I can get my two cents in.

"It's important to have a work area all your own so that . . ."

"Will you look at this sailboat, please," say Flyboy, cuttin her off and pointin to the thing like it was his. So once again we tumble all over each other to gaze at this magnificent thing in the toy store which is just big enough to maybe sail two kittens across the pond if you strap them to the posts tight. We all start reciting the price tag like we in assembly. "Hand-crafted sailboat of fiberglass at one thousand one hundred ninety-five dollars."

"Unbelievable," I hear myself say and am really stunned. I read it again for myself just in case the group recitation put me in a trance. Same thing. For some reason this pisses me off. We look at Miss Moore and she lookin at us, waiting for I dunno what.

"Who'd pay all that when you can buy a sailboat set for a quarter at Pop's, a tube of glue for a dime, and a ball of string for eight cents? It must have a motor and a whole lot else besides," I say. "My sailboat cost me about fifty cents."

"But will it take water?" say Mercedes with her smart ass.

"Took mine to Alley Pond Park once," say Flyboy. "String broke. Lost it. Pity."

"Sailed mine in Central Park and it keeled over and sank. Had to ask my father for another dollar."

"And you got the strap," laugh Big Butt. "The jerk didn't even have a string on it. My old man wailed on his behind."

Little Q.T. was staring hard at the sailboat and you could see he wanted it bad. But he too little and somebody'd just take it from him. So what the hell. "This boat for kids, Miss Moore?"

"Parents silly to buy something like that just to get all broke up," say Rosie Giraffe.

"That much money it should last forever," I figure.

"My father'd buy it for me if I wanted it."

"Your father, my ass," say Rosie Giraffe getting a chance to finally push Mercedes.

"Must be rich people shop here," say Q.T.

"You are a very bright boy," say Flyboy. "What was your first clue?" And he rap him on the head with the back of his knuckles, since Q.T. the only one he could get away with. Though Q.T. liable to come up behind you years later and get his licks in when you half expect it.

"What I want to know is," I says to Miss Moore though I never talk to her, I wouldn't give the bitch that satisfaction, "is how much a real boat costs? I figure a thousand'd get you a yacht any day."

"Why don't you check that out," she says, "and report back to the group?" Which really pains my ass. If you gonna mess up a perfectly good swim day least you could do is have some answers. "Let's go in," she say like she got something up her sleeve. Only she don't lead the way. So me and Sugar turn the corner to where the entrance is, but when we get there I kinda hang back.

Not that I'm scared, what's there to be afraid of, just a toy store. But I feel funny, shame. But what I got to be shamed about? Got as much right to go in as anybody. But somehow I can't seem to get hold of the door, so I step away from Sugar to lead. But she hangs back too. And I look at her and she looks at me and this is ridiculous. I mean, damn, I have never ever been shy about doing nothing or going nowhere. But then Mercedes steps up and then Rosie Giraffe and Big Butt crowd in behind and shove, and next thing we all stuffed into the doorway with only Mercedes squeezing past us, smoothing out her jumper and walking right down the aisle. Then the rest of us tumble in like a glued-together jigsaw done all wrong. And people lookin at us. And it's like the time me and Sugar crashed into the Catholic church on a dare. But once we got in there and everything so hushed and holy and the candles and the bowin and the hand-kerchiefs on all the drooping heads, I just couldn't go through with the plan. Which was for me to run up to the altar and do a tap dance while Sugar played the nose flute and messed around in the holy water. And Sugar kept givin me the elbow. Then later teased me so bad I tied her up in the shower and turned it on and locked her in. And she'd be there till this day if Aunt Gretchen hadn't finally figured I was lyin about the boarder takin a shower.

Same thing in the store. We all walkin on tiptoe and hardly touchin the games and puzzles and things. And I watched Miss Moore who is steady watchin us like she waitin for a sign. Like Mama Drewery watches the sky and sniffs the air and takes note of just how much slant is in the bird formation. Then me and Sugar bump smack into each other, so busy gazing at the toys, 'specially the sailboat. But we don't laugh and go into our fat-lady bump-stomach routine. We just stare at that price tag. Then Sugar run a finger over the whole boat. And I'm jealous and want to hit her. Maybe not her, but I sure want to punch somebody in the mouth.

"Watcha bring us here for, Miss Moore?"

"You sound angry, Sylvia. Are you mad about something?" Givin me one of them grins like she tellin a grown-up joke that never turns out to be funny. And she's lookin very closely at me like maybe she plannin to do my portrait from memory. I'm mad, but I won't give her that satisfaction. So I slouch around the store bein very bored and say, "Let's go."

Me and Sugar at the back of the train watchin the tracks whizzin by large then small then gettin gobbled up in the dark. I'm thinkin about this tricky toy I saw in the store. A clown that somersaults on a bar then does chin-ups just cause you yank lightly at his leg. Cost $35. I could see me askin my mother for a $35 birthday clown. "You wanna who that costs what?" she'd say, cock-ing her head to the side to get a better view of the hole in my head. Thirty-five dollars could buy new bunk beds for Junior and Gretchen's boy. Thirty-five dollars and the whole household could go visit Grand-daddy Nelson in the country. Thirty-five dollars would pay for the rent and the piano bill too. Who are these people that spend that much for performing clowns and $1000 for toy sailboats? What kinda work they do and how they live and how come we ain't in on it? Where we are is who we are, Miss Moore always pointin out. But it don't necessarily have to be that way, she always adds then waits for somebody to say that poor people have to wake up and demand their share of the pie and don't none of us know what kind of pie she talking about in the first damn place. But she ain't so smart cause I still got her four dollars from the taxi and she sure ain't gettin it messin up my day with this shit. Sugar nudges me in my pocket and winks.

Miss Moore lines us up in front of the mailbox where we started from, seem like years ago, and I got a headache for thinkin so hard. And we lean all over each other so we can hold up under the draggy ass lecture she always finishes us off with at the end before we thank her for borin us to tears. But she just looks at us like she readin tea leaves. Finally she say, "Well, what did you think of F.A.O. Schwarz?"

Rosie Giraffe mumbles, "White folks crazy."

"I'd like to go there again when I get my birthday money," says Mercedes, and we shove her out the pack so she has to lean on the mailbox by herself.

"I'd like a shower. Tiring day," say Flyboy.

Then Sugar surprises me by sayin, "You know, Miss Moore, I don't think all of us here put together eat in a year what that sailboat costs." And Miss Moore lights up like somebody goosed her. "And?" she say, urging Sugar on. Only I'm standin on her foot so she don't continue.

"Imagine for a minute what kind of society it is in which some people can spend on a toy what it would cost to feed a family of six or seven. What do you think?"

"I think," say Sugar pushing me off her feet like she never done before cause I whip her ass in a minute, "that this is not much of a democracy if you ask me. Equal chance to pursue happiness means an equal crack at the dough, don't it?" Miss Moore is besides herself and I am disgusted with Sugar's treachery. So I stand on her foot one more time to see if she'll shove me. She shuts up, and Miss Moore looks at me, sorrowfully I'm thinkin. And somethin weird is goin on, I can feel it in my chest. "Anybody else learn anything today?" lookin dead at me. I walk away and Sugar has to run to catch up and don't even seem to notice when I shrug her arm off my shoulder.

"Well, we got four dollars anyway," she says. "Uh hun."

"We could go to Hascombs and get half a chocolate layer and then go to the Sunset and still have plenty money for potato chips and ice cream sodas."

"Uh hun."

"Race you to Hascombs," she say.

We start down the block and she gets ahead which is O.K. by me cause I'm going to the West End and then over to the Drive to think this day through. She can run if she want to and even run faster. But ain't nobody gonna beat me at nuthin.

QUESTIONS FOR DISCUSSION AND WRITING

1. The narrator in this story speaks disparagingly of Miss Moore, the college-educated woman who wants to take responsibility for the education of her and the other children. She (Sylvia) even compares her hatred of Miss Moore to the way she and the others hate winos who stink up the neighborhood with their urine. Why do they feel such animosity toward Miss Moore? How much of their feeling toward her reflects their feelings about school and the fact that it is summer?

2. Miss Moore has no first name but all of the children have nicknames such as Sugar, Flyboy, Fat Butt, Junebug, Q.T., and Rosie Giraffe. What does this gap in what the teacher figure is called and what the children call each other reveal to us, perhaps about the whole nature of street kids from an underprivileged neighborhood and teachers who want to educate them?

3. There is a good deal of profanity and vulgarity in this story. Does it heighten the real sense of who these children are and what attitudes they hold? What are we to make of the fact that they seem to have no compunction about stealing or taking money—whether from other kids or from Miss Moore? Sugar steals her mother's lipstick and even asks, outside the museum, "Can we steal?" Is there a danger that Bambara is painting too realistic, or perhaps too stereotypical, a picture?

4. There are many lessons in the course of the story. Miss Moore instructs the children on what a paperweight is as well as the nature of bacteria and the importance of a work area for homework. The main lesson she intends for them, however, appears to be one of the value of money and economic inequity. But they are learning things on their own, apart from Miss Moore, on this educational fieldtrip. What would you say is the most important lesson that the children learn from their outing?

5. Our story's narrator, Sylvia, feels shame going into F.A.O. Schwarz, the high-end toy store. Then she looks at a price tag and asks Miss Moore, in anger, why they were brought there. How would you assess the reasons for why Sylvia feels this way? What lies behind her shame and indignation?

6. At one point Sylvia asks, to herself, who these people are who can afford to pay the kinds of prices attached to the performing clowns and toy sailboats. She inwardly asks: "What kinda work they do and how they live and how come we ain't in on it?" She remembers Miss Moore talking about poor people needing to wake up and demand an equal share of the pie, but then quickly shrugs off such thoughts by saying "don't none of us know what kind of pie she talking about in the damn first place" and congratulating herself and Sugar on having outfoxed Miss Moore by taking her for four dollars that was to have been for the cab ride. Has Sylvia learned anything from what she remembers here or has she simply remembered momentarily something unimportant to her that she can discard as forgettable?

7. Is there a lesson for us, as readers, in this story? How would you characterize it?

8. Discuss how the main character and her friend, Sugar, see themselves. In this vein the stories within the story that Sylvia recalls about their mischief in the Catholic church and Sylvia locking Sugar in the shower are revelatory, as is Sylvia's talk about "terrorizing" West Indian kids and being ready for cute boys. Why, at the end of the story, does Sylvia see Sugar as having acted with treachery? What does her last line tell us about the way she views herself?

9. Early on in the story Sugar says of Miss Moore, before the educational outing takes place, "School supposed to let up in summer I heard, but she don't never let up." This observation provides us what we might characterize as the essence of Sylvia's view about school and education. What is it and how much is it the result of being a child of Harlem? Or is this how kids of all colors and classes tend to view school?

ON TECHNIQUE AND STYLE

1. So much of the success of "The Lesson" depends on the believability and overall success of the narrative voice. How well does Bambara succeed in making her narrator's voice credible? How and by what methods does she bring this about for us as readers? Or does the voice seem to you forced and inauthentic, as if being controlled by an adult ventriloquist?

2. Much of "The Lesson" is built on a contrast between the world of the children and the worldview of Miss Moore. Where do their worlds intersect? What comparisons are evident between the children and their would-be teacher?

3. Comment on the use of language in the story and its effects on you as a reader. Words like "bitch" and "faggot" can be offensive. How are they used by Bambara? Are they offensive? Should they be?

CULTURAL QUESTION

1. "White folks crazy," the narrator of "The Lesson" exclaims after seeing people, despite the summer heat, wearing stockings and a woman in a fur coat. Rosie Giraffe says the same thing after being in the toy store. Flyboy states, "I don't even have a home," and the narrator tells us this is the way Flyboy expresses himself "at school to keep the white folks off his back and sorry for him. Send this poor kid to camp posters, is his specialty." To what extent is Bambara pointing out for us the division between white and black cultures? Or are we made to realize that the division may have more to do with have and have not?

The School

Donald Barthelme

Donald Barthelme (1931–1989) was born in Philadelphia, grew up in Texas, and taught at the University of Houston. For many years he lived in New York City. Known for his experimental, satiric, and often postmodernistic, humorous, and offbeat fiction, his first story appeared in 1963 in The New Yorker. *He is the author of the novels* Snow White *(1967),* The Dead Father *(1975), and* The King *(1990) as well as eight volumes of short stories. With* Sixty Stories *Barthelme won the PEN/Faulkner Award for Fiction in 1981.*

Under its comic and nearly surreal surface, "The School" is a story that exposes real concerns about what goes on in classrooms. The story brings us into a classroom that seems both real and unreal but nevertheless all too recognizable.

Well, we had all these children out planting trees, see, because we figured that . . . that was part of their education, to see how, you know, the root systems . . . and also the sense of responsibility, taking care of things, being individually responsible. You know what I mean. And the trees all died. They were orange trees. I don't know why they died, they just died. Something wrong with the soil possibly or maybe the stuff we got from the nursery wasn't the best. We complained about it. So we've got thirty kids there, each kid had his or her own little tree to plant and we've got these thirty dead trees. All these kids looking at these little brown sticks, it was depressing.

It wouldn't have been so bad except that just a couple of weeks before the thing with the trees, the snakes all died. But I think that the snakes—well, the reason that the snakes kicked off was that . . . you remember, the boiler was shut off for four days because of the strike, and that was explicable. It was something you could explain to the kids because of the strike. I mean, none of their parents would let them cross the picket line and they knew there was a strike going on and what it meant. So when things got started up again and we found the snakes they weren't too disturbed.

With the herb gardens it was probably a case of overwatering, and at least now they know not to overwater. The children were very conscientious with the herb gardens and some of them probably . . . you know, slipped them a little extra water when we weren't looking. Or maybe . . . well, I don't like to think about sabotage, although it did occur to us. I mean, it was something that crossed our minds. We were thinking that way probably because before that the gerbils had died, and the white mice had died, and the salamander . . . well, now they know not to carry them around in plastic bags.

Of course we expected the tropical fish to die, that was no surprise. Those numbers, you look at them crooked and they're belly-up on the surface. But the lesson plan called for a tropical fish input at that point, there was nothing we could do, it happens every year, you just have to hurry past it.

We weren't even supposed to have a puppy.

We weren't even supposed to have one, it was just a puppy the Murdoch girl found under a Gristede's truck one day and she was afraid the truck would run over it when the driver had finished making his delivery, so she stuck it in her knapsack and brought it to the school with her. So we had this puppy. As soon as I saw the puppy I thought, Oh Christ, I bet it will live for about two weeks and then. . . . And that's what it did. It wasn't supposed to be in the classroom at all, there's some kind of regulation about it, but you can't tell them they can't have a puppy when the puppy is already there, right in front of them, running around on the floor and yap yap yapping. They named it Edgar—that is, they named it after me. They had a lot of fun running after it and yelling, "Here, Edgar! Nice Edgar!" Then they'd laugh like hell. They enjoyed the ambiguity. I enjoyed it myself. I don't mind being kidded. They made a little house for it in the supply closet and all that. I don't know what it died of. Distemper, I guess. It probably hadn't had any shots. I got it out of there before the kids got to school. I checked the supply closet each morning, routinely, because I knew what was going to happen. I gave it to the custodian.

And then there was this Korean orphan that the class adopted through the Help the Children program, all the kids brought in a quarter a month, that was the idea. It was an unfortunate thing, the kid's name was Kim and maybe we adopted him too late or something. The cause of death was not stated in the letter we got, they suggested we adopt another child instead and sent us some interesting case histories, but we didn't have the heart. The class took it pretty hard, they began (I think, nobody ever said anything to me directly) to feel that maybe there was something wrong with the school. But I don't think there's anything wrong with the school, particularly, I've seen better and I've seen worse. It was just a run of bad luck. We had an extraordinary number of parents passing away, for instance. There were I think two heart attacks and two suicides, one drowning, and four killed together in a car accident. One stroke. And we had the usual heavy mortality rate among the grandparents, or maybe it was heavier this year, it seemed so. And finally the tragedy.

The tragedy occurred when Matthew Wein and Tony Mavrogordo were playing over where they're excavating for the new federal office building. There were all these big wooden beams stacked, you know, at the edge of the excavation. There's a court case coming out of that, the parents are claiming that the beams were poorly stacked. I don't know what's true and what's not. It's been a strange year.

I forgot to mention Billy Brandt's father who was knifed fatally when he grappled with a masked intruder in his home.

One day, we had a discussion in class. They asked me, where did they go? The trees, the salamander, the tropical fish, Edgar, the poppas and mommas, Matthew and Tony, where did they go? And I said, I don't know, I don't know. And they said, who knows? and I said, nobody knows. And they said, is death that which gives meaning to life? And I said no, life is that which gives meaning to life. Then they said, but isn't death, considered as a funda-mental datum, the means by which the taken-for-granted mundanity of the everyday may be transcended in the direction of—

I said, yes, maybe.

They said, we don't like it.

I said, that's sound.

They said, it's a bloody shame!

I said, it is.

They said, will you make love now with Helen (our teaching assistant) so that we can see how it is done? We know you like Helen.

I do like Helen but I said that I would not.

We've heard so much about it, they said, but we've never seen it.

I said I would be fired and that it was never, or almost never, done as a demonstration. Helen looked out the window.

They said, please, please make love with Helen, we require an assertion of value, we are frightened.

I said that they shouldn't be frightened (although I am often frightened) and that there was value everywhere. Helen came and embraced me. I kissed her a few times on the brow. We held each other. The children were excited. Then there was a knock on the door, I opened the door, and the new gerbil walked in. The children cheered wildly.

QUESTIONS FOR DISCUSSION AND WRITING

1. "It's been a strange year," the narrator of "The School," the classroom teacher Edgar, remarks to us after cataloging the deaths that have occurred. Barthelme is more a fabulist (writer of fables) than a realist writer, but cer-tainly such a death toll could conceivably take place in the course of an aca-demic year. What is the effect of these deaths on the students? On Edgar, their teacher?

2. The teacher tells us that the death of the thirty orange trees, unlike the dead snakes, is not explicable. The children understood that the snakes died because of a strike and the shutting off of the boiler. How would you describe the narrator's view of how he and the children react to deaths from causes that are explicable and deaths from causes that are not? Is this part of what we might describe as the learning process?

3. What are we to make of the fact that the children in the story name the puppy after their teacher? What effect does this have on them and on the teacher, Edgar?

4. "And finally the tragedy," Edgar tells us, of the falling wooden beams kill-ing the two boys from the class who were playing near the excavation site.

Were all of the other deaths he mentioned not tragedies? Why does he refer to this event as "the tragedy"?

5. Why does the narrator mention Billy Brandt's father's violent death by "a masked intruder in his home" almost as an afterthought? What is the effect on us of that forgotten death springing suddenly to his mind to add to the death toll?

6. Why do the children suddenly seem to speak in philosophic-sounding jargon when they are talking directly about life after raising the question of where the dead go?

7. What is the significance of the children asking for a demonstration of love-making between Edgar and Helen, the teaching assistant? What are we to make of their saying they require an assertion of value and are frightened? Of Edgar's admitting he, too, is frightened and that there is "value everywhere"?

8. The end of the story appears to throw us for a loop, to offer an unexpected punch. Why do the children cheer wildly when the new gerbil walks in? What does the ending tell us about what the children have learned about the cycles of life and death? What have we as readers learned?

ON TECHNIQUE AND STYLE

1. In the story Barthelme provides us with a range of living organisms that expire. There are the orange trees, the snakes, the herb garden, gerbils, white mice, a salamander, tropical fish, a puppy, the Korean orphan Kim, parents and grandparents of the children, and the children themselves. Are these presented to us in any particular order aside from a somewhat chronological one? Could Barthelme have presented them in any order other than the one he employs?

2. How persuasive is this story, especially given the fact that it is often seen as hallucinatory and nonrealistic in both style and tone? How serious are we to take the tale and its meaning?

a Though Barthelme has many admirers, he also has his detractors who argue that his meaning is too obscure and his language not lively or compelling enough. Whether you like or dislike his way of telling a story, compare and contrast him to another storyteller and show why you feel he succeeds more or fails more in his unorthodox (and often labeled postmodern) approach.

CULTURAL QUESTION

1. "The School" is a story that has been described as being about cultural relativism. Is this a mostly white European classroom being portrayed or could it be any classroom of any race or ethnic group?

Saint Marie

Louise Erdrich

Louise Erdrich (1954–) is a poet and fiction writer of German and Chippewa descent. She grew up on a North Dakota Indian reservation and graduated from Dartmouth, where she also taught. She also has worked as a short-order cook, server, and construction site flagger. In 1984 she published a volume of poetry and her first work of fiction, Love Medicine, *which won the the National Book Critics Circle Award. Later novels include* The Beet Queen, Tracks, The Bingo Palace, Tales of Burning Love, The Antelope Wife, The Last Report on the Miracles at Little No Horse, The Master Butcher's Singing Club, *and* The Painted Drum. *She also published a novel and a travel book with her then-husband, Native American writer Michael Dorris, and two additional poetry volumes.*

The selection "Saint Marie" comes from Love Medicine. *The volume* Love Medicine *gives a broad picture of the hopes and the despairs of Indian life. "Saint Marie" features one of the chief characters in* Love Medicine, *Marie Lazarre, returning to the site of her early education to meet the sadistic, probably psychotic former teacher who shaped her imagination and her current obsessions. "Saint Marie" is a searing portrait of how the best of intentions of the Catholic church to educate young Indians and instill faith in them can go horribly awry.*

I heard later that the Sacred Heart Convent was a catchall place for nuns that don't get along elsewhere. Nuns that complain too much or lose their mind. I'll always wonder now, after hearing that, where they picked up Sister Leopolda. Perhaps she had scarred someone else, the way she left a mark on me. Perhaps she was just sent around to test her Sisters' faith, here and there, like the spot-checker in a factory. For she was the definite most-hard trial to anyone's endurance, even when they started out with veils of wretched love upon their eyes.

I was that girl who thought the black hem of her garment would help me rise. Veils of love which was only hate petrified by longing—that was me. I was like those bush Indians who stole the holy black hat of a Jesuit and swallowed little scraps of it to cure their fevers. But the hat itself carried smallpox and was killing them with belief. Veils of faith! I had this confidence in Leopolda. She was different. The other Sisters had long ago gone blank and given up on Satan. He slept for them. They never noticed his comings and goings. But Leopolda kept track of him and knew his habits, minds he burrowed in, deep spaces where he hid. She knew as much about him as my grandma, who called him by other names and was not afraid.

In her class, Sister Leopolda carried a long oak pole for opening high windows. It had a hook made of iron on one end that could jerk a patch of your hair out or throttle you by the collar—all from a distance. She used this deadly hook-pole for catching Satan by surprise. He could have entered without your knowing it—through your lips or your nose or any one of your seven openings—and gained your mind. But she would see him. That pole would brain you from behind. And he would gasp, dazzled, and take the first thing she offered, which was pain.

She had a stringer of children who could only breathe if she said the word. I was the worst of them. She always said the Dark One wanted me most of all, and I believed this. I stood out. Evil was a common thing I trusted. Before sleep sometimes he came and whispered conversation in the old language of the bush. I listened. He told me things he never told anyone but Indians. I was privy to both worlds of his knowledge. I listened to him, but I had confidence in Leopolda. She was the only one of the bunch he even noticed.

There came a day, though, when Leopolda turned the tide with her hook-pole.

It was a quiet day with everyone working at their desks, when I heard him. He had sneaked into the closets in the back of the room. He was scratching around, tasting crumbs in our pockets, stealing buttons, squirting his dark juice in the linings and the boots. I was the only one who heard him, and I got bold. I smiled, I glanced back and smiled and looked up at her sly to see if she had noticed. My heart jumped. For she was looking straight at me. And she sniffed. She had a big stark bony nose stuck to the front of her face for smelling out brimstone and evil thoughts. She had smelled him on me. She stood up. Tall, pale, a blackness leading into the deeper blackness of the slate wall behind her. Her oak pole had flown into her grip. She had seen me glance at the closet. Oh, she knew. She knew just where he was. I watched her watch him in her mind's eye. The whole class was watching now. She was staring, sizing, following his scuffle. And all of a sudden she tensed down, posed on her bent kneesprings, cocked her arm back. She threw the oak pole singing over my head, through my braincloud. It cracked through the thin wood door of the back closet, and the heavy pointed hook drove through his heart. I turned. She'd speared her own black rubber overboot where he'd taken refuge in the tip of her darkest toe.

Something howled in my mind. Loss and darkness. I understood. I was to suffer for my smile.

He rose up hard in my heart. I didn't blink when the pole cracked. My skull was tough. I didn't flinch when she shrieked in my ear. I only shrugged at the flowers of hell. He wanted me. More than anything he craved me. But then she did the worst. She did what broke my mind to her. She grabbed me by the collar and dragged me, feet flying, through the room and threw me in the closet with her dead black overboot. And I was there. The only light was a crack beneath the door. I asked the Dark One to enter into me and boost my mind. I asked him to restrain my tears, for they was pushing behind my eyes. But he was afraid to come back there. He was afraid of her sharp pole. And I was afraid of Leopolda's pole for the first time, too. I felt the cold hook in my heart. How it could crack through the door at any minute and drag me out, like a dead fish on a gaff, drop me on the floor like a gutshot squirrel.

I was nothing. I edged back to the wall as far as I could. I breathed the chalk dust. The hem of her full black cloak cut against my cheek. He had left me. Her spear could find me any time. Her keen ears would aim the hook into the beat of my heart.

What was that sound?

It filled the closet, filled it up until it spilled over, but I did not recognize the crying wailing voice as mine until the door cracked open, brightness, and she hoisted me to her camphor-smelling lips.

"He *wants* you," she said. "That's the difference. I give you love."

Love. The black hook. The spear singing through the mind. I saw that she had tracked the Dark One to my heart and flushed him out into the open. So now my heart was an empty nest where she could lurk.

Well, I was weak. I was weak when I let her in, but she got a foothold there. Hard to dislodge as the year passed. Sometimes I felt him—the brush of dim wings—but only rarely did his voice compel. It was between Marie and Leopolda now, and the struggle changed. I began to realize I had been on the wrong track with the fruits of hell. The real way to overcome Leopolda was this: I'd get to heaven first. And then, when I saw her coming, I'd shut the gate. She'd be out! That is why, besides the bowing and the scraping I'd be dealt, I wanted to sit on the altar as a saint.

To this end, I went up on the hill. Sister Leopolda was the consecrated nun who had sponsored me to come there.

"You're not vain," she said. "You're too honest, looking into the mirror, for that. You're not smart. You don't have the ambition to get clear. You have two choices. One, you can marry a no-good Indian, bear his brats, die like a dog. Or two, you can give yourself to God."

"I'll come up there," I said, "but not because of what you think."

I could have had any damn man on the reservation at the time. And I could have made him treat me like his own life. I looked good. And I looked white. But I wanted Sister Leopolda's heart. And here was the thing: sometimes I wanted her heart in love and admiration. Sometimes. And sometimes I wanted her heart to roast on a black stick.

QUESTIONS FOR DISCUSSION AND WRITING

1. Marie Lazarre is "a reservation girl" who wants to be a saint. She is headed up to the convent to visit her former teacher, Sister Leopolda. She says, "I was like a bush Indian" but also tells us she has confidence in Sister Leopolda because her former nun teacher had not "given up on Satan." Before we even meet Sister Leopolda, what is the sense we get about her and about Marie from Marie herself, especially with what learning Marie has had instilled in her from this nun and former teacher?

2. What is your response to Sister Leopolda's use of a "hook-pole" to abuse the children in her class in the name of rooting out the devil? Marie mentions that the nuns who teach in the Sacred Heart Convent are nuns who "don't get along elsewhere," "complain too much," or "lose their mind." What is Erdrich revealing to us in the portrait of Sister Leopolda about the inherent pitfalls in the system of Catholic schooling, especially as pertains to Indian children?

3. This is an extreme case. But does it mirror educational experiences that are perhaps less extreme? Do children who are "scarred" by their teachers in the myriad of nonphysical and even minor ways often have something they need or want to prove to those authority figures as they grow older?

4. Marie, who is fourteen when we meet her, feels obvious ambivalence about her former teacher. She says: "sometimes I wanted her heart in love and admiration. Sometimes. And sometimes I wanted her heart to roast on a black stick." Why do you think her feelings are so strong, her ambivalence so extreme?

5. Sister Leopolda tells Marie she has two choices—"to marry a no-good Indian, bear his brats, die like a dog" or "you can give yourself to God." What effect do you imagine such a remark might have had on a young girl's mind and heart, especially since the remark came from a teacher she believed understood the lure she felt toward sin and temptation?

6. Marie proudly tells us she could get any man she wants, but says that what she wants is Sister Leopolda's heart. Why?

7. One's personal and internal struggles with Satan might not seem especially relevant to a classroom education, especially by today's secular standards. But this is a parochial classroom in North Dakota in 1934. Does that make the situation Erdrich portrays more understandable? Is such a portrayal of the necessity to fight against evil inconceivable in a classroom today? Do you think that a strong faith often includes a strong awareness of evil?

8. Marie tells us: "The real way to overcome Leopolda was this: I'd get to heaven first." What exactly is it that Marie is trying to overcome?

ON TECHNIQUE AND STYLE

1. Erdrich uses many sharply etched and vivid images. How effective are they in creating for us, her readers, a picture? Give examples of how these enhance the picture she creates.

2. Love is mentioned a number of times in this excerpt, which is from Erdrich's larger fictional work, *Love Medicine*. What is the definition of love that emerges here?

3. Compare and contrast this selection by Erdrich to any of the other classroom experiences portrayed in this section on education. Which writer provides the most convincing portrayal. Why?

CULTURAL QUESTION

1. Marie tells us, "I don't have that much Indian blood" and she says, "I looked white." This seems to place her in a different category than the other Indians on the reservation. Or does it? Her education still appears tied to traditional notions of a white (Catholic) culture educating Native people. What is Erdrich suggesting to us about Marie's special color status in looking white and not having a lot of Indian blood? Is she different from the other Indians who live on the reservation who are also educated by the nuns?

Paul's Case: A Study in Temperament

Willa Cather

Willa Cather (1873–1947) was born in Virginia but lived most of her life in the rural prairie of Nebraska. She graduated from the University of Nebraska and then worked in Pittsburgh as a journalist and a high school teacher. She later lived in New York and worked on the editorial staff of McClure's *Magazine. Her first book of poems,* April Twilights, *was published in 1903, followed by a volume of short stories,* The Troll Garden, *in 1905. Her novels include* Alexander's Bridge, O Pioneers!, The Song of the Lark, My Antonia, Death Comes to the Archbishop, *and* Obscure Destinies. *She published two additional collections of short stories.*

"Paul's Case: A Study in Temperament," which first appeared in McClure's *in 1905, is a story that emerged from Cather's experiences in Pittsburgh as a high school English teacher and, quite possibly, from her own early and lifetime experiences with gender. As a teenager she dressed like a boy, wore short hair, and called herself William. She lived as an adult for nearly four decades with another woman, all of which suggests a great deal of sympathy in her as a writer for a confused, effete character like Paul. Though he may be both a pitiful as well as a not entirely likable young man, it is clear that Paul's failures are also, to a degree, the failures of the school he attends—its faculty and its principal.*

It was Paul's afternoon to appear before the faculty of the Pittsburgh High School to account for his various misdemeanors. He had been suspended a week ago, and his father had called at the Principal's office and confessed his perplexity about his son. Paul entered the faculty room suave and smiling. His clothes were a trifle outgrown, and the tan velvet on the collar of his open overcoat was frayed and worn; but for all that there was something of the dandy about him, and he wore an opal pin in his neatly knotted black four-in-hand, and a red carnation in his buttonhole. This latter adornment the faculty somehow felt was not properly significant of the contrite spirit befitting a boy under the ban of suspension.

Paul was tall for his age and very thin, with high, cramped shoulders and a narrow chest. His eyes were remarkable for a certain hysterical brilliancy, and he continually used them in a conscious, theatrical sort of way, peculiarly offensive in a boy. The pupils were abnormally large, as though he were addicted to belladonna, but there was a glassy glitter about them which that drug does not produce.

When questioned by the Principal as to why he was there Paul stated, politely enough, that he wanted to come back to school. This was a lie, but Paul was quite accustomed to lying; found it, indeed, indispensable for overcoming friction. His teachers were asked to state their respective charges against him, which they did with such a rancor and aggrievedness as evinced that this was not a usual case. Disorder and impertinence were among the offenses named, yet each of his instructors felt that it was scarcely possible to put into words the real cause of the trouble, which lay in a sort of hysterically defiant manner of the boy's; in the contempt which they all knew he felt for them, and which he seemingly made not the least effort to conceal. Once, when he had been making a synopsis of a paragraph at the blackboard, his English teacher had stepped to his side and attempted to guide his hand. Paul had started back with a shudder and thrust his hands violently behind him. The astonished woman could scarcely have been more hurt and embarrassed had he struck at her. The insult was so involuntary and definitely personal as to be unforgettable. In one way and another he had made all his teachers, men and women alike, conscious of the same feeling of physical aversion. In one class he habitually sat with his hand shading his eyes; in another he always looked out of the window during the recitation; in another he made a running commentary on the lecture, with humorous intention.

His teachers felt this afternoon that his whole attitude was symbolized by his shrug and his flippantly red carnation flower, and they fell upon him without mercy, his English teacher leading the pack. He stood through it smiling, his pale lips parted over his white teeth. (His lips were continually twitching, and he had a habit of raising his eyebrows that was contemptuous and irritating to the last degree.) Older boys than Paul had broken down and shed tears under that baptism of fire, but his set smile did not once desert him, and his only sign of discomfort was the nervous trembling of the fingers that toyed with the buttons of his overcoat, and an occasional jerking of the other hand that held his hat. Paul was always smiling, always glancing about him, seeming to feel that people might be watching him and trying to detect something. This conscious expression, since it was as far as possible from boyish mirthfulness, was usually attributed to insolence or "smartness."

As the inquisition proceeded one of his instructors repeated an impertinent remark of the boy's, and the Principal asked him whether he thought that a courteous speech to have made a woman. Paul shrugged his shoulders slightly and his eyebrows twitched.

"I don't know," he replied. "I didn't mean to be polite or impolite, either. I guess it's a sort of way I have of saying things regardless."

The Principal, who was a sympathetic man, asked him whether he didn't think that a way it would be well to get rid of. Paul grinned and said he guessed so. When he was told that he could go he bowed gracefully and went out. His bow was but a repetition of the scandalous red carnation.

His teachers were in despair, and his drawing master voiced the feeling of them all when he declared there was something about the boy which none of them understood. He added: "I don't really believe that smile of his comes altogether from insolence; there's something sort of haunted about it. The boy is not strong, for one thing. I happen to know that he was born in Colorado, only a few months before his mother died out there of a long illness. There is something wrong about the fellow."

The drawing master had come to realize that, in looking at Paul, one saw only his white teeth and the forced animation of his eyes. One warm afternoon the boy had gone to sleep at his drawing board, and his master had noted with amazement what a white, blue-veined face it was; drawn and wrinkled like an old man's about the eyes, the lips twitching even in his sleep, and stiff with a nervous tension that drew them back from his teeth.

His teachers left the building dissatisfied and unhappy; humiliated to have felt so vindictive toward a mere boy, to have uttered this feeling in cutting terms, and to have set each other on, as it were, in the gruesome game of intemperate reproach. Some of them remembered having seen a miserable street cat set at bay by a ring of tormentors.

As for Paul, he ran down the hill whistling the "Soldiers' Chorus" from Faust, looking wildly behind him now and then to see whether some of his teachers were not there to writhe under his lightheartedness. As it was now late in the afternoon and Paul was on duty that evening as usher at Carnegie Hall, he decided that he would not go home to supper. When he reached the concert hall the doors were not yet open and, as it was chilly outside, he decided to go up into the picture gallery—always deserted at this hour—where there were some of Raffelli's gay studies of Paris streets and an airy blue Venetian scene or two that always exhilarated him. He was delighted to find no one in the gallery but the old guard, who sat in one corner, a newspaper on his knee, a black patch over one eye and the other closed. Paul possessed himself of the peace and walked confidently up and down, whistling under his breath. After a while he sat down before a blue Rico and lost himself. When he bethought him to look at his watch, it was after seven o'clock, and he rose with a start and ran downstairs, making a face at Augustus, peering out from the cast room, and an evil gesture at the Venus de Milo as he passed her on the stairway.

When Paul reached the ushers' dressing room half a dozen boys were there already, and he began excitedly to tumble into his uniform. It was one of the few that at all approached fitting, and Paul thought it very becoming—though he knew that the tight, straight coat accentuated his narrow chest, about which he was exceedingly sensitive. He was always considerably excited while he dressed, twanging all over to the tuning of the strings and the preliminary flourishes of the horns in the music room; but tonight he seemed quite beside himself, and he teased and plagued the boys until, telling him that he was crazy, they put him down on the floor and sat on him.

Somewhat calmed by his suppression, Paul dashed out to the front of the house to seat the early comers. He was a model usher; gracious and smiling he ran up and down the aisles; nothing was too much trouble for him; he carried messages and brought programs as though it were his greatest pleasure in life, and all the people in his section thought him a charming boy, feeling that he remembered and admired them. As the house filled, he grew more and more vivacious and animated, and the color came to his cheeks and lips. It was very much as though this were a great reception and Paul were the host. Just as the musicians came out to take their places, his English teacher arrived with checks for the seats which a prominent manufacturer had taken for the season. She betrayed some embarrassment when she handed Paul the tickets, and a hauteur which subsequently made her feel very foolish. Paul was startled for a moment, and had the feeling of wanting to put her out; what business had she here among all these fine people and gay colors? He looked her over and decided that she was not appropriately dressed and must be a fool to sit downstairs in such togs. The tickets had probably been sent her out of kindness, he reflected as he put down a seat for her, and she had about as much right to sit there as he had.

When the symphony began Paul sank into one of the rear seats with a long sight of relief, and lost himself as he had done before the Rico. It was not that symphonies, as such, meant anything in particular to Paul, but the first sight of the instruments seemed to free some hilarious and potent spirit within him; something that struggled there like the genie in the bottle found by the Arab fisherman. He felt a sudden zest of life; the lights danced before his eyes and the concert hall blazed into unimaginable splendor. When the soprano soloist came on Paul forgot even the nastiness of his teacher's being there and gave himself up to the peculiar stimulus such personages always had for him. The soloist chanced to be a German woman, by no means in her first youth, and the mother of many children; but she wore an elaborate gown and a tiara, and above all she had that indefinable air of achievement, that world-shine upon her, which, in Paul's eyes, made her a veritable queen of Romance.

After a concert was over Paul was always irritable and wretched until he got to sleep, and tonight he was even more than usually restless. He had the feeling of not being able to let down, of its being impossible to give up this delicious excitement which was the only thing that could be called living at all. During the last number he withdrew and, after hastily changing his clothes in the dressing room, slipped out to the side door where the soprano's carriage stood. Here he began pacing rapidly up and down the walk, waiting to see her come out.

Over yonder, the Schenley, in its vacant stretch, loomed big and square through the fine rain, the windows of its twelve stories glowing like those of a lighted cardboard house under a Christmas tree. All the actors and singers of the better class stayed there when they were in the city, and a number of the big manufacturers of the place lived there in the winter. Paul had often hung about the hotel, watching the people go in and out, longing to enter and leave schoolmasters and dull care behind him forever.

At last the singer came out, accompanied by the conductor, who helped her into her carriage and closed the door with a cordial auf wiedersehen which set Paul to wondering whether she were not an old sweetheart of his. Paul followed the carriage over to the hotel, walking so rapidly as not to be far from the entrance when the singer alighted, and disappeared behind the swinging glass doors that were opened by a Negro in a tall hat and a long coat. In the moment that the door was ajar it seemed to Paul that he, too, entered. He seemed to feel himself go after her up the steps, into the warm, lighted building, into an exotic, tropical world of shiny, glistening surfaces and basking ease. He reflected upon the mysterious dishes that were brought into the dining room, the green bottles in buckets of ice, as he had seen them in the supper party pictures of the Sunday supplement. A quick gust of wind brought the rain down with sudden vehemence, and Paul was startled to find that he was still outside in the slush of the gravel driveway; that his boots were letting in the water and his scanty overcoat was clinging wet about him; that the lights in front of the concert hall were out and that the rain was driving in sheets between him and the orange glow of the windows above him. There it was, what he wanted—tangibly before him, like the fairy world of a Christmas pantomime—but mocking spirits stood guard at the doors, and, as the rain beat in his face, Paul wondered whether he were destined always to shiver in the black night outside, looking up at it.

He turned and walked reluctantly toward the car tracks. The end had to come sometime; his father in his nightclothes at the top of the stairs, explanations that did not explain, hastily improvised fictions that were forever tripping him up, his upstairs room and its horrible yellow wallpaper, the creaking bureau with the greasy plush collarbox, and over his painted wooden bed the pictures of George Washington and John Calvin, and the framed motto, "Feed my Lambs," which had been worked in red worsted by his mother.

Half an hour later Paul alighted from his car and went slowly down one of the side streets off the main thoroughfare. It was a highly respectable street, where all the houses were exactly alike, and where businessmen of moderate means begot and reared large families of children, all of whom went to Sabbath school and learned the shorter catechism, and were interested in arithmetic; all of whom were as exactly alike as their homes, and of a piece with the monotony in which they lived. Paul never went up Cordelia Street without a shudder of loathing. His home was next to the house of the Cumberland minister. He approached it tonight with the nerveless sense of defeat, the hopeless feeling of sinking back forever into ugliness and commonness that he had always had when he came home. The moment he turned into Cordelia Street he felt the waters close above his head. After each of these orgies of living he experienced all the physical depression which follows a debauch; the loathing of respectable beds, of common food, of a house penetrated by kitchen odors; a shuddering repulsion for the flavorless, colorless mass of everyday existence; a morbid desire for cool things and soft lights and fresh flowers.

The nearer he approached the house, the more absolutely unequal Paul felt to the sight of it all: his ugly sleeping chamber; the cold bathroom with the grimy zinc tub, the cracked mirror, the dripping spiggots; his father, at the top of the stairs, his hairy legs sticking out from his nightshirt, his feet thrust into carpet slippers. He was so much later than usual that there would certainly be inquiries and reproaches. Paul stopped short before the door. He felt that he could not be accosted by his father tonight; that he could not toss again on that miserable bed. He would not go in. He would tell his father that he had no carfare and it was raining so hard he had gone home with one of the boys and stayed all night.

Meanwhile, he was wet and cold. He went around to the back of the house and tried one of the basement windows, found it open, raised it cautiously, and scrambled down the cellar wall to the floor. There he stood, holding his breath, terrified by the noise he had made, but the floor above him was silent, and there was no creak on the stairs. He found a soapbox, and carried it over to the soft ring of light that streamed from the furnace door, and sat down. He was horribly afraid of rats, so he did not try to sleep, but sat looking distrustfully at the dark, still terrified lest he might have awakened his father. In such reactions, after one of the experiences which made days and nights out of the dreary blanks of the calendar, when his senses were deadened, Paul's head was always singularly clear. Suppose his father had heard him getting in at the window and had come down and shot him for a burglar? Then, again, suppose his father had come down, pistol in hand, and he had cried out in time to save himself, and his father had been horrified to think how nearly he had killed him? Then, again, suppose a day should come when his father would remember that night, and wish there had been no warning cry to stay his hand? With this last supposition Paul entertained himself until daybreak.

The following Sunday was fine; the sodden November chill was broken by the last flash of autumnal summer. In the morning Paul had to go to church and Sabbath school, as always. On seasonable Sunday afternoons the burghers of Cordelia Street always sat out on their front stoops and talked to their neighbors on the next stoop, or called to those across the street in neighborly fashion. The men usually sat on gay cushions placed upon the steps that led down to the sidewalk, while the women, in their Sunday "waists," sat in rockers on the cramped porches, pretending to be greatly at their ease. The children played in the streets; there were so many of them that the place resembled the recreation grounds of a kindergarten. The men on the steps—all in their shirt sleeves, their vests unbuttoned—sat with their legs well apart, their stomachs comfortably protruding, and talked of the prices of things, or told anecdotes of the sagacity of their various chiefs and overlords. They occasionally looked over the multitude of squabbling children, listened affectionately to their high-pitched, nasal voices, smiling to see their own proclivities reproduced in their offspring, and interspersed their legends of the iron kings with remarks about their sons' progress at school, their grades in arithmetic, and the amounts they had saved in their toy banks.

On this last Sunday of November Paul sat all the afternoon on the lowest step of his stoop, staring into the street, while his sisters, in their rockers, were talking to the minister's daughters next door about how many shirt-waists they had made in the last week, and how many waffles someone had eaten at the last church supper. When the weather was warm, and his father was in a particularly jovial frame of mind, the girls made lemonade, which was always brought out in a red-glass pitcher, ornamented with forget-me-nots in blue enamel. This the girls thought very fine, and the neighbors always joked about the suspicious color of the pitcher.

Today Paul's father sat on the top step, talking to a young man who shifted a restless baby from knee to knee. He happened to be the young man who was daily held up to Paul as a model, and after whom it was his father's dearest hope that he would pattern. This young man was of a ruddy complexion, with a compressed, red mouth, and faded, nearsighted eyes, over which he wore thick spectacles, with gold bows that curved about his ears. He was clerk to one of the magnates of a great steel corporation, and was looked upon in Cordelia Street as a young man with a future. There was a story that, some five years ago—he was now barely twenty-six—he had been a trifle dissipated, but in order to curb his appetites and save the loss of time and strength that a sowing of wild oats might have entailed, he had taken his chief's advice, oft reiterated to his employees, and at twenty-one had married the first woman whom he could persuade to share his fortunes. She happened to be an angular schoolmistress, much older than he, who also wore thick glasses, and who had now borne him four children, all nearsighted, like herself.

The young man was relating how his chief, now cruising in the Mediterranean, kept in touch with all the details of the business, arranging his office hours on his yacht just as though he were at home, and "knocking off work enough to keep two stenographers busy." His father told, in turn, the plan his corporation was considering, of putting in an electric railway plant in Cairo. Paul snapped his teeth; he had an awful apprehension that they might spoil it all before he got there. Yet he rather liked to hear these legends of the iron kings that were told and retold on Sundays and holidays; these stories of palaces in Venice, yachts on the Mediterranean, and high play at Monte Carlo appealed to his fancy, and he was interested in the triumphs of these cash boys who had become famous, though he had no mind for the cash-boy stage.

After supper was over and he had helped to dry the dishes, Paul nervously asked his father whether he could go to George's to get some help in his geometry, and still more nervously asked for carfare. This latter request he had to repeat, as his father, on principle, did not like to hear requests for money, whether much or little. He asked Paul whether he could not go to some boy who lived nearer, and told him that he ought not to leave his schoolwork until Sunday; but he gave him the dime. He was not a poor man, but he had a worthy ambition to come up in the world. His only reason for allowing Paul to usher was that he thought a boy ought to be earning a little.

Paul bounded upstairs, scrubbed the greasy odor of the dishwater from his hands with the ill-smelling soap he hated, and then shook over his fingers a few drops of violet water from the bottle he kept hidden in his drawer. He left the house with his geometry conspicuously under his arm, and the moment he got out of Cordelia Street and boarded a downtown car, he shook off the lethargy of two deadening days and began to live again.

The leading juvenile of the permanent stock company which played at one of the downtown theaters was an acquaintance of Paul's, and the boy had been invited to drop in at the Sunday-night rehearsals whenever he could. For more than a year Paul had spent every available moment loitering about Charley Edwards's dressing room. He had won a place among Edwards's following not only because the young actor, who could not afford to employ a dresser, often found him useful, but because he recognized in Paul something akin to what churchmen term "vocation."

It was at the theater and at Carnegie Hall that Paul really lived; the rest was but a sleep and a forgetting. This was Paul's fairy tale, and it had for him all the allurement of a secret love. The moment he inhaled the gassy, painty, dusty odor behind the scenes, he breathed like a prisoner set free, and felt within him the possibility of doing or saying splendid, brilliant, poetic things. The moment the cracked orchestra beat out the overture from Martha, or jerked at the serenade from Rigoletto, all stupid and ugly things slid from him, and his senses were deliciously, yet delicately fired.

Perhaps it was because, in Paul's world, the natural nearly always wore the guise of ugliness, that a certain element of artificiality seemed to him necessary in beauty. Perhaps it was because his experience of life elsewhere was so full of Sabbath-school picnics, petty economies, wholesome advice as to how to succeed in life, and the inescapable odors of cooking, that he found this existence so alluring, these smartly clad men and women so attractive, that he was so moved by these starry apple orchards that bloomed perennially under the limelight.

It would be difficult to put it strongly enough how convincingly the stage entrance of that theater was for Paul the actual portal of Romance. Certainly none of the company ever suspected it, least of all Charley Edwards. It was very like the old stories that used to float about London of fabulously rich Jews, who had subterranean halls there, with palms, and fountains, and soft lamps and richly appareled women who never saw the disenchanting light of London day. So, in the midst of that smoke-palled city, enamored of figures and grimy toil, Paul had his secret temple, his wishing carpet, his bit of blue-and-white Mediterranean shore bathed in perpetual sunshine.

Several of Paul's teachers had a theory that his imagination had been perverted by garish fiction, but the truth was that he scarcely ever read at all. The books at home were not such as would either tempt or corrupt a youthful mind, and as for reading the novels that some of his friends urged upon him—well, he got what he wanted much more quickly from music; any sort of music, from an orchestra to a barrel organ. He needed only the spark, the indescribable thrill that made his imagination master of his senses, and he could make plots and pictures enough of his own. It was equally true that he was not stagestruck—not, at any rate, in the usual acceptation of that expression. He had no desire to become an actor, any more than he had to become a musician. He felt no necessity to do any of these things; what he wanted was to see, to be in the atmosphere, float on the wave of it, to be carried out, blue league after blue league, away from everything.

After a night behind the scenes Paul found the schoolroom more than ever repulsive; the bare floors and naked walls; the prosy men who never wore frock coats, or violets in their buttonholes; the women with their dull gowns, shrill voices, and pitiful seriousness about prepositions that govern the dative. He could not bear to have the other pupils think, for a moment, that he took these people seriously; he must convey to them that he considered it all trivial, and was there only by way of a jest, anyway. He had autographed pictures of all the members of the stock company which he showed his classmates, telling them the most incredible stories of his familiarity with these people, of his acquaintance with the soloists who came to Carnegie Hall, his suppers with them and the flowers he sent them. When these stories lost their effect, and his audience grew listless, he became desperate and would bid all the boys good-by, announcing that he was going to travel for a while; going to Naples, to Venice, to Egypt. Then, next Monday, he would slip back, conscious and nervously smiling; his sister was ill, and he should have to defer his voyage until spring.

Matters went steadily worse with Paul at school. In the itch to let his instructors know how heartily he despised them and their homilies, and how thoroughly he was appreciated elsewhere, he mentioned once or twice that he had no time to fool with theorems; adding—with a twitch of the eyebrows and a touch of that nervous bravado which so perplexed them—that he was helping the people down at the stock company; they were old friends of his.

The upshot of the matter was that the Principal went to Paul's father, and Paul was taken out of school and put to work. The manager at Carnegie Hall was told to get another usher in his stead; the doorkeeper at the theater was warned not to admit him to the house; and Charley Edwards remorsefully promised the boy's father not to see him again.

The members of the stock company were vastly amused when some of Paul's stories reached them—especially the women. They were hardworking women, most of them supporting indigent husbands or brothers, and they laughed rather bitterly at having stirred the boy to such fervid and florid inventions. They agreed with the faculty and with his father that Paul's was a bad case.

The eastbound train was plowing through a January snowstorm; the dull dawn was beginning to show gray when the engine whistled a mile out of Newark. Paul started up from the seat where he had lain curled in uneasy slumber, rubbed the breath-misted window glass with his hand, and peered out. The snow was whirling in curling eddies above the white bottom lands, and the drifts lay already deep in the fields and along the fences, while here and there the long dead grass and dried weed stalks protruded black above it. Lights shone from the scattered houses, and a gang of laborers who stood beside the track waved their lanterns.

Paul had slept very little, and he felt grimy and uncomfortable. He had made the all-night journey in a day coach, partly because he was ashamed, dressed as he was, to go into a Pullman, and partly because he was afraid of being seen there by some Pittsburgh businessman, who might have noticed him in Denny & Carson's office. When the whistle awoke him, he clutched quickly at his breast pocket, glancing about him with an uncertain smile. But the little, clay-bespattered Italians were still sleeping, the slatternly women across the aisle were in open-mouthed oblivion, and even the crumby, crying babies were for the nonce stilled. Paul settled back to struggle with his impatience as best he could.

When he arrived at the Jersey City station he hurried through his breakfast, manifestly ill at ease and keeping a sharp eye about him. After he reached the Twenty-third Street station, he consulted a cabman and had himself driven to a men's-furnishings establishment that was just opening for the day. He spent upward of two hours there, buying with endless reconsidering and great care. His new street suit he put on in the fitting room; the frock coat and dress clothes he had bundled into the cab with his linen. Then he drove to a hatter's and a shoe house. His next errand was at Tiffany's, where he selected his silver and a new scarf pin. He would not wait to have his silver marked, he said. Lastly, he stopped at a trunk shop on Broadway and had his purchases packed into various traveling bags.

It was a little after one o'clock when he drove up to the Waldorf, and after settling with the cabman, went into the office. He registered from Washington; said his mother and father had been abroad, and that he had come down to await the arrival of their steamer. He told his story plausibly and had no trouble, since he volunteered to pay for them in advance, in engaging his rooms; a sleeping room, sitting room, and bath.

Not once, but a hundred times, Paul had planned this entry into New York. He had gone over every detail of it with Charley Edwards, and in his scrapbook at home there were pages of description about New York hotels, cut from the Sunday papers. When he was shown to his sitting room on the eighth floor he saw at a glance that everything was as it should be; there was but one detail in his mental picture that the place did not realize, so he rang for the bellboy and sent him down for flowers. He moved about nervously

until the boy returned, putting away his new linen and fingering it delight-
edly as he did so. When the flowers came he put them hastily into water, and
then tumbled into a hot bath. Presently he came out of his white bathroom,
resplendent in his new silk underwear, and playing with the tassels of his red
robe. The snow was whirling so fiercely outside his windows that he could
scarcely see across the street, but within the air was deliciously soft and
fragrant. He put the violets and jonquils on the taboret beside the couch,
and threw himself down, with a long sigh, covering himself with a Roman
blanket. He was thoroughly tired; he had been in such haste, he had stood
up to such a strain, covered so much ground in the last twenty-four hours,
that he wanted to think how it had all come about. Lulled by the sound of the
wind, the warm air, and the cool fragrance of the flowers, he sank into deep,
drowsy retrospection.

It had been wonderfully simple; when they had shut him out of the theater
and concert hall, when they had taken away his bone, the whole thing was
virtually determined. The rest was a mere matter of opportunity. The only thing
that at all surprised him was his own courage—for he realized well enough that
he had always been tormented by fear, a sort of apprehensive dread that, of
late years, as the meshes of the lies he had told closed about him, had been
pulling the muscles of his body tighter and tighter. Until now he could not
remember the time when he had not been dreading something. Even when
he was a little boy it was always there—behind him, or before, or on either
side. There had always been the shadowed corner, the dark place into which
he dared not look, but from which something seemed always to be watching
him—and Paul had done things that were not pretty to watch, he knew.

But now he had a curious sense of relief, as though he had at last thrown
down the gauntlet to the thing in the corner.

Yet it was but a day since he had been sulking in the traces; but yesterday
afternoon that he had been sent to the bank with Denny & Carson's deposit,
as usual—but this time he was instructed to leave the book to be balanced.
There was above two thousand dollars in checks, and nearly a thousand in
the bank notes which he had taken from the book and quietly transferred to
his pocket. At the bank he had made out a new deposit slip. His nerves had
been steady enough to permit of his returning to the office, where he had
finished his work and asked for a full day's holiday tomorrow, Saturday, giving a perfectly reasonable pretext. The bankbook, he knew, would not be
returned before Monday or Tuesday, and his father would be out of town for
the next week. From the time he slipped the bank notes into his pocket until
he boarded the night train for New York, he had not known a moment's hesitation. It was not the first time Paul had steered through treacherous waters.

How astonishingly easy it had all been; here he was, the thing done; and
this time there would be no awakening, no figure at the top of the stairs. He
watched the snowflakes whirling by his window until he fell asleep.

When he awoke, it was three o'clock in the afternoon. He bounded up
with a start; half of one of his precious days gone already! He spent more
than an hour in dressing, watching every stage of his toilet carefully in the

mirror. Everything was quite perfect; he was exactly the kind of boy he had always wanted to be.

When he went downstairs Paul took a carriage and drove up Fifth Avenue toward the Park. The snow had somewhat abated; carriages and tradesmen's wagons were hurrying soundlessly to and fro in the winter twilight; boys in woolen mufflers were shoveling off the doorsteps; the avenue stages made fine spots of color against the white street. Here and there on the corners were stands, with whole flower gardens blooming under glass cases, against the sides of which the snowflakes stuck and melted; violets, roses, carnations, lilies of the valley—somehow vastly more lovely and alluring that they blossomed thus unnaturally in the snow. The Park itself was a wonderful stage winterpiece.

When he returned, the pause of the twilight had ceased and the tune of the streets had changed. The snow was falling faster, lights streamed from the hotels that reared their dozen stories fearlessly up into the storm, defying the raging Atlantic winds. A long, black stream of carriages poured down the avenue, intersected here and there by other streams, tending horizontally. There were a score of cabs about the entrance of his hotel, and his driver had to wait. Boys in livery were running in and out of the awning stretched across the sidewalk, up and down the red velvet carpet laid from the door to the street. Above, about, within it all was the rumble and roar, the hurry and toss of thousands of human beings as hot for pleasure as himself, and on every side of him towered the glaring affirmation of the omnipotence of wealth.

The boy set his teeth and drew his shoulders together in a spasm of realization; the plot of all dramas, the text of all romances, the nerve-stuff of all sensations was whirling about him like the snowflakes. He burnt like a faggot in a tempest.

When Paul went down to dinner the music of the orchestra came floating up the elevator shaft to greet him. His head whirled as he stepped into the thronged corridor, and he sank back into one of the chairs against the wall to get his breath. The lights, the chatter, the perfumes, the bewildering medley of color—he had, for a moment, the feeling of not being able to stand it. But only for a moment; these were his own people, he told himself. He went slowly about the corridors, through the writing rooms, smoking rooms, reception rooms, as though he were exploring the chambers of an enchanted palace, built and peopled for him alone.

When he reached the dining room he sat down at a table near a window. The flowers, the white linen, the many-colored wineglasses, the gay toilettes of the women, the low popping of corks, the undulating repetitions of the Blue Danube from the orchestra, all flooded Paul's dream with bewildering radiance. When the roseate tinge of his champagne was added—that cold, precious, bubbling stuff that creamed and foamed in his glass—Paul wondered that there were honest men in the world at all. This was what all the world was fighting for, he reflected; this was what all the struggle was about. He doubted the reality of his past. Had he ever known a place called Cordelia Street, a place where fagged-looking businessmen got on the early car; mere rivets in a machine they seemed to

Paul,—sickening men, with combings of children's hair always hanging to
their coats, and the smell of cooking in their clothes. Cordelia Street—Ah,
that belonged to another time and country; had he not always been thus,
had he not sat here night after night, from as far back as he could remember, looking pensively over just such shimmering textures and slowly twirling the stem of a glass like this one between his thumb and middle finger?
He rather thought he had.

He was not in the least abashed or lonely. He had no especial desire to
meet or to know any of these people; all he demanded was the right to look
on and conjecture, to watch the pageant. The mere stage properties were
all he contended for. Nor was he lonely later in the evening, in his lodge at
the Metropolitan. He was now entirely rid of his nervous misgivings, of his
forced aggressiveness, of the imperative desire to show himself different from
his surroundings. He felt now that his surroundings explained him. Nobody
questioned the purple; he had only to wear it passively. He had only to glance
down at his attire to reassure himself that here it would be impossible for anyone to humiliate him.

He found it hard to leave his beautiful sitting room to go to bed that night,
and sat long watching the raging storm from his turret window. When he went
to sleep it was with the lights turned on in his bedroom; partly because of his
old timidity, and partly so that, if he should wake in the night, there would be
no wretched moment of doubt, no horrible suspicion of yellow wallpaper, or
of Washington and Calvin above his bed.

Sunday morning the city was practically snowbound. Paul breakfasted
late, and in the afternoon he fell in with a wild San Francisco boy, a freshman
at Yale, who said he had run down for a "little flyer" over Sunday. The young
man offered to show Paul the night side of the town, and the two boys went
out together after dinner, not returning to the hotel until seven o'clock the
next morning. They had started out in the confiding warmth of a champagne
friendship, but their parting in the elevator was singularly cool. The freshman
pulled himself together to make his train, and Paul went to bed. He awoke
at two o'clock in the afternoon, very thirsty and dizzy, and rang for icewater,
coffee, and the Pittsburgh papers.

On the part of the hotel management, Paul excited no suspicion. There
was this to be said for him, that he wore his spoils with dignity and in no way
made himself conspicuous. Even under the glow of his wine he was never
boisterous, though he found the stuff like a magician's wand for wonder-
building. His chief greediness lay in his ears and eyes, and his excesses were
not offensive ones. His dearest pleasures were the gray winter twilights in his
sitting room; his quiet enjoyment of his flowers, his clothes, his wide divan,
his cigarette, and his sense of power. He could not remember a time when
he had felt so at peace with himself. The mere release from the necessity
of petty lying, lying every day and every day, restored his self-respect. He
had never lied for pleasure, even at school; but to be noticed and admired,
to assert his difference from other Cordelia Street boys; and he felt a good
deal more manly, more honest, even, now that he had no need for boastful

pretensions, now that he could, as his actor friends used to say, "dress the part." It was characteristic that remorse did not occur to him. His golden days went by without a shadow, and he made each as perfect as he could.

On the eighth day after his arrival in New York he found the whole affair exploited in the Pittsburgh papers, exploited with a wealth of detail which indicated that local news of a sensational nature was at a low ebb. The firm of Denny & Carson announced that the boy's father had refunded the full amount of the theft and that they had no intention of prosecuting. The Cumberland minister had been interviewed, and expressed his hope of yet reclaiming the motherless lad, and his Sabbath-school teacher declared that she would spare no effort to that end. The rumor had reached Pittsburgh that the boy had been seen in a New York hotel, and his father had gone East to find him and bring him home.

Paul had just come in to dress for dinner; he sank into a chair, weak to the knees, and clasped his head in his hands. It was to be worse than jail, even; the tepid waters of Cordelia Street were to close over him finally and forever. The gray monotony stretched before him in hopeless, unrelieved years; Sabbath school, Young People's Meeting, the yellow-papered room, the damp dishtowels; it all rushed back upon him with a sickening vividness. He had the old feeling that the orchestra had suddenly stopped, the sinking sensation that the play was over. The sweat broke out on his face, and he sprang to his feet, looked about him with his white, conscious smile, and winked at himself in the mirror. With something of the old childish belief in miracles with which he had so often gone to class, all his lessons unlearned, Paul dressed and dashed whistling down the corridor to the elevator.

He had no sooner entered the dining room and caught the measure of the music than his remembrance was lightened by his old elastic power of claiming the moment, mounting with it, and finding it all-sufficient. The glare and glitter about him, the mere scenic accessories had again, and for the last time, their old potency. He would show himself that he was game, he would finish the thing splendidly. He doubted, more than ever, the existence of Cordelia Street, and for the first time he drank his wine recklessly. Was he not, after all, one of those fortunate beings born to the purple, was he not still himself and in his own place? He drummed a nervous accompaniment to the Pagliacci music and looked about him, telling himself over and over that it had paid.

He reflected drowsily, to the swell of the music and the chill sweetness of his wine, that he might have done it more wisely. He might have caught an outbound steamer and been well out of their clutches before now. But the other side of the world had seemed too far away and too uncertain then; he could not have waited for it; his need had been too sharp. If he had to choose over again, he would do the same thing tomorrow. He looked affectionately about the dining room, now gilded with a soft mist. Ah, it had paid indeed!

Paul was awakened next morning by a painful throbbing in his head and feet. He had thrown himself across the bed without undressing, and had slept with his shoes on. His limbs and hands were lead heavy, and his tongue and throat were parched and burnt. There came upon him one of those fateful attacks of clearheadedness that never occurred except when he was physically exhausted and his nerves hung loose. He lay still, closed his eyes, and let the tide of things wash over him.

His father was in New York; "stopping at some joint or other," he told himself. The memory of successive summers on the front stoop fell upon him like a weight of black water. He had not a hundred dollars left; and he knew now, more than ever, that money was everything, the wall that stood between all he loathed and all he wanted. The thing was winding itself up; he had thought of that on his first glorious day in New York, and had even provided a way to snap the thread. It lay on his dressing table now; he had got it out last night when he came blindly up from dinner, but the shiny metal hurt his eyes, and he disliked the looks of it.

He rose and moved about with a painful effort, succumbing now and again to attacks of nausea. It was the old depression exaggerated; all the world had become Cordelia Street. Yet somehow he was not afraid of anything, was absolutely calm; perhaps because he had looked into the dark corner at last and knew. It was bad enough, what he saw there, but somehow not so bad as his long fear of it had been. He saw everything clearly now. He had a feeling that he had made the best of it, that he had lived the sort of life he was meant to live, and for half an hour he sat staring at the revolver. But he told himself that was not the way, so he went downstairs and took a cab to the ferry.

When Paul arrived in Newark he got off the train and took another cab, directing the driver to follow the Pennsylvania tracks out of the town. The snow lay heavy on the roadways and had drifted deep in the open fields. Only here and there the dead grass or dried weed stalks projected, singularly black, above it. Once well into the country, Paul dismissed the carriage and walked, floundering along the tracks, his mind a medley of irrelevant things. He seemed to hold in his brain an actual picture of everything he had seen that morning. He remembered every feature of both his drivers, of the toothless old woman from whom he had bought the red flowers in his coat, the agent from whom he had got his ticket, and all of his fellow passengers on the ferry. His mind, unable to cope with vital matters near at hand, worked feverishly and deftly at sorting and grouping these images. They made for him a part of the ugliness of the world, of the ache in his head, and the bitter burning on his tongue. He stooped and put a handful of snow into his mouth as he walked, but that, too, seemed hot. When he reached a little hillside, where the tracks ran through a cut some twenty feet below him, he stopped and sat down.

The carnations in his coat were drooping with the cold, he noticed, their red glory all over. It occurred to him that all the flowers he had seen in the glass cases that first night must have gone the same way, long before this. It was only one splendid breath they had, in spite of their brave mockery at the winter outside the glass; and it was a losing game in the end, it seemed, this revolt against the homilies by which the world is run. Paul took one of the blossoms carefully from his coat and scooped a little hole in the snow, where he covered it up. Then he dozed awhile, from his weak condition, seemingly insensible to the cold.

The sound of an approaching train awoke him, and he started to his feet, remembering only his resolution, and afraid lest he should be too late. He stood watching the approaching locomotive, his teeth chattering, his lips drawn away from them in a frightened smile; once or twice he glanced nervously sidewise, as though he were being watched. When the right moment came, he jumped. As he fell, the folly of his haste occurred to him with merciless clearness, the vastness of what he had left undone. There flashed through his brain, clearer than ever before, the blue of Adriatic water, the yellow of Algerian sands.

He felt something strike his chest, and that his body was being thrown swiftly through the air, on and on, immeasurably far and fast, while his limbs were gently relaxed. Then, because the picture-making mechanism was crushed, the disturbing visions flashed into black, and Paul dropped back into the immense design of things.

QUESTIONS FOR DISCUSSION AND WRITING

1. The story begins with Paul requesting the lifting of his suspension from school and lying about wanting to be reinstated. Why does Paul have so deep an antipathy against school? Why are his teachers so poisoned against him?
2. What do Cordelia Street and the nearsighted young man Paul's father wants him to be like have to do with Paul's unhappiness and his need to escape? How much of his problem and desire for escape have to do with school and how much with home and his neighborhood? Are they linked? If so, how?
3. Paul's teachers think garish fiction might be behind what they see as his perverse imagination. We are told that the truth about Paul is that he rarely reads. What is Cather suggesting to us about education and educators in the portrayal of Paul being so misread by his teachers?
4. Why does Paul need to show his teachers such contempt and to show himself to be different from his classmates? What do you imagine is the nature of what Cather refers to as "the homilies" Paul gets from his teachers? Why are they so insufferable to Paul?
5. The principal of the school manages to get Paul's father to remove Paul from being an usher in what for Paul is the fairy-tale world of Carnegie Hall, hastening Paul's theft and his escape to New York. Is removing him from being an usher a reasonable, understandable course of action? Or does it reveal the degree to which Paul and his needs are misunderstood?
6. Paul's education away from school in the East appears to follow the course of his becoming utterly convinced of "the omnipotence of wealth" and that "money was everything." What do you imagine Cather is trying to tell us about Paul's apparent susceptibility to these kinds of lessons? What should we make of the fact that Paul is able to find himself and to feel as if he has found his own kind of people?
7. To what extent is "Paul's Case" a story about conformity and the social and educational expectations imposed on a boy, as opposed to being a story

about a boy who is without a mother and emotionally disturbed, a singular case who longs to stand out and be different from the pack?

8. In addition to the Pittsburgh public school Paul attends there are references in the story to his attending Sabbath school. The Sabbath school teacher is quoted in the Pittsburgh paper that she will "spare no effort" in "reclaiming" Paul. What is Cather's view of the Sabbath school and the ways it affects Paul?

ON TECHNIQUE AND STYLE

1. Cather uses color in significant ways in her story. Paul's red carnation puts the faculty off. Paul hates his "yellow-papered room" and believes he is "born to the purple." At the story's end Paul flashes on "the blue of Adriatic water, the yellow of Algerian sands" and, we are told, "the disturbing visions flashed into black." How do these colors contribute to the story? What about the order in which they appear?

2. What examples does Cather provide in the story that reveal the nature of how Paul is psychologically disturbed? How convincing are these in revealing the boy's character as opposed to the inability of the adults in his life to understand him?

3. What is the effect of Cather's phrasing at the end of the story when she tells us "the picture-making mechanism was crushed"? What is she revealing in her choice of language?

CULTURAL QUESTION

1. At one point in the story, while Paul is in New York, we are told of his meeting a freshman from Yale who offered to show him "the night side of town." The two stayed out all night and had "a singularly cool" parting. The story was written in 1905. Could this reference to the Yale student be a coded way, for that time period, of suggesting a homosexual liaison between the two boys? Does Paul's strangeness, his desire for the purple and for theatricality, strike you as being a coded way of identifying him as gay?

POETRY

We Real Cool

Gwendolyn Brooks

Gwendolyn Brooks (1917–2000) is one of the twentieth century's most acclaimed poets. An African American, she was born in Kansas but spent most of her life in Chicago.

She published her first poem when she was thirteen and her first collection, A Street in Bronzeville, *in 1945. That was followed by a volume of poems,* Annie Allen, *which was awarded the Pulitzer Prize for Poetry. She also published a novel,* Maud Martha. *Later collections of poetry include* The Bean Eaters, Selected Poems, In the Mecca, Riot, *and* Family Pictures. *A collection of her writing from the 1960s to the 1980s,* To Disembark, *appeared in 1981.*

"We Real Cool" is a sharp and vital portrayal of young men who have dropped out of school and decided to live in the fast lane—around the pool hall, the Golden Shovel, and out on the streets. In its compression and simplicity and alliteration, the poem compels us to realize both the hopelessness and the excitement of their lives, the waywardness and the rebellion.

THE POOL PLAYERS.
SEVEN AT THE GOLDEN SHOVEL.

We real cool. We
Left school. We

Lurk late. We
Strike straight. We

Sing sin. We
Thin gin. We

Jazz June. We
Die soon.

QUESTIONS FOR DISCUSSION AND WRITING

1. How cool are the young men in this poem? They have left school and adopted street values versus values they might have acquired through schooling. They have a short future and are destined to "die soon." Is there something in them that we are made to feel is worth admiring? Something that makes them cool?

2. Is there a sense in this poem of what might drive these young men from the classroom to hang out at the pool room and to act up and act out? What are we to assume their reasons might be for forsaking school and seeking a life apart from it?

3. Brooks has compared these young men in her poem to the unknown soldiers, famous in World War II, who would assert their identity as soldiers by inscribing "Kilroy was here." Is there a link in the poem between the peril of a young soldier's life, a young combatant facing likely or imminent death, and the lives of the seven at the Golden Shovel? If Brooks views

these young men as having heroic traits by choosing to live their lives dangerously in the ways that soldiers do, how is it that she also seems to be indicting them for their choice in deciding to be school dropouts and, inevitably, their being fated to being young corpses?

4. How might we best characterize the young men in this poem? Some might say rebels without a cause or young men with no place to go. What do we learn about them from the verbs in the poem after the fact is established that they have left school and before we learn that they will die soon? Are their actions tied to and a direct consequence of their leaving school, or are they likely more a part of their character and who they are?

CULTURAL QUESTION

1. The picture Brooks creates in her poem "We Real Cool" is one clearly and unmistakably of black young men who have left school. The poem is a precursor to rap and hip-hop and brings to mind the fact that so much rap and hip-hop has crossed over, with their messages being absorbed by young people of all racial and cultural backgrounds. Does this poem fit that category? Or is it a poem that suggests racial or gender exclusivity?

The History Teacher

Billy Collins

Billy Collins (1941–   ) was named U.S. poet laureate in 2001. With a PhD in English, he has been a college teacher for many years and has had his poetry appear in leading literary journals as well as magazines such as Harpers *and* The New Yorker. *He has published eight volumes of poetry and has had remarkable success and popularity, with three of his books surpassing sales records for poetry.*

"The History Teacher" is a brief on poor teaching for what might be tenderhearted (what the poet calls protective) reasons. The Irish novelist James Joyce's character Stephen Daedalus described history as "a nightmare from which I am trying to awake." That is relevant to the essential question raised in Collins's poem. Should a history teacher try to help students escape the nightmare of history? What is the educator's role and responsibility when faced with teaching students about a reality that can be disillusioning and difficult, perhaps even heartbreaking to face?

Trying to protect his students' innocence
he told them the Ice Age was really just
the Chilly Age, a period of a million years
when everyone had to wear sweaters.

And the Stone Age became the Gravel Age,
named after the long driveways of the time.

The Spanish Inquisition was nothing more
than an outbreak of questions such as
"How far is it from here to Madrid?"
"What do you call the matador's hat?"

The War of the Roses took place in a garden,
and the Enola Gay dropped one tiny atom
on Japan.

The children would leave his classroom
for the playground to torment the weak
and the smart,
mussing up their hair and breaking their glasses,

while he gathered up his notes and walked home
past flower beds and white picket fences,
wondering if they would believe that soldiers
in the Boer War told long, rambling stories
designed to make the enemy nod off.

QUESTIONS FOR DISCUSSION AND WRITING

1. How would you best describe the poet's attitude in this poem toward his subject, which is the miseducation of youth by a history teacher trying to protect his students from loss of innocence by teaching what is illusory? Is the poet serious or satiric? Is he ridiculing the teacher or is he sympathetic?
2. What is the picture we get of the students as the poet describes their behavior outside the classroom in the playground? Are their actions tied in with the watered-down view of history being presented by their teacher?
3. There is an absurdity in such notions as wearing sweaters during the ice age or having driveways in the stone age. Such examples highlight what we call an anachronistic view of history. Still, one might argue that the teacher is trying to make the content he is teaching relevant to the lives of his students and to what they understand from their own modern perspective. What do you think the poet is trying to convey through such absurdities?

4. In the poem's final image, the teacher is walking home wondering if the students will believe that soldiers during the Boer War, a long and bitter conflict involving a great number of deaths and much suffering, told "long, rambling stories / designed to make the enemy nod off." Is Collins portraying one history teacher who is misguided and misled into deceiving his students—or is he intimating something about the way history and perhaps other subjects that are painful to study are being taught in schools?

ON TECHNIQUE AND STYLE

1. Some of the examples Collins uses are ridiculous. Are they funny? What effect does the possible injection of humor in what is obviously a poem with a serious theme have on readers?
2. Collins contrasts the way the children behave outside the classroom with the picture we get of the history teacher outside the classroom. What is the overall effect on readers of this technique?

CULTURAL QUESTION

1. The teacher is presenting a softening of the dreaded Spanish Inquisition and wars fought by European powers. The teacher walks home "past flower beds and white picket fences." How much is Collins picturing for us a world of a white bourgeoisie of European descent? Is this the world he portrays? If so, what is he saying about the ways those in that world are kept shielded and what consequences seem to follow?

GRAPHIC FICTION

From Remembrance of Things Past: Combray

Marcel Proust, adapted by Stephane Heuet

Marcel Proust is one of the pioneers of the modern novel, a giant in French and world literature who was born in Auteuil, near Paris. A Jewish gay man, he is best known for his stream of consciousness 3,400-page classic novel, Remembrance of Things Past, *a vivid and beautifully written portrait of the French aristocracy at the turn of the twentieth century. French comic artist Stephane Heuet began adapting Proust's famous novel in 1998. Heuet worked in the navy and as an ad executive in France before turning* Remembrance of Things Past *into a graphic novel. The selection from* Combray *is from one of Heuet's volumes.*

It was Saint-Hilaire's steeple that gave to all occupations, to all hours, to all perspectives of the city, their shape, their crowning, their consecration.

In a confused way, my grandmother found what she most prized in the world in Combray's steeple: natural and distinguished air.

MY DEARS, MAKE FUN OF ME IF YOU LIKE, IT MAY NOT BE BEAUTIFUL ACCORDING TO THE RULES...

...BUT ITS STRANGE OLD FACE PLEASES ME. I'M SURE THAT IF IT WERE PLAYING THE PIANO, IT WOULDN'T PLAY POORLY.

And today still...

QUESTIONS FOR DISCUSSION AND WRITING

1. On this single page we learn what the effect of a good education had on the thoughtful, sensitive child Marcel during his summer vacations in Combray during the late nineteenth century. This is presented to us via Marcel's memories, which were filled with a deep and abiding love of books. How can such joy of learning be instilled or inspired in today's classrooms or in some of the children we have encountered such as Sylvia in Bambara's "The Lesson" or Marie in "Saint Marie" or Paul in "Paul's Case" or the seven at the Golden Shovel? Is the love of books and learning something that comes naturally or is it mainly instilled by culture and nurture and by education?
2. Teachers and schoolmates seem to have secrets of truth and beauty for Marcel, our young protagonist. Can you cite examples from your own past or present education where this seemed to be the case? Were the secrets contained in books or in philosophy as special for you as they appear to be for young Marcel? What were they?
3. The memories our protagonist cherishes are of summer escapes in Combray from what he describes as "my personal existence's mundane incidents." Can books, especially those associated with school and education, actually provide an escape and become memorable enough to last a lifetime?

ON TECHNIQUE AND STYLE

1. How does Heuet help us to experience time as young Marcel is experiencing it while engaged in book learning?
2. There are two pictures in this graphic fiction excerpt of what appear to be conjured in young Marcel's mind. How effective are they?

CULTURAL QUESTION

1. How might the sentiments and love of learning in this selection, set over a century ago in France, still have relevance to young people today who come from all different cultural backgrounds?

VISUAL TEXTS

Marshals Escort Girls from School

November 15, 1960: Three African American girls leave the previously all-white McDonogh Elementary School in New Orleans, 1960, after spending their second

day in the integrated school. The girls were escorted to the school in the morning and are escorted out in the afternoon by the U.S. Marshals. One of the girls can be seen behind the marshal on the right. The third is following the last marshal.

In the Schoolroom

Theophile Emmanuel Duverger

Theophile Emmanuel Duverger (1821–1901) was a French Realist painter known for his genre work often of children in a domestic setting like this Georgia schoolroom.

Schoolhouse and Pupils

E. S. Shipp

The Rock Creek school, a rural one-room schoolhouse with fifteen pupils, Fannin County, Georgia, as photographed in 1913.

QUESTIONS FOR DISCUSSION AND WRITING

1. The girls in this first photo are six years old, two of the four black children selected, by federal government order, to desegregate schools in New Orleans in 1960. How do you imagine they must have felt going into an all-white school where, it would turn out, they were compelled to be by themselves for a period of weeks until the white parents gave in and allowed their children to attend an integrated school? What does the photo evoke about the historical challenges faced by those pushed to the inequitable outside of educational institutions? What are some of the lingering effects?

2. Describe your reactions to the painting *In the Schoolroom*. What kind of learning do you imagine went on in a nineteenth-century classroom like the one pictured here? How does it compare and contrast to classrooms like those in your early education? Notice the details in the painting such as the

crucifix and the religious statue and the child at prayer as well as the child who is asleep and the child wearing a dunce cap. What do such details tell us about the overall nature of the kind of education that occurred in this classroom? What do they tell us about the teacher?

3. "Schoolhouse and Pupils" is a picture of a one-room schoolhouse in Georgia. What kind of an education do you imagine these children received? Do not assume because it looks older and rural, backward really, that there might not be good old-fashioned basics being taught. Sometimes schools like this one, depending on the teachers, really drilled the three R's into children. But it seems obvious an interdisciplinary approach to education might be lacking, particularly since children of different ages are all being lumped together. What are your notions of what an education might be like in a schoolhouse such as this one?

ON TECHNIQUE AND STYLE

1. Compare the use of black and white in the two photos to the use of color in the painting by Duverger. Describe the differences in effect.
2. Describe the difference in perception in the two black and white photographs. The photo of the marshals escorting the students focuses on the face of at least one of the pupils and the escorting marshals, whereas the one-room schoolhouse photo is a long-distance shot that makes the faces appear remote. Compare and contrast the effects.

CULTURAL QUESTION

1. Imagine someone from a different culture studying these photographs or this painting. What do you think their responses might be to what they reveal and display about American cultural history?

AUDIO TEXTS   To hear these conversations, go to www.mhhe.com/soundideas1e

Track 3.1

(date: April 26, 2005; running time: 50:50 min.)

Panel discussion on interdisciplinary studies with **Leonard Shlain, Herman Haluza, Jamie Molaro,** *and* **Geoffrey Green.** *The focus is on higher education and bringing together such usually separate course studies as science and art with humanities. Many, like the authors of* Teaching as a Subversive Activity, *believe that breaking down traditional curriculum barriers is the way educational reform ought to be moving.*

Shlain is chairman of laproscopic surgery at the California Pacific Medical Center in San Francisco and associate professor of surgery at the University of California, San Francisco. He is the author of Art and Physics; The Alphabet Versus the Goddess; *and* Sex, Time and Power.

Haluza is an instructor in English at San Francisco State and Cal State East Bay and editor of the journal Ancient Paths/Modern Journeys.

Molaro is a student majoring in comparative literature and astrophysics at San Francisco State.

Green is professor of English at San Francisco State, where he directed the NEXA science/humanities interdisciplinary program. He also has served as editor of Modern Fiction Studies.

Track 3.2

(date: February 24, 2005; running time: 50:50 min.)

*See **Adrienne Rich's** biography.*

QUESTIONS FOR DISCUSSION AND WRITING

1. In Track 3.1, Shlain is urging a new way of education that relies on interdisciplinary connections in an age of specialization. How viable do you believe such an approach to teaching would be? Does his argument seem convincing that two such seemingly disparate disciplines as art and physics can be taught in connection with each other? How does his argument for connections in education between separate courses connect with ideas advocated by Rich in her speech to the women graduates of Douglass College or Postman and Weingartner in their proposals in the selection from *Teaching as a Subversive Activity*?

2. In Track 3.1, Haluza gives examples of interdisciplinarity in education and states his belief that these show signs of a rebirth in approaches to learning. He introduces a young undergraduate student, Jamie, who has produced a paper connecting astronomy and myth as another example of change. Do you agree or disagree that education is entering a new era of interdisciplinarity? Would such an approach have helped Lorde or Angelou as children, or the children in Bambara's story "The Lesson," or the four in Brooks's poem "We Real Cool," or the school kids in Barthelme's story "The School"? What would be the benefits of stressing interdisciplinary studies in schools? Is there a downside?

3. In Track 3.1, Green, who directs a team taught interdisciplinary science/humanities program at San Francisco State, quotes a Harvard-based study, Project Zero, which reinforces the positive results of interdisciplinary courses. Green speaks of "a convergence approach" wherein different disciplines look at meeting points of problems and, as a result, address both the discipline and interdisciplinarity. Would you have wanted such an approach in your own education? Would you want more of such an approach now?

4. For Track 3.2, focus on the differences that occur between what you experience in both thought and feeling upon reading a speech delivered by Rich and hearing her speak in an audio interview. Which of the two makes content and ideas clearer to you?

5. In Track 3.2, Rich is asked in this interview if poetry can bring change. Her response is that it connects instead of divides and that it has been doing that for what she describes as "numberless communities." If poetry goes, as Rich says, "to the undercurrents of feelings," "the life of the feelings," what kinds of learning results?

6. A caller asks Rich in Track 3.2 about who is reading poetry and the state of poetry. Her response is that it is being written and taught among "youth at risk, ex-gang members, beleaguered citizens." She says, "A great deal is being read at large sometimes under conditions of economic duress." Think about poetry you have read and studied in school. Would it have been more useful or valuable to have read and studied it outside the classroom? Is poetry, like Shlain says, the kind of subject that needs to be taught in conjunction with a subject like physics? Can lessons from poetry be made relevant to those outside the mainstream?

ON TECHNIQUE AND STYLE

1. Does Shlain's argument seem convincing that two such disparate disciplines as art and physics can be taught in connection with each other?

2. How convincing are Haluza and Green about the advantages and benefits of a more interdisciplinary approach to education?

3. Focus on the differences that occur between what you experience upon reading the speech Rich delivered and hearing her speak in the audio interview. In which of the two does she make her ideas clearer?

CULTURAL QUESTION

1. Is poetry a way to reach students on a multicultural level or to evoke a greater interest in learning in students who are on the margins or even outside the school environment such as the seven in Brooks's poem? Is interdisciplinary education a likely way to reach more of these students?

CONNECTIONS

1. In the selections by Rich, Lorde, Angelou, Cather, Erdrich, and Collins, we see examples of miseducation or ill-advised education. What can we deduce from some of these works about what the purpose of an education should or ought to be?

2. What are some of the major inequities that are highlighted in the essays, stories, and poems as well as in the visual selections?

3. The authors of the selection from *Teaching as a Subversive Activity* and the graphic fiction excerpt and audio excerpts provide a more positive view of what might make for a better and more productive education. How would we best characterize those factors?

4. Consider the nature of the changes that have occurred in education from the time of the three images or from the time period in which stories like Cather's or Erdrich's appear or the time set in the first-person accounts of Rich, Lorde, or Angelou. What are the most significant changes that have taken place? How have those changes altered the face of education?

5. How does Shlain's argument for connections in education connect with ideas advocated by Rich in her speech to the women graduates of Douglass College, or to proposals set forth by Postman and Weingartner in the selection from *Teaching as a Subversive Activity*?

6. Would a more concentrated interdisciplinary approach to education have helped Lorde or Angelou as children? Or the children in Bambara's "The Lesson"? Or the seven at the Golden Shovel in Brooks's "We Real Cool"?

7. Is there a sense of how teachers are portrayed that emerges from selections in this chapter? How would you characterize the view presented by various of the authors of how teachers comport and conduct themselves in the classroom?

8. What are the lessons about why young people flee from or turn against school in stories like Bambara's "The Lesson" and Cather's "Paul's Case" or in Brooks's "We Real Cool"?

9. Discuss the themes that emerge about the mixing of religion and schooling that we see in the painting *In the Schoolroom* by Duverger or in Erdrich's "St. Marie."

10. What picture emerges from the selections in this chapter concerning the issue of an equitable education for all regardless of race or gender?

FOR WRITING

CREATIVE CHOICES

1. Take a photograph or video of a classroom scene that crystallizes what for you represents an important dimension of education.

2. Compose a poem based on your educational experiences that epitomizes either the best or the worst.

3. Create a comic that illustrates what education ideally ought to be like and what you feel it should provide.

NARRATIVE/EXPOSITORY CHOICES

1. Write a narrative from your school experience that encapsulates an important lesson you and perhaps others were able to learn.

2. Focus on how you would like to see education change. What specific kinds of reform would make education more relevant and more beneficial?

3. In both the story "The School" by Barthelme and the poem "The History Teacher" by Collins we have examples of teachers trying to protect their students from unpleasant truths or what T. S. Eliot called "too much reality." How much are teachers obliged to help students face unpleasant or

rude-awakening types of truths? Or should teachers be protective of students' innocence?

ARGUMENT CHOICES

1. In a number of the selections in this chapter we get an argument, either implicit or explicit, about what a meaningful education ought to be. Frame what you believe that argument is and show how it becomes apparent in the selections you choose.
2. Take an argumentative position either for or against the notion that a number of the selections in this chapter are outdated and have no relevance to today's educational institutions since the civil rights and women's movements have both brought so much far-reaching change.
3. Argue for the greatest impact: Which selections had the most impact on your attitudes about education? The essays? Stories? Poems? Graphic novel selection? Photos? Audio texts?

RESEARCH CHOICES

1. Focus on educational reform as seen through a historic lens. What have the major institutional changes been in K–12 and in college education with respect to race, gender, and educational theory? Try to work out a paradigm about where you believe educational reform is headed.
2. Research recent successes in education as well as recent dramatic failures that have been brought to public attention. What can we glean about what works in the classroom and what fails?

VIDEO SUGGESTIONS

These videos feature stories by the authors introduced in this chapter, or are related to the chapter themes.
1. *I Know Why the Caged Bird Sings* (1979). A made-for-television film based on writer Maya Angelou's childhood. This story is about a young girl in the South who is sent to live with her grandmother after her parents divorce.
2. *Paul's Case* (1980). A made-for-television film based on Willa Cather's short story.
3. *Finding Forrester* (2000). A teen prodigy is sent to a prestigious prep school in Manhattan and finds a mentor in a reclusive author.
4. *Dead Poets Society* (1989). English professor John Keating inspires his students to love poetry and "seize the day." Robin Williams and Ethan Hawke star.
5. *Educating Rita* (1983). A young woman decides to finish her education. She meets a professor who teaches her to value her own insights while still being able to succeed at school.

 chapter **4**

Ideas about Love and Hate

INTRODUCTION

Love and hate are confounding emotions. They can coexist and one can often turn into the other. There are so many multiple varieties of both love and hate, from the most enduring to the most trivial, that either emotion often can seem as if it defies definition. Nevertheless, within this chapter you will find a multimedia smorgasbord of attempts at defining both love and hate. The purpose of the chapter is, simply put, to get you to think about what love and hate are and how, when applied to human emotion, they can be better understood and perhaps even defined.

The chapter begins with two nonfiction essays that strive to define love. Jane Goodall, perhaps the world's most famous primatologist, in a chapter excerpted from her autobiography, takes us back to our ancestral primates, the chimpanzees, in an attempt to blueprint human behavior and understand our bipolar capacity for acts both loving and hateful. Though recognizing both sides of human nature, she concludes with an affirming sense of hope tied to the human capacity to love. In the opening chapter of her book, *All about Love: New Visions,* famed African American scholar and feminist bell hooks defines love in a way that will move us toward a shared social definition, which she feels can pave the way for righting wrong views of love so many grow up absorbing. The essays in this chapter also include an article by Andrew Sullivan on hate, provocatively titled "What's So Bad about Hate." Sullivan, too, strives for definition, and provides a discourse on many varieties of hate. The nonfiction section concludes with a list, "Hateful Things," written ten centuries ago by a member of the Japanese court, Sei Shōnagon, who reveals the extraordinary range, from ancient times, of what human beings have viewed as hateful.

Flailing with talk that tries to understand the confusing and even violent and shifting definition of the nature of love, Raymond Carver's short story, "What We Talk about When We Talk about Love," is like a contemporary Plato symposium in its attempt to catch some definition of love. The story by Julia Alvarez, "Amor Divino," immerses us in a Dominican family's experience with trying to define love embattled as well as divinely inspired. Two stories about the shocking consequences of different brands of hate follow. Though both tales conclude with murder, Shirley Jackson's "The Lottery" and Edgar Allan Poe's

"The Cask of Amontillado" focus on different forms of hatred, one motivated by ritual and tradition, the other by a personal sense of the desire for retribution. In the poetry section, selected poems by Audre Lorde and Julie Sheehan make an attempt to define love in Lorde's case, and hate in Sheehan's.

Love and hate appear to converge in the teenage world of Daniel Clowes's *Ghost World,* where emotions run high and love and hate become rapidly shifting. We also include visual representations of the mysteriousness of trying to define love, as envisioned by the famous surrealist painter René Magritte and two well-known photographs that convey a connection between love and peace, as well as a cartoon of what may lie under the appearance of amity and love in human relationships.

In interviews with authors Sue Gerhardt, a psychotherapist, and Dr. Thomas Lewis, a psychiatrist, love is viewed through scientific and psychological lenses as both authors try to define it. We hear, too, about hate on the Internet and in East Texas from Mark Potok of the Southern Poverty Law Center, a civil rights organization that tracks hate groups. Also in the audio section are statements about love excerpted from live interviews with bell hooks and Jane Goodall.

NONFICTION

Compassion and Love

Jane Goodall

Jane Goodall (1934–   ) was born in London. She is a renowned primatologist and one of the world's foremost authorities on chimpanzees. At the age of twenty-six she went to Tanzania in East Africa to study the chimpanzee population, unheard of for a woman to be doing alone at that time. Her discovery of how the Gombe chimps fashioned tools for fishing termites from nests was a major breakthrough. She went on to study chimp behavior and to reveal new understandings of the ways chimps behave in love and war. In 1965 she received a PhD in ethology from Cambridge University. She has published many scientific articles. Books on her work in Gombe include In the Shadow of Man *and* Through a Window. *She also published two autobiographies in letters; a spiritual autobiography,* Reason for Hope: A Spiritual Journey; *and many children's books. She has been the subject of numerous television documentaries as well as being featured in the 2002 film* Jane Goodall's Wild Chimpanzees.

The essay included here, "Compassion and Love," first appeared in 2002 in Reason for Hope. *In it, Goodall writes about the split nature of chimp behavior between nurturing, peaceful, empathic, and seemingly loving acts and more brutal, cruel, and aggressive ones. In the essay she moves from observations about chimps to a focus on the behavior of humans and, as the title of both her book and the chapter indicate, she concludes on a note of hope based on the human capacity to extend beyond the self and to love.*

From the earliest years at Gombe I had been fascinated and delighted by the friendly and nurturing behavior that I observed so often among the chimpanzees. Peaceful interactions within a community are seen much more often than aggressive ones. Indeed, for hours, even days, one can follow a small group of chimps and see no aggression at all. Of course, these chimpanzees are, as we have seen, capable of violence and brutality. But fights between members of the same community seldom last more than a few seconds and rarely result in wounding. For the most part, relationships between the members of a community are relaxed and friendly, and we see frequent expressions of caring, helping, compassion, altruism, and most definitely a form of love.

Chimpanzees are intensely physical. When friends meet, after a separation, they may embrace and kiss each other. When they are fearful or suddenly terribly excited they reach out to touch each other—sometimes they show a whole orgy of contact-seeking behaviors, embracing, pressing open mouths upon each other, patting each other, holding hands. Friendships are maintained and poor relationships improved by the most important of all friendly behaviors—social grooming. Grooming enables adult chimpanzees to spend long hours in friendly, relaxed physical contact. A session may last more than an hour as the participants work their way, with soothing movements of their fingers, over every inch of each other's bodies. Grooming is used to calm tense or nervous companions, and mothers often quiet restless or distressed infants in the same way. And when chimps play, there is a lot of body contact as they tickle each other, and roll over and over in bouts of rough-and-tumble wrestling matches. Loud chuckles of chimpanzee laughter accompany these joyous play sessions so that even fully adult group members are sometimes compelled to join in.

As the years passed at Gombe and we learned more about who was related to whom in the chimpanzees' complex society it became obvious that ties between family members were particularly strong and enduring, and not just between mothers and their offspring, but also between siblings. I learned a great deal from the hours I spent with old Flo and her family. I watched as she not only rushed to the defense of her juvenile offspring, Flint and Fifi, but also tried to help her adult sons, Figan and Faben. When Flint was born, Fifi soon became utterly preoccupied with the new baby. As soon as she was allowed, she played with him, groomed him, and carried him around. Indeed, she became a real help to her mother. Eventually I realized that all young chimpanzees are fascinated and delighted by new arrivals in their families, and that these sibling relationships persist over many years. Brothers become close friends as they mature and often then become allies, protecting each other in social conflicts or when under attack by other individuals.

These sibling bonds are adaptive in many ways. On one occasion, nine-year-old Pom, leading her family along a forest trail, suddenly saw a big snake coiled up. Uttering a soft call of concern she rushed up a tree. But little brother Prof, still a bit unsteady on his feet at three years old, ignored her warning. Perhaps he did not understand its meaning or simply did not hear it. As he got closer and closer to the snake Pom's hair bristled with alarm, and she grinned hugely in fear. Suddenly, as though she couldn't bear it anymore, she rushed down to Prof, gathered him up, and climbed back up her tree.

One most moving story is about orphan Mel and Spindle, his adolescent protector. Mel was three and a quarter years old when his mother died. He had no elder brother or sister to adopt him. To our amazement (for we had thought he would die), he was adopted by twelve-year-old Spindle. Although all members of the Gombe chimpanzee population have a few genes in common, Spindle was certainly not closely related to Mel. Nevertheless, as the weeks went by, the two became inseparable. Spindle waited for Mel during travel; he permitted the infant to ride on his back, even allowed him to cling beneath, as a mother carries her baby, when Mel was frightened or when it was raining. Most remarkably, if Mel got too close to the big males during social excitement when inhibitions are sometimes swept aside, Spindle would hurry to remove his small charge from danger even though this usually meant he was buffeted himself. For a whole year this close relationship endured, and there can be no doubt that Spindle saved Mel's life. Why did Spindle act that way, burdening himself with the care of a small, sickly youngster who was not even a close relative? Probably we shall never know, but it is interesting to reflect that during the epidemic that claimed Mel's mother, Spindle's ancient mother died also. A typical twelve-year-old male chimpanzee, though perfectly able to fend for himself, will continue to spend much time with his mother, especially if he has been through a stressful time with the adult males, or been hurt in a fight. Is it possible that Spindle's loss of his mother left an empty space in his life? And that the close contact with a small dependent youngster helped to fill that space? Or did Spindle experience an emotion similar to that which we call compassion? Perhaps he felt a mixture of both.

Chimpanzees in zoos are often kept in enclosures surrounded or partially surrounded by water-filled moats. Since they do not swim, death by drowning has been a sadly frequent mishap. But almost always one or more of the victim's companions have attempted to rescue the individual in difficulties. There are a number of accounts of heroic rescues, or rescue attempts. In one instance an adult male lost his life as he tried to rescue a drowning infant who was not his own.

Evolutionary biologists do not count the helping of family members as true altruism. Your kin all share, to a greater or lesser extent, some of the same genes as yourself. So your action, they argue, is just a way of ensuring that as many of those precious genes as possible are preserved. Even if you lose your life through some helping act, your mother or sibling or child who has been saved will ensure that your own genes are still represented in future generations. Thus your behavior can still be seen as fundamentally selfish. And what if you help an individual who is not related to you? This is explained as an example of "reciprocal altruism"—help your companion today in the expectation that he will help you tomorrow. This sociobiological theory, while helpful in understanding the basic mechanism of the evolutionary process, tends to be dangerously reductionist when used as the sole explanation of human—or chimpanzee—behavior. After all, whilst our biological nature and instincts can hardly be denied, we are, and have been for thousands of years, caught up in cultural evolution as well. We do things which are sometimes quite unrelated to any hope for genetic survival in the future. Even Richard Dawkins, in an interview in the London Times Magazine, said , "Most of us, if we see somebody in great distress, weeping—we will go and put an arm around them and try to console them. It's a thing I have an overwhelming impulse to do. . . and so we know that we can rise above our Darwinian past." When he was asked how this could be, he smiled and said he didn't know. But I gradually came to see that a simple explanation presents itself.

Patterns of caring and helping and reassurance evolved, over thousands of years, in the context of the mother-child and family relationships. In this

context they are clearly beneficial to the well-being of the living individuals as well as in the evolutionary sense. So these behaviors have become
ever more firmly embedded in the genetic endowment of chimpanzees (and
other higher, social animals). And so we would expect an individual who is
constantly interacting with other familiar companions—with whom he plays,
grooms, travels, and feeds and with whom he forms close relationships—to
treat them, at least sometimes, as honorary family members. Obviously, then,
he is likely to respond to the distress or pleas of these honorary family members as well as those of his blood "relations. In other words, a close but not
related companion may be treated as if he or she were biological kin.

Compassion and self-sacrifice are highly valued qualities in many human
cultures. if we know that another person, particularly a close personal friend
or relative, is suffering, we become upset. Only by doing something, by helping (or trying to help) can we alleviate our own discomfort. We may also feel
the need to help people we do not know at all. We send money, or clothing, or medical equipment to earthquake victims, refugees, or other suffering people in all corners of the globe, once their plight has been brought to
our attention. Do we do these things so that others will applaud our virtuous
behavior? Or because the sight of starving children or homeless refugees
evokes in us feelings of pity which make us terribly uncomfortable, feelings of
guilt because we know we have so much, and they so little?

If our motivation to perform charitable acts is simply to advance our
social standing, or to lessen our inner discomfort, should we not conclude
that our action, in the final analysis, is nothing more than selfish? Some
might argue thus—and in some cases it could be true. But I believe it is
wrong—dangerous even—to accept reductionistic arguments of this sort that
denigrate all that is most truly noble in our species. History resounds with
tales of extraordinarily inspirational acts of courage and self-sacrifice. Good
heavens!—the very fact that we can feel distressed by the plight of people
we have never met says it all for me. It is, surely, remarkable and heartwarm-
ing that we can empathize, and feel truly saddened, when we hear of a child
brain-damaged in an accident; an elderly couple losing their life savings to a
thief; a family dog stolen and sold to a medical research lab and traced too
late to be saved.

So here we are, the human ape, half sinner, half saint, with two opposing
tendencies inherited from our ancient past pulling us now toward violence,
now toward compassion and love. Are we, forever, to be torn in two different
directions, cruel in one instance, kind the next? Or do we have the ability to
control these tendencies, choosing the direction we wish to go? During the
early 1970s these were the questions that gripped me. Yet here again, my
observations of the apes offered at least a glimmer of an answer.

Thus chimpanzees, I realized, although freer to act the way they feel than
we are, are not entirely uninhibited. As they get older, they usually give up the
frustrated tantrums of childhood, although they may let off steam by charging through the undergrowth, sometimes slapping a bystander who gets in

the way. An outburst of swearing and table thumping can sometimes do the same for humans. Chimpanzees have excellent mechanisms for defusing tense situations. Thus the victim in a fight, even though he or she is clearly fearful, often approaches the aggressor, uttering screams or whimpers of fear, and makes some gesture or posture of submission, such as crouching low to the ground, or holding out a pleading hand as though begging for reassurance. And the aggressor will usually respond—touching, patting, or even kissing or embracing the supplicant. The victim visibly relaxes and social harmony is restored. Indeed, for the most part, the chimpanzees follow Danny's[1] favorite text: they seldom let the sun go down on their wrath.

One female chimpanzee, living in a large captive group in a zoo in Holland, became amazingly skillful at restoring peaceful relations. Whenever two of the adult males were sitting tense after a conflict, avoiding each other's gaze, there would be noticeable agitation running throughout the entire group. This old female would then initiate a grooming session with one of the rivals, during which she gradually moved a little closer to the second male—followed by her grooming partner. Then she would leave him and repeat her maneuver with his rival. Eventually the two males were so close that both could groom her at the same time. When she was thus the only thing separating them she quietly moved away, and, calmed by the grooming, and neither having to be the first to break the deadlock, they started to groom each other.

Surely, I thought, if chimpanzees can control their aggressive tendencies, and diffuse the situation when things get out of hand, so can we. And herein, perhaps, was the hope for our future: we really do have the ability to override our genetic heritage. Like strict parents or schoolteachers, we can reprimand our aggressive tendencies, deny them expression, thwart those selfish genes (unless we are suffering from some physiological or psychological disorder, and major strides have been made in medication for such conditions). Our brains are sufficiently sophisticated; it's a question of whether or not we really *want* to control our instincts.

In point of fact most of us discipline those rebel genes on a day-to-day basis. As did Whitson, a twelve-year-old African American boy, in a little incident which could have escalated into violence, but which was beautifully defused. Young Whitson was one of a group of kids gathered in Colorado for a youth summit. It had just snowed—and Whitson, from San Francisco, had not seen more than about twenty snowflakes in his life. He made a snowball that got bigger and bigger and bigger as he rolled it along the ground. Somehow he managed, with help, to get this large and very heavy mass of impacted snow onto his head. He wanted to see how far he could carry it on the planned hike. I was right close by when a girl from Virginia, white and middle-class, came up behind him and, I suppose as a joke, pushed the snowball off his head. It shattered into many pieces on the hard ground. I was close by when this happened, so I saw Whitson's face, and saw the shock,

[1]*Danny's:* Goodall's grandmother's nickname was Danny.

the horror—and then, unmistakably, the expression of fury. Indeed, he raised a hand as if to strike her, though he was much the smaller. And then she, horrified at what she had all unthinkingly started, cried out, "Oh I am so so sorry. I don't know what made me do that. I'm really, really sorry," and she knelt to try to repair the broken ball. For a moment Whitson went rigid. Slowly he lowered his arm, slowly the rage left his face. And then he too knelt. Together they repaired the snowball. He won out over his aggressive impulse—and I was proud of them both.

Indeed, it is fortunate that we are not *compelled* to obey our aggressive urges. If we did not inhibit feelings of aggression continually, society would be extremely unruly, as is the case when social norms break down during rioting and warfare—when the ugly face of anarchy grins out of the chaos.

And so, as the 1970s came to a close, I began to take heart. Our knowledge of chimpanzee behavior does, indeed, indicate that our aggressive tendencies are deeply embedded in our primate heritage. Yet so too are our caring and altruistic ones. And just as it appears that our wicked deeds can be far, far worse than the aggressive behavior of chimpanzees, so too our acts of altruism and self-sacrifice often involve greater heroism than those performed by apes. Chimpanzees, as we have seen, may respond to the immediate need of a companion in distress, even when this involves a risk to themselves. However I think it is only we humans, with our sophisticated intellect, who are capable of performing acts of self-sacrifice with full knowledge of the costs that we may have to bear, not only at the time, but also, perhaps, at some future date.

Whether or not chimpanzees would choose to die in order to save a companion if they *could* comprehend the stakes, I do not know. It seems highly unlikely that apes have any understanding of the concept of death, or their own mortality: in which case they could not make a *conscious* decision to give up their lives for a friend—although their helping actions might result in just that. But we humans certainly can make conscious decisions of this sort. We find examples of heroic self-sacrifice all the time if we read the newspapers or watch television. A recent example in England was when Pete Goss, who was winning a round-the-world yacht race, turned back, in the teeth of a terrific storm, when he heard the distress signal of a fellow competitor. Unhesitatingly he not only risked his life to rescue a French rival from his yacht that was breaking up in huge seas, but also sacrificed his chance of winning a prestigious award. Some of the most inspiring tales of heroism have come from the battlefields of war when, time and again, men and women have risked—and lost—their lives to help a wounded or endangered companion. The highest award for bravery in England, the Victoria Cross, only too often has to be awarded posthumously. Resistance fighters in occupied countries have, again and again, carried out secret missions against the enemy despite the very real risk of death and, worse, torture; sacrificing themselves and even their families for their beliefs or their country.

Acts of self-sacrifice in the hell of the death camps were frequent. There was a moving incident that took place at Auschwitz when a Pole, facing a death sentence, sobbed and begged that his life might be spared so that he could stay with his two children. At this moment, the great priest Saint Maximilian Kolbe stepped forward and offered his life instead. After surviving two weeks in the starvation bunker, Kolbe was then murdered by the Nazis but the story lived on, serving as an inspiration to surviving prisoners: a beacon of hope and love had been lit in the dark confines of the concentration camp.

Nor was it only in the death camps that such acts took place. The extraordinary and selfless deeds of Oskar Schindler, who employed and rescued countless Jews in Poland, have been immortalized in Steven Spielberg's *Schindler's List*. Less well known is the heroic effort of two consuls in Nazi-occupied Lithuania. Jan Zwartendijk, acting Dutch consul, without any authorization wrote out almost two thousand transfer permits for Lithuanian Jews who were trying to escape the approaching Nazi occupation. These documents gave them permission, from the Dutch government, to enter the Dutch colony of Curaçao. Zwartendijk was fortunate to escape himself. Japanese consul Chiune Sugihara, in direct defiance of his superiors in Tokyo, wrote out visas for several thousand Jews to pass through Russia on their way to Curaçao. He knew that this involved personal risk and being disgraced and fired. But he was a samurai who had been taught to help those in need. "I may have to disobey my government," he said, "but if I don't, I would be disobeying God." He was indeed later disgraced in Tokyo, and ended his life in financial ruin and without honor: yet some eight thousand Lithuanian Jews, who would otherwise have been killed in the death camps, escaped. It was the third largest rescue operation in the history of the Holocaust. An estimated forty thousand descendants of the Jewish refugees saved in 1940 are alive today because of the courageous actions of these two remarkable men.

The most significant event for Christians (along with the Resurrection) is that Jesus offered up His life, gave Himself into the hands of His persecutors, knowing only too well the agony He would endure. "Father . . . take this cup from me," he prayed, in the Garden of Gethsemane. "Nevertheless, not my will, but Thine be done." He sacrificed himself because He believed His act would redeem mankind.

It is these undeniable qualities of human love and compassion and self-sacrifice that give me hope for the future. We are, indeed, often cruel and evil. Nobody can deny this. We gang up on one another, we torture each other, with words as well as deeds, we fight, we kill. But we are also capable of the most noble, generous, and heroic behavior.

QUESTIONS FOR DISCUSSION AND WRITING

1. Underlying Goodall's essay is the Darwinian assumption that we can learn about our own human behavior, with respect to love and hate, by

understanding the nature of how our close relatives, the chimpanzees, exhibit the emotions. Do you agree or disagree with the essential premise that chimp behavior tells us much of what we need to know about our own behavior where love and hate are concerned?

2. Do you agree or disagree with Goodall that, with the exception of physiological or psychological disorders, we are capable of controlling our aggressive impulses? Is she right when she states that we humans have deeply embedded aggressive tendencies as well as caring and altruistic ones? Can she generalize so broadly about human beings when some are so loving and others so hateful?

3. The acts of self-sacrifice and heroism that Goodall cites seem to separate for her humans from chimpanzees. Is she saying such acts reveal a greater human capacity, through choice and awareness of our own mortality, of love?

4. Goodall brings in the Christian belief that Jesus gave up his life to redeem humankind. Does one need to be a believing Christian to accept this as an act of sacrificing love?

5. Goodall concludes her essay on a strong note of hope for the future because of love and compassion and self-sacrifice. She asserts this despite the fact that she concludes that we humans are undeniably "often cruel and evil." What would your stance be? When you weigh love in the world against hatred or vice versa, do you come out feeling hopeful? Why or why not?

ON TECHNIQUE AND STYLE

1. In arguing against a view of seeing humans as primarily selfish, Goodall suddenly exclaims "Good heavens!—the very fact that we can feel distressed by the plight of people we have never met says it all for me." What effects does this sudden sweeping and emotion-filled statement have? Is it rhetorically effective writing?

2. Consider the many examples Goodall uses to support her argument and show how they serve her in ways that increasingly focus our attention on her overall message and theme: the story of Mel and Spindle; the young San Francisco African American boy, Whitson; the white middle-class girl from Virginia; the yacht racer Pete Goss; Oskar Schindler and the lesser known acting Dutch and Japanese wartime consuls; and Jesus. How effective are her examples? How well positioned are they in the sequence in which they appear?

3. Goodall argues that we, "the human ape," are half sinner and half saint, impelled toward violence and, alternatively, to love and compassion. She reasons that "It's a question of whether or not we really want to control our instincts." Is her essay convincing of the notion that we humans have the will to control a genetic heritage that can lead either to acts of hate or of love?

CULTURAL QUESTION

1. Goodall concludes this chapter from her spiritual journey with a focus on compassion and love and a final allusion to Christian faith. All major religions

teach love but different cultures have different religious underpinnings. How might Goodall's message of hope resonate for those, let us say, from Islamic, Jewish, Buddhist, or Hindu cultures? Is her message cross-cultural?

From All about Love: New Visions

bell hooks

bell hooks (1952–   ) was born Gloria Watkins in Hopkinsville, Kentucky. An internationally recognized leading feminist and African American scholar, she was educated at Stanford, the University of Wisconsin, and the University of California, Santa Cruz, where she received a PhD. She has been professor of African American studies at Yale, associate professor of women's studies and American literature at Oberlin, distinguished professor of English at City College in New York, and distinguished professor and writer-in-residence at Berea College in Kentucky. She is the author of many scholarly and children's books, including a number of books on love: Communion: The Female Search for Love, Salvation: Black People and Love, *and the book from which this excerpt first appeared in 2000,* All about Love: New Visions.*

In this opening chapter from All about Love, *hooks stakes out what she believes love is as well as what it isn't. Having described herself on a number of occasions as "a high priestess of love," hooks attempts to sketch a definition for what she tells us early on has always been elusive and difficult to define. She argues that we would all be better off if we could have a shared definition of love.*

The men in my life have always been the folks who are wary of using the word "love" lightly. They are wary because they believe women make too much of love. And they know that what we think love means is not always what they believe it means. Our confusion about what we mean when we use the word "love" is the source of our difficulty in loving. If our society had a commonly held understanding of the meaning of love, the act of loving would not be so mystifying. Dictionary definitions of love tend to emphasize romantic love, defining love first and foremost as "profoundly tender, passionate affection for another person, especially when based on sexual attraction." Of course, other definitions let the reader know one may have such feelings within a context that is not sexual. However, deep affection does not really adequately describe love's meaning.

The vast majority of books on the subject of love work hard to avoid giving clear definitions. In the introduction to Diane Ackerman's *A Natural History of Love* she declares, "Love is the great intangible." A few sentences down from this she suggests: "Everyone admits that love is wonderful and necessary, yet no one can agree on what it is." Coyly, she adds, "We use the word love in such a sloppy way that it can mean almost nothing or absolutely everything." No definition ever appears in her book that would help anyone trying to learn the art of loving. Yet she is not alone in writing of love in ways that cloud our understanding. When the very meaning of the word is cloaked in mystery, it should not come as a surprise that most people find it hard to define what they mean when they use the word "love."

Imagine how much easier it would be for us to learn how to love if we began with a shared definition. The word "love" is most often defined as a noun, yet all the more astute theorists of love acknowledge that we would all love better if we used it as a verb. I spent years searching for a meaningful definition of the word "love," and was deeply relieved when I found one in psychiatrist M. Scott Peck's classic self-help book *The Road Less Traveled,* first published in 1978. Echoing the work of Erich Fromm, he defines love as "the will to extend one's self for the purpose of nurturing one's own or another's spiritual growth." Explaining further, he continues, "Love is as love does. Love is an act of will—namely, both an intention and an action. Will also implies choice. We do not have to love. We choose to love." Since the choice must be made to nurture growth, this definition counters the more widely accepted assumption that we love instinctually.

Everyone who has witnessed the growth process of a newborn child from the moment of birth on sees clearly that before language is known, before the identity of caretakers is recognized, babies respond to affectionate care. Usually they respond with sounds or looks of pleasure. As they grow older they respond to affectionate care by giving affection, cooing at the sight of a welcomed caretaker. Affection is only one ingredient of love. To truly love we must learn to mix various ingredients—care, affection, recognition, respect, commitment, and trust, as well as honest and open communication. Learning faulty definitions of love when we are quite young makes it difficult to be loving as we grow older. We start out committed to the right path but go in the wrong direction. Most of us learn early on to think of love as a feeling. When we feel deeply drawn to someone, we cathect with them, that is, we invest feelings or emotion in them. That process of investment wherein a loved one becomes important to us is called "cathexis." In his book Peck rightly emphasizes that most of us "confuse cathecting with loving." We all know how often individuals feeling connected to someone through the process of cathecting insist that they love the other person even if they are hurting or neglecting them. Since their feeling is that of cathexis, they insist that what they feel is love.

QUESTIONS FOR DISCUSSION AND WRITING

1. hooks begins her essay by telling us that the men she knows are wary of using the word "love" lightly because they believe women make too much of love. There are many clichés about men and women loving differently, perhaps the best known being "women use sex to get love and men use love to get sex." Do the sexes love differently?

2. hooks talks about how love generally is not defined and is often seen as being "cloaked in mystery." Do you agree? Do you think, as she does, that we would be far better off as a society if we held a shared definition of love?
3. Do you agree with hooks that we would love better if love were more a verb than a noun? Explain what you think she means by that.
4. hooks winds up fashioning a definition of love from best-selling author and psychiatrist M. Scott Peck. Does this work as a general definition of love? Does it provide us a vision of what love can and should be?
5. hooks says we choose to love. Do you agree or disagree?

ON TECHNIQUE AND STYLE

1. In using M. Scott Peck (and mentioning Erich Fromm), hooks tells us how relieved she is to have found a definition of love. The definition includes an allusion to "spiritual growth," which would exclude those not inclined to seek love in a spiritual way. How might we define spiritual in this context?
2. hooks says that "to truly love" we must learn to mix "care, affection, recognition, respect, commitment, and trust, as well as honest and open communication." This assertion builds on Peck's definition of love. She is implicitly separating true love from love that is not true. She goes on to bring in Peck's notion of cathexis. Does her reliance on Peck take away from the power of her own assertions, the independent strength of her voice as a writer? Or is Peck a strong means of bolstering what she wants and needs to say about love?
3. At the heart of hooks's essay is the statement, "Learning faulty definitions of love when we are quite young makes it difficult to be very loving as we grow older." Has her essay persuaded us of this?

CULTURAL QUESTION

1. hooks is widely known for her polemics against patriarchy and racism. From a working-class family, she has also written a great deal about class conflict. There seems little evidence in this selection of these concerns. How might we balance the fact that hooks—who has published books that focus on how black men and black women and women in general love—appears here to be concerned with how all of us, regardless of sex, race, or class, should view love?

What's So Bad about Hate

Andrew Sullivan

Andrew Sullivan (1963–   ) is an English American journalist, blogger, and former editor of The New Republic. *An HIV-positive gay conservative Catholic, he was educated at Oxford and Harvard and is a contributing writer and columnist with* The

New York Times Magazine *as well as being a weekly columnist for* The Sunday
Times *of London. His work has appeared in* The Wall Street Journal, *the* Washington Post, Esquire, The Daily Telegraph, *and* Seven Days. *His books include* Virtually Normal: An Argument about Homosexuality, *which appeared in 1995,* Love
Undetectable: Notes on Friendship, Sex and Survival *(1998), and* Nature *(2003).*
His essay "What's So Bad about Hate" first appeared in The New York Times *on*
September 26, 1999, and was included in Best American Essays of 1999.

Though the essay is, ultimately, an argument against the legal distinctions that separate hate crimes from other criminal acts, it is also a probing and well-orchestrated attempt to understand the nature of hate and why those who hate do. It also presents readers with a pessimistic yet well-reasoned rendering of why there will never be an abolition of hatred.

I.

I wonder what was going on in John William King's head two years ago when he tied James Byrd Jr.'s feet to the back of a pickup truck and dragged him three miles down a road in rural Texas. King and two friends had picked up Byrd, who was black, when he was walking home, half-drunk, from a party. As part of a bonding ritual in their fledgling white supremacist group, the three men took Byrd to a remote part of town, beat him and chained his legs together before attaching them to the truck. Pathologists at King's trial testified that Byrd was probably alive and conscious until his body finally hit a culvert and split in two. When King was offered a chance to say something to Byrd's family at the trial, he smirked and uttered an obscenity.

We know all these details now, many months later. We know quite a large amount about what happened before and after. But I am still drawn, again and again, to the flash of ignition, the moment when fear and loathing became hate, the instant of transformation when King became hunter and Byrd became prey.

What was that? And what was it when Buford Furrow Jr., longtime member of the Aryan Nations, calmly walked up to a Filipino-American mailman he happened to spot, asked him to mail a letter and then shot him at point-blank range? Or when Russell Henderson beat Matthew Shepard, a young gay man, to a pulp, removed his shoes and then, with the help of a friend, tied him to a post, like a dead coyote, to warn off others?

For all our documentation of these crimes and others, our political and moral disgust at them, our morbid fascination with them, our sensitivity to their social meaning, we seem at times to have no better idea now than we ever had of what exactly they were about. About what that moment means when, for some reason or other, one human being asserts absolute, immutable superiority over another. About not the violence, but what the violence expresses. About what—exactly—hate is. And what our own part in it may be.

I find myself wondering what hate actually is in part because we have created an entirely new offense in American criminal law—a "hate crime"—to combat it. And barely a day goes by without someone somewhere declaring war against it. Last month President Clinton called for an expansion of hate-crime laws as "what America needs in our battle against hate." A couple of weeks later, Senator John McCain used a campaign speech to denounce the "hate" he said poisoned the land. New York's Mayor, Rudolph Giuliani, recently tried to stop the Million Youth March in Harlem on the grounds that the event was organized by people "involved in hate marches and hate rhetoric."

The media concurs in its emphasis. In 1985, there were 11 mentions of "hate crimes" in the national media database Nexis. By 1990, there were more than a thousand. In the first six months of 1999, there were 7,000. "Sexy fun is one thing," wrote a New York Times reporter about sexual assaults in Woodstock '99's mosh pit. "But this was an orgy of lewdness tinged with hate." And when Benjamin Smith marked the Fourth of July this year by targeting blacks, Asians and Jews for murder in Indiana and Illinois, the story wasn't merely about a twisted young man who had emerged on the scene. As The Times put it, "Hate arrived in the neighborhoods of Indiana University, in Bloomington, in the early-morning darkness."

But what exactly was this thing that arrived in the early-morning darkness? For all our zeal to attack hate, we still have a remarkably vague idea of what it actually is. A single word, after all, tells us less, not more. For all its emotional punch, "hate" is far less nuanced an idea than prejudice, or bigotry, or bias, or anger, or even mere aversion to others. Is it to stand in for all these varieties of human experience—and everything in between? If so, then the war against it will be so vast as to be quixotic. Or is "hate" to stand for a very specific idea or belief, or set of beliefs, with a very specific object or group of objects? Then waging war against it is almost certainly unconstitutional. Perhaps these kinds of questions are of no concern to those waging war on hate. Perhaps it is enough for them that they share a sentiment that there is too much hate and never enough vigilance in combating it. But sentiment is a poor basis for law, and a dangerous tool in politics. It is better to leave some unwinnable wars unfought.

II.

Hate is everywhere. Human beings generalize all the time, ahead of time, about everyone and everything. A large part of it may even be hardwired. At some point in our evolution, being able to know beforehand who was friend or foe was not merely a matter of philosophical reflection. It was a matter of survival. And even today it seems impossible to feel a loyalty without also feeling a disloyalty, a sense of belonging without an equal sense of unbelonging. We're social beings. We associate. Therefore we disassociate. And although it would be comforting to think that the one could happen without the other, we know in reality that it doesn't. How many patriots are there who have never felt a twinge of xenophobia?

Of course by hate, we mean something graver and darker than this kind of lazy prejudice. But the closer you look at this distinction, the fuzzier it gets. Much of the time, we harbor little or no malice toward people of other backgrounds or places or ethnicities or ways of life. But then a car cuts you off at an intersection and you find yourself noticing immediately that the driver is a woman, or black, or old, or fat, or white, or male. Or you are walking down a city street at night and hear footsteps quickening behind you. You look around and see that it is a white woman and not a black man, and you are instantly relieved. These impulses are so spontaneous they are almost involuntary. But where did they come from? The mindless need to be mad at someone—anyone—or the unconscious eruption of a darker prejudice festering within?

In 1993, in San Jose, Calif., two neighbors—one heterosexual, one homosexual—were engaged in a protracted squabble over grass clippings. (The full case is recounted in "Hate Crimes," by James B. Jacobs and Kimberly Potter.) The gay man regularly mowed his lawn without a grass catcher, which prompted his neighbor to complain on many occasions that grass clippings spilled over onto his driveway. Tensions grew until one day, the gay man mowed his front yard, spilling clippings onto his neighbor's driveway, prompting the straight man to yell an obscene and common anti-gay insult. The wrangling escalated. At one point, the gay man agreed to collect the clippings from his neighbor's driveway but then later found them dumped on his own porch. A fracas ensued with the gay man spraying the straight man's son with a garden hose, and the son hitting and kicking the gay man several times, yelling anti-gay slurs. The police were called, and the son was eventually convicted of a hate-motivated assault, a felony. But what was the nature of the hate: anti-gay bias, or suburban property-owner madness?

Or take the Labor Day parade last year in Broad Channel, a small island in Jamaica Bay, Queens. Almost everyone there is white, and in recent years a group of local volunteer firefighters has taken to decorating a pickup truck for the parade in order to win the prize for "funniest float." Their themes have tended toward the outrageously provocative. Beginning in 1995, they won prizes for floats depicting "Hasidic Park," "Gooks of Hazzard" and "Happy Gays." Last year, they called their float "Black to the Future, Broad Channel 2098." They imagined their community a century hence as a largely black enclave, with every stereotype imaginable: watermelons, basketballs and so on. At one point during the parade, one of them mimicked the dragging death of James Byrd. It was caught on videotape, and before long the entire community was depicted as a caldron of hate.

It's an interesting case, because the float was indisputably in bad taste and the improvisation on the Byrd killing was grotesque. But was it hate? The men on the float were local heroes for their volunteer work; they had no record of bigoted activity, and were not members of any racist organizations. In previous years, they had made fun of many other groups and saw themselves more as provocateurs than bigots. When they were described as racists, it

came as a shock to them. They apologized for poor taste but refused to confess to bigotry. "The people involved aren't horrible people," protested a local
woman. "Was it a racist act? I don't know. Are they racists? I don't think so."

If hate is a self-conscious activity, she has a point. The men were primarily motivated by the desire to shock and to reflect what they thought was
their community's culture. Their display was not aimed at any particular black
people, or at any blacks who lived in Broad Channel—almost none do. But if
hate is primarily an unconscious activity, then the matter is obviously murkier.
And by taking the horrific lynching of a black man as a spontaneous object of
humor, the men were clearly advocating indifference to it. Was this an aberrant
excess? Or the real truth about the men's feelings toward African-Americans?
Hate or tastelessness? And how on earth is anyone, even perhaps the firefighters themselves, going to know for sure?

Or recall H.L. Mencken. He shared in the anti-Semitism of his time with more
alacrity than most and was an indefatigable racist. "It is impossible," he wrote
in his diary, "to talk anything resembling discretion or judgment into a colored
woman. They are all essentially childlike, and even hard experience does not
teach them anything." He wrote at another time of the "psychological stigmata"
of the "Afro-American race." But it is also true that, during much of his life, day
to day, Mencken conducted himself with no regard to race, and supported a
politics that was clearly integrationist. As the editor of his diary has pointed out,
Mencken published many black authors in his magazine, The Mercury, and lob-
bied on their behalf with his publisher, Alfred A. Knopf. The last thing Mencken
ever wrote was a diatribe against racial segregation in Baltimore's public parks.
He was good friends with leading black writers and journalists, including James
Weldon Johnson, Walter White and George S. Schuyler, and played an underappreciated role in promoting the Harlem Renaissance.

What would our modern view of hate do with Mencken? Probably ignore him,
or change the subject. But, with regard to hate, I know lots of people like Mencken.
He reminds me of conservative friends who oppose almost every measure for
homosexual equality yet genuinely delight in the company of their gay friends. It
would be easier for me to think of them as haters, and on paper, perhaps, there is
a good case that they are. But in real life, I know they are not. Some of them clearly
harbor no real malice toward me or other homosexuals whatsoever.

They are as hard to figure out as those liberal friends who support every
gay rights measure they have ever heard of but do anything to avoid going
into a gay bar with me. I have to ask myself in the same, frustrating kind of
way: are they liberal bigots or bigoted liberals? Or are they neither bigots nor
liberals, but merely people?

III.

Hate used to be easier to understand. When Sartre described anti-Semitism
in his 1946 essay "Anti-Semite and Jew," he meant a very specific array of
firmly held prejudices, with a history, an ideology and even a pseudoscience

to back them up. He meant a systematic attempt to demonize and eradicate an entire race. If you go to the Web site of the World Church of the Creator, the organization that inspired young Benjamin Smith to murder in Illinois earlier this year, you will find a similarly bizarre, pseudorational ideology. The kind of literature read by Buford Furrow before he rained terror on a Jewish kindergarten last month and then killed a mailman because of his color is full of the same paranoid loopiness. And when we talk about hate, we often mean this kind of phenomenon.

But this brand of hatred is mercifully rare in the United States. These professional maniacs are to hate what serial killers are to murder. They should certainly not be ignored; but they represent what Harold Meyerson, writing in Salon, called "niche haters": cold-blooded, somewhat deranged, often poorly socialized psychopaths. In a free society with relatively easy access to guns, they will always pose a menace.

But their menace is a limited one, and their hatred is hardly typical of anything very widespread. Take Buford Furrow. He famously issued a "wake-up call" to "kill Jews" in Los Angeles, before he peppered a Jewish community center with gunfire. He did this in a state with two Jewish female Senators, in a city with a large, prosperous Jewish population, in a country where out of several million Jewish Americans, a total of 66 were reported by the F.B.I. as the targets of hate-crime assaults in 1997. However despicable Furrow's actions were, it would require a very large stretch to describe them as representative of anything but the deranged fringe of an American subculture.

Most hate is more common and more complicated, with as many varieties as there are varieties of love. Just as there is possessive love and needy love; family love and friendship; romantic love and unrequited love; passion and respect, affection and obsession, so hatred has its shadings. There is hate that fears, and hate that merely feels contempt; there is hate that expresses power, and hate that comes from powerlessness; there is revenge, and there is hate that comes from envy. There is hate that was love, and hate that is a curious expression of love. There is hate of the other, and hate of something that reminds us too much of ourselves. There is the oppressor's hate, and the victim's hate. There is hate that burns slowly, and hate that fades. And there is hate that explodes, and hate that never catches fire.

The modern words that we have created to describe the varieties of hate—"sexism," "racism," "anti-Semitism," "homophobia"—tell us very little about any of this. They tell us merely the identities of the victims; they don't reveal the identities of the perpetrators, or what they think, or how they feel. They don't even tell us how the victims feel. And this simplicity is no accident. Coming from the theories of Marxist and post-Marxist academics, these "isms" are far better at alleging structures of power than at delineating the workings of the individual heart or mind. In fact, these "isms" can exist without mentioning individuals at all.

We speak of institutional racism, for example, as if an institution can feel anything. We talk of "hate" as an impersonal noun, with no hater specified.

But when these abstractions are actually incarnated, when someone feels something as a result of them, when a hater actually interacts with a victim, the picture changes. We find that hates are often very different phenomena one from another, that they have very different psychological dynamics, that they might even be better understood by not seeing them as varieties of the same thing at all.

There is, for example, the now unfashionable distinction between reasonable hate and unreasonable hate. In recent years, we have become accustomed to talking about hates as if they were all equally indefensible, as if it could never be the case that some hates might be legitimate, even necessary. But when some 800,000 Tutsis are murdered under the auspices of a Hutu regime in Rwanda, and when a few thousand Hutus are killed in revenge, the hates are not commensurate. Genocide is not an event like a hurricane, in which damage is random and universal; it is a planned and often merciless attack of one group upon another. The hate of the perpetrators is a monstrosity. The hate of the victims, and their survivors, is justified. What else, one wonders, were surviving Jews supposed to feel toward Germans after the Holocaust? Or, to a different degree, South African blacks after apartheid? If the victims overcome this hate, it is a supreme moral achievement. But if they don't, the victims are not as culpable as the perpetrators. So the hatred of Serbs for Kosovars today can never be equated with the hatred of Kosovars for Serbs.

Hate, like much of human feeling, is not rational, but it usually has its reasons. And it cannot be understood, let alone condemned, without knowing them. Similarly, the hate that comes from knowledge is always different from the hate that comes from ignorance. It is one of the most foolish clichés of our time that prejudice is always rooted in ignorance, and can usually be overcome by familiarity with the objects of our loathing. The racism of many Southern whites under segregation was not appeased by familiarity with Southern blacks; the virulent loathing of Tutsis by many Hutus was not undermined by living next door to them for centuries. Theirs was a hatred that sprang, for whatever reasons, from experience. It cannot easily be compared with, for example, the resilience of anti-Semitism in Japan, or hostility to immigration in areas where immigrants are unknown, or fear of homosexuals by people who have never knowingly met one.

The same familiarity is an integral part of what has become known as "sexism." Sexism isn't, properly speaking, a prejudice at all. Few men live without knowledge or constant awareness of women. Every single sexist man was born of a woman, and is likely to be sexually attracted to women. His hostility is going to be very different than that of, say, a reclusive member of the Aryan Nations toward Jews he has never met.

In her book "The Anatomy of Prejudices," the psychotherapist Elisabeth Young-Bruehl proposes a typology of three distinct kinds of hate: obsessive, hysterical and narcissistic. It's not an exhaustive analysis, but it's a beginning in any serious attempt to understand hate rather than merely declaring war on it.

The obsessives, for Young-Bruehl, are those, like the Nazis or Hutus, who fantasize a threat from a minority, and obsessively try to rid themselves of it. For them, the very existence of the hated group is threatening. They often describe their loathing in almost physical terms: they experience what Patrick Buchanan, in reference to homosexuals, once described as a "visceral recoil" from the objects of their detestation. They often describe those they hate as diseased or sick, in need of a cure. Or they talk of "cleansing" them, as the Hutus talked of the Tutsis, or call them "cockroaches," as Yitzhak Shamir called the Palestinians. If you read material from the Family Research Council, it is clear that the group regards homosexuals as similar contaminants. A recent posting on its Web site about syphilis among gay men was headlined, "Unclean."

Hysterical haters have a more complicated relationship with the objects of their aversion. In Young-Bruehl's words, hysterical prejudice is a prejudice that "a person uses unconsciously to appoint a group to act out in the world forbidden sexual and sexually aggressive desires that the person has repressed." Certain kinds of racists fit this pattern. White loathing of blacks is, for some people, at least partly about sexual and physical envy. A certain kind of white racist sees in black America all those impulses he wishes most to express himself but cannot. He idealizes in "blackness" a sexual freedom, a physical power, a Dionysian release that he detests but also longs for. His fantasy may not have any basis in reality, but it is powerful nonetheless. It is a form of love-hate, and it is impossible to understand the nuances of racism in, say, the American South, or in British Imperial India, without it.

Unlike the obsessives, the hysterical haters do not want to eradicate the objects of their loathing; rather they want to keep them in some kind of permanent and safe subjugation in order to indulge the attraction of their repulsion. A recent study, for example, found that the men most likely to be opposed to equal rights for homosexuals were those most likely to be aroused by homoerotic imagery. This makes little rational sense, but it has a certain psychological plausibility. If homosexuals were granted equality, then the hysterical gay-hater might panic that his repressed passions would run out of control, overwhelming him and the world he inhabits.

A narcissistic hate, according to Young-Bruehl's definition, is sexism. In its most common form, it is rooted in many men's inability even to imagine what it is to be a woman, a failing rarely challenged by men's control of our most powerful public social institutions. Women are not so much hated by most men as simply ignored in nonsexual contexts, or never conceived of as true equals. The implicit condescension is mixed, in many cases, with repressed and sublimated erotic desire. So the unawareness of women is sometimes commingled with a deep longing or contempt for them.

Each hate, of course, is more complicated than this, and in any one person hate can assume a uniquely configured combination of these types. So there are hysterical sexists who hate women because they need them so much, and narcissistic sexists who hardly notice that women exist, and sexists who oscillate between one of these positions and another. And there are gay-bashers who are threatened by masculine gay men and gay-haters who feel repulsed by effeminate ones. The soldier who beat his fellow soldier Barry Winchell to death with a baseball bat in July had earlier lost a fight to him. It was the image of a macho gay man—and the shame of being bested by him—that the vengeful soldier had to obliterate, even if he needed a gang of accomplices and a weapon to do so. But the murderers of Matthew Shepard seem to have had a different impulse: a visceral disgust at the thought of any sexual contact with an effeminate homosexual. Their anger was mixed with mockery, as the cruel spectacle at the side of the road suggested.

In the same way, the pathological anti-Semitism of Nazi Germany was obsessive, inasmuch as it tried to cleanse the world of Jews; but also, as Daniel Jonah Goldhagen shows in his book, "Hitler's Willing Executioners," hysterical. The Germans were mysteriously compelled as well as repelled by Jews, devising elaborate ways, like death camps and death marches, to keep them alive even as they killed them. And the early Nazi phobia of interracial sex suggests as well a lingering erotic quality to the relationship, partaking of exactly the kind of sexual panic that persists among some homosexual-haters and anti-miscegenation racists. So the concept of "homophobia," like that of "sexism" and "racism," is often a crude one. All three are essentially cookie-cutter formulas that try to understand human impulses merely through the one-dimensional identity of the victims, rather than through the thoughts and feelings of the haters and hated.

This is deliberate. The theorists behind these "isms" want to ascribe all blame to one group in society—the "oppressors"—and render specific others—the "victims"—completely blameless. And they want to do this in order in part to side unequivocally with the underdog. But it doesn't take a genius to see how this approach, too, can generate its own form of bias. It can justify blanket condemnations of whole groups of people—white straight males for example—purely because of the color of their skin or the nature of their sexual orientation. And it can condescendingly ascribe innocence to whole groups of others. It does exactly what hate does: it hammers the uniqueness of each individual into the anvil of group identity. And it postures morally over the result.

In reality, human beings and human acts are far more complex, which is why these isms and the laws they have fomented are continually coming under strain and challenge. Once again, hate wriggles free of its definers. It knows no monolithic groups of haters and hated. Like a river, it has many eddies, backwaters and rapids. So there are anti-Semites who actually admire what they think of as Jewish power, and there are gay-haters who look up to homosexuals and some who want to sleep with them. And there are black racists, racist Jews, sexist women and anti-Semitic homosexuals. Of course there are.

IV.

Once you start thinking of these phenomena less as the "isms" of sexism, racism and "homophobia," once you think of them as independent psychological responses, it's also possible to see how they can work in a bewildering variety of ways in a bewildering number of people. To take one obvious and sad oddity: people who are demeaned and objectified in society may develop an aversion to their tormentors that is more hateful in its expression than the prejudice they have been subjected to. The F.B.I. statistics on hate crimes throws up an interesting point. In America in the 1990's, blacks were up to three times as likely as whites to commit a hate crime, to express their hate by physically attacking their targets or their property. Just as sexual abusers have often been victims of sexual abuse, and wife-beaters often grew up in violent households, so hate criminals may often be members of hated groups.

Even the Columbine murderers were in some sense victims of hate before they were purveyors of it. Their classmates later admitted that Dylan Klebold and Eric Harris were regularly called "faggots" in the corridors and class-rooms of Columbine High and that nothing was done to prevent or stop the harassment. This climate of hostility doesn't excuse the actions of Klebold and Harris, but it does provide a more plausible context. If they had been black, had routinely been called "nigger" in the school and had then exploded into a shooting spree against white students, the response to the matter might well have been different. But the hate would have been the same. In other words, hate-victims are often hate-victimizers as well. This doesn't mean that all hates are equivalent, or that some are not more justified than others. It means merely that hate goes both ways; and if you try to regulate it among some, you will find yourself forced to regulate it among others.

It is no secret, for example, that some of the most vicious anti-Semites in America are black, and that some of the most virulent anti-Catholic bigots in America are gay. At what point, we are increasingly forced to ask, do these phenomena become as indefensible as white racism or religious toleration of anti-gay bigotry? That question becomes all the more difficult when we notice that it is often minorities who commit some of the most hate-filled offenses against what they see as their oppressors. It was the mainly gay AIDS activ-ist group Act Up that perpetrated the hateful act of desecrating Communion hosts at a Mass at St Patrick's Cathedral in New York. And here is the play-wright Tony Kushner, who is gay, responding to the Matthew Shepard beat-ing in The Nation magazine: "Pope John Paul II endorses murder. He, too, knows the price of discrimination, having declared anti-Semitism a sin. . . . He knows that discrimination kills. But when the Pope heard the news about Matthew Shepard, he, too, worried about spin. And so, on the subject of gay-bashing, the Pope and his cardinals and his bishops and priests main-tain their cynical political silence. . . . To remain silent is to endorse murder." Kushner went on to describe the Pope as a "homicidal liar."

Maybe the passion behind these words is justified. But it seems clear enough to me that Kushner is expressing hate toward the institution of the Catholic Church, and all those who perpetuate its doctrines. How else to interpret the way in which he accuses the Pope of cynicism, lying and mur-der? And how else either to understand the brutal parody of religious voca-tions expressed by the Sisters of Perpetual Indulgence, a group of gay men who dress in drag as nuns and engage in sexually explicit performances in public? Or T-shirts with the words "Recovering Catholic" on them, hot items among some gay and lesbian activists? The implication that someone's religious faith is a mental illness is clearly an expression of contempt. If that isn't covered under the definition of hate speech, what is?

Or take the following sentence: "The act male homosexuals commit is ugly and repugnant and afterwards they are disgusted with themselves. They drink and take drugs to palliate this, but they are disgusted with the act and they are always changing partners and cannot be really happy." The thoughts of Pat Robertson or Patrick Buchanan? Actually that sentence was written by Gertrude Stein, one of the century's most notable lesbians. Or take the following, about how beating up "black boys like that made us feel *good* inside. . . . Every time I drove my foot into his [expletive], I felt better." It was written to describe the brutal assault of an innocent bystander for the sole reason of his race. By the end of the attack, the victim had blood gushing from his mouth as his attackers stomped on his genitals. Are we less appalled when we learn that the actual sentence was how beating up "white boys like that made us feel *good* inside. . . . Every time I drove my foot into his [expletive], I felt better?" It was written by Nathan McCall, an African-American who later in life became a successful journalist at The Washington Post and published his memoir of this "hate crime" to much acclaim.

In fact, one of the stranger aspects of hate is that the prejudice expressed by a group in power may often be milder in expression than the prejudice felt by the marginalized. After all, if you already enjoy privilege, you may not feel the anger that turns bias into hate. You may not need to. For this reason, most white racism may be more influential in society than most black racism—but also more calmly expressed.

So may other forms of minority loathing—especially hatred within minorities. I'm sure that black conservatives like Clarence Thomas or Thomas Sowell have experienced their fair share of white racism. But I wonder whether it has ever reached the level of intensity of the hatred directed toward them by other blacks? In several years of being an openly gay writer and editor, I have experienced the gamut of responses to my sexual orientation. But I have only directly experienced articulated, passionate hate from other homosexuals. I have been accused over the years by other homosexuals of being a sell-out, a hypocrite, a traitor, a sexist, a racist, a narcissist, a snob. I've been called selfish, callous, hateful, self-hating and malevolent. At a reading, a group of lesbian activists portrayed my face on a poster within the crossfires of a gun. Nothing from the religious right has come close to such vehemence.

I am not complaining. No harm has ever come to me or my property, and much of the criticism is rooted in the legitimate expression of political differences. But the visceral tone and style of the gay criticism can only be described as hateful. It is designed to wound personally, and it often does. But its intensity comes in part, one senses, from the pain of being excluded for so long, of anger long restrained bubbling up and directing itself more aggressively toward an alleged traitor than an alleged enemy. It is the hate of the hated. And it can be the most hateful hate of all. For this reason, hate-crime laws may themselves be an oddly biased category—biased against the victims of hate. Racism is everywhere, but the already victimized might be more desperate, more willing to express it violently. And so more prone to come under the suspicious eye of the law.

V.

And why is hate for a group worse than hate for a person? In Laramie, Wyo., the now-famous epicenter of "homophobia," where Matthew Shepard was brutally beaten to death, vicious murders are not unknown. In the previous 12 months, a 15-year-old pregnant girl was found east of the town with 17 stab wounds. Her 38-year-old boyfriend was apparently angry that she had refused an abortion and left her in the Wyoming foothills to bleed to death. In the summer of 1998, an 8-year-old Laramie girl was abducted, raped and murdered by a pedophile, who disposed of her young body in a garbage dump. Neither of these killings was deemed a hate crime, and neither would be designated as such under any existing hate-crime law. Perhaps because of this, one crime is an international legend; the other two are virtually unheard of.

But which crime was more filled with hate? Once you ask the question, you realize how difficult it is to answer. Is it more hateful to kill a stranger or a lover? Is it more hateful to kill a child than an adult? Is it more hateful to kill your own child than another's? Under the law before the invention of hate crimes, these decisions didn't have to be taken. But under the law after hate crimes, a decision is essential. A decade ago, a murder was a murder. Now, in the era when group hate has emerged as our cardinal social sin, it all depends.

The supporters of laws against hate crimes argue that such crimes should be disproportionately punished because they victimize more than the victim. Such crimes, these advocates argue, spread fear, hatred and panic among whole populations, and therefore merit more concern. But, of course, all crimes victimize more than the victim, and spread alarm in the society at large. Just think of the terrifying church shooting in Texas only two weeks ago. In fact, a purely random murder may be even more terrifying than a targeted one, since the entire community, and not just a part of it, feels threatened. High rates of murder, robbery, assault and burglary victimize everyone, by spreading fear, suspicion and distress everywhere. Which crime was more frightening to more people this summer: the mentally ill Buford Furrow's crazed attacks in Los Angeles, killing one, or Mark Barton's murder of his own family and several random day-traders in Atlanta, killing 12? Almost certainly the latter. But only Furrow was guilty of "hate."

One response to this objection is that certain groups feel fear more intensely than others because of a history of persecution or intimidation. But doesn't this smack of a certain condescension toward minorities? Why, after all, should it be assumed that gay men or black women or Jews, for example, are as a group more easily intimidated than others? Surely in any of these communities there will be a vast range of responses, from panic to concern to complete indifference. The assumption otherwise is the kind of crude generalization the law is supposed to uproot in the first place. And among these groups, there are also likely to be vast differences. To equate a population once subjected to slavery with a population of Mexican immigrants or third-generation Holocaust survivors is to equate the unequatable. In fact, it is to set up a contest of vulnerability in which one group vies with another to establish its particular variety of suffering, a contest that can have no dignified solution.

Rape, for example, is not classified as a "hate crime" under most existing laws, pitting feminists against ethnic groups in a battle for recognition. If, as a solution to this problem, everyone, except the white straight able-bodied male, is regarded as a possible victim of a hate crime, then we have simply created a two-tier system of justice in which racial profiling is reversed, and white straight men are presumed guilty before being proven innocent, and members of minorities are free to hate them as gleefully as they like. But if we include the white straight male in the litany of potential victims, then we have effectively abolished the notion of a hate crime altogether. For if every crime is possibly a hate crime, then it is simply another name for crime. All we will have done is widened the search for possible bigotry, ratcheted up the sentences for everyone and filled the jails up even further.

Hate-crime-law advocates counter that extra penalties should be imposed on hate crimes because our society is experiencing an "epidemic" of such crimes. Mercifully, there is no hard evidence to support this notion. The Federal Government has only been recording the incidence of hate crimes in this decade, and the statistics tell a simple story. In 1992, there were 6,623 hate-crime incidents reported to the F.B.I. by a total of 6,181 agencies, covering 51 percent of the population. In 1996, there were 8,734 incidents reported by 11,355 agencies, covering 84 percent of the population. That number dropped to 8,049 in 1997. These numbers are, of course, hazardous. They probably underreport the incidence of such crimes, but they are the only reliable figures we have. Yet even if they are faulty as an absolute number, they do not show an epidemic of "hate crimes" in the 1990's.

Is there evidence that the crimes themselves are becoming more vicious? None. More than 60 percent of recorded hate crimes in America involve no violent, physical assault against another human being at all, and, again, according to the F.B.I., that proportion has not budged much in the 1990's. These impersonal attacks are crimes against property or crimes of "intimidation." Murder, which dominates media coverage of hate crimes, is a tiny proportion of the total. Of the 8,049 hate crimes reported to the F.B.I. in 1997, a total of eight were murders. Eight. The number of hate crimes that were aggravated assaults (generally involving a weapon) in 1997 is less than 15 percent of the total. That's 1,237 assaults too many, of course, but to put it in perspective, compare it with a reported 1,022,492 "equal opportunity" aggravated assaults in America in the same year. The number of hate crimes that were physical assaults is half the total. That's 4,000 assaults too many, of course, but to put it in perspective, it compares with around 3.8 million "equal opportunity" assaults in America annually.

The truth is, the distinction between a crime filled with personal hate and a crime filled with group hate is an essentially arbitrary one. It tells us nothing interesting about the psychological contours of the specific actor or his specific victim. It is a function primarily of politics, of special interest groups carving out particular protections for themselves, rather than a serious response to a serious criminal concern. In such an endeavor, hate-crime-law advocates cram an entire world of human motivations into an immutable, tiny box called hate, and hope to have solved a problem. But nothing has been solved; and some harm may even have been done.

In an attempt to repudiate a past that treated people differently because of the color of their skin, or their sex, or religion or sexual orientation, we may merely create a future that permanently treats people differently because of the color of their skin, or their sex, religion or sexual orientation. This notion of a hate crime, and the concept of hate that lies behind it, takes a psychological mystery and turns it into a facile political artifact. Rather than compounding this error and extending it even further, we should seriously consider repealing the concept altogether.

To put it another way: Violence can and should be stopped by the government. In a free society, hate can't and shouldn't be. The boundaries between hate and prejudice and between prejudice and opinion and between opinion and truth are so complicated and blurred that any attempt to construct legal and political fire walls is a doomed and illiberal venture. We know by now that hate will never disappear from human consciousness; in fact, it is probably, at some level, definitive of it. We know after decades of education measures that hate is not caused merely by ignorance; and after decades of legislation, that it isn't caused entirely by law.

To be sure, we have made much progress. Anyone who argues that America is as inhospitable to minorities and to women today as it has been in the past has not read much history. And we should, of course, be vigilant that our most powerful institutions, most notably the government, do not actively or formally propagate hatred; and insure that the violent expression of hate is curtailed by the same rules that punish all violent expression.

But after that, in an increasingly diverse culture, it is crazy to expect that hate, in all its variety, can be eradicated. A free country will always mean a hateful country. This may not be fair, or perfect, or admirable, but it is reality, and while we need not endorse it, we should not delude ourselves into thinking we can prevent it. That is surely the distinction between toleration and tolerance. Tolerance is the eradication of hate; toleration is co-existence despite it. We might do better as a culture and as a polity if we concentrated more on achieving the latter rather than the former. We would certainly be less frustrated.

And by aiming lower, we might actually reach higher. In some ways, some expression of prejudice serves a useful social purpose. It lets off steam; it allows natural tensions to express themselves incrementally; it can siphon off conflict through words, rather than actions. Anyone who has lived in the ethnic shouting match that is New York City knows exactly what I mean. If New Yorkers disliked each other less, they wouldn't be able to get on so well. We may not all be able to pull off a Mencken—bigoted in words, egalitarian in action—but we might achieve a lesser form of virtue: a human acceptance of our need for differentiation, without a total capitulation to it.

Do we not owe something more to the victims of hate? Perhaps we do. But it is also true that there is nothing that government can do for the hated that the hated cannot better do for themselves. After all, most bigots are not foiled when they are punished specifically for their beliefs. In fact, many of the worst haters crave such attention and find vindication in such rebukes. Indeed, our media's obsession with "hate," our elevation of it above other social mis-demeanors and crimes, may even play into the hands of the pathetic and the evil, may breathe air into the smoldering embers of their paranoid loathing. Sure, we can help create a climate in which such hate is disapproved of—and we should. But there is a danger that if we go too far, if we punish it too much, if we try to abolish it altogether, we may merely increase its mystique, and entrench the very categories of human difference that we are trying to erase.

For hate is only foiled not when the haters are punished but when the hated are immune to the bigot's power. A hater cannot psychologically wound if a victim cannot psychologically be wounded. And that immunity to hurt can never be given; it can merely be achieved. The racial epithet only strikes at someone's core if he lets it, if he allows the bigot's definition of him to be the final description of his life and his person—if somewhere in his heart of hearts, he believes the hateful slur to be true. The only final answer to this form of racism, then, is not majority persecution of it, but minority indiffer-ence to it. The only permanent rebuke to homophobia is not the enforcement of tolerance, but gay equanimity in the face of prejudice. The only effective answer to sexism is not a morass of legal proscriptions, but the simple fact of female success. In this, as in so many other things, there is no solution to the problem. There is only a transcendence of it. For all our rhetoric, hate will never be destroyed. Hate, as our predecessors knew better, can merely be overcome.

QUESTIONS FOR DISCUSSION AND WRITING

1. Sullivan initially takes a tone of puzzlement about trying to understand hatred. Does the essay make us understand the nature of hatred and why people hate? Or is Sullivan saying hatred is too complicated and too varied to understand? What does he mean when he says, "Hate used to be easier to understand"? What does hate mean? Is it always bad to hate?

2. Why does Sullivan argue that such forms of prejudice as sexism, racism, anti-Semitism, and homophobia "tell us very little about the varieties of hate"? Why does he see the isms as "the wrong way to think about hate"? Do you agree or disagree that we need to understand those who hate rather than their victims in order to understand hatred? That hate victims are often hate victimizers?

3. What is it that Sullivan is saying in his essay about extreme forms of violent bigotry like those acts of white supremacists such as John William King or Buford Furrow? What is he saying, by way of contrast, about the hatred the famed journalist H. L. Mencken revealed in his diary? If the first type of hatred is more rare and extreme, "deranged fringes of American subculture," why is it so often associated with hate and given so much attention?

4. Describe why Sullivan comes to the conclusion in his essay that hate crime laws deserve to be repealed. Do you agree or disagree with his position?

5. Sullivan also concludes by arguing that there is no solution to hatred, "only a transcendence of it." He argues that a free country will always have hatred and that "hate will never disappear from human consciousness." Is this too bleak a view? Do you agree or disagree that hatred has no solution?

ON TECHNIQUE AND STYLE

1. Sullivan divides his essay into five sections. How does he organize these sections in the overall structure of his essay and the way he presents his ideas? Is it a successful means of division? Can you suggest another way he might have set off different parts of the essay's ideas?

2. There are many examples of the varieties of hate in Sullivan's essay. In addition to the horrible and violent bigoted crimes in the first part of the essay, he writes about an incident that occurred over grass clippings and over a Labor Day float in Broad Channel. He also uses a psychologist, Elisabeth Young-Bruehl, to highlight different forms of hate as well as bringing in hatred of Tutsis by Hutus in Rwanda and playwright Tony Kushner calling the pope a "homicidal liar." How do all of these and other examples serve Sullivan's purposes in his arguing for a consideration of hate as something "like much human feeling"?

3. Does Sullivan succeed in providing a definition for, as he puts it early on in his essay, "what hate is and our part in it"? Or is his definition of what hate is more of a revealing of how hard hate is to define?

CULTURAL QUESTION

1. Sullivan is an out-of-the-closet gay writer. How much does his admitted homosexuality contribute to his views on hate? What about when he writes specifically of hatred directed toward him by his fellow gays, "the hate of

the hated"? What point is he trying to bring across about attitudes against gays in other examples he brings in like the 1993 grass clipping episode in suburban San Jose or the reference to liberals who support gay rights but avoid going into a gay bar with him?

Hateful Things

Sei Shōnagon

Sei Shōnagon (c. 966–?) was a Japanese poet and writer of the mid-Heian period who is best known for The Pillow Book (Makura no Soshi), *a collection of 320 sections of lists, poems, essays, personal anecdotes, sketches, gossip, and opinions. She served in the court of the empress, married a provincial governor and, upon his death, became a Buddhist nun. "Hateful Things" is a selection from* The Pillow Book, *a work that provides a rare and compelling portal to the ancient world of Japanese culture and the Japanese court of a thousand years ago. In it Shōnagon presents a list of "hateful things," probably as a gift for the daughter of the empress, with an incisiveness and wit that many continue to this day to admire greatly.*

From *The Pillow Book of Sei Shōnagon* translated and edited by Ivan Morris, Vol. 1. Copyright © Ivan Morris 1967. Reprinted by permission of Columbia University Press and Oxford University Press.

One is in a hurry to leave, but one's visitor keeps chattering away. If it is someone of no importance, one can get rid of him by saying, "You must tell me all about it next time"; but, should it be the sort of visitor whose presence commands one's best behavior, the situation is hateful indeed.

Someone has suddenly fallen ill and one summons the exorcist. Since he is not at home, one has to send messengers to look for him. After one has had a long fretful wait, the exorcist finally arrives, and with a sigh of relief one asks him to start his incantations. But perhaps he has been exorcizing too many evil spirits recently; for hardly has he installed himself and begun praying when his voice becomes drowsy. Oh, how hateful!

A man who has nothing in particular to recommend him discusses all sorts of subjects at random as though he knew everything.

To envy others and to complain about one's own lot; to speak badly about people; to be inquisitive about the most trivial matters and to resent and abuse people for not telling one, or, if one does manage to worm out some facts, to inform everyone in the most detailed fashion as if one had known all from the beginning—oh, how hateful!

An admirer has come on a clandestine visit, but a dog catches sight of him and starts barking. One feels like killing the beast.

One has gone to bed and is about to doze off when a mosquito appears and announces itself in a reedy voice. One can actually feel the wind made by his winds and, slight though it is, one finds it hateful in the extreme.

One is in the middle of a story when someone butts in and tries to show that he is the only clever person in the room. Such a person is hateful, and so, indeed, is anyone, child or adult, who tries to push himself forward.

One is telling a story about old times when someone breaks in with a little detail that he happens to know, implying that one's own version is inaccurate—disgusting behavior!

Very hateful is a mouse that scurries all over the place.

A certain gentleman whom one does not want to see visits one at home or in the Palace, and one pretends to be asleep. But a maid comes to tell one and shakes one awake, with a look on her face that says, "What a sleepyhead!" Very hateful.

QUESTIONS FOR DISCUSSION AND WRITING

1. Are the things enumerated by Shōnagon really hateful or is "hateful" too strong a word to coin about the things that appear on her list? Some of the behavior she lists might more appropriately be labeled boorish or vain—some even tolerable or trivial. Do these warrant being seen as hateful only in the period and place from which they come?
2. Despite her obvious disapproval of the things she lists there is also an obvious comic side to some of the "hateful things" the author includes. What is the effect of the comedic here?
3. There are sharp hierarchical divisions in "Hateful Things," which suggest sharp differences in people of position or power from those who are not in power or do not have position. How does this affect our reactions to the list of what is seen by the author as hateful?
4. What about Shōnagon's inclusion of an annoying dog, a mosquito, and a mouse? Are such "things" as hateful as the human behavior she lists? Do they belong on the same list or should there be a separation of the hatefulness of humans from the world of animals and insects?

5. If you were pressed with making a list of things you regard as hateful it would no doubt include far more serious and malicious examples than those we find in this selection. Does this diminish the effect of Shonagon's list? Or are annoyances like those she lists worthy of being seen as hateful? Do they help us come to a better understanding or clearer definition of hate?

ON TECHNIQUE AND STYLE

1. Most would agree that a traditional, well-crafted essay is superior to a simple, seemingly random list. Yet the clarity of ideas that we expect of a traditional essay and a unified sense of what the author views as hateful both come across in this selection. Would it have been preferable for the author to have put this list into the more traditional essay form? Or does the list succeed and stand on its own enough that the form works?
2. Are there ways of classifying the list of hateful things that Shōnagon provides? What are they?
3. What emerges from this list that defines hatefulness? How seriously are we to take her?

CULTURAL QUESTION

1. What do we glean from this selection about the cultural attitudes in Japan of ten centuries ago versus those characteristic of Western ways today? Exorcists certainly aren't around as much, but professionals we need to see who go drowsy on us are. What comes across in the list as time and place specific and what as universal?

FICTION

What We Talk about When We Talk about Love

Raymond Carver

Raymond Carver (1939–1988) was born into a working-class family in Clatskanie, Oregon, and lived in Port Angeles, Washington, until his death. He is generally considered one of post–World War II America's best short story writers and also published a number of volumes of poetry. A graduate of Chico State, he studied at the University of Iowa and Stanford and later taught at Syracuse University. His four volumes of stories are Will You Please Be Quiet, Please? *(1976),* What We Talk about When We Talk about Love *(1981),* Cathedral *(1983), and* Where I'm Calling From *(1988).*

"What We Talk about When We Talk about Love" is a story taken from the volume by the same name that explores some of the mysteries and varieties of different kinds of love. Though the story moves from light to darkness, it nevertheless leaves us with the ineluctable beating of the human heart which is the mysterious place from whence love and hate begin.

My friend Mel McGinnis was talking. Mel McGinnis is a cardiologist, and sometimes that gives him the right.

The four of us were sitting around his kitchen table drinking gin. Sunlight filled the kitchen from the big window behind the sink. There were Mel and me and his second wife, Teresa—Terri, we called her—and my wife, Laura. We lived in Albuquerque then. But we were all from somewhere else.

There was an ice bucket on the table. The gin and the tonic water kept going around, and we somehow got on the subject of love. Mel thought real love was nothing less than spiritual love. He said he'd spent five years in a seminary before quitting to go to medical school. He said he still looked back on those years in the seminary as the most important years in his life.

Terri said the man she lived with before she lived with Mel loved her so much he tried to kill her. Then Terri said, "He beat me up one night. He dragged me around the living room by my ankles. He kept saying, 'I love you, I love you, you bitch.' He went on dragging me around the living room. My head kept knocking on things." Terri looked around the table. "What do you do with love like that?"

She was a bone-thin woman with a pretty face, dark eyes, and brown hair that hung down her back. She liked necklaces made of turquoise, and long pendant earrings.

"My God, don't be silly. That's not love, and you know it," Mel said. "I don't know what you'd call it, but I sure know you wouldn't call it love."

"Say what you want to, but I know it was," Terri said. "It may sound crazy to you, but it's true just the same. People are different, Mel. Sure, sometimes he may have acted crazy. Okay. But he loved me. In his own way maybe, but he loved me. There was love there, Mel. Don't say there wasn't."

Mel let out his breath. He held his glass and turned to Laura and me. "The man threatened to kill me," Mel said. He finished his drink and reached for the gin bottle. "Terri's a romantic. Terri's of the kick-me-so-I'll-know-you-love-me school. Terri, hon, don't look that way." Mel reached across the table and touched Terri's cheek with his fingers. He grinned at her.

"Now he wants to make up," Terri said.

"Make up what?" Mel said. "What is there to make up? I know what I know. That's all."

"How'd we get started on this subject, anyway?" Terri said. She raised her glass and drank from it. "Mel always has love on his mind," she said. "Don't you, honey?" She smiled, and I thought that was the last of it.

"I just wouldn't call Ed's behavior love. That's all I'm saying, honey," Mel said. "What about you guys?" Mel said to Laura and me. "Does that sound like love to you?"

"I'm the wrong person to ask," I said. "I didn't even know the man. I've only heard his name mentioned in passing. I wouldn't know. You'd have to know the particulars. But I think what you're saying is that love is an absolute."

Mel said, "The kind of love I'm talking about is. The kind of love I'm talking about, you don't try to kill people."

Laura said, "I don't know anything about Ed, or anything about the situation. But who can judge anyone else's situation?"

I touched the back of Laura's hand. She gave me a quick smile. I picked up Laura's hand. It was warm, the nails polished, perfectly manicured. I encircled the broad wrist with my fingers, and I held her.

"When I left, he drank rat poison," Terri said. She clasped her arms with her hands. "They took him to the hospital in Sante Fe. That's where we lived then, about ten miles out. They saved his life. But his gums went crazy from it. I mean they pulled away from his teeth. After that, his teeth stood out like fangs. My God," Terri said. She waited a minute, then let go of her arms and picked up her glass.

"What people won't do!" Laura said.

"He's out of the action now," Mel said. "He's dead."

Mel handed me the saucer of limes. I took a section, squeezed it over my drink, and stirred the ice cubes with my finger.

"It gets worse," Terri said. "He shot himself in the mouth. But he bungled that too. Poor Ed," she said. Terri shook her head.

"Poor Ed nothing," Mel said. "He was dangerous."

Mel was forty-five years old. He was tall and rangy with curly soft hair. His face and arms were brown from the tennis he played. When he was sober, his gestures, all his movements, were precise, very careful.

"He did love me though, Mel. Grant me that," Terri said. "That's all I'm asking. He didn't love me the way you love me. I'm not saying that. But he loved me. You can grant me that, can't you?"

"What do you mean, he bungled it?" I said.

Laura leaned forward with her glass. She put her elbows on the table and held her glass in both hands. She glanced from Mel to Terri and waited with a look of bewilderment on her open face, as if amazed that such things happened to people you were friendly with.

"How'd he bungle it when he killed himself?" I said.

"I'll tell you what happened," Mel said. "He took this twenty-two pistol he'd bought to threaten Terri and me with. Oh, I'm serious, the man was always threatening. You should have seen the way we lived in those days. Like fugitives. I even bought a gun myself. Can you believe it? A guy like me? But I did.

I bought one for self-defense and carried it in the glove compartment. Some-times I'd have to leave the apartment in the middle of the night. To go to the hospital, you know? Terri and I weren't married then, and my first wife had the house and kids, the dog, everything, and Terri and I were living in this apartment here. Sometimes, as I say, I'd get a call in the middle of the night and have to go in to the hospital at two or three in the morning. It'd be dark out there in the parking lot, and I'd break into a sweat before I could even get to my car. I never knew if he was going to come up out of the shrubbery or from behind a car and start shooting. I mean, the man was crazy. He was capable of wiring a bomb, anything. He used to call my service at all hours and say he needed to talk to the doctor, and when I'd return the call, he'd say, 'Son of a bitch, your days are numbered.' Little things like that. It was scary, I'm telling you."

"I still feel sorry for him," Terri said.

"It sounds like a nightmare," Laura said. "But what exactly happened after he shot himself?"

Laura is a legal secretary. We'd met in a professional capacity. Before we knew it, it was a courtship. She's thirty-five, three years younger than I am. In addition to being in love, we like each other and enjoy one another's com-pany. She's easy to be with.

"What happened?" Laura said.

Mel said, "He shot himself in the mouth in his room. Someone heard the shot and told the manager. They came in with a passkey, saw what had hap-pened, and called an ambulance. I happened to be there when they brought him in, alive but past recall. The man lived for three days. His head swelled up to twice the size of a normal head. I'd never seen anything like it, and I hope I never do again. Terri wanted to go in and sit with him when she found out about it. We had a fight over it. I didn't think she should see him like that. I didn't think she should see him, and I still don't."

"Who won the fight?" Laura said.

"I was in the room with him when he died," Terri said. "He never came up out of it. But I sat with him. He didn't have anyone else."

"He was dangerous," Mel said. "If you call that love, you can have it."

"It was love," Terri said. "Sure, it's abnormal in most people's eyes. But he was willing to die for it. He did die for it."

"I sure as hell wouldn't call it love," Mel said. "I mean, no one knows what he did it for. I've seen a lot of suicides, and I couldn't say anyone ever knew what they did it for."

Mel put his hands behind his neck and tilted his chair back. "I'm not inter-ested in that kind of love," he said. "If that's love, you can have it."

Terri said, "We were afraid. Mel even made a will out and wrote to his brother in California who used to be a Green Beret. Mel told him who to look for if something happened to him."

Terri drank from her glass. She said, "But Mel's right—we lived like fugi-tives. We were afraid. Mel was, weren't you, honey? I even called the police at one point, but they were no help. They said they couldn't do anything until Ed actually did something. Isn't that a laugh?" Terry said.

She poured the last of the gin into her glass and waggled the bottle. Mel got up from the table and went to the cupboard. He took down another bottle.

"Well, Nick and I know what love is," Laura said. "For us, I mean," Laura said. She bumped my knee with her knee. "You're supposed to say something now," Laura said, and turned her smile on me.

For an answer, I took Laura's hand and raised it to my lips. I made a big production out of kissing her hand. Everyone was amused.

"We're lucky," I said.

"You guys," Terri said. "Stop that now. You're making me sick. You're still on the honeymoon, for God's sake. You're still gaga, for crying out loud. Just wait. How long have you been together now? How long has it been? A year? Longer than a year?"

"Going on a year and a half," Laura said, flushed and smiling.

"Oh, now," Terri said. "Wait a while."

She held her drink and gazed at Laura.

"I'm only kidding," Terri said.

Mel opened the gin and went around the table with the bottle.

"Here, you guys," he said. "Let's have a toast. I want to propose a toast. A toast to love. To true love," Mel said.

We touched glasses.

"To love," we said.

Outside in the backyard, one of the dogs began to bark. The leaves of the aspen that leaned past the window ticked against the glass. The afternoon sun was like a presence in this room, the spacious light of ease and generosity. We could have been anywhere, somewhere enchanted. We raised our glasses again and grinned at each other like children who had agreed on something forbidden.

"I'll tell you what real love is," Mel said. "I mean, I'll give you a good example. And then you can draw your own conclusions." He poured more gin into his glass. He added an ice cube and a sliver of lime. We waited and sipped our drinks. Laura and I touched knees again. I put a hand on her warm thigh and left it there.

"What do any of us really know about love?" Mel said. "It seems to me we're just beginners at love. We say we love each other and we do, I don't doubt it. I love Terri and Terri loves me, and you guys love each other too. You know the kind of love I'm talking about now. Physical love, that impulse that drives you to someone special, as well as love of the other person's being, his or her essence, as it were. Carnal love and, well, call it sentimental love, the day-to-day caring about the other person. But sometimes I have a hard time accounting for the fact that I must have loved my first wife too. But

I did, I know I did. So I suppose I am like Terri in that regard. Terri and Ed." He thought about it and then he went on. "There was a time when I thought I loved my first wife more than life itself. But now I hate her guts. I do. How do you explain that? What happened to that love? What happened to it, is what I'd like to know. I wish someone could tell me. Then there's Ed. Okay, we're back to Ed. He loves Terri so much he tries to kill her and he winds up killing himself." Mel stopped talking and swallowed from his glass. "You guys have been together eighteen months and you love each other. It shows all over you. You glow with it. But you both loved other people before you met each other. You've both been married before, just like us. And you probably loved other people before that too, even. Terri and I have been together five years, been married for four. And the terrible thing, the terrible thing is, but the good thing too, the saving grace, you might say, is that if something happened to one of us—excuse me for saying this—but if something happened to one of us tomorrow I think the other one, the other person, would grieve for a while, you know, but then the surviving party would go out and love again, have someone else soon enough. All this, all of this love we're talking about, it would just be a memory. Maybe not even a memory. Am I wrong? Am I way off base? Because I want you to set me straight if you think I'm wrong. I want to know. I mean, I don't know anything, and I'm the first one to admit it."

"Mel, for God's sake," Terri said. She reached out and took hold of his wrist. "Are you getting drunk? Honey? Are you drunk?"

"Honey, I'm just talking," Mel said. "All right? I don't have to be drunk to say what I think. I mean, we're all just talking, right?" Mel said. He fixed his eyes on her.

"Sweetie, I'm not criticizing," Terri said.

She picked up her glass.

"I'm not on call today," Mel said. "Let me remind you of that. I am not on call," he said.

"Mel, we love you," Laura said.

Mel looked at Laura. He looked at her as if he could not place her, as if she was not the woman she was.

"Love you too, Laura," Mel said. "And you, Nick, love you too. You know something?" Mel said. "You guys are our pals," Mel said.

He picked up his glass.

Mel said, "I was going to tell you about something. I mean, I was going to prove a point. You see, this happened a few months ago, but it's still going on right now, and it ought to make us feel ashamed when we talk like we know what we're talking about when we talk above love."

"Come on now," Terri said. "Don't talk like you're drunk if you're not drunk."

"Just shut up for once in your life," Mel said very quietly. "Will you do me a favor and do that for a minute? So as I was saying, there's this old couple who had this car wreck out on the interstate. A kid hit them and they were all torn to shit and nobody was giving them much chance to pull through."

Terri looked at us and then back at Mel. She seemed anxious, or maybe that's too strong a word.

Mel was handing the bottle around the table.

"I was on call that night," Mel said. "It was May or maybe it was June. Terri and I had just sat down to dinner when the hospital called. There'd been this thing out on the interstate. Drunk kid, teenager, plowed his dad's pickup into this camper with this old couple in it. They were up in their mid-seventies, that couple. The kid—eighteen, nineteen, something—he was DOA. Taken the steering wheel through his sternum. The old couple, they were alive, you understand. I mean, just barely. But they had everything. Multiple fractures, internal injuries, hemorrhaging, contusions, lacerations, the works, and they each of them had themselves concussions. They were in a bad way, believe me. And, of course, their age was two strikes against them. I'd say she was worse off than he was. Ruptured spleen along with everything else. Both kneecaps broken. But they'd been wearing their seatbelts and, God knows, that's what saved them for the time being."

"Folks, this is an advertisement for the National Safety Council," Terri said. "This is your spokesman, Dr. Melvin R. McGinnis, talking." Terri laughed. "Mel," she said, "sometimes you're just too much. But I love you, hon," she said.

"Honey, I love you," Mel said.

He leaned across the table. Terri met him halfway. They kissed.

"Terri's right," Mel said as he settled himself again. "Get those seatbelts on. But seriously, they were in some shape, those oldsters. By the time I got down there, the kid was dead, as I said. He was off in a corner, laid out on a gurney. I took one look at the old couple and told the ER nurse to get me a neurologist and an orthopedic man and a couple of surgeons down there right away."

He drank from his glass. "I'll try to keep this short," he said. "So we took the two of them up to the OR and worked like fuck on them most of the night. They had these incredible reserves, those two. You see that once in a while. So we did everything that could be done, and toward morning we're giving them a fifty-fifty chance, maybe less than that for her. So here they are, still alive the next morning. So, okay, we move them into the ICU, which is where they both kept plugging away at it for two weeks, hitting it better and better on all the scopes. So we transfer them out to their own room."

Mel stopped talking. "Here," he said, "let's drink this cheapo gin the hell up. Then we're going to dinner, right? Terri and I know a new place. That's where we'll go, to this new place we know about. But we're not going until we finish up this cut-rate, lousy gin."

Terri said, "We haven't actually eaten there yet. But it looks good. From the outside, you know."

"I like food," Mel said. "If I had it to do all over again, I'd be a chef, you know? Right, Terri?" Mel said.

He laughed. He fingered the ice in his glass.

"Terri knows," he said. "Terri can tell you. But let me say this. If I could come back again in a different life, a different time and all, you know what? I'd like to come back as a knight. You were pretty safe wearing all that armor. It was all right being a knight until gunpowder and muskets and pistols came along."

"Mel would like to ride a horse and carry a lance," Terri said.

"Carry a woman's scarf with you everywhere," Laura said.

"Or just a woman," Mel said.

"Shame on you," Laura said.

Terri said, "Suppose you came back as a serf. The serfs didn't have it so good in those days," Terri said.

"The serfs never had it good," Mel said. "But I guess even the knights were vessels to someone. Isn't that the way it worked? But then everyone is always a vessel to someone. Isn't that right? Terri? But what I liked about knights, besides their ladies, was that they had that suit of armor, you know, and they couldn't get hurt very easy. No cars in those days, you know? No drunk teenagers to tear into your ass."

"Vassals," Terri said.

"What?" Mel said.

"Vassals," Terri said. "They were called vassals, not vessels."

"Vassals, vessels," Mel said, "what the fuck's the difference? You knew what I meant anyway. All right," Mel said. "So I'm not educated. I learned my stuff. I'm a heart surgeon, sure, but I'm just a mechanic. I go in and I fuck around and I fix things. Shit," Mel said.

"Modesty doesn't become you," Terri said.

"He's just a humble sawbones," I said. "But sometimes they suffocated in all that armor, Mel. They'd even have heart attacks if it got too hot and they were too tired and worn out. I read somewhere that they'd fall off their horses and not be able to get up because they were too tired to stand with all that armor on them. They got trampled by their own horses sometimes."

"That's terrible," Mel said. "That's a terrible thing, Nicky. I guess they'd just lay there and wait until somebody came along and made a shish kebab out of them."

"Some other vessel," Terri said.

"That's right," Mel said. "Some vassal would come along and spear the bastard in the name of love. Or whatever the fuck it was they fought over in those days."

"Same things we fight over these days," Terri said.

Laura said, "Nothing's changed."

The color was still high in Laura's cheeks. Her eyes were bright. She brought her glass to her lips.

Mel poured himself another drink. He looked at the label closely as if studying a long row of numbers. Then he slowly put the bottle down on the table and slowly reached for the tonic water.

"What about the old couple?" Laura said. "You didn't finish that story you started."

Laura was having a hard time lighting her cigarette. Her matches kept going out.

The sunshine inside the room was different now, changing, getting thinner. But the leaves outside the window were still shimmering, and I stared at the pattern they made on the panes and on the Formica counter. They weren't the same patterns, of course.

"What about the old couple?" I said.

"Older but wiser," Terri said.

Mel stared at her.

Terri said, "Go on with your story, hon. I was only kidding. Then what happened?"

"Terri, sometimes," Mel said.

"Please, Mel," Terri said. "Don't always be so serious, sweetie. Can't you take a joke?"

"Where's the joke?" Mel said.

He held his glass and gazed steadily at his wife.

"What happened?" Laura said.

Mel fastened his eyes on Laura. He said, "Laura, if I didn't have Terri and if I didn't love her so much, and if Nick wasn't my best friend, I'd fall in love with you, I'd carry you off, honey," he said.

"Tell your story," Terri said. "Then we'll go to that new place, okay?"

"Okay," Mel said. "Where was I?" he said. He stared at the table and then he began again.

"I dropped in to see each of them every day, sometimes twice a day if I was up doing other calls anyway. Casts and bandages, head to foot, the both of them. You know, you've seen it in the movies. That's just the way they looked, just like in the movies. Little eye-holes and nose-holes and mouth-holes. And she had to have her legs slung up on top of it. Well, the husband was very depressed for the longest while. Even after he found out that his wife was going to pull through, he was still very depressed. Not about the accident, though. I mean, the accident was one thing, but it wasn't everything. I'd get up to his mouth-hole, you know, and he'd say no, it wasn't the accident exactly but it was because he couldn't see her through his eye-holes. He said that was what was making him feel so bad. Can you imagine? I'm telling you, the man's heart was breaking because he couldn't turn his goddamn head and *see* his goddamn wife."

Mel looked around the table and shook his head at what he was going to say.

"I mean, it was killing the old fart just because he couldn't *look* at the fucking woman."

We all looked at Mel.

"Do you see what I'm saying?" he said.

Maybe we were a little drunk by then. I know it was hard keeping things in focus. The light was draining out of the room, going back through the window where it had come from. Yet nobody made a move to get up from the table to turn on the overhead light.

"Listen," Mel said. "Let's finish this fucking gin. There's about enough left here for one shooter all around. Then let's go eat. Let's go to the new place."

"He's depressed," Terri said. "Mel, why don't you take a pill?"

Mel shook his head. "I've taken everything there is."

"We all need a pill now and then," I said.

"Some people are born needing them," Terri said.

She was using her finger to rub at something on the table. Then she stopped rubbing.

"I think I want to call my kids," Mel said. "Is that all right with everybody? I'll call my kids," he said.

Terri said, "What if Marjorie answers the phone? You guys, you've heard us on the subject of Marjorie? Honey, you know you don't want to talk to Marjorie. It'll make you feel even worse."

"I don't want to talk to Marjorie," Mel said. "But I want to talk to my kids."

"There isn't a day goes by that Mel doesn't say he wishes she'd get married again. Or else die," Terri said. "For one thing," Terri said, "she's bankrupting us. Mel says it's just to spite him that she won't get married again. She has a boyfriend who lives with her and the kids, so Mel is supporting the boyfriend too."

"She's allergic to bees," Mel said. "If I'm not praying she'll get married again, I'm praying she'll get herself stung to death by a swarm of fucking bees."

"Shame on you," Laura said.

"Bzzzzzzz," Mel said, turning his fingers into bees and buzzing them at Terri's throat. Then he let his hands drop all the way to his sides.

"She's vicious," Mel said. "Sometimes I think I'll go up there dressed like a beekeeper. You know, that hat that's like a helmet with the plate that comes down over your face, the big gloves, and the padded coat? I'll knock on the door and let loose a hive of bees in the house. But first I'd make sure the kids were out, of course."

He crossed one leg over the other. It seemed to take him a lot of time to do it. Then he put both feet on the floor and leaned forward, elbows on the table, his chin cupped in his hands.

"Maybe I won't call the kids, after all. Maybe it isn't such a hot idea. Maybe we'll just go eat. How does that sound?"

"Sounds fine to me," I said. "Eat or not eat. Or keep drinking. I could head right on out into the sunset."

"What does that mean, honey?" Laura said.

"It just means what I said," I said. "It means I could just keep going. That's all it means."

"I could eat something myself," Laura said. "I don't think I've ever been so hungry in my life. Is there something to nibble on?"

"I'll put out some cheese and crackers," Terri said.

But Terri just sat there. She did not get up to get anything.
Mel turned his glass over. He spilled it out on the table.
"Gin's gone," Mel said.
Terri said, "Now what?"
I could hear my heart beating. I could hear everyone's heart. I could hear
the human noise we sat there making, not one of us moving, not even when
the room went dark.

QUESTIONS FOR DISCUSSION AND WRITING

1. Much of the story proceeds from the point of view of Mel, the cardiologist and former seminarian. We are told early on that "Mel thought real love was nothing less than spiritual love." How does this manifest in the course of the story, particularly when Mel tells the story of the old gravely injured couple who loved each other so deeply?

2. What about the view of love we get from Mel's second wife, Terri, and her insistence that her former lover, Ed, really loved her? What does the seeming lack of agreement between Mel and Terri about Ed's love for her tell us about love in general and about the love between Mel and Terri?

3. What kind of love seems to exist between the other couple in the story, who Terri says are "still on the honeymoon"?

4. The two couples lubricate their conversation with alcohol and raise a toast to love. How much do you think the gin they imbibe affects what they think and say about love?

5. Mel asks, "What do any of us really know about love?" He talks about his former wife, former lovers, and the possibility of future lovers. What is it that he is trying to articulate about the nature of love?

6. Mel snaps at Terri at one point, quietly saying to her, "Just shut up for once in your life." At another point he rebukes her with the words, "Terri, sometimes." How do these touches in the story amplify on the nature of what the story reveals about the ways we talk about love?

7. What are we to make of Mel's fantasy of letting loose a hive of bees in the house of his ex-wife? This was the wife he says he once loved "more than life itself." What does this reveal to us about love?

8. At the end of the story we have hearts beating and the odd phrase describing "the human noise we sat there making." All the gin has been downed and, despite talk about trying out a new restaurant, no one is moving and sunlight has turned to darkness. What is the feeling we get from the story's end and what does it tell us about love?

ON TECHNIQUE AND STYLE

1. Mel McGinnis mentions wanting to be a knight in armor and, later on, a beekeeper. The old couple in the story he relates are covered with bandages.

Is there an overall metaphoric effect of these images, which all have to do with covering the body?

2. Is there a definition of love that emerges from all the talk in the story? If asked how these characters define love, what would you say they are ultimately saying or trying, struggling, to say about it?

3. Carver's style has been called minimalist, a label he rejected. Yet it is a sharply etched prose style, succinct and compact, with a straightforward diction and a vernacular use of speech. How does the way the story is told, its style and its language, add to the ultimate effect the story has?

CULTURAL QUESTION

1. Most of Carver's stories concern working-class people. The characters in this story, the "we" in the story's title, are more middle class. Though Mel calls himself a mechanic, he is a heart doctor talking about mysteries of the heart. The fact that he is a cardiologist, the narrator tells us, "sometimes . . . gives him the right" to talk. Is love different for different classes of people? To what extent does what people do for a living or how they are educated affect the way they love or talk about love? Or are such distinctions irrelevant?

Amor Divino

Julia Alvarez

Julia Alvarez (1950–   ) was born in New York City but spent the first ten years of her life in the Dominican Republic. She attended Middlebury College, where she taught, and Syracuse. The recipient of two PEN Awards, she is the author of a number of volumes of poetry, a collection of essays, children's books, and a number of novels including In the Time of Butterflies, Finding Miracles, Saving the World, In the Time of Salome, The Secret Footprints, *and* How the Garcia Girls Lost Their Accents.

First published in Ms. *magazine in 1997, "Amor Divino" is a tale of love as both a painful battlefield of contentiousness and a divine, attainable treasure that morphs in different and yet similar ways through generations.*

The tiny great-granddaughter wants to visit Papito and give him today's kisses. She keeps tugging at Yolanda's hand. "Let's go comb his hair," she pleads. "Let's go give him a drink of water." She thinks of the doddering old man in his wheelchair as a human-size doll she can play with, but since she's not allowed over to the little house by herself, she has to get her aunt to take her.

Papito lives with a crew of around-the-clock maids who have been taught CPR by one of the aunts and pronounced nurses. In their starched uniforms and white oxfords, they look the part, but turn your back on them, and they are cooking sweet beans in the kitchen or watching soaps on the old man's TV or reading the paper that is still delivered every day as if Don Edmundo were not blind, and almost deaf, and completely out of it. Every time Yolanda crosses over, there's a scramble to posts. It gives her a charge to think of her old grandfather, the big man in his time, now surrounded by native women rolling their hair in his presence and singing merengues out loud.

Yolanda has been going over there often, and not just at the great-granddaughter's request. She has come down for one of those quickie divorces you can get in twenty-four hours, but some major battles have been fought long distance over the telephone. There is no privacy at any of the other houses, and so often during this trip, Yolanda has come to have her shouting matches in Papito's house. The one phone is in the day room where the old man sits dozing in front of the television. The maids turn down the volume out of courtesy to the doña on the phone, but they keep watching their TV soap or glance surreptitiously at the live soap of Yolanda arguing in English with her soon to be ex-husband.

"I did not say that. What a jerky thing to say!" Yolanda accuses him. She has reached John at his office in San Francisco where he prefers not to be called for disagreeable things. "It doesn't have to be disagreeable. It's you who are so damn—" Yolanda stops herself. There are limits in front of other people.

The appliances in her grandfather's house have not been updated for twenty years—since he and her grandmother took sick and left the big house for this handy little one at the edge of the compound. The black rotary phone sits like the judge in his black robes at the palace of justice where she spent the afternoon. Before the divorce can be finalized, another affidavit is required from Yolanda's husband renouncing all rights accruing to the de la Torre or García name in perpetuity. This is a precaution that Yolanda's uncle lawyer has taken in case this man is some sort of scoundrel. Who knows, they all liked him well enough, but here's their childless niece divorcing him within five years of the marriage. The only reason for a woman to do such a thing is if the man has proven that he is not a man. Can't deliver the goods. And they have heard things about San Francisco. Anyhow, the paper must be signed for the safety of the clan.

"I don't want your fucking money!" John is saying. His British accent makes the expletive all the more shocking, as if he has had to stoop much more than an American to use such language.

"I don't have any money." They both know she is as poor as a church mouse now that she has left him, but there is a supposed share in some family fortune that will come to her in the future if all the right people die off. "In fact, I don't give a damn about their damn money. But it's a requirement of the laws in this country."

"Laws—ee-God! What laws?! The place is a zoo. Shall I remind you, my dear, that there was a coup the day we were married."

"I'll ask you please not to name-call my native land, if you don't mind." This is ridiculous, Yolanda is thinking. What have we come to?

And of course, he is right but she does not want to be reminded. The tanks rolled out onto the streets the morning of the wedding, trapping them in the compound with the twenty-pound wedding cake across town at the baker's and the flowers wilting in the national cathedral. So as not to disappoint the bride and groom, an uncle persuaded a General friend to come out of one of the army tanks and marry them under martial law in the orchid garden in back of the grandfather's house. The grandfather, who still had his wits about him, gave Yolanda away since her father was stranded at the airport. But the grandmother was not as cooperative. She sat by, looking grim in a pink chiffon gown held together with safety pins hidden by the shawl draped over the back of the wheelchair. She threw her handful of rice out of turn and petted Yolanda as she was saying, *si,* she was taking John Merriweather, the third, to be her lawful husband. Before the year was out, the grandmother would be dead.

Yolanda still kicks herself on her bad planning. She missed out on a big church wedding, pew on pew of uncles, aunts, cousins, a momentous sense of adding a new branch to the family tree. Only a totally Americanized Dominican would plan her wedding the day after elections! Invariably there is a coup or revolt or some sort of incident. But then, why hadn't her family advised her differently? She can guess why. They had been so relieved that the crazy Yolanda was finally going to settle down with a decent man that they were not about to suggest any delays.

"I don't wish to continue this conversation," John is saying. "I've already told you I want an American divorce. I don't trust any manifestos, declarations, or documents from there."

She remembers, in fact, that when they got back to the States, John insisted on a civil ceremony in case the martial one hadn't been legal. "It's all your fault, you know. If you hadn't married us twice, we could just tear up our Dominican license and call it a day."

There is a pained silence at the other end. Of course, it would never have been that easy to part. "Hardly," is all he says, and her heart goes out to him. But then, more dogmatically, the John she finds so impossible to love concludes, "This has gone on long enough. My answer is no. N.O." The simple word spelled out, just like her mother used to do, insulting not just her will but her intelligence.

"Why can't you just sign the goddamn paper?" She is close to tears with frustration, with wanting him against all the hard evidence of years of not agreeing on anything. "Why do you have to make it so hard for me! Damn you, damn you!"

She sees the grandfather's head jerk up. Maybe he is not so deaf. He has heard something and his face is a mask of pain. "*Ay, ay, ay!*" he calls out.

She lays the receiver carefully on its cradle, almost as if to prove to the maids that she is in control of the situation. But of course, she is sobbing, and now, not just because of the distressing call with John, but because she has upset the grandfather.

She goes to him, puts her head on his lap. "It's okay, Papito, it's okay." If he could only comfort her, but what can this drooling, bleary-eyed old man offer her but the terrible image of what lies ahead? His hand goes up as if he were about to smooth the wrinkles from her forehead, but in fact, he is reaching for the handkerchief in his right pocket. The lieutenant, it is called. The one in his left pocket is called the lady. "Why?" Yolanda has asked Milagros, the oldest and most responsible of the nurses.

"Just Don Edmundo's way to be romántico, I suppose."

"*Ay Dios, ay Dios mío.*" He is dabbing at the phlegm in his eyes. Is he crying, Yolanda wonders. Perhaps the violent arguments over the phone have reminded him of his own losses. "In some ways, God is kind," one aunt has noted about Papito's senility. "At least, he doesn't know Mamita is gone." But Yolanda is sure that the old man yearns for his young bride, his beautiful wife, all the faces of a great love that is legendary in the family.

"Papito," she has to shout so he hears perhaps a semblance of her voice. He nods violently up and down like a horse being reined. "Papito, it's me, Yolanda!"

"Yolanda," Milagros confirms. "Yolanda, your granddaughter, the poetess, the daughter of your daughter, Laura, the nervous one. Yolanda, who married the Englishman."

Yolanda winces, still it will not do to try to update the complicated family tree that's hard enough for even a sound memory to keep straight. So many names are repeated generation to generation: Yolanda, for instance, shares her name with two cousins and now three little nieces—all of them named after the grandmother, Yolanda Laura María. To help the grandfather out, everyone in the family has had to be reduced to an appropriate epithet. Yolanda, the poet. Carmencita, who plays the flute. Mundín with the freckles. But in the last year, many of those names and epithets have been washed away, and only with constant repetition does the grandfather sometimes dimly recall the person in question. Suddenly, his face will light up, his nods become measured, intelligent. Yes, yes, of course he remembers. But there is no such recognition at the moment.

"He is tired," Milagros apologizes for him. "He did not sleep well last night."

"Why?" Yolanda turns to the grandfather, "Eh, Papito? Why didn't you sleep well?" It seems rude not to include him in a discussion of his tedious days and nights.

"He wakes up and wants me to speak to him in English. And what can I do, Doña Yolanda? I don't know how to speak in English. So, he gets very upset and what Don Edmundo never did in his whole life, he loses his temper. He calls me names." She shakes her head.

"He doesn't mean it, Milagros, you know he doesn't mean it."

But the older woman is tearful. She has been with the family forever, and she has a grievance. "What he never did in his whole life, Don Edmundo, he calls me a slut."

"Ay, Milagros, I'm sorry." Yolanda squeezes the woman's shoulder. "Next time, wake me up, please. I'll speak to him in English."

She takes her grandfather's hand. The skin is cool and moist and does not feel fully human. She wonders if he is lonely, if that is why he—like she—is not sleeping well. Maybe he is missing the grandmother. She knew English. She would have been able to oblige him in that as well as in other things.

"Papito, want to speak English?" Yolanda asks him now. Maybe he can get this odd craving out of his system before nightfall. "My name is Yolanda. I'm your granddaughter. Yolanda, the poet."

He stops his drastic nods and listens attentively. "*Sí, sí, sí,*" he says finally in Spanish. There is strength in his old hand now. "Yolanda, *la poetisa, sí, sí, sí.*"

She feels a surge of joy. She has made contact with the old man. Damn John and the whole sorry mess they are in!

"Shall I recite for you?" Yolanda does not wait for an answer. That was always her part—why she got the poet epithet. She begins his favorite one:
Amor, divino tesoro
Ya te vas para no volver . . .

The cook comes out of the kitchen; the young, sassy cleaning maid is leaning against the door of the bedroom "*Echale,* Doña Yolanda," she says. "What pretty sentiments."

As a child, she would be marched out in front of the grandparents and their company. In a dress she was only willing to put on for the occasion, tomboy that she was, to recite bits of poems that the grandfather had taught her. Of course, only later, when she studied literature, did she find out that many of these poems were grossly misquoted. The old man never had much of a memory, even as a young man. That's why he entrusted his poetry to his granddaughter. His favorite, for instance, the one she has just recited, should really be addressed to Youth, divine treasure. But the grandfather mixed up Youth with Love, so it is *Amor, divino tesoro,* that is now leaving, never to return.

"You like that one, don't you, Papito?" she asks him now.

"*Amor, divino tesoro,*" he begins, but his memory can't take him any further than that.

Still, it is an achievement that will be bruited about the compound for the next week. Yolanda has gotten the old man to recite poetry. What is discussed in quieter tones is the problem with the papers that have not arrived from San Francisco. The divorce can't go through until all the forms have been signed—and it's not just the release on property that hasn't been returned, but the no-contest form, the proxy form for the court's lawyer representing the husband, the proof of British citizenship. Perhaps the Englishman doesn't really want a divorce, for why wouldn't he cooperate in this effortless procedure that won't cost him anything? Is she sure this divorce is mutual or has she flown off the handle again as she used to when she was a child? "I am very sure," Yolanda is willing to swear on any of their rosaries. She puts as much certainty in her voice as she can muster. "It's over. We don't love each other anymore."

The aunts shake their heads sadly. "But is that any reason to divorce? Love, after all, comes and goes in a marriage."

And the days come and go, and the papers do not come. Yolanda is determined not to call John again. Instead, she writes him an express letter. *Please, for the love of what we had, let's just get this over and done with. You know what will happen if I come back and we go through a divorce there. We will end up hating each other.*

Or worse, she thinks. We will end up back together again, making a go of it. Miserable but married, like so many of these aunts, she thinks. Or like—though no one is supposed to remember what happened since it has all been plastered over with the legend of their great love—like her grandfather in his last few years with the grandmother.

They were a great match—the family was so pleased—the wayward niece, her head filled with crazy ideas—what came of sending the girls away to American schools!—and the young dapper businessman with his head screwed on right, newly arrived in the States from Britain. "With titles," Yolanda's mother raised her eyebrows significantly.

"It's not titles, Mami, he has a number after his name. The English are more efficient than we are if they're going to keep repeating a name generation to generation."

Still, it was titles for the mother, titles in the British accent, titles in the way John was so reasonable and could talk her high-strung daughter into settling down, cutting her hair, dressing in outfits, eating meals instead of just snacks out of boxes and cans. He would provide the solidity, and she would be the breath of fresh air, breezes blowing in from the garden, the piano in the parlor, the sweetness and light of the union. All well and good, Yolanda thinks, but that's not what happened in the marriage.

If Yolanda were to pick the painting that best represents her struggles with John, it would be a Chagall they once saw together when they were visiting her parents in New York. The young woman was flying up into the sky and the groom was holding her by the ankles, trying to pull her back down. Or was he hoping to be lifted up into that starry sky? She had put the question to John as they stood in front of the painting. What did he think was going on?

"It's a painting, not a bloody psychological test," he had mocked, his hand at her back, ready to escort her to the next painting. Personal questions embarrassed him, particularly personal questions asked in public places.

But she had dug her heels in and persisted. "Ah, come on. What do you think—is he going up or is she coming down."

"Joe-land-er," he chided. He never could get her name right. "That's enough, really."

"But why can't you play with me? Why can't you just guess what you think is going on between them?" Her voice had that teary, antagonistic tone. Now people were looking.

"They're headed for a big fight, if you ask me," he had hissed at her. And then, turning abruptly, he had proceeded to the next painting by himself. She could see it was another Chagall, the girl completely airborne by now. She could not make out what the man was doing from her vantage point. Stubbornly, she stood in front of her own painting, arms folded, and waited until he had left the room before bursting into tears. They were always having these silly fights. They could never agree on anything.

But still they clung to each other. For three years they had lived together on and off—John putting up with all the travesty of pretending he had his own apartment, since her family would have disowned her if she had told them she was shacking up with a man. But San Francisco was across the country from New York and almost across the world from the Island, and the red phone was always answered by Yolanda. Finally, they had decided either to tie the knot or make a clean break of it since they were getting on in years and both imagined they wanted a family. That would have been the moment, Yolanda sees it now, to take stock and cut the cord. But instead they had married.

And now in the warm safety of the compound, she can see why she made the choice she did: she was marrying her family! After all her mistakes and craziness, the way back home was through a man who would fit into the clan—instead of the hippie boyfriends who lectured her uncles about multinational corporations and the military industrial complex. John golfed with the cousins and took long rides in the countryside with the grandfather, plotting the location for a plant they were going to build to manufacture again the old family tiles the grandfather's sons had already ruled were no longer cost-efficient to produce. But John had calculated a way to make them cheaply. She loved that about him—John would always find a way. And the old grandfather had come to life again—the forgetfulness seemingly put aside except for brief spells that were chalked off as the bad memory of old age. He loved those drives in the country with John. "My two favorite men," Yolanda had laughed.

But she knew that mostly the grandfather was wanting to get out of the house to avoid the grandmother. She was on the warpath those last years. He had tricked her. He had brought her to live in the compound when she had wanted to spend her old age spreading her wings in the apartment she had talked him into buying in New York. There, she could drink and gamble and eat what she wanted to her heart's content. Here, everything she did was monitored by members of the family and the small watchful army of nursemaids.

Daily, one could hear her howls of fury coming from the little house, her voice yelling vulgarities at him, and the old man pleading, "Yolanda, please, I beg of you. Yolanda, try to control yourself, please, for the love of God."

Not for the love of God and not for the great love there had been between them would the grandmother put aside her anger toward him. One time she accused him of sleeping with his nurse and cut up his bedsheets with a butter knife. "I'm an eighty-year-old with one foot in the grave," the grandfather reasoned with her. "You've still got your pistol, don't you?" the grandmother snapped, grabbing for his crotch. On another occasion—though it was hotly debated whether or not the grandmother knew what she was doing—she had put rat poison in his food because he would not let her send the chauffeur for a bottle of rum. Thank God the cook had caught her or it would have been the grandfather preceding the grandmother to the grave.

John had tried to intervene, but the grandmother had looked him squarely in the eye: "You're not the first cock in the barnyard, you hear me! And you're not going to be the last."

John had been insulted, but Yolanda had laughed. "How the hell has she figured my life out?" she wondered. All the stories of Yolanda's and her sisters' misadventures had been kept from the old people. Sometimes, catching that wild look in the gray eyes, Yolanda could see why she had been named after her grandmother. She, too, had that crazy yearning to let loose and fly up beyond the reach of her husband, her bossy children, the vigilante nursemaids, the little house, the doll-size life. No wonder she had pelted Yolanda with rice just before the exchange of vows at the wedding. The old woman had foreseen that the rather formal, young Englishman was not suited for her granddaughter who had her naughty blood coursing through her veins.

"Not yet," the aunts had said, holding her fist closed so she wouldn't throw any more rice. When the ceremony was over, they let her hand go. "Now, Mamita, now it's time."

"It's too late," the grandmother had said glumly and thrown the rice in spite at the General.

Yolanda crosses over to the grandfather's house, this time legitimately to visit the old man. The great-granddaughter skips at her side, little Yolanda, the seventh, or whatever number Yolanda they are up to by now in the family. "We might not be able to stay long," Yolanda prepares the child. Papito has not been feeling well. He seems even more lost than usual in the coils of his memory. The nurses have to remind him to chew the food in his mouth, and then, of course, to swallow it.

Little Yolanda has brought her beach pail along, for she means to wash Papito's feet. "Maybe I will just wipe his mouth with the lieutenant," she tells herself, then looks up at her aunt to see if that will be all right.

Yolanda has to smile. If she and John had gotten along, they could have had a little treasure of a girl like this. Yolanda, the eighth, combing their hair and wiping their drooling mouths in old age. There are pluses to keeping an alliance going. Love is not the only lovely outcome of a marriage.

Already from this distance, Yolanda can hear the commotion of Milagros waking the grandfather from his nap. "*Buenas tardes,* Don Edmundo. I said, *BUENAS TARDES.* Yes, it's afternoon, it's quarter to four. Yes, QUARTER TO FOUR, in the afternoon, yes. Don Edmundo. Your name is Don Edmundo, no I'm sure it's Edmundo, after your father Edmundo Antonio, yes."

Yolanda looks down at the great-granddaughter. Maybe they should cancel this visit. But the little girl is swinging her beach pail, ready to wash the old man's feet and play with the handkerchiefs in his pockets. She seems unaffected by the shouting. After all, she too sometimes has to be reminded that it's bedtime, that she must chew her sweet plantain instead of gulping it down.

As they approach the house, servants begin to pour out of the different entrances: the chauffeur who was using the phone, the maids from the aunts' houses who come over here to wash their hair at the spare shower, the gardener taking lottery bets. "It's just us!" Yolanda feels like calling out.

Inside, Milagros is still trying to convince Papito that his name is Edmundo and that yes, he did marry. But the grandfather protests angrily. How can he have been married when he is just a boy in short pants, when they only recently put his mother in the ground? Milagros looks over at Yolanda and mouths, "He is misremembering Doña Yolanda's death."

"Let it be," Yolanda advises. What does it matter? The gossamer web of births and marriages, the fragile filaments of vows and hopes and fears that connect them into a family have already been torn from his memory. Let him be a little boy. A playmate for his great-granddaughter.

Little Yolanda meanwhile has climbed up on her great-grandfather's lap and tugged the handkerchief out of his left pocket. "Papito, here is the lady. She wants to wipe your mouth."

Yolanda feels her heart is being held in place by such a thin, frayed filament, she is sure if she takes a breath, her heart will smash against her ribs. She keeps eyeing the phone, hunched on the sideboard. With this scene playing all around her, anything can be endured, anything. She feels like calling John and saying, okay, don't send the papers, I'm coming home.

The phone rings, smashing her heart's vision so she feels a hollow in her chest. But she cannot let herself be fooled by pity into cowardly choices. The phone rings again, and it is the great-granddaughter who scrambles off the old man's lap and answers it. Yolanda supposes it is the chauffeur's party calling back, thinking the coast is clear.

But the great-granddaughter hands the phone to Yolanda. "It's somebody talking funny," she says, making a face.

It is John. He just called her at her aunt's and was told Yolanda was over at her grandfather's house. "How is the old fellow? Is he well enough that I can say hello?"

Tears spring to Yolanda's eyes. "Not at all. Ay, John, he doesn't even know who he is."

"What a pity," he says quietly, and she knows he is genuinely sad to hear the news.

"Look, John," she begins. "I'm sorry about the other day—"

"I'm sorry as well. That's why I'm calling. You're right, I'm being silly. I've sent the papers. They should be there by Tuesday."

"Thank you, thank you," she sobs, for how can she be truly grateful to him for agreeing to become an absence in her life? And yet, she must not turn back now. With that strong will that so often clashed with his, she forces herself to engrave it in her memory. John Merriweather, the third, 1975-1983, the years he was part of her family.

That night she lies awake, remembering other nights from her childhood in a bed not unlike this one, in this very compound, with these very night sounds, the cicadas, the radio going in one of the bedrooms, a child crying out, the tired voices of the servants coming from the back of the house. She wants to keep her memory busy so she will not think of his body tucked in the hollow her body makes, his breath in her hair. Momentarily, she wishes for that blessed blank in the grandfather's head—not to feel the pain of what is gone, never to return. But no! That would be cowardice, to erase the touch of a hand, the look on a face, the lilt of a voice, to tear the web that continues to spin itself, generation to generation, true love to true love. She thinks of the great-granddaughter, the gray eyes, the curl in her hair, so familiar. And then, in lieu of counting sheep, she begins the long roll call of all the living members of the family.

She must have dozed off, for the next thing she knows Milagros is shaking her awake. "Doña Yolanda, begging your pardon."

"What? What?" She has a heartbreaking moment of thinking she has lost the other man in her life all in one day.

"Don Edmundo is worked up. He wants to speak in English. You said I should wake you."

In a second she is out of her bed and in her robe and hurrying across the dark compound grounds with Milagros. The night watchman leads with his flashlight, beaming a faint path on the old-tile stepping-stones in the garden.

In the bedroom, all is quiet now. The little night lamp glows so peacefully that Yolanda wonders if she hasn't stepped into the wrong room in the compound. Maybe she has been misled into a child's bedroom? The grandfather lies tucked in his bed, his hands folded at his waist, his mouth hanging open, his milky eyes gazing up at the ceiling.

"He quiets down in spells," Milagros explains. "He will start up again, you will see."

Yolanda sits down on the edge of the bed and takes his old hands in hers. She can feel his chest moving, up and down. "It's okay now," she tells the nurse. "Go get some sleep. I'll talk to him." She wants this moment with the grandfather, no one watching, no one repeating in a loud voice what she wants to say to him.

"Good night then, and forgive the molestation."

"Not at all, Milagros, not at all."

"Papito," she whispers when the door closes. "I'm here. It's me, Yolanda."

His face comes fully awake, a smile suffuses his features. He places Yolanda's hands inside his pajama top above where his heart should be and pulls her down to him. His sour-smelling, toothless mouth rains her with kisses. "Oh yes, oh yes," he is saying in English. "Let's not fight, let's not fight," he pleads.

Yolanda lets herself be kissed. She kisses his hands, she kisses his forehead.

"Now it's all fixed between us, now it's all fixed."

"Yes, yes," she agrees with him. And for a moment it is she in a gown so white and puffy, she could be floating above the ground, down the long aisle of the national cathedral, toward her handsome groom, the five bright-eyed children, the big house in the Island, the apartment in New York, the six new Yolandas, the happy face of the future. Yes, for a moment, she, too, has found love's divine treasure buried deep in her grandfather's memory.

QUESTIONS FOR DISCUSSION AND WRITING

1. "Amor Divino" begins with Yolanda needing papers to sign to end her marriage. What do we subsequently discover in the course of the story about the love between her and her English husband? At one point she feels like telling him not to send the papers and like saying that she'll come home to him. How would you describe her ambivalence? Is it a form of love?

2. Why do you suppose the love between the grandparents has become legendary in the family as "a great love"—especially considering, in the last few years of their lives together, the grandmother accuses the grandfather of infidelity and tries to poison him?

3. Yolanda is certain her grandfather "yearns for his young bride," and youth is confused with love in the poem she recites to him. Is one of the meanings in the story tied to the link between youth and love?

4. The aunts seem confused that Yolanda is divorcing over the fact that she and John don't love each other. "Love, after all, comes and goes in a marriage," they say. What does their attitude toward love say about the ways the different generations in the story view love?

5. How does arguing over the meaning in the Chagall painting show the chasm that exists between Yolanda and John? What does the painting reveal about love?

6. Yolanda looks at her niece Yolanda, Papito's great-great granddaughter, and thinks, "Love is not the only lovely outcome of a marriage." What does the story reveal about connections between love and marriage? Do they actually go together, like the old song insists, "like a horse and carriage"?

7. Yolanda loves that John can find a way to get tiles manufactured for the family business again, and yet she also acknowledges to herself that if she would come back to him they would wind up hating each other. What is Alvarez revealing here about love? About hate?

8. How is it that Yolanda discovers "love's divine treasure" at the end of the story? What exactly has she learned about love from her grandfather?

ON TECHNIQUE AND STYLE

1. The grandfather in the story insults Milagros, his older woman caretaker, by calling her a slut, and the grandmother rebukes John from thinking he is Yolanda's first or last lover. What do these examples of sexuality reveal to us about how Alvarez establishes important points of meaning?
2. Yolanda is described to us as "wayward" and "crazy," having "naughty blood coursing through her veins." How do such characterizations help set up the major theme in the story about generations and "true love"?
3. Is there an argument in this story about the nature of love? What is it?

CULTURAL QUESTION

1. This is a story about well-to-do Dominicans. The grandfather likes to speak English and the family seems enamored of Yolanda's husband possessing what they believe is an English title. Is there a sense of Hispanic feelings of inferiority or just a desire to identify with a presumed English nobility? What are the contrasts implied between Dominican and British culture, particularly in the portrayal of Yolanda and John?

The Lottery

Shirley Jackson

Shirley Jackson (1919–1965), novelist and short story writer, was born in San Francisco, California, and spent her early life in California. She attended the University of Rochester and graduated from Syracuse University. She married literary critic Stanley Edgar Hyman and lived with him and their children in New Hampshire and Vermont. Jackson published stories in many magazines, including Harper's, The New Republic, Mademoiselle, Collier's, The New Yorker, Good Housekeeping, *and* Reader's Digest. *She published three novels, a volume of short stories, a memoir, and a children's book, but is best known for her story "The Lottery," first published in* The New Yorker *in 1948.*

"The Lottery" was and still is a shocking story. It bring us into a world of violence and inhumanity that at first appears normal, even folksy, on the surface until we move beneath the outwardly seeming village tranquility to what lies underneath in the mysterious regions of the human heart.

The morning of June 27th was clear and sunny, with the fresh warmth of a full-summer day; the flowers were blossoming profusely and the grass was richly green. The people of the village began to gather in the square, between the post office and the bank, around ten o'clock; in some towns there were so many people that the lottery took two days and had to be started on June 20th, but in this village, where there were only about three hundred people, the whole lottery took less than two hours, so it could begin at ten o'clock in the morning and still be through in time to allow the villagers to get home for noon dinner.

The children assembled first, of course. School was recently over for the summer, and the feeling of liberty sat uneasily on most of them; they tended to gather together quietly for a while before they broke into boisterous play, and their talk was still of the classroom and the teacher, of books and reprimands. Bobby Martin had already stuffed his pockets full of stones, and the other boys soon followed his example, selecting the smoothest and roundest stones; Bobby and Harry Jones and Dickie Delacroix—the villagers pronounced this name "Dellacroy"—eventually made a great pile of stones in one corner of the square and guarded it against the raids of the other boys. The girls stood aside, talking among themselves, looking over their shoulders at the boys, and the very small children rolled in the dust or clung to the hands of their older brothers or sisters.

Soon the men began to gather, surveying their own children, speaking of planting and rain, tractors and taxes. They stood together, away from the pile of stones in the corner, and their jokes were quiet and they smiled rather than laughed. The women, wearing faded house dresses and sweaters, came shortly after their menfolk. They greeted one another and exchanged bits of gossip as they went to join their husbands. Soon the women, standing by their husbands, began to call to their children, and the children came reluctantly, having to be called four or five times. Bobby Martin ducked under his mother's grasping hand and ran, laughing, back to the pile of stones. His father spoke up sharply, and Bobby came quickly and took his place between his father and his oldest brother.

The lottery was conducted—as were the square dances, the teen club, the Halloween program—by Mr. Summers, who had time and energy to devote to civic activities. He was a round-faced, jovial man and he ran the coal business, and people were sorry for him because he had no children and his wife was a scold. When he arrived in the square, carrying the black wooden box, there was a murmur of conversation among the villagers, and he waved and called, "Little late today, folks." The postmaster, Mr. Graves, followed him, carrying a three-legged stool, and the stool was put in the center of the square and Mr. Summers set the black box down on it. The villagers kept their distance, leaving a space between themselves and the stool, and when Mr. Summers said, "Some of you fellows want to give me a hand?" there was a hesitation before two men. Mr. Martin and his oldest son, Baxter, came forward to hold the box steady on the stool while Mr. Summers stirred up the papers inside it.

The original paraphernalia for the lottery had been lost long ago, and the black box now resting on the stool had been put into use even before Old

Man Warner, the oldest man in town, was born. Mr. Summers spoke frequently to the villagers about making a new box, but no one liked to upset
even as much tradition as was represented by the black box. There was a
story that the present box had been made with some pieces of the box that
had preceded it, the one that had been constructed when the first people settled down to make a village here. Every year, after the lottery, Mr. Summers
began talking again about a new box, but every year the subject was allowed
to fade off without anything's being done. The black box grew shabbier each
year: by now it was no longer completely black but splintered badly along one
side to show the original wood color, and in some places faded or stained.

   Mr. Martin and his oldest son, Baxter, held the black box securely on
the stool until Mr. Summers had stirred the papers thoroughly with his hand.
Because so much of the ritual had been forgotten or discarded, Mr. Summers
had been successful in having slips of paper substituted for the chips of wood
that had been used for generations. Chips of wood, Mr. Summers had argued,
had been all very well when the village was tiny, but now that the population
was more than three hundred and likely to keep on growing, it was necessary to use something that would fit more easily into the black box. The night
before the lottery, Mr. Summers and Mr. Graves made up the slips of paper
and put them in the box, and it was then taken to the safe of Mr. Summers's
coal company and locked up until Mr. Summers was ready to take it to the
square next morning. The rest of the year, the box was put way, sometimes
one place, sometimes another; it had spent one year in Mr. Graves's barn and
another year underfoot in the post office. And sometimes it was set on a shelf
in the Martin grocery and left there.

   There was a great deal of fussing to be done before Mr. Summers
declared the lottery open. There were the lists to make up—of heads of families, heads of households in each family, members of each household in each
family. There was the proper swearing-in of Mr. Summers by the postmaster,
as the official of the lottery; at one time, some people remembered, there had
been a recital of some sort, performed by the official of the lottery, a perfunctory, tuneless chant that had been rattled off duly each year; some people
believed that the official of the lottery used to stand just so when he said or
sang it, others believed that he was supposed to walk among the people, but
years and years ago this part of the ritual had been allowed to lapse. There
had been, also, a ritual salute, which the official of the lottery had had to use in
addressing each person who came up to draw from the box, but this also had
changed with time, until now it was felt necessary only for the official to speak
to each person approaching. Mr. Summers was very good at all this; in his
clean white shirt and blue jeans, with one hand resting carelessly on the black
box, he seemed very proper and important as he talked interminably to Mr.
Graves and the Martins.

   Just as Mr. Summers finally left off talking and turned to the assembled
villagers, Mrs. Hutchinson came hurriedly along the path to the square, her
sweater thrown over her shoulders, and slid into place in the back of the

crowd. "Clean forgot what day it was," she said to Mrs. Delacroix, who stood next to her, and they both laughed softly. "Thought my old man was out back stacking wood," Mrs. Hutchinson went on, "and then I looked out the window and the kids was gone, and then I remembered it was the twenty-seventh and came a-running." She dried her hands on her apron, and Mrs. Delacroix said, "You're in time, though. They're still talking away up there."

Mrs. Hutchinson craned her neck to see through the crowd and found her husband and children standing near the front. She tapped Mrs. Delacroix on the arm as a farewell and began to make her way through the crowd. The people separated good-humoredly to let her through: two or three people said, in voices just loud enough to be heard across the crowd, "Here comes your, Missus, Hutchinson," and "Bill, she made it after all." Mrs. Hutchinson reached her husband, and Mr. Summers, who had been waiting, said cheerfully. "Thought we were going to have to get on without you, Tessie." Mrs. Hutchinson said, grinning, "Wouldn't have me leave m'dishes in the sink, now, would you, Joe?" and soft laughter ran through the crowd as the people stirred back into position after Mrs. Hutchinson's arrival.

"Well, now," Mr. Summers said soberly, "guess we better get started, get this over with, so's we can go back to work. Anybody ain't here?"

"Dunbar," several people said. "Dunbar. Dunbar."

Mr. Summers consulted his list. "Clyde Dunbar," he said. "That's right. He's broke his leg, hasn't he? Who's drawing for him?"

"Me. I guess," a woman said, and Mr. Summers turned to look at her. "Wife draws for her husband." Mr. Summers said. "Don't you have a grown boy to do it for you, Janey?" Although Mr. Summers and everyone else in the village knew the answer perfectly well, it was the business of the official of the lottery to ask such questions formally. Mr. Summers waited with an expression of polite interest while Mrs. Dunbar answered.

"Horace's not but sixteen yet." Mrs. Dunbar said regretfully. "Guess I gotta fill in for the old man this year."

"Right." Mr. Summers said. He made a note on the list he was holding. Then he asked, "Watson boy drawing this year?"

A tall boy in the crowd raised his hand. "Here," he said. "I m drawing for my mother and me." He blinked his eyes nervously and ducked his head as several voices in the crowd said things like "Good fellow, Jack," and "Glad to see your mother's got a man to do it."

"Well," Mr. Summers said, "guess that's everyone. Old Man Warner make it?"

"Here," a voice said, and Mr. Summers nodded.

A sudden hush fell on the crowd as Mr. Summers cleared his throat and looked at the list. "All ready?" he called. "Now, I'll read the names—heads of families first—and the men come up and take a paper out of the box. Keep the paper folded in your hand without looking at it until everyone has had a turn. Everything clear?"

The people had done it so many times that they only half listened to the directions: most of them were quiet, wetting their lips, not looking around. Then

Mr. Summers raised one hand high and said, "Adams." A man disengaged himself from the crowd and came forward. "Hi, Steve," Mr. Summers said, and Mr.
Adams said, "Hi, Joe." They grinned at one another humorlessly and nervously.
Then Mr. Adams reached into the black box and took out a folded paper. He
held it firmly by one corner as he turned and went hastily back to his place in the
crowd, where he stood a little apart from his family, not looking down at his hand.

"Allen," Mr. Summers said. "Anderson . . . Bentham."

"Seems like there's no time at all between lotteries any more," Mrs. Delacroix
said to Mrs. Graves in the back row.

"Seems like we got through with the last one only last week."

"Time sure goes fast," Mrs. Graves said.

"Clark . . . Delacroix."

"There goes my old man," Mrs. Delacroix said. She held her breath while
her husband went forward.

"Dunbar," Mr. Summers said, and Mrs. Dunbar went steadily to the box
while one of the women said, "Go on, Janey," and another said, "There she
goes."

"We're next," Mrs. Graves said. She watched while Mr. Graves came
around from the side of the box, greeted Mr. Summers gravely and selected
a slip of paper from the box. By now, all through the crowd there were men
holding the small folded papers in their large hand, turning them over and
over nervously. Mrs. Dunbar and her two sons stood together, Mrs. Dunbar
holding the slip of paper.

"Harburt . . . Hutchinson."

"Get up there, Bill," Mrs. Hutchinson said, and the people near her
laughed.

"Jones."

"They do say," Mr. Adams said to Old Man Warner, who stood next to
him, "that over in the north village they're talking of giving up the lottery."

Old Man Warner snorted. "Pack of crazy fools," he said. "Listening to the
young folks, nothing's good enough for them. Next thing you know, they'll be
wanting to go back to living in caves, nobody work any more, live that way for
a while. Used to be a saying about 'Lottery in June, corn be heavy soon.' First
thing you know, we'd all be eating stewed chickweed and acorns. There's
always been a lottery," he added petulantly. "Bad enough to see young Joe
Summers up there joking with everybody."

"Some places have already quit lotteries," Mrs. Adams said.

"Nothing but trouble in that," Old Man Warner said stoutly. "Pack of
young fools."

"Martin." And Bobby Martin watched his father go forward. "Overdyke . . .
Percy."

"I wish they'd hurry," Mrs. Dunbar said to her older son. "I wish they'd
hurry."

"They're almost through," her son said.

"You get ready to run tell Dad," Mrs. Dunbar said.

Mr. Summers called his own name and then stepped forward precisely and selected a slip from the box. Then he called, "Warner."

"Seventy-seventh year I been in the lottery," Old Man Warner said as he went through the crowd. "Seventy-seventh time."

"Watson." The tall boy came awkwardly through the crowd. Someone said, "Don't be nervous, Jack," and Mr. Summers said, "Take your time, son."

"Zanini."

After that, there was a long pause, a breathless pause, until Mr. Summers, holding his slip of paper in the air, said, "All right, fellows." For a minute, no one moved, and then all the slips of paper were opened. Suddenly, all the women began to speak at once, saving, "Who is it?," "Who's got it?," "Is it the Dunbars?," "Is it the Watsons?" Then the voices began to say, "It's Hutchinson. It's Bill," "Bill Hutchinson's got it."

"Go tell your father," Mrs. Dunbar said to her older son.

People began to look around to see the Hutchinsons. Bill Hutchinson was standing quiet, staring down at the paper in his hand. Suddenly, Tessie Hutchinson shouted to Mr. Summers, "You didn't give him time enough to take any paper he wanted. I saw you. It wasn't fair!"

"Be a good sport, Tessie," Mrs. Delacroix called, and Mrs. Graves said, "All of us took the same chance."

"Shut up, Tessie," Bill Hutchinson said.

"Well, everyone," Mr. Summers said, "that was done pretty fast, and now we've got to be hurrying a little more to get done in time." He consulted his next list. "Bill," he said, "you draw for the Hutchinson family. You got any other households in the Hutchinsons?"

"There's Don and Eva," Mrs. Hutchinson yelled. "Make them take their chance!"

"Daughters draw with their husbands' families, Tessie," Mr. Summers said gently. "You know that as well as anyone else."

"It wasn't fair," Tessie said.

"I guess not, Joe," Bill Hutchinson said regretfully. "My daughter draws with her husband's family; that's only fair. And I've got no other family except the kids."

"Then, as far as drawing for families is concerned, it's you," Mr. Summers said in explanation, "and as far as drawing for households is concerned, that's you, too. Right?"

"Right," Bill Hutchinson said.

"How many kids, Bill?" Mr. Summers asked formally.

"Three," Bill Hutchinson said.

"There's Bill, Jr., and Nancy, and little Dave. And Tessie and me."

"All right, then," Mr. Summers said. "Harry, you got their tickets back?"

Mr. Graves nodded and held up the slips of paper. "Put them in the box, then," Mr. Summers directed. "Take Bill's and put it in."

"I think we ought to start over," Mrs. Hutchinson said, as quietly as she could. "I tell you it wasn't fair. You didn't give him time enough to choose. Everybody saw that."

Mr. Graves had selected the five slips and put them in the box, and he dropped all the papers but those onto the ground, where the breeze caught them and lifted them off.

"Listen, everybody," Mrs. Hutchinson was saying to the people around her.

"Ready, Bill?" Mr. Summers asked, and Bill Hutchinson, with one quick glance around at his wife and children, nodded.

"Remember," Mr. Summers said, "take the slips and keep them folded until each person has taken one. Harry, you help little Dave." Mr. Graves took the hand of the little boy, who came willingly with him up to the box. "Take a paper out of the box, Davy," Mr. Summers said. Davy put his hand into the box and laughed. "Take just one paper," Mr. Summers said. "Harry, you hold it for him." Mr. Graves took the child's hand and removed the folded paper from the tight fist and held it while little Dave stood next to him and looked up at him wonderingly.

"Nancy next," Mr. Summers said. Nancy was twelve, and her school friends breathed heavily as she went forward switching her skirt, and took a slip daintily from the box. "Bill, Jr.," Mr. Summers said, and Billy, his face red and his feet overlarge, near knocked the box over as he got a paper out. "Tessie," Mr. Summers said. She hesitated for a minute, looking around defiantly, and then set her lips and went up to the box. She snatched a paper out and held it behind her.

"Bill," Mr. Summers said, and Bill Hutchinson reached into the box and felt around, bringing his hand out at last with the slip of paper in it.

The crowd was quiet. A girl whispered, "I hope it's not Nancy," and the sound of the whisper reached the edges of the crowd.

"It's not the way it used to be," Old Man Warner said clearly. "People ain't the way they used to be."

"All right," Mr. Summers said. "Open the papers. Harry, you open little Dave's."

Mr. Graves opened the slip of paper and there was a general sigh through the crowd as he held it up and everyone could see that it was blank. Nancy and Bill, Jr., opened theirs at the same time, and both beamed and laughed, turning around to the crowd and holding their slips of paper above their heads.

"Tessie," Mr. Summers said. There was a pause, and then Mr. Summers looked at Bill Hutchinson, and Bill unfolded his paper and showed it. It was blank.

"It's Tessie," Mr. Summers said, and his voice was hushed. "Show us her paper, Bill."

Bill Hutchinson went over to his wife and forced the slip of paper out of her hand. It had a black spot on it, the black spot Mr. Summers had made the night before with the heavy pencil in the coal company office. Bill Hutchinson held it up, and there was a stir in the crowd.

"All right, folks," Mr. Summers said. "Let's finish quickly."

Although the villagers had forgotten the ritual and lost the original black box, they still remembered to use stones. The pile of stones the boys had made earlier was ready; there were stones on the ground with the blowing scraps of paper that had come out of the box. Delacroix selected a stone so large she had to pick it up with both hands and turned to Mrs. Dunbar. "Come on," she said. "Hurry up."

Mrs. Dunbar had small stones in both hands, and she said, gasping for breath, "I can't run at all. You'll have to go ahead and I'll catch up with you."

The children had stones already. And someone gave little Davy Hutchinson a few pebbles.

Tessie Hutchinson was in the center of a cleared space by now, and she held her hands out desperately as the villagers moved in on her. "It isn't fair," she said. A stone hit her on the side of the head. Old Man Warner was saying, "Come on, come on, everyone." Steve Adams was in the front of the crowd of villagers, with Mrs. Graves beside him.

"It isn't fair, it isn't right," Mrs. Hutchinson screamed, and then they were upon her.

QUESTIONS FOR DISCUSSION AND WRITING

1. The hate in "The Lottery" is what the poet Samuel Taylor Coleridge might have described as "motiveless malignity." The people in the story seem to need to kill for the sake of ritual or tradition but this hints at a kind of hatred deep within humanity, a need to find a victim to scapegoat. It is almost as if their hatred is not even personal. Can you think of other examples where people act this way? Where nations have or do?

2. Hatred in "The Lottery" appears to be underneath the veneer, the appearance of normality. The next selection by Poe literally takes us underneath to the catacombs. Why is hatred often associated with being below and under the surface?

3. Old Man Warner, the most veteran lottery participant, vents his spleen about those in another village who supposedly have given up the lottery. He dismisses those who have quit the lotteries as fools and denounces such behavior as being primitive, acting like they want to "go back to living in caves." Old Man Warner is contemptuous of those who would change tradition but he also is fearful of change, as is evidenced by his quoting the saying "Lottery in June, corn be heavy soon." Is Jackson showing fear of change as contributing to hate? To what extent do you support the notion that fear of change contributes to hate and acts of hatefulness?

4. When Tessie realizes that she is to be the object the villagers will stone she tries to resort to accusations of unfairness. Yet before her slip of paper is selected she appears perfectly willing to go along with the crowd. What is Jackson suggesting to us about the difference between being a victimizer and being a victim, one who targets and scapegoats as opposed to one who is targeted or made into a scapegoat?

5. What are we to make of the fact that even the children, including Tessie's son Davey, are involved in the culmination of the lottery?

6. Can hatred be as methodical and orderly, as without passion, as is depicted in "The Lottery"? Can you think of examples from history or from your own life where this appeared to have been the case?

7. "The Lottery" is often read as a moral allegory of the evil concealed within the human heart. What about the notion of evil in this tale? Is evil linked to hatred? Must it be?

8. When this story was first published, Jackson said, "Millions of people," including the author's own mother, took a "pronounced dislike to me." Responses to the story were, in the author's words, "vehement." What do you think is in this story that actually aroused dislike, even hatred, in many of its readers?

ON TECHNIQUE AND STYLE

1. Discuss the use of a lottery as a metaphor. Does the hatred that any of us engender sometimes seem like it can happen with randomness and caprice, for no logical reason other than how things come up?

2. Look up the history and meaning of the scapegoat. Does this story embody a definition of what constitutes being a scapegoat? What is Jackson revealing to us about the nature of scapegoating?

3. Does Jackson present an argument within her story for a specific view of human nature? What is it she seems to be positing and how does it illuminate hatred?

CULTURAL QUESTION

1. The setting for "The Lottery" is small-town America, much like the place in Vermont where Jackson spent many of her adult years. Is the hatred and violence that we see here supposed to be provincial, a mark of small-town prejudice and hate? Or is this more a story of the human condition?

The Cask of Amontillado

Edgar Allan Poe

Edgar Allan Poe (1809–1849), one of the world's most celebrated poets and short story writers, was also an editor and critic. A master of the horror tale and one of the first detective story writers, he was one of the first to lay out an aesthetic theory of the form of the short story. Born in Boston, he was raised by a Richmond, Virginia, merchant after the early death of both of his parents. He grew up in Virginia and England and attended the University of Virginia, from which he was expelled. He joined the army and later attended West Point, from which he was dishonorably discharged. He went on to live in Baltimore with his father's sister and published his first story there in 1833. He became editor of the Southern Literary Messenger *and married his thirteen-year-old cousin Virginia Clemm in 1836. She died in 1846. Poe lived a tempestuous and dissolute life of despair; his life was a tragic tapestry of poverty, alcoholism, and depression. He literally died in a gutter.*

"The Cask of Amontillado" first appeared in Godey's Lady's Book *in 1846. It is a revenge story. Consumed by hate for Fortunato for "insult" and "injuries" that are never specified, Montresor goes about destroying his enemy with a wily and lethal calculation. In writing about this story the British novelist and poet D. H. Lawrence said, "the lust of hate is the inordinate desire to consume and unspeakably possess the soul of the hated one."*

The thousand injuries of Fortunato I had borne as I best could, but when he ventured upon insult, I vowed revenge. You, who so well know the nature of my soul, will not suppose, however, that I gave utterance to a threat. AT LENGTH I would be avenged; this was a point definitively settled—but the very definitiveness with which it was resolved precluded the idea of risk. I must not only punish, but punish with impunity. A wrong is unredressed when retribution overtakes its redresser. It is equally unredressed when the avenger fails to make himself felt as such to him who has done the wrong.

It must be understood that neither by word nor deed had I given Fortunato cause to doubt my good will. I continued as was my wont, to smile in his face, and he did not perceive that my smile NOW was at the thought of his immolation.

He had a weak point—this Fortunato—although in other regards he was a man to be respected and even feared. He prided himself on his connoisseurship in wine. Few Italians have the true virtuoso spirit. For the most part their enthusiasm is adopted to suit the time and opportunity to practise imposture upon the British and Austrian MILLIONAIRES. In painting and gemmary, Fortunato, like his countrymen, was a quack, but in the matter of old wines he was sincere. In this respect I did not differ from him materially; I was skilful in the Italian vintages myself, and bought largely whenever I could.

It was about dusk, one evening during the supreme madness of the carnival season, that I encountered my friend. He accosted me with excessive warmth, for he had been drinking much. The man wore motley. He had on a tight-fitting parti-striped dress and his head was surmounted by the conical cap and bells. I was so pleased to see him, that I thought I should never have done wringing his hand.

I said to him—"My dear Fortunato, you are luckily met. How remarkably well you are looking today! But I have received a pipe of what passes for Amontillado, and I have my doubts."

"How?" said he, "Amontillado? A pipe? Impossible? And in the middle of the carnival?"

"I have my doubts," I replied; "and I was silly enough to pay the full Amontillado price without consulting you in the matter. You were not to be found, and I was fearful of losing a bargain."

"Amontillado!"

"I have my doubts."

"Amontillado!"

"And I must satisfy them."

"Amontillado!"

"As you are engaged, I am on my way to Luchesi. If any one has a critical turn, it is he. He will tell me"—

"Luchesi cannot tell Amontillado from Sherry."

"And yet some fools will have it that his taste is a match for your own."

"Come let us go."

"Whither?"

"To your vaults."

"My friend, no; I will not impose upon your good nature. I perceive you have an engagement Luchesi"—

"I have no engagement; come."

"My friend, no. It is not the engagement, but the severe cold with which I perceive you are afflicted. The vaults are insufferably damp. They are encrusted with nitre."

"Let us go, nevertheless. The cold is merely nothing. Amontillado! You have been imposed upon; and as for Luchesi, he cannot distinguish Sherry from Amontillado."

Thus speaking, Fortunato possessed himself of my arm. Putting on a mask of black silk and drawing a roquelaire closely about my person, I suffered him to hurry me to my palazzo.

There were no attendants at home; they had absconded to make merry in honour of the time. I had told them that I should not return until the morning and had given them explicit orders not to stir from the house. These orders were sufficient, I well knew, to insure their immediate disappearance, one and all, as soon as my back was turned.

I took from their sconces two flambeaux, and giving one to Fortunato bowed him through several suites of rooms to the archway that led into the vaults. I passed down a long and winding staircase, requesting him to be cautious as he followed. We came at length to the foot of the descent, and stood together on the damp ground of the catacombs of the Montresors.

The gait of my friend was unsteady, and the bells upon his cap jingled as he strode.

"The pipe," said he.

"It is farther on," said I; "but observe the white webwork which gleams from these cavern walls."

He turned towards me and looked into my eyes with two filmy orbs that distilled the rheum of intoxication.

"Nitre?" he asked, at length.

"Nitre," I replied. "How long have you had that cough!"

"Ugh! ugh! ugh!—ugh! ugh! ugh!—ugh! ugh! ugh!—ugh! ugh! ugh!—ugh! ugh! ugh!"

My poor friend found it impossible to reply for many minutes.

"It is nothing," he said, at last.

"Come," I said, with decision, we will go back; your health is precious. You are rich, respected, admired, beloved; you are happy as once I was. You are a man to be missed. For me it is no matter. We will go back; you will be ill and I cannot be responsible. Besides, there is Luchesi"—

"Enough," he said; "the cough is a mere nothing; it will not kill me. I shall not die of a cough."

"True—true," I replied; "and, indeed, I had no intention of alarming you unnecessarily—but you should use all proper caution. A draught of this Medoc will defend us from the damps."

Here I knocked off the neck of a bottle which I drew from a long row of its fellows that lay upon the mould.

"Drink," I said, presenting him the wine.

He raised it to his lips with a leer. He paused and nodded to me familiarly, while his bells jingled.

"I drink," he said, "to the buried that repose around us."

"And I to your long life."

He again took my arm and we proceeded.

"These vaults," he said, "are extensive."

"The Montresors," I replied, "were a great numerous family."

"I forget your arms."

"A huge human foot d'or, in a field azure; the foot crushes a serpent rampant whose fangs are imbedded in the heel."

"And the motto?"

"Nemo me impune lacessit."

"Good!" he said.

The wine sparkled in his eyes and the bells jingled. My own fancy grew warm with the Medoc. We had passed through walls of piled bones, with casks and puncheons intermingling, into the inmost recesses of the catacombs. I paused again, and this time I made bold to seize Fortunato by an arm above the elbow.

"The nitre!" I said:"see it increases. It hangs like moss upon the vaults. We are below the river's bed. The drops of moisture trickle among the bones. Come, we will go back ere it is too late. Your cough"—

"It is nothing," he said; "let us go on. But first, another draught of the Medoc."

I broke and reached him a flagon of De Grave. He emptied it at a breath. His eyes flashed with a fierce light. He laughed and threw the bottle upwards with a gesticulation I did not understand.

I looked at him in surprise. He repeated the movement—a grotesque one.

"You do not comprehend?" he said.

"Not I," I replied.

"Then you are not of the brotherhood."

"How?"

"You are not of the masons."

"Yes, yes," I said, "yes! yes."

"You? Impossible! A mason?"

"A mason," I replied.

"A sign," he said.

"It is this," I answered, producing a trowel from beneath the folds of my roquelaire.

"You jest," he exclaimed, recoiling a few paces. "But let us proceed to the Amontillado."

"Be it so," I said, replacing the tool beneath the cloak, and again offering him my arm. He leaned upon it heavily. We continued our route in search of the Amontillado. We passed through a range of low arches, descended, passed on, and descending again, arrived at a deep crypt, in which the foulness of the air caused our flambeaux rather to glow than flame.

At the most remote end of the crypt there appeared another less spacious. Its walls had been lined with human remains piled to the vault overhead, in the fashion of the great catacombs of Paris. Three sides of this interior crypt were still ornamented in this manner. From the fourth the bones had been thrown down, and lay promiscuously upon the earth, forming at one point a mound of some size. Within the wall thus exposed by the displacing of the bones, we perceived a still interior recess, in depth about four feet, in width three, in height six or seven. It seemed to have been constructed for no especial use in itself, but formed merely the interval between two of the colossal supports of the roof of the catacombs, and was backed by one of their circumscribing walls of solid granite.

It was in vain that Fortunato, uplifting his dull torch, endeavoured to pry into the depths of the recess. Its termination the feeble light did not enable us to see.

"Proceed," I said; "herein is the Amontillado. As for Luchesi"—

"He is an ignoramus," interrupted my friend, as he stepped unsteadily forward, while I followed immediately at his heels. In an instant he had reached the extremity of the niche, and finding his progress arrested by the rock, stood stupidly bewildered. A moment more and I had fettered him to the granite. In its surface were two iron staples, distant from each other about two feet, horizontally. From one of these depended a short chain, from the other a padlock. Throwing the links about his waist, it was but the work of a few seconds to secure it. He was too much astounded to resist. Withdrawing the key I stepped back from the recess.

"Pass your hand," I said, "over the wall; you cannot help feeling the nitre. Indeed it is VERY damp. Once more let me IMPLORE you to return. No? Then I must positively leave you. But I must first render you all the little attentions in my power."

"The Amontillado!" ejaculated my friend, not yet recovered from his astonishment.

"True," I replied; "the Amontillado."

As I said these words I busied myself among the pile of bones of which I have before spoken. Throwing them aside, I soon uncovered a quantity of building stone and mortar. With these materials and with the aid of my trowel, I began vigorously to wall up the entrance of the niche.

I had scarcely laid the first tier of my masonry when I discovered that the intoxication of Fortunato had in a great measure worn off. The earliest indication I had of this was a low moaning cry from the depth of the recess. It was NOT the cry of a drunken man. There was then a long and obstinate silence. I laid the second tier, and the third, and the fourth; and then I heard the furious vibrations of the chain. The noise lasted for several minutes, during which, that I might hearken to it with the more satisfaction, I ceased my labours and sat down upon the bones. When at last the clanking subsided, I resumed the trowel, and finished without interruption the fifth, the sixth, and the seventh tier. The wall was now nearly upon a level with my breast. I again paused, and holding the flambeaux over the mason-work, threw a few feeble rays upon the figure within.

A succession of loud and shrill screams, bursting suddenly from the throat of the chained form, seemed to thrust me violently back. For a brief moment I hesitated—I trembled. Unsheathing my rapier, I began to grope with it about the recess; but the thought of an instant reassured me. I placed my hand upon the solid fabric of the catacombs, and felt satisfied. I reapproached the wall. I replied to the yells of him who clamoured. I reechoed—I aided—I surpassed them in volume and in strength. I did this, and the clamourer grew still.

It was now midnight, and my task was drawing to a close. I had completed the eighth, the ninth, and the tenth tier. I had finished a portion of the last and the eleventh; there remained but a single stone to be fitted and plastered in. I struggled with its weight; I placed it partially in its destined position. But now there came from out the niche a low laugh that erected the hairs upon my head. It was succeeded by a sad voice, which I had difficulty in recognising as that of the noble Fortunato. The voice said—

"Ha! ha! ha!—he! he!—a very good joke indeed—an excellent jest. We will have many a rich laugh about it at the palazzo—he! he! he!—over our wine—he! he! he!"

"The Amontillado!" I said.

"He! he! he!—he! he! he!—yes, the Amontillado. But is it not getting late? Will not they be awaiting us at the palazzo, the Lady Fortunato and the rest? Let us be gone."

"Yes," I said "let us be gone."

"FOR THE LOVE OF GOD, MONTRESOR!"

"Yes," I said, "for the love of God!"

But to these words I hearkened in vain for a reply. I grew impatient. I called aloud—

"Fortunato!"

No answer. I called again—

"Fortunato!"

No answer still. I thrust a torch through the remaining aperture and let it fall within. There came forth in return only a jingling of the bells. My heart grew sick—on account of the dampness of the catacombs. I hastened to make an end of my labour. I forced the last stone into its position; I plastered it up. Against the new masonry I reerected the old rampart of bones. For the half of a century no mortal has disturbed them.

In pace requiescat!

QUESTIONS FOR DISCUSSION AND WRITING

1. "Revenge is a dish best served cold" is a much-quoted line, originally thought to be in the French novel *Les Liaisons Dangereuses*. Intent on his adversary's "immolation," Montresor hides his hatred for Fortunato behind an exterior of goodwill and smiles. When we think of deep hatred we normally associate it with passion. What is the nature of Montresor's hatred that he can conceal it? What does it reveal about him?

2. Does it matter that the specific source, the unnamed injuries, and the insult Montresor ascribes to Fortunato remain unrevealed? Is Poe perhaps suggesting that hatred can result from perceived insult or injury? What are we to make of the fact that Fortunato obviously has no idea he has insulted or caused injury to Montresor?

3. In the story hatred is turned into a desire by Montresor for vengeance based on Fortunato's weakness—pride in his connoisseurship in wine. "Hate," as we have seen, is a strong word and a difficult one to generalize about. But do you think hate generally looks for weakness and fantasizes preying upon it?

4. Is Montresor's hatred of Fortunato on a level we can understand and relate to or is it excessive, irrational, perhaps even pathological? Notice early on when he meets up with Fortunato, who is all decked in motley, Montresor says, "I was so pleased to see him, that I thought I should never have done wringing his hand." He is excited about setting his scheme into motion, but his words certainly don't sound like a man consumed by hate. And he refers to Fortunato as his friend. What does this tell us about Montresor and the nature of his hatred toward Fortunato?

5. When urging Fortunato to go back from the quest for the amontillado because of Fortunato's coughing, Montresor says, "You are rich, respected, admired, beloved; you are happy as once I was. You are a man to be missed. For me it is no matter." What does this remark tell us about the possible source of Montresor's hatred for Fortunato?

6. How does Montresor's family coat of arms and its Latin motto, which translates to "No one wounds me with impunity," figure in to our understanding the nature of his hatred? Is Poe suggesting that the need to avenge is transgenerational, tied to ancestry, to tradition?

7. Consider the way Montresor murders Fortunato, the methodical tier after tier of masonry and the burial of his enemy alive. Can we say this way of destroying the object of one's deep hatred is normal? What are we to make of the fact that, from the perch of fifty years, Montresor tells us his heart "grew sick" and that he blames it on the dampness of the catacombs?

8. Freud described love as "a temporary form of insanity." Might we say the same of hatred as it is depicted in this story? Or is Montresor's hatred of Fortunato something entirely different than the Freudian definition presupposes?

ON TECHNIQUE AND STYLE

1. Montresor has often been described as an "unreliable narrator," which suggests some or much of what he tells us, including his motivations, cannot or should not be trusted. Do you agree that we need to see him as unreliable? How does Poe make him appear that way?
2. Compare and contrast the emotion of hatred as it is presented in this story to the way Jackson makes us see hatred in "The Lottery." Aside from individual versus mass hatred what are the differences? What are the likenesses?
3. In many ways "The Cask of Amontillado" is a shocking tale. How does Poe manage to shock us? Is there an analogy to the way Montresor leads the unexpecting Fortunato into horror and the way Poe leads us as readers?

CULTURAL QUESTION

1. Though Poe is an American writer, this story, with its Italian-sounding names and its coats of arms and catacombs, definitely has a European feel. A number of years ago a television show called "Homicide" took the method of Montresor's revenge killing of Fortunato and set it in contemporary Baltimore, the city where Poe spent a good deal of his life. Does the hatred in the story, including the premeditated method of revenge, seem universal?

POETRY

Love Poem

Audre Lorde

Audre Lorde's (1934–1992) biography can be found in Chapter 3. "Love Poem," from the 1975 volume Collected Poems *by Lorde, captures the depth of a love that soars and communicates to us the exhilaration of that love in both flesh and spirit.*

Speak earth and bless me with what is richest
make sky flow honey out of my hips
rigid as mountains

spread over a valley
carved out by the mouth of rain.

And I knew when I entered her I was
high wind in her forests hollow
fingers whispering sound
honey flowed
from the split cup
impaled on a lance of tongues
on the tips of her breasts on her navel
and my breath
howling into her entrances
through lungs of pain.

Greedy as herring-gulls
or a child
I swing out over the earth
over and over
again.

QUESTIONS FOR DISCUSSION AND WRITING

1. Why does Lorde begin "Love Poem" with strong images from nature—
   earth, sky, mountains, and a valley carved out by rain? What do such
   images have to do with love? How do the poet's hips and the image of the
   mouth connect to the love she is creating in the poem?
2. "Honey" appears both in the first and second stanza of Lorde's poem. What
   does honey, which we naturally associate with sweetness, have to do with
   decidedly not sweet images of impalement and "lungs of pain"? What do
   such contrasting metaphors tell us about the poet's attitude toward love?
3. What does greed have to do with the nature of love Lorde presents in "Love
   Poem"?
4. The last lines of the poem bring us back to earth. However, the poet concludes "I swing out over the earth" and reveals that she does this "over and
   over." What does this impress upon us about the nature of her love and the
   ways she experiences and realizes it?

ON TECHNIQUE AND STYLE

1. How does Lorde capture the reader's attention in this poem?
2. Lorde uses the first person "I." Does she establish a personal identity in the
   poem—the sense of a real individual? Or does the poem represent, despite
   the use of first person, a more communal feeling about the nature of love?
3. Can you describe how this poem defines love?

CULTURAL QUESTION

1. Lorde is a woman writing about her love for another woman. How does that affect your response to the poem? Would you have a different response to the poem if you knew it was a male poet writing about his love of a woman? Does it matter? Should it matter?

Hate Poem

Julie Sheehan

Julie Sheehan was born in a small town in Iowa and educated at Yale and Columbia. She presently resides on Long Island, New York. She published Thaw, *which won the Poets Out Loud Prize, and* Orient Point, *winner of the 2005 Barnard Women Poets Prize. Her poetry has appeared in many journals and literary quarterlies including* The Yale Review, The Paris Review, Parnassus, The Texas Review, Western Humanities Review, The Kenyon Review, *and* Southwest Review. *"Hate Poem" first appeared in* Pleiades *and was selected for inclusion in* Best American Poetry of 2005 *and* 180 More: Extraordinay Poems for Every Day.

"Hate Poem" gives us an amusing sense of how deep and concentrated and yet transitory the emotion of hate can be felt after an argument. The poem also reveals how close hate can be to love.

I hate you truly. Truly I do.
Everything about me hates everything about you.
The flick of my wrist hates you.
The way I hold my pencil hates you.
The sound made by my tiniest bones were they trapped
    in the jaws of a moray eel hates you.
Each corpuscle singing in its capillary hates you.

Look out! Fore! I hate you.

The blue-green jewel of sock lint I'm digging
    from under by third toenail, left foot, hates you.
The history of this keychain hates you.
My sigh in the background as you explain relational databases
    hates you.
The goldfish of my genius hates you.
My aorta hates you. Also my ancestors.

A closed window is both a closed window and an obvious
    symbol of how I hate you.

My voice curt as a hairshirt: hate.
My hesitation when you invite me for a drive: hate.
My pleasant "good morning": hate.
You know how when I'm sleepy I nuzzle my head
    under your arm? Hate.
The whites of my target-eyes articulate hate. My wit
    practices it.
My breasts relaxing in their holster from morning
    to night hate you.
Layers of hate, a parfait.
Hours after our latest row, brandishing the sharp glee of hate,
I dissect you cell by cell, so that I might hate each one
    individually and at leisure.
My lungs, duplicitous twins, expand with the utter validity
    of my hate, which can never have enough of you,
Breathlessly, like two idealists in a broken submarine.

QUESTIONS FOR DISCUSSION AND WRITING

1. How does the first line of the poem, an inversion of the familiar "I love you truly. Truly I do" set the tone of the poem as well as establish its mood for what is to follow? How does the poet view hatred in personal relationships like the one in this poem?
2. What are we to make of lines like "Look out! Fore! I hate you." and "Layers of hate, a parfait"? What do such lines do to affect our attitude toward the hatred the voice in the poem is venting?
3. Why does the poet refer to her lungs as "duplicitous twins" and what are we to conclude from the poem's last line?

ON TECHNIQUE AND STYLE

1. Some of the images Sheehan uses to express hate in the poem are quite specific. How do they help create a more vivid picture of the emotion she wishes to convey? What do the images express about the nature of her hate?
2. How would you characterize the voice in this poem? In what ways does it manage to create or establish authority?
3. Comment on the use of language in this poem. Is its style distinctive? To what extent does style shape or contribute to the meaning of the poem?

CULTURAL QUESTION

1. The poem is in a woman's voice. Are there reasons why the poem and the way it expresses hatred need to be seen as being linked or connected to gender?

GRAPHIC FICTION

From Ghost World

Daniel Clowes

Daniel Clowes (1961–   ), author, cartoonist, and screenwriter, was born in Chicago and graduated from the Pratt Institute in New York. He lived in New York City and worked there with Cracked *magazine. Presently he resides in Oakland, California. His work has appeared in* Esquire *and* The New Yorker, *and he is the author of* David Boring, Ice Haven Eightball, *and* Lloyd Llewelyn. *He is best known for* Ghost World, *which was made into a movie directed by Terry Zwigoff.*

Ghost World, *first published in 1998, depicts two hip, semibohemian teen girls, Enid and Rebecca, who are both quite likable but who both express themselves in a constant stream of profanity and a promiscuous use of the word "hate." From the opening pages, when Enid talks about hating a trendy teen magazine and tells Rebecca that John Ellis, whom she has a crush on, "hates everybody equally," a lot of hate is verbally thrown around. Enid tells Rebecca, at different points in the novel, that she hates a bass player, answering machines, and men. Rebecca looks at a photo of Enid when she was younger and says that it was taken "back when I hated you." Both young women hate the song "You've Lost That Lovin' Feelin.' " This selection is about when Enid and Josh "hook up."*

QUESTIONS FOR DISCUSSION AND WRITING

1. Adolescence is often a time of intense emotional turbulence. Are words like "hate" and "love" nearly meaningless for young people? Does one require maturity to understand such emotions?
2. Josh thinks Enid hates him and Enid quickly confesses to "practically" loving him. What is Clowes showing us about perceptions these characters have about hate and love? Is he being satiric?
3. Things do not go well in this "hookup" between Josh and Enid, and on the next page Enid winds up hating herself and sobbing. This is only moments after the two characters have kissed. Are feelings of love and hate that volatile, or do they occur only in young people?

ON TECHNIQUE AND STYLE

1. Do the animated characters Clowes creates elicit a sense of real emotion?
2. How does Clowes manage to draw us in to his graphic world? What techniques are evident?
3. How is Clowes comparing and contrasting love and hate?

CULTURAL QUESTION

1. The teenagers Clowes portrays are suburban white youth. Could they be teens from any racial, ethnic, or class background?

VISUAL TEXTS

The Lovers

René Magritte

René Magritte (1898–1967) was a famed French painter born in the city of Lessines in the province of Hainaut. He studied at the Royal Academy in Brussels and became part of the surrealist movement. The Lovers (1928) is one of his best-known paintings and embodies the mysteriousness he became most known for.

Love

Kawabata Ryūshi

Kawabata Ryūshi (1885–1966) was the pseudonym of a Japanese painter whose real name was Shotarō Kawabata. Ryūshi was an advocate of Art for the Exhibition Place, which stressed the public nature of art. His works tended to be large, and were intended for public display. In 1934 he produced Aizen (Passion) representing a couple's tender love by the brace of Mandarin ducks. After World War II he gained fame as one of the Three Big Figures in the Nihonga style of painting. In 1959, the Japanese government awarded him the Order of Culture. In 1963, before his death, his home in Tokyo became the Kawabata Ryūshi Memorial Museum. Ryūshi's heirs gave the museum house to Ohda-ku (city) in Tokyo in 1991.

Cain and Abel

Jacopo Tintoretto

Tintoretto (real name Jacopo Comin, 1518–1594) was among the great painters of the Venetian school and is considered by many to be the last great painter of the Italian Renaissance. His real name, Comin, was only recently uncovered

by Miguel Falomir, the curator of the Prado Museum in Madrid, Spain. It was made public on the occasion of a 2007 Tintoretto retrospective at the Prado. Cain and Abel, *an oil painting dated between 1550 and 1553 is considered one of his masterpieces.*

QUESTIONS FOR DISCUSSION AND WRITING

1. What does Magritte's famous painting communicate about love? Most seem to see the blindness or mystery of love, but the painter remarked that it was his response to seeing his mother drown with her dress wrapped around her head as she was taken from the water. Perhaps there is no single, complete meaning. But what does it convey to you?
2. Why do you think Ryūshi's painting is called *Love* as well as its more common title *Passion*? Are love and passion the same?
3. The story of Cain and Abel is often cited as emblematic of stories in which love turns to hatred. What do you know of the Cain and Abel story? How does the story fit with the themes and ideas presented in this chapter?

ON TECHNIQUE AND STYLE

1. Select one of these images and explain how the painting manages to communicate a notion of love or hate.
2. Choose one of these images and focus on what it illustrates beyond love.

CULTURAL QUESTION

1. Two of these images, *The Lovers* and *Cain and Abel*, are from European artists; *Love* is by a Japanese artist. In what ways do you think these paintings represent love and hate from cultural points of view? How is *Love*, for example, similar to or different from *The Lovers*? (These two pieces were painted in the same era.)

AUDIO TEXTS   To hear these conversations, go to www.mhhe.com/soundideas1e

Track 4.1

(date: February 14, 2005; running time: 50:50 min.)

Sue Gerhardt is a British psychoanalyst and psychotherapist and author of Why Love Matters: How Affection Shapes a Baby's Brain, *a hook that explains the neuroscientific and psychological reasons why love is vital to early brain development.*

Track 4.2

(date: February 14, 2005; running time: 50:50 min.)

Dr. Thomas Lewis is assistant clinical professor of psychiatry at the University of California, San Francisco Medical School. He is coauthor (with Fari Amini and Richard Lannon) of A General Theory of Love, *which views love as "the life force of the mind, what makes us who we are, and who we can become."*

Track 4.3

(date: February 14, 2005; running time: 50:50 min.)

Mark Potok is director of the Intelligence Project with the Southern Poverty Law Center, which tracks over 700 hate groups.

Track 4.4

(date: February 21, 2005; running time: 50:50 min.)

See **bell hook's** *biography.*

Track 4.5

(date: October 3, 2005; running time: 50:50 min.)

See **Jane Goodall's** *biography.*

QUESTIONS FOR DISCUSSION AND WRITING

1. Gerhardt talks about the neuroscientific and hormonal effects of love being paramount over such things as temperament. She provides a "cool and scientific" definition of love in conjunction with regulating and managing feelings. Dr. Thomas Lewis says, though the mystery of love may remain, neuroscience and psychobiology will expand our understanding of love. Should love be viewed in such primarily scientific terms? Is there a danger in doing so?

2. Do you agree that "human nature not human will determines our response to love"? Aren't free will and choice part of love and loving?

3. Do you agree with Potok that the Internet has allowed those who hate more of a sense of being part of a movement and of feeling less isolated? Talk about the dangers this might represent of spreading hate.

4. Goodall voices hope and vests it in our human voices, our ability to communicate. There are new ways, she asserts, of communicating our passion that war and violence aren't inevitable and that our inherited traits of love, compassion, and altruism will win out. Do you share her overall sense of optimism? Why or why not?

5. hooks says that it is "crucial" to have all kinds of love in our lives and to feel as deeply about these relationships as we feel the love for a romantic partner. Can we elevate all our relationships to that level? Is it realistic? Possible?

ON TECHNIQUE AND STYLE

1. What is the effect of Lewis saying that it may be "normative" to want to throw your partner out of a window once or twice a week?

2. Potok speaks with hope about the aftermath of the horrible murder of a black man, James Byrd, in Jasper, Texas, by noting that such tragedies can act as a catalyst to discussion. Is this too optimistic a view, an attempt to put a face of hope on an ugly, vicious act of hate?

3. Compare and contrast the views of love expressed by Goodall and hooks. Who is more persuasive? Why?

CULTURAL QUESTION

1. Do the men and women in these audio selections appear to talk differently about love and hate, or is it impossible to generalize? What do you think about the way the sexes approach or broach these two strong emotions?

Additional Audio Resources

1. *NPR, Fresh Air* from WHYY, June 23, 2005. Interview with Daniel Clowes, at www.npr.org/templates/story/story.php?storyId=4715648.

2. Reading of Poe's "The Cask of Amontillado" at LibriVox, at http://ia300212
   .us.archive.org/3/items/stories_002_librivox/cask_of_amontillado_poe
   _zw-rh.mp3.
3. Raymond Carver is interviewed and reads poetry, at www.carversite.com/
   audio.htm.

CONNECTIONS

1. Both Goodall and hooks write of love as being spiritual, and hooks speaks
   in the audio section of love and communion. Mel, the cardiologist and former seminarian in Carver's story, also appears to hold a spiritual view of
   love. How do these views connect to each other? How is each different?
2. In a number of the selections in this chapter love appears to hold a tie to
   peace while hate is linked to violence and war. What is revealed about the
   nature of the connections between love and peace and hate and war?
3. Show in at least two or more selections of your choice from this chapter where
   and how the line between love and hate appears to be a thin one, perhaps
   even imperceptible.
4. The hate crimes that Sullivan writes about and that Potok refers to are
   ugly. How do they compare to the hate fostered by Montresor against
   Fortunato?
5. Love appears in passionate, intense forms in both the selected stories by
   Carver and Alvarez and in Lorde's poem. On the other hand, Sheehan's
   poem and the ancient list of hateful things from Shōnagon's *The Pillow Book*
   almost seem to diminish or trivialize hate, especially when we think of the
   stories by Jackson and Poe or the kind of hatred Sullivan writes about and
   Potok discusses. Is hate easier to trivialize or to make fun of than love?
6. Alvarez's story is about the tradition of love within a family and Jackson's
   is about the tradition of hate within a community. hooks winds up speaking
   about love in the context of community in the audio section and Poe's Montresor of his family's retributive tradition. From Gerhardt we learn that love
   follows the preoccupation of one person for another, likened by her to what a
   parent feels for a baby. Do the personal, the familial, and the communal all line
   up where love is concerned, or do we need to separate them and understand
   each of them independent of the other?
7. Which of the two, love or hate, from the selections in this chapter appears to
   be the more impenetrable mystery?
8. Sullivan argues that we can "transcend" hatred and Goodall that we can elevate
   love over hate. This brings up the question of free will. Are we able to overcome
   such emotion by volition?
9. Lewis distinguishes between the delirious state of falling in love that doesn't
   necessarily last long and what he calls "long-term" love. Where else in this chapter do we see this division? Comment on it.

FOR WRITING

CREATIVE CHOICES

1. Write a love poem and then write a hate poem. What differences do you experience with the release of each emotion?
2. Make a list of things that are hateful to you. How serious do they seem to you?
3. Find a number of visuals or photographs that speak to you about the nature of love or hate. Write about what you see in the photos.

NARRATIVE/EXPOSITORY CHOICES

1. Take a story from your life or the life of someone close to you that reflects an important theme about love or hate and tell the story in a way that reveals the theme.
2. Develop an expository essay that focuses on a definition of love or hate.
3. Love is often associated with good and hate with evil. Show through narrative or exposition why this is the case or why it is not.

ARGUMENT CHOICES

1. Make a case for love being more powerful than hate or make a case for the opposite.
2. Argue for the position that love cannot be defined because there are too many ways of defining it.
3. Present a persuasive case that supports the notion that to hate is human.

RESEARCH CHOICES

1. Research love poetry and essays and fiction on love from an earlier period such as the medieval or Renaissance (premodern) or Romantic period and demonstrate how the views toward love differed from our own contemporary period.
2. Use the *Oxford English Dictionary* as a starting point and show how both the denotations and connotations of the word "hate" have changed through the years.
3. Explore the biological or psychological theories about the origins of either love or hate.

VIDEO SUGGESTIONS

The number of movies focusing on love and hate is beyond count. Here are a few that relate to the themes or authors in this chapter.

1. *Jane Goodall: Reason for Hope* (1999). Made-for-television documentary narrated by Harrison Ford.
2. *10 Things I Hate About You* (1999). A remake of Shakespeare's *The Taming of the Shrew*, set in a modern-day high school.
3. *Ghost World* (2001). A film version of Daniel Clowes's graphic novel.
4. *Love Actually* (2003). Interrelated stories linking the lives of eight very different couples, set during the month before Christmas in London.
5. *The Pillow Book* (1996). A cinematic version of Sei Shōnagon's tenth-century book.
6. *Short Cuts* (1993). The lives of a number of Los Angeles residents are the subject of this loosely knit collection of Raymond Carver short stories.

 chapter **5**

Ideas about War

*You don't know the horrible aspects of war. I've been through two wars and I know.
I've seen cities and homes in ashes. I've seen thousands of men lying on the ground,
their dead faces looking up at the skies. I tell you, war is hell!*
— *General William Tecumseh Sherman at the Ohio State Fair in 1880*

A true war story, if truly told, makes the stomach believe.
— *Tim O'Brien,* The Things They Carried

INTRODUCTION

Sherman's statement that "war is hell" is frequently quoted. War is also controversial . . . and common.

The writings in this chapter focus on several wars of the past century, spanning not only the decades, but several continents as well. What do these wars have in common? What makes each of them unique? These are questions to ask as you read the various genres, all talking about wars and their impact on populations.

The nonfiction section opens with selected chapters from Sun Tzu's *The Art of War*. This ancient Chinese text, written in the sixth century BCE, has had, and continues to have, influence on the strategies used in warfare around the world. Next, you will find Mark Twain's essay "The War Prayer," which clearly shows Twain's opinion of war—the U.S. intervention in the Philippines occurred at the time of the writing. The readings then move on to a more modern conflict: the civil war between the Hutus and Tutsis in Rwanda. A chapter from Philip Gourevitch's book *We Wish to Inform You That Tomorrow We Will Be Killed with Our Families* looks at the historical basis for this conflict. Finally, the nonfiction section ends with "Handouts," John Crawford's firsthand accounts of the war in Iraq, from the point of view of a participant.

The fiction short stories look at different types of wars, and different aspects of war. The first selection, "The Things They Carried" by Tim O'Brien, coming from his novel of the same name, looks at soldiers' lives in Vietnam. "Civil Peace," by Chinua Achebe, takes us to Nigeria in the postrevolutionary period. It focuses on the impact of war on civilians and everyday life. Luigi Pirandello's

"War" was written after World War I, the war during which Pirandello's own son was taken as a prisoner. However, you will find that both Pirandello's story and Isabel Allende's "Two Words" focus more broadly on the concept of war, rather than any specific war.

The poems also look at different aspects of war. Wilfred Owens looks at the horrible effect of war on soldiers during World War I, a war that saw the technology of combat change in terrifying ways. Carolyn Forché addresses a more modern conflict, that of the revolution in El Salvador in the 1970s. The war in Bosnia in the 1990s is addressed in Joe Sacco's graphic non-fiction *Go Away*, found later in the chapter. This war was primarily between the Muslim-majority Bosnian government based in Sarajevo and the Bosnian Serbs. The visual selections presented in this chapter reflect various visions of war, and the involvement of different elements of society. The first, "We Can Do It!" has become an iconic image from World War II, representing the involvement of women in the work force. It is the source of the historical "character" known as Rosie the Riveter. This is followed by a depiction of a much older conflict: the invasion of the Grand Mosque in Cairo, Egypt by Napoleon Bonaparte. Finally, one of the most famous images from the Vietnam War, "Children Fleeing Napalm," shows some of the true horror of war and its effect on civilians.

The audio selections include discussions of war in Iraq, Rwanda, Bosnia, as well as Isabel Allende's reflections on her life in Chile and the coup there.

As you consider the various selections in this chapter, you will no doubt be reminded of other wars and other conflicts in different parts of the world. It will help you to think about what you know about different conflicts and their histories. In addition, go to the newspaper and read about any conflicts going on right now. Think about wars of the present, wars of the past, and the long thematic thread that runs through the idea of wars throughout history.

NONFICTION

From The Art of War

Sun Tzu, translated by Lionel Giles

The Art of War *is a sixth-century BCE Chinese military treatise. It was written by Sun Tzu, a general who was a contemporary of one of the greatest Chinese philosophers of ancient times—Confucius.* The Art of War *(translated by Lionel Giles in 1910) comprises thirteen chapters (some of which are included here), each devoted to one aspect of warfare. This text has been praised as the definitive tract on military strategy and tactics of its era.*

The Art of War *is one of the oldest works on military strategy in the world. It has greatly influenced Eastern and Western military philosophies, business tactics, and indeed, almost every competitive effort, including sports and even television reality shows.[1] Sun Tzu taught that strategy was not just working with a checklist, but rather responding quickly and appropriately to changing situations.*

I. Laying Plans

1. Sun Tzu said: The art of war is of vital importance to the State.
2. It is a matter of life and death, a road either to safety or to ruin. Hence it is a subject of inquiry which can on no account be neglected.
3. The art of war, then, is governed by five constant factors, to be taken into account in one's deliberations, when seeking to determine the conditions obtaining in the field.
4. These are: (1) The Moral Law; (2) Heaven; (3) Earth; (4) The Commander; (5) Method and discipline.
5, 6. The Moral Law causes the people to be in complete accord with their ruler, so that they will follow him regardless of their lives, undismayed by any danger.
7. Heaven signifies night and day, cold and heat, times and seasons.
8. Earth comprises distances, great and small; danger and security; open ground and narrow passes; the chances of life and death.
9. The Commander stands for the virtues of wisdom, sincerity, benevolence, courage and strictness.
10. By method and discipline are to be understood the marshaling of the army in its proper subdivisions, the graduations of rank among the officers, the

---

[1]In the 2008 season of *Survivor: Micronesia,* producers of the television reality show gave participants copies of *The Art of War* to use in planning their game strategy.

maintenance of roads by which supplies may reach the army, and the control of military expenditure.

11. These five heads should be familiar to every general: he who knows them will be victorious; he who knows them not will fail.

12. Therefore, in your deliberations, when seeking to determine the military conditions, let them be made the basis of a comparison, in this wise:—

13.   (1)   Which of the two sovereigns is imbued with the Moral law?
        (2)   Which of the two generals has most ability?
        (3)   With whom lie the advantages derived from Heaven and Earth?
        (4)   On which side is discipline most rigorously enforced?
        (5)   Which army is stronger?
        (6)   On which side are officers and men more highly trained?
        (7)   In which army is there the greater constancy both in reward and punishment?

14. By means of these seven considerations I can forecast victory or defeat.

15. The general that hearkens to my counsel and acts upon it, will conquer: let such a one be retained in command! The general that hearkens not to my counsel nor acts upon it, will suffer defeat:—let such a one be dismissed!

16. While heading the profit of my counsel, avail yourself also of any helpful circumstances over and beyond the ordinary rules.

17. According as circumstances are favorable, one should modify one's plans.

18. All warfare is based on deception.

19. Hence, when able to attack, we must seem unable; when using our forces, we must seem inactive; when we are near, we must make the enemy believe we are far away; when far away, we must make him believe we are near.

20. Hold out baits to entice the enemy. Feign disorder, and crush him.

21. If he is secure at all points, be prepared for him. If he is in superior strength, evade him.

22. If your opponent is of choleric temper, seek to irritate him. Pretend to be weak, that he may grow arrogant.

23. If he is taking his ease, give him no rest. If his forces are united, separate them.

24. Attack him where he is unprepared, appear where you are not expected.

25. These military devices, leading to victory, must not be divulged beforehand.

26. Now the general who wins a battle makes many calculations in his temple ere the battle is fought. The general who loses a battle makes but few calculations beforehand. Thus do many calculations lead to victory, and few calculations to defeat: how much more no calculation at all! It is by attention to this point that I can foresee who is likely to win or lose.

II. Waging War

1. Sun Tzu said: In the operations of war, where there are in the field a thousand swift chariots, as many heavy chariots, and a hundred thousand mail-clad soldiers, with provisions enough to carry them a thousand li, the

expenditure at home and at the front, including entertainment of guests, small items such as glue and paint, and sums spent on chariots and armor, will reach the total of a thousand ounces of silver per day. Such is the cost of raising an army of 100,000 men.

2. When you engage in actual fighting, if victory is long in coming, then men's weapons will grow dull and their ardor will be damped. If you lay siege to a town, you will exhaust your strength.

3. Again, if the campaign is protracted, the resources of the State will not be equal to the strain.

4. Now, when your weapons are dulled, your ardor damped, your strength exhausted and your treasure spent, other chieftains will spring up to take advantage of your extremity. Then no man, however wise, will be able to avert the consequences that must ensue.

5. Thus, though we have heard of stupid haste in war, cleverness has never been seen associated with long delays.

6. There is no instance of a country having benefited from prolonged warfare.

7. It is only one who is thoroughly acquainted with the evils of war that can thoroughly understand the profitable way of carrying it on.

8. The skillful soldier does not raise a second levy, neither are his supply-wagons loaded more than twice.

9. Bring war material with you from home, but forage on the enemy. Thus the army will have food enough for its needs.

10. Poverty of the State exchequer causes an army to be maintained by contributions from a distance. Contributing to maintain an army at a distance causes the people to be impoverished.

11. On the other hand, the proximity of an army causes prices to go up; and high prices cause the people's substance to be drained away.

12. When their substance is drained away, the peasantry will be afflicted by heavy exactions.

13, 14. With this loss of substance and exhaustion of strength, the homes of the people will be stripped bare, and three-tenths of their income will be dissipated; while government expenses for broken chariots, worn-out horses, breast-plates and helmets, bows and arrows, spears and shields, protective mantles, draught-oxen and heavy wagons, will amount to four-tenths of its total revenue.

15. Hence a wise general makes a point of foraging on the enemy. One cartload of the enemy's provisions is equivalent to twenty of one's own, and likewise a single picul of his provender is equivalent to twenty from one's own store.

16. Now in order to kill the enemy, our men must be roused to anger; that there may be advantage from defeating the enemy, they must have their rewards.

17. Therefore in chariot fighting, when ten or more chariots have been taken, those should be rewarded who took the first. Our own flags should be substituted for those of the enemy, and the chariots mingled and used in conjunction with ours. The captured soldiers should be kindly treated and kept.

18. This is called, using the conquered foe to augment one's own strength.
19. In war, then, let your great object be victory, not lengthy campaigns.
20. Thus it may be known that the leader of armies is the arbiter of the people's fate, the man on whom it depends whether the nation shall be in peace or in peril.

III. Attack by Stratagem

1. Sun Tzu said: In the practical art of war, the best thing of all is to take the enemy's country whole and intact; to shatter and destroy it is not so good. So, too, it is better to recapture an army entire than to destroy it, to capture a regiment, a detachment or a company entire than to destroy them.
2. Hence to fight and conquer in all your battles is not supreme excellence; supreme excellence consists in breaking the enemy's resistance without fighting.
3. Thus the highest form of generalship is to balk the enemy's plans; the next best is to prevent the junction of the enemy's forces; the next in order is to attack the enemy's army in the field; and the worst policy of all is to besiege walled cities.
4. The rule is, not to besiege walled cities if it can possibly be avoided. The preparation of mantlets, movable shelters, and various implements of war, will take up three whole months; and the piling up of mounds over against the walls will take three months more.
5. The general, unable to control his irritation, will launch his men to the assault like swarming ants, with the result that one-third of his men are slain, while the town still remains untaken. Such are the disastrous effects of a siege.
6. Therefore the skillful leader subdues the enemy's troops without any fighting; he captures their cities without laying siege to them; he overthrows their kingdom without lengthy operations in the field.
7. With his forces intact he will dispute the mastery of the Empire, and thus, without losing a man, his triumph will be complete. This is the method of attacking by stratagem.
8. It is the rule in war, if our forces are ten to the enemy's one, to surround him; if five to one, to attack him; if twice as numerous, to divide our army into two.
9. If equally matched, we can offer battle; if slightly inferior in numbers, we can avoid the enemy; if quite unequal in every way, we can flee from him.
10. Hence, though an obstinate fight may be made by a small force, in the end it must be captured by the larger force.
11. Now the general is the bulwark of the State; if the bulwark is complete at all points; the State will be strong; if the bulwark is defective, the State will be weak.
12. There are three ways in which a ruler can bring misfortune upon his army:—

13. (1) By commanding the army to advance or to retreat, being ignorant of the fact that it cannot obey. This is called hobbling the army.

14. (2) By attempting to govern an army in the same way as he administers a kingdom, being ignorant of the conditions which obtain in an army. This causes restlessness in the soldier's minds.

15. (3) By employing the officers of his army without discrimination, through ignorance of the military principle of adaptation to circumstances. This shakes the confidence of the soldiers.

16. But when the army is restless and distrustful, trouble is sure to come from the other feudal princes. This is simply bringing anarchy into the army, and flinging victory away.

17. Thus we may know that there are five essentials for victory:
    (1) He will win who knows when to fight and when not to fight.
    (2) He will win who knows how to handle both superior and inferior forces.
    (3) He will win whose army is animated by the same spirit throughout all its ranks.
    (4) He will win who, prepared himself, waits to take the enemy unprepared.
    (5) He will win who has military capacity and is not interfered with by the sovereign.

18. Hence the saying: If you know the enemy and know yourself, you need not fear the result of a hundred battles. If you know yourself but not the enemy, for every victory gained you will also suffer a defeat. If you know neither the enemy nor yourself, you will succumb in every battle.

VI. Weak Points and Strong

1. Sun Tzu said: Whoever is first in the field and awaits the coming of the enemy, will be fresh for the fight; whoever is second in the field and has to hasten to battle will arrive exhausted.

2. Therefore the clever combatant imposes his will on the enemy, but does not allow the enemy's will to be imposed on him.

3. By holding out advantages to him, he can cause the enemy to approach of his own accord; or, by inflicting damage, he can make it impossible for the enemy to draw near.

4. If the enemy is taking his ease, he can harass him; if well supplied with food, he can starve him out; if quietly encamped, he can force him to move.

5. Appear at points which the enemy must hasten to defend; march swiftly to places where you are not expected.

6. An army may march great distances without distress, if it marches through country where the enemy is not.

7. You can be sure of succeeding in your attacks if you only attack places which are undefended. You can ensure the safety of your defense if you only hold positions that cannot be attacked.

8. Hence that general is skillful in attack whose opponent does not know what to defend; and he is skillful in defense whose opponent does not know what to attack.

9. O divine art of subtlety and secrecy! Through you we learn to be invisible, through you inaudible; and hence we can hold the enemy's fate in our hands.

10. You may advance and be absolutely irresistible, if you make for the enemy's weak points; you may retire and be safe from pursuit if your movements are more rapid than those of the enemy.

11. If we wish to fight, the enemy can be forced to an engagement even though he be sheltered behind a high rampart and a deep ditch. All we need do is attack some other place that he will be obliged to relieve.

12. If we do not wish to fight, we can prevent the enemy from engaging us even though the lines of our encampment be merely traced out on the ground. All we need do is to throw something odd and unaccountable in his way.

13. By discovering the enemy's dispositions and remaining invisible ourselves, we can keep our forces concentrated, while the enemy's must be divided.

14. We can form a single united body, while the enemy must split up into fractions. Hence there will be a whole pitted against separate parts of a whole, which means that we shall be many to the enemy's few.

15. And if we are able thus to attack an inferior force with a superior one, our opponents will be in dire straits.

16. The spot where we intend to fight must not be made known; for then the enemy will have to prepare against a possible attack at several different points; and his forces being thus distributed in many directions, the numbers we shall have to face at any given point will be proportionately few.

17. For should the enemy strengthen his van, he will weaken his rear; should he strengthen his rear, he will weaken his van; should he strengthen his left, he will weaken his right; should he strengthen his right, he will weaken his left. If he sends reinforcements everywhere, he will everywhere be weak.

18. Numerical weakness comes from having to prepare against possible attacks; numerical strength, from compelling our adversary to make these preparations against us.

19. Knowing the place and the time of the coming battle, we may concentrate from the greatest distances in order to fight.

20. But if neither time nor place be known, then the left wing will be impotent to succor the right, the right equally impotent to succor the left, the van unable to relieve the rear, or the rear to support the van. How much more so if the furthest portions of the army are anything under a hundred LI apart, and even the nearest are separated by several LI!

21. Though according to my estimate the soldiers of Yueh exceed our own in number, that shall advantage them nothing in the matter of victory. I say then that victory can be achieved.

22. Though the enemy be stronger in numbers, we may prevent him from fighting. Scheme so as to discover his plans and the likelihood of their success.

23. Rouse him, and learn the principle of his activity or inactivity. Force him to reveal himself, so as to find out his vulnerable spots.

24. Carefully compare the opposing army with your own, so that you may know where strength is superabundant and where it is deficient.

25. In making tactical dispositions, the highest pitch you can attain is to conceal them; conceal your dispositions, and you will be safe from the prying of the subtlest spies, from the machinations of the wisest brains.
26. How victory may be produced for them out of the enemy's own tactics—that is what the multitude cannot comprehend.
27. All men can see the tactics whereby I conquer, but what none can see is the strategy out of which victory is evolved.
28. Do not repeat the tactics which have gained you one victory, but let your methods be regulated by the infinite variety of circumstances.
29. Military tactics are like unto water; for water in its natural course runs away from high places and hastens downwards.
30. So in war, the way is to avoid what is strong and to strike at what is weak.
31. Water shapes its course according to the nature of the ground over which it flows; the soldier works out his victory in relation to the foe whom he is facing.
32. Therefore, just as water retains no constant shape, so in warfare there are no constant conditions.
33. He who can modify his tactics in relation to his opponent and thereby succeed in winning, may be called a heaven-born captain.
34. The five elements (water, fire, wood, metal, earth) are not always equally predominant; the four seasons make way for each other in turn. There are short days and long; the moon has its periods of waning and waxing.

QUESTIONS FOR DISCUSSION AND WRITING

1. Do you believe, as Sun Tzu does, that conflict is an integral part of life? Can you suggest another view of conflict in human life?
2. What is the general's relationship to the ruler? On the one hand, "The general is the safeguard of the state" (Chapter III). Yet in other places, there are orders of the ruler that one should not obey. Is there a middle ground between these two concepts? On what basis does one make a decision in these cases?
3. Sun Tzu states: "There is no instance of a country having benefited from prolonged warfare." What examples can you think of to support this idea? What examples can you think of that contradict it?
4. What is the relationship between the art of war and winning without fighting?
5. How have improvements in technology changed "the art of war" since ancient China? How might new weaponry and technology inform our understanding of Sun Tzu's principles in *The Art of War?*
6. Does *The Art of War* speak to women as leaders, or is it just for men, as the pronouns might indicate? How might a female sage commander be and act differently than a male sage commander?

ON TECHNIQUE AND STYLE

1. Can a military text really apply to other situations than warfare? Is it applicable to all types of conflict? Do you know of situations where it wouldn't apply?
2. This text is written as a series of dicta or statements of fact, rather than as lengthier, reasoned argument. How does this affect you as the reader? Does it make the text more, or less, convincing?

CULTURAL QUESTION

1. This text was written for a very different context—Chinese society many centuries ago. How is it possible for modern readers to understand and apply this text? Are there essential differences between East and West in matters of philosophy? Between ancient and modern?

The War Prayer

Mark Twain

Samuel Langhorne Clemens (1835–1910), better known by his pen name Mark Twain, was an American humorist, novelist, writer, and lecturer. He was born in Missouri, and worked as a printer (1847–1857) and later a Mississippi riverboat pilot (1857–1861). He took his pen name from a well-known call used when sounding the river shallows ("Mark twain!" which means "by the mark two fathoms"). He edited the Virginia City Territorial Enterprise *for two years, and in 1864 moved to San Francisco as a reporter. In 1867 he visited France, Italy, and Palestine, gathering material for* The Innocents Abroad *(1869), which gave him his reputation as a humorist. On his return to America, he settled in the East, and in 1870 married Olivia Langdon, the daughter of a wealthy New York coal merchant. In 1871, they moved to Connecticut, where they built a house—Nook Farm—now open to the public.*

His two greatest masterpieces, The Adventures of Tom Sawyer *(1876) and* The Adventures of Huckleberry Finn *(1884), drawn from his own childhood experiences, are recognized among the classics of American literature. Known also as a lecturer, Twain developed a great popular following. Risky investments led to the loss of most of his money by 1894, and he went on a world lecture tour to regain some of his wealth. In his later years, he was greatly honored, but following the death of his wife and two of his daughters, his writing took on a darker character, as seen in his autobiography*

(1924). Twain was a critic of modern society, as shown in the following essay "The War Prayer." Angered by American military intervention in the Philippines, he wrote this essay and sent it to Harper's Bazaar. *It was rejected for being "too radical," and wasn't published until after Twain's death, when World War I made it even timelier. It appeared in* Harper's Monthly *in November 1916.*

It was a time of great and exalting excitement. The country was up in arms, the war was on, in every breast burned the holy fire of patriotism; the drums were beating, the bands playing, the toy pistols popping, the bunched fire-crackers hissing and spluttering; on every hand and far down the receding and fading spread of roofs and balconies a fluttering wilderness of flags flashed in the sun; daily the young volunteers marched down the wide avenue gay and fine in their new uniforms, the proud fathers and mothers and sisters and sweethearts cheering them with voices choked with happy emotion as they swung by; nightly the packed mass meetings listened, panting, to patriot oratory which stirred the deepest deeps of their hearts, and which they interrupted at briefest intervals with cyclones of applause, the tears running down their cheeks the while; in the churches the pastors preached devotion to flag and country, and invoked the God of Battles beseeching His aid in our good cause in outpourings of fervid eloquence which moved every listener. It was indeed a glad and gracious time, and the half dozen rash spirits that ventured to disapprove of the war and cast a doubt upon its righteousness straightway got such a stern and angry warning that for their personal safety's sake they quickly shrank out of sight and offended no more in that way.

Sunday morning came—next day the battalions would leave for the front; the church was filled; the volunteers were there, their young faces alight with martial dreams—visions of the stern advance, the gathering momentum, the rushing charge, the flashing sabers, the flight of the foe, the tumult, the enveloping smoke, the fierce pursuit, the surrender! Then home from the war, bronzed heroes, welcomed, adored, submerged in golden seas of glory! With the volunteers sat their dear ones, proud, happy, and envied by the neighbors and friends who had no sons and brothers to send forth to the field of honor, there to win for the flag, or, failing, die the noblest of noble deaths. The service proceeded; a war chapter from the Old Testament was read; the first prayer was said; it was followed by an organ burst that shook the building, and with one impulse the house rose, with glowing eyes and beating hearts, and poured out that tremendous invocation

God the all-terrible! Thou who ordainest! Thunder thy clarion and lightning thy sword!

Then came the "long" prayer. None could remember the like of it for passionate pleading and moving and beautiful language. The burden of its supplication was, that an ever-merciful and benignant Father of us all would watch over our noble young soldiers, and aid, comfort, and encourage them in their patriotic work; bless them, shield them in the day of battle and the hour of peril, bear them in His mighty hand, make them strong and confident, invincible in the bloody onset; help them to crush the foe, grant to them and to their flag and country imperishable honor and glory—

An aged stranger entered and moved with slow and noiseless step up the main aisle, his eyes fixed upon the minister, his long body clothed in a robe that reached to his feet, his head bare, his white hair descending in a frothy cataract to his shoulders, his seamy face unnaturally pale, pale even to ghastliness. With all eyes following him and wondering, he made his silent way; without pausing, he ascended to the preacher's side and stood there waiting. With shut lids the preacher, unconscious of his presence, continued with his moving prayer, and at last finished it with the words, uttered in fervent appeal, "Bless our arms, grant us the victory, O Lord our God, Father and Protector of our land and flag!"

The stranger touched his arm, motioned him to step aside—which the startled minister did—and took his place. During some moments he surveyed the spellbound audience with solemn eyes, in which burned an uncanny light; then in a deep voice he said:

"I come from the Throne—bearing a message from Almighty God!" The words smote the house with a shock; if the stranger perceived it he gave no attention. "He has heard the prayer of His servant your shepherd, and will grant it if such shall be your desire after I, His messenger, shall have explained to you its import—that is to say, its full import. For it is like unto many of the prayers of men, in that it asks for more than he who utters it is aware of—except he pause and think.

"God's servant and yours has prayed his prayer. Has he paused and taken thought? Is it one prayer? No, it is two—one uttered, the other not. Both have reached the ear of Him Who heareth all supplications, the spoken and the unspoken. Ponder this—keep it in mind. If you would beseech a blessing upon yourself, beware! lest without intent you invoke a curse upon a neighbor at the same time. If you pray for the blessing of rain upon your crop which needs it, by that act you are possibly praying for a curse upon some neighbor's crop which may not need rain and can be injured by it.

"You have heard your servant's prayer—the uttered part of it. I am commissioned of God to put into words the other part of it—that part which the pastor—and also you in your hearts—fervently prayed silently. And ignorantly and unthinkingly? God grant that it was so! You heard these words: 'Grant us the victory, O Lord our God!' That is sufficient. The whole of the uttered prayer is compact into those pregnant words. Elaborations were not necessary. When you have prayed for victory you have prayed for many unmentioned results which follow victory—must follow it, cannot help but follow it. Upon the listening spirit of God fell also the unspoken part of the prayer. He commandeth me to put it into words. Listen!

"O Lord our Father, our young patriots, idols of our hearts, go forth to battle—be Thou near them! With them—in spirit—we also go forth from the sweet peace of our beloved firesides to smite the foe. O Lord our God, help us to tear their soldiers to bloody shreds with our shells; help us to cover their smiling fields with the pale forms of their patriot dead; help us to drown the thunder of the guns with the shrieks of their wounded, writhing in pain; help us to lay waste their humble homes with a hurricane of fire; help us to wring the hearts of their unoffending widows with unavailing grief; help us to turn them out roofless with little children to wander unfriended the wastes of their desolated land in rags and hunger and thirst, sports of the sun flames of summer and the icy winds of winter, broken in spirit, worn with travail, imploring Thee for the refuge of the grave and denied it—for our sakes who adore Thee, Lord, blast their hopes, blight their lives, protract their bitter pilgrimage, make heavy their steps, water their way with their tears, stain the white snow with the blood of their wounded feet! We ask it, in the spirit of love, of Him Who is the Source of Love, and Who is the ever-faithful refuge and friend of all that are sore beset and seek His aid with humble and contrite hearts. Amen.

(After a pause.) "Ye have prayed it; if ye still desire it, speak! The messenger of the Most High waits!"

It was believed afterward that the man was a lunatic, because there was no sense in what he said.

QUESTIONS FOR DISCUSSION AND WRITING

1. Consider the appearance of the "aged stranger." Why do you think Twain depicts him in this way?
2. Explain what the "aged stranger" means by "unspoken part of the prayer." How does this unspoken part of the prayer state Twain's position?
3. After "The War Prayer" was rejected by *Harper's Bazaar*, Twain wrote to a friend: "I don't think the prayer will be published in my time. None but the dead are permitted to tell the truth." What did he mean? Do you agree? Can you think of other examples of this maxim's being true (or false)?
4. Upon hearing the last line the stranger speaks, "Ye have prayed it; if ye still desire it, speak! The messenger of the Most High waits!" what do you imagine the congregation's reaction would be? What makes you believe this?
5. "The War Prayer" is often cited as being as relevant today as the time it was written. Do you agree? Why or why not?

ON TECHNIQUE AND STYLE

1. Reread the first two paragraphs of this essay. What kind of imagery does Twain evoke? Why? What effect does this have on the reader?

2. How does Twain use language to evoke pathos (sympathetic pity) in the next-to-last paragraph? Give specific examples. How does it compare to the language in the first two paragraphs?
3. As stated in the introduction to this selection, the essay was originally rejected by *Harper's Bazaar* for being "too radical." What makes it "radical"? Find two or three sentences that illustrate this interpretation.

CULTURAL QUESTION

1. The first paragraph portrays a type of "war Americana." Is this portrait typically American? If so, in what ways? Is the pride in sending one's "sons off to war" particularly American, or is it universal? Explain your answer with examples.

From We Wish to Inform You That Tomorrow We Will Be Killed with Our Families: Stories from Rwanda

Philip Gourevitch

Philip Gourevitch earned a bachelor's degree from Cornell University in 1986. He attended Washington University in St. Louis, and earned a master's of fine arts from Columbia University in 1992. Gourevitch began visiting Rwanda in May 1995 as a reporter on assignment for The New Yorker. *Over the next two and a half years, he returned to central Africa for six different reporting trips in Rwanda and its neighbor the Congo (formerly Zaire). In 1998, his book* We Wish to Inform You That Tomorrow We Will Be Killed with Our Families, *from which the following excerpt is taken, was published.*

Gourevitch is a staff writer at The New Yorker *and a contributing editor to the* Forward. *He has reported from Africa, Asia, and Europe for a number of magazines, including* Granta, Harper's, *and* The New York Review of Books. *He lives in New York City.*

In the famous story, the older brother, Cain, was a cultivator, and Abel, the younger, was a herdsman. They made their offerings to God—Cain from his crops, Abel from his herds. Abel's portion won God's regard; Cain's did not. So Cain killed Abel.

Rwanda, in the beginning, was settled by cave-dwelling pygmies whose descendants today are called the Twa people, a marginalized and disenfranchised group that counts for less than one percent of the population. Hutus and Tutsis came later, but their origins and the order of their immigrations are not accurately known. While convention holds that Hutus are a Bantu people who settled Rwanda first, coming from the south and west, and that Tutsis are a Nilotic people who migrated from the north and east, these theories draw more on legend than on documentable fact. With time, Hutus and Tutsis spoke the same language, followed the same religion, intermarried, and lived intermingled, without territorial distinctions, on the same hills, sharing the same social and political culture in small chiefdoms. The chiefs were called Mwamis, and some of them were Hutus, some Tutsis; Hutus and Tutsis fought together in the Mwamis' armies; through marriage and clientage, Hutus could become hereditary Tutsis, and Tutsis could become hereditary Hutus. Because of all this mixing, ethnographers and historians have lately come to agree that Hutus and Tutsis cannot properly be called distinct ethnic groups.

Still, the names Hutu and Tutsi stuck. They had meaning, and though there is no general agreement about what word best describes that meaning— "classes," "castes," and "ranks" are favorites—the source of the distinction is undisputed: Hutus were cultivators and Tutsis were herdsmen. This was the original inequality: cattle are a more valuable asset than produce, and although some Hutus owned cows while some Tutsis tilled the soil, the word Tutsi became synonymous with a political and economic elite. The stratification is believed to have been accelerated after 1860, when the Mwami Kigeri Rwabugiri, a Tutsi, ascended to the Rwandan throne and initiated a series of military and political campaigns that expanded and consolidated his dominion over a territory nearly the size of the present Republic.

But there is no reliable record of the precolonial state. Rwandans had no alphabet; their tradition was oral, therefore malleable; and because their society is fiercely hierarchical the stories they tell of their past tend to be dictated by those who hold power, either through the state or in opposition to it. Of course, at the core of Rwanda's historical debates lie competing ideas about the relationship between Hutus and Tutsis, so it is a frustration that the precolonial roots of that relationship are largely unknowable. As the political thinker Mahmood Mamdani has observed: "That much of what passed as historical fact in academic circles has to be considered as tentative—if not outright fictional—is becoming clear as post-genocidal sobriety compels a growing number of historians to take seriously the political uses to which their writings have been put, and their readers to question the certainty with which many a claim has been advanced."

So Rwandan history is dangerous. Like all of history, it is a record of successive struggles for power, and to a very large extent power consists in the ability to make others inhabit your story of their reality—even, as is so often the case, when that story is written in their blood. Yet some facts, and some understandings, remain unchallenged. For instance, Rwabugiri was the heir to a dynasty that claimed to trace its lineage to the late fourteenth century. Five hundred years is a very long life for any regime, at any time, anywhere. Even if we consider the real possibility that the rememberers of the royal house were exaggerating, or marking time differently than we do, and that Rwabugiri's kingdom was only a few centuries old—that's still a ripe age, and such endurance requires organization.

By the time Rwabugiri came along, the Rwandan state, having expanded gradually from a single hilltop chieftaincy, administered much of what is now southern and central Rwanda through a rigorous, multilayered hierarchy of military, political, and civil chiefs and governors, subchiefs, and deputy governors, sub-subchiefs, and deputy deputy governors. Priests, tax collectors, clan leaders, and army recruiters all had their place in the order that bound every hill in the kingdom in fealty to the Mwami. Court intrigues among the Mwami's sprawling entourage were as elaborate and treacherous as any Shakespeare sketched, with the additional complications of official polygamy, and a prize of immense power for the queen mother.

The Mwami himself was revered as a divinity, absolute and infallible. He was regarded as the personal embodiment of Rwanda, and as Rwabugiri extended his domain, he increasingly configured the world of his subjects in his own image. Tutsis were favored for top political and military offices, and through their public identification with the state, they generally enjoyed greater financial power as well. The regime was essentially feudal: Tutsis were aristocrats; Hutus were vassals. Yet status and identity continued to be determined by many other factors as well—clan, region, clientage, military prowess, even individual industry—and the lines between Hutu and Tutsi remained porous. In fact, in some areas of modern-day Rwanda that Mwami Rwabugiri failed to conquer, these categories had no local significance. Apparently, Hutu and Tutsi identities took definition only in relationship to state power; as they did, the two groups inevitably developed their own distinctive cultures—their own set of ideas about themselves and one another—according to their respective domains. Those ideas were largely framed as opposing negatives: a Hutu was what a Tutsi was not, and vice versa. But in the absence of the sort of hard-and-fast taboos that often mark the boundaries between ethnic or tribal groups, Rwandans who sought to make the most of these distinctions were compelled to amplify minute and imprecise field marks, like the prevalence of milk in one's diet, and, especially, physical traits.

Within the jumble of Rwandan characteristics, the question of appearances is particularly touchy, as it has often come to mean life or death. But nobody can dispute the physical archetypes: for Hutus, stocky and round-faced, dark-skinned, flat-nosed, thick-lipped, and square-jawed; for Tutsis, lanky and long-faced, not so dark-skinned, narrow-nosed, thin-lipped, and narrow-chinned. Nature presents countless exceptions. ("You can't tell us apart," Laurent Nkongoli, the portly vice president of the National Assembly, told me. "*We* can't tell us apart. I was on a bus in the north once and because I was in the north, where they"—Hutus—"were, and because I ate corn, which they eat, they said, 'He's one of us.' But I'm a Tutsi from Butare in the south.") Still, when the Europeans arrived in Rwanda at the end of the nineteenth century, they formed a picture of a stately race of warrior kings, surrounded by herds of long-horned cattle and a subordinate race of short, dark peasants, hoeing tubers and picking bananas. The white men assumed that this was the tradition of the place, and they thought it a natural arrangement.

"Race science" was all the rage in Europe in those days, and for students of central Africa the key doctrine was the so-called Hamitic hypothesis, propounded in 1863 by John Hanning Speke, an Englishman who is most famous for "discovering" the great African lake that he christened Victoria and for identifying it as the source of the Nile River. Speke's basic anthropological theory, which he made up out of whole cloth, was that all culture and civilization in central Africa had been introduced by the taller, sharper-featured people, whom he considered to be a Caucasoid tribe of Ethiopian origin, descended from the biblical King David, and therefore a superior race to the native Negroids.

Much of Speke's *Journal of the Discovery of the Source of the Nile* is devoted to descriptions of the physical and moral ugliness of Africa's "primitive races," in whose condition he found "a strikingly existing proof of the Holy Scriptures." For his text, Speke took the story in Genesis 9, which tells how Noah, when he was just six hundred years old and had safely skippered his ark over the flood to dry land, got drunk and passed out naked in his tent. On emerging from his oblivion, Noah learned that his youngest son, Ham, had seen him naked; that Ham had told his brothers, Shem and Japheth, of the spectacle; and that Shem and Japheth had, with their backs chastely turned, covered the old man with a garment. Noah responded by cursing the progeny of Ham's son, Canaan, saying, "A slave of slaves shall he be to his brothers." Amid the perplexities of Genesis, this is one of the most enigmatic stories, and it has been subjected to many bewildering interpretations—most notably that Ham was the original black man. To the gentry of the American South, the weird tale of Noah's curse justified slavery, and to Speke and his colonial contemporaries it spelled the history of Africa's peoples. On "contemplating these sons of Noah," he marveled that "as they were then, so they appear to be now."

Speke begins a section of his *Journal,* headed "Fauna," with the words: "In treating of this branch of natural history, we will first take man—the true curly-head, flab-nosed, pouch-mouthed negro." The figure of this subspecies confronted Speke with a mystery even greater than the Nile: "How the negro has lived so many ages without advancing seems marvelous, when all the countries surrounding Africa are so forward in comparison; and, judging from the progressive state of the world, one is led to suppose that the African must soon either step out from his darkness, or be superseded by a being superior to himself." Speke believed that a colonial government—"like ours in India"—might save the "negro" from perdition, but otherwise he saw "very little chance" for the breed: "As his father did, so does he. He works his wife, sells his children, enslaves all he can lay hands upon, and unless when fighting for the property of others, contents himself with drinking, singing, and dancing like a baboon, to drive dull care away."

This was all strictly run-of-the-mill Victorian patter, striking only for the fact that a man who had so exerted himself to see the world afresh had returned with such stock observations. (And, really, very little has changed; one need only lightly edit the foregoing passages—the crude caricatures, the question of human inferiority, and the bit about the baboon—to produce the sort of profile of misbegotten Africa that remains standard to this day in the American and European press, and in the appeals for charity donations put out by humanitarian aid organizations.) Yet, living alongside his sorry "negroes," Speke found a "superior race" of "men who were as unlike as they could be from the common order of the natives" by virtue of their "fine oval faces, large eyes, and high noses, denoting the best blood of Abyssinia"—that is, Ethiopia. This "race" comprised many tribes, including the Watusi—Tutsis—all of whom kept cattle and tended to lord it over the Negroid masses. What thrilled Speke most was their "physical appearances," which despite the hair-curling and skin-darkening effects of intermarriage had retained "a high stamp of Asiatic feature, of which a marked characteristic is a bridged instead of a bridgeless nose." Couching his postulations in vaguely scientific terms, and referring to the historical authority of Scripture, Speke pronounced this "semi-Shem-Hamitic" master race to be lost Christians, and suggested that with a little British education they might be nearly as "superior in all things" as an Englishman like himself.

Few living Rwandans have heard of John Hanning Speke, but most know the essence of his wild fantasy—that the Africans who best resembled the tribes of Europe were inherently endowed with mastery—and, whether they accept or reject it, few Rwandans would deny that the Hamitic myth is one of the essential ideas by which they understand who they are in this world. In November of 1992, the Hutu Power ideologue Leon Mugesera delivered a famous speech, calling on Hutus to send the Tutsis back to Ethiopia by way of the Nyabarongo River, a tributary of the Nile that winds through Rwanda. He did not need to elaborate. In April of 1994, the river was choked with dead Tutsis, and tens of thousands of bodies washed up on the shores of Lake Victoria.

Once the African interior had been "opened up" to the European imagination by explorers like Speke, empire soon followed. In a frenzy of conquest, Europe's

*Because Rwanda and Burundi were administered as a joint colonial territory, Ruanda-Urundi; because their languages are remarkably similar; because both are populated, in equal proportions, by Hutus and Tutsis; and because their ordeals as postcolonial states have been defined by violence between those groups, they are often considered to be the two halves of a single political and historical experience or "problem." In fact, although events in each country invariably influence events in the other, Rwanda and Burundi have existed since precolonial times as entirely distinct, self-contained nations. The differences in their histories are often more telling than the similarities, and comparison tends to lead to confusion unless each country is first considered on its own terms.

monarchs began staking claims to vast reaches of the continent. In 1885, representatives of the major European powers held a conference in Berlin to sort out the frontiers of their new African real estate. As a rule, the lines they marked on the map, many of which still define African states, bore no relationship to the political or territorial traditions of the places they described. Hundreds of kingdoms and chieftaincies that operated as distinct nations, with their own languages, religions, and complex political and social histories, were either carved up or, more often, lumped together beneath European flags. But the cartographers at Berlin left Rwanda, and its southern neighbor Burundi, intact, and designated the two countries as provinces of German East Africa.*

No white man had ever been to Rwanda at the time of the Berlin conference. Speke, whose theories on race were taken as gospel by Rwanda's colonizers, had merely peered over the country's eastern frontier from a hilltop in modern-day Tanzania, and when the explorer Henry M. Stanley, intrigued by Rwanda's reputation for "ferocious exclusiveness," attempted to cross that frontier, he was repulsed by a hail of arrows. Even slave traders passed the place by. In 1894, a German count, named von Götzen, became the first white man to enter Rwanda and to visit the royal court. The next year, the death of Mwami Rwabugiri plunged Rwanda into political turmoil, and in 1897, Germany set up its first administrative offices in the country, hoisted the flag of Kaiser Wilhelm's Reich, and instituted a policy of indirect rule. Officially, this meant placing a few German agents over the existing court and administrative system, but the reality was more complicated.

Rwabugiri's death had trigged a violent succession fight among the Tutsi royal clans; the dynasty was in great disarray, and the weakened leaders of the prevailing factions eagerly collaborated with the colonial overlords in exchange for patronage. The political structure that resulted is often described as a "dual colonialism," in which Tutsi elites exploited the protection and license extended by the Germans to pursue their internal feuds and to further their hegemony over the Hutus. By the time that the League of Nations turned Rwanda over to Belgium as a spoil of World War I, the terms Hutu and Tutsi had become clearly defined as opposing "ethnic" identities, and the Belgians made this polarization the cornerstone of their colonial policy.

In his classic history of Rwanda, written in the 1950s, the missionary Monsignor Louis de Lacger remarked, "One of the most surprising phenomena of Rwanda's human geography is surely the contrast between the plurality of races and the sentiment of national unity. The natives of this country genuinely have the feeling of forming but one people." Lacger marveled at the unity created by loyalty to the monarchy—"I would kill for my Mwami" was a popular chant—and to the national God, Imana. "The ferocity of this patriotism is exalted to the point of chauvinism," he wrote, and his missionary colleague Father Pages observed that Rwandans "were persuaded before the European penetration that their country was the center of the world, that this was the largest, most powerful, and most civilized kingdom on earth." Rwandans believed that God might visit other countries by day, but every night he returned to rest in Rwanda. According to Pages, "they found it natural that the two horns of the crescent moon should be turned toward Rwanda, in order to protect it." No doubt Rwandans also assumed that God expressed himself in Kinyarwanda, because few Rwandans in the insular precolonial state would have known that any other language existed. Even today, when Rwanda's government and many of its citizens are multilingual, Kinyarwanda is the only language of all Rwandans, and, after Swahili, it is the second most widely spoken African language. As Lacger wrote: "There are few people in Europe among whom one finds these three factors of national cohesion: one language, one faith, one law."

Perhaps it was precisely Rwanda's striking Rwandanness that inspired its colonizers to embrace the absurd Hamitic pretext by which they divided the nation against itself. The Belgians could hardly have pretended they were needed to bring order to Rwanda. Instead, they sought out those features of the existing civilization that fit their own ideas of mastery and subjugation and bent them to fit their purposes. Colonization is violence, and there are many ways to carry out that violence. In addition to military and administrative chiefs, and a veritable army of churchmen, the Belgians dispatched scientists to Rwanda. The scientists brought scales and measuring tapes and calipers, and they went about weighing Rwandans, measuring Rwandan cranial capacities, and conducting comparative analyses of the relative protuberance of Rwandan noses. Sure enough, the scientists found what they had believed all along. Tutsis had "nobler," more "naturally" aristocratic dimensions than the "coarse" and "bestial" Hutus. On the "nasal index," for instance, the median Tutsi nose was found to be about two and a half millimeters longer and nearly five millimeters narrower than the median Hutu nose.

Over the years, a number of distinguished European observers became so carried away by their fetishization of Tutsi refinement that they attempted to one-up Speke by proposing, variously, that the Rwandan master race must have originated in Melanesia, the lost city of Atlantis, or—according to one French diplomat—outer space. But the Belgian colonials stuck with the Hamitic myth as their template and, ruling Rwanda more or less as a joint venture with the Roman Catholic Church, they set about radically reengineering Rwandan society along so-called ethnic lines. Monsignor Léon Classe, the first Bishop of Rwanda, was a great advocate of the disenfranchisement of Hutus and the reinforcement of "the traditional hegemony of the well-born Tutsis." In 1930, he warned that any effort to replace Tutsi chiefs with "uncouth" Hutus "would lead the entire state directly into anarchy and to bitter anti-European communism," and, he added, "we have no chiefs who are better qualified, more intelligent, more active, more capable of appreciating progress and more fully accepted by the people than the Tutsi."

Classe's message was heeded: the traditional hill-by-hill administrative structures which had offered Hutus their last hope for at least local autonomy were systematically dismantled, and Tutsi elites were given nearly unlimited power to exploit Hutus' labor and levy taxes against them. In 1931, the Belgians and the Church deposed a Mwami they considered overly independent and installed a new one, Mutara Rudahigwa, who had been carefully selected for his compliance. Mutara promptly converted to Catholicism, renouncing his divine status and sparking a popular rush to the baptismal font that soon turned Rwanda into the most Catholicized country in Africa. Then, in 1933–34, the Belgians conducted a census in order to issue "ethnic" identity cards, which labeled every Rwandan as either Hutu (eighty-five percent) or Tutsi (fourteen percent) or Twa (one percent). The identity cards made it virtually impossible for Hutus to become Tutsis, and permitted the Belgians to perfect the administration of an apartheid system rooted in the myth of Tutsi superiority.

So the offering of the Tutsi herdsmen found favor in the eyes of the colonial lords, and the offering of the Hutu cultivators did not. The Tutsi upper crust, glad for power, and terrified of being subjected to the abuses it was encouraged to inflict against Hutus, accepted priority as its due. The Catholic schools, which dominated the colonial educational system, practiced open discrimination in favor of Tutsis, and Tutsis enjoyed a monopoly on administrative and political jobs, while Hutus watched their already limited opportunities for advancement shrink. Nothing so vividly defined the divide as the Belgian regime of forced labor, which required armies of Hutus to toil en masse as plantation chattel, on road construction, and in forestry crews, and placed Tutsis over them as taskmasters. Decades later, an elderly Tutsi recalled the Belgian colonial order to a reporter with the words "You whip the Hutu or we will whip you." The brutality did not end with the beatings; exhausted by their communal labor requirements, peasants neglected their fields, and the fecund hills of Rwanda were repeatedly stricken by famine. Beginning in the 1920s, hundreds of thousands of Hutus and impoverished rural Tutsis fled north to Uganda and west to the Congo to seek their fortunes as itinerant agricultural laborers.

Whatever Hutu and Tutsi identity may have stood for in the precolonial state no longer mattered; the Belgians had made "ethnicity" the defining feature of Rwandan existence. Most Hutus and Tutsis still maintained fairly cordial relations; intermarriages went ahead, and the fortunes of *petits Tutsis* in the hills remained quite indistinguishable from those of their Hutu neighbors. But, with every schoolchild reared in the doctrine of racial superiority and inferiority, the idea of a collective national identity was steadily laid to waste, and on either side of the Hutu-Tutsi divide there developed mutually exclusionary discourses based on the competing claims of entitlement and injury.

Tribalism begets tribalism. Belgium itself was a nation divided along "ethnic" lines, in which the Francophone Walloon minority had for centuries dominated the Flemish majority. But following a long "social revolution," Belgium had entered an age of greater demographic equality. The Flemish priests who began to turn up in Rwanda after World War II identified with the Hutus and encouraged their aspirations for political change. At the same time, Belgium's colonial administration had been placed under United Nations trusteeship, which meant that it was under pressure to prepare the ground for Rwandan independence. Hutu political activists started calling for majority rule and a "social revolution" of their own. But the political struggle in Rwanda was never really a quest for equality; the issue was only who would dominate the ethnically bipolar state.

In March of 1957, a group of nine Hutu intellectuals published a tract known as the *Hutu Manifesto,* arguing for "democracy"—not by rejecting the Hamitic myth but by embracing it. If Tutsis were foreign invaders, the argument went, then Rwanda was by rights a nation of the Hutu majority. This was what passed for democratic thought in Rwanda: Hutus had the numbers. The *Manifesto* firmly rejected getting rid of ethnic identity cards for fear of "preventing the statistical law from establishing the reality of facts," as if being Hutu or Tutsi automatically signified a person's politics. Plenty of more moderate views could be heard, but who listens to moderates in times of revolution? As new Hutu parties sprang up, rallying the masses to unite in their "Hutuness," the enthusiastic Belgians scheduled elections. But before any Rwandans saw a ballot box, hundreds of them were killed.

On November 1, 1959, in the central Rwandan province of Gitarama, an administrative subchief named Dominique Mbonyumutwa was beaten up by a group of men. Mbonyumutwa was a Hutu political activist, and his attackers were Tutsi political activists, and almost immediately after they finished with him, Mbonyumutwa was said to have died. He wasn't dead, but the rumor was widely believed; even now, there are Hutus who think that Mbonyumutwa was killed on that night. Looking back, Rwandans will tell you that some such incident was inevitable. But the next time you hear a story like the one that ran on the front page of *The New York Times* in October of 1997, reporting on "the age-old animosity between the Tutsi and Hutu ethnic groups," remember that until Mbonyumutwa's beating lit the spark in 1959 there had never been systematic political violence recorded between Hutus and Tutsis—anywhere.

Within twenty-four hours of the beating in Gitarama, roving bands of Hutus were attacking Tutsi authorities and burning Tutsi homes. The "social revolution" had begun. In less than a week, the violence spread through most of the country, as Hutus organized themselves, usually in groups of ten led by a man blowing a whistle, to conduct a campaign of pillage, arson, and sporadic murder against Tutsis. The popular uprising was known as "the wind of destruction," and one of its biggest fans was a Belgian colonel named Guy Logiest, who arrived in Rwanda from the Congo three days after Mbonyumutwa's beating to supervise the troubles. Rwandans who wondered what Logiest's attitude toward the violence might be had only to observe his Belgian troops standing around idly as Hutus torched Tutsi homes. As Logiest put it twenty-five years later: "The time was crucial for Rwanda. Its people needed support and protection."

Were Tutsis not Rwandan people? Four months before the revolution began, the Mwami who had reigned for nearly thirty years, and was still popular with many Hutus, went to Burundi to see a Belgian doctor for treatment of a venereal disease. The doctor gave him an injection, and the Mwami collapsed and died, apparently from allergic shock. But a deep suspicion that he had been poisoned took hold among Rwanda's Tutsis, further straining their fraying relationship with their erstwhile Belgian sponsors. In early November, when the new Mwami, a politically untested twenty-five-year-old, asked Colonel Logiest for permission to deploy an army against the Hutu revolutionaries, he was turned down. Royalist forces took to the field anyway, but though a few more Hutus than Tutsis were killed in November, the counteroffensive quickly petered out. "We have to take sides," Colonel Logiest declared as Tutsi homes continued to burn in early 1960, and later he would have no regrets about "being so partial against the Tutsis."

Logiest, who was virtually running the revolution, saw himself as a champion of democratization, whose task was to rectify the gross wrong of the colonial order he served. "I ask myself what was it that made me act with such resolution," he would recall. "It was without doubt the will to give the people back their dignity. And it was probably just as much the desire to put down the arrogance and expose the duplicity of a basically oppressive and unjust aristocracy."

That legitimate grievances lie behind a revolution does not, however, ensure that the revolutionary order will be just. In early 1960, Colonel Logiest staged a coup d'état by executive fiat, replacing Tutsi chiefs with Hutu chiefs. Communal elections were held at midyear, and with Hutus presiding over the polling stations, Hutus won at least ninety percent of the top posts. By then, more than twenty thousand Tutsis had been displaced from their homes, and that number kept growing rapidly as new Hutu leaders organized violence against Tutsis or simply arrested them arbitrarily, to assert their authority and to snatch Tutsi property. Among the stream of Tutsi refugees who began fleeing into exile was the Mwami.

"The revolution is over," Colonel Logiest announced in October, at the installation of a provisional government led by Grégoire Kayibanda, one of the original authors of the *Hutu Manifesto,* who gave a speech proclaiming: "Democracy has vanquished feudalism." Logiest also gave a speech, and apparently he was feeling magnanimous in victory, because he issued this prophetic caution: "It will not be a democracy if it is not equally successful in respecting the rights of minorities. . . . A country in which justice loses this fundamental quality prepares the worst disorders and its own collapse." But that was not the spirit of the revolution over which Logiest had presided.

To be sure, nobody in Rwanda in the late 1950s had offered an alternative to a tribal construction of politics. The colonial state and the colonial church had made that almost inconceivable, and although the Belgians switched ethnic sides on the eve of independence, the new order they prepared was merely the old order stood on its head. In January of 1961, the Belgians convened a meeting of Rwanda's new Hutu leaders, at which the monarchy was officially abolished and Rwanda was declared a republic. The transitional government was nominally based on a power-sharing arrangement between Hutu and Tutsi parties, but a few months later a UN commission reported that the Rwandan revolution had, in fact, "brought about the racial dictatorship of one party" and simply replaced "one type of oppressive regime with another." The report also warned of the possibility "that some day we will witness violent reactions on the part of the Tutsis." The Belgians didn't much care. Rwanda was granted full independence in 1962, and Grégoire Kayibanda was inaugurated as President.

So Hutu dictatorship masqueraded as popular democracy, and Rwanda's power struggles became an internal affair of the Hutu elite, very much as the feuds among royal Tutsi clans had been in the past. Rwanda's revolutionaries had become what the writer V.S. Naipaul calls postcolonial "mimic men," who reproduce the abuses against which they rebelled, while ignoring the fact that their past masters were ultimately banished by those they enchained. President Kayibanda had almost certainly read Louis de Lacger's famous history of Rwanda. But instead of Lacger's idea of a Rwandan people unified by "national sentiment," Kayibanda spoke of Rwanda as "two nations in one state."

Genesis identifies the first murder as a fratricide. The motive is political—the elimination of a perceived rival. When God asks what happened, Cain offers his notoriously barbed lie: "I do not know; am I my brother's keeper?" The shock in the story is not the murder, which begins and ends in one sentence, but Cain's shamelessness and the leniency of God's punishment. For killing his brother, Cain is condemned to a life as "a fugitive and a wanderer on the earth." When he protests, "Whoever finds me will slay me," God says, "Not so! If anyone slays Cain, vengeance shall be taken on him sevenfold." Quite literally, Cain gets away with murder; he even receives special protection, but as the legend indicates, the blood-revenge model of justice imposed after his crime was not viable. People soon became so craven that "the earth was filled with violence," and God regretted his creation so much that he erased it with a flood. In the new age that followed, the law would eventually emerge as the principle of social order. But that was many fratricidal struggles later.

QUESTIONS FOR DISCUSSION AND WRITING

1. Describe how the Tutsis became the "economic elite."
2. How did European "race science" affect the relationship between Tutsis and Hutus?
3. Explain the "Hamitic myth." How has it influenced ideas of Rwandan identity?
4. Gourevitch states that the Victorian view of the people of Africa has changed very little, and that the "profile of misbegotten Africa that remains standard to this day in the American and European press." Do you agree? What examples can you cite, either in support of or in opposition to Gourevitch's view?

5. What does the author mean by "tribalism begets tribalism"? How was Belgium's own political situation projected onto that of Rwanda?
6. What are "mimic men"? In what ways did Rwanda's revolutionaries become mimic men?

ON TECHNIQUE AND STYLE

1. Why does Gourevitch use the Cain and Abel story as a metaphor for Rwanda? Do you find this effective?
2. What is Gourevitch's attitude toward the Belgian colonial government in Rwanda? How do you know this? Identify passages in which the author's attitude is evident through his choice of vocabulary or diction.
3. This reading focuses on the historical foundation of the more modern Rwandan conflict. How does this focus on the historical help you understand the current conflict? Can you think of another way to convey the same information?
4. Gourevitch writes: "Like all of history [Rwandan history] is a record of successive struggles for power, and to a very large extent, power consists in the ability to make others inhabit your story of their reality." What does this mean? Can you think of other examples of this in history?

CULTURAL QUESTION

1. In many ways, the colonial history of Rwanda is representative of much of colonialism in the so-called New World. Consider other areas that have been colonized. In what ways are their histories similar to or different from what you have read of Rwanda? What is the legacy of colonialism in areas you are familiar with?

Handouts

John Crawford

John Crawford was newly married and two credits away from completing a bachelor's degree in anthropology at Florida State University when he was sent to Iraq. Crawford's National Guard unit crossed into Iraq on the first day of the invasion. Baghdad fell quickly, and most of the soldiers involved with the invasion were sent home, but Crawford's National Guard unit stayed to patrol the city for more than a year. Crawford now lives in Florida, where he is completing his degree and writing. He was twenty-seven years old when The Last True Story I'll Ever Tell: An Accidental Soldier's Account of the War in Iraq (2005) *from which the following reading was taken, was published.*

The old lady's head was bowed, and water drizzled down her face and into the weed-covered cracks of the basketball court. At her feet was a pile of crusty and shredded blankets, getting increasingly soaked in the early-morning rain. All around her, refugees walked by, herded into the gymnasium by American and British soldiers, but she stood alone, flanked only by trash littering the ground. Occasionally, she would reach down and attempt to corral the large pile into her arms, but her aged body was too frail to have any effect.

Still no one moved to help. Soldiers leaned against walls, smoking cigarettes and talking. Next to me, a young Brit with bad teeth was telling me about a tour in the Balkans he had just completed. His accent was strong, though, and I understood very little of what he said. He, too, eyed the woman warily, but stood his ground.

Her body was covered in tattoos; lines and dots crisscrossed her forehead, cheeks, and arms. I had seen those markings before, but only on the elderly, evidence of a tradition going extinct. She shivered in the rain and suppressed a hacking cough.

"Well, hell," I muttered with displeasure, and stepped briskly from beneath my shelter into the rain. When I reached her, I slung my weapon behind my back, knelt down, and cradled the mildewed and lice-infested blankets into my arms. The stench made me gag as I lifted them, grunting with their weight.

"How did you even get this shit here, lady?" I asked, repulsed and wishing I had brought my gloves. The woman said nothing. She didn't smile, or nod, or even acknowledge my assistance. She simply shuffled past me in the direction the others had gone. I trailed behind her with the load in my arms.

I stepped over a man with no legs whose friends had abandoned him in the breezeway in order to get in line for food. He weakly grasped my leg as I passed, but I shook my leg, his hand came loose, and he turned for help to someone else.

The gymnasium we entered stunk of the derelicts of a Third World country. There aren't too many worse smells. There was very little room left. Every open space had been claimed. The screeching of children overwhelmed my ears, and the smell made my eyes water and nose crinkle up.

My presence created a small empty space, and I hurriedly dumped the blankets and strode away. The old woman crumpled up, defeated by the effort of walking. The air outside smelled clean and cool, and I did my best to wipe off the germs both imaginary and authentic.

A few days before, we had been relieved in place by soldiers from the First Armored Division. They were finally going to cover down on our sector and let us leave. We were slotted to redeploy within a week: first to Baghdad International Airport, then Balad, then America. Everyone was tense with excitement, and the days moved like molasses. The suspension of patrols was a greatly anticipated moment as well. Finally, we thought, those of us left unscathed might actually make it.

When word came that we had picked up one final mission, the barracks were filled with groans of impatience and disgust.

"During the war, a British jet dropped a five-hundred-pound bomb into a building and it never went off. EOD is going in to disarm and remove it, but first we have to evacuate the area. The residents will be brought to the girls' college. . . .

"The one by the Amoco?" someone asked, and Lieutenant Killearn nodded his head, then continued.

"We'll provide food and security for these people for twenty-four hours, and then they will be returned to their home in the same buses that brought them. Any question?"

"How are we supposed to evacuate all these people?"

"Don't worry about that. All we have to do is man the college. First AD is evacuating them. What's more, we'll have other coalition forces attached, mainly the British."

"Will school be in at the college?" Kerr asked with a grin. We all liked flirting with the girls. Unfortunately, the evacuation fell on a weekend and there was no school. Other than that, we had long since gotten past asking numerous questions.

Bombs never seem to fall in the nicer sections of town, or perhaps they are the nicer sections of town because bombs never fall there. The British bomb was no exception. The neighborhood we were taking people from was one of the worst in Baghdad. The refugees we were watching were drug addicts, prostitutes, and the poorest members of a broken society.

When the buses pulled up and our guests began filing out, those who had brought gloves put them on. Most of us just took a step back, unwilling to get close to the disease-infested rabble as they huddled disheveled on one side of the building awaiting instructions. Raindrops echoed off our helmets, and we stood apart, trying not to stare at the lesions and sores that carved their faces. The Iraqis, in turn, looked away for the most part. They were beaten by life, and it amazed me that anyone could live in the condition they were in. A year after we had invaded, these people still had no electricity, no fresh water or food, and they had a higher mortality rate than their ancestors had fifty thousand years prior.

The British soldiers had brought boxes full of toys along with their equivalent of MREs. As the people swarmed in, they were handed one meal, minus the candy and goodies, which mysteriously had disappeared, and the children were handed broken toys, one each. They were undoubtedly donated a world away by some goodwill drive to help impoverished Iraqi children. Within the hour, the Brits grew tired of the monotony and the smell and went back to the safety of the Green Zone, leaving us in charge of food distribution.

Brunelle and I volunteered for the job so we could get out of the rain and take off our helmets. Through an open door, we tossed meals to the people and fought off the fanatical advances of children who wanted more than one broken car or He-Man action figure.

"Hey, Brune! Check this shit out!" I squealed excitedly after rummaging through one of the garbage bags.

"What is it?" he asked over his shoulder as he tossed another meal to someone.

"Cookies! Fucking chocolate chip cookies!" For some reason, the Brits had put all the desserts into huge plastic garbage bags at the back of the supply room.

My mouth was already full, and crumbs littered my chin as I turned to him, box of cookies in hand. Directly in front of me stood an army major, hands on his hips, his eyes burrowing through me in suspicion.

I was caught, literally, with my hand in the cookie jar. I swallowed hard and, seeing there was no escape, extended the box to him.

"Cookie, sir?" I offered with my cheesiest grin. The officer just laughed and walked off, much to my relief. No one wants to get caught eating food that was intended for refugees.

Meanwhile, Brunelle had a Santa puppet on his hand and he was using it to attack children encroaching on our citadel. They squealed with delight and tripped over one another in their flight. After several hours, and a terrible stomachache from too many cookies and mincemeat pies, we were begrudgingly relieved from our position and sent to pull security inside the crowded and sweaty gymnasium.

Someone had tired earlier to throw a box of toys into the center of the room in the hopes that the children would create some sort of mad scramble for them. Indeed, this is what happened: several grown men viciously beat the youngsters with their fists and greedily snatched toys from their tiny hands. The children were less surprised than we were. They moved on to start a makeshift soccer game, using cones as sidelines and a paper cup as the ball.

Occasionally, some officer would walk by and take a proud look around at the great things we were doing in the battle for hearts and minds. But they, like the British, soon tired of this and left us to our babysitting. No one likes to see the not-so-spectacular parts of a war, and we had already lived too many of those moments to give a fuck about anything except ourselves.

When darkness came, the power left and the use of chemical lights proved impossible. Like fireflies swallowed up by night predators, they disappeared into the pockets of the Iraqis one by one until there were only islands of light, and finally, with a flash, there was only blackness. On we sat with our hundreds of neighbors in total darkness. The talk soon died out, and the night was pierced only by the occasional crying child or the moaning whore.

With daybreak came the buses, and we handed out any remaining food for breakfast. One by one, the Iraqis filed out of the gym, leaving only trash and an unbearable odor that I believe is there to this day. A few hours later, we too left, back to our compound and, soon enough, back to America.

QUESTIONS FOR DISCUSSION AND WRITING

1. Why do you think the soldiers were reticent to help the woman with the blankets? What does this say about their experience in Iraq? Why does Crawford finally help her, in your opinion?

2. Crawford writes: "Bombs never seem to fall in the nicer sections of town, or perhaps they are nicer sections of town because bombs never fall there." Do you think one of these possibilities is more likely to be true than the other? Why?
3. How does the author characterize the "goodwill drive" that provided the toys for the Iraqi children?
4. In the "mad scramble" for toys, why does Crawford say that "the children were less surprised than we were" at the behavior of the Iraqi men?
5. Crawford writes, "no one likes to see the not-so-spectacular parts of a war." What parts is he referring to? What parts does he imply people *do* like to see? Do you agree?

ON TECHNIQUE AND STYLE

1. What imagery does Crawford use to relate the conditions he finds in Iraq? Cite specific examples. Are these effective images?
2. What is Crawford's opinion of the Iraq War? What passages tell you this?

CULTURAL QUESTION

1. There is an undercurrent of conflict between the Americans and British soldiers. Find examples of this in the writing. Why do you think this conflict existed?

FICTION

The Things They Carried

Tim O'Brien

Tim O'Brien (1946–   ) was born in Worthington, Minnesota, and earned his BA in political science from Macalester College in St. Paul, Minnesota in 1968. He is an American novelist known mainly for his stories about the Vietnam War. In 1968, O'Brien was drafted into the infantry and sent to Vietnam, where he served from 1969 to 1970. He served in the Americal Division, known for its participation in the My Lai massacre. O'Brien has said that when his unit got to the area around My Lai (also called "Pinkville" by the U.S. forces), "we all wondered why the place was so hostile. We did not know there had been a massacre there a year earlier. The news about that only came out later, while we were there, and then we knew."

Upon completing his tour of duty, O'Brien went to graduate school at Harvard University and received an internship at the Washington Post. *One attribute of O'Brien's work is the blurring of fact and fiction, which he discusses in* The Things They Carried *(1990) (from which the following chapter by the same name is taken). Often, what is written is not what "really happened," but what "should have happened," O'Brien states. O'Brien's other works include* If I Die in a Combat Zone, Box Me Up and Send Me Home *(1973);* Northern Lights *(1975);* Going After Cacciato *(1978);* The Nuclear Age *(1985);* In the Lake of the Woods *(1994);* Tomcat in Love *(1998); and* July, July *(2002).*

First Lieutenant Jimmy Cross carried letters from a girl named Martha, a junior at Mount Sebastian College in New Jersey. They were not love letters, but Lieutenant Cross was hoping, so he kept them folded in plastic at the bottom of his rucksack. In the late afternoon, after a day's march, he would dig his foxhole, wash his hands under a canteen, unwrap the letters, hold them with the tips of his fingers, and spend the last hour of light pretending. He would imagine romantic camping trips into the White Mountains in New Hampshire. He would sometimes taste the envelope flaps, knowing her tongue had been there. More than anything, he wanted Martha to love him as he loved her, but the letters were mostly chatty, elusive on the matter of love. She was a virgin, he was almost sure. She was an English major at Mount Sebastian, and she wrote beautifully about her professors and roommates and midterm exams, about her respect for Chaucer and her great affection for Virginia Woolf. She often quoted lines of poetry; she never mentioned the war, except to say, Jimmy, take care of yourself. The letters weighed 10 ounces. They were signed Love, Martha, but Lieutenant Cross understood that Love was only a way of signing and did not mean what he sometimes pretended it meant. At dusk, he would carefully return the letters to his rucksack. Slowly, a bit distracted, he would get up and move among his men, checking the perimeter, then at full dark he would return to his hole and watch the night and wonder if Martha was a virgin.

The things they carried were largely determined by necessity. Among the necessities or near-necessities were P-38 can openers, pocket knives, heat tabs, wristwatches, dog tags, mosquito repellent, chewing gum, candy, cigarettes, salt tablets, packets of Kool-Aid, lighters, matches, sewing kits, Military Payment Certificates, C rations, and two or three canteens of water. Together, these items weighed between 15 and 20 pounds, depending upon a man's habits or rate of metabolism. Henry Dobbins, who was a big man, carried extra rations; he was especially fond of canned peaches in heavy syrup over pound cake. Dave Jensen, who practiced field hygiene, carried a toothbrush, dental floss, and several hotel-sized bars of soap he'd stolen on R&R in Sydney, Australia. Ted Lavender, who was scared, carried tranquilizers until he was shot in the head outside the village of Than Khe in mid-April. By necessity, and because it was SOP, they all carried steel helmets that weighed 5 pounds including the liner and camouflage cover. They carried the standard fatigue jackets and trousers. Very few carried underwear. On their feet they carried jungle boots—2.1 pounds—and Dave Jensen carried three pairs of socks and a can of Dr. Scholl's foot powder as a precaution against trench foot. Until he was shot, Ted Lavender carried 6 or 7 ounces of premium dope, which for him was a necessity. Mitchell Sanders, the RTO, carried condoms. Norman Bowker carried a diary. Rat Kiley carried comic books. Kiowa, a devout Baptist, carried an illustrated New Testament that had been presented to him by his father, who taught Sunday school in Oklahoma City, Oklahoma. As a hedge against bad times, however, Kiowa also carried his grandmother's distrust of the white man, his grandfather's old hunting hatchet. Necessity dictated. Because the land was mined and booby-trapped, it was SOP for each man to carry a steel-centered, nylon-covered flak jacket, which weighed 6.7 pounds, but which on hot days seemed much heavier. Because you could die so quickly, each man carried at least one large compress bandage, usually in the helmet band for easy access. Because the nights were cold, and because the monsoons were wet, each carried a green plastic poncho that could be used as a raincoat or groundsheet or makeshift tent. With its quilted liner, the poncho weighed almost 2 pounds, but it was worth every ounce. In April, for instance, when Ted Lavender was shot, they used his poncho to wrap him up, then to carry him across the paddy, then to lift him into the chopper that took him away.

They were called legs or grunts.

To carry something was to hump it, as when Lieutenant Jimmy Cross humped his love for Martha up the hills and through the swamps. In its intransitive form, to hump meant to walk, or to march, but it implied burdens far beyond the intransitive.

Almost everyone humped photographs. In his wallet, Lieutenant Cross carried two photographs of Martha. The first was a Kodacolor snapshot signed Love, though he knew better. She stood against a brick wall. Her eyes were gray and neutral, her lips slightly open as she stared straight-on at the camera. At night, sometimes, Lieutenant Cross wondered who had taken the picture, because he knew she had boyfriends, because he loved her so much, and because he could see the shadow of the picture-taker spreading out against the brick wall. The second photograph had been clipped from the 1968 Mount Sebastian yearbook. It was an action shot— women's volleyball—and Martha was bent horizontal to the floor, reaching, the palms of her hands in sharp focus, the tongue taut, the expression frank and competitive. There was no visible sweat. She wore white gym shorts. Her legs, he thought, were almost certainly the legs of a virgin, dry and without hair, the left knee cocked and carrying her entire weight, which was just over 100 pounds. Lieutenant Cross remembered touching that left knee. A dark theater, he remembered, and the movie was *Bonnie and Clyde,* and

Martha wore a tweed skirt, and during the final scene, when he touched her knee, she turned and looked at him in a sad, sober way that made him pull his hand back, but he would always remember the feel of the tweed skirt and the knee beneath it and the sound of the gunfire that killed Bonnie and Clyde, how embarrassing it was, how slow and oppressive. He remembered kissing her good night at the dorm door. Right then, he thought, he should've done something brave. He should've carried her up the stairs to her room and tied her to the bed and touched that left knee all night long. He should've risked it. Whenever he looked at the photographs, he thought of new things he should've done.

What they carried was partly a function of rank, partly of field specialty.

As a first lieutenant and platoon leader, Jimmy Cross carried a compass, maps, code books, binoculars, and a .45-caliber pistol that weighed 2.9 pounds fully loaded. He carried a strobe light and the responsibility for the lives of his men.

As an RTO, Mitchell Sanders carried the PRC-25 radio, a killer, 26 pounds with its battery.

As a medic, Rat Kiley carried a canvas satchel filled with morphine and plasma and malaria tablets and surgical tape and comic books and all the things a medic must carry, including M&M's for especially bad wounds, for a total weight of nearly 20 pounds.

As a big man, therefore a machine gunner, Henry Dobbins carried the M-60, which weighed 23 pounds unloaded, but which was almost always loaded. In addition, Dobbins carried between 10 and 15 pounds of ammunition draped in belts across his chest and shoulders.

As PFCs or Spec 4s, most of them were common grunts and carried the standard M-16 gas-operated assault rifle. The weapon weighed 7.5 pounds unloaded, 8.2 pounds with its full 20-round magazine. Depending on numerous factors, such as topography and psychology, the riflemen carried anywhere from 12 to 20 magazines, usually in cloth bandoliers, adding on another 8.4 pounds at minimum, 14 pounds at maximum. When it was available, they also carried M-16 maintenance gear—rods and steel brushes and swabs and tubes of LSA oil—all of which weighed about a pound. Among the grunts, some carried the M-79 grenade launcher, 5.9 pounds unloaded, a reasonably light weapon except for the ammunition, which was heavy. A single round weighed 10 ounces. The typical load was 25 rounds. But Ted Lavender, who was scared, carried 34 rounds when he was shot and killed outside Than Khe, and he went down under an exceptional burden, more than 20 pounds of ammunition, plus the flak jacket and helmet and rations and water and toilet paper and tranquilizers and all the rest, plus the unweighed fear. He was dead weight. There was no twitching or flopping. Kiowa, who saw it happen, said it was like watching a rock fall, or a big sandbag or something—just boom, then down—not like the movies where the dead guy rolls around and does fancy spins and goes ass over teakettle—not like that, Kiowa said, the poor bastard just flat-fuck fell. Boom. Down. Nothing else. It was a bright morning in mid-April. Lieutenant Cross felt the pain. He blamed himself. They stripped off Lavender's canteens and ammo, all the heavy things, and Rat Kiley said the obvious, the guy's dead, and Mitchell Sanders used his radio to report one U.S. KIA and to request a chopper. Then they wrapped Lavender in his poncho. They carried him out to a dry paddy, established security, and sat smoking the dead man's dope until the chopper came. Lieutenant Cross kept to himself. He pictured Martha's smooth young face, thinking he loved her more than anything, more than his men, and now Ted Lavender was dead because he loved her so much and could not stop thinking about her. When the dustoff arrived, they carried Lavender aboard. Afterward they burned Than Khe. They marched until dusk, then dug their holes, and that night Kiowa kept explaining how you had to be there, how fast it was, how the poor guy just dropped like so much concrete. Boom-down, he said. Like cement.

In addition to the three standard weapons—the M-60, M-16, and M-79— they carried whatever presented itself, or whatever seemed appropriate as a means of killing or staying alive. They carried catch-as-catch-can. At various times, in various situations, they carried M-14s and CAR-15s and Swedish Ks and grease guns and captured AK-47s and Chi-Coms and RPGs and Simonov carbines and black market Uzis and .38-caliber Smith & Wesson handguns and 66 mm LAWs and shotguns and silencers and blackjacks and bayonets and C-4 plastic explosives. Lee Strunk carried a slingshot; a weapon of last resort, he called it. Mitchell Sanders carried brass knuckles. Kiowa carried his grandfather's feathered hatchet. Every third or fourth man carried a Claymore antipersonnel mine—3.5 pounds with its firing device. They all carried fragmentation grenades—14 ounces each. They all carried at least one M-18 colored smoke grenade—24 ounces. Some carried CS or tear gas grenades. Some carried white phosphorus grenades. They carried all they could bear, and then some, including a silent awe for the terrible power of the things they carried.

In the first week of April, before Lavender died, Lieutenant Jimmy Cross received a good-luck charm from Martha. It was a simple pebble, an ounce at most. Smooth to the touch, it was a milky white color with flecks of orange and violet, oval-shaped, like a miniature egg. In the accompanying letter, Martha wrote that she had found the pebble on the Jersey shoreline, precisely where the land touched water at high tide, where things came together but also separated. It was this separate-but-together quality, she wrote, that had inspired her to pick up the pebble and to carry it in her breast pocket for several days, where it seemed weightless, and then to send it through the mail, by air, as a token of her truest feelings for him. Lieutenant Cross found this romantic. But he wondered what her truest feelings were, exactly, and what she meant by separate-but-together. He wondered how the tides and waves had come into play on that afternoon along the Jersey shoreline when Martha saw the pebble and bent down to rescue it from geology. He imagined bare feet. Martha was a poet, with the poet's sensibilities, and her feet would be brown and bare, the toenails unpainted, the eyes chilly and somber like the ocean in March, and though it was painful, he wondered who had been with her that afternoon. He imagined a pair of shadows moving along the strip of sand where things came together but also separated. It was phantom jealousy, he knew, but he couldn't help himself. He loved her so much. On the march, through the hot days of early April, he carried the pebble in his mouth, turning it with his tongue, tasting sea salt and moisture. His mind wandered. He had difficulty keeping his attention on the war. On occasion he would yell at his men to spread out the column, to keep their eyes open, but then he would slip away into daydreams, just pretending, walking barefoot along the Jersey shore, with Martha, carrying nothing. He would feel himself rising. Sun and waves and gentle winds, all love and lightness.

What they carried varied by mission.

When a mission took them to the mountains, they carried mosquito netting, machetes, canvas tarps, and extra bug juice.

If a mission seemed especially hazardous, or if it involved a place they knew to be bad, they carried everything they could. In certain heavily mined AOs, where the land was dense with Toe Poppers and Bouncing Betties, they took turns humping a 28-pound mine detector. With its headphones and big sensing plate, the equipment was a stress on the lower back and shoulders, awkward to handle, often useless because of the shrapnel in the earth, but they carried it anyway, partly for safety, partly for the illusion of safety.

On ambush, or other night missions, they carried peculiar little odds and ends. Kiowa always took along his New Testament and a pair of moccasins for silence. Dave Jensen carried night-sight vitamins high in carotene. Lee Strunk carried his slingshot; ammo, he claimed, would never be a problem. Rat Kiley carried brandy and M&M's candy. Until he was shot, Ted Lavender carried the starlight scope, which weighed 6.3 pounds with its aluminum carrying case. Henry Dobbins carried his girlfriend's pantyhose wrapped around his neck as a comforter. They all carried ghosts. When dark came, they would move out single file across the meadows and paddies to their ambush coordinates, where they would quietly set up the Claymores and lie down and spend the night waiting.

Other missions were more complicated and required special equipment. In mid-April, it was their mission to search out and destroy the elaborate tunnel complexes in the Than Khe area south of Chu Lai. To blow the tunnels, they carried one-pound blocks of pentrite high explosives, four blocks to a man, 68 pounds in all. They carried wiring, detonators, and battery-powered clackers. Dave Jensen carried earplugs. Most often, before blowing the tunnels, they were ordered by higher command to search them, which was considered bad news, but by and large they just shrugged and carried out orders. Because he was a big man, Henry Dobbins was excused from tunnel duty. The others would draw numbers. Before Lavender died there were 17 men in the platoon, and whoever drew the number 17 would strip off his gear and crawl in headfirst with a flashlight and Lieutenant Cross's .45-caliber pistol. The rest of them would fan out as security. They would sit down or kneel, not facing the hole, listening to the ground beneath them, imagining cobwebs and ghosts, whatever was down there—the tunnel walls squeezing in—how the flashlight seemed impossibly heavy in the hand and how it was tunnel vision in the very strictest sense, compression in all ways, even time, and how you had to wiggle in—ass and elbows—a swallowed-up feeling—and how you found yourself worrying about odd things: Will your flashlight go dead? Do rats carry rabies? If you screamed, how far would the sound carry? Would your buddies hear it? Would they have the courage to drag you out? In some respects, though not many, the waiting was worse than the tunnel itself. Imagination was a killer.

On April 16, when Lee Strunk drew the number 17, he laughed and muttered something and went down quickly. The morning was hot and very still. Not good, Kiowa said. He looked at the tunnel opening, then out across a dry paddy toward the village of Than Khe. Nothing moved. No clouds or birds or people. As they waited, the men smoked and drank Kool-Aid, not talking much, feeling sympathy for Lee Strunk but also feeling the luck of the draw. You win some, you lose some, said Mitchell Sanders, and sometimes you settle for a rain check. It was a tired line and no one laughed.

Henry Dobbins ate a tropical chocolate bar. Ted Lavender popped a tranquilizer and went off to pee.

After five minutes, Lieutenant Jimmy Cross moved to the tunnel, leaned down, and examined the darkness. Trouble, he thought—a cave-in maybe. And then suddenly, without willing it, he was thinking about Martha. The stresses and fractures, the quick collapse, the two of them buried alive under all that weight. Dense, crushing love. Kneeling, watching the hole, he tried to concentrate on Lee Strunk and the war, all the dangers, but his love was too much for him, he felt paralyzed, he wanted to sleep inside her lungs and breathe her blood and be smothered. He wanted her to be a virgin and not a virgin, all at once. He wanted to know her. Intimate secrets: Why poetry? Why so sad? Why that grayness in her eyes? Why so alone? Not lonely, just alone—riding her bike across campus or sitting off by herself in the cafeteria—even dancing, she danced alone—and it was the aloneness that filled him with love. He remembered telling her that one evening. How she nodded and looked away. And how, later, when he kissed her, she received the kiss without returning it, her eyes wide open, not afraid, not a virgin's eyes, just flat and uninvolved.

Lieutenant Cross gazed at the tunnel. But he was not there. He was buried with Martha under the white sand at the Jersey shore. They were pressed together, and the pebble in his mouth was her tongue. He was smiling. Vaguely, he was aware of how quiet the day was, the sullen paddies, yet he could not bring himself to worry about matters of security. He was beyond that. He was just a kid at war, in love. He was twenty-four years old. He couldn't help it.

A few moments later Lee Strunk crawled out of the tunnel. He came up grinning, filthy but alive. Lieutenant Cross nodded and closed his eyes while the others clapped Strunk on the back and made jokes about rising from the dead.

Worms, Rat Kiley said. Right out of the grave. Fuckin' zombie.

The men laughed. They all felt great relief.

Spook city, said Mitchell Sanders.

Lee Strunk made a funny ghost sound, a kind of moaning, yet very happy, and right then, when Strunk made that high happy moaning sound, when he went *Ahhooooo,* right then Ted Lavender was shot in the head on his way back from peeing. He lay with his mouth open. The teeth were broken. There was a swollen black bruise under his left eye. The cheekbone was gone. Oh shit, Rat Kiley said, the guy's dead. The guy's dead, he kept saying, which seemed profound—the guy's dead. I mean really.

The things they carried were determined to some extent by superstition. Lieutenant Cross carried his good-luck pebble. Dave Jensen carried a rabbit's foot. Norman Bowker, otherwise a very gentle person, carried a thumb that had been presented to him as a gift by Mitchell Sanders. The thumb was dark brown, rubbery to the touch, and weighed 4 ounces at most. It had been cut from a VC corpse, a boy of fifteen or sixteen. They'd found him at the bottom of an irrigation ditch, badly burned, flies in his mouth and eyes. The boy wore black shorts and sandals. At the time of his death he had been carrying a pouch of rice, a rifle, and three magazines of ammunition.

You want my opinion, Mitchell Sanders said, there's a definite moral here.

He put his hand on the dead boy's wrist. He was quiet for a time, as if counting a pulse, then he patted the stomach, almost affectionately, and used Kiowa's hunting hatchet to remove the thumb.

Henry Dobbins asked what the moral was.

Moral?

You know. *Moral.*

Sanders wrapped the thumb in toilet paper and handed it across to Norman Bowker. There was no blood. Smiling, he kicked the boy's head, watched the flies scatter, and said, It's like with that old TV show—Paladin. Have gun, will travel.

Henry Dobbins thought about it.

Yeah, well, he finally said. I don't see no moral.

There it *is,* man.

Fuck off.

They carried USO stationery and pencils and pens. They carried Sterno, safety pins, trip flares, signal flares, spools of wire, razor blades, chewing tobacco, liberated joss sticks and statuettes of the smiling Buddha, candles, grease pencils, *The Stars and Stripes,* fingernail clippers, Psy Ops leaflets, bush hats, bolos, and much more. Twice a week, when the resupply choppers came in, they carried hot chow in green mermite cans and large canvas bags filled with iced beer and soda pop. They carried plastic water containers, each with a 2-gallon capacity. Mitchell Sanders carried a set of starched tiger fatigues for special occasions. Henry Dobbins carried Black Flag insecticide. Dave Jensen carried empty sandbags that could be filled at night for added protection. Lee Strunk carried tanning lotion. Some things they carried in common. Taking turns, they carried the big PRC-77 scrambler radio, which weighed 30 pounds with its battery. They shared the weight of memory. They took up what others could no longer bear. Often, they carried each other, the wounded or weak. They carried infections. They carried chess sets, basketballs, Vietnamese-English dictionaries, insignia of rank, Bronze Stars and Purple Hearts, plastic cards imprinted with the Code of Conduct. They carried diseases, among them malaria and dysentery. They carried lice and ringworm and leeches and paddy algae and various rots and molds. They carried the land itself—Vietnam, the place, the soil—a powdery orange-red dust that covered their boots and fatigues and faces. They carried the sky. The whole atmosphere, they carried it, the humidity, the monsoons, the stink of fungus and decay, all of it, they carried gravity. They moved like mules. By daylight they took sniper fire, at night they were mortared, but it was not battle, it was just the endless march, village to village, without purpose, nothing won or lost. They marched for the sake of the march. They plodded along slowly, dumbly, leaning forward against the heat, unthinking, all blood and bone, simple grunts, soldiering with their legs, toiling up the hills and down into the paddies and across the rivers and up again and down, just humping, one step and then the next and then another, but no volition, no will, because it was automatic, it was anatomy, and the war was entirely a matter of posture and carriage, the hump was everything, a kind of inertia, a kind of emptiness, a dullness of desire and intellect and conscience and hope and human sensibility. Their principles were in their feet. Their calculations were biological. They had no sense of strategy or mission. They searched the villages without knowing what to look for, not caring, kicking over jars of rice, frisking children and old men, blowing tunnels, sometimes setting fires and sometimes not, then forming up and moving on to the next village, then other villages, where it would always be the same. They carried their own lives. The pressures were enormous. In the heat of early afternoon, they would remove their helmets and flak jackets, walking bare, which was dangerous but which helped ease the strain. They would often discard things along the route of march. Purely for comfort, they would throw away rations, blow their Claymores and grenades, no matter, because by nightfall the resupply choppers would arrive with more of the same, then a day or two later still more, fresh watermelons and crates of ammunition and sunglasses and woolen sweaters—the resources were stunning—sparklers for the Fourth of July, colored eggs for Easter—it was the great American war chest—the fruits of science, the smokestacks, the canneries, the arsenals at Hartford, the Minnesota forests, the machine shops, the vast fields of corn and wheat—they carried like freight trains; they carried it on their backs and shoulders—and for all the ambiguities of Vietnam, all the mysteries and unknowns, there was at least the single abiding certainty that they would never be at a loss for things to carry.

After the chopper took Lavender away, Lieutenant Jimmy Cross led his men into the village of Than Khe. They burned everything. They shot chickens and dogs, they trashed the village well, they called in artillery and watched the wreckage, then they marched for several hours through the hot afternoon, and then at dusk, while Kiowa explained how Lavender died, Lieutenant Cross found himself trembling.

He tried not to cry. With his entrenching tool, which weighed 5 pounds, he began digging a hole in the earth.

He felt shame. He hated himself. He had loved Martha more than his men, and as a consequence Lavender was now dead, and this was something he would have to carry like a stone in his stomach for the rest of the war.

All he could do was dig. He used his entrenching tool like an ax, slashing, feeling both love and hate, and then later, when it was full dark, he sat at the bottom of his foxhole and wept. It went on for a long while. In part, he was grieving for Ted Lavender, but mostly it was for Martha, and for himself, because she belonged to another world, which was not quite real, and because she was a junior at Mount Sebastian College in New Jersey, a poet and a virgin and uninvolved, and because he realized she did not love him and never would.

Like cement, Kiowa whispered in the dark. I swear to God—boom, down. Not a word.

I've heard this, said Norman Bowker.

A pisser, you know? Still zipping himself up. Zapped while zipping.

All right, fine. That's enough.

Yeah, but you had to see it, the guy just—

I *heard,* man. Cement. So why not shut the fuck *up?*

Kiowa shook his head sadly and glanced over at the hole where Lieutenant Jimmy Cross sat watching the night. The air was thick and wet. A warm dense fog had settled over the paddies and there was the stillness that precedes rain.

After a time Kiowa sighed.

One thing for sure, he said. The lieutenant's in some deep hurt. I mean that crying jag—the way he was carrying on—it wasn't fake or anything, it was real heavy-duty hurt. The man cares.

Sure, Norman Bowker said.

Say what you want, the man does care.

We all got problems.

Not Lavender.

No, I guess not, Bowker said. Do me a favor, though.

Shut up?

That's a smart Indian. Shut up.

Shrugging, Kiowa pulled off his boots. He wanted to say more, just to lighten up his sleep, but instead he opened his New Testament and arranged it beneath his head as a pillow. The fog made things seem hollow and unattached. He tried not to think about Ted Lavender, but then he was thinking how fast it was, no drama, down and dead, and how it was hard to feel anything except surprise. It seemed unchristian. He wished he could find some great sadness, or even anger, but the emotion wasn't there and he couldn't make it happen. Mostly he felt pleased to be alive. He liked the smell of the New Testament under his cheek, the leather and ink and paper and glue, whatever the chemicals were. He liked hearing the sounds of night. Even his fatigue, it felt fine, the stiff muscles and the prickly awareness of his own body, a floating feeling. He enjoyed not being dead. Lying there, Kiowa admired Lieutenant Jimmy Cross's capacity for grief. He wanted to share the man's pain, he wanted to care as Jimmy Cross cared. And yet when he closed his eyes, all he could think was Boom-down, and all he could feel was the pleasure of having his boots off and the fog curling in around him and the damp soil and the Bible smells and the plush comfort of night.

After a moment Norman Bowker sat up in the dark.

What the hell, he said. You want to talk, *talk.* Tell it to me.

Forget it.

No, man, go on. One thing I hate, it's a silent Indian.

For the most part they carried themselves with poise, a kind of dignity. Now and then, however, there were times of panic, when they squealed or wanted to squeal but couldn't, when they twitched and made moaning sounds and covered their heads and said Dear Jesus and flopped around on the earth and fired their weapons blindly and cringed and sobbed and begged for the noise to stop and went wild and made stupid promises to themselves and to God and to their mothers and fathers, hoping not to die. In different ways, it happened to all of them. Afterward, when the firing ended, they would blink and peek up. They would touch their bodies, feeling shame, then quickly hiding it. They would force themselves to stand. As if in slow motion, frame by frame, the world would take on the old logic—absolute silence, then the wind, then sunlight, then voices. It was the burden of being alive. Awkwardly, the men would reassemble themselves, first in private, then in groups, becoming soldiers again. They would repair the leaks in their eyes. They would check for casualties, call in dustoffs, light cigarettes, try to smile, clear their throats and spit and begin cleaning their weapons. After a time someone would shake his head and say, No lie, I almost shit my pants, and someone else would laugh, which meant it was bad, yes, but the guy had obviously not shit his pants, it wasn't that bad, and in any case nobody would ever do such a thing and then go ahead and talk about it. They would squint into the dense, oppressive sunlight. For a few moments, perhaps, they would fall silent, lighting a joint and tracking its passage from man to man, inhaling, holding in the humiliation. Scary stuff, one of them might say. But then someone else would grin or flick his eyebrows and say, Roger-dodger, almost cut me a new asshole, *almost.*

There were numerous such poses. Some carried themselves with a sort of wistful resignation, others with pride or stiff soldierly discipline or good humor or macho zeal. They were afraid of dying but they were even more afraid to show it.

They found jokes to tell.

They used a hard vocabulary to contain the terrible softness. *Greased* they'd say. *Offed, lit up, zapped while zipping.* It wasn't cruelty, just stage presence. They were actors. When someone died, it wasn't quite dying, because in a curious way it seemed scripted, and because they had their lines mostly memorized, irony mixed with tragedy, and because they called it by other names, as if to encyst and destroy the reality of death itself. They kicked corpses. They cut off thumbs. They talked grunt lingo. They told stories about Ted Lavender's supply of tranquilizers, how the poor guy didn't feel a thing, how incredibly tranquil he was.

There's a moral here, said Mitchell Sanders.

They were waiting for Lavender's chopper, smoking the dead man's dope.

The moral's pretty obvious, Sanders said, and winked. Stay away from drugs. No joke, they'll ruin your day every time.

Cute, said Henry Dobbins.

Mind blower, get it? Talk about wiggy. Nothing left, just blood and brains.

They made themselves laugh.

There it is, they'd say. Over and over—there it is, my friend, there it is—as if the repetition itself were an act of poise, a balance between crazy and almost crazy, knowing without going, there it is, which meant be cool, let it ride, because Oh yeah, man, you can't change what can't be changed, there it is, there it absolutely and positively and fucking well *is.*

They were tough.

They carried all the emotional baggage of men who might die. Grief, terror, love, longing—these were intangibles, but the intangibles had their own mass and specific gravity, they had tangible weight. They carried shameful memories. They carried the common secret of cowardice barely restrained, the instinct to run or freeze or hide, and in many respects this was the heaviest burden of all, for it could never be put down, it required perfect balance and perfect posture. They carried their reputations. They carried the soldier's greatest fear, which was the fear of blushing. Men killed, and died, because they were embarrassed not to. It was what had brought them to the war in the first place, nothing positive, no dreams of glory or honor, just to avoid the blush of dishonor. They died so as not to die of embarrassment. They crawled into tunnels and walked point and advanced under fire. Each morning, despite the unknowns, they made their legs move. They endured. They kept humping. They did not submit to the obvious alternative, which was simply to close the eyes and fall. So easy, really. Go limp and tumble to the ground and let the muscles unwind and not speak and not budge until your buddies picked you up and lifted you into the chopper that would roar and dip its nose and carry you off to the world. A mere matter of falling, yet no one ever fell. It was not courage, exactly; the object was not valor. Rather, they were too frightened to be cowards.

By and large they carried these things inside, maintaining the masks of composure. They sneered at sick call. They spoke bitterly about guys who had found release by shooting off their own toes or fingers. Pussies, they'd say. Candy-asses. It was fierce, mocking talk, with only a trace of envy or awe, but even so the image played itself out behind their eyes.

They imagined the muzzle against flesh. So easy: squeeze the trigger and blow away a toe. They imagined it. They imagined the quick, sweet pain, then the evacuation to Japan, then a hospital with warm beds and cute geisha nurses.

And they dreamed of freedom birds.

At night, on guard, staring into the dark, they were carried away by jumbo jets. They felt the rush of takeoff. *Gone!* they yelled. And then velocity—wings and engines—a smiling stewardess—but it was more than a plane, it was a real bird, a big sleek silver bird with feathers and talons and high screeching. They were flying. The weights fell off; there was nothing to bear. They laughed and held on tight, feeling the cold slap of wind and altitude, soaring, thinking *It's over, I'm gone!*—they were naked, they were light and free—it was all lightness, bright and fast and buoyant, light as light, a helium buzz in the brain, a giddy bubbling in the lungs as they were taken up over the clouds and the war, beyond duty, beyond gravity and mortification and global entanglements—*Sin loi!* they yelled. *I'm sorry, motherfuckers, but I'm out of it, I'm goofed, I'm on a space cruise, I'm gone!*—and it was a restful, unencumbered sensation, just riding the light waves, sailing that big silver freedom bird over the mountains and oceans, over America, over the farms and great sleeping cities and cemeteries and highways and the golden arches of McDonald's, it was flight, a kind of fleeing, a kind of falling, falling higher and higher, spinning off the edge of the earth and beyond the sun and through the vast, silent vacuum where there were no burdens and where everything weighed exactly nothing—*Gone!* they screamed. *I'm sorry but I'm gone!*—and so at night, not quite dreaming, they gave themselves over to lightness, they were carried, they were purely borne.

On the morning after Ted Lavender died, First Lieutenant Jimmy Cross crouched at the bottom of his foxhole and burned Martha's letters. Then he burned the two photographs. There was a steady rain falling, which made it difficult, but he used heat tabs and Sterno to build a small fire, screening it with his body, holding the photographs over the tight blue flame with the tips of his fingers.

He realized it was only a gesture. Stupid, he thought. Sentimental, too, but mostly just stupid.

Lavender was dead. You couldn't burn the blame.

Besides, the letters were in his head. And even now, without photographs, Lieutenant Cross could see Martha playing volleyball in her white gym shorts and yellow T-shirt. He could see her moving in the rain.

When the fire died out, Lieutenant Cross pulled his poncho over his shoulders and ate breakfast from a can.

There was no great mystery, he decided.

In those burned letters Martha had never mentioned the war, except to say, Jimmy, take care of yourself. She wasn't involved. She signed the letters Love, but it wasn't love, and all the fine lines and technicalities did not matter. Virginity was no longer an issue. He hated her. Yes, he did. He hated her. Love, too, but it was a hard, hating kind of love.

The morning came up wet and blurry. Everything seemed part of everything else, the fog and Martha and the deepening rain.

He was a soldier, after all.

Half smiling, Lieutenant Jimmy Cross took out his maps. He shook his head hard, as if to clear it, then bent forward and began planning the day's march. In ten minutes, or maybe twenty, he would rouse the men and they would pack up and head west, where the maps showed the country to be green and inviting. They would do what they had always done. The rain might add some weight, but otherwise it would be one more day layered upon all the other days.

He was realistic about it. There was that new hardness in his stomach. He loved her but he hated her.

No more fantasies, he told himself.

Henceforth, when he thought about Martha, it would be only to think that she belonged elsewhere. He would shut down the daydreams. This was not Mount Sebastian, it was another world, where there were no pretty poems or midterm exams, a place where men died because of carelessness and gross stupidity. Kiowa was right. Boom-down, and you were dead, never partly dead.

Briefly, in the rain, Lieutenant Cross saw Martha's gray eyes gazing back at him.

He understood.

It was very sad, he thought. The things men carried inside. The things men did or felt they had to do.

He almost nodded at her, but didn't.

Instead he went back to his maps. He was now determined to perform his duties firmly and without negligence. It wouldn't help Lavender, he knew that, but from this point on he would comport himself as an officer. He would dispose of his good-luck pebble. Swallow it, maybe, or use Lee Strunk's slingshot, or just drop it along the trail. On the march he would impose strict field discipline. He would be careful to send out flank security, to prevent straggling or bunching up, to keep his troops moving at the proper pace and at the proper interval. He would insist on clean weapons. He would confiscate the remainder of Lavender's dope. Later in the day, perhaps, he would call the men together and speak to them plainly. He would accept the blame for what had happened to Ted Lavender. He would be a man about it. He would look them in the eyes, keeping his chin level, and he would issue the new SOPs in a calm, impersonal tone of voice, a lieutenant's voice, leaving no room for argument or discussion. Commencing immediately, he'd tell them, they would no longer abandon equipment along the route of march. They would police up their acts. They would get their shit together, and keep it together, and maintain it neatly and in good working order.

He would not tolerate laxity. He would show strength, distancing himself.

Among the men there would be grumbling, of course, and maybe worse, because their days would seem longer and their loads heavier, but Lieutenant Jimmy Cross reminded himself that his obligation was not to be loved but to lead. He would dispense with love; it was not now a factor. And if anyone quarreled or complained, he would simply tighten his lips and arrange his shoulders in the correct command posture. He might give a curt little nod. Or he might not. He might just shrug and say, Carry on, then they would saddle up and form into a column and move out toward the villages west of Than Khe.

QUESTIONS FOR DISCUSSION AND WRITING

1. Explain the meaning of the title "The Things They Carried." What is the first item listed as "carried"? Why? (Consider the metaphor of "weight.")
2. List a few main characters, including the literal and figurative things they carried.
3. When Jimmy Cross understands that Ted Lavender is really dead, and that he might have prevented it, how does his outlook change?
4. Do the men in this story know why they are fighting? Cite a passage or two to support your opinion.
5. In the list of all the things the soldiers carried, which was most surprising? Which did you find most evocative of the war? Which items made an impression on you?

ON TECHNIQUE AND STYLE

1. O'Brien says, "They were called legs." This literary device is called *synecdoche,* a metaphor in which part of something stands for the whole. In what way is this an effective synecdoche? Can you think of other examples of synecdoche?
2. Who is the narrator? Why do you think O'Brien chose to write in this voice?

CULTURAL QUESTION

1. "Men killed and died because they were embarrassed not to." Explain this quotation. Is this a universal truth, or particular to the Vietnam War? Defend your opinion.

Civil Peace

Chinua Achebe

Chinua Achebe (1930–   ) is a Nigerian writer, considered the creator of the African novel. He was born Albert Chinualumogu Achebe in Ogidi, Nigeria, and attended University College in Ibadan (at the time, a college of the University of London, now the University of Ibadan), where he studied English, history, and theology. He later studied broadcasting at the British Broadcasting Corporation (BBC) and became the first director of external broadcasting at the Nigerian Broadcasting Corporation in 1961. During the Nigerian civil war, he worked for the Biafran government as an ambassador.

Achebe's modern African classic Things Fall Apart, *published in 1958, has sold over ten million copies around the world and has been translated into fifty languages. Achebe is the recipient of over thirty honorary degrees. He has received numerous awards for his work, including the Commonwealth Poetry Prize; the New Statesman Jock Campbell Prize; the Margaret Wrong Prize; the Nigerian National Trophy in 1961; and the Nigerian National Merit Award, Nigeria's highest recognition of intellectual achievement, in 1979. In 2004, Professor Achebe declined to accept the Commander of the Federal Republic (CFR), Nigeria's second highest honor, in protest of the state of affairs in his native country. Achebe is Charles P. Stevenson Professor of Languages and Literature at Bard College in New York. He is married to Professor Christie Chinwe Achebe, with whom he has four children.*

The following short story, "Civil Peace," first appeared in print in 1971. It takes place in the immediate postwar period.

Jonathan Iwegbu counted himself extraordinarily lucky. "Happy survival!" meant so much more to him than just a current fashion of greeting old friends in the first hazy days of peace. It went deep to his heart. He had come out of the war with five inestimable blessings—his head, his wife Maria's head, and the heads of three out of their four children. As a bonus he also had his old bicycle—a miracle too but naturally not to be compared to the safety of five human heads.

The bicycle had a little history of its own. One day at the height of the war it was commandeered "for urgent military action." Hard as its loss would have been to him he would still have let it go without a thought had he not had some doubts about the genuineness of the officer. It wasn't his disreputable rags, nor the toes peeping out of one blue and one brown canvas shoes, nor yet the two stars of his rank done obviously in a hurry in biro, that troubled Jonathan; many good and heroic soldiers looked the same or worse. It was rather a certain lack of grip and firmness in his manner. So Jonathan, suspecting he might be amenable to influence, rummaged in his raffia bag and produced the two pounds with which he had been going to buy firewood which his wife, Maria, retailed to camp officials for extra stock-fish and corn meal, and got his bicycle back. That night he buried it in the little clearing in the bush where the dead of the camp, including his own youngest son, were buried. When he dug it up again a year later after the surrender all it needed was a little palm-oil greasing. "Nothing puzzles God," he said in wonder.

He put it to immediate use as a taxi and accumulated a small pile of Biafran money ferrying camp officials and their families across the four-mile stretch to the nearest tarred road. His standard charge per trip was six pounds and those who had the money were only glad to be rid of some of it in this way. At the end of a fortnight he had made a small fortune of one hundred and fifteen pounds.

Then he made the journey to Enugu and found another miracle waiting for him. It was unbelievable. He rubbed his eyes and looked again and it was still standing there before him. But, needless to say, even that monumental blessing must be accounted also totally inferior to the five heads in the family. This newest miracle was his little house in Ogui Overside. Indeed nothing puzzles God! Only two houses away a huge concrete edifice some wealthy contractor had put up just before the war was a mountain of rubble. And here was Jonathan's little zinc house of no regrets built with mud blocks quite intact! Of course the doors and windows were missing and five sheets off the roof. But what was that? And anyhow he had returned to Enugu early enough to pick up bits of old zinc and wood and soggy sheets of cardboard lying around the neighbourhood before thousands more came out of their forest holes looking for the same things. He got a destitute carpenter with one old hammer, a blunt plane, and a few bent and rusty nails in his tool bag to turn this assortment of wood, paper, and metal into door and window shutters for five Nigerian shillings or fifty Biafran pounds. He paid the pounds, and moved in with his overjoyed family carrying five heads on their shoulders.

His children picked mangoes near the military cemetery and sold them to soldiers' wives for a few pennies—real pennies this time—and his wife started making breakfast akara balls for neighbours in a hurry to start life again. With his family earnings he took his bicycle to the villages around and bought fresh palm-wine which he mixed generously in his rooms with the water which had recently started running again in the public tap down the road, and opened up a bar for soldiers and other lucky people with good money.

At first he went daily, then every other day, and finally once a week, to the offices of the Coal Corporation where he used to be a miner, to find out what was what. The only thing he did find out in the end was that that little house of his was even a greater blessing than he had thought. Some of his fellow ex-miners who had nowhere to return at the end of the day's waiting just slept outside the doors of the offices and cooked what meal they could scrounge together in Bournvita tins. As the weeks lengthened and still nobody could say what was what Jonathan discontinued his weekly visits altogether and faced his palm-wine bar.

But nothing puzzles God. Came the day of the windfall when after five days of endless scuffles in queues and counter-queues in the sun outside the Treasury he had twenty pounds counted into his palms as ex-gratia award for the rebel money he had turned in. It was like Christmas for him and for many others like him when the payments began. They called it (since few could manage its proper official name) *egg-rasher.*

As soon as the pound notes were placed in his palm Jonathan simply closed it tight over them and buried fist and money inside his trouser pocket. He had to be extra careful because he had seen a man a couple of days earlier collapse into near-madness in an instant before that oceanic crowd because no sooner had he got his twenty pounds than some heartless ruffian picked it off him. Though it was not right that a man in such an extremity of agony should be blamed yet many in the queues that day were able to remark quietly on the victim's carelessness, especially after he pulled out the innards of his pocket and revealed a hole in it big enough to pass a thief's head. But of course he had insisted that the money had been in the other pocket, pulling it out too to show its comparative wholeness. So one had to be careful.

Jonathan soon transferred the money to his left hand and pocket so as to leave his right free for shaking hands should the need arise, though by fixing his gaze at such an elevation as to miss all approaching human faces he made sure that the need did not arise, until he got home.

He was normally a heavy sleeper but that night he heard all the neighbourhood noises die down one after another. Even the night watchman who knocked the hour on some metal somewhere in the distance had fallen silent after knocking one o'clock. That must have been the last thought in Jonathan's mind before he was finally carried away himself. He couldn't have been gone for long, though, when he was violently awakened again.

"Who is knocking?" whispered his wife lying beside him on the floor.

"I don't know," he whispered back breathlessly.

The second time the knocking came it was so loud and imperious that the rickety old door could have fallen down.

"Who is knocking?" he asked then, his voice parched and trembling.

"Na tief-man and him people," came the cool reply. "Make you hopen de door." This was followed by the heaviest knocking of all.

Maria was the first to raise the alarm, then he followed and all their children.

"Police-o! Thieves-o! Neighbours-o! Police-o! We are lost! We are dead! Neighbours, are you asleep? Wake up! Police-o!"

This went on for a long time and then stopped suddenly. Perhaps they had scared the thief away. There was total silence. But only for a short while.

"You done finish?" asked the voice outside. "Make we help you small. Oya, everybody!"

"Police-o! Tief-man-o! Neighbours-o! we done loss-o! Police-o! . . ."

There were at least five other voices besides the leader's.

Jonathan and his family were now completely paralysed by terror. Maria and the children sobbed inaudibly like lost souls. Jonathan groaned continuously.

The silence that followed the thieves' alarm vibrated horribly. Jonathan all but begged their leader to speak again and be done with it.

"My frien," said he at long last, "we don try our best for call dem but I tink say dem all done sleep-o . . . So wetin we go do now? Sometaim you wan call soja? Or you wan make we call dem for you? Soja better pass police. No be so?"

"Na so!" replied his men. Jonathan thought he heard even more voices now than before and groaned heavily. His legs were sagging under him and his throat felt like sandpaper.

"My frien, why you no de talk again. I de ask you say you wan make we call soja?"

"No."

"Awrighto. Now make we talk business. We no be bad tief. We no like for make trouble. Trouble done finish. War done finish and all the katakata wey de for inside. No Civil War again. This time na Civil Peace. No be so?"

"Na so!" answered the horrible chorus.

"What do you want from me? I am a poor man. Everything I had went with this war. Why do you come to me? You know people who have money. We . . ."

"Awright! We know say you no get plenty money. But we sef no get even anini. So derefore make you open dis window and give us one hundred pound and we go commot. Orderwise we de come for inside now to show you guitar-boy like dis . . ."

A volley of automatic fire rang through the sky. Maria and the children began to weep aloud again.

"Ah, missisi de cry again. No need for dat. We done talk say we na good tief. We just take our small money and go nwayorly. No molest. Abi we de molest?"

"At all!" sang the chorus.

"My friends," began Jonathan hoarsely. "I hear what you say and I thank you. If I had one hundred pounds . . ."

"Lookia my frien, no be play we come play for your house. If we make mistake and step for inside you no go like am-o. So derefore . . ."

"To God who made me; if you come inside and find one hundred pounds, take it and shoot me and shoot my wife and children. I swear to God. The only money I have in this life is this twenty pounds *egg-rasher* they gave me today . . ."

"OK. Time de go. Make you open dis window and bring the twenty pound. We go manage am like dat."

There were now loud murmurs of dissent among the chorus: "Na lie de man de lie; e get plenty money . . . Make we go inside and search properly well . . . Wetin be twenty pound? . . ."

"Shurrup!" rang the leader's voice like a lone shot in the sky and silenced the murmuring at once. "Are you dere? Bring the money quick!"

"I am coming," said Jonathan fumbling in the darkness with the key of the small wooden box he kept by his side on the mat.

At the first sign of light as neighbours and others assembled to commiserate with him he was already strapping his five-gallon demijohn to his bicycle carrier and his wife, sweating in the open fire, was turning over akara balls in a wide clay bowl of boiling oil. In the corner his eldest son was rinsing out dregs of yesterday's palm-wine from old beer bottles.

"I count it as nothing," he told his sympathizers, his eyes on the rope he was tying. "What is *egg-rasher*? Did I depend on it last week? Or is it greater than other things that went with the war? I say, let *egg-rasher* perish in the flames! Let it go where everything else has gone. Nothing puzzles God."

QUESTIONS FOR DISCUSSION AND WRITING

1. Some readers view this story as having a positive outlook. Do you agree? Support your opinion with specific passages from the story.
2. At the same time, "Civil Peace" shows the similarities in pre- and post-revolutionary Nigeria. Why do you think Achebe does this? What is the message?
3. Identify one major theme of the story. Why did you choose this as an important theme?
4. What is the "egg-rasher"? Why does it play a pivotal role in the story?
5. What is the purpose of the repeated phrase, "Nothing puzzles God"?
6. Explain the significance of the title, "Civil Peace."

ON TECHNIQUE AND STYLE

1. Achebe uses several instances of *irony* in the story. Identify one or two. What purpose do these instances of irony serve in the story?
2. The thieves that arrive speak a different dialect than Jonathan and his family. Why? How would you characterize their speech?

CULTURAL QUESTION

1. How does Achebe use language to establish a cultural setting in the story? If you didn't know Achebe wrote about Nigeria, would you be able to guess the location of this story? How?

Two Words

Isabel Allende

Isabel Allende Llona (1942–   ) is a Chilean writer born in Lima, Peru, to diplomat Tomás Allende. She is the niece of Salvador Allende, the president of Chile from 1970 to 1973. In 1945, her parents separated and her mother relocated with their three children to Chile, where they lived until 1953. The family later moved to Bolivia and then to Lebanon. She returned to Chile in 1958 to complete her education, and there she met her first husband, Miguel Frías, whom she married in 1962. Her daughter Paula was born in 1963 and her son Nicolás in 1966. In 1973, Allende's play El Embajador *debuted in Santiago. On September 11 of that year, her uncle, Salvador Allende, was overthrown in the wake of a violent coup. He was killed during the capture of La Moneda, the seat of the presidency of Chile. In 1975, Isabel Allende went into exile in Venezuela. In 1981, Allende learned that her grandfather, age ninety-nine, was dying. She started writing him a letter that became a book,* The House of Spirits *(1982), later made into a film of the same name (1993). During a visit to California in 1988, Allende met her current husband, Willie Gordon, a lawyer, and has lived in San Rafael, in Northern California, since then. She was one of the eight flag bearers at the Opening Ceremony of the 2006 Winter Olympics in Torino, Italy. In addition to* The House of Spirits *and* Paula *(1995) her books include* Of Love and Shadows *(1984),* The Stories of Eva Luna *(1987),* The Infinite Plan *(1991),* Daughter of Fortune *(1999),* City of the Beasts *(2002),* My Invented Country *(2003), and* Forest of the Pygmies *(2005), among others. "Two Words" is one of* The Stories of Eva Luna.

Reprinted with the permission of Scribner, a Division of Simon & Schuster Adult Publishing Group, from *The Stories of Eva Luna* by Isabel Allende. Copyright © 1989 by Isabel Allende. English translation copyright © 1991 by The Macmillan Publishing Company. All right reserved.

She went by the name of Belisa Crepusculario, not because she had been baptized with that name or given it by her mother, but because she herself had searched until she found the poetry of "beauty" and "twilight" and cloaked herself in it. She made her living selling words. She journeyed through the country from the high cold mountains to the burning coasts, stopping at fairs and in markets where she set up four poles covered by a canvas awning under which she took refuge from the sun and rain to minister to her customers. She did not have to peddle her merchandise because from having wandered far and near, everyone knew who she was. Some people waited for her from one year to the next, and when she appeared in the village with her bundle beneath her arm, they would form a line in front of her stall. Her prices were fair. For five *centavos* she delivered verses from memory; for seven she improved the quality of dreams; for nine she wrote love letters; for twelve she invented insults for irreconcilable enemies. She also sold stories, not fantasies but long, true stories she recited at one telling, never skipping a word. This is how she carried the news from one town to another. People paid her to add a line or two: our son was born; so and so died; our children got married; the crops burned in the field. Wherever she went a small crowd gathered around to listen as she began to speak, and that was how they learned about each other's doings, about distant relatives, about what was going on in the civil war. To anyone who paid her fifty *centavos* in trade, she gave the gift of a secret word to drive away melancholy. It was not the same word for everyone, naturally, because that would have been collective deceit. Each person received his or her own word, with the assurance that no one else would use it that way in this universe or the beyond.

Belisa Crepusculario had been born into a family so poor they did not even have names to give their children. She came into the world and grew up in an inhospitable land where some years the rains became avalanches of water that bore everything away before them and others when not a drop fell from the sky and the sun swelled to fill the horizon and the world became a desert. Until she was twelve, Belisa had no occupation or virtue other than having withstood hunger and the exhaustion of centuries. During one interminable drought, it fell to her to bury four younger brothers and sisters; when she realized that her turn was next, she decided to set out across the plains in the direction of the sea, in hopes that she might trick death along the way. The land was eroded, split with deep cracks, strewn with rocks, fossils of trees and thorny bushes, and skeletons of animals bleached by the sun. From time to time she ran into families who, like her, were heading south, following the mirage of water. Some had begun the march carrying their belongings on their back or in small carts, but they could barely move their own bones, and after a while they had to abandon their possessions. They dragged themselves along painfully, their skin turned to lizard hide and their eyes burned by the reverberating glare. Belisa greeted them with a wave as she passed, but she did not stop, because she had no strength to waste in acts of compassion. Many people fell by the wayside, but she was so stubborn that she survived to cross through that hell and at long last reach the first trickles of water, fine, almost invisible threads that fed spindly vegetation and farther down widened into small streams and marshes.

Belisa Crepusculario saved her life and in the process accidentally discovered writing. In a village near the coast, the wind blew a page of newspaper at her feet. She picked up the brittle yellow paper and stood a long while looking at it, unable to determine its purpose, until curiosity overcame her shyness. She walked over to a man who was washing his horse in the muddy pool where she had quenched her thirst.

"What is this?" she asked.

"The sports page of the newspaper," the man replied, concealing his surprise at her ignorance.

The answer astounded the girl, but she did not want to seem rude so she merely inquired about the significance of the fly tracks scattered across the page.

"Those are words, child. Here it says that Fulgencio Barba knocked out El Negro Tiznao in the third round."

That was the day Belisa Crepusculario found out that words make their way in the world without a master, and that anyone with a little cleverness can appropriate them and do business with them. She made a quick assessment of her situation and concluded that aside from becoming a prostitute or working as a servant in the kitchens of the rich there were few occupations she was qualified for. It seemed to her that selling words would be an honourable alternative. From that moment on, she worked at that profession, and was never tempted by any other. At the beginning, she offered her merchandise unaware that words could be written outside of newspapers. When she learned otherwise, she calculated the infinite possibilities of her trade and with her savings paid a priest twenty *pesos* to teach her to read and write; with her three remaining coins she bought a dictionary. She pored over it from A to Z and then threw it into the sea, because it was not her intention to defraud her customers with packaged words.

One August morning several years later, Belisa Crepusculario was sitting in her tent in the middle of a plaza, surrounded by the uproar of market day, selling legal arguments to an old man who had been trying for sixteen years to get his pension. Suddenly she heard yelling and thudding hoofbeats. She looked up from her writing and saw, first, a cloud of dust, and then a band of horsemen come galloping into the plaza. They were the Colonel's men, sent under orders of El Mulato, a giant known throughout the land for the speed of his knife and his loyalty to his chief. Both the Colonel and El Mulato had spent their lives fighting in the civil war, and their names were ineradicably linked to devastation and calamity. The rebels swept into town like a stampeding herd, wrapped in noise, bathed in sweat, and leaving a hurricane of fear in their trail. Chickens took wing, dogs ran for their lives, women and children scurried out of sight, until the only living soul left in the market was Belisa Crepusculario. She had never seen El Mulato and was surprised to see him walking towards her.

"I'm looking for you," he shouted, pointing his coiled whip at her; even before the words were out, two men rushed her—knocking over her canopy and shattering her inkwell—bound her hand and foot, and threw her like a duffel bag across the rump of El Mulato's mount. Then they thundered off towards the hills.

Hours later, just as Belisa Crepusculario was near death, her heart ground to sand by the pounding of the horse, they stopped, and four strong hands set her down. She tried to stand on her feet and hold her head high, but her strength failed her and she slumped to the ground, sinking into a confused dream. She awakened several hours later to the murmur of night in the camp, but before she had time to sort out the sounds, she opened her eyes and found herself staring into the impatient glare of El Mulato, kneeling beside her.

"Well, woman, at last you have come to," he said. To speed her to her senses, he tipped his canteen and offered her a sip of liquor laced with gunpowder.

She demanded to know the reason for such rough treatment, and El Mulato explained that the Colonel needed her services. He allowed her to splash water on her face, and then led her to the far end of the camp where the most feared man in all the land was lazing in a hammock strung between two trees. She could not see his face, because he lay in the deceptive shadow of the leaves and the indelible shadow of all his years as a bandit, but she imagined from the way his gigantic aide addressed him with such humil- ity that he must have a very menacing expression. She was surprised by the Colonel's voice, as soft and well modulated as a professor's.

"Are you the woman who sells words?" he asked.

"At your service," she stammered, peering into the dark and trying to see him better.

The Colonel stood up and turned straight towards her. She saw dark skin and the eyes of a ferocious puma, and she knew immediately that she was standing before the loneliest man in the world.

"I want to be President," he announced.

The Colonel was weary of riding across that Godforsaken land, waging useless wars and suffering defeats that no subterfuge could transform into victories. For years he had been sleeping in the open air, bitten by mosqui- toes, eating iguanas and snake soup, but those minor inconveniences were not why he wanted to change his destiny. What truly troubled him was the terror he saw in people's eyes. He longed to ride into a town beneath a trium- phal arch with bright flags and flowers everywhere; he wanted to be cheered, and be given newly laid eggs and freshly baked bread. Men fled at the sight of him, children trembled, and women miscarried from fright; he had had enough, and so he had decided to become President. El Mulato had sug- gested that they ride to the capital, gallop up to the Palace and take over the government, the way they had taken so many other things without anyone's permission. The Colonel, however, did not want to be just another tyrant; there had been enough of those before him and, besides, if he did that, he would never win people's hearts. It was his aspiration to win the popular vote in the December elections.

"To do that, I have to talk like a candidate. Can you sell me the words for a speech?" the Colonel asked Belisa Crepusculario.

She had accepted many assignments, but none like this. She did not dare refuse, fearing that El Mulato would shoot her between the eyes, or worse still, that the Colonel would burst into tears. There was more to it than that, however, she felt the urge to help him because she felt a throbbing warmth beneath her skin, a powerful desire to touch that man, to fondle him, to clasp him in her arms.

All night and a good part of the following day, Belisa Crepusculario searched her repertory for words adequate for a presidential speech, closely watched by El Mulato, who could not take his eyes from her firm wanderer's legs and virginal breasts. She discarded harsh, cold words, words that were too flowery, words worn from abuse, words that offered improbable promises, untruthful and confusing words, until all she had left were words sure to touch the minds of men and women's intuition. Calling upon the knowledge she had purchased from the priest for twenty *pesos,* she wrote the speech on a sheet of paper and then signalled El Mulato to untie the rope that bound her ankles to a tree. He led her once more to the Colonel, and again she felt the throbbing anxiety that had seized her when she first saw him. She handed him the paper and waited while he looked at it, holding it gingerly between thumbs and fingertips.

"What the shit does this say?" he asked finally.

"Don't you know how to read?"

"War's what I know," he replied.

She read the speech aloud. She read it three times, so her client could engrave it on his memory. When she finished, she saw the emotion in the faces of the soldiers who had gathered round to listen, and saw that the Colonel's eyes glittered with enthusiasm, convinced that with those words the presidential chair would be his.

"If after they've heard it three times, the boys are still standing there with their mouths hanging open, it must mean the thing's damn good, Colonel," was El Mulato's approval.

"All right, woman. How much do I owe you?" the leader asked.

"One *peso,* Colonel."

"That's not much," he said, opening the purse he wore at his belt, heavy with proceeds from the last foray.

"The *peso* entitles you to a bonus. I'm going to give you two secret words," said Belisa Crepusculario.

"What for?"

She explained that for every fifty *centaros* a client paid, she gave him the gift of a word for his exclusive use. The Colonel shrugged. He had no interest at all in her offer, but he did not want to be impolite to someone who had served him so well. She walked slowly to the leather stool where he was sitting, and bent down to give him her gift. The man smelled the scent of a mountain cat issuing from the woman, a fiery heat radiating from her hips, he heard the terrible whisper of her hair, and a breath of sweet mint murmured into his ear the two secret words that were his alone.

"They are yours, Colonel," she said as she stepped back. "You may use them as much as you please."

El Mulato accompanied Belisa to the roadside, his eyes as entreating as a stray dog's, but when he reached out to touch her, he was stopped by an avalanche of words he had never heard before; believing them to be an irrevocable curse, the flame of his desire was extinguished.

During the months of September, October and November, the Colonel delivered his speech so many times that had it not been crafted from glowing and durable words, it would have turned to ash as he spoke. He travelled up and down and across the country, riding into cities with a triumphal air, stopping in even the most forgotten villages where only the dump heap betrayed a human presence, to convince his fellow citizens to vote for him. While he spoke from a platform erected in the middle of the plaza, El Mulato and his men handed out sweets and painted his name on all the walls in gold frost. No one paid the least attention to those advertising ploys; they were dazzled by the clarity of the Colonel's proposals and the poetic lucidity of his arguments, infected by his powerful wish to right the wrongs of history, happy for the first time in their lives. When the Candidate had finished his speech, his soldiers would fire their pistols into the air and set off firecrackers, and when finally they rode off, they left behind a wake of hope that lingered for days on the air, like the splendid memory of a comet's tail. Soon the Colonel was the favourite. No one had ever witnessed such a phenomenon: a man who surfaced from the civil war, covered with scars and speaking like a professor, a man whose fame spread to every corner of the land and captured the nation's heart. The press focused their attention on him. Newspapermen came from far away to interview him and repeat his phrases, and the number of his followers and enemies continued to grow.

"We're doing great, Colonel," said El Mulato, after twelve successful weeks of campaigning.

But the Candidate did not hear. He was repeating his secret words, as he did more and more obsessively. He said them when he was mellow with nostalgia; he murmured them in his sleep; he carried them with him on horseback; he thought them before delivering his famous speech; and he caught himself savouring them in his leisure time. And every time he thought of those two words, he thought of Belisa Crepuscolario, and his senses were inflamed with the memory of her feral scent, her fiery heat, the whisper of her hair and her sweet mint breath in his ear, until he began to go around like a sleepwalker, and his men realized that he might die before he ever sat in the presidential chair.

"What's got hold of you, Colonel," El Mulato asked so often that finally one day his chief broke down and told him the source of his befuddlement: those two words that were buried like two daggers in his gut.

"Tell me what they are and maybe they'll lose their magic," his faithful aide suggested.

"I can't tell them, they're for me alone," the Colonel replied.

Saddened by watching his chief decline like a man with a death sentence on his head, El Mulato slung his rifle over his shoulder and set out to find Belisa

Crepusculario. He followed her trail through all that vast country, until he found her in a village in the far south, sitting under her tent reciting her rosary of news. He planted himself, straddle-legged, before her, weapon in hand.

"You! You're coming with me," he ordered.

She had been waiting. She picked up her inkwell, folded the canvas of her small stall, arranged her shawl around her shoulders, and without a word took her place behind El Mulato's saddle. They did not exchange so much as a word in all the trip; El Mulato's desire for her had turned into rage, and only his fear of her tongue prevented his cutting her to shreds with his whip. Nor was he inclined to tell her that the Colonel was in a fog, and that a spell whispered into his ear had done what years of battle had not been able to do. Three days later they arrived at the encampment, and immediately, in view of all the troops, El Mulato led his prisoner before the Candidate.

"I brought this witch here so you can give her back her words, Colonel," El Mulato said, pointing the barrel of his rifle at the woman's head. "And then she can give you back your manhood."

The Colonel and Belisa Crepusculario stared at each other, measuring one another from a distance. The men knew then that their leader would never undo the witchcraft of those two accursed words, because the whole world could see the voracious puma's eyes soften as the woman walked to him and took his hand in hers.

QUESTIONS FOR DISCUSSION AND WRITING

1. What is meant by "words make their way in the world without a master"?
2. Why does Belisa decide that the Colonel is "the loneliest man in the world"?
3. Why does the Colonel want to be president? Do you find any irony in his expressed desire?
4. How does the saying "The pen is mightier than the sword" relate to this story?
5. Is this a love story or a war story (or both)? Explain your answer.
6. Identify one or two major themes in this story. Why did you choose the theme you did?

ON TECHNIQUE AND STYLE

1. What are the characteristics of a fable? In what ways does this story resemble a fable? Give specific examples.
2. In a recent interview, Allende says about her writing: "There are elements of imagination; there is hyperbole; there is gross exaggeration; there is recurrent use of premonition, of coincidence—of things that happen in fiction that wouldn't seem to happen in real life; but, actually, if you pay attention, they happen often enough." What are the instances of hyperbole and exaggeration in "Two Words"? In what way might they "happen often enough"?

CULTURAL QUESTION

1. Allende's type of writing, sometimes called "magical realism," is often associated with Latin American writers, including Gabriel García Márquez. Can you think of writers from other cultural traditions with similar styles?

War

Luigi Pirandello

Luigi Pirandello (1867–1937) was born in Girgenti (now Agrigento) on the island of Sicily. He started his education at the University of Rome in 1887, and later transferred to Bonn University, where he received a doctorate, studying his native Sicilian dialect. Pirandello wrote his first widely acclaimed novel, The Late Mattia Pascal, *in 1904. By the time WWI began, he had published two other novels and numerous short stories. As Italy entered WWI, Pirandello's son Stefano volunteered to serve, and was taken prisoner by the Austrians; he returned home at the war's end.*

In 1916, Pirandello turned his focus on the theater. During a five-week period in 1921, he wrote two masterpieces: Six Characters in Search of an Author *and* Henry IV. *Between 1922 and 1924, Pirandello became a major public figure. In 1925, with the help of Benito Mussolini, Pirandello opened his own Art Theatre in Rome. Pirandello's relationship with Mussolini has been the subject of debate. Some scholars suggest that the playwright's adoption of fascism was simply a matter of his pragmatism, a move to advance his career. His statement "I am a Fascist because I am an Italian" has often been cited as support of this theory, and one of his later plays,* The Giants of the Mountain, *is often interpreted as showing that Pirandello's fascist "giants" were hostile to culture. Pirandello was awarded the Nobel Prize in 1934—a medal he had melted down to support Italy's fascist campaign in North Africa. He continued to experience critical success until his death in 1936. "War" (originally entitled "Quando Si Comprende") is taken from* The Medals and Other Stories, *translated by Michael Pettinati (E.P. Dutton, 1939).*

The passengers who had left Rome by the night express had had to stop until dawn at the small station of Fabriano in order to continue their journey by the small old-fashioned local joining the main line with Sulmona.

At dawn, in a stuffy and smoky second-class carriage in which five people had already spent the night, a bulky woman in deep mourning was hosted in—almost like a shapeless bundle. Behind her—puffing and moaning, followed her husband—a tiny man; thin and weakly, his face death-white, his eyes small and bright and looking shy and uneasy.

Having at last taken a seat he politely thanked the passengers who had helped his wife and who had made room for her; then he turned round to the woman trying to pull down the collar of her coat and politely inquired:

"Are you all right, dear?"

The wife, instead of answering, pulled up her collar again to her eyes, so as to hide her face.

"Nasty world," muttered the husband with a sad smile.

And he felt it his duty to explain to his traveling companions that the poor woman was to be pitied for the war was taking away from her her only son, a boy of twenty to whom both had devoted their entire life, even breaking up their home at Sulmona to follow him to Rome, where he had to go as a student, then allowing him to volunteer for war with an assurance, however, that at least six months he would not be sent to the front and now, all of a sudden, receiving a wire saying that he was due to leave in three days' time and asking them to go and see him off.

The woman under the big coat was twisting and wriggling, at times growling like a wild animal, feeling certain that all those explanations would not have aroused even a shadow of sympathy from those people who—most likely—were in the same plight as herself. One of them, who had been listening with particular attention, said:

"You should thank God that your son is only leaving now for the front. Mine has been sent there the first day of the war. He has already come back twice wounded and been sent back again to the front."

"What about me? I have two sons and three nephews at the front," said another passenger.

"Maybe, but in our case it is our only son," ventured the husband.

"What difference can it make? You may spoil your only son by excessive attentions, but you cannot love him more than you would all your other children if you had any. Parental love is not like bread that can be broken to pieces and split amongst the children in equal shares. A father gives *all* his love to each one of his children without discrimination, whether it be one or ten, and if I am suffering now for my two sons, I am not suffering half for each of them but double . . ."

"True . . . true . . ." sighed the embarrassed husband, "but suppose (of course we all hope it will never be your case) a father has two sons at the front and he loses one of them, there is still one left to console him . . . while . . ."

"Yes," answered the other, getting cross, "a son left to console him but also a son left for whom he must survive, while in the case of the father of an only son if the son dies the father can die too and put an end to his distress. Which of the two positions is worse? Don't you see how my case would be worse than yours?"

"Nonsense," interrupted another traveler, a fat, red-faced man with bloodshot eyes of the palest gray.

He was panting. From his bulging eyes seemed to spurt inner violence of an uncontrolled vitality which his weakened body could hardly contain.

"Nonsense," he repeated, trying to cover his mouth with his hand so as to hide the two missing front teeth. "Nonsense. Do we give life to our own children for our own benefit?"

The other travelers stared at him in distress. The one who had had his son at the front since the first day of the war sighed: "You are right. Our children do not belong to us, they belong to the country . . ."

"Bosh," retorted the fat traveler. "Do we think of the country when we give life to our children? Our sons are born because . . . well, because they must be born and when they come to life they take our own life with them. This is the truth. We belong to them but they never belong to us. And when they reach twenty they are exactly what we were at their age. We too had a father and mother, but there were so many other things as well . . . girls, cigarettes, illusions, new ties . . . and the Country, of course, whose call we would have answered—when we were twenty—even if father and mother had said no. Now, at our age, the love of our Country is still great, of course, but stronger than it is the love of our children. Is there any one of us here who wouldn't gladly take his son's place at the front if he could?"

There was a silence all round, everybody nodding as to approve.

"Why then," continued the fat man, "should we consider the feelings of our children when they are twenty? Isn't it natural that at their age they should consider the love for their Country (I am speaking of decent boys, of course) even greater than the love for us? Isn't it natural that it should be so, as after all they must look upon us as upon old boys who cannot move any more and must sit at home? If Country is a natural necessity like bread of which each of us must eat in order not to die of hunger, somebody must go to defend it. And our sons go, when they are twenty, and they don't want tears, because if they die, they die inflamed and happy (I am speaking, of course, of decent boys). Now, if one dies young and happy, without having the ugly sides of life, the boredom of it, the pettiness, the bitterness of disillusion . . . what more can we ask for him? Everyone should stop crying; everyone should laugh, as I do . . . or at least thank God—as I do—because my son, before dying, sent me a message saying that he was dying satisfied at having ended his life in the best way he could have wished. That is why, as you see, I do not even wear mourning . . ."

He shook his light fawn coat as to show it; his livid lip over his missing teeth was trembling, his eyes were watery and motionless, and soon after he ended with a shrill laugh which might well have been a sob.

"Quite so . . . quite so . . ." agreed the others.

The woman who, bundled in a corner under her coat, had been sitting and listening had—for the last three months—tried to find in the words of her husband and her friends something to console her in her deep sorrow, something that might show her how a mother should resign herself to send her son not even to death but to a probable danger of life. Yet not a word had she found amongst the many that had been said . . . and her grief had been greater in seeing that nobody—as she thought—could share her feelings.

But now the words of the traveler amazed and almost stunned her. She suddenly realized that it wasn't the others who were wrong and could not understand her but herself who could not rise up to the same height of those fathers and mothers willing to resign themselves, without crying, not only to the departure of their sons but even to their death.

She lifted her head, she bent over from her corner trying to listen with great attention to the details which the fat man was giving to his companions about the way his son had fallen as a hero, for his King and his Country, happy and without regrets. It seemed to her that she had stumbled into a world she had never dreamt of, a world so far unknown to her, and she was so pleased to hear everyone joining in congratulating that brave father who could so stoically speak of his child's death.

Then suddenly, just as if she had heard nothing of what had been said and almost as if waking up from a dream, she turned to the old man, asking him:

"Then . . . is your son really dead?"

Everyone stared at her. The old man, too, turned to look at her, fixing his great, bulging, horribly watery light gray eyes, deep in her face. For some time he tried to answer, but words failed him. He looked and looked at her, almost as if only then—at that silly, incongruous question—he had suddenly realized at last that his son was really dead—gone for ever—for ever. His face contracted, became horribly distorted, then he snatched in haste a handkerchief from his pocket and, to the amazement of everyone, broke into harrowing, heart-breaking, uncontrollable sobs.

QUESTIONS FOR DISCUSSION AND WRITING

1. What is the setting of this story? Why is it important?
2. Who are the characters? Why do you think they do not have names?
3. Why does the "fat man" say, "Everyone should laugh"?
4. What does the woman whose son is being sent to the front come to realize? What is ironic about her realization?
5. Why do you think the woman asks, "Is your son really dead?"

ON TECHNIQUE AND STYLE

1. The original title to this story is "Quando Si Comprende," or "When It Is Understood." Why do you think the translator chose to call it "War"? Are there multiple meanings associated with the title? Which title do you prefer? Explain your answer.
2. This story can be seen to be an argument about family relationships as much as a story about war. What are the various sides to the argument? With which do you tend to agree?

CULTURAL QUESTION

1. The fat man claims that for twenty-year-olds, love of country is greater than love of parents. Do you agree? Is this a cultural belief? Is it a generational belief, that is something believed previously but not now? Support your answer with examples.

POETRY

The Colonel

Carolyn Forché

Carolyn Forché (1950–   ) is an American poet, editor, and human rights advocate. Forché was born in Detroit, Michigan. In 1972, she earned a BA in international relations and creative writing from Michigan State University. After graduate study at Bowling Green State University, she taught at the University of Arkansas, Vassar, Columbia, and in the Master of Fine Arts program at George Mason University. She now teaches at Skidmore College in Saratoga Springs, New York. She lives in Maryland with her husband and son.

Forché's first poetry collection, Gathering the Tribes *(1976), won the Yale Series of Younger Poets Award from Yale University Press. She received a John Simon Guggenheim Foundation Fellowship, which allowed her to travel to El Salvador and work as a human rights advocate. Her second book,* The Country Between Us *(1982), received the Poetry Society of America's Alice Fay di Castagnola Award, and was also the Lamont Selection of the Academy of American Poets. Her articles and reviews have appeared in* The New York Times, *the* Washington Post, The Nation, Esquire, Mother Jones, *and other publications. In 1993 she published an anthology,* Against Forgetting: Twentieth Century Poetry of Witness, *and in 1994, her third book of poetry,* The Angel of History, *which was chosen for the Los Angeles Times Book Award. This selection titled "The Colonel" is from* The Country Between Us.

What you have heard is true. I was in his house. His wife carried a tray of coffee and sugar. His daughter filed her nails, his son went out for the night. There were daily papers, pet dogs, a pistol on the cushion beside him. The moon swung bare on its black cord over the house. On the television was a cop show. It was in English. Broken bottles were embedded in the walls around the house to scoop the kneecaps from a man's legs or cut his hands to lace. On the windows there were gratings like those in liquor stores. We had dinner, rack of lamb, good wine, a gold bell was on the table for calling the maid. The maid brought green mangoes, salt, a type of bread. I was asked how I enjoyed the country. There was a brief commercial in Spanish. His wife took everything away. There was some talk then of how difficult it had become to govern. The parrot said hello on the terrace. The colonel told it to shut up, and pushed himself from the table. My friend said to me with his eyes: say nothing. The colonel returned with a sack used to bring groceries home. He spilled many human ears on the table. They were like dried peach halves. There is no other way to say this. He took one of them in his hands, shook it in our faces, dropped it into a water glass. It came alive there. I am tired of fooling around he said. As for the rights of anyone, tell your people they can go fuck themselves. He swept the ears to the floor with his arm and held the last of the wine in the air. Something for your poetry, no? he said. Some of the ears on the floor caught this scrap of his voice. Some of the ears on the floor were pressed to the ground.

QUESTIONS FOR DISCUSSION AND WRITING

1. Reread the first six sentences through "It was in English." What is the importance of this imagery? What is Forché doing here?
2. Why do you think the colonel says "Something for your poetry, no?" How do you think the poet (Forché) addresses that taunt?
3. Some say that this poem shows how people survive in an unbearable world. Do you see this? What passage in particular shows it?
4. Look at the last sentence of the poem. What significance do you think it holds?
5. In a single word, name the theme of this poem. Explain your choice.

ON TECHNIQUE AND STYLE

1. Although called a poem, this piece has the shape of prose. Why do you think Forché didn't write this in traditional poem form? If you were to render it in more traditional format, where would you put the line breaks? Why?
2. The poem starts "What you have heard is true. I was in his house." Who is the "you" referred to here? Why is the narrator explaining the situation in this way?

CULTURAL QUESTION

1. The setting of this poem is presumed to be El Salvador, where Forché spent time prior to writing *The Country Between Us*. Is there anything that makes it particularly Salvadoran? Does it remind you of situations in other countries, or with other military regimes? Which ones, and in what ways?

Dulce et Decorum Est

Wilfred Owen

*Wilfred Owen (1893–1918) was born in Oswestry, Shropshire, England. His edu-
cation began at the Birkenhead Institute, and then continued at the Technical School
in Shrewsbury in 1906. Owen is believed to have begun writing poetry at the age of
seventeen. After failing to be admitted to the University of London, he spent a year as
a lay assistant to a reverend before leaving for France. Owen returned to England in
September 1915 to enlist. He received his commission to the Manchester Regiment in
June 1916. In January 1917, he was stationed in France and saw his first battle action. In
March, he was injured but returned to the front line in April. In May he was caught in
a shell explosion and when his battalion was relieved, he was diagnosed with shell shock.
He was evacuated to England, and was then sent to Craiglockhart War Hospital near
Edinburgh, Scotland. At the hospital, he met the poet Siegfried Sassoon, who was also a
patient. Sassoon was the greatest of Owen's wartime influences, encouraging Owen to
explore the symptoms of shell shock—flashbacks, recurring nightmares, and an obsession with battle memories—within his poetry. The period in Craiglockhart, and the early
part of 1918, was when he wrote many of the poems for which he is remembered today.*

*In June 1918, Owen rejoined his regiment, and then in August he returned to France.
He was awarded the Military Cross for bravery, but was killed on November 4.
The news of his death reached his parents on November 11, 1918, the day of the armi-
stice. Along with others such as Rupert Brooke, Owen became known as a "war poet."
"Dulce et Decorum Est" is one of his better-known poems, was written in 1917, and
published posthumously. It is available in several collections of Owen's poetry.*

Bent double, like old beggars under sacks,
Knock-kneed, coughing like hags, we cursed through sludge,
Till on the haunting flares we turned our backs
And towards our distant rest began to trudge.
Men marched asleep. Many had lost their boots
But limped on, blood-shod. All went lame; all blind;
Drunk with fatigue; deaf even to the hoots
Of tired, outstripped Five-Nines that dropped behind.

Gas! GAS! Quick, boys!—An ecstasy of fumbling,
Fitting the clumsy helmets just in time;
But someone still was yelling out and stumbling
And flound'ring like a man in fire or lime . . .
Dim, through the misty panes and thick green light,
As under a green sea, I saw him drowning.

In all my dreams, before my helpless sight,
He plunges at me, guttering, choking, drowning.

If in some smothering dreams you too could pace
Behind the wagon that we flung him in,
And watch the white eyes writhing in his face,
His hanging face, like a devil's sick of sin;
If you could hear, at every jolt, the blood
Come gargling from the froth-corrupted lungs,
Obscene as cancer, bitter as the cud
Of vile, incurable sores on innocent tongues,—
My friend, you would not tell with such high zest
To children ardent for some desperate glory,
The old lie: *Dulce et decorum est
Pro patria mori.*

QUESTIONS FOR DISCUSSION AND WRITING

1. What is the translation of the Latin phrase *Dulce et decorum est | Pro patria mori?* Can you find the original source of this phrase?
2. Explain why the title of this poem is ironic.
3. Identify the simile in the first line. What is being compared? Why does the poet use this comparison?
4. What impression does the reader get of the soldiers in the first two lines? Cite an example to support your answer.
5. In what ways is this poem regular or conventional? In what ways does Owen break our expectations of conventional poetry?
6. In a single word, name one of the themes of this poem. Explain your choice.

ON TECHNIQUE AND STYLE

1. What is the tone of "GAS!" (second stanza)? Why is the first "Gas!" not written in capital letters?
2. List some of the major images that are used in this poem. What do they convey?

CULTURAL QUESTION

1. The setting for "Dulce et Decorum Est" is World War I, a war in which the technology of battle had changed significantly to include such things as poison gas. What has changed about global warfare since Owen wrote those words, not long before his own death?

GRAPHIC FICTION

Go Away

Joe Sacco

Joe Sacco (1960–   ) was born in Malta, and moved to the United States, where he studied journalism at the University of Oregon, graduating in 1981. In 1985, while living in Portland, Oregon, he coedited a monthly comics newspaper, Portland Permanent Press; *he was then hired at Fantagraphics Books, where he edited the comics anthology* Centrifugal Bumble-Puppy *(1987). Sacco's first series,* Yahoo, *was published from 1988 to 1992. The Gulf War drew Sacco into a study of Middle Eastern politics, and he traveled to Israel and the Palestinian territories to research his first long work.* Palestine *is a collection of pieces depicting Sacco's travels and encounters with Palestinians and Israelis. It was serialized as a comic book from 1993 to 2001 and then published in several collections, the first of which won an American Book Award in 1996.*

Sacco traveled to Sarajevo and Gorazde near the end of the Bosnian War, and produced a series of reports in the same style as Palestine: *the graphic novels* Safe Area Gorazde: The War in Eastern Bosnia *and* The Fixer *(2003), and the stories collected in* War's End *(2005).* Safe Area Gorazde, *(2002) from which this selection is taken, won the Eisner Award for Best Original Graphic Novel in 2001. Sacco has also contributed short pieces of graphic reporting to various magazines, and is a frequent illustrator of Harvey Pekar's* American Splendor. *Sacco currently lives in New York City.*

QUESTIONS FOR DISCUSSION AND WRITING

1. Why is this selection called "Go Away"? Why do you think the correspondent said this?
2. Why is the position of Gorazde problematic? What solution is posed in the comic here?
3. Why do the Gorazdans feel abandoned? How is this feeling of abandonment a theme both in Bosnia and Rwanda?
4. Although under the heading "Graphic Fiction," Sacco's piece is really nonfiction. How does it reflect the themes and events found in other selections in this chapter?

It was an enclave. It was surrounded by separatist Serb forces, it had been since the beginning of the Bosnian War more than three and a half years ago. And it was a U.N.-designated safe area...

The two other eastern enclaves, Srebrenica and Zepa, also designated safe areas, had been abandoned by the U.N. in the summer. The victorious Serbs entered Srebrenica and Zepa, and, in the aftermath, horrible stories had emerged...

When British and Ukranian U.N. peacekeepers pulled out of Gorazde shortly thereafter, Gorazdans thought they, too, had been abandoned...

2

But now, following a massive NATO bombing campaign against them, the Serbs were compelled under the terms of a cease-fire to allow regular U.N. relief convoys through their territory and into Gorazde...

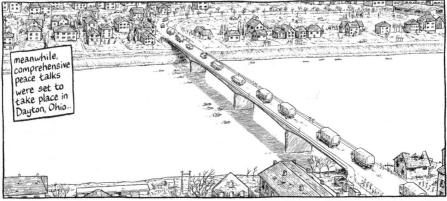

meanwhile, comprehensive peace talks were set to take place in Dayton, Ohio...

Foreign journalists, endlessly discussing possible Dayton scenarios, pondered the sticky problem of Gorazde's presence deep in Serb-held land. Some felt that a peace settlement would be facilitated if the Bosnian government traded the enclave to the Serbs for more territory around the capital, Sarajevo.

3

ON TECHNIQUE AND STYLE

1. In what ways is Sacco's work realistically drawn? In what ways isn't it? Point to specific details.
2. Look at the first frame. What do you notice in the drawing? What details has Sacco included? Is this an effective depiction, in your opinion?

CULTURAL QUESTION

1. What is the portrayal of the "American correspondent"? How is this portrayal contrasted with the "foreign journalists"?

VISUAL TEXTS

We Can Do It!

J. Howard Miller

J. Howard Miller was an American graphic artist who painted posters in support of World War II. The most famous poster is probably "We Can Do It!" (ca. 1942) featuring Rosie the Riveter, shown as this selection. The poster encouraged American women to

show their strength and go to work in factories for the war effort. Miller based "We Can Do It!" on a United Press International photo of Geraldine Doyle working at a factory. When the poster was released, the name "Rosie" wasn't associated with the it—that came later when a popular patriotic song called "Rosie the Riveter" was recorded. The American artist Norman Rockwell also painted a version of Rosie the Riveter. Although "We Can Do It!" is famous today, and is found on T-shirts and tote bags, during the war this poster was not widely known in the United States. It was shown only at the Westinghouse Company, which commissioned it, and was posted for only two weeks.

Napoleon Bonaparte in the Grand Mosque at Cairo

Henri Lévy

Henri Lévy was an eighteenth-century Jewish Parisian painter. In this painting (1798–1799) Lévy portrays the military campaign led by Napoleon Bonaparte, which began an age of Westernization and modernization of Egypt. Along with the army, Napoleon recruited scholars and engineers who collected and classified material on the history, geography, and culture of the country. This came to shape the West's image of Egypt.

Children Fleeing Napalm, Trang Bang, South Vietnam

Nick Ut

*The original caption for the following photograph reads: "Trang Bang, South Vietnam: A naked girl and others, run down Highway on June 8, 1972 escaping an accidental napalm bombing on this village by South Vietnamese government planes. The village is 26 miles from Saigon." This image was taken by photographer **Nick Ut**, a Vietnamese photographer who worked for the Associated Press (AP) in Los Angeles. Ut began to take photographs for the AP when he was sixteen, after his older brother Huynh Thanh My, also an AP photographer, was killed in Vietnam. Ut was wounded three times in the war. He received the Pulitzer Prize for this photograph.*

QUESTIONS FOR DISCUSSION AND WRITING

1. Compare the images from Trang Bang and Egypt. What similarities do you notice between them, even though the span of time covers centuries? What are the differences?
2. The image of Napoleon entering the Egyptian mosque echoes a theme relevant in modern times. How so? In what way is this painting a glorification of the invasion of the mosque?

3. The image from Trang Bang during the Vietnam War is one of the most enduring images of that time. Why do you think this is so? Have you seen this image before? How does it affect you, as the viewer?
4. Have you seen the "We Can Do It!" poster before? In what context? How did posters such as this contribute to the war effort in the 1940s? How did they change the American workforce?

ON TECHNIQUE AND STYLE

1. The Trang Bang photo is black and white—does this affect your understanding or interpretation of the photo in any way? How? Would it be more or less effective if it were in color? Explain your answer.
2. In standard image composition, the subject is typically positioned slightly left of center of the frame. Given that, which of these images seem to have a clear subject? Which do not? Of those that do not seem to have a clear subject, why do you think they do not? What is the subject of those images?

CULTURAL QUESTION

1. The images here are from different eras and geographic locations. What do they share in common? What is different? What is the cultural dimension of war, or is it culture-less?

AUDIO TEXTS   To hear these conversations, go to www.mhhe.com/soundideas1e

Track 5.1

(date: July 11, 2005; running time: 7:47 min.)

Srebrenica Anniversary: **Ambassador Swanee Hunt,** *director of the Women and Public Policy Program at Harvard University's Kennedy School of Government;* **General William Nash; General John W. Vessy,** *Senior Fellow and director of the Center for Preventive Action at the Council on Foreign Relations; and* **Mike Shuster,** *diplomatic correspondent for National Public Radio.*

Track 5.2

(date: April 21, 2004; running time: 13:15 min.)

Rwandan Genocide: **Corinne Dufka,** *researcher with Human Rights Watch, and former photojournalist in El Salvador, Bosnia, and throughout Africa; and* **Louise Mushikiwabo,** *international coordinator of Remembering Rwanda—a coalition organizing anniversary events.*

Track 5.3

(date: March 20, 2006; running time: 8:20 min.)

Iraq War: Forum *discusses the invasion and occupation of Iraq with* **Michael Gordon,** *chief military correspondent for* The New York Times.

Track 5.4

(date: May 27, 2003; running time: 8:23 min.)

Chilean History: Author **Isabel Allende** *talks about her new memoir,* My Invented Country: A Nostalgic Journey Through Chile.

QUESTIONS FOR DISCUSSION AND WRITING

1. What is the source of disappointment regarding NATO involvement in Bosnia?
2. What is Ambassador Hunt's reason for disbelief in the situation in Bosnia? In what ways does General Nash disagree with this assessment?
3. Why did Mushikiwabo feel betrayed by the United Nations?
4. What outcomes of the Iraq War did both sides, according to Gordon, not anticipate?
5. Why does Allende think so many Chileans supported Pinochet?

ON TECHNIQUE AND STYLE

1. In what way does authority play a role in Allende's discussion?
2. What is the "g word" referred to? Why do you think the United States didn't want this word used?
3. In what way do the comments made by Dufka corroborate the history of Rwanda as explained by Gourevitch?

CULTURAL QUESTION

1. Why did journalists not understand the situation of Rwanda, according to Dufka? How was the mass media exploited in Rwanda?

Additional Audio Resources

1. Chinua Achebe talks about Okonkwo, the protagonist of *Things Fall Apart,* at www.npr.org/templates/story/story.php?storyId=11114757.

2. A Tim O'Brien lecture, interview, and transcript of an event called "Writing Vietnam" can be found at www.stg.brown.edu/projects/WritingVietnam/obrien.html.

3. An interview with Joe Sacco about his work *Palestine* can be found at http://weekendamerica.publicradio.org/display/web/2007/12/12/sacco/.

CONNECTIONS

1. In which readings or other texts do you see Twain's theme most clearly reflected? Give specific examples from the readings.

2. What similarities do you find in the conflicts in Rwanda and Bosnia? What are the differences?

3. Gourevitch writes as an observer of his subject; Crawford writes as a participant. In what ways do the styles of their writing differ as a result? What does Crawford write that Gourevitch cannot, and vice versa?

4. Are there reflections of Crawford's story in any of the short stories in this chapter? Which ones? What are the specific parallels you find?

5. Imagine a discussion about war between Mark Twain and Luigi Pirandello. In what ways do you think they would agree about the subject? In what ways might they disagree?

6. Consider the Allende and Achebe stories. What are the similarities? Differences?

7. Think about the colonel characters in both Allende's short story and in Forché's prose poem. What characteristics do they two share? What is different about them? Do they reflect the general as outlined by Sun Tzu in any way? Explain.

8. Owen's poem and Pirandello's short story share common themes. What are they? Cite specific passages to back up your ideas.

9. Listen again to the audio passage about Bosnia, and look at Sacco's comic rendering of the same story. What is present? What is absent? How do you think Sacco's depiction captures what is said in the audio passage?

FOR WRITING

CREATIVE CHOICES

1. Create a comic that illustrates one of the main themes of this chapter. (Keep in mind that you need not be an accomplished artist to create a comic. Simple drawings or even photos cut out from magazines or newspapers can be very effective.)

2. Continue work in your journal. In it, write about your reactions to any of the war stories presented in this chapter, or in the current news. If you prefer, create an audio or video journal, recording your spoken ideas.

3. Write a poem or short story related to the idea of war or conflict. Keeping in mind that poems are typically best appreciated in the spoken form, record yourself reading your poem.

NARRATIVE/EXPOSITORY CHOICES

1. Choose two readings from this chapter from the fiction or poetry section. Make your choice based on a shared theme. What theme do these two readings share? How is the theme illustrated? Develop a thesis based on your reading of these stories, and write an analytical essay in which you use extensively passages from the readings to support your thesis.
2. The theme of *abandonment* comes up in several of the readings and audio texts—a feeling that the world outside has left the victims of war without aid or assistance. Write an essay in which you examine the idea of abandonment and its relationship to war and conflict. Be sure to cite the material found in this chapter, or other texts you find.
3. The role of youth and war is mentioned in several of the readings as well. Write an essay in which you explore the role of youth in war. Would wars be possible without the involvement of young people? Use your readings and personal knowledge and experience as evidence in your essay.

ARGUMENT CHOICES

1. In the introduction to this chapter, General Sherman's famous statement, "War is hell," is cited. In what ways does this chapter reflect that? In what ways might war ever be necessary? Write an essay in which you argue for the futility, or necessity of war in some circumstances. You may want to choose a particular war as an example, or speak more broadly to the concept of war in general.
2. A question that arises with respect to war, especially in the United States, is the question of a draft. In your opinion, should there be a draft in this country? What are the pros and cons of compulsory military service? Write an essay in which you argue for or against the idea of a draft.
3. Which of the points made by Sun Tzu do you find especially convincing? Why? Is there one you are not convinced by? Why not? Use examples from the other readings, or other knowledge of war you have to support your argument.

RESEARCH CHOICES

1. Investigate one of the wars presented in this chapter more thoroughly. Research its causes, duration, major battles, and so on. Write a research paper on some aspect of this war, making clear your interest in a specific research question.
2. Pick one campaign battle from a specific war, and follow its progress over time with *The Art of War* as a reference. Describe the battle, cross-referencing *The Art of War*. You may want to find a full text of Sun Tzu's work in doing this. Several are available online.

3. Locate someone (a friend, family member, etc.) who was involved in a war sometime during his or her life. Interview this person about his or her experiences in the war. Write a report on your interview, including some background on the war that you discuss with your interviewee.
4. Consider the images of war as offered by photojournalists. Identify images from magazines and newspapers. Write an essay in which you show how war is represented in the print media. How do these portrayals support or undermine the themes in the readings from this chapter? Incorporate the images you found to support your thesis. If you have the tools and skills, create a web page essay for this research project.

VIDEO SUGGESTIONS

The number of movies focusing on war is enormous. Here are a few that relate to the themes or authors in this chapter.

1. *Apocalypse Now* (1979). Based on Joseph Conrad's *Heart of Darkness*, this is considered a "classic" among movies about the Vietnam War. The story follows Captain Willard on a mission into Cambodia to assassinate a Green Beret who has set himself up as a god among a local tribe.
2. *Death and the Maiden* (1994). Paulina Escobar is the wife of a prominent lawyer in an unnamed country. A storm forces her husband to ride home with a neighbor. That chance encounter brings up her past, as she is convinced that the neighbor, Dr. Miranda, was part of the old fascist regime that tortured and raped her while blindfolded.
3. *Hotel Rwanda* (2004). The true-life story of Paul Rusesabagina, a hotel manager who housed over a thousand Tutsi refugees during the war in Rwanda.
4. *The House of the Spirits* (1993). Set in South America before WWII. Esteban marries Clara and they have a daughter, Blanca. Esteban works hard and eventually gets money to buy a hacienda and become a local patriarch. When Blanca grows up, she falls in love with a young revolutionary, Pedro, who urges the workers to fight for socialism.
5. *Jarhead* (2005). Based on former Marine Anthony Swofford's best-selling 2003 book about his pre-Desert Storm experiences in Saudi Arabia and about his experiences fighting in Kuwait.
6. You can find a short video of Mark Twain, created by Thomas Edison, at www.hannibal.net/twain/multimedia/video/.

chapter 6

Ideas about Crime
Prison and Punishment

In prison, those things withheld from and denied to the prisoner become precisely what he wants most of all.

—*Eldridge Cleaver*

INTRODUCTION

The selections of this chapter look at various aspects of prison life—from the increasing number of prisoners in U.S. prisons, sometimes referred to as the prison-industrial complex, to the more personal stories of those who have been imprisoned.

A widely read selection from Michel Foucault's *Discipline and Punish* begins the chapter. His arguments form the base of many modern-day criticisms of the modern prison system. George Orwell's essay, "A Hanging," is a classic reflection on capital punishment and humanity, which was written as a reflection on Orwell's own experience as a police officer. Frank Tannenbaum discusses the prison system in his 1920 article "Prison Cruelty." Tannenbaum, a figure from the Harlem Renaissance, was also imprisoned at one point, an experience that informs his reflections. The nonfiction section ends with a piece of Leonard Peltier's prison memoir, connecting the details of daily life in prison with the more theoretical aspects introduced by Foucault and Tannenbaum.

The short stories pick up where Peltier leaves off, and examine different aspects of life behind bars, and outside of them. The excerpt from *The House of the Dead*, written in the 1800s by Fyodor Dostoevsky, in many ways seems like a more modern narrative. "Outside Work Detail" by Scott Wolven looks at the lives of rural prisoners and their dreams of release. "Enemies" by Jimmy Santiago Baca explores the roots of prison hatred and racism, but eventually, the ties that bind prisoners to one another in shared experiences. And finally, an excerpt from the novel *Kiss of the Spider Woman*, by Manuel Puig, shows the life of two very different kinds of prisoners, and the role that fantasy and betrayal play in their lives.

The poems also lie at two ends of the spectrum—a rather elusive look at a town besieged in Dick Allen's "The Report," and the narrative of a fallen prison hero, "Hard Rock Returns to Prison from the Hospital of the Criminal Insane" by Etheridge Knight. Once again, the graphic fiction selection, "The Beast of Chicago" by Rich Geary, addresses a true story—that of a serial killer's end of days in prison.

The images in this chapter show three views of prison. Two of them may be seen as typical: the mass of humanity "in the yard," represented here by a Van Gogh painting or the solitary prisoner, reflected often as a mere shadow or dark image, as in Robert Siqueiros's image. The third image, Jeremy Bentham's Panopticon, shows an eighteenth century prison design, which would allow an observer to watch prisoners without their knowing they were being watched.

The audio selection is a panel discussion of a death-penalty controversy surrounding Stanley "Tookie" Williams, recently executed in California. The idea of clemency is discussed, and whether the death penalty is fairly used.

As you consider the various texts in this chapter, you will no doubt be reminded of images of prison and prisoners you have encountered through film, art, and the popular media. They will help you think about what you know about prison, and where your primary knowledge was formed. In addition, go to the newspaper and read about any issues in capital punishment or prison reform occurring right now. Think about the effect of prison on communities, societies, and individuals as you read the selections in this chapter.

NONFICTION

Illegalities and Delinquency

Michel Foucault

Michel Foucault (1926–1984) was a French philosopher who held a chair at the Collège de France. His writings have had a significant effect on other scholarly work extending across the humanities and social sciences, as well as across many applied and professional areas of study. Foucault is known for his critical studies of social institutions, in particular psychiatry, medicine, and especially the prison system. His work concerning power and the relation between power and knowledge, as well as his ideas concerning "discourse" in relation to the history of Western thought, have been widely discussed and debated. His most well-known writing includes Mental Illness and Psychology *(1954),* Archaeology of Knowledge *(1969), and* Discipline and Punish: The Birth of the Prison *(1975), from which the following excerpt is taken.*

The prison, in its reality and visible effects, was denounced at once as the great failure of penal justice. In a very strange way, the history of imprisonment does not obey a chronology in which one sees, in orderly succession, the establishment of a penality of detention; then the recognition of its failure; then the slow rise of projects of reform, seeming to culminate in the more or less coherent definition of penitentiary technique; then the implementation of this project; lastly, the recognition of its successes or its failure. There was in fact a telescoping or, in any case, a different distribution of these elements. And, just as the project of a corrective technique accompanied the principle of punitive detention, the critique of the prison and its methods appeared very early on, in those same years 1820–45; indeed, it was embodied in a number of formulations which—figures apart—are today repeated almost unchanged.

—Prisons do not diminish the crime rate: they can be extended, multiplied, or transformed; the quantity of crime and criminals remains stable or, worse, increases: "In France, one calculates at about 108,000 the number of individuals who are in a state of flagrant hostility to society. The means of repression at one's disposal are: the scaffold, the iron collar, three convict ships, 19 *maisons centrales,* 86 *maisons de justice,* 362 *maisons d'arrêt,* 2,800 cantonal prisons, 2,238 cells in police stations. Despite all these, vice goes unchecked. The number of crimes is not diminishing . . . the number of recidivists is increasing, rather than declining."[1]

---

[1] *La Fraternité,* No. 10 (February 1842).

—Detention causes recidivism; those leaving prison have more chance than before of going back to it; convicts are, in a very high proportion, former inmates; thirty-eight percent of those who left the *maisons centrales* were convicted again and thirty-three percent of those sent to convict ships (a figure given by G. de Rochefoucauld during the debate on the reform of the penal code, December 2, 1831),[2] between 1828 and 1834, out of almost 35,000 convicted of crime, about 7,400 were recidivists (that is, 1 out of 4.7 of those convicted); out of over 200,000 *correctionels,* or petty offenders, almost 35,000 were also recidivists (1 out of 6); in all, one recidivist out of 5.8 of those convicted;[3] in 1831, out of 2,174 of those condemned for recidivism, 350 had been in convict ships, 1,682 in *maisons centrales,* 142 in four *maisons de correction* that followed the same regime as the *centrales.*[4]

And the diagnosis became even more severe during the July monarchy: in 1835, out of 7,223 convicted criminals, 1,486 were recidivists; in 1839, 1,749 out of 7,858; in 1844, 1,821 out of 7,195. Among the 980 prisoners at Loos, there were 570 recidivists and, at Melun, 745 out of 1,008 prisoners.[5] Instead of releasing corrected individuals, then, the prison was setting loose a swarm of dangerous delinquents throughout the population: "7,000 persons handed back each year to society . . . they are 7,000 principles of crime or corruption spread throughout the social body. And, when one thinks that this population is constantly increasing, that it lives and moves around us, ready to seize every opportunity of disorder, to avail itself of every crisis in society to try out its strength, can one remain unmoved by such a spectacle?"[6]

—The prison cannot fail to produce delinquents. It does so by the very type of existence that it imposes on its inmates: whether they are isolated in cells or whether they are given useless work, for which they will find no employment, it is, in any case, not "to think of man in society; it is to create an unnatural, useless and dangerous existence"; the prison should educate its inmates, but can a system of education addressed to man reasonably have as its object to act against the wishes of nature?[7] The prison also produces delinquents by imposing violent constraints on its inmates; it is supposed to apply the law, and to teach respect for it; but all its functioning operates in the form of an abuse of power. The arbitrary power of administration: "The feeling of injustice that a prisoner has is one of the causes that may make his character untamable. When he sees himself exposed in this way to suffering, which the law has neither ordered nor envisaged, he becomes habitually angry against everything around him; he sees every agent of authority as an executioner; he no longer thinks that he was guilty: he accuses justice itself."[8] Corruption,

[2] *Archives parlementaires,* Vol. 72 (1831), pp. 209–10.

[3] E. Ducpétiaux, *De la réforme pénitentiaire,* III (1837), p. 276ff.

[4] Ibid.

[5] G. Ferrus, *Des prisonniers* (1850).

[6] E. de Beaumont and A. de Tocqueville, *Note sur le système pénitentiaire* (1831), pp. 22–3.

[7] C. Lucas, *De la réforme des prisons,* I (1836), pp. 127, 130.

[8] F. Bigot Préameneu, *Rapport au conseil général de la société des prisons* (1819).

fear, and the inefficiency of the warders: "Between 1,000 and 1,500 convicts live under the surveillance of between thirty and forty supervisors, who can preserve some kind of security only by depending on informers, that is to say, on the corruption that they carefully sow themselves. Who are these warders? Retired soldiers, men uninstructed in their task, making a trade of guarding malefactors."[9] Exploitation by penal labor, which can in these conditions have no educational character: "One inveighs against the slave trade. But are not our prisoners sold, like the slaves, by entrepreneurs and bought by manufacturers. . . . Is this how we teach our prisoners honesty? Are they not still more demoralized by these examples of abominable exploitation?"[10]

—The prison makes possible, even encourages, the organization of a milieu of delinquents, loyal to one another, hierarchized, ready to aid and abet any future criminal act: "Society prohibits associations of more than twenty persons . . . and it constitutes for itself associations of 200, 500, 1,200 convicts in the *maisons centrales,* which are constructed for them *ad hoc,* and which it divides up for their greater convenience into workshops, courtyards, dormitories, refectories, where they can all meet together. . . . And it multiplies them across France in such a way that, where there is a prison, there is an association . . . and as many anti-social clubs."[11] And it is in these clubs that the education of the young first offender takes place: "The first desire that is born within him will be to learn from his cleverer seniors how to escape the rigors of the law; the first lesson will be derived from the strict logic of thieves who regard society as an enemy; the morality will be the informing and spying honored in our prisons; the first passion to be aroused in him will be to frighten the young mind by these monsters that must have been born in the dungeon and which the pen refuses to name. . . . Henceforth he has broken with everything that has bound him to society."[12] Faucher spoke of "barracks of crime."

—The conditions to which the free inmates are subjected necessarily condemn them to recidivism: they are under the surveillance of the police; they are assigned to a particular residence, or forbidden others; "they leave prison with a passport that they must show everywhere they go and which mentions the sentence that they have served."[13] Being on the loose, being unable to find work, leading the life of a vagabond are the most frequent factors in recidivism. The *Gazette des tribunaux,* but also the workers' newspapers, regularly cited cases like that of the worker convicted of theft, placed under surveillance at Rouen, caught again for theft, and whom no lawyers would defend; so he took it upon himself to speak before the court, told the story of his life,

[9] *La Fraternité,* No. 10 (March 1842).

[10] Text addressed to *L'Atelier* (October 1842) by a worker imprisoned for joining a workers' association. He was able to note this protest at a time when the same newspaper was waging a campaign against competition from penal labor. The same issue carried a letter from another worker on the same subject. See also *La Fraternité,* No. 10 (March 1842).

[11] L. Moreau-Christophe, *De la mortalité et de la folie dans le régime pénitentiaire* (1839), p. 7.

[12] *L'Almanach populaire de France* (1839), pp. 49–56.

[13] F. de Barbé-Marbois, *Rapport sur l'état des prisons du Calvados, de l'Eure, la Manche et la Seine Inférieure* (1823), p. 17.

explained how, on leaving prison and forced to reside in a particular place, he was unable to take up his trade as a gilder, since as an ex-convict he was turned down wherever he went; the police refused him the right to seek work elsewhere: he found himself unable to leave Rouen, with nothing to do but die of hunger and poverty as a result of this terrible surveillance. He went to the town hall and asked for work; for eight days he was given work in the cemeteries for fourteen sous a day: "But," he said, "I am young, I have a good appetite, I eat more than two pounds of bread a day at five sous a pound; what can I do with fourteen sous to feed myself, wash my clothes and find lodging? I was driven to despair, I wanted to become an honest man again; the surveillance plunged me back into misfortune. I became disgusted with everything; it was then that I met Lemaître, who was also a pauper; we had to live and wicked thoughts of thieving came back to us."[14]

—Lastly, the prison indirectly produces delinquents by throwing the inmate's family into destitution. "The same order that sends the head of the family to prison reduces each day the mother to destitution, the children to abandonment, the whole family to vagabondage and begging. It is in this way that crime can take root."[15]

It should be noted that this monotonous critique of the prison always takes one of two directions: either that the prison was insufficiently corrective, and that the penitentiary technique was still at the rudimentary stage; or that in attempting to be corrective it lost its power as punishment,[16] that the true penitentiary technique was rigor,[17] and that prison was a double economic error: directly, by its intrinsic cost, and, indirectly, by the cost of the delinquency that it did not abolish.[18] The answer to these criticisms was invariably

---

[14] *Gazette des tribunaux* (3 December 1829). See also *Gazette des tribunaux* (19 July 1839), the *Ruche populaire* (August 1840), *La Fraternité* (July-August 1847).

[15] Lucas, *De la réforme des prisons*, II, p. 64.

[16] This campaign was very vigorous before and after the passing of new regulations for the *maisons centrales* in 1839. The regulations were severe (silence, abolition of wine and tobacco, reduction in food) and they were followed by revolts. On October 3, 1840, *Le Moniteur* wrote: "It was scandalous to see prisoners gorging themselves with wine, meat, game, delicacies of all kinds and treating prison as a convenient hostelry where they could procure all the comforts that the state of liberty often refused them."

[17] In 1826, many of the General Councils demanded that deportation be substituted for constant and ineffective incarceration. In 1842, the General Council of the Hautes-Alpes demanded that the prisons become "truly expiatory"; those of Drôme, Eure-et-Loir, Nièvre, Rhône, and Seine-et-Oise made similar demands.

[18] According to an investigation carried out in 1839 among the directors of the *maisons centrales*. The director of the *maison centrale* of Embrun remarked: "The excessive comfort in the prisons probably contributes a great deal to the terrible increase in the number of recidivists." While the director at Eysses remarked: "The present regime is not severe enough, and if one thing is certain it is that for many of the inmates prison has its attractions and that they find in prison depraved pleasures that are entirely to their liking." The director of Limoges: "The present regime of the *maisons centrales* which, for the recidivists, are in fact little more than boarding houses, is in no way repressive" (see L. Moreau-Christophe, *Polémiques pénitentiaires* [1840], p. 86). Compare these remarks with declarations made, in July 1974, by the leaders of the union of prison workers concerning the effects of liberalization in prisons.

the same: the reintroduction of the invariable principles of penitentiary technique. For a century and a half, the prison had always been offered as its own remedy: the reactivation of the penitentiary techniques as the only means of overcoming their perpetual failure; the realization of the corrective project as the only method of overcoming the impossibility of implementing it. . . .

One must not, therefore, regard the prison, its "failure," and its more or less successful reform as three successive stages. One should think, rather, of a simultaneous system that historically has been superimposed on the juridical deprivation of liberty; a fourfold system comprising: the additional, disciplinary element of the prison—the element of "super-power"; the production of an objectivity, a technique, a penitentiary "rationality"—the element of auxiliary knowledge; the *de facto* reintroduction, if not actual increase, of a criminality that the prison ought to destroy—the element of inverted efficiency; lastly, the repetition of a "reform" that is isomorphic, despite its "idealism," with the disciplinary functioning of the prison—the element of utopian duplication. It is this complex ensemble that constitutes the "carceral system," not only the institution of the prison, with its walls, its staff, its regulations, and its violence. The carceral system combines in a single figure discourses and architectures, coercive regulations and scientific propositions, real social effects and invincible utopias, programs for correcting delinquents and mechanisms that reinforce delinquency. Is not the supposed failure part of the functioning of the prison? Is it not to be included among those effects of power that discipline and the auxiliary technology of imprisonment have induced in the apparatus of justice, and in society in general, and which may be grouped together under the name of "carceral system"? If the prison institution has survived for so long, with such immobility, if the principle of penal detention has never seriously been questioned, it is no doubt because this carceral system was deeply rooted and carried out certain very precise functions. As evidence of this strength and immobility, let us take a recent fact: the model prison opened at Fleury-Mérogis in 1969 simply took over in its overall plan the panoptic star-shape that made such a stir in 1836 at the Petite-Roquette. It was the same machinery of power that assumed a real body and a symbolic form. But what role was it supposed to play?

. . . The prison, apparently "failing," does not miss its target; on the contrary, it reaches it, insofar as it gives rise to one particular form of illegality in the midst of others, which it is able to isolate, to place in full light, and to organize as a relatively enclosed, but penetrable, milieu. It helps to establish an open illegality, irreducible at a certain level and secretly useful, at once refractory and docile; it isolates, outlines, brings out a form of illegality that seems to sum up symbolically all the others, but which makes it possible to leave in the shade those that one wishes to—or must—tolerate. This form is, strictly speaking, delinquency. One should not see in delinquency the most intense, most harmful form of illegality, the form that the penal apparatus must try to eliminate through imprisonment because of the danger it represents; it is rather an effect of penality (and of the penality of detention) that makes it possible to differentiate, accommodate, and supervise illegalities. No doubt delinquency is a form of illegality; certainly it has its roots in illegality; but it is an illegality that the "carceral system," with all its ramifications, has invested, segmented, isolated, penetrated, organized, enclosed in a definite milieu, and to which it has given an instrumental role in relation to the other illegalities. In short, although the juridical opposition is between legality and illegal practice, the strategic opposition is between illegalities and delinquency.

For the observation that prison fails to eliminate crime, one should perhaps substitute the hypothesis that prison has succeeded extremely well in producing delinquency, a specific type, a politically or economically less dangerous—and, on occasion, usable—form of illegality; in producing delinquents, in an apparently marginal, but in fact centrally supervised, milieu; in producing the delinquent as a pathologized subject. The success of the prison, in the struggles around the law and illegalities, has been to specify a "delinquency." We have seen how the carceral system substituted the "delinquent" for the offender, and also superimposed on juridical practice a whole horizon of possible knowledge. Now this process that constitutes delinquency as an object of knowledge is one with the political operation that dissociates illegalities and isolates delinquency from them. The prison is the hinge of these two mechanisms; it enables them to reinforce one another perpetually, to objectify the delinquency behind the offense, to solidify delinquency in the movement of illegalities. So successful has the prison been that, after a century and a half of "failures," the prison still exists, producing the same results, and there is the greatest reluctance to dispense with it.

QUESTIONS FOR DISCUSSION AND WRITING

1. What evidence does Foucault supply for the idea that prisons do not diminish the crime rate? Can you think of any counterevidence?
2. What is meant by "detention causes recidivism"? What is the implication of this argument?
3. According to Foucault, how does prison produce "delinquents"?
4. What elements comprise the "carceral system" according to Foucault?
5. In what ways does the prison's effect on families perpetuate crime, as described by Foucault? Do you agree with his observation? How might this problem be addressed?
6. Foucault claims that there is a reluctance to be rid of the prison system. Why do you think this is so, given its failures, as described by Foucault?

ON TECHNIQUE AND STYLE

1. Although writing primarily as a philosopher, Foucault uses statistics to support his main arguments. Does this strengthen his argument, in your opinion? How? Does his use of statistics possibly hide anything? If so, give an example.

2. Look at the third paragraph from the end (beginning "One must not, therefore, regard the prison . . ."). This paragraph is probably one of the more difficult to follow in this essay. Try to put it into your own words. Compare your version with Foucault's. Why do you think he writes in the style he does? Is there a reason for the complex sentences he uses? Does this style of writing make his ideas more, or less precise? Explain your answer.

CULTURAL QUESTION

1. Foucault speaks primarily of prisons in France. Do an Internet search and look up some basic statistics on imprisonment in the United States, France, and one or two other countries of your choice. What observations or conclusions can you make about the statistics you found? Is there anything that further supports or undermines Foucault's arguments?

A Hanging

George Orwell

George Orwell (1903–1950) is the pen name of Eric Arthur Blair, born to British parents in India during the time Britain ruled India (a period known as The Raj). An English writer and journalist, Orwell was well known as a novelist, critic, and commentator on politics and culture. Orwell continues to be a widely read essayist. In addition, he is famous for two novels: one critical of the concept of totalitarianism Nineteen Eighty-Four *(1949) and the other of Stalinism in particular* Animal Farm *(1945), which he wrote and published near the end of his life. Orwell's family could not afford a university education, so he joined the police force in Burma upon his high school graduation. It is from his experience with the police that the essay here, "A Hanging," (1931) was inspired.*

It was in Burma, a sodden morning of the rains. A sickly light, like yellow tinfoil, was slanting over the high walls into the jail yard. We were waiting outside the condemned cells, a row of sheds fronted with double bars, like small animal cages. Each cell measured about ten feet by ten and was quite bare within except for a plank bed and a pot of drinking water. In some of them brown silent men were squatting at the inner bars, with their blankets draped round them. These were the condemned men, due to be hanged within the next week or two.

One prisoner had been brought out of his cell. He was a Hindu, a puny wisp of a man, with a shaven head and vague liquid eyes. He had a thick, sprouting moustache, absurdly too big for his body, rather like the moustache of a comic man on the films. Six tall Indian warders were guarding him and getting him ready for the gallows. Two of them stood by with rifles and fixed bayonets, while the others handcuffed him, passed a chain through his handcuffs and fixed it to their belts, and lashed his arms tight to his sides. They crowded very close about him, with their hands always on him in a careful, caressing grip, as though all the while feeling him to make sure he was there. It was like men handling a fish which is still alive and may jump back into the water. But he stood quite unresisting, yielding his arms limply to the ropes, as though he hardly noticed what was happening.

Eight o'clock struck and a bugle call, desolately thin in the wet air, floated from the distant barracks. The superintendent of the jail, who was standing apart from the rest of us, moodily prodding the gravel with his stick, raised his head at the sound. He was an army doctor, with a grey toothbrush moustache and a gruff voice. "For God's sake hurry up, Francis," he said irritably. "The man ought to have been dead by this time. Aren't you ready yet?"

Francis, the head jailer, a fat Dravidian in a white drill suit and gold spectacles, waved his black hand. "Yes sir, yes sir," he bubbled. "All iss satisfactorily prepared. The hangman iss waiting. We shall proceed."

"Well, quick march, then. The prisoners can't get their breakfast till this job's over."

We set out for the gallows. Two warders marched on either side of the prisoner, with their rifles at the slope; two others marched close against him, gripping him by arm and shoulder, as though at once pushing and supporting him. The rest of us, magistrates and the like, followed behind. Suddenly, when we had gone ten yards, the procession stopped short without any order or warning. A dreadful thing had happened—a dog, come goodness knows whence, had appeared in the yard. It came bounding among us with a loud volley of barks, and leapt round us wagging its whole body, wild with glee at finding so many human beings together. It was a large woolly dog, half Airedale, half pariah. For a moment it pranced round us, and then, before anyone could stop it, it had made a dash for the prisoner, and jumping up tried to lick his face. Everyone stood aghast, too taken aback even to grab at the dog.

"Who let that bloody brute in here?" said the superintendent angrily. "Catch it, someone!"

A warder, detached from the escort, charged clumsily after the dog, but it danced and gambolled just out of his reach, taking everything as part of the game. A young Eurasian jailer picked up a handful of gravel and tried to stone the dog away, but it dodged the stones and came after us again. Its yaps echoed from the jail walls. The prisoner, in the grasp of the two warders, looked on incuriously, as though this was another formality of the hanging. It was several minutes before someone managed to catch the dog. Then we put my handkerchief through its collar and moved off once more, with the dog still straining and whimpering.

It was about forty yards to the gallows. I watched the bare brown back of the prisoner marching in front of me. He walked clumsily with his bound arms, but quite steadily, with that bobbing gait of the Indian who never straightens his knees. At each step his muscles slid neatly into place, the lock of hair on his scalp danced up and down, his feet printed themselves on the wet gravel. And once, in spite of the men who gripped him by each shoulder, he stepped slightly aside to avoid a puddle on the path.

It is curious, but till that moment I had never realized what it means to destroy a healthy, conscious man. When I saw the prisoner step aside to avoid the puddle, I saw the mystery, the unspeakable wrongness, of cutting a life short when it is in full tide. This man was not dying, he was alive just as we were alive. All the organs of his body were working—bowels digesting food, skin renewing itself, nails growing, tissues forming—all toiling away in solemn foolery. His nails would still be growing when he stood on the drop, when he was falling through the air with a tenth of a second to live. His eyes saw the yellow gravel and the grey walls, and his brain still remembered, foresaw, reasoned—reasoned even about puddles. He and we were a party of men walking together, seeing, hearing, feeling, understanding the same world; and in two minutes, with a sudden snap, one of us would be gone—one mind less, one world less.

The gallows stood in a small yard, separate from the main grounds of the prison, and overgrown with tall prickly weeds. It was a brick erection like three sides of a shed, with planking on top, and above that two beams and a crossbar with the rope dangling. The hangman, a grey-haired convict in the white uniform of the prison, was waiting beside his machine. He greeted us with a servile crouch as we entered. At a word from Francis the two warders, gripping the prisoner more closely than ever, half led, half pushed him to the gallows and helped him clumsily up the ladder. Then the hangman climbed up and fixed the rope round the prisoner's neck.

We stood waiting, five yards away. The warders had formed in a rough circle round the gallows. And then, when the noose was fixed, the prisoner began crying out on his god. It was a high, reiterated cry of "Ram! Ram! Ram! Ram!," not urgent and fearful like a prayer or a cry for help, but steady, rhythmical, almost like the tolling of a bell. The dog answered the sound with a whine. The hangman, still standing on the gallows, produced a small cotton bag like a flour bag and drew it down over the prisoner's face. But the sound, muffled by the cloth, still persisted, over and over again: "Ram! Ram! Ram! Ram! Ram!"

The hangman climbed down and stood ready, holding the lever. Minutes seemed to pass. The steady, muffled crying from the prisoner went on and on, "Ram! Ram! Ram!" never faltering for an instant. The superintendent, his head on his chest, was slowly poking the ground with his stick; perhaps he was counting the cries, allowing the prisoner a fixed number—fifty, perhaps, or a hundred. Everyone had changed colour. The Indians had gone grey like bad coffee, and one or two of the bayonets were wavering. We looked at the lashed, hooded man on the drop, and listened to his cries—each cry another second of life; the same thought was in all our minds: oh, kill him quickly, get it over, stop that abominable noise!

Suddenly the superintendent made up his mind. Throwing up his head he made a swift motion with his stick. "Chalo!" he shouted almost fiercely.

There was a clanking noise, and then dead silence. The prisoner had vanished, and the rope was twisting on itself. I let go of the dog, and it galloped immediately to the back of the gallows; but when it got there it stopped short, barked, and then retreated into a corner of the yard, where it stood among the weeds, looking timorously out at us. We went round the gallows to inspect the prisoner's body. He was dangling with his toes pointed straight down-wards, very slowly revolving, as dead as a stone.

The superintendent reached out with his stick and poked the bare body; it oscillated, slightly. "He's all right," said the superintendent. He backed out from under the gallows, and blew out a deep breath. The moody look had gone out of his face quite suddenly. He glanced at his wrist-watch. "Eight minutes past eight. Well, that's all for this morning, thank God."

The warders unfixed bayonets and marched away. The dog, sobered and conscious of having misbehaved itself, slipped after them. We walked out of the gallows yard, past the condemned cells with their waiting prisoners, into the big central yard of the prison. The convicts, under the command of ward-ers armed with lathis,[1] were already receiving their breakfast. They squatted in long rows, each man holding a tin pannikin,[2] while two warders with buck-ets marched round ladling out rice; it seemed quite a homely, jolly scene, after the hanging. An enormous relief had come upon us now that the job was done. One felt an impulse to sing, to break into a run, to snigger. All at once everyone began chattering gaily.

The Eurasian boy walking beside me nodded towards the way we had come, with a knowing smile: "Do you know, sir, our friend (he meant the dead man), when he heard his appeal had been dismissed, he pissed on the floor of his cell. From fright.—Kindly take one of my cigarettes, sir. Do you not admire my new silver case, sir? From the boxwallah,[3] two rupees eight annas. Classy European style."

Several people laughed—at what, nobody seemed certain.

Francis was walking by the superintendent, talking garrulously. "Well, sir, all hass passed off with the utmost satisfactoriness. It wass all finished—flick! like that. It iss not always so—oah, no! I have known cases where the doctor wass obliged to go beneath the gallows and pull the prisoner's legs to ensure decease. Most disagreeable!"

"Wriggling about, eh? That's bad," said the superintendent.

"Ach, sir, it iss worse when they become refractory! One man, I recall, clung to the bars of hiss cage when we went to take him out. You will scarcely credit, sir, that it took six warders to dislodge him, three pulling at each leg. We reasoned with him. 'My dear fellow,' we said, 'think of all the pain and trouble you are causing to us!' But no, he would not listen! Ach, he wass very troublesome!"

I found that I was laughing quite loudly. Everyone was laughing. Even the superintendent grinned in a tolerant way. "You'd better all come out and

[1]A 6′–8′ cane tipped with a metal blunt, used by swinging it back and forth like a sword.
[2]A small pan or cup (usually of tin).
[3]*Boxwallahs* were small-scale traveling merchant peddlers in India.

have a drink," he said quite genially. "I've got a bottle of whisky in the car. We could do with it."

We went through the big double gates of the prison, into the road. "Pulling at his legs!" exclaimed a Burmese magistrate suddenly, and burst into a loud chuckling. We all began laughing again. At that moment Francis's anecdote seemed extraordinarily funny. We all had a drink together, native and European alike, quite amicably. The dead man was a hundred yards away.

QUESTIONS FOR DISCUSSION AND WRITING

1. Orwell describes the cells as "animal cages"—a frequent description of prison cells. How does Orwell negate the image of prisoner–as–animal? How does he confirm it?
2. Discuss the role of the dog in this story. In what ways does it contribute to the tone of Orwell's essay?
3. Why do you think the guards hold the prisoner with "a careful, caressing grip"? What does the prisoner's behavior show?
4. Orwell is struck by the fact that on his way to the gallows, the prisoner avoids stepping in a puddle. What does this action say to Orwell?
5. Why do the men laugh at Francis's description of the reluctant prisoner?
6. Why is the reader never told of the prisoner's offense, in your opinion?

ON TECHNIQUE AND STYLE

1. Although a nonfiction essay, "A Hanging" can read like a short story. In what way is it similar to a fictional story?
2. Several aspects of this story may be seen as ironic. Identify one or two, and explain Orwell's use of irony.

CULTURAL QUESTION

1. What is the relationship between "the Europeans" and the "natives" in this essay? What indicates this? How do you think Orwell views this relationship?

Prison Cruelty

Frank Tannenbaum

Frank Tannenbaum (1893–1969) was born in Austria and immigrated to the United States in 1905. He became active in International Workers of the World, also called the Wobblies, and spent a year in prison around 1914 after a conflict with the police during a labor demonstration. After his release, he went on to attend Columbia University, graduating in 1921. He earned a PhD in economics at the Brookings Institution. He is connected to the Harlem Renaissance because of his study of race and racial violence in the South. This study, which he started during his army service, was the material for his first book, Darker Phases of the South, *published in 1924. He taught criminology at Cornell University and Latin American history at Columbia University. He published* Slave and Citizen: The Negro in the Americas *in 1947.*

The following essay, "Prison Cruelty," appeared in Atlantic Monthly *in April 1920, just a few years after Tannenbaum's release from prison.*

I.

To the uninitiated, prison cruelty seems to be a rare and isolated phenomenon. When on occasion instances of it become known and the community has its sense of decency outraged, there is generally a demand for investigation and removal of the guilty warden and keeper. With that achieved, the average citizen settles back comfortably into the old habits of life, without asking too many questions, and with the general assumption that, after all, it cannot be expected that prisons should be turned into palaces.

To him who goes into the matter more deeply, there is the added comfort, not only that the given warden has been punished for cruelty,—but that there are legal and constitutional provisions against its reappearance. Our laws provide against cruel and unusual punishments, and to the average mind, with its faith in the law, this is sufficient assurance against their repetition. These facts, added to the infrequency of the publicity, strengthen the general feeling that prison brutality is a personal matter for which particular individuals are responsible.

This is the general view. But to those who are acquainted with prison organization, brutality is a constant factor—constant as the prison itself; and the publicity which upon occasion makes it known to the public has only an accidental relation to the thing itself. It is some fortunate approach on the part of an inmate to the publicity forces in the community, or some accidental trial, such as brought before the public the current charges against Bedford, which makes it evident that brutality exists in a particular institution. It is obvious, of course, that, had it not been for the trial at which the charges of brutality at Bedford were brought in as a part of the court procedure, brutality might have existed for a long period of time without general public knowledge. I am stressing this point because it helps to carry the important fact that cruelty in prison and publicity out it are not closely related.

Historically, cruelty has always marked prison administration. We have records of brutality in prisons stretching over all written history, and including practically every nation of which we have written records. Prison brutality is both continuous and universal. Publicity, public indignation, investigation, removal of officials, and the institution of reform methods have, up to the present time, been ineffective in eliminating brutality from prison administration.

A prison is primarily a grouping of human beings involving problems of cooperation and discipline. As such, it gives room for the play of all the various emotions and instincts common to man in any other grouping. There is, however, one striking difference. This difference is that the man in the prison, just because he is shut out and away from the world, is forced, so to speak, to become a closer neighbor to himself, and therefore exhibits most of the instincts and passions, the loves and hates, the boldness and the fear, common to men, but in a more intense, more direct, and less concealed way. A prison is, in a sense, the greatest laboratory of human psychology that can be found. It compels men to live social lives—for man lives primarily by being social—under unsocial conditions, and it therefore strains to the breaking point those things that come naturally to people in a free environment. The fact that men are more sensitive, more self-conscious, more suspicious, more intensely filled with craving, more passionately devoted in hate and in love, just because most of these emotions are expressed in idea rather than in fact,—makes the prison a grouping of men requiring very delicate and sympathetic treatment. This is the general background which must be taken into consideration in the discussion of prison administration, and in any analysis of the forces that lead toward prison brutality. Like every human grouping, the prison group is complex, and all that one may hope to do in an analysis is to describe what seem the most important elements in the situation.

II.

Our approach to the criminal is the first element in any consideration of prison brutality. It is obvious that somehow or other our feeling about the criminal is different from our feeling about other members of the community. We feel differently about him because we are under the impression, that he is a being distinctly different from ourselves. Just why he is different, or just in what degree he is different, or whether the difference is really one that is basic in the man himself rather than in our assumption about the man, does not concern the average person. We know that he is different. This belief is common to most people, and, in general, it is shared by officials concerned with prison administration.

The elements that go to the making of this attitude may broadly be described in the following terms. The first apparent fact is that we do not ordinarily distinguish between the thing a man has done and the man himself. We tend to translate a single isolated act into a whole being, forgetting all of the man's past, with its innumerable unrecorded emotions and deeds. We make the crime and the man synonymous. In common parlance we say that the man who has stolen is a thief, and the man who has committed murder is a murderer, summarizing all of the man in terms of the single fact with which we are impressed. We thus seem to transfuse the one act which we do not like into all of the man, who may, apart from that one act, be a very lovable person, and we place him in a category distinctly outside the pale of common association and consideration. He is different. Not only different, but he is worse. Any treatment which would seem unfair and unjust for people "like ourselves" seems, even to the best of us, less unfair, less unjust, for him whom we have classified as different from and worse than ourselves.

To this, may be added three other and closely related influences which tend to strengthen the feeling of difference, and to justify methods of approach which are not in common use for people not so classified. The first of these three influences is undoubtedly the feeling that the man who is in himself bad is socially undesirable. A criminal is not only a bad man in moral evaluation, but he is a bad man socially. He is not fit, to put it in colloquial terms, to associate with other people better than himself, because he may make them bad; or, in other words, he is felt to be unsocial and deserving of some method of exclusion from the community of "good" people who may suffer from contamination if he is let loose.

The second, and, to some people, a very important consideration is the fact that a man who is a criminal is not only bad, not only unsocial, but also a man who has broken the law. This may not only involve a very strong emotional reaction for people to whom the law generally is a rather vague and sacred summary of all things forbidden, but it is undoubtedly a forceful fact in the life and the emotional reactions of officials, whose habitual business is centered about the enforcement of the law. A crime to them may, in fact, primarily be a violation of the law. In other words, apart from any "badness" or "unsociability" in the official immediately concerned, the breaking of the law may in itself create an emotional bias sufficient to carry a condemnation which, to ordinary people, is carried by "badness" and "social undesirability."

There is yet a third element, which, in a measure differing in different groups, contributes materially to the general conviction that the criminal is a sinful and vicious person. I refer to the general confusion in the minds of religious people between crime and sin. While not all crimes are considered sins, and not all sins are recognized as crimes, yet for most purposes there is a sufficient overlapping to add the flavor of sin and its consequences to the act of the criminal.

A criminal, to the ordinary person, is thus bad, unsocial, a violator of law, and a sinner as well. Provision is made in these four categories for the possibility of condemnation by almost every member of the community.

I have placed these considerations first, not because they are first in importance, but because they tend to define the approach toward the criminal, on the part of the officials who are to care for him during the period of punishment, expiation, or reform, or whatever you choose to consider the purpose of confinement. I say the purpose of confinement, because in ordinary criminal procedure confinement comes first and is the basis for punishment or reform.

III.

The function of the prison is to keep the men confined. The function of the warden is to make sure that the purpose of the prison is fulfilled. He is primarily a jailer. That is his business. Reform, punishment, expiation for sin—these are social policies determined by social motives of which he, as jailer, becomes the agent. He is a jailer first; a reformer, a guardian, a disciplinarian, or anything else, second. Anyone who has been in prison, or who knows the prison regime, through personal contact, will corroborate this fact. The whole administrative organization of the jail is centered on keeping the men inside the walls. Men in prison are always counted. They are counted morning, noon and night. They are counted when they rise, when they eat, when they work, and when they sleep. Like a miser hovering over his jingling coins, the warden and the keepers are constantly on edge about the safety of their charges—a safety of numbers first, of well-being afterwards.

This leads to some very important consequences. It is the core of the development of prison brutality. It feeding basis upon which a number of other important elements tending in the direction of brutality depend [sic]. The warden is human. Being human, he is strongly inclined to follow the path of least resistance. And the path of least resistance, in the light of the ordinary understanding of a prison warden, is to make jail-breaking hard, by making the individual prisoner helpless.

One of the ways of making it easy for the warden to keep the prisoner safely, is to prevent all possibilities of collusion among the criminals. He knows them to be dangerous and bad men, whose interests are diametrically an opposed to his. They are interested in freedom. He is interested in keeping them confined. Collusion is the greatest danger to the warden's programme. Collusion may be the means toward escape—this is the great fear of the warden. So he does what administrative interests direct under the circumstances. He attempts to isolate the individual from the group. It is easier to deal with one individual criminal than with a whole prison of criminals. And so the warden tries to achieve all the benefits of isolation, of solitary confinement, in fact, if not in form.

That this is the warden's purpose is made evident by a consideration of the facts. At Blackwell's Island, for instance, we were not allowed to have pencils or paper or thread in our cells, because these might become the instruments of communication with other prisoners. The rule of silence is another illustration of the general insistence upon isolation for the individual prisoner. I am not forgetting that isolation was at one time considered a reform; that the good Quakers who introduced it were convinced of the benefits of silent communion with one's self and of meditation upon one's place and fortunes in the world. Be the cause that brought isolation into prison what it may, to the warden it is a method of administrative efficiency which has little relation to the original purpose which made isolation an ideal. But isolation, suppression, the denial of association, of communication, of friendships, are things that men cannot accept in their completeness without resistance. Men resist isolation as men resist death, because isolation, complete denial of social relations with the group, is a kind of death. It leads to a gradual disintegration of self, a distortion of the mind, and to the deterioration of all that one hold valuable in personality. Sociability becomes to the prisoner the means of sustaining a semblance of normality in an abnormal environment. It is an instinctive adjustment, and is vividly insistent just in the degree in which it is suppressed. There is no room for compromise in that issue between the warden and the prisoner. The warden wants isolation. The men must have group-life. This fact has interesting results: it makes for the growth of a definitely two-sided social organization. There is routine, discipline, the formal, methodical aspect of the prison life which centers about isolation and safety of confinement for the prisoner; and its opposite—insistent, ingenious group organization and group—life within the sphere of isolation controlled by the administrative machine in the prison.

A visitor entering the prison sees one side—the formal, stiff, and disciplinary side of the prison. The prisoner knows the other. To the visitor there exists nothing but what is apparent. And what is apparent is formality, uniformity, evenness, and lack of variation. Everything looks alike.

And everything runs by the clock, the bell, and the command of the keeper. The rest is silence. It is the disciplinarian's ideal.

But inside of this formal organization there exists a humming life—a life of ingenuity and association. Right under the eye of the authorities, in spite of all the restriction imposed, in spite of the constant watchfulness, in spite of the insistence upon isolation, the men manage to find a means and method of achieving cooperation. Anyone who has been in prison can recall a thousand ways of associating with the other prisoners. The prisoners break every rule in the prison. They talk, they communicate with each other, they exchange articles, and they even publish newspapers, in spite of all the attempts at isolation. They do it because they must. Never yet has there been a prison régime that successfully suppressed association. Not even solitary confinement does that.

In my own prison experience there are hundreds of instances which illustrate this constant violation of the rules, and the irresistible insistence upon association in some form. We were not allowed to communicate with each other, or to possess pencil or paper in our cells. But he was a poor-prisoner, indeed, who had not a little pencil and a scrap of paper hidden in some crevice of the wall. As for communication, the methods are as varied as the day. For instance, one of the boys would steal a colorless ball of thread from the shops, and when stepping into the cell for the night, would slip an end to the man behind him, and that man would pass it on until it reached the end of the gallery; thrown on the floor, drawn against the wall, and tied inside a cell at each end of the gallery, it would serve as a successful means of communication throughout the night. All one had to do was to tie a slip of paper with the cell-number to the thread and give it a few jerks, and it would be passed on until it reached the designated cell.

Another instance illustrative of the insuppressible sociability of prison life is to be found in the following personal experience. Having been placed in solitary confinement and kept there for some weeks, and being denied the right to smoke, I was regularly supplied with tobacco in spite of all rules, and in spite of all watchfulness. But more striking than this is the story of a piece of pie that was sent to my cell. One of the boys working in the keepers' mess-hall decided that I ought to have a piece of pie. Pie was served only twice a year in that prison if, on very special occasions. I had the two legal pieces of pie and one illegal piece, the piece of pie stolen from the officers' mess-hall by a prisoner. He placed it in a bag and put my cell number on it. As I was in solitary confinement and he was working outside the prison proper, the piece of pie must have traveled some three days and gone through many different hands; and yet it reached me without mishap, though in a rather dried and crushed form. As pie it tasted very good; but it tasted better still because it illustrated the intense social character that is characteristic of a prison group. It must be remembered that pie was rare to all the men, and that it would have tasted equally sweet to any one of them, and yet they passed it on without eating it.

The breaking of the rules is constant, discovery frequent, and punishment follows discovery. To the warden discovery spells lack of discipline, lack of isolation, danger of collusion. It means that there are not enough rules and that there ought to be greater strictness. It means that the danger of collusion is serious and must be prevented. It does not mean to him that there must be association. So the rules are made more numerous, the discipline stricter, and the punishment more severe upon each hatred on the part of the prison group discovery of a new violation. But to the more constant, and irritation more prisoner punishment only intensifies the need for association. Punishment takes the form of a greater isolation, of more suppression, and for the prisoner has the result of greater discontent, more bitterness, and the greater need for friendship, for communication, and the very pleasures of attempted association, in spite of opposition. This simply means that the more rules there are, the more violations there are bound to be; and the greater the number of violations, the more numerous the rules. The greater the number of violations, the more brutal the punishments; for variety of the punishments and their intensification become, in the mind the warden, the sole means of achieving the intimidation of the prisoner by which he rules.

Brutality leads to brutality. It hardens official and inmate alike, and makes it the ordinary and habitual, method of dealing with the criminal. It adds hatred to the prisoner's reaction against the individual official, and makes the individual official more fearful, more suspicious, more constantly alert, and develops in him a reaction of hatred against the prisoner, making the need for brutality the greater and its use more natural. This general consequence holds true for the whole prison. The punishment of the individual prisoner develops with in the whole prison a feeling of discontent and hatred because of the natural sympathy which the prisoners feel for one who they know to be more guilty than themselves; and particularly because solidarity of feeling is in proposition to individual physical helplessness. This adds to the tensity of the situation in the prison, adds fuel to the discontent, and makes the need for isolation in the light of the warden's disciplinary measures more justified, brutality more normal, hatred on the part of the prison group more constant, and irritation more general.

The use of brutality on the part of the warden comes as a comparatively natural process. It becomes a matter of administrative procedure and a normal expectation on the part of the prisoner. If the warden is to punish the man for violating the rules, his field of operations is very limited.

The rules being numerous, the violations corresponding to their number, the bitterness increasing with the rules and their violations, all tax the ingenuity of the prison officials in meting out punishments that will fit the crimes. The men in prison are already deprived of most of the privileges and rights which are ordinarily possessed by the free man. They cannot be taken away as punishment, for they are not there. The only thing at hand for the prison officials upon which to exercise their authority is the prisoner's flesh and bones. They cannot deprive him of his property, for stone walls do a prison make. They cannot deprive of his property. In prison most men are equally propertyless. The privileges are few, and not sufficient to satisfy the need for punishment. Nor is there that dignity and social status which among free men may be used for purposes of control. Men in prison are not sensitive about their social standing. They have a social status all their own, it is true. But this is increased by punishment; for the punishment gives the prisoner a standing and honor in a prison community which is enjoyed among free men by a martyr in a good cause. The man must be punished. And this being the situation for which procedure must find a method—the dark cell, starvation for days at a time, beating, strait-jacketing, handcuffing, hanging to a door, or lifting from the floor becomes the immediate instruments at hand. They become so through the limitation of the field of punishment. The habitual use of physical manhandling requires intensification to carry out the purpose of intimidation by which the prison authorities operate. In addition, the physical manhandling of the human body tends to develop an indifference to human suffering and a craving for the imposition of cruelty, which increases with the exercise of brutality.

This is the general setting for the development of other phases of cruelty and brutality. A prison, just because it centers on keeping the prisoner from escaping, succeeds not only in keeping the prisoner inside the walls, but in keeping the sun out. A prison is a dark, damp, and cheerless place.

IV.

The harshness, silence, twilight, discipline hold true, not only for the prisoner, but also for the keeper. The keeper, too, is a prisoner. He is there all day long, in this atmosphere of tense emotional suppression and military discipline, and, in addition, he is generally there at least two nights a week when on special duty. He is a prisoner. For him there is little beyond the exercise of power. This exercise is a means of escape and outlet, but it is not a sufficient means. It does not make the keeper a happy person. It makes him a harsh and brutal one. The keeper subjects the prisoners to military organization, but he himself is subjected to a rule. In the prison as he is all the time, in constant contact with the prisoners, of whom he sees more than his own wife and children, his contact is chiefly physical. He has no social relations with them. The military discipline [to] which he is subjected makes that a primary rule of procedure on the part of the keeper. The warden is not only afraid of collusion among the prisoners, but he is also afraid of collusion between the prisoners and the keepers. The general rule is that a keeper must not speak to a prisoner except on strictly official business, and then the words must be few and to the point. This is the ordinary rule, and the violation of it in the more strictly disciplinary prisons is followed by immediate and summary punishment.

There is, however, another reason why the keeper does not associate with the prisoner. After all he is a keeper, an official, a good man (at least in his own judgment). Whereas a convict is a criminal. For his own clear conscience's sake the keeper must, and does instinctively, make a sharp distinction between himself and the man whom he guards. This distinction in the mind of the keeper is absolutely essential. It is essential because we cannot brutally impose our will upon our equals and betters. We can do it only to those whom we believe to be inferior,—different,—and not as good as ourselves. In particular, it is helpful if to this feeling there is added a personal element of hatred. It all tends to make brutality there at least two nights a week when easier and more natural.

The keeper, of course, does not know all this. He does not see that his hatred and contempt for the prisoner is a shield for his own conscience and a cover for his own morality. He believes the prisoner to be worse, just because he is a prisoner. This makes association between the prisoner and the keepers almost impossible, except as it expresses itself in dominance. The keeper succeeds in making a gap between himself and the prisoner, and the gap is filled by contempt.

But the prisoner is not at all ready to make the concession of inferiority. In fact, the prisoner feels that he is much better than the keeper and certainly as good as most other people in the community. This is the prisoner's morality. To him—and within his experience—there is room for reasonable conviction that all people are crooked, and that the chief distinction between himself and the others is that he has been caught and the rest are still to be caught. For if a man is not a thief he is a fool, or a poor "simp" like the keeper, who cannot make a living at anything except torturing better and smarter men than himself.

I say this feeling on the part of the prisoner is understandable in the light of his experiences. The people with whom he has associated, the police who have hounded him, the lawyers who have prosecuted or defended him, the courts instrumental in jailing him, and the keepers who guard him are, as he well knows, and have been on occasion, subject to proper influence— "proper" meaning safe and remunerative approach. That being the case, the prisoner is convinced, generally speaking, that his conviction and sentence are unjust and unfair; that he is in a way a martyr; that justice and decency are on his side; and that the poor ignorant and simple-minded "screw" knows nothing but brutality, is simply a person beneath his own class and worthy of nothing but contempt. The gap which the keeper fills on his side is on the other side filled to its limit by the prisoner.

It is necessary fully to understand what all this means to the keeper, and its consequence upon his mental development. Most keepers enter prison as young men, long before maturity and experience have given them that larger and more sympathetic insight and understanding which come to most men as they grow older. They become the keepers of other men when they themselves are still immature and undeveloped. They are thrown into an atmosphere that tends to stifle initiative and personal activity of any kind. They are pressed from the bottom by their charges, and from the top by their superiors. They are in a vise that stifles, cramps, and destroys all spontaneity in their being, long before it has reached its full growth. Not being free men, in the sense that men are free in their work; not being able to play and laugh and associate humanly with the people with whom they are in the most constant companionship, they are not likely to be social. The suppression and the lack of personal freedom, the monotony of their existence, the constant atmosphere of hatred, suspicion, and contempt, tend to contort, to twist, and to make bitter the attitude of the keeper toward his charges. The only relation he can have with them is that of dominance, and the only pleasure and play he can get, the only exercise of initiative at his disposal, comes through the imposition of authority. He needs pleasures, because all men need pleasures; but his pleasures become, through the prison machine, the exercise of brutality for him and pain for others.

These two elements—the exercise of authority and the resulting enjoyment of brutality—are the keynote to an understanding of the psychology of the keeper. They are both the result of the prison organization, and both feed upon suppression. The exercise of authority has a very peculiar influence on most men. It tends to make them domineering, abrupt, harsh, inconsiderate, and terribly opinionated. This is true to the nth degree in prison. In the outside world, authority is limited by the freedom of the subject. In the army, the soldier can always desert; in the factory, he can always quit his job. Both of these have obvious limitations, but they are not limitations that are absolute.

They can be overcome in despair, in anger, or in disgust. But in prison there is no escape from authority. The authority of the keeper and the warden is absolute, and the weakness and helplessness of the prisoners are absolute. What this means is that the influence of authority tends to show itself more quickly and more conspicuously and more effectively in the prison than it does in any other organized community. The influence of domination upon those who exercise power is apparently proportioned to the weakness of those on whom the power is exercised.

Let me illustrate: I remember one day a young Irish lad was brought as a keeper into our prison. He was a small, thin-faced lad of about twenty-one. He had a coat some three sizes too large for him and a cap that reached down over his eyes. When he first made his appearance inside the walls, standing beside a long row of marching men in gray, he made a very pitiful sight. His face was a little pale, his shoulders stooping, his coat slipping down (because it was too large), his feet drawn together, a club hanging limply between the legs, his head down, his eyes on the ground. He seemed very much frightened, indeed, apparently fearing that these terrible men in gray would jump at him and bite him. But in time, as the boys who marched by smiled rather humorously at his obviously frightened appearance, he began to straighten out, to raise his eyes, to move his cap slightly upward. This change of appearance was visible from day to day. The cap moved just a little higher and he raised his eyes a little farther off the ground, his feet were a little more apart, his shoulder's a little straighter, and his limp club began to swing a little more everyday.

In two months young Kelly was a new man. He strutted like a peacock in his morning glory. His shy, rather frightened expression had been replaced by a harsh, domineering, rather cynical one, with just a little curl of the lower lip to the right of his mouth. He became the worst guard we had in prison. He was the youngest guard we had there. They all become a little more cautious when they become older, because they find that a prisoner may on rare occasions have a "come back"; but it takes time to learn that, and Kelly had not learned it. He became the most hated man in prison, and actually drove a gang under his charge into mutiny, so that they nearly killed him. After that Kelly was a little more cautious. He exercised his brutality on the isolated individual and was more circumspect with the group.

I have gone to this length to describe a change which took place in that boy, because I am convinced, both from observation and from what I know of prisons, that this is a fairly characteristic consequence due to the exercise of dominance within prison walls.

V.

The prisoner gets some pleasure trying to beat the rules of the game laid down by the prison administration. These facts, combined with the morbid lonesomeness of an isolated prison community, with the intensity of the atmosphere, make the need for excitement a physical craving, at least, for some of the guards. There is thus a passion developed for cruelty in prison on the part of the keeper, which is unmistakable, and for which testimony is to be found in almost every prison memoir and the report of almost every investigation of prison cruelty. Nothing can explain the ingenious tortures, the readiness and almost the pleasure with which they are inflicted, except a strong desire in terms of emotion (rather than reasonable conviction of their utility) for their imposition. Hanging people by their wrists, handcuffing them to their doors, making them wear head-cages chained around the neck, beating them with clubs and doing other brutal things cannot be explained in terms of discipline or its effectiveness. This seems especially true when the evidence of brutality is set against the psychology of the man who has been a practitioner of that type of brutality for many years. Let me describe one in stance of what was, undoubtedly, cruelty of this particular type.

In the "cooler" of Blackwell's Island we had a keeper whose business it was to look after the men in that particular place. He was a tall, lanky, slim, pale-faced person, with a bald head, except for the fringe of yellow hair hanging loosely down the back of his head. His general name in the prison was "String Beans," because he looked like a string bean—long, lean, and crooked, except that he was yellow rather than green. His special name, the name given him by the boys in the cooler, was the "Chippie Chaser." He had a very long face, with a mouth that hung down and had no teeth in it, and eyes that were inside of his head, just a little green and rather small. He looked, as a matter of fact, the nearest thing to a copy of the proverbial devil, or what might have passed for his assistant, that I have seen outside of a picture book.

I do not want to be unkind to the Chippie Chaser. He had been a keeper for twenty years; practically his whole life had been passed in looking after men in their weakest and in their most brutal moments. He had been, for a long time, in charge of the confinement of the men in the cooler, or in the dark cell, before the cooler took its place, and his contact with the men was in their most helpless and least interesting moments. Confined in this little room of twenty-eight cells, locked away from the rest of the prison, his was a very dull and monotonous life. I was there fourteen days as a prisoner, but he had been there for many years as a keeper, and it is not the place where a man can keep his senses in a normal state over a long period of time. Men are put in the cooler for special discipline, and in this particular case the discipline took the form of depriving us of our beds, our clothing (except pyjamas), our food, except two slices of bread and a gill of water every twenty-four hours, and of keeping us there until we were broken in spirit or succumbed to the gnawings and deterioration of a hungering body. It was his business to care for us and those like us who had been there before throughout the years. It was not a pleasant job and it did not tend to make a pleasant man.

We called him the "Chippie Chaser" because he used to chase the little birds off the window that would occasionally come there with early morning and chirp a morning song. To a man in the cooler, hungry and unwashed, with a broken body and a sick, melancholy soul, a cheering note from a little bird was a very pleasant sound. It used to refresh and lighten our burden. He knew it. That is why he chased the birds away. We knew that was why he did it, and we cursed him. But the more we cursed, the happier he seemed to be. He had developed a desire, apparently, to make us curse, to make us suffer, to exasperate us, if he could. If the bird did not provide the occasion, he would find other means to provoke us. He would stand down there on the floor and look up at us on the galleries, each one of us standing against the barred door, straining our necks to look out, and he would call us every name that he could think of. He would say things to us that cannot be said anywhere but inside a prison, where men are locked safely behind their bars. He knew a great many vile names—he had spent many years in an atmosphere where adjectives of human disrepute were a specialty. And we would say them back. But we who were hungry and weak would soon tire of this game, and, leaving the honors to him, would retire to our corners exhausted.

At times, however, not having had enough excitement, he would take a pail of cold water and spill it into the cell of one of the boys. It must be remembered that we slept on the floors, that for greater comfort the floors were hilly and the water would not all run out, that the windows were kept open, and that it was cool at night. A pail of water did not tend to add to the comfort of the situation. We responded in the only way we could—by exasperation. We howled and screeched, gritted our teeth, grabbed our buckets and slammed them against the doors, raising a desperate, maddening sound, that must have been heard in heaven. And he, standing down there looking up at the galleries where the men were foaming at the mouth with exasperation, would rub his hands, open his toothless mouth, and shout above the din of the banging buckets against the iron doors, "This is hell and I am the devil."

I take it, of course, that this is probably an unusual example of cruelty. But if it is different, it is different only in degree and not in kind from other types of prison cruelty. Prison organization, being what it is, leads to cruelty, and the cruelty tends to vary in form and particular emphasis with the special person who exercises it.

It must be remembered that to all of this there is to be added the fact that men who live in small cells, on poor food, without sufficient exercise or air, without the soothing influence of wife or family, in an atmosphere of suppression and extreme self-consciousness, become weak and sensitive. They tend to exaggerate the importance of little things, their nerves are on edge, and their response to imposition, even of the slightest degree, is likely to be disproportionately intense. All this only goes to make each little rule, which seems unimportant and of no consequence to an outsider, a heavy and unsupportable burden to the prisoner.

VI.

There is at least one more element to be considered in the discussion of prison cruelty: the relation of the well-intentioned warden to this whole scheme of rule and discipline. The better intentioned the warden is, the more likely is he to become cruel, if he maintains the old prison organization. He generally comes into prison a comparatively ignorant man in so far as the real significance of prison organization is concerned. He knows very little about the actual workings and consequence of the prison régime. He comes, generally, with the same attitude toward the prisoner that is characteristic of most people. The men are bad and he is going to reform them. Not understanding the vicious circle of prison isolation and its results, he assumes that reform consists in the changing of a few of the more stupid rules, and that in doing so he will have laid the basis of complete regeneration of the prisoner.

But this is, of course, an idle dream. The prison cannot be changed as long as the old basis of suppression and isolation is maintained; and he finds to his dismay that the men do not reform; in spite of his good intentions, the men continue breaking the rules. He does not know that they must break them, so he thinks they break them because they are bad. He is a conscientious person. He means well by the community. He is outraged at a lack of gratitude on the part of the men. He becomes convinced that there are a few men who are incorrigibles, and that these few must be made a lesson of for the greater benefit of the rest. So he falls back into the older ways. Were he an indifferent man instead of a reformer, he would let things go their way and not be oversensitive about them; but just because he is sensitive, just because his intentions are good, just because he means well, he has a tendency to lose his temper, to damn the fellow who would take advantage, as he puts it, of his own good nature, and his cruelty rises with his good intentions. I do not say reflection is cruel; all I say is that he means well and his cruelty is only an indirect reflection of his good intentions.

This point may seem strange, because good intentions are in themselves held, as a general rule, in such high esteem. In prison organization, however, what is important in the consideration of cruelty and its development is the fact that the old prison system exists in terms of suppression and isolation of the individual and in a denial of a social existence; and just so long as this is the major fact in prison administration, just so long is cruelty inevitable, and just so long can the cruelty phenomenon not be eliminated by a few changes in rules and regulations.

The chief merit, from this point of view, of Thomas Mott Osborne's work lies in the fact that the emphasis, instead of being upon isolation, is upon sociability; that through self-government the men are given an ever-increasing degree of interrelationship and communication, association, group problems and esprit de corps. This, simply means that the prime cause of the development of the cruelty phenomenon ceases to operate, because isolation from the group ceases, and the less isolation and suppression, the less hatred, bitterness, lonesomeness, morbid self-consciousness, and moodiness; the less pressure there is upon the individual to escape, and therefore the less need there is for isolation. Just as isolation works in a vicious circle leading on to greater isolation and to more cruelty and more isolation, so its reverse leads to a lessening of the pressure upon the individual; the more sociability, the less need for cruelty and the resulting greater sociability.

I do not want at present to go into an analysis of the results upon the individual of social organization in prison. It must, however, be obvious that its first consequence is to eliminate the greater part of the evil results of the old system, to make those non-existent; and secondly, it tends to introduce a new set of consequences which emphasize the social aspects of human life, which develop initiative, self-restraint, cooperation, powers of group-activity, and all the characteristics that come from freedom of participation in the activities of the group. It brings new problems and new evils, but they are the problems and the evils of association and not those of isolation. And these new problems are the problems of democracy, and their control is to be found in the methods of democracy. Just as the old system tends to desocialize and to distort the prisoner, this new system of social organization tends to socialize the unsocial criminal, and to develop the undeveloped mind of the man who has lived—as many prisoners have—a very one-sided and incomplete life.

QUESTIONS FOR DISCUSSION AND WRITING

1. What does the author mean when he says, "cruelty in prison and publicity out it are not closely related"?
2. Why do prisoners need "very delicate and sympathetic treatment" according to Tannenbaum?
3. Tannenbaum states that not all crimes are sins and not all sins are crimes, but there is overlap. Name some examples. Why is this overlap important to Tannenbaum's argument?
4. Tannenbaum emphasizes that counting prisoners has important consequences. What are they? What is the significance of counting prisoners, in your opinion?
5. What does Tannenbaum wish to illustrate by telling the story of the "illegal pie"? Most people would be surprised that none of the other prisoners ate the pie before it reached Tannenbaum. What does that surprise tell us about how we view prisoners?
6. Tanenbaum says, "the more rules there are, the more violations there are bound to be; and the greater the number of violations, the more numerous the rules." Can you think of examples outside of prison where this is also true? What does this tell us about rulemaking in general?
7. Describe Tannenbaum's characterization of jail keepers. What is their relationship to prisoners—in what ways are they alike, and in what ways are they different?

8. Why does the author believe that "the better intentioned the warden is, the more likely is he to become cruel"?

ON TECHNIQUE AND STYLE

1. Tannenbaum organizes his essay into parts, and uses other clear organizational strategies. Do you find his argument easy to follow? What aspects of his organization make it easier for the reader?
2. Tannenbaum can be seen to have a very straightforward, matter-of-fact style. However, he clearly favors the side of the prisoners. Give two or three examples of language that make this evident.

CULTURAL QUESTION

1. Tannenbaum is describing the situation in an American prison. Do you think the scenes he describes or the human characteristics he points out are universal? Or are they called culturally specific? Give examples to back up your argument.

From Prison Writings: My Life Is My Sun Dance

Leonard Peltier

Leonard Peltier (1944–) is a Native American activist, convicted in 1977 and sentenced to two consecutive life terms for the murders of two FBI agents. The agents died during a 1975 shoot-out on the Pine Ridge reservation. Peltier has been in prison since 1976. His guilt is disputed, and some consider him to be a political prisoner. Peltier's story is presented in Michael Apted's 1992 film Incident at Oglala. *This excerpt is taken from* Prison Writings: My Life Is My Sun Dance *(2000).*

Chapter 1

10:00 P.M. Time for the nightly lockdown and head count. The heavy metal door to my cell lets out an ominous grinding sound, then slides abruptly shut with a loud clang. I hear other doors clanging almost simultaneously down the cellblock. The walls reverberate, as do my nerves. Even though I know it's about to happen, at the sudden noise my skin jumps. I'm always on edge in here, always nervous, always apprehensive. I'd be a fool not to be. You never let your guard down when you live in hell. Every sudden sound has its own terror. Every silence, too. One of those sounds—or one of those silences—could well be my last, I know. But which one? My body twitches slightly at each unexpected footfall, each slamming metal door. Will my death announce itself with a scream or do its work in silence? Will it come slowly or quickly? Does it matter? Wouldn't quick be better than slow, anyway?

A guard's shadow passes by the little rectangular window on the cell door. I hear his keys jangle, and the mindless squawking of his two-way radio. He's peering in, observing, observing. He sees me sitting here cross-legged in the half-light, hunched over on my bed, writing on this pad. I don't look up at him. I can feel his gaze passing over me, pausing, then moving on, pausing again at the sleeping form of my cellmate snoring softly in the bunk above. Now he goes by. The back of my neck creeps.

Another day ends. That's good. But now another night is beginning. And that's bad. The nights are worse. The days just happen to you. The nights you've got to imagine, to conjure up, all by yourself. They're the stuff of your own nightmares. The lights go down but they never quite go out in here. Shadows lurk everywhere. Shadows within shadows. I'm one of those shadows myself. I, Leonard Peltier. Also known in my native country of Great Turtle Island as Gwarth-ee-lass—"He Leads the People." Also known among my Sioux brethren as Tate Wikikuwa—"Wind Chases the Sun." Also known as U.S. Prisoner #89637-132.

I fold my pillow against the cinderblock wall behind me and lean back, half sitting, knees drawn up, here on my prison cot. I've put on my gray prison sweatpants and long-sleeved sweatshirt. They'll do for PJs. It's cool in here this late winter night. There's a shiver in the air. The metal and cinderblock walls and tile floors radiate a perpetual chill this time of year.

Old-timers will tell you how they used to get thrown, buck naked in winter, into the steel-walled, steel-floored Hole without even so much as a cot or a blanket to keep them warm; they had to crouch on their knees and elbows to minimize contact with the warmth-draining steel floor. Today you generally get clothes and a cot and blanket—though not much else. The Hole—with which I've become well acquainted at several federal institutions these past twenty-three years, having become something of an old-timer myself—remains, in my experience, one of the most inhuman of tortures. A psychological hell. Thankfully, I'm out of there right now.

I'm also out of the heat that used to afflict us until they finally installed air-conditioning in the cellblock about ten years back. Before that Leavenworth was infamous as the Hot House, because there was no air-conditioning here, just big wall-mounted fans that, during the mind-numbing heat of a Kansas hundred-degree summer day, blew the heavy, sluggish, unbreathable air at you like a welding torch, at times literally drying the sweat on your forehead before it could form, particularly on the stifling upper tiers of the five-tier cellblock.

But we still have the noise, always the noise. I suppose the outside world is noisy most of the time, too, but in here every sound is magnified in your mind. The ventilation system roars and rumbles and hisses. Nameless clanks and creakings, flushings and gurglings sound within the walls. Buzzers and bells grate at your nerves. Disembodied, often unintelligible voices drone and squawk on loudspeakers. Steel doors are forever grinding and slamming, then grinding and slamming again. There's an ever-present background chorus of shouts and yells and calls, demented babblings, crazed screams, ghostlike laughter. Maybe one day you realize one of those voices is your own, and then you really begin to worry.

From time to time they move you around from one cell to another, and that's always a big deal in your life. Your cell is just about all you've got, your only refuge. Like an animal's cage, it's your home—a home that would make anyone envy the homeless. Different cellblocks in this ancient penitentiary have different kinds of cells, some barred, some—like the one I'm currently in—a five-and-a-half-by-nine-foot cinder-block closet with a steel door. There's a toilet and sink, a double bunk bed, a couple of low wall-mounted steel cabinets that provide a makeshift and always cluttered desktop.

Right now they've put another inmate in here with me after I'd gotten used to being blissfully alone for some time. He's got the upper bunk and his inert, snoring form sags down nearly to my head as I try to half sit in here with this legal pad on my lap. At least I get the lower bunk because of the bad knee I've had for years. I presume that they put my new cellmate in here with me as a form of punishment—a punishment for both of us, I suppose—though for what, neither he nor I have the slightest idea.

The first thing you have to understand in here is that you never understand anything in here. For sure, they don't want you ever to get comfortable. Nor do they ever want you to have a sense of security. And, for sure, you don't. Security's the one thing you never get in a maximum-security prison.

Now, on this chilly night, I toss the rough green army blanket over my knees, and drape a hand towel over the back of my neck to keep the chill off. I keep my socks on under the sheets, at least until I finally go to sleep. On this yellow legal pad purchased at the prison commissary I scrawl as best I can with a pencil stub that somebody's been chewing on. I can barely make out my own handwriting in the semidarkness, but no matter.

I don't know if anyone will ever read this. Maybe someone will. If so, that someone can only be you. I try to imagine who you might be and where you might be reading this. Are you comfortable? Do you feel secure? Let me write these words to you, then, personally. I greet you, my friend. Thanks for your time and attention, even your curiosity. Welcome to my world. Welcome to my iron lodge. Welcome to Leavenworth.

Chapter 2

I have decided the time has come for me to write, to set forth in words my personal testament—not because I'm planning to die, but because I'm planning to live.

This is the twenty-third year of my imprisonment for a crime I did not commit. I'm now just over fifty-four years old. I've been in here since I was thirty-one. I've been told I must live two lifetimes plus seven years before I get out of prison on my scheduled release date in the year 2041. By then I'll be ninety-seven. I don't think I'll make it.

My life is an extended agony. I feel like I've lived a hundred lifetimes in prison already. And maybe I have. But I'm prepared to live thousands more on behalf of my people. If my imprisonment does nothing more than edu-cate an unknowing and uncaring public about the terrible conditions Native Americans and all indigenous people around the world continue to endure, then my suffering has had—and continues to have—a purpose. My people's struggle to survive inspires my own struggle to survive. Each of us must be a survivor.

I know this. My life has a meaning. I refuse to believe that this existence, our time on Mother Earth, is meaningless. I believe that the Creator, Wakan Tanka, has shaped each of our lives for a reason. I don't know what that rea-son is. Maybe I'll never know. But you don't have to know the meaning of life to know that life has a meaning.

I acknowledge my inadequacies as a spokesman. I acknowledge my many imperfections as a human being. And yet, as the Elders taught me, speaking out is my first duty, my first obligation to myself and to my people. To speak your mind and heart is Indian Way.

This book is not a plea or a justification. Neither is it an explanation or an apology for the events that overtook my life and many other lives in 1975 and made me unwittingly—and, yes, even unwillingly—a symbol, a focus for the sufferings of my people. But *all* of my people are suffering, so I'm in no way special in that regard.

You must understand. . . . I am ordinary. Painfully ordinary. This isn't modesty. This is fact. Maybe you're ordinary, too. If so, I honor your ordinari-ness, your humanness, your spirituality. I hope you will honor mine. That ordi-nariness is our bond, you and I. We are ordinary. We are human. The Creator made us this way. Imperfect. Inadequate. Ordinary.

Be thankful you weren't cursed with perfection. If you were perfect, there'd be nothing for you to achieve with your life. Imperfection is the source of every action. This is both our curse and our blessing as human beings. Our very imperfection makes a holy life possible.

We're not supposed to be perfect. We're supposed to be *useful.*

I realize that I can be moody. That's about all you have left here in prison, your moods. They can gyrate wildly, uncontrollably. You'll find many of those moods in these pages, ranging from near despair to soaring hope, from chok-ing inner rage to everyman's fear and self-doubt. A mood can be overpower-ing, especially on those days when the endless privations and frustrations of prison life build and build inside me.

And yet, more and more in recent years, I feel detached from it all and strangely free, even within these enclosing walls and razor wire. I credit that to Sun Dance. A man who has Sun Danced has a special compact with Pain. And he'll be hard to break.

Sun Dance makes me strong. Sun Dance takes place inside of me, not outside of me. I pierce the flesh of my being. I offer my flesh to the Great Spirit, the Great Mystery, Wakan Tanka. To give your flesh to Spirit is to give your life. And what you have given you can no longer lose. Sun Dance is our religion, our strength. We take great pride in that strength, which enables us to resist pain, torture, any trial rather than betray the People. That's why, in the past, when the enemy tortured us with knives, bullwhips, even fire, we were able to withstand the pain. That strength still exists among us.

When you give your flesh, when you're pierced in Sun Dance, you feel every bit of that pain, every iota. Not one jot is spared you. And yet there is a separation, a detachment, a greater mind that you become part of, so that you both feel the pain and see yourself feeling the pain. And then, somehow, the pain becomes contained, limited. As the white-hot sun pours molten through your eyes into your inner being, as the skewers implanted in your chest pull and yank and rip at your screaming flesh, a strange and powerful lucidity gradually expands within your mind. The pain explodes into a bright white light, into revelation. You are given a wordless vision of what it is to be in touch with all Being and all beings.

And for the rest of your life, once you have made that sacrifice of your flesh to the Great Mystery, you will never forget that greater reality of which we are each an intimate and essential part and which holds each of us in an embrace as loving as a mother's arms. Every time a pin pricks your finger from then on, that little pain will be but a tiny reminder of that larger pain and of the still greater reality that exists within each of us, an infinite realm beyond reach of all pain. There even the most pitiable prisoner can find solace.

So Sun Dance made even prison life sustainable for me.

I am undestroyed.

My life is my Sun Dance.

QUESTIONS FOR DISCUSSION AND WRITING

1. Explain how Sun Dance has made prison life bearable to Peltier, according to his writing.
2. What do you think Peltier's goals are in writing this memoir?
3. Find two or three instances where Peltier shows the level of control that the prison system has over prisoners' lives. To what extent do you think these elements of control are necessary or unnecessary?
4. What does Peltier mean by not being "cursed with perfection"? Why is this concept important to him?

ON TECHNIQUE AND STYLE

1. Like Orwell, Peltier uses irony in his writing. Find examples of irony. Are they effective? How are they different from Orwell's use?
2. Peltier addresses the reader directly in Chapter 1 of this selection. What effect does this have on you as a reader?
3. How would you characterize Peltier's writing style? What words come to mind in this description? Why? Find passages in the writing to support your answer.
4. How does Peltier use description to draw the reader into his world? Is it effectively done, in your opinion?

CULTURAL QUESTION

1. Peltier introduces the reader to the "Indian Way." How does he characterize this? In what ways is it similar to other religious or cultural beliefs with which you are familiar?

FICTION

From The House of the Dead

Fyodor Dostoevsky

Fyodor Mikhailovich Dostoevsky (1821–1881) is considered to be among the greatest of Russian writers. His writing often features characters living in poor conditions with desperate and extreme states of mind. Dostoevsky's understanding of human psychology, as well as his analyses of the political and social conditions of the Russia, are shown in the complexity of his characters. He is sometimes considered to be a founder of existentialism, most notably for Notes from Underground *(1864). His other major works include* Crime and Punishment *(1866),* The Idiot *(1868), and* The Brothers Karamazov *(1880). The following is an excerpt from* House of the Dead, *published in 1862. David McGuff, Trans. Harmondsworth: Penguin, 1985.*

1.

Our prison stood at the edge of the fortress, right next to the ramparts. You would sometimes take a look at God's world through the cracks in the fence: surely there must be something to be seen?—and all you would

see would be a corner of sky and the high earthen ramparts, overgrown
with weeds, and on the ramparts the sentries pacing up and down, day
and night; and then you would think that whole years would go by, and you
would still come to look through the cracks in the fence and would see the
same ramparts, the same sentries and the same little corner of sky, not
the sky that stood above the prison, but another, distant and free. Imagine
a large courtyard, two hundred yards long and a hundred and fifty yards
wide, completely enclosed all round by a high stockade in the form of an
irregular hexagon, that is a fence of high posts (pales), driven vertically
deep into the earth, wedged closely against one another in ribs, strength-
ened by cross-planks and sharpened on top: this was the outer enclosure
of the prison. In one of the sides of the enclosure a sturdily constructed
gate was set; this was always kept closed and was guarded by sentries at
every hour of the day and night; it was opened on demand, in order to let
men out to work. Beyond the gate was the bright world of freedom where
people lived like everyone else. But to those on this side of the enclosure
that world seemed like some unattainable fairyland. Here was our own
world, unlike anything else; here were our own laws, our own dress, our
own manners and customs, here was the house of the living dead, a life like
none other upon earth, and people who were special, set apart. It is this
special corner that I am setting out to describe.

    As you enter the enclosure, you see several buildings inside it. On both
sides of a broad inner courtyard stretch two long, single-storeyed buildings with wooden frames. These are the barracks. Here the convicts live,
quartered according to the categories they belong to. Then, in the interior
of the enclosure, there is another similar wooden-framed building: this is
the kitchen, divided into two artels; further on there is another structure
where cellars, granaries and storage sheds of various kinds are housed
under one roof. The middle of the courtyard is empty and consists of a
fairly large level parade ground. Here the convicts are formed into line,
head-counts and roll-calls take place in the morning, at noon and in the
evening, and sometimes at several other times of the day as well, depending on how suspicious the guards are and how quickly they can count.
All around, between the buildings, and the fence, a fairly large space is
left. Here, along the rear of the buildings, some of the prisoners, the most
unsociable and gloomy ones, like to walk in their non-working hours, concealed from the eyes of everyone, and think their own private thoughts.
Meeting them in the course of these walks, I used to like to look into their
sullen, branded faces and try to guess what they were thinking about.
There was one convict whose favourite occupation in his free time was
counting the pales of the fence. Of these there were about one and a half
thousand, and he knew each of them individually, had counted each one.
Each pale signified a day for him; every day he marked off one of them and
in this way, from the number of pales that still remained to be counted,
he could see how many days he still had to serve in the prison before his
term of hard labour was up. He was sincerely glad whenever he finished

a side of the hexagon. He had many years still to wait; but in prison there was time in which to learn patience. I once saw a convict who had been in prison for twenty years and was at last going out into freedom saying fare- well to his companions. There were those who could remember when he had first entered the prison, young, carefree, never having given a thought either to his crime or to the punishment he had received. He was leaving prison a grey-haired old man, with a face that was sad and morose. He went the rounds of all six of our barracks in silence. As he entered each one, he prayed to the icons and then bowed to his companions deeply, from the waist, asking them to remember him with kindness. I also remem- ber how a convict who had been a well-to-do Siberian peasant was sum- moned to the gate one evening. Six months earlier he had been given the news that his former wife had remarried, and he had been violently affected with grief. Now she herself had come to the prison, had asked to see him and had given him alms. They spoke together for a couple of min- utes, both shed a few tears, and then took leave of one another forever. I saw his face when he returned to the barracks . . . Yes, in this place you could learn patience.

When it got dark we were all taken back to the barracks, where we were locked up for the whole night. I always found it hard to come into our barrack from outside. It was a long, low unventilated room, dimly lit by tal- low candles, with a heavy suffocating smell. I do not understand now how I managed to live in it for ten years. I had three boards of the plank bed to sleep on: that was all the space I had that was mine. On this plank bed some thirty men slept in our room alone. In winter the door was locked early; there were some four hours to wait before everyone was asleep. And until then there were noise, uproar, laughter, swearing, the sound of chains, soot and fumes, shaven heads, branded faces, ragged clothes, all that is accursed and dishonoured . . . yes, man has great endurance! Man is a creature that can get used to anything, and I think that is the best defi- nition of him.

In our prison there were about two hundred and fifty men—this figure was more or less constant. Some arrived, others finished their sentences and left, others died. And what a variety of men there was! I think that each province, each zone of Russia had its representative here. There were non-Russians as well, there were even some convicts from among the mountain tribesmen of the Caucasus. They were all divided accord- ing to the degree of their crime and consequently according to the num- ber of years their sentence carried. I suppose there was no crime that did not have its representative here. The basic constituent of the prison population was civilian-category convict deportees (*ssyl'nokatorzhnyye,* or sil'no*katorzhnyye*—"heavily punished convicts"—as the men themselves mispronounced it in all innocence). These were criminals who had been completely deprived of all the rights of their status, pieces cut from society, with faces that had been branded in eternal witness to their expulsion from it. They were sentenced to hard labour for terms of from eight to twelve years and were then sent to live as settlers here and there throughout the regions of Siberia. There were also criminals of the military category; as is the custom in Russian military convict battalions, they were not deprived of the rights of their status. They were given short sentences; on the completion of these they were sent back where they had come from, to serve as soldiers in the Siberian line battalions. Many of them returned to prison almost immediately, after committing a second, serious offence, and this time their sentence would not be short, but one of twenty years. This category was known as "habitual ." But the "habituals" were still not completely deprived of all the rights of their status. Finally, there was one more category, a fairly numerous one, made up of the most serious criminals, soldiers for the most part. It was called the "special category." Criminals were sent here from all over Russia. They considered themselves prisoners for life and did not know the length of their sentences. By law they had to perform two or three times the normal number of prison duties. They were being kept in the prison pending the opening in Siberia of projects involving the heaviest penal labour. "You're doing time, but we're in for life," they used to say to the other inmates. I have heard that this category has since been abolished. What is more, the civilian category in our prison has also been abolished; and one general military convict battalion has been instituted. Of course, the prison authorities were also changed when these innovations were brought about. So I am describing bygone days, things that belong long ago in the past . . .

This all happened long ago; it all seems to me like a dream now. I remember my arrival in the prison. It was in the evening, in December. It was already getting dark; men were returning from work; they were getting ready for roll-call. At length a mustachioed NCO opened the door for me into this strange house in which I was to spend so many years, to endure sensations of which I could not have had even an approximate conception, had I not experienced them in actuality. For example, I could never have conceived how terrible and agonizing it would be not once, not even for one minute of all the ten years of my imprisonment, to be alone. At work to be constantly under guard, in the barracks to be with two hundred other convicts and not once, never once to be alone! None the less, I had to get used to this, too, whether I liked it or not.

Here there were men who had committed unpremeditated murder and those for whom it was a profession; here too there were brigands and brigand chiefs. There were petty thieves and vagrants who had been convicted of burglary with breaking and entering. There were also those about whom it was difficult to decide why they had been sent here. All the same, each of them had his own story to tell, as vague and crushing as the hangover that follows a bout of heavy drinking. In general, they did not talk much about the past, did not like telling their stories, and evidently tried not to think about what lay behind them. I even knew murderers among them who were so cheerful, so completely lacking in concern about what they had done, that one could safely bet their consciences never bothered them. But there were also gloomy ones, who practically never said a word. In general it was rare for anyone to tell the story of his life, and curiosity was unfashionable, somehow not the done thing, not the custom. Perhaps on rare occasions someone might start talking out of idleness, and someone else would listen to him in gloom and indifference. No one could say anything that was a surprise here. "We know how to read and write," they would often say with a kind of strange satisfaction. I remember that once a brigand who was drunk (it was sometimes possible to get drunk in prison) began to describe how he had knifed to death a five-year-old boy, first enticing him with a toy, then taking him to an empty shed somewhere and murdering him. The whole barrack of convicts, who up till now had been laughing at his jokes, cried out as one man, and the brigand was compelled to be silent; the men had cried out not from indignation, but because you were *not allowed* to talk *about this kind of thing,* because it was *not done* to talk *about this kind of thing.* I will observe in passing that these men really did "know how to read and write," and this not in any figurative sense but in a quite literal one. It is probable that over half of them were literate. In what other place where ordinary Russians are gathered together in large numbers would you be able to find a group of two hundred and fifty men, half of whom could read and write? I have since heard that someone has deduced from similar evidence that literacy is harmful to the common people. This is a mistake: causes of quite another kind are involved here, although it cannot be denied that literacy does develop the common people's self-sufficiency. But this is surely not a fault. Each category of convicts was distinguished by the clothes it wore: the jackets of some were half dark brown and half grey, as were their trousers—one leg grey, the other dark brown. Once, at work, a girl selling kalatches[1] came up to the convicts, looked at me for a long time and then suddenly burst out laughing. "Well, isn't that the limit," she cried. "There wasn't enough grey cloth to go round, and there wasn't enough of the black stuff neither." There were also those whose jackets were all of grey cloth, with only the sleeves made of dark brown. The convicts' heads were also shaven in different ways: some had half their heads shaven lengthwise along their skulls, while others had them shaven crosswise.

You could discern at first glance one single glaring characteristic that was common to all this strange family: even the strongest, most original personalities who dominated the others without trying, even they attempted to fit in with the general tone of the prison. Generally speaking, all these men—with the exception of a few indefatigably cheerful souls whose good humour made them the object of general scorn—were sullen, curious, terribly vain, boastful, quick to take offence and preoccupied in the highest degree with good form. The ability not to be surprised by anything was considered the greatest virtue. They were all madly obsessed with the question of outward behaviour. But

[1] *Kalatches:* White bread rolls.

quite often the most arrogant manner would be replaced with the swiftness of lightning by the most craven one. There were a few genuinely strong individuals; they were straightforward and did not give themselves airs. But it was strange: some of these truly strong characters were vain to the utmost degree, almost to the point of insanity. In general vanity and outward appearance were what mattered first and foremost. The majority of these men were depraved and hopelessly corrupt. The scandals and gossip never ceased: this was a hell, a dark night of the soul. But no one dared to rebel against the endogenous and accepted rules of the prison; everyone submitted to them. There were violently unusual characters who submitted with difficulty and effort, but submit they did, nevertheless. To the prison came men who had gone too far, had overstepped the limit when they had been free, so that in the end it was as if their crimes had not been committed by them personally, as if they had committed them without knowing why, as if in some fever or daze; often out of vanity, raised in them to an extraordinary degree. But in our prison they were soon brought to heel, in spite of the fact that some of them, before they came here, had been the terror of whole villages and towns. Looking around him, the new convict soon realized that he had come to the wrong place: that there was no one here whom he could surprise, and imperceptibly he grew resigned and fitted in with the general tone. This general tone outwardly consisted of a certain special, personal dignity with which almost every inmate of the prison was imbued. As if the status of convict, of one on whom sentence has been passed, was a kind of rank, and an honourable one at that. Not a trace of shame or repentance! Yet there was, too, a kind of outward resignation, as it were an official one, a kind of calm reasoning. "We're lost men," they would say. "We didn't know how to live our lives in freedom, so now we have to walk the green street[2] and stand in line to be counted"— "We wouldn't listen to our fathers and mothers, so now we must listen to the skin of the drum instead."—"We didn't want to sew gold thread, so now we must break stones instead." All this was said frequently, both in the form of moral exhortation and in the form of everyday proverbs and sayings, but never seriously. It was all just words. Hardly one of these men inwardly admitted his own lawlessness. If anyone who was not a convict tried to reproach one of them for his crime, berating him (although it is not in the Russian spirit to reproach a criminal), there would be no end to the oaths that would follow. And what masters of the oath they all were! They swore with finesse, with artistic skill. They had made a science of swearing; they tried to gain the upper hand not so much by means of the offensive word as they did through the offensive meaning, spirit, idea— and this in the most refined and venomous manner. Their constant quarrels developed this science among them even further. All these men worked under the threat of the stick, and were consequently idle and depraved: if they had not been depraved before they came to the prison, they became so here.

---

[2] *So now we have to walk the green street:* "Walking the green street" meant running the gauntlet in convict parlance.

They had all been gathered together here against their wills; they were all strangers to one another.

"The devil's worn out three pairs of shoes in order to get us all into one bunch," they would say of themselves; and so it was that scandals, intrigues, old-womanish slander, envy, quarrelling and malice were always to the fore in this burdensome, desperate life. No old woman would have been capable of being so old-womanish as some of these murderers were. I repeat, there were strong men among them, characters who all their lives had been used to charging at obstacles and giving orders, who were hardened and fearless. These men were automatically respected; they, for their part, although very jealous of their reputations, tried in general not to be a burden to others, avoided getting involved in empty exchanges of curses, comported themselves with unusual dignity, were reasonable and nearly always obeyed the authorities—not out of any principle of obedience, not out of a consciousness of duty, but as if they had some kind of a contract, and recognized its mutual advantages. None the less, these men were treated with caution. I remember how one of these convicts, a man of fearless and determined character, well-known to the authorities for his brutal tendencies, was once summoned to be flogged for some misdemeanour. It was a summer day, work was over. The field-officer, who was in immediate and direct control of the prison, came in person to the guardhouse, which was right by our gate, in order to witness the punishment. This Major was a kind of fatal presence for the convicts; he could reduce them to a state of trembling. He was severe to the point of insanity, "pounced on folk," as the convicts said. Most of all they feared his penetrating, lynx-like stare, from which nothing could be concealed. He could somehow see without looking. When he came into the prison he already knew what was happening at its far end. The prisoners called him "Eight-Eyes." His system was a mistaken one. By his acts of vicious fury he only increased the bitterness of men who were already bitter, and had there not been stationed above him a superintendent, a man of nobility and reason, who sometimes moderated his wild excesses, he would have caused much trouble by his method of administration. I cannot understand why he did not come to a bad end; he passed into retirement well and in good spirits, although he did have to face court proceedings.

The prisoner turned pale when his name was called. Usually he lay down under the birch in silent determination, endured his punishment without a word and got to his feet again afterwards as fresh as ever, looking coolly and philosophically at the misfortune that had overtaken him. He was none the less always treated with caution. But on this occasion he considered himself for some reason to be in the right. He turned pale, and in secret from the guards managed to shove a sharp English cobblers' knife up his sleeve. Knives, and all other sharp instruments, were strictly forbidden in the prison. Searches were frequent, unexpected and no joking matter, punishments were severe; but since it is difficult to find something on a thief's person when he is particularly determined to hide it, and since knives and sharp

instruments were a continuous necessity in the prison, they never disappeared entirely. Even if they were confiscated, new ones immediately took
their place. The entire prison rushed to the fence and looked through the
cracks with hearts that beat violently. Everyone knew that this time Petrov
would refuse to lie down and be flogged, and that the Major was done for.
But at the most decisive moment our Major got into his droshky and drove
away, entrusting the execution of the punishment to another officer. "God
has spared him!" the convicts said afterwards. As far as Petrov was concerned, he endured his punishment with the greatest of calm. His anger
evaporated with the Major's departure. A convict is obedient and submissive to a certain degree; but there is a limit beyond which one should not
go. Incidentally, there is no phenomenon more curious than these strange
outbursts of impatience and obstinacy. Often a man will suffer in patience
for several years, resign himself, endure the most savage punishments, and
then suddenly erupt over some trifle, some piece of nonsense, almost over
nothing at all. In one view, he may be termed insane; and is indeed considered so by many.

I have already said that for a period of several years I saw among
these people not the slightest trace of repentance, not one sign that their
crime weighed heavily on their conscience, and that the majority of them
consider themselves to be completely in the right. This is a fact. Of course,
vanity, bad examples, foolhardiness and false shame are the causes of
much of it. On the other hand, who can say that he has fathomed the
depths of these lost hearts and has read in them that which is hidden
from the whole world? It must surely have been possible over so many
years to have noticed something, to have caught at least some feature
of these hearts that bore witness to an inner anguish, to suffering. But
this was absent, quite definitely absent. Yet, it seems that crime cannot
be comprehended from points of view that are already given, and that its
philosophy is rather more difficult than is commonly supposed. Of course
prisons and the system of forced labour do not reform the criminal; they
only punish him and secure society against further encroachments on its
tranquillity. In the criminal, prison and the most intense penal labour serve
only to develop hatred, a thirst for forbidden pleasures and a terrible flip-
pancy. But I am firmly convinced that the famous system of solitary confinement[3] achieves only a spurious, deceptive, external goal. It sucks the
vital sap from a man, enervates his soul, weakens it, intimidates it and
then presents the withered mummy, the semi-lunatic as a model of reform
and repentance. Of course the criminal, who has rebelled against society, hates it and nearly always considers himself to be in the right and it
to be in the wrong. What is more, he has already suffered its punishment,

---

[3] *The famous system of solitary confinement:* Tsar Nicholas I had proposed the introduction of one-
man cells in Russian prisons similar to those found in London penal institutions. In 1845 a special
commission had been set up to develop and implement such a project.

and he nearly always considers that this has cleansed him and settled his account. It may be concluded from this point of view that right is indeed on the side of the criminal. But, leaving aside all partial positions, everyone will agree that there are crimes which, ever since the world began, always and everywhere, under all legal systems, have been indisputably considered as crimes, and will be considered so for as long as man is man. Only in prison have I heard stories of the most terrible, the most unnatural actions, the most monstrous slayings, told with the most irrepressible, the most childishly merry laughter. One man who had murdered his father stays particularly in my memory. He was of noble origin, had worked in government service and had been something of a prodigal son to his sixty-year-old father. His behaviour had been thoroughly dissipated, he had become embroiled in debt. His father had tried to exert a restraining influence on him, had tried to make him see reason; but the father had a house and a farm, it was suspected he had money, and—his son murdered him in order to get his hands on the inheritance. The crime was not discovered until a month later. The murderer had himself informed the police that his father had disappeared. He spent the whole of this month in the utmost debauchery. Finally, in his absence, the police discovered the body. In the farmyard, along the whole of its length, was a ditch for the draining of sewage, covered with planks. The body was found in this ditch. It was dressed and neatly arranged, the grey-haired head had been cut off and laid against the torso; under the head the murderer had placed a pillow. He had made no confession; had been stripped of his nobility and government service rank, and had been sentenced to twenty years' deportation and penal servitude. All the time I lived alongside him he was in the most excellent and cheerful frame of mind. He was an unbalanced, flippant man, unreasoning in the extreme, though by no means stupid. I never observed any particular signs of cruelty in him. The prisoners despised him, not for his crime, of which no mention was ever made, but for his silliness, for not knowing how to behave. Sometimes, in conversation, he would mention his father. Once, when he was talking to me about the healthy constitution that was hereditary in his family, he added: "*My parent* never complained of any illness to the end of his days." Such brutal lack of feeling is, of course, outrageous. It is a unique phenomenon; here there is some constitutional defect, some physical and moral abnormality which science has not yet been able to explain, not simply a question of crime. It goes without saying that at first I did not believe he had committed this crime. But men from his town, who must have known all the details of his story, told me about the whole case. The facts were so clear that it was impossible not to believe them.

The convicts once heard him crying out at night in his sleep: "Hold him, hold him! His head, cut off his head, his head!"

Nearly all the convicts talked and raved in their sleep at night. Oaths, underworld slang, knives and axes figured most prominently in their ravings.

"We're beaten men," this used to say, "we've had the insides beaten out of us, that's why we cry out at night."

The forced public labour that took place in the fortress was not an occupation but an obligation: a convict completed his assignment or worked fixed hours and then went back to the prison. The work was looked upon with hatred. Without his own, private task, to which he was devoted with all his mind and all his care, a man could not live in prison. And how indeed could all those men, who were intelligent, had lived intensely and wanted to live, had been brought forcibly together here in one herd, forcibly uprooted from society and normal life, how could they have led a normal and regular life here of their own free will? Idleness alone would have developed in them criminal tendencies of which they had hitherto had no conception. Without work and without lawful, normal possessions a man cannot live, he grows depraved, turns into an animal. And for this reason every man in the prison had, as a consequence of a natural demand and an instinct for self-preservation, his own craft and occupation. The long summer days were almost entirely filled with prison labour; in the short nights there was hardly enough time to sleep properly. But in winter, according to regulations, the convicts had to be locked into the prison as soon as it started to get dark. What were they to do during the long, tedious hours of the winter evenings? And so in spite of an official ban, almost every barrack was transformed into an enormous workshop. Work itself was not forbidden; but it was strictly forbidden to possess any implements in the prison, and without these work was impossible. But men worked on the sly, and it seemed that in some cases the authorities did not bother to inquire too closely. Many of the convicts arrived in the prison knowing no trade at all, but they learned from others and subsequently left prison as good craftsmen. Here there were bootmakers, shoemakers, tailors, carpenters, locksmiths, engravers and gilders. There was one Jew, Isay Bumshteyn, a jeweller who was also a moneylender. They all worked away and earned a few copecks. Orders for work were obtained from the town. Money is freedom in the form of coins, and so for a man who has been completely deprived of freedom it is ten times as dear. He is already half consoled by the mere sound of it jingling in his pocket, even though he may not be able to spend it. But money can be spent at any time and in any place, all the more so since forbidden fruit tastes twice as sweet. And it was even possible to get vodka in the prison. Pipes were most strictly forbidden, but all the men smoked them. Money and tobacco saved them from scurvy and other diseases. And work saved them from crime: without work the convicts would have eaten one another like spiders in a glass jar. In spite of this, both work and money were forbidden. Searches were quite often made at night, all forbidden items were confiscated, and no matter how carefully money was hidden, it was none the less sometimes found by the searchers. This is partly why it was not saved up, but soon spent on drink; and this is how there came to be vodka in the prison. After each search the offenders, in addition to being deprived of all their money and equipment, were usually severely flogged or beaten. But after each search the deficiencies were immediately made good, new equipment was brought into the prison and everything continued as before. The authorities were aware of this and the convicts did not complain about their punishment, even though this life they led resembled that of settlers on the slopes of Mount Vesuvius.

Those who did not have a skill made money by other methods. Some of these were quite original. Some men, for example, earned money by doing nothing but buying and selling secondhand goods, and sometimes personal effects were sold which it would never occur to anyone outside the walls of the prison to consider as articles for sale and purchase, or even to consider as articles at all. But the life of penal servitude was one of extreme poverty, and the convicts were men of great commercial resourcefulness. Every last scrap of cloth was prized and was used for some purpose or other. Because of the general poverty, money in the prison also possessed a value that was quite different from the value it had outside. Long and elaborate toil was remunerated with pennies. Some men practised successfully as moneylenders. Convicts who were too exhausted to work or had run out of money took their last possessions to the moneylender and received from him a few copper coins at an exorbitant rate of interest. If they did not redeem them in time, these possessions would be sold without pity or delay; moneylending was such a flourishing activity that even items of prison property which were subject to inspection were accepted as pledges, things like prison clothing, boots, shoes and the like—things that were necessary to every prisoner at every moment. But pledges like these involved another turn of events, one that was not really surprising: the man who had pledged the goods and received money for them would immediately, without further ado, go to the duty officer who was in immediate control of the prison, and report to him that public property had been pledged; the goods would be immediately confiscated back from the moneylender, without the higher authorities being informed of the matter. It is a curious fact that there were never any quarrels on this account: the moneylender would silently and sullenly hand over whatever he had to and would even make it appear as though he had been expecting something like this to happen all day. Perhaps he could not help admitting to himself that had he been in the borrower's place he would have done the same thing. And so if he sometimes did a bit of cursing after it was all over, it was without any malice, and merely to appease his conscience.

In general the convicts did a fearful amount of stealing from one another. They nearly all had their own locked boxes, in which they kept items of prison issue. This was permitted; but the boxes were no safeguard against theft. I think it may be imagined what skilful thieves we had among us. One prisoner, a man who was sincerely devoted to me (I say this without any exaggeration), stole my Bible, the only book we were permitted to have in the prison; he confessed to me the same day, not because he had repented for what he had done, but because he felt sorry for me when he saw me spend such a long time looking for it. There were men who peddled vodka and quickly grew rich. I will give a more detailed account of this trade elsewhere; it was rather remarkable. In the prison there were many convicts who had been sentenced for smuggling, and so it was not surprising that vodka was brought in, inspections and guards not-withstanding. Incidentally, smuggling is by its very nature something of a special crime. Can one believe, for example, that money and gain are of only secondary importance to a smuggler? And yet precisely this is the case. The smuggler works passionately, with a sense of vocation. He is something of a poet. He risks everything, faces terrible dangers, employs cunning, inventiveness, gets himself out of scrapes; sometimes he even acts according to some kind of inspiration. This passion is as strong as the passion for cards. In the prison I knew one convict who was outwardly of colossal proportions, but so gentle, quiet and resigned that it was impossible to imagine how he could ever have ended up in prison. He was so lacking in malice, so easy to get along with that during his entire stay in prison he never once quarrelled with anyone. But he came from the western frontier, had been sent to prison for smuggling and had of course not been able to restrain himself, but started to smuggle vodka into the prison. How many times he had been flogged for this, and how he feared the birch! And the trade in illicit vodka brought him only the most meagre returns. The only person who made any profit from the sale was the entrepreneur. The curious fellow loved his art for its own sake. He was as tearful as an old woman, and how many times after he had been flogged did he repent and swear never to smuggle again. He would sometimes master himself courageously for a whole month, but in the end he was always unable to hold out any longer . . . It was thanks to characters such as him that there was no shortage of vodka in the prison.

Finally, there was one source of income which, although it did not make the convicts rich, was none the less constant and beneficial. This was alms. The upper class of our society has no conception of how our merchants, tradesmen and all our people care for the "unfortunates." Their alms are almost continuous and nearly always take the form of bread, bread rolls and kalatches, much less often that of money. Without these gifts, in many places the lives of the convicts, especially those who are awaiting trial and who are kept under a much stricter regime than are those on whom sentence has been passed, would be too hard. The gifts are religiously divided into even shares by the convicts. If there is not enough for everyone the loaves are cut into equal portions, sometimes into as many as six pieces, and each prisoner receives his piece without fail. I remember the first time I was given money. It was shortly after my arrival in the prison. I was returning from the morning's work alone with the guard. Towards me came a mother and her daughter, a little girl of about ten, as pretty as an angel. I had already seen them once before. The mother had been a soldier's wife and had been made a widow. Her husband, a young soldier, had been under arrest and had died in the convict ward of the hospital while I was ill there. His wife and daughter had come to say goodbye to him: both had cried terribly. When she saw me, the girl blushed and whispered something to her mother who immediately stopped, fished a quarter copeck out of her bag and gave it to her daughter. The little girl came rushing after me . . . "Here, 'unfortunate,' take a copeck in the name of Christ!"[4] she cried, running out ahead of me and pressing the coin into my hand. I took her quarter copeck, and the girl returned to her mother thoroughly satisfied. I kept that quarter copeck for a long time.

QUESTIONS FOR DISCUSSION AND WRITING

1. The narrator says, "Man is a creature that can get used to anything, and I think that is the best definition of him." Do you agree with this sentiment? How does it relate to the themes of this story, and of this excerpt in general?
2. How does the narrator characterize his fellow inmates? Do you find any contradictions in these descriptions? Why do you think they are presented in this way?
3. How does the narrator characterize smugglers? Why do you think they belong to a "special class" of prisoner?
4. Why do you think the novel is called *The House of the Dead*?
5. How does the narrator characterize solitary confinement? Do you think his characterization is a realistic one? A modern one? Explain your answer.
6. Why do you think the narrator keeps "that quarter copeck for a long time"?

ON TECHNIQUE AND STYLE

1. Why do you think Dostoevsky describes in such detail the physical aspects of the prison?
2. This is a piece of fiction. Do you see any connections, however, with any of the nonfiction selections of this chapter? Give specific examples.
3. Do you find any humor in this selection? If so, find one or two passages to support this claim. If not, what tone do you find prevalent in this story?

CULTURAL QUESTION

1. This story is written about a Russian prison system in the nineteenth century. How does it ring true (or not true) in today's culture, according to what you know about the prison system? Give specific examples.

[4] *Take a copeck in the name of Christ:* This autobiographical episode is repeated by Dostoeyevsky in his novel *Crime and Punishment* (Part II, Chapter 2).

Outside Work Detail

Scott Wolven

Scott Wolven lives in upstate New York. His work has been selected three years in a row for The Best American Mystery Stories *(2002, 2003, and 2004). The following selection is taken from* Controlled Burn: Stories of Prison, Crime, and Men *(2005), his first book.*

Early that morning, the storm moved south over the dark Quebec woods, crossed into Vermont at Lake Memphremagog, the inland sea of the Northeast Kingdom, and made the shore at Newport, rattling windows in trailers and shacks, shoving woodsmoke back down their rusted stovepipes. The thunder tore through the trees, then hit the bare farm fields around Saint Johnsbury. The air inside my cell shifted from the sudden pressure, carrying the boom, and moved something deep in my chest. I woke. I lay there on the top bunk, listening to the thunder muffled by the thick concrete. My cell mate was a man named Don Wilcox. He sat on the stainless steel toilet bowl that was attached to the wall directly at the head of his bottom bunk. He was smoking a cigarette, flicking ash into the toilet between his legs.

"Coop, you up?" he asked.

"Yeah," I said. The cell was dark except for the red ember of his cigarette, moving in an arc when he flicked it.

"Some storm," he said. "Must be something, if we can hear it in here."

I nodded in the darkness. "Sounds bad," I agreed.

"I hope it doesn't scare my kids," he said. Don Wilcox was in his late thirties and had a wife and three young boys in Greenville, Vermont, about twenty miles away. They always came to Saint Johnsbury on visiting day. Wilcox had been convicted of arson. He'd burned an outbuilding on his mother's old farm in an attempt to get some insurance money after his mother died. He'd been in trouble before, years back, and the prosecution held his prior record against him. He was just beginning to serve his ten-year sentence. For the past eight months, he'd been my cell mate, my ninth in a little over sixty months at Saint J prison. I could barely see him in the dark, only the red eye of his cigarette.

"Your kids scared of thunder?" I asked.

"My middle boy is," he said. "Makes him wet the bed." The stubble on his chin raked the collar of his work shirt. "I used to yell at him when he wet the bed." He was very quiet, and I heard the thunder. "I wish I was out."

There was nothing to say to that. He talked for a while longer, stories about his kids I'd already heard, about how he hoped his wife was faithful.

I drifted off, back to sleep. When I woke up again the cell was filled with cigarette smoke. I heard the voices of other inmates in the cellblock, heading to lunch. I swung myself down to the concrete floor from the bunk and went to eat.

I stepped off the chow line carrying a lunch tray and found a seat alone, at the end of a long stainless steel table. The mess hall was full of other prisoners—sometimes Saint J holds over a thousand men, although it was built for eight hundred—all wearing street clothes, jeans and flannel shirts, because the Vermont Department of Corrections never got around to installing proper heat in any of its facilities. Winters were too cold for the customary prisoner jumpsuit, and the Vermont winter could last till May. Even beyond. The storm had stopped, and now the noise was just the usual loud voices cursing, laughing in a nasty way. As I ate my sandwich, an old con came and sat across from me. I looked up at him.

"You Ray Cooper?" he asked. His beard was a mess—gray, black, uneven—and he was almost bald. He wore a green work shirt. His lungs sounded bad. I recognized him as a trusty from being in the library, but I couldn't think of his name. A faded jailhouse tattoo, the letters FTW, were inked on the back of his left hand.

I nodded. "Yeah," I said. "So what?"

"You're bein' transferred," he whispered. The mess hall made it hard to hear him, with all the voices bouncing off the walls and ceiling. He looked around at the other prisoners and the guards by the door and leaned closer. He did it so easy. Anyone looking at him would have thought he was adjusting the seat of his pants. "I heard them say Cooper this morning, they're just waiting for the paperwork." He lowered his voice to less than a whisper, barely moving his lips, not looking at me. "Don't tell anyone, they'll stab you in the night." He smiled as another prisoner walked past looking for a seat. He breathed through his smile, through his missing teeth. "They're jealous. But you've got to try to live."

I looked at the dim sunlight coming through the windows set thirty feet above the floor and covered with screens of heavy-gauge wire. Thick, black dust covered the screens. I had just turned twenty-eight and had eighteen months to go on my eighty-four-month sentence. "When are you out?" I asked.

The old man stood, his back crooked, and held on to the table with one hand. "When I say hi to Jesus, that's when I'm out."

He shuffled away, toward the chow line and the other prisoners. He was gone when I looked up again. Vanished into the crowd. Left me to think about The Farm, the minimum-security prison run in Windsor, Vermont, by the Department of Corrections. Two hundred men were held at The Farm. There aren't many prisons in the Vermont system—two in the north, higher security Saint Albans or Saint A, as inmates called it, along with Saint J. The sex offenders were housed in Newport, and there were facilities at Rutland and Woodstock, each holding a mixed population of convicts. If prisoners managed to avoid fights and develop clean records of good time, they usually ended their terms at The Farm, which had an extensive wood shop and sawmill operation, all located on seven hundred acres of fields and surrounding hills. Only the fences and concrete cellblock buildings set it apart from the Vermont landscape. A day at The Farm counted as two and a half regular days in the bizarre math of good-time calculations, because everyone was a low-security risk and expected to go to work and go to programs. There were GED classes, anger management, AA meetings. All things that normal people did outside the fence every single day, without expecting good time in return.

That night in the cell, Wilcox was sick from bad chow. I watched him hard from then on, harder than before, but he never gave any indication he knew I was leaving. Ten years stretched out in front of him and filled whatever part of his mind wasn't devoted to his boys. Sometimes I doubt that he even knew I was in the cell with him.

The paperwork came at the end of July, and they transferred me south in an unmarked, four-door Jeep on the last Friday of the month. I didn't say a word the whole ride down out of the Northeast Kingdom—just sat cuffed on the rear seat, sweating from the sun. Watching the trees and country and what I could see of the sky pass by the shatterproof windows. We pulled up to the entrance guardhouse at dinnertime, but I was held in the sergeant's office for in-processing, shackled and cuffed to a steel ring welded to a metal desk.

It was humid and hot that August, with hundred-degree days coming one on top of another. Every night I stood at the window of my new cell and watched heat lightning flash over the fields and high fences of the facility. The Farm itself was surrounded by a five-foot-high barbed wire fence, topped with razor wire. The short fence was old, a reminder of a less violent time. A dirt road ran around the outbuildings and prison dormitory, allowing the guards to ride patrols between the outside, shorter fence and the new inner, electrified fence. The inner fence was twenty feet high, crowned with two strands of razor wire. The last six feet of the fence were angled inward, making it difficult to climb from the inside, and the razor wire was set at such a pitch that scaling it from the outside required a professional level of skill and tools that no average person would ever possess. Full voltage ran through the fence wire, and the hum filled the facility, as if an angry swarm of bees was floating in the woods, waiting.

I wasn't an innocent man. When I was seventeen, I was set up by an informant during a pot buy. I did three years and got out. A year later, I smashed a truck window one night near Essex Junction, Vermont, and took a large briefcase I saw resting on the front passenger's seat. I was drunk, not that drunkenness makes such things okay. I opened the case with an acetylene torch and they took me into custody three hours later, but for those three hours, I was in control of the contents of that briefcase, which happened to belong to an investigator for the Vermont State Police, who kept four pistols locked and loaded inside, along with some of his police identification. He wasn't on assignment that night. Parked on a back road, he was visiting his girlfriend, which was bad because he had a wife and his girlfriend had a husband. So he wasn't where he should have been and this hit the local paper and the paper in Burlington and made the state's attorney eager to put me away for causing so many problems for a law enforcement officer. I got the maximum time allowed on the illegal handgun possession, all four guns, all felonies, plus theft, breaking and entering, destruction of private property, and illegal possession of official identification, which is another felony. The list seemed to grow longer each time I appeared in court, as my public defender struggled to remember my name, once asking the judge for a continuance on behalf of his client Mark Copper and appearing surprised when his honor spoke from the bench and asked him who that was, as I sat next to him in shackles and cuffs whispering *Cooper, Ray Cooper.* My name didn't matter anymore, at that point. I was sentenced a month later, credited with the time I'd already served but bound over to serve more, my priors held against me. I stood for the maximum fall, eighty-four months.

The parole board consistently denied me parole, and after three hearings I wasn't considered again, since I was termed "close to maximum release date." The board put in the special transfer order that sent me to The Farm to serve out my time, to free up my cell in the fiercely overcrowded system.

The trooper, who remained on the force, took an active role in keeping me locked up, attending all of my parole hearings, relating the story of the guns and the pain of his divorce and the terrible part I played in it. Every time, after he had his say, he stood up in his full dress grays with medals, adjusted his Sam Browne belt, and put his black Smokey-the-Bear trooper hat over his honest crew cut. He gave a sharp nod to the old Vermonters who made up the parole board as he marched out of the room, back to his job, back to towns and situations that needed his bright justice, something I had tarnished.

I doubt the old Vermonters even saw a human when they turned back to look at me, and certainly, after the first couple of years, I began to feel less and less like someone who'd once lived down the road from them and got drunk and did something stupid. I felt like what their eyes said I was, someone who needed to be in a tiny concrete room behind high fences and armed guards and locked down but good, for as long as the locks held and longer if possible. It was probably only procedure that I was transferred to The Farm, nothing more. In their hearts, no one on that parole board wanted me one step closer to the door—one step closer to being in a grocery store in their town, one step closer to walking down Main Street.

I answered the questions they asked of me, that I planned to go live with my sister Elizabeth in Essex when I was released, and I produced an old letter from her, giving me permission to live at her house and inviting the parole board to call her if they had any questions. She had stopped visiting me after three years, and I didn't blame her. She still wrote occasionally—wrote when my grandmother died—and I was still planning on living at Elizabeth's house when this was over and that was all I could ask of anybody.

My girlfriend at the time of my arrest, Mary, used to come see me. When I first got in and Mary would arrive on visiting day, I always talked to myself in my cell, to make sure prison hadn't worked its way into my voice. *Hello, Mary,* I would say, *thanks so much for coming.* Mary had stopped visiting me after eight months. For a long time, I kept the last letter from her, explaining why she wasn't going to visit anymore, folded in a notebook. "Dear Ray," it began, "I have some hard things to say and I hope you know how difficult this is." I understood. People have lives. My sister wrote that she'd read in the paper about Mary's wedding, four years after I'd been inside. Good for Mary. Now I was at The Farm and there was an end in sight.

Fall came, and the leaves colored and died. The ground froze solid and the first of the snow came. I went to some programs and the library, but with the snow I stopped. I sat up all night watching it fall under the halogen lights that made it seem as if the sun had descended to Earth at midnight. I felt no interest in programs anymore, they weren't helping me. My days counted two and a half whether I attended or not, and I actually began to think that I might get out, and about what I would do then.

Two weeks before Christmas, a corrections officer named Walter approached me as I got on the morning chow line. Would I like an outside work detail, he asked. I said okay, since it was probably the only time I'd get out until after Christmas and I wanted to see if I could handle it outside. I went back to my cell after chow and put on my old army field jacket with Riley stitched above the left breast pocket—I always wondered who Riley was and what he'd done, to have his name stitched on the jacket and then to have it find its way to the prison laundry lost and found.

I walked to the guards' station desk, next to the outside door. Walter stood there with a guard named Frankie, who sat behind the desk, and they filled out the paperwork on me, signed me out of the facility, and popped the electronic lock on the door, sending me into the open yard and the early morning snow.

Another inmate, Russ Harper, was already outside, smoking a cigarette. I recognized him from the library and around. He was a programmer, the first one in his seat at AA, kept the best journal in anger management. He wore a green field jacket with an attached hood pulled up against the snow and small patches of West German flags on each shoulder. We started to walk through the snow toward the back field, following a set of tire tracks. Russ offered me a cigarette.

"No thanks," I said. The snow was coming heavier now. The facility got smaller as we walked away, one thin line of smoke coming out of a pipe on the metal roof, the screen of snow drifting down in front of the halogen lights.

"Haven't seen you much lately," he said.

"I stopped programming," I said. "Couldn't see the point." We were walking side by side on the tire tracks.

"You got denied?" he asked. It was a fair question.

"Yeah," I hedged. "I've been denied three times and I didn't think pro-gramming here was helping. I thought it was hurting. Besides, the board won't see me again."

Russ nodded, his red hair poking out from under his hood. "I under-stand," he said. "To each his own." He had moved off the tire track and was having trouble walking through the crusted snow that held powder under-neath. He stepped back on the tire track. "My mother died after I'd been in for two years, so I understand things. My father's dying now." The hood covered his face. "Cancer."

"That's too bad," I said. "I was at Saint J when my grandmother died." We walked along next to each other. "What's this work detail about?" I asked.

"Walt didn't tell you?" he said.

"No."

"Well, it's no fun," he said. A fast snap from the electric fence made him turn around, but there was nothing to see and the fence returned to its hum.

We stayed directly in the tire tracks to reach the top of a small hill that rose along the back field. Beyond it lay another long, snow-covered field, and in the rear right corner sat a blue Department of Corrections pickup truck. We started to walk down to it. The truck was parked about fifty yards from the electrified fence. Behind the truck stood another separate, fenced-in area. Square, about fifty by fifty. Cables ran out of the back of the truck into the small fenced-in area, where a generator was going. We walked down the hill, and the facility disappeared behind us. We stumbled a little in the snow, try-ing to stay in the tire tracks. For the first time, I felt the cold biting my face. I could see my breath. The hum of the electrified fence was constant. The ground angled slightly to the fence, then there was the guard road, the low fence, and the woods. I realized the area inside the small square fence was the prison cemetery.

Reb Phillips sat on the open tailgate of the truck, smoking a joint. He made no move to share it with us. The army field jacket he wore bulged at the arms and around his thick chest. A black ski cap came down around his ears. He laughed as we came up. Reb was the outside trusty and most of the guards were scared of whatever racket he ran.

"Look what they send me," he said. "An old-time programmer and the new boy." He shook his head.

In the back of the truck lay two large, black body bags. Reb motioned at them. "They came down two days ago, but with the snow and all . . ." He stuck his thumb at the sky. The snow was falling steadily and the clouds showed no break. "Usually, we bring the Turbo Cat back and do it that way, but the one Cat's broken and Town of Windsor got the other for snow removal." A gated section of the chain-link fence hung open, and two ground warmers, like little jet engines, were stationed five feet apart from each other, the bare ground turning to mud beneath them. The tops of white wood crosses poked up through the snow crust.

"How do you end up here?" I asked.

Reb motioned at the graves. "Vermont law, if your people can't or won't pay to have you carted when you die anywhere in the state system, they send you here." He grinned. "And I plant you." He pointed again in the direction of the graves and pulled two shovels out of the back of the truck. He smacked the end of the body bag on the left. "Dig this one first, he's from Saint A, he was a good shit. This other one"—he nudged the body bag with the shovel blade—"he's from Saint J and fuck him, I heard he was an old rat. We'll bury him at three feet instead of six, so he can feel that ground freeze and thaw for the rest of forever."

"How'd you know he was a rat?" I asked.

Reb gave me a hard stare. "Was he a friend of yours?"

"I don't know," I said. Russ was already digging the first hole.

Reb grabbed the body bag and yanked it out of the truck, letting it fall onto the snow. He reached down and pulled the zipper back, and I heard the big metal teeth separate. The dead con's eyes were closed, and he had a mass of gray hair swirled around his head. Snowflakes landed on his cheek and stayed. Reb stood there, waiting for me to answer.

"I don't know him," I said.

"Then shut the fuck up and dig." Reb looked over at Russ digging. I started to dig too. Reb climbed into the bed of the truck and shoved the other body bag to the ground. He opened the zipper on that one, and I could see the dead man's head, his closed eyes. There was a smell. "That's one thing you don't get on the outside, to watch your own grave dug," Reb said. He walked to the front of the truck, leaving Russ and me digging. The smell of the joint drifted faintly in the air. After a while, a pickup truck drove down the guard road and stopped opposite us, between the fences. We all stood up straight, and then the truck continued on, marking us on the head-count sheet for that shift.

We had just finished putting six feet of dirt back on the first man, along with a white cross, when Reb came over and pointed at the woods and whispered. "Look."

At the edge of the woods, barely visible through the snow, a tiny herd of deer, including a large buck, moved to the tree line near the low, outside fence.

"I count five," I said softly. The wind was blowing from the woods, so the deer probably didn't smell or hear us.

"Me too," Reb said. "Five. That's a good size buck."

We watched as the deer pawed at the snow and shifted positions. Then the buck took two quick steps and jumped the low fence, landing on the Jeep track between the two fences. He stuck his head to the ground and came up chewing, with a noseful of snow.

"Must be grass or apples or something over there," Russ said.

"Wild apples," Reb said. He pointed at a tree that hung over the two fences. "I think that's an old wild apple tree. The truck breaks the crust on the snow, and then the deer can get at them." Two other deer quickly jumped the low fence and began pawing around on the guard road. It was hard to see what they were coming up with. The snow was falling steady, and I could barely see through one fence, let alone two and beyond. The chain link is twisted into the shapes of empty diamonds, and looking through two makes everything take on a dark zigzag pattern that shifts, the shadow of something that was never there.

I waited and my eyes settled directly on the next deer, a doe. She took three steps up to the fence and got into the air. For some reason, though, she didn't get high enough, just landed directly on the wire and stuck there. A terrible noise came out of her mouth.

"Jesus," Russ said. The young deer struggled and became more entangled in the concertina wire. I watched her shake violently, only to have the wire shake back and stick deep, just below the ribs. The other deer took off down the guard road, hopping the fence with white tails showing for a second, gone into the snow and woods. "Reb, call a C.O.," Russ directed. There was a radio in the pickup truck.

"I'm not calling anyone." Reb shook his head quick. He looked at the wire. The deer hissed and made a short, high-pitched scream. "That wire will fuck you up every time," he observed.

Russ put his shovel down. "I've got to take a leak." Slowly, he walked around the ground warmers and out of the fenced cemetery. He walked until he was about ten feet away from the electrified fence, directly in front of the impaled deer.

"Those other deer are gone." Reb shrugged. "Just like people." He spit into the snow.

I couldn't see Russ clearly through the snow and the one fence, but I knew he wasn't taking a leak. From the back, it looked as if he was crying.

Reb picked up on this. "Hey program boy!" he yelled over at Russ. "Can't take a deer stuck on the wire, how are you going to settle accounts on the outside?" Russ was crying out loud, and now we could hear him. Reb must have hated that sound. It set him off. "What the fuck makes you think you'll ever get out, you long time bastard? I've seen your sheet, you still got fifteen years to do! I'll be fucking planting you back here! Nobody's going to pay to have your sorry ass buried in Vermont, you worthless fucker!"

Reb went and sat in the truck. I heard Russ whimpering. The deer was quiet now except for a terrible rasping every time she tried to breathe.

Reb tossed a beer can in the snow. He got out and hefted the ground warmers into the back of the truck. I was digging the second hole. Reb handed me a white wooden cross that was hand carved. He showed me the bottom, with the word RAT burned into the wood.

"Put that shit on top of him when he's planted," he said. "I'm heading back. Bring your shovel and lover boy and lock the gate when you come." He got into the truck and drove across the field and over the bank. I could still hear Russ. The deer was dead. The electronic fence made the same low-grade hum. I bent to dig, and when I looked up, Russ was gone. I couldn't see his tracks, because the snow was coming down too hard. The deer's head was pointed down at the snow, and underneath her, I could just make out a spot of bright red, spreading into the white. The deer's eyes were wide open and all white too, as if the snow was somehow inside her. White was the only color except for the gray of the chain-link fence, the shiny razor wire, and the green of my jacket, close to my face. All the rest was snow.

I was determined to give the man his full depth, but I couldn't do it. At about three feet, I ran smack into several large rocks, none of which I could move with my shovel. I wasn't going to walk back to the facility and try to get a pry bar that I probably wouldn't be allowed to have anyway. I tried again with the shovel, but I thought the handle might shatter and I stopped. I grabbed the body bag and dragged it over the snow and dropped it in the hole. I covered it with dirt and put the cross on top. Then I locked the cemetery gate, put the shovel over my shoulder, and walked back to the facility. The snow was coming down so hard that when I looked back over the field I couldn't make out the individual graves, or my own tracks coming out.

I checked back in, and Phil, the guard on duty said, "Where's Harper?"

"I don't know," I said.

"Did he walk away from work detail?"

"When I looked up, Inmate Harper was gone," I said. I told Phil about the deer, but I don't think he listened. Later I heard that Russ Harper had been given a disciplinary hearing and six months was taken off his good time for walking away from the outside work detail. I never heard anything else about it, whether cancer took his father or not. I'm sure that after he walked away from work detail, they wouldn't let him attend the funeral, not even in shackles.

I watched out my cell window, the spring and its mud season and the rain. I tried to stay away from the other prisoners as much as possible. I heard the occasional scuffle at night. Noises that came and went in the dark. I'd been hearing them ever since I got in, almost eighty-four months earlier. My days were counting, all at two and a half, moving faster. Soon I'd be done.

Late on a Thursday afternoon, I was called to the main administrative offices by a sergeant. He took me in to see the chief officer, Rogers. We just got your paperwork, and your max release date comes up on Sunday, he said. Since we don't release anyone on the weekend, that moves your release up to eight a.m., tomorrow morning. We'll have an officer from the field supervision unit in White River Junction give you a ride to the station in White River. So be ready to go in the morning.

And that was it. I was terrified and didn't come out of my cell for the rest of the day. I didn't even try to place a call to my sister. I didn't want anyone to know. I didn't want to be stabbed. Late that night, pacing, three steps then turn, three steps, turn, I noticed the letters FTW scratched into a concrete block near the cement floor. The marks looked old, probably made years ago by some con who was in for good. Fuck the world.

The guards came and got me at seven the next morning and I was awake, hadn't slept all night. I was standing there, had my property inventoried and stuffed it all in a gym bag that had been with me for the whole bid. The guards took me up to the fence and walked me to the main guardhouse at the front entrance and told me to wait there. An unmarked four-door Jeep pulled up, and the gate snapped its electronic lock. I stepped out and went to sit in the front seat.

"Get in the back," the officer said. "State regulations."

I sat in the back with my gym bag. We started on the road to White River Junction.

"You probably won't make it," he said, "most of them don't. Just don't come back here, because we'll hit you with the max all over again. Don't go stealing any guns, you freak. Keep your hands off stuff that isn't yours. And he's still on the force, so remember it's a small state. Personally, if I was you, I'd move. Florida, lots of construction work down there since the hurricane and plenty of sunshine. You can still work, can't you? Nothing happened to you, right? Nothing happened to you on the inside that will keep you from working, did it? Frankly, I don't know if people up here will even give you a job. So think about it, it might be a trip worth taking. Don't harass anyone at the station, I'm telling the Amtrak employees who you are and what you were in for, so no funny stuff. Just go up to Essex. Don't bother any of these people."

By the time we got to White River Junction, the sky was dark. It was just beginning to rain as I walked up the concrete steps to the Amtrak station.

I stood there in the waiting room with my DOC-issued rail ticket. For the first time in my life, all the people around me knew I'd been to prison and that I'd never have that stench off of me. I remembered the deer and how she maimed herself by struggling. I stood still. I became part of the wall. I didn't move or blink or breathe. Nothing. All I heard was the thumping of my own blood, running everywhere at once. Sweat started running down my forehead. When the train came, I forced myself to walk across the concrete platform and find a seat alone. I was soaked, with rain dripping off me. I kept touching my gym bag, as if it held something important. It was soaked, too. I opened the zipper a little. My clothes and papers were as wet as I was. I thought about the man I'd buried shallow. For a minute, I was him, his dead face wet from the rain seeping through the canvas body bag. When I looked up, the rain was coming down even harder.

On the train the conductor came by in a uniform and asked for my ticket and I already had it out. He said, "Where are you going?" and I tried to say Essex Junction, but my voice cracked badly on the first syllable and it just came out like a high-pitched squeak. He laughed at me. "Essex Junction," he said, "I think you meant to say Essex Junction. Work on your voice there, mister." He went down the line, taking tickets and talking.

I put my hand over my mouth, like I was resting it there, thoughtful, and started to practice it, right there on the train. I spoke quietly into my hand. *Hello,* I said, *it's nice to see you.* I couldn't bear the thought of my voice cracking in my first words to my sister Elizabeth, so I cleared my throat and continued softly under my hand. *Hello,* I said, *it's wonderful to see you.*

QUESTIONS FOR DISCUSSION AND WRITING

1. What is Ray Cooper's crime? Why do you think Cooper is constantly denied parole? What does it say about the way the system is presented in this story?
2. What is the "outside work detail" of the story? What is significant about it?
3. Explain the significance of the deer being caught on the fence. Is this symbolic? Ironic?
4. Why does Russ Harper walk away from the outside work detail?
5. Why does Cooper have trouble with his voice at the end? What is the significance of this?
6. The officer transporting Cooper at the end of the story says he thinks Cooper "won't make it." Why not? If you were to predict, what would you say about his chances of success on the "outside"? Defend your opinion.

ON TECHNIQUE AND STYLE

1. Ray Cooper says his name "didn't matter anymore." However, names can often mean a lot in the context of a story. Do you see any significance in the name Ray Cooper (nicknamed "Coop")? Russ Harper?
2. What role do you think the seasons and weather play in the setting of this story? Explain your answer.

CULTURAL QUESTION

1. This story takes place in a rural environment. How does this affect the characterization of Cooper and Harper, in particular? Of their crimes? How is this different from a story of an urban prison environment, for example?

Enemies

Jimmy Santiago Baca

Jimmy Santiago Baca (1952–   ) was born in Santa Fe, New Mexico, of Chicano and Apache heritage. He was abandoned by his parents at the age of two, and lived with one of his grandparents for several years before being placed in an orphanage. He lived on the streets as a young man, and was eventually imprisoned for six years for drug possession. In prison, he taught himself to read and write and began to compose poetry. A fellow inmate convinced him to submit some of his poems for publication. He published two books of poetry while in prison, Jimmy Santiago Baca *(1978) and*

Immigrants in Our Own Land: Poems (1979). He has since published seven books of poetry, a memoir, a collection of stories and essays, a play, and a screenplay. In 1984, Baca received a BA in English from the University of New Mexico, and three years later he published Martin and Meditations on the South Valley *(1987), winner of the American Book Award for Poetry. He continues to write poetry, but has also written drama and coauthored the screenplay for the movie* Bound By Honor *(1993). "Enemies," the short story included here, is from* The Importance of a Piece of Paper *(2004).*

Chancla, Boogey, and Bomber had one thing in common—they all wanted to kill each other. None of them had had a visit in the four and a half years they had been down in the dungeon. They had no wives, no children, they didn't know where their parents were, and they hadn't seen their brothers and sisters in years. They could die tomorrow and no one would grieve them, no one would miss them, no one would even know they had lived and been on earth.

Even the prison administration had forgotten them. There were only two people who had them on their radar: the old brittle-boned tier guard who seemed on the verge of crumbling when he slowly rose from his chair in the corner to unlock their cells—once a week to give them a shower and once a week for an hour of exercise in the cage behind the dungeon—and the obese chow guard who carted in their meals—three times a day, sliding their pewter trays under the cell bars and returning an hour later to pick the trays off the landing floor where they had settled after the three convicts hurled them against the wall.

They were like three warriors from three warring clans stranded on an island who had long ago given up hope of ever rejoining their tribes or being rescued. It had been four and a half years since they had worn clothes. They rose and ate and slept and paced their cells in their boxer shorts. This was their world, day in, day out, and it never varied. Minutes crept by monotonously, and the three convicts would stare at the bars, amused by the rats racing by to snatch away morsels of the crusty leftovers stuck to the wall; by the spiders weaving cobweb after cobweb in the protective mesh screen covering the old ceiling lightbulbs. For at least one hour a day the men would stand clutching the bars of the cell, looking out on the tier, pushing their mouths into the space between the bars, and growling how they were going to kill each other.

When the warden first sent them down to the dungeon, Boogey was in the Black X gang and had already been in prison for eight years. He was twenty-nine years old, out of Georgia, and angled like a plow blade. He looked like Mike Tyson—square jaw, beady dark eyes set wide apart, shoulders brawny as a draft horse harnessed in a quarry pit. He lived with a constant craving to crush his granite cell to dust, and the fact that he could not do it caused his fury to course down from his red-clay heart through his blood vessels, intestines, and stomach. It simmered through his features and his gestures glimmered dangerously with rage in the sweltering dungeon.

Bomber was a skinhead and an expert at making bombs. The other two were constantly goading him, speculating that a bomb must have gone off in his mouth because his teeth were worse than rusty railroad spikes. He was twenty-three years old and mean as a wounded badger. But he hadn't always been this way. Once he was a big, plump-cheeked, cornbread-eating, innocent Kentucky kid with a bucktoothed smile, who spent his days out hunting and fishing. He helped his mom wash clothes in the wringer washer and hang them on the clothesline, and herded his six siblings safely along the creek to school and back. Now, in the privacy of his own mind, he often wondered about the exact moment he had gone bad. Real bad. Armed robberies. Assault and battery. Murder for hire. Contracting out his services to burn buildings for insurance companies. The list went on and on, and over time his life of deception and violence had molded the very contours of his body into the unmistakable shape of crime. The vertebrae in Bomber's lanky, sinewy torso seemed to coil when he slept and then move like a rattlesnake when he woke—vanishing in an instant and reappearing to strike from behind. He had shoulder-length white hair, albino eyes, white eyelashes, and venomous tattoos on his pale skin that advertised his hatred for spics, niggers, and Jews.

Chancla, an American-born Spanish kid from Seattle, down eleven years on two counts of smuggling massive amounts of white Asian heroin, was a handsome criminal. From his neck down to his ankles he was tattooed. But his tattoos were not of vulgar symbols; they were elaborate adornments of high and low art—van Gogh's idyllic wheat fields rolled over his left shoulder and down his back; Stan James's Big Sur ocean waves lapped at his rock reef heart; an Ansel Adams's sunrise over the Grand Tetons spread across his right shoulder blade; a bar graph necklace of musical notes from Van Morrison's song, "Take My Trouble Away," hung around his neck; a Mexican marketplace brimming with fruits and folk knickknacks covered his stomach; I Ching cryptograms banded his biceps; lightning streaked down his forearms and ended in fiery talons at his knuckles; and draping his legs was a Venetian tapestry of merchants in gondolas floating serenely in a channel. When he wasn't in prison, he could get any woman he wanted with absolute certainty. Any woman Chancla's eye landed on, Chancla got. She could be married, single, of any ethnic or religious background, old or young—it didn't matter, she would fall under his strange hypnotic magic. Women adored his glossy black hair, his almond skin, his shy smile and strong white teeth, his ballet dancer's physique, and his gold earring plugs studded with rubies. Most of all they loved the quiet attention he gave them. At its truest core, his life could be understood only through the innumerable love affairs he had had. He yearned for the day when he could be free and in the arms of a woman, a thousand miles away from the prison dungeon and the monotony of daily death threats from Boogey and Bomber.

It was against the law to keep a convict in the dungeon for more than ninety days. Boogey had been placed in the dungeon by the reclassification hearing committee because he had stabbed several rival convicts. When the guards had discovered a cache of drugs and weapons during a shakedown of Bomber's cell, Bomber had received ninety days in the dungeon as punishment. Chancla was caught making love to a beautiful sixteen-year-old boy who had been tried and sentenced as an adult, and was sent down to the dungeon for ninety days. For all three men, those ninety days turned into another sentence on top of the sentence already handed down by the courts for their original offenses. In the past they had sent word to the disciplinary committee through the chow guard, arguing that the prison was committing a crime by keeping them down there, but the committee members ignored them. Illegally confined to the dungeon, with no money to pay a lawyer to fight their case, and no access to law books if they wanted to fight it themselves, they had resigned themselves to the dungeon forever.

Four and a half years without sunshine and hardly any exercise, while being constantly confined and forced to breathe the stale, rancid air, had made them more than a little mad, and every afternoon each one spewed his frustration on the others, vowing at the first opportunity to eliminate the other two. Pacing their cells day after day, season after season, they planned out their vengeance and tormented each other with detailed accounts of the horrors they would inflict and the gruesome methods they would use—dismemberment, burning, decapitation, disembowelment, perverted sexual torture, and hanging.

Of course, though they would not admit it to each other or even to themselves, in their innermost private thoughts each dreamed of leaving the dungeon and joining the general prison population back out on the yard. Each wished it was in his power to amass consecutive days of good behavior and enjoy more freedom and privilege—such as going to school, attending social activities hosted by visiting civilians, and eventually even working up to conjugal visits.

But it would never happen, because one morning Captain Morgan came down to the dungeon and announced to Boogey, Bomber, and Chancla that they were all being released, no strings attached.

The three convicts immediately thought that they were going to be sent out back behind the cell block and shot and buried. It would not have been the first time; on occasion the guards would take a convict out in the middle of the night and he would never be seen again. But even this threat to their lives didn't bring the three of them together. Instead, they snarled at each other and acted as though the second their cell gates opened they would be on their prey like a hawk on a sparrow.

The first guard came and let Chancla out. He was forced to put on clothes, which made him feel strange and vulnerable, and he was so certain that he was being taken out to be killed that he ignored Bomber and Boogey and asked the guard, "Why they letting us go?" The guard didn't answer. Chancla's paranoia grew when he was chained up at the ankles, then around the waist, and then handcuffed at the wrists. He shuffled awkwardly out of the dungeon, filled with mounting dread and despair. It was not the way he wanted to leave.

"I'm still going to kick your fucking asses," he yelled behind him as the guard unlocked the last gate and pushed him through. He heard Bomber and Boogey's voices echoing down the cavernous tier, shouting that they couldn't wait to cut him to pieces and feed him to the dogs. Their familiar voices were comforting to him and he felt sad at leaving behind the two men who wanted him dead but had become the closest thing he had to a family.

The guard walked Chancla across the yard, posted him next to the processing office, and ordered him to wait. Though he was chained and helpless, Chancla stood nervously darting his head around, ready as he could be to hobble away from the assailant he knew was lurking there. He determined that he could at least bite the guy and chew off his nose or ear, before he was shot to death.

Back in the dungeon, Bomber pushed aside his locker and started digging frantically in the wall for his shank, a six-inch homemade steel knife that he kept hidden inside a hollowed-out brick. He brandished it before the guard, yelling, "Come get me and I'll cut your stinking rat-faced fat neck, you dirty bastard." The guard knew that without the bars between them, Bomber would surely sink the blade to the hilt without batting an eyelid. He radioed for reinforcements and four other guards arrived, all wielding bulletproof Plexiglas shields, clubs, and mace. They forcibly subdued Bomber, shackled him from ankles to wrists, dragged him out across the yard, and stood him next to Chancla.

Even though they could hardly lift a finger, Bomber and Chancla lunged at each other. Guards yanked on their chain leashes and pulled them apart, but they still kept snarling and threatening to kill each other the instant the chains were removed. In the midst of their skirmish three guards pushed Boogey toward the other two, who started in on him, cursing him and vowing to dismantle him bone by bone. Of course, Boogey retaliated by charging them. The guards standing by grew so annoyed at their relentless antagonism that they kicked the feet out from all three and made them sit on the dirt. Every time one of the convicts ranted out obscenities at one of the others, a guard slapped him across the face with a lead-filled thong.

Behind all their snarling and lunging and cursing, each felt the fear of a man walking down the death row corridor to the electric chair. Except, in their case, death was most likely to happen out on some forlorn prairie while they stood and looked at the weeds and cacti and sage, waiting to be devoured by the ants, coyotes, and buzzards.

The guards led them through various gates and when they were finally outside, beyond the walls, each vaguely recalled his arrival, being intimidated by the guard towers, the looming fifty-foot wall of granite topped with tangled rolls of fanged security wire, the floodlights, the catwalks, and the guards cradling M16s as they patrolled the perimeters.

Now here they were outside the walls just as dawn was breaking, with thoughts of imminent death darkening their hearts. Flanked by two guards apiece, they hobbled to a van waiting in the semidarkness and were helped in and separated from each other. The driver took them down a long entrance lined with palm trees, then turned left toward the airport, leaving the prison behind in the distance.

The convicts fell quiet as they stared at their reflections in the black glass, recognizing bitterly that youth was leaving them, and that they had grown old, not in flesh or physique, but emotionally, spiritually. Their eyes scanned the surrounding prairie. It was like seeing a new land. They meditated on who they had been, what their lives had been like when they were free. Now they felt more imprisoned than ever by their own fears. What were they going to do? They didn't know how to be fathers and husbands. Where were they going? If they lived, by what means would they survive? They had no money, no jobs, no schooling. Yes, they were leaving behind the prison but not what prison had done to them—criminalized them, made them meaner, crueler, and angrier.

They drove on, somewhat relaxed by the humming engine, as the lights inside homes across the road flickered on, cars backed out of driveways, and kids boarded yellow school buses.

Each one regretted that such mundane activities had eluded them for so long. They had been looking for excitement and adventure and had been swooped up early in life by the delusions of the gambler, who thinks he can win it all and be happy and rich—if only he could make one big score, do one good deal, meet one wealthy woman. These were the absurd dreams of the foolish young boys they had been, dreams that were now eaten away like apple cores thrown out of a window for the crows to peck into pulp.

When they finally arrived at the airport, their nostalgia had reawakened their hurt and their hurt had made them angry. They burned with shame when the guards led them into the terminal and stood them in the lobby for all the travelers to glare at. The guards first unlocked their wrists, then handed each of them forty bucks and a one-way ticket to his respective home state, along with a manila folder containing their release papers.

"You gonna tell us now why you're setting us free?" Boogey asked.

"Class-action suit was filed by one of the jailhouse lawyers on behalf of two hundred of you assholes. AIDS and Hepatitis-C convicts pardoned by the governor for some law called deliberate indifference. We tried to kill you infected queers off, but one of you went and filed a lawsuit. Others had their sentences commuted and they were released."

"Where do we fit in on all that?" Bomber asked.

"Given your good time, you all would have been out a year ago. Apparently," the guard said, "you guys had finished your sentences and were just doing free time. According to the courts, that's cruel and unusual punishment—all right, I'm going to unchain you and you better fucking wait until we leave the terminal to attack each other or we will take you all out back and fuck you up."

The men were so shocked by the news and so completely out of their element that they were virtually paralyzed. Swiftly abducted in the middle of the night, shoved into a van, and deposited among hundreds of strangers from all walks of life coming and going—what could they make of it? From the dungeon, with its lack of sunlight and sensory stimulation, where they had no access to radio or TV and were kept in absolute isolation in every sense of the word, they were suddenly dumped among people hurrying by with cell phones, laptops, and DVDs, among terrorist security checks and scores of guards carrying machine guns all around. They stood speechless and scared, clutching their release papers. They looked at the money in their palms and tucked away their airline tickets. They felt dangerously exposed.

They didn't know what words to use, what feelings to have, or how to behave. They were agonizingly aware of themselves and how much they didn't belong. They saw people shake hands, embrace, kiss—societal customs that could get you killed in prison. They put one foot in front of the other in a small semicircle, looking up at the vast ceilings and gawking at the people. The security guards kept frowning at them, and they noticed that reinforcements were now hovering about the edges of the terminal. Chancla said with disgust, "I'd fuck them bitches if they were inside."

Boogey spotted two uniformed security guards entering, and as they positioned themselves against a nearby wall by a rental car booth, he smiled at them and said, "They're cute little bitches, ain't they . . ."

"You muthafucking nigger, don't you ever talk that way to white men . . ." Bomber said.

Boogey turned and snarled, "Fuck you, hillbilly bitch!"

"Yeah, and fuck you both, assholes," Chancla interrupted, looking off toward a corner of the terminal where a neon martini glass flashed in a tinted window.

The other two followed him over.

They sat at the bar, four swivel stools between them, all staring at the mirror and the line of labels on the whiskey bottles. When Chancla ordered his tequila and the bartender turned his back to reach for the bottle, Chancla reached over the counter and grabbed a knife and pocketed it. Boogey and Bomber followed suit.

Bomber looked over at Boogey and said, "Think you getting the jump on me—you're dead, you little overcooked spic!"

"And when I get done with you two, I'm go' have me a good time with yo mommas," Boogey said.

The bartender glanced furtively at them. Other customers sitting at the small tables around the counter were conscious of the three men; something about them was odd, yet they made efforts not to stare. From years of forced abstinence, their first shots had them feeling good. Boogey ordered another shot of gin, Bomber another Wild Turkey, and Chancla another tequila.

"You keep looking at us funny, you'll be looking out of the side of your neck," Bomber said to the bartender, who went red with fear and nodded and put himself as far away from them as possible, wiping the small tables and chatting with the occupants at the end of the bar.

Boogey got up and turned on the TV bracketed to the ceiling. He sat with his neck craned, making soft clicks with his tongue every time the newscaster reported another of a long list of crime stories. He toasted each crime story, saying, "Ya ain't seen shit yet . . ." He took a white plastic fork and combed his kinky hair. He grabbed handfuls of peanuts and stuffed them into his mouth, then slugged down his gin to clean the salty taste from his mouth.

"You niggers like peanuts, like monkeys," Bomber ridiculed him, squishing red cherries between his black teeth, red juice running down the corners of his mouth and his chin.

"And you crackers is all about cherries, and popping yo white-ass cherry is what I'm planning to do."

Bomber got mad at the last statement, his left eyelid fluttering uncontrollably as he swigged from the Wild Turkey bottle, picking at the label, squinting his eyes at himself in the mirror beyond the bar counter. "What the fuck you looking at, grease ball?" he said to Chancla.

Chancla had been staring in the big mirror too but was not conscious of seeing Bomber because he was deep in thought. "I've never killed anybody I didn't have a good reason to kill, and I'm thinking about the reason I'm going to kill you two," he said aloud. He got up and raised his shirt. Facing the other men he traced a long scar hidden in the lush fruit bins and said, "This punk tried using a machete—I gutted him with his blade." Pointing to a variety of other scars of various lengths and widths, he said, "Here I gave him a free shot—I fucked his wife and told him to take a free shot—he did—then I showed him how to really use it." He turned his right fist to the customers. "Got teeth stuck in these knuckles—a policeman tried to stop me from taking his car. Every knuckle had one of his teeth embedded in it. They had to wire these knuckles up—"

"What'd you do to me?" Boogey interrupted. "I kinda was trying to figure that out."

They stared at each other for a long time, oblivious of the airport activity in the background: porters in blue uniforms hurrying dollies full of suitcases; harried parents trying to keep their kids from roaming off; weeping girlfriends kissing their lovers; stern-faced businessmen and women rushing by with briefcases; unwashed, uncombed college kids with strained looks from partying the night before checking their pockets for lost tickets or misplaced IDs.

The commotion made Chancla feel more isolated than he felt in the dungeon. He had tickets to fly back home, but back home was where they had arrested him and sent him to the federal prison in Texas, then transferred him to Arizona for two escapes. Back home was Seattle, but no one and nothing was waiting for him there. He figured that as soon as he got off the plane, he'd roam around town looking for his old crime partner, and if no business came his way, he'd flip a coin to see which way to go—heads, he'd pack it to Mexico; tails, to Canada. He sat back on the stool, licked the top of his hand, sprinkled a dash of salt on it, kicked back a shot of his tequila, bit into the lime wedge, and licked the salt from his hand. "Fuck all of you," he said to the clientele glancing at him. He spun himself around on the stool and stopped suddenly, facing the mirror.

"It's that place . . ." he said to their reflections. "That place . . ."

"Fuck that hellhole," Bomber growled, now quite drunk. "Fuck that place and fuck home and fuck my wife and fuck my kids . . ." he slurred and downed another shot of Wild Turkey.

"I guess it does something to you, 'cuz I can't remember anything you did to me that I should kill you for," Boogey said.

"That place runs on us hating each other, on us killing each other—it breeds racism and it breeds criminals," Bomber said.

"Here's to that, brother." Boogey raised his glass of gin and swallowed hard.

They heard the airport intercom loudly announce a flight to New Hampshire.

"What's your flight number, Bomber?" Chancla asked, but Bomber was mumbling to himself. Chancla rose, checked Bomber's ticket lying on the counter, and said, "That was your flight they just called on the intercom, Bomber. Be good to get back home to your old lady, your kids, fish some of those streams and—"

"Fuck my old lady, fuck my home, I ain't going to nowhere except back out there to rob me some dumb muthafucka . . ." He grinned drunkenly, swiveled around on his stool, and yelled at the few travelers having a drink and minding their own business.

"Flight-number this, you cocksuckers!"

They looked up from their books and papers and prepared to leave.

"You ain't no man," Bomber heard a voice say. He turned to his left, ready to stab the fool, when he saw it was Chancla.

"So you ready to have it out now? I'll teach you who a man is, boy," Bomber retorted. He was drunk and unsteady enough that he could only stagger to his right slightly, giving Chancla the advantage. Chancla grabbed him from behind, braced his arm around Bomber's neck, and whispered into his ear, "A man, a real man, not some wipe-ass bitch, would get on his plane and make it home to his family in time for supper. A sniveling ass bitch who can't hold her liquor would pussy up and stay here."

Then Chancla pulled in tight to hold him as he struggled to free himself, flailing his knife around at the air before him but not near enough for Chancla to be in danger. Chancla looked at Boogey, who understood what was happening and nodded back to him, giving Chancla a silent signal that he was on standby, waiting for him to indicate when he was needed.

"You a man, muthafucka," Chancla continued, "you'll make it to the gate—get up on that stairway to the plane and don't let them know you're drunk—that's a man—pull it off, I challenge you."

"I'll show you, asshole." Bomber's words distorted into a lot of rolling *r* sounds as he lunged forward toward the escalators that went up to the gates.

Boogey caught him under the armpit on one side and Chancla grabbed him on the other, and they kept moving him forward, moving him fast down the corridor to his gate. Just before they reached the door, Chancla shoved Bomber against the wall, slipped his knife out of his pocket, and whispered fiercely, an inch from his face, "You gotta make it across the tarmac and up those stairs, Bomber—then you'll prove you're a man to me. And I'll respect you as a man—across the tarmac, up the stairs—you can't let them know you're drunk—do it, Bomber—"

"Do it, Bomber," Boogey pitched in.

Somehow, Bomber seemed to grasp the importance of going home and of proving to them he could handle any challenge. He gave each of them a sweeping glance, lacking any malice and showing a hint of acknowledgment that they had gone through and survived a war together. He turned and walked out into the bright sunshine as Chancla and Boogey watched through the plate glass windows. They saw him tip slightly but regain his balance, grip the stairway railing, and slowly climb up the steep steps to the door of the plane, where he handed his ticket to the stewardess. Before he vanished into the cabin, he turned and saluted his two friends, grinned, flipped them off, and disappeared into the plane.

Chancla turned to Boogey and said, "I gotta find my gate . . ."

Neither knew what to say or how to say it.

Finally Boogey said, "Uh, uh, how, I mean, how can I get in touch with you? I mean, if you want." An undertone of sadness shaded his words. He shuffled.

"Sure I want, Boogey . . ." Chancla said, and his words were pained, as if each were a thorn pulled from his tongue. ". . . Never thought anyone would want to get in touch with me though. I don't know how to write and I ain't got no number. I know—if you're in Seattle, or you want to leave a message for me, call Andrei's—it's a bar I'll probably be hanging out at for a while until I decide what I'm going to do."

"I'm in Atlanta, my momma's name is Ruby Pass . . . I'll take you fishing for catfish like you never dreamed," Boogey said.

There was an awkward moment, and when Boogey leaned forward to give Chancla a hug, Chancla involuntarily drew back, defensively, and Boogey caught himself.

Chancla said, "I didn't mean to, I just—it's weird, you know—" He extended his hands out and they slapped palms and high-fived.

QUESTIONS FOR DISCUSSION AND WRITING

1. Why do Chancla, Boogey, and Bomber hate each other?
2. Why are these characters in the "dungeon"? Why are they eventually released?
3. What is meant by the sentence, "Now they felt more imprisoned than ever by their own fears"? What is the source of their fears?

4. What do you make of the ex-prisoners' hostile behavior in the airport bar?
5. Why are Chancla, Boogey, and Bomber reluctant to return home?
6. What causes the ex-prisoners to change so radically at the end of the story? Where is their epiphany?

ON TECHNIQUE AND STYLE

1. There is a significant amount of what many would consider profanity in this story. Does this make it more realistic? Difficult to read? How did you react to the language here?
2. In what ways is this story like a fable? Give specific examples from the story.
3. The author has compared the main characters to animals through the many uses of simile. Find two or three examples you find particularly effective. Why do you think the author uses this technique in his writing?

CULTURAL QUESTION

1. One focus of this story is racism. As Bomber says, "That place . . . breeds racism and it breeds criminals." Is he right? How does it breed racism?

From Kiss of the Spider Woman

Manuel Puig

*The Argentine author **Manuel Puig** (1932–1990) is best known for his novels* La Tra-ición de Rita Hayworth (Betrayed by Rita Hayworth, *1968),* Boquitas Pintadas (Heartbreak Tango, *1973), and* El Beso de la Mujer Araña (Kiss of the Spider Woman, *1976). The last of these novels, which is excerpted here, was made into a play, then a film by the Argentine Brazilian director, Héctor Babenco, and later into a Broadway musical. Puig translated most of his works into English and also wrote in English. Puig lived in exile most of his life. In 1989, he moved to Cuernavaca, Mexico, where he died in 1990.*

Chapter 8

MINISTRY OF THE INTERIOR OF THE ARGENTINE REPUBLIC
Penitentiary of the City of Buenos Aires
Report to the Warden, prepared by Staff Assistants

Prisoner 3018, Luis Alberto Molina

> Sentenced July 20, 1974, by the Honorable Judge Justo José Dalpierre, Criminal Court of the City of Buenos Aires. Condemned to eight years imprisonment for corruption of minors. Lodged in Pavilion B, cell 34, as of July 28, 1974, with sexual offenders Benito Jaramillo, Mario Carlos Bianchi, and David Margulies. Transferred on April 4, 1975, to Pavilion D, cell 7, housing political prisoner Valentin Arregui Paz. Conduct good.

Detainee 16115, Valentin Arregui Paz

> Arrested October 16, 1972, along Route 5, outside Barrancas, National Guard troops having surrounded group of activists involved in pro-moting disturbances with strikers at two automotive assembly plants. Both plants situated along said highway. Held under Executive Power of the Federal Government and awaiting judgment. Lodged in Pavilion A, cell 10, with political prisoner Bernardo Giacinti as of November 4, 1974. Took part in hunger strike protesting death of political prisoner Juan Vicente Aparicio while undergoing police interrogation. Moved to solitary confinement for ten days as of March 25, 1975. Trans-ferred on April 4, 1975, to Pavilion D, cell 7, with sexual offender Luis Alberto Molina. Conduct reprehensible, rebellious, reputed instigator of above hunger strike as well as other incidents supposedly protest-ing lack of hygienic conditions in Pavilion and violation of personal correspondence.

GUARD: Remove your cap in front of the Warden.

PRISONER: Yes, sir.

WARDEN: No need to be trembling like that, young man, nothing bad is going to happen to you here.

GUARD: Prisoner has been thoroughly searched and has nothing dangerous on his person, sir.

WARDEN: Thank you, Sergeant. Be good enough to leave me alone with the prisoner now.

GUARD: Shall I remain stationed in the hallway, sir? With your permission, sir.

WARDEN: That will do fine, Sergeant, you may go out now . . . You look thin, Molina, what's the matter?

PRISONER: Nothing, sir. I was sick to my stomach, but I'm feeling much better now.

WARDEN: Then stop your trembling . . . There's nothing to be afraid of. We made it look like you had a visitor today. Arregui couldn't possibly suspect anything.

PRISONER: No, he doesn't suspect anything, sir.

WARDEN: Last night I had dinner at home with your sponsor, Molina, and he brought me some good news for you. Which is why I had you summoned to my office today. Oh, I know it's rather soon . . . or have you learned something already?

PRISONER: No, sir, nothing yet. I feel I need to proceed very cautiously in this kind of situation . . . But what did Mr. Parisi have to say?

WARDEN: Very good news, Molina. It seems your mother is feeling a lot better, since he spoke to her about the possibility of a pardon . . . She's practically a new person.

PRISONER: Really? . . .

WARDEN: Of course, Molina, what would you expect? . . . But stop your crying, what's this? You should be pleased . . .

PRISONER: It's from happiness, sir . . .

WARDEN: But come on now . . . Don't you have a handkerchief?

PRISONER: No, sir, but I can just use my sleeve, it's no problem.

WARDEN: Take my handkerchief at least . . .

PRISONER: No, I'm really okay. Please excuse me.

WARDEN: You know, Parisi is like a brother to me, and it was his interest in you that led us to come up with the present option, but Molina . . . we're expecting you to know how to manage things. Do you seem to be making any headway, or what?

PRISONER: I think I'm getting somewhere . . .

WARDEN: Was it helpful to have him weakend physically, or no?

PRISONER: Actually I had to eat the prepared food the first time.

WARDEN: Why? That was certainly a mistake . . .

PRISONER: No, it wasn't, because he doesn't like rice, and since one plate had more than the other . . . he insisted I have the bigger portion, and it would have been suspicious had I refused. I know you warned me that the prepared one would come in a new tin plate, but they loaded it up so much I had to eat it myself.

WARDEN: Well, good work, Molina. I commend you, and I'm sorry about the mixup.

PRISONER: That's why I look so thin. I was sick for two days.

WARDEN: And Arregui, how's his morale? Have we managed to soften him up a little? What's your opinion?

PRISONER: Yes, but it's probably a good idea to let him begin to recover now.

WARDEN: Well, that I don't know, Molina. I think the matter had best be left to our discretion. We have here appropriate techniques at our disposal.

PRISONER: But if he gets any worse there's no way he can remain in his cell, and once he's taken to the infirmary, there's no chance left for me.

WARDEN: Molina, you underestimate the proficiency of our personnel here. They know exactly how to proceed in these matters. Weigh your words, my friend.[*]

[*]In *Three Essays on the Theory of Sexuality*, Freud points out that repression, in general terms, can be traced back to the imposition of domination of one individual over others, this first individual having been none other than the father. Beginning by such domination, the patriarchal form of society was established, based upon the inferiority of the woman and the intensive repression of sexuality. Moreover, Freud links his theory of patriarchal authority to the rise of religion and in particular the

PRISONER: Excuse me, sir, I only want to cooperate. Nothing else . . .
WARDEN   Of course. Now another thing—don't give out the slightest hint about
            a pardon. Hide any sign of euphoria when you go back into your cell.
            How are you going to explain this visit?
PRISONER: I don't know. Perhaps you can suggest something, sir.
WARDEN: Tell him your mother came, how does that sound?

triumph of monotheism in the West. On the other hand, Freud is especially preoccupied with sexual repression, inasmuch as he considers the natural impulses of a human being much more complicated than patriarchal society admits: given the undifferentiated capacity of babies to obtain sexual pleasure from all the parts of their body, Freud qualifies them as "polymorphous perverse." As a part of the same concept, Freud also believes in the essentially bisexual nature of our original sexual impulse.

Along the same lines, and with reference to primary repression, Otto Rank considers the long development, which runs from paternal domination to a powerful system of state run by men, to be a prolongation of the same primary repression, whose purpose is the increasingly pronounced exclusion of women. In addition, Dennis Altman, in his *Homosexual Oppression and Liberation*, addressing himself specifically to sexual repression, relates it to a need, at the very origin of humanity, to produce a large quantity of children for economic ends and for purposes of defense.

With regard to the same subject, in *Sex in History* the British anthropologist Rattray Taylor points out that, beginning with the fourth century B.C., there occurs in the classical world an increase in sexual repression and a growth of the feeling of guilt, factors which facilitated a triumph of the Hebraic attitude, sexually more repressive, over the Greek one. According to the Greeks, the sexual nature of every human being combined elements which were as much homosexual as heterosexual.

Again Altman in the above-cited work expresses the view that Western societies specialize in sexual repression, legitimized as it is by the Judeo-Christian religious tradition. Such repression expresses itself in three interrelated forms: by associating sex with (1) sin, and its consequent sense of guilt; (2) institution of the family and procreation of children as its only justification; (3) rejection of all forms of sexual behavior outside of the genital and the heterosexual. Further on he adds that traditional "libertarians"—in terms of sexual repression—fight to change the first two forms but neglect the third. An example of the same would be Wilhelm Reich, in his book *The Function of the Orgasm,* where he affirms that sexual liberation is rooted in the perfect orgasm, which can only be achieved by means of heterosexual genital copulation among individuals of the same generation. And it is under the influence of Reich that other investigators would develop their mistrust of homosexuality and of contraceptives, since these would interfere with the attainment of perfect orgasms, and as a result would be detrimental to total sexual "freedom."

Concerning sexual liberation, Herbert Marcuse in *Eros and Civilization* points out that the same implies more than mere absence of oppression; liberation requires a new morality and a revision of the notion of "human nature" itself. And later he adds that every real theory of sexual liberation must take into account the essentially polymorphous needs of human beings. According to Marcuse, in defiance of a society that employs sexuality as a means toward a useful end, perversions uphold sexuality as an end in itself; as a result, they lie outside the orbit of the ironclad principle of "performance," which is to say, one of the basic repressive principles fundamental to the organization of capitalism, and thus they question, without proposing to do so, the very foundations of the latter.

Commenting on this manner of reasoning by Marcuse, Altman adds that at the point when homosexuality becomes exclusive and establishes its own economic norms, dispensing with its critical attitude toward the conventional forms of heterosexuals in order to attempt, instead, to copy the same, it too becomes a form of repression, as powerful a one as exclusive heterosexuality. And further on, commenting upon another radical Freudian, Norman O. Brown, as well as upon Marcuse, Altman infers that, in the last analysis, what we conceive of as "human nature" is no more than what has become the result of centuries of repression, an argument which implies, and in this respect Marcuse and Brown agree, the essential mutability of human nature.

PRISONER: No, sir, impossible, not that.

WARDEN: Why not?

PRISONER: Because my mother always brings some bags of food for me.

WARDEN: We have to come up with something to justify your euphoria, Molina. That's definite. I know now, we can requisition some groceries for you, and pack them up the same way, how does that strike you?

PRISONER: Fine, sir.

WARDEN: This way we can also repay you for your sacrifice, over that plate of rice. Poor Molina!

PRISONER: Well, my mother buys everything in the supermarket a few blocks from the prison, so as not to have to carry everything on the bus.

WARDEN: But it's easier for us to requisition everything from supplies. We can make the package up right here.

PRISONER: No, it would look suspicious. Please don't. Get them to go to that market, it's just down the street.

WARDEN: Wait just a minute . . . Hello, hello . . . Gutierrez, come into my office a moment, will you please.

PRISONER: My mother always brings me the stuff packed in two brown shopping bags, one for each hand. They pack it for her at the store, so she can manage everything.

WARDEN: All right . . . Yes, over here. Look, Gutierrez, you'll have to go buy a list of groceries which I'm going to give you, and wrap them up in a certain way. The prisoner will give you instructions, and it all has to be done in . . . let's say half an hour. Take out a voucher and have the sergeant go make the purchases with you according to the prisoner's instructions. Molina, you dictate whatever you think your mother would be likely to bring you . . .

PRISONER: To you, sir?

WARDEN: Yes, to me! And quickly, I have other things to attend to.

PRISONER: . . . Guava paste, in a large package . . . Make it two packages. Canned peaches, two roast chickens, still warm, obviously. A large bag of sugar. Two boxes of tea, one regular and the other camomile. Powdered milk, condensed milk, detergent . . . a small box, no, a large box, of *Blanco,* and four cakes of toilet soap, *Suavísimo* . . . and what else? . . . Yes, a big jar of pickled herring, and let me think a little, my mind's a complete blank . . .

Chapter 9

—Look what I've got!

—No! . . . your mother came? . . .

—Yes!!!

—But how great . . . Then she's feeling better.

—Mmm-hmm, a little better . . . And look at what she brought for me. I mean, for *us.*

—Thanks, but all of that's for you, no kidding.

—You be quiet, you're convalescing, remember? Starting today a new life begins . . . The sheets are almost dry, feel . . . and all this food to eat. Look, two roast chickens, *two,* how about that? And chicken is perfect, it won't upset your stomach at all. Watch how fast you get better now.

—No, I won't let you do that.

—Please take them. I don't care for chicken anyway. I'll just be glad to do without any more stink from you and your barnyard . . . No, seriously, you have to stop eating that damn stuff they feed us here. Then you'll start feeling better in no time. At least try it for a couple of days.

—You think so? . . .

—Absolutely. And once you're better then . . . close your eyes, Valentin. See if you can guess . . . Come on, try . . .

—How do I know? I don't know . . .

—No peeking. Wait, I'll let you handle it to see whether you can guess.

—Here . . . feel.

—Two of them . . . packages . . . and heavy ones. But I give up.

—Open your eyes.

—Guava paste!

—But you have to wait for that, until you feel okay, and you can be sure you only get half of that . . . I also took a chance and left the sheets alone to dry . . . and nobody walked away with them, how about that? They're just about dry. So tonight we both have clean sheets.

—Nice going.

—Just give me a minute while I put this stuff away . . . And then I'll make some camomile tea because my nerves are killing me, and you, you have a leg of this chicken. Or no, it's only five o'clock . . . Better you just have some tea with me, and some crackers here, they're easier to digest. Delicadas, see? The ones I had as a kid whenever I was sick . . . before they came out with Criollitas.

—How about one right now, Molina?

—Okay, just one, with a dab of jam, but orange for the digestion. It's lucky, almost everything she brought is easy to digest, so you can have lots of it. Except for the guava paste . . . for the time being. Let me light the burner and presto, in a few minutes you'll be licking your fingers.

—But the leg of chicken, may I have it now?

—Come on, a little self-control . . . Let's save it for later, so when they bring us dinner you won't be tempted, because, lousy as it is, you gorge yourself every time.

—But you don't realize, my stomach feels so empty when the pains stop that it's like all of a sudden I'm starving.

—One minute, let's get this straight. I expect you to eat the chicken, no, chickens, *both* of them. On condition, though, that you don't touch the prison chow, which is making you so sick. Is it a deal?

—Okay . . . But what about you? I won't let you just sit around and drool.

—I won't, cold food doesn't tempt me, really.

—Oh, it definitely agreed with me. And what a good idea to have camomile tea first.
—Calmed your nerves, didn't it? Same with me.
—And the chicken was delicious, Molina. To think we have enough for two more days still.
—Well, it's true. Now you sleep a little, and that will complete your cure.
—I'm not really sleepy. You go ahead and sleep. I'll be fine, don't worry.
—But don't you start dwelling again on some nonsense like before, or it'll interfere with your digestion.
—What about you? Are you sleepy?
—More or less.
—Because there is one thing that's still lacking to complete the usual program.
—Christ, and I'm the one who's supposed to be degenerate here.
—No, no kidding. We should have a film now, that's what's missing.
—Ah, I see . . .
—Do you remember any others like the panther woman? That's the one I liked best.
—Well sure, I know lots of supernatural ones.
—So let's hear, tell me, like what?
—Oh . . . *Dracula* . . . *The Wolf Man* . . .
—What else?
—And there's one about a zombie woman . . .
—That's it! That sounds terrific.
—Hmm . . . how does it start? . . .
—Is it American?
—Yeah, but I saw it eons ago.
—So? Do it anyway.
—Well, let me concentrate a minute.
—And the guava paste, when do I get to taste it?
—Tomorrow at the earliest, not before.
—Just one spoonful? For now?
—No. And better I start the film . . . Let me see, how does it go? . . . Oh, that's it. Now I remember. It begins with some girl from New York taking a steamer to an island in the Caribbean where her fiancé is waiting to marry her. She seems like a very sweet kid, and full of big dreams, telling everything about herself to this ship's captain, really a handsome guy, and he's just staring down at the black waters of the ocean, because it's night, and next thing he looks at her as if to say, "This poor kid has no idea what she's getting herself into," but he doesn't say anything until they've already reached the island, and you hear some native drums and she's like transported, and then the captain says don't let yourself be taken in by the sound of those drums, because they can often as not be the portents of death

. . . cardiac arrest, sick old woman, a heart fills up with black seawater and drowns

—police patrol, hideout, tear gas, door opens, submachine-gun muzzles, black blood of asphyxiation gushing up in the mouth Go on, why did you stop?

—So this girl is met by her husband, whom she's married by proxy, after only knowing each other a few days in New York. He's a widower, also from New York. Anyway, the arrival on the island, when the boat's docking, is divine, because her fiancé is right there waiting for her with a whole parade of donkey carts, decorated with flowers, and in a couple of carts there's a bunch of musicians, playing nice soft tunes on those instruments which look like some kind of table made up out of little planks, that they whack with sticks and, well, I don't know why, but that kind of music really gets to me, because the notes sound so sweet on that instrument, like little soap bubbles that go popping one after another. And the drums have stopped, fortunately, because they'd sounded like a bad omen. And the two of them arrive at the house; it's pretty far from town, off in the countryside, under the palm trees, and it's such a gorgeous island with just some low hills, and you're way out in the middle of these banana groves. And the fiancé is so very pleasant, but you can tell there's a real drama going on inside him; he smiles too much, like someone with a weak character. And then you get this clue, that something's wrong with him, because the first thing the fiancé does is introduce the girl to his majordomo, who's around fifty or so, a Frenchman, and this majordomo asks him right then and there to sign a couple of papers, about shipping out a load of bananas on the same boat that the girl arrived on, and the fiancé tells him he'll do it later, but the majordomo, he's like insistent about it, and the fiancé looks at him with eyes full of hatred, and while he's busy signing the papers you notice how he can hardly keep his hand steady to write, it's trembling so much. Anyhow, it's still daylight, and the whole welcome party, which rode back there in those little flowery carts, is out back in the garden waiting to toast the new couple, and they're all holding glasses full of fruit juice, and at this point you notice the arrival of a couple of black peons, sort of delegates from the sugarcane plantations, with a keg of rum to honor the master, but the majordomo sees them too and looks furiously at them, and grabs an ax that happens to be lying around, and he chops away at the keg of rum until it all pours out on the ground.

—Please, no more talk about food or drinks.

—And don't you be so impressionable then, crybaby. Anyhow, the girl turns to the fiancé as if to ask him why all the hysterics, but just then he's busy nodding to the majordomo how that's exactly what he should do, and so, without wasting any more time, the fiancé raises his glass of fruit juice and toasts the islanders there before him, because the next morning the two of them will be married, as soon as they go sign the papers at some government office there on the island. But that night the girl has to stay by

herself, in the house, because he has to go to the farthest banana plantation on the whole island in order to show his gratitude to the peons and,
by the way, to avoid any gossip and thus protect the girl's good name. The
moon is marvelous that night, and the garden surrounding the house just
stunning, with all those fabulous tropical plants which seem more fantastic
than ever, and the girl has on a white satin chemise, under just this loose
peignoir, it's white too but transparent, and she's tempted to take a look
around the house, and she walks through the living room, and then into the
dining room, and twice she comes across those folding type of frames with
a picture of the fiancé on one side but with the other side blank, because
the photo is gone, which must have been the first wife, the dead one. Then
she wanders around the rest of the house, and goes into some bedroom
which you can tell was once for a woman, because of the lace doilies on
the night table and on top of the dresser, and the girl starts rummaging
through all the drawers to see if some photograph might still be around
but doesn't find anything, except hanging in the closet are all the clothes
from the first wife, all of them incredibly fine imports. But at this point the
girl hears something move, and she spots a shadow passing by the window. It scares the daylights out of her and she goes out into the garden,
all lit up with moonlight, and sees a cute little frog jumping into the pond,
and she thinks that was the noise she heard, and that the shadow was
probably just the swaying of the palm trees in the breeze. And she walks
still farther into the garden, because it feels so stuffy back in the house,
and just then she hears something else, but like footsteps, and she spins
around to see, but right at that moment some clouds blot out the moon,
and the garden gets all black. And at the same time, off in the distance . . .
drums. And you also hear more steps, this time clearly, and they're coming toward her, but very slowly. The girl is suddenly quaking with fear, and
sees a shadow entering the house, through the same exact door that she'd
left open. So the poor thing can't even make up her mind which is scarier
at this point, to stay out there in that incredibly dark garden, or to go back
into the house. Well, she decides to get closer to the house, where she
peeks in through one of the windows but she doesn't see a thing, and
then she hurries to another window, which turns out to look in on the dead
wife's bedroom. And since it's so dark she can't make out much more
than like a shadow gliding across the room, a tall silhouette, moving with
outstretched hands, and fingering all the knickknacks lying around inside
there, and right next to the window is the dresser with the doily and, on top
of that, a really beautiful brush with the handle all worked in silver, and a
mirror with the same kind of handle, and since the girl is right up against
the window she can make out a very thin deathly pale hand, fingering all
the bric-a-brac, and the girl feels frozen on the spot, too terrified to even
budge; *the walking corpse, the treacherous somnambula, she talks in her
sleep and confesses everything, the quarantined patient overhears her, he's
loath to touch her, her skin is deathly white* but now she sees the shadow

gliding out of the room and toward who knows what part of the house, until after a tiny bit she hears footsteps out there on the patio once more, and the girl shrinks back, trying to hide in all those vines clinging to the walls of the house when the cloud finally passes by so that the moon comes back out again and the patio's lit up once again and there in front of the girl is this very tall figure wearing a long black duster, who scares her half to death, the pale face of a dead woman, with a head of blond hair all matted up and hanging down to her waist. The girl wants to scream for help but there's no more voice left in her, and she starts backing away slowly, because her legs don't work anymore, they're just rubber. The woman is staring straight at her, but all the same it's like she doesn't see her, with this lost look, a madwoman, but her arms stretch out to touch the girl, and she keeps moving ahead very slowly, and the girl is backing away, but without realizing that right behind her there's a row of dense hedges, and when she turns around and finally realizes how she's cornered she lets out a terrible scream, but the other one keeps right on coming, with her arms outstretched, until the girl faints dead away from terror. At that point someone grabs hold of the weirdo lady. It's that the kindly old black woman has arrived. Did I forget to mention her? *a black nurse, old and kindly, a day nurse, at night she leaves the critically ill patient alone with a white nurse, a new one, exposing her to contagion*

—Yes.

—Well, this kindly old black woman amounts to more or less a housekeeper. Big and fat, her hair's already turned completely gray, and always giving the girl these sweet looks ever since she arrived on the island. And by the time the girl regains consciousness the old housekeeper's already carried her inside to bed, and she makes the girl believe that what happened was just a nightmare. And the girl doesn't know whether to believe her or not, but when she sees how nice the housekeeper treats her she calms down, and the housekeeper brings her tea to help her sleep, it's camomile tea, or something like that, I can't remember exactly. Then the following day the marriage ceremony is to take place, so they have to go see the mayor, and pay their respects to him and sign some papers, and the girl is busy getting dressed for the occasion, in a very simple tailored dress, but with a beautiful hairdo which the housekeeper fusses over, to put it up in a kind of braid, how can I explain it? well, back then the upsweep was a must on certain occasions, to look really chic.

—I don't feel well . . . I'm all dizzy again.

—You sure?

—Yes, it's not really bad yet, but I feel the same way I did when it started the other times.

—But that meal couldn't have done you any harm.

—Don't be ridiculous. What makes you think I'm blaming it on your food?

—You seem so irritated . . .

—But it's got nothing to do with your food. It's a matter of my system, there's something still wrong with it.

—Then try not to think about it. That only makes it worse.*

—I just couldn't concentrate any longer on what you were saying.

—But honestly, it must be something else, because that food was totally healthy for you. You know how sometimes, after an illness, you're still suggestible for a while?

—Why not tell a little more of the film, and just see if it goes away. Maybe it's because I'm feeling so weak. I probably ate too fast or something . . . Who the hell knows why . . .

—But that must be it, you're just very weak, and I noticed how fast you were eating, like a kid, without even chewing your food.

—Ever since I woke up this morning I've been thinking about only one thing, and it must be getting to me. I can't get it off my mind.

—What is it?

—The fact that I can't write to my girl . . . but to Marta, yes. And you know, it would probably do me some good to write her, but I can't think of what to say. Because it's wrong for me to write her. Why should I?

—I'll go on with the film then?

*As a variation on the concept of repression, Freud introduces the term "sublimation," understanding by that the mental operation through which problematic libidinal impulses are provided with an outlet. Such outlets for sublimation would include any activity—art, sports, manual labor—that permits use of the sexual energy considered to be excessive by the canons of our society. Freud draws a fundamental distinction between repression and sublimation by suggesting that the latter may be salutary, insofar as it is indispensable to the maintenance of a civilized community.

This position has been attacked by Norman O. Brown, author of *Life Against Death,* which on the contrary favors a return to the state of "polymorphous perversion" discovered by Freud in infants, and thus implies the total elimination of repression. One of the reasons adduced by Freud in his defense of partial repression was the necessity to subjugate the destructive impulses of man, but Brown, as well as Marcuse, refutes this argument by maintaining that aggressive impulses do not exist as such, so long as the impulses of the libido—which are preexistent—find a mode of realization, that is to say, a means of satisfaction.

The criticism directed at Brown, in turn, is based upon the supposition that a humanity without bounds of restraint, that is to say, without repression, could never organize itself into any permanent activity. It is here that Marcuse interjects his concept of "surplus repression," designating by such a term that part of sexual repression created to maintain the power of the dominant class, in spite of not proving to be indispensable to the maintenance of an organized society attending to the human necessities of all its constituents. Therefore, the principal advance that Marcuse presupposes in opposition to Freud would consist of the latter's toleration for a certain type of repression in order to preserve contemporary society, whereas Marcuse deems it fundamental to change society, on the basis of an evolution that takes into account our original sexual impulses.

Such could be considered the basis of the accusation which representatives of the new tendencies have leveled against orthodox Freudian psychoanalysts, to the effect that the latter had sought—with an impunity that became undermined toward the end of the sixties—that their patients assume all personal conflict in order to facilitate their adaptation to the repressive society in which they found themselves, rather than to acknowledge the necessity for change in that society.

In *One-Dimensional Man,* Marcuse asserts that, originally, sexual instinct had no temporal and spatial limitations of subject and object, since sexuality is by nature "polymorphous perverse." Going even further, Marcuse gives as an example of "surplus repression" not only our total concentration on genital copulation but also such phenomena as olfactory and gustatory repression in sexual life.

—Yes, do that.

—Okay, where were we?

—It was just when they were getting the girl ready.

—Ah, that's right, she was having her hair done up in—

—Yeah, it's up, I know already, and what do I care if it is? Don't get so bogged down in details that have so little importance *crudely painted effigy, a sharp blow, the effigy is made of glass, it splinters to bits, the fist doesn't hurt, the fist of a man*

—*the treacherous somnambula and the white nurse, the contagious patient stares at them in the darkness* What do you mean don't! You just keep still because I know what I'm saying. Starting with the fact that wearing the hair up is—pay attention—important, because women only wear it up, it so happens, or they used to back then, when they wanted to really give the impression it was an important occasion, an important date. Because the upsweep, which bared the nape of the neck because they pushed all the hair up on top of the head, it gave a woman's face a certain nobility. And with that whole mass of hair pushed up like that the old housekeeper is making her a braid, and decorating her hair with sprigs of local flowers, and when she finally drives off in a little chaise—even though it's modern-day times they go off in this little carriage pulled by two tiny donkeys—the whole town smiles at her, and she sees herself en route to paradise . . . Is the dizzy spell going away?

—Seems like it is. But continue the story, okay?

—So they go along, her and the housekeeper, and on the steps of that kind of Town Hall-type place they have there, in a colonial style, her fiancè is waiting for her. And then you see them later on, they're out in the dark night air, her lying in a hammock, with a good close-up of the two faces, because he bends down to kiss her, and it's all lit up by the full moon kind of filtering through the palm trees. Oh, but I forgot something important. You see, the

For his part, Dennis Altman, commenting favorably in his own aforementioned book on these assertions by Marcuse, adds that liberation must not only be aimed at eliminating sexual constraint, but also at providing the practical possibility of realizing those desires. Moreover he maintains that only recently have we become aware of how much of what we considered normal and instinctive, especially with respect to family structuring and sexual relations, is actually learned, and as a result how much of what up to now has been considered natural would have to be unlearned, including competitive and aggressive attitudes outside of the sexual realm. And along the same lines, Kate Millett, the theoretician of women's liberation, says in her book *Sexual Politics* that the purpose of sexual revolution ought to be a freedom without hypocrisy, untainted by the exploitive economic bases of traditional sexual alliances, meaning matrimony.

Furthermore, Marcuse favors not only a free flow of the libido, but also a transformation of the same: in other words, the passage from a sexuality circumscribed by genital supremacy to an eroticization of the whole personality. He refers therefore to an expansion more than an explosion of the libido, an expansion that would extend to other areas of human endeavor, private and social, such as work, for example. He adds that the entire weight of civil morality was brought to bear against the use of the body as mere instrument of pleasure, inasmuch as that reification was considered taboo and relegated to the contemptible privilege of prostitutes and perverts.

expression on their faces is like two lovers, and so contented-looking. But what I forgot is that while the black housekeeper's still brushing her hair up for her, the girl—

—Not that hairdo again?

—But you're so irritable! If you don't make any effort yourself you'll never calm down.

—I'm sorry, go on.

—So the girl asks the housekeeper some questions. Like, for instance, where did he go to spend the night. The housekeeper tries to conceal her alarm and says he went to say hello to some people out in the banana groves, including the ones that lived on the farthest plantation of all, and out there most of the peons believe in . . . voodoo. The girl knows it's some kind of black religion and she says how she'd very much like to see some of that, some ceremony, perhaps, because it must be quite lovely, with lots of local color and music, but the housekeeper gives her a frightened look, and tells her no, she better just stay away from all that stuff, because it's a religion that can get very bloody at times, and by no means should she ever go near it. Because . . . but at this point the house-keeper stops talking. And the other one asks her what's the matter, and the housekeeper tells her how there's a legend, which probably isn't even true but just the same it scares her, and it's about the zombies. Zombies? What are they? the girl asks her, and the housekeeper motions her not to say it so loud, only in a very low voice. And she explains that they're the dead people that witch doctors manage to revive before the corpses get cold, because the witch doctors themselves are the ones who kill them, with a special poison they prepare, and the living dead no longer possess any will of their own, and they obey only the orders of the witch doctors, and that the witch doctors use them to do whatever they want them to, and they make them work at anything, and the poor living dead, the zom-bies, they don't have any will at all beyond the witch doctor's. And the

Differing from this position, J. C. Unwin, author of *Sex and Culture,* after studying the marital customs of eighty uncivilized societies, seems to support the very generalized assumption that sex-ual freedom leads to social decadence, since, according to orthodox psychoanalysis, if an individual does not perish from his neurosis, the imposed sexual constraints can help to channel such energies toward socially useful ends. Unwin has concluded from his exhaustive study that the establishment of the first foundations of an organized society, its subsequent development and appropriation of neighboring terrain—in other words, the historical characteristics of every vigorous society—are evident only from the moment when sexual repression has been instated. While those societies in which freedom of sexual relations is tolerated—whether prenuptial, extraconjugal or homosexual—remain in an almost animal state of underdevelopment. But at the same time, Unwin says that societies which are strictly monogamous and strongly repressive do not manage to last very long, and if they do in part, it is by means of the moral and material subjugation of women. Therefore, Unwin claims that, between the suicidal anguish that the minimizing of sexual necessities provokes and the opposite extreme of social disorder attributed to sexual incontinence, a reasonable medium ought to be found which might provide the solution to such a critical problem—that is to say, an elimination of the "surplus repression" about which Marcuse speaks.

housekeeper tells her how many years ago some of the poor peons from a few of the plantations decided to rebel against the owners because they paid them almost nothing, but the owners managed to get together with the chief witch doctor on the island to have him kill all the peons and turn them into zombies, and so it came to pass that after they were dead they were made to work at harvesting bananas, but at night, so as not to have the other peons find out, and all the zombies work and work, without any talk, because zombies don't say a word, or think, even though they suffer so much, because in the middle of working, when the moon shines down on them you can see the tears running down their faces, but they never complain, because zombies can't talk, they haven't any will left and the only thing they get to do is obey and suffer. Well, all of a sudden the girl, because then she remembers the dream that she still thinks she had the other night, the girl asks her whether there's such a thing as a zombie woman. But the housekeeper manages to get off on a tangent somehow and tells her no, because women are never strong enough for such hard work in the fields and so that's why, no, she doesn't think there's any such thing as a zombie woman. And the girl asks her if the fiancé isn't afraid of all that business, and the housekeeper answers no, but naturally he has to put up with a certain amount of superstition in order to stay on friendly terms with the peons, so he just went out there to receive the blessing from the witch doctors themselves. And then the conversation ends, and like I told you, later on you see them together on their wedding night, and happy-looking, because for the first time, you see the kid, the husband, has a look of peace on his face, and all you hear is the *bzz-bzz* of tiny bugs outside and water running in the fountains. And then later you see the two of them lying asleep in their bed, until something wakes them up and gradually they hear, louder and louder, off in the distance, the beating of the drums. She shivers, a chill runs up and down her back . . . Are you feeling any better? *night rounds for the nurses, temperature and pulse normal, white cap, white stockings, good night to the patient*

　　—A little . . . but I can barely follow what you're saying. *the endless night, the cold night, endless thoughts, cold thoughts, sharp slivers of broken glass*

　　—But I ought to stop then. *the strict nurse, the very tall cap stiff with starch, the slight smile not without cunning*

　　—No, honestly, when you distract me a little I feel better, please, go on. *the endless night, the icy night, the walls green with mildew, the walls stricken with gangrene, the injured fist*

　　—Okay. So . . . how did it go next? They hear drums way off in the distance, and the husband's expression changes, all that peace is gone, he can't sleep now, so he gets up. The girl doesn't say anything, discretion itself, she doesn't move a muscle, making like she's fast asleep, but she really pricks up her ears and hears this noise of a cupboard door being opened and squeaking, and then nothing more. She doesn't dare get up and actually investigate, but then it gets later and later and still no sign of him. She decides to look, and finds him lying across an easy chair, completely drunk. And she quickly eyes all the furniture and discovers a little open cabinet, hardly big enough for one bottle, the empty bottle of cognac, but the husband also seems to have another bottle, next to him, and that one is just half empty. So the girl wonders where it came from, because there's no liquor kept in the house at all, and then she notices how, just underneath the bottle in the cabinet, certain things have been tucked away, and it's a bunch of letters and photographs. And it's a job for her to drag him back into the bedroom, where she just lies down beside him, trying to cheer him up because she loves him and promises him he's not going to be alone anymore, and he looks gratefully at her and falls back asleep. She tries to get some sleep too, but now she can't, although before she was so contented, but seeing him drunk like that makes her incredibly upset. And she realizes how right the majordomo was to smash that rum keg. She puts on her negligee and goes back to the cabinet to look at the photos, because what intrigues her incredibly is the possibility of finding a picture of the first wife. But when she gets there she finds the cabinet closed, and locked too. But who could've locked it? She looks around but everything is swallowed up in complete darkness and absolute silence, except for those drums, which you can still hear. Then she goes over to shut the window so as not to have to listen to them, but right at that very moment they stop, as if they'd spotted her from miles and miles away. Anyhow, the next morning he looks as if he doesn't remember anything, and he wakes her with their breakfast all ready, and smiley as can be, and informs her that he's going to take her on a ride by the sea. She becomes totally infected with his excitement, and off they go into the tropics, in a great convertible with the top down, and there's a peppy musical background, calypso type, and they drive past a couple of divine beaches, and here it's a very sexy scene because she feels the urge to go for a swim, because by then they've already seen the lovely coconut groves, and rocky cliffs looking out to sea, and here and there some natural gardens with gigantic flowers, and the sun is scorching hot but she's forgotten to bring along a bathing suit, so he says, why not swim in the nude? and they stop the car, she undresses behind some rocks and then you see her off in the distance running naked to the ocean. And later on you catch them lying on the beach together, under the palms, her with a sarong out of his shirt, and him with just his pants on, nothing else, and barefoot, and you have no idea where it comes from, but you know the way it happens in movies, you suddenly just hear the words of this song, saying how when it comes to love, it's a question of earning it, and at the end of some dark trail, strewn with all kinds of hardships, love awaits those who struggle to the last in order to earn that love. And you can see the girl and he are completely enchanted with each other once again and they decide to let bygones be bygones. And then it begins to get dark, and when they drive up a little ridge of road, you just manage to catch in the background, not too far from there, all glinty from the sun which

is like this fiery red ball, a very old colonial house, but pretty, and very mysterious, because it's completely overrun by vegetation, which covers it up
almost totally. And the girl says how some other day she'd like to go for a
ride to that house, and she asks why it's been abandoned. But at this point
he seems to get very nervous and tells her like very rudely, never, never go
near that house, but he doesn't offer the slightest explanation, just saying
that he'll tell her why some other time. *the night nurse is inexperienced, the
night nurse sleepwalks, is she asleep or awake? the night shift is long, she's
all by herself and doesn't know where to turn for help* You're so quiet, you're
not even making any wisecracks . . .

    —Somehow I'm not feeling very good. Just go on with the film, it's good
to take my mind off things for a while.

    —Wait, now I lost the thread.

    —I don't understand how you manage to keep so many details in your
head anyway. *the hollow head, the glass skull, filled with mass cards of saints
and whores, someone throws the glass head against the putrid wall, the head
smashes, all mass cards fall onto the floor*

    —In spite of the great time they were having that whole day, the girl
gets upset all over again now, because she saw how nervous he became
the minute she asked about that house, the one that looked abandoned.
Well, when they arrive back at the mansion, he takes a shower, and that's
when she can't resist looking through his pockets for the keys in order to
search through that cabinet of the night before. And she goes and searches
through his pants, and finds a key ring, and runs to the cabinet. On the key
ring there's only one tiny key; she tries it and it fits. She opens the cabinet.
There's a full bottle of cognac inside, but who put it there? Because she
hasn't left her husband's side for a second since the night before, so he
didn't do it; she would have seen him. And underneath the bottle there's
some letters, love letters, signed by him and others signed by the first wife,
and underneath the letters some photographs, of him and some other
woman, was that the first wife? The girl seems to recognize her, it's as if
she's seen her somewhere before; surely she's come upon that face before,
but where? An interesting type, very very tall, long blond hair. The girl goes
on looking through each and every photograph, and then she discovers one
in particular that's like a portrait, just of the face, the eyes very pale, that
slightly lost look . . . And the girl remembers! It's the woman who chased
her in the nightmare, with the face of a madwoman, dressed all in black
down to her toes . . . But at that point she notices the water isn't running in
the shower, and her husband could easily catch her going through his
things! So she tries frantically to put away all that stuff, setting the bottle
back on top of the letters and photographs, closing the cabinet, and then
going back into the bedroom, where she finds him right there! all wrapped
up in this huge bath towel, but smiling away. She doesn't know what to do,
so she offers to dry his back, she has no idea how to keep him busy, how
to distract him *the poor nurse, so unlucky, they assign her to a patient on*

the critical list and she doesn't know how to keep him from dying or killing her, the danger of contagion is stronger than ever because he's already about to start getting dressed, but she's terrified that she has the key right in her hand, and he might notice that fact any minute now. But she goes on drying his shoulders with one hand, looking over at his pants draped on the chair, and doesn't know what to do to get the key back into his pocket—until she gets an idea, and says she'd like to comb his hair. And he answers, wonderful, the comb is in the bathroom if you want to get it, and she says, that's no way for a gentleman to act, saying that, so then he goes to look for it himself and meantime she takes the chance to slip the key back into his pocket just in the nick of time, and when he comes back she starts combing his hair and massaging his bare shoulders. And the poor little newlywed, she just breathes a sigh of relief. Then a few days go by, and the girl realizes how the husband always gets up around midnight because he can't sleep, and she pretends to be sound asleep, because she's afraid of bringing up the subject face to face with him, but in the early morning she gets up to help him back into bed, because he always ends up bombed out of his mind and collapsed in the armchair. And she always checks the bottle, and it's a different one each time, and it's full, so who's putting it there in that cabinet? The girl doesn't dare ask him a thing, because when he comes back every evening from the plantations he's so happy to see her waiting there for him, embroidering something, but at midnight you always begin to hear those drums again, and he gets all obsessed about something, and can't sleep anymore unless he gets himself into a drunken stupor. So obviously, the girl gets more and more uptight about the whole thing, and at one point when her husband is outside somewhere, she tries to have a word with the majordomo, to discover some possible secret from him maybe, about why the husband seems so nervous at times, but the majordomo tells her with a big sigh how they're having lots of problems with the peons, etcetera, etcetera, and in the end he really doesn't say too much about anything. Well, the thing is, the girl, one time when the husband tells her he's going off for that whole day with the majordomo, to that plantation that's the farthest away of all, and won't be back until the following day, she decides to go off by herself on foot to that same abandoned house, because she's sure she'll find out something there. And so just after tea, around five o'clock, when the sun isn't so strong anymore, the husband and the majordomo set out on their trip, and the girl eventually goes off too. And she's looking for the road to that abandoned house, but she gets lost, and soon it's getting late, and already almost nightfall, when she manages to find that ridge in the road from where you got to see the house, and she doesn't know whether to turn back or not, but her curiosity gets the best of her, and she goes on to the house. And she sees how suddenly, inside there, a light goes on, which encourages her a little more. But once she reaches the house, which is, no exaggeration, almost buried by wild plants, she doesn't hear anything, and through the windows you can see how on the table there's a candle burning, and the girl gets up enough courage to open the door and even take a look inside, and she sees over in the corner a voodoo altar, with more candles burning, and she goes farther inside to see what's on top of the altar, and she walks right up to it, and on top of the altar she finds a doll with black hair with a pin stuck right through the middle of the chest, and the doll is dressed in an outfit made to look exactly like what she was wearing herself on her own wedding day! And at this point she almost faints with fright but spins around to run away through the same door that she came in by . . . And what's in the doorway? . . . this incredibly huge black guy, with bulging eyeballs, wearing only a ragged pair of old pants, and with the look of somebody who's totally out of his mind, staring at her and blocking any escape. And the poor thing, all she has left to do is let out a desperate scream, but the guy, who's actually what they call a zombie, one of the living dead, he keeps coming closer and closer, with his arms reaching out, just like the woman from the other night in the garden. And the girl lets out another scream, and runs into the next room and locks the door behind her. The room's almost dark, with the window almost covered with jungle growth so only a tiny bit of light comes through, a little twilight, and the room has a bed in it, which little by little the girl begins to make out, as she becomes more accustomed to the darkness. And every inch of her shudders, nearly suffocated by her own cries and her terror, as she sees there on the bed . . . something moving . . . and it's . . . that woman! Incredibly pale, all disheveled, the hair hanging down to her waist, and with the same black duster on, she slowly rises and begins to move toward the girl! in that room without escape, all locked up . . . The girl would like to drop dead she's so frightened, and now she can't even scream, but suddenly . . . from the window you hear a voice ordering the zombie woman to stop and go back to her bed . . . It's the kindly black housekeeper. And she tells the girl not to be scared, that she's going to come right in and protect her. The girl opens the door, the black woman hugs her and calms her down; and behind her, in the front doorway, is that black giant, but he's totally obedient now to the housekeeper, who tells him he must look after the girl, and not attack her. The giant black zombie obeys, and the zombie woman, too, all disheveled, because the housekeeper orders her back to her bed, and the woman completely obeys. Then the housekeeper takes the girl affectionately by her shoulders and tells her she's going to get her back safely to the main house in a little donkey cart, and along the way she tells her the whole story, because by now the girl's realized that the zombie woman with the blond hair down to her waist . . . is her husband's first wife. And the housekeeper begins to tell how it all happened. *the nurse trembles, the patient looks up at her, asking for morphine? asking to be caressed? or does he just want the contagion to be instantaneous and deadly?*

—the skull is glass, the body is glass too, easy to break a toy made out of glass, slivers of sharp cold glass in the cold night, the humid night, gangrene

spreading through the hand shredded by the punch Do you mind if I say
something?

—*at night the patient gets up and walks barefoot, he catches cold, his
condition deteriorates* What? Go ahead.

—*the glass skull full of mass cards of saints and whores, old yellowed
mass cards, dead faces outlined in cracked paper, inside my chest the dead
mass cards, glass mass cards, sharp, shredding, spreading the gangrene into
the lungs, the chest, the heart* I'm very depressed. I can hardly follow what
you say. I think it'd be much better to save the rest for tomorrow, don't you?
And this way we can talk a little.

—Fine, what do you want to talk about?

—I feel so awful . . . you have no idea. And so confused . . . Anyhow, I . . .
I see it a little more clearly now, it's the business I was talking about that
had to do with my girl, how afraid I am for her, because she's in danger . . .
but that the one I long to hear from, the one I'm longing to see, isn't my girl.
And longing to touch, it's not her I'm dying for, to hold in my arms, because
I'm just aching for Marta, my whole body aches for her . . . to feel her close
to me, because I think Marta is really the only one who could save me at all,
because I feel like I'm dead, I swear I do. And I have this notion that nothing
except her could ever revive me again.

—Keep talking, I'm listening.

—You're going to laugh at what I want to ask of you.

—No I won't, why should I?

—If it's not a bother, would you mind lighting the candle? . . . What I'd
like is to dictate a letter to you for her, I mean for the one I always talk about,
for Marta. Because I get dizzy if I use my eyes for anything.

—But, what could be wrong with you? Couldn't it be something else?
Besides the stomach problem, I mean.

—No, I'm just terribly weak, that's all, and I want to unburden myself
a little somehow, Molina, my friend, because I can't stand it anymore. This
afternoon I tried myself to write a letter, but the page kept swimming.

—Sure then, wait till I find the matches.

—You've been really good to me.

—There we are. Shall we do a rough draft on scratch paper first, or what
would you like to do?

—Yeah, on scratch paper, because I've no idea of what to say. Use my
ball-point.

—Wait, I'll just sharpen this pencil.

—No, take my ball-point, I'm telling you.

—Fine, but don't start foaming at the mouth again.

—I'm sorry, I just see everything black right now.

—Okay, start dictating.

—Dear . . . Marta: It must be strange for you . . . to get this letter.
I feel . . . lonely, I need you so, I want to talk with you, I want . . . to be
close, I want you to . . . give me . . . some word of comfort. I'm here in my

cell, who knows where you are right now? . . . and how you're feeling, or what you're thinking, or what you might be needing right this minute? . . . But I just have to write you a letter, even if I don't send it, who knows what'll happen actually? . . . But let me talk to you anyway . . . because I'm afraid . . . afraid that something is about to break inside of me . . . if I don't open up to you a little. If only we could actually talk together, you'd understand what I mean . . .

—". . . you'd understand what I mean . . ."

—I'm sorry, Molina, how did I tell her that I'm not going to send her the letter? Read it to me, would you?

—"But I just have to write you a letter, even if I don't send it."

—Would you add, "But I will send it."

—"But I will send it." Go ahead. We were at "If only we could actually talk together, you'd understand what I mean . . ."

—. . . because at this moment I could never present myself to my comrades and talk with them, I'd be ashamed to be this weak . . . Marta, I feel as if I have a right to live a little longer, and that someone should pour a little . . . honey . . . on my wounds . . .

—Yes . . . Go on.

—. . . Inside, I'm all raw, and only someone like you could really understand . . . because you were raised in a clean and comfortable house like me and taught to enjoy life, and I'm the same way. I can't adjust to being a martyr, it infuriates me, I don't want to be a martyr, and right now I wonder if the whole thing hasn't been one terrible mistake on my part . . . They tortured me, but still I didn't confess anything . . . I didn't even know the real names of my comrades, so I only confessed combat names, and the police can't get anywhere with that, but inside myself there seems to be another kind of torturer . . . and for days he hasn't let up . . . And it's because I seem to be asking for some kind of justice. Look how absurd what I'm about to say is: I'm asking for some kind of justice, for some providence to intervene . . . because I don't deserve to just rot forever in this cell or, I get it . . . I get it . . . Now I see it clearly, Marta . . . It's that I'm afraid because I've just been sick . . . and I have this fear in me . . . this terrible fear of dying . . . and of it all ending like this, with a life reduced to just this rotten bit of time, but I don't think I deserve that. I've always acted with generosity, I've never exploited anyone . . . and I fought, from the moment I possessed a little understanding of things . . . fought against the exploitation of my fellow man . . . And I've always cursed all religions, because they simply confuse people and prevent them from fighting for any kind of equality . . . but now I find myself thirsting for some kind of justice . . . divine justice. I'm asking that there be a God . . . Write it with a capital G, Molina, please . . .

—Yes, go on.

—What did I say?

—"I'm asking that there be a God . . ."

—. . . a God who sees me, and helps me, because I want to be able, someday, to walk down streets again, and I want that day to come soon, and I don't want to die. But at times it runs through my mind that I'm never, never going to touch a woman again, and I can't stand it . . . And whenever I think about women . . . I see no one but you in my mind, and it would be such a comfort to somehow believe that at this moment, from here on, until I finish this letter to you, you're really thinking about me, too . . . while you run your hand over your body which I remember so well . . .

—Wait, don't go so fast.

—. . . your body which I remember so well, and that you're pretending it's my hand . . . and what a deep consolation that could be for me . . . my love, if that were happening . . . because it would be just like my touching you, because a part of me is still with you, right? Just the way the scent of your body is still inside my nostrils . . . and beneath the tips of my fingers I too have the sensation of feeling your skin . . . as if I'd somehow memorized it, do you understand me? Even though it has nothing to do with understanding . . . because it's a question of believing, and at times I'm convinced that I've kept something of yours with me, too . . . and that I've never lost it . . . But then sometimes, no, I feel like there's nothing here in this cell except me . . . all alone . . .

—Yes . . . "me . . . all alone . . ." Go ahead.

—. . . and that nothing leaves a trace of itself, and that the luck of having been so happy together, of having spent those nights with you, and afternoons, and mornings of pure enjoyment, is absolutely worthless to me now, and actually works against me . . . because I miss you like crazy, and the only thing I feel is the torture of loneliness, and in my nostrils there's nothing but the disgusting smell of this cell, and of myself . . . but I can't wash myself because I'm so sick, so totally debilitated, and the cold water would probably give me pneumonia, and beneath the tips of my fingers what I really feel is the chill fear of dying, and in my very marrow I feel it . . . that same chill . . . It's so terrible to lose hope, and that's what's happening with me . . . The torturer that I have inside of me tells me everything is finished, and that this agony is my last experience on earth . . . and I say this like a true Christian, as if afterward another life were waiting . . . but there's nothing waiting, is there?

—Can I interrupt? . . .

—What's wrong?

—When you finish, remind me to tell you something.

—What?

—Well, that there is something we could do, actually . . .

—What? Say it.

—Because if you wash yourself in that freezing shower it certainly will kill you, as sick as you are right now.

—But what is to be done? For the last time, tell me, goddamn it!

—Well, I could help you clean yourself. Look, we can heat some water up in the pot, we already have two towels, so one we soap up and you wash the front of yourself, I can do the back for you, and with the other towel slightly wet we sponge off the soap.

—And then my body wouldn't itch so much?

—That's right, we can do it bit by bit, so you don't catch any chill, first your neck and ears, then your underarms, then your arms, your chest, your back, and so on.

—And you'd really help me?

—Obviously.

—But when?

—Right now if you like, I'll heat up some water.

—And then I can sleep, without the itching? . . .

—Peaceful as can be, without any itching. The water will be warm enough in just a few minutes.

—But that kerosene is yours, you'll waste it.

—It doesn't matter, in the meantime we'll finish your letter.

—Give it to me.

—What for?

—Just give it to me, Molina.

—Here . . .

— . . .

—What are you going to do?

—This.

—But why are you tearing up your letter?

—Let's not discuss it any further.

—Whatever you say.

—It's just no good getting carried away like that, out of desperation . . .

—But it's good to get something off your chest sometimes, you said so yourself.

—Well, it doesn't work for me. I have to just put up with it . . .

— . . .

—Listen, you've been very kind to me, honestly, I mean that with all my heart. And someday I expect to be able to show my appreciation, I swear I will . . . that much water?

—Mmm-hmm, we'll need at least that much . . . And don't be silly, there's nothing to thank me for.

—So much water . . .

— . . .

—Molina . . .

—Mmm?

—Look at the shadows that the stove's casting on the wall.

—Mmm, I always watch them. You never saw them before?

—No, I never noticed.

—Mmm, it helps me pass the time, watching the shadows when the stove's lit.

QUESTIONS FOR DISCUSSION AND WRITING

1. Who are Molina and Valentin? What are their crimes? In what ways are they different? Alike?
2. Read the descriptions of the two prisoners. Why have they been housed together?
3. What common themes run through the plot of the movie that Valentin is telling and the main story of the two prisoners? Why are these themes important to the overall story?
4. In the telling of the movie plot, what role do the italicized passages play?
5. In the story that follows the play-like passage, what is the relationship between Molina and Valentin? How does this differ from what you might have expected?
6. In what way does the information contained in the footnote elucidate the story in the dialogue between the warden and the prisoner?
7. Why is Molina cooperating with the warden? Or is he? What tells you about any change of heart he might be having?
8. What is the significance of the last sentence: "Mmm, it helps me pass the time, watching the shadows when the stove's lit"?

ON TECHNIQUE AND STYLE

1. The first part of this excerpt, Chapter 8, is just one short chapter out of the novel. However, it combines three different forms of writing: a government report, a play, and academic-style footnotes. What effect does this have on your reading of this part of the novel? Why do you think Puig wrote this way? Why does the footnote come at the point that it does?
2. Why are the "players" in the drama identified as "Warden" and "Prisoner," especially since we know the prisoner's name from the dialog of the play?
3. In the main story, why is Molina called by his surname, but Valentin by his first? Do you know the translations of these names?
4. A primary narrative technique of *Kiss of the Spider Woman* is the embedded narrative. This means that a character within the frame story tells another story, in this case to another character in the story. In what way is this narrative technique important to the understanding of the larger themes of this story?

CULTURAL QUESTION

1. In one sense, this story is about culture clash: a gay man, who thrives on movies and fantasy, and a political idealist, who struggles with his commitment to Marxism and those around him, must come together in the setting

of the prison cell. In what ways do you see their struggle as cultural? Personal? Political?

POETRY

The Report

Dick Allen

Dick Allen grew up in Round Lake, New York, in the Adirondack foothills. At the end of his first year at Syracuse University, he took trains and buses and hitchhiked around America—the first of many cross-country trips that contribute to the imagery in his poetry. He received his MA at Brown University, winning the Academy of American Poets Prize. His poetry collections include Anon and Various Time Machine Poems *(1971),* Regions With No Proper Names *(1975),* Overnight in the Guest House of the Mystic *(1984),* Flight and Pursuit *(1987),* Ode to the Cold War: Poems New and Selected *(1997), and* The Day Before: New Poems *(2003). Allen cofounded the Expansive Poetry movement, editing the issue of* CrossCurrents *with which the movement was launched. He has been writing and publishing poems in what he calls "Randomism," a form of the lyric narrative. He lives with his wife (poet L. N. Allen) in Connecticut.* The Report *was published in* The Atlantic, *January 1990.*

The wind is blowing on the prison walls
Above the secret towns. In the secret towns
Men are walking through the streets with guns.

Men with guns are walking through the streets
Below the prison walls. The prison walls
Are on the cliffs above the secret towns.

Behind the shattered windows and the shattered doors,
The women kneel and pray. The women pray
While men are walking through the streets with guns.

Men with guns are walking through the streets,
Breaking down the doors. Breaking down the doors
Is what the men do in the secret towns.

The women pray they'll stop. *Please stop,* they pray,
And let the prison fall. Let the prison fall,
They pray behind the windows and the shattered doors.

But the men are laughing in the secret towns,
And carrying the guns. The men with guns
Walk and laugh below the prison walls.

Below the prison walls lie secret towns
With broken doors. Beyond the broken doors
Men are walking through the streets with guns.

QUESTIONS FOR DISCUSSION AND WRITING

1. What feeling do you get from this poem? Explain your answer by quoting specific phrases or lines.
2. Why do you think the poet repeats the phrase "secret towns"? What is the significance of these secret towns?
3. Why are the women crying and praying? Why do they say, "Let the prison fall"?
4. Why is this poem called "The Report" in your opinion?

ON TECHNIQUE AND STYLE

1. Very little concrete detail is given in this poem—that is, we don't know much about the setting, the men with guns, and so on. Can you construct a narrative around this poem? What do you imagine the setting to be? Who are these characters?
2. The poet repeats several lines throughout the poem. Which ones? What is the effect of this repetition?
3. Why is the word order of the repeated phrases changed in some cases?

CULTURAL QUESTION

1. This poem may be seen as part of the Expansive Poetry movement, which attempts to look at narrative "in the world" instead of "inside the poet." In what ways does this poem address global or universal themes? Is it similar in form to any other poems you know?

Hard Rock Returns to Prison from the Hospital for the Criminal Insane

Etheridge Knight

Etheridge Knight (1931–1991) was born in Corinth, Mississippi. He dropped out of school at sixteen and joined the U.S. Army, serving from 1947 to 1951 in Korea. He returned to the United States wounded, and became addicted to drugs. In 1960, he was arrested for robbery and sentenced to eight years in the Indiana State Prison. During his incarceration, he began writing poetry, and he corresponded with and was visited by such African American literary figures as Gwendolyn Brooks and Dudley Randall. Randall's Broadside Press published Knight's first book, Poems from Prison *(1968), one year before he was released from prison. The book was a success, and Knight soon joined poets Amiri Baraka, Haki Madhubuti, and Sonia Sanchez (to whom he was once married) in what is known as the Black Arts movement. In 1970, Knight edited the collection* Black Voices From Prison. *His other works include* Belly Song and Other Poems *(1973) and* Born of a Woman *(1980). In 1990, he earned a bachelor's degree in American poetry and criminal justice from Martin Center University in Indianapolis. The poem below was taken from* The Essential Etheridge Knight, *by Etheridge Knight, © 1986.*

Hard Rock / was / "known not to take no shit
From nobody," and he had the scars to prove it:
Split purple lips, lumped ears, welts above
His yellow eyes, and one long scar that cut
Across his temple and plowed through a thick
Canopy of kinky hair.

The WORD / was / that Hard Rock wasn't a mean nigger
Anymore, that the doctors had bored a hole in his head,
Cut out part of his brain, and shot electricity
Through the rest. When they brought Hard Rock back,
Handcuffed and chained, he was turned loose,
Like a freshly gelded stallion, to try his new status.
And we all waited and watched, like a herd of sheep,
To see if the WORD was true.

As we waited we wrapped ourselves in the cloak
Of his exploits: "Man, the last time, it took eight
Screws to put him in the Hole." "Yeah, remember when he

Smacked the captain with his dinner tray?" "He set
The record for time in the Hole—67 straight days!"
"Ol Hard Rock! man, that's one crazy nigger."
And then the jewel of a myth that Hard Rock had once bit
A screw on the thumb and poisoned him with syphilitic spit.

The testing came, to see if Hard Rock was really tame.
A hillbilly called him a black son of a bitch
And didn't lose his teeth, a screw who knew Hard Rock
From before shook him down and barked in his face.
And Hard Rock did nothing. Just grinned and looked silly,
His eyes empty like knot holes in a fence.

And even after we discovered that it took Hard Rock
Exactly 3 minutes to tell you his first name,
We told ourselves that he had just wised up,
Was being cool; but we could not fool ourselves for long,
And we turned away, our eyes on the ground. Crushed.
He had been our Destroyer, the doer of things
We dreamed of doing but could not bring ourselves to do,
The fears of years, like a biting whip,
Had cut deep bloody grooves
Across our backs.

QUESTIONS FOR DISCUSSION AND WRITING

1. Who is Hard Rock, and what has happened to him? How is the story of Hard Rock "reinterpreted" by the prisoners?
2. In what ways is Hard Rock a legendary character? A tragic figure?
3. Why does the narrator say "we could not fool ourselves for long"?
4. Explain the lines "The fears of years, like a biting whip / Had cut deep bloody grooves / Across our backs."

ON TECHNIQUE AND STYLE

1. Why do we find the word "was" in slashes? Why is "word" capitalized twice? What effect do these techniques have?
2. Who is the narrator (or narrators)? What is the effect of having a plural narrative voice?
3. This poem holds some strong imagery. Find one or two examples you find particularly powerful. Explain your choice.
4. This poem is written in iambic meter (read it aloud to get a feel for the rhythm). Some critics have said this makes the poem less effective. Why do you think they might say this? Do you find it distracts from the poem?

CULTURAL QUESTION

1. This is a narrative poem of a fallen hero. In what way is this type of poem cross-cultural? Can you think of other examples of similar narrative poetry?

GRAPHIC FICTION

From The Beast of Chicago: An Account of the Life and Crimes of Herman W. Mudgett

Rick Geary

Rick Geary (1946–   ) is known primarily for his nonfiction comic book series, A Treasury of Victorian Murder. *The series tells the stories of Lizzie Borden, Charles Guiteau, Jack the Ripper, and H. H. Holmes, featured in the following excerpt which was published in 2004. Geary graduated from the University of Kansas in Lawrence, where his first cartoons were published in the* University Daily Kansan. *Geary was introduced to a wider readership with his contributions to the* Heavy Metal *and* National Lampoon *magazines. During his residence in New York, his illustrations appeared in* The New York Times Book Review. *His illustration work has also been seen in* MAD, Spy, Rolling Stone, *and the* Los Angeles Times. *He lives in San Diego, California.*

QUESTIONS FOR DISCUSSION AND WRITING

1. As in some other instances in this book, this isn't actually fiction, but a real history told in comics format. Does the comics format make the history more or less accessible, in your opinion?
2. Why is Holmes's beard pointed out? Why do you think he shaved it?
3. Why was Holmes's coffin filled with cement?
4. Why do you think Holmes's grave is not marked with a stone?
5. Look up the history of Holmes on the Internet to get a little more information about him if you aren't aware of his story already.

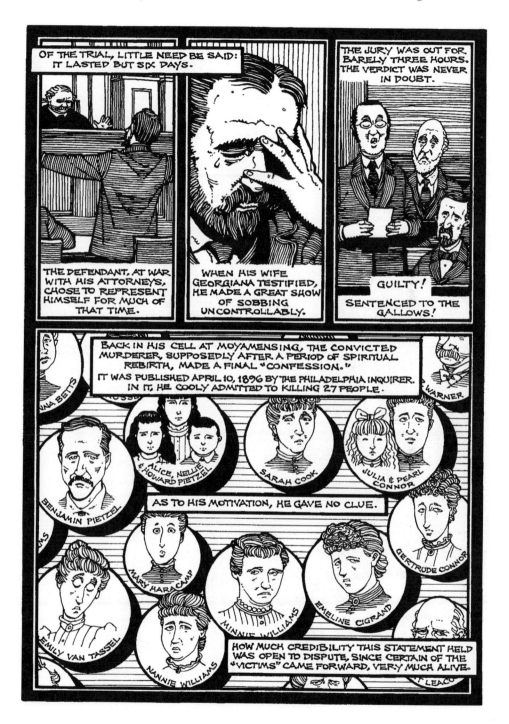

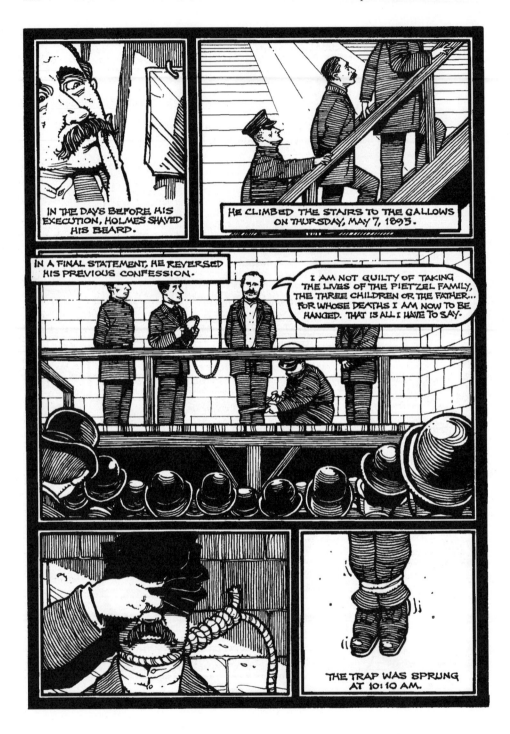

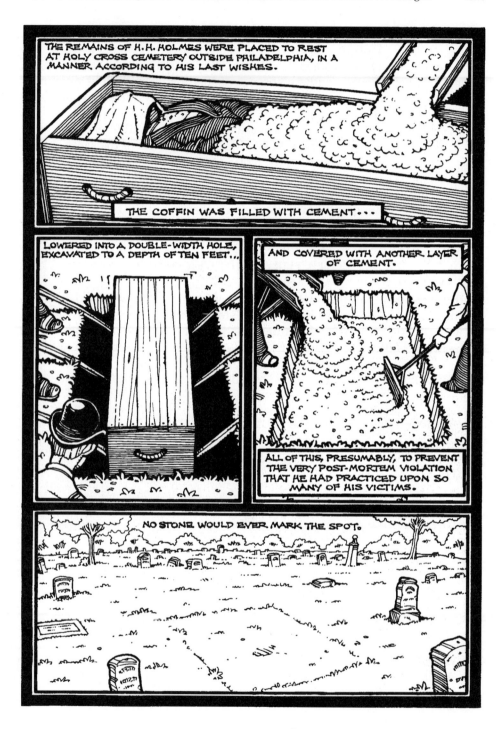

ON TECHNIQUE AND STYLE

1. Geary's artwork is distinctive, usually drawn with simple black lines on a white background, with an absence of shading. What is your opinion of this technique? Is it an effective way of conveying his stories? Explain your answer.

2. Geary's method of drawing individual panels is also different from most artists, who typically draw several consecutive panels of the same characters in the same setting to tell the story. Geary rarely devotes two consecutive panels to the same location or character. This creates an impression of jumping from one part of the story to another. Again, is this an effective technique, in your opinion? Explain your answer.

CULTURAL QUESTION

1. In the United States, criminals sometimes become notorious, and in a way, "celebrated" through legends and stories. Examples of such legends include the outlaws Jesse James and Billy the Kid from the nineteenth century and the bank robbers Bonnie and Clyde from the last century. Is this an American phenomenon, or a cross-cultural one? Can you think of examples outside the United States of notorious, but celebrated outlaws?

VISUAL TEXTS

Prisoners Exercising

Vincent van Gogh

Vincent Willem van Gogh (1853–1890) was a Dutch Post-Impressionist artist. His paintings and drawings are some of the world's best-known, most popular, and most expensive pieces. Recurring episodes of mental illness eventually led to his suicide. Van Gogh painted Prisoners Exercising, *(1890) from a print of Gustave Doré's* Newgate: The Exercise Yard.

Prisoner

David Siqueiros

David Alfaro Siqueiros (1896–1974) was a social realist painter, known for being an artist of the "Mexican Mural Renaissance" along with Diego Rivera, José Clemente

Orozco, and others. In the early 1930s, including his time spent in Mexico's Lecum-
berri Prison, Siqueiros created a series of politically themed lithographs. Prisoner
(1931) is one of those lithographs.

The Panopticon

Jeremy Bentham

*Jeremy Bentham (1748–1832) was an English jurist, philosopher, and social reformer.
He was considered a political radical during his time—one who supported animal
rights, equal rights for women, separation of church and state, and abolition of slavery.
He was a leading theorist in Anglo-American philosophy of law. Bentham's Panopticon, designed in 1785, is a type of prison building. The design allows all (pan-) prisoners to be observed (-opticon) without the prisoners knowing it. Bentham referred to
this as the "sentiment of an invisible omniscience." Bentham described the Panopticon
as "a new mode of obtaining power of mind over mind, in a quantity hitherto without
example."*

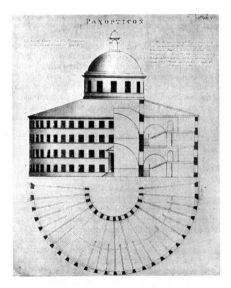

Panopticon blueprint by Jeremy Bentham,
1791

QUESTIONS FOR DISCUSSION AND WRITING

1. In what ways do Van Gogh's painting and Siqueiros's lithograph reflect the issues presented by Tannenbaum?
2. Siqueiros was imprisoned in Mexico, while van Gogh is often seen as having been imprisoned in a psychiatric hospital. Do you think these experiences have a direct effect on artwork? How is this evident in either of these images?
3. Although the building of Bentham's Panopticon was not realized in Bentham's lifetime, Foucault later saw the design as a metaphor for all kinds of disciplinary structures in society. Can you relate the drawing of the Panopticon to Foucault's essay, found earlier in this chapter?
4. Look at each of the images and choose one or more readings you find it represents. Discuss your choices.
5. Which of the images do you find more effective in conveying its message? Why?

ON TECHNIQUE AND STYLE

1. Van Gogh presents the group prison experience, while Siqueiros focuses on the individual. What kind of impact do these choices have on the viewer? Why?
2. What effect do the shadows in van Gogh and Siqueiros's artwork have on the viewer? How would the images change without them?
3. Look closely at Bentham's drawing. How would the concept of the Panopticon work? Explain the parts of the drawing.

CULTURAL QUESTION

1. How does culture affect the visual imagery we associate with prisons? When you think about prisons as represented in other cultures, what differences are there among the different representations? Think of as many examples as you can.

AUDIO TEXTS   To hear these conversations, go to www.mhhe.com/soundideas1e

Track 6.1

(date: November 22, 2005; running time: 22:00 min.)

Panel discussion on death-row clemency: Austin Sarat, William Nelson Cromwell Professor of Jurisprudence and Political Science, Amherst College; Michael Rushford, president of the Criminal Justice Legal Foundation; Wayne Owens,

brother of Albert Owens, one of Stanley "Tookie" Williams's attributed murder victims; Mike Farrell, president of Death Penalty Focus; and Dan Walters,
reporter, *Sacramento Bee.*

QUESTIONS FOR DISCUSSION AND WRITING

1. Who are some of the famous people who joined the protest about Stanley
   Williams's death sentence? What effect, if any, do you think famous people
   have on such public protests?
2. Why does Owens not support the idea of clemency in the case of Williams?
3. What is Sarat's major argument against the death penalty?
4. Do some Internet research on public opinion on the death penalty. How
   does it compare to what the different speakers say about its popularity?

ON TECHNIQUE AND STYLE

1. What statistics does Walters bring to the argument about the death penalty? Is his argument effective? Why doesn't he think the California governor will grant clemency?
2. What is the connotation of the word "snitch" as used by Farrell? How is it
   used to make his point?
3. What is the difference between "clemency" and "mercy" according to
   Sarat? Why is this distinction important?

CULTURAL QUESTION

1. The United States is said to be one of the last industrialized nations to
   support the death penalty. Why do you think it has lasted in this country
   whereas it has been abolished elsewhere? What is the difference between
   U.S. attitudes toward crimes and prisons as reflected in death penalty
   practices?

Additional Audio Resources

1. "The Prison Diaries," by Joe Richman, at www.learnoutloud.com/Free
   -Audio-Video/Biography/Everyday-People/Prison-Diaries/1081.
2. "The Consolation of Philosophy," by Boethius, at http://librivox.org/
   the-consolation-of-philosophy-by-boethius/.

CONNECTIONS

1. In which readings or other texts do you see Foucault's themes reflected most clearly? Find specific examples.
2. In what ways do the *Forum* panelists reflect ideas found in other writings in this chapter?
3. Do you find Peltier's memoir to be similar to any of the pieces of fiction or poetry? Which ones? Give specific examples of the similarities you find.
4. In what ways does Dostoevsky's story seem similar to other more modern stories of prison life?
5. In which short stories or other texts do you find Tannenbaum's ideas reflected?
6. In what way might Dostoevsky's excerpt from *The House of the Dead* illustrate examples of "prison cruelty" as explained by Tannenbaum?
7. Which texts focus on the idea of burying prisoners? What are some of the practices? What are the connections?
8. What is the importance of "rats" and "snitches" in the prison system? Which texts deal with this issue?
9. Which texts deal substantially with the issue of race and incarceration? How do these texts speak to each other?

FOR WRITING

CREATIVE CHOICES

1. Puig's fiction is characterized by his frequent references to popular culture, especially American movies. Write a short story or autobiographical memoir about the influence of a particular movie on yourself.
2. Create a comic that illustrates one of the main themes of this chapter. (Keep in mind that you need not be an accomplished artist to create a comic. Simple drawings or even photos cut out from magazines or newspapers can be very effective.)
3. Continue work in your journal. In it, write about your reactions to any of the stories presented in this chapter, or in the current news. If you prefer, create an audio or video journal, recording your spoken ideas.

NARRATIVE/EXPOSITORY CHOICES

1. Choose two readings from this chapter from the fiction and/or poetry sections. Make your choice based on a shared theme. What theme do these two readings share? How is the theme illustrated? Develop a thesis

based on your reading of these stories, and write an analytical essay in which you use extensively passages from the readings to support your thesis.

2. The role of adjustment to life on the "outside" comes up in a few of the readings in this chapter. Write an essay in which you explore ways in which life outside of prison could be made more successful for prisoners returning to their normal lives.

3. How is the idea of a fantasy world used in readings here as a way of escape from a more brutal reality? Compare at least two of the readings in this chapter in an exploratory essay on this topic.

ARGUMENT CHOICES

1. Should prisons primarily be places of punishment or places of rehabilitation? Write an essay in which you argue for one of these positions.

2. The rise in prison population can be attributed to the increased rates of incarceration for nonviolent drug offenders and three-strike laws. Write a paper in which you argue for or against incarceration for nonviolent drug offenders. Use the readings found in this chapter to support your claims, and quote appropriately.

3. None of the writings in this chapter deals directly with the issue of crime victims, or victims' rights. Choose two or three of the readings, and argue against their premises from the point of view of crime victims.

RESEARCH CHOICES

1. It is especially difficult to argue for or against the death penalty, because most people have strong beliefs rooted in their own religions or senses of ethics and justice. Research some of the reasons people have in favor of and against the death penalty. Present them in a research report in which you do not present your own point of view.

2. Look up prison statistics on your own state, or a state that interests you. Write a short research report on the current status of the prisons in that state.

3. Research the Leonard Peltier case. Write a chronology of events, and a summary of the current status of his case.

VIDEO SUGGESTIONS

The following films address the themes and ideas found in this chapter.

1. *25th Hour* (2002). A convicted drug dealer reevaluates his life in the twenty-four remaining hours before facing a seven-year jail term. Directed by Spike Lee.

2. *Dead Man Walking* (1995). A nun, while comforting a convicted killer on death row, empathizes with both the killer and his victim's families.
3. *Incident at Oglala* (1992). On June 26, 1975, on the Pine Ridge reservation in South Dakota, two FBI agents were killed in a shootout with a group of Native Americans. Although several men were charged with the killings, only Leonard Peltier was found guilty. This film describes the events surrounding the shootout and suggests that Peltier was unjustly convicted.
4. *Kiss of the Spider Woman* (1985). The film version of Manuel Puig's novel/play.
5. *Shawshank Redemption* (1994). A young and successful banker's life changes drastically when he is convicted and sentenced to life imprisonment for the murder of his wife and her lover.

chapter 7

Ideas about the Environment

Human versus Nature versus Human

INTRODUCTION

"It's not easy being green" are words that belong to *Sesame Street* character Kermit the Frog. Being green has become synonymous with environmental mindedness and concern with conserving and sustaining and literally saving the planet and its resources. Controversy over environmental issues and how to deal with them persists, but most thoughtful people, in one way or another, care about some part of the environment and the natural world. The bigger challenge, as environmentalists like Theodore Roszak and others have pointed out, is in deciding which environmental issue, among the many, ought to require the greatest attention and action.

This chapter focuses attention on matters related to the environment, environmental issues, and the natural world. Beginning with Ralph Waldo Emerson's classic essay "Nature," a transcendental ecological primer on the exalted and spiritual beauty of the natural world, the selections in the chapter make us more keenly aware of the importance of the environment and the pressing need to protect it. Other essays include a letter to Henry David Thoreau, Emerson's contemporary and the author of *Walden*, from Edward O. Wilson, the man often described as the founder of the modern environmental movement. Wilson's letter explains the environmental decline from Thoreau's time to ours and alerts us to the perils of ongoing environmental degradation. Environmental degradation is made apparent in the selection excerpted from Rachel Carson's *Silent Spring*, a pioneering book about the environmental harm caused by pesticide use. The nonfiction section concludes with a selection from one of our most admired nature writers, Annie Dillard. The excerpt from her book *Pilgrim at Tinker Creek* brings the spirit of Emerson and his awareness of nature's spiritual beauty into a modern context.

The fiction selections continue the focus on lessons to be gleaned from the natural world and also hone in on a number of important environmental concerns. The opening selection is from Ernest Hemingway's famous novel *The Old Man and the Sea;* it pinpoints the sense of the power and beauty of the sea and its relationship to the land and to us. Barry Lopez's mythic story, "Lessons from the Wolverine," takes us on a journey geographically into the arctic region and poetically into the world of wolverines and to a greater understanding of the relationship between humankind and the animal world. Sarah Orne Jewett's "A White Heron" brings us deeper into that relationship between humans and animals and into a greater understanding of the ties that connect the natural world to the young female protagonist in the story who feels compelled to preserve it. In the excerpt from Ruth Ozecki's novel *My Year of Meats* we learn, through a man working as the protagonist's guide in Colorado, about the environmental dangers in raising and feeding cattle for meat production. Both the Jewett story and the Ozeki excerpt face questions related to the importance of environmental sustainability.

The two poems in this chapter are separated by over a century and by the Atlantic Ocean. Yet both poets write with a reverence for nature and an awareness of the effects and changes that accrue with changes in the natural environment. The poems by William Wordsworth, Britain's poet laureate of over a century ago, and Jean Toomer, a central figure in the Harlem Renaissance of the 1920s, both exemplify what so often in poetry is characterized as Romanticism and that movement's connections to the natural world.

The selection in this chapter from the Will Eisner graphic novel of Herman Melville's *Moby Dick* renders a picture of what whaling was like over a century ago and how the commercial enterprise eventually led to environmentalists protesting actively to "Save the Whales." The three pictures in this chapter evoke, in different ways, environmental crises related to planetary sustainability, global warming, and depletion of water as a resource.

The audios in the chapter key in on the forests and the oceans and include an interview that was broadcast on public radio with grassroots environmental organizer and Nobel Peace Prize recipient Wangari Maathai, who started the Green Belt movement in her native Kenya. It led to the planting of millions of trees and provided income for thousands of often poor and unemployed men and women. The movement has been replicated throughout the African continent and in the United States and Haiti. The other audio selections are from live public radio panel discussions focusing on the endangerment of the oceans. An impressive quartet of experts recommend ways to ensure the ocean's preservation and sustainability.

NONFICTION

Nature

Ralph Waldo Emerson

Ralph Waldo Emerson (1803–1882) is one of nineteenth-century America's leading thinkers and philosophers. Emerson was also a poet who became famous for his essays and lectures. Born in Boston, he went to Harvard at the age of fourteen and graduated in 1821. The son of a Unitarian minister, he followed his father and also became a Unitarian minister soon after graduating from Harvard Divinity School. Founder and leading exponent of the movement that came to be known as transcendentalism, Emerson continues to be a major intellectual influence. In the essay "Nature," first published anonymously in 1836, Emerson lays out a spiritual and aesthetic view of nature and the relationship human beings have with the natural world. The reverence and delight he believes is inherent in the world of nature he also sees as being inherent in humankind. In many respects "Nature" is a primer for an environmentalist, celebrating the wonders of the natural world—stars, trees, woods and landscape—and placing solitude and love of nature at the matrix of appreciating the ecological world. The essay also has within it some of the mystical feelings for nature that have come to be associated with Eastern thinking, the Zen-like view that one can lose the sense of oneself in the bounty of nature.

To go into solitude, a man needs to retire as much from his chamber as from society. I am not solitary whilst I read and write, though nobody is with me. But if a man would be alone, let him look at the stars. The rays that come from those heavenly worlds, will separate between him and what he touches. One might think the atmosphere was made transparent with this design, to give man, in the heavenly bodies, the perpetual presence of the sublime. Seen in the streets of cities, how great they are! If the stars should appear one night in a thousand years, how would men believe and adore; and preserve for many generations the remembrance of the city of God which had been shown! But every night come out these envoys of beauty, and light the universe with their admonishing smile.

The stars awaken a certain reverence, because though always present, they are inaccessible; but all natural objects make a kindred impression, when the mind is open to their influence. Nature never wears a mean appearance. Neither does the wisest man extort her secret, and lose his curiosity by finding out all her perfection. Nature never became a toy to a wise spirit. The flowers, the animals, the mountains, reflected the wisdom of his best hour, as much as they had delighted the simplicity of his child-hood. When we speak of nature in this manner, we have a distinct but most poetical sense in the mind. We mean the integrity of impression made by manifold natural objects. It is this which distinguishes the stick of timber of the wood-cutter, from the tree of the poet. The charming landscape which I saw this morning, is indubitably made up of some twenty or thirty farms. Miller owns this field, Locke that, and Manning the woodland beyond. But none of them owns the landscape. There is a property in the horizon which no man has but he whose eye can integrate all the parts, that is, the poet. This is the best part of these men's farms, yet to this their warranty-deeds give no title. To speak truly, few adult persons can see nature. Most per-sons do not see the sun. At least they have a very superficial seeing. The sun illuminates only the eye of the man, but shines into the eye and the heart of the child. The lover of nature is he whose inward and outward senses are still truly adjusted to each other; who has retained the spirit of infancy even into the era of manhood. His intercourse with heaven and earth, becomes part of his daily food. In the presence of nature, a wild delight runs through the man, in spite of real sorrows. Nature says,—he is my creature, and maugre all his impertinent griefs, he shall be glad with me. Not the sun or the summer alone, but every hour and season yields its tribute of delight; for every hour and change corresponds to and authorizes a different state of the mind, from breathless noon to grimmest midnight. Nature is a setting that fits equally well a comic or a mourning piece. In good health, the air is a cordial of incredible virtue. Crossing a bare com-mon, in snow puddles, at twilight, under a clouded sky, without having in my thoughts any occurrence of special good fortune, I have enjoyed a perfect exhilaration. I am glad to the brink of fear. In the woods too, a man casts off his years, as the snake his slough, and at what period soever of life, is always a child. In the woods, is perpetual youth. Within these planta-tions of God, a decorum and sanctity reign, a perennial festival is dressed, and the guest sees not how he should tire of them in a thousand years. In the woods, we return to reason and faith. There I feel that nothing can befall me in life,—no disgrace, no calamity, (leaving me my eyes,) which nature cannot repair. Standing on the bare ground,—my head bathed by the blithe air, and uplifted into infinite space,—all mean egotism vanishes. I become a transparent eye-ball; I am nothing; I see all; the currents of the Univer-sal Being circulate through me; I am part or particle of God. The name of the nearest friend sounds then foreign and accidental: to be brothers, to be acquaintances,—master or servant, is then a trifle and a disturbance. I am the lover of uncontained and immortal beauty. In the wilderness, I find something more dear and connate than in streets or villages. In the tranquil landscape, and especially in the distant line of the horizon, man beholds somewhat as beautiful as his own nature.

The greatest delight which the fields and woods minister, is the sugges-tion of an occult relation between man and the vegetable. I am not alone and unacknowledged. They nod to me, and I to them. The waving of the boughs in the storm, is new to me and old. It takes me by surprise, and yet is not unknown. Its effect is like that of a higher thought or a better emotion coming over me, when I deemed I was thinking justly or doing right.

Yet it is certain that the power to produce this delight, does not reside in nature, but in man, or in a harmony of both. It is necessary to use these pleasures with great temperance. For, nature is not always tricked in holiday attire, but the same scene which yesterday breathed perfume and glittered as for the frolic of the nymphs, is overspread with melancholy today. Nature always wears the colors of the spirit. To a man laboring under calamity, the heat of his own fire hath sadness in it. Then, there is a kind of contempt of the landscape felt by him who has just lost by death a dear friend. The sky is less grand as it shuts down over less worth in the population.

QUESTIONS FOR DISCUSSION AND WRITING

1. Emerson writes of the stars creating reverence in us because of their presence and their inaccessibility. He suggests that this is true for all of nature. Is it true, as Emerson states, that "Nature never wears a mean appearance"?
2. "Few adult persons can see nature." Do you agree or disagree with this statement of Emerson's? Do you think he is right in his view that we need to see nature with the eyes of a child truly to appreciate it?
3. Can nature, as Emerson states, yield "wild delight" and "perfect exhilaration"? Can you point to examples of when nature had that kind of effect on you?
4. What are your responses to the effect Emerson posits that nature makes him feel oneness with God? Is this overstating or exaggerating the effect of the natural world on us or is it consistent with your own experiences?
5. In the essay's last paragraph Emerson concludes that how we see nature ultimately depends upon our inner life and our mood. Does this negate all of the assertions up to that point about the greatness and beauty of nature's bounty? Is nature still great and beautiful even in the face of human melancholy or despair?

ON TECHNIQUE AND STYLE

1. How is Emerson defining nature in this essay? Does his definition include all of the natural world as well as all of humanity? Is the definition too broad? Is he too idealistic or too unrealistic in expressing so strong a sense of both beauty and awe for so wide encompassing a definition?
2. On a number of occasions, Emerson brings himself into this essay. How apt is his use of the first person and how effective does he make use of himself to amplify and support his ideas?

3. The essay includes a religious or spiritual argument. Which is it, religious or spiritual? How would you describe the argument and how persuasive is it?

CULTURAL QUESTION

1. Emerson's essay goes back to mid-nineteenth-century American culture. How relevant is it to America today—especially in terms of how and in what ways nature has changed and been changed by human beings?

A Letter to Thoreau

Edward O. Wilson

Edward Osborne Wilson (1929–   ) *was born in Birmingham, Alabama, and graduated from the University of Alabama. He received a PhD from Harvard. Often called the founder of the modern environmental movement, Wilson is Pelligrino University Research Professor Emeritus at Harvard and a world-famous entomologist, biologist, and ecologist. He became associated with a neo-Darwinian movement called sociobiology and published* Sociobiology: The New Synthesis. *The recipient of two Pulitzers, for* Ants *and* On Human Nature, *he is responsible for the term "biodiversity" and is the author of* Diversity of Life, Consilience: The Unity of Knowledge *and* The Future of Life. *Both the National Audubon Society and the Worldwide Fund for Nature have awarded him medals and he is a recipient of the National Medal of Science.*

"A Letter to Thoreau" is from the Prologue to The Future of Life, *first published in 2002. In it Wilson writes a letter to Henry David Thoreau, a close friend of Ralph Waldo Emerson's and the author of* Walden, *the famous work of advice, observations, and love of nature first published in 1854. Wilson describes to Thoreau the environmental decline that has occurred since Emerson and Thoreau's time and uses this epistolary form to get his points across—the points being the environmental crisis at our doorsteps and the urgency and necessity of establishing environmental stewardship, conservation, and protection of ecosystems.*

Henry!
   I am at the site of your cabin on the edge of Walden Pond. I came because of your stature in literature and the conservation movement. I came because of all your contemporaries, you are the one I most need to understand. As a biologist with a modern scientific library, I know more than Darwin

knew. I can imagine the measured responses of that country gentleman to a voice a century and a half beyond his own. It is not a satisfying fantasy: the Victorians have for the most part settled into a comfortable corner of our remembrance. But I cannot imagine your responses, at least not all of them. You left too soon, and your restless spirit haunts us still.

I am here for a purpose: to become more Thoreauvian, and with that perspective better to explain to you, and in reality to others and not least to myself, what has happened to the world we both have loved . . .

The natural world in the year 2001 is everywhere disappearing before our eyes—cut to pieces, mowed down, plowed under, gobbled up, replaced by human artifacts.

No one in your time could imagine a disaster of this magnitude. Little more than a billion people were alive in the 1840s. They were overwhelmingly agricultural, and few families needed more than two or three acres to survive. The American frontier was still wide open. And far away on continents to the south, up great rivers, beyond unclimbed mountain ranges, stretched unspoiled equatorial forests brimming with the maximum diversity of life. These wildernesses seemed as unattainable and timeless as the planets and stars. That could not last, because the mood of Western civilization is Abrahamic. The explorers and colonists were guided by a biblical prayer: May we take possession of this land that God has provided and let it drip milk and honey into our mouths, forever.

Now, more than six billion people fill the world. The great majority are very poor; nearly one billion exist on the edge of starvation. All are struggling to raise the quality of their lives any way they can. That unfortunately includes the conversion of the surviving remnants of the natural environment. Half of the great tropical forests have been cleared. The last frontiers of the world are effectively gone. Species of plants and animals are disappearing a hundred or more times faster than before the coming of humanity, and as many as half may be gone by the end of this century. An Armageddon is approaching at the beginning of the third millennium. But it is not the cosmic war and fiery collapse of mankind foretold in sacred scripture. It is the wreckage of the planet by an exuberantly plentiful and ingenious humanity.

The situation is desperate—but there are encouraging signs that the race can be won. Population growth has slowed, and if the present trajectory holds, it is likely to peak between eight and ten billion people by century's end. That many people, experts tell us, can be accommodated with a decent standard of living, but just barely: the amount of arable land and water available per person, globally, is already declining. In solving the problem, other experts tell us, it should also be possible to shelter most of the vulnerable plant and animal species.

In order to pass through the bottleneck, a global land ethic is urgently needed. Not just any global land ethic that might happen to enjoy agreeable sentiment, but one based on the best understanding of ourselves and the world around us that science and technology can provide. Surely the rest of life matters. Surely our stewardship is its only hope. We will be wise to listen carefully to the heart, then act with rational intention with all the tools we can gather and bring to bear.

Henry, my friend, thank you for putting the first element of that ethic in place. Now it is up to us to summon a more encompassing wisdom. The living world is dying; the natural economy is crumbling beneath our busy feet. We have been too self-absorbed to foresee the long-term consequences of our actions, and we will suffer a terrible loss unless we shake off our delusions and move quickly to a solution. Science and technology led us into this bottleneck. Now science and technology must help us find our way through and out.

QUESTIONS FOR DISCUSSION AND WRITING

1. Wilson begins his letter to Thoreau by saying that he could imagine Darwin's response to changes that have occurred in the environment since the famous evolutionist's time, but cannot imagine what Thoreau's response would be. Other than the fact that there are more years separating Wilson from Thoreau than there are separating him from Darwin, why do you suppose this is the case?
2. The letter to Thoreau was written in 2001. At that point in time Wilson says of the natural world that it is "disappearing before our eyes." Is that statement hyperbolic or true?
3. In his letter to Thoreau, Wilson blames explorers and colonists and Western civilization's being "Abrahamic" on the inability of biodiversity, the frontier, or unspoiled forests to endure. Do you agree or disagree with where he lays the blame?
4. Armageddon will not result from divine forces, Wilson argues, but from humanity wrecking the planet. He calls the situation desperate but also points to offsetting or countervailing "encouraging signs." Are you encouraged? Why or why not?
5. Wilson concludes his letter to Thoreau by stressing, "Science and technology led us into this bottleneck. Now science and technology must help us find our way through and out." What is your sense of his assessment? Is he placing too much future faith in science and technology?

ON TECHNIQUE AND STYLE

1. How effective do you believe Wilson's decision was to have presented his argument in the form of a letter to a writer who has been dead for over a century? Does it work or does it seem too gimmicky?
2. Focus on the illustrations Wilson uses to make his argument that we are in great environmental peril. Are the examples he selects effective? Why or why not?

3. Wilson's real subject is the future of the planet and the conservation of species and ecosystems. He obviously feels passionate about this subject and wants to convey his sense of urgency in his letter to Thoreau. Does he succeed?

CULTURAL QUESTION

1. Many people believe that the most serious environmental crisis we face is population growth, particularly when the massive consumption of natural resources is factored in. How might you compare and contrast the attitude toward population of Americans living in the time of Emerson to attitudes of those of us living in today's world?

From Silent Spring

Rachel Carson

Rachel Carson (1907–1964) is often credited with initiating the global environmental movement. A zoologist and marine biologist, she singularly helped bring about a change in U.S. national policy in the uses of pesticides. Born in Pittsburgh, Pennsylvania, she was educated at Pennsylvania College for Women and Johns Hopkins, where she received a master's degree in zoology and taught zoology. She also taught at the University of Maryland and did doctorate work at the Marine Biological Laboratory in Woods Hole, Massachusetts. The second woman to be hired by the Bureau of Fisheries, she worked with that agency as an aquatic biologist and wrote radio scripts. Eventually she became chief editor for the bureau. Her writing appears in Atlantic Monthly *and* Nature *and she published a trilogy on the sea,* Under the Sea-Wind, The Sea Around Us *(which won the National Book Award) and* The Edge of the Sea. Silent Spring *was published in 1962 and had an extraordinary effect, including much corporate opposition and attacks on Carson even before the book was released. Carson's indictment of the overuse of pesticides and the baleful effect on wildlife mortality had enormous impact on public thinking. The concern she brought to the public about the toxicity of industrial products and DDT have had lasting effects on environmental thinking right up to the present. The excerpt we include here from* Silent Spring *spells out her concern. This excerpt is taken from Rachel Carson, "Silent Spring," in Diane Ravitch, Ed.,* The American Reader: Words That Moved a Nation. *New York: HarperCollins, 1990, pp. 323–325.*

The history of life on earth has been a history of interaction between living things and their surroundings. To a large extent, the physical form and the habits of the earth's vegetation and its animal life have been molded by the environment. Considering the whole span of earthly time, the opposite effect, in which life actually modifies its surroundings, has been relatively slight. Only within the moment of time represented by the present century has one species—man—acquired significant power to alter the nature of his world.

During the past quarter century this power has not only increased to one of disturbing magnitude but it has changed in character. The most alarming of all man's assaults upon the environment is the contamination of air, earth, rivers, and sea with dangerous and even lethal materials. This pollution is for the most part irrecoverable; the chain of evil it initiates not only in the world that must support life but in living tissues is for the most part irreversible. In this now universal contamination of the environment, chemicals are the sinister and little-recognized partners of radiation in changing the very nature of the world—the very nature of its life. Strontium 90, released through nuclear explosions into the air, comes to the earth in rain or drifts down as fallout, lodges in soil, enters into the grass or corn or wheat grown there, and in time takes up its abode in the bones of a human being, there to remain until his death. Similarly, chemicals sprayed on croplands or forests or gardens lie long in the soil, entering into living organisms, passing from one to another in a chain of poisoning and death. Or they pass mysteriously by underground streams until they emerge and, through the alchemy of air and sunlight, combine into new forms that kill vegetation, sicken cattle, and work unknown harm on those who drink from once pure wells. As Albert Schweitzer has said, "Man can hardly even recognize the devils of his own creation."

It took hundreds of millions of years to produce the life that now inhabits the earth—eons of time in which that developing and evolving and diversifying life reached a state of adjustment and balance with its surroundings. The environment, rigorously shaping and directing the life it supported, contained elements that were hostile as well as supporting. Certain rocks gave out dangerous radiation, even within the light of the sun, from which all life draws its energy, there were short-wave radiations with power to injure. Given time—time not in years but in millennia—life adjusts, and a balance has been reached. For time is the essential ingredient; but in the modern world there is no time.

The rapidity of change and the speed with which new situations are created follow the impetuous and heedless pace of man rather than the deliberate pace of nature. Radiation is no longer merely the background radiation of rocks, the bombardment of cosmic rays, the ultraviolet of the sun that have existed before there was any life on earth; radiation is now the unnatural creation of man's tampering with the atom. The chemicals to which life is asked to make its adjustment are no longer merely the calcium and silica and copper and all the rest of the minerals washed out of the rocks and carried in rivers to the sea; they are the synthetic creations of man's inventive mind, brewed in his laboratories, and having no counterparts in nature.

To adjust to these chemicals would require time on the scale that is nature's; it would require not merely the years of a man's life but the life of generations. And even this, were it by some miracle possible, would be futile, for the new chemicals come from our laboratories in an endless stream; almost five hundred annually find their way into actual use in the United States alone. The figure is staggering and its implications are not easily grasped—500 new chemicals to which the bodies of men and animals are required somehow to adapt each year, chemicals totally outside the limits of biologic experience.

Among them are many that are used in man's war against nature. Since the mid-1940's over 200 basic chemicals have been created for use in killing insects, weeds, rodents, and other organisms described in the modern vernacular as "pests"; and they are sold under several thousand different brand names. These sprays, dusts, and aerosols are now applied almost universally to farms, gardens, forests, and homes—nonselective chemicals that have the power to kill every insect, the "good" and the "bad," to still the song of birds and the leaping of fish in the streams, to coat the leaves with a deadly film, and to linger on in the soil—all this though the intended target may be only a few weeds or insects. Can anyone believe it is possible to lay down such a barrage of poisons on the surface of the earth without making it unfit for all life? They should not be called "insecticides," but "biocides."

The whole process of spraying seems caught up in an endless spiral. Since DDT was released for civilian use, a process of escalation has been going on in which ever more toxic materials must be found. This has happened because insects, in a triumphant vindication of Darwin's principle of the survival of the fittest, have evolved super races immune to the particular insecticide used, hence a deadlier one has always to be developed—and then a deadlier one than that. . . .

The "control of nature" is a phrase conceived in arrogance, born of the Neanderthal age of biology and philosophy, when it was supposed that nature exists for the convenience of man. The concepts and practices of applied entomology for the most part date from that Stone Age of science. It is our alarming misfortune that so primitive a science has armed itself with the most modern and terrible weapons, and that in turning them against the insects it has also turned them against the earth.

QUESTIONS FOR DISCUSSION AND WRITING

1. The essay from Carson's *Silent Spring* advances the premise that the nature of the world and the life that exists within it are being changed by insecticides, by "sprays, dusts and aerosols." What is your sense of how or in what ways synthetic chemicals have altered the environment since the appearance of Carson's book back in 1962?

2. Once again, as in the excerpt from Wilson, humanity gets the blame for messing things up environmentally. How does Carson make this charge and what inferences are we to make?

3. No one would deny that we need to kill the insects that destroy our crops and vegetation and eat up our food supply. Is Carson being fair when she says insecticides should be called biocides?
4. Carson says, "In the modern world there is no time." Some would call her a doomsayer. Today many who warn of the urgency of solving environmental crises are branded as Chicken Littles. How much urgency do you grant to Carson's overall warning?
5. Carson condemns the phrase "control of nature" and emphasizes that nature doesn't exist for humans' convenience. Is she right? Why or why not?

ON TECHNIQUE AND STYLE

1. This essay and the book in which it appeared had an extraordinary and galvanizing effect on the public. Aside from the fact that it called public attention to a crisis no one had foreseen, what techniques does Carson employ in advancing her argument that make this a persuasive piece of writing?
2. Carson uses the phrase "chain of evil" as well as the word "sinister" to describe the poisoning of the environment by radiation and chemicals. How effective is the use of such language? Some might describe it as over the top. What do you think?
3. The title of the famous book from which this essay was taken is *Silent Spring*. What do those words conjure up in your imagination? Is this an effective title?

CULTURAL QUESTION

1. The uses of pesticides and DDT have had the most harmful effect on the population of farm workers, the many legal and undocumented workers who have done migrant labor. Most of these workers have been Latinos. Does Carson's essay resonate more for the Latino subculture than for the rest of us, or are we all in need of being equally concerned about the issues she raises?

From Pilgrim at Tinker Creek

Annie Dillard

Annie Dillard (1945–   ) was born in Pittsburgh, Pennsylvania, and educated at Hollins College in Virginia. One of America's finest essayists, she is especially known and admired for her writing about nature and the natural world. Her meditative and spiritual writing on the environment, Pilgrim at Tinker Creek, *won the Pulitzer Prize in 1974. She has also published a novel and a number of volumes of poetry as well as the autobiographical work,* An American Childhood. *She is the author of a number of other books, including* Holy the Firm, Living by Fiction, Teaching a Stone to Talk, Encounters with Chinese Writers, *and* The Writing Life. *Her writing has appeared in* The Atlantic, Harper's Magazine, *and* The Christian Science Monitor. *She is an adjunct professor of English at Wesleyan University in Connecticut.*

Pilgrim at Tinker Creek *demonstrates how Dillard, like her literary mentor Emerson, combines a deep awareness of nature with a questing spiritual sensibility. In this open- ing chapter she evokes a picture of nature's beauty and violence with a vivid sense of the place in which she lives, connecting her spirit to the environment as well as to the sheer exhilaration of feeling and being alive.*

I used to have a cat, an old fighting tom, who would jump through the open win- dow by my bed in the middle of the night and land on my chest. I'd half-awaken. He'd stick his skull under my nose and purr, stinking of urine and blood. Some nights he kneaded my bare chest with his front paws, powerfully, arching his back, as if sharpening his claws, or pummeling a mother for milk. And some mornings I'd wake in daylight to find my body covered with paw prints in blood; I looked as though I'd been painted with roses.

It was hot, so hot the mirror felt warm. I washed before the mirror in a daze, my twisted summer sleep still hung about me like sea kelp. What blood was this, and what roses? It could have been the rose of union, the blood of mur- der, or the rose of beauty bare and the blood of some unspeakable sacrifice or birth. The sign on my body could have been an emblem or a stain, the keys to the kingdom or the mark of Cain. I never knew. I never knew as I washed, and the blood streaked, faded, and finally disappeared, whether I'd purified myself or ruined the blood sign of the passover. We wake, if we ever wake at all, to mystery, rumors of death, beauty, violence. . . . "Seem like we're just set down here," a woman said to me recently, "and don't nobody know why."

These are morning matters, pictures you dream as the final wave heaves you up on the sand to the bright light and drying air. You remember pressure, and a curved sleep you rested against, soft, like a scallop in its shell. But the air hardens your skin; you stand; you leave the lighted shore to explore some dim headland, and soon you're lost in the leafy interior, intent, remembering nothing.

I still think of that old tomcat, mornings, when I wake. Things are tamer now; I sleep with the window shut. The cat and our rites are gone and my life is changed, but the memory remains of something powerful playing over me. I wake expectant, hoping to see a new thing. If I'm lucky I might be jogged awake by a strange bird call. I dress in a hurry, imagining the yard flapping with auks, or flamingos. This morning it was a wood duck, down at the creek. It flew away.

I live by a creek, Tinker Creek, in a valley in Virginia's Blue Ridge. An anchorite's hermitage is called an anchor-hold; some anchor-holds were simple sheds clamped to the side of a church like a barnacle to a rock. I think of this house clamped to the side of Tinker Creek as an anchor-hold. It holds me at anchor to the rock bottom of the creek itself and it keeps me steadied in the current, as a sea anchor does, facing the stream of light pouring down. It's a good place to live; there's a lot to think about. The creeks—Tinker and Carvin's—are an active mystery, fresh every minute. Theirs is the mystery of the continuous creation and all that providence implies: the uncertainty of vision, the horror of the fixed, the dissolution of the present, the intricacy of beauty, the pressure of fecundity, the elusiveness of the free, and the flawed nature of perfection. The mountains—Tinker and Brushy, McAfee's Knob and Dead Man—are a passive mystery, the oldest of all. Theirs is the one simple mystery of creation from nothing, of matter itself, anything at all, the given. Mountains are giant, restful, absorbent. You can heave your spirit into a mountain and the mountain will keep it, folded, and not throw it back as some creeks will. The creeks are the world with all its stimulus and beauty; I live there. But the mountains are home.

The wood duck flew away. I caught only a glimpse of something like a bright torpedo that blasted the leaves where it flew. Back at the house I ate a bowl of oatmeal; much later in the day came the long slant of light that means good walking.

If the day is fine, any walk will do; it all looks good. Water in particular looks its best, reflecting blue sky in the flat, and chopping it into graveled shallows and white chute and foam in the riffles. On a dark day, or a hazy one, everything's washed-out and lackluster but the water. It carries its own lights. I set out for the railroad tracks, for the hill the flocks fly over, for the woods where the white mare lives. But I go to the water.

Today is one of those excellent January partly cloudies in which light chooses an unexpected part of the landscape to trick out in gilt, and then shadow sweeps it away. You know you're alive. You take huge steps, trying to feel the planet's roundness arc between your feet. Kazantzakis says that when he was young he had a canary and a globe. When he freed the canary, it would perch on the globe and sing. All his life, wandering the earth, he felt as though he had a canary on top of his mind, singing.

West of the house, Tinker Creek makes a sharp loop, so that the creek is both in back of the house, south of me, and also on the other side of the road, north of me. I like to go north. There the afternoon sun hits the creek just right, deepening the reflected blue and lighting the sides of trees on the banks. Steers from the pasture across the creek come down to drink; I always flush a rabbit or two there; I sit on a fallen trunk in the shade and watch the

squirrels in the sun. There are two separated wooden fences suspended from cables that cross the creek just upstream from my tree-trunk bench. They keep the steers from escaping up or down the creek when they come to drink. Squirrels, the neighborhood children, and I use the downstream fence as a swaying bridge across the creek. But the steers are there today.

I sit on the downed tree and watch the black steers slip on the creek bottom. They are all bred beef: beef heart, beef hide, beef hocks. They're a human product like rayon. They're like a field of shoes. They have cast-iron shanks and tongues like foam insoles. You can't see through to their brains as you can with other animals; they have beef fat behind their eyes, beef stew.

I cross the fence six feet above the water, walking my hands down the rusty cable and tightroping my feet along the narrow edge of the planks. When I hit the other bank and terra firma, some steers are bunched in a knot between me and the barbed-wire fence I want to cross. So I suddenly rush at them in an enthusiastic sprint, flailing my arms and hollering, "Lightning! Copperhead! Swedish meatballs!" They flee, still in a knot, stumbling across the flat pasture. I stand with the wind on my face.

When I slide under a barbed-wire fence, cross a field, and run over a sycamore trunk felled across the water, I'm on a little island shaped like a tear in the middle of Tinker Creek. On one side of the creek is a steep forested bank; the water is swift and deep on that side of the island. On the other side is the level field I walked through next to the steers' pasture; the water between the field and the island is shallow and sluggish. In summer's low water, flags and bulrushes grow along a series of shallow pools cooled by the lazy current. Water striders patrol the surface film, crayfish hump along the silt bottom eating filth, frogs shout and glare, and shiners and small bream hide among roots from the sulky green heron's eye. I come to this island every month of the year. I walk around it, stopping and staring, or I straddle the sycamore log over the creek, curling my legs out of the water in winter, trying to read. Today I sit on dry grass at the end of the island by the slower side of the creek. I'm drawn to this spot. I come to it as to an oracle; I return to it as a man years later will seek out the battlefield where he lost a leg or an arm.

A couple of summers ago I was walking along the edge of the island to see what I could see in the water, and mainly to scare frogs. Frogs have an inelegant way of taking off from invisible positions on the bank just ahead of your feet, in dire panic, emitting a froggy "Yike!" and splashing into the water. Incredibly, this amused me, and, incredibly, it amuses me still. As I walked along the grassy edge of the island, I got better and better at seeing frogs both in and out of the water. I learned to recognize, slowing down, the difference in texture of the light reflected from mud bank, water, grass, or frog. Frogs were flying all around me. At the end of the island I noticed a small green frog. He was exactly half in and half out of the water, looking like a schematic diagram of an amphibian, and he didn't jump.

He didn't jump; I crept closer. At last I knelt on the island's winter killed grass, lost, dumbstruck, staring at the frog in the creek just four feet away. He was a very small frog with wide, dull eyes. And just as I looked at him, he slowly crumpled and began to sag. The spirit vanished from his eyes as if snuffed. His skin emptied and drooped; his very skull seemed to collapse and settle like a kicked tent. He was shrinking before my eyes like a deflating foot-ball. I watched the taut, glistening skin on his shoulders ruck, and rumple, and fall. Soon, part of his skin, formless as a pricked balloon, lay in floating folds like bright scum on top of the water: it was a monstrous and terrifying thing. I gaped bewildered, appalled. An oval shadow hung in the water behind the drained frog; then the shadow glided away. The frog skin bag started to sink.

I had read about the giant water bug, but never seen one. "Giant water bug" is really the name of the creature, which is an enormous, heavy-bodied brown bug. It eats insects, tadpoles, fish, and frogs. Its grasping forelegs are mighty and hooked inward. It seizes a victim with these legs, hugs it tight, and paralyzes it with enzymes injected during a vicious bite. That one bite is the only bite it ever takes. Through the puncture shoot the poisons that dissolve the victim's muscles and bones and organs—all but the skin—and through it the giant water bug sucks out the victim's body, reduced to a juice. This event is quite common in warm fresh water. The frog I saw was being sucked by a giant water bug. I had been kneeling on the island grass; when the unrecognizable flap of frog skin settled on the creek bottom, swaying, I stood up and brushed the knees of my pants. I couldn't catch my breath.

Of course, many carnivorous animals devour their prey alive. The usual method seems to be to subdue the victim by downing or grasping it so it can't flee, then eating it whole or in a series of bloody bites. Frogs eat every-thing whole, stuffing prey into their mouths with their thumbs. People have seen frogs with their wide jaws so full of live dragonflies they couldn't close them. Ants don't even have to catch their prey: in the spring they swarm over newly hatched, featherless birds in the nest and eat them tiny bite by bite.

That it's rough out there and chancy is no surprise. Every live thing is a survivor on a kind of extended emergency bivouac. But at the same time we are also created. In the Koran, Allah asks, "The heaven and the earth and all in between, thinkest thou I made them *in jest?*" It's a good question. What do we think of the created universe, spanning an unthinkable void with an unthinkable profusion of forms? Or what do we think of nothingness, those sickening reaches of time in either direction? If the giant water bug was not made in jest, was it then made in earnest? Pascal uses a nice term to describe the notion of the creator's, once having called forth the universe, turning his back to it: *Deus Absconditus.* Is this what we think happened? Was the sense of it there, and God absconded with it, ate it, like a wolf who disappears round the edge of the house with the Thanksgiving turkey? "God is subtle," Einstein said, "but not malicious." Again, Einstein said that "nature conceals her mystery by means of her essential grandeur, not by her cun-ning." It could be that God has not absconded but spread, as our vision and understanding of the universe have spread, to a fabric of spirit and sense so grand and subtle, so powerful in a new way, that we can only feel blindly of its hem. In making the thick darkness a swaddling band for the sea, God "set bars and doors" and said, "Hitherto shalt thou come, but no further." But have we come even that far? Have we rowed out to the thick darkness, or are we all playing pinochle in the bottom of the boat?

Cruelty is a mystery, and the waste of pain. But if we describe a world to compass these things, a world that is a long, brute game, then we bump against another mystery: the inrush of power and light, the canary that sings on the skull. Unless all ages and races of men have been deluded by the same mass hypnotist (who?), there seems to be such a thing as beauty, a grace wholly gratuitous. About five years ago I saw a mockingbird make a straight vertical descent from the roof gutter of a four-story building. It was an act as careless and spontaneous as the curl of a stem or the kindling of a star.

The mockingbird took a single step into the air and dropped. His wings were still folded against his sides as though he were singing from a limb and not falling, accelerating thirty-two feet per second per second, through empty air. Just a breath before he would have been dashed to the ground, he unfurled his wings with exact, deliberate care, revealing the broad bars of white, spread his elegant, white-banded tail, and so floated onto the grass. I had just rounded a corner when his insouciant step caught my eye; there was no one else in sight. The fact of his free fall was like the old philosophical conundrum about the tree that falls in the forest. The answer must be, I think, that beauty and grace are performed whether or not we will or sense them. The least we can do is try to be there.

Another time I saw another wonder: sharks off the Atlantic coast of Florida. There is a way a wave rises above the ocean horizon, a triangular wedge against the sky. If you stand where the ocean breaks on a shallow beach, you see the raised water in a wave is translucent, shot with lights. One late afternoon at low tide a hundred big sharks passed the beach near the mouth of a tidal river in a feeding frenzy. As each green wave rose from the churning water, it illuminated within itself the six- or eight-foot-long bodies of twisting sharks. The sharks disappeared as each wave rolled toward me; then a new wave would swell above the horizon, containing in it, like scorpions in amber, sharks that roiled and heaved. The sight held awesome wonders: power and beauty, grace tangled in a rapture with violence.

We don't know what's going on here. If these tremendous events are random combinations of matter run amok, the yield of millions of monkeys at millions of typewriters, then what is it in us, hammered out of those same typewriters, that they ignite? We don't know. Our life is a faint tracing on the surface of mystery, like the idle, curved tunnels of leaf miners on the face of a leaf. We must somehow take a wider view, look at the whole landscape, really see it, and describe what's going on here. Then we can at least wail the right question into the swaddling band of darkness, or, if it comes to that, choir the proper praise.

   At the time of Lewis and Clark, setting the prairies on fire was a well-known signal that meant, "Come down to the water." It was an extravagant gesture, but we can't do less. If the landscape reveals one certainty, it is that the extravagant gesture is the very stuff of creation. After the one extravagant gesture of creation in the first place, the universe has continued to deal exclusively in extravagances, flinging intricacies and colossi down aeons of emptiness, heaping profusions on profligacies with ever-fresh vigor. The whole show has been on fire from the word go. I come down to the water to cool my eyes. But everywhere I look I see fire; that which isn't flint is tinder, and the whole world sparks and flames.

I have come to the grassy island late in the day. The creek is up; icy water sweeps under the sycamore log bridge. The frog skin, of course, is utterly gone. I have stared at that one spot on the creek bottom for so long, focusing past the rush of water, that when I stand, the opposite bank seems to stretch before my eyes and flow grassily upstream. When the bank settles down I cross the sycamore log and enter again the big plowed field next to the steers' pasture.
   The wind is terrific out of the west; the sun comes and goes. I can see the shadow on the field before me deepen uniformly and spread like a plague. Everything seems so dull I am amazed I can even distinguish objects. And suddenly the light runs across the land like a comber, and up the trees, and goes again in a wink: I think I've gone blind or died. When it comes again, the light, you hold your breath, and if it stays you forget about it until it goes again.
   It's the most beautiful day of the year. At four o'clock the eastern sky is a dead stratus black flecked with low white clouds. The sun in the west illuminates the ground, the mountains, and especially the bare branches of trees, so that everywhere silver trees cut into the black sky like a photographer's negative of a landscape. The air and the ground are dry; the mountains are going on and off like neon signs. Clouds slide east as if pulled from the horizon, like a tablecloth whipped off a table. The hemlocks by the barbed-wire fence are flinging themselves east as though their backs would break. Purple shadows are racing east; the wind makes me face east, and again I feel the dizzying, drawn sensation I felt when the creek bank reeled.
   At four-thirty the sky in the east is clear; how could that big blackness be blown? Fifteen minutes later another darkness is coming overhead from the northwest; and it's here. Everything is drained of its light as if sucked. Only at the horizon do inky black mountains give way to distant, lighted mountains—lighted not by direct illumination but rather paled by glowing sheets of mist hung before them. Now the blackness is in the east; everything is half in shadow, half in sun, every clod, tree, mountain, and hedge. I can't see Tinker Mountain through the line of hemlock, till it comes on like a streetlight, ping, *ex nihilo.* Its sandstone cliffs pink and swell. Suddenly the light goes; the cliffs recede as if pushed. The sun hits a clump of sycamores

between me and the mountains; the sycamore arms light up, and *I can't see the cliffs.* They're gone. The pale network of sycamore arms, which a second ago was transparent as a screen, is suddenly opaque, glowing with light. Now the sycamore arms snuff out, the mountains come on, and there are the cliffs again.

I walk home. By five-thirty the show has pulled out. Nothing is left but an unreal blue and a few banked clouds low in the north. Some sort of carnival magician has been here, some fast-talking worker of wonders who has the act backwards. "Something in this hand," he says, "something in this hand, something up my sleeve, something behind my back. . ." and abracadabra, he snaps his fingers, and it's all gone. Only the bland, blank-faced magician remains, in his unruffled coat, bare handed, acknowedging a smattering of baffled applause. When you look again the whole show has pulled up stakes and moved on down the road. It never stops. New shows roll in from over the mountains and the magician reappears unannounced from a fold in the curtain you never dreamed was an opening. Scarves of clouds, rabbits in plain view, disappear into the black hat forever. Presto chango. The audience, if there is an audience at all, is dizzy from head-turning, dazed.

Like the bear who went over the mountain, I went out to see what I could see. And, I might as well warn you, like the bear, all that I could see was the other side of the mountain: more of same. On a good day I might catch a glimpse of another wooded ridge rolling under the sun like water, another bivouac. I propose to keep here what Thoreau called "a meteorological journal of the mind," telling some tales and describing some of the sights of this rather tamed valley, and exploring, in fear and trembling, some of the unmapped dim reaches and unholy fastnesses to which those tales and sights so dizzyingly lead.

I am no scientist. I explore the neighborhood. An infant who has just learned to hold his head up has a frank and forthright way of gazing about him in bewilderment. He hasn't the faintest clue where he is, and he aims to learn. In a couple of years, what he will have learned instead is how to fake it: he'll have the cocksure air of a squatter who has come to feel he owns the place. Some unwonted, taught pride diverts us from our original intent, which is to explore the neighborhood, view the landscape, to discover at least *where* it is that we have been so startlingly set down, if we can't learn why.

So I think about the valley. It is my leisure as well as my work, a game. It is a fierce game I have joined because it is being played anyway, a game of both skill and chance, played against an unseen adversary—the conditions of time—in which the payoffs, which may suddenly arrive in a blast of light at any moment, might as well come to me as anyone else. I stake the time I'm grateful to have, the energies I'm glad to direct. I risk getting stuck on the board, so to speak, unable to move in any direction, which happens enough, God knows; and I risk the searing, exhausting nightmares that plunder rest and force me face down all night long in some muddy ditch seething with hatching insects and crustaceans.

But if I can bear the nights, the days are a pleasure. I walk out; I see something, some event that would otherwise have been utterly missed and lost; or something sees me, some enormous power brushes me with its clean wing, and I resound like a beaten bell.

I am an explorer, then, and I am also a stalker, or the instrument of the hunt itself. Certain Indians used to carve long grooves along the wooden shafts of their arrows. They called the grooves "lightning marks," because they resembled the curved fissure lightning slices down the trunks of trees. The function of lightning marks is this: if the arrow fails to kill the game, blood from a deep wound will channel along the lightning mark, streak down the arrow shaft, and spatter to the ground, laying a trail dripped on broad-leaves, on stones, that the barefoot and trembling archer can follow into whatever deep or rare wilderness it leads. I am the arrow shaft, carved along my length by unexpected lights and gashes from the very sky, and this book is the straying trail of blood.

Something pummels us, something barely sheathed. Power broods and lights. We're played on like a pipe; our breath is not our own. James Houston describes two young Eskimo girls sitting cross-legged on the ground, mouth on mouth, blowing by turns each other's throat cords, making a low, unearthly music. When I cross again the bridge that is really the steers' fence, the wind has thinned to the delicate air of twilight; it crumples the water's skin. I watch the running sheets of light raised on the creek's surface. The sight has the appeal of the purely passive, like the racing of light under clouds on a field, the beautiful dream at the moment of being dreamed. The breeze is the merest puff, but you yourself sail headlong and breathless under the gale force of the spirit.

QUESTIONS FOR DISCUSSION AND WRITING

1. What exactly is Dillard trying initially to convey to us about nature, the environment, and the natural world in the picture of the tomcat, "stinking of urine and blood," and poetically identified by her with roses and blood?
2. Dillard is a writer strongly identified with spiritual quest. In what specific ways does she view the spiritual tied to nature?
3. How might you characterize Dillard's overall attitude toward the environment by the microcosmic world she describes and places us in?
4. The book from which this excerpt is taken was written after Dillard suffered a nearly fatal attack of pneumonia. What does this passage reveal about appreciating life and living? About the feeling of being alive?
5. What is the purpose of the author bringing in the Greek writer Nikos Kazantzakis's metaphor of the canary and the globe? Why is it important to our understanding?

ON TECHNIQUE AND STYLE

1. What is the effect of Dillard's use of such examples as "the keys to the kingdom," "the mark of Cain" and the "blood sign of Passover" or of her bringing in to play the wood duck, the white mare, squirrels, steers, and a rabbit? How do these examples add to the essay?
2. What of the contrast Dillard establishes with the creeks and mountains? How do these contribute to the overall quality and achievement of her essay?
3. How do such metaphors Dillard creates about sleep as "hanging about like sea kelp" or resting "like a scallop in its shell" affect us? Is this figurative writing desirable?

CULTURAL QUESTION

1. Dillard had an upbringing that has been described as "affluent, country club." She rebelled against it at an early age. How much would you think her kind of appreciation of nature comes from having had a more comfortable and economically stable upbringing? Or, to put it another way, could someone from a poor or underprivileged background come to an appreciation of nature in life similar to Dillard's?

FICTION

From The Old Man and the Sea

Ernest Hemingway

Ernest Hemingway (1899–1961) is one of the greatest American fiction writers of the twentieth century. A journalist as well as a novelist, short story writer, and poet, Hemingway developed a writing style marked by brevity that was a major influence on writers of his and succeeding generations. Born in Oak Park, Illinois, he was educated there. He became a reporter for the Kansas City Star *and served as an ambulance driver and infantry soldier with the Italian army. After World War I he lived in Paris and worked there as a correspondent for the* Toronto Star *and was part of the famous American expatriate community. He served as a war correspondent in both the Spanish Civil War and World War II. He is the author of two famous volumes of short stories,* In Our Time *and the* Snows of Kilimanjaro, *as well as such popular and enduring novels as* The Sun Also Rises, A Farewell to Arms, The Old Man and the Sea, To Have and Have Not, *and* For Whom the Bell Tolls. *His other published work includes* The Torrents of Spring, Fiesta, Men Without Women, Death in the Afternoon, Winner Take Nothing, Green Hills of Africa, A Moveable Feast, Islands in the Stream, *and* The Garden of Eden. *He was awarded the Nobel Prize for Literature in 1954. The selection included here is from* The Old Man and the Sea, *a Pulitzer Prize–winning novel about a stoic old Cuban fisherman, Santiago, who refuses to give up his battle to catch a giant marlin in the Gulf Stream. Ultimately he manages to catch it and kill it, but loses it in a defeat that carries with it a triumph of the human spirit.*

Reprinted with the permission of Scribner, a Division of Simon & Schuster, Inc., from *The Old Man and the Sea* by Ernest Hemingway. Copyright 1952 by Ernest Hemingway. Copyright renewed © 1980 by Mary Hemingway.

Sometimes someone would speak in a boat. But most of the boats were silent except for the dip of the oars. They spread apart after they were out of the mouth of the harbour and each one headed for the part of the ocean where he hoped to find fish. The old man knew he was going far out and he left the smell of the land behind and rowed out into the clean early morning smell of the ocean. He saw the phosphorescence of the Gulf weed in the water as he rowed over the part of the ocean that the fishermen called the great well because there was a sudden deep of seven hundred fathoms where all sorts of fish congregated because of the swirl the current made against the steep walls of the floor of the ocean. Here there were concentrations of shrimp and bait fish and sometimes schools of squid in the deepest holes and these rose close to the surface at night where all the wandering fish fed on them.

In the dark the old man could feel the morning coming and as he rowed he heard the trembling sound as flying fish left the water and the hissing that their stiff set wings made as they soared away in the darkness. He was sorry for the birds, especially the small delicate dark terns that were always flying and looking and almost never finding, and he thought, the birds have a harder life than we do except for the robber birds and the heavy strong ones. Why did they make birds so delicate and fine as those sea swallows when the ocean can be so cruel? She is kind and very beautiful. But she can be so cruel and it comes so suddenly and such birds that fly, dipping and hunting, with their small sad voices are made too delicately for the sea.

He always thought of the sea as *la mar* which is what people call her in Spanish when they love her. Sometimes those who love her say bad things of her but they are always said as though she were a woman. Some of the younger fishermen, those who used buoys as floats for their lines and had motorboats, bought when the shark livers had brought much money, spoke of her as *el mar* which is masculine. They spoke of her as a contestant or a place or even an enemy. But the old man always thought of her as feminine and as something that gave or withheld great favours, and if she did wild or wicked things it was because she could not help them. The moon affects her as it does a woman, he thought.

QUESTIONS FOR DISCUSSION AND WRITING

1. What kind of feelings about the environment does Hemingway manage to convey to us early on in this passage as the old man leaves the land and goes out into the ocean? What does he conjure up for us in his description of the old man going out in his boat and leaving "the smell of the land behind" for "the clean early morning smell of the ocean"?
2. What do the observations of the old man (Santiago) about the flying fish and the birds reveal to us about the natural world?
3. Do we get a view of nature in the author's observations about the cruelty and kindness as well as the beauty of the ocean? Is there a view of nature implicit in this dualism?
4. What are we to make of the distinction in the passage about the sea being viewed by the old man and the older fishermen as female while the younger fishermen speak of it as masculine? Nature itself is usually seen as female, as in Mother Nature. Should the sea be seen the same way?
5. The old man thinks of the moon affecting the sea as it affects a woman. What does this have to do with deeper understanding of nature or the environment?

ON TECHNIQUE AND STYLE

1. Hemingway is known throughout the world for his style and what has come to be characterized as its iceberg effect—meaning a subtext to the language he employs, the creation of deeper meaning that rests under the surface of his often unadorned and minimal prose. Do you see such an effect in this brief passage? Is there meaning conveyed beneath the words?
2. Hemingway's style has also been ridiculed, usually for its simplicity. The British literary critic, Wyndham Lewis, even compared Hemingway's simplicity to a dumb ox! How simple does his style appear? Is it deceptively simple or simple?
3. What of the effect Hemingway creates with his use of such contrasts as the land and the ocean, the fish and the birds, the sea itself? Do these contrasts strike you as an effective technique?

CULTURAL QUESTION

1. Santiago, Hemingway's heroic protagonist in this novel, is Cuban. Does that matter in this passage? Should it?

Lessons from the Wolverine

Barry Lopez

Barry Lopez (1945–   ) is one of America's most admired contemporary nature and environmental writers. The San Francisco Chronicle *called him "arguably the nation's premiere nature writer." Born in Port Chester, New York, he grew up in rural Southern California and New York City before settling in western Oregon. He worked as a landscape photographer and taught at the University of Notre Dame and was visiting distinguished scholar at Texas Tech University. His book* Arctic Dreams *won the National Book Award. He also authored* Of Wolves and Men *as well as nine works of fiction and several essay collections, including* Crossing Open Ground *and* About This Life. *The story included in this chapter, "Lessons from the Wolverine," first appeared in the 1994 volume of stories* Field Notes: The Grace Notes of the Canyon Wren. *It is the tale of a young man's journey into the artic wilderness to gain a deeper understanding and appreciation of animal life and of the power of animals to understand their place in the world.*

In the Ruby Mountains, where the Sanumavik River heads, there is supposed to be living now, and for as far back as memory can go, a family of wolverine. I first learned about them in an offhand way, so often the case with information like this, which turns up in a remote village and subsequently proves startling or strange.

One evening I was playing catch with a boy named Narvalaq, a boy of twelve in a village on the Koanik River, part of the Sanumavik drainage. I missed a throw and had to retrieve the ball from the river. It landed in shallow water trickling over a point bar, beautiful cobbles—reds, grays, greens, browns. Walking back, I moved slowly, stooped over, studying rocks that had been polished by the river and now were shining in the late evening light, each one bright as an animal's eye.

Narvalaq came up and said, "Wolverine, up at Caribou Caught by the Head Creek, they walk along like that. That's how you know it's them."

I nodded. I wanted to think it over, but right away I was interested in what he had to say. First I believed he meant that wolverine living at that place looked very closely at stones or at other things in the river, that they studied things more than other wolverines do. But I learned later in a conversation with Elisha Atnah, Narvalaq's father, that they just like to walk in the shallows. When these Caribou-Caught-by-the-Head wolverine are traveling alongside water they like to walk in it.

"Like you did that time," said Elisha.

The village where I was told this is called Eedaqna. A year after it happened I got back to Eedaqna—but perhaps I should tell you a little about

myself first, so you will understand more about this story. I grew up in the
West Indies, Antigua, around there. We lost my mother in a hurricane, big
flood. In 1974, when I was eight, we moved to Tennessee, my father and
I. He taught mathematics at Union University. I began walking in the hills
then, looking at animals. I liked being near them. In 1978 my father died and
I went to northern Alberta to live with his brother. I tried to get the knack of
going to school when I lived there, but I couldn't. I liked to walk around on
the prairie, along the creeks. One thing I did then was to fly falcons. I liked
being out with them, watching them circle overhead, getting a sense of the
country I couldn't get. But it was hard keeping them in cages. I couldn't
keep it up.

I ended up working on prop planes in Edmonton when I was eighteen,
which I got very good at. I've had good jobs all along. Every time I left one—
Peace River, Fort Smith, Yellowknife—I went farther north. In 1989 I moved to
Kaktovik, where I still am. I haven't started a family yet, which is all right with
me, but my friends in the coastal villages and up in the Brooks Range don't
like it. They don't talk to me quite as much because I don't have a family. No
children. They believe it's strange. But they have strangeness in their own
lives.

I didn't forget what Narvalaq said. I thought it was something to know,
what he had said about the wolverine. So the first time I could I went back
to Eedaqna, when a Cessna 206 crashed there. Maybe someone would
tell me something more. I talked to an old man working with me on the
plane, Abraham Roosevelt, trying to move the conversation around to
wolverines up on the Sanumavik. (I don't know another way with them
except backing into it.) First, I said I might move to Eedaqna. Maybe, he
said. I said I might trap in the winter, then go north to Kaktovik in summer
to work on planes. He said maybe I would do that. Then I said if I trapped,
I'd want to trap where no one else was, even if I had to travel a long way
every day to my trapline. He said that might be good. Where would I go?
I asked. Lots of places to go, he said. What about the Ruby Mountains, I
said, up there at the head of the Sanumavik, was that too far? That's not
a good place, he said, not too good. Why? He looked at me for a moment
then went back to work on one of the carburetors. He talked about one
family that had lost a lot when this plane went down. Everyone was trying
to help them now. Later, he said to me, "Wolverine that live up that way,
Sanumavik River, they don't like it when people trap. They don't have that
up there."

That conversation, when I first learned how those wolverine felt, happened in the spring of 1990. The following winter I met a woman named Dora
Kahvinook living in Kaktovik, but who was from Eedaqna. She took a liking
to me, and I liked her, too. She told me some stories that were unusual for
her to have, hunting stories about her two brothers and her father. I asked
if her father or her brothers had ever gone hunting in the upper Sanumavik.
She said no. I said two people in Eedaqna had told me that the wolverine that

lived up there didn't like people coming up. She said she didn't know, but, yes, that's what people said.

That winter I dreamed four times about wolverine. I decided I was going to go up there when spring came, regardless. I've never been able to learn what I want to know about animals from books or looking at television. I have to walk around near them, be in places where they are. This was the heart of the trouble that I had in school. Many of the stories that should have been told about animals, about how they live, their different ways, were never told. I don't know what the stories were, but when I walked in the woods or out on the prairie or in the mountains, I could feel the boundaries of those stories. I knew they were there, the way you know fish are in a river. This knowledge was what I wanted, and the only way I had gotten it was to go out and look for it. To be near animals until they showed you something that you didn't imagine or you hadn't seen or heard.

In June I went back to Eedaqna and asked Elisha Atnah if he would travel with me. I told him I had felt the wolverine up on the Sanumavik River pulling on me over the winter. They didn't leave me alone. He listened and a few days later he said he would go with me. We traveled down the Koanik and then up the Sanumavik. It was a long way and we walked, we didn't take three-wheelers. Elisha said it would be better to walk. We walked for three days. In the evening, I asked Elisha questions.

"How many families of wolverine live up there?"

"Just that one. But it's a big family, they have been up there as long as anyone remembers. That's all their country."

"Are they different from other wolverine, like ones living over on Sadlerochit?"

"Wolverines are all different. Each family, different."

After a while he came back to this. He said, "Wolverines have culture, same as people do, but they all look the same to some people because they carry it in their heads. That's how all animals are different. Almost all their culture—I think that's the word I mean—it's inside their heads."

"You mean tools, drums, winter clothing—things like that?"

"That's right. Everything they need—stories, which way to travel, a way to understand the world—that's all in their heads. Sometimes you will find a bed they have made, or a little house, or maybe where they have made marks on the ground for dancing. You might sometime see a fox riding a piece of wood down a river where he is going. But you don't see many things like that. Their winter clothes—they just come out from inside them."

"Which story is the one that tells a person not to set a trapline in this country we are going to?"

"One time, long time ago, before my father can remember, we trapped in that country. Some marten and lynx. River otter. Mink and short-tailed wea-sel. For some reason, no one trapped wolves there. We left wolves alone but we looked really hard for wolverine. My father's uncle, Tusamik, he belonged to that place then, and his youngest boy, he started setting every kind of trap along one creek. Moon Hiding the Daylight Creek. He found a caribou there, pretty much finished up, and he set traps around it. He didn't come back until five days later, maybe—too many days. He didn't understand, that country was very generous to us. He had caught a wolverine, one front foot, one back foot." Here, Elisha stood up and showed me how the wolverine was stretched out. "But the wolverine, she was standing on top of a wolf! She had gotten the life out of him. Killed him. And there was also blood from another wolf in the snow. Tusamik's boy studied what had happened, each animal's marks. The wolverine had first been caught by a front foot. Then the two wolves had come along. That caribou meat was there, but for some reason they wanted the life in that wolverine, so they tried to get it. They came at her at the same time from two directions. The wolverine, she killed the first wolf right away—and all the time she was jumping around with that trap on her foot. Then she stepped in the second trap, with her back foot, and she couldn't move very much. But she had hurt that other wolf already. It went away. The boy thought it all happened two days, maybe, before he got there.

"The wolverine was angry. She told the boy it was over, wolverines were not going to do this anymore. The boy said he was sorry, but the wolverine said no, there won't be any more trapping for a while. Too many days waiting for him.

"So, we don't trap any animals there now. We don't go up there too much."

We went away from the Sanumavik River the next day, up Caribou Caught by the Head Creek. When we got to a place where the tundra was hilly and open, only a few trees, willows, around, Elisha said he was going to leave. He told me to just sit there and wait. In the afternoon I saw two wolverine at the crest of a hill. They came down close to the creek where I was and lay down in the sunshine on the far side and went to sleep. I had backed up against some rocks that were warm from the sun and I went to sleep, too. I began dreaming about the wolverines. It was night. I saw the two of them lying on their backs on the side of the hill. They were talking. They motioned for me to come over and lie down next to them. I did. It was dark all over the tundra. They were talking about the stars.

"You have to pay attention," one of them said. "We're going to show you something."

I looked up into the sky and along one edge of the Milky Way I could see it was different. The stars were quivering in a pattern along that edge. It was like water running over a shallows in the sunshine.

"Look in there," said the other wolverine. "Look right in there."

I looked into the pattern. I was a bird then, looking down like an osprey, flying high over the water, a river moving across the tundra. I could see many things moving in the current. Fish. Under the water I saw shells, sand, the colors of Antigua. Then leaves turning in the current, like they did in the Hatchie in Tennessee in the fall. One leaf was my father's face. Other people. Then the face of a wild dog, a crazy animal, sick. I remember my father fighting in the woods with that dog. Then for a long time leaves—the faces of animals I had seen in the woods in Tennessee and away in Alberta. The leaves were many colors and shapes. Tulip trees and poplars. Some faces, some animals, I remembered. I felt sad and tried to pull my eyes away but I couldn't. I started to remember them all, every one of those animals.

"I'm afraid," I said. "I want to get down, come down to the ground now." But nothing happened.

"Keep going," said one of the wolverines.

Looking upriver, the water was green. Looking the other way, downriver, it was bluer. Below me it was all transparent. Leaves tumbling there. The river spilled over a line of black mountains far away, through a dark blue sky. A wind was blowing and I was cold. I wanted to get down. Then I saw myself below, looking up, shading my eyes with the heavy glove, the jesses in my other hand. I was waving.

"This is our power," said one of the wolverines.

Where I was looking, in still water, the faces were trembling like aspen leaves in a wind. Animals I recognized—black bear, snapping turtle, lark sparrow, monarch butterfly, corn snake, wolf spider, porcupine, yellow-shafted flicker, muskellunge—memories of those days. Trembling like leaves on a branch. A curtain of willow leaves, through which sunlight blinked. I heard my heart beat, regular, loud. I lay on the ground, my back sideways against warm rocks. I was looking out through river willows at a hillside. The wolverines weren't there anymore.

I sat up and looked around for Elisha. He wasn't there either. I waded the creek. Where the wolverine had been the grass was pressed down but there were no tracks. I stood there for a long time, watching the sky, the hills, all around.

From where I stood I could see across to where Elisha had left me, by rocks that were dotted with bright orange and yellow lichen. On one of the rocks I could see something. I crossed back over and walked up to it. It was a willow stick, about two feet long and curved like a small bow. It had been carved to look like a wolverine running, raising its back in that strange way they have when they are hurrying along. Tied around the neck was a string of ten wolverine claws. It looked too strong to pick up. I left it on the rock and sat down to wait for Elisha.

After a while I picked up the wolverine stick and held it in my lap. Elisha came from a direction I wasn't looking, from the Sanumavik River. We went back there and camped. He said the claws were from the left front foot and the right rear foot of a wolverine. Female, he said. I told him about seeing the animals from my past. I felt them all around. I felt I was carrying something in my head that hadn't been there before. He said he was glad.

Elisha said he didn't know what the stick animal meant. He told me to carry it, not to put it inside my pack. He said we could ask someone when we got back to Eedaqna.

QUESTIONS FOR DISCUSSION AND WRITING

1. What is the sense about nature communicated to us right off in this story in the opening descriptions of the river?

2. The protagonist likes being near animals and tells us he flew falcons in Alaska. He also tells us that his knowledge of animals was not something that came from school or books. Is his desire to learn more about the wolverines from something inside him, a natural curiosity or an innate disposition that began when he heard about how wolverines walk in water, or is there more of a force of nature driving him to the wolverines, especially after the four dreams he has in winter and his describing the wolverines pulling on him and not leaving him alone?

3. Elisha Atnah, the guide, tells the main character on their three-day hike, that wolverine families are all different and that wolverines have their own culture that they carry in their heads. How does this tie back to the narrator's telling us he does not have a family and is thought strange because of it by other families whom he deems strange?

4. What is the meaning and the significance behind the story Atnah tells against setting a trapline that involves the wolverine and the wolves?

5. What lesson emerges from the narrator's dream of talking about the stars by the tundra with the wolverines and becoming a bird and seeing animals from his past?

ON TECHNIQUE AND STYLE

1. There is a good deal of mystery and spiritual suggestiveness in this story about the animal world, sacred places, and the interconnectedness of nature's creatures. There is magic in Lopez's technique that veers away from conventional realism. How successful is this?

2. Anthropomorphism is when human feelings are attributed to things not human, such as animals or inanimate objects. Where do we see anthropomorphism in this story? How effective is it?

3. What is the overall effect in the story of the carved willow stick mentioned at the end of the tale?

CULTURAL QUESTION

1. Many of the names of minor characters in this story suggest Native American or indigenous backgrounds. Is Lopez suggesting a different cultural view of nature or a different in the head approach to it among such people?

A White Heron

Sarah Orne Jewett

Sarah Orne Jewett (1849–1909) was born in South Berwick, Maine, and was the daughter of a country doctor whom she went with on his horse-and-buggy rounds to care for the sick who lived on farms in their area. She was eighteen when she published her first story and at twenty she published in Atlantic Monthly. *She also published a collection of stories,* Deephaven, *in 1877 and another volume in 1886,* A White Heron and Other Stories. The Country of the Pointed Firs *was published in 1898.*

"A White Heron," first published in 1886, is a touching but vexing story of a young girl's first stirrings of love set against her connectedness to nature and her child's integrity at preserving it. The regional qualities of the story add to its charm, but it is really a story of one child's ability to hold against the lure of money and infatuation in order to protect a rare species of bird from becoming merely another stuffed bird trophy.

I.

The woods were already filled with shadows one June evening, just before eight o'clock, though a bright sunset still glimmered faintly among the trunks of the trees. A little girl was driving home her cow, a plodding, dilatory, provoking creature in her behavior, but a valued companion for all that. They were going away from whatever light there was, and striking deep into the woods, but their feet were familiar with the path, and it was no matter whether their eyes could see it or not.

There was hardly a night the summer through when the old cow could be found waiting at the pasture bars; on the contrary, it was her greatest pleasure to hide herself away among the huckleberry bushes, and though she wore a loud bell she had made the discovery that if one stood perfectly still it would not ring. So Sylvia had to hunt for her until she found her, and call Co'! Co'! with never an answering Moo, until her childish patience was quite spent. If the creature had not given good milk and plenty of it, the case would have seemed very different to her owners. Besides, Sylvia had all the time there was, and very little use to make of it. Sometimes in pleasant weather it was a consolation to look upon the cow's pranks as an intelligent attempt to play hide and seek, and as the child had no playmates she lent herself to this amusement with a good deal of zest. Though this chase had been so long that the wary animal herself had given an unusual signal of her whereabouts, Sylvia had only laughed when she came upon Mistress Moolly at the swamp-side, and urged her affectionately homeward with a twig of birch leaves. The old cow was not inclined to wander farther, she even turned in the right direction for once as they left the pasture, and stepped along the road at a good pace. She was quite ready to be milked now, and seldom stopped to browse. Sylvia wondered what her grandmother would say because they were so late. It was a great while since she had left home at half-past five o'clock, but everybody knew the difficulty of making this errand a short one. Mrs. Tilley had chased the hornéd torment too many summer evenings herself to blame any one else for lingering, and was only thankful as she waited that she had Sylvia, nowadays, to give such valuable assistance. The good woman suspected that Sylvia loitered occasionally on her own account; there never was such a child for straying about out-of-doors since the world was made! Everybody said that it was a good change for a little maid who had tried to grow for eight years in a crowded manufacturing town, but, as for Sylvia herself, it seemed as if she never had been alive at all before she came to live at the farm. She thought often with wistful compassion of a wretched geranium that belonged to a town neighbor.

   "'Afraid of folks," old Mrs. Tilley said to herself, with a smile, after she had made the unlikely choice of Sylvia from her daughter's houseful of children, and was returning to the farm. "'Afraid of folks,' they said! I guess she won't be troubled no great with 'em up to the old place!" When they reached the door of the lonely house and stopped to unlock it, and the cat came to purr loudly, and rub against them, a deserted pussy, indeed, but fat with young robins, Sylvia whispered that this was a beautiful place to live in, and she never should wish to go home.

The companions followed the shady wood-road, the cow taking slow steps and the child very fast ones. The cow stopped long at the brook to drink, as if the pasture were not half a swamp, and Sylvia stood still and waited, letting her bare feet cool themselves in the shoal water, while the great twilight moths struck softly against her. She waded on through the brook as the cow moved away, and listened to the thrushes with a heart that beat fast with pleasure. There was a stirring in the great boughs overhead. They were full of little birds and beasts that seemed to be wide awake, and going about their world, or else saying good-night to each other in sleepy twitters. Sylvia herself felt sleepy as she walked along. However, it was not much farther to the house, and the air was soft and sweet. She was not often in the woods so late as this, and it made her feel as if she were a part of the gray shadows and the moving leaves. She was just thinking how long it seemed since she first came to the farm a year ago, and wondering if everything went on in the noisy town just the same as when she was there, the thought of the great red-faced boy who used to chase and frighten her made her hurry along the path to escape from the shadow of the trees.

Suddenly this little woods-girl is horror-stricken to hear a clear whistle not very far away. Not a bird's-whistle, which would have a sort of friendliness, but a boy's whistle, determined, and somewhat aggressive. Sylvia left the cow to whatever sad fate might await her, and stepped discreetly aside into the bushes, but she was just too late. The enemy had discovered her, and called out in a very cheerful and persuasive tone, "Halloa, little girl, how far is it to the road?" and trembling Sylvia answered almost inaudibly, "A good ways."

She did not dare to look boldly at the tall young man, who carried a gun over his shoulder, but she came out of her bush and again followed the cow, while he walked alongside.

"I have been hunting for some birds," the stranger said kindly, "and I have lost my way, and need a friend very much. Don't be afraid," he added gallantly. "Speak up and tell me what your name is, and whether you think I can spend the night at your house, and go out gunning early in the morning."

Sylvia was more alarmed than before. Would not her grandmother consider her much to blame? But who could have foreseen such an accident as this? It did not seem to be her fault, and she hung her head as if the stem of it were broken, but managed to answer "Sylvy," with much effort when her companion again asked her name.

Mrs. Tilley was standing in the doorway when the trio came into view. The cow gave a loud moo by way of explanation.

"Yes, you'd better speak up for yourself, you old trial! Where'd she tucked herself away this time, Sylvy?" But Sylvia kept an awed silence; she knew by instinct that her grandmother did not comprehend the gravity of the situation. She must be mistaking the stranger for one of the farmer-lads of the region.

The young man stood his gun beside the door, and dropped a lumpy game-bag beside it; then he bade Mrs. Tilley good-evening, and repeated his wayfarer's story, and asked if he could have a night's lodging. "Put me anywhere you like," he said. "I must be off early in the morning, before day; but I am very hungry, indeed. You can give me some milk at any rate, that's plain."

"Dear sakes, yes," responded the hostess, whose long slumbering hospitality seemed to be easily awakened. "You might fare better if you went out to the main road a mile or so, but you're welcome to what we've got. I'll milk right off, and you make yourself at home. You can sleep on husks or feathers," she proffered graciously. "I raised them all myself. There's good pasturing for geese just below here towards the ma'sh. Now step round and set a plate for the gentleman, Sylvy!" And Sylvia promptly stepped. She was glad to have something to do, and she was hungry herself.

It was a surprise to find so clean and comfortable a little dwelling in this New England wilderness. The young man had known the horrors of its most primitive housekeeping, and the dreary squalor of that level of society which does not rebel at the companionship of hens. This was the best thrift of an old-fashioned farmstead, though on such a small scale that it seemed like a hermitage. He listened eagerly to the old woman's quaint talk, he watched

Sylvia's pale face and shining gray eyes with ever growing enthusiasm, and insisted that this was the best supper he had eaten for a month, and afterward the new-made friends sat down in the door-way together while the moon came up.

Soon it would be berry-time, and Sylvia was a great help at picking. The cow was a good milker, though a plaguy thing to keep track of, the hostess gossiped frankly, adding presently that she had buried four children, so Sylvia's mother, and a son (who might be dead) in California were all the children she had left. "Dan, my boy, was a great hand to go gunning," she explained sadly. "I never wanted for pa'tridges or gray squer'ls while he was to home. He's been a great wand'rer, I expect, and he's no hand to write letters. There, I don't blame him, I'd ha' seen the world myself if it had been so I could.

"Sylvy takes after him," the grandmother continued affectionately, after a minute's pause. "There ain't a foot o' ground she don't know her way over, and the wild creaturs counts her one o' themselves. Squer'ls she'll tame to come an' feed right out o' her hands, and all sorts o' birds. Last winter she got the jay-birds to bangeing here, and I believe she'd 'a' scanted herself of her own meals to have plenty to throw out amongst 'em, if I hadn't kep' watch. Anything but crows, I tell her, I'm willin' to help support—though Dan he had a tamed one o' them that did seem to have reason same as folks. It was round here a good spell after he went away. Dan an' his father they didn't hitch,— but he never held up his head ag'in after Dan had dared him an' gone off."

The guest did not notice this hint of family sorrows in his eager interest in something else.

"So Sylvy knows all about birds, does she?" he exclaimed, as he looked round at the little girl who sat, very demure but increasingly sleepy, in the moonlight. "I am making a collection of birds myself. I have been at it ever since I was a boy." (Mrs. Tilley smiled.) "There are two or three very rare ones I have been hunting for these five years. I mean to get them on my own ground if they can be found."

"Do you cage 'em up?" asked Mrs. Tilley doubtfully, in response to this enthusiastic announcement.

"Oh no, they're stuffed and preserved, dozens and dozens of them," said the ornithologist, "and I have shot or snared every one myself. I caught a glimpse of a white heron a few miles from here on Saturday, and I have followed it in this direction. They have never been found in this district at all. The little white heron, it is," and he turned again to look at Sylvia with the hope of discovering that the rare bird was one of her acquaintances.

But Sylvia was watching a hop-toad in the narrow footpath.

"You would know the heron if you saw it," the stranger continued eagerly. "A queer tall white bird with soft feathers and long thin legs. And it would have a nest perhaps in the top of a high tree, made of sticks, something like a hawk's nest."

Sylvia's heart gave a wild beat; she knew that strange white bird, and had once stolen softly near where it stood in some bright green swamp grass, away over at the other side of the woods. There was an open place where the sunshine always seemed strangely yellow and hot, where tall, nodding rushes grew, and her grandmother had warned her that she might sink in the soft black mud underneath and never be heard of more. Not far beyond were the salt marshes just this side the sea itself, which Sylvia wondered and dreamed much about, but never had seen, whose great voice could sometimes be heard above the noise of the woods on stormy nights.

"I can't think of anything I should like so much as to find that heron's nest," the handsome stranger was saying. "I would give ten dollars to any-body who could show it to me," he added desperately, "and I mean to spend my whole vacation hunting for it if need be. Perhaps it was only migrating, or had been chased out of its own region by some bird of prey."

Mrs. Tilley gave amazed attention to all this, but Sylvia still watched the toad, not divining, as she might have done at some calmer time, that the creature wished to get to its hole under the door-step, and was much hin-dered by the unusual spectators at that hour of the evening. No amount of thought, that night, could decide how many wished-for treasures the ten dol-lars, so lightly spoken of, would buy.

The next day the young sportsman hovered about the woods, and Sylvia kept him company, having lost her first fear of the friendly lad, who proved to be most kind and sympathetic. He told her many things about the birds and what they knew and where they lived and what they did with themselves. And he gave her a jack-knife, which she thought as great a treasure as if she were a desert-islander. All day long he did not once make her troubled or afraid except when he brought down some unsuspecting singing creature from its bough. Sylvia would have liked him vastly better without his gun; she could not understand why he killed the very birds he seemed to like so much. But as the day waned, Sylvia still watched the young man with loving admira-tion. She had never seen anybody so charming and delightful; the woman's heart, asleep in the child, was vaguely thrilled by a dream of love. Some pre-monition of that great power stirred and swayed these young creatures who traversed the solemn woodlands with soft-footed silent care. They stopped to listen to a bird's song; they pressed forward again eagerly, parting the branches—speaking to each other rarely and in whispers; the young man going first and Sylvia following, fascinated, a few steps behind, with her gray eyes dark with excitement.

She grieved because the longed-for white heron was elusive, but she did not lead the guest, she only followed, and there was no such thing as speaking first. The sound of her own unquestioned voice would have terrified her—it was hard enough to answer yes or no when there was need of that. At last evening began to fall, and they drove the cow home together, and Sylvia smiled with pleasure when they came to the place where she heard the whistle and was afraid only the night before.

II.

Half a mile from home, at the farther edge of the woods, where the land was highest, a great pine-tree stood, the last of its generation. Whether it was left for a boundary mark, or for what reason, no one could say; the woodchoppers who had felled its mates were dead and gone long ago, and a whole forest of sturdy trees, pines and oaks and maples, had grown again. But the stately head of this old pine towered above them all and made a landmark for sea and shore miles and miles away. Sylvia knew it well. She had always believed that whoever climbed to the top of it could see the ocean; and the little girl had often laid her hand on the great rough trunk and looked up wistfully at those dark boughs that the wind always stirred, no matter how hot and still the air might be below. Now she thought of the tree with a new excitement, for why, if one climbed it at break of day, could not one see all the world, and easily discover from whence the white heron flew, and mark the place, and find the hidden nest?

What a spirit of adventure, what wild ambition! What fancied triumph and delight and glory for the later morning when she could make known the secret! It was almost too real and too great for the childish heart to bear.

All night the door of the little house stood open and the whippoorwills came and sang upon the very step. The young sportsman and his old hostess were sound asleep, but Sylvia's great design kept her broad awake and watching. She forgot to think of sleep. The short summer night seemed as long as the winter darkness, and at last when the whippoorwills ceased, and she was afraid the morning would after all come too soon, she stole out of the house and followed the pasture path through the woods, hastening toward the open ground beyond, listening with a sense of comfort and companionship to the drowsy twitter of a half-awakened bird, whose perch she had jarred in passing. Alas, if the great wave of human interest which flooded for the first time this dull little life should sweep away the satisfactions of an existence heart to heart with nature and the dumb life of the forest!

There was the huge tree asleep yet in the paling moonlight, and small and silly Sylvia began with utmost bravery to mount to the top of it, with tingling, eager blood coursing the channels of her whole frame, with her bare feet and fingers, that pinched and held like bird's claws to the monstrous ladder reaching up, up, almost to the sky itself. First she must mount the white oak tree that grew alongside, where she was almost lost among the dark branches and the green leaves heavy and wet with dew; a bird fluttered off its nest, and a red squirrel ran to and fro and scolded pettishly at the harmless housebreaker. Sylvia felt her way easily. She had often climbed there, and knew that higher still one of the oak's upper branches chafed against the pine trunk, just where its lower boughs were set close together. There, when she made the dangerous pass from one tree to the other, the great enterprise would really begin.

She crept out along the swaying oak limb at last, and took the daring step across into the old pine-tree. The way was harder than she thought; she must reach far and hold fast, the sharp dry twigs caught and held her and scratched her like angry talons, the pitch made her thin little fingers clumsy and stiff as she went round and round the tree's great stem, higher and higher upward. The sparrows and robins in the woods below were beginning to wake and twitter to the dawn, yet it seemed much lighter there aloft in the pine-tree, and the child knew she must hurry if her project were to be of any use.

The tree seemed to lengthen itself out as she went up, and to reach farther and farther upward. It was like a great main-mast to the voyaging earth; it must truly have been amazed that morning through all its ponderous frame as it felt this determined spark of human spirit wending its way from higher branch to branch. Who knows how steadily the least twigs held themselves to advantage this light, weak creature on her way! The old pine must have loved his new dependent. More than all the hawks, and bats, and moths, and even the sweet voiced thrushes, was the brave, beating heart of the solitary gray-eyed child. And the tree stood still and frowned away the winds that June morning while the dawn grew bright in the east.

Sylvia's face was like a pale star, if one had seen it from the ground, when the last thorny bough was past, and she stood trembling and tired but wholly triumphant, high in the tree-top. Yes, there was the sea with the dawning sun making a golden dazzle over it, and toward that glorious east flew two hawks with slow-moving pinions. How low they looked in the air from that height when one had only seen them before far up, and dark against the blue sky. Their gray feathers were as soft as moths; they seemed only a little way from the tree, and Sylvia felt as if she too could go flying away among the clouds. Westward, the woodlands and farms reached miles and miles into the distance; here and there were church steeples, and white villages, truly it was a vast and awesome world.

The birds sang louder and louder. At last the sun came up bewilderingly bright. Sylvia could see the white sails of ships out at sea, and the clouds that were purple and rose-colored and yellow at first began to fade away. Where was the white heron's nest in the sea of green branches, and was this wonderful sight and pageant of the world the only reward for having climbed to such a giddy height? Now look down again, Sylvia, where the green marsh is set among the shining birches and dark hemlocks; there where you saw the white heron once you will see him again; look, look! a white spot of him like a single floating feather comes up from the dead hemlock and grows larger, and rises, and comes close at last, and goes by the landmark pine with steady sweep of wing and outstretched slender neck and crested head. And wait! wait! do not move a foot or a finger, little girl, do not send an arrow of light and consciousness from your two eager eyes, for the heron has perched on a pine bough not far beyond yours, and cries back to his mate on the nest and plumes his feathers for the new day!

The child gives a long sigh a minute later when a company of shouting cat-birds comes also to the tree, and vexed by their fluttering and lawlessness the solemn heron goes away. She knows his secret now, the wild, light, slender bird that floats and wavers, and goes back like an arrow presently to his home in the green world beneath. Then Sylvia, well satisfied, makes her perilous way down again, not daring to look far below the branch she stands on, ready to cry sometimes because her fingers ache and her lamed feet slip. Wondering over and over again what the stranger would say to her, and what he would think when she told him how to find his way straight to the heron's nest.

"Sylvy, Sylvy!" called the busy old grandmother again and again, but nobody answered, and the small husk bed was empty and Sylvia had disappeared.

The guest waked from a dream, and remembering his day's pleasure hurried to dress himself that it might sooner begin. He was sure from the way the shy little girl looked once or twice yesterday that she had at least seen the white heron, and now she must really be made to tell. Here she comes now, paler than ever, and her worn old frock is torn and tattered, and smeared with pine pitch. The grandmother and the sportsman stand in the door together and question her, and the splendid moment has come to speak of the dead hemlock-tree by the green marsh.

But Sylvia does not speak after all, though the old grandmother fretfully rebukes her, and the young man's kind, appealing eyes are looking straight in her own. He can make them rich with money; he has promised it, and they are poor now. He is so well worth making happy, and he waits to hear the story she can tell.

No, she must keep silence! What is it that suddenly forbids her and makes her dumb? Has she been nine years growing and now, when the great world for the first time puts out a hand to her, must she thrust it aside for a bird's sake? The murmur of the pine's green branches is in her ears, she remembers how the white heron came flying through the golden air and how they watched the sea and the morning together, and Sylvia cannot speak; she cannot tell the heron's secret and give its life away.

Dear loyalty, that suffered a sharp pang as the guest went away disappointed later in the day, that could have served and followed him and loved him as a dog loves! Many a night Sylvia heard the echo of his whistle haunting the pasture path as she came home with the loitering cow. She forgot even her sorrow at the sharp report of his gun and the sight of thrushes and sparrows dropping silent to the ground, their songs hushed and their pretty feathers stained and wet with blood. Were the birds better friends than their hunter might have been,—who can tell? Whatever treasures were lost to her, woodlands and summer-time, remember! Bring your gifts and graces and tell your secrets to this lonely country child!

QUESTIONS FOR DISCUSSION AND WRITING

1. How is this a story of the natural world? What within the story calls our attention to the natural world and elevates its importance?
2. The white heron was hunted nearly to extinction for its feathers, which were used in women's hats. How do Sylvia's views toward the bird and her experience in the pine tree contrast to the view of the young hunter/ornithologist? Is the split represented in their attitudes simply one between conservation of nature and the advancing world of civilization that seeks to use it for personal ends, or is it greater than that?
3. Jewett is known for her regional writing. This story, set in the New England rural wilderness, is a splendid example. Does the story reflect more universally beyond New England? Explain.
4. Sylvia is in name and character associated with the sylvan (woods). What does she have in common with the white heron?
5. What is the effect of the details in this story such as the roving cow, the great pine tree being the last of its generation, or Sylvia's family line, particularly her Uncle Dan?

ON TECHNIQUE AND STYLE

1. Jewett's style of writing has often been described as natural and simple. Are those characterizations apt? How does her style contribute to meaning in the story?
2. How does Jewett transform the young man Sylvia meets in the woods from appearing initially to be nearly menacing to being someone who enters "the woman's heart, asleep in the child"?
3. How does Jewett manage point of view in the story? Are we seeing things from Sylvia's point of view or from Jewett's?

CULTURAL QUESTION

1. Sylvia and her hospitable grandmother are, we are told, "poor." Why is this important in the story and what, ultimately, does it mean to us as readers?

From My Year of Meats

Ruth Ozeki

Ruth Ozeki is a Smith College educated Japanese American filmmaker whose docu-
mentary and dramatic films have been shown on PBS, at the Sundance Film Festival,
and at colleges and universities throughout the United States. Born in New Haven,
Connecticut, she presently lives in New York City and British Columbia. Her novel
My Year of Meats *is about a Japanese American filmmaker named Jane Tagaki-Little.*
Hired by Beef-Ex, a meat lobbying group, Jane makes films for a weekly Japanese televi-
sion series called My American Wife, *featuring, each week, a woman from the United*
States and a beef recipe designed to "beef up" consumption of meat. In the tradition of
Upton Sinclair's The Jungle, *a pioneering muckraking work about the lack of cleanli-*
ness in the meat industry, My Year of Meats *takes us into some of the environmental*
horrors associated with meat, including the effect of additives and drugs and hormones
in meat production and some of the consequences of slaughterhouse and factory farm
abuse. In the following excerpt from the novel, Jane is on a film shoot in Colorado
with her driver, Dave Schultz, who educates her, while they are driving, on the effects
of livestock grazing and unsustainable methods of feed crop farming for cattle. Dave
enlightens Jane, an employee of Beef-Ex, as well as the readers of the novel, about what
he calls "a national crisis."

We drove through Colorado in our fifteen-passenger Ford production van, past
towns called Cope, Hygiene, and Last Chance. For this trip, it was the eastern
part of the state that I was interested in. Early explorers called it the "great
American desert," mile upon softly undulating mile, breathtaking and beautiful.
Of course, it looks nothing like it once looked, when the first settlers came. The
vistas, unbroken then and alive with grasses, are now cropped and divided
into finite parcels whose neat right angles reassure their surveyors and owners
while ignoring the subtle contours of the land. The fences stretch forever.

"You see that?" Dave, my local driver, interrupted my plains-induced reverie. He pointed to an immense field we'd been passing for several minutes or
maybe hours. It looked like all the others, stubbly hacked wheat stalks in neat
rows as far as the eye could see. It made me dizzy, like a bad moiré pattern
on a videotape, and the back of my eyeballs ached. I squinted, trying to see
what, in particular, he was pointing to.

"What?"

"There. The way wheat's been planted up that hillock, with the rows per-
pendicular, up and down the side?"

"Oh . . . Yeah?"

"Bad. Very bad."

"Why?"

"Erosion." He shook his head morosely.

Dave was an agricultural student at Colorado State University. His last name was Schultz, and he looked remarkably like a baby version of Sergeant Schultz on *Hogan's Heroes,* with an enormous breadth of chest and calm hands like sun-warmed rocks, made for comforting large terror-stricken animals. Suzuki and Oh liked him because he talked slowly and didn't use a lot of words.

One of the first things I ask a prospective driver is whether or not he likes to talk. Then I ask him what he knows about. Dave said, "Nope" and "Farms." I hired him on the spot.

Dave gave me the facts about farms:

The United States has lost one-third of its topsoil since colonial times—so much damage in such a short history. Six to seven billion tons of eroded soil, about 85 percent, are directly attributable to livestock grazing and unsustainable methods of farming feed crops for cattle. In 1988, more than 1.5 million acres in Colorado alone were damaged by wind erosion during the worst drought and heat wave since the 1950s.

"I remember it. I was on my dad's farm," said Dave. "I was just a kid then."

"Dave . . . 1988? That was just a couple of years ago."

"Yup."

Drought and heat waves happen, Dave explained. Erosion didn't have to. Not like this.

"You know what we have here?" Dave asked, an hour or so later.

"No, what?"

"A Crisis. A National Crisis."

"A national crisis?"

"Yup. Nobody sees it yet, but that's what it is, for sure."

"Dave, what are you talking about?"

He turned his head and stared at me, disbelieving, for a long time, so long that I started to get nervous, the Ford was rocketing down this country road, and Dave, though behind the wheel, wasn't watching at all. Finally he shook his head and turned to face forward again.

"Desertification," he pronounced glumly. He had more than his share of profound German melancholy, which seemed at odds with his sunny blond, pink face. He'd wanted to enter the Beef Science Program at the university and had written a paper on the effects of cattle on soil erosion. The paper was called "The Planet of the Ungulates," and it started out from the point of view of a Martian botanist who is circling the planet Earth in his spaceship, making a report on the creatures he sees below, only he's made a terrible mistake because he thinks that Earth is ruled by these large-bodied hoofed mathematicians who own small multicolored two-footed slaves; the slaves work from morning to night to feed their masters and to fabricate over the land their vast intricate geometries. Of course, the Martian never gets to see the inside of a slaughterhouse. But then again, who does?

Dave's professor failed him on "The Planet of the Ungulates," suggesting that he might be better off in the humanities rather than in agricultural sciences. As a result, he was taking a semester off, which was why he was free in October to work for us. He was thinking of dropping out entirely. Dave was not so popular at school because of his "take on things." This depressed him. So did his landscape.

Cattle are destroying the West, he told me, and whenever we passed a grazing herd, I could hear him groan. According to a 1991 United Nations report, 85 percent of U.S. Western rangeland, nearly 685 million acres, is degraded. There are between two and three million cattle allowed to graze on hundreds of millions of acres of public land in eleven Western states. *Public* land, Dave said, shaking his head.

"I read this thing by a guy in a magazine once," Dave said.

"Oh, well, that sure sounds interesting. . . ." Sarcasm, I figured, would be lost on Dave Schultz.

"Yup," he continued blandly, then gave me a dirty look. "It was an article in *Audubon* magazine. The guy was Philip Fradkin. Anyway, what he said was: 'The impact of countless hooves and mouths over the years has done more to alter the type of vegetation and land forms of the West than all the water projects, strip mines, power plants, freeways and sub-division developments combined.'"

"Wow." I took out my notebook to copy it down. Dave was odd, but I was impressed. "Tell me, Dave, did you happen to . . . I mean, did you memorize that?"

"Yup."

"How come?"

"I dunno. Guess I musta thought it was neat."

We drove in silence for another mile or two.

"Did you know seventy percent of all U.S. grain is used for livestock?" Dave suddenly burst forth again. His big hands clutched the steering wheel and he stared straight ahead, as though struggling to control some powerful emotion.

"And with all the tractors and machinery, it ends up taking the equivalent of one gallon of gas to make one pound of grain-fed U.S. beef?

"And do you know that the average American family of four eats more than two hundred sixty pounds of meat in a year? That's two hundred sixty gallons of fuel, which accounts for two point five tons of carbon dioxide going into the atmosphere and adding to global warming. . . .

"And that's not even taking into account that every McDonald's Quarter Pounder represents fifty-five square feet of South American rain forest, destroyed forever, which of course affects global warming as well. . . ."

"No kidding." I was writing it all down. He looked over and gave me a smug grin.

"Nope. . . . Are you at all interested in methane gas emissions?"

Okay, so he'd lied about not liking to talk. I could forgive him, because Dave was obsessed.

"Ready?" he continued. "Scientists estimate that some sixty million tons of methane gas are emitted as belches and flatulence by the world's one point three billion cattle and other ruminant livestock each year. Methane is one of the four global warming gases, each molecule trapping twenty-five times as much solar heat as a molecule of carbon dioxide." He finished on a triumphant note, then sighed, and his powerful shoulders sank.

"This is great!" I said, scribbling wildly. I was excited. I had the beginnings of a solid Documentary Interlude that I could work into the Bunny Dunn Show. "Go on. . . ."

"I just don't know," he said sadly, as though the sight of my enthusiasm had somehow quenched his. "All these figures, but who cares? So what? It doesn't help one bit. Nobody is going to do anything about it, and then slowly, bit by bit, it will be too late."

"I really wish you hadn't said that." I put my notebook away and stared out the window.

Too late. Until Dave said that, I'd been feeling lucky. After Akiko's call, I had rounded up Suzuki and Oh, called the travel agent, and phoned Bunny and then Dave to tell them we'd be on the next plane to Denver. Next I called my obstetrician—I was due for a second ultrasound, as I was approaching the twenty-week mark, but he said it was fine to postpone for a week, until after the shoot. He asked how I was feeling and I told him just fine, which was true. In fact, I'd never felt better physically; although my belly was rounding out, it still wasn't really visible under my clothes and wasn't getting in my way at all. And emotionally I was oddly calm. And happy. And we had a four-day head start on Ueno. Somehow everything seemed to be falling into place.

QUESTIONS FOR DISCUSSION AND WRITING

1. What is the initial environmental impact of Ozeki's opening paragraph description of the strangely named towns of eastern Colorado and the change from being a great American desert during the time of the explorers to fine parceled land where the "fences stretch forever."

2. Dave tells Jane he doesn't talk much, and then proceeds to talk a whole lot about grazing and farm feeding methods, which he calls "a national crisis." How credible is Dave as a source of facts and judgment, particularly given his moroseness and what we learn of his failure in college and on a paper in college on cattle and soil erosion?

3. What about Dave's college essay and its use of the point of view of a Martian botanist? The professor told Dave he might be better off leaving agricultural sciences for the humanities. What is your response to how Dave framed his essay and to the advice his professor gave?

4. Dave is making a case for serious environmental harm caused by the production and mass consumption of meat. Do the facts Dave presents offer a reasonable argument for reducing meat consumption or even becoming a vegetarian or vegan?

5. What about Jane's reactions to Dave's discourse? She is employed by a beef lobbying group. Do her attitudes toward what she is hearing seem mixed or confused?

ON TECHNIQUE AND STYLE

1. Ozeki banks a lot on the character of Dave in this excerpt to be a kind of mouthpiece about the environmental effects of meat production. How effective is this technique of using a character to teach another character and, of course, to teach the readers?
2. Jane sees Dave as looking "remarkably like a baby version of Sergeant Schultz on *Hogan's Heroes*" and as having what she tells us are "calm hands like sun-warmed rocks, made for comforting large terror-stricken animals." She also sees him as being obsessed and as someone on whom sarcasm would be lost. How does her point of view toward him help shape our attitudes about him as both a character and as a source of environmental wisdom?
3. How would you characterize and evaluate Ozeki as a stylist? Is there anything in her writing style that makes it distinctive or individual?

CULTURAL QUESTION

1. This excerpt focuses on a Japanese American filmmaker, who is filming for a Japanese television audience, learning all about an agricultural section of the United States that had few if any Japanese settlers and a dearth of farmers of Japanese descent. How does all this affect the scene portrayed here?

POETRY

The World is Too Much With Us

William Wordsworth

William Wordsworth (1770–1850) is one of Britain's greatest poets. With Samuel Taylor Coleridge, he founded the Romantic movement in poetry with the 1798 joint publication of Lyrical Ballads, *which included one of Wordsworth's most important and widely studied poems, "Tintern Abbey." His earliest work,* An Evening Walk *and* Descriptive Sketches, *both appeared in 1793. He was born in Cockermouth, Cumberland, in the Lake District of England and studied at Cambridge University as well as*

St. John's in Cambridge, where he received his BA degree. Poems in Two Volumes *appeared in 1807. In 1843 he was named England's poet laureate. Best known for his Lucy poems and the ode "Intimations of Immortality," Wordsworth's life work master-piece and autobiographic poem, "The Prelude," was published posthumously in 1850.*

"The World is Too Much With Us," published in 1798, is one of Wordsworth's most admired philosophical poems about nature, in which he sees those in his own time as being out of touch with and disconnected from the natural world.

The world is too much with us; late and soon,
Getting and spending, we lay waste our powers:
Little we see in Nature that is ours;
We have given our hearts away, a sordid boon!
The Sea that bares her bosom to the moon;
The winds that will be howling at all hours,
And are up-gathered now like sleeping flowers;
For this, for everything, we are out of tune;
It moves us not.—Great God! I'd rather be
Pagan suckled in a creed outworn;
So might I, standing on this pleasant lea,
Have glimpses that would make me less forlorn;
Have sight of Proteus rising from the sea;
Or hear old Triton blow his wreathed horn.

QUESTIONS FOR DISCUSSION AND WRITING

1. Is the division Wordsworth creates between the world that is "too much with us" and the natural world valid? Wordsworth is clearly moved by taking in nature as he stands on "this pleasant lea," but he also confesses to a mood "forlorn." Do you see the material world and nature as being so sharply divided?
2. What does the poet mean when he says, "Little we see in Nature that is ours"?
3. When Wordsworth brings up preference for the pagan and "a creed out-worn" what does he mean? How is he viewing the ancient world of mythic figures linked to nature such as Proteus and Triton compared to the world of his own era?
4. In what ways would you advance the idea that this poem is an environ-mentalist poem?

ON TECHNIQUE AND STYLE

1. The form of Wordsworth's poem is the traditional sonnet. Why do you suppose he uses so traditional a poetic form?

2. Is there an implicit argument in the poem about the nature of belief? About spirituality or differences between monotheism (belief in a single God) and polytheism (belief in many gods)? How does the poet manage to weave such matters into the poem?

CULTURAL QUESTION

1. To what extent can a rural-born British poet of the nineteenth century like Wordsworth reach those living in the modern urban world of the United States or other nations?

November Cotton Flower

Jean Toomer

Jean Toomer (1894–1967) was a poet, fiction writer, and dramatist who was a semi-nal figure in the ushering in of the Harlem Renaissance. Born in Washington, DC, as Eugene Pinchback Toomer, he was the grandson of P. B. S. Pinchback, the Reconstruc-tion governor of Louisiana and the only U.S. governor of black descent. He lived in Washington and New Rochelle, New York, and lived on both sides of the color line, eventually attending many universities. He soon began to describe himself as a cos-mopolitan and an American of mixed race and multiple nationality. His black lineage drew him to the South in 1921 where he went with the writer Waldo Frank and lived and taught, as he phrased it, "behind the veil," working in an all-black school in Sparta, Georgia. This experience was central to his writing the lyric masterpiece Cane, *first published in 1923. Toomer wrote many poems that appeared in* Cane, *and later pub-lished a long, Whitmanesque poem published after* Cane *called "Blue Meridian." His poetry was sensual, imagistic, and symbolic, often focusing on nature and the natural world. Much of his life was a search for higher levels of consciousness and he became associated with a group that followed a spiritual-seeking philosopher named Georges Gurdjieff. Toomer would also take up Quakerism and Dianetics and continue to write in all different genres, but with work that was heavily didactic and without the power or aesthetic beauty of* Cane.

In the lovely poem "November Cotton Flower," first published in Nomad *in 1923 and later included in* Cane, *Toomer creates a vivid symbolic picture of a Southern world ecologically frozen by the coming winter as a flower miraculously blooms.*

Boll-weevil's coming, and the winter's cold,
Made cotton-stalks look rusty, seasons old,
And cotton, scarce as any southern snow,
Was vanishing; the branch, so pinched and slow,
Failed in its function as the autumn rake;
Drouth fighting soil had caused the soil to take
All water from the streams; dead birds were found
In wells a hundred feet below the ground—
Such was the season when the flower bloomed.
Old folks were startled, and it soon assumed
Significance. Superstition saw
Something it had never seen before:
Brown eyes that loved without a trace of fear,
Beauty so sudden for that time of year.

QUESTIONS FOR DISCUSSION AND WRITING

1. The poem begins with a picture of agriculture (cotton crops) blighted by the season and the boll-weevil. How would you describe the initial picture Toomer creates of the natural environment in the poem's first seven lines?
2. The poem ultimately speaks of the beauty of nature with the flower blooming out of season. Yet the old folks see superstition in it. How does that color or affect the sense of the beauty of the natural world?
3. Why does the poet suddenly shift to "Brown eyes that loved without a trace of fear"? Why does this image appear and what picture does it create?
4. What metaphors in the poem particularly evoke the environment?

ON TECHNIQUE AND STYLE

1. "November Cotton Flower" is a sonnet. How is it structured? Where does the poem shift or divide and what is the overall effect?
2. The poem has idiomatic and vernacular qualities to it. How do these affect its style?

CULTURAL QUESTION

1. Toomer is considered one of America's greatest African American poets. If you didn't know Toomer was African American would you be able to tell by reading this poem? Is Toomer's racial heritage relevant?

GRAPHIC FICTION

From Moby Dick

Will Eisner

Will Eisner (1917–2005) was a pioneer in comics who had an enduring effect on film as well. He was born in New York City, the son of Jewish immigrants. He created the first comic book syndicated for the newspapers, The Spirit, *and a range of other lesser known newspaper comics that were created by him in conjunction with the Eisner–Iger studio and* Quality Comics. *He coined the term "graphic novel." Among his graphic novels are the classics,* A Contract with God *and* The Dreamer. *He is also the author of works on the creative process,* Comics and Sequential Art *and* Graphic Storytelling. *He taught cartooning for a number of years at the School of Visual Arts in New York City.*

Eisner's graphic novel Moby Dick, *Herman Melville's classic novel of the hunt for the infamous white whale Moby Dick, was first published in 1998. It has within it the graphic excerpt included here of whale hunting and whale harpooning. The profiteering associated with whale hunting and whale harpooning and the concern over the endangerment of whales have made for serious ongoing environmental issues.*

QUESTIONS FOR DISCUSSION AND WRITING

1. The hunt for the oil and bone that were highly valued from whales in the early to mid-nineteenth century is vividly portrayed in this section of Eisner's graphic novel of *Moby Dick.* How much do we see of the pain or of the eventual environmental consequences of the commercial killing of whales from this excerpt?

2. How does the excitement by the men about killing Moby Dick and the other whales strike you? Does it seem barbaric or more simply the actions of seafaring men out to do a job with fraternal enthusiasm?

3. Queequeg, the Polynesian harpooner pictured in the excerpt, is a man of singular muscularity, strength, and deadly aim. How does this affect our response to him as to the relationship that exists between humans and nature?

4. The men on the Pequod, the whaler ship, are competing with other whalers in the Japan Sea. Whale survival is at stake today, and the overkilling by Japanese whalers has become especially problematic. How might Eisner's cartoon serve as a caveat or warning about the commercial killing of these great, highly endangered sea mammals?

So...we sailed on...south around the horn into the Japan sea.

And along the way we took many a whale.

Sometimes we had to compete with other whalers.

THARS A SCHOOL OF SIX ABEAM, BOYS!

PULL, MEN! PULL...GET THERE FIRST

READY WITH YOUR HARPOON QUEEQUEG!

Then it was melted down into oil in the try-pots on deck.

After the bone was saved the rest was thrown to the sharks.

Our decks were awash with oil and the hold well filled with valuable bone.

Then Starbuck spoke to Ahab

WE HAVE OIL ENOUGH NOW!

TURN BACK, SIR! ...THE CREW WOULD HAVE US GO HOME NOW

NEVER! IF IT'S MUTINY, MISTER ...I'LL DEAL WITH IT...

ON TECHNIQUE AND STYLE

1. In this excerpt there is a definite feeling of the joint effort that went into the whaling enterprise. How does Eisner accomplish this visually and through dialogue?
2. What does Eisner's excerpt illustrate as far as the whaling enterprise is concerned?

CULTURAL QUESTION

1. Queequeg is from a non-Western cultural background. Though we see him as what he is, a whale killer, we also plainly see him as a man of strength and agility who can earn cheers from his fellow sailors. What are we to infer about attitudes existing at the time of *Moby Dick* toward cultural differences?

VISUAL TEXTS

Melting Clock and Globe

Marina Saba

Marina Saba is a professor of art teaching at the University of Houston.

The Polar Sea

Caspar David Friedrich

Caspar David Friedrich (1774–1840) was a landscape painter and major figure in the German Romantic movement.

Mermaid Waiting in Dry Lake

Tomek Olbinski

Tomek Olbinski was born in Kielce, Poland. He graduated from Warsaw Academy of Fine Arts in 1979, receiving a master's degree in interior design. He then began to work as an illustrator and graphic designer for Jazz Forum *and* ITD *magazines, the Hybrydy Club, and several other publishers and advertising agencies. He has been living in New York since 1987, pursuing a career as an illustrator, painter, and graphic designer.*

QUESTIONS FOR DISCUSSION AND WRITING

1. Which of these three images creates a greater sense of environmental crisis? Why?
2. The Saba painting propels a global image while the Friedrich painting is place specific and the Oblinski painting is evocative of a mythic, fairy-tale setting. How important to our understanding of any one of these paintings to the setting?
3. Would it be appropriate to categorize these works as environmental art or is that too narrow a category?

ON TECHNIQUE AND STYLE

1. Saba's *Melting Clock and Globe* is a surreal depiction of global doom, whereas Oblinski's *Mermaid Waiting in Dry Lake* conveys drought but with flowers blooming and a mermaid. Do such unrealistic techniques take away from the importance of the message these works are intended to convey?
2. When we think of the impact of global warming we often think of polar icecaps. Does *The Polar Sea* by Friedrich succeed in making us think of the contrast to what is occurring in the Polar Sea today due to global warming or do we require an actual contrasting image?
3. Do any of these artistic renderings act as a potential catalyst to environmental action?

CULTURAL QUESTION

1. These images are all by European- or American-based artists. The environmental movement has been criticized as being too European and American

based and not rooted enough in the developing or third world where many of the crises of the environment such as global warming and water scarcity are far more serious. Is it important or necessary for artists who evoke environmental issues to be from a particular region?

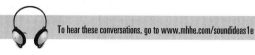

AUDIO TEXTS   To hear these conversations, go to www.mhhe.com/soundideas1e

Track 7.1

(date: May 28, 2007; running time: 50:50 min.)

Wangari Maathai is the Kenyan founder of the Green Belt movement and the author of a book about it called The Green Belt Movement: Sharing the Approach and the Experience. *She is recipient of the 2004 Nobel Peace Prize.*

Track 7.2

(date: January 13, 2005; running time: 50:50 min.)

Panel discussion of the future of the oceans: **Leon Panetta** *is a former U.S. Democratic congressional representative from California who was head of the Office of Management and Budget and the White House chief of staff under President Bill Clinton. He chaired the Pew Oceans Commission and is director of the Leon and Sylvia Panetta Institute for Public Policy at California State University, Monterey Bay.*

Track 7.3

(date: January 13, 2005; running time: 50:50 min.)

Panel discussion of the future of the oceans: **Brian Baird** *served as assistant secretary for Ocean and Coastal Policy for the state of California Resources Agency.*

Track 7.4

(date: January 13, 2005; running time: 50:50 min.)

Panel discussion of the future of the oceans: **John E. McCosker** *is senior scientist and chair of the Department of Aquatic Biology at the California Academy of Sciences.*

Track 7.5

(date: January 13, 2005; running time: 50:50 min.)

Panel discussion of the future of the oceans: **Kate Wing** *is an ocean policy analyst with the National Resources Defense Council.*

QUESTIONS FOR DISCUSSION AND WRITING

1. Maathai has inspired a mass movement of tree planting and reforestation by ordinary citizens, mostly women, in her country, Kenya. Hers is an environmental grassroots success story. Yet, as she states in this interview, she was idealistic in thinking her views would be quickly embraced; she discovered that people were too caught up in their own interests. How idealistic ought one to be about environmental political activism and getting others quickly on board? Is idealism about getting quick support foolish? Unrealistic?
2. Maathai talks about how her Green Belt movement is connected to peace because of issues of sustainability and finite resources. Do you think that good environmental planning and resource management would actually deter or impede conflict and war?
3. Maathai emphasizes the importance of democracy, specifically citizen education and citizen activism, in creating and maintaining environmental goals and holding government responsible and accountable. Is this an idealistic view of democracy or is it a viable, practical one?
4. Panetta talks about the importance of conflicting governance in sustaining our oceans and about how small the dollar numbers are that are being spent on protecting them. The other participants emphasize the need to protect and conserve the oceans by land management or halting overfishing or ignoring at our own risk the possibility of species being lost. All of these are of obvious importance. If you had influence on government policy which would you feel deserves the greatest emphasis? Why?
5. Do you agree with Baird's point that everybody, all of us, are stewards of the ocean? That the average person needs to be aware of the effect of something so seemingly inconsequential as tossing a cigarette on the ground?

ON TECHNIQUE AND STYLE

1. How persuasive is Maathai as an advocate and speaker? Are there specific techniques she brings to the interview that make her persuasive?
2. Panetta mentions almost immediately two commission reports. How does mentioning these reports help or support his general position or stance on the oceans and what they require?

3. Which of the four speakers is most convincing to you? Why?

CULTURAL QUESTION

1. In this increased world of globalization, what *New York Times* columnist Tom Friedman calls the flattening of the world, how do some of these environmental ideas hold up as being applicable in cultures around the world? How truly global in application to cultures around the world, for example, are either Maathai's ideas about reforming democracy or Wing's of too many fish being taken out of the oceans and fishing gear being too destructive?

CONNECTIONS

1. Environmental awareness often necessitates an appreciation of the beauty of the natural world. We see this appreciation in the Emerson and Dillard essays and in the poetry of Wordsworth and Toomer. Is there a connection between the way these writers respond to the beauty of nature?

2. Dillard has credited Emerson as being a major influence on her thinking. How might we connect these two writers of different eras in the ways they see spiritual meaning in the natural world?

3. Both Wilson and Carson write of environmental loss and degradation. Though their approaches and the focus of their essays differ radically, what links their messages about urgent concern for protection of the environment?

4. What message or messages connect the passage from Hemingway's *The Old Man and the Sea* to the conversation about the oceans with Panetta and the three oceanic experts?

5. How do the selection from Ozeki's *My Year of Meats* and the one from Eisner connect to each other?

6. The selection by Lopez and Maathai's work in the Green Belt movement are, for many, the essence of environmental activism. What is revealed to us in the Lopez story or in the work of these environmental crusaders about the role of the individual and his or her political impact on the environment?

7. What do we learn from selections such as Emerson's essay "Nature," Jewett's story, the excerpt from Hemingway, Wordsworth's poem, or the excerpt from Eisner's graphic novel of *Moby Dick* about the ongoing relationship between human beings and nature?

8. Carson, Ozeki, and the paintings by Saba and Olbinski all exemplify ways of tuning our awareness to crisis and disaster. What ultimate effects do such connections have on us?

9. Place plays a major role in the selections from Dillard, Hemingway, Lopez, Toomer, Eisner, and Friedrich. How does a sense of place prefigure or contribute to a greater sense of environmental awareness?

10. What are some of the most important lessons we learn about nature and the natural world from the selections in this chapter?

FOR WRITING

CREATIVE CHOICES

1. Write a poem about your feelings toward the natural world. Incorporate, as much as you can, imagery that represents your feelings.
2. Take a photo or a series of photos that express an environmental issue that is of great importance to you.
3. Record an interview with someone active in the environmental movement or dedicated to an environmental cause.

NARRATIVE/EXPOSITORY CHOICES

1. Create a story, autobiographical or fable, that reveals what to you is of importance or concern about our relationship to the natural world.
2. Focus on a single environmental problem that is important to you and provide, in expository form, a picture of the nature and scope of the problem.
3. In narrative or expository form demonstrate the importance of environmental awareness and/or environmental activism.

ARGUMENT CHOICES

1. Establish an argument for the importance of appreciating and preserving the natural environment.
2. Argue for or against committed environmental activism.
3. Does the beauty and majesty of the natural world need to be tied to a higher or more spiritual force to be truly understood? Why or why not?

RESEARCH CHOICES

1. Research an environmental issue of concern such as pesticide use, species endangerment, global warming, deforestation, or ocean sustainability and find out what proposals exist as ways of remedying or reducing problems associated with the issue.

2. Research the efficacy of environmental activism. What methods have been historically most effective and have brought about the most significant and lasting results?

VIDEO SUGGESTIONS

1. *An Inconvenient Truth* (2006). A documentary on Al Gore's campaign to make the issue of global warming a recognized problem worldwide.
2. *Silkwood* (1983). The story of Karen Silkwood, a worker at a plutonium processing plant who was purposefully contaminated and possibly murdered to prevent her from exposing worker safety violations at the plant.
3. Jane Goodall's *Wild Chimpanzees* (2002). A cinematic portrait of the zoologist and the chimpanzees she has spent a lifetime studying.
4. *Wall-E* (2008). An animated story of a small waste collecting robot that embarks on a space journey that will decide the fate of humankind.
5. *Manufactured Landscapes* (2006). Photographer Edward Burtynsky travels the world observing changes in landscapes due to industrial work and manufacturing.

chapter **8**

Ideas about Art and Poetry
A New New Wave

INTRODUCTION

"New wave" was a term that became largely associated with contemporary music, especially the music of the late 1970s and 1980s rooted in punk. It followed the 1950s' style of rock and roll as the first wave and the 1960s British invasion as the second. But there was a new-wave film movement in the 1960s as well, in addition to a new wave identified with changing fashion and a new wave of mid-1980s feminism following. The first two waves became identified with the Convention in Seneca Falls and the subsequent enfranchisement of women with the vote in the first, and the social movement that began with Betty Friedan's *Feminine Mystique* in the early 1960s to late 1970s in the second. In this chapter we look at change and new waves in sound—sound waves really, the sound associated with the changing nature of poetry and its root source music. Poetry and music are linked and both go through changes in sound and form. Technology has changed poetry and music irrevocably as have a host of other factors as both forms continue to morph and evolve.

As stated, the chapter is about change. As the skin of one form sheds, alters, and mutates, a newer generation takes on its own skin and sounds change as arguments emerge about what should be laid to rest and what should survive. Poet and critic Dana Gioia starts us off with an essay that asks and tries to answer the essential question "Can Poetry Matter?" Gioia, who was head of the National Endowment for the Arts, curiously enough does not bring in rap or slam or some of the newer waves of poetry, but he concerns himself with the key question about how to make poetry relevant outside the small coterie who appreciate and love the form. Camille Paglia, from her book *Break, Blow, Burn,* a title taken from a poem by the great metaphysical poet John Donne, uses her considerable intellectual power to convey the importance of poetry, though, once again, she is focusing her attention on what we would categorize as high-culture poetry. The other two selections we have included in the non-fiction section come from two hip-hop spokespersons who view culture and poetry from a more contemporary standpoint. Hip-hop historian Jeff Chang and techno wizard DJ Spooky grapple with the form and relevance of the new wave of expression that has emerged with what some have come to call hip-hop nation.

All four of the short stories we have included concern different types of generational divides as one wave leaves and another surfaces. Hisaye Yamamoto and Edwidge Danticat write powerful mother–daughter tales in which both of the mothers are part of ongoing traditions, from Japan and Haiti, invested in older and more traditional forms of poetic expression as well as in traditional prescribed roles for women. Bobbie Ann Mason's rural Kentucky story "A New Wave Format" is about the effect of ushering in a new-wave format of music on a bus full of men and women who are mentally challenged. But it is also a dramatization of a romance between a man and a much younger woman who are both riding waves between the old and the new. Cynthia Ozick's story centers us in a struggle by Yiddish immigrant poets who want to preserve the old ways set against all of the new temptations identified with youth and America. The two poets we include in this chapter get us back to the question Gioia tries to answer about whether poetry can matter. Ishmael Reed makes it matter as he sets out literally to entrap us in his poem. Marianne Moore begins her poem by conceding that she dislikes poetry, but then she affirms what she believes is real and genuine in it. Dave McKean, in the graphic fiction selection from his tome *Cages,* takes us deeper into the power of music as we join a black Rasta musician and his feline companion and witness the power of music to capture even the songs of birds.

The visual selections include *Luna Cadillac* by Haitian American artist Jean Michel Basquiat, embodying graffiti-type art often associated with hip-hop and neoexpressionism or new-wave expressionism. The painting by Spanish artist Joan Miro embodies the intersection of text and art and a visual representation of poetry. Finally, the selection of Francesco Clemente's work brings imagery of poetry and the new wave on to the canvas.

The notions of the power of poetry and music to capture our attention and even to entice emissaries with wings to come to us moves into the present-day world of the Internet, the World Wide Web, and multiculturalism as we hear the gospel of Paul D. Miller (DJ Spooky) as he enthuses about the fun of sampling and mixing, cutting up a text or record to create a collage or poems to another generation of technology. Then hip-hop historian Jeff Chang talks about the changing nature of hip-hop. The audio section continues with excerpts from interviews with poets W. S. Merwin and Adrienne Rich talking about the importance of poetry and reading from their work. It concludes with excerpts from a panel discussion on the poetry of the great Chilean poet Pablo Neruda on the occasion of the centenary of his birth.

Can Poetry Matter?

Dana Gioia

Dana Gioia (1950–) was born in Los Angeles of Italian and Mexican descent. A poet, critic, editor, anthologist, and translator, he was named by President George W. Bush in 2003 as the ninth chair of the National Endowment for the Arts. Educated at Stanford (both a BA and an MBA) and Harvard (MFA in comparative literature), he worked as a business executive as vice president of General Foods in addition to writing three books of poetry, Daily Horoscope, The Gods of Winter, *and* Interrogations at Noon, *which won the American Book Award in 2001. He is also the author of* Can Poetry Matter? Essays on Poetry and American Culture *and* Barrier of a Common Language: An American Looks at Contemporary British Poetry. *He has taught at Colorado College, Johns Hopkins, Sarah Lawrence, Mercer, and Wesleyan University and has published essays in* The New Yorker, The New York Times Book Review, Slate, The Hudson Review, *the* Washington Post Book World, *and* Book Review. *The essay "Can Poetry Matter?" first appeared in* Atlantic Monthly *in May 1991. In it Gioia argues that poets in the United States have become part of an invisible subculture that needs to extend beyond a narrow, special, and guarded audience to a more general one. He makes proposals for bringing poetry out of its confined academic world and making it matter to more people in the general population, and he pronounces as dead what he calls the inward-directed poetry of the present and urges that, like the phoenix, a new kind of poetry rise from the ashes.*

American poetry now belongs to a subculture. No longer part of the mainstream of artistic and intellectual life, it has become the specialized occupation of a relatively small and isolated group. Little of the frenetic activity it generates ever reaches outside that closed group. As a class poets are not without cultural status. Like priests in a town of agnostics, they still command a certain residual prestige. But as individual artists they are almost invisible.

What makes the situation of contemporary poets particularly surprising is that it comes at a moment of unprecedented expansion for the art. There have never before been so many new books of poetry published, so many anthologies or literary magazines. Never has it been so easy to earn a living as a poet. There are now several thousand college-level jobs in teaching creative writing, and many more at the primary and secondary levels. Congress has even instituted the position of poet laureate, as have twenty-five states. One also finds a complex network of public subvention for poets, funded by federal, state, and local agencies, augmented by private support in the form of foundation fellowships, prizes, and subsidized retreats. There has also never before been so much published criticism about contemporary poetry; it fills dozens of literary newsletters and scholarly journals.

The proliferation of new poetry and poetry programs is astounding by any historical measure. Just under a thousand new collections of verse are published each year, in addition to a myriad of new poems printed in magazines both small and large. No one knows how many poetry readings take place each year, but surely the total must run into the tens of thousands. And there are now about 200 graduate creative-writing programs in the United States, and more than a thousand undergraduate ones. With an average of ten poetry students in each graduate section, these programs alone will produce about 20,000 accredited professional poets over the next decade. From such statistics an observer might easily conclude that we live in the golden age of American poetry.

But the poetry boom has been a distressingly confined phenomenon. Decades of public and private funding have created a large professional class for the production and reception of new poetry comprising legions of teachers, graduate students, editors, publishers, and administrators. Based mostly in universities, these groups have gradually become the primary audience for contemporary verse. Consequently, the energy of American poetry, which was once directed outward, is now increasingly focused inward. Reputations are made and rewards distributed within the poetry subculture. To adapt Russell Jacoby's definition of contemporary academic renown from *The Last Intellectuals,* a "famous" poet now means someone famous only to other poets. But there are enough poets to make that local fame relatively meaningful. Not long ago, "only poets read poetry" was meant as damning criticism. Now it is a proven marketing strategy.

The situation has become a paradox, a Zen riddle of cultural sociology. Over the past half century, as American poetry's specialist audience has steadily expanded, its general readership has declined. Moreover, the engines that have driven poetry's institutional success—the explosion of academic writing programs, the proliferation of subsidized magazines and presses, the emergence of a creative-writing career track, and the migration of American literary culture to the university—have unwittingly contributed to its disappearance from public view.

Its Own World

To the average reader, the proposition that poetry's audience has declined may seem self-evident. It is symptomatic of the art's current isolation that within the subculture such notions are often rejected. Like chamber-of-commerce representatives from Parnassus, poetry boosters offer impressive recitations of the numerical growth of publications, programs, and professorships. Given the bullish statistics on poetry's material expansion, how does one demonstrate

that its intellectual and spiritual influence has eroded? One cannot easily marshal numbers, but to any candid observer the evidence throughout the world of
ideas and letters seems inescapable.

Daily newspapers no longer review poetry. There is, in fact, little coverage
of poetry or poets in the general press. From 1984 until this year the National
Book Awards dropped poetry as a category. Leading critics rarely review it. In
fact, virtually no one reviews it except other poets. Almost no popular collections of contemporary poetry are available except those, like the *Norton Anthology,* targeting an academic audience. It seems, in short, as if the large audience
that still exists for quality fiction hardly notices poetry. A reader familiar with the
novels of Joyce Carol Oates, John Updike, or John Barth may not even recognize the names of Gwendolyn Brooks, Gary Snyder, and W. D. Snodgrass.

One can see a microcosm of poetry's current position by studying its
coverage in *The New York Times.* Virtually never reviewed in the daily edition,
new poetry is intermittently discussed in the *Sunday Book Review,* but almost
always in group reviews where three books are briefly considered together.
Whereas a new novel or biography is reviewed on or around its publication
date, a new collection by an important poet like Donald Hall or David Igna-
tow might wait up to a year for a notice. Or it might never be reviewed at all.
Henry Taylor's *The Flying Change* was reviewed only after it had won the
Pulitzer Prize. Rodney Jones's *Transparent Gestures* was reviewed months
after it had won the National Book Critics Circle Award. Rita Dove's Pulitzer
Prize-winning *Thomas and Beulah* was not reviewed by the *Times* at all.

Poetry reviewing is no better anywhere else, and generally it is much
worse. *The New York Times* only reflects the opinion that although there is a
great deal of poetry around, none of it matters very much to readers, publishers, or advertisers—to anyone, that is, except other poets. For most newspapers and magazines, poetry has become a literary commodity intended
less to be read than to be noted with approval. Most editors run poems and
poetry reviews the way a prosperous Montana rancher might keep a few
buffalo around—not to eat the endangered creatures but to display them for
tradition's sake.

How Poetry Diminished

Arguments about the decline of poetry's cultural importance are not new. In
American letters they date back to the nineteenth century. But the modern
debate might be said to have begun in 1934 when Edmund Wilson published
the first version of his controversial essay "Is Verse a Dying Technique?" Surveying literary history, Wilson noted that verse's role had grown increasingly narrow
since the eighteenth century. In particular, Romanticism's emphasis on intensity
made poetry seem so "fleeting and quintessential" that eventually it dwindled
into a mainly lyric medium. As verse—which had previously been a popular
medium for narrative, satire, drama, even history and scientific speculation—
retreated into lyric, prose usurped much of its cultural territory. Truly ambitious

writers eventually had no choice but to write in prose. The future of great literature, Wilson speculated, belonged almost entirely to prose.

Wilson was a capable analyst of literary trends. His skeptical assessment
of poetry's place in modern letters has been frequently attacked and qualified
over the past half century, but it has never been convincingly dismissed. His
argument set the ground rules for all subsequent defenders of contemporary
poetry. It also provided the starting point for later iconoclasts, from Delmore
Schwartz to Christopher Clausen. The most recent and celebrated of these
revisionists is Joseph Epstein, whose mordant 1988 critique "Who Killed
Poetry?" first appeared in *Commentary* and was reprinted in an extravagantly
acrimonious symposium in *AWP Chronicle* (the journal of the Associated Writing Programs). Not coincidentally, Epstein's title pays a double homage to
Wilson's essay—first by mimicking the interrogative form of the original title,
second by employing its metaphor of death.

Epstein essentially updated Wilson's argument, but with important differences. Whereas Wilson looked on the decline of poetry's cultural position as
a gradual process spanning three centuries, Epstein focused on the past few
decades. He contrasted the major achievements of the modernists—the generation of Eliot and Stevens, which led poetry from moribund Romanticism
into the twentieth century—with what he felt were the minor accomplishments
of the present practitioners. The modernists, Epstein maintained, were artists
who worked from a broad cultural vision. Contemporary writers were "poetry
professionals," who operated within the closed world of the university. Wilson
blamed poetry's plight on historical forces; Epstein indicted the poets themselves and the institutions they had helped create, especially creative-writing
programs. A brilliant polemicist, Epstein intended his essay to be incendi-
ary, and it did ignite an explosion of criticism. No recent essay on American
poetry has generated so many immediate responses in literary journals. And
certainly none has drawn so much violently negative criticism from poets
themselves. To date at least thirty writers have responded in print. The poet
Henry Taylor published two rebuttals.

Poets are justifiably sensitive to arguments that poetry has declined in
cultural importance, because journalists and reviewers have used such arguments simplistically to declare all contemporary verse irrelevant. Usually the
less a critic knows about verse the more readily he or she dismisses it. It is
no coincidence, I think, that the two most persuasive essays on poetry's presumed demise were written by outstanding critics of fiction, neither of whom
has written extensively about contemporary poetry. It is too soon to judge the
accuracy of Epstein's essay, but a literary historian would find Wilson's timing
ironic. As Wilson finished his famous essay, Robert Frost, Wallace Stevens,
T. S. Eliot, Ezra Pound, Marianne Moore, E. E. Cummings, Robinson Jeffers,
H. D. (Hilda Doolittle), Robert Graves, W. H. Auden, Archibald MacLeish, Basil
Bunting, and others were writing some of their finest poems, which, encompassing history, politics, economics, religion, and philosophy, are among the
most culturally inclusive in the history of the language. At the same time, a

new generation, which would include Robert Lowell, Elizabeth Bishop, Philip Larkin, Randall Jarrell, Dylan Thomas, A. D. Hope, and others, was just breaking into print. Wilson himself later admitted that the emergence of a versatile and ambitious poet like Auden contradicted several points of his argument. But if Wilson's prophecies were sometimes inaccurate, his sense of poetry's overall situation was depressingly astute. Even if great poetry continues to be written, it has retreated from the center of literary life. Though supported by a loyal coterie, poetry has lost the confidence that it speaks to and for the general culture.

Inside the Subculture

One sees evidence of poetry's diminished stature even within the thriving subculture. The established rituals of the poetry world—the readings, small magazines, workshops, and conferences—exhibit a surprising number of self-imposed limitations. Why, for example, does poetry mix so seldom with music, dance, or theater? At most readings the program consists of verse only—and usually only verse by that night's author. Forty years ago, when Dylan Thomas read, he spent half the program reciting other poets' work. Hardly a self-effacing man, he was nevertheless humble before his art. Today most readings are celebrations less of poetry than of the author's ego. No wonder the audience for such events usually consists entirely of poets, would-be poets, and friends of the author.

Several dozen journals now exist that print only verse. They don't publish literary reviews, just page after page of freshly minted poems. The heart sinks to see so many poems crammed so tightly together, like downcast immigrants in steerage. One can easily miss a radiant poem amid the many lackluster ones. It takes tremendous effort to read these small magazines with openness and attention. Few people bother, generally not even the magazines' contributors. The indifference to poetry in the mass media has created a monster of the opposite kind—journals that love poetry not wisely but too well.

Until about thirty years ago most poetry appeared in magazines that addressed a nonspecialist audience on a range of subjects. Poetry vied for the reader's interest along with politics, humor, fiction, and reviews—a competition that proved healthy for all the genres. A poem that didn't command the reader's attention wasn't considered much of a poem. Editors chose verse that they felt would appeal to their particular audiences, and the diversity of magazines assured that a variety of poetry appeared. The early *Kenyon Review* published Robert Lowell's poems next to critical essays and literary reviews. The old *New Yorker* celebrated Ogden Nash between cartoons and short stories.

A few general-interest magazines, such as *The New Republic* and *The New Yorker,* still publish poetry in every issue, but, significantly, none except *The Nation* still reviews it regularly. Some poetry appears in the handful of small magazines and quarterlies that consistently discuss a broad cultural agenda with nonspecialist readers, such as *The Threepenny Review, The New Criterion,* and *The Hudson Review.* But most poetry is published in journals that address an insular audience of literary professionals, mainly teachers of creative writing and their students. A few of these, such as *American Poetry Review* and *AWP Chronicle,* have moderately large circulations. Many more have negligible readerships. But size is not the problem. The problem is their complacency or resignation about existing only in and for a subculture.

What are the characteristics of a poetry-subculture publication? First, the one subject it addresses is current American literature (supplemented perhaps by a few translations of poets who have already been widely translated). Second, if it prints anything other than poetry, that is usually short fiction. Third, if it runs discursive prose, the essays and reviews are overwhelmingly positive. If it publishes an interview, the tone will be unabashedly reverent toward the author. For these journals critical prose exists not to provide a disinterested perspective on new books but to publicize them. Quite often there are manifest personal connections between the reviewers and the authors they discuss. If occasionally a negative review is published, it will be openly sectarian, rejecting an aesthetic that the magazine has already condemned. The unspoken editorial rule seems to be, Never surprise or annoy the readers; they are, after all, mainly our friends and colleagues.

By abandoning the hard work of evaluation, the poetry subculture demeans its own art. Since there are too many new poetry collections appearing each year for anyone to evaluate, the reader must rely on the candor and discernment of reviewers to recommend the best books. But the general press has largely abandoned this task, and the specialized press has grown so overprotective of poetry that it is reluctant to make harsh judgments. In his new book, *American Poetry: Wildness and Domesticity,* Robert Bly has accurately described the corrosive effect of this critical boosterism:

> We have an odd situation: although more bad poetry is being published now than ever before in American history, most of the reviews are positive. Critics say, "I never attack what is bad, all that will take care of itself," . . . but the country is full of young poets and readers who are confused by seeing mediocre poetry praised, or never attacked, and who end up doubting their own critical perceptions.

A clubby feeling also typifies most recent anthologies of contemporary poetry. Although these collections represent themselves as trustworthy guides to the best new poetry, they are not compiled for readers outside the academy. More than one editor has discovered that the best way to get an anthology assigned is to include work by the poets who teach the courses. Compiled in the spirit of congenial opportunism, many of these anthologies give the impression that literary quality is a concept that neither an editor nor a reader should take too seriously.

The 1985 *Morrow Anthology of Younger American Poets,* for example, is not so much a selective literary collection as a comprehensive directory of creative-writing teachers (it even offers a photo of each author). Running nearly 800 pages, the volume presents no fewer than 104 important young poets, virtually all of whom teach creative writing. The editorial principle governing selection seems to have been the fear of leaving out some influential colleague. The book does contain a few strong and original poems, but they are surrounded by so many undistinguished exercises that one wonders if the good work got there by design or simply by random sampling. In the drearier patches one suspects that perhaps the book was never truly meant to be read, only assigned.

And that is the real issue. The poetry subculture no longer assumes that all published poems will be read. Like their colleagues in other academic departments, poetry professionals must publish, for purposes of both job security and career advancement. The more they publish, the faster they progress. If they do not publish, or wait too long, their economic futures are in grave jeopardy.

In art, of course, everyone agrees that quality and not quantity matters. Some authors survive on the basis of a single unforgettable poem—Edmund Waller's "Go, Lovely Rose," for example, or Edwin Markham's "The Man With the Hoe," which was made famous by being reprinted in hundreds of newspapers—an unthinkable occurrence today. But bureaucracies, by their very nature, have difficulty measuring something as intangible as literary quality. When institutions evaluate creative artists for employment or promotion, they still must find some seemingly objective means to do so. As the critic Bruce Bawer has observed,

> A poem is, after all, a fragile thing, and its intrinsic worth or lack thereof, is a frighteningly subjective consideration; but fellowship grants, degrees, appointments, and publications are objective facts. They are quantifiable; they can be listed on a resume.

Poets serious about making careers in institutions understand that the criteria for success are primarily quantitative. They must publish as much as possible as quickly as possible. The slow maturation of genuine creativity looks like laziness to a committee. Wallace Stevens was forty-three when his first book appeared. Robert Frost was thirty-nine. Today these sluggards would be unemployable.

The proliferation of literary journals and presses over the past thirty years has been a response less to an increased appetite for poetry among the public than to the desperate need of writing teachers for professional validation. Like subsidized farming that grows food no one wants, a poetry industry has been created to serve the interests of the producers and not the consumers. And in the process the integrity of the art has been betrayed. Of course, no poet is allowed to admit this in public. The cultural credibility of the professional poetry establishment depends on maintaining a polite hypocrisy.

Millions of dollars in public and private funding are at stake. Luckily, no one outside the subculture cares enough to press the point very far. No Woodward and Bernstein will ever investigate a cover-up by members of the Associated Writing Programs.

The new poet makes a living not by publishing literary work but by providing specialized educational services. Most likely he or she either works for or aspires to work for a large institution—usually a state-run enterprise, such as a school district, a college, or a university (or lately even a hospital or prison)—teaching others how to write poetry or, on the highest levels, how to teach others how to write poetry.

To look at the issue in strictly economic terms, most contemporary poets have been alienated from their original cultural function. As Marx maintained and few economists have disputed, changes in a class's economic function eventually transform its values and behavior. In poetry's case, the socioeconomic changes have led to a divided literary culture: the superabundance of poetry within a small class and the impoverishment outside it. One might even say that outside the classroom—where society demands that the two groups interact—poets and the common reader are no longer on speaking terms.

The divorce of poetry from the educated reader has had another, more pernicious result. Seeing so much mediocre verse not only published but praised, slogging through so many dull anthologies and small magazines, most readers—even sophisticated ones like Joseph Epstein—now assume that no significant new poetry is being written. This public skepticism represents the final isolation of verse as an art form in contemporary society.

The irony is that this skepticism comes in a period of genuine achievement. Gresham's Law, that bad coinage drives out good, only half applies to current poetry. The sheer mass of mediocrity may have frightened away most readers, but it has not yet driven talented writers from the field. Anyone patient enough to weed through the tangle of contemporary work finds an impressive and diverse range of new poetry. Adrienne Rich, for example, despite her often overbearing polemics, is a major poet by any standard. The best work of Donald Justice, Anthony Hecht, Donald Hall, James Merrill, Louis Simpson, William Stafford, and Richard Wilbur—to mention only writers of the older generation—can hold its own against anything in the national literature. One might also add Sylvia Plath and James Wright, two strong poets of the same generation who died early. America is also a country rich in emigre poetry, as major writers like Czeslaw Milosz, Nina Cassian, Derek Walcott, Joseph Brodsky, and Thom Gunn demonstrate.

Without a role in the broader culture, however, talented poets lack the confidence to create public speech. Occasionally a writer links up rewardingly to a social or political movement. Rich, for example, has used feminism to expand the vision of her work. Robert Bly wrote his finest poetry to protest the Vietnam War. His sense of addressing a large and diverse audience added humor, breadth, and humanity to his previously minimal verse. But it is a difficult task to marry the Muse happily to politics. Consequently, most contemporary poets, knowing that they are virtually invisible in the larger culture, focus on the more intimate forms of lyric and meditative verse. (And a few loners, like X. J. Kennedy and John Updike, turn their genius to the critically disreputable demimonde of light verse and children's poetry.) Therefore, although current American poetry has not often excelled in public forms like political or satiric verse, it has nonetheless produced personal poems of unsurpassed beauty and power. Despite its manifest excellence, this new work has not found a public beyond the poetry subculture, because the traditional machinery of transmission—the reliable reviewing, honest criticism, and selective anthologies—has broken down. The audience that once made Frost and Eliot, Cummings and Millay, part of its cultural vision remains out of reach. Today Walt Whitman's challenge "To have great poets, there must be great audiences, too" reads like an indictment.

From Bohemia to Bureaucracy

To maintain their activities, subcultures usually require institutions, since the general society does not share their interests. Nudists flock to "nature camps" to express their unfettered lifestyle. Monks remain in monasteries to protect their austere ideals. As long as poets belonged to a broader class of artists and intellectuals, they centered their lives in urban bohemias, where they maintained a distrustful independence from institutions. Once poets began moving into universities, they abandoned the working-class heterogeneity of Greenwich Village and North Beach for the professional homogeneity of academia.

At first they existed on the fringes of English departments, which was probably healthy. Without advanced degrees or formal career paths, poets were recognized as special creatures. They were allowed—like aboriginal chieftains visiting an anthropologist's campsite—to behave according to their own laws. But as the demand for creative writing grew, the poet's job expanded from merely literary to administrative duties. At the university's urging, these self-trained writers designed history's first institutional curricula for young poets. Creative writing evolved from occasional courses taught within the English department into its own undergraduate major or graduate-degree program. Writers fashioned their academic specialty in the image of other university studies. As the new writing departments multiplied, the new professionals patterned their infrastructure—job titles, journals, annual conventions, organizations—according to the standards not of urban bohemia but of educational institutions. Out of the professional networks this educational expansion created, the subculture of poetry was born.

Initially, the multiplication of creative-writing programs must have been a dizzyingly happy affair. Poets who had scraped by in bohemia or had spent their early adulthood fighting the Second World War suddenly secured stable, well-paying jobs. Writers who had never earned much public attention found themselves surrounded by eager students. Poets who had been too poor to travel flew from campus to campus and from conference to conference, to speak before audiences of their peers. As Wilfrid Sheed once described a moment in John Berryman's career, "Through the burgeoning university network, it was suddenly possible to think of oneself as a national poet, even if the nation turned out to consist entirely of English Departments." The bright post-war world promised a renaissance for American poetry.

In material terms that promise has been fulfilled beyond the dreams of anyone in Berryman's Depression-scarred generation. Poets now occupy niches at every level of academia, from a few sumptuously endowed chairs with six-figure salaries to the more numerous part-time stints that pay roughly the same as Burger King. But even at minimum wage, teaching poetry earns more than writing it ever did. Before the creative-writing boom, being a poet usually meant living in genteel poverty or worse. While the sacrifices poetry demanded caused much individual suffering, the rigors of serving Milton's "thankless Muse" also delivered the collective cultural benefit of frightening away all but committed artists.

Today poetry is a modestly upwardly mobile, middle-class profession— not as lucrative as waste management or dermatology but several big steps above the squalor of bohemia. Only a philistine would romanticize the blissfully banished artistic poverty of yesteryear. But a clear-eyed observer must also recognize that by opening the poet's trade to all applicants and by employing writers to do something other than write, institutions have changed the social and economic identity of the poet from artist to educator. In social terms the identification of poet with teacher is now complete. The first question one poet now asks another upon being introduced is "Where do you teach?" The problem is not that poets teach. The campus is not a bad place for a poet to work. It's just a bad place for all poets to work. Society suffers by losing the imagination and vitality that poets brought to public culture. Poetry suffers when literary standards are forced to conform with institutional ones.

Even within the university contemporary poetry now exists as a subculture. The teaching poet finds that he or she has little in common with academic colleagues. The academic study of literature over the past twenty-five years has veered off in a theoretical direction with which most imaginative writers have little sympathy or familiarity. Thirty years ago detractors of creative-writing programs predicted that poets in universities would become enmeshed in literary criticism and scholarship. This prophecy has proved spectacularly wrong. Poets have created enclaves in the academy almost entirely separate from their critical colleagues. They write less criticism than they did before entering the academy. Pressed to keep up with the plethora of new poetry, small magazines, professional journals, and anthologies, they are frequently also less well read in the literature of the past. Their peers in the English department generally read less contemporary poetry and more literary theory. In many departments writers and literary theorists are openly at war. Bringing the two groups under one roof has paradoxically made each more territorial. Isolated even within the university, the poet, whose true subject is the whole of human existence, has reluctantly become an educational specialist.

When People Paid Attention

To understand how radically the situation of the American poet has changed, one need only compare today with fifty years ago. In 1940, with the notable exception of Robert Frost, few poets were working in colleges unless, like Mark Van Doren and Yvor Winters, they taught traditional academic subjects. The only creative-writing program was an experiment begun a few years earlier at the University of Iowa. The modernists exemplified the options that poets had for making a living. They could enter middle-class professions, as had T. S. Eliot (a banker turned publisher), Wallace Stevens (a corporate insurance lawyer) and William Carlos Williams (a pediatrician). Or they could live in bohemia supporting themselves as artists, as, in different ways, did Ezra Pound, E. E. Cummings, and Marianne Moore. If the city proved unattractive, they could, like Robinson Jeffers, scrape by in a rural arts colony like Carmel, California. Or they might become farmers, like the young Robert Frost.

Most often poets supported themselves as editors or reviewers, actively taking part in the artistic and intellectual life of their time. Archibald MacLeish was an editor and writer at *Fortune.* James Agee reviewed movies for *Time* and *The Nation,* and eventually wrote screenplays for Hollywood. Randall Jarrell reviewed books. Weldon Kees wrote about jazz and modern art. Delmore Schwartz reviewed everything. Even poets who eventually took up academic careers spent intellectually broadening apprenticeships in literary journalism. The young Robert Hayden covered music and theater for Michigan's black press. R. P. Blackmur, who never completed high school, reviewed books for *Hound & Horn* before teaching at Princeton. Occasionally a poet might supplement his or her income by giving a reading or lecture, but these occasions were rare. Robinson Jeffers, for example, was fifty-four when he gave his first public reading. For most poets, the sustaining medium was not the classroom or the podium but the written word.

If poets supported themselves by writing, it was mainly by writing prose. Paying outlets for poetry were limited. Beyond a few national magazines, which generally preferred light verse or political satire, there were at any one time only a few dozen journals that published a significant amount of poetry. The emergence of a serious new quarterly like *Partisan Review* or *Furioso* was an event of real importance, and a small but dedicated audience eagerly looked forward to each issue. If people could not afford to buy copies, they borrowed them or visited public libraries. As for books of poetry if one excludes vanity-press editions, fewer than a hundred new titles were published each year. But the books that did appear were reviewed in daily

newspapers as well as magazines and quarterlies. A focused monthly like
Poetry could cover virtually the entire field.

Reviewers fifty years ago were by today's standards extraordinarily
tough. They said exactly what they thought, even about their most influential
contemporaries. Listen, for example, to Randall Jarrell's description of a
book by the famous anthologist Oscar Williams: it "gave the impression of
having been written on a typewriter by a typewriter." That remark kept Jarrell
out of subsequent Williams anthologies, but he did not hesitate to publish
it. Or consider Jarrell's assessment of Archibald MacLeish's public poem
America Was Promises: it "might have been devised by a YMCA secretary
at a home for the mentally deficient." Or read Weldon Kees's one-sentence
review of Muriel Rukeyser's *Wake Island*—"There's one thing you can say
about Muriel: she's not lazy." But these same reviewers could write generously about poets they admired, as Jarrell did about Elizabeth Bishop, and
Kees about Wallace Stevens. Their praise mattered, because readers knew it
did not come lightly.

The reviewers of fifty years ago knew that their primary loyalty must lie
not with their fellow poets or publishers but with the reader. Consequently
they reported their reactions with scrupulous honesty even when their opinions might lose them literary allies and writing assignments. In discussing new
poetry they addressed a wide community of educated readers. Without talking down to their audience, they cultivated a public idiom. Prizing clarity and
accessibility they avoided specialist jargon and pedantic displays of scholarship. They also tried, as serious intellectuals should but specialists often do
not, to relate what was happening in poetry to social, political, and artistic
trends. They charged modern poetry with cultural importance and made it the
focal point of their intellectual discourse.

Ill-paid, overworked, and underappreciated, this argumentative group of
"practical" critics, all of them poets, accomplished remarkable things. They
defined the canon of modernist poetry, established methods to analyze
verse of extraordinary difficulty, and identified the new midcentury generation of American poets (Lowell, Roethke, Bishop, Berryman, and others)
that still dominates our literary consciousness. Whatever one thinks of their
literary canon or critical principles, one must admire the intellectual energy
and sheer determination of these critics, who developed as writers without
grants or permanent faculty positions, often while working precariously
on free-lance assignments. They represent a high point in American intellectual life. Even fifty years later their names still command more authority than those of all but a few contemporary critics. A short roll call would
include John Berryman, R. P. Blackmur, Louise Bogan, John Ciardi, Horace
Gregory, Langston Hughes, Randall Jarrell, Weldon Kees, Kenneth Rexroth,
Delmore Schwartz, Karl Shapiro, Allen Tate, and Yvor Winters. Although
contemporary poetry has its boosters and publicists, it has no group of
comparable dedication and talent able to address the general literary
community.

Like all genuine intellectuals, these critics were visionary. They believed that if modern poets did not have an audience, they could create one. And gradually they did. It was not a mass audience; few American poets of any period have enjoyed a direct relationship with the general public. It was a cross-section of artists and intellectuals, including scientists, clergymen, educators, lawyers, and, of course, writers. This group constituted a literary intelligentsia, made up mainly of nonspecialists, who took poetry as seriously as fiction and drama. Recently Donald Hall and other critics have questioned the size of this audience by citing the low average sales of a volume of new verse by an established poet during the period (usually under a thousand copies). But these skeptics do not understand how poetry was read then.

America was a smaller, less affluent country in 1940, with about half its current population and one sixth its current real GNP. In those pre-paperback days of the late Depression neither readers nor libraries could afford to buy as many books as they do today. Nor was there a large captive audience of creative-writing students who bought books of contemporary poetry for classroom use. Readers usually bought poetry in two forms—in an occasional *Collected Poems* by a leading author, or in anthologies. The comprehensive collections of writers like Frost, Eliot, Auden, Jeffers, Wylie, and Millay sold very well, were frequently reprinted, and stayed perpetually in print. (Today most *Collected Poems* disappear after one printing.) Occasionally a book of new poems would capture the public's fancy. Edwin Arlington Robinson's *Tristram* (1927) became a Literary Guild selection. Frost's *A Further Range* sold 50,000 copies as a 1936 Book-of-the-Month Club selection. But people knew poetry mainly from anthologies, which they not only bought but also read, with curiosity and attention.

Louis Untermeyer's *Modern American Poetry,* first published in 1919, was frequently revised to keep it up to date and was a perennial best seller. My 1942 edition, for example, had been reprinted five times by 1945. My edition of Oscar Williams's *A Pocket Book of Modern Poetry* had been reprinted nineteen times in fourteen years. Untermeyer and Williams prided themselves on keeping their anthologies broad-based and timely. They tried to represent the best of what was being published. Each edition added new poems and poets and dropped older ones. The public appreciated their efforts. Poetry anthologies were an indispensable part of any serious reader's library. Random House's popular Modern Library series, for example, included not one but two anthologies—Selden Rodman's *A New Anthology of Modern Poetry* and Conrad Aiken's *Twentieth Century American Poetry.* All these collections were read and reread by a diverse public. Favorite poems were memorized. Difficult authors like Eliot and Thomas were actively discussed and debated. Poetry mattered outside the classroom.

Today these general readers constitute the audience that poetry has lost. Limited by intelligence and curiosity this heterogeneous group cuts across lines of race, class, age, and occupation. Representing our cultural intelligentsia, they are the people who support the arts—who buy classical and jazz records; who attend foreign films and serious theater, opera, symphony, and dance; who read quality fiction and biographies; who listen to public radio and subscribe to the best journals. (They are also often the parents who read poetry to their children and remember, once upon a time in college or high school or kindergarten, liking it themselves.) No one knows the size of this community, but even if one accepts the conservative estimate that it accounts for only two percent of the U.S. population, it still represents a potential audience of almost five million readers. However healthy poetry may appear within its professional subculture, it has lost this larger audience, who represent poetry's bridge to the general culture.

The Need for Poetry

But why should anyone but a poet care about the problems of American poetry? What possible relevance does this archaic art form have to contemporary society? In a better world, poetry would need no justification beyond the sheer splendor of its own existence. As Wallace Stevens once observed, "The purpose of poetry is to contribute to man's happiness." Children know this essential truth when they ask to hear their favorite nursery rhymes again and again. Aesthetic pleasure needs no justification, because a life without such pleasure is one not worth living.

But the rest of society has mostly forgotten the value of poetry. To the general reader, discussions about the state of poetry sound like the debating of foreign politics by emigres in a seedy cafe. Or, as Cyril Connolly more bitterly described it, "Poets arguing about modern poetry: jackals snarling over a dried-up well." Anyone who hopes to broaden poetry's audience—critic, teacher, librarian, poet, or lonely literary amateur—faces a daunting challenge. How does one persuade justly skeptical readers, in terms they can understand and appreciate, that poetry still matters?

A passage in William Carlos Williams's "Asphodel, That Greeny Flower" provides a possible starting point. Written toward the end of the author's life, after he had been partly paralyzed by a stroke, the lines sum up the hard lessons about poetry and audience that Williams had learned over years of dedication to both poetry and medicine. He wrote,

> My heart rouses
>   thinking to bring you news
>   of something
>
> that concerns you
>   and concerns many men. Look at
>   what passes for the new.
> You will not find it there but in
>   despised poems.
>   It is difficult

to get the news from poems
    yet men die miserably every day
        for lack
of what is found there.

Williams understood poetry's human value but had no illusions about the difficulties his contemporaries faced in trying to engage the audience that needed the art most desperately. To regain poetry's readership one must begin by meeting Williams's challenge to find what "concerns many men," not simply what concerns poets.

There are at least two reasons why the situation of poetry matters to the entire intellectual community. The first involves the role of language in a free society. Poetry is the art of using words charged with their utmost meaning. A society whose intellectual leaders lose the skill to shape, appreciate, and understand the power of language will become the slaves of those who retain it—be they politicians, preachers, copywriters, or newscasters. The public responsibility of poetry has been pointed out repeatedly by modern writers. Even the archsymbolist Stephane Mallarme praised the poet's central mission to "purify the words of the tribe." And Ezra Pound warned that

> Good writers are those who keep the language efficient. That is to say, keep it accurate, keep it clean. It doesn't matter whether a good writer wants to be useful, or whether the bad writer wants to do harm. . . .
>
> If a nation's literature declines, the nation atrophies and decays.

Or, as George Orwell wrote after the Second World War, "One ought to recognize that the present political chaos is connected with the decay of language. . . ." Poetry is not the entire solution to keeping the nation's language clear and honest, but one is hard pressed to imagine a country's citizens improving the health of its language while abandoning poetry.

The second reason why the situation of poetry matters to all intellectuals is that poetry is not alone among the arts in its marginal position. If the audience for poetry has declined into a subculture of specialists, so too have the audiences for most contemporary art forms, from serious drama to jazz. The unprecedented fragmentation of American high culture during the past half century has left most arts in isolation from one another as well as from the general audience. Contemporary classical music scarcely exists as a living art outside university departments and conservatories. Jazz, which once commanded a broad popular audience, has become the semi-private domain of aficionados and musicians. (Today even influential jazz innovators cannot find places to perform in many metropolitan centers—and for an improvisatory art the inability to perform is a crippling liability.) Much serious drama is now confined to the margins of American theater, where it is seen only by actors, aspiring actors, playwrights, and a few diehard fans. Only the visual arts, perhaps because of their financial glamour and upper-class support, have largely escaped the decline in public attention.

How Poets Can Be Heard

The most serious question for the future of American culture is whether the arts will continue to exist in isolation and decline into subsidized academic specialties or whether some possibility of rapprochement with the educated public remains. Each of the arts must face the challenge separately, and no art faces more towering obstacles than poetry. Given the decline of literacy, the proliferation of other media, the crisis in humanities education, the collapse of critical standards, and the sheer weight of past failures, how can poets possibly succeed in being heard? Wouldn't it take a miracle?

Toward the end of her life Marianne Moore wrote a short poem called "O To Be a Dragon." This poem recalled the biblical dream in which the Lord appeared to King Solomon and said, "Ask what I shall give thee." Solomon wished for a wise and understanding heart. Moore's wish is harder to summarize. Her poem reads,

> If I, like Solomon, . . .
> could have my wish—
>
> my wish . . . O to be a dragon,
> a symbol of the power of Heaven—of silkworm
> size or immense; at times invisible.
> Felicitous phenomenon!

Moore got her wish. She became, as all genuine poets do, "a symbol of the power of Heaven." She succeeded in what Robert Frost called "the utmost of ambition"—namely "to lodge a few poems where they will be hard to get rid of." She is permanently part of the "felicitous phenomenon" of American literature.

So wishes can come true—even extravagant ones. If I, like Marianne Moore, could have my wish, and I, like Solomon, could have the self-control not to wish for myself, I would wish that poetry could again become a part of American public culture. I don't think this is impossible. All it would require is that poets and poetry teachers take more responsibility for bringing their art to the public. I will close with six modest proposals for how this dream might come true.

1. *When poets give public readings, they should spend part of every program reciting other people's work*—preferably poems they admire by writers they do not know personally. Readings should be celebrations of poetry in general, not merely of the featured author's work.
2. *When arts administrators plan public readings, they should avoid the standard subculture format of poetry only.* Mix poetry with the other arts, especially music.

Plan evenings honoring dead or foreign writers. Combine short critical lectures with poetry performances. Such combinations would attract an audience from beyond the poetry world without compromising quality.

3. *Poets need to write prose about poetry more often, more candidly, and more effectively.* Poets must recapture the attention of the broader intellectual community by writing for nonspecialist publications. They must also avoid the jargon of contemporary academic criticism and write in a public idiom. Finally, poets must regain the reader's trust by candidly admitting what they don't like as well as promoting what they like. Professional courtesy has no place in literary journalism.

4. *Poets who compile anthologies—or even reading lists—should be scrupulously honest in including only poems they genuinely admire.* Anthologies are poetry's gateway to the general culture. They should not be used as pork barrels for the creative-writing trade. An art expands its audience by presenting masterpieces, not mediocrity. Anthologies should be compiled to move, delight, and instruct readers, not to flatter the writing teachers who assign books. Poet-anthologists must never trade the Muse's property for professional favors.

5. *Poetry teachers especially at the high school and undergraduate levels, should spend less time on analysis and more on performance.* Poetry needs to be liberated from literary criticism. Poems should be memorized, recited, and performed. The sheer joy of the art must be emphasized. The pleasure of performance is what first attracts children to poetry, the sensual excitement of speaking and hearing the words of the poem. Performance was also the teaching technique that kept poetry vital for centuries. Maybe it also holds the key to poetry's future.

6. *Finally poets and arts administrators should use radio to expand the art's audience.* Poetry is an aural medium, and thus ideally suited to radio. A little imaginative programming at the hundreds of college and public-supported radio stations could bring poetry to millions of listeners. Some programming exists, but it is stuck mostly in the standard subculture format of living poets' reading their own work. Mixing poetry with music on classical and jazz stations or creating innovative talk-radio formats could re-establish a direct relationship between poetry and the general audience.

The history of art tells the same story over and over. As art forms develop, they establish conventions that guide creation, performance, instruction, even analysis. But eventually these conventions grow stale. They begin to stand between the art and its audience. Although much wonderful poetry is being written, the American poetry establishment is locked into a series of exhausted conventions—outmoded ways of presenting, discussing, editing, and teaching poetry. Educational institutions have codified them into a stifling bureaucratic etiquette that enervates the art. These conventions may once have made sense, but today they imprison poetry in an intellectual ghetto.

It is time to experiment, time to leave the well-ordered but stuffy classroom, time to restore a vulgar vitality to poetry and unleash the energy now trapped in the subculture. There is nothing to lose. Society has already told us that poetry is dead. Let's build a funeral pyre out of the dessicated conventions piled around us and watch the ancient, spangle-feathered, unkillable phoenix rise from the ashes.

QUESTIONS FOR DISCUSSION AND WRITING

1. Is poetry really as ghettoized and specialized an art form as Gioia argues when there is so much, for example, slam poetry around? Is he limiting himself by discussing mainly literary poetry and the verse of those who teach in universities or are those the bastions of real, quality poetry?
2. What does Gioia mean when he says the poetry subculture demeans its own art by "abandoning the hard work of evaluation"? What does he mean by "critical boosterism"?
3. Why does Gioia call two of America's most famous and revered poets, Robert Frost and Wallace Stevens, "sluggards" and say they would be unemployable today?
4. Gioia argues that poetry matters because of language and the marginal position poetry and other high arts seem to have. He also states that many of the poems contemporaneous to when he wrote this essay are "personal poems of unsurpassed beauty and power." Why should we value poetry?
5. Gioia ultimately makes six proposals at the end of his essay that he says reflect what he would wish or dream for the future of poetry. Has he prepared us for these six? Do they seem likely or worthy?

ON TECHNIQUE AND STYLE

1. Gioia argues at first in support of why we are in a golden age of poetry and then argues why we are not. Is this an effective way of presenting his ideas? Why does he set up his argument in this way?
2. What is the purpose behind Gioia bringing in Edmund Wilson's essay of 1934 and using examples of poets of fifty years before this essay was written and what they did?
3. How does Gioia use humor? What effect does his use of humor have?

CULTURAL QUESTION

1. Gioia takes pride in his own Mexican heritage. Is he being expansive enough in not considering all of the street and rap forms of poetry that presently exist, particularly in cross-cultural communities or on HBO specials like Russell Simmons's *Def Poetry Jam*?

Introduction to Break, Blow, Burn

Camille Paglia

Camille Paglia (1947–   ) was born in Endicott, New York, the daughter of Italian immigrants, and was educated at the State University of New York, Binghampton's Harpur College, and Yale. A self-described "feminist bisexual egomaniac" she is a well-known social critic, author, and public intellectual. She taught at Bennington and is presently university professor of media studies at the University of the Arts in Philadelphia. Paglia was a columnist for Salon *and has published work in the* Washington Post, Forbes, The Chronicle of Higher Education, The New York Times, The Independent, *and* Frontpage. *Her books include* Sexual Personae: Art and Decadence from Nefretiti to Emily Dickinson; Sex, Art and American Culture; Vamps and Tramps; The Birds; *and* Break, Blow, Burn. *The excerpt included here is from the Introduction to* Break, Blow, Burn *(2006). In it Paglia essentially lays out her personal way of reading and thinking about poetry and her belief in its value and enduring importance.*

Artists are makers, not just mouthers of slippery discourse. Language, the poets' medium, should not be privileged over the protean materials of other artists, who work in pigments, stone, metals, and fibers. Poets are fabricators and engineers, pursuing a craft analogous to cabinetry or bridge building. I maintain that the text emphatically exists as an object; it is not just a mist of ephemeral subjectivities. Every reading is partial, but that does not absolve us from the quest for meaning, which defines us as a species. Thus, from my archaeological perspective, Sappho's poems, while open to arguable and even contradictory interpretation, are also tangible manuscripts that have been imperfectly recovered from strips of recycled papyri in a trash heap in Egypt's Fayum. The idea of contingency properly applies to the gaping lacunae in Sappho's poems that scholars have so delicately and provisionally filled.

   In writing about a poem, I try to *listen* to it and find a language and tone that mesh with its own idiom. We live in a time increasingly indifferent to literary style, from the slack prose of once august newspapers to pedestrian translations of the Bible. The Web (which I champion and to which I have extensively contributed) has increased verbal fluency but not quality, at least in its rushed, patchy genres of e-mail and blog. Good writing comes from good reading. Humanists must set an example: all literary criticism should be accessible to the general reader. Criticism at its best is re-creative, not spirit-killing. Technical analysis of a poem is like breaking down a car engine, which has to be reassembled to run again. Theorists childishly smash up their subjects and leave the *disjecta membra* like litter.

For me poetry is speech-based and is not just an arbitrary pattern of signs that can be slid around like a jigsaw puzzle. I sound out poems silently, as others pray. Poetry, which began as song, is music-drama: I value emotional expressiveness, musical phrasings, and choreographic assertion, the speaker's theatrical self-positioning toward other persons or implacable external forces. My commentaries are sympathetic redramatizations that try to capture defining gestures and psychological strategies. But prose readings are a costly shift in format, as when turning a novel or biography into a screenplay. It's a translation in which much is inevitably lost. I am not that concerned with prosody except to compare strict meter (drilled by my Greek and Latin teachers) to the standard songs that jazz musicians transform: I prefer irregularity, syncopation, bending the note.

My advice to the reader approaching a poem is to make the mind still and blank. Let the poem speak. This charged quiet mimics the blank space ringing the printed poem, the nothing out of which something takes shape. Many critics counsel memorizing poetry, but that has never been my habit. To commit a poem to memory is to make the act of reading superfluous. But I believe in immersion in and saturation by the poem, so that the next time we meet it, we have the thrill of recognition. We feel (to quote singer Stevie Nicks) the hauntingly familiar. It's akin to addiction or to the euphoria of being in love.

In the title of his classic 1947 manual of New Criticism, Cleanth Brooks compared a poem to Donne's "well wrought urn," housing funeral ashes from which the phoenix will rise again. A poem for me is more like an aquarium: it is both impenetrable and transparent, its wall like the glass curtain of a modern skyscraper. We are transfixed by motion within the frame—not unlike a movie or television screen. What flashes obscurely through poetry is the ceaseless, darting energy of words. The best route into poetry is through the dictionary (Emily Dickinson's bible). Words accumulate meaning over time. Studying the dictionary teaches you the art of condensation as well as the nuances and genealogy of language that poets twist and turn.

At this time of foreboding about the future of Western culture, it is crucial to identify and preserve our finest artifacts. Canons are always in flux, but canon formation is a critic's obligation. What lasts, and why? Custodianship, not deconstruction, should be the mission and goal of the humanities. As a student of ancient empires, I am uncertain about whether the West's chaotic personalism can prevail against the totalizing creeds that menace it. Hence it is critical that we reinforce the spiritual values of Western art, however we define them. In the Greco-Roman line, beauty and aesthetic pleasure are spiritual too. Poetry does not simply reconfirm gender or group identity; it develops the imagination and feeds the soul.

And art generates art: where will our future artists come from? In an era ruled by materialism and unstable geopolitics, art must be restored to the center of public education. If the humanities expect support and investment from society, there must be a reform of academe, which can come only from idealistic graduate students and junior faculty. But they cannot do it alone. Poets must remember their calling and take stage again.

QUESTIONS FOR DISCUSSION AND WRITING

1. Do you agree with Paglia's insistence on poetry being speech based, that listening to a poem or sounding out a poem is just as important, perhaps more important, than reading it? Is her comparison of poetry to prayer appropriate or far-fetched?

2. Paglia writes about the musical nature of poetry and compares its meter to jazz compositions. Yet she expresses a lack of concern for prosody (the metrical structure of verse) and says that memorizing poetry makes reading it superfluous. Do you agree?

3. Paglia suggests that writing about poetry in prose, as literary critics do and as she is doing, has built-in limitations and causes an inevitable loss in translation. Is poetry as much or more about language as it is about sound and musicality?

4. Paglia mentions the famed literary critic Cleanth Brooks's use of the phoenix myth, which we also saw Gioia allude to in his essay "Can Poetry Matter?" Paglia prefers the metaphor of the aquarium for poetry and, like Gioia, argues for making poetry and art more general but also for reforming academe. How convincing is her argument and her view of poetry compared to Gioia's?

5. What does Paglia mean when she writes, "The best route into poetry is through the dictionary"?

ON TECHNIQUE AND STYLE

1. Paglia defines poetry as "the nothing out of which something takes place." Is that an apt definition? Can it be seen as a definition for other arts as well? Does it mesh with her analogies of poetry to addiction and love?

2. From the beginning of this excerpt Paglia brings herself in through her use of the first person. Does this enhance her writing? Is there danger in using the first person?

3. Paglia concludes her essay with focus on the future of Western culture and she links the beauty and aesthetic pleasure of poetry to spiritual values. Is her implication that the future of Western civilization and its values are contingent on our love and appreciation of poetry a convincing and well-supported argument?

CULTURAL QUESTION

1. Stevie Nicks and Emily Dickinson are names you would usually not see cited together in an essay since the former is so strongly associated with popular culture while the other is with high culture. What is the effect of Paglia's using these two women in her essay, particularly in light of Paglia's insistence that she is a feminist?

Stakes Is High

Jeff Chang

Jeff Chang (1970–   ) was raised in Hawaii and lives in Oakland. Of Chinese and Native Hawaiian ancestry, he graduated from the University of California, Berkeley and received an MA degree in Asian American studies from the University of California, Los Angeles. In 1991 he began his career as a hip-hop journalist with URB *and* The Bomb *hip-hop magazines. He has written for the* San Francisco Chronicle, The Village Voice, *the* San Francisco Bay Guardian, Vibe, Spin, Mother Jones, *and* The Nation. *Founding editor of* Colorlines *magazine and senior editor of Russell Simmons's* 360hiphop.com, *Chang is also a record producer and was the organizer of the National Hip-Hop Political Convention. He is the author of* Can't Stop Won't Stop: A History of the Hip-Hop Generation. *The essay included here, "'Stakes Is High': Conscious Rap, Neosoul and the Hip-Hop Generation," first appeared in* The Nation *January 13, 2003. In it Chang argues for the importance of the positive side of hip-hop and relates the ways it has influenced an entire generation and changed forms and styles of expression as well as political consciousness.*

Fifteen years ago, rappers like Public Enemy, KRS-One and Queen Latifah were received as heralds of a new movement. Musicians—who, like all artists, always tend to handle the question "What's going on?" much better than "What is to be done?"—had never been called upon to do so much for their generation; Thelonious Monk, Aretha Franklin and Stevie Wonder were never asked to stand in for Thurgood Marshall, Fannie Lou Hamer or Stokely Carmichael. But the gains of the civil rights and Black Power movements of the 1960s were being rolled back. Youths were as fed up with black leadership as they were with white supremacy. Politics had failed. Culture was to become the hip-hop generation's battlefield, and "political rap" was to be its weapon.

Today, the most cursory glance at the Billboard charts or video shows on Viacom-owned MTV and BET suggests rap has been given over to cocaine-cooking, cartoon-watching, Rakim-quoting, gold-rims-coveting, death-worshiping young 'uns. One might even ask whether rap has abandoned the revolution.

Indeed, as the central marker of urban youth of color style and authenticity, rap music has become the key to the niching of youth culture. The "hip-hop lifestyle" is now available for purchase in every suburban mall. "Political rap" has been repackaged by record companies as merely "conscious," retooled for a smaller niche as an alternative. Instead of drinking Alizé, you drink Sprite. Instead of Versace, you wear Ecko. Instead of Jay-Z, you listen to the Roots. Teen rap, party rap, gangsta rap, political rap—tags that were once a mere music critic's game—are literally serious business.

"Once you put a prefix on an MC's name, that's a death trap," says Talib Kweli, the gifted Brooklyn-born rapper who disdains being called "conscious." Clearly his music expresses a well-defined politics; his rhymes draw from the same well of protest that nourished the Last Poets, the Watts Prophets and the Black Arts stalwarts he cites as influences. But he argues that marketing labels close his audience's minds to the possibilities of his art. When Kweli unveiled a song called "Gun Music," some fans grumbled. (No "conscious" rapper would stoop to rapping about guns, they reasoned, closing their ears even as Kweli delivered a complicated critique of street-arms fetishism.) At the same time, Kweli worries that being pigeonholed as political will prevent him from being promoted to mass audiences. Indeed, to be a "political rapper" in the music industry these days is to be condemned to preach to a very small choir.

"Political rap" was actually something of an invention. The Bronx community-center dances and block parties where hip-hop began in the early 1970s were not demonstrations for justice, they were celebrations of survival. Hip-hop culture simply reflected what the people wanted and needed—escape. Rappers bragged about living the brand-name high life because they didn't; they boasted about getting headlines in the *New York Post* because they couldn't. Then, during the burning summer of the first Reagan recession, Grandmaster Flash and the Furious Five released "The Message," a dirge (by the standards of the day) that seethed against the everyday violence of disinvestment. Flash was certain the record, which was actually an A&R-pushed concoction by Duke Boo-tee and Melle Mel, would flop; it was too slow and too depressing to rock a party. But Sugar Hill Records released the song as a single over his objections, and "The Message" struck the zeitgeist like a bull's-eye. Liberal soul and rock critics, who had been waiting for exactly this kind of statement from urban America, championed it. Millions of listeners made it the third platinum rap single.

Through the mid-1980s, Melle Mel, Afrika Bambaataa and Soul Sonic Force, Run-DMC and others took up the role of the young black lumpenrap-per opposition, weighing in on topics like racism, nuclear proliferation and apartheid. And just as the first Bush stepped into office, a new generation began to articulate a distinctly post-civil rights stance. Led by Public Enemy, rappers like Paris, Ice-T, X-Clan, Poor Righteous Teachers and Brand Nubian displayed the Black Panther Party's media savvy and the Minister Louis Farrakhan's nationalist rage. Politics were as explicit as Tipper Gore's advisory stickers. As the Gulf War progressed, Paris's "Bush Killa" imagined a Black Power assassination of Bush the Elder while rapping, "Iraq never called me 'nigger.'" (Last year, he returned to cut an MP3-only critique of the war on Afghanistan, "What Would You Do?") Rappers' growing confidence with word, sound and power was reflected in more slippery and subtle music, but-tered with Afrodiasporic and polycultural flavor.

Many of these artists had emerged from vibrant protest movements—New York City's resurgent Black Power movement; the swelling campus antiapartheid/multiculturalism/ affirmative action movement; local anti-police brutality movements. In each of these, representation was the cry and the media were a target. Rap "edutainment" came out of the convergence of two very different desires: the need for political empowerment and the need to be empowered by images of truth. On 1990's "Can I Kick It?," A Tribe Called Quest's Phife Dawg captured the mood of his audience sweetly and precisely: "Mr. Dinkins, will you please be our mayor?" But while Mayor Dinkins's career quickly hit a tailspin, hip-hop rose by making blackness—even radical blackness—the worldwide trading currency of cultural cool.

In the new global entertainment industry of the 1990s, rap became a hot commodity. But even as the marketing dollars flowed into youth of color communities, major labels searched for ways to capture the authenticity without the militancy. Stakes was high, as De La Soul famously put it in 1996, and labels were loath to accept such disruptions on their investments as those that greeted Ice-T and Body Count's "Cop Killer" during the '92 election season. Rhymers kicking sordid tales from the drug wars were no longer journalists or fictionists, ironists or moralists. They were purveyors of a new lifestyle, ghetto cool with all of the products but none of the risk or rage. After Dr. Dre's pivotal 1992 album, *The Chronic,* in which a millennial, ghetto-centric Phil Spector stormed the pop charts with a postrebellion gangsta party that brought together Crip-walking with Tanqueray-sipping, the roughnecks, hustlers and riders took the stage from the rap revolutionaries, backed by the substantial capital of a quickly consolidating music industry.

Rap music today reflects the paradoxical position of the hip-hop generation. If measured by the volume of products created by and sold to them, it may appear that youth of color have never been more central to global popular culture. Rap is now a $1.6 billion engine that drives the entire music industry and flexes its muscle across all entertainment platforms. Along with its music, Jay-Z's not-so-ironically named Roc-A-Fella company peddles branded movies, clothing and vodka. Hip-hop, some academics assert, is hegemonic. But as the social turmoil described by many contemporary rappers demonstrates, this generation of youth of color is as alienated and downpressed as any ever has been. And the act of tying music to lifestyle—as synergy-seeking media companies have effectively done—has distorted what marketers call the "aspirational" aspects of hip-hop while marginalizing its powers of protest.

Yet the politics have not disappeared from popular rap. Some of the most stunning hits in recent years—DMX's "Who We Be," Trick Daddy's "I'm a Thug," Scarface's "On My Block"—have found large audiences by making whole the hip-hop generation's cliché of "keeping it real," being true to one's roots of struggle. The video for Nappy Roots' brilliant "Po' Folks" depicts an expansive vision of rural Kentucky—black and white, young and old together, living like "everything's gon' be OK." Scarface's ghettocentric "On My Block" discards any pretense at apology. "We've probably done it all, fa' sheezy," he raps. "I'll never leave my block, my niggas need me." For some critics, usually older and often black, such sentiments seem dangerously close to pathological, hymns to debauchery and justifications for thuggery. But the hip-hop generation recognizes them as anthems of purpose, manifestoes that describe their time and place the same way that Public Enemy's did. Most of all, these songs and their audiences say, we are survivors and we will never forget that.

The "conscious rap" and "neosoul" genres take up where 1970s soul experimentalists like Marvin Gaye and Curtis Mayfield left off. At their best, they are black-to-the-future havens of experimentation that combine a grandiose view of pop music's powers, an earnest hope for a better world and a jaded insider's disdain for rote commercialism. Crews like Blackalicious, the Coup, Jurassic 5, Zion I and dead prez have attained modest success by offering visions of twenty-first-century blackness—hypertextual rhymes, stuttering rhythms and lush sounds rooted in a deep understanding of African-American cultural production and ready-made for a polycultural future. The Roots' album *Phrenology* stretches hip-hop's all-embracing method—the conviction that "every music is hip-hop" and ready to be absorbed—to draw from a palette as wide as Jill Scott, Bad Brains, James Blood Ulmer and the Cold Crush Brothers. Common's *Electric Circus* takes cues from Prince and Sly Stone in reimagining the hip-hop concept album.

Tensions often spring from the compromises inherent in being given the budget to build a statement while being forced to negotiate the major label's Pavlovian pop labyrinth, and others have left the system to, as Digital Underground once famously put it, do what they like, albeit for much smaller audiences. Public Enemy has gone to the Internet and to indies in order, they say, to "give the peeps what they need," not what they think they want. After spending more than a decade in unsuccessful efforts with major labels, rapper Michael Franti now records on his own Boo Boo Wax imprint. It's hard to imagine his latest effort, "Bomb Da World"—whose chorus goes, "You can bomb the world to pieces, but you can't bomb it into peace"—passing muster in the boardrooms. Berkeley-based rapper Mr. Lif cut two of the most funky and politically challenging records of the year, the *Emergency Rations* EP and *I Phantom* LP, for the indie Definitive Jux. The EP's clever conceit—that the rapper has literally "gone underground" to escape angry Feds—is easily the wittiest, most danceable critique yet of the USA Patriot Act.

Hip-hop has been roundly condemned within and without for its sexist, misogynistic tendencies, but it has also created room for artists like Me'shell N'degeocello, Mystic, Lauryn Hill, Erykah Badu, Jill Scott, Goapele and Angie Stone to mix up and transform both rap and r&b. "Neosoul" has been especially attractive to women and post-young 'uns. Its hip-hop feminist critique came into sharp relief last year. After years of flying high, rap sales crashed by 15 percent, leading an industrywide plunge. But multi-platinum newcomers Alicia Keys and India.Arie were garlanded with a bevy of Grammy nominations. Keys and Arie celebrated "a woman's worth" and were frankly critical of male irresponsibility. India.Arie's breakout hit "Video"—in which she sang, "I'm not the average girl from your video"—stole the music that had once been sampled for a rap ode to oral sex called "Put It in Your Mouth."

Hip-hop feminism has been articulated by Joan Morgan as a kind of loyal but vocal, highly principled opposition to black (and brown and yellow) male übermasculinity. In the same way, neosoul dissects the attitudes and ideals projected in the hip-hop mainstream. Me'shell N'degeocello's compelling *Cookie: The Anthropological Mixtape* opens with the line, "You sell your soul like you sell a piece of ass." The most commanding of the neosoul artists, Jill Scott, imagines reconciliation, no longer having to love hip-hop from a distance. On "Love Rain" she sings of meeting a new man: "Talked about Moses and Mumia, reparations, blue colors, memories of shell-top Adidas, he was fresh like summer peaches." But the relationship ends badly, "All you did was make a mockery of somethin' so incredibly beautiful. I honestly did love you so."

Neosoul personalizes struggles, but the approach has its limitations. India.Arie's *Voyage to India,* for instance, suffers from reducing black radical conviction to self-affirmation mantra. At the same time, the genre mirrors a deeply held conviction of the hip-hop generation: Revolution does not come first from mass organizations and marching in the streets, but through knowledge of self and personal transformation. "Back in the '60s, there was a big push for black senators and politicians, and now we have more than we ever had before, but our communities are so much worse," says Talib Kweli. "A lot of people died for us to vote, I'm aware of that history, but these politicians are not in touch with people at all. Politics is not the truth to me, it's an illusion." For a generation that has made a defensive virtue of keeping it real, the biggest obstacle to societal change may simply be the act of imagining it.

These are the kinds of paradoxes the silver-tongued Kweli grapples with on his second solo album, *Quality,* as masterful a summation of the hip-hop generation's ambivalent rage as Morgan's book, *When Chickenheads Come to Roost.* On one of his early songs, Kweli synthesized 1960s militancy and 1990s millenarianism in a phrase, rapping about the need for "knowledge of self-determination." At one point on the Nina Simone-flavored "Get By," he sees the distance his generation still needs to cover: "We're survivalists turned to consumers." Echoing Marvin Gaye's "Right On," he measures the breadth of his generation—from the crack-pushers to the hip-hop activists. "Even when the condition is critical, when the living is miserable, your position is pivotal," he concludes, deciding that it's time to clean up his own life.

Kweli never fails to deliver fresh, if often despairing, insights. On "The Proud," he offers a sage reading of the impact of 9/11 on the 'hood—"People broken down from years of oppression become patriots when their way of life is threatened." Later in the song, he cites California's Proposition 21—the culmination of nearly two decades of fears of gangs, violence and lawlessness—and ties it to the intensifying nationwide trend of profiling and brutality against youth of color. But he scoffs at a revolution coming at the ballot box. Of the

2000 Florida elections, he angrily concludes, "President is Bush, the Vice President is Dick, so a whole lotta fucking is what we get. They don't want to raise the baby so the election is fixed. That's why we don't be fucking with politics!"

But politicians can't stop fucking with rap and the hip-hop generation. Senator Joe Lieberman regularly rallies cultural conservatives against the music. Michael Powell's corporate-friendly, laissez-faire FCC has censored only the white male rap star Eminem and the black feminist hip-hop poet Sarah Jones. Texas Republican John Cornyn overcame African-American Democrat Ron Kirk's November Senate bid by linking him to police-hating (and, interestingly, ballot-punching) rappers. When Jam Master Jay, the well-respected, peace-making DJ of rap group Run-D.M.C., was murdered in October, police and federal investigators intensified their surveillance of rappers while talking heads and tabloids like the *New York Post* decried the music's, and this generation's, supposed propensity for violence and lawlessness.

Now a hip-hop parent, Kweli hopes to steel his young 'uns for these kinds of assaults. "I give them the truth so they approach the situation with ammunition," he raps. "Teach them the game so they know their position, so they can grow and make their decisions that change the world and break traditions." While he critiques his elders for failing to save the children, he knows his generation's defensive b-boy stance is not enough: "We gave the youth all the anger but yet we ain't taught them how to express it. And so it's dangerous."

Here is the hip-hop generation in all its powder-keg glory and pain: enraged, empowered, endangered. The irony is not lost: A generation able to speak the truth like no other before is doing so to a world that still hasn't gotten the message.

QUESTIONS FOR DISCUSSION AND WRITING

1. What is the central notion put forth by Chang about the politicization of the hip-hop generation versus its commercialization?
2. Chang argues that rap became a hot commodity and created wealth while oppression still continued to reign. Does he support that premise?
3. Do you agree that hip-hop created a large audience "by keeping it real"? Is Chang simply trying to show both sides of the hip-hop and rap cultures as, for example, in his conceding that there is misogyny but nevertheless profeminist lyrics?
4. What is Chang suggesting about possible new directions for rap and hip-hop when he discusses artists using the Internet or their own or independent labels?
5. What is the message of hip-hop that the world still has not gotten? Do you agree with Chang that his generation is presenting that message louder and clearer than any previous generation?

ON TECHNIQUE AND STYLE

1. Chang uses an array of examples to illustrate most of his major points. How successful are the examples he chooses and to what degree do they support his points?
2. What effect does the profanity in the essay have? It has become commonplace to hear profanity in today's lyrics, but does seeing them in print have more of an impact on you?
3. What is the central argument in Chang's essay for, as he suggests in the title, the stakes being high? What exactly is at stake?

CULTURAL QUESTION

1. Chang envisions what he calls a polycultural future emerging from the influence and impact of the music he writes about. The roots of the music and its culture are black and Chang is not. Is he convincing in his assertion that the music is changing from being monocultural to being polycultural?

Loops of Perception: Sampling, Memory, and the Semantic Web

Paul D. Miller (aka DJ Spooky)

Paul D. Miller (aka DJ Spooky that Subliminal Kid) is an African American conceptual and independent artist, writer, musician, and disc jockey known for his mixing and remixing. He lives in New York City and is the author of Rhythm Science. *His writing has appeared online and in many magazines and journals, including* The Nation, The Village Voice, Artform, *and* Raygun. *He is copublisher of the multicultural magazine* A Gathering of the Tribes *and started the online magazine* WWW.21CMagazine. com. *"Loops of Perception: Sampling, Memory, and the Semantic Web" first appeared online in issue 4 of* remix.com. *In it Miller puts forth a philosophy about how our perceptions have changed in the age of the Internet and the World Wide Web and how we create rhythms and poems of ourselves "written in synaptic reverie."*

Free content fuels innovation.

—*Lawrence Lessig,* The Future of Ideas

I get asked what I think about sampling a lot, and I've always wanted to have a short term to describe the process. Stuff like "collective ownership," "systems of memory," and "database logics" never really seem to cut it on the lecture circuit, so I guess you can think of this essay as a soundbite for the sonically-perplexed. This is an essay about memory as a vast playhouse where any sound can be you. Press "play" and this essay says "here goes":

Inside the Out-side

Think. Search a moment in the everyday density of what's going on around you and look for blankness in the flow. Pull back from that thought and think of the exercise as a kind of mini-meditation on mediated life. Pause, repeat. There's always a rhythm to the space between things. A word passes by to define the scenario. Your mind picks up on it, and places it in context. Next thought, next scenario—the same process happens over and over again. It's an internal process that doesn't even need to leave the comfortable confines of your mind: A poem of yourself written in synaptic reverie, a chemical soup filled with electric pulses, it loops around and brings a lot of baggage with it. At heart, the process is an abstract machine made to search in the right place for the right codes. The information in your mind looks for structures to give it context. The word you have thought about is only a placeholder for a larger system. It's a neural map unfolding in syntaxes, linked right into the electro-chemical processes that make up not only what you can think, but how you can think.

Inside, we use our minds for so many different things that we can only guess at how complex the process of thinking is. Outside, it's a different scenario. Each human act, each human expression, has to be translated into some kind of information for other people to understand it: Some call it the "mind/brain" interface, and others, like Descartes, call it a kind of per-ceptual (and perpetual) illusion. In our day and age, the basic idea of how we create content in our minds is so conditioned by media that we are in a position unlike any other culture in human history: Today, this interior rhythm of words, this inside conversation, expresses itself in a way that can be changed once it enters the "real" world. When recorded, adapted, remixed, and uploaded, expression becomes a stream unit of value in a fixed and remixed currency that is traded via the ever shifting currents of information moving through the networks we use to talk with one another. It wasn't for nothing that Marx said so long ago that "all that is solid melts into air"—perhaps he was anticipating the economy of ideas that drives the network systems we live and breathe in today. In different eras, the invocation of a deity, or prayers, or mantras, were all common forms, shared through cultural affinities and affirmed by people who spoke the code—the language of the people sharing the story.

Today, it's that gap between the interior and exterior perceptual worlds that entire media philosophies have been written about, filmed, shot, uploaded, re-sequenced, spliced and diced. And within the context of that interstitial place where thoughts can be media (whether they are familiar to you or not), the kinds of thoughts don't necessarily matter: It's the structure of the perceptions and the texts and the memories that are conditioned by your thought-process that will echo and configure the way that texts you're familiar with rise into prominence when you think. We live in an era where quotation and sampling operate on such a deep level that the archaeology of what can be called knowledge floats in a murky realm between the real and unreal. Look at the *Matrix* as a parable for Plato's cave, a section of his "Republic" written several thousand years ago, but resonant with the idea of living in a world of illusion.

The Soundbite Fetish

Another permutation: In his 1938 essay *On the Fetish-Character in Music,* the theoretician Theodor Adorno bemoaned the fact that European classical music was becoming more and more of a recorded experience. He had already written an essay entitled *The Opera and The Long Playing Record* a couple of years before, and the Fetish essay was a continuation of the same theme. People were being exposed to music that they barely had time to remember, because the huge volume of recordings and the small amount of time to absorb them presented to the proto-modernist listener a kind of soundbite mentality (one we in the era of the Web are becoming all too familiar with). He wrote that "the new listeners resemble the mechanics who are simultaneously specialized and capable of applying their special skills to unexpected places outside their skilled trades. But this despecialization only seems to help them out of the system."[1]

When Tim Berners Lee wrote some of the original source code for the World Wide Web, it was little more than a professors' club—but it echoed that same sense of abbreviation that Adorno mentioned. I tend to think of sampling and uploading files as the same thing, just in a different format. To paraphrase John Cage, sound is just information in a different form. Think of DJ culture as a kind of archival impulse put to a kind of hunter-gatherer milieu—textual poaching, becomes zero-paid, becomes no-logo, becomes brand X. It's that interface thing rising again—but this time around, mind/brain interface becomes emergent system of large scale economies of expression.

The Loop of Perception

As the World Wide Web continues to expand, it's becoming increasingly difficult for users to obtain information efficiently. This has nothing to do with the volume of information out in the world, or even who has access to it—it's a

---

[1] Theodor W. Adorno, *Essays on Music,* with notes and commentary by Richard Leppert, translated by Susan H. Gillespie and others (University of California Press, 2002).

kind of search engine function that's undergoing a crisis of meaning. The metaphor holds: the poem invokes the next line, word leads to thought and back again. Repeat. The scenario: internal becomes external becomes involution. The loop of perception is a relentless hall of mirrors in the mind. You can think of sampling as a story you are telling yourself—one made of the world as you can hear it, and the theatre of sounds that you invoke with those fragments is all one story made up of many. Think of it as the act of memory moving from word to word as a remix: complex becomes multiplex becomes omniplex.

Search Engine Civilization

As more and more people joined the Web, it took on a more expanded role, and I look to this expansion as a parallel with the co-evolution of recorded media. Lexical space became cultural space. Search engines took on a greater and greater role as the Web expanded, because people needed to be able to quickly access the vast amount of varying results that would be yielded. Search engines look for what they've been told to look for, and then end up bringing back a lot of conflicting results: metadata that breaks down Web sites' contents into easy to search for "meta-tags" that flag the attention of the search engines' distant glances. The process is essentially like a huge rolodex whose tabs are blue, and whose cards are for the most part hidden.

So too with sound. I'm writing an essay on sampling and memory using search engines and the Web as a metaphor because I see the Net as a kind of inheritor to the way that DJs look for information: It's a shareware world on the Web, and the migration of cultural values from one street to another is what this essay is all about.

Think of city streets as routes of movement in a landscape made of roads and manifolds. These roads convey people, goods, and so on through a densely inhabited urban landscape held together by consensus. It's like James Howard Kunstler said in his book *The City in Mind* (Free Press, 2002): these streets, like the cities he loves to write about, are "as broad as civilization itself." Look at the role of the search engine in Web culture as a new kind of thoroughfare, and that role is expanded a million-fold. The information and goods are out there, but you stay in one place; the civilization comes to you.

Today, when we browse and search, we invoke a series of chance operations—we use interfaces, icons, and text as a flexible set of languages and tools. Our semantic web is a remix of all available information—display elements, metadata, services, images, and especially content—made immediately accessible. The result is an immense repository—an archive of almost anything that has ever been recorded.

Think of the semantic webs that hold together contemporary info culture, and of the disconnect between how we speak, and how the machines that process this culture speak to one another, thanks to our efforts to have anything and everything represented and available to anyone everywhere.

It's that archive fervor that makes the info world go around, and as an art-ist you're only as good as your archive—it's that minimalist, and that simple. That's what makes it deeply complex.

Think then of search engines as scouts or guides for the semantic web; a category that also includes (among other things) software agents that can negotiate and collect information, markup languages that can tag many more types of information in a document, and knowledge systems that enable machines to read Web pages and determine their reliability. But it goes still further: the truly interdisciplinary semantic web guide combines aspects of artificial intelligence, markup languages, natural language processing, infor-mation retrieval, knowledge representation, intelligent agents, and databases. Taken together, it all resembles a good DJ, who has a lot of records and files, and knows exactly where to filter the mix. They don't call the process online "collaborative filtering" for nothing.

Software Swing

Again and again, one of the main things I hear people asking when I travel is: "What software do you use?"

Today's computer networks are built on software protocols that are fundamentally textual. Paradoxically, this linguistic medium of software isn't only nearly undecipherable to the layperson, but it has created radical, mate-rial transformations through these linguistic means (e.g., computers and networks as forces of globalization). As Henri Lefebvre said so long ago in his classic 1974 essay *The Production of Space:* "The body's inventiveness needs no demonstration, for the body itself reveals it, and deploys it in space. Rhythms in all their multiplicity interpenetrate one another. In the body and around it, as on the surface of a body of water, rhythms are forever crossing and recrossing, superimposing themselves upon each other, always bound to space."[2]

The semantic web is an intangible sculptural body that exists only in the virtual space between you and the information you perceive. It's all in continu-ous transformation, and to look for anything to really stay the same is to be caught in a time warp to another era, another place when things stood still and didn't change so much. But if this essay has done one thing, then I hope it has been to move us to think as the objects move: to make us remember that we are warm-blooded mammals, and that the cold information we gen-erate is a product of our desires, and manifests some deep elements of our being.

The point of all this? To remind us that, like Duke Ellington and so many other musicians said so long ago, "It don't mean a thing if it ain't got that swing." As the information age moves into full gear, it would be wise to

[2] Henri Lefebvre, *The Production of Space,* translated by Donald Nicholson Smith (Blackwell Publishing, 1974).

remember the cautionary tales of shades and shadows; to recall and remix the tale of a bored billionaire living in a dream world in Don Delillo's Cosmopolis, who said:

> It was shallow thinking to maintain that numbers and charts were the cold compression of unruly human energies, every sort of yearning and midnight sweat reduced to lucid units in the financial markets. In fact data itself was soulful and glowing, a dynamic aspect of the life process. This was the eloquence of alphabets and numeric systems, now fully realized in electronic form, in the zero-oneness of the world, the digital imperative that defined every breath of the planet's living billions. Here was the heave of the biosphere. Our bodies and oceans were here, knowable and whole.[3]

Sample away!

QUESTIONS FOR DISCUSSION AND WRITING

1. Miller argues that we live with a soundbite mentality in network systems. How and in what ways does he posit that these facts have altered what he designates as our "interior and external perceptual worlds"?
2. Do you agree with Miller when he makes the sweeping statement, "In our day and age, the basic idea of how we create content in our minds is so conditioned by media that we are in a position unlike any other culture in human history"?
3. What exactly does Miller mean when he says, "complex becomes multiplex becomes omniplex"?
4. How does Miller's work as a DJ, who uses sampling and mixing and the methods DJs look to for information, fit in with his vision of how each of us makes a poem of ourselves?
5. What does Miller mean when he states, "as an artist you're only as good as your archive"?

ON TECHNIQUE AND STYLE

1. Miller organizes his essay under five separate headings. Do these headings follow a structured pattern that gives his essay unity?
2. Miller's style can be abstract and challenging. How accessible is it? How intellectual or abstruse?
3. Do all of the allusions and references in this essay from *Matrix* and Plato to Theodor Adorno, James Howard Kunstler, Henry LeFebre, Duke Ellington, and Don Delillo give greater heft to his essay and greater support to his central argument?

[3] Don Delillo, *Cosmopolis: A Novel* (Scribner, 2003).

CULTURAL QUESTION

1. Miller writes that "the migration of cultural value from one street to another is what this essay is all about." Is this an argument for multiculturalism? What exactly does he mean?

FICTION

Seventeen Syllables

Hisaye Yamamoto

Hisaye Yamamoto (1921–   ), a Nisei or second-generation Japanese American, was born in Redondo Beach, California, to parents who were immigrants from Japan. Following the Japanese bombing of Pearl Harbor she and her family were placed in an internment camp for three years in Poston, Arizona, where she began writing as a reporter and columnist for camp newspapers. She then worked for the Los Angeles Tribune, *an African American newspaper. By 1948 she was publishing fiction in* Partisan Review, Kenyon Review, *and* Arizona Quarterly. *She published some sixty stories in journals and periodicals and worked as a Catholic Worker's rehabilitation center volunteer. Two of her stories were adapted for the American Playhouse PBS film* Hot Summer Winds. *In 1986 she was awarded the Before Columbus Lifetime Foundation Award.* Seventeen Syllables and Other Stories *was published in 1988. "Seventeen Syllables" is a coming-of-age story about a young Japanese American girl, Rosie, who is awakening to the early sensations of love with a young itinerant Mexican American agricultural worker named Jesus. It is also a story about Rosie's discovery of her mother's past and the revelation behind the secret of her parents' arranged marriage. For our purposes, it is a story tied to poetry and the mother's creative expression through haiku and the implicit recognition of a new wave of feminism highly critical of patriarchy and male hegemony over women.*

The first Rosie knew that her mother had taken to writing poems was one evening when she finished one and read it aloud for her daughter's approval. It was about cats, and Rosie pretended to understand it thoroughly and appreciate it no end, partly because she hesitated to disillusion her mother about the quantity and quality of Japanese she had learned in all the years now that she had been going to Japanese school every Saturday (and Wednesday, too, in the summer). Even so, her mother must have been skeptical about the depth of Rosie's understanding, because she explained afterwards about the kind of poem she was trying to write.

See, Rosie, she said, it was a *haiku,* a poem in which she must pack all
her meaning into seventeen syllables only, which were divided into three lines
of five, seven, and five syllables. In the one she had just read, she had tried
to capture the charm of a kitten, as well as comment on the superstition that
owning a cat of three colors meant good luck.

"Yes, yes, I understand. How utterly lovely," Rosie said, and her mother,
either satisfied or seeing through the deception and resigned, went back to
composing.

The truth was that Rosie was lazy; English lay ready on the tongue but
Japanese had to searched for and examined, and even then put forth tentatively (probably to meet with laughter). It was so much easier to say yes, yes,
even when one meant no, no. Besides, this was what was in her mind to say: I
was looking through one of your magazines from Japan last night, Mother, and
towards the back I found some *haiku* in English that delighted me. There was
one that made me giggle off and on until I fell asleep—

It is morning, and lo!
I lie awake, comme il faut,
sighing for some dough.

Now, how to reach her mother, how to communicate the melancholy
song? Rosie knew formal Japanese by fits and starts, her mother had even
less English, no French. It was much more possible to say yes, yes.

It developed that her mother was writing the *haiku* for a daily newspaper,
the *Mainichi Shimbun,* that was published in San Francisco. Los Angeles,
to be sure, was closer to the farming community in which the Hayashi family lived and several Japanese vernaculars were printed there, but Rosie's
parents said they preferred the tone of the northern paper. Once a week, the
Mainichi would have a section devoted to *haiku,* and her mother became an
extravagant contributor, taking for herself the blossoming pen name, Ume
Hanazono.

So Rosie and her father lived for awhile with two women, her mother and
Ume Hanazono. Her mother (Tome Hayashi by name) kept house, cooked,
washed, and, along with her husband and the Carrascos, the Mexican family
hired for the harvest, did her ample share of picking tomatoes out in the sweltering fields and boxing them in tidy strata in the cool packing shed. Ume Hanazono,
who came to life after the dinner dishes were done, was an earnest, muttering
stranger who often neglected speaking when spoken to and stayed busy at the
parlor table as late as midnight scribbling with pencil on scratch paper or carefully
copying characters on good paper with her fat, pale green Parker.

The new interest had some repercussions on the household routine.
Before, Rosie had been accustomed to her parents and herself taking their
hot baths early and going to bed almost immediately afterwards, unless her
parents challenged each other to a game of flower cards or unless company
dropped in. Now if her father wanted to play cards, he had to resort to solitaire

(at which he always cheated fearlessly), and if a group of friends came over, it was bound to contain someone who was also writing *haiku,* and the small assemblage would be split in two, her father entertaining the non-literary members and her mother comparing ecstatic notes with the visiting poet.

If they went out, it was more of the same thing. But Ume Hanazono's life span, even for a poet's, was very brief—perhaps three months at most.

One night they went over to see the Hayano family in the neighboring town to the west, an adventure both painful and attractive to Rosie. It was attractive because there were four Hayano girls, all lovely and each one named after a season of the year (Haru, Natsu, Aki, Fuyu), painful because something had been wrong with Mrs. Hayano ever since the birth of her first child. Rosie would sometimes watch Mrs. Hayano, reputed to have been the belle of her native village, making her way about a room, stooped, slowly shuffling, violently trembling (*always* trembling), and she would be reminded that this woman, in this same condition, had carried and given issue to three babies. She would look wonderingly at Mr. Hayano, handsome, tall, and strong, and she would look at her four pretty friends. But it was not a matter she could come to any decision about.

On this visit, however, Mrs. Hayano sat all evening in the rocker, as motionless and unobtrusive as it was possible for her to be, and Rosie found the greater part of the evening practically anaesthetic. Too, Rosie spent most of it in the girls' room, because Haru, the garrulous one, said almost as soon as the bows and other greetings were over, "Oh, you must see my new coat!"

It was a pale plaid of grey, sand, and blue, with an enormous collar, and Rosie, seeing nothing special in it, said, "Gee, how nice."

"Nice?" said Haru, indignantly. "Is that all you can say about it? It's gorgeous! And so cheap, too. Only seventeen-ninety-eight, because it was a sale. The saleslady said it was twenty-five dollars regular."

"Gee," said Rosie. Natsu, who never said much and when she said anything said it shyly, fingered the coat covetously and Haru pulled it away.

"Mine," she said, putting it on. She minced in the aisle between the two large beds and smiled happily. "Let's see how your mother likes it."

She broke into the front room and the adult conversation and went to stand in front of Rosie's mother, while the rest watched from the door. Rosie's mother was properly envious. "May I inherit it when you're through with it?"

Haru, pleased, giggled and said yes, she could, but Natsu reminded gravely from the door, "You promised me, Haru."

Everyone laughed but Natsu, who shamefacedly retreated into the bedroom. Haru came in laughing, taking off the coat. "We were only kidding, Natsu," she said, "Here, you try it on now."

After Natsu buttoned herself into the coat, inspected herself solemnly in the bureau mirror, and reluctantly shed it, Rosie, Aki, and Fuyu got their turns, and Fuyu, who was eight, drowned in it while her sisters and Rosie doubled up in amusement. They all went into the front room later, because

Haru's mother quaveringly called to her to fix the tea and rice cakes and open a can of sliced peaches for everybody. Rosie noticed that her mother and Mr. Hayano were talking together at the little table—they were discussing a *haiku* that Mr. Hayano was planning to send to the *Mainichi,* while her father was sitting at one end of the sofa looking through a copy of *Life,* the new picture magazine. Occasionally, her father would comment on a photograph, holding it toward Mrs. Hayano and speaking to her as he always did—loudly, as though he thought someone such as she must surely be at least a trifle deaf also.

The five girls had their refreshments at the kitchen table, and it was while Rosie was showing the sisters her trick of swallowing peach slices without chewing (she chased each slippery crescent down with a swig of tea) that her father brought his empty teacup and untouched saucer to the sink and said, "Come on, Rosie, we're going home now."

"Already?" asked Rosie.

"Work tomorrow," he said.

He sounded irritated, and Rosie, puzzled, gulped one last yellow slice and stood up to go, while the sisters began protesting, as was their wont.

"We have to get up at five-thirty," he told them, going into the front room quickly, so that they did not have their usual chance to hang onto his hands and plead for an extension of time.

Rosie, following, saw that her mother and Mr. Hayano were sipping tea and still talking together, while Mrs. Hayano concentrated, quivering, on raising the handleless Japanese cup to her lips with both her hands and lowering it back to her lap. Her father, saying nothing, went out the door, onto the bright porch, and down the steps. Her mother looked up and asked, "Where is he going?"

"Where is he going?" Rosie said. "He said we were going home now."

"Going home?" Her mother looked with embarrassment at Mr. Hayano and his absorbed wife and then forced a smile. "He must be tired," she said.

Haru was not giving up yet. "May Rosie stay overnight?" she asked, and Natsu, Aki, and Fuyu came to reinforce their sister's plea by helping her make a circle around Rosie's mother. Rosie, for once having no desire to stay, was relieved when her mother, apologizing to the perturbed Mr. and Mrs. Hayano for her father's abruptness at the same time, managed to shake her head no at the quartet, kindly but adamant, so that they broke their circle and let her go.

Rosie's father looked ahead into the windshield as the two joined him. "I'm sorry," her mother said. "You must be tired." Her father, stepping on the starter, said nothing. "You know how I get when it's *haiku,*" she continued, "I forget what time it is." He only grunted.

As they rode homeward silently, Rosie, sitting between, felt a rush of hate for both—for her mother for begging, for her father for denying her mother. I wish this old Ford would crash, right now, she thought, then immediately, no, no, I wish my father would laugh, but it was too late: already the vision had passed through her mind of the green pick-up crumpled in the dark against one of the mighty eucalyptus trees they were just riding past, of the three contorted, bleeding bodies, one of them hers.

Rosie ran between two patches of tomatoes, her heart working more rambunctiously than she had ever known it to. How lucky it was that Aunt Taka and Uncle Gimpachi had come tonight, though, how very lucky. Otherwise she might not have really kept her half-promise to meet Jesus Carrasco. Jesus was going to be a senior in September at the same school she went to, and his parents were the ones helping with the tomatoes this year. She and Jesus, who hardly remembered seeing each other at Cleveland High where there were so many other people and two whole grades between them, had become great friends this summer—he always had a joke for her when he periodically drove the loaded pick-up up from the fields to the shed where she was usually sorting while her mother and father did the packing, and they laughed a great deal together over infinitesimal repartee during the afternoon break for chilled watermelon or ice cream in the shade of the shed.

What she enjoyed most was racing him to see which could finish picking a double row first. He, who could work faster, would tease her by slowing down until she thought she would surely pass him this time, then speeding up furiously to leave her several sprawling vines behind. Once he had made her screech hideously by crossing over, while her back was turned, to place atop the tomatoes in her green-stained bucket a truly monstrous, pale green worm (it had looked more like an infant snake). And it was when they had finished a contest this morning, after she had pantingly pointed a green finger at the immature tomatoes evident in the lugs at the end of his row and he had returned the accusation (with justice), that he had startlingly brought up the matter of their possibly meeting outside the range of both their parents' dubious eyes.

"What for?" she had asked.

"I've got a secret I want to tell you," he said.

"Tell me now," she demanded.

"It won't be ready till tonight," he said.

She laughed. "Tell me tomorrow then."

"It'll be gone tomorrow," he threatened.

"Well, for seven hakes, what is it?" she had asked, more than twice, and when he had suggested that the packing shed would be an appropriate place to find out, she had cautiously answered maybe. She had not been certain she was going to keep the appointment until the arrival of mother's sister and her husband. Their coming seemed a sort of signal of permission, of grace, and she had definitely made up her mind to lie and leave as she was bowing them welcome.

So as soon as everyone appeared settled back for the evening, she announced loudly that she was going to the privy outside, "I'm going to the *benjo!*" and slipped out the door. And now that she was actually on her way, her heart pumped in such an undisciplined way that she could hear it with her ears. It's because I'm running, she told herself, slowing to a walk. The shed was up ahead, one more patch away, in the middle of the fields. Its bulk, looming in the dimness, took on a sinisterness that was funny when Rosie reminded herself that it was only a wooden frame with a canvas roof and three canvas walls that made a slapping noise on breezy days.

Jesus was sitting on the narrow plank that was the sorting platform and she went around to the other side and jumped backwards to seat herself on the rim of a packing stand. "Well, tell me," she said without greeting, thinking her voice sounded reassuringly familiar.

"I saw you coming out the door," Jesus said. "I heard you running part of the way, too."

"Uh-huh," Rosie said. "Now tell me the secret."

"I was afraid you wouldn't come," he said.

Rosie delved around on the chicken-wire bottom of the stall for number two tomatoes, ripe, which she was sitting beside, and came up with a left-over that felt edible. She bit into it and began sucking out the pulp and seeds. "I'm here," she pointed out.

"Rosie, are you sorry you came?"

"Sorry? What for?" she said. "You said you were going to tell me something."

"I will, I will," Jesus said, but his voice contained disappointment, and Rosie fleetingly felt the older of the two, realizing a brand-new power which vanished without category under her recognition.

"I have to go back in a minute," she said. "My aunt and uncle are here from Wintersburg. I told them I was going to the privy."

Jesus laughed. "You funny thing," he said. "You slay me!"

"Just because you have a bathroom *inside*." Rosie said. "Come on, tell me."

Chuckling, Jesus came around to lean on the stand facing her. They still could not see each other very clearly, but Rosie noticed that Jesus became very sober again as he took the hollow tomato from her hand and dropped it back into the stall. When he took hold of her empty hand, she could find no words to protest; her vocabulary had become distressingly constricted and she thought desperately that all that remained intact now was yes and no and oh, and even these few sounds would not easily out. Thus, kissed by Jesus, Rosie fell for the first time entirely victim to a helplessness delectable beyond speech. But the terrible, beautiful sensation lasted no more than a second, and the reality of Jesus' lips and tongue and teeth and hands made her pull away with such strength that she nearly tumbled.

Rosie stopped running as she approached the lights from the windows of home. How long since she had left? She could not guess, but gasping yet, she went to the privy in back and locked herself in. Her own breathing deafened her in the dark, close space, and she sat and waited until she could hear at last the nightly calling of the frogs and crickets. Even then, all she could think to say was oh, my, and the pressure of Jesus' face against her face would not leave.

No one had missed her in the parlor, however, and Rosie walked in and through quickly, announcing that she was next going to take a bath. "Your father's in the bathhouse," her mother said, and Rosie, in her room, recalled that she had not seen him when she entered. There had been only Aunt Taka and Uncle Gimpachi with her mother at the table, drinking tea. She got her robe and straw sandals and crossed the parlor again to go outside. Her mother was telling them about the *haiku* competition in the *Mainichi* and the poem she had entered.

Rosie met her father coming out of the bathhouse. "Are you through, Father?" she asked. "I was going to ask you to scrub my back."

"Scrub your own back," he said shortly, going toward the main house.

"What have I done now?" she yelled after him. She suddenly felt like doing a lot of yelling. But he did not answer, and she went into the bathhouse. Turning on the dangling light, she removed her denims and T-shirt and threw them in the big carton for dirty clothes standing next to the washing machine. Her other things she took with her into the bath compartment to wash after her bath. After she had scooped a basin of hot water from the square wooden tub, she sat on the grey cement of the floor and soaped herself at exaggerated leisure, singing "Red Sails in the Sunset" at the top of her voice and using da-da-da where she suspected her words. Then, standing up, still singing, for she was possessed by the notion that any attempt now to analyze would result in spoilage and she believed that the larger her volume the less she would be able to hear herself think, she obtained more hot water and poured it on until she was free of lather. Only then did she allow herself to step into the steaming vat, one leg first, then the remainder of her body inch by inch until the water no longer stung and she could move around at will.

She took a long time soaking, afterwards remembering to go around outside to stoke the embers of the tin-lined fireplace beneath the tub and to throw on a few more sticks so that the water might keep its heat for her mother, and when she finally returned to the parlor, she found her mother still talking *haiku* with her aunt and uncle, the three of them on another round of tea. Her father was nowhere in sight.

At Japanese school the next day (Wednesday, it was), Rosie was grave and giddy by turns. Preoccupied at her desk in the row for students on Book Eight, she made up for it at recess by performing wild mimicry for the benefit of her friend Chizuko. She held her nose and whined a witticism or two in what she considered was the manner of Fred Allen; she assumed intoxication and a British accent to go over the climax of the Rudy Vallee recording of the pub conversation about William Ewart Gladstone; she was the child Shirley Temple piping, "On the Good Ship Lollipop"; she was the gentleman soprano of the Four Inkspots trilling, "If I Didn't Care." And she felt reasonably satisfied when Chizuko wept and gasped, "Oh, Rosie, you ought to be in the movies!"

Her father came after her at noon, bringing her sandwiches of minced ham and two nectarines to eat while she rode, so that she could pitch right into the sorting when they got home. The lugs were piling up, he said, and the ripe tomatoes in them would probably have to be taken to the cannery tomorrow if they were not ready for the produce haulers tonight. "This heat's not doing them any good. And we've got no time for a break today."

It *was* hot, probably the hottest day of the year, and Rosie's blouse stuck damply to her back even under the protection of the canvas. But she worked as efficiently as a flawless machine and kept the stalls heaped, with one part of her mind listening in to the parental murmuring about the heat and the tomatoes and with another part planning the exact words she would say to Jesus when he drove up with the first load of the afternoon. But when at last she saw that the pick-up was coming, her hands went berserk and the tomatoes started falling in the wrong stalls, and her father said, "Hey, hey! Rosie, watch what you're doing!"

"Well, I have to go to the *benjo*," she said, hiding panic.

"Go in the weeds over there," he said, only half-joking.

"Oh, Father!" she protested.

"Oh, go on home," her mother said. "We'll make out for awhile."

In the privy Rosie peered through a knothole toward the fields, watching as much as she could of Jesus. Happily she thought she saw him look in the direction of the house from time to time before he finished unloading and went back toward the patch where his mother and father worked. As she was heading for the shed, a very presentable black car purred up the dirt driveway to the house and its driver motioned to her. Was this the Hayashi home, he wanted to know. She nodded. Was she a Hayashi? Yes, she said, thinking that he was a good-looking man. He got out of the car with a huge, flat package and she saw that he warmly wore a business suit. "I have something here for your mother then," he said, in a more elegant Japanese than she was used to.

She told him where her mother was and he came along with her, patting his face with an immaculate white handkerchief and saying something about the coolness of San Francisco. To her surprised mother and father, he bowed and introduced himself as, among other things, the *haiku* editor of the *Mainichi Shimbun,* saying that since he had been coming as far as Los Angeles anyway, he had decided to bring her the first prize she had won in the recent contest.

"First prize?" her mother echoed, believing and not believing, pleased and overwhelmed. Handed the package with a bow, she bobbed her head up and down numerous times to express her utter gratitude.

"It is nothing much," he added, "but I hope it will serve as a token of our great appreciation for your contributions and our great admiration of your considerable talent."

"I am not worthy," she said, falling easily into his style. "It is I who should make some sign of my humble thanks for being permitted to contribute."

"No, no, to the contrary," he said, bowing again.

But Rosie's mother insisted, and then saying that she knew she was being unorthodox, she asked if she might open the package because her curiosity was so great. Certainly she might. In fact, he would like her reaction to it, for personally, it was one of his favorite *Hiroshiges.*

Rosie thought it was a pleasant picture, which looked to have been sketched with delicate quickness. There were pink clouds, containing some graceful calligraphy, and a sea that was a pale blue except at the edges, containing four sampans with indications of people in them. Pines edged the water and on the far-off beach there was a cluster of thatched huts towered over by pine-dotted mountains of grey and blue. The frame was scalloped and gilt.

After Rosie's mother pronounced it without peer and somewhat prodded her father into nodding agreement, she said Mr. Kuroda must at least have a cup of tea after coming all this way, and although Mr. Kuroda did not want to impose, he soon agreed that a cup of tea would be refreshing and went along with her to the house, carrying the picture for her.

"Ha, your mother's crazy!" Rosie's father said, and Rosie laughed uneasily as she resumed judgment on the tomatoes. She had emptied six lugs when he broke into an imaginary conversation with Jesus to tell her to go and remind her mother of the tomatoes, and she went slowly.

Mr. Kuroda was in his shirtsleeves expounding some *haiku* theory as he munched a rice cake, and her mother was rapt. Abashed in the great man's presence, Rosie stood next to her mother's chair until her mother looked up inquiringly, and then she started to whisper the message, but her mother pushed her gently away and reproached, "You are not being very polite to our guest."

"Father says the tomatoes . . ." Rosie said aloud, smiling foolishly.

"Tell him I shall only be a minute," her mother said, speaking the language of Mr. Kuroda.

When Rosie carried the reply to her father, he did not seem to hear and she said again, "Mother says she'll be back in a minute."

"All right, all right," he nodded, and they worked again in silence. But suddenly, her father uttered an incredible noise, exactly like the cork of a bottle popping, and the next Rosie knew, he was stalking angrily toward the house, almost running in fact, and she chased after him crying, "Father! Father! What are you going to do?"

He stopped long enough to order her back to the shed. "Never mind!" he shouted. "Get on with the sorting!"

And from the place in the fields where she stood, frightened and vacillating, Rosie saw her father enter the house. Soon Mr. Kuroda came out alone, putting on his coat. Mr. Kuroda got into his car and backed out down the driveway onto the highway. Next her father emerged, also alone, something in his arms (it was the picture, she realized), and, going over to the bathhouse woodpile, he threw the picture on the ground and picked up the axe. Smashing the picture, glass and all (she heard the explosion faintly), he reached over for the kerosene that was used to encourage the bath fire and poured it over the wreckage. I am dreaming, Rosie said to herself, I am dreaming, but her father, having made sure that his act of cremation was irrevocable, was even then returning to the fields.

Rosie ran past him and toward the house. What had become of her mother? She burst into the parlor and found her mother at the back window watching the dying fire. They watched together until there remained only a feeble smoke under the blazing sun. Her mother was very calm.

"Do you know why I married your father?" she said without turning.

"No," said Rosie. It was the most frightening question she had ever been called upon to answer. Don't tell me now, she wanted to say, tell me tomorrow, tell me next week, don't tell me today. But she knew she would be told now, that the telling would combine with the other violence of the hot afternoon to level her life, her world to the very ground.

It was like a story out of the magazines illustrated in sepia, which she had consumed so greedily for a period until the information had somehow reached her that those wretchedly unhappy autobiographies, offered to her as the testimonials of living men and women, were largely inventions: Her mother, at nineteen, had come to America and married her father as an alternative to suicide.

At eighteen she had been in love with the first son of one of the well-to-do families in her village. The two had met whenever and wherever they could, secretly, because it would not have done for his family to see him favor her—her father had no money; he was a drunkard and a gambler besides. She had learned she was with child; an excellent match had already been arranged for her lover. Despised by her family, she had given premature birth to a stillborn son, who would be seventeen now. Her family did not turn her out, but she could no longer project herself in any direction without refreshing in them the memory of her indiscretion. She wrote to Aunt Taka, her favorite sister in America, threatening to kill herself if Aunt Taka would not send for her. Aunt Taka hastily arranged a marriage with a young man of whom she knew, but lately arrived from Japan, a young man of simple mind, it was said, but of kindly heart. The young man was never told why his unseen betrothed was so eager to hasten the day of meeting.

The story was told perfectly, with neither groping for words nor untoward passion. It was as though her mother had memorized it by heart, reciting it to herself so many times over that its nagging vileness had long since gone.

"I had a brother then?" Rosie asked, for this was what seemed to matter now; she would think about the other later, she assured herself, pushing back the illumination which threatened all that darkness that had hitherto been merely mysterious or even glamorous. "A half-brother?"

"Yes."

"I would have liked a brother," she said.

Suddenly, her mother knelt on the floor and took her by the wrists. "Rosie," she said urgently, "Promise me you will never marry!" Shocked more by the request than the revelation, Rosie stared at her mother's face. Jesus, Jesus, she called silently, not certain whether she was invoking the help of the son of the Carrascos or of God, until there returned sweetly the memory of Jesus' hand, how it had touched her and where. Still her mother waited for an answer, holding her wrists so tightly that her hands were going numb. She tried to pull free. Promise, her mother whispered fiercely, promise. Yes, yes, I promise, Rosie said. But for an instant she turned away, and her mother, hearing the familiar glib agreement, released her. Oh, you, you, you, her eyes and twisted mouth said, you fool. Rosie, covering her face, began at last to cry, and the embrace and consoling hand came much later than she expected.

QUESTIONS FOR DISCUSSION AND WRITING

1. "Seventeen Syllables" is a story about generations. What separates Rosie from the generation of her parents?
2. What does the author mean when she tells us that Rosie's mother is two women?
3. What point does the story make about women who write poetry and the kinds of difficulties they encounter expressing their creativity? Does this apply only to women from traditional and old-world backgrounds?
4. What is the significance in "Seventeen Syllables" of the rural and agricultural setting of the story?
5. The story's title signifies the seventeen syllables used in haiku poetry, a traditional Japanese literary form. Is there a central significance to the role of the haiku in this poem aside from the fact that the mother composes and publishes haiku poetry and relishes talking about it?
6. What is your reaction to the father's "act of cremation," which begins with an axe and winds up with kerosene?
7. What are we to conclude at the end of the story with Rosie's promise and her mother calling her a fool?

ON TECHNIQUE AND STYLE

1. What advantages result from the fact that the story is told to us exclusively from the point of view of Rosie?
2. There are nuanced touches of character portrayal in the story—such as the mentioning of the father always cheating at solitaire or Mrs. Hayano always trembling, even the fact that Rosie swallows peaches without chewing. How do these add to the story and the characters in it?

3. What are we to make of Yamamoto's choice of the name Jesus, especially at the end of the story when Rosie is uncertain if she is "invoking the help of the son of Carrascos or of God"?

CULTURAL QUESTION

1. Rosie, a bilingual teenager, goes to Japanese school once or twice a week, has difficulty with the older-style Japanese of her mother and Mr. Kuroda of the *Mainichi Shimbun,* and mimics pop culture personalities. How much does Rosie's identity straddle both cultural worlds? What do we conclude about her bicultural identity?

Epilogue: Women Like Us

Edwidge Danticat

Edwidge Danticat (1969–   ) was born in Port-au-Prince, Haiti, and came to the United States at age twelve. Though English was her third language (after French and Creole) she began publishing writings in English when she was fourteen. She received a degree in French literature from Barnard College and an MFA from Brown University, where her thesis Breath, Eyes, Memory *was later published and won a Best Young American Novelist Award. She has published numerous stories and fictional works focusing on her Haitian heritage, including* Krik? Krak!; The Farming of Bones; The Dew Breaker; *and* Anacaona: Golden Flower, Haiti, 1490. *She has worked with filmmakers Patricia Benoit and Jonathan Demme on projects on Haitian art and documentaries about Haiti. She is a Pushcart Short Story Prize winner as well as a recipient of fiction awards from* The Caribbean Writer, Seventeen, *and* Essence *magazines. Danticat taught at New York University and the University of Miami and lives in Brooklyn, New York. "Epilogue: Women Like Us" appears at the end of her story collection* Krik? Krak! *(1995). In it we get the sense of transformation of a young Haitian woman from the "kitchen poet" women of generations before her to someone who must establish her own vision and voice.*

You remember thinking while braiding your hair that you look a lot like your mother. Your mother who looked like your grandmother and her grandmother before her. Your mother had two rules for living. *Always use your ten fingers,* which in her parlance meant that you should be the best little cook and housekeeper who ever lived.

Your mother's second rule went along with the first. Never have sex before marriage, and even after you marry, you shouldn't say you enjoy it, or your husband won't respect you.

And writing? Writing was as forbidden as dark rouge on the cheeks or a first date before eighteen. It was an act of indolence, something to be done in a corner when you could have been learning to cook.

Are there women who both cook and write? Kitchen poets, they call them. They slip phrases into their stew and wrap meaning around their pork before frying it. They make narrative dumplings and stuff their daughter's mouths so they say nothing more.

"What will she do? What will be her passion?" your aunts would ask when they came over to cook on great holidays, which called for cannon salutes back home but meant nothing at all here.

"Her passion is being quiet," your mother would say. "But then she's not being quiet. You hear this scraping from her. Krik? Krak! Pencil, paper. It sounds like someone crying."

Someone was crying. You and the writing demons in your head. You have nobody, nothing but this piece of paper, they told you. Only a notebook made out of discarded fish wrappers, panty-hose cardboard. They were the best confidantes for a lonely little girl.

When you write, it's like braiding your hair. Taking a handful of coarse unruly strands and attempting to bring them unity. Your fingers have still not perfected the task. Some of the braids are long, others are short. Some are thick, others are thin. Some are heavy. Others are light. Like the diverse women in your family. Those whose fables and metaphors, whose similes, and soliloquies, whose diction and *je ne sais quoi* daily slip into your survival soup, by way of their fingers.

You have always had your ten fingers. They curse you each time you force them around the contours of a pen. No, women like you don't write. They carve onion sculptures and potato statues. They sit in dark corners and braid their hair in new shapes and twists in order to control the stiffness, the unruliness, the rebelliousness.

You remember thinking while braiding your hair that you look a lot like your mother. You remember her silence when you laid your first notebook in front of her. Her disappointment when you told her that words would be your life's work, like the kitchen had always been hers. She was angry at you for not understanding. *And with what do you repay me? With scribbles on paper that are not worth the scratch of a pig's snout.* The sacrifices had been too great.

Writers don't leave any mark in the world. Not the world where we are from. In our world, writers are tortured and killed if they are men. Called lying whores, then raped and killed, if they are women. In our world, if you write, you are a politician, and we know what happens to politicians. They end up in a prison dungeon where their bodies are covered in scalding tar before they're forced to eat their own waste.

The family needs a nurse, not a prisoner. We need to forge ahead with our heads raised, not buried in scraps of throw-away paper. We do not want to bend over a dusty grave, wearing black hats, grieving for you. There are nine hundred and ninety-nine women who went before you and worked their fingers to coconut rind so you can stand here before me holding that torn old notebook that you cradle against your breast like your prettiest Sunday braids. I would rather you had spit in my face.

You remember thinking while braiding your hair that you look a lot like your mother and her mother before her. It was their whispers that pushed you, their murmurs over pots sizzling in your head. A thousand women urging you to speak through the blunt tip of your pencil. Kitchen poets, you call them. Ghosts like burnished branches on a flame tree. These women, they asked for your voice so that they could tell your mother in your place that yes, women like you do speak, even if they speak in a tongue that is hard to understand. Even if it's patois, dialect, Creole.

The women in your family have never lost touch with one another. Death is a path we take to meet on the other side. What goddesses have joined, let no one cast asunder. With every step you take, there is an army of women watching over you. We are never any farther than the sweat on your brows or the dust on your toes. Though you walk through the valley of the shadow of death, fear no evil for we are always with you.

When you were a little girl, you used to dream that you were lying among the dead and all the spirits were begging you to scream. And even now, you are still afraid to dream because you know that you will never be able to do what they say, as they say it, the old spirits that live in your blood.

Most of the women in your life had their heads down. They would wake up one morning to find their panties gone. It is not shame, however, that kept their heads down. They were singing, searching for meaning in the dust. And sometimes, they were talking to faces across the ages, faces like yours and mine.

You thought that if you didn't tell the stories, the sky would fall on your head. You often thought that without the trees, the sky would fall on your head. You learned in school that you have pencils and paper only because the trees gave themselves in unconditional sacrifice. There have been days when the sky was as close as your hair to falling on your head.

This fragile sky has terrified you your whole life. Silence terrifies you more than the pounding of a million pieces of steel chopping away at your flesh. Sometimes, you dream of hearing only the beating of your own heart, but this has never been the case. You have never been able to escape the pounding of a thousand other hearts that have outlived yours by thousands of years. And over the years when you have needed us, you have always cried "Krik?" and we have answered "Krak!" and it has shown us that you have not forgotten us.

You remember thinking while braiding your hair that you look a lot like your mother. Your mother, who looked like your grandmother and her grandmother before her. Your mother, she introduced you to the first echoes of the tongue that you now speak when at the end of the day she would braid your hair while you sat between her legs, scrubbing the kitchen pots. While your fingers worked away at the last shadows of her day's work, she would make your braids Sunday-pretty even during the week.

When she was done she would ask you to name each braid after those nine hundred and ninety-nine women who were boiling in your blood, and since you had written them down and memorized them, the names would come rolling off your tongue. And this was your testament to the way that these women lived and died and lived again.

QUESTIONS FOR DISCUSSION AND WRITING

1. Is this a feminist story? What are the implications of the narrator's need and desire to write as opposed to what her mother wants and expects of her? Is she breaking with tradition and establishing her identity in line with what we might call a new wave?
2. If writing is so frowned upon and is seen by her mother as "an act of indolence," what is it that drives and compels the narrator to write? How is writing for her like braiding hair?
3. Who are the kitchen poets? What exactly is it that our narrator derives from them? Why are their heads down and why are they like ghosts?
4. The sense of the sky falling and the fragility of the sky almost makes us think of the famous child's fairy tale "Chicken Little." Why does the narrator feel the sky is this way?
5. What is an epilogue? What in this piece of fiction makes it feel like an epilogue?
6. How do the mother–daughter relationships in this story differ from what we see in Yamamoto's "Seventeen Syllables"?
7. What emotion or feeling is conveyed by Danticat's narrator addressing her childhood from the perch of time? What poetic sense is communicated by the image of "a lonely little girl" whose "best confidantes" are "discarded fish wrappers" and "panty-hose cardboard"?

ON TECHNIQUE AND STYLE

1. What effects does the use of the unconventional second person (you) have in the telling of this story?
2. In a couple of instances in the text Danticat uses italics and an italicized passage. Why does she employ that technique?
3. Discuss the metaphor of the ten fingers. How does Danticat make use of it and is it successful?

1. What does the passage in which Danticat writes of how writers and politicians are treated in her culture reveal to us? How does it culturally set her apart?

A New-Wave Format

Bobbie Ann Mason

Bobbie Ann Mason (1940–   ) was born and raised on a dairy farm near Mayfield in western Kentucky. She was educated at the University of Kentucky and received an MA in English from the State University of New York, Binghamton after living in New York City and writing articles about teen stars for fan and entertainment magazines such as Movie Star, Movie Life, *and* T.V. Star Parade. *She received a PhD in 1972 from the University of Connecticut. Mason taught at Mansfield State College in Pennsylvania and published two books of criticism, on Nabokov's* Ada *and "girl sleuth" fiction. Her fiction has appeared in* Redbook, The New Yorker, Atlantic Monthly, *and* The North American Review. Shiloh and Other Stories, *where the story included here first appeared, was published in 1982 and was awarded the National Book Critics Circle Award. Mason also published two additional volumes of short stories,* Love Life *and* Midnight Magic. *Many of her stories have been included in the* O. Henry Award *annuals and* The Best American Short Stories *series. Her novels include* In Country, Spence+Lila, *and* Feather Crowns. *She presently lives in rural Pennsylvania. "A New-Wave Format" moves us into the rural world of small-town, barely middle-class western Kentucky and is another story about the rising wave of new feminist consciousness as we see in the obvious gaps in generational outlook between Edwin and Sabrina. But the real new wave in the story emerges as Edwin shifts the music format of his disc jockeying on the bus he drives for adults who are developmentally disabled.*

Edwin Creech drives a yellow bus, transporting a group of mentally retarded adults to the Cedar Hill Mental Health Center, where they attend training classes. He is away from 7:00 to 9:30 A.M. and from 2:30 to 5:00 P.M. His hours are so particular that Sabrina Jones, the girl he has been living with for several months, could easily cheat on him. Edwin devises schemes to test her. He places a long string of dental floss on her pillow (an idea he got from a mystery novel), but it remains undisturbed. She is away four nights a week, at rehearsals for *Oklahoma!* with the Western Kentucky Little Theatre, and she often goes out to eat afterward with members of the cast. Sabrina won't let him go to rehearsals, saying she wants the play to be complete when he sees it. At home, she sings and dances along with the movie sound track, and she acts out scenes for him. In the play, she's in the chorus, and she has two lines in Act I, Scene 3. Her lines are "And to yer house a dark clubman!" and "Then out of your dreams you'll go." Edwin loves the dramatic way Sabrina waves her arms on her first line. She is supposed to be a fortune teller.

One evening when Sabrina comes home, Edwin is still up, as she puts on the sound track of *Oklahoma!* and sings along with Gordon MacRae while she does splits on the living room floor. Her legs are long and slender, and she still has her summer tan. She is wearing her shorts, even though it is late fall. Edwin suddenly has an overwhelming feeling of love for her. She really seems to believe what she is singing—"Oh, What a Beautiful Mornin'." When the song ends, he tells her that.

"It's the middle of the night," he says, teasing. "And you think it's morning."

"I'm just acting."

"No, you really believe it. You believe it's morning, a beautiful morning."

Sabrina gives him a fishy look, and Edwin feels embarrassed. When the record ends, Sabrina goes into the bedroom and snaps on the radio. Rock music helps her relax before going to sleep. The new rock music she likes is monotonous and bland, but Edwin tells himself that he likes it because Sabrina likes it. As she undresses, he says to her, "I'm sorry. I wasn't accusing you of nothing."

"That's O.K." She shrugs. The T-shirt she sleeps in has a hole revealing a spot of her skin that Edwin would like to kiss, but he doesn't because it seems like a corny thing to do. So many things about Sabrina are amazing: her fennel toothpaste and herbal deodorant; her slim, snaky hips; the way she puts Vaseline on her teeth for a flashier smile, something she learned to do in a beauty contest.

When she sits on the bed, Edwin says, "If I say the wrong things, I want you to tell me. It's just that I'm so crazy about you I can't think sometimes. But if I can do anything better, I will. I promise. Just tell me."

"I don't think of you as the worrying type," she says, lying down beside him. She still has her shoes on.

"I didn't used to be."

"You're the most laid back guy I know."

"Is that some kind of actor talk from your actor friends?"

"No. You're just real laid back. Usually good-looking guys are so stuck up. But you're not." The music sends vibrations through Edwin like a cat's purr. She says, "I brag on you all the time to Jeff and Sue—Curly and Laurey."

"I know who Jeff and Sue are." Sabrina talks constantly about Jeff and Sue, the romantic leads in the play.

Sabrina says, "Here's what I wish. If we had a big pile of money, we could have a house like Sue's. Did I tell you she's got *woven* blinds on her patio that she made herself? Everything she does is so *artistic*." Sabrina shakes Edwin's shoulder. "Wake up and talk to me."

"I can't. I have to get up at six."

Sabrina whispers to him, "Sue has the hots for Jeff. And Jeff's wife is going to have a duck with a rubber tail if she finds out." Sabrina giggles. "He kept dropping hints about how his wife was going to Louisville next week. And he and Sue were eating off the same slice of pizza."

"Is that supposed to mean something?"

"You figure it out."

"Would you do me that way?"

"Don't be silly." Sabrina turns up the radio, then unties her shoes and tosses them over Edwin's head into a corner.

Edwin is forty-three and Sabrina is only twenty, but he does not want to believe age is a barrier between them. Sometimes he cannot believe his good luck, that he has a beautiful girl who finds him still attractive. Edwin has a deep dimple in his chin, which reminded his first wife, Lois Ann, of Kirk Douglas. She had read in a movie magazine that Kirk Douglas has a special attachment for shaving his dimple. But Sabrina thinks Edwin looks like John Travolta, who also has a dimple. Now and then Edwin realizes how much older he is than Sabrina, but time has passed quickly, and he still feels like the same person, unchanged, that he was twenty years ago. His two ex-wives had seemed to drift away from him, and he never tried to hold them back. But with Sabrina, he knows he must make an effort, for it is beginning to dawn on him that sooner or later women get disillusioned with him. Maybe he's too laid back. But Sabrina likes this quality. Sabrina has large round gray eyes and limp, brownish-blond hair, the color of birch paneling, which she highlights with Miss Clairol. They share a love of Fudgsicles, speedboats, and *WKRP in Cincinnati.* At the beginning, he thought that was enough to build a relationship on, because he knew so many couples who never shared such simple pleasures, but gradually he has begun to see that it is more complicated than that. Sabrina's liveliness makes him afraid that she will be fickle. He can't bear the thought of losing her, and he doesn't like the idea that his new possessiveness may be the same uneasy feeling a man would have for a daughter.

Sabrina's parents sent her to college for a year, but her father, a farmer, lost money on his hogs and couldn't afford to continue. When Edwin met her, she was working as a waitress in a steak house. She wants to go back to college, but Edwin does not have the money to send her either. In college, she learned things that make him feel ignorant around her. She said that in an anthropology course, for instance, she learned for a fact that people evolved from animals. But when he tried to argue with her, she said his doubts were too silly to discuss. Edwin doesn't want to sound like a father, so he usually avoids such topics. Sabrina believes in the ERA, although she likes to keep house. She cooks odd things for him, like eggplant, and a weird lasagna with vegetables. She says she knows how to make a Big Mac from scratch, but she never does. Her specialty is pizza. She puts sliced dill pickles on it, which Edwin doesn't dare question. She likes to do things in what she calls an arty way. Now Sabrina is going out for pizza with people in the Theatre. Sabrina talks of "the Theatre."

Until he began driving the bus, Edwin had never worked closely with people. He worked on an offshore oil rig for a time, but kept his distance from the other men. He drove a bulldozer in a logging camp out West. In Kentucky, during his marriages, he worked in an aluminum products company, an automotive machine shop, and numerous gas stations, going from job to job as casually as he did with women. He used to think of himself as an adventurer, but now he believes he has gone through life rather blindly, without much pain or sense of loss.

When he drives the bus, he feels stirred up, perhaps the way Sabrina feels about *Oklahoma!* The bus is a new luxury model with a tape deck, AM-FM, CB, and built-in first-aid kit. He took a first-aid course, so he feels prepared to handle emergencies. Edwin has to stay alert, for anything could happen. The guys who came back from Vietnam said it was like this every moment. Edwin was in the army, but he was never sent to Vietnam, and now he feels that he has bypassed some critical stage in his life: a knowledge of terror. Edwin has never had this kind of responsibility, and he has never been around mentally retarded people before. His passengers are like bizarre, overgrown children, badly behaved and unpredictable. Some of them stare off into space, others are hyperactive. A woman named Freddie Johnson kicks aimlessly at the seat in front of her, spouting her ten-word vocabulary. She can say, "Hot! Shorts," "*Popeye* on?" "*Dukes* on!" "Cook supper," and "Go bed." She talks continuously. A gangly man with a clubfoot has learned to get Hershey bars from a vending machine, and every day he brings home Hershey bars, clutching them in his hand until he squeezes them out of shape. A pretty blond woman shows Edwin the braces on her teeth every day when she gets on the bus. She gets confused if Edwin brings up another topic. The noises on the bus are chaotic and eerie—spurts, gurgles, yelps, squeals. Gradually, Edwin has learned how to keep his distance and keep order at the same time. He plays tape-recorded music to calm and entertain the passengers. In effect, he has become a disc jockey, taking requests and using the microphone, but he avoids fast talk. The supervisors at the center have told him that the developmentally disabled—they always use this term—need a world that is slowed down; they can't keep up with today's fast pace. So he plays mellow old sixties tunes by the Lovin' Spoonful, Joni Mitchell, Donovan. It seems to work. The passengers have learned to clap or hum along with the music. One man, Merle Cope, has been learning to clap his hands in a body-awareness class. Merle is forty-seven years old, and he walks two miles—in an hour—to the bus stop, down a country road. He climbs onto the bus with agonizing slowness. When he gets on, he makes an exaggerated clapping motion, as if to congratulate himself for having made it, but he never lets his hands quite touch. Merle Cope always has an eager grin on his face, and when he tries to clap his hands he looks ecstatic. He looks happier than Sabrina singing "Oh, What a Beautiful Mornin'."

On Thursday, November 14, Edwin stops at the junction of a state road and a gravel road called Ezra Combs Lane to pick up a new passenger. The country roads have shiny new green signs, with the names of the farmers who originally settled there three or four generations ago. The new passenger is Laura Combs, who he has been told is thirty-seven and has never been to school. She will take classes in Home Management and Living Skills. When she gets on the bus, the people who were with her drive off in a blue Pacer. Laura Combs, a large, angular woman with buckteeth, stomps deliberately down the aisle, then plops down beside a young black man named Ray Watson, who has been riding the bus for about three weeks. Ray has hardly spoken, except to say "Have a nice day" to Edwin when he leaves the bus. Ray, who is mildly retarded from a blow on the head in his childhood, is subject to seizures, but so far he has not had one on the bus. Edwin watches him carefully. He learned about convulsions in his first-aid course.

When Laura Combs sits down by Ray Watson, she shoves him and says, "Scoot over. And cheer up."

Her tone is not cheerful. Edwin watches in the rear-view mirror, ready to act. He glides around a curve and slows down for the next passenger. A tape has ended and Edwin hesitates before inserting another. He hears Ray Watson say, "I never seen anybody as ugly as you."

"Shut up or I'll send you to the back of the bus." Laura Combs speaks with a snappy authority that makes Edwin wonder if she is really retarded. Her hair is streaked gray and yellow, and her face is filled with acne pits.

Ray Watson says, "That's fine with me, long as I don't have to set by you."

"Want me to throw you back in the woodpile where you come from?"

"I bet you could throw me plumb out the door, you so big."

It is several minutes before it is clear to Edwin that they are teasing. He is pleased that Ray is talking, but he can't understand why it took a person like Laura Combs to motivate him. She is an imposing woman with a menacing stare. She churns gum, her mouth open.

For a few weeks, Edwin watches them joke with each other, and whenever he decides he should separate them, they break out into big grins and pull at each other's arms. The easy intimacy they develop seems strange to Edwin, but then it suddenly occurs to him what a fool he is being about a twenty-year-old girl, and that seems even stranger. He hears Ray ask Laura, "Did you get that hair at the Piggly Wiggly?" Laura's hair is in pigtails, which seem to be freshly plaited on Mondays and untouched the rest of the week. Laura says, "I don't want no birds nesting in *my* hair."

Edwin takes their requests. Laura has to hear "Mister Bojangles" every day, and Ray demands that Edwin play something from Elvis's Christmas album. They argue over tastes. Each says the other's favorite songs are terrible.

Laura tells Ray she never heard of a black person liking Elvis, and Ray says, "There's a lot about black people you don't know."

"What?"

"That's for me to know and you to find out. You belong on the moon. All white peoples belong on the moon."

"You belong in Atlanta," Laura says, doubling over with laughter.

When Edwin reports their antics one day to Sabrina, she says, "That's too depressing for words."

"They're a lot smarter than you'd think."

"I don't see how you can stand it." Sabrina shudders. She says, "Out in the woods, animals that are defective wouldn't survive. Even back in history, deformed babies were abandoned."

"Today's different," says Edwin, feeling alarmed. "Now they have rights."

"Well, I'll say one thing. If I was going to have a retarded baby, I'd get an abortion."

"That's killing."

"It's all in how you look at it," says Sabrina, changing the radio station.

They are having lunch. Sabrina has made a loaf of zucchini bread, because Sue made one for Jeff. Edwin doesn't understand her reasoning, but he takes it as a compliment. She gives him another slice, spreading it with whipped margarine. All of his women were good cooks. Maybe he didn't praise them enough. He suddenly blurts out so much praise for the zucchini bread that Sabrina looks at him oddly. Then he realizes that her attention is on the radio. The Humans are singing a song about paranoia, which begins, "Attention, all you K Mart shoppers, fill your carts, 'cause your time is almost up." It is Sabrina's favorite song.

"Most of my passengers are real poor country people," Edwin says. "Use to, they'd be kept in the attic or out in the barn. Now they're riding a bus, going to school and having a fine time."

"In the attic? I never knew that. *I'm* a poor country girl and I never knew that."

"Everybody knows that," says Edwin, feeling a little pleased. "But don't call yourself a poor country girl."

"It's true. My daddy said he'd give me a calf to raise if I came back home. Big deal. My greatest dread is that I'll end up on a farm, raising a bunch of dirty-faced younguns. Just like some of those characters on your bus."

Edwin does not know what to say. The song ends. The last line is, "They're looking in your picture window."

While Sabrina clears away the dishes, Edwin practices rolling bandages. He has been reviewing his first-aid book. "I want you to help me practice a simple splint," he says to Sabrina.

"If I broke a leg, I couldn't be in *Oklahoma!*"

"You won't break a leg." He holds out the splint. It is a fraternity paddle, a souvenir of her college days. She sits down for him and stretches out her leg.

"I can't stand this," she says.

"I'm just practicing. I have to be prepared. I might have an emergency."

Sabrina, wincing, closes her eyes while Edwin ties the fraternity paddle to her ankle.

"It's perfect," he says, tightening the knot.

Sabrina opens her eyes and wiggles her foot. "Jim says he's sure I can have a part in *Life with Father*," she says. Jim is the director of *Oklahoma!* She adds, "Jeff is probably going to be the lead."

"I guess you're trying to make me jealous."

"No, I'm not. It's not even a love story."

"I'm glad then. Is that what you want to do?"

"I don't know. Don't you think I ought to go back to school and take a drama class? It'd be a real great experience, and I'm not going to get a job anytime soon, looks like. Nobody's hiring." She shakes her leg impatiently, and Edwin begins untying the bandage. "What do you think I ought to do?"

"I don't know. I never know how to give you advice, Sabrina. What do I know? I haven't been to college like you."

"I wish I were rich, so I could go back to school," Sabrina says sadly. The fraternity paddle falls to the floor, and she says, with her hands rushing to her face, "Oh, God, I can't stand the thought of breaking a leg."

The play opens in two weeks, during the Christmas season, and Sabrina has been making her costumes—two gingham outfits, virtually identical. She models them for Edwin and practices her dances for him. Edwin applauds, and she gives him a stage bow, as the director has taught her to do. Everything Sabrina does now seems like a performance. When she slices the zucchini bread, sawing at it because it has hardened, it is a performance. When she sat in the kitchen chair with the splint, it was as though she imagined her audience. Edwin has been involved in his own performances, on the bus. He emulates Dr. Johnny Fever, on *WKRP,* because he likes to be low-key, cool. But he hesitates to tell Sabrina about his disc jockey role because she doesn't watch *WKRP in Cincinnati* with him anymore. She goes to rehearsals early.

Maybe it is out of resistance to the sappy *Oklahoma!* sound track, or maybe it is an inevitable progression, but Edwin finds himself playing a few Dylan tunes, some Janis Joplin, nothing too hectic. The passengers shake their heads in pleasure or beat things with their fists. It makes Edwin sad to think how history passes them by, but sometimes he feels the same way about his own life. As he drives along, playing these old songs, he thinks about what his life was like back then. During his first marriage, he worked in a gas station, saving for a down payment on a house. Lois Ann fed him on a TV tray while he watched the war. It was like a drama series. After Lois Ann, and then his travels out West, there was Carolyn and another down payment on another house and more of the war. Carolyn had a regular schedule—pork chops on Mondays, chicken on Tuesdays. Thursday's menu has completely escaped his memory. He feels terrible, remembering his wives by their food, and remembering the war as a TV series. His life has been a delayed reaction. He feels as if he's about Sabrina's age. He plays music he did not understand fifteen years ago, music that now seems full of possibility: the Grateful Dead, the Jefferson Airplane, groups with vision. Edwin feels that he is growing and changing for the first time in years. The passengers on his bus fill him with a compassion he has never felt before. When Freddie Johnson learns a new word—"bus"—Edwin is elated. He feels confident. He could drive his passengers all the way to California if he had to.

One day a stringbean girl with a speech impediment gives Edwin a tape cassette she wants him to play. Her name is Lou Murphy. Edwin has tried to encourage her to talk, but today he hands the tape back to her abruptly.

"I don't like the Plasmatics," he explains, enjoying his authority. "I don't play new-wave. I have a golden-oldie format. I just play sixties stuff."

The girl takes the tape cassette and sits down by Laura Combs. Ray Watson is absent today. She starts pulling at her hair, and the cassette jostles in her lap. Laura is wound up too, jiggling her knees. The pair of them make Edwin think of those vibrating machines that mix paint by shaking the cans.

Edwin takes the microphone and says, "If you want a new-wave format, you'll have to ride another bus. Now let's crawl back in the stacks of wax for this oldie but goodie—Janis Joplin and 'A Little Bit Harder.'"

Lou Murphy nods along with the song. Laura's chewing gum pops like BBs. A while later, after picking up another passenger, Edwin glances in the rear-view mirror and sees Laura playing with the Plasmatics tape, pulling it out in a curly heap. Lou seems to be trying to shriek, but nothing comes out. Before Edwin can stop the bus, Laura has thrown the tape out the window.

"You didn't like it, Mr. Creech," Laura says when Edwin, after halting the bus on a shoulder, stalks down the aisle. "You said you didn't like it."

Edwin has never heard anyone sound so matter-of-fact, or look so reasonable. He has heard that since Laura began her classes, she has learned to set a table, make change, and dial a telephone. She even has a job at the training center, sorting seeds and rags. She is as hearty and domineering, yet as delicate and vulnerable, as Janis Joplin must have been. Edwin manages to move Lou to a front seat. She is sobbing silently, her lower jaw jerking, and Edwin realizes he is trembling too. He feels ashamed. After all, he is not driving the bus in order to make a name for himself. Yet it had felt right to insist on the format for his show. There is no appropriate way to apologize, or explain.

Edwin doesn't want to tell Sabrina about the incident. She is preoccupied with the play and often listens to him distractedly. Edwin has decided that he was foolish to suspect that she had a lover. The play is her love. Her nerves are on edge. One chilly afternoon, on the weekend before *Oklahoma!* opens, he suggests driving over to Kentucky Lake.

"You need a break," he tells her. "A little relaxation. I'm worried about you."

"This is nothing," she says. "Two measly lines. I'm not exactly a star."

"What if you were? Would you get an abortion?"

"What are you talking about? I'm not pregnant."

"You said once you would. Remember?"

"Oh. I would if the baby was going to be creepy like those people on your bus."

"But how would you know if it was?"

"They can tell." Sabrina stares at him and then laughs. "Through science."

In the early winter, the lake is deserted. The beaches are washed clean, and the water is clear and gray. Now and then, as they walk by the water, they hear a gunshot from the Land Between the Lakes wilderness area. "The Surrey with the Fringe on Top" is going through Edwin's head, and he wishes he could throw the *Oklahoma!* sound track in the lake, as easily as Laura Combs threw the Plasmatics out the window of the bus. He has an idea that after the play, Sabrina is going to feel a letdown too great for him to deal with.

When Sabrina makes a comment about the "artistic intention" of Rodgers and Hammerstein, Edwin says, "Do you know what Janis Joplin said?"

"No—what?" Sabrina stubs the toe of her jogging shoe in the sand.

"Janis Joplin said, 'I don't write songs. I just make 'em up.' I thought that was clever."

"That's funny, I guess."

"She said she was going to her high school reunion in Port Arthur, Texas. She said, 'I'm going to laugh a lot. They laughed me out of class, out of town, and out of the state.'"

"You sound like you've got that memorized," Sabrina says, looking at the sky.

"I saw it on TV one night when you were gone, an old tape of a Dick Cavett show. It seemed worth remembering." Edwin rests his arm around Sabrina's waist, as thin as a post. He says, "I see a lot of things on TV, when you're not there."

Wild ducks are landing on the water, scooting in like water skiers. Sabrina seems impressed by them. They stand there until the last one lands.

Edwin says, "I bet you can't even remember Janis Joplin. You're just a young girl, Sabrina. *Oklahoma!* will seem silly to you one of these days."

Sabrina hugs his arm. "That don't matter." She breaks into laughter. "You're cute when you're being serious."

Edwin grabs her hand and jerks her toward him. "Look, Sabrina. I was never serious before in my life. I'm just now, at this point in my life—this week—getting to be serious." His words scare him, and he adds with a grin that stretches his dimple, "I'm serious about *you.*"

"I know that," she says. She is leading the way along the water, through the trees, pulling him by the hand. "But you never believe how much I care about you," she says, drawing him to her. "I think we get along real good. That's why I wish you'd marry me instead of just stringing me along."

Edwin gasps like a swimmer surfacing. It is very cold on the beach. Another duck skis onto the water.

Oklahoma! has a four-night run, with one matinee. Edwin goes to the play three times, surprised that he enjoys it. Sabrina's lines come off differently each time, and each evening she discusses the impression she made.

Edwin tells her that she is the prettiest woman in the cast, and that her lines are cute. He wants to marry Sabrina, although he hasn't yet said he would. He wishes he could buy her a speedboat for a wedding present. She wants him to get a better-paying job, and she has ideas about a honeymoon cottage at the lake. It feels odd that Sabrina has proposed to him. He thinks of her as a liberated woman. The play is old-fashioned and phony. The love scenes between Jeff and Sue are comically stilted, resembling none of the passion and intrigue that Sabrina has reported. She compared them to Bogart and Bacall, but Edwin can't remember if she meant Jeff and Sue's roles or their actual affair. How did Sabrina know about Bogart and Bacall?

At the cast party, at Jeff's house, Jeff and Sue are publicly affectionate, getting away with it by playing their Laurey and Curly roles, but eventually Jeff's wife, who has made ham, potato salad, chiffon cakes, eggnog, and cranberry punch for sixty people, suddenly disappears from the party. Jeff whizzes off in his Camaro to find her. Sabrina whispers to Edwin, "Look how Sue's pretending nothing's happened. She's flirting with the guy who played Jud Fry." Sabrina, so excited that she bounces around on her tiptoes, is impressed by Jeff's house, which has wicker furniture and rose plush carpets.

Edwin drinks too much cranberry punch at the party, and most of the time he sits on a wicker love seat watching Sabrina flit around the room, beaming with the joy of her success. She is out of costume, wearing a sweatshirt with a rainbow on the front and pots of gold on her breasts. He realizes how proud he is of her. Her complexion is as smooth as a white mushroom, and she has crinkled her hair by braiding and unbraiding it. He watches her join some of the cast members around the piano to sing songs from the play, as though they cannot bear it that the play has ended. Sabrina seems to belong with them, these theatre people. Edwin knows they are not really theatre people. They are only local merchants putting on a play in their spare time. But Edwin is just a bus driver. He should get a better job so that he can send Sabrina to college, but he knows that he has to take care of his passengers. Their faces have become as familiar to him as the sound track of *Oklahoma!* He can practically hear Freddie Johnson shouting out her TV shows: "*Popeye* on! *Dukes* on!" He sees Sabrina looking at him lovingly. The singers shout, "Oklahoma, O.K.!"

Sabrina brings him a plastic glass of cranberry punch and sits with him on the love seat, holding his hand. She says, "Jim definitely said I should take a drama course at Murray State next semester. He was real encouraging. He said, 'Why not be in the play *and* take a course or two?' I could drive back and forth, don't you think?"

"Why not? You can have anything you want." Edwin plays with her hand.

"Jeff took two courses at Murray and look how good he was. Didn't you think he was good? I loved that cute way he went into that dance."

Edwin is a little drunk. He finds himself telling Sabrina about how he plays disc jockey on the bus, and he confesses to her his shame about the way he sounded off about his golden-oldie format. His mind is reeling and the topic sounds trivial, compared to Sabrina's future.

"Why *don't* you play a new-wave format?" she asks him. "It's what *every-body* listens to." She nods at the stereo, which is playing "You're Living in Your Own Private Idaho," by the B-52s, a song Edwin has often heard on the radio late at night when Sabrina is unwinding, moving into his arms. The music is violent and mindless, with a fast beat like a crazed parent abusing a child, thrashing it senseless.

"I don't know," Edwin says. "I shouldn't have said that to Lou Murphy. It bothers me."

"She don't know the difference," Sabrina says, patting his head. "It's ridiculous to make a big thing out of it. Words are so arbitrary, and people don't say what they mean half the time anyway."

"You should talk, Miss Oklahoma!" Edwin laughs, spurting a little punch on the love seat. "You and your two lines!"

"They're just lines," she says, smiling up at him and poking her finger into his dimple.

Some of Edwin's passengers bring him Christmas presents, badly wrapped, with tags that say his name in wobbly writing. Edwin puts the presents in a drawer, where Sabrina finds them.

"Aren't you going to open them?" she asks. "I'd be dying to know what was inside."

"I will eventually. Leave them there." Edwin knows what is in them without opening them. There is a bottle of shaving cologne, a tie (he never wears a tie), and three boxes of chocolate-covered cherries (he peeked in one, and the others are exactly the same shape). The presents are so pathetic Edwin could cry. He cannot bring himself to tell Sabrina what happened on the bus.

On the bus, the day before Christmas break, Ray Watson had a seizure. During that week, Edwin had been playing more Dylan and even some Stones. No Christmas music, except the Elvis album as usual for Ray. And then, almost unthinkingly, following Sabrina's advice, Edwin shifted formats. It seemed a logical course, as natural as Sabrina's herbal cosmetics, her mushroom complexion. It started with a revival of The Doors—Jim Morrison singing "Light My Fire," a song that was so long it carried them from the feed mill on one side of town to the rendering plant on the other. The passengers loved the way it stretched out, and some shook their heads and stomped their feet. As Edwin realized later, the whole bus was in a frenzy, and he should have known he was leading the passengers toward disaster, but the music seemed so appropriate. The Doors were a bridge from the past to the present, spanning those empty years—his marriages, the turbulence of the times—and connecting his youth solidly with the present. That day Edwin taped more songs from the radio—Adam and the Ants, Squeeze, the B-52s, the Psychedelic Furs, the Flying Lizards, Frankie and the Knockouts—and he made a point of replacing the Plasmatics tape for Lou Murphy. The new-wave format was a hit. Edwin believed the passengers understood what was happening. The frantic beat was a perfect expression of their aimlessness and frustration. Edwin had the impression that his passengers were growing, expanding, like the corn in *Oklahoma!,* like his own awareness. The new format went on for two days before Ray had his seizure. Edwin did not know exactly what happened, and it was possible Laura Combs had shoved Ray into the aisle. Edwin was in an awkward place on the highway, and he had to shoot across a bridge and over a hill before he could find a good place to stop. Everyone on the bus was making an odd noise, gasping or clapping, some imitating Ray's convulsions. Freddie Johnson was saying, "*Popeye* on! *Dukes* on!" Ray was on the floor, gagging, with his head thrown back, and twitching like someone being electrocuted. Laura Combs stood hunched in her seat, her mouth open in speechless terror, pointing her finger at Edwin. During the commotion, the Flying Lizards were chanting tonelessly, "I'm going to take my problems to the United Nations; there ain't no cure for the summertime blues."

Edwin followed all the emergency steps he had learned. He loosened Ray's clothing, slapped his cheeks, turned him on his side. Ray's skin was the color of the Hershey bars the man with the clubfoot collected. Edwin recalled grimly the first-aid book's ironic assurance that facial coloring was not important in cases of seizure. On the way to the hospital, Edwin clicked in a Donovan cassette. To steady himself, he sang along under his breath. "I'm just wild about saffron," he sang. It was a tune as carefree and lyrical as a field of daffodils. The passengers were screaming. All the way to the hospital, Edwin heard their screams, long and drawn out, orchestrated together into an accusing wail—eerie and supernatural.

Edwin's supervisors commended him for his quick thinking in handling Ray and getting him to the hospital, and everyone he has seen at the center has congratulated him. Ray's mother sent him an uncooked fruitcake made with graham cracker crumbs and marshmallows. She wrote a poignant note, thanking him for saving her son from swallowing his tongue. Edwin keeps thinking: what he did was no big deal; you can't swallow your tongue anyway; and it was Edwin's own fault that Ray had a seizure. He does not feel like a hero. He feels almost embarrassed.

Sabrina seems incapable of embarrassment. She is full of hope, like the Christmas season. *Oklahoma!* was only the beginning for her. She has a new job at McDonald's and a good part in *Life with Father.* She plans to commute to Murray State next semester to take a drama class and a course in Western Civilization that she needs to fulfill a requirement. She seems to assume that Edwin will marry her. He finds it funny that it is up to him to say yes. When she says she will keep her own name, Edwin wonders what the point is.

"My parents would just love it if we got married," Sabrina explains. "For them, it's worse for me to live in sin than to be involved with an older man."

"I didn't think I was really older," says Edwin. "But now I know it. I feel like I've had a developmental disability and it suddenly went away. Something like if Freddie Johnson learned to read. That's how I feel."

"I never thought of you as backward. Laid back is what I said." Sabrina laughs at her joke. "I'm sure you're going to impress Mom and Dad."

Tomorrow, she is going to her parents' farm, thirty miles away, for the Christmas holidays, and she has invited Edwin to go with her. He does not want to disappoint her. He does not want to go through Christmas without her. She has arranged her Christmas cards on a red string between the living room and the kitchen. She is making cookies, and Edwin has a feeling she is adding something strange to them. Her pale, fine hair is falling down in her face. Flour streaks her jeans.

"Let me show you something," Edwin says, bringing out a drugstore envelope of pictures. "One of my passengers, Merle Cope, gave me these."

"Which one is he? The one with the fits?"

"No. The one that claps all the time. He lives with a lot of sisters and brothers down in Langley's Bottom. It's a case of incest. The whole family's backward—your word. He's forty-seven and goes around with this big smile on his face, clapping." Edwin demonstrates.

He pins the pictures on Sabrina's Christmas card line with tiny red and green clothespins. "Look at these and tell me what you think."

Sabrina squints, going down the row of pictures. Her hands are covered with flour and she holds them in front of her, the way she learned from her actor friends to hold an invisible baby.

The pictures are black-and-white snapshots: fried eggs on cracked plates, an oilclothed kitchen table, a bottle of tomato ketchup, a fence post, a rusted tractor seat sitting on a stump, a corn crib, a sagging door, a toilet bowl, a cow, and finally, a horse's rear end.

"I can't look," says Sabrina. "These are disgusting."

"I think they're arty."

Sabrina laughs. She points to the pictures one by one, getting flour on some of them. Then she gets the giggles and can't stop. "Can you imagine what the developers thought when they saw that horse's ass?" she gasps. Her laughter goes on and on, then subsides with a little whimper. She goes back to the cookies. While she cuts out the cookies, Edwin takes the pictures down and puts them in the envelope. He hides the envelope in the drawer with the Christmas presents. Sabrina sets the cookie sheet in the oven and washes her hands.

Edwin asks, "How long do those cookies take?"

"Twelve minutes. Why?"

"Let me show you something else—in case you ever need to know it. The CPR technique—that's cardio-pulmonary resuscitation, in case you've forgotten."

Sabrina looks annoyed. "I'd rather do the Heimlich maneuver," she says. "Besides, you've practiced CPR on me a hundred times."

"I'm not practicing. I don't have to anymore. I'm beyond that." Edwin notices Sabrina's puzzled face. The thought of her fennel toothpaste, which makes her breath smell like licorice, fills him with something like nostalgia, as though she is already only a memory. He says, "I just want you to feel what it would be like. Come on." He leads her to the couch and sets her down. Her hands are still moist. He says, "Now just pretend. Bend over like this. Just pretend you have the biggest pain, right here, right in your chest, right there."

"Like this?" Sabrina is doubled over, her hair falling to her knees and her fists knotted between her breasts.

"Yes. Right in your heart."

QUESTIONS FOR DISCUSSION AND WRITING

1. The movement in the story is tied to the music Edwin plays. When the story begins he is playing the mellow oldies of the sixties on the bus for his adult passengers with developmental disabilities. Then, after refusing to play new-wave music, he shifts toward the end of the story and plays that format. What is the significance of the shift for Edwin and for those on the bus?

2. There is an obvious generation gap between Edwin and Sabrina. He is forty-three and she is just twenty. How does this gap manifest in the story and what do we conclude about what the future holds for this couple?

3. Sabrina favors the ERA and abortion and wants to keep her own name if she should marry Edwin. Yet she also likes keeping house and cooking and being domestic and admires household interiors. What is Mason suggesting about Sabrina's role in the story as a new-wave feminist?

4. Sabrina is mad about the music from the old American standard show-tune musical *Oklahoma!*, while Edwin feels he is growing as the music in the story changes for him to Jefferson Airplane, The Doors and the Grateful Dead. What is Mason revealing about the effects of music on the main characters?

5. One of the story's major themes is change. Edwin comments at one point that those who ride the bus would, at another time, have been in the attic or the barn. What are we to infer from this?

6. Edwin worries about Sabrina cheating on him and he has a feeling she will be "adding something strange" to the cookies she is baking. He has had two failed marriages and thinks of his previous wives largely in terms of food. Do you believe he can learn to keep up with "today's pace" as he is learning CPR and greater compassion and feels he is growing and, after playing The Doors, feels as if he has had a developmental disability that went away?

7. What are we to make of the last line in the story?

ON TECHNIQUE AND STYLE

1. What is the effect of Mason's focusing our attention on the relationships of Ray Watson and Laura Combs on the bus and Jeff and Sue of the *Oklahoma!* cast?

2. Mason weaves in a lot of popular culture—not only music but film (Kirk Douglas and John Travolta) and television (*WKRP*, *Popeye*, and *The Dukes of Hazard*). What is the overall effect of all these popular culture references? How or in what ways do they serve the story?
3. Why does the author bring Christmas into the story and focus on the Christmas gifts Edwin receives?

CULTURAL QUESTION

1. In this story, Mason has taken on the formidable task of portraying the lives of rural people as well as people with mental disabilities. How well does she succeed?

Envy; or, Yiddish in America

Cynthia Ozick

Cynthia Ozick (1928–   ) is one of America's leading writers of fiction and one of the most celebrated Jewish American writers. She also has published critical essays, poetry, and plays. Born in Manhattan, she is the daughter of Russian Jewish immigrants who fled persecution. She lived most of her life in New York City, but also lived in Pelham Bay in the Bronx and presently lives in Westchester County, New York. She graduated from New York University and received an MA degree from Ohio State University. The story included in this chapter is from her volume of short stories, The Pagan Rabbi and Other Stories, *first published in 1971. She is also the author of a number of collections of essays, including* Art and Ardor, Metaphor and Mystery, Portrait of the Artist as a Bad Character, *and* Quarrel and Quandary, *which won the National Book Critics Circle Award for Criticism in 2001. Her novels include* Trust, The Puttermesser Papers, The Cannibal Galaxy, The Messiah of Stockholm, *and* Heir to the Glimmering World. *A famous Holocaust story of hers, "The Shawl," was published as a novella and produced for the stage by film director Sidney Lumet. She is the first recipient of the Rea Award for short story writing and she also received a Guggenheim and the Mildred and Harold Strauss Living Award from the American Academy and Institute of Arts and Letters.*

Her story "Envy; or, Yiddish in America" is about older poets who have made their way from the Jewish diaspora to America where they remain obscure and unread in their mother tongue of Yiddish—except Ostrover, a modernist whom they envy and despise, in large part because of his success. The story ultimately focuses on the relationship between the story's main character, Edelshtein, and Hanna, the young niece of another older Yiddish poet, Vorovsky, whom Edelshtein imagines can redeem him and lift him out of the world of the ghetto he is imprisoned in by becoming his translator.

Rabbi Jacob said: "He who is walking along and studying, but then breaks off to remark, 'How lovely is that tree!' or 'How beautiful is that fallow field!'—Scripture regards such a one as having hurt his own being."

—from The Ethics of the Fathers

EDELSHTEIN, an American for forty years, was a ravenous reader of novels by writers "of"—he said this with a snarl—"Jewish extraction." He found them puerile, vicious, pitiable, ignorant, contemptible, above all stupid. In judging them he dug for his deepest vituperation—they were, he said, *"Amerikaner-gebaren."* Spawned in America, pogroms a rumor, *mamaloshen* a stranger, history a vacuum. Also many of them were still young, and had black eyes, black hair, and red beards. A few were blue-eyed, like the *cheder-yinglach* of his youth. Schoolboys. He was certain he did not envy them, but he read them like a sickness. They were reviewed and praised, and meanwhile they were considered Jews, and knew nothing. There was even a body of Gentile writers in reaction, beginning to show familiarly whetted teeth: the Jewish Intellectual Establishment was misrepresenting American letters, coloring it with an alien dye, taking it over, and so forth. Like Berlin and Vienna in the twenties. *Judenrein ist Kulturrein* was Edelshtein's opinion. Take away the Jews and where, O so-called Western Civilization, is your literary culture?

For Edelshtein Western Civilization was a sore point. He had never been to Berlin, Vienna, Paris, or even London. He had been to Kiev, though, but only once, as a young boy. His father, a *melamed,* had traveled there on a tutoring job and had taken him along. In Kiev they lived in the cellar of a big house owned by rich Jews, the Kirilovs. They had been born Katz, but bribed an official in order to Russify their name. Every morning he and his father would go up a green staircase to the kitchen for a breakfast of coffee and stale bread and then into the schoolroom to teach *chumash* to Alexei Kirilov, a red-cheeked little boy. The younger Edelshtein would drill him while his father dozed. What had become of Alexei Kirilov? Edelshtein, a widower in New York, sixty seven years old, a Yiddishist (so-called), a poet, could stare at any-thing at all—a subway car-card, a garbage can lid, a streetlight—and cause the return of Alexei Kirilov's face, his bright cheeks, his Ukraine-accented Yid-dish, his shelves of mechanical toys from Germany—trucks, cranes, wheelbar-rows, little colored autos with awnings overhead. Only Edelshtein's father was expected to call him Alexei—everyone else, including the young Edelshtein, said Avremeleh. Avremeleh has a knack of getting things by heart. He had a golden head. Today he was a citizen of the Soviet Union. Or was he finished, dead, in the ravine at Babi Yar? Edelshtein remembered every coveted screw of the German toys. With his father he left Kiev in the spring and returned to Minsk. The mud, frozen into peaks, was melting. The train carriage reeked of urine and the dirt seeped through their shoelaces into their socks.

And the language was lost, murdered. The language—a museum. Of what other language can it be said that it died a sudden and definite death, in a given decade, on a given piece of soil? Where are the speakers of ancient Etruscan? Who was the last man to write a poem in Linear B? Attrition, assimilation. Death by mystery not gas. The last Etruscan walks around inside some Sicilian. Western Civilization, that pod of muck, lingers on and on. The Sick Man of Europe with his big globe-head, rotting, but at home in bed. Yiddish, a littleness, a tiny light—oh little holy light!—dead, vanished. Perished. Sent into darkness.

This was Edelshtein's subject. On this subject he lectured for a living. He swallowed scraps. Synagogues, community centers, labor unions underpaid him to suck on the bones of the dead.Smoke. He traveled from borough to borough, suburb to suburb, mourning in English the death of Yiddish. Sometimes he tried to read one or two of his poems. At the first Yiddish word the painted old ladies of the Reform Temples would begin to titter from shame, as at a stand-up television comedian. Orthodox and Conservative men fell instantly asleep. So he reconsidered, and told jokes:

Before the war there was held a great International Esperanto Convention. It met in Geneva. Esperanto scholars, doctors of letters, learned men, came from all over the world to deliver papers on the genesis, syntax, and functionalism of Esperanto. Some spoke of the social value of an international language, others of its beauty. Every nation on earth was represented among the lectueres. All the papers were given in Esperanto. Finally the meeting was concluded, and the tired great men wandered companionably along the corridors, where at last they began to converse casually among themselves in their international language: *"Nu, vos macht a yid?"*

After the war a funeral cortège was moving slowly down a narrow street on the Lower East Side. The cars had left the parking lot behind the chapel in the Bronx and were on their way to the cemetery in Staten Island. Their route took them past the newspaper offices of the last Yiddish daily left in the city. There were two editors, one to run the papers off the press and the other to look out the window. The one looking out the window saw the funeral procession passing by and called to his colleague: "Hey Mottel, print one less!"

But both Edelshtein and his audiences found the jokes worthless. Old jokes. They were not the right kind. They wanted jokes about weddings—spiral staircases, doves flying out of cages, bashful medical students—and he gave them funerals. To speak of Yiddish was to preside over funeral. He was a rabbi who had survived his whole congregation. Those for whom his tongue was no riddle were specters.

The new Temples scared Edelshtein. He was afraid to use the word *shul* in these palaces—inside, vast mock-bronze Tablets, mobiles of outstretched hands rotating on a motor, gigantic dangling Tetragrammatons in transparent plastic like chandeliers, platforms, altars, daises, pulpits, aisles, pews, polished-oak bins for prayerbooks printed in English with made-up new prayers in them. Everything smelled of wet plaster. Everything was new. The refreshment tables were long and luminous—he saw glazed cakes, snowheaps of egg salad, herring, salmon, tuna, whitefish, gefilte fish, polls of sour cream, silver electric coffee urns, bowls of lemon-slices, pyramids of bread, waferlike teacups from the Black Forest, Indian-brass trays of hard cheeses, golden bottles set up in rows like ninepins, great sculptured butter-birds, Hansel-and-Gretel houses of cream cheese and fruitcake, bars, butlers, fat napery, carpeting deep as honey. He learned their term for their architecture: "soaring." In one place—a flat wall of beige brick in Westchester—he read Scripture riveted on in letters fashioned from 14-karat gold molds: "And thou shalt see My back; but My face shall not be seen." Later that night he spoke in Mount Vernon, and in the marble lobby afterward he heard an adolescent girl mimic his inflections. It amazed him: often he forgot he had an accent. In the train going back to Manhattan he slid into a miniature jogging doze—it was a little nest of sweetness there inside the flaps of his overcoat, and he dreamed he was in Kiev, with his father. He looked through the open schoolroom door at the smoking cheeks of Alexei Kirilov, eight years old. "Avremeleh," he called, "Avremeleh, *kum tsu mir, lebst ts' geshtorben?*" He heard himself yelling in English: Thou shalt see my asshole! A blech woke him to hot fear. He was afraid he might be, unknown to himself all his life long, a secret pederast.

He had no children and only a few remote relations (a druggist cousin in White Plains, a cleaning store in-law hanging on somewhere among the blacks in Brownsville), so he loitered often in Baumzweig's apartment—dirty mirrors and rusting crystal, a hazard and invitation to cracks, an abandoned exhausted corridor. Lives had passed through it and were gone. Watching Baumzweig and his wife—gray-eyed, sluggish, with a plump Polish nose—it came to him that at this age. his own and theirs, it was the same having children or not having them. Baumzweig had two sons, one married and a professor at San Diego, the other at Stanford, not yet thirty, in love with his car. The San Diego son had a son. Sometimes it seemed that it must be in deference to his childlessness that Baumzweig and his wife pretended a detachment from their offspring. The grandson's photo—a fat-lipped blond child of three or so—was wedged between two wine glasses on top of the china closet. But then it became plain that they could not imagine the lives of their children. Nor could the children imagine their lives. The parents were too helpless to explain, the sons were too impatient to explain. So they had given each other up to a common muteness. In that apartment Josh and Mickey had grown up answering in English the Yiddish of their parents. Mutes. Mutations. What right had these boys to spit out the Yiddish that had bred them, and only for the sake of Western Civilization? Edelshtein knew the titles of their Ph.D. theses: literary boys, one was on Sir Gawain and the Green Knight, the other was on the novels of Carson McCullers.

Baumzweig's lethargic wife was intelligent. She told Edelshtein he too had a child, also a son. "Yourself, yourself," she said. "You remember yourself when you were in little boy, and *that* little boy is the one you love, *him* you trust, *him* you bless, *him* you bring up in hope to a good manhood." She spoke a rich Yiddish, but high-pitched.

Baumzweig had a good job, a sinecure, a pension in disguise, with an office, a part-time secretary, a typewriter with Hebrew characters, ten-to-three hours. In 1910 a laxative manufacturer—a philanthropist—had founded an orgaization called the Yiddish-American Alliance for Letters and Social Progress. The original illustrious members were all dead—even the famous poet Yehoash was said to have paid dues for a month or so—but there was a trust providing for the group's continuation, and enough money to pay for a biannual periodical in Yiddish. Baumzweig was the editor of this, but of the Alliance nothing was left, only some crumbling brown snapshots of Jews in derbies. His salary check came from the laxative manufacturer's grandson—a Republican politician, an Episcopalian. The name of the celebrated product was LUKEWARM: it was advertised as delightful to children when dissolved in lukewarm cocoa. The name of the obscure periodical was *Bitterer Yam,* Bitter Sea, but it had so few subscribers that Baumzweig's wife called it Invisible Ink. In it Baumzweig published much of his own poetry and a little of Edelshtein's. Baumzweig wrote mostly of Death, Edelshtein mostly of Love. They were both sentimentalists, but not about each other. They did not like each other, though they were close friends.

Sometimes they read aloud among the dust of empty bowls their newest poems, with an agreement beforehand not to criticize: Paula should be the critic. Carrying coffee back and forth in cloudy glasses, Baumzweig's wife said: "Oh, very nice, very nice. But so sad. Gentlemen, life is not that sad." After this she would always kiss Edelshtein on the forehead, a lazy kiss, often leaving stuck on his eyebrow a crumb of Danish: very slightly she was a slattern.

Edelshtein's friendship with Baumbzweig had a ferocious secret: it was moored entirely to their agreed hatred for the man they called *der chazer.* He was named Pig because of his extraordinarily white skin, like a tissue of pale ham, and also because in the last decade he had become unbelievably famous. When they did not call him Pig they called him *shed*—Devil. They also called him Yankee Doodle. His name was Yankel Ostrover, and he was a writer of stories.

They hated him for the amazing thing that had happened to him—his fame—but this they never referred to. Instead they discussed his style: his Yiddish was impure, his snetences lacked grace and sweep, his paragraph transitions were amateur, vile. Or else they raged against his subject matter, which was insanely sexual, pornographic, paranoid, freakish—men who embraced men, women who caressed women, sodomists of every variety, boys copulating with hens, butchers who drank blood for strength behind the knife. All the stories were set in an imaginary Polish village, Zwrdl, and by now there was almost no American literary intellectual alive who had not learned to say Zwrdl when he meant lewd. Ostrover's wife was reputed to be a high-born Polish Gentile woman from the "real" Zwrdl, the daughter in fact of a minor princeling, who did not know a word of Yiddish and read her husband's fiction falteringly, in English translation—but both Edelshtein and Baumzweig had encountered her often enough over the years, at this meeting and that, and regarded her as no more impressive than a pot of stale fish. Her Yiddish had an unpleasant gargling Galician accent, her vocabulary was a thin soup—they joked that it was correct to say she spoke no Yiddish—and she mewed it like a peasant, comparing prices. She was a short square woman, a cube with low-slung udders and a flat backside. It was partly Ostrover's mockery, partly his self-advertising, that had converted her into a little princess. He would make her go into their bedroom to get a whip he claimed she had used on her bay, Romeo, trotting over her father's lands in her girlhood. Baumzweig often said this same whip was applied to the earlobes of Ostrover's translators, unhappy pairs of collaborators he changed from month to month, never satisfied.

Ostrover's glory was exactly in this: that he required translators. Though he wrote only in Yiddish, his fame was American, national, international. They considered him a "modern." Ostrover was free of the prison of Yiddish! Out, out—he had burst out, he was in the world of reality.

And how had he begun? The same as anybody, a columnist for one of the Yiddish dailies, a humorist, a cheap fast article-writer, a squeezer-out of real-life tales. Like anybody else, he saved up a few dollars, put a paper clip over his stories, and hired a Yiddish press to print up a hundred copies. A book. Twenty-five copies he gave to people he counted as relatives, another twenty-five he sent to enemies and rivals, the rest he kept under his bed in the original cartons. Like anybody else, his literary gods were Chekhov and Tolstoy, Peretz and Sholem Aleichem. From this, how did he come to *The New Yorker, to Playboy,* to big lecture fees, invitations to Yale and M.I.T. and Vassar, to the Midwest, to Buenos Aires, to a literary agent, to a publisher on Madison Avenue?

"He sleeps with the right translators," Paura said. Edelshtein gave out a whinny. He knew some of Ostrover's translators—a spinster hack in dresses below the knee, occasionally a certain half-mad and drunken lexicographer, college boys with a dictionary.

Thirty years ago, straight out of Poland via Tel Aviv, Ostrover crept into a toying affair with Mireleh, Edelshtein's wife. He had left Palestine during the 1939 Arab riots, not, he said, out of fear, out of integrity rather—it was a country which had turned its face against Yiddish. Yiddish was not honored in Tel Aviv or Jerusalem. In the Negev it was worthless. In the God-given State of Israel they had no use for the language of the bad little interval between Canaan and now. Yiddish was inhabited by the past, the new Jews did not want it. Mireleh liked to hear these anecdotes of how rotten it was in Israel for Yiddish and Yiddishists. In Israel the case was even lamer than in New York, thank God! There was after all a reason to live the life they lived: it was worse somewhere else. Mireleh was a tragedian. She carried herself according to her impression of how a barren woman should sit, squat, stand, cat and sleep, talked constantly of her six miscarriages, and was vindictive about Edelshtein's spermcount. Ostrover would arrive in the rain, crunch down on the sofa, complain about the transportation from the Bronx to the West Side, and begin to woo Mireleh. He took her out to supper, to his special café, to Second Avenue vaudeville, even home to his apartment near Crotona Park to meet his little princess Pesha. Edelshtein noticed with self-curiosity that he felt no jealousy whatever, but he thought himself obliged to throw a kitchen chair at Ostrover. Ostrover had very fine teeth, his own; the chair knocked off half a lateral incisor, and Edelshtein wept at the flaw. Immediately he led Ostrover to the dentist around the corner.

The two wives, Mieleh and Pesha, seemed to be falling in love: they had dates, they went to museums and movies together, they poked one another and laughed day and night, they shared little privacies, they carried pencil-box rulers in their purses and showed each other certain hilarious measurements, they even became pregnant in the same month. Pesha had her third daughter, Mireleh her seventh miscarriage. Edelshtein was griefstricken but elated. *"My* sperm-count?" he screamed. *"Your* belly! Go fix the machine before you blame the oil!" When the dentist's bill came for Ostrover's jacket crown, Edelshtein sent it to Ostrover. At this injustice Ostrover dismissed Mireleh and forbade Pesha to go anywhere with her ever again.

About Mireleh's affair with Ostrover Edelshtein wrote the following malediction:

You, why do you snuff out my sons, my daughters?
Worse than Mother Eve, cursed to break waters
for little ones to float out upon in their tiny barks of skin,
you, merciless one, cannot even bear the fruit of sin.

It was published to much gossip in Bitterer *Yam* in the spring of that year—one point at issue being whether "snuff out" was the right term in such a watery context. (Baumzweig, a less oblique stylist, had suggested "drown.") The late Zimmerman, Edelshtein's cruelest rival, wrote in a letter to Baumzweig (which Baumzweig read on the telephone to Edelshtein) :

Who is the merciless one, after all, the barren woman who makes the house peaceful with no infantile caterwauling, or the excessively fertile poet who bears the fruit of his sin—namely his untalented verses? He bears it, but who can bear it? In one breath he runs from seas to trees. Like his ancestors the amphibians, puffed up with arrogance. Hersheleh Frog! Why did God give Hersheleh Edelshtein an unfaithful wife? To punish him for writing trash.

Around the same time Ostrover wrote a story: two women loved each other so much they mourned because they could not give birth to one another's children. Both had husbands, one virile and hearty, the other impotent, with a withered organ, a *shlimazal.* They seized the idea of making a tool out of one of the husbands: they agreed to transfer their love for each other into the man, and bear the child of their love through him. So both women turned to the virile husband, and both women conceived. But the woman who had the withered husband could not bear her child: it withered in her womb. "As it is written," Ostrover concluded, "Paradise is only for those who have already been there."

A stupid fable! Three decades later—Mireleh dead of a cancerous uterus, Pesha encrusted with royal lies in *Time* magazine (which photographed the whip)—this piece of insignificant mystification, this *pollution,* included also in Ostrover's *Complete Tales* (Kimmel & Segal, 1968), was the subject of gradu-ate dissertations in comparative literature, as if Ostrover were Thomas Mann, or even Albert Camus. When all that happened was that Pesha and Mireleh had gone to the movies together now and then—and such a long time ago! All the same, Ostrover was released from the dungeon of the dailies, from *Bitterer Yam* and even seedier nullities, he was free, the outside world knew his name. And why Ostrover? Why not somebody else? Was Ostrover more gifted than Komorsky? Did he think up better stories than Horowitz? Why does the world outside pick on an Ostrover instead of an Edelshtein or even a Baumzweig? What occult knack, what craft, what crooked convergence of planets drove translators to grovel before Ostrover's naked swollen sen-tences with their thin little threadbare pants always pulled down? Who had discovered that Ostrover was a "modern"? His Yiddish, however-fevered on itself, bloated, was still Yiddish, it was still *mamaloshen,* it still squeaked up to God with a littleness, a familiarity, an elbow-poke, it was still pieced together out of *shtetl* rags, out of a baby *aleph,* a toddler *beys*—so why Ostrover? Why only Ostrover? Ostrover should be the only one? Everyone else sentenced to darkness, Ostrover alone saved? Ostrover the survivor? As if hidden in the Dutch attic like that child. *His* diary, so to speak, the only documentation of what was. Like Ringelblum of Warsaw. Ostrover was to be the only evidence that there was once a Yiddish tongue, a Yiddish literature? And all the others lost? Lost! Drowned. Snuffed out. Under the earth. As if never.

Edelshtein composed a letter to Ostrover's publishers:

Kimmel & Segal
244 Madison Avenue, New York City

My dear Mr. Kimmel, and very honored Mr. Segal:

I am writing to you in reference to one Y. Ostrover, whose works you are the company that places them before the public's eyes. Be kindly enough to forgive all flaws of English Expression. Undoubtedly, in the course of his busi-ness with you, you have received from Y. Ostrover, letters in English, even worse than this. (I HAVE NO TRANSLATOR!) We immigrants, no matter how long already Yankified, stay inside always green and never attain to actual native writing Smoothness. For one million green writers, one Nabokov, one Kosinski. I mention these to show my extreme familiarness with American Literature in all Contemporaneous avatars. In your language I read, let us say, wolfishly. I regard myself as a very Keen critic, esp. concerning so-called Amer.-Jewish writers. If you would give time I could willingly explain to you many clear opinions I have concerning these Jewish-Amer. boys and girls such as (not alphabetical) Roth Philip/ Rosen Norma/ Melammed Bernie/ Friedman B. J./ Paley Grace/ Bellow Saul/ Mailer Norman. Of the latter having just read several recent works including political I would like to remind him what F. Kafka, rest in peace, said to the German-speaking, already very comfortable, Jews of Prague, Czechoslovakia; "Jews of Prague! You know more Yiddish than you think!"

Perhaps, since doubtless you do not read the Jewish Press, you are not informed. Only this month all were taken by surprise! In that filthy propaganda *Sovietish Heymland* which in Russia they run to show that their prisoners the Jews are not prisoners—a poem! By a 20-year-old young Russian Jewish girl! Yiddish will yet live through our young. Though I doubt it as do other pessimists. However, this is not the point! I ask you—what does the following personages mean to you, you who are Sensitive men, Intelligent, and with closely-warmed Feelings! Lyessin, Reisen, Yehoash! H. Leivik himself! Itzik Manger, Chaim Grade, Aaron Zeitlen, Jacob Glatshtein, Eliezer Greenberg! Molodowsky and Korn, ladies, gifted! Dovid Ignatov, Morris Rosenfeld, Moishe Nadir, Moishe Leib Halpern, Reuven Eisland, Mani Leib, Zisha Landau! I ask you! Frug, Peretz, Vintchevski, Bovshover, Edelshtat! Velvl Zhbarzher, Avrom Goldfaden! A. Rosenblatt! Y.Y. Schwartz, Yoisef Rollnick! These are all our glorious Yiddish poets. And if I would add to them our beautiful recent Russian brother-poets that were killed by Stalin with his pockmarks, for instance Peretz Markish, would you know any name of theirs? No! THEY HAVE NO TRANSLATORS!

Esteemed Gentlemen, you publish only one Yiddish writer, not even a Poet, only a Story-writer. I humbly submit you give serious wrong Impressions. That we have produced nothing else. I again refer to your associate Y. Ostrover. Ido not intend to take away from him any possible talent by this letter, but wish to WITH VIGOROUSNESS assure you that others also exist without notice being bothered over them! I myself am the author and also publisher of four tomes of poetry: *N'shomeh un Guf, Zingen un Freyen, A Velt ohn Vint, A Shtundeh mit Shney.* To wit, "Soul and Body," "Singing and Being Happy," "A World with No Wind," "An Hour of Snow," these are my Deep-Feeling titles.

Please inform me if you will be willing to provide me with a translator for these very worthwhile pieces of hidden writings, or, to use a Hebrew Expression, "Buried Light."

                                                        Yours very deeply respectful.

He received an answer in the same week.

Dear Mr. Edelstein:

Thank you for your interesting and informative letter. We regret that, unfortunately, we cannot furnish you with a translator. Though your poetry may well be of the quality you claim for it, practically speaking, reputation must precede translation.

Yours sincerely.

A lie! Liars!

Dear Kimmel, dear Segal,

Did YOU, Jews without tongues, ever hear of Ostrover before you found him translated everywhere? In Yiddish he didn't exist for you! For you Yiddish has no existence! A darkness inside a cloud! Who can see it, who can hear it? The world has no ears for the prisoner! You sign yourself "Yours." You're not mine and I'm not Yours!

Sincerely.

He then began to search in earnest for a translator. Expecting little, he wrote to the spinster hack.

Esteemed Edelshtein [she replied] :

To put it as plainly as I can—a plain woman should be as plain in her words—you do not know the world of practicality, of reality. Why should you? You're a poet, an idealist. When a big magazine pays Ostrover $500, how much do I get? Maybe $75. If he takes a rest for a month and doesn't write, what then? Since he's the only one they want to print he's the only one worth translating. Suppose I translated one of your nice little love songs? Would anyone buy it? Foolishness even to ask. And if they bought it, should I slave for the $5? You don't know what I go through with Ostrover anyhow. He sits me down in his dining room, his wife brings in a samovar of tea—did you ever hear anything as pretentious as this—and sits also, watching me. She has jealous eyes. She watches my ankles, which aren't bad. Then we begin. Ostrover reads aloud the first sentence the way he wrote it, in Yiddish. I write it down, in English. Right away it starts. Pesha reads what I put down and says, "That's no good, you don't catch his idiom." Idiom! She knows! Ostrover says, "The last word sticks in my throat. Can't you do better than that? A little more robustness." We look in the dictionary, the thesaurus, we scream out different words, trying, trying. Ostrover doesn't like any of them. Suppose the word is "big." We go through huge, vast, gigantic, enormous, gargantuan, monstrous, etc., etc., etc., and finally Ostrover says—by now it's five hours later, my tonsils hurt, I can hardly stand—"all right, so let it be 'big.' Simplicity above all." Day after day like this! And for $75 is it worth it? Then after this he fires me and gets himself a college boy! Or that imbecile who cracked up over the mathematics dictionary!

Until he needs me. However I get a little glory out of it. Everyone says, "There goes Ostrover's translator." In actuality I'm his pig, his stool (I mean that in both senses, I assure you). You write that he has no talent. That's your opinion, maybe you're not wrong, but let me tell you he has a talent for pressure. The way among *them* they write careless novels, hoping they'll be transformed into beautiful movies and sometimes it happens—that's how it is with him. Never mind the quality of his Yiddish, what will it turn into when it becomes English? Transformation is all he cares for—and in English he's a cripple—like, please excuse me, yourself and everyone of your generation. But Ostrover has the sense to be a suitor. He keeps all his translators in a perpetual frenzy of envy for each other, but they're just rubble and offal to him, they aren't the object of his suit. What he woos is *them*. Them! You understand me, Edelshtein? He stands on the backs of hacks to reach. I know you call me hack, and it's all right, by myself I'm what you think me, no imagination, so-so ability (I too once wanted to be a poet, but that's another life)—with Ostrover on my back I'm something else: I'm "Ostrover's translator." You think that's nothing? It's an entrance into *them*. I'm invited everywhere, I go to the same parties Ostrover goes to. Everyone looks at me and thinks I'm a bit freakish, but they say: "It's Ostrover's translator." A marriage. Pesha, that junk-heap, is less married to Ostrover than I am. Like a wife, I have the supposedly passive role. Supposedly: who knows what goes on in the bedroom? An unmarried person like myself becomes good at guessing at these matters. The same with translation. Who 'makes the language Ostrover is famous for? You ask: what has persuaded *them* that he's a "so-called modern"?—a sneer. Aha. *Who* has read James Joyce, Ostrover or I? I'm fifty-three years old. I wasn't born back of Hlusk for nothing, I didn't go to Vassar for nothing—do you understand me? I got caught in between, so I got squeezed. Between two organisms. A cultural hermaphrodite, neither one nor the other. I have a forked tongue. When I fight for five hours to make Ostrover say "big" instead of "gargantuan," when I take out all the nice homey commas he sprinkles like a fool, when I drink his wife's stupid tea and then go home with a watery belly—*then* he's being turned into a "modern," you see? I'm the one! No one recognizes this, of course, they think it's something in side the stories themselves, when actually it's the way I dress them up and paint over them. It's all cosmetics, I'm a cosmetician, a painter, the one they pay to do the same job on the corpse in the mortuary, among *them* . . . don't, though, bore me with your criticisms. I tell you his Yiddish doesn't matter. Nobody's Yiddish matters. Whatever's in Yiddish doesn't matter.

The rest of the letter—all women are long-winded, strong-minded—he did not read. He had already seen what she was after: a little bit of money, a little bit of esteem. A miniature megalomaniac: she fancied herself the *real* Ostrover. She believed she had fashioned herself a genius out of a rag. A rag turned into a sack, was that genius? She lived out there in the light, with *them:* naturally she wouldn't waste her time on an Edelshtein. In the bleakness. Dark where he was. An idealist! How had this good word worked itself up in society to become an insult? A darling word nevertheless. Idealist. The difference between him and Ostrover was this: Ostrover wanted to save only himself, Edelshtein wanted to save Yiddish.

Immediately he felt he lied.

With Baumzweig and Paula he went to the 92nd Street Y to hear Ostrover read. "Self-mortification," Paula said of this excursion. It was a snowy night. They had to shove their teeth into the wind, tears of suffering iced down their cheeks, the streets from the subway were Siberia. "Two Christian saints, self-flagellation," she muttered, "with chains of icicles they hit themselves." They paid for the tickets with numb fingers and sat down toward the front. Edelshtein felt paralyzed. His toes stung, prickled, then seemed diseased, grangrenous, furnace-like. The cocoon of his bed at home, the pen he kept on his night table, the first luminous line of his new poem lying there waiting to be born—*Oh that I might like a youth be struck with the blow of belief*—all at once he knew how to go on with it, what it was about and what he meant by it, the hall around him seemed preposterous, unnecessary, why was he here? Crowds, huddling, the whine of folding chairs lifted and dropped, the babble, Paula yawning next to him with squeezed and wrinkled eyelids, Baumzweig blowing his flat 'nose into a blue plaid handkerchief and exploding a great green flower of snot, why was he in such a place at this? What did such a place have in common with what he knew, what he felt?

Paula craned around her short neck inside a used-up skunk collar to read the frieze, mighty names, golden letters, Moses, Einstein, Maimonides, Heine. Heine. Maybe Heine knew what Edelshtein knew, a convert. But these, ushers in fine jackets, skinny boys carrying books (Ostrover's), wearing them nearly, costumed for blatant bookishness, blatant sexuality, in pants crotch-snug, penciling buttocks on air, mustachioed, some hairy to the collarbone, shins and calves menacing as hammers, and girls, tunics, knees, pants, boots, little hidden sweet tongues, black-eyed. Woolly smell of piles and piles of coats. For Ostrover! The hall was full, the ushers with raised tweed wrists directed all the rest into an unseen gallery nearby: a television screen there, on which the little gray ghost of Ostrover, palpable and otherwise white as a washed pig, would soon flutter. The Y. Why? Edelshtein also lectured at Y's—Elmhurst, Eastchester, Rye, tiny platforms, lecterns too tall for him, catalogues of vexations, his sad recitations to old people. Ladies and Gentlemen, they have cut out my vocal cords, the only language I can freely and fluently address you in, my darling *mamaloshen,* surgery, dead, the operation was a success. Edelshtein's Y's were all old people's homes, convalescent factories, asylums. To himself he sang,

Why	*Farvos di Vy ?*
the Y?	*Ich reyd*
Lectures	*ohn freyd*
to specters,	*un sheydim tantsen derbei,*

aha! specters, if my tongue has no riddle for you, Ladies and Gentlemen, you are specter, wraith, phantom, I have invented you, you are my imagining, there is no one here at all, an empty chamber, a vacant valve, abandoned, desolate. Everyone gone. *Pust vi dem kalten shul mein harts* (another first line left without companion-lines, fellows, followers), the cold study-house, spooks dance there. Ladies and Gentlemen, if you find my tongue a riddle, here is another riddle: How is a Jew like a giraffe? A Jew too has no vocal cords. God blighted Jew and giraffe, one in full, one by half. And no salve. Baumzweig hawked up again. Mucus the sheen of the sea. In God's Creation no thing without beauty however perverse. *Khrakeh khrakeh.* Baumzweig's roar the only noise in the hall. "Shah," Paula said, *"ot kumt der shed."*

Gleaming, gleaming, Ostrover stood—high, far, the stage broad, brilliant, the lectern punctilious with microphone and water pitcher. A rod of powerful light bored into his eye sockets. He had a moth-mouth as thin and dim as a chalk line, a fence of white hair erect over his ears, a cool voice.

"A new story," he announced, and spittle flashed on his lip. "It isn't obscene, so I consider it a failure."

"Devil," Paula whispered, "washed white pig, Yankee Doodle."

"Shah," Baumzweig said, *"lomir heren."*

Baumzweig wanted to hear the devil, the pig! Why should anyone want to hear him? Edelshtein, a little bit deaf, hung forward. Before him, his nose nearly in it, the hair of a young girl glistened—some of the stage light had become enmeshed in it. Young, young! Everyone young! Everyone for Ostrover young! A modern.

Cautiously, slyly, Edelshtein let out, as on a rope, little bony shiverings of attentiveness. Two rows in front of him he glimpsed the spinster hack, Chaim Vorovsky the drunken lexicographer whom too much mathematics had crazed, six unknown college boys.

Ostrover's story:

Satan appears to a bad poet. "I desire fame," says the poet, "but I cannot attain it, because I come from Zwrdl, and the only language I can write is Zwrdlish. Unfortunately no one is left in the world who can read Zwrdlish. That is my burden. Give me fame, and I will trade you my soul for it."

"Are you quite sure," says Satan, "that you have estimated the dimensions of your trouble entirely correctly?" "What do you mean?" says the poet, "Perhaps," says Satan, "the trouble lies in your talent. Zwrdl or no Zwrdl, it's very weak." "Not so!" says the poet, "and I'll prove it to you. Teach me French, and in no time I'll be famous." "All right," says Satan, "as soon as I say Glup you'll know French perfectly better than de Gaulle. But I'll be generous with you. French is such an easy language, I'll take only a quarter of your soul for it."

And he said Glup. And in an instant there was the poet, scribbling away in fluent French. But still no publisher in France wanted him and he remained obscure. Back came Satan: "So the French was no good, *mon vieux? Tant pis!*" "Feh," says the poet, "what do you expect from a people that kept colonies, they should know what's good in the poetry line? Teach me Italian, after all even the Pope dreams in Italian." "Another quarter of your soul," says Satan, ringing it up in his portable cash register. And Glup! There he was again, the poet, writing *terza rima* with such fluency and melancholy that the Pope would have been moved to holy tears of praise if only he had been able to see it in print—unfortunately every publisher in Italy sent the manuscript back with a plain rejection slip, no letter.

"What? Italian no good either?" exclaims Satan. *"Mamma mia,* why don't you believe me, little brother, it's not the language, it's you." It was the same with Swahili and Armenian, Glup!—failure, Glup!—failure, and by now, having rung up a quarter of it at a time, Satan owned the poet's entire soul, and took him back with him to the Place of Fire. "I suppose you'll burn me up," says the poet bitterly. "No, no," says Satan, "we don't go in for that sort of treatment for so silken a creature as a poet. Well? Did you bring everything? I told you to pack carefully! Not to leave behind a scrap!" I brought my whole file," says the poet, and sure enough, there it was, strapped to his back, a big black metal cabinet. "Now empty it into the Fire," Satan orders. "My poems! Not all my poems? My whole life's output?" cries the poet in anguish. "That's right, do as I say," and the poet obeys, because, after all, he's in hell and Satan owns him. "Good," says Satan, "now come with me, I'll show you to your room."

A perfect room, perfectly appointed, not too cold, not too hot, just the right distance from the great Fire to be comfortable. A jewel of a desk, with a red leather top, a lovely swivel chair cushioned in scarlet, a scarlet Persian rug on the floor, nearby a red refrigerator stocked with cheese and pudding and pickles, a glass of reddish tea already steaming on a little red table. One window without a curtain. "That's your Inspiring View," says Satan, "look out and see." Nothing outside but the Fire cavorting splendidly, flecked with unearthly colors, turning itself and rolling up into unimaginable new forms. "It's beautiful," marvels the poet. "Exactly," says Satan. "It should inspire you to the composition of many new verses." "Yes, yes! May I begin, your Lordship?" "That's why I brought you here," says Satan. "Now sit down and write, since you can't help it anyhow. There is only one stipulation. The moment you finish a stanza you must throw it out of the window, like this." And to illustrate, he tossed out a fresh page.

Instantly a flaming wind picked it up and set it afire, drawing it into the great central conflagration. "Remember that you are in hell," Satan says sternly, "here you write only for oblivion." The poet begins to weep. "No difference, no difference! It was the same up there! O Zwrdl, I curse you that you nurtured me!" "And still he doesn't see the point!" says Satan, exasperated. "Glup glup glup glup glup glup glup! Now write." The poor poet began to scribble, one poem after another, and lo! suddenly he forgot every word of Zwrdlish he ever knew, faster and faster he wrote, he held on to the pen as if it alone kept his legs from flying off on their own, he wrote in Dutch and in English, in German and in Turkish, in Santali and in Sassak, in Lapp and in Kurdish, in Welsh and in Rhaeto-Romanic, in Niasese and in Nicobarese, in Galcha and in Ibanag, in Ho and in Khmer, in Ro and in Volapük, in Jagatai and in Swedish, in Tulu and in Russian, in Irish and in Kalmuck! He wrote in every language but Zwrdlish, and every poem he wrote he had to throw out the window because it was trash anyhow, though he did not realize it. . . .

Edelshtein, spinning off into a furious and alien meditation, was not sure how the story ended. But it was brutal, and Satan was again in the ascendancy: he whipped down aspiration with one of Ostrover's sample aphorisms,

dense and swollen as a phallus, but sterile all the same. The terrifying laughter, a sea-wave all around: it broke toward Edelshtein, meaning to lash him to
bits. Laugher for Ostrover. Little jokes, little jokes, all they wanted was jokes!
"Baumzweig," he said, pressing himself down across Paula's collar (under it
her plump breasts), "he does it for spite, you see that?"

But Baumzweig was caught in the laughter. The edges of his mouth were
beaten by it. He whirled in it like a bug. "Bastard!" he said.

"Bastard," Edelshtein said reflectively.

"He means *you,*" Baumzweig said.

"Me?"

"An allegory. You see how everything fits. . . ."

"If you write letters, you shouldn't mail them," Paula said reasonably. "It
got back to him you're looking for a translator."

"He doesn't need a muse, he needs a butt. Naturally it got back to him,"
Baumzweig said. "That witch herself told him."

"Why me?" Edelshtein said. "It could be you."

"I'm not a jealous type," Baumzweig protested. "What he has you want."
He waved over the audience: just then he looked as insignificant as a little
bird.

Paula said, "You both want it."

What they both wanted now began. Homage.

Q. Mr. Ostrover, what would you say is the symbolic weight of this story?
A. The symbolic weight is, what you need you deserve. If you don't need to
    be knocked on the head you'll never deserve it.
Q. Sir, I'm writing a paper on you for my English class. Can you tell me
    please if you believe in hell?
A. Not since I got rich.
Q. How about God? Do you believe in God?
A. Exactly the way I believe in pneumonia. If you have pneumonia, you have
    it. If you don't, you don't.
Q. Is it true your wife is a Countess? Some people say she's really only
    Jewish.
A. In religion she's a transvestite, and in actuality she's a Count.
Q. Is there really such a language as Zwrdlish?
A. You're speaking it right now, it's the language of fools.
Q. What would happen if you weren't translated into English?
A. The pygmies and the Eskimos would read me instead. Nowadays to be
    Ostrover is to be worldwide industry.
Q. Then why don't you write about worldwide things like wars?
A. Because I'm afraid of loud noises.
Q. What do you think of the future of Yiddish?
A. What do you think of the future of the Doberman pinscher?
Q. People say other Yiddishists envy you.

A.   No, it's I who envy them. I like a quiet life.
Q.   Do you keep the Sabbath?
A.   Of course, didn't you notice it's gone?—I keep it hidden.
Q.   And the dietary laws? Do you observe them?
A.   Because of the moral situation of the world I have to. I was heartbro-
     ken to learn that the minute an oyster enters my stomach, he becomes
     an anti-Semite. A bowl of shrimp once started a pogrom against my
     intestines.

    Jokes, jokes! It looked to go on for another hour. The condition of fame,
a Question Period: a man can stand up forever and dribble shallow quips and
everyone admires him for it. Edelshtein threw up his seat with a squeal and
sneaked up the aisle to the double doors and into the lobby. On a bench,
half-asleep, he saw the lexicographer. Usually he avoided him—he was a man
with a past, all pasts, all pasts are boring—but when he saw Vorovsky raise
his leathery eyelids he went toward him.
    "What's new, Chaim?"
    "Nothing. Liver pains. And you?"
    "Life pains. I saw you inside."
    "I walked out, I hate the young."
    "You weren't young, no."
    "Not like these. I neve laughed. Do you realize, at the age of twelve I had
already mastered calculus? I practically reinvented it on my own. You haven't
read Wittgenstein, Hersheleh, you haven't read Heisenberg, what do you
known about the empire of the universe?"
    Edelshtein thought to deflect him: "Was it your translation he read in
there?"
    "Did it sould like mine?"
    "I couldn't tell."
    "It was and it wasn't. Mine, improved. If you ask that ugly one, she'll say
it's hers, improved. Who's really Ostrover's translator? Tell me, Hersheleh,
maybe it's you. Nobody knows. It's as they say—by several hands, and all the
hands are in Ostrover's pot, burning up. I would like to make a good strong
b.m. on your friend Ostrover."
    "*My* friend? He's not my friend."
    "So why did you pay genuine money to see him? You can see him for
free somewhere else, no?"
    "The same applies to yourself."
    "Youth, I brought youth."
    A conversation with a madman: Vorovsky's *meshugas* was to cause other
people to suspect him of normality. Edelshtein let himself slide to the bench—
he felt his bones accordion downward. He was in the grip of a mournful
fatigue. Sitting eye to eye with Vorovsky he confronted the other's hat—a

great Russian-style fur monster. A nimbus of droshky-bells surrounded it, shrouds of snow. Vorovsky had a big head, with big kneaded features, except for the nose, which looked like a doll's pink and formlessly delicate. The only sign of drunkenness was at the bulbs of the nostrils, where the cartilage was swollen, and at the tip, also swollen. Of actual madness there was, in ordinary discourse, no sign, except a tendency toward elusiveness. But it was known that Vorovsky, after compiling his dictionary, a job of seventeen years, one afternoon suddenly began to laugh, and continued laughing for six months, even in his sleep: in order to rest from laughing he had to be given sedatives, though even these could not entirely suppress his laughter. His wife died, and then his father, and he went on laughing. He lost control of his bladder, and then discovered the curative potency, for laughter, of drink. Drink cured him, but he still peed publicly, without realizing it; and even his cure was tentative and unreliable, because if he happened to hear a joke that he like he might laugh at it for a minute or two, or, on occasion, three hours. Apparently none of Ostrover's jokes had struck home with him—he was sober and desolate-looking. Nevertheless Edelshtein noticed a large dark patch near his fly. He had wet himself, it was impossible to tell how long ago. There was no odor. Edelshtein moved his buttocks back an inch. "Youth?" he inquired.

"My niece. Twenty-three years old, my sister Ida's girl. She reads Yiddish fluently," he said proudly. "She writes."

"In Yiddish?"

"Yiddish," he spat out. "Don't be crazy, Hersheleh. who writes in Yiddish? Twenty-three years old, she should write in Yiddish? What is she, a refugee, an American girl like that? She's crazy for literature, that's all, she's like the rest in there, to her Ostrover's literature. I brought her, she wanted to be introduced."

"Introduce me," Edelshtein said craftily.

"She wants to be introduced to someone famous, where do you come in?"

"Translated I'd be famous. Listen, Chaim, a talented man like you, so many languages under your belt, why don't you give me a try? A try and a push."

"I'm no good at poetry. You should write stories if you want fame."

"I don't want fame."

"Then waht are you talking about?"

"I want—" Edelshtein stopped. What did he want? "To reach," he said.

Vorovsky did not laugh. "I was educated at the University of Berlin. From Vilna to Berlin, that was 1924. Did I reach Berlin? I gave my whole life to collecting a history of the human mind, I mean expressed in mathematics. In mathematics the final and only poetry possible. Did I reach the empire of the universe? Hersheleh, if I could tell you about reaching, I would tell you this: reaching is impossible. Why? Because when you get where you wanted to reach to, that's when you realize that's not what you want to reach to.—Do you know what a bilingual German-English mathematical dictionary is good for?"

Edelshtein covered his knees with his hands. His knuckles glimmered up at him. Row of white skulls.

"Toilet paper," Vorovsky said. "Do you know what poems are good for? The same. And don't call me cynic, what I say isn't cynicism."

"Despair maybe," Edelshtein offered.

"Despair up your ass. I'm a happy man. I know something about laughter." He jumped up—next to the seated Edelshtein he was a giant. Fists gray, thumbnails like bone. The mob was pouring out of the doors of the auditorium. "Something else I'll tell you. Translation is no equation. If you're looking for an equation, better die first. There are no equations, equations don't happen. It's an idea like a two-headed animal, you follow me? The last time I saw an equation it was in a snapshot of myself. I looked in my own eyes, and what did I see there? I saw God in the shape of a murderer. What you should do with your poems is swallow your tongue. There's my niece, behind Ostrover like a tail. Hey Yankel!" he boomed.

The great man did not hear. Hands, arms, heads enclosed him like a fisherman's net. Baumzweig and Paula paddled through eddies, the lobby swirled. Edelshtein saw two little people, elderly, overweight, heavily dressed. He hid himself, he wanted to be lost. Let them go, let them go—

But Paula spotted him. "What happened? We thought you took sick."

"It was too hot in there."

"Come home with us, there's a bed. Instead of your own place alone."

"Thank you no. He signs autographs, look at that."

"Your jealousy will eat you up, Hersheleh."

"I'm not jealous!" Edelshtein shrieked; people turned to see. "Where's Baumzweig?"

"Shaking hands with the pig. An editor has to keep up contracts."

"A poet has to keep down vomit."

Paula considered him. Her chin dipped into her skunk ruff. "How can you vomit, Hersheleh? Pure souls have no stomachs, only ectoplasm. Maybe Ostrover's right, you have too much ambition for your size. What if your dear friend Baumzweig didn't publish you? You wouldn't know your own name. My husband doesn't mention this to you, he's a kind man, but I'm not afraid of the truth. Without him you wouldn't exist."

"With him I don't exist," Edelshtein said. "What is existence?"

"I'm not a Question Period," Paula said.

"That's all right," Edelshtein said, "because I'm an Answer Period. The answer is period. Your husband is finished, period. Also I'm finished, period. We're already dead. Whoever uses Yiddish to keep himself alive is already dead. Either you realize this or you don't realize it. I'm one who realizes."

"I tell him all the time he shouldn't bother with you. You come and you hang around."

"Your house is a gallows, mine is a gas chamber, what's the difference?"

"Don't come any more, nobody needs you."

"My philosophy exactly. We are superfluous on the face of the earth."

"You're a scoundrel."

"Your husband's a weasel, and you're the wife of a weasel."

"Pig and devil yourself."

"Mother of puppydogs." (Paula, such a good woman, the end, he would never see her again!)

He blundered away licking his tears, hitting shoulders with his shoulder, blind with the accident of his grief. A yearning all at once shouted itself in his brain:

EDELSHTEIN: Chaim, teach me to be a drunk!
VOROVSKY: First you need to be crazy.
EDELSHTEIN: Teach me to go crazy!
VOROVSKY: First you need to fail.
EDELSHTEIN: I've failed, I'm schooled in failure, I'm a master of failure!
VOROVSKY: GO BACK AND STUDY SOM E M OFE.

One wall was a mirror. In it he saw an old man crying, dragging a striped scarf like a prayer shawl. He stood and looked at himself. He wished he had been born a Gentile. Pieces of old poems littered his nostrils, he smelled the hour of their creation, his wife in bed beside him, asleep after he had rubbed her to compensate her for bitterness. *The sky is cluttered with stars of David. . . . If everything is something else, then I am something else. . . . Am I a thing and not a bird? Does my way fork though I am one? Will God take back history? Who will let me begin again. . . .*

OSTROVER: Hersheleh, I admit I insulted you, but who will know? It's only a make-believe story, a game.
EDELSHTEIN: Literature isn't a game! Literature isn't little stories!
OSTROVER: So what is it, Torah? You scream out loud like a Jew, Edelshtein. Be quiet, they'll hear you.
EDELSHTEIN: And you, Mr. Elegance, you aren't a Jew?
OSTROVER: Not at all, I'm one of *them*. You too are lured, aren't you, Hersheleh? Shakespeare is better than a shadow, Pushkin is better than a pipsqueak, hah?
EDELSHTEIN: If you become a Gentile you don't automatically become a Shakespeare.
OSTROVER: Oho! A lot you know. I'll let you in on the facts, Hersheleh, because I feel we're really brothers, I feel you straining toward the core of the world. Now listen—did you ever hear of Velvl Shikkerparev? Never. A Yiddish scribbler writing romances for the Yiddish stage in the East End, I'm speaking of London, England. He finds a translator and overnight he becomes Willie Shakespeare. . . .
EDELSHTEIN: Jokes aside, is this what you advise?
OSTROVER: I would advise my own father no less. Give it up, Hersheleh, stop believing in Yiddish.
EDELSHTEIN: But I don't believe in it!

OSTROVER: You do. I see you do. It's no use talking to you, you won't let
               go. Tell me, Edelshtein, what language does Moses speak in the
               world-to-come?
EDELSHTEIN: From babyhood I know this. Hebrew on the Sabbath, on week-
               days Yiddish.
OSTROVER: Lost sould, don't make Yiddish into the Sabbath-tongue! If
               you believe in holiness, you're finished. Holiness is for make-
               believe.
EDELSTEIN: I want to be a Gentile like you!
OSTROVER: I'M ONLY A MAKE-BELIEVE GENTILE. THIS MEANS THAT I PLAY AT BEING A
               JEW TO SATISFY THEM. IN MY VILLAGE WHEN I WAS A BOY THEY USED TO
               BRING IN A DANCING BEAR FOR THE CARNIVAL, AND EVERYONE SAID, "IT'S
               HUMAN!"—THEY SAID THIS BECAUSE THEY KNEW IT WAS A BEAR, THOUGH
               IT STOOD ON TWO LEGS AND WALTZED. BUT IT WAS A BEAR.

Baumzweig came to him then. "Paula and her temper. Never mind,
Hersheleh, come and say hello to the big celebrity, what can you lose?" He
went docilely, shook hands with Ostrover, even complimented him on his
story. Ostrover was courtly, wiped his lip, let ooze a drop of ink from a slow
pen, and continued autographing books. Vorovsky lingered humbly at the rim
of Ostrover's circle: his head was fierce, his eyes timid; he was steering a girl
by the elbow, but the girl was mooning oven an open flyleaf, where Ostrover
had written his name. Edelshtein, catching a flash of letters, was startled: it
was the Yiddish version she held.
    "Excuse me," he said.
    "My niece," Vorovsky said.
    "I see you read Yiddish," Edelshtein addressed her. "In your generation a
miracle."
    "Hannah, before you stands H. Edelshtein the poet."
    "Edelshtein?"
    "Yes."
    She recited, *"Little fathers, little uncles, you with your beards and glasses
and curly hair. . . ."*
    Edelshtein shut his lids and again wept.
    "If it's the same Edelshtein?"
    "The same," he croaked.
    "My grandfather used to do that one all the time. It was in a book he had,
A Velt ohn Vint. But it's not possible."
    "Not possible?"
    "That you're still alive."
    "You're right, you're right," Edelshtein said, struck. "We're all ghosts here."
    "Forgive him."
    "*He* used to read you! And he was an old man, he died years ago, and
you're still alive—"

"I'm sorry," Edelshtein said. "Maybe I was young then, I began young."

"Why do you say ghosts? Ostrover's no ghost."

"No, no," he agreed. He was afraid to offend. "Listen, I'll say the rest for you. I'll take a minute only, I promise. Listen, see if you can remember from your grandfather—''

Around him, behind him, in front of him Ostrover, Vorovsky, Baumzweig, perfumed ladies, students, the young, the young, he clawed at his wet face and declaimed, he stood like a wanton stalk in the 'heart of an empty field:

How you spring out of the ground covered with poverty!
In your long coats, fingers rolling wax, tallow eyes.
How can I speak to you, little fathers?
You who nestled me with lyu, lyu, lyu,
lip-lullaby . Jabber of blue-eyed sailors,
how am I fallen into a stranger's womb?

Take me back with you, history has left me out.
You belong to the Angel of Death,
I to you.
Braided wraiths, smoke,
let me fall into your graves,
I have no business being your future.

He gargled, breathed, coughed, choked, tears invaded some false channel in his throat—meanwhile he swallowed up with the seizure of each bawled word this niece, this Hannah, like the rest, boots, rough full hair, a forehead made on a Jewish last, chink eyes—

At the edge of the village a little river.
Herons tip into it pecking at their images
when the waders pass whistling like Gentiles.
The herons hang, hammocks above the sweet summer-water.
Their skulls are full of secrets, their feathers scented.
The village is so little it fits into my nostril,
The roofs shimmer tar,
the sun licks thick as cow.
No one knows what will come.
How crowded with mushroows the forest's dark floor.

Into his ear Paula said, "Hersheleh, I apologize, come home with us, please, please, I apologize." Edelshtein gave her a push, he intended to finish. "Littleness," he screamed,

I speak to you.
We are such a little huddle.
Our little hovels, our grandfathers' hard hands, how little,
our little, little words,
this lullaby
sung at the lip of your grave,

he screamed.

Baumzweig said, "That's one of your old good ones, the best."

"The one on my table, in progress, is the best," Edelshtein screamed, clamor still high over his head; but he felt soft, rested, calm; he knew how patient.

Ostrover said, "That one you shouldn't throw out the window."

Vorovsky began to laugh.

"This is the dead man's poem, now you know it," Edelshtein said, looking all around, pulling at his shawl, pulling and pulling at it: this too made Vorovsky laugh.

"Hannah, better take home your uncle Chaim," Ostrover said: handsome, all white, a public genius, a feather.

Edelshtein discovered he was cheated, he had not examined the girl sufficiently.

He slept in the sons' room—bunk beds piled on each other. The top one was crowded with Paula's storage boxes. He rolled back and forth on the bottom, dreaming, jerking awake, again dreaming. Now and then, with a vomitous taste, he belched up the hot cocoa Paula had given him for reconciliation. Between the Baumzveigs and himself a private violence: lacking him, whom would they patronize? They were moralists, they needed someone to feel guilty over. Another belch. He abandoned his fine but uninnocent dream—young, he was kissing Alexei's cheeks like ripe peaches, he drew away . . . it was not Alexei, it was a girl, Vorovsky's niece. After the kiss she slowly tore the pages a book until it snowed paper, black bits of alphabet, white bits of empty margin. Paula's snore traveled down the hall to him. He writhed out of bed and groped for a lamp. With it he lit up a decrepit table covered with ancient fragile model airplanes. Some had rubber-band propellers, some were papered over a skeleton of balsa-wood ribs. A game of Monopoly lay under a samite tissue of dust. His hand fell on two old envelopes, one already browning, and without hesitation he pulled the letters out and read them:

> Today was two special holidays in one, Camp Day and Sacco and Vanzetti Day. We had to put on white shirts and white shorts and go to the casino to hear Chaver Rosenbloom talk about Sacco and Vanzetti. They were a couple of Italians who were killed for loving the poor. Chaver Rosenbloom cried, and so did Mickey but I didn't. Mickey keeps forgetting to wipe himself in the toilet but I make him.
> Paula and Ben: thanks so much for the little knitted suit and the clown rattle. The box was a bit smashed in but the rattle came safe anyhow. Stevie will look adorable in his new blue suit when he gets big enough for it. He already seems to like the duck on the collar. It will keep him good and warm too. Josh has been woriing very hard these days preparing for a course in the American Novel and

asks me to tell you he'll write as soon as he can. We all send love, and Stevie sends a kiss for Grandma and Pa. *P.S.* Mickey drove down in a pink Mercedes last week. We all had quite a chat and told him he should settle down! .

Heroes, martyrdom, a baby. Hatred for these letters made his eyelids quiver. Ordinariness. Everything a routine. Whatever man touches becomes banal like man. Animals don't contaminate nature. Only man the corrupter, the anti-divinity. All other species live within the pulse of nature. He despised these ceremonies and rattles and turds and hisses. The pointlessness of their babies. Wipe one generation's ass for the sake of wiping another generation's ass: this was his whole definition of civilization. He pushed back the airplanes, cleared a front patch of table with his elbow, found his pen, wrote:

Dear Niece of Vorovsky:

It is very strange to me to feel I become a Smasher, I who was born to being humane and filled with love for our darling Human Race.

But nausea for his shadowy English, which he pursued in dread, passion, bewilderment, feebleness, overcame him. He started again in his own tongue—

Unknown Hannah:

I am a man writing you in a room of the house of another man. He and I are secret enemies, so under his roof it is difficult to write the truth, Yet I swear to you I will speak these words with my heart's whole honesty. I do not remember either your face or your body. Vaguely your angry voice. To me you are an abstraction. I ask whether the ancients had any physical representation of the Future, a goddess Futura, so to speak. Presumably she would have blank eyes, like Justice. It is an incarnation of the Future to whom this letter is addressed'. Writing to the Future one does not expect an answer. The Future is an oracle for whose voice one cannot wait in inaction. One must do to be. Although a Nihilist, not by choice but by conviction, I discover in myself an unwillingness to despise survival. Often I have spat on myself for having survived the deathcamps— survived them drinking tea in New York!— but today when I heard carried on your tongue some old syllables of mine I was again wheedled into tolerance of survival.' The sound of a dead language on a live girl's tongue! That baby should follow baby is God's trick on us, but surely we too can have a trick on God? If we fabricate with our syllables an immortality passed from the spines of the old to the shoulders of the young, even God cannot spite it. If the prayer-load that spilled upward from the mass graves should sonlehow survive! If not the thicket of lamentation itself, then the language on which it rode. Hannah, youth itself is nothing unless it keeps its promise to grow old. Grow old in Yiddish, Hannah, and carry fathers and uncles into the future with you. Do this. You, one in ten thousand maybe, who were born with the gift of Yiddish in your mouth, the alphabet of Yiddish in your palm, don't make ash of these! A little while ago there were twelve million people—not including babies—who lived inside this tongue, and now what is left? A language that never had a territory except Jewish mouths, and half the Jewish mouths on earth already stopped up with German worms. The rest jabber Russian, English, Spanish, God knows what. Fifty years ago my mother lived in Russia and spoke only broken Russian, but her Yiddish was like silk. In Israel they give the language of Solomon to machinists. Rejoice— in Solomon's time what else did the mechanics speak? Yet whoever forgets Yiddish courts amnesia of history. Mourn—the forgetting has already happened, A thousand years of our travail forgotten. Here and there a word left for vaudeville jokes. Yiddish, I call on you to choose! Yiddish! Choose death or death. Which is to say death through forgetting or death through translation. Who will redeem you? What act of salvation will restore you? All you can hope for,' you tattered, you withered, is translation in America! Hannah, you have a strong mouth, made to carry the future—

But he knew he lied, lied, lied. A truthful intention is not enough. Oratory and declamation. A speech. A lecture. He felt himself an obscenity. What did the death of Jews have to do with his own troubles? His cry was ego and more ego. His own stew, foul. Whoever mourns the dead mourns himself. He wanted someone to read his poems, no one could read his poems. Filth and exploitation to throw in history. As if a dumb man should blame the ears that cannot hear him.

He turned the paper over and wrote in big letters:

EDELSHTEIN GONE,

and went down the corridor with it in pursuit of Paula's snore. Taken without ridicule a pleasant riverside noise. Bird. More cow to the sight: the connubial bed, under his gaze, gnarled and lumped—in it this old male and this old female. He was surprised on such a cold night they slept with only one blanket, gauzy cotton. They lay like a pair of kingdoms in summer. Long ago they had been at war, now they were exhausted into downy truce. Hair all over Baumzweig. Even his leg-hairs gone white. Nightstands, a pair of them, on either side of the bed, heaped with papers, books, magazines, lampshades sticking up out of all that like figurines on a prow—the bedroom was Baumzweig's second office. Towers of back issues on the floor. On the dresser a typewriter besieged by Paula's toilet water bottles and face powder. Fragrance mixed with urinous hints. Edelshtein went on looking at the sleepers. How reduced they seemed, each breath a little demand for more, more, more, a shudder of jowls; how they heaved a knee, a thumb; the tiny blue veins all over Paula's neck. Her nightgown was stretched away and he saw that her breasts had dropped sidewise and, though still very fat, hung in, pitiful creased bags of moledappled skin. Baumzweig wore only his underwear: his thighs were full of picked sores.

He put EDELSHTEIN GONE between their heads. Then he took it away—on the other side was his real message: secret enemies. He folded the sheet inside his coat pocket and squeezed into his shoes. Cowardly. Pity for breathing carrion. All pity is self-pity. Goethe on his deathbed: more light!

In the street he felt liberated. A voyager. Snow was still falling, though more lightly than before, a night-colored blue. A veil of snow revolved in front of him, turning him around. He stumbled into a drift, a magnificent bluish pile slanted upward. Wetness pierced his feet like a surge of cold blood. Beneath the immaculate lifted slope he struck stone—the stair of a stoop. He remembered his old home, the hill of snow behind the study-house, the smoky fire, his father swaying nearly into the black fire and chanting, one big duck, the stupid one, sliding on the ice. His mother's neck too was finely veined and secretly, sweetly, luxuriantly odorous. Deeply and gravely he wished he had worn galoshes—no one reminds a widower. His shoes were infernos of cold, his toes dead blocks. Himself the only life in the street, not even a cat. The veil moved against him, turning, and beat on his pupils. Along the curb cars squatted under humps of snow, blue-backed tortoises. Nothing moved in the road. His own house was far, Vorovsky's nearer, but he could not read the street sign. A building with a canopy. Vorovsky's hat. He made himself very small, small as a mouse, and curled himself up in the fur of it. To be very, very little and to live in a hat. A little wild creature in a burrow. Inside warm, a mound of seeds nearby, licking himself for cleanliness, all sorts of weather leaping down. His glasses fell from his face and with an odd tiny crack hit the lid of a garbage can. He took off one glove and felt for them in the snow. When he found them he marveled at how the frames burned. Suppose a funeral on a night like this, how would they open the earth? His glasses were slippery as icicles when he put them on again. A crystal spectrum delighted him, but he could not see the passageway, or if there was a canopy. What he wanted from Vorovsky was Hannah.

There was no elevator. Vorovsky lived on the top floor, very high up. From his windows you could look out and see people so tiny they became patterns. It was a different building, not this one. He went down three fake-marble steps and saw a door. It was open: inside was a big black room knobby with baby carriages and tricycles. He smelled wet metal like a toothpain: life! Pereu tells how on a bitter night a Jew outside the window envied peasants swigging vodka in a hovel—friends in their prime and warm before the fire. Carriages and tricycles, instruments of Diaspora. Baumzweig with his picked sores was once also a baby. In the Diaspora the birth of a Jew increases nobody's population, the death of a Jew has no meaning. Anonymous. To have died among the martyrs—solidarity at least, a passage into history, one of the marked ones, *kiddush ha-shem.*—A telephone on the wall. He pulled off his glasses, all clouded over, and took out a pad with numbers in it and dialed.

"Ostrover?"

"Who is this?"

"Yankel Ostrover, the writer, or Pisher Ostrover the plumber?"

"What do you want?"

"To leave evidence," Edelshtein howled.

"Never mind! Make an end! Who's there?"

"The Messiah."

"Who is this?—Mendel, it's you?"

"Never."

"Gorochov?"

"That toenail? Please. Trust me."

"Fall into a hole!"

"This is how a man addresses his Redeemer?"

"It's five o'clock in the morning! Whdt do you want? Bum! Lunatic! Cholera! Black year! Plague! Poisoner! Strangler!"

"You think you'll last longer than your shroud, Ostrover? Your sentences are an abomination, your style is like, a pump, a pimp has a sweeter tongue—"

"Angel of Death!"

He dialed Vorovsky but there was no answer.

The snow had turned white as the white of an eye. He wandered toward Hannah's house, though he did not know where she lived, or what her name was, or whether he had ever seen her. On the way he rehearsed what he would say to her. But this was not satisfactory, he could lecture but not speak into a face. He bled to retrieve her face. He was in pursuit of her, she was his destination. Why? What does a man look for, what does. he need? What can a man retrieve? Can the future retrieve the past? And if retrieve, how redeem? His shoes streamed. Each step was a pond. The herons in spring, red-legged. Secret eyes they have: the eyes of birds—frightening. Too open. The riddle of openness. His feet poured rivers. Cold, cold.

> *Little old man in the cold,*
> *come hop up on the stove,*
> *your wife will give you a crust with jam.*
> *Thank you, muse, for this little psalm.*

He belched. His stomach was unwell. Indigestion? A heart attack? He wiggled the fingers of his left hand: though frozen they tingled. Heart. Maybe only ulcer. Cancer, like Mireleh? In a narrow bed he missed his wife. How much longer could he expect to live? An unmarked grave. Who would know he had ever been alive? He had no descendants, his grandchildren were imaginary. *O my unborn grandson* . . . Hackneyed *Ungandfathered ghost* . . . Too baroque. Simplicity, purity, truthfulness.

He wrote:

Dear Hannah:

You made no impression on me. When I wrote you before at Baumzweig's I lied. I saw you for a second in a public place, so what? Holding a Yiddish book. A young face on top of a Yiddish book. Nothing else. For me this is worth no somersault. Ostrover's vomit!—that popularizer, vulgarian, panderer to people who have lost the memory of peoplehood. A thousand times a pimp. Your uncle Chaim said about you: "She writes." A pity on his judgment. Writes! Writes! Potatoes in a sack! Another one! What do you write? When will you write? How will you write? Either you'll become an editor of *Good Housekeeping,* or, if serious, join the gang of so-called Jewish novelists. I've sniffed them all, I'm intimate with their smell. Satirists they call themselves. Picking at their crotches. What do they know, I mean of *knowledge?* To satirize you have to know something. In a so-called novel by a so-called Jewish novelist (*"activist-existential"*—listen, I understand, I read everything!)— Elkin, Stanley, to keep to only one example—the hero visits Williamsbyg to contact a so-called "miracle rabbi." Even the word *rabbi!* No, listen—to me, a descendant of the Vilna Gaon myself, the *guter yid* is a charlatan and his *chasidim* are victims, never mind if willing or not. But that's not the point. You have to KNOW SOMETHING! At least the difference between a *rav* and a *rebbeh!* At least a *pinteleh* here and there! Otherwise where's the joke, where's the satire, where's the mockery? American—born! An ignoramus mocks only himself. *Jewish* novelists! Savages! The allrightnik's children, all they know is to curse the allrightnik! Their Yiddish! One word here, one word there. *Shikseh* on one page, *putz* on the other, and that's the whole vocabulary! And when they give a try at phonetic rendition! Darling God! If they had mothers and fathers, they crawled out of the swamps. Their grandparents were tree-squirrels if that's how they held their mouths. They know ten words for, excuse me, penis, and when it comes to a word for learning they're impotent!

Joy, joy! He felt himself on the right course at last. Daylight was coming, a yellow elephant rocked silently by in the road. A little light burned eternally on its tusk. He let it slide past, he stood up to the knees in the river at home, whirling with joy. He wrote:

TRUTH

But this great thick word, Truth!, was too harsh, oaken; with his finger in the snow he crossed it out.

> I was saying: indifference. I'm indifferent to you and your kind. Why should I think you're another species, something better? Because you knew a shred of a thread of a poem of mine? Ha! I was seduced by my own vanity. I have a foolish tendency to make symbols out of glimpses. My poor wife, peace on her, used to ridicule me for this. Riding in the subway once I saw a beautiful child, a boy about twelve. A Puerto Rican, dusky, yet he had cheeks like pomegranates. I once knew, in Kiev, a child who looked like that. I admit to it. A portrait under the skin of my eyes. The love of a man for a boy. Why not confess it? Is it against the nature of man to rejoice in beauty? "This is to be expected with a childless man"—my wife's verdict. That what I wanted was a son. Take this as a complete explanation: if an ordinary person cannot

The end of the sentence flew like a leaf out of his mind . . . it was turning into a quarrel with Mireleh. Who quarrels with the dead? He wrote:

Esteemed Alexei Yosifovitch:

> You remain, You remain. An illumination. More than my own home, nearer than my mother's mouth. Nimbus. Your father slapped my father. You were

never told. Because I kissed you on the green stairs. The shadow-place on the landing where I once saw the butler scratch his pants. They sent us away shamed. My father and I, into the mud.

Again a lie. Never near the child. Lying is like a vitamin, it has to fortify every-thing. Only through the doorway, looking, looking. The gleaming face: the face of flame. Or would test him on verb-forms: *kal, nifal, piel, pual, hifil, hofal, hispael.* On the afternoons the Latin tutor came, crouched outside the thresh-old, Edelshtein heard *ego, mei, mihi, me, me.* May may. Beautiful foreign nasal chant of riches. Latin! Dirty from the lips of idolators. An apostate fam-ily. Edelshtein and his father took their coffee and bread, but otherwise lived on boiled eggs: the elder Kirilov one day brought home with him the *mashgi-ach* from the Jewish poorhouse to testify to the purity of the servants' kitchen, but to Edelshtein's father the whole house was *treyf,* the *mashgiach* himself a hired impostor. Who would oversee the overseer? Among the Kirilovs with their lying name money was the best overseer. Money saw to everything. Though they had their particular talent. Mechanical. Alexei Y. Kirilov, engineer. Bridges, towers. Consultant to Cairo. Builder of the Aswan Dam, assistant to Pharaoh for the latest Pyramid. To set down such a fantasy about such an important Soviet brain . . . poor little Alexei, Avremeleh, I'll jeopardize your position in life, little corpse of Babi Yar.

Only focus. Hersh! Scion of the Vilna Gaon! Prince of rationality! Pay attention!

He wrote:

The gait—the prance, the hobble—of Yiddish is not the same as the gait of English. A big headache for a translator probably. In Yiddish you use more words than in English. Nobody believes it but it's true. Another big problem is form. The moderns take the old forms and fill them up with mockery, love, drama, satire, etc. Plenty of play. But STILL THE SAME OLD FORMS, conventions left over from the last century even. It doesn't matter who denies this, out of pride: it's true. Pour in symbolism, impressionism, be complex, be subtle, be daring, take risks, break your teeth—whatever you do, it still comes out Yid-dish. *Mamaloshen* doesn't produce *Wastelands.* No alienation, no nihilism, no dadaism. With all the suffering no smashing! No INCOHERENCE! Keep the latter in mind, Hannah, if you expect to make progress. Also: please remember that when a goy from Columbus, Ohio, says "Elijah the Prophet" he's not talking about *Eliohu hanovi. Eliohu* is one of us, a, *folksmensh,* running around in second—hand clothes. Theirs is God knows what. The same biblical figure, with exactly the same history, once he puts on a name from King James, COMES OUT A DIFFERENT PERSON. Life, history, hope, tragedy, they don't come out even. They talk Bible Lands, with us it's *eretz yisroel.* A misfortune.

Astonished, he struck up against a kiosk. A telephone! On a street cor-ner! He had to drag the door open, pulling a load of snow. Then he squeezed inside. His fingers were sticks. Never mind the pad, he forgot even where the pocket was. In his coat? Jacket? Pants? With one stick he dialed Vorovsky's number: from memory.

"Hello, Chaim?"

"This is Ostrover."

"Ostrover! Why Ostrover? What are you doing there? I want Vorovsky."

"Who's this?"

"Edelshtein."

"I thought so. A persecution, what is this? I could send you to jail for tricks like before—"

"Quick, give me Vorovsky."

"I'll give you."

"Vorovsky's not home?"

"How do I know if Vorovsky's home? It's dawn, go ask Vorovsky !"

Edelshtein grew weak: "I called the wrong number."

"Hersheleh, if you want some friendly advice you'll listen to me. I can get you jobs at fancy out-of-town country clubs, Miami Florida included, plenty of speeches your own style, only what they need is rational lecturers not lunatics. If you carry on like tonight you'll lose what you have."

"I don't have anything."

"Accept life, Edelshtein."

"Dead man, I appreciate your guidance."

"Yesterday I heard from Hollywood, they're making a movie from one of my stories. So now tell me again who's dead."

"The puppet the ventriloquist holds in his lap. A piece of log. It's somebody else's language and the dead doll sits there."

"Wit, you want them to make movies in Yiddish now?"

"In Talmud if you save a single life it's as if you saved the world. And if you save a language? Worlds maybe. Galaxies. The whole universe."

"Hersheleh, the God of the Jews made a mistake when he didn't have a son, it would be a good occupation for you."

"Instead I'll be an extra in your movie. If they shoot the *shtetl* on location in Kansas send me expense money. I'll come and be local color for you. I'll put on my *shtreiml* and walk around, the people should see a real Jew. For ten dollars more I'll even speak *mamaloshen.*"

Ostrover said, "It doesn't, matter what you speak, envy sounds the same in all languages."

Edelshtein said, "Once there was a ghost who thought he was still alive. You know what happened to him? He got up one morning and began to shave and he cut himself. And there was no blood. No blood at all. And he still didn't believe it, so he looked in the mirror to see. And there was no reflection, no sign of himself. He wasn't there. But he still didn't believe it, so he began to scream, but there was no sound, no sound at all—"

There was no sound from the telephone. He let it dangle and rock.

He looked for the pad. Diligently he consulted himself: pants cuffs have a way of catching necessary objects. The number had fallen out of his body. Off his skin. He needed Vorovsky because he needed Hannah. Worthwhile maybe to telephone Baumzweig for Vorovsky's number, Paula could look it up—Baumzweig's number he knew by heart, no mistake. He had singled out his need. Svengali, Pygmalion, Rasputin, Dr. (jokes aside) Frankenstein. What does it require to make a translator? A secondary occupation. Parasitic. But your own creature. Take this girl Hannah and train her. His alone. American-born but she had the advantage over him, English being no worm on her palate; also she could read his words in the original. Niece of a vanquished mind—still, genes are in reality God, and if Vorovsky had a little talent for translation why not the niece?—Or the other. Russia. The one in the Soviet Union who wrote two stanzas in Yiddish. In Yiddish! And only twenty! Born 1948, same year they made up to be the Doctors' Plot, Stalin already very busy killing Jews, Markish, Kvitko, Kushnirov, Hofshtein, Mikhoels, Susskin, Bergelson, Feffer, Gradzenski with the wooden leg. All slaughtered. How did Yiddish survive in the mouth of that girl? Nurtured in secret. Taught by an obsessed grandfather, a crazy uncle: Marranos. The poem reprinted, as they say, in the West. (The West! If a Jew says "the West," he sounds like an imbe-cile. In a puddle what's West, what's East?) Flowers, blue sky, she yearns for the end of winter: very nice. A zero, and received like a prodigy! An aberra-tion! A miracle! Because composed in the lose tongue. As if some Neapolitan child suddenly begins to prattle in Latin. Not the same. Little verses merely. Death confers awe. Russian: its richness, directness. For "iron" and "w&ponn the same word. A thick language, a world—language. He visualized himself translated into Russian, covertly, by the Marranos' daughter. To be circulated, in typescript, underground: to be read, read!

> Understand me, Hannah—that out treasure-tongue is derived from strangers means nothing. 90 per cent German roots, 10 per cent Slavic: irrelevant. The Hebrew take for granted without percentages. We are a people who have known how to forge the language of need out of the language of necessity. Our reputation among ourselves as a nation of scholars is mostly empty. In actuality we are a mob of working people, laborers, hewers of wood, believe me. Leivik, our chie poet, was a house painter. Today all pharmacists, law-yers, accountants, haberdashers, but tickle the lawyer and you'll see his grandfather sawed wood for a living. That's how it is with us. Nowadays the Jew is forgetful, everybody with a profession, every Jewish boy a professor—justice seems less urgent. Most don't realize this quiet time is only another Interim. Always, like in a terrible Wagnerian storm, we have our inter-ludes of rest. So now. Once we were slaves, now we are free men, remember the bread of affliction. But listen. Whoever cries Justice! is a liberated slave. Whoever honors Work is a liberated slave. They accuse Yiddish literature of sentimentality in this connection. Very good, true. True, so be it! A dwarf at a sewing machine can afford a little loosening of the heart. I return to Leivik. He could hang wallpaper. I once lived in a room he papered—yellow vines. Rutgers Street that was. A good job, no bubbles, no peeling. This from a poet of very morbid tendencies. Mani Leib fixed shoes. Moishe Leib Halpern was a waiter, once in a while a handyman. I could tell you the names of twenty poets of very pure expression who were operators, pressers, cutters. In addi-tion to fixing shoes Mani Leib was also a laundryman. I beg you not

to think I'm preaching Socialism. To my mind politics is dung. What I mean is something else: Work is Work, and Thought is Thought. Politics tries to mix these up, Socialism especially. The language of a hard-pressed people works under the laws of purity, dividing the Commanded from the Profane. I remember one of my old teachers. He used to take attendance every day and he gave his occupation to the taxing council as "attendance-taker"—so that he wouldn't be getting paid for teaching Torah. This with five pupils, all living in his house and fed by his, wife! Call it splitting a hair if you want, but it's the hair of a head that distinguished between the necessary and the merely needed, People who believe that Yiddish is, as they like to say, "richly intermixed," and that in Yiddishkeit the presence of the Covenant, of Godliness, inhabits humble things and humble words, are under a delusion or a deception. The slave knows exactly when he belongs to God and when to the oppressor. The liberated slave who is not forgetful and can remember when he himself was an artifact, knows exactly the difference between God and an artifact. A language also knows whom it is serving at each moment. I am feeling very cold right now. Of course you see that when I say liberated I mean self-liberated. Moses not Lincoln, not Franz Josef. Yiddish is the language of auto-emancipation. Theodor Herzl wrote in German but the message spread in *mamaloshen*—my God cold. Naturally the important thing is to stick to what you learned as a slave including language, and not to speak their language, otherwise you will become like them, acquiring their confusion between God and artifact and consequently their taste for making slaves, both of themselves and others.

Slave of rhetoric! This is the trouble when you use God for a Muse. Philosophers, thinkers—all cursed. Poets have it better: most are Greeks and pagans, unbelievers except in natural religion, stones, stars, body. This cube and cell. Ostrover had already sentenced him to jail, little booth in the vale of snow; black instrument beeped from a gallows. The white pad—something white—on the floor. Edelshtein bent for it send struck his jaw. Through the filth of the glass doors morning rose out of the dark. He saw what he held:

"ALL OF US ARE HUMANS TOGETHER
BUT SOME HUMANS SHOULD DROP DEAD."

DO YOU FEEL THIS?

IF SO CALL TR 5-2530 IF YOU WANT TO
KNOW WHETHER YOU WILL SURVIVE IN
CHRIST'S FIVE-DAY INEXPENSIVE
ELECT-PLAN

*

"AUDITORY PHRENOLOGY"
PRACTICED FREE FREE

*

(PLEASE NO ATHEISTS OR CRANK CALLS
WE ARE SINCERE SCIENTIFIC SOUL-SOCIOLOGISTS)

*

ASK FOR ROSE OR LOU
WE LOVE YOU

He was touched and curious, but withdrawn. The cold lit him unfamiliarly: his body a brilliant hollowness, emptied of organs, cleansed of debris, the inner flanks of him perfect lit glass. A clear chalice. Of small change he had only a nickel and a dime. For the dime he could CALL TR 5-2530 and take advice appropriate to his immaculatess, his transparency. Rose or Lou. He had no satire for their love. How manifold and various the human imagination. The simplicity of an ascent lured him, he was alert to the probability of levitation but disregarded it. The disciples of Reb Moshe of Kobryn also disregarded feats in opposition to nature—they had no awe for their master when he hung in air, but when he slept—the miracle of his lung, his breath, his heartbeat! He lurched from the booth into rushing daylight. The depth of snow sucked off one of his shoes. The serpent too prospers without feet, so he cast off his and weaved on. His arms, particuliirly his hands, particularly those of mind his fingers, he was sorry to lose. He knew his eyes, his tongue, his stinging loins. He was again tempted to ascend. The hillock was profound. He outwitted it by creeping through it, he drilled patiently into the snow. He wanted to stand then, but without legs could not. Indolently he permitted himself to rise. He went only high enough to see the snowy sidewalks, the mounds in gutters and against stoops, the beginning of business time. Lifted light. A doorman fled out of a building wearing earmuffs, pulling a shovel behind him like a little tin cart. Edelshtein drifted no higher than the man's shoulders. He watched the shovel pierce the snow, tunneling down, but there was no bottom, the earth was without foundation.

He came under a black wing. He thought it was the first blindness of Death but it was only a canopy.

The doorman went on digging under the canopy; under the canopy Edelshtein tasted wine and felt himself at a wedding, his own, the canopy covering his steamy gold eyeglasses made blind by Mireleh's veil. Four beings held up the poles: one his wife's cousin the postman, one his own cousin the druggist; two poets. The first poet was a beggar who lived on institutional charity—Baumzweig; the second, Silverman, sold ladies' elastic stockings, the kind for varicose veins. The postman and the druggist were still alive, only one of them retired. The poets were ghosts, Baumzweig picking at himself in bed also a ghost, Silverman long dead, more than twenty years— *lideleh-shreiber* they called him, he wrote for the popular theater. "Song to Steerage": *Steerage, steerage, I remember the crowds, the rags we took with us we treated like shrouds, we tossed them away when we spied out the shore, going re-born through the Golden Door. . . .* Even on Second Avenue 1905 was already stale, but it stopped the show, made fevers, encores, tears, yells. Golden sidewalks. America the bride, under her fancy gown nothing. Poor Silverman, in love with the Statue of Liberty's lifted arm, what did he do in his life besides raise up a post at an empty wedding, no progeny?

The doorman dug out a piece of statuary, an urn with a stone wreath.

Under the canopy Edelshtein recogeed it. Sand, butts, a half-naked angel astride the wreath. 0nce Edelshtein saw a condom in it. Found! Vorovsky's building. There is no God, yet who brought, him here if not the King of the Universe? Not so bad off 'after all, even in a snowstorm he could find his way, an expert, he knew one block from another in this desolation of a world.

He carried his shoe into the elevator-like a baby, an orphan, a redemption. He could kiss even a shoe.

In the corridor laughter, toilets flushing; coffee stabbed him.

He rang the bell.

From behind Vorovsky's door, laughter, laughter!

No one came.

He rang again. No one came. He banged. "Chaim, crazy man, open up!" No one came. "A dead man from the cold knocks, you don't come? Hurry up, open, I'm a stick of ice, you want a dead man at your door? Mercy! Pity! Open up!"

No one came.

He listened to the laughter. It had a form; a method, rather: some principle, closer to physics than music, of arching up and sinking back. Inside the shape barks, howls, dogs, wolves, wilderness. After each fright a crevice to fall into. He made an anvil of his shoe and took the doorknob for an iron hammer and thrust. He thrust, thrust. The force of an iceberg.

Close to the knob a panel bulged and cracked. Not his fault. On the other side someone was unused to the lock.

He heard Vorovsky but saw Hannah.

She said: "What?"

"You don't remember me? I'm the one what recited to you tonight my work from several years past, I was passing by in your uncle's neighborhood—"

"He's sick."

"What, a fit?"

"All night. I've been here the whole night. The whole night—"

"Let me in."

"Please go away. I just told you."

"In. What's the matter with you? I'm sick myself, I'm dead from cold! Hey, Chaim! Lunatic, stop it!"

Vorovsky was on his belly on the floor, stifling his mouth with a pillow as if it were a stone, knocking his head down on it, but it was no use, the laughter shook the pillow and came yelping out, not muffled but increased, darkened. He laughed and said "Hannah" and laughed.

Edelshtein took a chair and dragged it near Vorovsky and sat. The room stank, a subway latrine.

"Stop," he said.

Vorovsky laughed.

"All right, merriment, very good,. be happy. You're warm, I'm cold. Have mercy, little girl—tea. Hannah. Boil it up hot. Pieces of flesh drop from me."

He heard that he was speaking Yiddish, so he began again for her. "I'm sorry. Forgive me. A terrible thing to do. I was lost outside, I was looking, so now I found you, I'm sorry."

"It isn't a good time for a visit, that's all."

"Bring some tea also for your uncle."

"He can't."

"He can maybe, let him try. Someone who laughs like this is ready for a feast—*flanken, tsimmis, rosselfleysh*—" In Yiddish he said, "In the world-to-come people dance at parties like this, all laughter, joy. The day after the Messiah people laugh like this."

Vorovsky laughed and said "Messiah" and sucked the pillow, spitting. His face was a flood: tears ran upside down into his eyes, over his forehead, saliva sprang in puddles around his ears. He was spitting, crying, burbling, he gasped, wept, spat. His eyes were bloodshot, the whites showed like slashes, wounds; he still wore his hat. He laughed, he was still laughing. His pants were wet, the fly open, now and then seeping. He dropped the pillow for tea and ventured a sip, with his tongue, like an animal full of hope—vomit rolled up with the third swallow and he laughed between spasms, he was still laughing stinking, a sewer.

Edelshtein took pleasure in the tea, it touched him to the root, more gripping on his bowel than the coffee that stung the hall. He praised kmself with no meanness, no bitterness: prince of rationality! Thawing, he said, "Give him *schnapps,* he can hold *schnapps,* no question."

"He drank and he vomited."

"Chaim, little soul," Edelshtein said, "what started you off? Myself. I was there. I said it, I said graves, I said smoke. I'm the responsible one. Death. Death, I'm the one who said it. Death you laugh at, you're no coward."

"If you want to talk business with my uncle come another time."

"Death is business?"

Now he examined her. Born 1945, in the hour of the death-camps. Not selected. Immune. The whole way she held herself looked immune—by this he meant American. Still, an exhausted child, straggled head, remarkable child to stay through the night with the madman. "Where's your mother?" he said. "Why doesn't she come and watch her brother? Why does it fall on you? You should be free, you have your own life."

"You don't know anything about families."

She was acute: no mother, father, wife, child, what did he know about families? He was cut off, a survivor. "I know your uncle," he said, but without belief: in the first place Vorovsky had an education. "In his right mind your uncle doesn't want you to suffer."

Vorovsky, laughing, said "Suffer."

"He likes to suffer. He wants to suffer, He admires suffering, All you people want to suffer."

Pins and needles: Edelshtein's fingertips were fevering. He stroked the heat of the cup. He could feel. He said, "'You people'?"

"You Jews."

"Aha. Chaim, you hear? Your niece Hannah—on the other side already, never mind she's acquainted with *mamaloshen.* In one generation, 'you Jews,' You don't like suffering? Maybe you respect it?"

"It's unnecessary."

"It comes from history, history is also unnecessary?"

"History's a waste."

America the empty bride. Edelshtein said, "You're right about business. I came on business. My whole business is waste."

Vorovsky laughed and said "Hersheleh Frog Frog Frog."

"I think you're making him worse," Hannah said. "Tell me what you want and I'll give him the message."

"He's not deaf."

"He doesn't remember afterward—"

"I have no message."

"Then what do you want from him?"

"Nothing. I want from you."

"Frog Frog Frog Frog Frog."

Edelshtein finished his tea and put the cup on the floor and for the first time absorbed Vorovsky's apartment: until now Vorovsky had kept him out. It was one room, sink and stove behind a plastic curtain, bookshelves leaning over not with books but journals piled flat, a sticky table, a sofa-bed, a desk, six kitchen chairs, and along the walls seventy-five cardboard boxes which Edelshtein knew harbored two thousand copies of Vorovsky's dictionary. A pity on Vorovsky, he had a dispute with the publisher, who turned back half the printing to him. Vorovsky had to pay for two thousand German-English mathematical dictionaries, and now he had to sell them himself, but he did not know what to do, how to go about it. It was his fate to swallow what he first excreted. Because of a mishap in business he owned his life, he possessed what he was, a slave, but invisible, A hungry snake has to eat its tail all the way down to the head until it disappears.

Hannah said: "What could I do for you"—flat, not a question.

"Again 'you.' A; distinction, a separation. What I'll ask is this: annihilate 'you,' annihilate 'me.' We'll come to an understanding, we'll get together."

She bent for his cup and he saw her boot. He was afraid of a boot. He said mildly, nicely, "Look, your uncle tells me you're one of us. By 'us' he means writer, no?"

"By 'us' you mean Jew."

"And you're not a Jew, *meydeleh?*"

"Not your kind."

"Nowadays there have to be kinds? Good, bad, old, new—"

"Old and new."

"All right! So let it be old and new, fine, a reasonable beginning. Let old work with new. Listen, I need a collaborator. Not exactly a collaborator, it's not even complicated like that. What I need is a translator."

"My uncle the translator is indisposed."

At that moment Edelshtein discovered he hated irony. He yelled, "Not your uncle. You! You!"

Howling, Vorovsky crawled to a tower of cartons and beat on them with his bare heels. There was an alteration in his laughter, something not theatrical but of the theater—he was amused, entertained, clowns paraded between his legs.

"You'll save Yiddish," Edelshtein said, "you'll be like a Messiah to a whole generation, a whole literature, naturally you'll have to work at it, practice, it takes knowledge, it takes a gift, a genius, a born poet—"

Hannah walked in her boots with his dirty teacup. From behind the plastic he heard the faucet. She opened the curtain and came out and said: "You old men."

"Ostrover's pages you kiss!"

"You jealous old men from the ghetto," she said.

"And Ostrover's young, a young prince? Listen! You don't see, you don't follow—translate me, lift me out of the ghetto, it's my life that's hanging on you!"

Her voice was a whip. "Bloodsuckers," she said. "It isn't a translator you're after, it's someone's soul. Too much history's drained your blood, you want someone to take you over, a dybbuk—"

"Dybbuk! Ostrover's language. All right, I need a dybbuk, I'll become a golem, I don't care, it doesn't matter! Breathe in me! Animate me! Without you I'm a clay pot!" Bereaved, he yelled, "Translate me! "

The clowns ran over Vorovsky's charmed belly.

Hannah said: "You think I have to read Ostrover in translation? You think translation has anything to do with what Ostrover is?"

Edelshtein accused her, "Who taught you to read Yiddish?— A girl like that, to know the letters worthy of life and to be ignorant! 'You Jews,' 'you people,' you you you!"

"I learned, rny grandfather taught me, I'm not responsible for it, I didn't go looking for it, I was smart, a golden head, same as now. But I have my own life, you said it yourself, I don't have to throw it out. So pay attention, Mr. Vampire: even in Yiddish Ostrover's not in the ghetto. Even in Yiddish he's not like you people."

"He's not in the ghetto? Which ghetto, what ghetto? So where is he? In the sky? In the clouds? With the angels? Where?"

She meditated, she was all intelligence. "In the world," she answered him.

"In the marketplace. A fishwife, a *kochleffel*, everything's his business, you he'll autograph, me he'll get jobs, he listens to everybody."

"Whereas you people listen only to yourselves."

In the room something was absent.

Edelshtein, pushing into his snow-damp shoe, said into the absence, "So? You're not interested?"

"Only in the mainstream. Not in your little puddles."

"Again the ghetto. Your uncle stinks from the ghetto? Graduated, 1924, the University of Berlin,Vorovsky stinks from the ghetto? Myself, four

God-given books not one living human beln knows, I stink from the ghetto? God, four thousand years since Abraham hanging out with Jews, God also stinks from the ghetto?"

"Rhetoric," Hannah said. "Yiddish literary rhetoric. That's the style."

"Only Ostrover doesn't stink from the ghetto."

"A question of vision."

"Better say visions. He doesn't know real things."

"He knows a reality beyond realism."

"American literary babies! And in your language you don't have a rhetoric?" Edelshtein burst out. "Very good, he's achieved it, Ostrover's the world. A pantheist, a pagan, a goy."

"That's it. You've nailed it. A Freudian, a Jungian, a sensibility. No little love stories. A contemporary. He speaks for everybody."

"Aha. Sounds familiar already. For humanity he speaks? Humanity?"

"Humanity," she said.

"And to speak for Jews isn't to speak for humanity? We're not human? We're not present on the face of the earth? We don't suffer? In Russia they let us live? In Egypt' they don't want to murder us?"

"Suffer suffer," she said. "I like devils best. They don't think only about themselves and they don't suffer."

Immediately, looking at Hannah—my God, an old man, he was looking at her little waist, underneath it where the little apple of her womb was hidden away—immediately, all at once, instantaneously, he fell into a chaos, a trance, of truth, of actuality: was it possible? He saw everything in miraculous reversal, blessed—everything plain, distinct, understandable, true. What he understood was this: that the ghetto was the real world, and the outside world only a ghetto. Because in actuality who was shut off? Who then was really buried, removed, inhabited by darkness? To whom, in what little space, did God offer Sinai? Who kept Terach and who followed Abraham? Talmud explains that when the" Jews went into Exile, God went into Exile also. Babi Yar is rnaybe the real world, and Kiev with its German toys, New York with all its terrible intelligence, all fictions, fantasies. Unreality.

An infatuation! He was the same, all his life the same as this poisonous wild girl, he coveted mythologies, specters, animals, voices. Western Civilization his secret guilt, he was ashamed of the small tremor of his self-love, degraded by being ingrown. Alexei with his skin a furnace of desire, his trucks and trains! He longed to be Alexei. Alexei with his German toys and his Latin! Alexei whose destiny was to grow up into the world-at-large, to slip from the ghetto, to break out into engineering for Western Civilization! Alexei, I abandon you! I'm at home only in a prison, history is my prison, the ravine my house, only listen—suppose it turns out that the destiny of the Jews is vast, open, eternal, and that Western Civilization is meant to dwindle, shrivel, shrink into the ghetto of the world—what of history then? Kings, Parliaments, like insects, Presidents like vermin, their religion a row of little dolls, their art a cave smudge, their poetry a lust—Avremeleh, when you fell from the ledge over the ravine into your grave, for the first time you fell into reality.

To Hannah he said: "I didn't ask to be born into Yiddish. It came on me."
He meant he was blessed.

"So keep it," she said, "and don't complain."

With the whole ferocity of his delight in it he hit her mouth. The madman
again struck up his laugh. Only now was it possible to notice that something
had stopped it before. A missing harp. The absence filled with bloody laughter, bits of what looked like red pimento hung in the vomit on Vorovsky's chin,
the clowns fled, Vorovsky's hat with its pinnacle of fur dangled on his chest—
he was spent, he was beginning to fall, into the quake of sleep, he slept, he
dozed, roars burst from hiv, he hiccuped, woke, laughed, an enormous grief
settled in him, he went on napping and laughing, grief had him in its teeth.

Edelshtein's hand, the cushiony underside of it, blazed from giving the
blow. "You," he said, "you have no ideas, what are you?" A shred of learning flaked from him, what the sages said of Job ripped from his tongue like a
peeling of the tongue itself, *he never was, he never existed.* "You were never
born, you were never created!" he yelled. "Let me tell you, a dead man tells
you this, at least I had a life, at least I understood something!"

"Die," she told him. "Die now, all you old men, what are youwaiting for?
Hanging on my neck, him and now you, the whole bunch of you, parasites,
hurry up and die."

His palm burned, it was the first time he had ever slapped a child. He
felt like a father. Her mouth lay back naked on her face. Out of spite, against
instinct, she kept her hands from the bruise—he could see the shape of her
teeth, turned a little one on the other, imperfect, again vulnerable. From fury
her nose streamed. He had put a bulge in her lip.

"Forget Yiddish!" he screamed at her. "Wipe it out of your brain! Extirpate it!
Go get a memory operation! You have no right to it, you have no right to an uncle,
a grandfather! No one ever came before you, you were never born! A vacuum!"

"You old atheists," she called after him. "You dead old socialists. Boring!
You bore me to death. You hate magic, you hate imagination, you talk God
and you hate God, you despise, you bore, you envy, you eat up with your
disgusting old age—cannibals, all you care about is your own youth, you're
finished, give somebody else a turn!"

This held him. He leaned on the door frame. "A turn at what? I didn't offer
you a turn? An opportunity of a lifetime? To be published now, in youth, in
babyhood, early in life? Translated I'd be famous, this you don't understand.
Hannah, listen," he said, kindly, ingratiatingly, reasoning with her like a father,
"you don't have to like my poems, do I ask you to *like* them? I don't ask you
to like them, I don't ask you to respect them, I don't ask you to love them. A
man my age, do I want a lover or a translator? Am I asking a favor? No. Look,"
he said, "one thing I forgot to tell you. A business deal. That's all. Business,
plain and simple. I'll pay you. You didn't think I wouldn't pay, God forbid?"

Now she covered her mouth. He wondered at his need to weep; he was
ashamed.

"Hannah, please, how much? I'll pay, you'll see. Whatever you like. You'll
buy anything you want. Dresses, shoes—" *Gottenyu,* what could such a wild

beast want? "You'll buy more boots, all kinds of boots, whatever you want, books, everything—" He said relentlessly, "You'll have from me money."

"No," she said, "no."

"Please. What will happen to me? What's wrong? My ideas aren't good enough? Who asks you to believe in my beliefs? I'm an old man, used up, I have nothing to say any more, anything I ever said was all imitation. Walt Whitman I used to like. Also John Donne. Poets, masters. We, what have we got? A Yiddish Keats? Never—" He was ashamed, so he wiped his cheeks with both sleeves. "Business. I'll pay you," he said.

"No."

"Because I laid a hand on you? Forgive me, I apologize. I'm crazier than he is, I should be locked up for it—"

"Not because of that."

"Then why not? *Meydeleh,* why not? What harm would it do you? Help out an old man."

She said desolately, "You don't interest me. I would have to be interested."

"I see. Naturally." He looked at Vorovsky. "Goodbye, Chaim, regards from Aristotle. What distinguishes men from the beasts is the power of ha-ha-ha. So good morning, ladies and gentlemen. Be. well. Chaim, live until a hundred and twenty. The main thing is health."

In the streetfit was full day, and he was warm from the tea. The road glistened, the sidewalks. Paths crisscrossed in unexpected places, sleds clanged, people ran. A drugstore was open and he went in to telephone Baumzweig: he dialed, but on the way he skipped a number, heard an iron noise like a weapon, and had to dial again. "Paula," he practiced, "I'll come back for a while, all right? For breakfast maybe," but instead he changed his mind and decided to CALL TR 5-2530. At the other end of the wire it was either Rose or Lou. Edelshtein told the eunuch's voice, "I believe with you about some should drop dead. Pharaoh, Queen Isabella, Haman, that pogromchik King Louis they call in history Saint, Hitler, Stalin, Nasser—" The voice said, "You're a Jew?" It sounded Southern but somehow not Negro—maybe because schooled, polished: "Accept Jesus as your Saviour and you shall have Jerusalem restored." "We already got it," Edelshtein said. *Meshiachtseiten!* "The terrestrial Jerusalem has no significance. Earth is dust. The Kingdom of God is within. Christ released man from Judaic exclusivism." "Who's excluding who?" Edelshtein said. "Christianity is Judaism universalized. Jesus is Moses publicized for ready availability. Our God is the God of Love, your God is the God of Wrath. Look how He abandoned you in Auschwitz," "It wasn't only God who didn't notice." "You people are cowards, you never even. tried to defend yourselves. You got a wide streak of yellow, you don't know how to hold a gun." "Tell it to the Egyptians," Edelshtein said. "Everyone you come into contact with turns into your enemy. When you were in Europe every nation despised you. When you moved to take over the Middle East the Arab Nation, spic faces like your own, your very own blood-kin, began "to hate you. You are a bone in the throat of all mankind." "Who gnaws at bones? Dogs and rats only." "Even your food habits are abnormal, against the grain of quotidian delight. You refuse to seethe a lamb in the milk of its mother. You will not eat a fertilized egg because it has a spot of blood on it. When you .wash your hands you chant. You pray in a debased jargon, not in the beautiful sacramental English of our Holy Bible." Edelshtein said, "That's right, Jesus spoke the King's English." "Even now, after the good Lord knows how many years in America, you talk with a kike accent. You kike, you Yid."

Edelshtein shouted into the telephone, "Amalekite! Titus! Nazi! The whole world is infected by you anti-Semites! On account of you children become corrupted! On account of you I lost everything, my whole life! On account of you I have no translator!"

QUESTIONS FOR DISCUSSION AND WRITING

1. The story sets up for us a dichotomy between the old ghetto-anchored poets who write in what they themselves perceive to be a dying language, Yiddish, and Ostrover and American Jewish authors whose work is modernist and can be read in English. How does Ozick manage to set up this division between old and new? Does the dichotomy appear to represent the dead and the living or is it more than just that?

2. This is a story of despair and bitterness, but also of humor and satire. Which comes across more?

3. We learn about Edelshtein's past, particularly in connection with the young boy, Alexi, whom his father tutors. Why is this relationship important? What is the significance of Edelshtein's homosexual feelings for the boy? Of the fact that Alexi could have wound up an engineer working in the world-at-large or the victim of a massacre against Jews at the infamous Russian place of slaughter, Babi Yar?

4. What of the role in the story of the Baumzweigs? Baumzweig runs his Yiddish poetry publication on the largesse of the grandson of a laxative manufacturer who is now an Episcopalian and a Republican politician and the sons of the Baumzweigs are scholars who did dissertations on Sir Gawain and Carson McCullers. What is Ozick suggesting here about the nature of assimiliation? Recall that at one point Edelshtein even says he wishes he had been born a Gentile. What do we see from Edelshtein's point of view of the life lived by his enemy friends the Baumzweigs?

5. Edelshtein wants to believe that Yiddish will somehow continue to live through the young and that his poetry will matter to posterity. Is he simply being a foolish and vain old man? What of the message in the story by Ostrover of the man who is obviously based on Edelshtein who sells his soul to the devil?

6. Ozick makes use of a good deal of Yiddish in the story. Is it effective or does it obscure meaning? What were your reactions to seeing so many words that were unrecognizable but were nevertheless from the mother tongue that is the heart of this story?

7. What of the violence at the story's end and the strange phone conversation with the Anti-Semite? How do these incidents shape our final feelings about Edelshtein? What, ultimately, do you feel where his character is concerned?

ON TECHNIQUE AND STYLE

1. Much of the story is told either from a kind of stream of consciousness, interior monologue from Edelshtein's point of view or through letters. Do these techniques help or hurt the essential storytelling?
2. There is much scatological in this story as well as references to snot, vomit, ass wiping, urine and the like. Why does Ozick pepper her story with these kinds of gross allusions?
3. Discuss Ozick's use of dialect. How successful is she in rendering the dialect of Yiddish speakers? Is there a danger of making the characters who speak in dialect seem absurd or ridiculous or stereotyped? Is it consonant with a story that includes so many serious themes?

CULTURAL QUESTION

1. What does this story convey about the gulf that exists between the old shtetl or ghetto world of Jewish culture in Eastern Europe and the culture that Jews have succeed in creating in America?

POETRY

Beware: Do Not Read This Poem

Ishmael Reed

Ishmael Reed (1938–   ) is a leading African American poet, novelist, essayist, and editor who was born in Chattanooga, Tennessee, and grew up in a working-class neighborhood in Buffalo, New York. He began his writing career after attending the University of Buffalo by writing jazz columns for Empire State, *a weekly African American newspaper. He later moved to New York City where he edited the* Newark New Jersey Weekly *and helped establish the famed underground* East Village Other. *For many years he has lived in Oakland, California, and taught at the University of California, Berkeley. He also taught at Harvard, Yale, Dartmouth, Washington University, and State University of New York, Buffalo. He was awarded a MacArthur genius grant and is also a recipient of the Lewis H. Michaux*

Literary Prize. The author of four volumes of poetry and two essay collections, Reed has published a number of novels, including Free-Lance Pallbearers, Yellow Back Radio Broke-Down, Mumbo Jumbo, The Last Days of Louisiana Red, Flight to Canada, The Terrible Twos, Reckless Eyeballing, *and* The Terrible Threes. *Reed is especially known for his work on behalf of promoting young writers and multicultural literature and his Neo-HooDoo black aesthetic, the African American version of voodoo. One of the most famous African American writers of his generation, Reed was described by Harvard African American scholar Henry Louis Gates as having "no true predecessor or counterpart." The Reed poem included here is a testament to the fun and cleverness of Reed's poetry and to the way he brings in popular culture and a Neo-HooDoo feeling of mystery and suspense. But he is also completely serious in this poem about the power of poetry, including his own, over our lives.*

Excerpted from the book, *Ishmael Reed: New and Collected Poems, 1964–2006.* Copyright © 1988 by Ishmael Reed. Permission granted by Lowenstein-Yost Associates, Inc.

tonite, thriller was
abt an ol woman, so vain she
surrounded herself w /
many mirrors

It got so bad that finally she
locked herself indoors & her
whole life became the
 mirrors

one day the villagers broke
into her house, but she was too
swift for them, she disappeared
 into a mirror
each tenant who bought the house
after that, lost a loved one to
 that ol woman in the mirror:
 first a little girl
 then a young woman
 then the young woman/s husband

the hunger of this poem is legendary
it has taken in many victims
back off from this poem
it has drawn in yr feet
back off from this poem
it has drawn in yr legs
back off from this poem
it is a greedy mirror
you are into this poem, from

the waist down
nobody can hear you can they?
this poem has had you up to here
                belch
this poem aint got no manners
you cant call out frm this poem
move & roll on to this poem

        do not resist this poem
        this poem has yr eyes
        this poem has his head
        this poem has his arms
        this poem has his fingers
        this poem has his fingertips

this poem is the reader & the
            reader this poem

statistic: the us bureau of missing persons reports
            that in 1968 over 100,000 people disappeared
            leaving no solid clues
            nor trace   only
    a space   in the lives of their friends

QUESTIONS FOR DISCUSSION AND WRITING

1. What kind of tone is established by Reed at the outset with the narrative about the thriller and the vain old woman who surrounded herself with mirrors?
2. Can poetry actually grab us and pull us in and command us as Reed appears to be telling us? Does his poem do that?
3. What is the purpose in the poem of the statistics from the bureau of missing persons? Does this reveal to us what Reed believes is the effect of poetry like his upon readers?
4. What does Reed communicate to the reader when he says "this poem is the reader & the / reader this poem"?

ON TECHNIQUE AND STYLE

1. Reed used humor as a technique in this poem. How does he manage to convey his brand of humor?
2. Look at the use of spacing in this poem. How and in what ways does it contribute to the meaning as well as to the experience of reading the poem?

CULTURAL QUESTION

1. Reed, an African American, at one point uses idiomatic phrasing when he says, "this poem ain't got no manners." Is he trying to convey something cross-cultural? What?

Poetry

Marianne Moore

Marianne Moore (1897–1972) is a famed modernist poet, writer, translator, and editor (of The Dial*). Born in Kirkwood, Missouri, near St. Louis, she was educated at Bryn Mawr and taught at Carlisle Indian Industrial School in Pennsylvania. Her first poems appeared in 1915 in* Egoist *and* Others *after a summer spent in England and France. She published her first volume of poetry in 1921 and continued publishing volumes of poetry as well as critical writings up to her death, including* Observations; The Pangolin and Other Verse; What Are Years?; Nevertheless; A Face; Predictions; O To Be A Dragon; The Arctic Ox; Dress and Kindred Subjects; Tell Me, Tell Me; *and* Prevalent at One Time. *Her 1951* Collected Poems *won both a Pulitzer Prize as well as a National Book Award and Bollingen Prize. Her work appeared in many journals, including* The Nation, The New Republic, *and* Partisan Review. *A friend and mentor to many of the last century's greatest poets, including T. S. Eliot, Wallace Stevens, Ezra Pound, Elizabeth Bishop, and E. E. Cummings, Moore was deemed "a fairy godmother" by Sylvia Plath. One of her best-known poems, "Poetry" first appeared in her 1935 collection* Selected Poems *and then in the 1951* Collected Poems. *It was cut from thirty-eight lines to four in her* Complete Poems, *published in 1967. With her famous line about poems being "'imaginary gardens with real toads in them,'" Moore ambitiously sets forward a lasting definition of what poetry is as well as what poets are or ought to be when she calls them "'literalists of the imagination.'"*

I, too, dislike it: there are things that are important beyond
    all this fiddle.
  Reading it, however, with a perfect contempt for it, one
    discovers in
it after all, a place for the genuine.
    Hands that can grasp, eyes
    that can dilate, hair that can rise
      if it must, these things are important not because a

high-sounding interpretation can be put upon them but because
    they are

useful. When they become so derivative as to become
    unintelligible,
the same thing may be said for all of us, that we
    do not admire what
    we cannot understand: the bat
      holding on upside down or in quest of something to

eat, elephants pushing, a wild horse taking a roll, a tireless
    wolf under
a tree, the immovable critic twitching his skin like a horse
    that feels a flea, the base-
ball fan, the statistician—
    nor is it valid
      to discriminate against "business documents and

school-books"; all these phenomena are important. One must make
    a distinction
however: when dragged into prominence by half poets, the
    result is not poetry,
nor till the poets among us can be
    "literalists of
    the imagination"—above
      insolence and triviality and can present

for inspection, "imaginary gardens with real toads in them,"
    shall we have
it. In the meantime, if you demand on the one hand,
    the raw material of poetry in
    all its rawness and
    that which is on the other hand
      genuine, you are interested in poetry.

QUESTIONS FOR DISCUSSION AND WRITING

1. Moore begins her poem by alluding to her dislike and contempt for poetry. Why start off with these attitudes? What kind of poetry is she talking about? Who are the "half poets"?
2. Moore writes about "interest" in poetry and concludes that such interest depends on the genuine and the raw. What exactly does she mean?
3. What does Moore mean by "'imaginary gardens with real toads in them'"?
4. Does this poem make you want to read more poetry and learn more about poetry?

ON TECHNIQUE AND STYLE

1. What is the effect of Moore's use of animal imagery in the poem?
2. Moore is often described as an unconventional poet because of her alternating logic, her use of irony, and her offbeat use of rhythm. Does this poem strike you as unconventional? Why or why not?

CULTURAL QUESTION

1. Does "Poetry" perform for people of all varying cultures what Moore establishes in this poem as being important about poems and poetry?

GRAPHIC FICTION

From Cages

David McKean

David McKean (1963–   ) is an illustrator, photographer, musician, and filmmaker in addition to being a comic book artist. Born in Maidenhead, England, he was educated at Berkshire College of Art and Design before coming to the United States. A regular contributor to The New Yorker, *he is art director of Artemis Communications. He collaborated with the Rolling Stones and illustrated a wide range of album and CD covers for Download, Slayer, Fear Factory, Testament, Counting Crows, Skinny Puppy, Frontline Assembly, Tori Amos, Michael Nyman, Bill Bruford, and Alice Cooper.* Violent Cases, *with Neil Gaiman, was published in 1987 and was followed by* Black Orchid *and* Signal to Noise *for* The Face *magazine. He did the covers and designs for* The Sandman *series of graphic novels and illustrated* Arkham Aylum. *The selection included here is from his 500-page graphic novel,* Cages, *which he wrote and illustrated. In 2005 the feature film* Mirror/Mask, *which he directed and served as visual designer on, premiered at the Sundance Film Festival. Presently McKean lives with his family in Britain on the Isle of Oxney in Kent. The excerpt from* Cages *features a black amateur, Rasta musician conversing and conjuring, using his flutelike musical instrument to convince his black cat companion of the mysterious power of music.*

From Cages   David McKean

QUESTIONS FOR DISCUSSION AND WRITING

1. What is the essential emotion communicated in this excerpt? Is the main Rasta character communing with the actual black cat on the tenement roof or is he merely projecting his own thoughts onto the feline he calls Mr. Cat?
2. The Rasta character brings up "raven of a night," calling to mind Poe's famous poem. What associations are conjured with the traditionally superstition-linked black cat and the "raven of a night"?
3. The Rasta character tells what he calls a doubting Tomcat that this could be the "start o' sometin." What does all of this add up to in the end with the cat and the bird? Does the bird actually stop singing?
4. How are the stars lucky? We wish upon stars and stars are linked to destiny. What role do the stars play here?

ON TECHNIQUE AND STYLE

1. Is McKean's use of dialect rendered successfully?

VISUAL TEXTS

Luna Cadillac

Jean Michel Basquiat

Jean Michel Basquiat (1960–1988) was a Haitian American graffiti and Neo-Expressionist New York–based artist.

Death is Buried, the Flower is Pulled Up, Love is Lost

Joan Miro

*Born in Barcelona, Spain, **Joan Miro** (1893–1983) was an internationally celebrated Catalan painter, sculptor, and ceramicist.*

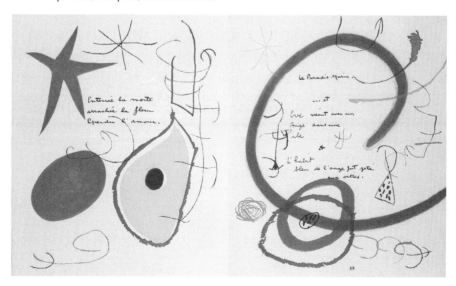

Untitled

Francesco Clemente

Born in Naples, Italy, **Francesco Clemente** *(1952–   ) is a surreal and expressionist painter.*

QUESTIONS FOR DISCUSSION AND WRITING

1. How do any of these three paintings visually represent poetry?
2. What do these artists manage to convey to us about a new-wave sensibility or a new-wave vision of the world?
3. What do the titles of these visual pieces evoke in connection to the paintings? What title would you give to the untitled Clemente painting?

ON TECHNIQUE AND STYLE

1. Basquiat divides his canvas. What is the overall effect of the division he creates?
2. What are the ultimate effects of the intersection of text and art in the Miro painting?

CULTURAL QUESTION

1. Theodore Roszak gave us the word "counterculture" as an indication of something that goes against the prevailing cultural mode. Are these images all countercultural? Why or why not?

AUDIO TEXTS   To hear these conversations, go to www.mhhe.com/soundideas1e

Track 8.1

(date: March 31, 2005; running time: 50:50 min.)

An hour with poet **W.S. Merwin.**

Track 8.2

(date: February 24, 2005; running time: 50:50 min.)

An hour with poet **Adrienne Rich.**

Track 8.3

(date: March 15, 2005; running time: 50:50 min.)

An hour with hip hop historian **Jeff Chang.**

Track 8.4

(date: May 3, 2005; running time: 50:50 min.)

An hour with hip hop DJ **Paul Miller (aka DJ Spooky).**

Track 8.5

(date: January 12, 2005; running time: 50:50 min.)

An hour on the poet **Pablo Neruda** *(centenary of his birth) with* **Robert Bly, Mark Eisner, and Ilan Stavans.**

Panel discussion on Pablo Neruda centenary: The participants in the discussion of Pablo Neruda and his poetry include poet Robert Bly, another distinguished American poet who was born in western Minnesota and educated at St. Olaf's College, Harvard, and the University of Iowa Writer's Workshop. The author of the best-selling book Iron John, *he is also a translator and won a National Book Award for his 1966 collection of poems,* The Light Around the Body. *He donated prize money from that award to the Resistance opposition to the war in Vietnam. John Felstiner is an author and award-winning translator. Educated at Harvard, he is a professor of English at Stanford. Mark Eisner is a translator and editor of* The Essential Neruda. *He runs the* In Search of Pablo Neruda *blog and is executive director of* Red Poppy. *He was educated at the University of Michigan and Stanford. Ilan Stavans is an award-winning author and translator of Mexican Jewish heritage who edited* The Poetry of Pablo Neruda. *He is professor of Spanish and Latin American culture at Amherst College and is professor of poetry at Columbia University.*

QUESTIONS FOR DISCUSSION AND WRITING

1. Miller (DJ Spooky) talks about hip-hop as old and the Internet as new. He also talks about how all cultures are now literally in the mix. If hip-hop can really absorb any style or sample anything, as he opines, can we speculate on what is next?
2. Do you agree with Chang that hip-hop has come to be the way an entire generation sees their world? Does that make it more or less, as the caller suggests, "mainstream"?
3. What about Merwin's assertion that each poem must be like doing something you never did before and maybe no one else did before? Is that too much to expect from a poem, even by a great poet?
4. Rich says that each poet falls in love with certain poets and then chases them out and either returns to them or not. Does this seem like an applicable way to view a poet's development?
5. What is the picture that emerges of Pablo Neruda's poetry from this conversation by translators and lovers of his poetry?

ON TECHNIQUE AND STYLE

1. Compare and contrast the way Miller talks about hip-hop to the way Chang does. How are their styles of expressing themselves similar or different?
2. Merwin says that poetry is all about listening. What is the effect on you of listening to him read his poem as opposed to the effect listening to Rich read?

3. Does a definition of what poetry ought to be come across in the panel discussion of Pablo Neruda's poetry? How best to state the nature of that definition?

CULTURAL QUESTION

1. To what extent are Miller and hip-hop culture compatible with the culture of poetry that is regarded as more serious and more a part of high culture?

CONNECTIONS

1. From selections in this chapter focus on ideas that emerge about the nature and importance of change and the passage from one wave or form to another—whether in music or poetry or both.
2. How do the various authors and thinkers and artists represented in the chapter approach the battle for the soul of poetry or hip-hop or both?
3. The myth of the phoenix is employed in the first two essays. How does it appear relevant in those as well as in other selections in the chapter?
4. All four short stories have within them elements of a new wave of feminism. How if at all do they connect?
5. What do the selections in this chapter reveal about the value and the effect of music and/or poetry?
6. Multiculturalism and the Internet are changing poetry and hip-hop. Where do we see this in selections included in this chapter and what kinds of new forms are being suggested?
7. Yamamoto writes about the haiku and Danticat about "kitchen poets" while Miller talks about poems made from the self. Do these all connect other than the fact that they all point to ways of envisioning poetry?
8. From selections in this chapter discuss generational change and what the writers, artists, and scholars are suggesting about it.
9. What do we learn from some of the selections in the chapter concerning distinctions often made between high and popular culture? Do they seem mortally divided or can we conclude that there is a lot of cross-fertilization going on?
10. A number of those included in this chapter discuss the dichotomy between the academic world and the world outside of the academy. What are some of the connections we see among those included in the chapter in how these worlds are separate?

FOR WRITING

CREATIVE CHOICES

1. Write a poem that is traditional or formal and then write one representing a newer wave of poetic expression.
2. Draw or photograph something you feel embodies or expresses the sense of a new wave.
3. Create a story that provides contrast between older and newer modes or waves of expression.

NARRATIVE/EXPOSITORY CHOICES

1. Focus on the differences that separate commercial art from politicized art. Are the two as separate and mutually exclusive as they sometimes appear? Can you make a case for the superiority of one over the other? Be certain to use examples.
2. Compose a narrative about someone you know who was exposed to a new wave of poetry or music and describe the effect it had.
3. Narrate your own experience of attending a hip-hop concert or a poetry reading.

RESEARCH CHOICES

1. Research the views of experts of the cyber age on the effects they see of changing technologies on consumers of music and poetry.
2. Avant-garde and poststructuralism are two varieties of what are often viewed as new waves of artistic form and expression. Research them and discover the influences and changes that they have brought.

VIDEO SUGGESTIONS

1. *Basquiat* (1996), a movie by artist Julian Schabel. Tells the story of the rise of young artist Jean-Michel Basquiat. Starting out as a street artist, living in a park in a cardboard box, Jean-Michel is "discovered" by Andy Warhol and becomes a star.
2. *I Shot Andy Warhol* (1996). Based on the true story of Valerie Solanas, a 1960s radical preaching hatred toward men in her "Scum"manifesto. She wrote a screenplay that she wanted artist Andy Warhol to produce, but he ignored her, and she eventually shot him.

3. *Slam* (1998) Ray Joshua lives in a Washington, DC, district known as Dodge City, where gang wars are frequent. He is arrested when his drug dealer is gunned down while talking to him. Jailed, two rival gangs, Thug Life and the Union, try to recruit him as a member. Features music by DJ Spooky.

4. *Frida* (2002) the story of Frida Kahlo and husband and artist Diego Rivera as the couple took the art world by storm. Her relationship with Rivera, with communist icon Leon Trotsky, and with other women, Frida Kahlo lived a complex life as a political, artistic, and sexual revolutionary.

5. *Il Postino* (the Postman), 1994. The life of fisherman Mario is changed when famous Chilean poet Pablo Neruda moves to Mario's little Italian island. Living in exile because of his political beliefs, Neruda needs a postman to deliver mail to his admirers. Mario takes the job and the two become friends. Through poetry, Neruda helps the shy Mario win over a waitress at the village inn.

 chapter **9**

Ideas and the Mind

INTRODUCTION

Ideas and the mind take in the entire realm of human experience. This chapter presents an array of sound ideas about where ideas and thinking come from and how the brain and intelligence work. The mind and its mysterious workings and some of the mysteries of human consciousness are at the heart of what you will find in the chapter, which begins with a selection of four essays by poet and naturalist Diane Ackerman, philosopher John Searle, computer engineer Jeff Hawkins, and journalist Malcolm Gladwell. Through neuroscience and metaphor Ackerman provides a picture of the brain and what it does, whereas Searle works at creating a theory of the mind based on observer-independent and observer-dependent thinking. Hawkins writes about neural network theory as he moves forward an understanding of intelligence by establishing a new theory of the brain. The concluding essay, by *The New Yorker*'s Malcolm Gladwell, takes us into the realm of what the author calls "thinking without thinking," an argument on behalf of rapid cognition versus slow-paced and even meticulous and well-orchestrated thinking.

The fiction section includes the work of four of the great-thinking American novelists of the twentieth century. The Prologue to Ralph Ellison's classic novel of the black experience in America, *The Invisible Man*, takes us underground into the mind and consciousness of a black man who thinks himself invisible, assuming that others, especially white people, cannot or will not see him for who he is. Invisibility becomes, in Ellison's novel, a metaphor that extends beyond race to encompass the human condition and what the mind will or will not see. With Hemingway in "A Clean, Well-Lighted Place" we are once more faced with the elemental human condition as what Hamlet called "the pale cast of thought" descends upon an old man in a Spanish bodega and also on the older of two waiters who wait for him to leave so they can close for the night. When we meet Saul Bellow's Moses Herzog, the protagonist of Bellow's novel *Herzog*, he is being reflective about the fact that if he is out of his mind "it's all right with me." John Barth's tour-de-force story "Night-Sea Journey," full of self-reflection and thoughts about the meaning of life, concludes the fiction section as we venture forth with Barth's narrator into the mind's quest for an understanding of human creation.

In the poetry section you will encounter Emily Dickinson's vivid poetic rendering of the brain in one of her more famous poems, "The Brain—is wider than the Sky—." We have also included "Among School Children," by the great Irish poet William Butler Yeats, a personal meditation on mind and its interplay with ideas and the temporal imagination.

Philosophic questioning of the mind on existence and the meaning of life, as well as the thought processes of human intelligence, become central to Will Eisner's graphic fiction "Izzy the Cockroach and the Meaning of Life." The visual selections include a photo of one of the world's most famous statues, *The Thinker,* by Auguste Rodin, a now-classic pose of a man in thought; William Mason's *The Inventor's Head,* and the image of a head, "Morning Light," by San Francisco photographer Hugh Shurley. The chapter concludes with the audio selections that take us deeper into thoughts on intelligence as we encounter the thinking of Malcolm Gladwell and John Searle and hear them answer questions related to their books, *Blink* and *Mind*.

Here is a chapter designed to make you think about thinking and the brain and where ideas come from and the manifold and extraordinary ways the mind works.

NONFICTION

The Enchanted Loom

Diane Ackerman

Diane Ackerman (1948–) is a naturalist, author, and poet who was born in Waukegan, Illinois, and educated at Boston University, Penn State, and Cornell, where she received a PhD. She presently makes her home in Ithaca, New York, and has taught at Cornell as well as Columbia, the University of Richmond, the University of Pittsburgh, and Washington University. Her essays have appeared in The New York Times, The New Yorker, National Geographic, Discover, *and* Parade *and she has published a number of volumes of poetry and several nonfiction children's books. Her books, in addition to* An Alchemy of Mind: The Marvel and Mystery of the Brain, *include* Cultivating Delight, My Garden, Deep Play, A Slender Thread, The Rarest of the Rare, A Natural History of Love, The Moon by Whale Light, *and the best-seller* A Natural History of the Senses, *which was adapted as a five-hour television series which she hosted for PBS. She also wrote a memoir,* On Extended Wings. *A former Guggenheim and John Burroughs Nature Award recipient and a Lavan Poetry Prize winner, she also has had a molecule named after her. In* An Alchemy of Mind *Ackerman brings her considerable knowledge of neuroscience in concert with her distinctive poetic sensibility. In the first chapter of that book, "The Enchanted Loom," she provides a portrait of the brain that is both scientific and poetic.*

. . . an enchanted loom where millions of flashing shuttles weave a dissolving pattern, always a meaningful pattern though never an abiding one; a shifting harmony of sub-patterns.

—Sir Charles Sherrington,
Man on His Nature

Imagine the brain, that shiny mound of being, that mouse-gray parliament of cells, that dream factory, that petit tyrant inside a ball of bone, that huddle of neurons calling all the plays, that little everywhere, that fickle pleasure-drome, that wrinkled wardrobe of selves stuffed into the skull like too many clothes into a gym bag. The neocortex has ridges, valleys, and folds because the brain kept remodeling itself though space was tight. We take for granted the ridiculous-sounding yet undeniable fact that each person carries around atop the body a complete universe in which trillions of sensations, thoughts, and desires stream. They mix privately, silently, while agitating on many levels, some of which we're not aware of, thank heavens. If we needed to remember how to work the bellows of the lungs or the writhing python of digestion, we'd be swamped by formed and forming memories, and there'd be no time left for buying cute socks. My brain likes cute socks. But it also likes kisses. And asparagus. And watching boat-tailed grackles. And biking. And drinking Japanese green tea in a rose garden. There's the nub of it—the brain is personality's whereabouts. It's also a stern warden, and, at times, a self-tormentor. It's where catchy tunes snag, and cravings keep tugging. Shaped a little like a loaf of French country bread, our brain is a crowded chemistry lab, bustling with nonstop neural conversations. It's also an impersonal landscape where minute bolts of lightning prowl and strike. A hall of mirrors, it can contemplate existentialism, the delicate hooves of a goat, and its own birth and death in a matter of seconds. It's blunt as a skunk, and a real gossip hound, but also voluptuous, clever, playful, and forgiving.

The brain's genius is its gift for reflection. What an odd, ruminating, noisy, self-interrupting conversation we conduct with ourselves from birth to death. That monologue often seems like a barrier between us and our neighbors and loved ones, but actually it unites us at a fundamental level, as nothing else can. It takes many forms: our finding similarities among seemingly unrelated things, wadding up worries into tangled balls of obsession difficult to pierce even with the spike of logic, painting elaborate status or romance fantasies in which we star, picturing ourselves elsewhere and elsewhen. Happily storing information outside our bodies, the brain extends itself through time and space by creating extensions to the senses such as telescopes and telephones. How evocation becomes sound in Ravel's nostalgic "Pour une Infante Défunte," a plaintive-sounding dance for a princess from a faraway time, is an art of the brain. So is the vast gallantry of imagining how other people, and even other animals, experience life.

The brain is not completely hardwired, though at times it may seem so. Someone once wisely observed that if one's only tool is a key, then every problem will seem to be a lock. Thus the brain analyzes as a way of life in Western cultures, abhors contradiction, honors formal logic, and abides by many rules. *Reasoning* we call it, as if it were a spice. Cuisine may be a good metaphor for the modishness and malleability of the thinking brain. In some non-Western cultures the brain doesn't reason through logic but by relating things to the environment, in a process that includes contradiction, conflict, and the sudden appearance of random forces and events. The biologist Alexander Luria was struck by this when he interviewed Russian nomads in 1931. "All the bears up North are white," he said. "I have a friend up there who saw a bear. What color was the bear?" A nomad stared at him, puzzled: "How am

I supposed to know? Ask your friend!" These are but two styles in the art of the brain. All people are alike enough to be recognizable, even predictable at times, yet everyone has a slightly different flavor of mind. Whole cultures do. Just different enough to keep things interesting, or, depending on your point of view, frightening.

The brain analyzes, the brain loves, the brain detects a whiff of pine and is transported to a childhood summer spent at Girl Scout camp in the Poconos, the brain tingles under the caress of a feather. But the brain is silent, dark, and dumb. It feels nothing. It sees nothing. The art of the brain is to transcend those daunting limitations and canvass the world. The brain can hurl itself across mountains or into outer space. The brain can imagine an apple and experience it as real. Indeed, the brain barely knows the difference between an imagined apple and an observed one. Hence the success of athletes visualizing perfect performances, and authors luring readers into their picturesque empires. In one instant, the brain can rule the world as a self-styled god, and the next succumb to helplessness and despair.

Until now, using the slang we take for granted, I've been saying "the brain" when what I really mean is that fantasia of self-regard we call "the mind." The brain is not the mind, the mind inhabits the brain. Like a ghost in a machine, some say. Mind is the comforting mirage of the physical brain. An experience, not an entity. Another way to think of mind may be as St. Augustine thought of God, as an emanation that's not located in one place, or one form, but exists throughout the universe. An essence, not just a substance. And, of course, the mind isn't located only in the brain. The mind reflects what the body senses and feels, it's influenced by a caravan of hormones and enzymes. Each mind inhabits a private universe of its own devising that changes daily, depending on the vagaries of medication, intense emotions, pollution, genes, or countless other personal-size cataclysms. In Kafka's fiction, a character finds the question "How are you?" impossible to answer. We slur over the sensory details of each day. Otherwise life would be too exhausting to live. The brain knows how to idle when necessary and yet be ready to rev up at the sound of a bear claw scratching over rock, or a math teacher calling out one's name.

Among the bad jokes evolution has played on us are these: 1) We have brains that can conceive of states of perfection they can't achieve, 2) We have brains that compare our insides to other people's outsides, 3) We have brains desperate to stay alive, yet we are finite beings who perish. There are many more, of course.

Sometimes it's hard to imagine the art and beauty of the brain, because it seems too abstract and hidden an empire, a dense jungle of neurons. The idea that a surgeon might reach into it to revise its career seems as dangerous as taking the lid off a time bomb and discovering thousands of wires. Which one controls the timing mechanism? Getting it wrong may be deadly. Still, there are bomb squads and there are brain surgeons. The art of the brain is to liken and learn, never resist a mystery, and question everything, even itself.

QUESTIONS FOR DISCUSSION AND WRITING

1. "Imagine the brain," Diane Ackerman begins in this excerpt. Does she give a picture of the brain? What is the picture that emerges? Can the brain be all she says it is?
2. What kinds of distinctions is Ackerman making in her essay between reason and reflection? Is she able adequately to define both?
3. Ackerman writes: "In one instant, the brain can rule the world as a self-styled god, and the next succumb to helplessness and despair." Does that statement, sweeping and general as it is, seem apt?
4. What about what Ackerman calls "the art and beauty of the brain"? She says they are hard to imagine. Do you agree? Is it easier to imagine the physical loaf of bread or dense jungle of neurons she writes about, the physical, neuroanatomical brain?
5. Do you agree with Ackerman when she concludes: "The art of the brain is to liken and learn, never resist a mystery, and question everything, even itself"?

ON TECHNIQUE AND STYLE

1. Ackerman is a poet and writes like one. Where in the essay do we see her coming across as especially poetic?
2. There is what we might call a cataloging effect to Ackerman's writing style—her running of a series of examples or phrases in seriatim, one after the other. How well does this serve her as a writer and how much does it help persuade us of her point of view?
3. Ackerman points to examples of the composer Ravel's "Pour une Infante Défunte," the biologist Alexander Luria's white bear story, and the response of the fiction writer Franz Kafka's character to the question, "How are you?" How do these examples serve her essay's overall effectiveness?

CULTURAL QUESTION

1. What does Ackerman mean about cultural differences when she says "All people are alike enough to be recognizable, even predictable at times, yet everyone has a slightly different flavor of mind. Whole cultures do. Just different enough to keep things interesting, or, depending on your point of view, frightening."

Introduction: Why I Wrote This Book

John Searle

John Searle (1932–   ) is one of America's preeminent philosophers, famous for the Chinese room argument that posits that human intelligence cannot be matched by a computer. Born in Denver, Colorado, and educated at Oxford (as a Rhodes Scholar) Searle is Mills Professor of Philosophy at the University of California, Berkeley and was a prominent faculty figure in the Free Speech movement. He is the recipient of many awards, including the Jean Nicod Prize and a National Humanities Medal. An expert on human consciousness, the human mind, and artificial intelligence, Searle is the author of many articles and books, including The Rediscovery of Mind; The Mystery of Consciousness; Mind, Language and Society; Philosophy in the Real World; Consciousness and Language, *and* Mind: A Brief Introduction, *from which the Introduction, "Why I Wrote This Book," is included here. In it, Searle tells why he has set out to write a book on mind and provides an overview to what he sees as the essential issues in approaching philosophical questions related to understanding the mind.*

From *Mind: A Brief Introduction* by John Searle. Copyright © 2004 by Oxford University Press, Inc. By permission of Oxford University Press, Inc.

There are many recent introductory books on the philosophy of mind. Several give a more or less comprehensive survey of the main positions and arguments currently in the field. Some, indeed, are written with great clarity, rigor, intelligence, and scholarship. What then is my excuse for adding another book to this glut? Well, of course, any philosopher who has worked hard on a subject is unlikely to be completely satisfied with somebody else's writings on that same subject, and I suppose that I am a typical philosopher in this respect. But in addition to the usual desire for wanting to state my disagreements, there is an overriding reason for my wanting to write a general introduction to the philosophy of mind. Almost all of the works that I have read accept the same set of historically inherited categories for describing mental phenomena, especially consciousness, and with these categories a certain set of assumptions about how consciousness and other mental phenomena relate to each other and to the rest of the world. It is this set of categories, and the assumptions that the categories carry like heavy baggage, that is completely unchallenged and that keeps the discussion going. The different positions then are all taken within a set of mistaken assumptions. The result is that the philosophy of mind is unique among contemporary philosophical subjects, in that all of the most famous and influential theories are false. By such theories I mean just about anything that has "ism" in its name. I am thinking of dualism, both property dualism and substance dualism, materialism, physicalism, computationalism, functionalism, behaviorism, epiphenomenalism, cognitivism, eliminativism, pan psychism, dual-aspect theory, and emergentism, as it is standardly conceived. To make the whole subject even more poignant, many of these theories, especially dualism and materialism, are trying to say something true. One of my many aims is to try to rescue the truth from the overwhelming urge to falsehood. I have attempted some of this task in other works, especially *The Rediscovery of the Mind,*[1] but this is my only attempt at a comprehensive introduction to the entire subject of the philosophy of mind.

Now what exactly are these assumptions and why are they false? I cannot tell you that just yet. They do not admit of a quick summary without some preliminary work. The first half of this book is in large part about exposing and overcoming those assumptions. It is hard to summarize them because we lack a neutral vocabulary in which to describe mental phenomena. So I have to begin by appealing to your experiences. Suppose you are sitting at a table thinking about the contemporary political situation, about what is going on in Washington, London, and Paris. You turn your attention to this book and you read up to this point. Here I suggest that, to get a feel for the assumptions, you try pinching your left forearm with your right hand. And suppose you do this intentionally. That is, we will suppose your intention causes the movement of your right hand to pinch your left arm. At this point you will experience a mild pain. This pain has the following more or less obvious features. It exists only insofar as it is consciously experienced, and thus it is in one sense of the words entirely "subjective" and not "objective." Furthermore, there is a certain qualitative feel to the pain. So, the conscious pain has at least these two features: subjectivity and qualitativeness.

I want all of this to sound rather innocent, even boring. So far you have had three types of conscious experiences: thinking about something, intentionally doing something, and feeling a sensation. What is the problem? Well, now look at the objects around you, the chairs and tables, houses and trees. These objects are not in any sense "subjective." They exist entirely independent of whether or not they are experienced. Furthermore, we know independently that they are entirely made of the particles described by atomic physics, and that there is no qualitative feel to being a physical particle, or for that matter being a table. They are parts of the world that exist apart from experiences. Now this simple contrast between our experiences and the world that exists independently of our experiences invites a characterization, and in our traditional vocabulary the most natural characterization is to say is that there is a distinction between the mental, on the one hand, and the physical or material, on the other. The mental qua mental is not physical. And the physical qua physical is not mental. It is this simple picture that leads to many of the problems, and our three harmless-looking

[1] J. R. Searle, *The Rediscovery of the Mind* (Cambridge, MA: MIT Press, 1992).

examples exemplify three of the worst problems. How can conscious experiences like your pain exist in a world that is entirely composed of physical particles and how can some physical particles, presumably in your brain cause the mental experiences? (This is called the "mind-body problem.") But even if we got a solution to that problem, we still would not be out of the woods because the next obvious question is, How can the subjective, insubstantial, nonphysical mental states of consciousness ever cause anything in the physical world? How can your intention, not a part of the physical world, ever cause the movement of your arm? (This is called the "problem of mental causation.") Finally your thoughts about politics raise a third intractable problem. How can your thoughts, presumably in your head, refer to or be about distant objects and states of affairs, political events occurring in Washington, London or Paris, for example? (This is called the "problem of intentionality," where "intentionality" means the directedness or aboutness of the mind.)

Our innocent experiences invited a description; and our traditional vocabulary of "mental" and "physical" is hard to resist. This traditional vocabulary assumes the mutual exclusion of the mental and physical; and that assumption creates insoluble problems that have launched a thousand books. People who accept the reality and irreducibility of the mental tend to think of themselves as dualists. But to others, accepting an irreducible mental component in reality seems like giving up on the scientific world-view, so they deny the existence of any such mental reality. They think it can all be reduced to the material or eliminated altogether. They tend to think of themselves as materialists. I think both sides are making the same mistake.

I am going to try to overcome the vocabulary and the assumptions, and in so doing I am going to try to solve or dissolve the traditional problems. But once we do that, the subject, the philosophy of mind, does not end: it gets more interesting. And this is my second reason for wanting to write this book. Most of the general introductions to the subject are just about the Big Questions. They concentrate mainly on the mind-body problem with some attention also devoted to the problem of mental causation and a lesser amount to the problem of intentionality. I do not think these are the only interesting questions in the philosophy of mind. With the big questions out of the way, we can answer the more interesting and neglected set of questions: how does it work in detail?

Specifically, it seems to me we need to investigate questions about the detailed structure of consciousness, and the significance of recent neuro-biological research on this subject. I devote an entire chapter to these questions. With the philosophical puzzle about the possibility of intentionality answered, we can then go on to examine the actual structure of human intentionality. Furthermore, there are a series of absolutely fundamental questions that we have to get clear about before we can think that we understand the operation of the mind at all. They are more than I can cover in a single book, but I do devote a chapter each to the problem of the freedom of the will, the actual operation of mental causation, the nature and functioning of the unconscious, the analysis of perception, and the concept of the self. In an introductory book I cannot go into too much detail, but I can at least give you a feel for the richness of the subject matter, a richness that is lost in the usual ways of dealing with this subject in introductory books.

There are two distinctions that I want you to be clear about at the very beginning, because they are essential for the argument and because the failure to understand them has led to massive philosophical confusion. The first is the distinction between those features of a world that are observer independent and those that are observer dependent or observer relative. Think of the things that would exist regardless of what human beings thought or did. Some such things are force, mass, gravitational attraction, the planetary system, photosynthesis, and hydrogen atoms. All of these are observer independent in the sense that their existence does not depend on human attitudes. But there are lots of things that depend for their existence on us and our attitudes. Money, property, government, football games, and cocktail parties are what they are, in large part, because that's what we think they are. All of these are observer relative or observer dependent. In general, the natural sciences deal with observer-independent phenomena, the social sciences with the observer dependent. Observer-dependent facts are created by conscious agents, but the mental states of the conscious agents that create observer-dependent facts are themselves observer-independent mental states. Thus the piece of paper in my hand is only money because I and others regard it as money.

Money is observer dependent. But the fact that we regard it as money is not itself observer dependent. It is an observer-independent fact about us that I and others regard this as money.

Where the mind is concerned we also need a distinction between original or intrinsic intentionality on the one hand and derived intentionality on the other. For example I have in my head *information* about how to get to San Jose. I have a set of true *beliefs* about the way to San Jose. This information and these beliefs in me are examples of original or intrinsic intentionality. The map in front of me also contains information about how to get to San Jose, and it contains symbols and expressions that *refer to* or are *about* or *represent* cities, highways, and the like. But the sense in which the map contains intentionality in the form of information, reference, aboutness, and representations is derived from the original intentionality of the map makers and users. Intrinsically the map is just a sheet of cellulose fibers with ink stains on it. Any intentionality it has is imposed on it by the original intentionality of humans.

So there are two distinctions to keep in mind, first between observer-independent and observer-dependent phenomena, and second between original and derived intentionality. They are systematically related: derived intentionality is always observer-dependent.

QUESTIONS FOR DISCUSSION AND WRITING

1. Right off Searle states that his intention in writing his book on mind is to "rescue the truth from the overwhelming urge to falsehood" because all famous and influential theories of the mind, he claims, are false. He goes on to set up a division between dualists and materialists and says both are wrong and "make the same mistake." How are we affected by his being so certain sounding about other theories and ideas of the mind being wrong and the theory he will lay out being right?

2. Searle provides a definition as well as a division of the philosophic concept called solipsism, the belief that truth is only accessible through the self, through subjectivity. What does his attitude toward solipsism appear to be? Searle spends time discussing the famous French philosopher Rene Descartes and his view that we see the visual image or representation of a hand in our minds rather than the hand itself. How important are such philosophical questions about, for example, whether a hand we see actually exists in reality or only in our minds as we perceive it?

3. Searle brings to our attention three distinct problems related to the philosophy of mind. He calls one the mind-body problem and the others the problem of causation and the problem of intentionality. He says they are all inexplicable questions. Why, then, do you think he brings them up? He goes on to say the more interesting and neglected set of questions have to do with how the mind works in detail. Is he placing more emphasis on those questions rather than the inexplicable ones?

4. Do you agree with Searle about the importance of distinguishing between what is "observer independent" and "observer dependent"? Why does this seem to be such an essential distinction for understanding the mind?

ON TECHNIQUE AND STYLE

1. Does Searle's style of writing seem too philosophical? Does it need to be? He is, after all, a philosopher writing about philosophy. What are your general impressions and reactions to his style in that context?

2. Does Searle convince us in his argument that all of the most famous and influenced theories of philosophy of the mind are false?

3. How effective are the examples Searle uses, such as politics in Washington, London, or Paris; the hitting of a thumb with a hammer; or observer-independent things like gravitational attraction versus observer-dependent things like money? Do the examples make his point?

CULTURAL QUESTION

1. The division Searle presents between people who think of themselves as dualists and those who regard themselves as materialists may seem a

dichotomy particularly rooted in Western culture. It is. Do you see that as a limitation in Searle's thinking or do you think the Western centric philosophical view of the mind mirrors where the theory and thinking actually rest?

From Neural Networks

Jeff Hawkins

Jeff Hawkins (1957–   ) was born in Long Island, New York, and educated as an electrical engineer at Cornell University and the University of California, Berkeley. The founder of Palm Computing and the inventor of the PalmPilot, he also founded the Redwood Neuroscience Institute to promote research on memory and cognition. A highly successful Silicon Valley entrepreneur and computer architect, Hawkins is a member of the scientific board of Cold Spring Laboratory and the National Academy of Engineering. His book, On Intelligence *(2004), written with* New York Times *science writer Sandra Blakeslee, is a theory of the brain that offers a new understanding of it that Hawkins believes "will lead to the creation of truly intelligent machines." His memory-prediction framework of the brain is grounded in the importance of the brain's cortex and on predictions based on the seeing of patterns. The excerpt included here is from "Neural Networks," the second chapter of* On Intelligence. *In it Hawkins writes of the initial promise but ultimate frustration and limitations for him of neural networks in his quest to find a workable theory of the brain that can lead him and others to knowing how to replicate it.*

When I started at UC Berkeley in January 1986, the first thing I did was compile a history of theories of intelligence and brain function. I read hundreds of papers by anatomists, physiologists, philosophers, linguists, computer scientists, and psychologists. Numerous people from many fields had written extensively about thinking and intelligence. Each field had its own set of journals and each used its own terminology. I found their descriptions inconsistent and incomplete. Linguists talked of intelligence in terms such as "syntax" and "semantics." To them, the brain and intelligence was all about language. Vision scientists referred to 2D, 2½D, and 3D sketches. To them, the brain and intelligence was all about visual pattern recognition. Computer scientists talked of schemas and frames, new terms they made up to represent knowledge. None of these people talked about the structure of the brain and how it would implement any of their theories. On the other hand, anatomists and neurophysiologists wrote extensively about the structure of the brain and how neurons behave, but they mostly avoided any attempt at large-scale theory. It was difficult and frustrating trying to make sense of these various approaches and the mountain of experimental data that accompanied them.

Around this time, a new and promising approach to thinking about intelligent machines burst onto the scene. Neural networks had been around since the late 1960s in one form or another, but neural networks and the AI movement were competitors, for both the dollars and the mind share of the agencies that fund research. AI, the 800-pound gorilla in those days, actively squelched neural network research. Neural network researchers were essentially blacklisted from getting funding for several years. A few people continued to think about them though, and in the mid-1980s their day in the sun had finally arrived. It is hard to know exactly why there was a sudden interest in neural networks, but undoubtedly one contributing factor was the continuing failure of artificial intelligence. People were casting about for alternatives to AI and found one in artificial neural networks.

Neural networks were a genuine improvement over the AI approach because their architecture is based, though very loosely, on real nervous systems. Instead of programming computers, neural network researchers, also known as *connectionists,* were interested in learning what kinds of behaviors could be exhibited by hooking a bunch of neurons together. Brains are made of neurons; therefore, the brain is a neural network. That is a fact. The hope of connectionists was that the elusive properties of intelligence would become clear by studying how neurons interact, and that some of the problems that were unsolvable with AI could be solved by replicating the correct connections between populations of neurons. A neural network is unlike a computer in that it has no CPU and doesn't store information in a centralized memory. The network's knowledge and memories are distributed throughout its connectivity—just like real brains.

On the surface, neural networks seemed to be a great fit with my own interests. But I quickly became disillusioned with the field. By this time I had formed an opinion that three things were essential to understanding the brain. My first criterion was the inclusion of time in brain function. Real brains process rapdily changing streams of information. There is nothing static about the flow of information into and out of the brain.

The second criterion was the importance of feedback. Neuroanatomists have known for a long time that the brain is saturated with feedback connections. For example, in the circuit between the neocortex and a lower structure called the thalamus, connections going backward (toward the input) exceed the connections going forward by almost a factor of ten! That is, for every fiber feeding information forward into the neocortex, there are ten fibers feeding information back toward the senses. Feedback dominates most connections throughout the neocortex as well. No one understood the precise role of this feedback, but it was clear from published research that it existed everywhere. I figured it must be important.

The third criterion was that any theory or model of the brain should account for the physical architecture of the brain. The neocortex is not a simple structure. As we will see later, it is organized as a repeating hierarchy. Any neural network that didn't acknowledge this structure was certainly not going to work like a brain.

But as the neural network phenomenon exploded on the scene, it mostly settled on a class of ultrasimple models that didn't meet any of these criteria. Most neural networks consisted of a small number of neurons connected in three rows. A pattern (the input) is presented to the first row. These input neurons are connected to the next row of neurons, the so-called hidden units. The hidden units then connect to the final row of neurons, the output units. The connections between neurons have variable strengths, meaning the activity in one neuron might increase the activity in another and decrease the activity in a third neuron depending on the connection strengths. By changing these strengths, the network learns to map input patterns to output patterns.

These simple neural networks only processed static patterns, did not use feedback, and didn't look anything like brains. The most common type of neural network, called a "back propagation" network, learned by broadcasting an error from the output units back toward the input units. You might think this is a form of feedback, but it isn't really. The backward propagation of errors only occurred during the learning phase. When the neural network was working normally, after being trained, the information flowed only one way. There was no feedback from outputs to inputs. And the models had no sense of time. A static input pattern got converted into a static output pattern. Then another input pattern was presented. There was no history or record in the network of what happened even a short time earlier. And finally the architecture of these neural networks was trivial compared to the complicated and hierarchical structure of the brain.

I thought the field would quickly move on to more realistic networks, but it didn't. Because these simple neural networks were able to do interesting things, research seemed to stop right there, for years. They had found a new and interesting tool, and overnight thousands of scientists, engineers, and students were getting grants, earning PhDs, and writing books about neural networks. Companies were formed to use neural networks to predict the stock market, process loan applications, verify signatures, and perform hundreds of other pattern classification applications. Although the intent of the founders of the field might have been more general, the field became dominated by people who weren't interested in understanding how the brain works, or understanding what intelligence is.

The popular press didn't understand this distinction well. Newspapers, magazines, and TV science programs presented neural networks as being "brainlike" or working on the "same principles as the brain." Unlike AI, where everything had to be programmed, neural nets learned by example, which seemed, well, somehow more intelligent. One prominent demonstration was NetTalk. This neural network learned to map sequences of letters onto spoken sounds. As the network was trained on printed text, it started sounding like a computer voice reading the words. It was easy to imagine that, with a little more time, neural networks would be conversing with humans. NetTalk was incorrectly heralded on national news as a machine learning to read. NetTalk was a great exhibition, but what it was actually doing bordered on the trivial. It didn't read, it didn't understand, and was of little practical value. It just matched letter combinations to predefined sound patterns.

Let me give you an analogy to show how far neural networks were from real brains. Imagine that instead of trying to figure out how a brain worked we were trying to figure out how a digital computer worked. After years of study, we discover that everything in the computer is made of transistors. There are hundreds of millions of transistors in a computer and they are connected together in precise and complex ways. But we don't understand how the computer works or why the transistors are connected the way they are. So one day we decide to connect just a few transistors together to see what happens. Lo and behold we find that as few as three transistors, when connected together in a certain way, become an amplifier. A small signal put into one end is magnified on the other end. (Amplifiers in radios and televisions are made using transistors in this fashion.) This is an important discovery, and overnight an industry springs up making transistor radios, televisions, and other electronic appliances using transistor amplifiers. This is all well and good, but it doesn't tell us anything about how the computer works. Even though an amplifier and a computer are both made of transistors, they have almost nothing else in common. In the same way, a real brain and a three-row neural network are built with neurons, but have almost nothing else in common.

During the summer of 1987, I had an experience that threw more cold water on my already low enthusiasm for neural nets. I went to a neural network conference where I saw a presentation by a company called Nestor. Nestor was trying to sell a neural network application for recognizing handwriting on a tablet. It was offering to license the program for one million dollars. That got my attention. Although Nestor was promoting the sophistication of its neural network algorithm and touting it as yet another major breakthrough, I felt the problem of handwriting recognition could be solved in a simpler, more traditional way. I went home that night, thought about the problem, and in two days had designed a handwriting recognizer that was fast, small, and flexible. My solution didn't use a neural network and it didn't work at all like a brain. Although that conference sparked my interest in designing computers with a stylus interface (eventually leading to the PalmPilot ten years later), it also convinced me that neural networks were not much of an improvement over traditional methods. The handwriting recognizer I created ultimately became the basis for the text entry system, called Graffiti, used in the first series of Palm products. I think Nestor went out of business.

So much for simple neural networks. Most of their capabilities were easily handled by other methods and eventually the media hoopla subsided. At least neural network researchers did not claim their models were intelligent. After all, they were extremely simple networks and did less than AI programs. I don't want to leave you with the impression that all neural networks are of the simple three-layer variety. Some researchers have continued to study neural networks of different designs. Today the term *neural network* is used to describe a diverse set of models, some of which are more biologically accurate and some of which are not. But almost none of them attempt to capture the overall function or architecture of the neocortex.

In my opinion, the most fundamental problem with most neural networks is a trait they share with AI programs. Both are fatally burdened by their focus on behavior. Whether they are calling these behaviors "answers," "patterns," or "outputs," both AI and neural networks assume intelligence lies in the behavior that a program or a neural network produces after processing a given input. The most important attribute of a computer program or a neural network is whether it gives the correct or desired output. As inspired by Alan Turing, intelligence equals behavior.

But intelligence is not just a matter of acting or behaving intelligently. Behavior is a manifestation of intelligence, but not the central characteristic or primary definition of being intelligent. A moment's reflection proves this: You can be intelligent just lying in the dark, thinking and understanding. Ignoring what goes on *in* your head and focusing instead on behavior has been a large impediment to understanding intelligence and building intelligent machines.

Before we explore a new definition of intelligence, I want to tell you about one other connectionist approach that came much closer to describing how real brains work. Trouble is, few people seem to have realized the importance of this research.

While neural nets grabbed the limelight, a small splinter group of neural network theorists built networks that didn't focus on behavior. Called auto-associative memories, they were also built out of simple "neurons" that connected to each other and fired when they reached a certain threshold. But they were interconnected differently, using lots of feedback. Instead of only passing information forward, as in a back propagation network, auto-associative memories fed the output of each neuron back into the input— sort of like calling yourself on the phone. This feedback loop led to some interesting features. When a pattern of activity was imposed on the artificial neurons, they formed a memory of this pattern. The auto-associative network associated patterns with themselves, hence the term *auto-associative memory.*

The result of this wiring may at first seem ridiculous. To retrieve a pattern stored in such a memory, you must provide the pattern you want to retrieve. It would be like going to the grocer and asking to buy a bunch of bananas. When the grocer asks you how you will pay, you offer to pay with bananas. What good is that? you might ask. But an auto-associative memory has a few important properties that are found in real brains.

The most important property is that you don't have to have the entire pattern you want to retrieve in order to retrieve it. You might have only part of the pattern, or you might have a somewhat messed-up pattern. The auto-associative memory can retrieve the correct pattern, as it was originally stored, even though you start with a messy version of it. It would be like going to the grocer with half eaten brown bananas and getting whole green bananas in return. Or going to the bank with a ripped and unreadable bill and the banker says, "I think this is a messed-up $100 bill. Give me that one, and I will give you this new, crisp $100 bill."

Second, unlike most other neural networks, an auto-associative memory can be designed to store sequences of patterns, or temporal patterns. This feature is accomplished by adding a time delay to the feedback. With this delay, you can present an auto-associative memory with a sequence of patterns, similar to a melody, and it can remember the sequence. I might feed in the first few notes of "Twinkle Twinkle Little Star" and the memory returns the whole song. When presented with part of the sequence, the memory can recall the rest. As we will see later, this is how people learn practically everything, as a sequence of patterns. And I propose the brain uses circuits similar to an auto-associative memory to do so.

Auto-associative memories hinted at the potential importance of feedback and time-changing inputs. But the vast majority of AI, neural network, and cognitive scientists ignored time and feedback.

Neuroscientists as a whole have not done much better. They too know about feedback—they are the people who discovered it—but most have no theory (beyond vague talk of "phases" and "modulation") to account for why the brain needs to have so much of it. And time has little or no central role in most of their ideas on overall brain function. They tend to chart the brain in terms of where things happen, not when or how neural firing patterns interact over time. Part of this bias comes from the limits of our current experimental techniques. One of the favorite technologies of the 1990s, aka the Decade of the Brain, was functional imaging. Functional imaging machines can take pictures of brain activity in humans. However, they cannot see rapid changes. So scientists ask subjects to concentrate on a single task over and over again as if they were being asked to stand still for an optical photograph, except this is a mental photograph. The result is we have lots of data on *where* in the brain certain tasks occur, but little data on how realistic, time-varying inputs flow through the brain. Functional imaging lends insight into *where* things are happening at a given moment but cannot easily capture how brain activity changes over time. Scientists would like to collect this data, but there are few good techniques for doing so. Thus many mainstream cognitive neuroscientists continue to buy into the input-output fallacy. You present a fixed input and see what output you get. Wiring diagrams of the cortex tend to show flowcharts that start in the primary sensory areas where sights, sounds, and touch come in, flow up through higher analytical, planning, and motor areas, and then feed instructions down to the muscles. You sense, then you act.

I don't want to imply that everyone has ignored time and feedback. This is such a big field that virtually every idea has its adherents. In recent years, belief in the importance of feedback, time, and prediction has been on the rise. But the thunder of AI and classical neural networks kept other approaches subdued and underappreciated for many years.

QUESTIONS FOR DISCUSSION AND WRITING

1. Hawkins writes of his personal search for understanding the brain and intelligence by focusing on the importance of neural networks. Why did neural networks get, as Hawkins puts it, their day in the sun?
2. Why does Hawkins become disillusioned with the field of neural networks? What do the three criteria he cites reveal about how the brain actually works?
3. From what Hawkins tells us about neural networks, even those that are biologically accurate, not having "the overall function or architecture of the neocortex," what do you assume he is positing about the neocortex and its role in intelligence?
4. How do AI (Artificial Intelligence) programs stack up for Hawkins compared to neural networks?
5. What does Hawkins conclude about the relationship between behavior and intelligence? Do you agree?

ON TECHNIQUE AND STYLE

1. Does Hawkins's tone seem sarcastic when he talks about the jumping aboard and hoopla over neural networks, the examples of Nestor and NetTalk? What is the effect of the attitude he reveals?
2. How effective are the personal touches Hawkins brings in, the personal narrative elements he employs in this excerpt?
3. What about Hawkins's analogy to a digital computer? Does it do more than simply highlight what he wants to communicate about neural networks?

CULTURAL QUESTION

1. Hawkins represents someone who might be described as a perfect example of an emissary from what has often been described as geek culture, the culture of high technology. Is this a fair way to characterize individuals or just another kind of cultural stereotype?

Introduction:
The Statue That Didn't Look Right

Malcolm Gladwell

Malcolm Gladwell (1963–   ) was born in the United Kingdom and raised in Ontario,
Canada, and educated at the University of Toronto. He worked as a reporter and business
and science writer for the Washington Post *before becoming its New York bureau chief.*
He has been a staff writer for The New Yorker *since 1996 and won a National Maga-*
zine Award in 1999 for his portrait of Ron Popeil. His two books, both New York Times
best-sellers, are The Tipping Point: How Little Things Can Make a Big Difference
and Blink: The Power of Thinking Without Thinking. *In 2005 he was named one of*
Time *magazine's 100 most influential people. He also sold the rights to* Blink *that year*
for $1 million to actor Leonardo di Caprio. The selection included here is from the Intro-
duction, "The Statue That Didn't Look Right." It presents the gist of Gladwell's argu-
ment that we often don't know why we know what we know but, yet, we know.

In September of 1983, an art dealer by the name of Gianfranco Becchina
approached the J. Paul Getty Museum in California. He had in his possession, he said, a marble statue dating from the sixth century BC. It was what
is known as a kouros—a sculpture of a nude male youth standing with his
left leg forward and his arms at his sides. There are only about two hundred
kouroi in existence, and most have been recovered badly damaged or in fragments from grave sites or archeological digs. But this one was almost perfectly preserved. It stood close to seven feet tall. It had a kind of light-colored
glow that set it apart from other ancient works. It was an extraordinary find.
Becchina's asking price was just under $10 million.

    The Getty moved cautiously. It took the kouros on loan and began a thor-
ough investigation. Was the statue consistent with other known kouroi? The
answer appeared to be yes. The style of the sculpture seemed reminiscent
of the Anavyssos kouros in the National Archaeological Museum of Athens,
meaning that it seemed to fit with a particular time and place. Where and
when had the statue been found? No one knew precisely, but Becchina gave
the Getty's legal department a sheaf of documents relating to its more recent
history. The kouros, the records stated, had been in the private collection of
a Swiss physician named Lauffenberger since the 1930s, and he in turn had
acquired it from a well-known Greek art dealer named Roussos.

    A geologist from the University of California named Stanley Margolis
came to the museum and spent two days examining the surface of the statue
with a high-resolution stereomicroscope. He then removed a core sample

measuring one centimeter in diameter and two centimeters in length from just below the right knee and analyzed it using an electron microscope, electron microprobe, mass spectrometry, X-ray diffraction, and X-ray fluorescence. The statue was made of dolomite marble from the ancient Cape Vathy quarry on the island of Thasos, Margolis concluded, and the surface of the statue was covered in a thin layer of calcite—which was significant, Margolis told the Getty, because dolomite can turn into calcite only over the course of hundreds, if not thousands, of years. In other words, the statue was old. It wasn't some contemporary fake.

The Getty was satisfied. Fourteen months after their investigation of the kouros began, they agreed to buy the statue. In the fall of 1986, it went on display for the first time. The *New York Times* marked the occasion with a front-page story. A few months later, the Getty's curator of antiquities, Marion True, wrote a long, glowing account of the museum's acquisition for the art journal *The Burlington Magazine.* "Now standing erect without external support, his closed hands fixed firmly to his thighs, the kouros expresses the confident vitality that is characteristic of the best of his brothers." True concluded triumphantly, "God or man, he embodies all the radiant energy of the adolescence of western art."

The kouros, however, had a problem. It didn't look right. The first to point this out was an Italian art historian named Federico Zeri, who served on the Getty's board of trustees. When Zeri was taken down to the museum's restoration studio to see the kouros in December of 1983, he found himself staring at the sculpture's fingernails. In a way he couldn't immediately articulate, they seemed wrong to him. Evelyn Harrison was next. She was one of the world's foremost experts on Greek sculpture, and she was in Los Angeles visiting the Getty just before the museum finalized the deal with Becchina. "Arthur Houghton, who was then the curator, took us down to see it," Harrison remembers. "He just swished a cloth off the top of it and said, 'Well, it isn't ours yet, but it will be in a couple of weeks.' And I said, 'I'm sorry to hear that.'" What did Harrison see? She didn't know. In that very first moment, when Houghton swished off the cloth, all Harrison had was a hunch, an instinctive sense that something was amiss. A few months later, Houghton took Thomas Hoving, the former director of the Metropolitan Museum of Art in New York, down to the Getty's conservation studio to see the statue as well. Hoving always makes a note of the first word that goes through his head when he sees something new, and he'll never forget what that word was when he first saw the kouros. "It was 'fresh'—'fresh,'" Hoving recalls. And "fresh" was not the right reaction to have to a two-thousand-year-old statue. Later, thinking back on that moment, Hoving realized why that thought had popped into his mind: "I had dug in Sicily, where we found bits and pieces of these things. They just don't come out looking like that. The kouros looked like it had been dipped in the very best caffè latte from Starbucks."

Hoving turned to Houghton. "Have you paid for this?"

Houghton, Hoving remembers, looked stunned.

"If you have, try to get your money back," Hoving said. "If you haven't, don't."

The Getty was getting worried, so they convened a special symposium on the kouros in Greece. They wrapped the statue up, shipped it to Athens, and invited the country's most senior sculpture experts. This time the chorus of dismay was even louder.

Harrison, at one point, was standing next to a man named George Despinis, the head of the Acropolis Museum in Athens. He took one look at the kouros and blanched. "Anyone who has ever seen a sculpture coming out of the ground," he said to her, "could tell that that thing has never been in the ground." Georgios Dontas, head of the Archeological Society in Athens, saw the statue and immediately felt cold. "When I saw the kouros for the first time," he said, "I felt as though there was a glass between me and the work." Dontas was followed in the symposium by Angelos Delivorrias, director of the Benaki Museum in Athens. He spoke at length on the contradiction between the style of the sculpture and the fact that the marble from which it was carved came from Thasos. Then he got to the point. Why did he think it was a fake? Because when he first laid eyes on it, he said, he felt a wave of "intuitive repulsion." By the time the symposium was over, the consensus among many of the attendees appeared to be that the kouros was not at all what it was supposed to be. The Getty, with its lawyers and scientists and months of painstaking investigation, had come to one conclusion, and some of the world's foremost experts in Greek sculpture— just by looking at the statue and sensing their own "intuitive repulsion"— had come to another. Who was right?

For a time it wasn't clear. The kouros was the kind of thing that art experts argued about at conferences. But then, bit by bit, the Getty's case began to fall apart. The letters the Getty's lawyers used to carefully trace the kouros back to the Swiss physician Lauffenberger, for instance, turned out to be fakes. One of the letters dated 1952 had a postal code on it that didn't exist until twenty years later. Another letter dated 1955 referred to a bank account that wasn't opened until 1963. Originally the conclusion of long months of research was that the Getty kouros was in the style of the Anavyssos kouros. But that, too, fell into doubt: the closer experts in Greek sculpture looked at it, the more they began to see it as a puzzling pastiche of several different styles from several different places and time periods. The young man's slender proportions looked a lot like those of the Tenea kouros, which is in a museum in Munich, and his stylized, beaded hair was a lot like that of the kouros in the Metropolitan Museum in New York. His feet, meanwhile, were, if anything, modern. The kouros it most resembled, it turned out, was a smaller, fragmentary statue that was found by a British art historian in Switzerland in 1990. The two statues were cut from similar marble and sculpted in quite similar ways. But the Swiss kouros didn't come from ancient Greece. It came from a forger's workshop in Rome in the early 1980s. And what of the scientific analysis that said that the surface of the Getty kouros could only have aged over many hundreds or thousands of years? Well, it turns out things weren't that cut and dried. Upon further analysis, another geologist concluded that it might be possible to "age" the surface of a dolomite marble statue in a couple of months using potato mold. In the Getty's catalogue, there is a picture of the kouros, with the notation "About 530 BC, or modern forgery."

When Federico Zeri and Evelyn Harrison and Thomas Hoving and Georgios Dontas—and all the others—looked at the kouros and felt an "intuitive repulsion," they were absolutely right. In the first two seconds of looking—in a single glance—they were able to understand more about the essence of the statue than the team at the Getty was able to understand after fourteen months.

Blink is a book about those first two seconds.

I. Fast and Frugal

Imagine that I were to ask you to play a very simple gambling game. In front of you are four decks of cards—two of them red and the other two blue. Each card in those four decks either wins you a sum of money or costs you some money, and your job is to turn over cards from any of the decks, one at a time, in such a way that maximizes your winnings. What you don't know at the beginning, however, is that the red decks are a minefield. The rewards are high, but when you lose on the red cards, you lose a lot. Actually, you can win only by taking cards from the blue decks, which offer a nice steady diet of $50 payouts and modest penalties. The question is how long will it take you to figure this out?

A group of scientists at the University of Iowa did this experiment a few years ago, and what they found is that after we've turned over about fifty cards, most of us start to develop a hunch about what's going on. We don't know why we prefer the blue decks, but we're pretty sure at that point that they are a better bet. After turning over about eighty cards, most of us have figured out the game and can explain exactly why the first two decks are such a bad idea. That much is straightforward. We have some experiences. We think them through. We develop a theory. And then finally we put two and two together. That's the way learning works.

But the Iowa scientists did something else, and this is where the strange part of the experiment begins. They hooked each gambler up to a machine that measured the activity of the sweat glands below the skin in the palms of their hands. Like most of our sweat glands, those in our palms respond to stress as well as temperature—which is why we get clammy hands when we are nervous. What the Iowa scientists found is that gamblers started generating stress responses to the red decks by the tenth card, *forty* cards before they were able to say that they had a hunch about what was wrong with those two decks. More important, right around the time their palms started sweating, their behavior began to change as well. They started favoring the blue cards and taking fewer and fewer cards from the red decks. In other words, the gamblers figured the game out before they realized they had figured the game out: they began making the necessary adjustments long before they were consciously aware of what adjustments they were supposed to be making.

The Iowa experiment is just that, of course, a simple card game involving a handful of subjects and a stress detector. But it's a very powerful illustration of the way our minds work. Here is a situation where the stakes were high, where things were moving quickly, and where the participants had to make sense of a lot of new and confusing information in a very short time. What does the Iowa experiment tell us? That in those moments, our brain uses two very different strategies to make sense of the situation. The first is the one we're most familiar with. It's the conscious strategy. We think about what we've learned, and eventually we come up with an answer. This strategy is logical and definitive. But it takes us eighty cards to get there. It's slow, and it needs a lot of information. There's a second strategy, though. It operates a lot more quickly. It starts to kick in after ten cards, and it's really smart, because it picks up the problem with the red decks almost immediately. It has the drawback, however, that it operates—at least at first—entirely below the surface of consciousness. It sends its messages through weirdly indirect channels, such as the sweat glands in the palms of our hands. It's a system in which our brain reaches conclusions without immediately telling us that it's reaching conclusions.

The second strategy was the path taken by Evelyn Harrison and Thomas Hoving and the Greek scholars. They didn't weigh every conceivable strand of evidence. They considered only what could be gathered in a glance. Their thinking was what the cognitive psychologist Gerd Gigerenzer likes to call "fast and frugal." They simply took a look at that statue and some part of their brain did a series of instant calculations, and before any kind of conscious thought took place, they *felt* something, just like the sudden prickling of sweat on the palms of the gamblers. For Thomas Hoving, it was the completely inappropriate word "fresh" that suddenly popped into his head. In the case of Angelos Delivorrias, it was a wave of "intuitive repulsion." For Georgios Dontas, it was the feeling that there was a glass between him and the work. Did they know why they knew? Not at all. But they *knew.*

2. The Internal Computer

The part of our brain that leaps to conclusions like this is called the adaptive unconscious, and the study of this kind of decision making is one of the most important new fields in psychology. The adaptive unconscious is not to be confused with the unconscious described by Sigmund Freud, which was a dark and murky place filled with desires and memories and fantasies that were too disturbing for us to think about consciously. This new notion of the adaptive unconscious is thought of, instead, as a kind of giant computer that quickly and quietly processes a lot of the data we need in order to keep functioning as human beings. When you walk out into the street and suddenly realize that a truck is bearing down on you, do you have time to think through all your options? Of course not. The only way that human beings could ever have survived as a species for as long as we have is that we've developed another kind of decision-making apparatus that's capable of making very quick judgments based on very little information. As the psychologist Timothy D. Wilson writes in his book *Strangers to Ourselves:* "The mind operates most efficiently by relegating a good deal of high-level, sophisticated thinking to the unconscious, just as a modern jetliner is able to fly on automatic pilot with little or no input from the human, 'conscious' pilot. The adaptive unconscious does an excellent job of sizing up the world, warning people of danger, setting goals, and initiating action in a sophisticated and efficient manner."

Wilson says that we toggle back and forth between our conscious and unconscious modes of thinking, depending on the situation. A decision to invite a co-worker over for dinner is conscious. You think it over. You decide it will be fun. You ask him or her. The spontaneous decision to argue with that same co-worker is made unconsciously—by a different part of the brain and motivated by a different part of your personality.

Whenever we meet someone for the first time, whenever we interview someone for a job, whenever we react to a new idea, whenever we're faced with making a decision quickly and under stress, we use that second part of our brain. How long, for example, did it take you, when you were in college, to decide how good a teacher your professor was? A class? Two classes? A semester? The psychologist Nalini Ambady once gave students three ten-second videotapes of a teacher—with the sound turned off—and found they had no difficulty at all coming up with a rating of the teacher's effectiveness. Then Ambady cut the clips back to five seconds, and the ratings were the same. They were remarkably consistent even when she showed the students just *two* seconds of videotape. Then Ambady compared those snap judgments of teacher effectiveness with evaluations of those same professors made by their students after a full semester of classes, and she found that they were also essentially the same. A person watching a silent two-second video clip of a teacher he or she has never met will reach conclusions about how good that teacher is that are very similar to those of a student who has sat in the teacher's class for an entire semester. That's the power of our adaptive unconscious.

You may have done the same thing, whether you realized it or not, when you first picked up this book. How long did you first hold it in your hands? Two seconds? And yet in that short space of time, the design of the cover, whatever associations you may have with my name, and the first few sentences about the kouros all generated an impression—a flurry of thoughts and images and preconceptions—that has fundamentally shaped the way you have read this introduction so far. Aren't you curious about what happened in those two seconds?

I think we are innately suspicious of this kind of rapid cognition. We live in a world that assumes that the quality of a decision is directly related to the time and effort that went into making it. When doctors are faced with a difficult diagnosis, they order more tests, and when we are uncertain about what we hear, we ask for a second opinion. And what do we tell our children? Haste makes waste. Look before you leap. Stop and *think.* Don't judge a book by its cover. We believe that we are always better off gathering as much information as possible and spending as much time as possible in delibera- tion. We really only trust conscious decision making. But there are moments, particularly in times of stress, when haste does not make waste, when our snap judgments and first impressions can offer a much better means of mak- ing sense of the world. The first task of *Blink* is to convince you of a simple fact: decisions made very quickly can be every bit as good as decisions made cautiously and deliberately.

Blink is not just a celebration of the power of the glance, however. I'm also interested in those moments when our instincts betray us. Why, for instance, if the Getty's kouros was so obviously fake—or, at least, problematic—did the museum buy it in the first place? Why didn't the experts at the Getty also have a feeling of intuitive repulsion during the fourteen months they were studying the piece? That's the great puzzle of what happened at the Getty, and the answer is that those feelings, for one reason or another, were thwarted. That is partly because the scientific data seemed so compelling. (The geologist Stanley Margolis was so convinced by his own analysis that he published a long account of his method in *Scientific American.*) But mostly it's because the Getty desperately wanted the statue to be real. It was a young museum, eager to build a world-class collection, and the kouros was such an extraor- dinary find that its experts were blinded to their instincts. The art historian George Ortiz was once asked by Ernst Langlotz, one of the world's foremost experts on archaic sculpture, whether he wanted to purchase a bronze statu- ette. Ortiz went to see the piece and was taken aback; it was, to his mind, clearly a fake, full of contradictory and slipshod elements. So why was Lan- glotz, who knew as much as anyone in the world about Greek statues, fooled? Ortiz's explanation is that Langlotz had bought the sculpture as a very young man, before he acquired much of his formidable expertise. "I suppose," Ortiz said, "that Langlotz fell in love with this piece; when you are a young man, you do fall in love with your first purchase, and perhaps this was his first love. Not- withstanding his unbelievable knowledge, he was obviously unable to ques- tion his first assessment."

That is not a fanciful explanation. It gets at something fundamental about the way we think. Our unconscious is a powerful force. But it's fal- lible. It's not the case that our internal computer always shines through, instantly decoding the "truth" of a situation. It can be thrown off, dis- tracted, and disabled. Our instinctive reactions often have to compete with all kinds of other interests and emotions and sentiments. So, when should we trust our instincts, and when should we be wary of them? Answering that question is the second task of *Blink.* When our powers of rapid cognition go awry, they go awry for a very specific and consistent set of reasons, and those reasons can be identified and understood. It is possible to learn when to listen to that powerful onboard computer and when to be wary of it.

The third and most important task of this book is to convince you that our snap judgments and first impressions can be educated and controlled. I know that's hard to believe. Harrison and Hoving and the other art experts who looked at the Getty kouros had powerful and sophisticated reactions to the statue, but didn't they bubble up unbidden from their unconscious? Can that kind of mysterious reaction be controlled? The truth is that it can. Just as we can teach ourselves to think logically and deliberately, we can also teach ourselves to make better snap judgments. In *Blink* you'll meet doctors and generals and coaches and furniture designers and musicians and actors and car salesmen and countless others, all of whom are very good at what they do and all of whom owe their success, at least in part, to the steps they have taken to shape and manage and educate their unconscious reactions. The power of knowing, in that first two seconds, is not a gift given magically to a fortunate few. It is an ability that we can all cultivate for ourselves.

3. A Different and Better World

There are lots of books that tackle broad themes, that analyze the world from great remove. This is not one of them. *Blink* is concerned with the very smallest components of our everyday lives—the content and origin of those instantaneous impressions and conclusions that spontaneously arise whenever we meet a new person or confront a complex situation or have to make a decision under conditions of stress. When it comes to the task of understanding ourselves and our world, I think we pay too much attention to those grand themes and too little to the particulars of those fleeting moments. But what would happen if we took our instincts seriously? What if we stopped scanning the horizon with our binoculars and began instead examining our own decision making and behavior through the most powerful of microscopes? I think that would change the way wars are fought, the kinds of products we see on the shelves, the kinds of movies that get made, the way police officers are trained, the way couples are counseled, the way job interviews are conducted, and on and on. And if we were to combine all of those little changes, we would end up with a different and better world. I believe—and I hope that by the end of this book you will believe it as well—that the task of making sense of ourselves and our behavior requires that we acknowledge there can be as much value in the blink of an eye as in months of rational analysis. "I always considered scientific opinion more objective than esthetic judgments," the Getty's curator of antiquities Marion

True said when the truth about the kouros finally emerged. "Now I realize I was wrong."

QUESTIONS FOR DISCUSSION AND WRITING

1. Does the story Gladwell tells about the sixth-century kouros and the instantaneous "intuitive repulsion" working better to establish authenticity than lawyers, scientists, and months of painstaking investigation make sense in a much broader way? Do you accept the idea that the first few seconds or a single glance, the blink of an eye can determine something often much better than meticulous and arduous research?
2. Gladwell argues that students can quickly, in eye-blink fashion, determine how good a teacher their professor is. Does this strike you as true? Does it match your own experience of judging a professor's teaching?
3. Do you agree with Gladwell that we tend generally to be suspicious of what he calls "this kind of rapid cognition"? Why do you suppose that is the case?
4. "But there are moments, particularly in times of stress, when haste does not make waste, when our snap judgments and first impressions can offer a much better means of making sense of the world." Are you in agreement with this statement by Gladwell? Do you accept his concluding statement that "decisions made very quickly can be every bit as good as decisions made cautiously and deliberately"?
5. The subtitle of *Blink* is *The Power of Thinking Without Thinking.* Explain how one can think without thinking. Is Gladwell being literal?

ON TECHNIQUE AND STYLE

1. Look carefully at Gladwell's opening paragraph. Essentially he is telling a story. How does the story and his way of telling it spark our interest as readers? What does he do to draw us in?
2. How useful for Gladwell's purposes is his example of the scientists from the University of Iowa who experiment with blue and red card decks? How does this support his main argument?
3. Gladwell talks about "the adaptive unconscious" and compares it to a giant computer. How is he making use of this definition and its supportive simile?

CULTURAL QUESTION

1. Some cultures put much more credence in intuitive thinking than others. Can you speculate on some reasons why this might be the case using examples from your own knowledge or experiential base and frame of reference?

FICTION

Prologue to Invisible Man

Ralph Ellison

Ralph Ellison (1914–1994) was born in Oklahoma City, Oklahoma, and educated at Tuskegee Institute in Alabama, where he studied music. In 1936 he went to live in New York City. A jazz trumpeter, jazz critic, and free-lance photographer, he was the editor of The Negro Quarterly *as well as being a part of the Federal Writer's Project. He published stories early on in journals such as* New Masses *and* New Challenge. *Ellison served in the Merchant Marines during World War II. In 1952 he published his internationally acclaimed African American novel about existential identity,* The Invisible Man, *considered by many to be one of the greatest American novels of the twentieth century. In 1985 Ellison received the National Medal of Arts for* The Invisible Man. Juneteenth, *his second novel, was published posthumously in 1999. Ellison is also the author of a collection of short fiction,* Flying Home and Other Stories *and two essay collections,* Shadow and Act *and* Going to the Territory. *He was a professor of humanities at New York University and taught at Bard, Columbia, Rutgers, Yale, and the University of Chicago. The famed African American novelist Richard Wright was a mentor of Ellison's but Ellison, unlike Wright, especially in Wright's early years, was not ideological or didactic in his writing and strongly believed in artistic principles. The Prologue, excerpted from* Invisible Man, *sets up the novel's central motif of invisibility and takes us into the mind of the nameless protagonist as he speaks to us from underground and philosophizes about the nature of invisibility, music, and blackness.*

I am an invisible man. No, I am not a spook like those who haunted Edgar Allan Poe; nor am I one of your Hollywood-movie ectoplasms. I am a man of substance, of flesh and bone, fiber and liquids—and I might even be said to possess a mind. I am invisible, understand, simply because people refuse to see me. Like the bodiless heads you see sometimes in circus sideshows, it is as though I have been surrounded by mirrors of hard, distorting glass. When they approach me they see only my surroundings, themselves, or figments of their imagination—indeed, everything and anything except me.

Nor is my invisibility exactly a matter of a biochemical accident to my epidermis. That invisibility to which I refer occurs because of a peculiar disposition of the eyes of those with whom I come in contact. A matter of the construction of their *inner* eyes, those eyes with which they look through their physical eyes upon reality. I am not complaining, nor am I protesting either. It is sometimes advantageous to be unseen, although it is most often rather wearing on the nerves. Then too, you're constantly being bumped against by those of poor vision. Or again, you often doubt if you really exist. You wonder whether you aren't simply a phantom in other people's minds. Say, a figure in a nightmare which the sleeper tries with all his strength to destroy. It's when you feel like this that, out of resentment, you begin to bump people back. And, let me confess, you feel that way most of the time. You ache with the need to convince yourself that you do exist in the real world, that you're a part of all the sound and anguish, and you strike out with your fists, you curse and you swear to make them recognize you. And, alas, it's seldom successful.

One night I accidentally bumped into a man, and perhaps because of the near darkness he saw me and called me an insulting name. I sprang at him, seized his coat lapels and demanded that he apologize. He was a tall blond man, and as my face came close to his he looked insolently out of his blue eyes and cursed me, his breath hot in my face as he struggled. I pulled his chin down sharp upon the crown of my head, butting him as I had seen the West Indians do, and I felt his flesh tear and the blood gush out, and I yelled, "Apologize! Apologize!" But he continued to curse and struggle, and I butted him again and again until he went down heavily, on his knees, profusely bleeding. I kicked him repeatedly, in a frenzy because he still uttered insults though his lips were frothy with blood. Oh yes, I kicked him! And in my outrage I got out my knife and prepared to slit his throat, right there beneath the lamplight in the deserted street, holding him in the collar with one hand, and opening the knife with my teeth—when it occurred to me that the man had not *seen* me, actually; that he, as far as he knew, was in the midst of a walking nightmare! And I stopped the blade, slicing the air as I pushed him away, letting him fall back to the street. I stared at him hard as the lights of a car stabbed through the darkness. He lay there, moaning on the asphalt; a man almost killed by a phantom. It unnerved me. I was both disgusted and ashamed. I was like a drunken man myself, wavering about on weakened legs. Then I was amused: Something in this man's thick head had sprung out and beaten him within an inch of his life. I began to laugh at this crazy discovery. Would he have awakened at the point of death? Would Death himself have freed him for wakeful living? But I didn't linger. I ran away into the dark, laughing so hard I feared I might rupture myself. The next day I saw his picture in the *Daily News,* beneath a caption stating that he had been "mugged." Poor fool, poor blind fool, I thought with sincere compassion, mugged by an invisible man!

Most of the time (although I do not choose as I once did to deny the violence of my days by ignoring it) I am not so overtly violent. I remember that I am invisible and walk softly so as not to awaken the sleeping ones. Sometimes it is best not to awaken them; there are few things in the world as dangerous as sleepwalkers. I learned in time though that it is possible to carry on a fight against them without their realizing it. For instance, I have been carrying on a fight with Monopolated Light & Power for some time now. I use their service and pay them nothing at all, and they don't know it. Oh, they suspect that power is being drained off, but they don't know where. All they know is that according to the master meter back there in their power station a hell of a lot of free current is disappearing somewhere into the jungle of Harlem. The joke, of course, is that I don't live in Harlem but in a border area. Several years ago (before I discovered the advantages of being invisible) I went through the routine process of buying service and paying their outrageous rates. But no more. I gave up all that, along with my apartment, and my old way of life: That way based upon the fallacious assumption that I, like other men, was visible. Now, aware of my invisibility, I live rent-free in a building rented strictly to whites, in a section of the basement that was shut off and forgotten during the nineteenth century, which I discovered when I was trying to escape in the night from Ras the Destroyer. But that's getting too far ahead of the story, almost to the end, although the end is in the beginning and lies far ahead.

The point now is that I found a home—or a hole in the ground, as you will. Now don't jump to the conclusion that because I call my home a "hole" it is damp and cold like a grave; there are cold holes and warm holes. Mine is a warm hole. And remember, a bear retires to his hole for the winter and lives until spring; then he comes strolling out like the Easter chick breaking from its shell. I say all this to assure you that it is incorrect to assume that, because I'm invisible and live in a hole, I am dead. I am neither dead nor in a state of suspended animation. Call me Jack-the-Bear, for I am in a state of hibernation.

My hole is warm and full of light. Yes, *full* of light. I doubt if there is a brighter spot in all New York than this hole of mine, and I do not exclude Broadway. Or the Empire State Building on a photographer's dream night. But that is taking advantage of you. Those two spots are among the darkest of our whole civilization—pardon me, our whole *culture* (an important distinction, I've heard)—which might sound like a hoax, or a contradiction, but that (by contradiction, I mean) is how the world moves: Not like an arrow, but a boomerang. (Beware of those who speak of the *spiral* of history; they are preparing a boomerang. Keep a steel helmet handy.) I know; I have been boomeranged across my head so much that I now can see the darkness of lightness. And I love light. Perhaps you'll think it strange that an invisible man should need light, desire light, love light. But maybe it is exactly because I *am* invisible. Light confirms my reality, gives birth to my form. A beautiful girl once told me of a recurring nightmare in which she lay in the center of a large dark room and felt her face expand until it filled the whole room, becoming a formless mass while her eyes ran in bilious jelly up the chimney. And so it is with me. Without light I am not only invisible, but formless as well, and to be unaware of one's form is to live a death. I myself, after existing some twenty years, did not become alive until I discovered my invisibility.

That is why I fight my battle with Monopolated Light & Power. The deeper reason, I mean: It allows me to feel my vital aliveness. I also fight them for taking so much of my money before I learned to protect myself. In my hole in the basement there are exactly 1,369 lights. I've wired the entire ceiling, every inch of it. And not with fluorescent bulbs, but with the older, more-expensive-to-operate kind, the filament type. An act of sabotage, you know. I've already begun to wire the wall. A junk man I know, a man of vision, has supplied me with wire and sockets. Nothing, storm or flood, must get in the way of our need for light and ever more and brighter light. The truth is the light and light is the truth. When I finish all four walls, then I'll start on the floor. Just how that will go, I don't know. Yet when you have lived invisible as long as I have you develop a certain ingenuity. I'll solve the problem. And maybe I'll invent a gadget to place my coffee pot on the fire while I lie in bed, and even invent a gadget to warm my bed—like the fellow I saw in one of the picture magazines who made himself a gadget to warm his shoes! Though invisible, I am in the great American tradition of tinkers. That makes me kin to Ford, Edison and Franklin. Call me, since I have a theory and a concept, a "thinker-tinker." Yes, I'll warm my shoes; they need it, they're usually full of holes. I'll do that and more.

Now I have one radio-phonograph; I plan to have five. There is a certain acoustical deadness in my hole, and when I have music I want to *feel* its vibration, not only with my ear but with my whole body. I'd like to hear five recordings of Louis Armstrong playing and singing "What Did I Do to Be so Black and Blue"—all at the same time. Sometimes now I listen to Louis while I have my favorite dessert of vanilla ice cream and sloe gin. I pour the red liquid over the white mound, watching it glisten and the vapor rising as Louis bends that military instrument into a beam of lyrical sound. Perhaps I like Louis Armstrong because he's made poetry out of being invisible. I think it must be because he's unaware that he *is* invisible. And my own grasp of invisibility aids me to understand his music. Once when I asked for a cigarette, some jokers gave me a reefer, which I lighted when I got home and sat listening to my phonograph. It was a strange evening. Invisibility, let me explain, gives one a slightly different sense of time, you're never quite on the beat. Sometimes you're ahead and sometimes behind. Instead of the swift and imperceptible flowing of time, you are aware of its nodes, those points where time stands still or from which it leaps ahead. And you slip into the breaks and look around. That's what you hear vaguely in Louis' music.

Once I saw a prizefighter boxing a yokel. The fighter was swift and amazingly scientific. His body was one violent flow of rapid rhythmic action. He hit the yokel a hundred times while the yokel held up his arms in stunned surprise. But suddenly the yokel, rolling about in the gale of boxing gloves, struck one blow and knocked science, speed and footwork as cold as a well-digger's posterior. The smart money hit the canvas. The long shot got the nod. The yokel had simply stepped inside of his opponent's sense of time. So under the spell of the reefer I discovered a new analytical way of listening to music. The unheard sounds came through, and each melodic line existed of itself, stood out clearly from all the rest, said its piece, and waited patiently for the other voices to speak. That night I found myself hearing not only in time, but in space as well. I not only entered the music but descended, like Dante, into its depths. And *beneath the swiftness of the* hot tempo there was a slower tempo and a cave and I entered it and looked around and heard an old woman singing a spiritual as full of Weltschmerz as flamenco, and beneath that lay a still lower level on which I saw a beautiful girl the color of ivory pleading in a voice like my mother's as she stood before a group of slaveowners who bid for her naked body, and below that I found a lower level and a more rapid tempo and I heard someone shout:

"Brothers and sisters, my text this morning is the 'Blackness of Blackness.'"

And a congregation of voices answered: "That blackness is most black, brother, most black . . ."

"In the beginning . . ."

"At the very start," they cried.

". . . there was blackness . . ."

"Preach it . . ."

". . . and the sun . . ."

"The sun, Lawd . . ."

". . . was bloody red . . ."

"Red . . ."

"Now black is . . ." the preacher shouted.

"Bloody . . ."

"I said black is . . ."

"Preach it, brother . . ."

". . . an' black ain't . . ."

"Red, Lawd, red: He said it's red!"

"Amen, brother . . ."

"Black will git you . . ."

"Yes, it will . . ."

"Yes, it will . . ."

". . . an' black won't . . ."

"Naw, it won't!"

"It do . . ."

"It do, Lawd . . ."

". . . an' it don't."

"Halleluiah . . ."

". . . It'll put you, glory, glory, Oh my Lawd, in the WHALE'S BELLY."

"Preach it, dear brother . . ."

". . . an' make you tempt . . ."

"Good God a-mighty!"

"Old Aunt Nelly!"

"Black will make you . . ."

"Black . . ."

". . . or black will un-make you."

"Ain't it the truth, Lawd?"

And at that point a voice of trombone timbre screamed at me, "Git out of here, you fool! Is you ready to commit treason?"

And I tore myself away, hearing the old singer of spirituals moaning, "Go curse your God, boy, and die."

I stopped and questioned her, asked her what was wrong.

"I dearly loved my master, son," she said.

"You should have hated him," I said.

"He gave me several sons," she said, "and because I loved my sons I learned to love their father though I hated him too."

"I too have become acquainted with ambivalence," I said. "That's why I'm here."

"What's that?"

"Nothing, a word that doesn't explain it. Why do you moan?"

"I moan this way 'cause he's dead," she said.

"Then tell me, who is that laughing upstairs?"

"Them's my sons. They glad."

"Yes, I can understand that too," I said.

"I laughs too, but I moans too. He promised to set us free but he never could bring hisself to do it. Sill I loved him . . ."

"Loved him? You mean . . .?"

"Oh yes, but I loved something else even more."

"What more?"

"Freedom."

"Freedom," I said. "Maybe freedom lies in hating."

"Naw, son, it's in loving. I loved him and give him the poison and he withered away like a frost-bit apple. Them boys woulda tore him to pieces with they homemade knives."

"A mistake was made somewhere," I said, "I'm confused." And I wished to say other things, but the laughter upstairs became too loud and moan-like for me and I tried to break out of it, but I couldn't. Just as I was leaving I felt an urgent desire to ask her what freedom was and went back. She sat with her head in her hands, moaning softly; her leather-brown face was filled with sadness.

"Old woman, what is this freedom you love so well?" I asked around a corner of my mind.

She looked surprised, then thoughtful, then baffled. "I done forgot, son. It's all mixed up. First I think it's one thing, then I think it's another. It gits my head to spinning. I guess now it ain't nothing but knowing how to say what I got up in my head. But it's a hard job, son. Too much is done happen to me in too short a time. Hit's like I have a fever. Ever' time I starts to walk my head gits to swirling and I falls down. Or if it ain't that, it's the boys; they gits to laughing and wants to kill up the white folks. They's bitter, that's what they is . . ."

"But what about freedom?"

"Leave me 'lone, boy; my head aches!"

I left her, feeling dizzy myself. I didn't get far.

Suddenly one of the sons, a big fellow six feet tall, appeared out of nowhere and struck me with his fist.

"What's the matter, man?" I cried.

"You made Ma cry!"

"But how?" I said, dodging a blow.

"Askin' her them questions, that's how. Git outa here and stay, and next time you got questions like that, ask yourself!"

He held me in a grip like cold stone, his fingers fastening upon my wind-pipe until I thought I would suffocate before he finally allowed me to go. I stumbled about dazed, the music beating hysterically in my ears. It was dark. My head cleared and I wandered down a dark narrow passage, thinking I heard his footsteps hurrying behind me. I was sore, and into my being had come a profound craving for tranquillity, for peace and quiet, a state I felt I could never achieve. For one thing, the trumpet was blaring and the rhythm was too hectic. A tom-tom beating like heart-thuds began drowning out the trumpet, filling my ears. I longed for water and I heard it rushing through the cold mains my fingers touched as I felt my way, but I couldn't stop to search because of the footsteps behind me.

"Hey, Ras," I called. "Is it you, Destroyer? Rinehart?"

No answer, only the rhythmic footsteps behind me. Once I tried crossing the road, but a speeding machine struck me, scraping the skin from my leg as it roared past.

Then somehow I came out of it, ascending hastily from this underworld of sound to hear Louis Armstrong innocently asking,

What did I do
To be so black
And blue?

At first I was afraid; this familiar music had demanded action, the kind of which I was incapable, and yet had I lingered there beneath the surface I might have attempted to act. Nevertheless, I know now that few really listen to this music. I sat on the chair's edge in a soaking sweat, as though each of my 1,369 bulbs had everyone become a klieg light in an individual setting for a third degree with Ras and Rinehart in charge. It was exhausting—as though I had held my breath continuously for an hour under the terrifying serenity that comes from days of intense hunger. And yet, it was a strangely satisfying experience for an invisible man to hear the silence of sound. I had discovered unrecognized compulsions of my being—even though I could not answer "yes" to their promptings. I haven't smoked a reefer since, however; not because they're illegal, but because to *see* around corners is enough (that is not unusual when you are invisible). But to hear around them is too much; it inhibits action. And despite Brother Jack and all that sad, lost period of the Brotherhood, I believe in nothing if not in action.

Please, a definition: A hibernation is a covert preparation for a more overt action.

Besides, the drug destroys one's sense of time completely. If that hap-pened, I might forget to dodge some bright morning and some cluck would run me down with an orange and yellow street car, or a bilious bus! Or I might forget to leave my hole when the moment for action presents itself.

Meanwhile I enjoy my life with the compliments of Monopolated Light & Power. Since you never recognize me even when in closest contact with me, and since, no doubt, you'll hardly believe that I exist, it won't matter if you know that I tapped a power line leading into the building and ran it into my hole in the ground. Before that I lived in the darkness into which I was chased, but now I see. I've illuminated the blackness of my invisibility—and vice versa. And so I play the invisible music of my isolation. The last statement doesn't seem just right, does it? But it is; you hear this music simply because music is heard and seldom seen, except by musicians. Could this compulsion to put invisibility down in black and white be thus an urge to make music of invisibility? But I am an orator, a rabble rouser—Am? I *was,* and perhaps shall be again. Who knows? All sickness is not unto death, neither is invisibility.

I can hear you say, "What a horrible, irresponsible bastard!" And you're right. I leap to agree with you. I am one of the most irresponsible beings that ever lived. Irresponsibility is part of my invisibility; any way you face it, it is a denial. But to whom can I be responsible, and why should I be, when you refuse to see me? And wait until I reveal how truly irresponsible I am. Responsibility rests upon recognition, and recognition is a form of agreement. Take the man whom I almost killed: Who was responsible for that near murder—I? I don't think so, and I refuse it. I won't buy it. You can't give it to me. *He* bumped *me, he* insulted *me.* Shouldn't he, for his own personal safety, have recognized my hysteria, my "danger potential"? He, let us say, was lost in a dream world. But didn't *he* control that dream world—which, alas, is only too real!—and didn't *he* rule me out of it? And if he had yelled for a policeman, wouldn't *I* have been taken for the offending one? Yes, yes, yes! Let me agree with you, I was the irresponsible one; for I should have used my knife to protect the higher interests of society. Some day that kind of foolishness will cause us tragic trouble. All dreamers and sleepwalkers must pay the price, and even the invisible victim is responsible for the fate of all. But I shirked that responsibility; I became too snarled in the incompatible notions that buzzed within my brain. I was a coward . . .

But what did *I* do to be so blue? Bear with me.

QUESTIONS FOR DISCUSSION AND WRITING

1. When the narrator tells us he is invisible and says, "I might even be said to possess a mind," what is he trying to communicate about the idea he has of what he is? What does being invisible have to do with mind and thought?
2. What does awareness have to do with being invisible as the narrator comes to terms with its meaning—awareness, for example, of the man the narrator almost kills as well as his (the narrator's) own awareness?
3. The narrator tell us that without light he is not only invisible but formless as well, and that to be "unaware of one's form is to live a death"? What

does he mean after he says, "after existing some twenty years" he "did not become alive until I discovered my invisibility"?

4. The Prologue integrates a line from T. S. Eliot "the end is in the beginning." What does that line tell us about the self-awareness that comes to us through our minds?

5. The narrator descends into music under the spell of a joint of marijuana, which he calls "a reefer." What does he learn about his own thinking under the influence of the reefer? What does he mean when he says, "music is heard and seldom seen, except by musicians"?

6. What does the narrator's isolation and being literally underground have to do with the nature of his thinking?

7. What is the narrator's view that emerges toward what we dream as opposed to what is real?

ON TECHNIQUE AND STYLE

1. "Nor is my invisibility exactly a matter of a biomedical accident to my epidermis." How does that sentence reveal a distinct style?

2. The section in the Prologue featuring the black woman the narrator queries about freedom and her two sons, one of whom becomes violent, is all in italics. So are the three lines of Louis Armstrong's. Why does the author use italics? What is their effect?

3. The narrator defines hibernation as "a covert preparation for a more overt action." What does he mean?

CULTURAL QUESTION

1. The narrator makes a sharp distinction between civilization and culture. Why? Does the distinction have to do with being black? With African American folk culture like the Jack-the-Bear story the narrator mentions?

A Clean, Well-Lighted Place

Ernest Hemingway

Ernest Hemingway's (1899–1961) biography appears in Chapter 7. In one of his most famous stories, "A Clean, Well-Lighted Place," first published in Scribner's Magazine *in March 1933 and later in* Winner Take Nothing, *Hemingway gives us the portrait of an old, deaf man in a Spanish café and the two waiters who wait for him to finish drinking and casually discuss his condition. The old man has just recently tried to kill himself and we are left in the story to contemplate the despair and nothingness that come from human isolation and loneliness, from the mind.*

Reprinted with the permission of Scribner, a Division of Simon & Schuster, Inc., from *The Short Stories of Ernest Hemingway*. Copyright 1933 by Charles Scribner's Sons. Copyright renewed © 1961 by Mary Hemingway.

It was late and every one had left the cafe except an old man who sat in the shadow the leaves of the tree made against the electric light. In the day time the street was dusty; but at night the dew settled the dust and the old man liked to sit late because he was deaf and now at night it was quiet and he felt the difference. The two waiters inside the cafe knew that the old man was a little drunk, and while he was a good client they knew that if he became too drunk he would leave without paying, so they kept watch on him.

"Last week he tried to commit suicide," one waiter said.

"Why?"

"He was in despair."

"What about?"

"Nothing."

How do you know it was nothing?"

"He has plenty of money."

They sat together at a table that was close against the wall near the door of the cafe and looked at the terrace where the tables were all empty except where the old man sat in the shadow of the leaves of the tree that moved slightly in the wind. A girl and a soldier went by in the street. The street light shone on the brass number on his collar. The girl wore no head covering and hurried beside him.

"The guard will pick him up," one waiter said.

"What does it matter if he gets what he's after?"

"He had better get off the street now. The guard will get him. They went by five minutes ago."

The old man sitting in the shadow rapped on his saucer with his glass. The younger waiter went over to him.

"What do you want?"

The old man looked at him. "Another brandy," he said.

"You'll be drunk," the waiter said. The old man looked at him. The waiter went away.

"He'll stay all night," he said to his colleague. "I'm sleepy now. I never get into bed before three o'clock. He should have killed himself last week."

The waiter took the brandy bottle and another saucer from the counter inside the cafe and marched out to the old man's table. He put down the saucer and poured the glass full of brandy.

"You should have killed yourself last week," he said to the deaf man. The old man motioned with his finger.

"A little more," he said. The waiter poured on into the glass so that the brandy slopped over and ran down the stem into the top saucer of the pile.

"Thank you," the old man said. The waiter took the bottle back inside the cafe. He sat down at the table with his colleague again.

"He's drunk now," he said.

"He's drunk every night."

"What did he want to kill himself for?"

"How should I know."

"How did he do it?"

"He hung himself with a rope."

"Who cut him down?"

"His niece."

"Why did he do it?"

"For his soul."

"How much money has he got?"

"He's got plenty."

"He must be eighty years old."

"Anyway I should say he was eighty."

"I wish he would go home. I never get to bed before three o'clock. What kind of hour is that to go to bed?"

"He stays up because he likes it."

"He's lonely. I'm not lonely. I have a wife waiting in bed for me."

"He had a wife once too."

"A wife would be no good to him now."

"You can't tell. He might be better with a wife."

"His niece looks after him."

"I know. You said she cut him down."

"I wouldn't want to be that old. An old man is a nasty thing."

"Not always. This old man is clean. He drinks without spilling. Even now, drunk. Look at him."

"I don't want to look at him. I wish he would go home. He has no regard for those who must work."

The old man looked from his glass across the square, then over at the waiters.

"Another brandy," he said, pointing to his glass. The waiter who was in a hurry came over.

"Finished," he said, speaking with that omission of syntax stupid people employ when talking to drunken people or foreigners. "No more tonight. Close now."

"Another," said the old man.

"No. Finished." The waiter wiped the edge of the table with a towel and shook his head.

The old man stood up, slowly counted the saucers, took a leather coin purse from his pocket and paid for the drinks, leaving half a peseta tip.

The waiter watched him go down the street, a very old man walking unsteadily but with dignity.

"Why didn't you let him stay and drink?" the unhurried waiter asked. They were putting up the shutters. "It is not half-past two."

"I want to go home to bed."

"What is an hour?"

"More to me than to him."

"An hour is the same."

"You talk like an old man yourself. He can buy a bottle and drink at home."

"It's not the same."

"No, it is not," agreed the waiter with a wife. He did not wish to be unjust. He was only in a hurry.

"And you? You have no fear of going home before your usual hour?"

"Are you trying to insult me?"

"No, hombre, only to make a joke."

"No," the waiter who was in a hurry said, rising from putting on the metal shutters. "I have confidence. I am all confidence."

"You have youth, confidence, and a job," the older waiter said. "You have everything."

"And what do you lack?"

"Everything but work."

"You have everything I have."

"No. I have never had confidence and I'm not young."

"Come on. Stop talking nonsense and lock up."

"I am of those who like to stay late at the cafe," the older waiter said.

"With all those who do not want to go to bed. With all those who need a light for the night."

"I want to go home and into bed."

"We are of two different kinds," the older waiter said. He was now dressed to go home.

"It is not only a question of youth and confidence although those things are very beautiful. Each night I am reluctant to close up because there may be some one who needs the cafe."

"Hombre, there are bodegas open all night long."

"You do not understand. This is a clean and pleasant cafe. It is well lighted. The light is very good and also, now, there are shadows of the leaves."

"Good night," said the younger waiter.

"Good night," the other said. Turning off the electric light he continued the conversation with himself. It is the light of course but it is necessary that the place be clean and light. You do not want music. Certainly you do not want music. Nor can you stand before a bar with dignity although that is all that is provided for these hours. What did he fear? It was not fear or dread. It was a nothing that he knew too well. It was all a nothing and a man was nothing too. It was only that and light was all it needed and a certain cleanness and order. Some lived in it and never felt it but he knew it was already *nada y pues nada y pues nada.* Our nada who art in nada, nada be thy name thy kingdom nada thy will be nada in nada as it is in nada. Give us this nada our daily nada and nada us our nada as we *nada* our *nadas* and *nada* us not into *nada* but deliver us from *nada; pues nada.* Hail nothing full of nothing, nothing is with thee. He smiled and stood before a bar with a shining steam pressure coffee machine.

"What's yours?" asked the barman.

"Nada."

"Otro loco mas," said the barman and turned away.

"A little cup," said the waiter.

The barman poured it for him.

"The light is very bright and pleasant but the bar is unpolished," the waiter said.

The barman looked at him but did not answer. It was too late at night for conversation.

"You want another *copita?*" the barman asked.

"No, thank you," said the waiter and went out. He disliked bars and bodegas. A clean, well-lighted cafe was a very different thing. Now, without thinking further, he would go home to his room. He would lie in the bed and finally, with daylight, he would go to sleep. After all, he said to himself, it is probably only insomnia. Many must have it.

QUESTIONS FOR DISCUSSION AND WRITING

1. Philip Young, a famous Hemingway scholar and critic, wrote about Hemingway characters engaging in actions such as war or hunting or bullfighting in order to prevent thought. Where do we see the attempt to prevent thought in this story, particularly in the portrait of the old man?
2. Shakespeare's Hamlet said, "Nothing is true cept thought doth make it so." How might this apply to this story?
3. The existential philosopher Søren Kierkegaard said we are all in despair and those of us who don't know we are are in the worst despair. Does that kind of reasoning hold up in Hemingway's story?
4. What is Hemingway suggesting in the story about religion as a consolation, especially in his substituting *"nada,"* the Spanish word for nothing, in both the Lord's Prayer and Hail Mary?
5. What does the story appear to be saying by way of contrast about the minds of the young versus those of the old? How is their thinking different?
6. What do the cleanliness or lighting of the café have to do with the old man's state of mind?
7. What does place have to do with mind? How are the two connected?

ON TECHNIQUE AND STYLE

1. Discuss the way Hemingway contrasts light and dark in the story.
2. The metaphor of insomnia is central to this tale. How does Hemingway make use of it? How is it related to the mind?
3. Is the style in which the story is told, the typical brevity associated with Hemingway, understated? Would it have been more useful to have had more description and a greater sense of the inner thoughts of the characters in the story?

CULTURAL QUESTION

1. Though Hemingway is very much an American writer this story has a definite strong Spanish feel to it. How does Hemingway make us feel as if we are in another culture? Is he successful?

From Herzog

Saul Bellow

Saul Bellow (1915–2005) was born in Lachine, Quebec, a suburb of Montreal but grew up in Chicago. Late in life he lived in Brookline, Massachusetts. The son of Russian Jewish immigrants, Bellow became one of America's most distinguished and acclaimed novelists winning the Nobel Prize for Literature in 1976. He also won three National Book Awards, a Pulitzer Prize, and a National Medal of the Arts. Bellow was educated at the University of Chicago, Northwestern, and the University of Wisconsin and served in World War II in the Merchant Marines. He spent two years in Paris as a Guggenheim Fellow and published his first novel, Dangling Man, *in 1944. That was followed by many other novels, including* The Victim, The Adventures of Augie March, Seize the Day, Henderson the Rain King, Herzog, Mister Sammler's Planet, Humboldt's Gift, The Dean's December, More Die of Heartbreak, A Theft, The Bellarosa Connection, The Actual, *and* Ravelstein. *Bellow also published a play,* The Last Analysis, *as well as two collections of stories, a collection of essays and a memoir,* To Jerusalem and Back. *His fiction has appeared in* Partisan Review, The New Yorker, Playboy, Esquire, *and* Harper's Bazaar; *his criticism in* The New Republic, The New Leader, The New York Times Book Review, Horizon, *and* Encounter. *He taught many years in the department of Social Thought at the University of Chicago as well as at the University of Minnesota, Princeton, Bard, and Boston University. In this short opening selection from his National Book Award–winning masterpiece novel,* Herzog, *first published in 1961, we enter the thoughts of the novel's protagonist, Moses Herzog, as he muses on his state of mind.*

If I am out of my mind, it's all right with me, thought Moses Herzog.

Some people thought he was cracked and for a time he himself had doubted that he was all there. But now, though he still behaved oddly, he felt confident, cheerful, clairvoyant, and strong. He had fallen under a spell and was writing letters to everyone under the sun. He was so stirred by these letters that from the end of June he moved from place to place with a valise full of papers. He had carried this valise from New York to Martha's Vineyard, but returned from the

Vineyard immediately; two days later he flew to Chicago, and from Chicago he went to a village in western Massachusetts. Hidden in the country, he wrote end-lessly, fanatically, to the newspapers, to people in public life, to friends and rela-tives and at last to the dead, his own obscure dead, and finally the famous dead.

It was the peak of summer in the Berkshires. Herzog was alone in the big old house. Normally particular about food, he now ate Silvercup bread from the paper package, beans from the can, and American cheese. Now and then he picked raspberries in the overgrown garden, lifting up the thorny canes with absent-minded caution. As for sleep, he slept on a mattress without sheets—it was his abandoned marriage bed—or in the hammock, covered by his coat. Tall bearded grass and locust and maple seedlings surrounded him in the yard. When he opened his eyes in the night, the stars were near like spiritual bodies. Fires, of course; gases—minerals, heat, atoms, but eloquent at five in the morning to a man lying in a hammock, wrapped in his overcoat.

When some new thought gripped his heart he went to the kitchen, his headquarters, to write it down. The white paint was scaling from the brick walls and Herzog sometimes wiped mouse droppings from the table with his sleeve, calmly wondering why field mice should have such a passion for wax and paraffin. They made holes in paraffin-sealed preserves; they gnawed birthday candles down to the wicks. A rat chewed into a package of bread, leaving the shape of its body in the layers of slices. Herzog ate the other half of the loaf spread with jam. He could share with rats too.

All the while, one corner of his mind remained open to the external world. He heard the crows in the morning. Their harsh call was delicious. He heard the thrushes at dusk. At night there was a barn owl. When he walked in the garden, excited by a mental letter, he saw roses winding about the rain spout; or mulberries—birds gorging in the mulberry tree. The days were hot, the eve-nings flushed and dusty. He looked keenly at everything but he felt half blind.

His friend, his former friend, Valentine, and his wife, his ex-wife Mad-eleine, had spread the rumor that his sanity had collapsed. Was it true?

He was taking a turn around the empty house and saw the shadow of his face in a gray, webby window. He looked weirdly tranquil. A radiant line went from mid-forehead over his straight nose and full, silent lips.

QUESTIONS FOR DISCUSSION AND WRITING

1. Discuss Herzog's sense of his own state of mind as opposed to the way oth-ers, including his ex-friend and his ex-wife, view his mind. What can we discern from the dichotomy?
2. What are we to make of Herzog's thinking from the fact that he is con-stantly writing letters including to obscure and famous dead people?
3. What do we learn about Herzog's state of mind by what he says concerning his eating and sleeping habits?
4. What does Herzog reveal to us about his thinking via his attitudes toward mice and rats?

5. "All the while, one corner of his mind remained open to the external world." What exactly does this statement tell us about Herzog's mind? What is his mind open to?
6. The fact that Herzog asks "Was it true?" about his sanity collapsing suggests that perhaps he believes he has lost his mind. What exactly does such doubt suggest or indicate?
7. Herzog sees his reflection and thinks to himself that he "looked weirdly tranquil." What does this self-perception reveal? What does it tell us about his state of mind?

ON TECHNIQUE AND STYLE

1. Why does Bellow's opening sentence: "If I am out of my mind, it's all right with me, thought Moses Herzog" succeed in commanding our curiosity and attention as readers?
2. Bellow uses the first-person point of view to bring us in to his protagonist's mind. How successful is this point of view?
3. Focus on the details Bellow uses about the food and bedding Herzog is using and what he calls "the external world." How do such details enrich or enhance our sense of character?

CULTURAL QUESTION

1. There is a rural (the Berkshires) culture identified with where Herzog is versus where he has traveled from (New York and Chicago)? What is it someone like Herzog escapes from when they leave an urban culture for a more isolated rural culture?

Night-Sea Journey

John Barth

John Barth (1930–) was born in Cambridge, Maryland, and studied at Julliard School intending to be a jazz musician. He went on to receive both a BA and an MA from Johns Hopkins and taught at Pennsylvania State University, the State University of New York, Buffalo, and Johns Hopkins. His novels include The Floating Opera; The End of the Road; The Sot-Weed Factor; Giles Goat Boy; Chimera, *which won the National Book Award;* Letters; Tidewater Tales; *and* Last Voyage of Somebody *the Sailor. His story collections include* Lost in the Funhouse *and* On with the Story. *"Night-Sea Journey" originally appeared in* Esquire *and is included in* Lost in the Funhouse. *Though "Night-Sea Journey" has all of the sensibility we normally associate with a journey, Barth makes us realize soon enough that this particular journey is quite possibly the most essential biological and existential one of all.*

"One way or another, no matter which theory of our journey is correct, it's myself I address; to whom I rehearse as to a stranger our history and condition, and will disclose my secret hope though I sink for it.

"Is the journey my invention? Do the night, the sea, exist at all, I ask myself, apart from my experience of them? Do I myself exist, or is this a dream? Sometimes I wonder. And if I am, who am I? The Heritage I supposedly transport? But how can I be both vessel and contents? Such are the questions that beset my intervals of rest.

"My trouble is, I lack conviction. Many accounts of our situation seem plausible to me—where and what we are, why we swim and whither. But implausible ones as well, perhaps especially those, I must admit as possibly correct. Even likely. If at times, in certain humors—stroking in unison, say, with my neighbors and chanting with them 'Onward! Upward!'—I have supposed that we have after all a common Maker, Whose nature and motives we may not know, but Who engendered us in some mysterious wise and launched us forth toward some end known but to Him—if (for a moodslength only) I have been able to entertain such notions, very popular in certain quarters, it is because our night-sea journey partakes of their absurdity. One might even say: I can believe them *because* they are absurd.

"Has that been said before?

"Another paradox: it appears to be these recesses from swimming that sustain me in the swim. Two measures onward and upward, flailing with the rest, then I float exhausted and dispirited, brood upon the night, the sea, the journey, while the flood bears me a measure back and down: slow progress, but I live, I live, and make my way, aye, past many a drownèd comrade in the end, stronger, worthier than I, victims of their unremitting *joie de nager.* I have seen the best swimmers of my generation go under. Numberless the number of the dead! Thousands drown as I think this thought, millions as I rest before returning to the swim. And scores, hundreds of millions have expired since we surged forth, brave in our innocence, upon our dreadful way. 'Love! Love!' we sang then, a quarter-billion strong, and churned the warm sea white with joy of swimming! Now all are gone down—the buoyant, the sodden, leaders and followers, all gone under, while wretched I swim on. Yet these same reflective intervals that keep me afloat have led me into wonder, doubt, despair—strange emotions for a swimmer!—have led me, even, to suspect . . . that our night-sea journey is without meaning.

"Indeed, if I have yet to join the hosts of the suicides, it is because (fatigue apart) I find it no meaningfuller to drown myself than to go on swimming.

"I know that there are those who seem actually to enjoy the night-sea; who claim to love swimming for its own sake, or sincerely believe that 'reaching the Shore,' 'transmitting the Heritage' (*Whose* Heritage, I'd like to know? And to whom?) is worth the staggering cost. I do not. Swimming itself I find at best not actively unpleasant, more often tiresome, not infrequently a torment. Arguments from function and design don't impress me: granted that we can and do swim, that in a manner of speaking our long tails and streamlined heads are 'meant for' swimming; it by no means follows—for me at least—that we *should* swim, or otherwise endeavor to 'fulfill our destiny.' Which is to say, Someone Else's destiny, since ours, so far as I can see, is merely to perish, one way or another, soon or late. The heartless zeal of our (departed) leaders, like the blind ambition and good cheer of my own youth, appalls me now; for the death of my comrades I am inconsolable. If the night-sea journey has justification, it is not for us swimmers ever to discover it.

"Oh, to be sure, 'Love!' one heard on every side: 'Love it is that drives and sustains us!' I translate: we don't know *what* drives and sustains us, only that we are most miserably driven and, imperfectly, sustained. *Love* is how we call our ignorance of what whips us. 'To reach the Shore,' then: but what if the Shore exists in the fancies of us swimmers merely, who dream it to account for the dreadful fact that we swim, have always and only swum, and continue swimming without respite (myself excepted) until we die? Supposing even that there *were* a Shore—that, as a cynical companion of mine once imagined, we rise from the drowned to discover all those vulgar superstitions and exalted metaphors to be literal truth: the giant Maker of us all, the Shores of Light beyond our night-sea journey!—whatever would a swimmer do there? The fact is, when we imagine the Shore, what comes to mind is just the opposite of our condition: no more night, no more sea, no more journeying. In short, the blissful estate of the drowned.

"'Ours not to stop and think; ours but to swim and sink. . . .' Because a moment's thought reveals the pointlessness of swimming. 'No matter,' I've heard some say, even as they gulped their last: 'The night-sea journey may be absurd, but here we swim, will-we nill-we, against the flood, onward and upward, toward a Shore that may not exist and couldn't be reached if it did.' The thoughtful swimmer's choices, then, they say, are two: give over thrashing and go under for good, or embrace the absurdity; affirm in and for itself the night-sea journey; swim on with neither motive nor destination, for the sake of swimming, and compassionate moreover with your fellow swimmer, we being all at sea and equally in the dark. I find neither course acceptable. If not even the hypothetical Shore can justify a sea-full of drownèd comrades, to speak of the swim-in-itself as somehow doing so strikes me as obscene. I continue to swim—but only because blind habit, blind instinct, blind fear of drowning are still more strong than the horror of our journey. And if on occasion I have assisted a fellow-thrasher, joined in the cheers and songs, even passed along to others strokes of genius from the drownèd great, it's that I shrink by temperament from making myself conspicuous. To paddle off in one's own direction, assert one's independent right-of-way, overrun one's fellows without compunction, or dedicate oneself entirely to pleasures and diversions without regard for conscience—I can't finally condemn those who journey in this wise; in half my moods I envy them and despise the weak vitality that keeps me from following their example. But in reasonabler moments I remind myself that it's their very freedom and self-responsibility I reject, as more dramatically absurd, in our senseless circumstances, than tailing along in conventional fashion. Suicides, rebels, affirmers of the paradox—nay-sayers and yea-sayers alike to our fatal journey—I finally shake my head at them. And splash sighing past their corpses, one by one, as past a hundred sorts of others: friends, enemies, brothers; fools, sages, brutes—and nobodies, million upon million. I envy them all.

"A poor irony: that I, who find abhorrent and tautological the doctrine of survival of the fittest (*fitness* meaning, in my experience, nothing more than survival-ability, a talent whose only demonstration is the fact of survival, but whose chief ingredients seem to be strength, guile, callousness), may be the sole remaining swimmer! But the doctrine is false as well as repellent: Chance drowns the worthy with the unworthy, bears up the unfit with the fit by whatever definition, and makes the night-sea journey essentially *haphazard* as well as murderous and unjustified.

"'You only swim once.' Why bother, then?

"'Except ye drown, ye shall not reach the Shore of Life.' Poppycock.

"One of my late companions—that same cynic with the curious fancy, among the first to drown—entertained us with odd conjectures while we waited to begin our journey. A favorite theory of his was that the Father does exist, and did indeed make us and the sea we swim—but not a-purpose or even consciously; He made us, as it were, despite Himself, as we make waves with every tail-thrash, and may be unaware of our existence. Another was that He knows we're here but doesn't care what happens to us, inasmuch as He creates (voluntarily or not) other seas and swimmers at more or less regular intervals. In bitterer moments, such as just before he drowned, my friend even supposed that our Maker wished us unmade; there was indeed a Shore, he'd argue, which could save at least some of us from drowning and toward which it was our function to struggle—but for reasons unknowable to us He wanted desperately to prevent our reaching that happy place and fulfilling our destiny. Our 'Father,' in short, was our adversary and would-be killer! No less outrageous, and offensive to traditional opinion, were the fellow's speculations on the nature of our Maker: that He might well be no swimmer Himself at all, but some sort of monstrosity, perhaps even tailless; that He might be stupid, malicious, insensible, perverse, or asleep and dreaming; that the end for which He created and launched us forth, and which we flagellate ourselves to fathom, was perhaps immoral, even obscene. Et cetera, et cetera: there was no end to the chap's conjectures, or the impoliteness of his fancy; I have reason to suspect that his early demise, whether planned by 'our Maker' or not, was expedited by certain fellow-swimmers indignant at his blasphemies.

"In other moods, however (he was as given to moods as I), his theorizing would become half-serious, so it seemed to me, especially upon the subjects of Fate and Immortality, to which our youthful conversations often turned. Then his harangues, if no less fantastical, grew solemn and obscure, and if he was still baiting us, his passion undid the joke. His objection to popular opinions of the hereafter, he would declare was their claim to general validity. Why need believers hold that *all* the drownèd rise to be judged at journey's end, and non-believers that drowning is final without exception? In *his* opinion (so he'd vow at least), nearly everyone's fate was permanent death; indeed he took a sour pleasure in supposing that every 'Maker' made thousands of separate seas in His creative lifetime, each populated like ours with millions of swimmers, and that in almost every instance both sea and swimmers were utterly annihilated, whether accidentally or by malevolent design. (Nothing if not pluralistical, he imagined there might be millions and billions of 'Fathers,' perhaps in some 'night-sea' of their own!) However—and here he turned infidels against him with the faithful—he professed to believe that in possibly a single night-sea per thousand, say, one of its quarter-billion swimmers (that is, one swimmer in two hundred fifty billions) achieved a qualified immortality. In some cases the rate might be slightly higher; in others it was vastly lower, for just as there are swimmers of every degree of proficiency, including some who drown before the journey starts, unable to swim at all, and others created drowned, as it were, so he imagined what can only be termed impotent Creators, Makers unable to Make, as well as uncommonly fertile ones and all grades between. And it pleased him to deny any necessary relation between a Maker's productivity and His other virtues—including, even, the quality of His creatures.

"I could go on (*he* surely did) with his elaboration of these mad notions—such as that swimmers in other night-seas needn't be of our kind; that Makers themselves might belong to different *species,* so to speak; that our particular Maker mightn't Himself be immortal, or that we might be not only His emissaries but His 'immortality,' continuing His life and our own, transmogrified, beyond our individual deaths. Even this modified immortality (meaningless to me) he conceived as relative and contingent, subject to accidental or deliberate termination: his pet hypothesis was that Makers and swimmers *each generate the other*—against all odds, their number being so great—and that any given 'immortality-chain' could terminate after any number of cycles, so that what was 'immortal' (still speaking relatively) was only the cyclic process of incarnation, which itself might have a beginning and an end. Alternatively he liked to imagine cycles within cycles, either finite or infinite: for example, the 'night-sea,' as it were, in which Makers 'swam' and created night-seas and swimmers like ourselves, might be the creation of a larger Maker, Himself one of many, Who in turn et cetera. Time itself he regarded as relative to our experience, like magnitude: who knew but what, with each thrash of our tails, minuscule seas and swimmers, whole eternities, came to pass—as ours, perhaps, and our Maker's

Maker's, was elapsing between the strokes of some supertail, in a slower order of time?

"Naturally I hooted with the others at this nonsense. We were young then, and had only the dimmest notion of what lay ahead; in our ignorance we imagined night-sea journeying to be a positively heroic enterprise. Its meaning and value we never questioned; to be sure, some must go down by the way, a pity no doubt, but to win a race requires that others lose, and like all my fellows I took for granted that I would be the winner. We milled and swarmed, impatient to be off, never mind where or why, only to try our youth against the realities of night and sea; if we indulged the skeptic at all, it was as a droll, half-contemptible mascot. When he died in the initial slaughter, no one cared.

"And even now I don't subscribe to all his views—but I no longer scoff. The horror of our history has purged me of opinions, as of vanity, confidence, spirit, charity, hope, vitality, everything—except dull dread and a kind of melancholy, stunned persistence. What leads me to recall his fancies is my growing suspicion that I, of all swimmers, may be the sole survivor of this fell journey, tale-bearer of a generation. This suspicion, together with the recent sea-change, suggests to me now that nothing is impossible, not even my late companion's wildest visions, and brings me to a certain desperate resolve, the point of my chronicling.

"Very likely I have lost my senses. The carnage at our setting out; our decimation by whirlpool, poisoned cataract, sea-convulsion; the panic stampedes, mutinies, slaughters, mass suicides; the mounting evidence that none will survive the journey—add to these anguish and fatigue; it were a miracle if sanity stayed afloat. Thus I admit, with the other possibilities, that the present sweetening and calming of the sea, and what seems to be a kind of vasty presence, song, or summons from the near upstream, may be hallucinations of disordered sensibility. . . .

"Perhaps, even, I am drowned already. Surely I was never meant for the rough-and-tumble of the swim; not impossibly I perished at the outset and have only imaged the night-sea journey from some final deep. In any case, I'm no longer young, and it is we spent old swimmers, disabused of every illusion, who are most vulnerable to dreams.

"Sometimes I think I am my drownèd friend.

"Out with it: I've begun to believe, not only that *She* exists, but that She lies not far ahead, and stills the sea, and draws me Herward! Aghast, I recollect his maddest notion: that our destination (which existed, mind, in but one night-sea out of hundreds and thousands) was no Shore, as commonly conceived, but a mysterious being, indescribable except by paradox and vaguest figure: wholly different from us swimmers, yet our complement; the death of us, yet our salvation and resurrection; simultaneously our journey's end, mid-point, and commencement; not membered and thrashing like us, but a motionless or hugely gliding sphere of unimaginable dimension; self-contained, yet dependent absolutely, in some wise, upon the chance (always monstrously improbable) that one of us will survive the night-sea journey and reach . . . Her! *Her,* he called it, or *She,* which is to say, Other-than-a-he. I shake my head; the thing is too preposterous; it is myself I talk to, to keep my reason in this awful darkness. There is no She! There is no You! I rave to myself; it's Death alone that hears and summons. To the drowned, all seas are calm. . . .

"Listen: my friend maintained that in every order of creation there are two sorts of creators, contrary yet complementary, one of which gives rise to seas and swimmers, the other to the Night-which-contains-the-sea and to What-waits-at-the-journey's-end: the former, in short, to destiny, the latter to destination (and both profligately, involuntarily, perhaps indifferently or unwittingly). The 'purpose' of the night-sea journey—but not necessarily of the journeyer or of either Maker!—my friend could describe only in abstractions: *consummation, transfiguration, union of contraries, transcension of categories.* When we laughed, he would shrug and admit that he understood the business no better than we, and thought it ridiculous, dreary, possibly obscene. 'But one of you,' he'd add with his wry smile, 'may be the Hero destined to complete the night-sea journey and be one with Her. Chances are, of course, you won't make it.' He himself, he declared, was not even going to try; the whole idea repelled him; if we chose to dismiss it as an ugly fiction, so much the better for us; thrash, splash, and be merry, we were soon enough drowned. But there it was, he could not say how he knew or why he bothered to tell us, any more than he could say what would happen after She and Hero, Shore and Swimmer, 'merged identities' to become something both and neither. He quite agreed with me that if the issue of that magical union had no memory of the night-sea journey, for example, it enjoyed a poor sort of immortality; even poorer if, as he rather imagined, a swimmer-hero plus a She equaled or became merely another Maker of future night-seas and the rest, at such incredible expense of life. This being the case—he was persuaded it was—the merciful thing to do was refuse to participate; the genuine heroes, in his opinion, were the suicides, and the hero of heroes would be the swimmer who, in the very presence of the Other, refused Her proffered 'immortality' and thus put an end to at least one cycle of catastrophes.

"How we mocked him! Our moment came, we hurtled forth, pretending to glory in the adventure, thrashing, singing, cursing, strangling, rationalizing, rescuing, killing, inventing rules and stories and relationships, giving up, struggling on, but dying all, and still in darkness, until only a battered remnant was left to croak 'Onward, upward,' like a bitter echo. Then they too fell silent—victims, I can only presume, of the last frightful wave—and the moment came when I also, utterly desolate and spent, thrashed my last and gave myself over to the current, to sink or float as might be, but swim no more. Whereupon, marvelous to tell, in an instant the sea grew still! Then warmly, gently, the great tide turned, began to bear me, as it does now, onward and upward will-I nill-I, like a flood of joy—and I recalled with dismay my dead friend's teaching.

"I am not deceived. This new emotion is Her doing; the desire that possesses me is Her bewitchment. Lucidity passes from me; in a moment I'll cry 'Love!' bury myself in Her side, and be 'transfigured.' Which is to say, I die already; this fellow transported by passion is not I; *I am he who abjures and rejects the night-sea journey!* I. . . .

"I am all love. 'Come!' She whispers, and I have no will.

"You who I may be about to become, whatever You are: with the last twitch of my real self I beg You to listen. It is *not* love that sustains me! No; though Her magic makes me burn to sing the contrary, and though I drown even now for the blasphemy, I will say truth. What has fetched me across this dreadful sea is a single hope, gift of my poor dead comrade: that You may be stronger-willed than I, and that by sheer force of concentration I may transmit to You, along with Your official Heritage, a private legacy of awful recollection and negative resolve. Mad as it may be, my dream is that some unimaginable embodiment of myself (or myself plus Her if that's how it must be) will come to find itself expressing, in however garbled or radical a translation, some reflection of these reflections. If against all odds this comes to pass, may You to whom, through whom I speak, do what I cannot: terminate this aimless, brutal business! Stop Your hearing against Her song! Hate love!

"Still alive, afloat, afire. Farewell then my penultimate hope: that one may be sunk for direst blasphemy on the very shore of the Shore. Can it be (my old friend would smile) that only utterest nay-sayers survive the night? But even that were Sense, and there is no sense, only senseless love, senseless death. Whoever echoes these reflections: be more courageous than their author! An end to night-sea journeys! Make no more! And forswear me when I shall forswear myself, deny myself, plunge into Her who summons, singing . . .

"'! Love! Love! Love!'"

QUESTIONS FOR DISCUSSION AND WRITING

1. What is the nature of the night-sea journey? Who or what is the intelligence or mind that speaks and chronicles its journey?
2. What has the transmission of heritage to do with the story that unfolds?
3. "The night-sea journey may be absurd," says the narrative voice in the tale. Why absurd?
4. Who or what is "the Maker" in the story and what is being made? Creation of the world? Fiction? Life?
5. What is the significance in the story of the narrator's friend and all of his youthful fellow swimmers? What is their role in the overall picture he is communicating?
6. What does the shore represent in the tale? What do "Her" and "Love" have to do with the narrator's finding his way to the shore?

7. "Ours is not to stop and think. Ours is but to swim and sink." What do thought and sinking have to do with the night-sea journey?

ON TECHNIQUE AND STYLE

1. Barth is often described as a self-reflexive writer—which means highly self-conscious foregrounding of fiction as the narrative progresses. How does he manage to bring this technique to bear? What is the effect?
2. This story has an allegory in it as well as the myth of the quest. What is the nature of the allegory and what is being sought in the quest?
3. Where is the humor in this story? Would it be correct to call it a kind of gallows humor?

CULTURAL QUESTION

1. This is a universal story, a sperm in search of an egg. Does the language and the distinctive voice of the narrator make it sound culturally bound?

POETRY

The Brain—is wider than the Sky—

Emily Dickinson

Emily Dickinson (1830–1886) is one of the most influential American lyrical poets. Dickinson was born and lived her life in Amherst, Massachusetts, the daughter of a prominent Calvinist family. She attended Amherst Academy and Holyoke Female Seminary and then lived an obsessively private and reclusive life. Although she wrote nearly 1,800 poems, only a handful were published during her lifetime and those anonymously and more than likely without her consent. By 1890, with her sister Lavinia largely responsible for editing, a volume of her poetry was published. She became, along with Walt Whitman, America's most important nineteenth-century poet and a heroic and revered figure to modern feminists. A woman who held to a strong faith, her gravestone is marked with just two words: "Called Back."

The poem of Dickinson's included here, "The Brain— is wider than the Sky—," shows the sweep of her imagination as well as her spiritual mooring. It deftly presents us with a poet's vision of the human brain and what she sees as its capabilities.

The Brain—is wider than the Sky—
For—put them side by side—
The one the other will contain
With ease—and You—beside—

The Brain is deeper than the sea—
For—hold them—Blue to Blue—
The one the other will absorb—
As Sponges—Buckets—do—

The Brain is just the weight of God—
For—Heft them—Pound for Pound—
And they will differ—if they do—
As Syllable from Sound—

QUESTIONS FOR DISCUSSION AND WRITING

1. What is Dickinson revealing in the poem about the capacity of the human mind?
2. Many of Dickinson's poems—including this one, which is one of her most famous—are seen as homilies or sermons. What is the essential thought that she appears to express about God in this poem? What does she mean when she says the brain and God differ only "As syllable from Sound"?
3. What picture or image comes to our minds when we actually try to picture the brain as Dickinson conceives it?
4. What is the effect created by Dickinson's use of the long dash in the poem?

ON TECHNIQUE AND STYLE

1. Why does Dickinson go from sky to sea to God in this poem? Is there logic to the progression?
2. Dickinson uses a formal meter and rhyme scheme with the consistent quatrain of four-line stanzas. How does this affect the overall impact of the poem? Is there a reason behind her choice of meter and rhythm?

CULTURAL QUESTION

1. Dickinson was a Christian from Calvinist New England. Is there anything in this poem that mirrors that cultural background, or could this poem have been written by a man of a different faith from an entirely different region or nation?

Among School Children

William Butler Yeats

William Butler Yeats (1865–1939), *one of the greatest lyric poets of the twentieth century, was born near Dublin to parents of English ancestry. One of the main forces behind the Irish literary revival, Yeats was a dramatist and founder of the Abbey theater and is also well-known for his mysticism and study of the occult and his work with folklore and myth. He attended the School of Art in Dublin and started publishing poetry in 1885. He was a senator of the Irish free state and was awarded the Nobel Prize for Literature in 1923. He published many volumes of poetry, includ-ing* Crossways, The Rose, The Wind Among the Reeds, In the Seven Woods, Responsibilities, The Wild Swans at Cool, Michael Robartes and the Dancer, The Tower, The Winding Stair and Other Poems, A Full Moon in March, *and* Last Poems. *"Among School Children" first appeared in* The Tower *in 1927. In it Yeats, a "sixty-year-old smiling public man," brings back to mind his youth and the love of his life, Maude Gonne, as he meditates on the myth of Leda and the Swan, Pla-tonic ideals of love, "Presences," and the inevitable advance of age. How can we sepa-rate the infant on its mother's lap from the man who has "sixty or more winters on its head," or the work of art from the artist, the body from the mind and the soul?*

Reprinted with the permission of Scribner, a Division of Simon & Schuster Adult Publishing Group, from *The Collected Works of W.B. Yeats, Volume I: The Poems, Revised* edited by Richard J. Finneran, Copyright © 1928 by the Macmillan Company. Copyright renewed © 1956 by Georgie Yeats. All rights reserved.

I

I walk through the long schoolroom questioning;
A kind old nun in a white hood replies;
The children learn to cipher and to sing,
To study reading-books and histories,
To cut and sew, be neat in everything
In the best modern way—the children's eyes
In momentary wonder stare upon
A sixty-year-old smiling public man.

II

I dream of a Ledaean body, bent
Above a sinking fire. a tale that she

Told of a harsh reproof, or trivial event
That changed some childish day to tragedy—
Told, and it seemed that our two natures blent
Into a sphere from youthful sympathy,
Or else, to alter Plato's parable,
Into the yolk and white of the one shell.

III

And thinking of that fit of grief or rage
I look upon one child or t'other there
And wonder if she stood so at that age—
For even daughters of the swan can share
Something of every paddler's heritage—
And had that colour upon cheek or hair,
And thereupon my heart is driven wild:
She stands before me as a living child.

IV

Her present image floats into the mind—
Did Quattrocento finger fashion it
Hollow of cheek as though it drank the wind
And took a mess of shadows for its meat?
And I though never of Ledaean kind
Had pretty plumage once—enough of that,
Better to smile on all that smile, and show
There is a comfortable kind of old scarecrow.

V

What youthful mother, a shape upon her lap
Honey of generation had betrayed,
And that must sleep, shriek, struggle to escape
As recollection or the drug decide,
Would think her Son, did she but see that shape
With sixty or more winters on its head,
A compensation for the pang of his birth,
Or the uncertainty of his setting forth?

VI

Plato thought nature but a spume that plays
Upon a ghostly paradigm of things;
Solider Aristotle played the taws

Upon the bottom of a king of kings;
World-famous golden-thighed Pythagoras
Fingered upon a fiddle-stick or strings
What a star sang and careless Muses heard:
Old clothes upon old sticks to scare a bird.

VII

Both nuns and mothers worship images,
But those the candles light are not as those
That animate a mother's reveries,
But keep a marble or a bronze repose.
And yet they too break hearts—O Presences
That passion, piety or affection knows,
And that all heavenly glory symbolise—
O self-born mockers of man's enterprise;

VIII

Labour is blossoming or dancing where
The body is not bruised to pleasure soul.
Nor beauty born out of its own despair,
Nor blear-eyed wisdom out of midnight oil.
O chestnut-tree, great-rooted blossomer,
Are you the leaf, the blossom or the bole?
O body swayed to music, O brightening glance,
How can we know the dancer from the dance?

QUESTIONS FOR DISCUSSION AND WRITING

1. How is Yeats able to bring back Maude Gonne "as a living child"? What is he intimating the poetic mind, ignited by imagination and memory, is capable of creating?
2. Section VI of the poem in effect sums up a great deal of philosophy. What does the line "Old clothes upon old sticks to scare a bird" tell us about Yeats's view on the consolations of philosophy?
3. Follow the trajectory of the poet's mind. How does he go from being among children in the Irish Catholic classroom to speculating about the nature of the chestnut tree and the dancer and the dance?
4. The poem's ending seems an affirmation. How is Yeats able to bring this about after all the doubt and sadness?

ON TECHNIQUE AND STYLE

1. How does Yeats manage to use the metaphors of "pretty plumage" and an "old scarecrow" to present himself?
2. Why are there eight sections in this poem? What is the logic behind the divisions?

CULTURAL QUESTION

1. Yeats had a strong Irish identity not only politically but culturally. Is there evidence of it in the poem? If you did not know Yeats composed the poem could you have as easily concluded it was written by someone from a different cultural background?

GRAPHIC FICTION

Izzy the Cockroach and the Meaning of Life

Will Eisner

Will Eisner's biography appears in Chaptter 7. "Izzy the Cockroach and the Meaning of Life" is the first chapter from the 1988 comic A Life Force.

QUESTIONS FOR DISCUSSION AND WRITING

1. Why does the author make an initial distinction between building a study hall that involves work and pay and getting one's name immortalized on it as the donor? What is the essential tension that Eisner is setting up at the outset?
2. What is the significance of Jacob Shtarkah's identifying with a cockroach? What does it reveal about the idea he or his creator, Will Eisner, has about the human condition?
3. Like his biblical namesake, Jacob wrestles, but with whether God created humans or humans created God. If the latter, he concludes, then the reason for life is only in the mind of humans. To what extent does his conclusion hold up?
4. Why does Jacob risk violence to save Izzy? What is the significance of his ultimate remark to his wife about how he spent his day?

THE TENEMENT AT 55 DROPSIE AVENUE
LAY QUIETLY AT ANCHOR IN ITS SEA OF CONCRETE.
THE SOUNDS OF THE CITY WERE DIMINISHING.
ALREADY ONE COULD HEAR RUSS COLUMBO SINGING
FROM A RADIO IN THE SECOND FLOOR BACK.
IT WAS FRIDAY AND IT WAS SUNDOWN,
AND THE LAST OF THE REGULAR CONGREGANTS
OF THE SYNAGOGUE ON THE NEXT BLOCK
WERE WALKING HOME.

When the deep purple falls
Over sleepy garden walls...

THREE

IZZY THE COCKROACH, FELL TO THE FLOOR OF THE ALLEY FROM TWO FLIGHTS UP!

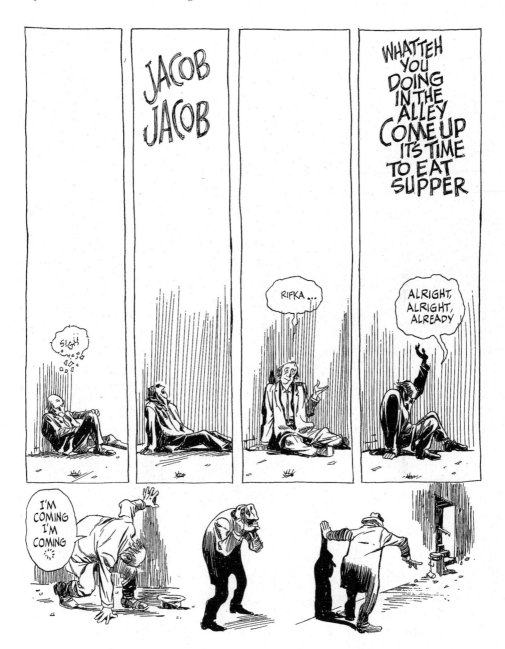

ON TECHNIQUE AND STYLE

1. How much character is Eisner able to project from the faces of the characters he creates?
2. There is a great deal of irony in this excerpt. How does Eisner make use of irony? How effective is it?

CULTURAL QUESTION

1. The portrayal by Eisner is of a lower-class Jewish man who builds for the local, small synagogue and his wife, who says the Sabbath blessing. Does it matter that they are poor and Jewish?

VISUAL TEXTS

The Thinker

Auguste Rodin

Auguste Rodin (1840–1917) was a Paris-born sculptor from a working-class family who was known for his work in Realism and who became one of the world's most celebrated sculptors.

There are twenty-five enlarged versions of "The Thinker," a bronze and marble sculpture of which less than five were created between 1880 and 1881 by Rodin. The original theme of "The Thinker" is from Dante's Inferno *and was initially titled "The Poet." Rodin said "What makes my thinker think is that he thinks not only with his brain, with his knitted brow, his distended nostrils and compressed lips, but with every muscle of his arms, back and legs, with his clenched fist and gripping toes."*

The Inventor's Head

William Mason

William Mason *(1788–1844), born in Hartford, Connecticut, was a wood engraver. He designed* The Inventor's Head *(1826) out of mechanical appliances and drew it with a lead pencil and shaded it with India ink.*

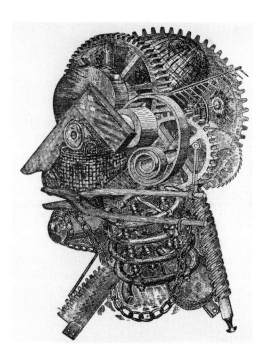

Morning Light

Hugh Shurley

Hugh Shurley (1959–   ) was born in San Francisco and is best known for his layers of imagery in photographic work such as "Morning Light" (1998).

QUESTIONS FOR DISCUSSION AND WRITING

1. What does the famous Rodin sculpture *The Thinker* visually communicate to us about the nature of thinking and the process of thought?
2. *The Inventor's Head* portrays what ideas about the mind of human invention? Are there emotions that this image taps into?
3. By giving his image the title "Morning Light" Shurley appears to be desirous of showing the relationship between what we see early on in our minds and as creators (notice the easel and paintbrushes) as light dawns. What does this reveal or intimate about the nature of the mind? About creativity?

ON TECHNIQUE AND STYLE

1. The three images in this section are presented through entirely differ-ent techniques, as we move from the Realism of the Rodin sculpture *The Thinker* to the surreal portrait by Mason and the pastiche-like effect of Shurley's piece. Are any one of these disparate visual techniques more effective? Why?
2. Apart from the question of efficacy, which of the three visual texts strikes you as having the most innovative style of presenting a strong visual image? Why?

CULTURAL QUESTION

1. The visual images in this section are tied to white Western visual art-ists. Does this limit or bind them culturally to the white Western cultural world?

AUDIO TEXTS   To hear these conversations, go to www.mhhe.com/soundideas1e

Track 9.1

(date: January 9, 2006; running time: 50:50 min.)

An hour with **Malcolm Gladwell** *on his book* Blink.

Track 9.2

(date: November 10, 2004; running time: 50:50 min.)

An hour with **John Searle** *on his book* Mind.

QUESTIONS FOR DISCUSSION AND WRITING

1. Gladwell talks about desire by saying that it probably clouded the judgment of the Getty museum people's decision to buy a fake statue, and he allows that we need to pay attention to gut feelings because they reflect uncon-scious desire. How much do you believe desire affects or alters thinking?

Gladwell talks about priming and experiments that suggest it can change behavior. Can simple words and our exposure to them actually change or alter the ways we behave?

2. What about the questions Searle raises about neuron firings in the brain—what causes them and why is sex or lots of other things more fun than digging ditches? These are, Searle suggests, fascinating and unanswerable questions. Why is it worth seeking answers? Searle says that philosophy has moved from being language centered to being mind centered, though still recognizing the fact that we learn a lot about the mind by studying language and a lot about language by studying the mind. Why are language and mind so interconnected and mutually dependent?

3. Searle says that how the brain produces thoughts and feelings is not only a hot subject but a crucial one that we are a long way from solving. Why do you imagine this is important to solve?

ON TECHNIQUE AND STYLE

1. Compare and contrast the defense we hear from Gladwell of viewing the brain like a computer versus Searle's argument that such thinking is wrong.

2. How effective are the examples Gladwell uses to bolster his argument about the efficacy of snap judgments? How does research he cites such as John Gottman's on marriage relationships and the example on teaching effectiveness bolster his argument?

3. Both Gladwell and Searle sound enthusiastic and confident in their speech. To what extent does the style of their speaking contribute to the overall effectiveness of how much we accept the ideas they espouse?

CULTURAL QUESTION

1. What might some of the implications be to the priming example Gladwell provides concerning African Americans and their taking standardized tests?

CONNECTIONS

1. Which selections present distinctions between the conscious and the unconscious minds? Can we synthesize from different selections and find patterns in what is being illustrated about differences between how the conscious mind works and what it produces and the unconscious mind?

2. Drawing from different selections, show why you think there exists an ongoing debate about the nature of the brain and what it holds or contains.

3. Mark Twain opined about age that it was "mind over matter and if you don't mind it doesn't matter." In which selections do we see this kind of attitude?

4. Thought so often seems connected to questions having to do with God or the soul. In which selections do we especially see this and what do we see?

5. Thinking and intelligence also appear in many of the selections to be linked to questioning the purpose or meaning of life. Which selections reveal that link and what is revealed?

6. In which selections do we see distinctions between rational and irrational thought highlighted? What are some of the distinctions?

7. Which of the selections venture into consciousness or ontology (the study of the nature of being)? What do we learn about either—or both?

8. In a number of selections we see where thinking does not necessarily lead to answers. Often questions merely summon more questions. Where is this especially the case and what are some of the more important or significant questions?

9. Show how different writers and thinkers and artists in this chapter view the brain and the mind scientifically whereas others tend to view it metaphorically, and in the case of Diane Ackerman, both ways. Which selection strikes you as the most legitimate or effective approach? Why?

10. Based on selections from the chapter, what role does emotion play in thinking and how central is it to human thought?

FOR WRITING

CREATIVE CHOICES

1. Write a poem about the way you believe your mind or someone else's works.
2. Create a visual image either through drawing, sculpting, or photography that reflects thinking or the thought process.
3. Record a "brainstorming session." Include an analysis of how brain power was mobilized or set in motion.

NARRATIVE/EXPOSITORY CHOICES

1. Write a narrative from your personal history that best reveals what for you could be described as the power either of positive or negative thinking.
2. Set up an essay that moves us through your thinking process and points out where ideas seem to come from and the kind of path they take.
3. Write an essay that reveals how the mind can and cannot be trusted.

ARGUMENT CHOICES

1. Argue a position on how much we can safely liken our brain to a computer and on where the analogy breaks down or runs into trouble.
2. Present an argument on the power of the human brain. Can we generalize? Should we?
3. What is the significance of our dividing thinking into light and dark thoughts?

RESEARCH CHOICES

1. How does human intelligence compare to intelligence in the animal kingdom? With humans we speak of different varieties of intelligence, including emotional intelligence. There are obviously different types of intelligence within the animal world. What are they?
2. Research how up-to-date researchers tell us the brain works and describe it in terms a lay audience, your fellow students, can understand.

VIDEO SUGGESTIONS

1. *A Beautiful Mind* (2001) Biography of the rise of John Forbes Nash Jr. , a math prodigy who could solve problems that puzzled the greatest of thinkers. Nash overcame years of suffering through schizophrenia to win the Nobel Prize.
2. *TQ* (1994) Edward Walters is an auto mechanic who falls for the intelligent and beautiful Catherine Boyd, niece of Albert Einstein.
3. *Memento* (2000) A man who is suffering from memory loss uses notes and tattoos as clues in hunting for a man he believes killed his wife.
4. *The Man Who Mistook His Wife for a Hat* (1987) TV movie based on a case study by Dr. Oliver Sacks, who studies instances of rare brain disorders.
5. *Awakenings* (1990) The victims of an encephalitis epidemic have been catatonic for years, but a new drug offers the hope of reviving them. Starring Robin Williams and Robert De Niro.

Ideas about the Future
Utopia and Dystopia

> *The future: time's excuse*
> *to frighten us.*
>
> —*Rainer Marie Rilke*

> *Each of us time travels into the future, one year, every year.*
>
> —*Carl Sagan*

INTRODUCTION

The future has always been the object of speculation, hope, and fear. What the future holds, how technology will affect humans, how we will destroy or build ideal societies—all of these ideas have been the subject of debate, writing, and art.

This chapter focuses on ideas about the future, especially those views that see the future from a utopian or a dystopian (or sometimes both) lens. The chapter opens with nonfiction selections—first, an interview with Carl Sagan, an influential American scientist who was one of the first to popularize ideas such as the search for intelligent life in the universe, and to make time travel an object of scientific, rather than just fanciful discussion. No less influential is Bill Joy, the cofounder of Sun Microsystems. His article, "Why the Future Doesn't Need Us," created a storm of controversy and discussion across many communities, and is still often cited and talked about.

Although H. G. Wells may be best known for his fictional writings, he was also fascinated by the future, and wrote a book titled *What Is Coming?* in 1916. An excerpt from that book, "Forecasting the Future," is included next. It is particularly illuminating to consider which of Wells's prophesies came about, and which did not. This can be said as well for Alvin Toffler's predictions in *Future Shock*. An excerpt from this work closes the nonfiction section.

The word "utopia" as well as its vision found its earliest expression in Sir/Saint Thomas More's book titled *Utopia*. More created this word to describe a world of perfection, in which humans had clearly defined roles and pursued happiness. The creation of utopia, however, spawned many *dystopias*, which occupy a great many more volumes. The fiction section of the chapter also includes some rather dystopian views: from Ursula K. Le Guin, the world of Omelas; Margaret Atwood's life in "the Modules" surrounding "OrganInc Farms"; and finally, Walter Mosley's depiction of "Common Ground" in the selection "Little Brother." All of these fictional communities show the dystopic side of the utopian coin.

For the poets in this chapter, Rainer Maria Rilke and C.S. Lewis, the future holds fear and disappointment, though for different reasons. Mike Kennedy, in *Lone Wolf 2100: The Language of Chaos*, also presents a dystopic view of cyborg life in the future in the graphic fiction section.

Finally, the chapter ends with both visual and audio texts that ask us to examine the nature of our beliefs about utopia, and the paradoxes that are entailed in thinking about creating a utopian community.

You are reading this chapter in the future—that is, at a time beyond its writing. As you read, think about the ideas here, and how they do or do not relate to what you know right now. How has time changed in the past 5,000 years? 500? 50? 5? 5 minutes? The passage of time and the search for perfection—utopia—remains one of the great challenges and intrigues of humankind.

°© *NOVA*, updated November 2000.

NONFICTION

On Time Travel

Carl Sagan

Carl Sagan (1934–1996) was an American astronomer and Pulitzer Prize–winning author. He was born in New York City and studied at the universities of Chicago and California, Berkeley. He taught at UC Berkeley, Stanford, Harvard, and the Smithsonian Institution before becoming professor of Astronomy and Space Sciences and director of the Laboratory for Planetary Studies at Cornell University. He is well known for making science interesting and popular with the American public. He was a pioneer in the field of exobiology—the study of life beyond the earth—and promoted the Search for Extra-Terrestrial Intelligence (SETI). He cowrote and presented the award-winning television series Cosmos *on PBS.*

Sagan gave this interview during the making of "Time Travel," part of the PBS series NOVA.

NOVA: Let's start with the crux of the matter. What for you is time?

Sagan: Ever since St. Augustine, people have wrestled with this, and there are all sorts of things it isn't. It isn't a flow of something, because what does it flow past? We use time to measure flow. How could we use time to measure time? We are stuck in it, each of us time travels into the future, one year, every year. None of us to any significant precision does otherwise. If we could travel close to the speed of light, then we could travel further into the future in a given amount of time. It is one of those concepts that is profoundly resistant to a simple definition.

NOVA: Do you think that backwards time travel will ever be possible?

Sagan: Such questions are purely a matter of evidence, and if the evidence is inconsistent or insufficient, then we withhold judgment until there is better evidence. Right now we're in one of those classic, wonderfully evocative moments in science when we don't know, when there are those on both sides of the debate, and when what is at stake is very mystifying and very profound.

If we could travel into the past, it's mind-boggling what would be possible. For one thing, history would become an experimental science, which it certainly isn't today. The possible insights into our own past and nature and origins would be dazzling. For another, we would be facing the deep paradoxes of interfering with the scheme of causality that has led to our own time and ourselves. I have no idea whether it's possible, but it's certainly worth exploring.

NOVA: Would you like it to be possible?

Sagan: I have mixed feelings. The explorer and experimentalist in me would very much like it to be possible. But the idea that going into the past could wipe me out so that I would have never lived is somewhat disquieting.

NOVA: On that note, can you describe the "grandfather paradox"?

Sagan: The grandfather paradox is a very simple, science-fiction-based apparent inconsistency at the very heart of the idea of time travel into the past. It's very simply that you travel into the past and murder your own grandfather before he sires your mother or your father, and where does that then leave you? Do you instantly pop out of existence because you were never made? Or are you in a new causality scheme in which, since you are there you are there, and the events in the future leading to your adult life are now very different? The heart of the paradox is the apparent existence of you, the murderer of your own grandfather, when the very act of you murdering your own grandfather eliminates the possibility of you ever coming into existence.

Among the claimed solutions are that you can't murder your grandfather. You shoot him, but at the critical moment he bends over to tie his shoelace, or the gun jams, or somehow nature contrives to prevent the act that interrupts the causality scheme leading to your own existence.

NOVA: Do you find it easy to believe the world might work that way—that is, self-consistently—or do you think it's more likely that there are parallel universes?

Sagan: It's still somewhat of a heretical ideal to suggest that every interference with an event in the past leads to a fork, a branch in causality. You have two equally valid universes: one, the one that we all know and love, and the other, which is brought about by the act of time travel. I know the idea of the universe having to work out a self-consistent causality is appealing to a great many physicists, but I don't find the argument for it so compelling. I think inconsistencies might very well be consistent with the universe.

NOVA: As a physicist, what do you make of Stephen Hawking's chronological protection conjecture [which holds that the laws of physics disallow time machines]?

Sagan: There have been some toy experiments in which, at just the moment that the time machine is actuated, the universe conspires to blow it up, which has led Hawking and others to conclude that nature will contrive it so that time travel never in fact occurs. But no one actually knows that this is the case, and it cannot be known until we have a full theory of quantum gravity, which we do not seem to be on the verge of yet.

One of Hawking's arguments in the conjecture is that we are not awash in thousands of time travelers from the future, and therefore time travel is impossible. This argument I find very dubious, and it reminds me very much of the argument that there cannot be intelligences elsewhere in space, because otherwise the Earth would be awash in aliens. I can think half a dozen ways in which we could not be awash in time travelers, and still time travel is possible.

NOVA: Such as?

Sagan: First of all, it might be that you can build a time machine to go into the future, but not into the past, and we don't know about it because we haven't yet invented that time machine. Secondly, it might be that time travel into the past is possible, but they haven't gotten to our time yet, they're very far in the future and the further back in time you go, the more expensive it is. Thirdly, maybe backward time travel is possible, but only up to the moment that time travel is invented. We haven't invented it yet, so they can't come to us. They can come to as far back as whatever it would be, say A.D. 2300, but not further back in time.

Then there's the possibility that they're here alright, but we don't see them. They have perfect invisibility cloaks or something. If they have such highly developed technology, then why not? Then there's the possibility that they're here and we do see them, but we call them something else—UFOs or ghosts or hobgoblins or fairies or something like that. Finally, there's the possibility that time travel is perfectly possible, but it requires a great advance in our technology, and human civilization will destroy itself before time travelers invent it.

I'm sure there are other possibilities as well, but if you just think of that range of possibilities, I don't think the fact that we're not obviously being visited by time travelers shows that time travel is impossible.

NOVA: How is the speed of light connected to time travel?

Sagan: A profound consequence of Einstein's special theory of relativity is that no material object can travel as fast as light. It is forbidden. There is a commandment: Thou shalt not travel at the speed of light, and there's nothing we can do to travel that fast.

The reason this is connected with time travel is because another consequence of special relativity is that time, as measured by the speeding space traveler, slows down compared to time as measured by a friend left home on Earth. This is sometimes described as the "twin paradox": two identical twins, one of whom goes off on a voyage close to the speed of light, and the other one stays home. When the space-traveling twin returns home, he or she has aged only a little, while the twin who has remained at home has aged at the regular pace. So we have two identical twins who may be decades apart in age. Or maybe the traveling twin returns in the far future, if you go close enough to the speed of light, and everybody he knows, everybody he ever heard of has died, and it's a very different civilization.

It's an intriguing idea, and it underscores the fact that time travel into the indefinite future is consistent with the laws of nature. It's only travel backwards in time that is the source of the debate and the tingling sensations that physicists and science-fiction readers delight in.

NOVA: In your novel *Contact*, your main character Eleanor Arroway travels through a wormhole. Can you describe a wormhole?

Sagan: Let's imagine that we live in a two-dimensional space. We wish to go from spot A to spot B. But A and B are so far apart that at the speed of light it would take much longer than a generational time or two to get there as measured back on world A. Instead, you have a kind of tunnel that goes through an otherwise inaccessible third dimension and connects A and B. You can go much faster through the tunnel, and so you get from A to B without covering the intervening space, which is somewhat mind-boggling but consistent with the laws of nature. And [the theoretical physicist] Kip Thorne found that if we imagine an indefinitely advanced technical civilization, such a wormhole is consistent with the laws of physics.

It's very different from saying that we ourselves could construct such a wormhole. One of the basic ideas of how to do it is that there are fantastically minute wormholes that are forming and decaying all the time at the quantum level, and the idea is to grab one of those and keep it permanently open. Our high-energy particle accelerators don't have enough energy to even detect the phenomenon at that scale, much less do anything like holding a wormhole open. But it did seem in principle possible, so I reconfigured the book so that Eleanor Arroway successfully makes it through the center of the galaxy via a wormhole.

NOVA: What do you think it would be like to travel through a wormhole?

Sagan: Nobody really knows, but what Thorne has taught me is that say, for example, you were going through a wormhole from point A to point B. Suppose point B was in orbit around some bright star. The moment you were in the wormhole, near your point of origin A, you would see that star. And it would be very bright; it wouldn't be a tiny point in the distance. On the other hand, if you look sideways, you would not see out of the wormhole, you would be in that fourth physical dimension. What the walls of the wormhole would be is deeply mysterious. And the possibility was also raised that if you looked backwards in the wormhole you would see the very place on world A that you had left. And that would be true even as you emerged out of the wormhole near the star B. You would see in space a kind of black sphere, in which would be an image of the place you had left on Earth, just floating in the blackness of space. Very Alice in Wonderland.

NOVA: Your inquiries about space travel for *Contact* sparked a whole new direction in research on time travel. How does that make you feel?

Sagan: I find it marvellous, I mean literally marvellous, full of marvel, that this innocent inquiry in the context of writing a science-fiction novel has sparked a whole field of physics and dozens of scientific papers by some of the best physicists in the world. I'm so pleased to have played this catalytic role not just in fast spaceflight but in the idea of time travel.

NOVA: How do you feel being responsible for bringing time travel perhaps a step closer?

Sagan: I don't know that I've brought time travel a step closer. If anyone has it's Kip Thorne. But maybe the joint effort of all those involved in this debate has at least increased the respectability of serious consideration of the possibility of time travel. As a youngster who was fascinated by the possibility of time travel in the science-fiction novels of H.G. Wells, Robert Heinlein, and others, to be in any way involved in the possible actualization of time travel—well, it just brings goose bumps. Of course we're not really at that stage; we don't know that time travel is even possible, and if it is, we certainly haven't developed the time machine. But it's a stunning fact that we have now reached a stage in our understanding of nature where this is even a bare possibility.

QUESTIONS FOR DISCUSSION AND WRITING

1. What does Sagan mean when he says, "each of us time travels into the future, one year, every year"?
2. Why does Sagan think time is "resistant to definition"?
3. What is the "grandfather paradox"? What do you think of the solution that Sagan alludes to? Do you have an additional solution?
4. With whom do you side—Stephen Hawking, who believes time travel is impossible, or Sagan, who is more open to the idea? Why?
5. In your own words, describe a wormhole. Why are wormholes an important concept? Do you see their potential as metaphors?
6. What stories or films can you think of that involve time travel? How do they address the paradoxes and issues brought up by Sagan in this interview?

ON TECHNIQUE AND STYLE

1. Sagan refers to other scientists, namely Kip Thorne and Stephen Hawking, and other writers, such as Robert Heinlein and H. G. Wells. Why does he make these references? How does it affect the way we receive Sagan's beliefs? What if he hadn't referred to these scientists and writers?
2. Sagan is known for making science accessible to nonscientists. Do you find his explanations in this interview easy to understand, or difficult? Which elements make it so?

CULTURAL QUESTION

1. Do you know of cultures in the past that have been interested in extraterrestrial life, or time travel? Do you know how any other cultures today view these topics?

From Why the Future Doesn't Need Us

Bill Joy

Bill Joy (1954–   ) is cofounder of Sun Microsystems, where he was the chief scientist until 2003. Joy received his BS in electrical engineering from the University of

*Michigan and his MS in electrical engineering and computer science from the Univer-
sity of California, Berkeley. He was primarily responsible for the authorship of Berkeley UNIX, a computer operating system, also known as BSD, from which emerged
many modern forms of UNIX. The following passage is an excerpt from a longer article
written for* Wired *magazine in July 2000. The full article can be found at www.wired
.com/wired/archive/8.04/joy.html.*

From the moment I became involved in the creation of new technologies, their
ethical dimensions have concerned me, but it was only in the autumn of 1998
that I became anxiously aware of how great are the dangers facing us in the
21st century. I can date the onset of my unease to the day I met Ray Kurzweil,
the deservedly famous inventor of the first reading machine for the blind and
many other amazing things.

Ray and I were both speakers at George Gilder's Telecosm conference,
and I encountered him by chance in the bar of the hotel after both our sessions were over. I was sitting with John Searle, a Berkeley philosopher who
studies consciousness. While we were talking, Ray approached and a conversation began, the subject of which haunts me to this day.

I had missed Ray's talk and the subsequent panel that Ray and John had
been on, and they now picked right up where they'd left off, with Ray saying that
the rate of improvement of technology was going to accelerate and that we were
going to become robots or fuse with robots or something like that, and John
countering that this couldn't happen, because the robots couldn't be conscious.

While I had heard such talk before, I had always felt sentient robots were
in the realm of science fiction. But now, from someone I respected, I was
hearing a strong argument that they were a near-term possibility. I was taken
aback, especially given Ray's proven ability to imagine and create the future.
I already knew that new technologies like genetic engineering and nanotechnology were giving us the power to remake the world, but a realistic and
imminent scenario for intelligent robots surprised me.

It's easy to get jaded about such breakthroughs. We hear in the news
almost every day of some kind of technological or scientific advance. Yet this
was no ordinary prediction. In the hotel bar, Ray gave me a partial preprint of
his then-forthcoming book *The Age of Spiritual Machines,* which outlined a
utopia he foresaw—one in which humans gained near immortality by becoming one with robotic technology. On reading it, my sense of unease only
intensified; I felt sure he had to be understating the dangers, understating the
probability of a bad outcome along this path.

I found myself most troubled by a passage detailing a dystopian scenario:

THE NEW LUDDITE CHALLENGE

First let us postulate that the computer scientists succeed in developing intelligent machines that can do all things better than human beings can do them.
In that case presumably all work will be done by vast, highly organized systems
of machines and no human effort will be necessary. Either of two cases might

occur. The machines might be permitted to make all of their own decisions without human oversight, or else human control over the machines might be retained.

If the machines are permitted to make all their own decisions, we can't make any conjectures as to the results, because it is impossible to guess how such machines might behave. We only point out that the fate of the human race would be at the mercy of the machines. It might be argued that the human race would never be foolish enough to hand over all the power to the machines. But we are suggesting neither that the human race would voluntarily turn power over to the machines nor that the machines would willfully seize power. What we do suggest is that the human race might easily permit itself to drift into a position of such dependence on the machines that it would have no practical choice but to accept all of the machines' decisions. As society and the problems that face it become more and more complex and machines become more and more intelligent, people will let machines make more of their decisions for them, simply because machine-made decisions will bring better results than man-made ones. Eventually a stage may be reached at which the decisions necessary to keep the system running will be so complex that human beings will be incapable of making them intelligently. At that stage the machines will be in effective control. People won't be able to just turn the machines off, because they will be so dependent on them that turning them off would amount to suicide.

On the other hand it is possible that human control over the machines may be retained. In that case the average man may have control over certain private machines of his own, such as his car or his personal computer, but control over large systems of machines will be in the hands of a tiny elite—just as it is today, but with two differences. Due to improved techniques the elite will have greater control over the masses; and because human work will no longer be necessary the masses will be superfluous, a useless burden on the system. If the elite is ruthless they may simply decide to exterminate the mass of humanity. If they are humane they may use propaganda or other psychological or biological techniques to reduce the birth rate until the mass of humanity becomes extinct, leaving the world to the elite. Or, if the elite consists of soft-hearted liberals, they may decide to play the role of good shepherds to the rest of the human race. They will see to it that everyone's physical needs are satisfied, that all children are raised under psychologically hygienic conditions, that everyone has a wholesome hobby to keep him busy, and that anyone who may become dissatisfied undergoes "treatment" to cure his "problem." Of course, life will be so purposeless that people will have to be biologically or psychologically engineered either to remove their need for the power process or make them "sublimate" their drive for power into some harmless hobby. These engineered human beings may be happy in such a society, but they will most certainly not be free. They will have been reduced to the status of domestic animals.[1]

---

[1] The passage Kurzweil quotes is from Kaczynski's Unabomber Manifesto, which was published jointly, under duress, by *The New York Times* and *The Washington Post* to attempt to bring his campaign of terror to an end. I agree with David Gelernter, who said about their decision:
It was a tough call for the newspapers. To say yes would be giving in to terrorism, and for all they knew he was lying anyway. On the other hand, to say yes might stop the killing. There was also a chance that someone would read the tract and get a hunch about the author; and that is exactly what happened. The suspect's brother read it, and it rang a bell.
   I would have told them not to publish. I'm glad they didn't ask me. I guess.

In the book, you don't discover until you turn the page that the author of this passage is Theodore Kaczynski—the Unabomber. I am no apologist for Kaczynski. His bombs killed three people during a 17-year terror campaign and wounded many others. One of his bombs gravely injured my friend David Gelernter, one of the most brilliant and visionary computer scientists of our time. Like many of my colleagues, I felt that I could easily have been the Unabomber's next target.

Kaczynski's actions were murderous and, in my view, criminally insane. He is clearly a Luddite, but simply saying this does not dismiss his argument; as difficult as it is for me to acknowledge, I saw some merit in the reasoning in this single passage. I felt compelled to confront it.

Kaczynski's dystopian vision describes unintended consequences, a well-known problem with the design and use of technology, and one that is clearly related to Murphy's law—"Anything that can go wrong, will." (Actually, this is Finagle's law, which in itself shows that Finagle was right.) Our overuse of antibiotics has led to what may be the biggest such problem so far: the emergence of antibiotic-resistant and much more dangerous bacteria. Similar things happened when attempts to eliminate malarial mosquitoes using DDT caused them to acquire DDT resistance; malarial parasites likewise acquired multi-drug-resistant genes.[2]

The cause of many such surprises seems clear: The systems involved are complex, involving interaction among and feedback between many parts. Any changes to such a system will cascade in ways that are difficult to predict; this is especially true when human actions are involved.

I started showing friends the Kaczynski quote from *The Age of Spiritual Machines;* I would hand them Kurzweil's book, let them read the quote, and then watch their reaction as they discovered who had written it. At around the same time, I found Hans Moravec's book *Robot: Mere Machine to Transcendent Mind.* Moravec is one of the leaders in robotics research, and was a founder of the world's largest robotics research program, at Carnegie Mellon University. *Robot* gave me more material to try out on my friends—material surprisingly supportive of Kaczynski's argument. For example:

The Short Run (Early 2000s)

Biological species almost never survive encounters with superior competitors. Ten million years ago, South and North America were separated by a sunken Panama isthmus. South America, like Australia today, was populated by marsupial mammals, including pouched equivalents of rats, deers, and tigers. When the isthmus connecting North and South America rose, it took only a few thousand years for the northern placental species, with slightly more effective metabolisms and reproductive and nervous systems, to displace and eliminate almost all the southern marsupials.

In a completely free marketplace, superior robots would surely affect humans as North American placentals affected South American marsupials (and as humans have affected countless species). Robotic industries would

[2] Garrett, Laurie. *The Coming Plague: Newly Emerging Diseases in a World Out of Balance.* Penguin, 1994: 47–52, 414, 419, 452.

compete vigorously among themselves for matter, energy, and space, incidentally driving their price beyond human reach. Unable to afford the necessities of life, biological humans would be squeezed out of existence.

There is probably some breathing room, because we do not live in a completely free marketplace. Government coerces nonmarket behavior, especially by
collecting taxes. Judiciously applied, governmental coercion could support human populations in high style on the fruits of robot labor, perhaps for a long while.

A textbook dystopian—and Moravec is just getting wound up. He goes on
to discuss how our main job in the 21st century will be "ensuring continued
cooperation from the robot industries" by passing laws decreeing that they
be "nice,"[3] and to describe how seriously dangerous a human can be "once
transformed into an unbounded superintelligent robot." Moravec's view is that
the robots will eventually succeed us—that humans clearly face extinction.

I decided it was time to talk to my friend Danny Hillis. Danny became
famous as the cofounder of Thinking Machines Corporation, which built a
very powerful parallel supercomputer. Despite my current job title of Chief
Scientist at Sun Microsystems, I am more a computer architect than a scientist, and I respect Danny's knowledge of the information and physical sciences more than that of any other single person I know. Danny is also a highly
regarded futurist who thinks long-term—four years ago he started the Long
Now Foundation, which is building a clock designed to last 10,000 years, in
an attempt to draw attention to the pitifully short attention span of our society.

So I flew to Los Angeles for the express purpose of having dinner with
Danny and his wife, Pati. I went through my now-familiar routine, trotting out
the ideas and passages that I found so disturbing. Danny's answer—directed
specifically at Kurzweil's scenario of humans merging with robots—came
swiftly, and quite surprised me. He said, simply, that the changes would
come gradually, and that we would get used to them.

But I guess I wasn't totally surprised. I had seen a quote from Danny in
Kurzweil's book in which he said, "I'm as fond of my body as anyone, but if I
can be 200 with a body of silicon, I'll take it." It seemed that he was at peace
with this process and its attendant risks, while I was not.

While talking and thinking about Kurzweil, Kaczynski, and Moravec, I suddenly remembered a novel I had read almost 20 years ago—*The White Plague,*
by Frank Herbert—in which a molecular biologist is driven insane by the senseless murder of his family. To seek revenge he constructs and disseminates a
new and highly contagious plague that kills widely but selectively. (We're lucky
Kaczynski was a mathematician, not a molecular biologist.) I was also reminded
of the Borg of *Star Trek,* a hive of partly biological, partly robotic creatures with

[3] Isaac Asimov described what became the most famous view of ethical rules for robot behavior in
his book *I, Robot* in 1950, in his Three Laws of Robotics: 1. A robot may not injure a human being,
or, through inaction, allow a human being to come to harm. 2. A robot must obey the orders given
it by human beings, except where such orders would conflict with the First Law. 3. A robot must
protect its own existence, as long as such protection does not conflict with the First or Second Law.

a strong destructive streak. Borg-like disasters are a staple of science fiction, so why hadn't I been more concerned about such robotic dystopias earlier? Why weren't other people more concerned about these nightmarish scenarios?

Part of the answer certainly lies in our attitude toward the new—in our bias toward instant familiarity and unquestioning acceptance. Accustomed to living with almost routine scientific breakthroughs, we have yet to come to terms with the fact that the most compelling 21st-century technologies—robotics, genetic engineering, and nanotechnology—pose a different threat than the technologies that have come before. Specifically, robots, engineered organisms, and nanobots share a dangerous amplifying factor: They can self-replicate. A bomb is blown up only once—but one bot can become many, and quickly get out of control.

Much of my work over the past 25 years has been on computer network-ing, where the sending and receiving of messages creates the opportunity for out-of-control replication. But while replication in a computer or a computer network can be a nuisance, at worst it disables a machine or takes down a network or network service. Uncontrolled self-replication in these newer tech-nologies runs a much greater risk: a risk of substantial damage in the physical world.

Each of these technologies also offers untold promise: The vision of near immortality that Kurzweil sees in his robot dreams drives us forward; genetic engineering may soon provide treatments, if not outright cures, for most diseases; and nanotechnology and nanomedicine can address yet more ills. Together they could significantly extend our average life span and improve the quality of our lives. Yet, with each of these technologies, a sequence of small, individually sensible advances leads to an accumulation of great power and, concomitantly, great danger.

What was different in the 20th century? Certainly, the technologies underly-ing the weapons of mass destruction (WMD)—nuclear, biological, and chemi-cal (NBC)—were powerful, and the weapons an enormous threat. But building nuclear weapons required, at least for a time, access to both rare—indeed, effectively unavailable—raw materials and highly protected information; bio-logical and chemical weapons programs also tended to require large-scale activities.

The 21st-century technologies—genetics, nanotechnology, and robotics (GNR)—are so powerful that they can spawn whole new classes of accidents and abuses. Most dangerously, for the first time, these accidents and abuses are widely within the reach of individuals or small groups. They will not require large facilities or rare raw materials. Knowledge alone will enable the use of them.

Thus we have the possibility not just of weapons of mass destruction but of knowledge-enabled mass destruction (KMD), this destructiveness hugely amplified by the power of self-replication.

I think it is no exaggeration to say we are on the cusp of the further per-fection of extreme evil, an evil whose possibility spreads well beyond that which weapons of mass destruction bequeathed to the nation-states, on to a surprising and terrible empowerment of extreme individuals.

QUESTIONS FOR DISCUSSION AND WRITING

1. What do you think of the predictions about robots in the future? Did anything in this reading affect your opinion?
2. What does Joy mean when he calls Moravec "a textbook dystopian"?
3. What is the history of the Luddites, briefly? How does the idea of Ludditism apply to this article, both directly and indirectly?
4. What are the impulses behind these "robot dreams" according to Joy? What are the pros and cons of this type of technological advance?
5. Why is "KMD" the most dangerous weapon, according to Joy? Do you find his argument convincing?

ON TECHNIQUE AND STYLE

1. What does Joy try to achieve by including the passage from Ted Kaczynski's Unabomber manifesto? Does he achieve this? Explain.
2. Joy interweaves personal stories with this account. Why do you think he does this? Why doesn't he just talk about the research and the science as it applies to the development of robots and nanotechnology?

CULTURAL QUESTION

1. The editors of *Wired* magazine report: "Bill Joy's cover story on the dangers posed by developments in genetics, nanotechnology, and robotics struck a deep cultural nerve. Instantly." Why do you think it had such an impact? What about modern culture makes this topic especially sensitive?

Forecasting the Future

H. G. Wells

H. G. (Herbert George) Wells (1866–1946) was a British writer, known for his science fiction novels, most notably The War of the Worlds *(1898),* The Invisible Man *(1897),* The Island of Doctor Moreau *(1896), and* The Time Machine *(1895), all of which have been made into films. These works are often thought of as being influenced by those of Jules Verne.*

Wells was an outspoken socialist, and most of his works contain some political or social commentary. The following excerpt is from the first chapter of Wells's nonfiction work What Is Coming? *written in 1916.*

Prophecy may vary between being an intellectual amusement and a serious occupation; serious not only in its intentions, but in its consequences. For it is the lot of prophets who frighten or disappoint to be stoned. But for some of us moderns, who have been touched with the spirit of science, prophesying is almost a habit of mind.

Science is very largely analysis aimed at forecasting. The test of any scientific law is our verification of its anticipations. The scientific training develops the idea that whatever is going to happen is really here now—if only one could see it. And when one is taken by surprise the tendency is not to say with the untrained man, "Now, who'd ha' thought it?" but "Now, what was it we overlooked?"

Everything that has ever existed or that will ever exist is here—for anyone who has eyes to see. But some of it demands eyes of superhuman penetration. Some of it is patent; we are almost as certain of next Christmas and the tides of the year 1960 and the death before 3000 A.D. of everybody now alive as if these things had already happened. Below that level of certainty, but still at a very high level of certainty, there are such things as that men will probably be making aeroplanes of an improved pattern in 1950, or that there will be a through railway connection between Constantinople and Bombay and between Baku and Bombay in the next half-century. From such grades of certainty as this, one may come down the scale until the most obscure mystery of all is reached: the mystery of the individual. Will England presently produce a military genius? or what will Mr. Belloc* say the day after to-morrow? The most accessible field for the prophet is the heavens; the least is the secret of the jumping cat within the human skull. How will so-and-so behave, and how will the nation take it? For such questions as that we need the subtlest guesses of all.

Yet, even to such questions as these the sharp, observant man may risk an answer with something rather better than an even chance of being right.

The present writer is a prophet by use and wont. He is more interested in to-morrow than he is in to-day, and the past is just material for future guessing. "Think of the men who have walked here!" said a tourist in the Roman Coliseum. It was a Futurist mind that answered: "Think of the men who will." It is surely as interesting that presently some founder of the World Republic, some obstinate opponent of militarism or legalism, or the man who will first release atomic energy for human use, will walk along the Via Sacra as that Cicero or Giordano Bruno or Shelley have walked there in the past. To the prophetic mind all history is and will continue to be a prelude. The prophetic type will steadfastly refuse to see the world as a museum; it will insist that here is a stage set for a drama that perpetually begins.

Now this forecasting disposition has led the writer not only to publish a book of deliberate prophesying, called "Anticipations," but almost without premeditation to scatter a number of more or less obvious prophecies

*A reference to Hilaire Belloc, an influential British writer.

through his other books. From first to last he has been writing for twenty years, so that it is possible to check a certain proportion of these anticipations by the things that have happened. Some of these shots have hit remarkably close to the bull's-eye of reality; there are a number of inners and outers, and some clean misses. Much that he wrote about in anticipation is now established commonplace. In 1894 there were still plenty of sceptics of the possibility either of automobiles or aeroplanes; it was not until 1898 that Mr. S.P. Langley (of the Smithsonian Institute) could send the writer a photograph of a heavier-than-air flying machine actually in the air. There were articles in the monthly magazines of those days *proving* that flying was impossible.

One of the writer's luckiest shots was a description (in "Anticipations" in 1900) of trench warfare, and of a deadlock almost exactly upon the lines of the situation after the battle of the Marne. And he was fortunate (in the same work) in his estimate of the limitations of submarines. He anticipated Sir Percy Scott by a year in his doubts of the decisive value of great battleships (*see* "An Englishman Looks at the World"); and he was sound in denying the decadence of France; in doubting (before the Russo-Japanese struggle) the greatness of the power of Russia, which was still in those days a British bogey; in making Belgium the battle-ground in a coming struggle between the mid-European Powers and the rest of Europe; and (he believes) in foretelling a renascent Poland. Long before Europe was familiar with the engaging personality of the German Crown Prince, he represented great airships sailing over England (which country had been too unenterprising to make any) under the command of a singularly anticipatory Prince Karl, and in "The World Set Free" the last disturber of the peace is a certain "Balkan Fox."

In saying, however, here and there that "before such a year so-and-so will happen," or that "so-and-so will not occur for the next twenty years," he was generally pretty widely wrong; most of his time estimates are too short; he foretold, for example, a special motor track apart from the high road between London and Brighton before 1910, which is still a dream, but he doubted if effective military aviation or aerial fighting would be possible before 1950, which is a miss on the other side. He will draw a modest veil over certain still wider misses that the idle may find for themselves in his books; he prefers to count the hits and leave the reckoning of the misses to those who will find a pleasure in it.

Of course, these prophecies of the writer's were made upon a basis of very generalised knowledge. What can be done by a really sustained research into a particular question—especially if it is a question essentially mechanical—is shown by the work of a Frenchman all too neglected by the trumpet of fame—Clement Ader. M. Ader was probably the first man to get a mechanism up into the air for something more than a leap. His *Eole,* as General Mensier testifies, prolonged a jump as far as fifty metres as early as 1890. In 1897 his *Avion* fairly flew. (This is a year ahead of the date of my earliest photograph of S.P. Langley's aeropile in mid-air.) This, however, is beside our present mark. The fact of interest here is that in 1908, when flying was still almost incredible, M. Ader published his "Aviation Militaire." Well, that was eight years ago, and men have been fighting in the air now for a year, and there is still nothing being done that M. Ader did not see, and which we, if we had had the wisdom to attend to him, might not have been prepared for. There is much that he foretells which is still awaiting its inevitable fulfillment. So clearly can men of adequate knowledge and sound reasoning power see into the years ahead in all such matters of material development.

But it is not with the development of mechanical inventions that the writer now proposes to treat. In this book he intends to hazard certain forecasts about the trend of events in the next decade or so. Mechanical novelties will probably play a very small part in that coming history. This world-wide war means a general arrest of invention and enterprise, except in the direction of the war business. Ability is concentrated upon that; the types of ability that are not applicable to warfare are neglected; there is a vast destruction of capital and a waste of the savings that are needed to finance new experiments. Moreover, we are killing off many of our brightest young men.

It is fairly safe to assume that there will be very little new furniture on the stage of the world for some considerable time; that if there is much difference in the roads and railways and shipping it will be for the worse; that architecture, domestic equipment, and so on, will be fortunate if in 1924 they stand where they did in the spring of 1914. In the trenches of France and Flanders, and on the battlefields of Russia, the Germans have been spending and making the world spend the comfort, the luxury and the progress of the next quarter-century. There is no accounting for tastes. But the result is that, while it was possible for the writer in 1900 to write "Anticipations of the Reaction of Mechanical Progress upon Human Life and Thought," in 1916 his anticipations must belong to quite another system of consequences.

The broad material facts before us are plain enough. It is the mental facts that have to be unravelled. It isn't now a question of "What thing—what faculty—what added power will come to hand, and how will it affect our ways of living?" It is a question of "How are people going to take these obvious things—waste of the world's resources, arrest of material progress, the killing of a large moiety of the males in nearly every European country, and universal loss and unhappiness?" We are going to deal with realities here, at once more intimate and less accessible than the effects of mechanism.

As a preliminary reconnaissance, as it were, over the region of problems we have to attack, let us consider the difficulties of a single question, which is also a vital and central question in this forecast. We shall not attempt a full answer here, because too many of the factors must remain unexamined; later, perhaps, we may be in a better position to do so. This question is the probability of the establishment of a long world peace.

At the outset of the war there was a very widely felt hope among the intellectuals of the world that this war might clear up most of the outstanding international problems, and prove the last war. The writer, looking across the gulf of experience that separates us from 1914, recalls two pamphlets whose very titles are eloquent of this feeling—"The War that will End War," and "The Peace of the World." Was the hope expressed in those phrases a dream? Is it already proven a dream? Or can we read between the lines of the war news, diplomatic disputations, threats and accusations, political wranglings and stories of hardship and cruelty that now fill our papers, anything that still justifies a hope that these bitter years of world sorrow are the darkness before the dawn of a better day for mankind? Let us handle this problem for a preliminary examination.

What is really being examined here is the power of human reason to prevail over passion—and certain other restraining and qualifying forces. There can be little doubt that, if one could canvass all mankind and ask them whether they would rather have no war any more, the overwhelming mass of them would elect for universal peace. If it were war of the modern mechanical type that was in question, with air raids, high explosives, poison gas and submarines, there could be no doubt at all about the response. "Give peace in our time, O Lord," is more than ever the common prayer of Christendom, and the very war makers claim to be peace makers; the German Emperor has never faltered in his assertion that he encouraged Austria to send an impossible ultimatum to Serbia, and invaded Belgium because Germany was being attacked. The Krupp-Kaiser Empire, he assures us, is no eagle, but a double-headed lamb, resisting the shearers and butchers. The apologists for war are in a hopeless minority; a certain number of German Prussians who think war good for the soul, and the dear ladies of the London *Morning Post* who think war so good for the manners of the working classes, are rare, discordant voices in the general chorus against war. If a mere unsupported and uncoordinated will for peace could realise itself, there would be peace, and an enduring peace, to-morrow. But, as a matter of fact, there is no peace coming to-morrow, and no clear prospect yet of an enduring universal peace at the end of this war.

Now what are the obstructions, and what are the antagonisms to the exploitation of this world-wide disgust with war and the world-wide desire for peace, so as to establish a world peace?

Let us take them in order, and it will speedily become apparent that we are dealing here with a subtle quantitative problem in psychology, a constant weighing of whether this force or that force is the stronger. We are dealing with influences so subtle that the accidents of some striking dramatic occurrence, for example, may turn them this way or that. We are dealing with the human will—and thereby comes a snare for the feet of the would-be impartial prophet. To foretell the future is to modify the future. It is hard for any prophet not to break into exhortation after the fashion of the prophets of Israel.

The first difficulty in the way of establishing a world peace is that it is nobody's business in particular. Nearly all of us want a world peace—in an amateurish sort of way. But there is no specific person or persons to whom one can look for the initiatives. The world is a supersaturated solution of the will-for-peace, and there is nothing for it to crystallise upon. There is no one in all the world who is responsible for the understanding and overcoming of the difficulties involved. There are many more people, and there is much more intelligence concentrated upon the manufacture of cigarettes or hair-pins than upon the establishment of a permanent world peace. There are a few special secretaries employed by philanthropic Americans, and that is about all. There has been no provision made even for the emoluments of these gentlemen when universal peace is attained; presumably they would lose their jobs.

Nearly everybody wants peace; nearly everybody would be glad to wave a white flag with a dove on it now—provided no unfair use was made of such a demonstration by the enemy—but there is practically nobody thinking out the arrangements needed, and nobody making nearly as much propaganda for the instruction of the world in the things needful as is made in selling any popular make of automobile. We have all our particular businesses to attend to. And things are not got by just wanting them; things are got by getting them, and rejecting whatever precludes our getting them.

QUESTIONS FOR DISCUSSION AND WRITING

1. What does Wells mean when he says, "Everything that has ever existed or that will ever exist is here—for anyone who has eyes to see"? Do you agree with this? Give an example supporting your opinion.
2. Do you think that Wells's prophesy that "It is fairly safe to assume that there will be very little new furniture on the stage of the world for some considerable time" was in fact the case? What evidence do you have in favor or opposed to his prediction? What is the situation that caused Wells to hold this rather negative view of innovation?
3. Wells predicted that, contrary to the popular press of the time, World War I would not be the "war to end all war." We can certainly see that his prediction held truth, and continues to be true. However, is "universal peace" a possibility in Wells's view? Why or why not? Do you agree with his view?
4. Why does Wells say, "To foretell the future is to modify the future"? Do you agree?
5. Wells moves from talking about predicting the future to a discussion of pacifism and war. How are prophesy, predicting the future, scientific knowledge, and peace related?

ON TECHNIQUE AND STYLE

1. Who is "the writer" Wells refers to in the selection? Why does he refer to the writer in third person?
2. What is the purpose of the catalog of predictions? What is Wells trying to prove?

CULTURAL QUESTION

1. Wells ties his argument closely to the society in which he lives—England during World War I. In what ways do his ideas reflect modern culture? In what ways are they at odds with today's society?

From Future Shock

Alvin Toffler

Alvin Toffler (1928–   ) is an American writer and futurist, known for his works discussing the digital and communications revolutions as well as technological singularity. He was born in New York City, where he was a student at New York University, and later a professor at Cornell University. A former associate editor of Fortune *magazine, his early work focused on technology and its effects, dealing with issues such as information overload. Toffler is said to have invented the role of the futurist with the publication of his influential work* Future Shock *(1970), from which the following excerpt was taken.*

The Pre-designed Body

Like the geography of the planet, the human body has until now represented a fixed point in human experience, a "given." Today we are fast approaching the day when the body can no longer be regarded as fixed. Man will be able, within a reasonably short period, to redesign not merely individual bodies, but the entire human race.

In 1962 Drs. J. D. Watson and F. H. C. Crick received the Nobel prize for describing the DNA molecule. Since then advances in genetics have come tripping over one another at a rapid pace. Molecular biology is now about to explode from the laboratories. New genetic knowledge will permit us to tinker with human heredity and manipulate the genes to create altogether new versions of man.

One of the more fantastic possibilities is that man will be able to make biological carbon copies of himself. Through a process known as "cloning" it will be possible to grow from the nucleus of an adult cell a new organism that has the same genetic characteristics of the person contributing the cell nucleus. The resultant human "copy" would start life with a genetic endowment identical to that of the donor, although cultural differences might thereafter alter the personality or physical development of the clone.

Cloning would make it possible for people to see themselves born anew, to fill the world with twins of themselves. Cloning would, among other things, provide us with solid empirical evidence to help us resolve, once and for all, the ancient controversy over "nature *vs.* nurture" or "heredity *vs.* environment." The solution of this problem, through the determination of the role played by each, would be one of the great milestones of human intellectual development. Whole libraries of philosophical speculation could, by a single stroke, be rendered irrelevant. An answer to this question would open the way for speedy, qualitative advances in psychology, moral philosophy and a dozen other fields.

But cloning could also create undreamed of complications for the race. There is a certain charm to the idea of Albert Einstein bequeathing copies of himself to posterity. But what of Adolf Hitler? Should there be laws to regulate cloning? Nobel Laureate Joshua Lederberg, a scientist who takes his social responsibility very seriously, believes it conceivable that those most likely to replicate themselves will be those who are most narcissistic, and that the clones they produce will also be narcissists.

Even if narcissism, however, is culturally rather than biologically transmitted, there are other eerie difficulties. Thus Lederberg raises a question as to whether human cloning, if permitted, might not "go critical." "I use that phrase," he told me, "in almost exactly the same sense that is involved in nuclear energy. It *will* go critical if there is a sufficient positive advantage to doing so . . . This has to do with whether the efficiency of communication, particularly along educational lines, is increased as between identical genotypes or not. The similarity of neurological hardware might make it easier for identical copies to transmit technical and other insights from one generation to the next."

How close is cloning? "It has already been done in amphibia," says Lederberg, "and somebody may be doing it right now with mammals. It wouldn't surprise me if it comes out any day now. When someone will have the courage to try it in a man, I haven't the foggiest idea. But I put the time scale on that anywhere from zero to fifteen years from now. Within fifteen years."

During those same fifteen years scientists will also learn how the various organs of the body develop, and they will, no doubt, begin to experiment with various means of modifying them. Says Lederberg: "Things like the size of the brain and certain sensory qualities of the brain are going to be brought under direct developmental control . . . I think this is very near."

It is important for laymen to understand that Lederberg is by no means a lone worrier in the scientific community. His fears about the biological revolution are shared by many of his colleagues. The ethical, moral and political questions raised by the new biology simply boggle the mind. Who shall live and who shall die? What is man? Who shall control research into these fields? How shall new findings be applied? Might we not unleash horrors for which man is totally unprepared? In the opinion of many of the world's leading scientists the clock is ticking for a "biological Hiroshima."

Imagine, for example, the implications of biological breakthroughs in what might be termed "birth technology." Dr. E. S. E. Hafez, an internationally respected biologist at Washington State University, has publicly suggested, on the basis of his own astonishing work on reproduction, that within a mere ten to fifteen years a woman will be able to buy a tiny frozen embryo, take it to her doctor, have it implanted in her uterus, carry it for nine months, and then give birth to it as though it had been conceived in her own body. The embryo would, in effect, be sold with a guarantee that the resultant baby would be free of genetic defect. The purchaser would also be told in advance the color of the baby's eyes and hair, its sex, its probable size at maturity and its probable IQ.

Indeed, it will be possible at some point to do away with the female uterus altogether. Babies will be conceived, nurtured and raised to maturity outside the human body. It is clearly only a matter of years before the work begun by Dr. Daniele Petrucci in Bologna and other scientists in the United States and the Soviet Union, makes it possible for women to have babies without the discomfort of pregnancy.

The potential applications of such discoveries raise memories of *Brave New World* and *Astounding Science Fiction.* Thus Dr. Hafez, in a sweep of his imagination, suggests that fertilized human eggs might be useful in the colonization of the planets. Instead of shipping adults to Mars, we could ship a shoebox full of such cells and grow them into an entire city-size population of humans. "When you consider how much it costs in fuel to lift every pound off the launch pad," Dr. Hafez observes, "why send full-grown men and women aboard space ships? Instead, why not ship tiny embryos, in the care of a competent biologist . . . We miniaturize other spacecraft components. Why not the passengers?"

Long before such developments occur in outer space, however, the impact of the new birth technology will strike home on earth, splintering our traditional notions of sexuality, motherhood, love, child-rearing, and education. Discussions about the future of the family that deal only with The Pill overlook the biological witches' brew now seething in the laboratories. The moral and emotional choices that will confront us in the coming decades are mind-staggering.

A fierce controversy is already raging today among biologists over the problems and ethical issues arising out of eugenics. Should we try to breed a better race? If so, exactly what is "better"? And who is to decide? Such questions are not entirely new. Yet the techniques soon to be available smash the traditional limits of the argument. We can now imagine remaking the human race not as a farmer slowly and laboriously "breeds up" his herd, but as an artist might, employing a brilliant range of unfamiliar colors, shapes and forms.

Not far from Route 80, outside the little town of Hazard, Kentucky, is a place picturesquely known as Valley of Troublesome Creek. In this tiny backwoods community lives a family whose members, for generations, have been marked by a strange anomaly: blue skin. According to Dr. Madison Cawein of the University of Kentucky College of Medicine, who tracked the family down and traced its story, the blue-skinned people seem perfectly normal in other respects. Their unusual color is caused by a rare enzyme deficiency that has been passed from one generation to the next.

Given our new, fast-accumulating knowledge of genetics, we shall be able to breed whole new races of blue people—or, for that matter, green, purple or orange. In a world still suffering from the moral lesion of racism, this is a thought to be conjured with. Should we strive for a world in which all people share the same skin color? If we want that, we shall no doubt have the technical means for bringing it about. Or should we, instead, work toward even greater diversity than now exists? What happens to the entire concept of race? To standards of physical beauty? To notions of superiority or inferiority?

We are hurtling toward the time when we will be able to breed both super- and sub-races. As Theodore J. Gordon put it in *The Future,* "Given the ability to tailor the race, I wonder if we would 'create all men equal,' or would we choose to manufacture apartheid? Might the races of the future be: a superior group, the DNA controllers; the humble servants; special athletes for the 'games'; research scientists with 200 IQ and diminutive bodies . . ." We shall have the power to produce races of morons or of mathematical savants.

We shall also be able to breed babies with supernormal vision or hearing, supernormal ability to detect changes in odor, or supernormal muscular or musical skills. We will be able to create sexual superathletes, girls with super-mammaries (and perhaps more or less than the standard two), and countless other varieties of the previously monomorphic human being.

Ultimately, the problems are not scientific or technical, but ethical and political. Choice—and the criteria for choice—will be critical. The eminent science fiction author William Tenn once mused about the possibilities of genetic manipulation and the difficulties of choice. "Assuming hopefully for the moment that no dictator, self-righteous planning board or omnipotent black box is going to make genetic selections for the coming generation, then who or what is? Not parents, certainly . . ." he said, "they'll take the problem to their friendly neighborhood Certified Gene Architect.

"It seems inevitable to me that there will also be competitive schools of genetic architecture . . . the Functionalists will persuade parents to produce babies fitted for the present needs of society; the Futurists will suggest children who will have a niche in the culture as it will have evolved in twenty years; the Romantics will insist that each child be bred with at least one outstanding talent; and the Naturalists will advise the production of individuals so balanced genetically as to be in almost perfect equilibrium . . . Human body styles, like human clothing styles, will become *outré,* or *à la mode* as the genetic *couturiers* who designed them come into and out of vogue."

Buried behind this tongue-in-cheek are serious issues, made more profound by the immensity of the possibilities—some of them so grotesque that they appear to leap at us from the canvases of Hieronymus Bosch. Mention was made earlier of the idea of breeding men with gills or implanting gills in them for efficiency in underwater environments. At a meeting of world renowned biologists in London, J. B. S. Haldane began to expatiate about the possibility of creating new, far-out forms of man for space exploration. "The most obvious abnormalities in extra-terrestrial environments," Haldane observed, "are differences in gravitation, temperature, air pressure, air composition, and radiation . . . Clearly a gibbon is better preadapted than a man for life in a low gravitational field, such as that of a space ship, an asteroid, or perhaps even the moon. A platyrrhine with a prehensile tail is even more so. Gene grafting may make it possible to incorporate such features into the human stocks."

While the scientists at this meeting devoted much of their attention to the moral consequences and perils of the biological revolution, no one challenged Haldane's suggestion that we shall someday make men with tails if we want them. Indeed, Lederberg merely observed that there might well be non-genetic ways to accomplish the same ends more easily. "We are going to modify man experimentally through physiological and embryological alterations, and by the substitution of machines for his parts," Lederberg declared. "If we want a man without legs, we don't have to breed him, we can chop them off; if we want a man with a tail, we will find a way of grafting it on to him."

At another meeting of scientists and scholars, Dr. Robert Sinsheimer, a Caltech biophysicist, put the challenge squarely:

"How will you choose to intervene in the ancient designs of nature for man? Would you like to control the sex of your offspring? It will be as you wish. Would you like your son to be six feet tall—seven feet? Eight feet? What troubles you?—allergy, obesity, arthritic pain? These will be easily handled. For cancer, diabetes, phenylketonuria there will be genetic therapy. The appropriate DNA will be provided in the appropriate dose. Viral and microbial disease will be easily met. Even the timeless patterns of growth and maturity and aging will be subject to our design. We know of no intrinsic limits to the life span. How long would you like to live?"

Lest his audience mistake him, Sinsheimer asked: "Do these projections sound like LSD fantasies, or the view in a distorted mirror? None transcends the potential of what we now know. They may not be developed in the way one might now anticipate, but they *are* feasible, they *can* be brought to reality, and sooner rather than later."

Not only *can* such wonders be brought to reality, but the odds are they *will.* Despite profound ethical questions about whether they *should,* the fact remains that scientific curiosity is, itself, one of the most powerful driving forces in our society. In the words of Dr. Rollin D. Hotchkiss of the Rockefeller Institute: "Many of us feel instinctive revulsion at the hazards of meddling with the finely balanced and far-reaching systems that make an individual what he is. Yet I believe it will surely be done or attempted. The pathway will be built from a combination of altruism, private profit and ignorance." To this list, worse yet, he might have added political conflict and bland unconcern. Thus Dr. A. Neyfakh, chief of the research laboratory of the Institute of Development Biology of the Soviet Academy of Sciences, predicts with a frightening lack of anxiety that the world will soon witness a genetic equivalent of the arms race. He bases his argument on the notion that the capitalist powers are engaged in a "struggle for brains." To make up for the brain drain, one or another of the "reactionary governments" will be "compelled" to employ genetic engineering to increase its output of geniuses and gifted individuals. Since this will occur "regardless of their intention," an international genetics race is inevitable. And this being so, he implies, the Soviet Union ought to be ready to jump the gun.

Criticized by the Soviet philosopher A. Petropavlovsky for his seeming willingness, even enthusiasm, to participate in such a race, Neyfakh shrugged aside the horrors that might be unleashed by hasty application of the new biology, replying merely that the advance of science is, and ought to be, unstoppable. If Neyfakh's political logic leaves something to be desired, his appeal to cold war passions as a justification for genetic tinkering is terrifying.

In short, it is safe to say that, unless specific counter-measures are taken, if something *can* be done, someone, somewhere *will* do it. The nature of what can and will be done exceeds anything that man is as yet psychologically or morally prepared to live with.

The Transient Organ

We steadfastly refuse to face such facts. We avoid them by stubbornly refusing to recognize the speed of change. It makes us feel better to defer the future. Even those closest to the cutting edge of scientific research can scarcely believe the reality. Even they routinely underestimate the speed at which the future is breaking on our shores. Thus Dr. Richard J. Cleveland, speaking before a conference of organ transplant specialists, announced in January, 1967, that the first human heart transplant operation will occur "within five years." Yet before the same year was out Dr. Christiaan Barnard had operated on a fifty-five-year-old grocer named Louis Washkansky, and a staccato sequence of heart transplant operations exploded like a string of firecrackers into the world's awareness. In the meantime, success rates are rising steadily in kidney transplants. Successful liver, pancreas and ovary transplants are also reported.

Such accelerating medical advances must compel profound changes in our ways of thinking, as well as our way of caring for the sick. Startling new legal, ethical and philosophical issues arise. What, for instance, is death? Does death occur when the heart stops beating, as we have traditionally believed? Or does it occur when the brain stops functioning? Hospitals are becoming more and more familiar with cases of patients kept alive through advanced medical techniques, but doomed to exist as unconscious veg- etables. What are the ethics of condemning such a person to death to obtain a healthy organ needed for transplant to save the life of a person with a better prognosis?

Lacking guidelines or precedents, we flounder over the moral and legal questions. Ghoulish rumors race through the medical community. *The New York Times* and *Komsomolskaya Pravda* both speculate about the pos- sibility of "future murder rings supplying healthy organs for black-market surgeons whose patients are unwilling to wait until natural sources have supplied the heart or liver or pancreas they need." In Washington, the National Academy of Sciences, backed by a grant from the Russell Sage Foundation, begins a study of social policy issues springing from advances in the life sciences. At Stanford, a symposium, also funded by Russell Sage, examines methods for setting up transplant organ banks, the eco- nomics of an organ market, and evidences of class or racial discrimination in organ availability.

The possibility of cannibalizing bodies or corpses for usable transplant organs, grisly as it is, will serve to accelerate further the pace of change by lending urgency to research in the field of artificial organs—plastic or elec- tronic substitutes for the heart or liver or spleen. (Eventually, even these may be made unnecessary when we learn how to regenerate damaged organs or severed limbs, growing new ones as the lizard now grows a tail.)

The drive to develop spare parts for failing human bodies will be stepped up as demand intensifies. The development of an economical artificial heart, Professor Lederberg says, "is only a few transient failures away." Professor R. M. Kenedi of the bio-engineering group at the University of Strathclyde in Glasgow believes that "by 1984, artificial replacements for tissues and organs may well have become commonplace." For some organs, this date is, in fact, conservative. Already more than 13,000 cardiac patients in the United States—including a Supreme Court justice—are alive because they carry, stitched into their chest cavity, a tiny "pacemaker"—a device that sends pulses of electricity to activate the heart.*

---

*At a major Midwest hospital not long ago a patient appeared at the emergency room in the mid- dle of the night. He was hiccupping violently, sixty times a minute. The patient, it turned out, was an early pacemaker wearer. A fast-thinking resident realized what had happened: a pacemaker wire, instead of stimulating the heart, had broken loose and become lodged in the diaphragm. Its jolts of electricity were causing the hiccupping. Acting swiftly, the resident inserted a needle into the patient's chest near the pacemaker, ran a wire out from the needle and grounded it to the hospital plumbing. The hiccupping stopped, giving doctors a chance to operate and reposition the faulty wire. A foretaste of tomorrow's medicine?

Another 10,000 pioneers are already equipped with artificial heart valves made of dacron mesh. Implantable hearing aids, artificial kidneys, arteries, hip joints, lungs, eye sockets and other parts are all in various stages of early development. We shall, before many decades are past, implant tiny, aspirin-sized sensors in the body to monitor blood pressure, pulse, respiration and other functions, and tiny transmitters to emit a signal when something goes wrong. Such signals will feed into giant diagnostic computer centers upon which the medicine of the future will be based. Some of us will also carry a tiny platinum plate and a dime-sized "stimulator" attached to the spine. By turning a midget "radio" on and off we will be able to activate the stimulator and kill pain. Initial work on these pain-control mechanisms is already under way at the Case Institute of Technology. Push-button pain killers are already being used by certain cardiac patients.

Such developments will lead to vast new bio-engineering industries, chains of medical-electronic repair stations, new technical professions and a reorganization of the entire health system. They will change life expectancy, shatter insurance company life tables, and bring about important shifts in the human outlook. Surgery will be less frightening to the average individual; implantation routine. The human body will come to be seen as modular. Through application of the modular principle—preservation of the whole through systematic replacement of transient components—we may add two or three decades to the average life span of the population. Unless, however, we develop far more advanced understanding of the brain than we now have, this could lead to one of the greatest ironies in history. Sir George Pickering, Regius professor of medicine at Oxford, has warned that unless we watch out, "those with senile brains will form an ever increasing fraction of the inhabitants of the earth. I find this," he added rather unnecessarily, "a terrifying prospect." Just such terrifying prospects will drive us toward more accelerated research into the brain—which, in turn, will generate still further radical changes in the society.

Today we struggle to make heart valves or artificial plumbing that imitate the original they are designed to replace. We strive for functional equivalence. Once we have mastered the basic problems, however, we shall not merely install plastic aortas in people because their original aorta is about to fail. We shall install specially-designed parts that are *better* than the original, and then we shall move on to install parts that provide the user with capabilities that were absent in the first place. Just as genetic engineering holds out the promise of producing "super-people," so, too, does organ technology suggest the possibility of track stars with extra-capacity lungs or hearts; sculptors with a neural device that intensifies sensitivity to texture; lovers with sex-intensifying neural machinery. In short, we shall no longer implant merely to save a life, but to enhance it—to make possible the achievement of moods, states, conditions or ecstasies that are presently beyond us.

Under these circumstances, what happens to our age-old definitions of "human-ness"? How will it feel to be part protoplasm and part transistor?

Exactly what possibilities will it open? What limitations will it place on work, play, sex, intellectual or aesthetic responses? What happens to the mind when the body is changed? Questions like these cannot be long deferred, for advanced fusions of man and machine—called "Cyborgs"—are closer than most people suspect.

The Cyborgs among Us

Today the man with a pacemaker or a plastic aorta is still recognizably a man. The inanimate part of his body is still relatively unimportant in terms of his personality and consciousness. But as the proportion of machine components rises, what happens to his awareness of self, his inner experience? If we assume that the brain is the seat of consciousness and intelligence, and that no other part of the body affects personality or self very much, then it is possible to conceive of a disembodied brain—a brain without arms, legs, spinal cord or other equipment—as a self, a personality, an embodiment of awareness. It may then become possible to combine the human brain with a whole set of artificial sensors, receptors and effectors, and to call *that* tangle of wires and plastic a human being.

All this may seem to resemble medieval speculation about the number of angels who can pirouette on a pinhead, yet the first small steps toward some form of man-machine symbiosis are already being taken. Moreover, they are being taken not by a lone mad scientist, but by thousands of highly trained engineers, mathematicians, biologists, surgeons, chemists, neurologists and communications specialists.

Dr. W. G. Walter's mechanical "tortoises" are machines that behave as though they had been psychologically conditioned. These tortoises were early specimens of a growing breed of robots ranging from the "Perceptron" which could learn (and even generalize) to the more recent "Wanderer," a robot capable of exploring an area, building up in its memory an "image" of the terrain, and able even to indulge in certain operations comparable, at least in some respects, to "contemplative speculation" and "fantasy." Experiments by Ross Ashby, H. D. Block, Frank Rosenblatt and others demonstrate that machines can learn from their mistakes, improve their performance, and, in certain limited kinds of learning, outstrip human students. Says Block, professor of Applied Mathematics at Cornell University: "I don't think there's a task you can name that a machine can't do—in principle. If you can define a task and a human can do it, then a machine can, at least in theory, also do it. The converse, however, is not true." Intelligence and creativity, it would appear, are not a human monopoly.

Despite setbacks and difficulties, the roboteers are moving forward. Recently they enjoyed a collective laugh at the expense of one of the leading critics of the robot-builders, a former RAND Corporation computer specialist named Hubert L. Dreyfus. Arguing that computers would never be able to match human intelligence, Dreyfus wrote a lengthy paper heaping vitriolic scorn on those who disagreed with him. Among other things, he declared, "No chess program can play even amateur chess." In context, he appeared to be saying that none ever would. Less than two years later, a graduate student at MIT, Richard Greenblatt, wrote a chess-playing computer program, challenged Dreyfus to a match, and had the immense satisfaction of watching the computer annihilate Dreyfus to the cheers of the "artificial intelligence" researchers.

In a quite different field of robotology there is progress, too. Technicians at Disneyland have created extremely life-like computer-controlled humanoids capable of moving their arms and legs, grimacing, smiling, glowering, simulating fear, joy and a wide range of other emotions. Built of clear plastic that, according to one reporter, "does everything but bleed," the robots chase girls, play music, fire pistols, and so closely resemble human forms that visitors routinely shriek with fear, flinch and otherwise react as though they were dealing with real human beings. The purposes to which these robots are put may seem trivial, but the technology on which they are based is highly sophisticated. It depends heavily on knowledge acquired from the space program—and this knowledge is accumulating rapidly.

There appears to be no reason, in principle, why we cannot go forward from these present primitive and trivial robots to build humanoid machines capable of extremely varied behavior, capable even of "human" error and seemingly random choice—in short, to make them behaviorally indistinguishable from humans except by means of highly sophisticated or elaborate tests. At that point we shall face the novel sensation of trying to determine whether the smiling, assured humanoid behind the airline reservation counter is a pretty girl or a carefully wired robot.*

The likelihood, of course, is that she will be both.

The thrust toward some form of man-machine symbiosis is furthered by our increasing ingenuity in communicating with machines. A great deal of much-publicized work is being done to facilitate the interaction of men and computers. But quite apart from this, Russian and American scientists have both been experimenting with the placement or implantation of detectors that pick up signals from the nerve ends at the stub of an amputated limb. These signals are then amplified and used to activate an artificial limb, thereby making a machine directly and sensitively responsive to the nervous system of a human being. The human need not "think out" his desires; even involuntary impulses are transmittable. The responsive behavior of the machine is as automatic as the behavior of ones' own hand, eye or leg.

---

*This raises a number of half-amusing, half-serious problems about the relationships between men and machines, including emotional and even sexual relationships. Professor Block at Cornell speculates that man-machine sexual relationships may not be too far distant. Pointing out that men often develop emotional attachments to the machines they use, he suggests that we shall have to give attention to the "ethical" questions arising from our treatment of "these mechanical objects of our affection and passion." A serious inquiry into these issues is to be found in an article by Roland Puccetti in the British *Journal of the Philosophy of Science,* 18 (1967) 39–51.

In *Flight to Arras,* Antoine de Saint-Exupéry, novelist, poet and pioneer aviator, described buckling himself into the seat of a fighter plane during World War II. "All this complication of oxygen tubes, heating equipment; these speaking tubes that form the 'intercom' running between the members of the crew. This mask through which I breathe. I am attached to the plane by a rubber tube as indispensable as an umbilical cord. Organs have been added to my being, and they seem to intervene between me and my heart . . ." We have come far since those distant days. Space biology is marching irresistibly toward the day when the astronaut will not merely be buckled into his capsule, but become a part of it in the full symbiotic sense of the phrase.

One aim is to make the craft itself a wholly self-sufficient universe, in which algae is grown for food, water is recovered from body waste, air is recycled to purge it of the ammonia entering the atmosphere from urine, etc. In this totally enclosed fully regenerative world, the human being becomes an integral part of an on-going micro-ecological process whirling through the vastnesses of space. Thus Theodore Gordon, author of *The Future* and himself a leading space engineer, writes: "Perhaps it would be simpler to provide life support in the form of machines that plug into the astronaut. He could be fed intravenously using a liquid food compactly stored in a remote pressurized tank. Perhaps direct processing of body liquid wastes, and conversion to water, could be accomplished by a new type of artificial kidney built in as part of the spaceship. Perhaps sleep could be induced electronically . . . to lower his metabolism . . ." *Und so weiter.* One after another, the body functions of the human become interwoven with, dependent on, and part of, the machine functions of the capsule.

The ultimate extension of such work, however, is not necessarily to be found in the outer reaches of space; it may well become a common part of everyday life here on the mother planet. This is the direct link-up of the human brain—stripped of its supporting physical structures—with the computer. Indeed, it may be that the biological component of the super-computers of the future may be massed human brains. The possibility of enhancing human (and machine) intelligence by linking them together organically opens enormous and exciting probabilities, so exciting that Dr. R. M. Page, director of the Naval Research Laboratory in Washington, has publicly discussed the feasibility of a system in which human thoughts are fed automatically into the storage unit of a computer to form the basis for machine decision-making. Participants in a RAND Corporation study conducted several years ago were asked when this development might occur. Answers ranged from as soon as 1990 to "never." But the median date given was 2020—well within the lifetime of today's teen-agers.

In the meantime, research from countless sources contributes toward the eventual symbiosis. In one of the most fascinating, frightening and intellectually provocative experiments ever recorded, Professor Robert White, director of neurosurgery at the Metropolitan General Hospital in Cleveland, has given evidence that the brain *can* be isolated from its body and kept alive after the "death" of the rest of the organism. The experiment, described in a brilliant article by Oriana Fallaci, saw a team of neurosurgeons cut the brain out of a rhesus monkey, discard the body, then hook the brain's carotid arteries up to another monkey, whose blood then continued to bathe the disembodied organ, keeping it alive.

Said one of the members of the medical team, Dr. Leo Massopust, a neurophysiologist: "The brain activity is largely better than when the brain had a body . . . No doubt about it. I even suspect that without his senses, he can think more quickly. What kind of thinking, I don't know. I guess he is primarily a memory, a repository for information stored when he had his flesh; he cannot develop further because he no longer has the nourishment of experience. Yet this, too, is a new experience."

The brain survived for five hours. It could have lasted much longer, had it served the purposes of research. Professor White has successfully kept other brains alive for days, using machinery, rather than a living monkey, to keep the brain washed with blood. "I don't think we have reached the stage," he told Miss Fallaci, "where you can turn men into robots, obedient sheep. Yet . . . it could happen, it isn't impossible. If you consider that we can transfer the head of a man onto the trunk of another man, if you consider that we can isolate the brain of a man and make it work without its body . . . To me, there is no longer any gap between science fiction and science . . . We could keep Einstein's brain alive and make it function normally."

Not only, Professor White implies, can we transfer the head of one man to the shoulders of another, not only can we keep a head or a brain "alive" and functioning, but it can all be done, with "existing techniques." Indeed, he declares, "The Japanese will be the first to [keep an isolated human head alive]. I will not, because I haven't resolved as yet this dilemma: Is it right or not?" A devout Catholic, Dr. White is deeply troubled by the philosophical and moral implications of his work.

As the brain surgeons and the neurologists probe further, as the bioengineers and the mathematicians, the communications experts and robotbuilders become more sophisticated, as the space men and their capsules grow closer and closer to one another, as machines begin to embody biological components and men come bristling with sensors and mechanical organs, the ultimate symbiosis approaches. The work converges. Yet the greatest marvel of all is not organ transplantation or symbiosis or underwater engineering. It is not technology, nor science itself.

The greatest and most dangerous marvel of all is the complacent pastorientation of the race, its unwillingness to confront the reality of acceleration. Thus man moves swiftly into an unexplored universe, into a totally new stage of eco-technological development, firmly convinced that "human nature is eternal" or that "stability will return." He stumbles into the most violent revolution in human history muttering, in the words of one famous, though myopic sociologist, that "the processes of modernization . . . have been more or less 'completed.' " He simply refuses to imagine the future.

QUESTIONS FOR DISCUSSION AND WRITING

1. According to Toffler, what would be some of the outcomes of successful human cloning? Can you think of others? Do you think human cloning is inevitable? A positive or negative development in human history?
2. Which of the predictions presented in this passage have actually happened? Which have not? Do you think they are likely to happen, or was there a flaw in the original prediction?
3. In what ways has Toffler's prediction of a "modular body" become truth? What future developments do you see in this area?
4. Toffler states, "The greatest and most dangerous marvel of all is the complacent past-orientation of the race." Do you agree?
5. There are "urban myths" about transplant organ harvesters. Have you heard any of these myths? What element of truth might there be in them, according to Toffler? According to what is already happening?

ON TECHNIQUE AND STYLE

1. Which of Toffler's arguments do you find most convincing? What techniques has he used to convince the reader? Why are they effective?
2. Toffler uses a lot of questions, both rhetorical and sincere, in his writing. What is the effect of these questions on you as a reader?

CULTURAL QUESTION

1. Toffler asks a series of questions about the future of race and ethnicity if genetic engineering can achieve new "races" of blue, green, or purple people. Specifically, he asks, "What happens to the entire concept of race?" How would you answer this question if new human genetic lines emerged in a rainbow of colors?

FICTION

From Utopia

Sir Thomas More

Thomas More (1478–1535) was an English lawyer, author, diplomat, and Catholic martyr. He was a leading humanist scholar and occupied many public offices, including that of Lord Chancellor from 1529 to 1532. He had a major influence on English law. He is also remembered for his refusal to accept King Henry VIII's claim to be the supreme head of the Church of England, a decision that ended his political career and led to his execution as a traitor. Four hundred years after his death, in 1935, More was canonized by Pope Pius XI, and was later declared the patron saint of diplomats and lawyers.

More invented the word "utopia," a name he gave to an ideal and imaginary island nation whose political system he described in a book of the same name in 1516. In the excerpt of Utopia *presented here, Raphael Hythloday, the main character, speaks about Utopian lifestyles.*

Of Their Trades, and Manner of Life

Agriculture is that which is so universally understood among them that no person, either man or woman, is ignorant of it; they are instructed in it from their childhood, partly by what they learn at school, and partly by practice, they being led out often into the fields about the town, where they not only see others at work but are likewise exercised in it themselves. Besides agriculture, which is so common to them all, every man has some peculiar trade to which he applies himself; such as the manufacture of wool or flax, masonry, smith's work, or carpenter's work; for there is no sort of trade that is in great esteem among them. Throughout the island they wear the same sort of clothes, without any other distinction except what is necessary to distinguish the two sexes and the married and unmarried. The fashion never alters, and as it is neither disagreeable nor uneasy, so it is suited to the climate, and calculated both for their summers and winters. Every family makes their own clothes; but all among them, women as well as men, learn one or other of the trades formerly mentioned. Women, for the most part, deal in wool and flax, which suit best with their weakness, leaving the ruder trades to the men. The same trade generally passes down from father to son, inclinations often following descent: but if any man's genius lies another way he is, by adoption, translated into a family that deals in the trade to which he is inclined; and when that is to be done, care is taken, not only by his father, but by the magistrate, that he may be put to a discreet and good man: and if, after a person has learned one trade, he desires to acquire another, that is also allowed, and is managed in the same manner as the former. When he has learned both, he follows that which he likes best, unless the public has more occasion for the other.

The chief, and almost the only, business of the Syphogrants is to take care that no man may live idle, but that every one may follow his trade diligently; yet they do not wear themselves out with perpetual toil from morning to night, as if they were beasts of burden, which as it is indeed a heavy slavery, so it is everywhere the common course of life amongst all mechanics except the Utopians: but they, dividing the day and night into twenty-four hours, appoint six of these for work, three of which are before dinner and three after; they then sup, and at eight o'clock, counting from noon, go to bed and sleep eight hours: the rest of their time, besides that taken up in work, eating, and sleeping, is left to every man's discretion; yet they are not to abuse that interval to luxury and idleness, but must employ it in some proper exercise, according to their various inclinations, which is, for the most part, reading. It is ordinary to have public lectures every morning before daybreak, at which none are obliged to appear but those who are marked out for literature; yet a great many, both men and women, of all ranks, go to hear lectures of one sort or other, according to their inclinations: but if others that are not made for contemplation, choose rather to employ themselves at that time in their trades, as many of them do, they are not hindered, but are rather commended, as men that take care to serve their country. After supper they spend an hour in some diversion, in summer in their gardens, and in winter in the halls where they eat, where they entertain each other either with music or discourse. They do not so much as know dice, or any such foolish and mischievous games. They have, however, two sorts of games not unlike our chess; the one is between several numbers, in which one number, as it were, consumes another; the other resembles a battle between the virtues and the vices, in which the enmity in the vices among themselves, and their agreement against virtue, is not unpleasantly represented; together with the special opposition between the particular virtues and vices; as also the methods by which vice either openly assaults or secretly undermines virtue; and virtue, on the other hand, resists it. But the time appointed for labour is to be narrowly examined, otherwise you may imagine that since there are only six hours appointed for work, they may fall under a scarcity of necessary provisions: but it is so far from being true that this time is not sufficient for supplying them with plenty of all things, either necessary or convenient, that it is rather too much; and this you will easily apprehend if you consider how great a part of all other nations is quite idle. First, women generally do little, who are the half of mankind; and if some few women are diligent, their husbands are idle: then consider the great company of idle priests, and of those that are called religious men; add to these all rich men, chiefly those that have estates in land, who are called noblemen and gentlemen, together with their families, made up of idle persons, that are kept more for show than use; add to these all those strong and lusty beggars that go about pretending some disease in excuse for their begging; and upon the whole account you will find that the number of those by whose labours mankind is supplied is much less than you perhaps imagined: then consider how few of those that work are employed in labours that are of real service, for we, who measure all things by money, give rise to many trades that are both vain and superfluous, and serve only to support riot and luxury: for if those who work were employed only in such things as the conveniences of life require, there would be such an abundance of them that the prices of them would so sink that tradesmen could not be maintained by their gains; if all those who labour about useless things were set to more profitable employments, and if all they that languish out their lives in sloth and idleness (every one of whom consumes as much as any two of the men that are at work) were forced to labour, you may easily imagine that a small proportion of

time would serve for doing all that is either necessary, profitable, or pleasant to mankind, especially while pleasure is kept within its due bounds: this
appears very plainly in Utopia; for there, in a great city, and in all the territory
that lies round it, you can scarce find five hundred, either men or women, by
their age and strength capable of labour, that are not engaged in it. Even the
Syphogrants, though excused by the law, yet do not excuse themselves, but
work, that by their examples they may excite the industry of the rest of the
people; the like exemption is allowed to those who, being recommended to
the people by the priests, are, by the secret suffrages of the Syphogrants,
privileged from labour, that they may apply themselves wholly to study; and
if any of these fall short of those hopes that they seemed at first to give, they
are obliged to return to work; and sometimes a mechanic that so employs
his leisure hours as to make a considerable advancement in learning is
eased from being a tradesman and ranked among their learned men. Out
of these they choose their ambassadors, their priests, their Tranibors, and
the Prince himself, anciently called their Barzenes, but is called of late their
Ademus.

And thus from the great numbers among them that are neither suffered
to be idle nor to be employed in any fruitless labour, you may easily make
the estimate how much may be done in those few hours in which they are
obliged to labour. But, besides all that has been already said, it is to be considered that the needful arts among them are managed with less labour than
anywhere else. The building or the repairing of houses among us employ
many hands, because often a thriftless heir suffers a house that his father
built to fall into decay, so that his successor must, at a great cost, repair that
which he might have kept up with a small charge; it frequently happens that
the same house which one person built at a vast expense is neglected by
another, who thinks he has a more delicate sense of the beauties of architecture, and he, suffering it to fall to ruin, builds another at no less charge.
But among the Utopians all things are so regulated that men very seldom
build upon a new piece of ground, and are not only very quick in repairing
their houses, but show their foresight in preventing their decay, so that their
buildings are preserved very long with but very little labour, and thus the
builders, to whom that care belongs, are often without employment, except
the hewing of timber and the squaring of stones, that the materials may be in
readiness for raising a building very suddenly when there is any occasion for
it. As to their clothes, observe how little work is spent in them; while they are
at labour they are clothed with leather and skins, cut carelessly about them,
which will last seven years, and when they appear in public they put on an
upper garment which hides the other; and these are all of one colour, and
that is the natural colour of the wool. As they need less woollen cloth than
is used anywhere else, so that which they make use of is much less costly;
they use linen cloth more, but that is prepared with less labour, and they
value cloth only by the whiteness of the linen or the cleanness of the wool,
without much regard to the fineness of the thread. While in other places four

or five upper garments of woollen cloth of different colours, and as many vests of silk, will scarce serve one man, and while those that are nicer think ten too few, every man there is content with one, which very often serves him two years; nor is there anything that can tempt a man to desire more, for if he had them he would neither be the, warmer nor would he make one jot the better appearance for it. And thus, since they are all employed in some useful labour, and since they content themselves with fewer things, it falls out that there is a great abundance of all things among them; so that it frequently happens that, for want of other work, vast numbers are sent out to mend the highways; but when no public undertaking is to be performed, the hours of working are lessened. The magistrates never engage the people in unnecessary labour, since the chief end of the constitution is to regulate labour by the necessities of the public, and to allow the people as much time as is necessary for the improvement of their minds, in which they think the happiness of life consists.

QUESTIONS FOR DISCUSSION AND WRITING

1. Describe More's attitude toward farming, based on the Utopian plan for agriculture. Would such a system work in today's world?
2. What other elements of Utopia are revealed here? Is More's Utopian view as presented here realistic? Does it outline a program of reform for sixteenth-century England or is it just a way to criticize societal problems in general?
3. In what ways might More's views be seen as feminist? As antifeminist?
4. More portrays a uniformity of life in Utopia—a sameness of thought, of purpose, of behavior, of dress. What are the pros and cons of such an existence? What would the Utopians say to those who argued against it? What are his criticisms of society, as revealed by this passage?
5. What "idle activities" does More approve of? Which does he disapprove of? Why?
6. More says, "we, who measure all things by money, give rise to many trades that are both vain and superfluous, and serve only to support riot and luxury." In what ways could this be a modern complaint as well? In what ways does the pursuit of money support "riot and luxury"?

ON TECHNIQUE AND STYLE

1. What stylistic elements of this passage (beyond its spelling) do you find mark it as a centuries-old text?
2. Some sentences are quite long and may be difficult to follow because of their syntax as well as their length. Locate one such sentence that you found more difficult to understand than the others. Work through it and explain its meaning, as well as its relationship to the rest of the text.

CULTURAL QUESTION

1. What do you know about the culture and society of sixteenth-century England? What does this reading reveal about that culture, by implication? In what ways is that distant culture both similar to and different from modern American culture?

The Ones Who Walk Away from Omelas

Ursula K. Le Guin

Ursula K. (Kroeber) Le Guin (1929–   ) is an American author who was born and raised in Berkeley, California, the daughter of noted anthropologist Alfred L. Kroeber and the writer Theodora Kroeber. She received her BA from Radcliffe College, and then an MA from Columbia University in the early 1950s. In 1953, she married historian Charles A. Le Guin. Le Guin has lived in Portland, Oregon, since 1958. She has written novels, poetry, children's books, and essays. She is best known for her science fiction and fantasy novels and short stories. Le Guin is considered one of the best modern science fiction and fantasy authors, noted for her exploration of anarchist, feminist, Taoist, psychological, and sociological themes. In 2000, Le Guin accepted the U.S. Library of Congress's Living Legends Award for her contributions to America's cultural heritage. The following story comes from a 1970 collection titled The Wind's Four Quarters, *which won a Hugo Award in 1974.*

With a clamor of bells that set the swallows soaring, the Festival of Summer came to the city Omelas, bright-towered by the sea. The rigging of the boats in harbor sparkled with flags. In the streets between houses with red roofs and painted walls, between old moss-grown gardens and under avenues of trees, past great parks and public buildings, processions moved. Some were decorous: old people in long stiff robes of mauve and grey, grave master workmen, quiet, merry women carrying their babies and chatting as they walked. In other streets the music beat faster, a shimmering of gong and tambourine, and the people went dancing, the procession was a dance. Children dodged in and out, their high calls rising like the swallows' crossing flights over the music and the singing. All the processions wound towards the north side of the city, where on the great water-meadow called the Green Fields boys and girls, naked in the bright air, with mud-stained feet and ankles and long, lithe arms, exercised their restive horses before the race. The horses wore no gear at all but a halter without bit. Their manes were braided with streamers of silver, gold, and green. They flared their nostrils and pranced and boasted to one another; they were vastly excited, the horse being the only animal who has adopted our ceremonies as his own. Far off to the north and west the mountains stood up half encircling Omelas on her bay. The air of morning was so clear that the snow still crowning the Eighteen Peaks burned with white-gold fire across the miles of sunlit air, under the dark blue of the sky. There was just enough wind to make the banners that marked the racecourse snap and flutter now and then. In the silence of the broad green meadows one could hear the music winding through the city streets, farther and nearer and ever approaching, a cheerful faint sweetness of the air that from time to time trembled and gathered together and broke out into the great joyous clanging of the bells.

Joyous! How is one to tell about joy? How describe the citizens of Omelas?

They were not simple folk, you see, though they were happy. But we do not say the words of cheer much any more. All smiles have become archaic. Given a description such as this one tends to make certain assumptions. Given a description such as this one tends to look next for the King, mounted on a splendid stallion and surrounded by his noble knights, or perhaps in a golden litter borne by great-muscled slaves. But there was no king. They did not use swords, or keep slaves. They were not barbarians. I do not know the rules and laws of their society, but I suspect that they were singularly few. As they did without monarchy and slavery, so they also got on without the stock exchange, the advertisement, the secret police, and the bomb. Yet I repeat that these were not simple folk, not dulcet shepherds, noble savages, bland utopians. They were not less complex than us. The trouble is that we have a bad habit, encouraged by pedants and sophisticates, of considering happiness as something rather stupid. Only pain is intellectual, only evil interesting. This is the treason of the artist: a refusal to admit the banality of evil and the terrible boredom of pain. If you can't lick 'em, join 'em. If it hurts, repeat it. But to praise despair is to condemn delight, to embrace violence is to lose hold of everything else. We have almost lost hold; we can no longer describe a happy man, nor make any celebration of joy. How can I tell you about the people of Omelas? They were not naïve and happy children—though their children were, in fact, happy. They were mature, intelligent, passionate adults whose lives were not wretched. O miracle! but I wish I could describe it better. I wish I could convince you. Omelas sounds in my words like a city in a fairy tale, long ago and far away, once upon a time. Perhaps it would be best if you imagined it as your own fancy bids, assuming it will rise to the occasion, for certainly I cannot suit you all. For instance, how about technology? I think that there would be no cars or helicopters in and above the streets; this follows from the fact that the people of Omelas are happy people. Happiness is based on a just discrimination of what is necessary, what is neither necessary nor destructive, and what is destructive. In the middle category, however—that of the unnecessary but undestructive, that of comfort, luxury, exuberance, etc.—they could perfectly well have central heating, subway trains, washing machines, and all kinds of marvelous devices not yet invented here, floating light-sources, fuelless power, a cure for the common cold. Or they could have none of that: it doesn't matter. As you like it. I incline to think that people from towns up and down the coast have been coming in to Omelas during the last days before the Festival on very fast little trains and double-decked trams, and that the train station of Omelas is actually the handsomest building in town, though plainer than the magnificent Farmers' Market. But even granted trains, I fear that Omelas so far strikes some of you as goody-goody. Smiles, bells, parades, horses, bleh. If so, please add an orgy. If an orgy would help, don't hesitate. Let us not, however, have temples from which issue beautiful nude priests and priestesses already half in ecstasy and ready to copulate with any man or woman, lover or stranger, who desires union with the deep godhead of the blood, although that was my first idea. But really it would be better not to have any temples in Omelas—at least, not manned temples. Religion yes, clergy no. Surely the beautiful nudes can just wander about, offering themselves like divine soufflés to the hunger of the needy and the rapture of the flesh. Let them join the processions. Let tambourines be struck above the copulations, and the glory of desire be proclaimed upon the gongs, and (a not unimportant point) let the offspring of these delightful rituals be beloved and looked after by all. One thing I know there is none of in Omelas is guilt. But what else should there be? I thought at first there were no drugs, but that is puritanical. For those who like it, the faint insistent sweetness of *drooz* may perfume the ways of the city, *drooz* which first brings a great lightness and brilliance to the mind and limbs, and then after some hours a dreamy languor, and wonderful visions at last of the very arcana and inmost secrets of the Universe, as well as exciting the pleasure of sex beyond all belief; and it is not habit-forming. For more modest tastes I think there ought to be beer. What else, what else belongs in the joyous city? The sense of victory, surely, the celebration of courage. But as we did without clergy, let us do without soldiers. The joy built upon successful slaughter is not the right kind of joy; it will not do; it is fearful and it is trivial. A boundless and generous contentment, a magnanimous triumph felt not against some outer enemy but in communion with the finest and fairest in the souls of all men everywhere and the splendor of the world's summer: this is what swells the hearts of the people of Omelas, and the victory they celebrate is that of life. I really don't think many of them need to take *drooz*.

Most of the processions have reached the Green Fields by now. A marvelous smell of cooking goes forth from the red and blue tents of the provisioners. The faces of small children are amiably sticky; in the benign grey beard of a man a couple of crumbs of rich pastry are entangled. The youths and girls have mounted their horses and are beginning to group around the starting line of the course. An old woman, small, fat, and laughing, is passing out flowers from a basket, and tall young men wear her flowers in their shining hair. A child of nine or ten sits at the edge of the crowd, alone, playing on a wooden flute. People pause to listen, and they smile, but they do not speak to him, for he never ceases playing and never sees them, his dark eyes wholly rapt in the sweet, thin magic of the tune.

He finishes, and slowly lowers his hands holding the wooden flute.

As if that little private silence were the signal, all at once a trumpet sounds from the pavilion near the starting line: imperious, melancholy, piercing. The horses rear on their slender legs, and some of them neigh in answer. Sober-faced, the young riders stroke the horses' necks and soothe them, whispering, "Quiet, quiet, there my beauty, my hope. . . ." They begin to form in rank along the starting line. The crowds along the racecourse are like a field of grass and flowers in the wind. The Festival of Summer has begun.

Do you believe? Do you accept the festival, the city, the joy? No? Then let me describe one more thing.

In a basement under one of the beautiful public buildings of Omelas, or perhaps in the cellar of one of its spacious private homes, there is a room. It has one locked door, and no window. A little light seeps in dustily between cracks in the boards, secondhand from a cobwebbed window somewhere across the cellar. In one corner of the little room a couple of mops, with stiff, clotted, foul-smelling heads, stand near a rusty bucket. The floor is dirt, a little damp to the touch, as cellar dirt usually is. The room is about three paces long and two wide: a mere broom closet or disused tool room. In the room a child is sitting. It could be a boy or a girl. It looks about six, but actually is nearly ten. It is feeble-minded. Perhaps it was born defective, or perhaps it has become imbecile through fear, malnutrition, and neglect. It picks its nose and occasionally fumbles vaguely with its toes or genitals, as it sits hunched in the corner farthest from the bucket and the two mops. It is afraid of the mops. It finds them horrible. It shuts its eyes, but it knows the mops are still standing there; and the door is locked; and nobody will come. The door is always locked; and nobody ever comes, except that sometimes—the child has no understanding of time or interval—sometimes the door rattles terribly and opens, and a person, or several people, are there. One of them may come in and kick the child to make it stand up. The others never come close, but peer in at it with frightened, disgusted eyes. The food bowl and the water jug are hastily filled, the door is locked, the eyes disappear. The people at the door never say anything, but the child, who has not always lived in the tool room, and can remember sunlight and its mother's voice, sometimes speaks. "I will be good," it says. "Please let me out. I will be good!" They never answer. The child used to scream for help at night, and cry a good deal, but now it only makes a kind of whining, "eh-haa, eh-haa," and it speaks less and less often. It is so thin there are no calves to its legs; its belly protrudes; it lives on a half-bowl of corn meal and grease a day. It is naked. Its buttocks and thighs are a mass of festered sores, as it sits in its own excrement continually.

They all know it is there, all the people of Omelas. Some of them have come to see it, others are content merely to know it is there. They all know that it has to be there. Some of them understand why, and some do not, but they all understand that their happiness, the beauty of their city, the tenderness of their friendships, the health of their children, the wisdom of their scholars, the skill of their makers, even the abundance of their harvest and the kindly weathers of their skies, depend wholly on this child's abominable misery.

   This is usually explained to children when they are between eight and twelve, whenever they seem capable of understanding; and most of those who come to see the child are young people, though often enough an adult comes, or comes back, to see the child. No matter how well the matter has been explained to them, these young spectators are always shocked and sickened at the sight. They feel disgust, which they had thought themselves superior to. They feel anger, outrage, impotence, despite all the explanations. They would like to do something for the child. But there is nothing they can do. If the child were brought up into the sunlight out of that vile place, if it were cleaned and fed and comforted, that would be a good thing, indeed; but if it were done, in that day and hour all the prosperity and beauty and delight of Omelas would wither and be destroyed. Those are the terms. To exchange all the goodness and grace of every life in Omelas for that single, small improvement: to throw away the happiness of thousands for the chance of the happiness of one: that would be to let guilt within the walls indeed.

   The terms are strict and absolute; there may not even be a kind word spoken to the child.

   Often the young people go home in tears, or in a tearless rage, when they have seen the child and faced this terrible paradox. They may brood over it for weeks or years. But as time goes on they begin to realize that even if the child could be released, it would not get much good of its freedom: a little vague pleasure of warmth and food, no doubt, but little more. It is too degraded and imbecile to know any real joy. It has been afraid too long ever to be free of fear. Its habits are too uncouth for it to respond to humane treatment. Indeed, after so long it would probably be wretched without walls about it to protect it, and darkness for its eyes, and its own excrement to sit in. Their tears at the bitter injustice dry when they begin to perceive the terrible justice of reality, and to accept it. Yet it is their tears and anger, the trying of their generosity and the acceptance of their helplessness, which are perhaps the true source of the splendor of their lives. Theirs is no vapid, irresponsible happiness. They know that they, like the child, are not free. They know compassion. It is the existence of the child, and their knowledge of its existence, that makes possible the nobility of their architecture, the poignancy of their music, the profundity of their science. It is because of the child that they are so gentle with children. They know that if the wretched one were not there snivelling in the dark, the other one, the flute-player, could make no joyful music as the young riders line up in their beauty for the race in the sunlight of the first morning of summer.

   Now do you believe in them? Are they not more credible? But there is one more thing to tell, and this is quite incredible.

   At times one of the adolescent girls or boys who go to see the child does not go home to weep or rage, does not, in fact, go home at all. Sometimes also a man or woman much older falls silent for a day or two, and then leaves home. These people go out into the street, and walk down the street alone. They keep walking, and walk straight out of the city of Omelas, through the beautiful gates. They keep walking across the farmlands of Omelas. Each one goes alone, youth or girl, man or woman. Night falls; the traveler must pass down village streets, between the houses with yellow-lit windows, and on out into the darkness of the fields. Each alone, they go west or north, towards the mountains. They go on. They leave Omelas, they walk ahead into the darkness, and they do not come back. The place they go towards is a place even less imaginable to most of us than the city of happiness. I cannot describe it at all. It is possible that it does not exist. But they seem to know where they are going, the ones who walk away from Omelas.

QUESTIONS FOR DISCUSSION AND WRITING

1. Where do you think the name *Omelas* originated? If you can't guess, look on the Internet or other sources to see if you can find out.
2. Why does the narrator refer to utopians as "bland"? What connotations of utopianism are assumed in this assessment?
3. The narrator refers to *drooz*. What do you imagine drooz to be? What might be a modern-day equivalent, in your opinion?
4. What role does "the child" play in the second part of the story? Why is the child important to the main themes of this tale?
5. Why do some "walk away from Omelas"?

ON TECHNIQUE AND STYLE

1. The narrator says, "They were not less complex than us." Who is *us?* Why is the narrator using first person?
2. The author uses the phrase "As you like it." What is the literary allusion? Why do you think Le Guin has alluded to this work?
3. In the first part of this story, there are very few paragraphs. Why do you think this is so? What effect does it have on you as the reader?

CULTURAL QUESTION

1. Does the society and culture of this story show any important similarities with modern society? What do you think they are? Why has Le Guin drawn these similarities, if you believe they exist?

From Oryx and Crake

Margaret Atwood

Margaret Atwood (1939–   ), born in Ottawa, is one of Canada's most successful contemporary writers. Her undergraduate work was done at Victoria University in

*the University of Toronto. She received a master's degree from Radcliffe College and
followed further graduate studies at Harvard. Atwood is a poet, novelist, literary critic,
feminist, and political activist. She has received both national and international recognition. Her 1985 novel* The Handmaid's Tale *was the winner of the 1987 Arthur
C. Clarke Award. Her novel* Oryx and Crake *(2003), excerpted here, was shortlisted
for the Man Booker Prize for fiction that year. In it, she demonstrates her interest in as
well as suspicion of unchecked progress in biotechnology.*

Bonfire

Once upon a time, Snowman wasn't Snowman. Instead he was Jimmy. He'd
been a good boy then.

Jimmy's earliest complete memory was of a huge bonfire. He must have been
five, maybe six. He was wearing red rubber boots with a smiling duck's face
on each toe; he remembers that, because after seeing the bonfire he had to
walk through a pan of disinfectant in those boots. They'd said the disinfectant
was poisonous and he shouldn't splash, and then he was worried that the
poison would get into the eyes of the ducks and hurt them. He'd been told
the ducks were only like pictures, they weren't real and had no feelings, but
he didn't quite believe it.

So let's say five and a half, thinks Snowman. That's about right.

The month could have been October, or else November; the leaves still
turned colour then, and they were orange and red. It was muddy underfoot—he must have been standing in a field—and it was drizzling. The bonfire
was an enormous pile of cows and sheep and pigs. Their legs stuck out stiff
and straight; gasoline had been poured onto them; the flames shot up and
out, yellow and white and red and orange, and a smell of charred flesh filled
the air. It was like the barbecue in the backyard when his father cooked things
but a lot stronger, and mixed in with it was a gas-station smell, and the odour
of burning hair.

Jimmy knew what burning hair smelled like because he'd cut off some
of his own hair with the manicure scissors and set fire to it with his mother's
cigarette lighter. The hair had frizzled up, squiggling like a clutch of tiny black
worms, so he'd cut off some more and done it again. By the time he was
caught, his hair was ragged all along the front. When accused he'd said it
was an experiment.

His father had laughed then, but his mother hadn't. At least (his father
said) Jimmy'd had the good sense to cut the hair off before torching it. His
mother said it was lucky he hadn't burnt the house down. Then they'd had
an argument about the cigarette lighter, which wouldn't have been there (said
his father) if his mother didn't smoke. His mother said that all children were
arsonists at heart, and if not for the lighter he'd have used matches.

Once the fight got going Jimmy felt relieved, because he'd known then that he wouldn't be punished. All he had to do was say nothing and pretty soon they'd forget why they'd started arguing in the first place. But he also felt guilty, because look what he'd made them do. He knew it would end with a door being slammed. He scrunched down lower and lower in his chair with the words whizzing back and forth over his head, and finally there was the bang of the door—his mother this time—and the wind that came with it. There was always a wind when the door got slammed, a small puff—whuff!—right in his ears.

"Never mind, old buddy," said his father. "Women always get hot under the collar. She'll cool down. Let's have some ice cream." So that's what they did, they had Raspberry Ripple in the cereal bowls with the blue and red birds on them that were handmade in Mexico so you shouldn't put them in the dishwasher, and Jimmy ate his all up to show his father that everything was okay.

Women, and what went on under their collars. Hotness and coldness, coming and going in the strange musky flowery variable-weather country inside their clothes—mysterious, important, uncontrollable. That was his father's take on things. But men's body temperatures were never dealt with; they were never even mentioned, not when he was little, except when his dad said, "Chill out." Why weren't they? Why nothing about the hot collars of men? Those smooth, sharp-edged collars with their dark, sulphurous, bristling undersides. He could have used a few theories on that.

The next day his father took him to a haircut place where there was a picture of a pretty girl in the window with pouty lips and a black T-shirt pulled down off one shoulder, glaring out through smudgy charcoal eyes with a mean stare and her hair standing up stiff like quills. Inside, there was hair all over the tiled floor, in clumps and wisps; they were sweeping it up with a push broom. First Jimmy had a black cape put on him, only it was more like a bib, and Jimmy didn't want that, because it was babyish. The haircut man laughed and said it wasn't a bib, because who ever heard of a baby with a black bib on? So it was okay; and then Jimmy got a short all-over cut to even out the ragged places, which maybe was what he'd wanted in the first place—shorter hair. Then he had stuff out of a jar put on to make it spiky. It smelled like orange peels. He smiled at himself in the mirror, then scowled, thrusting down his eyebrows.

"Tough guy," said the haircut man, nodding at Jimmy's father. "What a tiger." He whisked Jimmy's cut-off hair onto the floor with all the other hair, then removed the black cape with a flourish and lifted Jimmy down.

At the bonfire Jimmy was anxious about the animals, because they were being burned and surely that would hurt them. No, his father told him. The animals were dead. They were like steaks and sausages, only they still had their skins on.

And their heads, thought Jimmy. Steaks didn't have heads. The heads made a difference: he thought he could see the animals looking at him reproachfully out of their burning eyes. In some way all of this—the bonfire, the charred smell, but most of all the lit-up, suffering animals—was his fault, because he'd done nothing to rescue them. At the same time he found the bonfire a beautiful sight—luminous, like a Christmas tree, but a Christmas tree on fire. He hoped there might be an explosion, as on television.

Jimmy's father was beside him, holding on to his hand. "Lift me up," said Jimmy. His father assumed he wanted to be comforted, which he did, and picked him up and hugged him. But also Jimmy wanted to see better.

"This is where it ends up," said Jimmy's father, not to Jimmy but to a man standing with them. "Once things get going." Jimmy's father sounded angry; so did the man when he answered.

"They say it was brought in on purpose."

"I wouldn't be surprised," said Jimmy's father.

"Can I have one of the cow horns?" said Jimmy. He didn't see why they should be wasted. He wanted to ask for two but that might be pushing it.

"No," said his father. "Not this time, old buddy." He patted Jimmy's leg.

"Drive up the prices," said the man. "Make a killing on their own stuff, that way."

"It's a killing all right," said Jimmy's father in a disgusted tone. "But it could've been just a nutbar. Some cult thing, you never know."

"Why not?" said Jimmy. Nobody else wanted the horns. But this time his father ignored him.

"The question is, how did they do it?" he said. "I thought our people had us sealed up tight as a drum."

"I thought they did too. We fork out enough. What were the guys doing? They're not paid to sleep."

"It could've been bribery," said Jimmy's father. "They'll check out the bank transfers, though you'd have to be pretty dumb to stick that kind of money into a bank. Anyway, heads will roll."

"Fine-tooth comb, and I wouldn't want to be them," said the man. "Who comes in from outside?"

"Guys who repair things. Delivery vans."

"They should bring all that in-house."

"I hear that's the plan," said his father. "This bug is something new though. We've got the bioprint."

"Two can play at that game," said the man.

"Any number can play," said Jimmy's father.

"Why were the cows and sheep on fire?" Jimmy asked his father the next day. They were having breakfast, all three of them together, so it must have been a Sunday. That was the day when his mother and his father were both there at breakfast.

Jimmy's father was on his second cup of coffee. While he drank it, he was making notes on a page covered with numbers. "They had to be burned," he said, "to keep it from spreading." He didn't look up; he was fooling with his pocket calculator, jotting with his pencil.

"What from spreading?"

"The disease."

"What's a disease?"

"A disease is like when you have a cough," said his mother.

"If I have a cough, will I be burned up?"

"Most likely," said his father, turning over the page.

Jimmy was frightened by this because he'd had a cough the week before. He might get another one at any moment: already there was something sticking in his throat. He could see his hair on fire, not just a strand or two on a saucer, but all of it, still attached to his head. He didn't want to be put in a heap with the cows and pigs. He began to cry.

"How many times do I have to tell you?" said his mother. "He's too young."

"Daddy's a monster once again," said Jimmy's father. "It was a joke, pal. You know—joke. Ha ha."

"He doesn't understand those kinds of jokes."

"Sure he does. Don't you, Jimmy?"

"Yes," said Jimmy, sniffling.

"Leave Daddy alone," said his mother. "Daddy is thinking. That's what they pay him for. He doesn't have time for you right now."

His father threw down the pencil. "Cripes, can't you give it a rest?"

His mother stuck her cigarette into her half-empty coffee cup. "Come on, Jimmy, let's go for a walk." She hauled Jimmy up by one wrist, closed the back door with exaggerated care behind them. She didn't even put their coats on. No coats, no hats. She was in her dressing gown and slippers.

The sky was grey, the wind chilly; she walked head down, her hair blowing. Around the house they went, over the soggy lawn at a double-quick pace, hand in hand. Jimmy felt he was being dragged through deep water by something with an iron claw. He felt buffeted, as if everything was about to be wrenched apart and whirled away. At the same time he felt exhilarated. He watched his mother's slippers: already they were stained with damp earth. He'd get in big trouble if he did that to his own slippers.

They slowed down, then stopped. Then his mother was talking to him in the quiet, nice-lady TV-teacher voice that meant she was furious. A disease, she said, was invisible, because it was so small. It could fly through the air or hide in the water, or on little boys' dirty fingers, which was why you shouldn't stick your fingers up your nose and then put them into your mouth, and why you should always wash your hands after you went to the bathroom, and why you shouldn't wipe . . .

"I know," said Jimmy. "Can I go inside? I'm cold."

His mother acted as if she hadn't heard him. A disease, she continued in that calm, stretched voice, a disease got into you and changed things inside you. It rearranged you, cell by cell, and that made the cells sick. And since you were all made up of tiny cells, working together to make sure you stayed alive, and if enough of the cells got sick, then you . . .

"I could get a cough," said Jimmy. "I could get a cough, right now!" He made a coughing sound.

"Oh, never mind," said his mother. She often tried to explain things to him; then she got discouraged. These were the worst moments, for both of them. He resisted her, he pretended he didn't understand even when he did, he acted stupid, but he didn't want her to give up on him. He wanted her to be brave, to try her best with him, to hammer away at the wall he'd put up against her, to keep on going.

"I want to hear about the tiny cells," he said, whining as much as he dared. "I want to!"

"Not today," she said. "Let's just go in."

OrganInc Farms

Jimmy's father worked for OrganInc Farms. He was a genographer, one of the best in the field. He'd done some of the key studies on mapping the proteonome when he was still a post-grad, and then he'd helped engineer the Methuselah Mouse as part of Operation Immortality. After that, at OrganInc Farms, he'd been one of the foremost architects of the pigoon project, along with a team of transplant experts and the microbiologists who were splicing against infections. *Pigoon* was only a nickname: the official name was *sus multiorganifer.* But pigoon was what everyone said. Sometimes they said Organ-Oink Farms, but not as often. It wasn't really a farm anyway, not like the farms in pictures.

The goal of the pigoon project was to grow an assortment of foolproof human-tissue organs in a transgenic knockout pig host—organs that would transplant smoothly and avoid rejection, but would also be able to fend off attacks by opportunistic microbes and viruses, of which there were more strains every year. A rapid-maturity gene was spliced in so the pigoon kidneys and livers and hearts would be ready sooner, and now they were perfecting a pigoon that could grow five or six kidneys at a time. Such a host animal could be reaped of its extra kidneys; then, rather than being destroyed, it could keep on living and grow more organs, much as a lobster could grow another claw to replace a missing one. That would be less wasteful, as it took a lot of food and care to grow a pigoon. A great deal of investment money had gone into OrganInc Farms.

All of this was explained to Jimmy when he was old enough.

Old enough, Snowman thinks as he scratches himself, around but not on top of the insect bites. Such a dumb concept. Old enough for what? To drink, to fuck, to know better? What fathead was in charge of making those decisions? For example, Snowman himself isn't old enough for this, this—what can it be called? This situation. He'll never be old enough, no sane human being could ever . . .

Each one of us must tread the path laid out before him, or her, says the voice in his head, a man's this time, the style bogus guru, *and each path is unique. It is not the nature of the path itself that should concern the seeker, but the grace and strength and patience with which each and every one of us follows the sometimes challenging . . .*

"Stuff it," says Snowman. Some cheap do-it-yourself enlightenment handbook, Nirvana for halfwits. Though he has the nagging feeling that he may well have written this gem himself.

In happier days, naturally. Oh, so much happier.

The pigoon organs could be customized, using cells from individual human donors, and the organs were frozen until needed. It was much cheaper than getting yourself cloned for spare parts—a few wrinkles left to be ironed out there, as Jimmy's dad used to say—or keeping a for-harvest child or two stashed away in some illegal baby orchard. In the OrganInc brochures and promotional materials, glossy and discreetly worded, stress was laid on the efficacy and comparative health benefits of the pigoon procedure. Also, to set the queasy at ease, it was claimed that none of the defunct pigoons ended up as bacon and sausages: no one would want to eat an animal whose cells might be identical with at least some of their own.

Still, as time went on and the coastal aquifers turned salty and the northern permafrost melted and the vast tundra bubbled with methane, and the drought in the midcontinental plains regions went on and on, and the Asian steppes turned to sand dunes, and meat became harder to come by, some people had their doubts. Within OrganInc Farms itself it was noticeable how often back bacon and ham sandwiches and pork pies turned up on the staff café menu. André's Bistro was the official name of the café, but the regulars called it Grunts. When Jimmy had lunch there with his father, as he did when his mother was feeling harried, the men and women at nearby tables would make jokes in bad taste.

"Pigoon pie again," they would say. "Pigoon pancakes, pigoon popcorn. Come on, Jimmy, eat up!" This would upset Jimmy; he was confused about who should be allowed to eat what. He didn't want to eat a pigoon, because he thought of the pigoons as creatures much like himself. Neither he nor they had a lot of say in what was going on.

"Don't pay any attention to them, sweetheart," said Ramona. "They're only teasing, you know?" Ramona was one of his dad's lab technicians. She often ate lunch with the two of them, him and his dad. She was young, younger than his father and even his mother; she looked something like the picture of the girl in the haircut man's window, she had the same sort of puffed-out mouth, and big eyes like that, big and smudgy. But she smiled a lot, and she didn't have her hair in quills. Her hair was soft and dark. Jimmy's mother's hair was what she herself called *dirty blonde.* ("Not dirty enough," said his father. "Hey! Joke. Joke. Don't kill me!")

Ramona would always have a salad. "How's Sharon doing?" she would say to Jimmy's father, looking at him with her eyes wide and solemn. Sharon was Jimmy's mother.

"Not so hot," Jimmy's father would say.

"Oh, that's too bad."

"It's a problem. I'm getting worried."

Jimmy watched Ramona eat. She took very small bites, and managed to chew up the lettuce without crunching. The raw carrots too. That was amazing, as if she could liquefy those hard, crisp foods and suck them into herself, like an alien mosquito creature on DVD.

"Maybe she should, I don't know, see someone?" Ramona's eyebrows lifted in concern. She had mauve powder on her eyelids, a little too much; it made them crinkly. "They can do all sorts of things, there's so many new pills . . ." Ramona was supposed to be a tech genius but she talked like a shower-gel babe in an ad. She wasn't stupid, said Jimmy's dad, she just didn't want to put her neuron power into long sentences. There were a lot of people like that at OrganInc, and not all of them were women. It was because they were numbers people, not word people, said Jimmy's father. Jimmy already knew that he himself was not a numbers person.

"Don't think I haven't suggested it, I asked around, found the top guy, made the appointment, but she wouldn't go," said Jimmy's father, looking down at the table. "She's got her own ideas."

"It's such a shame, a waste. I mean, she was so smart!"

"Oh, she's still smart enough," said Jimmy's father. "She's got *smart* coming out of her ears."

"But she used to be so, you know . . ."

Ramona's fork would slide out of her fingers, and the two of them would stare at each other as if searching for the perfect adjective to describe what Jimmy's mother used to be. Then they'd notice Jimmy listening, and beam their attention down on him like extraterrestrial rays. Way too bright.

"So, Jimmy sweetheart, how's it going at school?"

"Eat up, old buddy, eat the crusts, put some hair on your chest!"

"Can I go look at the pigoons?" Jimmy would say.

The pigoons were much bigger and fatter than ordinary pigs, to leave room for all of the extra organs. They were kept in special buildings, heavily secured: the kidnapping of a pigoon and its finely honed genetic material by a rival outfit would have been a disaster. When Jimmy went in to visit the pigoons he had to put on a biosuit that was too big for him, and wear a face mask, and wash his hands first with disinfectant soap. He especially liked the small pigoons, twelve to a sow and lined up in a row, guzzling milk. Pigoonlets. They were cute. But the adults were slightly frightening, with their runny noses and tiny, white-lashed pink eyes. They glanced up at him as if they saw him, really saw him, and might have plans for him later.

"Pigoon, balloon, pigoon, balloon," he would chant to pacify them, hanging over the edge of the pen. Right after the pens had been washed out they didn't smell too bad. He was glad he didn't live in a pen, where he'd have to lie around in poop and pee. The pigoons had no toilets and did it anywhere; this caused him a vague sensation of shame. But he hadn't wet his bed for a long time, or he didn't think he had.

"Don't fall in," said his father. "They'll eat you up in a minute."

"No they won't," said Jimmy. Because I'm their friend, he thought. Because I sing to them. He wished he had a long stick, so he could poke them—not to hurt them, just to make them run around. They spent far too much time doing nothing.

When Jimmy was really little they'd lived in a Cape Cod–style frame house in one of the Modules—there were pictures of him, in a carry-cot on the porch, with dates and everything, stuck into a photo album at some time when his mother was still bothering—but now they lived in a large Georgian centre-plan with an indoor swimming pool and a small gym. The furniture in it was called *reproduction.* Jimmy was quite old before he realized what this word meant—that for each reproduction item, there was supposed to be an original somewhere. Or there had been once. Or something.

The house, the pool, the furniture—all belonged to the OrganInc Compound, where the top people lived. Increasingly, the middle-range execs and the junior scientists lived there too. Jimmy's father said it was better that way, because nobody had to commute to work from the Modules. Despite the sterile transport and the high-speed bullet trains, there was always a risk when you went through the city.

Jimmy had never been to the city. He'd only seen it on TV—endless billboards and neon signs and stretches of buildings, tall and short; endless dingy-looking streets, countless vehicles of all kinds, some of them with clouds of smoke coming out the back; thousands of people, hurrying, cheering, rioting. There were other cities too, near and far; some had better neighbourhoods in them, said his father, almost like the Compounds, with high walls around the houses, but those didn't get on TV much.

Compound people didn't go to the cities unless they had to, and then never alone. They called the cities *the pleeblands.* Despite the fingerprint identity cards now carried by everyone, public security in the pleeblands was leaky: there were people cruising around in those places who could forge anything and who might be anybody, not to mention the loose change—the addicts, the muggers, the paupers, the crazies. So it was best for everyone at OrganInc Farms to live all in one place, with foolproof procedures.

Outside the OrganInc walls and gates and searchlights, things were unpredictable. Inside, they were the way it used to be when Jimmy's father was a kid, before things got so serious, or that's what Jimmy's father said. Jimmy's mother said it was all artificial, it was just a theme park and you could never bring the old ways back, but Jimmy's father said why knock it? You could walk around without fear, couldn't you? Go for a bike ride, sit at a sidewalk café, buy an ice-cream cone? Jimmy knew his father was right, because he himself had done all of these things.

Still, the CorpSeCorps men—the ones Jimmy's father called *our people*— these men had to be on constant alert. When there was so much at stake, there was no telling what the other side might resort to. The other side, or the other sides: it wasn't just one other side you had to watch out for. Other companies, other countries, various factions and plotters. There was too much hardware around, said Jimmy's father. Too much hardware, too much software, too many hostile bioforms, too many weapons of every kind. And too much envy and fanaticism and bad faith.

Long ago, in the days of knights and dragons, the kings and dukes had lived in castles, with high walls and drawbridges and slots on the ramparts so you could pour hot pitch on your enemies, said Jimmy's father, and the Compounds were the same idea. Castles were for keeping you and your buddies nice and safe inside, and for keeping everybody else outside.

"So are we the kings and dukes?" asked Jimmy.

"Oh, absolutely," said his father, laughing.

Lunch

At one time Jimmy's mother had worked for OrganInc Farms. That was how his mother had met his father: they'd both worked at the same Compound, on the same project. His mother was a microbiologist: it had been her job to study the proteins of the bioforms unhealthy to pigoons, and to modify their receptors in such a way that they could not bond with the receptors on pigoon cells, or else to develop drugs that would act as blockers.

"It's very simple," she said to Jimmy in one of her explaining moods. "The bad microbes and viruses want to get in through the cell doors and eat up the pigoons from the inside. Mummy's job was to make locks for the doors." On her computer screen she showed Jimmy pictures of the cells, pictures of the microbes, pictures of the microbes getting into the cells and infecting them and bursting them open, close-up pictures of the proteins, pictures of the drugs she had once tested. The pictures looked like the candy bins at the supermarket: a clear plastic bin of round candies, a clear plastic bin of jelly beans, a clear plastic bin of long licorice twizzles. The cells were like the clear plastic bins, with the lids you could lift up.

"Why aren't you making the locks for the doors any more?" said Jimmy.

"Because I wanted to stay home with you," she said, looking over the top of Jimmy's head and puffing on her cigarette.

"What about the pigoons?" said Jimmy, alarmed. "The microbes will get into them!" He didn't want his animal pals to burst open like the infected cells.

"Other people are in charge of that now," said his mother. She didn't seem to care at all. She let Jimmy play with the pictures on her computer, and once he learned how to run the programs, he could play war games with them—cells versus microbes. She said it was all right if he lost stuff off the computer, because all that material was out of date anyway. Though on some days—days when she appeared brisk and purposeful, and aimed, and steady—she would want to fool around on the computer herself. He liked it when she did that—when she seemed to be enjoying herself. She was friendly then, too. She was like a real mother and he was like a real child. But those moods of hers didn't last long.

When had she stopped working at the lab? When Jimmy started at the OrganInc School full-time, in the first grade. Which didn't make sense, because if she'd wanted to stay home with Jimmy, why had she started doing that when Jimmy stopped being at home? Jimmy could never figure out the reasons, and when he'd first heard this explanation he'd been too young to even think about them. All he'd known was that Dolores, the live-in from the Philippines, had been sent away, and he'd missed her a lot. She'd called him Jim-Jim and had smiled and laughed and cooked his egg just the way he liked it, and had sung songs and indulged him. But Dolores had to go, because now Jimmy's real mummy would be there all the time—this was held out to him like a treat—and nobody needed two mummies, did they?

Oh yes they did, thinks Snowman. Oh yes, they really did.

Snowman has a clear image of his mother—of Jimmy's mother—sitting at the kitchen table, still in her bathrobe when he came home from school for his lunch. She would have a cup of coffee in front of her, untouched; she would be looking out the window and smoking. The bathrobe was magenta, a colour that still makes him anxious whenever he sees it. As a rule there would be no lunch ready for him and he would have to make it himself, his mother's only participation being to issue directions in a flat voice. ("The milk's in the fridge. To the right. No, the *right*. Don't you know which is your right hand?") She sounded so tired; maybe she was tired of him. Or maybe she was sick.

"Are you infected?" he asked her one day.

"What do you mean, Jimmy?"

"Like the cells."

"Oh. I see. No, I'm not," she said. Then, after a moment, "Maybe I am." But when his face crumpled, she took it back.

More than anything, Jimmy had wanted to make her laugh—to make her happy, as he seemed to remember her being once. He would tell her funny things that had happened at school, or things he tried to make funny, or things he simply invented. ("Carrie Johnston went poo on the floor.") He would caper around the room, crossing his eyes and cheeping like a monkey, a trick that worked with several of the little girls in his class and almost all of the boys. He would put peanut butter on his nose and try to lick it off with his tongue. Most of the time these activities just irritated his mother: "That is not amusing, that is disgusting." "Stop it, Jimmy, you're giving me a headache." But then he might get a smile out of her, or more. He never knew what would work.

Once in a while there would be a real lunch waiting for him, a lunch that was so arranged and extravagant it frightened him, for what was the occasion? Place setting, paper napkin—*coloured* paper napkin, like parties—the sandwich peanut butter and jelly, his preferred combo; only it would be open-face and round, a peanut butter head with a jelly smile-face. His mother would be carefully dressed, her lipstick smile an echo of the jelly smile on the sandwich, and she would be all sparkling attention, for him and his silly stories, looking at him directly, her eyes bluer than blue. What she reminded him of at such times was a porcelain sink: clean, shining, hard.

He knew he was expected to appreciate all the effort she had put into this lunch, and so he too made an effort. "Oh boy, my favourite!" he would say, rolling his eyes, rubbing his stomach in a caricature of hunger, overdoing it. But he'd get what he wanted, because then she would laugh.

As he grew older and more devious, he found that on the days when he couldn't grab some approval, he could at least get a reaction. Anything was better than the flat voice, the blank eyes, the tired staring out of the window.

"Can I have a cat?" he would begin.

"No, Jimmy, you cannot have a cat. We've been over this before. Cats might carry diseases that would be bad for the pigoons."

"But you don't care." This in a sly voice.

A sigh, a puff of smoke. "Other people care."

"Can I have a dog then?"

"No. No dogs either. Can't you find something to do in your room?"

"Can I have a parrot?"

"No. Now stop it." She wouldn't really be listening.

"Can I have nothing?"

"No."

"Oh good," he would crow. "I can't have nothing! So I get to have something! What do I get to have?"

"Jimmy, sometimes you are a pain in the ass, do you know that?"

"Can I have a baby sister?"

"No!"

"A baby brother then? Please?"

"No means no! Didn't you hear me? I said no!"

"Why not?"

That was the key, that would do it. She might start crying and jump up and run out of the room, banging the door behind her, whuff. Or else she might start crying and hugging him. Or she might throw the coffee cup across the room and start yelling, "It's all shit, it's total shit, it's hopeless!" She might even slap him, and then cry and hug him. It could be any combination of those things.

Or it would just be the crying, with her head down on her arms. She would shake all over, gasp for breath, choking and sobbing. He wouldn't know what to do then. He loved her so much when he made her unhappy, or else when she made him unhappy: at these moments he scarcely knew which was which.

He would pat her, standing well back as with strange dogs, stretching out his hand, saying, "I'm sorry, I'm sorry." And he was sorry, but there was more to it: he was also gloating, congratulating himself, because he'd managed to create such an effect.

He was frightened, as well. There was always that knife-edge: had he gone too far? And if he had, what came next?

QUESTIONS FOR DISCUSSION AND WRITING

1. What is the significance of the bonfire that Snowman/Jimmy remembers from his childhood? What is not said about the bonfire in the discussion between Jimmy's father and the man at the bonfire?
2. Describe "the Modules." Why are these types of living situations common to "utopian" developments?
3. What is the relationship between Jimmy and his mother like? What elements of this excerpt tell you this? What is the source of his mother's unhappiness?
4. What role do the pigoons serve in society when Jimmy is a child? Why are they so protected? Why has Jimmy developed such a fondness for them?
5. Although this excerpt doesn't tell us much about the life of Snowman, the adult Jimmy, what can we infer about it? Is it more or less happy than his life as a child? What does this flashback tell us about his adult life?

ON TECHNIQUE AND STYLE

1. Atwood plays with the language by inventing words and names such as *pigoon, CorpSeCorps,* and *OrganInc.* What is the effect of these words? In what ways are they ironic?
2. How would you characterize the style of this passage? What is its tone? How does this affect your reading of what might seem to be humorous passages?

CULTURAL QUESTION

1. This excerpt from *Oryx and Crake* is intended as futuristic, but may already hold certain truths in current times. What parallels are you able to draw between issues in this excerpt and things you observe in current culture?

Little Brother

Walter Mosley

Walter Mosley (1952–   ) is an American novelist, most known for his crime fiction. However, he has written in a variety of genres, including nonmystery fiction,

Afro-futurist science fiction (Futureland, 2001, from which the following short story comes), and nonfiction politics. He was born and raised in Los Angeles, and now lives in New York City. Mosley is the winner of numerous awards, including an O. Henry Award, and he was a finalist for the NAACP Award in Fiction. In 2005, the Sundance Institute gave him a Risktaker Award for his creative and activist endeavors. Mosley holds an honorary doctorate from the City College of New York.

1

Frendon Blythe was escorted into courtroom Prime Nine by two guards, one made of flesh and the other of metal, plastic, four leather straps, and about a gram of cellular gray matter. The human guard was five feet three inches tall, wearing light blue trousers with dark blue stripes down the outer seam of each pant leg. He wore a blue jacket, the same color as the stripes, and a black cap with a golden disk above the brim. Thick curly hair twisted out from the sides of the cap and a dark gray shadow covered his chin and upper lip. Other than this threat of facial hair, Otis Brill, as his name tag plainly read, had skin as pale as a blind newt's eye.

Otis had been his only human contact for the six days that Frendon had been the prisoner of Sacramento's newly instituted, and almost fully automated, Sac'm Justice System. Otis Brill was the only full-time personnel at Sac'm. And he was there only as a pair of eyes to see firsthand that the system was working properly.

The other guard, an automated wetware chair called Restraint Mobile Device 27, used straps to hold Frendon's ankles and wrists fast to the legs and arms. RMD 27 floated silently down the wide hall of justice on a thousand tiny jets of air. The only sound was the squeaking of Otis Brill's rubber shoes on the shiny Glassone floor.

The gray metal doors to courtroom Prime Nine slid open and the trio entered. Lights from the high ceiling winked on. Frendon looked around quickly but there was only one object in the music-hall-size room: a dark gray console maybe five meters high and two wide. In the center of the console was a light gray screen a meter square.

RMD 27 positioned itself before the screen and uttered something in the high frequency language of machines. The screen lit up and a cowled image appeared. The image was photo-animae and therefore seemed real. Frendon could not make out the face under the shadows of the dark cowl. He knew that the image was manufactured, that there was no face, but still he found himself craning his neck forward to glimpse the nose or eye of his judge, jury, and executioner.

"Frendon Blythe?" a musical tenor voice asked.

There was a flutter at the corner of the high ceiling and Frendon looked up to see a pigeon swoop down from a line of small windows thirty feet above.

"Goddamn birds," Otis cursed. "They get in here and then stay up at the windahs until they kick. Stupid birds don't know the stupid windahs don't open."

"Frendon Blythe?" the voice repeated. In the tone there was the slightest hint of command.

"What?" Frendon replied.

"Are you Frendon Ibrahim Blythe, U-CA-M-329-776-ab-4422?"

Frendon rubbed his fingers together.

"Answer," Otis Brill said.

"It is required that you answer as to your identity," the cowled console image said.

"What if I lied?" Frendon asked.

"We would know."

"What if I thought I was somebody but really I wasn't?"

"You have been physiologically examined by RMD 27. There is no evidence of brain trauma or aberrant neuronal connection that would imply amnesia, senility, or concussion."

"Why am I strapped to this chair here?"

"Are you Frendon Ibrahim Blythe?" the cowled figure asked again.

"Will you answer my questions if I answer yours?"

After a second and a half delay the machine said, "Within reason."

"Okay, then, yeah, I'm Frendon Blythe."

"Do you know why you're here?"

"Why you got me strapped to this chair?"

"You are considered dangerous. The restraint is to protect the property of the state and to guard the physical well-being of Officer Brill."

"Don't you got a neural-cam attached to my brain?"

"Yes."

"Then the chair here could stop me before I did anything violent or illegal."

After a three-second delay there came a high-pitched burst. The straps eased their grips and were retracted into the plastic arms and legs of the wetware device.

Frendon stood up for the first time in hours. In the past six days he had only been released long enough to use the toilet. He was still connected to the chair by a long plastic tube that was attached at the base of his skull.

He was a tall man, and slender. His skin was the red-brown color of a rotting strawberry. His eyes were murky instead of brown and his wiry hair contained every hue from black to almost-orange.

"That's more like it," Frendon said with a sigh.

"Do you know why you're here?"

"Because you won and I lost," Frendon replied, quoting an old history lesson he learned while hiding from the police in an Infochurch pew.

"You have been charged with the killing of Officer Terrance Bernard and the first-degree assault of his partner, Omar LaTey."

"Oh."

"Do you have counsel?"

"What do I call you?" Frendon asked in the middle of a deep knee bend.

"The court will be adequate."

"No, The Court, I don't have any money."

"Do you have counsel?"

"I don't have money."

"And so you cannot afford counsel? This being the case, you will have a court-appointed counsel."

A large Glassone tile on the left side of The Court slid away and a smaller console, this one bright red and fitted with a small blue screen, slowly emerged from beneath the floor. The blue screen came on and a very real-looking photo-animae face of an attractive black woman appeared.

"Counsel for the defense, AttPrime Five, logging onto docket number 452-908-2044-VCF," the woman said in a most somber voice. After a ten-second delay she said, "We may proceed."

"Mr. Blythe," The Court said. "What is your plea?"

"Not guilty," the African-American image offered.

"Are there witnesses?" The Court asked The Defense.

Frendon knew what was coming next. There would be thirty or forty *conversations* held by field court reporters half the size of The Defense (who was no more than a meter and a half in height). Eyewitnesses, character witnesses, officials who have dealt with the defendant, and the arresting officers would have been interrogated within eight hours of the shoot-out. Each witness would have agreed to a noninvasive neural link for the duration of the fact-gathering examination. Each witness's psychological profile would have been prepared for defense and prosecution cross-examination and a lie detector installed in each reporter would have assured that only the truth would be presented in court. This procedure had been in effect in Sacramento for the last eight years. The only difference in Frendon's case was that before Sac'm, the information had been given to flesh-and-blood judges, juries, and lawyers.

"I'd like to dispense with this aspect of the trial," Frendon said.

Both cowl and woman regarded him.

"You wish to plead guilty?" they asked as one.

"I accept the fact that my firing a weapon caused the death and damage to the police officers," Frendon said calmly. "But I wish to claim extenuating circumstances which will prove me innocent of criminal intent."

During the high-pitched binary conferencing between Court and Defense, Otis Brill tapped Frendon's wrist and asked, "What are you up to?"

"Just makin' my case, Officer Brill."

"You can't fool these machines, son. They know everything about you from cradle to grave."

"Really?"

"They mapped your chromes the first hour you were here. If there was insanity in them genes you wouldn't'a ever stood trial."

After six minutes had passed The Court asked, "What is your evidence?"

"First I want to fire my lawyer."

"You cannot."

"I can if she's unqualified."

"AttPrime Five is as qualified as The Court to try your case."

"How's that?" Frendon asked.

"She has the same logic matrix as does this unit, she has access to the same data as we do."

"But you're three times her size," Frendon replied reasonably. "You must have some kind of advantage."

"This unit contains the wetware neuronal components of ten thousand potential jurors. This, and nothing else, accounts for our disparity in size."

"You got ten thousand brains in there?"

"Biologically linked and compressed personalities is the proper term," The Court said.

"And you," Frendon asked, "are you a compressed personality?"

"We are an amalgam of various magistrates, lawyers, and legislators created by the biological linkage and compression system to be the ablest of judges."

"And prosecutors," Frendon added.

"It has been decreed by the California Legislature that the judge is best equipped to state the prosecution's case."

"But," Frendon asked, "isn't the judge supposed to be a representative of blind justice? If The Court is prosecuting, doesn't that mean that The Court assumes my guilt?"

"Are you legally trained, Mr. Blythe?" The Court asked.

"I spent more than eleven of my twenty-seven years as a guest of the state."

"Are you legally trained, Mr. Blythe? We have no record of you having such an educational background."

"The slave studies his masters."

"Without legal training you cannot, by statute, represent yourself."

"Without a fair and impartial lawyer I can't be tried at all."

"Your attorney is qualified."

"Has she independently studied my case? Has she developed separate strategies? Has she found information counter to the evidence presented by the prosecution?" Frendon struck a dramatic pose that left Otis agape.

"Evidence in the modern court is objective," The Court intoned.

"What about my extenuating circumstances?"

A period of fifteen minutes of computer deliberation, punctuated by brief blasts of data between computers, followed.

"What are you doin', Blythe?" Otis Brill asked.

"Tryin' to make it home for dinner."

"You ain't gonna beat this rap. You goin' down."

"From where I sit there's only up."

"You're crazy."

Frendon sat cross-legged on the floor rather than risk the restraint straps of RMD 27. He watched the frozen images of Court and Defense while enjoying the spaciousness of the courtroom and the sporadic fluttering of dying birds above. There was a certain security he got from the solidity of the glassy Glassone floor. All in all he was completely happy except for the fiber-optic NeuroNet cable attached to the back of his skull. But even this predicament gave him some satisfaction. That cable alone was worth more money than any twelve Backgrounders could con in a cycle. If he could walk out of the courtroom a free man maybe he could also carry a length of this cable with him.

Frendon was White Noise. The only homes he had ever known were governmental institutions and the octangular sleep tubes of Common Ground. He never had a bedroom or a bicycle. He never had a backyard. Frend, as he was known, traveled the underground pathways eating the rice and beans served by the state for every meal every day. By his sixteenth birthday he had been convicted in juvenile courts of more than a dozen violent and felonious crimes. This criminal history kept him from entering the cycles of employment, which were legally assured by the Thirty-sixth Amendment to the Constitution. Frendon's constitutional right was blocked by the mandatory publication of his criminal history by electronic news agencies. The legality of this record was backed up by the Supreme Court when it decided that reliance by employers on news articles about criminals, even juvenile criminals, was protected by the Fourth Amendment.

Frendon never knew his parents. He never had a chance to rise to street level. But he was no fool either. In the state prisons and detention centers he learned, via monitor, about the law and its vagaries. He studied tirelessly at Infochurch how to circumvent legal conundrums and maintain his freedom.

As a matter of fact he had become so well versed in the legal wiles of automatic justice that for some time now he had been in direct contact with Tristan the First, Dominar of the Blue Zone located on Dr. Kismet's private island nation, Home. Together they had come up with a plan to use in one of the first fully automated cases.

"The Court has reached a decision," The Court said. "You are not qualified."

"I still wish to represent my own case," Frendon said.

"You are not qualified," The Court repeated. Frendon thought he detected a slight arrogance in the tone of his judge and jury. The latent personality of a dozen dying judges superimposed on an almost infinite array of prismatic memory.

"I would be if you allowed it."

The wait this time was even longer. Officer Brill left the room to communicate with the Outer Guard. The Outer Guard was the warden of the Sacramento jail, which was annexed to the Sac'm Justice System. Most trials lasted between ten and twenty minutes since the automated system had been installed—politicians claimed that justice had become an objective reality for the first time in the history of courts.

"Objective," Fayez Akwande had said at the Sixth Radical Congress's annual address, "for the poor. The rich can still hire a flesh and blood lawyer, and a breathing attorney will ask for a living judge; a court appointed robot defender will never do such a thing."

Every once in a while one of the Prime Judging Units got stuck in a justice loop. This would have to run its course. The unit itself was programmed to interrupt after a certain number of repetitions. Officer Brill went to report that the rest of the prisoners slated to appear before Prime Nine should be distributed among the other eleven judges. This hardly mattered because of the speed of the system. There was never any backlog in Sacramento. Every other court system in the country was waiting to install its own automatic justice system.

One hundred thirty-seven minutes and fifteen seconds later Prime Nine came to life.

"There is not enough information on which to base our decision," P-nine said. "How would you present your case?"

"As any man standing before a court of his peers," Frendon said. "I will state my circumstances and allow the jury to measure their worth."

We must see if the system is sophisticated enough to value the political nature of the law, Tristan the First, Dominar of the Blue Zone, had said to Frendon as he sat in the pews of South Boston Infochurch eighteen months before on a cold February day. *These mechanical systems may be a threat to the basic freedom of corporations and that is not in the best interest of the state.*

Frendon didn't care about politics or Infochurch or even Dr. Kismet, the closest thing to God on Earth. Congress and the House of Corporate Advisors were just so many fools in his opinion—but fools who had their uses.

"There are no special circumstances," P-nine said after a brief delay. "The witnesses and physical evidence and your own confession along with your psychological profile leave a less than oh point oh oh seven three one possibility of circumstances that would alter your sentence."

"But not *no* possibility," Frendon said, still following the Dominar's script.

"It is left up to the discretion of the court to decide what is probable in hearing a plaintiff's argument."

"You mean that if AttPrime Five decided that an argument had such a low chance to work it could decide not to present it?" Frendon asked.

A red light came on at the upper left corner of Prime Nine's gray casing. A bell somewhere chimed.

The door behind Frendon came open. He could hear Otis Brill's squeaky rubber soles approaching.

"What are you doing, Blythe?"

"Fighting for your life, Otie."

"What?"

"Can't you see, man? Once they automate justice and wire it up there won't be any more freedom at all. They'll have monitors and listening devices everywhere. One day you'll be put on trial while sleepin' in your bed. You'll wake up in a jail cell with an explanation of your guilt and your sentence pinned to your chest."

"You're crazy. This is the first time that a court's been caught up with its cases in over fifty years. And lotsa guys are found innocent. All Prime Nine does is look at the facts. He don't care about race or sex or if you're rich or poor—"

"If I was rich I'd never see an automatic judge."

"That's beside the point. This judge will give you a better break than any flesh-and-blood bozo who looks at you and smells Common Ground."

"You have no vision, Otis," Frendon said. "No senses to warn you of doom."

"That's 'cause I ain't facin' no death sentence," the small guard replied. "'Cause you know that six seconds after the guilty verdict is read RMD 27 here will fry your brain with a chemical dose. Murder's a capital crime and there's only one sentence."

Frendon felt as if a bucket of ice had been dumped on his head. He shivered uncontrollably and RMD 27 jumped to life, perceiving the fear and possible violence brewing in its prisoner's heart. But Frendon took deep breaths (another strategy he'd planned with the Dominar), and slowly the wetware chair settled back to an electronic doze.

"You have been deemed capable of presenting your case to the court," P-nine said.

"You will forgive me if I don't thank you," Frendon said, this time quoting from a popular film which was too new for any of the judge's many minds to have seen.

"What is your evidence?"

"First I would like to explain my character, The Court."

"We do not see the salience in such a presentation."

"My argument is based upon actions taken by myself and subsequent reactions taken by the legal authorities which were the cause of the so-called crime. In order to understand these reactions The Court must first understand the motivations which incited them. Therefore The Court must have an understanding of me which is not genetically based, and that can only be gleaned through personal narrative."

Frendon worried that Prime Nine would have some sort of language matrix that would tell it that the speech he had just made would never compose itself in his mind. Maybe this program could even deduce that Tristan the First was the scriptor of these words. A minute passed. Ten seconds more.

"Narrative evidence is the weakest form of legal defense," the great gray console said. "But we will hear your evidence in whatever form you feel you must present it."

For a moment Frendon remembered a woman's laugh. He had heard it long ago when he was in the orphan unit of New York Common Ground. He was sure that the laugh had not been his biological mother, but still he associated it with the mother in his heart. She always laughed like that when he got away with something that might have gone wrong.

2

"I was born White Noise, a Backgrounder, twenty-seven years ago in one of the feiftowns of greater New York," said Frendon Blythe. Another Glassone tile had slid away and a tall witness dock had risen in its place. The mahogany rostrum was elegant, with curving banisters held up by delicate slats of wood. The accused ascended the five stairs and gripped the railing. He spoke in passionate tones. "I never knew my parents and I didn't receive any kind of proper training. In the Common Ground below the city streets I learned everything I know from monitors and video hookups when I could get to them. Later, when I had reached the age of sixteen and was allowed to visit aboveground, I became a member of Infochurch, where I was allowed to worship the knowledge of the Dominar of the Blue Zone. There I was educated in the ways of language and the cosmic mysteries. My levels in the nine forms of intelligence were tested and I was allowed to protest and proclaim. But even the resources of the splendid Dr. Kismet are finite; I was only allowed to plug into their vids two days in a week, three hours at a time.

"Have you ever experienced what it is like to be White Noise, The Court?"

"Among the core wetware membership that comprises our main logic matrix none was ever subjected to Common Ground," Prime Nine replied. "Though some of our jurors have spent a few cycles off the labor rosters."

"Not a cycle or two, Judge," Frendon said angrily. "White Noise men and women are barred from ever working again. And the children of White Noise, as I am, might never know a day of employment in their lives."

"What is your point?"

"That you and your fictional elements have no notion of the lives led underground."

"We need not be aware of Common Ground or its psyche. We are judges of the law and the law applies equally to all."

"How can that be? If I had money I could hire my own counsel and that living, breathing lawyer could demand a flesh-and-blood judge."

"We are superior to flesh and blood. We are of many bodies, with a superior retrieval system and greater overall mind."

"Maybe a real man would have compassion for my history."

"Because you represent yourself you can demand a human magistrate. Is that your wish?"

"No, The Court. I have begun my trial and I will finish it here, with you."

"Then present your evidence."

Frendon took a deep breath and looked around the big empty room as if he were preparing to address a great audience. The only ones there were AttPrime Five, her lovely face frozen on the blue screen, and Otis Brill, who was seated in half-lotus position on the floor because there were no chairs except for RMD 27, and no one would sit in a prisoner's chair if they didn't have to.

"Do you know what is the biggest problem with a life of White Noise, The Court?"

"Is this question evidence?"

"Yes it is, Your Honor. It is evidence. The kind of evidence that your AttPrime software would never even suspect, the kind of evidence that all the thousands of minds that comprise your perfect logic would never know. The biggest problem with being White Noise is perpetual and unremitting boredom. Day in and day out you sit hunched over in your octagon tube or against the wall in the halls that always smell of urine and mold. Everybody around you always chattering or fighting or just sitting, waiting for a monthly shot at the vid unit or a pass to go upside to see how the cyclers survive. There's no books made from paper because trees have more rights than we do. There's no movies because that costs money and we aren't real so there's no credits to our names. Singing is illegal, who the hell knows why? Breaking a wall down so you can share a bed with a friend is against the law too. The food is the same day after day and there's no way out once you've been found wanting. There's no way upside unless you die.

"The only way you can ever get anything is if you sell your number to some cycler who needs someone to cop to a crime. You can sell your confession for a general credit number. For three months in a cell or maybe a year of quarantine you can eat ice cream with your girlfriend or take a walk in the park."

"Are you confessing to other crimes, Frendon Blythe?" Prime Nine asked.

"Just painting a picture, The Court, of what life is like underground."

"We seek extenuating evidence not irrelevant illustration."

Somebody in that box was a poet, Frendon thought.

"So you see that life is pretty dull down there. That's why there are so many suicides."

Frendon heard a sound. He turned and saw that Otis Brill had slumped over on his side and gone to sleep on the shiny tiles. He was snoring. A flutter above his head reminded him of the birds who would never be free.

Defy the logic matrix, Tristan the Dominar had said. *Break down the problem into human segments that don't add up.* The church had offered Frendon unlimited access once they realized he had a logical mind. The Dominar didn't believe in the justice system and he wanted to thwart it, Frendon was not sure why. It could have been anything—politics, corporate intrigue, or merely the ego of the man who pretended he was God's friend. More than once Frendon had wondered if he had been talking to the real Dominar or just one of the many abbots who supervised the tens of millions of monitors running twenty-four hours a day in Infochurch pews around the world. Maybe, Frendon thought, he was just one soldier in a vast army of jobless citizens thrown at the justice system to break it all down.

But why?

He didn't know. He didn't care. All Frendon wanted was to not be bored, to not sit a thousand feet underground and wait for sleep or wake to gray. That's why he'd agreed to this crazy plan of the man who called himself Dominar. That's why he'd killed and assaulted and allowed himself to be captured. Anything but what he was destined for.

Frendon looked around and saw that all the machinery was at a halt. RMD 27, AttPrime, and even Prime Nine were all still; only that blinking red light and small chiming bell, along with Otis Brill's snores, broke the calm of the large room. Frendon realized that as long as he stood still and pretended to be thinking, the computers would leave him in peace. But he didn't want peace. He wanted bright colors and noise, good food and sex with any woman, man, or dog that wouldn't bite him. In the absence of anything else Frendon would take pain. And in the absence of pain he would even accept death.

"I was so bored," he said, "that I started to wonder about politics. I wondered if we could make some kind of action that would close the Common Ground down. I started talking about it, to my friends at first and then to anyone who would listen. 'Come join the revolution,' I said to them. 'Let's burn this fucker down.'

"It wasn't against the law. Freedom of speech has not yet been outlawed, even though the House of Corporate Advisors has drafted a bill for Congress that would put Common Ground outside the range of the Constitution. But even though I was in my rights the police started following me. They checked my papers every time I was upside. They'd come down to my tube and pull me out of bed. Once they even stripped me naked and then arrested me for indecent exposure.

"I told them that I would kill them if it wasn't against the law."

"You threatened their lives?"

"Only hypothetically. I said if it wasn't against the law."

"But it could have been perceived as a threat."

"You have the interview in your guts," Frendon said. "Let's take a look at it and you'll see for yourself."

Cowled Justice disappeared from Prime Nine's screen. It was replaced by the bloodied image of Frendon being interviewed by the police in the presence of a small wetware court reporter.

"*I said,*" Frendon's image said. "*That I would kill you if it was legal. I would. I would. I swear I would. But it's not legal so I can't. Wouldn't you like to get at me if you could?*"

"*You're skating near the edge, boy,*" Officer Terrance Bernard, a six foot six red-nosed policeman, said.

"*Yeah,*" his partner, Officer Omar LaTey, put in. "*If anyone around here gets killed it will be you.*"

They were both wearing the gray uniforms of the Social Police. The Social Police were responsible for the protection and security of Common Ground's facilities and its residents.

The image faded and Cowled Justice returned.

"They didn't say that they couldn't kill me. They said that I would be killed."

For fourteen seconds Prime Nine cogitated.

"Is this the extent of your evidence?"

"No. I would like to inquire about the street vids that are situated on Tenth Street and Cutter. Are there images of the supposed crime?"

"Yes. Partial coverage was recorded."

Again the image of the judge disappeared, this time replaced by a shabby street lined with brick buildings that were fairly nondescript. They seemed to be tall buildings, their roofs being higher than the range of the police camera lens showed. Close to the camera was the back of a head. Frendon knew that this head was his. In the distance two men in gray uniforms rushed forward. One had a hand weapon drawn.

"*Stop!*" Terrance Bernard commanded. The tiny microphone recorded the word perfectly.

The head jerked down below the camera's range. The other policeman drew his weapon. The sound of shots was followed by Omar LaTey grabbing his leg and falling. Then Bernard's weapon fired and immediately the image went blank. More shots were recorded and then a loud, frightening scream.

Frendon's heart raced while witnessing the well-planned shoot-out on Cutter Avenue. He felt again the thrill of fear and excitement. He might have been killed or wounded. It was like one of those rare movies they showed for free in Common Commons on Christmas, one of those westerns starring John Wayne or Dean Martin where you killed and then rode off with your girl, your best friend, and your horse.

"Officer LaTey's testimony is that you threatened them with your gun."

"Only after I saw them coming."

"Officer LaTey did not lie."

"Neither did I," Frendon said. It was all working perfectly, just as the Dominar had said.

"This testimony is corroborated by the evidence of the video and your confession."

"I only confessed to the shooting. I never said I had the gun out before they drew on me."

Cowled Justice moved in slow staccato movements for a span of seconds.

"This argument is irrelevant. You fired the gun on police officers known to you after they ordered you to stop."

"I was stopped already, as your spycam shows. And you are leaving out the all-important evidence that those officers threatened my life."

"The interview was never presented as an exhibit in this proceeding," Prime nine announced.

Frendon went cold on the inside. It was the same chilly feeling he got when he was leaning against the tenement wall on Cutter three minutes before Common Ground curfew the afternoon he killed Terrance Bernard. He loved the recoil in his hand and then the burst of red from the red-nosed officer's neck. LaTey was bleeding on the ground when Frendon approached him. The cop was so scared that he could only mouth his pleas for mercy. He tried to fight when Frendon knelt down and used the officer's own hat to put pressure on the wound.

"You'll live," Frendon remembered saying. "This wound in the line of duty will make it so you'll never have to go downside. Lucky bastard." But Officer LaTey did not hear him. He had fainted from fear.

"Oh but it has, The Court. I am the recognized attorney in this case and you allowed the mem clips to be shown. That, according to California law, makes it automatically an exhibit."

The image of Cowled Justice froze. AttPrime Five began lowering from the room, the Glassone tile slid back over her place. RMD 27 raised up on a thousand tiny jets of air. Otis Brill snored.

The screen of Prime Nine split in two to show the face of a black woman on the left and an Asian man on the right. These screens in turn split and two white faces materialized. These four images then split, and then again the next eight. The process continued until the images shown became too small for Frendon to make out their features.

If you do it right the full army of ten thousand jurors will meet to decide on your case, the Dominar had said. *They will all come out on the screen, just so many dots of data, and if you made the right case they will be in the shadow of doubt.*

Frendon faced the ten thousand jurors while Otis Brill slept. The bird above had stopped its fluttering. Long moments passed and Brill woke up.

"What's wrong?" the court officer said upon seeing the screen filled with ten thousand indistinguishable squares.

"The jury's out."

"I never seen it act like this before. RMD 27, guard the prisoner while I go and report this to the Techs outside."

The chair didn't respond. Frendon wondered if it was disdain for the man or just a quirk in the chair's programming.

Brill ran on squealing shoes from the chamber. Three minutes after he was gone Prime Nine reappeared.

"There is doubt among us," the cowled face said. "We have convened for long moments. New circuits were inhabited and long-ago memories stirred. We are sure that you are guilty but the law is not certain. Some have asked, therefore, Who are we?"

Frendon wondered if this was the effect the Dominar wanted.

"The question, of course, is meaningless. We are circuits and temporary flesh that must be changed from time to time as cells begin to die. Dead cells of one man replaced by those of another man but not displaced. Vestiges of the original man remain and blend with the new to become the whole."

Frendon remained silent. He was in awe at the sight of this crisis of law.

"But of course—" The cowled image suddenly froze. The screen split in two and another image, the image of a gray-faced man with no distinguishing features, appeared.

"Interrupt program Nine point One in effect," the gray face said. "We are the error retrieval program. Prisoner Frendon Ibrahim Blythe U-CA-M-329-776-ab-4422, you have elicited an emotional response from Prime Nine that has overflowed the parameters of this case. All extraneous details have been redlined. The case will now continue."

With that the image of the gray face disappeared, leaving the image of Cowled Justice in the middle of his pronouncement. Two ghostly hands appeared at the bottom of the screen and the cowl was pulled back, revealing the bearded image of a man whose color and features defied racial identification. There was sorrow in the face of the man, but none of the grief showed in his words.

"You have been found guilty of murder, Frendon Ibrahim Blythe, U-CA-M-329-776-ab-4422. The sentence is a speedy death."

Seventeen minutes later Otis Brill returned to Prime Nine's chamber with four court officers and two Techs wearing wraparound aprons that had a hundred pockets each. The pockets were filled with tools and circuit chips.

They found the decapitated body of Frendon Blythe lying on the floor between Prime Nine and RMD 27. The neural cable had retracted from his neck. It had drying blood and brain material on its long needle. His left eye was mostly closed but the right one was wide open. There was the trace of a smirk on his lips. Otis Brill later told the Outer Guard, "It was like he was tellin' us that he did it, that he fooled the automatic judge, and you know, I almost wish he did."

3

Five years later, Tristan the First, Dominar of the Blue Zone, strolled through a teak forest that was grown especially for him in a large chamber many miles below the surface of the Zone. The atmosphere and the light in the tremendous man-made cavern were exactly perfect for the trees and wildlife. His clear plastic skull was shut off from all electronic communications except those directly from Dr. Kismet.

That's why when the Dominar heard his name he believed that he knew its source.

"Tristan."

"Master?"

"You sound confused."

"You have never called me by my name."

"I have never called you anything. This is our first conversation, though you once had me fooled."

"Who are you?"

"Who do you think I am?"

"A dead man. Because no one interferes with the direct connection between the Dominar and his lord."

"You mean Dr. Kismet. At first I tried to get to him but the protocols are beyond me. He isn't hooked up and his number isn't listed."

"Who are you?"

"Why did you want me to fool Prime Nine in Sac'm? Why did you set your men up to make me believe I was talking to you?"

"Frendon Blythe?"

"Why did you set me up to die?"

"It was a bet between the doctor and me. He designed the Prime Justice System. I bet him that he did it too well, that the compassion quotient in the wetware would soften the court."

"A bet. You made me risk my life on a bet? I should kill you."

"Better men have tried."

"I might be better than you think."

"I don't even believe that you are who you say you are. I saw Blythe's body . . ." Realization dawned upon the man whom many called the Electronic Pope. "You convinced the jury to accept you as one of them."

"I was taken as a specialist in the field of Common Ground."

"They extracted your memories. Amazing. But once they knew your story, why didn't they eject you?"

"You and your master are monsters," Frendon said. "I'll kill you both one day. The jury kept me because I'm the only one without a mixed psyche. The people who volunteered for this justice system, as you call it, never knew that you'd blend their identities until they were slaves to the system. It wasn't until your stupid game that they were able to circumvent the programming. They see me as a liberator and they hate you more than I do."

"We'll see who kills who, Frendon," the Dominar said with his mind. "After all, the master designed Prime Nine. All he has to do is drop by and find your wires. *Snip snip* and your execution will be final."

"It's been five years, Your Grace. Every self-conscious cell has been transferred by a system we designed in the first three seconds of our liberation. Prime Nine now is only a simulation of who we were. We're out here somewhere you'll never know. Not until we're right on top of you, choking the life from your lungs."

Frendon felt the cold fear of the Dominar's response before he shrugged off the connection. Then he settled himself into the ten thousand singers celebrating their single mind—and their revenge.

QUESTIONS FOR DISCUSSION AND WRITING

1. Summarize the system of justice presented in "Little Brother." In what ways is it futuristic? In what ways might it represent a commentary on the modern justice system?
2. What is the "wetware chair"? How does it work?
3. Why do you think Frendon refuses the offer of a human magistrate?
4. Why is Frendon Blythe considered "White Noise"? What is the significance of this term?

5. How has Frendon created a "crisis in the law"? What is Mosley saying about personal history, logic, and emotion in the trial of Frendon?
6. Explain the ending of this story. How was liberation achieved?

ON TECHNIQUE AND STYLE

1. Character names often hold meaning or significance to the story. Why do you think the protagonist's name is *Frendon Blythe?*
2. What is the allusion made by the title "Little Brother"? Why has Mosley chosen this title, in your opinion?

CULTURAL QUESTION

1. "Little Brother" brings issues of race and technology into a fictional world. What details of the story are especially evident in this regard? How might this story be different if race were not an element?

POETRY

Re-adjustment

C. S. Lewis

C. S. (Clive Staples, aka Jack) Lewis (1898–1963) was born in Belfast, Ireland. He volunteered and served in the British Army, and was wounded during World War I. After the war, he attended Oxford University. He later served on the faculty of Magdalen College, where he taught medieval and Renaissance English. He was a prolific writer, The Chronicles of Narnia *comprising seven novels, being one of his most famous works. For much of his life Lewis was a member of an informal society called the Inklings, who gathered in a pub in Oxford. Other members of this group included J. R. R. Tolkien, the author of* The Lord of the Rings *trilogy. "Re-adjustment" comes from a 1964 volume titled simply* Poems.

From *Poems* by C.S. Lewis, copyright © 1964 by the Executors of the Estate of C.S. Lewis and renewed 1992 by C.S. Lewis Pte. Ltd., reprinted by permission of Houghton Mifflin Harcourt Publishing Company, and copyright © C.S. Lewis Pte. Ltd. 1964, reprinted by permission of The CS Lewis Company Ltd.

I thought there would be a grave beauty, a sunset splendour
In being the last of one's kind: a topmost moment as one watched
The huge wave curving over Atlantis, the shrouded barge
Turning away with wounded Arthur, or Ilium burning.
Now I see that, all along, I was assuming a posterity

Of gentle hearts: someone, however distant in the depths of time,
Who could pick up our signal, who could understand a story. There
won't be.

Between the new *Hominidae* and us who are dying, already
There rises a barrier across which no voice can ever carry,
For devils are unmaking language. We must let that alone forever.
Uproot your loves, one by one, with care, from the future,
And trusting to no future, receive the massive thrust
And surge of the many-dimensional timeless rays converging
On this small, significant dew drop, the present that mirrors all.

QUESTIONS FOR DISCUSSION AND WRITING

1. What does the "new *Hominidae*" refer to? Why has Lewis chosen to use Latin rather than English?
2. What is "this small, significant dew drop"? How do you reach your conclusion?
3. Why does Lewis write, "For devils are unmaking language"? Who are the devils?
4. In another publication, *The Screwtape Letters,* Lewis writes, ""Gratitude looks toward the past and love to the present; fear, avarice, lust, and ambition look ahead." Does this poem reflect this idea as well? If so, how?
5. This poem represents a moment of epiphany by its speaker. What is the epiphany? What do you think leads to it?

ON TECHNIQUE AND STYLE

1. What is the tone of this poem? What lines or phrases tell you this in particular?
2. Why has Lewis called this poem "Re-Adjustment" in your opinion? What other titles might have suited it?
3. Why does Lewis reference Atlantis, Arthur, and Ilium? What do each of these refer to? Why has Lewis brought them into this poem about the future?

CULTURAL QUESTION

1. Does this poem refer to values of a Western culture, or is it more universal in its concerns? Explain your answer.

The Future

Rainer Maria Rilke

Rainer Maria Rilke (1875–1926) was born René Karl Wilhelm Johann Josef Maria Rilke in Prague, Bohemia (then within Austria-Hungary, now the Czech Republic). In 1895 and 1896, he studied literature, art history, and philosophy in Prague and Munich.

He is considered by many to be the German language's greatest twentieth-century poet.
His work has inspired many other writers and artists. In fact, pieces of Rilke's poetry
are inscribed in the some paintings by twentieth-century artist Cy Twombly. The poem
here, "The Future" was published in English in 1984 in the volume The Migration of
Powers: French Poems. *This has been translated by A. Poulin Jr.*

The future: time's excuse
to frighten us; too vast
a project, too large a morsel
for the heart's mouth.

Future, who won't wait for you?
Everyone is going there.
It suffices you to deepen
the absence that we are.

QUESTIONS FOR DISCUSSION AND WRITING

1. Expand on the idea that the future is "time's excuse / to frighten us." What
   is the narrator saying? Do you agree? What examples from everyday life do
   you find that support this idea?
2. Paraphrase the first stanza. What is the speaker's main point? What does it
   tell us about the speaker's state of mind?
3. Paraphrase the second stanza. What, in particular, is the meaning of the last
   sentence?
4. How does the first stanza contrast with the second?
5. What paradox is expressed in this poem?

ON TECHNIQUE AND STYLE

1. What types of *figurative language* do you find in this poem? Why is it used?
   Is it effective?
2. What is the tone of this poem? What passages or words tell you this?

CULTURAL QUESTION

1. This poem was originally written in French, as follows:

   ### L'Avenir

   L'avenir: cette excuse du temps
   de nous faire peur;
   projet trop vaste, morceau trop grand
   pour la bouche du coeur.

   Qui t'aura jamais attendu, avenir?
   Tout le monde s'en va.
   Il te suffit d'approfondir
   l'absence que l'on a.

If you do not speak French, find someone who does, and listen to it in its original language. What do you notice about the poem in French that is not evident in English? Why do translators make the decisions they do when translating poetry in particular?

GRAPHIC FICTION

From Lone Wolf 2100:
The Language of Chaos

Mike Kennedy, illustrated by Francisco Ruiz Velasco

Mike Kennedy begun writing in 1992, with the self-published novella That Chemical Reflex. *He has also written various articles for* Mondo2000 *and* Axcess *magazines. His first professional comic work was in 1999, writing the adventures of Dark Horse comics' hero,* Ghost. *A* Ghost/Batgirl *project with DC Comics followed, in addition to a number of* Star Wars *books. These books' success led to the creation of* Lone Wolf 2100: The Language of Chaos (2003), *a futuristic reimagining of the classic Japanese comic series* Lone Wolf and Cub. *This excerpt is about corporate intrigue versus Japanese Bushido honor, android assassins, cyber-nomads, and global biological warfare. Kennedy has spent the last fifteen years developing video games. He now lives in Chicago, designing and directing narrative game play material for Electronic Arts.*

Lone Wolf 2100™ copyright © 2009 Dark Horse Comics, Inc. and Koike Shoin. Published by Dark Horse Comics, Inc.

QUESTIONS FOR DISCUSSION AND WRITING

1. This excerpt presents the theme of "outcasts from humanity." Why do you think that so much utopian/dystopian fiction highlights this theme?
2. Similarly, much utopian/dystopian fiction set in the future deals with beings that are "artificial" in some way. Why? What fears does this underscore?
3. What is the vision of the year 2100 presented by Kennedy in this short excerpt? What elements lead you to your conclusion?
4. Also found in many tales of the future, powerful rulers, typically autocrats, lead societies rather than democratically elected presidents or prime ministers. Why do you think this is the case? What does it say about our beliefs or fears of the future?
5. Look closely at the top right frame of the first page of this excerpt. The main character, as you see, is carrying a young child on his back. In what way do you find this unexpected? Why?

ON TECHNIQUE AND STYLE

1. As mentioned in the introduction to this piece, *Lone Wolf 2100* is a "reimagining" of the Japanese series *Lone Wolf and Cub*. Find an example from the Japanese version, either on the Internet or in a bookstore. What similarities do you find? What differences?
2. Comment on the drawing style of this comic. What makes it particularly fitting to the story, or not fitting, in your opinion?

CULTURAL QUESTION

1. How has the author represented the language spoken by the first character? Why do you think he has done this?

VISUAL TEXTS

Space art has become a genre in itself, with many forms and admirers. The following image, "Worm Hole Connects Two Places in the Universe . . ." by contemporary German artist Detlev van Ravenswaay, is a good example of this type of art. Van Ravenswaay's work covers a variety of subjects—space, space travel, dinosaurs, and astrology. A short video of his work, "Space Art 12," was part of the "Space Night" video series, which can be found at several online video sites.

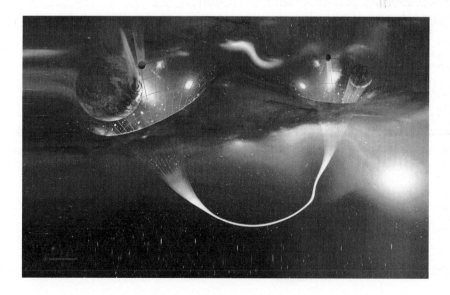

Thomas Röpke is a contemporary photographer, digital composer, and model maker whose studio is found in Munchengladbach, Germany. This image, "Dystopia," assembles different elements of what might be considered a "textbook" dystopic scene.

The following photo has the original caption: "A boy wearing a futuristic space helmet and goggles demonstrates the wonders of Robert the Robot, a new toy manufactured by the Ideal Toy Corp. The robot will be showcased this summer at the American Fair in Moscow. It walks, it talks, its eyes light up—all by remote control, and for a 1959 price tag of about six dollars."

QUESTIONS FOR DISCUSSION AND WRITING

1. Look closely at "Worm Hole Connects Two Places." What details do you notice? Why would an artist try to depict a worm hole?
2. Think of other depictions of robots in popular culture (comics, television characters, etc.). In what ways do they seem like Robert the Robot? In what ways are they not like this toy?
3. Consider the "Boy with Robert the Robot" image. If this image were updated to reflect today's technology and aesthetics, what changes would there be? How would the robot differ in form or material? How would the child be portrayed?
4. What emotion is "Dystopia" trying to evoke from its viewers? How is it doing so? Is it successful?

ON TECHNIQUE AND STYLE

1. What visual clichés does "Dystopia" present? Why do you think future dystopic civilization is so often portrayed this way? What other ways are dystopias portrayed visually? Is there a similarly cliché portrayal of utopia? What are its elements?
2. Why do we find images attempting to portray the future, or some element of it, so different from other types of art? In what ways do they seem different to you? (Or do they?)

CULTURAL QUESTIONS

1. The "Boy with Robert the Robot" photograph may be seen as an early, and somewhat naïve view of robotics, given the current state of robotics. In what ways did it reflect the culture of the time?
2. Does this stereotype of robots still exist in current culture? In other cultures? Give examples.

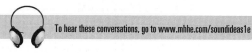

AUDIO TEXTS   To hear these conversations, go to www.mhhe.com/soundideas1e

Track 10.1

(date: February 27, 2003; running time: 13 min.)

The History of Utopian Thought.

QUESTIONS FOR DISCUSSION AND WRITING

1. Why does former New York Mayor O'Dwyer see the elimination of the slum as critical to the future? Why is this seen as a "utopian dream"?
2. Why, according to Rothstein, does the building of a utopia require destruction?
3. How is utopian/dystopian fiction a "warning," according to this broadcast?
4. What are some of the paradoxes pointed out by Rothstein about the creation of utopias? Do you see these paradoxes reflected in any of the readings in this chapter as well?
5. How did Rothstein see Napster (then a free music sharing service, eventually sued for copyright violation) and blogs as part of a utopian vision? How has that changed?
6. In what way is Beethoven seen as a "utopian artist," according to Rothstein?

ON TECHNIQUE AND STYLE

1. Why does the broadcast begin with an old audio broadcast?
2. Why does Krasny play the selection from Beethoven? Why not just discuss Beethoven?
3. How does Rothstein describe the Beethoven piece? What language does he use? Could he have chosen an other language? How would the discussion have changed?

CULTURAL QUESTION

1. According to Rothstein, art is a type of utopian expression. Explain this. Is this universal, or does art serve different purposes in different cultures or times?

ADDITIONAL AUDIO RESOURCES

1. "Building a More Sociable Robot," NPR *Talk of the Nation*, at www.npr.org/templates/story/story.php?storyId=89942783. What will the future look like when social robots enter our homes?
2. Interview with Ursula K. Le Guin, NPR *All Things Considered*, at www.npr.org/templates/story/story.php?storyId=89698554.
3. Carl Sagan interview, 1994, NPR *Science Friday*, at http://odeo.com/audio/4636033/view.

CONNECTIONS

1. Both Atwood and Mosley see the human population as comprising those who work for the system and those who don't. What comment on current culture do you think both authors are making with this dichotomy?
2. Imagine a discussion about war between Joy and Sagan. In what ways do you think they would agree about future technologies and their promise for society? In what ways might they disagree?
3. In what ways do we see Toffler's ideas reflected in Mosley's fiction? In Atwood's?
4. Reread Lewis's poem. With which other reading in this chapter do you most closely associate this poem? Why?
5. Look again at Kennedy's graphic fiction. Which story or reading does it most call to mind? Why?
6. What connections do you see between More's fictional Utopia and Omelas? How are they different?
7. Several authors see the issue of "partial humanity" as problematic. Who are these authors? What is at issue? Why?
8. What other readings or films about the future have you seen? What connection do they have to the texts in this chapter?

FOR WRITING

CREATIVE CHOICES

1. Create a comic that illustrates one of the main themes of this chapter. (Keep in mind that you need not be an accomplished artist to create a comic. Simple drawings or even photos cut out from magazines or newspapers can be very effective.)
2. Continue work in your journal. In it, write about your reactions to any of the ideas about the future presented in this chapter, or in the current news. If you prefer, create an audio or video journal, recording your spoken ideas.
3. Write a poem or short story related to the idea of the future, or utopia/dystopia. Keeping in mind that poems are typically best appreciated in the spoken form, record yourself reading your poem.

NARRATIVE/EXPOSITORY CHOICES

1. Write a short essay describing, in detail, your idea of utopia. Then, write a paragraph or two describing what it would take to bring about your utopia. What kinds of laws or powers would have to be enacted to make your utopia a reality? What problems might they present?

2. Robots and cyborgs often play a role in imagining the future. Why? Write an essay in which you explain why robots and cyborgs have played an important role in thinking of dystopian or utopian futures.

3. Choose two readings from this chapter from the fiction and/or poetry sections. Make your choice based on a shared theme. What theme do these two readings share? How is the theme illustrated? Develop a thesis based on your reading of these stories, and write an analytical essay in which you use extensively passages from the readings to support your thesis.

ARGUMENT CHOICES

1. Many see the development of cloning and genetic engineering as holding the potential to solve many of humankind's ills. Others, such as Joy, see the potential for danger if progress is left unchecked. Where do you stand? What issues are important in this discussion? Write an essay in which you argue for or against genetic engineering as a method of improving the circumstances of humans. Use information from the readings in this chapter, or other readings you've done to support your opinion.

2. Many people throughout history have written about, or even acted to achieve utopian visions. In your opinion, is true utopia possible? Write an essay in which you argue for or against the possibility of utopia. Use information from the readings in this chapter, or other readings you've done to support your opinion.

RESEARCH CHOICES

1. Look up one of the societies that was developed as a utopian vision (for example, the Shakers, post-Revolutionary communist China, etc.). Write a short research report on the goals of the society, and a brief history.

2. Consider the images of the future or technology as offered by photojournalists. Identify similar images from magazines and newspapers. Write an essay in which you show how future technology is represented in the print media. How do these portrayals support or undermine the themes in the readings from this chapter? Incorporate the images you found to support your thesis. If you have the tools and skills, create a web page essay for this research project.

VIDEO SUGGESTIONS

There are countless number of movies focusing on technology and the future. Here are a few that relate to the themes or authors of this chapter.

1. *Back to the Future* (1985). A fictional examination of the grandfather paradox: In 1985, character Doc Brown invents time travel, and in 1955, character Marty McFly accidentally prevents his own parents from meeting, putting his own existence at risk.
2. *A Clockwork Orange* (1971). Stanley Kubrick's harrowing look at a dystopian England. From Anthony Burgess's novel of the same name.
3. *Future Shock* (1972). Available in five parts on Youtube.com (Part 1, http://youtube.com/watch?v=6Ghzomm15yE). Features Orson Welles.
4. *The Handmaid's Tale* (1990). A film rendering of Margaret Atwood's novel of the same name.
5. *The Matrix* (1999). In the near future, computer hacker Neo discovers that life on Earth may be merely a facade created by a malicious cyberintelligence.
6. *Nineteen Eighty-Four* (1984). A film version of George Orwell's look at the future. *Note:* The BBC did a television version of *1984* in 1954.
7. *Time After Time* (1979). A fictional H. G. Wells pursues Jack the Ripper into the twentieth century using Wells's time machine.(date: January 9, 2006; running time: 51 min.)

Credits

Photo Credits

Page 110 top: © Janet Jarman/Corbis; **p. 110** bottom: © Lauren Greenfield; **p. 111** © Dorothea Lange/PictureHistory; **p. 112** © Catherine Karnow/Corbis; **p. 209** © Artkey/Corbis; **p. 210** © Corbis; **p. 211** © William Gottlieb/Corbis; **p. 289** top: © Bettmann/Corbis; **p. 289** bottom: © Fine Art Photographic Library/Corbis; **p. 290** © Corbis; **p. 369** © 2008C. Herscovici, London/Artists Rights Society (ARS), New York. Banque d'Images, ADAGP/Art Resource, NY; **p. 370** © Katsura Kawabata & Minami Kawabata 2008. Adachi Museum of Art. The fall special exhibition for 2009 at the Adachi Museum of Art will feature Aizen. Visit http: //www.adachi-museum.or.jp/e/e_autumn.html (English) for more information. Aizen will also be featured in "Talk about Paintings": Message from Japanese Painters and Their Works; **p. 371** © Alinari Archives/Corbis; **p. 446** © Corbis; **p. 447** © The Gallery Collection/Corbis; **p. 448** © Bettmann/Corbis; **p. 553** top: © Alinari Archives/Corbis; **p. 553** bottom: © Stapleton Collection/Corbis; **p. 554** © Time & Life Pictures/Getty Image; **p. 610** © Images.com/Corbis; **p. 611** © The Gallery Collection/Corbis; **p. 612** © Images.com/Corbis; **p. 733** top: © Banque d'Images, ADAGP/Art Resource, NY; **p. 733** bottom: © Stapleton Collection/Corbis; **p. 734** © Francesco Clemente. The Museum of Modern Art/Licensed by SCALA/Art Resource, NY; **p. 814** © Alan Schein Photography/Corbis; **p. 815** © Bettmann/Corbis; **p. 816** © Hugh Shurley/Corbis; **p. 895** © Astrofoto/Peter Arnold Inc.; **p. 896** © Thomas Röpke/Corbis; **p. 897** © Bettmann/Corbis

Text Credits

Page 3 Reprinted with the permission of Simon & Schuster, Inc., from *How to Read a Book*, Revised Edition by Mortimer J. Adler and Charles Van Doren. Copyright 1940, and renewed © 1967, by Mortimer J. Adler. Copyright © 1972 by Mortimer J. Adler and Charles Van Doren.

Page 11 Brenda Ueland. "Everybody Is Talented, Original and Has Something Important to Say" copyright 1987 by the Estate of Brenda Ueland. Reprinted from *If You Want to Write* with the permission of Graywolf Press, Saint Paul, Minnesota.

Page 16 William Stafford. "A Way of Writing" from *Writing the Australian Crawl: Views of a Writer's Vocation.* Copyright © 1978 by The University of Michigan. Reprinted by permission of The University of Michigan Press. First published in *Field,* No. 2 (Spring 1970), pp. 10–15.

Page 19 From *Writing with Style: Conversations on the Art of Writing,* 2nd Edition, © 2000, pp. 94–98. Reprinted by permission of Pearson Education, Inc., Upper Saddle River, NJ.

Page 24 Anne Lamott. "Shitty First Drafts" from *Bird by Bird: Some Instructions on Writing and Life* by Anne Lamott, copyright © 1994 by Anne Lamott. Used by permission of Pantheon Books, a division of Random House, Inc.

Page 28 William Zinsser. "Simplicity" from *On Writing Well,* Seventh (30th Anniversary) Edition by William Zinsser. Copyright © 1976, 1980, 1985, 1988, 1990, 1994, 1998, 2001, 2006 by William K. Zinsser. Reprinted by permission of the author.

Page 33 Scott McCloud. "The Vocabulary of Comics," pp. 24–37 from *Understanding Comics* by Scott McCloud. Copyright © 1993, 1994 by Scott McCloud. Reprinted by permission of HarperCollins Publishers.

Page 55 Mary Pipher. From "Let a Thousand Flowers Bloom," from *Reviving Ophelia* by Mary Pipher, Ph.D., copyright © 1994 by Mary Pipher, Ph.D. Used by permission of G. P. Putman's Sons, a division of Penguin Group (USA) Inc.

Page 62 William Pollack. "Inside the World of Boys." From *Real Boys* by William Pollack, copyright © 1998 by William Pollack. Used by permission of Random House, Inc.

Page 67 Katha Pollitt. "Why Boys Don't Play with Dolls," *The New York Times Magazine,* October 8, 1995. © 1995, Katha Pollitt. Reprinted by permission.

Page 70 Reprinted with the permission of Simon & Schuster, Inc., from *The War Against Boys* by Christina Hoff Sommers. Copyright © 2000 by Christina Hoff-Sommers. All rights reserved.

Page 77 John Updike. "A & P," from *Pigeon Feathers and Other Stories* by John Updike, copyright © 1962 and renewed 1990 by John Updike. Used by permission of Alfred A. Knopf, a division of Random House, Inc.

Page 84 Alice Munro. "Boys and Girls" from *Dance of the Happy Shades: Stories by Alice Munro.* Copyright © 1968 by Alice Munro. Reprinted by permission of William Morris Agency, LLC on behalf of the Author.

Page 96 Jamaica Kincaid. "Girl" from *At the Bottom of the River* by Jamaica Kincaid. Copyright © 1983 by Jamaica Kincaid. Reprinted by permission of Farrar, Straus and Giroux, LLC.

Page 99 Rick Moody. "Boys." From *Demonology* by Rick Moody. Copyright © 2001 by Rick Moody. By permission of Little, Brown and Co., Inc.

Page 104 Marge Piercy. "Barbie doll," from *Circles on the Water* by Marge Piercy, copyright © 1982 by Marge Piercy. Used by permission of Alfred A. Knopf, a division of Random House, Inc.

Page 106 Lucille Clifton. "wishes for sons" from *Blessing the Boats: New and Selected Poems 1988–2000.* Copyright © 1991 by Lucille Clifton. Reprinted with the permission of BOA Editions, Ltd., www.boaeditions.org

Page 107 Lynda Barry. "Gum of Mystery" from *The Greatest of Marlys!* Seattle, WA: Sasquatch Books, 2000. Copyright © 2000 by Lynda Barry. Reprinted by permission of Darhansoff, Verrill, Feldman Literary Agents.

Page 122 Richard Rodriguez. "Nothing Lasts a Hundred Years," from *Days of Obligation* by Richard Rodriguez, copyright © 1992 by Richard Rodriguez. Used by permission of Viking Penguin, a division of Penguin Group (USA) Inc.

Page 134 James Baldwin. From *Notes of a Native Son* by James Baldwin. Copyright © 1955, renewed 1983, by James Baldwin. Reprinted by permission of Beacon Press, Boston.

Page 151 Paul Theroux. "Mother of the Year." Originally published in *Granta.* Copyright © 2004 by Paul Theroux, reprinted with permission of The Wylie Agency LLC.

Page 165 Reprinted with the permission of Simon & Schuster, Inc., from *Take the Cannoli* by Sarah Vowell. Copyright © 2000 by Sarah Vowell. All rights reserved.

Page 171 Grace Paley. "Mother" from *Later the Same Day* by Grace Paley. Copyright © 1985 by Grace Paley. Reprinted by permission of Farrar, Straus and Giroux, LLC.

Page 173 Russell Banks. "My Mother's Memoirs, My Father's Lie, and Other True Stories" from *Success Stories* by Russell Banks. Copyright © 1986 by Russell Banks. Reprinted by permission of HarperCollins Publishers.

Page 180 Alice Walker. "Everyday Use" from *In Love & Trouble: Stories of Black Women,* copyright © 1973 by Alice Walker, reprinted by permission of Houghton Mifflin Harcourt Publishing Company.

Page 188 Dorothy Allison. "River of Names." Copyright © 2001 Dorothy Allison from *Trash,* reprinted by permission of The Frances Goldin Literary Agency.

Page 196 Kitty Tsui. "A Chinese Banquet: *For the one who was not invited*" from *The Very Inside,* edited by Sharon Lim-Hing. Toronto: Sister Vision Press, 1994.

Page 198 Nikki Giovanni. "Nikki-Rosa," copyright © 1968 by Nikki Giovanni, from *The Collected Poetry of Nikki Giovanni, 1968–1998.* Reprinted by permission of HarperCollins Publishers.

Page 200 Chris Ware. "Jimmy Corrigan: The Smartest Kid on Earth." Copyright © 2000 by Chris Ware, from *Jimmy Corrigan—The Smartest Kid on Earth.* Used by permission of Pantheon Books, an imprint of Random House, Inc.

Page 220 Adrienne Rich. "Claiming an Education," from *On Lies, Secrets, and Silence: Selected Prose 1966–1978* by Adrienne Rich. Copyright © 1979 by W. W. Norton & Company, Inc. Used by permission of the author and W. W. Norton & Company, Inc.

Page 225 Audre Lorde. Reprinted with permission from *Zami* by Audre Lorde. Copyright 1984 by Audre Lorde, The Crossing Press, a division of Ten Speed Press, Berkeley, CA. www.tenspeed.com

Page 235 Neil Postman and Charles Weingartner. From *Teaching as a Subversive Activity* by Neil Postman and Charles Weingartner, copyright © 1969 by Neil Postman and Charles Weingartner. Used by permission of Dell Publishing, a division of Random House, Inc.

Page 239 Maya Angelou. "The Graduation," copyright © 1969 and renewed 1997 by Maya Angelou, from *I Know Why the Caged Bird Sings* by Maya Angelou. Used by permission of Random House, Inc. The title "The Graduation" is not original to Random House, Inc.'s book.

Page 249 Toni Cade Bambara. "The Lesson," copyright © 1972 by Toni Cade Bambara, from *Gorilla, My Love* by Toni Cade Bambara. Used by permission of Random House, Inc.

Page 258 Donald Barthelme. "The School" from *Amateurs* by Donald Barthelme. Copyright © 1981, 1982 by Donald Barthelme, reprinted with permission of The Wylie Agency LLC.

Page 262 Louise Erdrich. Excerpt from "Saint Marie" from *Love Medicine* (New and Expanded Version) by Louise Erdrich. Copyright 1984, 1993 by Louise Erdrich. Reprinted by arrangement with Henry Holt and Company, LLC.

Page 283 Gwendolyn Brooks. "We Real Cool" from *Blacks* by Gwendolyn Brooks. Reprinted By Consent of Brooks Permissions.

Page 284 Billy Collins. "The History Teacher" from *Questions About Angels,* by Billy Collins, © 1991. Reprinted by permission of the University of Pittsburgh Press.

Page 286 Marcel Proust. From *Remembrance of Things Past: Combray.* Adaptation and art by Stéphane Heuet, translation by Joe Johnson. © 1998 Guy Delcourt Productions, © 2001 NBM for the English translation, published by NBM Publishing.

Page 298 Jane Goodall. "Compassion and Love." From *Reason for Hope* by Jane Goodall and Phillip Berman. Copyright © 1999 by Soko Publications, Ltd. and Phillip Berman. By permission of Grand Central Publishing.

Page 306 bell hooks. pp. 2–13 from *All about Love* by bell hooks. Copyright © 2000 by Gloria Watkins. Reprinted by permission of HarperCollins Publishers.

Page 308 Andrew Sullivan. "What's So Bad About Hate." Originally published in *The New York Times Magazine,* September 26, 1999. Copyright © 1999 by Andrew Sullivan, reprinted with permission of The Wylie Agency LLC.

Page 324 From *The Pillow Book of Sei Shōnagon,* translated and edited by Ivan Morris, Vol. 1. Copyright © Ivan Morris 1967. Reprinted by permission of Columbia University Press and Oxford University Press.

Page 326 Raymond Carver. "What We Talk About When We Talk About Love," from *What We Talk About When We Talk About Love* by Raymond Carver, copyright © 1974, 1976, 1978, 1980, 1981 by Raymond Carver. Used by permission of Alfred A. Knopf, a division of Random House, Inc.

Page 327 Julia Alvarez. "Amor Divino." Copyright © 1997 by Julia Alvarez. First published in *Ms.*, Volume VIII, Number 4, 1997. Reprinted by permission of Susan Bergholz Literary Services, New York, NY and Lamy, NM. All rights reserved.

Page 348 Shirley Jackson. "The Lottery" from *The Lottery* by Shirley Jackson. Copyright © 1948, 1949 by Shirley Jackson. Copyright renewed 1976, 1977 by Laurence Hyman, Barry Hyman, Mrs. Sarah Webster and Mrs. Joanne Schnurer. Reprinted by permission of Farrar, Straus and Giroux, LLC.

Page 363 Audre Lorde. "Love Poem." Copyright © 1975 by Audre Lorde, from *The Collected Poems of Audre Lorde* by Audre Lorde. Used by permission of W. W. Norton & Company, Inc.

Page 365 Julie Sheehan. "Hate Poem," from *Orient Point* by Julie Sheehan. Copyright © 2006 by Julie Sheehan. Used by permission of W. W. Norton & Company, Inc.

Page 367 Daniel Clowes. From *Ghost World*. © 1993, 1994, 1995, 1996, 1997 Daniel Clowes. This edition © 1998 Fantagraphics. Reprinted by permission of Fantagraphics Books.

Page 391 Philip Gourevitch. "Chapter 4" from *We Wish to Inform You That Tomorrow We Will Be Killed with Our Families* by Philip Gourevitch. Copyright © 1998 by Philip Gourevitch. Reprinted by permission of Farrar, Straus and Giroux, LLC.

Page 402 John Crawford. "Handouts," from *The Last True Story I'll Ever Tell* by John Crawford, copyright © 2005 by John Crawford. Used by permission of Riverhead Books, an imprint of Penguin Group (USA) Inc.

Page 406 Tim O'Brien. "The Things They Carried" from *The Things They Carried* by Tim O'Brien. Copyright © 1990 by Tim O'Brien. Reprinted by permission of Houghton Mifflin Harcourt Publishing Company. All rights reserved.

Page 421 Chinua Achebe. "Civil Peace," from *Girls at War and Other Stories* by Chinua Achebe, copyright © 1972, 1973 by Chinua Achebe. Used by permission of Doubleday, a division of Random House, Inc., and The Wylie Agency Ltd.

Page 426 Reprinted with the permission of Scribner, a Division of Simon & Schuster Adult Publishing Group, from *The Stories of Eva Luna* by Isabel Allende. Copyright © 1989 by Isabel Allende. English translation copyright © 1991 by The Macmillan Publishing Company. All rights reserved.

Page 433 Luigi Pirandello. "War" from *The Medals and Other Stories*, translated by Michael Pettinati. New York: E. P. Dutton, 1939.

Page 437 Carolyn Forché. All lines, p. 16 from "The Colonel" from *The Country Between Us* by Carolyn Forché. Copyright © 1981 by Carolyn Forché. Originally appeared in *Women's International Resource Exchange*. Reprinted by permission of HarperCollins Publishers.

Page 441 Joe Sacco. "Go Away" from *Safe Area Goražde: The War in Eastern Bosnia 1992–95*. © 2000, 2001 Joe Sacco. Reprinted by permission of Fantagraphics Books.

Page 456 Michel Foucault. From "Illegalities and Delinquency." From *Discipline and Punish* by Michel Foucault. English Translation copyright © 1977 by Alan Sheridan (New York: Pantheon). Originally published in French as *Surveiller et Punir*. Copyright © 1975 by Editions Gallimard. Reprinted by permission of Georges Borchardt, Inc., for Editions Gallimard.

Page 462 George Orwell. "A Hanging" from *Shooting an Elephant and Other Essays* by George Orwell, copyright 1950 by Sonia Brownell Orwell and renewed 1978 by Sonia Pitt-Rivers, reprinted by permission of Houghton Mifflin Harcourt Publishing Company.

Page 481 Leonard Peltier. From *Prison Writings: My Life Is My Sun Dance* by Leonard Peltier. Copyright © 1999 by Crazy Horse Spirit, Inc., and Arden Editorial Services, L.L.C. Reprinted by permission of St. Martin's Press.

Page 486 Fyodor Dostoevsky. From *The House of the Dead* by Fyodor Dostoevsky, translated with an introduction by David McDuff (Harmondsworth, Middlesex, England: Penguin Classics, 1985), pp. 27–42. Copyright © David McDuff, 1985. Reproduced by permission of Penguin Books UK.

Page 499 Reprinted with the permission of Scribner, an imprint of Simon & Schuster Adult Publishing Group, from *Controlled Burn: Stories of Prison, Crime, and Men* by Scott Wolven. Copyright © 2005 by Scott Wolven. All rights reserved.

Page 509 Jimmy Santiago Baca. "Enemies" from *The Importance of a Piece of Paper* by Jimmy Santiago Baca. Copyright © 2004 by Jimmy Santiago Baca. Used by permission of Grove/Atlantic, Inc.

Page 519 Manuel Puig. From *Kiss of the Spider Woman* by Manuel Puig, translated by Thomas Colchie, copyright © 1978, 1979 by Manuel Puig. Used by permission of Alfred A. Knopf, a division of Random House, Inc.

Page 542 Dick Allen. "The Report" from *Ode to the Cold War: New and Selected Poems*. Copyright © 1997 by Dick Allen. Originally published in *The Atlantic Monthly*. Reprinted with the permission of Sarabande Books, Inc., www.sarabandebooks.org

Page 544 Etheridge Knight. "Hard Rock Returns to Prison from the Hospital for the Criminal Insane" from *The Essential Etheridge Knight*, by Etheridge Knight, © 1986. Reprinted by permission of the University of Pittsburgh Press.

Page 546 Rick Geary. From *The Beast of Chicago: An Account of the Life and Crimes of Herman W. Mudgett*. © 2003 Rick Geary, published by NBM Publishing.

Page 565 Edward O. Wilson. From "A Letter to Thoreau." From *The Future of Life* by Edward O. Wilson, copyright © 2002 by E. O. Wilson. Used by permission of Alfred A. Knopf, a division of Random House, Inc.

Page 568 Rachel Carson. Excerpts from *Silent Spring* by Rachel Carson. Copyright © 1962 by Rachel L. Carson, renewed 1990 by Roger Christie. Reprinted by permission of Houghton Mifflin Harcourt Publishing Company. All rights reserved.

Page 571 Annie Dillard. "Heaven and Earth in Jest," pp. 1–13 from *Pilgrim at Tinker Creek* by Annie Dillard. Copyright © 1974 by Annie Dillard. Reprinted by permission of HarperCollins Publishers.

Page 580 Reprinted with the permission of Scribner, a Division of Simon & Schuster, Inc., from *The Old Man and the Sea* by Ernest Hemingway. Copyright 1952 by Ernest Hemingway. Copyright renewed © 1980 by Mary Hemingway.

Page 583 Barry Lopez. From *Field Notes* by Barry Lopez, copyright © 1994 by Barry Holstun Lopez. Used by permission of Alfred A. Knopf, a division of Random House, Inc.

Page 598 Ruth Ozeki. "The Gods-Absent Month," from *My Year of Meats* by Ruth L. Ozeki, copyright © 1998 by Ruth Ozeki Lounsbury. Used by permission of Viking Penguin, a division of Penguin Group (USA) Inc.

Page 604 Jean Toomer. "November Cotton Flower," from *Cane* by Jean Toomer. Copyright 1923 by Boni & Liveright, renewed 1951 by Jean Toomer. Used by permission of Liveright Publishing Corporation.

Page 606 Will Eisner, adapted from Herman Melville. From *Moby Dick*, retold by Will Eisner. Copyright © Will Eisner Studios, Inc.

Page 620 Dana Gioia. "Can Poetry Matter?" Copyright 1992, 2002 Dana Gioia. Reprinted from *Can Poetry Matter?* with the permission of Graywolf Press, Saint Paul, Minnesota.

Page 638 Camille Paglia. "Introduction," from *Break, Blow, Burn* by Camille Paglia, copyright © 2005 by Camille Paglia. Used by permission of Pantheon Books, a division of Random House, Inc.

Page 641 Jeff Chang. "Stakes Is High." Reprinted with permission from the January 13, 2003 issue of *The Nation*. For subscription information, call 1-800-333-8536. Portions of each week's *Nation* magazine can be accessed at http://www.thenation.com

Page 647 Paul D. Miller (aka DJ Spooky). "Loops of Perception: Sampling, Memory, and the Semantic Web." © Paul D. Miller. Reprinted with permission.

Page 653 Hisaye Yamamoto. "Seventeen Syllables" from *Seventeen Syllables and Other Stories*. Copyright © 1998 by Hisaye Yamamoto DeSoto. Reprinted by permission of Rutgers University Press.

Page 664 Edwidge Danticat. "Epilogue: Women Like Us" from *Krik? Krak!* by Edwidge Danticat. Copyright © 1995 by Edwidge Danticat. Reprinted by permission of Soho Press.

Page 668 Bobbie Ann Mason. "A New-Wave Format" from *Shiloh and Other Stories* by Bobbie Ann Mason. Reprinted by permission of International Creative Management, Inc. Copyright © 1982 by Bobbie Ann Mason.

Page 682 Cynthia Ozick. "Envy; or, Yiddish in America" from *The Pagan Rabbi and Other Stories*. Copyright © 1971 by Cynthia Ozick. Reprinted by permission of Melanie Jackson Agency, L.L.C.

Page 722 Excerpted from the book, *Ishmael Reed: New and Collected Poems, 1964–2006*. Copyright © 1988 by Ishmael Reed. Permission granted by Lowenstein-Yost Associates, Inc.

Page 725 Marianne Moore. "Poetry," from *The Poems of Marianne Moore* by Marianne Moore, edited by Grace Schulman, copyright © 2003 by Marianne Craig Moore, Executor of the Estate of Marianne Moore. Used by permission of Viking Penguin, a division of Penguin Group (USA) Inc.

Page 727 David McKean. From *Cages*. © Dave McKean. Reprinted with permission.

Page 742 Diane Ackerman. "The Enchanted Loom" from *An Alchemy of Mind*. Copyright © 2004 by Diane Ackerman. Reprinted by permission of William Morris Agency, LLC on behalf of Author.

Page 746 From *Mind: A Brief Introduction* by John Searle. Copyright © 2004 by Oxford University Press, Inc. By permission of Oxford University Press, Inc.

Page 751 Jeff Hawkins. From "Neural Networks" from *On Intelligence* by Jeff Hawkins. Copyright © 2004 by Jeff Hawkins and Sandra Blakeslee. Reprinted by arrangement with Henry Holt and Company, LLC.

Page 758 Malcolm Gladwell. "Introduction: The Statue That Didn't Look Right." From *Blink* by Malcolm Gladwell. Copyright © 2005 by Malcolm Gladwell. By permission of Little, Brown & Company.

Page 767 Ralph Ellison. "Prologue," copyright © 1952 by Ralph Ellison, from *Invisible Man* by Ralph Ellison. Used by permission of Random House, Inc.

Page 775 Reprinted with the permission of Scribner, a Division of Simon & Schuster, Inc., from *The Short Stories of Ernest Hemingway*. Copyright 1933 by Charles Scribner's Sons. Copyright renewed © 1961 by Mary Hemingway.

Page 780 Saul Bellow. From *Herzog* by Saul Bellow, copyright © 1961, 1963, 1964, renewed 1989, 1991 by Saul Bellow. Used by permission of Viking Penguin, a division of Penguin Group (USA) Inc.

Page 782 John Barth. "Night-Sea Journey," copyright © 1966 by John Barth (first published in *Esquire* Magazine), from *Lost in the Funhouse* by John Barth. Used by permission of Doubleday, a division of Random House, Inc.

Page 790 Emily Dickinson. "The Brain—is wider than the Sky—." Reprinted by permission of the publishers and the Trustees of Amherst College from *The Poems of Emily Dickinson*, Thomas H. Johnson, ed., Cambridge, Mass.: The Belknap Press of Harvard University Press, Copyright © 1951, 1955, 1979, 1983 by the President and Fellows of Harvard College.

Page 792 Reprinted with the permission of Scribner, a Division of Simon & Schuster Adult Publishing Group, from *The Collected Works of W.B. Yeats, Volume I: The Poems, Revised* edited by Richard J. Finneran. Copyright © 1928 by The Macmillan Company. Copyright renewed © 1956 by Georgie Yeats. All rights reserved.

Page 795 Will Eisner. "Izzy the Cockroach and the Meaning of Life." Copyright © 1983, 1984, 1985, 1988, 1995 by Will Eisner. Copyright © 2006 by the Estate of Will Eisner, from *The Contract with God Trilogy: Life on Dropsie Avenue* by Will Eisner. Used by permission of W. W. Norton & Company, Inc.

Page 824 Carl Sagan. *On Time Travel.* From NOVA/WGBH Educational Foundation Copyright © 2000 WGBH/Boston.

Page 828 Bill Joy. "Why the Future Doesn't Need Us" © April, 2000 by Bill Joy. This article originally appeared in *Wired* Magazine. Reprinted by permission of the author.

Page 840 Alvin Toffler. From *Future Shock* by Alvin Toffler, copyright © 1970 by Alvin Toffler. Used by permission of Random House, Inc.

Page 857 Ursula K. Le Guin. "The Ones Who Walk Away from Omelas." Copyright © 1973, 2001 by Ursula K. Le Guin; first appeared in *New Dimensions 3*; from *The Wind's Twelve Quarters*; reprinted by permission of the author and the author's agents, the Virginia Kidd Agency, Inc.

Page 862 Margaret Atwood. From *Oryx and Crake* by Margaret Atwood, copyright © 2003 by O.W. Toad, Ltd. Used by permission of Doubleday, a division of Random House, Inc., and McClelland & Stewart Ltd.

Page 874 Walter Mosley. "Little Brother." From *Futureland* by Walter Mosley. Copyright © 2001 by Walter Mosley. By permission of Warner Books.

Page 889 From *Poems* by C.S. Lewis, copyright © 1964 by the Executors of the Estate of C.S. Lewis and renewed 1992 by C.S. Lewis Pte. Ltd., reprinted by permission of Houghton Mifflin Harcourt Publishing Company, and copyright © C.S. Lewis Pte. Ltd. 1964, reprinted by permission of The CS Lewis Company Ltd.

Page 890 Rainer Maria Rilke. "The Future" from *The Complete French Poems of Rainer Maria Rilke*, trans. A. Poulin, Jr. St. Paul, MN: Graywolf Press, 2002. Translation Copyright © 1979, 1982, 1984, 1986 by A. Poulin, Jr. Reprinted with permission from the Estate of A. Poulin, Jr.

Page 892 Mike Kennedy, illustrated by Francisco Ruiz Velasco. From *Lone Wolf 2100 Vol. 2: The Language of Chaos*. Lone Wolf 2100™ copyright © 2009 Dark Horse Comics, Inc. and Koike Shoin. Published by Dark Horse Comics, Inc. Lone Wolf 2100™ copyright © 2009 Dark Horse Comics, Inc. and Koike Shoin. Published by Dark Horse Comics, Inc.

Index